Your Health Today
Choices in a Changing Society

Eighth Edition

Your Health Today
Choices in a Changing Society

Eighth Edition

Michael Teague
University of Iowa

Sara Mackenzie
University of Washington

David Rosenthal
Columbia University

YOUR HEALTH TODAY: CHOICES IN A CHANGING SOCIETY, EIGHTH EDITION

Published by McGraw-Hill LLC, 1325 Avenue of the Americas, New York, NY 10121. Copyright ©2022 by McGraw-Hill LLC. All rights reserved. Printed in the United States of America. Previous editions ©2019, 2017, and 2015. No part of this publication may be reproduced or distributed in any form or by any means, or stored in a database or retrieval system, without the prior written consent of McGraw-Hill LLC, including, but not limited to, in any network or other electronic storage or transmission, or broadcast for distance learning

Some ancillaries, including electronic and print components, may not be available to customers outside the United States.

This book is printed on acid-free paper.

1 2 3 4 5 6 7 8 9 LWI 24 23 22 21

ISBN   978-1-260-26033-5 (bound edition)
MHID   1-260-26033-X (bound edition)
ISBN   978-1-260-58004-4 (loose-leaf edition)
MHID   1-260-58004-0 (loose-leaf edition)

Vice President, Portfolio: *Katie Stevens*
Product Development Manager: *Dawn Groundwater*
Portfolio Manager: *Erika Lo*
Product Developer: *Elisa Adams*
Senior Marketing Manager: *Meredith Leo Digiano*
Content Project Managers: *Sherry Kane/Katie Reuter*
Senior Buyer: *Susan K. Culbertson*
Designer: *Beth Blech*
Lead Content Licensing Specialist: *Brianna Kirschbaum*
Cover Image: *©Photodisc/Getty Images*
Compositor: *Aptara, Inc.*

All credits appearing on page or at the end of the book are considered to be an extension of the copyright page.

Library of Congress Cataloging-in-Publication Data

Names: Teague, Michael, author. | Mackenzie, Sara L. C., author. |
   Rosenthal, David M., author.
Title: Your health today : choices in a changing society / Michael Teague,
   University of Iowa, Sara Mackenzie, University of Washington, David
   Rosenthal, Columbia University.
Description: Eighth edition. | New York, NY : McGraw-Hill Education, [2021]
   | Includes index.
Identifiers: LCCN 2020031756 | ISBN 9781260260335 (hardcover) | ISBN
   9781260580044 (spiral bound) | ISBN 9781260580068 (ebook)
Subjects: LCSH: Health education. | Health promotion.
Classification: LCC RA440 .T43 2021 | DDC 362.1—dc23
LC record available at https://lccn.loc.gov/2020031756

The Internet addresses listed in the text were accurate at the time of publication. The inclusion of a website does not indicate an endorsement by the authors or McGraw-Hill LLC, and McGraw-Hill LLC does not guarantee the accuracy of the information presented at these sites.

mheducation.com/highered

Dear Readers,

The story of this book began over 20 years ago when three friends—a health educator, a family physician, and a family therapist—had a conversation about their beliefs about teaching health. While our clinical and academic paths differed, we found that we shared a fundamental belief that, although the individual plays a role in the wellness process, society has a responsibility to promote the well-being of all individuals. Many personal health books at the time focused on personal responsibility for health. That is indeed a major part of health, but we wanted to emphasize a model where individuals make health decisions within the context of their relationships, cultures, communities, policies, and physical surroundings. What eventually came of that conversation was the decision to create a book that emphasizes putting personal health in context.

Since we started working on the first edition of what became *Your Health Today*, we have visited health educators across the country and learned from their many different approaches to teaching personal health. Recently we have also been confronted with a public health crisis (COVID-19) that has confirmed our focus on public and personal health. As always, we have tried to incorporate a range of those experiences, strategies, and resources into our revisions and our own personal health courses.

Like instructors who use our book, we too have been challenged through the years by the dynamic nature of health. The world is changing—interpersonally, financially, politically, and environmentally—so, what does that mean to personal health? How do students of the 21st century learn best, and where does their current understanding of personal health come from? What will be the health priorities of the future? What skills will today's students need 20 years from now to maintain a healthy lifestyle? Examining history and our own beliefs about those questions encouraged us to incorporate several health topics that are not traditionally covered (or covered only briefly) in other personal health books. As learners, we also believe that today's students generally do not need to memorize facts so much as learn how to access and assess health information, critically consider implications, and respond. In essence, our program fills the need for an approach to personal health that balances individual and cultural responsibility.

Our mission and passion for this endeavor has remained true years later. We continue to learn how to create small change in personal, professional, and community lives in an attempt to improve the health outcomes for all future generations. We hope that the eighth edition will challenge students to think of themselves as agents of change. Students can make personal changes in lifestyle behaviors that affect their own health, and they can also influence communities to make changes in response to social, political, and economic factors that affect the health of broader segments of the population.

Michael Teague
Sara Mackenzie
David Rosenthal

Courtesy of Maria Richter

University of Washington School of Public Health

Courtesy of Rebecca Sale

Brief Contents

Contents

p. 3

Who knew so many
things influence the
choices you make?

(BJI/Blue Jean Images/Getty Images)

p. 67
Friendship matters to
your health.

(Susanne Walstrom/Getty Images)

p. 167

Physical activity benefits your physical, cognitive, and emotional health.

(Adam Pretty/Getty Images)

p. 198

Many body types and sizes can be associated with good health.

(WENN Ltd/ Alamy Stock Photo)

p. 264

Should recreational use of marijuana be legal?

(Yarygin/Shutterstock)

p. 337

How does hand-washing protect us from disease?

(princessdlaf/Getty Images)

p. 384

How does physical activity support cardiovascular health?

(Adam Hester/Getty Images)

p. 437

How loud is too loud?

(Orchid24/Shutterstock)

p. 507

What can and can't be recycled?

(jonya/Getty Images)

Learn Without Limits

Your Health Today teaches personal health from a perspective of social responsibility. While each of us has a unique set of individual characteristics that shape our health, environmental factors have an impact on our well-being, too. *Your Health Today* incorporates the individual, interpersonal, and broader social factors that affect our health, acting as a guide for healthy living in college and beyond.

The student-focused features in the eighth edition of *Your Health Today* highlight current topics, illustrate concepts with new photos and graphs, and invite dialogue among personal health students. These features serve as entry points to classroom discussion, critical thought, and practical application of health concepts to students' lives. Many also have accompanying assignable online activities within Connect.

Connect Is Proven Effective

 **McGraw-Hill Connect®** is a digital teaching and learning environment that improves performance over a variety of critical outcomes; it is easy to use, and it is proven effective. Connect® empowers students by continually adapting to deliver precisely what they need, when they need it, and how they need it, so your class time is more engaging and effective. Connect for Personal Health offers a wealth of interactive online content, including health labs and self-assessments, video activities on timely health topics, and practice quizzes with immediate feedback.

New to this edition, Application-Based Activities help your student assess their own health and behavior. Twelve new self-assessments and five new Portfolio Health Profiles include privacy controls to protect student data.

Personalized Learning

 Available within Connect, **SmartBook®** makes study time as productive and efficient as possible by identifying and closing knowledge gaps. SmartBook identifies what an individual student knows and doesn't know based on the student's confidence level, responses to questions, and other factors. SmartBook builds an optimal, personalized learning path for each student, so students spend less time on concepts they already understand and more time on those they don't. As a student engages with SmartBook, the reading experience continuously adapts by highlighting the most impactful content a student needs to learn at that moment in time. This ensures that every minute spent with SmartBook is returned to the student as the most value-added minute possible. The result? More confidence, better grades, and greater success.

SmartBook is optimized for phones and tablets and accessible for students with disabilities using interactive features.

Writing Assignment

McGraw-Hill's new Writing Assignment tool delivers a learning experience that improves students' written communication skills and conceptual understanding with every assignment. Assign, monitor, and provide feedback on writing more efficiently and grade assignments within McGraw-Hill Connect®. Writing Assignment gives students an all-in-one place interface, so you can provide feedback more efficiently.

Features include:

- Saved and reusable comments (text and audio).
- Ability to link to resources in comments.
- Rubric building and scoring.
- Ability to assign draft and final deadline milestones.
- Tablet ready and tools for all learners.

Dietary Analysis Tool

NutritionCalc Plus is a suite of powerful dietary self-assessment tools that help students track their food intake and activity and analyze their diet and health goals. Students and instructors can trust the reliability of the ESHA database while interacting with a robust selection of reports. This tool is provided at no additional charge inside Connect for *Your Health Today*.

Features of *Your Health Today*

Action Skill-Builders present manageable first steps in making meaningful behavior changes and show that a small change can make a big difference. Topics include moving toward healthier eating, getting a better night's sleep, overcoming barriers to physical activity, and discussing contraception.

Consumer Clipboards show students how to weigh information, evaluate product claims, and make savvy health-related choices in a world full of misinformation and gimmicks. Topics include getting the most out of menu labeling, evaluating online health information, and selecting a pair of running shoes.

Public Health Is Personal boxes highlight broader community factors that influence personal health. They ask students to consider how systemic factors and policies that might seem remote—free early childhood education, community-sponsored needle-exchange programs, or community walkability—can have a profound impact on individual health choices and priorities.

Who's at Risk? boxes highlight data that show inequities in health outcomes and trends among diverse groups of people: for example, causes of death by geographic region and race, drinking problems by gender, or illicit drug use by geographic region. Featuring graphs and visuals, these boxes invite students to consider and critically discuss systemic reasons for these trends.

Life Stories boxes feature lively and relatable stories that personalize chapter concepts and show how topics play out in real life. Among the topics covered are online genetic testing, unintended pregnancy, culture and eating habits, and sexual assault.

Starting the Conversation boxes are designed to invite meaningful classroom discussion. Each box poses a question, presents information to inform the discussion, and ends with two critical thinking questions. Topics in the eighth edition include the role of voting in affecting public policy, the reason asthma rates are rising, and proposals to lower the legal limit for driving under the influence.

You Make the Call features present the facts behind a contentious social issue, followed by the pros and cons of two opposing positions. Topics include health insurance access, marijuana legalization, vaccination requirements for college students, mandatory calorie counts on menus, and digital connectivity.

A **Personal Health Portfolio** activity accompanies each chapter and can be completed on paper or online. Each includes a self-assessment or journaling activity and self-reflection questions. Students explore their personal health strengths and challenges and reflect on how friends, family, culture, community, and policy influence their personal health decisions. Activities include developing a family health tree; monitoring sleep, food, and activity levels; and assessing personal levels of stress.

Chapter-by-Chapter Changes—Informed by Student Data

Changes to the eighth edition include new research findings, updated statistics, and current hot topics that affect students' health choices and challenges. We have used inclusive language whenever possible. New pictures were added to chapters for relevance. Personal Health Portfolios were updated as necessary and remain as appendices at the end of chapters for convenient student access.

Chapter 1: Self, Family, and Community

- Reorganized discussion of health equities and socioecological model. Heredity and creating a family health tree now make up the last section of the chapter.
- Updated discussion of population health and health equity, with international comparison.
- New discussion about a single-payer system for health care coverage.

Chapter 2: Mental Health and Stress

- Updated references.
- Updated prevalence statistics about mental illness and health.
- Mention of ketamine as a potential treatment for anxiety disorders.
- New figure showing average stress levels in the United States in 2018.
- Added Web-based and virtual reality PTSD interventions.

Chapter 3: Social Connections

- Updated references.
- New emphasis on the importance of social support.
- Expanded discussion of gender identities such as cisgender.
- New Action Skill-Builder box: Learning to be supportive of non-binary individuals.

Chapter 4: Sleep

- New You Make the Call box on whether fatal or injurious accidents caused by sleep deprivation should be viewed as criminal acts in the judicial system.
- New Life Stories box on managing indoor and outdoor light for sleep.
- New Consumer Clipboard box on sleep-tracking apps.
- Added discussion of sleep and thyroid gland.
- Expanded Starting the Conversation box to address in more depth how caffeine crash affects students' academic work.

Chapter 5: Nutrition

- New figure showing beverage nutrient ratings from the Beverage Guidance Panel.
- New Action Skill-Builder box on whether smoothies are really healthy.
- Added discussion of cell-cultured (plant-based) meat.
- New topic whether black pepper is healthy.
- New topic on gluten sensitivity's effects on the thyroid gland.
- New section on microwaving food and potential nutrient loss.
- New topic on the safety of professional/college concession food.
- New Starting the Conversation box on the future of food.

Chapter 6: Fitness

- Added section on posterior muscle training to offset anterior/posterior muscle imbalance.
- Expanded discussion of neuromuscular fitness to explain slow, mindful movement.
- New Action Skill-Builder box on neuroplasticity training.
- New section on conscious movement, which combines t'ai chi and mindful exercise.
- New section on micro-workouts such as face gym, pump, and kegel.
- Extensive new section on the exercise recovery industry (e.g., float tanks and blood flushing).
- New Action Skill-Builder box on urine charts and hydration.
- New box on cold therapy for exercise recovery.
- New You Make the Call box on use of student fees to build elaborate campus recreation centers.

Chapter 7: Body Weight and Body Composition

- Increased sensitivity to the role of language and bias in discussions of body composition.
- Updated and expanded discussion of the multifactorial effect of genes on body composition.

- Revised approach to types of diets that emphasize critical thinking about their characteristics and individual dieting goals.
- Increased emphasis on a holistic approach to body composition and health.
- New section on the role of gut microbiome and body composition.

Chapter 8: Body Image

- Continued focus on positive body image development and resiliency.
- Increased inclusion of gender identity and sexual identity formation.
- Updates on media role, incorporating social media and media literacy.
- Updated data on and discussion of body art and cosmetic surgery.

Chapter 9: Alcohol and Tobacco

- New section on safety of vaping.
- New section on pot-infused alcohol.
- Update on new alcohol fads, such as vodka eyeballing and vodka tampons.
- New section on whether Millennials and Generation Z are drinking less alcohol than previous generations.
- Update on law enforcement efforts to confront fake identification cards.

Chapter 10: Drugs

- Updated references and data.
- Updated information about uses of specific drugs.
- Description of use of ketamine for the treatment of depression.
- Updated and expanded You Make the Call box on marijuana legalization.

Chapter 11: Sexual Health

- New sections on intersex anatomy, orgasm gap, and sexual noncordance.
- A new Public Health Is Personal box on cybersexing as a public health issue.
- A new section on sex recission by Millennials and Generation Z.
- A new Action Skill-Builder box on dating apps and services as well as sexual predators.
- A new Starting the Conversation box on sex doll brothels.

Chapter 12: Reproductive Choices

- Reorganized presentation of contraceptives to emphasize long-acting reversible contraceptives.
- New Starting the Conversation box exploring access to reproductive health care.
- More inclusive language and data on sexual-minority and gender-minority reproductive health.
- New You Make the Call box exploring options to support early childhood development.

Chapter 13: Infectious Diseases

- New discussion of SARS-CoV2 and the COVID-19 disease pandemic.
- Updated Starting the Conversation box about influenza and COVID-19.
- Updated figure about the adult immunization schedule.
- Updated and expanded discussion of antibiotic resistance in both the chapter and the Public Health Is Personal box introducing the One Health model.
- Updated statistics and focus on prevention of HIV, including new sections on treatment as prevention (TasP), postexposure prophylaxis (PEP), and preexposure prophylaxis (PrEP).

Chapter 14: Cardiovascular Disease, Diabetes, Chronic Lung Diseases, and Dementia

- "Promoting Cardiovascular Health" focuses on the Life's Simple 7, behaviors and factors that promote cardiovascular health.
- Updated data on and impact of chronic diseases.
- New section discussing dementia.

Chapter 15: Cancer

- Updated cancer diagnosis and death data.
- New Starting the Conversation box exploring the role of racism as it relates to cancer.

Chapter 16: Injury and Violence

- New section on electric scooter safety.
- New section on ride-sharing services and sexual assault.
- New Starting the Conversation box on whether the sexual assault investigation process is biased against men of color.
- More in-depth discussion of the moral and legal clarity of the #MeToo movement's effects on sexual harassment.
- Updated discussion of children and vehicular heat stroke and the Hot Car Act.
- Revised personal health portfolio on injury.

Mc Graw Hill connect   Chapter 17: **Complementary and Integrative Medicine**

- Revisions throughout to reflect the National Center for Complementary and Alternative Medicine's name change to the National Center for Complementary and Integrative Health.

- New You Make the Call box exploring whether the U.S. government should regulate drug prices.

Mc Graw Hill connect   Chapter 18: **Environmental Issues**

- New You Make the Call box on whether plastic straws should be banned.

- Updated discussions of how ocean acidification and warming oceans affect sea life behavior and coral reef erosion.

- Updates on Trump administration's legislative actions on renewable and nonrenewable energy resources.

- Updated Personal Health Portfolio activity with more personal assessment instruments on carbon, water, and lifestyle footprints.

- New section on light pollution's effects on ecosystems and human biochemical rhythms, and how and why some communities are going dark.

- New in-depth discussion of climate change and wildfires, particularly pyro-C tornado vortex.

- Discussion of how climate change is affecting the polar vortex.

- New section on what the weather in U.S. towns will look like in 2080.

- More in-depth discussion of microplastic pollution in the world's oceans.

- Use of IPCC reports to update major environmental issues.

Your Course, Your Way

McGraw-Hill Create® is a self-service website

that allows you to create customized course materials using McGraw-Hill Education's comprehensive, cross-disciplinary content and digital products. You can even access third-party content such as readings, articles, cases, videos, and more.

- Select and arrange content to fit your course scope and sequence.
- Upload your own course materials.
- Select the best format for your students—print or eBook.
- Select and personalize your cover.
- Edit and update your materials as often as you'd like.

Experience how McGraw-Hill Education's Create empowers you to teach your students your way: http://create.mheducation.com.

Campus

McGraw-Hill Campus® is a groundbreaking service

that puts world-class digital learning resources just a click away for all faculty and students. All faculty—whether or not they use a McGraw-Hill title—can instantly browse, search, and access the entire library of McGraw-Hill instructional resources and services, including eBooks, test banks, PowerPoint slides, animations, and learning objects—from any Learning Management System (LMS), at no additional cost to an institution. Users also have single sign-on access to McGraw-Hill digital platforms, including Connect, Create, and Tegrity, a fully automated lecture caption solution.

Instructor Resources

Your Health Today offers an array of instructor resources for the personal health course:

Instructor's manual. The instructor's manual provides a wide variety of tools and resources for presenting the course, including learning objectives and ideas for lectures and discussions.

Test bank. By increasing the rigor of the test bank development process, McGraw-Hill has raised the bar for student assessment. Each question has been tagged for level of difficulty, Bloom's taxonomy, and topic coverage. Organized by chapter, the questions are designed to test factual, conceptual, and higher order thinking.

Test Builder. New to this edition and available within Connect, Test Builder is a cloud-based tool that enables instructors to format tests that can be printed and administered within a Learning Management System. Test Builder offers a modern, streamlined interface for easy content configuration that matches course needs, without requiring a download.

Test Builder enables instructors to:

- Access all test bank content from a particular title.
- Easily pinpoint the most relevant content through robust filtering options.
- Manipulate the order of questions or scramble questions and/or answers.
- Pin questions to a specific location within a test.
- Determine your preferred treatment of algorithmic questions.
- Choose the layout and spacing.
- Add instructions and configure default settings.

PowerPoint. The PowerPoint presentations highlight the key points of the chapter and include supporting visuals. All slides are WCAG compliant.

Acknowledgments

Thanks to the reviewers who provided feedback and suggestions for enhancing *Your Health Today. Special gratitude for Jessica Hille, Indiana University, for her contribution as a gender specialist.*

Claire Belles, Central Piedmont Community College

Matt Belles, Central Piedmont Community College

Tia Bennett, Northeastern State University

Deborah Blair, Sacramento City College

Debra Blanchard, Victor Valley College

William P. Brown, Victor Valley College

Clara Butler, Jackson State University

Tim Curry, College of Western Idaho

Matt Elbert, Northeastern State University

Katie Fitzgerald, Western Michigan University

Lisa-Marie Hamill, The Citadel

Dina Hayduk, Kutztown University

Brian Hickey, Tallahassee Community College

Tonya Huff, Riverside City College

Rich Hughes, Bakersfield College

Joan Humphrey, Youngstown State University

Jacqueline Jackson, Jackson State University

Lindsay Jackson, The Citadel

Karla Jones, Central Piedmont Community College

Michelle Lomonaco, The Citadel

Janice Lung, College of Western Idaho

Pamela MacKay, Victor Valley College

Mia Richter, University of Iowa

Keisha Robinson, Youngstown State University

Richard Szwaja, Western Michigan University

Nigel Thomas, Bronx Community College

Bob Vezeau, Kalamazoo Valley Community College

Natasha Woods, Mississippi Valley State University

Self, Family, and Community

1

Ever Wonder...

why it's so hard to break a bad habit?

how much your parents' health predicts your own?

how your neighborhood influences your health?

As individuals, we are all responsible for our own health. Each of us makes choices about how we live—about whether to be physically active, whether to eat a healthy diet, whether to get enough sleep, and whether to see a doctor. And yet to talk about health only as a matter of individual choice assumes that we are always aware of the choices we are making and that we are always "free" to make them. The truth is that there are differences in the way we live and the contexts in which we make decisions.

In this book, we explore personal health within the context of our social, cultural, and physical environment. We recognize that individuals are ultimately responsible for their own health, but we also know that people make healthier choices when the environment in which they live, learn, work, and play supports those choices. Our goal is to challenge and empower individuals to enact personal and collective change to improve their health and the health of their communities.

YOUR HEALTH IN CONTEXT

To begin, we explore the terms *health* and *well-being,* and then we explore the personal and community factors that shape and influence our personal health.

Qualities associated with well-being include self-confidence, optimism, a sense of humor, an active mind, vitality, and joy in life. *(Stockbyte/Getty Images)*

Health and Well-Being

health
A state of complete physical, mental, social, and spiritual well-being.

Traditionally, people were considered "healthy" if they did not have symptoms of disease. In 1947, the World Health Organization (WHO) broke new ground with its positive definition of **health** as a state of complete physical, mental, and social well-being, not merely the absence of disease and infirmity. *Physical health* refers to the biological integrity of the individual. *Mental health* includes emotional and intellectual capabilities, or the individual's subjective sense of well-being. *Social health* means the ability of the individual to interact effectively with other people and the social environment.[1]

More recently, a *spiritual domain* has been added to the WHO definition, reflecting the idea that people's value systems or beliefs have an impact on their overall health. Spiritual health does not require participation in a particular organized religion but suggests a belief in (or a search for) some type of greater or higher power that gives meaning and purpose to life. Spiritual health implies a connectedness to self, to significant others, and to the community.

How do you know whether you are healthy? Does your body physically do what you want it to do? Can you actively participate in daily life? Are your physical needs for food and shelter met? Do you awake feeling rested, mentally sharp, calm, and peaceful? Do you have a network of supportive family, friends, and colleagues? Are you active in your community? Does your life have meaning and purpose? Answers to these questions are connected to well-being—a sense of how you think and feel your life is going. Well-being is a relative state in which you maximize your physical and emotional functioning to live a full and satisfying life.

Throughout this book you will have many opportunities to assess your individual health. Self-assessment is a common tool to explore personal health and to discover whether there are areas of your health and well-being you want to improve. Surveys, such as the Personal Health Portfolio: Physical and Mental Health Assessment at the end of this chapter, can help you explore physical and mental functioning. Monitoring behaviors is another way to assess your physical and mental health, and you will have opportunities throughout the Personal Health Portfolios to journal and analyze such behaviors as sleep, physical activity, and nutrition. Sometimes biomarkers or laboratory findings are used to help individuals assess their health when an illness or disease has no symptoms, or to help identify why someone has symptoms. Recommended screening tests will be included as relevant in respective chapters. At other times, you can screen for risk factors—behaviors or markers—that increase your risk for developing a health problem down the road. Identifying these early can help you make changes to prevent illness and promote well-being.[2]

Your individual health and well-being are strongly influenced by the context in which you live, work, and play. Your community promotes or reduces your capacity for good health.

What Determines Health?

Because this is a personal health book, our focus will be on your personal behavior. However, it is impossible to ignore the fact that individual behavior occurs in a context—we do not all have the same social, economic, environmental, and structural opportunities to be healthy. As shown in Figure 1.1,

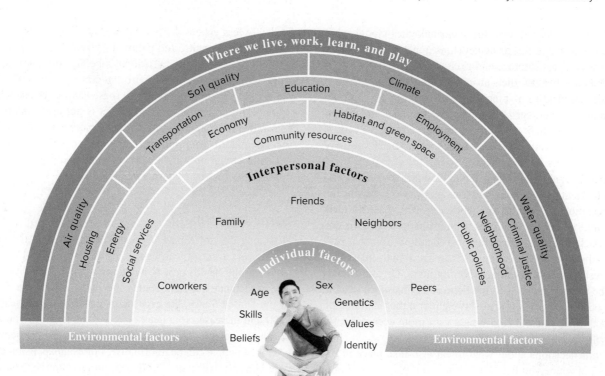

figure 1.1 **The socioecological model of health.**
Our health is shaped both by our unique set of individual characteristics and by the context in which we live. *(BJI/Blue Jean Images/Getty Images)*
Source: Rudolph, L., Caplan, J., Ben-Moshe, K., & Dillon, L. (2013). *Health in all policies: A guide for state and local governments.* Washington, DC, and Oakland, CA: American Public Health Association and Public Health Institute.

the **socioecological model of health** identifies the complex levels and interrelationships that influence your health. We can use it not only to understand differences in health outcomes between people but also as a framework to consider how to take action to improve health outcomes.

You are situated in the center as an individual. Your unique set of characteristics—genetics, age, sex, gender, sexual identity, economics, race, and ethnicity— along with your knowledge, beliefs, values, and skills frame the way you experience the world and guide the decisions you make about how to live your life. But you do not live in isolation—you live within social and physical environments. These environments include your relationships with other people, community resources, the physical and built environment, and the public policies that affect each. These complex environments can either create opportunities for you to achieve your full health potential or limit your ability to do so. Our communities have historical context with norms, values, opportunities, and sanctions.

According to the socioecological model, friends, family, community norms, economic, social and public policy, and even global events such as climate change affect your health opportunities. In addition, society's practices shape your environment in ways that increase or decrease your opportunities for making health or unhealthy choices. For example, if your neighborhood has sidewalks and safe parks, you are more likely to get out and walk. If affordable housing is located near good

schools, you are more likely to receive a better education, which prepares you for a better job. The complex external factors that influence an individual's and a population's health are known as the **social determinants of health**. This term highlights that the conditions in which you are born, grow, live, work, and age influence the options you have and the choices you make. Social determinants include income, economic status, educational attainment, literacy, employment status, working conditions, housing, transportation, social support networks, and access to health care services.[3,4,5]

Environmental factors that influence your health can be divided into built and natural factors. The *built* environment—human-made components such as housing, traffic flow, schools, sanitation, and transportation systems—and factors in the *natural* environment—such as air and water quality, weather, proximity to environmental hazards, and access to parks and natural settings—all affect your health.[6,7]

How does the socioecological model play out in your life? As an example, let's say you decide you want to have a

socioecological model of health
A framework that recognizes the interrelationship between individuals and their environment; emphasizes that where we live, work, and play strongly influences our health.

social determinants of health
Societal conditions that affect health and can potentially be altered by social and health policies and programs.

healthier diet. According to the socioecological model, what influences your ability to achieve this goal? First, consider your knowledge, attitudes, and skills—knowledge about what constitutes a healthy diet, attitudes toward different foods and diets, and skills at preparing and cooking. In addition, depending on your genetic predisposition, age, and health conditions, you may need to pay extra attention to certain components of your diet, such as salt or sugars if you have high blood pressure or diabetes.

Next, consider how your family, friends, coworkers, and peers influence your eating patterns. As you were growing up, you became familiar with the foods your family ate. In turn, your family's food preferences were influenced by their cultural background and geographical location. You may still prefer those foods. Your friends may like to eat out at fast-food restaurants, and you may go with them. Or your friends may be vegetarian, so you find yourself eating more vegetarian foods. If your friends are overweight or if they gain weight, it's likely that you will find weight gain more acceptable for yourself.[8,9]

Your decisions about what to eat also take place in the context of where you live, work, learn, and play. Your dining hall may have fresh salad bars or only serve fried foods. Your church may serve fruit or donuts after services. In your neighborhood, you may have opportunities to buy local fresh fruits and vegetables, or you may have a corner store that only stocks candy and liquor. Your income also significantly affects your diet because fast foods and packaged and processed foods are less expensive than fresh fruits, vegetables, meats, and nuts. Local, state, and national laws influence the safety of the food you eat, its nutritional labeling, and its cost. Finally, global climate and environmental changes influence the world food supply.[10] When all these factors are taken into account, it is clear that a healthy diet is not just a matter of your individual choices—though the choices you make within the context of your environment are critical. Promoting healthful eating options locally and nationally provides the opportunity for you to have a healthy diet.

Population Health

How long do you expect to live? Life expectancy, the number of years a person can expect to live, is a key tool used in assessing the health of a population or group of individuals. Life expectancy has significantly increased around the world. In the United States, life expectancy at birth was 50 years in 1900 and increased to a peak of 78.9 years in 2015. You may be pleased about this trend. However, comparing between groups of people can be informative. For example, if you compare U.S. life expectancy to that of other countries, you may be surprised. In 1960, the United States had the highest life expectancy among high-income countries. But since 1980, we have gradually fallen behind improvements in other countries. If there had been a "health Olympics" in 2018, the United States would have placed 36th for life expectancy, behind countries such as Chile, Lebanon, and Cuba[11,12] (Figure 1.2).

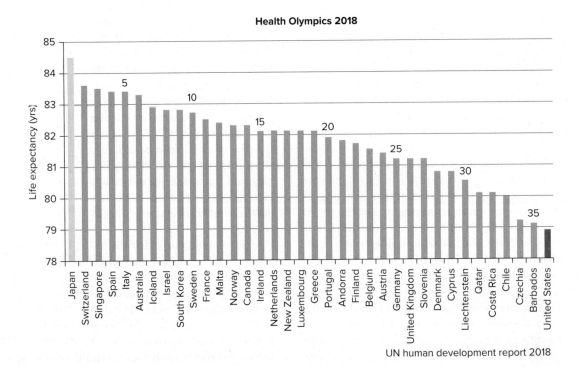

Health Olympics 2018

UN human development report 2018

figure 1.2   **Health Olympics 2018, life expectancy in 36 countries.**
Sources: University of Washington, School of Public Health. (2019). Retrieved from http://depts.washington.edu/eqhlth/; United Nations Development Program. (2019). Table 1, *Human development report.* Retrieved from http://www.hdr.undp.org/sites/default/files/2019_human_development_statistical_update.pdf

Even more concerning, between 2015 and 2017, we saw a decrease in U.S. life expectancy for the first time. In 2018, the decline appears to have stopped.[13] To understand and address this growing disadvantage, we must explore population health.

Population health is the study of health outcomes in or between groups of individuals. The populations (or groups of individuals) of interest might be people living in one country versus another, as shown in Figure 1.2, or comparisons between people living in urban and rural areas. Other **demographics**, statistical information about groups of people, that researchers consider include gender, age, sexual orientation, ability or disability, race/ethnicity, educational attainment, socioeconomic status, and geographical location. As an individual, you belong to many different "populations," and the intersecting advantages and disadvantages of each population will influence your health. Measuring differences in health outcomes between populations allows us to document and investigate why health gains are not equally shared, and it creates opportunity for intervention.

Health Equity

Over the past 100 years, advances in medical technology, living conditions, and environmental protections have produced significant health gains around the world. These advances, however, have not produced equal health benefits for all. Differences in health outcomes between specific populations, such as differences between racial or ethnic groups, are **health disparities**. Such differences can exist across a multitude of dimensions such as gender, sexual orientation, disability status, geographical residence, economic status, and educational attainment. Disparities can result from systemic and avoidable social and economic practices and policies that create barriers to opportunity for some groups. **Health equity** occurs when all people have the equal opportunity to attain their full health potential.[14] The "Who's at Risk?" boxes will highlight differences in risk factors or health outcomes throughout each chapter. We encourage you to consider the complex factors at the individual, interpersonal, community, and policy levels that contribute to differences in health outcomes. To start, let's consider a few—geography, ethnicity and race, socioeconomic status, health care, and age—as they can affect opportunity and health.

Geography Life expectancy is not the only measure in which the United States has fallen behind peer countries. In comparison to 16 other high-income countries (Australia, Austria, Canada, Denmark, Finland, France, Germany, Italy, Japan, Norway, Portugal, Spain, Sweden, Switzerland, the Netherlands, and the United Kingdom), the following facts apply:

- U.S. children are more likely to die at birth and less likely to live to age 5.

- U.S. adolescents are more likely to die from homicide and motor vehicle crashes and have higher rates of unplanned pregnancy and sexually transmitted infections.

- U.S. adults lose more years to alcohol and drug addiction.

- U.S. adults have the highest rates of obesity and diabetes.

Overall, compared to those in peer countries, people in the United States have the lowest probability of surviving to age 50. If they do survive to 50, they have higher rates of lung disease, cardiovascular disease, and disability.[15] Within the United States, health gains have not been shared equally. In urban areas, life expectancy is two years longer than that in rural areas, which should lead us to ask why. What is the cause of these differences?

We can look at rates of specific diseases and risk factors for diseases. Rural areas have higher rates of heart disease, cancer, unintentional injury, tobacco use, and obesity.[16] What causes the differences in risk factors? We see different rates of educational attainment and job opportunities. We should again ask why. Then we will notice that there are policies leading to differences in economics, social networks, and resource distribution based on geography that all affect opportunities. This practice of looking at all causes helps us examine the complexity of factors that influence individual health.

Approximately 86 percent of the U.S. population now lives in urban centers. Migration into urban areas has been the common trend, but we are seeing a slight shift in the pattern since 2016. Now people are moving toward non-metropolitan areas.[17] When we take a closer look within states and counties, we see that health outcomes can differ between neighboring zip codes. For example, life expectancy in the north end of Seattle is 14 years longer than in the south end of Seattle. Neighboring residential areas differ in opportunities for employment, education, safety, and public service.[18]

population health
The health outcomes of a group of individuals, including the distribution of those outcomes within the group.

demographics
The statistical characteristics of a population in terms of such categories as age, gender, ethnicity and race, income, disability, geographical location, and migration patterns.

health disparities
Differences in health outcomes between populations.

health equity
When all people have the opportunity to attain their full health potential.

Ethnicity and Race The United States has always been a multicultural country, and it will become even more diverse as the 21st century unfolds. Immigration currently accounts for approximately 50 percent of population growth in the United States. According to the U.S. Census Bureau, the primary racial/ethnic groups in the country are Black or African American, American Indian and Alaska Native, Asian, Native Hawaiian and Other Pacific Islander, and white. Hispanic origin is treated as a separate category because people of Hispanic origin may be of any race or ethnic group. Within each group, there is tremendous diversity: Asian Americans, for example, include people from China, Japan, Korea,

Who's at Risk?
Variations in Causes of Death Among Americans

Equity in health is achieved when all people have the same opportunity to live healthy lives. Comparing groups of people (or populations) is a way to explore if there are differences in health outcomes between groups and creates an opportunity to ask what factors may be contributing to inequities. Throughout the book, we will identify differences in health outcomes between certain groups of people—sometimes by race, economic status, gender, or sexual identity—as follows:

- The rate of diagnosis of diabetes is twice as high among American Indian/Alaska Native adults than among whites.

- Rates of hospitalization for asthma in children under the age of 5 are five times higher among Blacks and Hispanics than among non-Hispanic whites.

- The rate of maternal mortality (dying related to a complication of pregnancy) is three times as high among non-Hispanic Black women as that for non-Hispanic white women.

Can you hypothesize factors that may be contributing to these differences? Think about each level of the socioecological model. What social, economic, political, or cultural components may be involved?

Sources: Centers for Disease Control and Prevention. (2016). *Strategies for reducing health disparities—selected CDC sponsored interventions—U.S. 2016. MMWR Supplement, 65*(1); Centers for Disease Control and Prevention. (2019). Vital signs: Pregnancy-related deaths, U.S. 2011-2015, and Strategies for Prevention, 13 states, 2013–2017. *MMWR, 68.*

---

ethnicity
The sense of identity an individual draws from national, religious, tribal, language, and cultural origins.

race
A term used in the social sciences to describe ethnic groups based on physical characteristics; race does not exist as a biological reality.

Vietnam, Laos, Cambodia, the Philippines, and many other countries. In 2018, approximately 39 percent of the population consisted of members of racial or ethnic minority groups. In Hawaii, California, New Mexico, Texas, the District of Columbia, Nevada, Puerto Rico, and other states, minorities are the new majority—that is, non-Hispanic whites now make up less than 50 percent of the population.[19]

Ethnicity refers to the sense of identity individuals draw from a common ancestry, as well as from common national, religious, tribal, language, and cultural origins. Ethnic identity nurtures a sense of social belonging, helping to shape how we think, feel, and behave both within and outside our group. Ethnicity is often confused with **race**, a term used to describe ethnic groups based on physical characteristics such as skin color or facial features. Although classifying people by race has been a common practice, the fact is that biologically distinct and separate races do not exist within the human species. Genetic traits are inherited individually, not in groups or "races." Thus, it is more accurate to view race as a social category than a biological one and to think of similarities or differences among people as a matter of culture or ethnicity.[15,20]

When we look at rates of illness and death for ethnic and racial minority populations, we see differences in health outcomes that should lead us to ask why. For example, in the United States, Black and American Indian/Alaska Native women are 3.3 and 2.5 times more likely to die in childbirth, respectively, than white women.[21] Many minorities have higher rates of cancer, diabetes, cardiovascular disease, infant mortality, alcoholism, drug abuse, unintentional injury, and

premature death than the general population does (see the box, "Who's at Risk? Variations in Causes of Death Among Americans"). When we consider racial/ethnic differences (or differences among any marginalized group), we have to consider the role of racism and discrimination at the individual and systemic levels. At the individual level, racism and discrimination lead to chronic stress. At the systemic level, historical and ongoing discriminatory practices in housing, criminal justice, and educational systems perpetuate and exacerbate the problem of limited access to social, economic, and environmental resources and to opportunity.[15,20,22]

Socioeconomic Status Complicating, or perhaps explaining, geographical and racial/ethnic differences is socioeconomic status. It has possibly the most significant impact on health outcomes, with worse health status being strongly associated with poverty. Poverty creates a vicious cycle as it limits access to education, job opportunities, safe housing, food, and transportation. Low socioeconomic status

■ Health disparities between racial and ethnic groups are largely attributable to social and economic conditions. A poor neighborhood does not provide the same opportunities for a healthy life as a more affluent neighborhood.
(Filadendron/E+/Getty Images)

increases overall stress levels. People are more vulnerable if something goes wrong—such as unexpected medical expenses or a car that breaks down. Living in lower-income communities exposes children and families to increased levels of violence. The absence or existence of policies such as minimum wage requirements, parental leave legislation, and residential zoning laws can either perpetuate cycles of poverty or create opportunities for families to have equitable access to factors that influence health.[20,23]

Income inequality—the gap between rich and poor within a population—also has a strong negative impact on health. This is particularly disconcerting in the United States because, since the 1980s, we have experienced unprecedented increases in income inequality. Compared to communities with low levels of income inequality, those with higher levels have worse health outcomes in almost all areas: shorter life expectancy, more physical and mental health problems, increased violence, weaker community ties, and decreased trust.[24,25]

Health Care In the United States, we spend nearly twice as much per person on health care than any other country in the world, amounting to nearly 20 percent of our gross domestic product (GDP). Yet, based on what we have explored so far, we do not appear to be getting our money's worth, with shorter life expectancy and poorer health outcomes in many areas than other high-income countries. We differ from other high-income countries in that all other countries provide universal access to health care in some form, but we actually use health care services at the same rate as other countries. The price of medications and the cost to administer our health care system appear to be the main drivers of expenses.[26]

While health care is important, it is responsible for only an estimated 10 percent of health outcomes. Health behavior, genetics, and social and environmental factors play a much larger role. As you consider your personal and community health, consider the social, economic, and environmental factors outside the health care system.[26,27]

Age A life-course approach to health is important because our health trajectory plays out over our life span and even across generations. Higher rates of chronic illness are expected in older populations, making awareness of the age distribution in a population important for health and community planning. If we look at the overall leading causes of death for all ages, we see that the major health concerns are chronic diseases—heart disease, cancer, stroke, diabetes, chronic respiratory diseases—and the lifestyle behaviors that contribute to them. The overall makeup of the U.S. population is changing in terms of age. With the large baby boomer generation (those born between 1946 and 1964) reaching retirement age, the nation is aging. This profile places complex new pressures on society and the economy as the number of people in retirement facilities increases quickly while the number of people in the workforce decreases.

Given the relationship between age and health, perhaps the more important concept in a life-course approach is recognizing that there are critical phases in your life during which healthy or harmful environments have the potential for greater impact. It is increasingly clear that early adverse childhood experiences (ACEs) significantly affect long-term health. The United States has more children growing up in poverty and with less social mobility than in peer countries. Children raised in poverty experience higher rates of poor nutrition, greater exposure to toxins, and fewer educational opportunities. Children with ACEs have higher rates of mental and physical illness and participate in more risky behaviors (such as substance use, smoking, and unsafe sex). Every dollar invested early saves money down the road by preventing worse health outcomes. Family-leave policies and early childhood programming have been shown to improve health outcomes, for instance. Adolescence is another critical transitional period during which completion of high school, college education, and healthy behaviors can improve life-course trajectory.[23,28]

YOUR HEALTH AND YOUR COMMUNITY'S HEALTH

By now you should be aware that your community influences you and that you will have opportunities to influence aspects of your community. Responsibility for health and well-being extends beyond the individual to public health practices and policies.

Natural disasters affect whole populations. Forest fires, for instance, can necessitate the evacuation of entire communities. Preparing for, and responding to, their needs falls into the domain of public health.
(Elmer Frederick Fischer/Corbis)

Public Health Is Personal

What Is Public Health?

The benefits of public health are all around you, reducing your risk for disease and injury and helping you live a healthier life.

When you get up in the morning, you brush your teeth with the water from your tap. In general, you don't worry about contracting an infectious disease from tap water in the United States because your local health department monitors the water in an attempt to keep it safe. You have had fewer cavities and dental problems than people did a century ago because the tap water you drink contains fluoride, which strengthened your teeth when you were younger.

If you drive to campus, you buckle your seat belt out of habit. Your state has seat belt laws in place to reduce traffic fatalities, and even if you would prefer not to buckle up, you do not want to get a ticket. If you bike to campus, you can avoid dodging cars by taking the bike lane, which has been put in place to protect bicyclists. You meet a friend for a bagel and cream cheese before class. You don't worry about eating the food from a coffee shop because sanitation inspectors ensure that all restaurants follow regulations that reduce incidences of foodborne illness.

After breakfast, you continue your commute to school, past "clean buses" that run on emissions-controlled diesel as part of your city's green energy campaign. A road worker directs you around a lane closure, where construction workers are wearing helmets and hearing protection, following occupational safety and health laws.

You enter your class building, where the air you breathe is fresh and smoke-free. Because tobacco smoke has been recognized as a health hazard, your campus follows regulations that prohibit smoking within 25 feet of public buildings.

After class, you head to the campus health center to pick up a month's worth of contraceptive supplies. You and your partner are not ready for pregnancy; you're planning to delay starting a family until after you finish school. While at the center, you pass signs promoting HIV/AIDS awareness and a supply of free condoms. Free vaccinations are available as part of a campaign to reduce students' risk of illness during the approaching flu season.

Later in the day, you go for a run on a trail in a city park near your home. People are out walking their dogs and obeying the signs to clean up after them in compliance with local ordinances. On your way home, you stop at a local grocery store to pick up some fruit and packaged foods for dinner. You assume the ingredients list printed on the packaged foods accurately reflects what is in them because food-labeling laws have been in place your whole life. When you get home, you know you need to wash the fruit you bought, just as you know you should wash your hands frequently. The wealth of information you have about keeping yourself well and safe comes from the health education you have received in your schools and community.

Ten great public health achievements in the past century include vaccination, motor vehicle safety, safer workplaces, control of infectious diseases, safer and healthier foods, healthier mothers and babies, family planning, fluoridation of drinking water, the recognition of tobacco as a health hazard, and reduced deaths from heart attacks and stroke. Beyond these achievements, innumerable other developments and advances have contributed to your health, including health education initiatives and campaigns. In this book, you can learn more about public health from the "Public Health Is Personal" boxes that appear in each chapter and draw your attention to the different ways that your personal health depends on public health.

McGraw Hill connect

Source: Centers for Disease Control and Prevention. (1999; updated 2013). Ten great public health achievements— United States, 1900–1999. *Morbidity and Mortality Weekly Reports, 48*(12), 241–243. Retrieved from http://www.cdc.gov/about/history/tengpha.htm

Public Health

public health
The study and practice of health promotion and disease prevention at the population level.

health promotion
Public health–related actions designed to maintain a current healthy state or advance to a more desirable state.

disease prevention
Public health–related actions designed to ward off or protect against specific diseases.

Your health is inherently linked to the health of the people around you. **Public health** is a discipline that focuses on the health of populations of people (in contrast, the discipline of medicine focuses on the health of individuals). Public health efforts include both health promotion and disease prevention. **Health promotion** consists of actions designed to maintain a current health state or encourage a more desirable one (such as campaigns to promote physical activity). **Disease prevention** focuses on defensive actions to ward off specific diseases and their consequences (such as food and water safety standards, physical distancing requirements, recommendations to wear masks, or flu shot campaigns). Public health measures can improve the health of populations through education, engineering, and enforcement (see the box "Public Health Is Personal: What Is Public Health?"). Public health initiatives must balance the needs and rights of individuals against the needs and rights of other members of the population.

Community Health

Public health systems are public (government), private, and voluntary agencies that work together to ensure the health and safety of society. In the United States, multiple federal agencies work in partnership to promote and protect health. Housed within the Department of Health and Human Services, these include the Centers for Disease Control and Prevention (CDC), which works nationally and internationally to assess, monitor, and act to protect health; the Food and Drug Administration (FDA), which is responsible for promoting and protecting the food systems and regulating tobacco and medication safety; the National Institute for Health (NIH), which supports research for innovation; and the Indian Health Services (IHS), which is responsible for providing federal health services to American Indians and Alaska Natives as per treaties and laws. The states, tribes, and territories have the authority to carry out monitoring, reporting, and enforcement of health-related policies and procedures. They work with county health departments or health districts that perform essential services, including diagnosing and investigating disease outbreaks, monitoring community health status, organizing health promotion campaigns, and establishing and enforcing local policies. In addition, they lead and establish partnerships with other nongovernmental groups in the community.[29,30]

A healthy community provides services that support the health and wellness of community members. As an example, green spaces, sidewalks, and trails encourage physical activity. *(miljko/E+/Getty Images)*

Nongovernmental organizations promote population health by researching, educating people about, and advocating for a range of health-related issues, including environmental rights, women's health, economic development, health care, and cancer research. An increasing need for work by agencies and organizations not traditionally considered health-related has arisen due to the vital role of social determinants in health.[31] For example, city planners may not consider themselves in a health-related field, but parks and community walkability directly influence health and are determined by zoning and planning decisions.

Community implies an interdependence between people and organizations within a defined region. A community has historically been defined by geographical boundaries rather than by people with shared characteristics, and it specifically recognizes ties and connections within the community. **Community health** refers to activities directed toward improving the health of those people, or activities employing resources shared by the members of the community. For example, the health department in a town (the community) with a large immigrant population may decide as part of its COVID-19 pandemic response to design messages in different languages to reach all members of the community. Ideally, the health department would create partnerships with members of the various groups within the town to ensure cultural sensitivity, relevance, and engagement. Research suggests that a healthy community is one that meets the basic needs of *all* its members, offering adequate housing; transportation; access to quality schools, health care, healthy foods, and parks; job opportunities and living wages; and opportunities for civic engagement and social cohesion free from violence.[31]

Communities can plan their services better when they understand population trends (demographics) that affect their members. For example, the growth of Hispanic populations in non-metropolitan areas suggests that services in rural areas increasingly need to be bilingual or multilingual.[23] Knowing the composition of communities helps community members address the needs of all.

community health Issues, events, and activities related to the health of a whole community, as well as activities directed toward bettering the health of the public and/or activities employing resources available in common to members of the community.

The *Healthy People* Initiative

Another example of government role and interest in the health of the population is the *Healthy People* initiative, an effort among federal, state, and territorial governments and community partners (private and public) to set health objectives for the United States. The objectives identify the significant preventable threats to health and establish goals for improving the quality of life for all.[32] The U.S. government issued the first *Healthy People* report in 1980 and has issued revised reports every 10 years since then.

Healthy People 2030 continues to envision "a society in which all people can achieve their full potential for health and well-being across the lifespan" and sets the following broad national health goals[33]:

- Attain healthy, thriving lives free of preventable disease, disability, injury, and premature death

- Achieve health equity, eliminate disparities, and achieve health literacy to improve the health of all

- Create social, physical, and economic environments that promote attaining full potential health and well-being for all

- Promote healthy development, healthy behaviors, and well-being across all life stages

Healthy People emphasizes "health determinants"—factors that affect the health of individuals, communities, or entire populations. Using the same concepts as the socioecological model, the report focuses on the range of personal, social, economic, and environmental factors that affect health. It also takes a life-stages focus by recognizing that risk factors are different at different life stages, so interventions are more effective at different critical moments. The report emphasizes the importance of reducing health disparities—differences in health outcomes between populations. We see again that race or ethnicity, socioeconomic status, gender, sexual identity, age, and geographical location can all contribute to differences in health outcomes.

The *Healthy People* initiative identifies the nation's "leading health indicators"—a set of priority public health issues that can be targeted and measured—as follows:

- Nutrition, physical activity, and obesity

- Maternal, infant, and child health

- Tobacco

- Substance abuse

- Reproductive and sexual health

- Mental health

- Injury and violence

- Environmental quality

- Clinical preventive services (such as immunizations)

- Access to health care

- Oral health

- Social determinants of health[32]

These indicators are intended to motivate individuals and communities to take action by helping identify areas where action is necessary.

Individual Choice Versus Societal Responsibility

The socioecological model shows us how individual and societal factors are involved in creating outcomes in everyday life. Within this context, some thorny ethical questions arise:

- To what extent are individuals responsible for their choices, given the powerful influence of environment? Does someone who drinks excessively to suppress memories of childhood poverty and trauma have the same right to a liver transplant as a child with liver cancer?

- To what extent should individuals be held accountable if their choices pose a cost to society, such as the cost of fighting a fire caused by someone smoking in bed, the cost of EMTs at the scene of a motorcycle crash where the rider wasn't wearing a helmet, or the cost of medical care for a heart attack patient who ignored advice to lose weight and exercise?

- To what extent is government justified in enacting laws, regulations, and policies to "nudge" individuals toward better choices, such as requiring masks, vaccinations or adding taxes on tobacco, alcohol, or sugary beverages?

- What are the responsibilities of society to protect individuals and those around them from poor choices, such as drinking and driving? When should society take action to prevent individuals from participating in risky behaviors? When are violations of confidentiality or restrictions on individual rights justified for the sake of the "greater good," such as reporting sexually transmitted infections and requiring quarantine for people who have had close contact to someone with COVID-19?

- To what extent is health a basic right? Should all people be assured access to food, shelter, safety, and health care? Given the rising costs of health care, how do we distribute services—by ability to pay or by ensuring all have access to certain services? How do we prioritize community safety nets to buffer the effects of economic and social conditions?

Your life is influenced by policies related to questions like these. Your behavior is constrained by certain policies—think of seat belt laws, speed limits, drinking age laws, and gun control laws—because your choices have effects on others and on society. When you are making decisions, whether choosing a personal behavior or supporting or opposing a public policy, consider this complex web of relationships and interactions. In particular, ask yourself the following: How great a risk does this behavior pose for the individual and for the community? How strongly do individuals oppose restrictions on their ability to participate in the behavior? How much evidence is there that imposing a restriction will affect behavior? Are there social or environmental factors that limit the options available for an individual's "choice"? Are some populations more or less affected by policies? Use these questions to inform your thinking and guide you in making reasoned, responsible decisions.

YOUR PERSONAL HEALTH CHOICES

Now that you understand something about factors that influence your health, let's consider choices you can make that affect how it all plays out in your life. The sociological model makes it clear that there are many levels at which you can affect your health. In this section, we look at how your behavior choices affect your health and how you might change unhealthy behaviors.

Health-Related Behavior Choices

Your health-related behavior choices (or lifestyle choices) are actions you take and decisions you make that affect your individual health (and, possibly, the health of your immediate family members, friends, and community). They include choices concerning your physical, mental, social, and spiritual well-being—what you eat, how much you exercise, whether you spend time developing meaningful relationships, and so on. For example, having an apple instead of a bag of chips is a healthy behavior choice, as is quitting smoking. Other examples are getting enough sleep, practicing safer sex, wearing a seat belt in a car, finding effective ways to manage stress, drinking alcohol in moderation if at all, and getting regular health checkups.

Interesting questions arise when we consider why people make choices that don't enhance their health and why they don't change behaviors they know are hurting them. Psychologists have proposed many theories about health behavior choice and change. The Health Belief Model and the Stages of Change Model are especially useful.

The Health Belief Model

The **Health Belief Model** was developed in the 1950s as a framework for understanding why people make the health choices they do. According to the model, health behaviors are influenced by four perceptions[34]:

- *Perceived susceptibility.* Do you believe you are at risk for a problem?

- *Perceived seriousness of consequences.* Do you perceive the problem as serious if it were to occur?

- *Perceived benefits of specific action.* If you change behavior, do you believe it will reduce the threat?

- *Perceived barriers to taking action.* What factors will get in the way of your making a change, such as environment, time, money, or beliefs? Think of the socioecological model!

To illustrate how this works, imagine that you are a smoker in a family where people are prone to heart disease. Your uncle and your grandfather died from heart disease at relatively young ages. You know that your smoking habit increases your risk for this disease (*perceived susceptibility*) and that your continuing the habit could lead to an early death (*perceived seriousness of consequences*). If you quit, you reduce your risk for heart disease within a few years and you don't have to go outside to smoke because smoking is banned in the residence hall (*perceived benefit of specific action*). However, most of your friends smoke, and it would be hard to hang out with them and resist a cigarette (*perceived barrier to taking action*). According to the Health Belief Model, all these considerations enter into your decision-making process when you think about quitting smoking.

In the chapters to come, you will encounter information and ideas that may prompt you to consider changing your health behavior in one way or another. You will examine a variety of factors that affect your health, such as the nutritional content of your favorite foods, the amount of exercise you get, and your choices around alcohol and drugs. You will be asked to consider how community resources and policies create barriers or benefits. You might even begin to consider how your future voting patterns, community work, or career choice might influence those barriers or benefits. One way to organize your decision-making process is by using the concepts offered by the Health Belief Model.

The Stages of Change Model

Developed in the 1990s by psychologists James Prochaska and Carlo Di-Clemente, the **Stages of Change Model**, or Transtheoretical Model (TTM), is another widely accepted framework for understanding individual health behavior change. The model recognizes that change happens as a process, not a one-time event. It takes into account not only a person's knowledge but also his or her feelings, behaviors, relationships, and perceived **self-efficacy**, or the belief that he or she can perform a certain task. The stages of change are as follows:

Health Belief Model A model of behavior change that uses the constructs of perceived susceptibility, seriousness of consequences, benefits of action, and barriers to action.

Stages of Change Model A model of behavior change that focuses on stages of change.

self-efficacy An internal state in which you feel competent to perform a specific task.

- *Precontemplation.* In this stage, you have no motivation to change a behavior. In fact, you may not even realize or acknowledge that you have a problem. You just want people to quit bothering you about your behavior. Discrepancies between your behaviors and your goals may make you move to contemplation.

- *Contemplation.* You realize you have a problem behavior. You think you should make a change in the near future (within six months). You try to understand the problem and may search for solutions. You weigh the pros and cons of making a change. Self-efficacy is important because you are more likely to prepare for change if you believe in yourself and the fact that you can change.

- *Preparation.* The pros win and you have a plan for change. You set goals and a start date. You increase your sense of self-efficacy by building your skill set and finding tools to help support the change.

- *Action.* You implement behavior change. You commit time and energy to make it work. From this point forward, you support your efforts to change by rewarding yourself for change, avoiding environments that trigger the unhealthy behavior, and enlisting the help of friends and family.

- *Maintenance.* You have been doing the new behavior for at least six months. You are working to prevent yourself from falling back into old habits. You are well on your way! This can be a long, ongoing stage—sometimes lasting a lifetime.

- *Termination.* The new behavior has become such a part of your life that you have no temptation to return to the old behavior, and you have 100 percent confidence in your ability to maintain the new behavior.[34,35]

relapse
A backslide into a former health state.

Understanding that change is a process with different stages is important because you may need different information or different types of support, depending on where you are in the process (some examples are included in the list of stages). It's also important to realize that change is not a steady upward climb. You can get on or off any step in the process, and you may slip on some or all of the steps and have to repeat them (Figure 1.3). Most of us have to try several times to make a change before it really sticks. **Relapse** is the rule rather than the exception. You should see it not as failure but as a normal part of the process. The important thing is to keep trying and not get discouraged.

Let's consider an example of the stages of change. Say you are determined to get better grades this term, especially in psychology, your major. To improve, you've been studying a lot in the afternoons and drinking coffee and energy drinks to stay focused. Unfortunately, you keep oversleeping and missing your 8:00 a.m. psych class, where surprise quizzes are often given. Because you've missed several quizzes, your grade is suffering. The reason you're oversleeping is that you're having trouble falling asleep at night, which you've been attributing to stress. You don't make the connection between the caffeine you're consuming in the afternoon and your insomnia. This sort of behavior marks the precontemplation stage, in which you do not recognize that your caffeine consumption may be causing you a problem.

(Mark Dierker/McGraw-Hill Education)

When a friend mentions that you might sleep better if you cut out the caffeine, your first thought is that you really enjoy those drinks in the afternoon and might not be able to study without them. But then you start to weigh the benefits of caffeine (you feel sharper, you can concentrate more easily) against the problem of insomnia (you oversleep and miss class). This thought process marks the contemplation stage, in which you weigh the pros and cons of behavior change.

You decide to try decaffeinated coffee and see what happens. You buy some decaf at the grocery store (preparation) and make a switch the following week, at the same time cutting out energy drinks (action). Although you feel fuzzier and less focused at first, and you have a pounding headache for a day, you are able to get to sleep more easily and start making it to class. You ace some of the quizzes, so you know your grade will be going up. You also notice how much better you feel, and how much sharper your mind is, when you get enough sleep.

A few weeks later, you're at a friend's house and she offers you regular coffee. Your sleep problems seem to be over, so you drink it. You lie awake until 3 a.m. that night and have to force yourself out of bed in the morning. Though not a full-blown relapse, this slip reminds you of why you wanted to make this behavior change. It's not as hard to get back on track, skipping the caffeine, as it was to give it up in the first place. You are on your way to the maintenance stage.

Have you ever had an experience like this one? If so, were you able to make the necessary connections and stick with the behavior change you made?

Creating a Behavior Change Plan

Research has given us a great deal of information about how behavior change occurs. How can you use this information to change your own behavior? The first step is accepting responsibility for your health and making a commitment to change. Ask yourself these questions:

- *Is there a health behavior I would like to change?* It could be smoking, overeating, procrastinating, being sedentary, eating too much sugar, or a host of other behaviors.

- *Why do I want to change this behavior?* There can be many reasons and motivations, but it's best if you want to change for yourself.

- *What barriers am I likely to encounter?* Consider relationships, community resources, and environmental

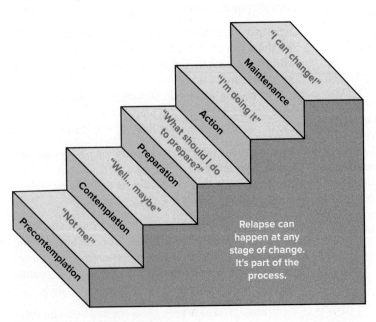

figure 1.3   **The stages of change.**

factors that hinder or help. Having a plan to deal with barriers will increase your chances of success.

- *Am I ready to change the behavior?* Beginning a behavior change plan when you haven't fully committed to it will likely result in relapse.

You can also ask all these questions about other levels in the socioecological model. Although making an initial commitment is an important step, it isn't enough to carry you through the process of change. For enduring change, you need a systematic behavior change plan. Once you have identified a behavior (or pattern) you would like to change, assessed your readiness to change, and made a commitment to change, follow the steps in the box, "Action Skill-Builder: Change to a New Behavior."

Action Skill-Builder

Change to a New Behavior

1. Set goals. Make them Specific, Measurable, Attainable, Realistic, and Time-bound (SMART goals). An example of a SMART goal might be: "I will increase my consumption of vegetables, especially dark green and orange vegetables, to 3 cups per day over the next four weeks, reaching my goal by October 30."

2. Develop action steps for attaining goals within a set time frame. For example, "I will include baby carrots in my lunch starting October 1."

3. Identify benefits associated with the behavior change. For example, "Eating more vegetables will help me lose weight, improve my complexion, and be healthier overall."

4. Identify positive enablers (skills, physical and emotional capabilities, resources) that will help you overcome barriers. An important capability is a sense of self-efficacy. Another capability might be the confidence that comes from having succeeded at behavior change in the past, along with skills that were used at that time. For example, "I was able to cut out caffeine last semester. I think I'll be able to improve my diet now."

5. Sign a behavior change contract to put your commitment in writing. Ask a friend or family member to witness your contract to increase your commitment. Signing a behavior change contract is one of the most effective strategies for change. An example of a behavior change contract is provided in one of the Personal Health Portfolio activities for Chapter 1 at the end of the chapter.

6. Create benchmarks to recognize and reward interim goals. Particularly when a goal is long term, it is useful to have rewards for short-term goals reached along the way. Reward yourself with something that particularly appeals to you (e.g., spend an afternoon with friends at the park, go to a movie).

7. Assess your accomplishment of goals and, if necessary, revise the plan.

Although behavior change theories offer valuable insights into the change process, they also have limitations. The major limitation of the behavior change approach is that it does not take into account health factors beyond the control of the individual, primarily the kinds of social environmental factors in the outer layers of the socioecological model illustrated in Figure 1.1. Another complicating factor is the glut of health-related information that inundates us daily, especially through social media and the Internet. Some of this information is confusing, some is contradictory, and some is even misleading or wrong. To make good choices, you need skills that allow you to access accurate health information, to understand the evidence underlying health recommendations, and to evaluate important health issues in society.

Being an Informed Consumer of Health Information

Part of taking responsibility for your health is learning how to evaluate health information, navigating health systems, and sorting the reputable and credible from the disreputable and unsubstantiated—in other words, becoming an informed consumer of health information.

Developing Health Literacy Do you read and understand the labels on foods you buy? Do you know which clinics are covered by your health insurance plan? If you learn that your dad is taking Lipitor, do you know how to find out more about the medication and its associated risks? These are all questions that relate to **health literacy**—the ability to read, understand, and act on health information. Health literacy includes the ability to critically evaluate health information, to understand medical instructions and directions, and to navigate the health care system. If you lack these skills, you have an increased risk for poor health outcomes, such as mistakes in using medications, higher rates of hospitalization, and delayed use of health services. Literacy becomes increasingly important as we receive more conflicting health information from a variety of sources such as websites and social media.[36,37]

Evaluating health information is complicated by the fact that we process information not just logically but also emotionally, and our emotional responses can affect the way we interpret and react to that information. Interpreting our **health risk**, defined as the probability that exposure to a hazard can result in negative consequences, can be especially difficult. Many factors contribute to our health risk for a particular condition, including age, gender, behaviors, family history, income, education, geographical location, and other factors that make us unique. So, for example, if you have a family history of breast cancer and you learn that 13 percent of women will develop breast cancer in their lifetime, you may feel alarmed and anxious about your risk based on that information. If you don't have a

health literacy
The ability to read, understand, and act on health information.

health risk
The probability of an exposure to a hazard that can result in negative consequences.

Consumer Clipboard
Evaluating Health Information on the Internet

You can find accurate health information on the Internet—but you can also find information that's misleading or just plain wrong. Ask yourself these questions to evaluate and deconstruct health messages you find on websites:

What techniques are used to catch your attention?
Dramatic images and language are frequently used to make you pay attention. How are the creators trying to influence you, either overtly or covertly?

What evidence is cited?
Reliable information is based on scientific research, not opinion. Be cautious if the "evidence" consists of personal stories or testimonials, and be wary about "miracle cures." A healthy dose of skepticism is helpful when assessing health information.

Is the information current?
Information about health and medicine is always changing. Use sources of information that are current and frequently updated. Remember that websites can stay on the Internet unchanged for years.

Who sponsors the website or advertises on it?
Ads give you another clue about the possible bias of the information and its providers. Is someone trying to sell you something?

Who created the website?
Look for the organization or individuals providing the information and consider whether there is an agenda, bias, or hidden message. The most reliable sources of health information are

Source: National Library of Medicine

government organizations, educational institutions, and nonprofits (URLs ending in .gov, .edu, or .org).

What values, lifestyles, or points of view are represented (or omitted) in the message?
Look for clues about the site's targeted audience in terms of gender, age, ethnicity, educational level, income, and political persuasion. If you identify with the audience, you may be more likely to overlook bias.

Sources: National Network of Libraries of Medicine. (n.d.). *Health literacy.* Retrieved from http://www.nnlm.gov/outreach/consumer/hlthlit.html; Tompkins, G. L. (2010). *Literacy for the 21st century* (5th ed.). Boston: Allyn & Bacon; Centers for Disease Control and Prevention. (2010). *CDC health literacy. National action plan to improve health literacy.* Washington, DC: U.S. Department of Health and Human Services, Office of Disease Prevention and Health Promotion. Retrieved from http://www.cdc.gov/healthliteracy/learn/index.html

family history of breast cancer and learn the same information, you may feel relieved and reassured about your risk. Recognizing the part played by your emotions can help you assess your risk in more balanced ways.[38]

Like other skills, health literacy can be developed, and this book will help you develop your own health literacy. Each chapter will introduce you to basic health and medical language related to the topic, coach you on how to find accurate information, and encourage you to apply your critical thinking skills. For some general guidelines related to health literacy, see the box, "Consumer Clipboard: Evaluating Health Information on the Internet."

Understanding Medical Research Studies Being an informed consumer also means understanding research studies, which inform most of the health recommendations you hear about on the news or in health journals or magazines. Most sources will cite the study, the researcher, and the journal in which the study appeared, and very often you can look

up the study online and read the original article or a summary of it.

There is a push for all research studies using human subjects to be registered in an accessible database and for researchers to release results from all studies in a timely fashion. This is important because otherwise there can be bias in results that are reported—results may be more likely to be published if they support the researchers' expectations or the study funder's interests.[39] Research studies follow a specific design and test a specific hypothesis. The research process should be described clearly enough in the study that other researchers can replicate it and confirm the results themselves.

There are many possible ways to categorize research studies. Formal studies can generally be of three types, with different methods and different goals:

* *Basic medical research.* This type of research typically conducts work on a cellular level or in animals. It contributes

14

(Portra/DigitalVision/Getty Images)

to a baseline of scientific knowledge, which then can be applied to humans in clinical or epidemiological research.

- *Epidemiological studies.* In this type of research, scientists use interviews, surveys, and measurements to study large groups of people (cohorts). The purpose is to identify and explore the relationships between potential risk factors and disease (or health) over time.

- *Clinical studies.* In this type of research, scientists study people who have received a particular treatment, screening, diagnostic test, or other intervention. The purpose is to identify whether a drug, a product, a behavior, or some other kind of intervention produces a particular effect.

Research studies can serve as credible supporting sources for news stories, product endorsements, and your own personal health decisions, as long as you know the limitations and goals of each type. When you are considering a health recommendation and the study that supports it, ask these questions:

- *Is the recommendation based on a formal research study, or is it simply an expert opinion?* Sources often cite experts when no clinical research is available to guide recommendations or when current research results are conflicting. Keep in mind that an expert's opinion hasn't necessarily been subjected to any formal testing and may contain bias.

- *If it was a formal clinical study, was it randomized and double-blind?* Randomized, double-blind studies are considered the gold standard. In such research, study participants are randomly assigned to either the group that receives the intervention or the group that receives a placebo. Neither the participants nor the researchers know until the end of the study who got what. If the study was randomized, you can be more confident that the results were not influenced by factors outside the treatment, such as differences between participants at the outset of the study. If it was a double-blind study, you can be more confident that the results weren't unduly influenced by the placebo effect or researcher bias.

- *Were the people in the study similar to you?* If the participants were different from you in some significant way—for example, if they were all over the age of 65 and you are 20—the results are less likely to apply to you than if they were similar to you. Sometimes the way people are categorized in study data can leave some populations completely out of the study. For example, if a study included only binary gender (male and female) subjects, then someone who identifies as trans will be excluded from the data.

- *How many participants were studied?* Larger studies with many participants are generally more reliable than investigations relying on only a small population sample.

- *Who sponsored or funded the study?* Some sponsors stand to benefit from certain results, such as drug companies. The most impartial sponsors are usually research institutes and government agencies.

- *Was the study published in a reputable, peer-reviewed medical or health journal?* Such a study has been evaluated by other researchers in the field, who are in a position to judge the strength of the methods and the accuracy of the results.

The answers to these questions affect how much credence you can put in the research results. Keep in mind that scientists typically consider individual studies stepping-stones in the ongoing search for answers to complex questions.

YOUR HEALTH AND YOUR FAMILY HEALTH HISTORY

Are you the way you are because of your genetic endowment or because of your experiences? This is the classic question of "nature versus nurture," and the answer isn't black and white. Who we are as individuals is the result of a complex, ongoing interaction among (1) environmental factors of many kinds (including our first environment—in utero),[40] (2) our lifestyle choices, and (3) our genetic inheritance. These influences are woven together in life, although in this chapter we treat them separately—socioecological context first, then lifestyle choices, and finally genetic inheritance.

At conception, you received what is perhaps your biggest inheritance, your genetic makeup. Your genetic inheritance plays a key role in establishing some of the parameters of what you can be and do in your life, but it does not determine everything. It gives you the potential to be tall or short; apple-shaped or pear-shaped; brown-eyed or blue-eyed; blonde, brunette, or bald. It gives you a unique bundle of strengths, vulnerabilities, and physical characteristics. You can think of genetic inheritance as your blueprint, or starting point. The blueprint is filled in and actualized over the course of your entire life.

Genetics used to be confined to the realm of scientists. Now, however, the language of genetics has entered the realm of everyday conversation. You will need to understand some basic genetic concepts to engage in personal health decisions, public debates, and policy decisions.

deoxyribonucleic acid (DNA)
A nucleic acid molecule that contains the encoded, heritable instructions for all of a cell's activities; DNA is the genetic material passed from one generation to the next.

genome
The total set of an organism's DNA.

chromosome
The gene-carrying structure found in the nucleus of a cell, composed of tightly wound molecules of DNA.

DNA and Genes: The Basis of Heredity

Our bodies are made up of about 260 different types of cells, each performing different, specific tasks. Except for red blood cells, every cell in the body contains one nucleus that acts as the control center. Within the nucleus, the entire set of genetic instructions is stored in the form of tightly coiled, threadlike molecules called **deoxyribonucleic acid (DNA)**. If we were to uncoil the DNA and magnify it thousands of times, we would find it consists of two long strands arranged in a double helix—a kind of spiraling ladder (Figure 1.4). DNA has four building blocks, or bases, called adenine (A), guanine (G), cytosine (C), and thymine (T). The two strands of DNA are held together with bonds between the building blocks; an A on one strand always connects to a T on the opposite strand, and a G on one strand connects to a C on the opposite strand. The consistent pairing is important—each strand is an image of the other (see Figure 1.4).

The complete set of a person's DNA is called his or her **genome**. Within the nucleus of a cell, DNA is divided into 23 pairs of **chromosomes**; one set of each pair comes from each parent. One pair of chromosomes—the sex chromosomes—is slightly different and is labeled with an X or a Y rather than a number. Biological females have two X chromosomes; biological males have an X and a Y chromosome.

DNA is the body's instruction book. The four bases are like a four-letter alphabet. Just as the letters in our 26-letter alphabet can be arranged to make thousands of words with different meanings, a series of thousands or millions of A-T-G-C combinations can be arranged to form a distinct message; this message is a gene. Each chromosome contains hundreds or thousands of genes located at precise points along the chromosome. Approximately 21,000 of these genes (about 2 percent of total DNA) serve as protein-coding templates, meaning they are transcribed into ribonucleic acid (RNA), which carries the template out of the nucleus to the cell sites where proteins are made. The sequence of RNA is translated into a precise sequence of amino acids, creating a protein with a specific composition, shape, and role. Different proteins make up structural components of the body and help direct the activities of cells and body processes. Much of the rest of the genome had been thought to contain "junk" DNA, also known as

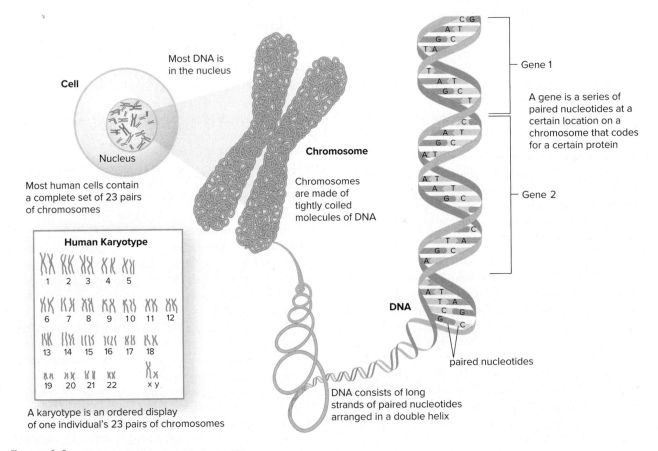

figure 1.4   **Chromosomes, genes, and DNA.**

noncoding DNA because it does not code for proteins. But it is now known that about 80 percent of DNA is playing a role in regulatory functions and thus is not "junk." Many genes are transcribed into noncoding types of RNA, which in turn are believed to play vital roles in cell function and regulation.[41,42,43]

Although our cells contain the same full set of genes, most of the cells in our body become specialized—that is, they take on characteristic shapes or functions, such as skin, bone, nerve, or muscle. Genes turn on or off to regulate this activity in a process called **differentiation**. Once a cell is differentiated, it can no longer become other cell types (it is as if certain "chapters" of the DNA instruction book are locked shut). Unspecialized cells, called **stem cells**, are present in an embryo (embryonic stem cells) and are retained within tissues (adult stem cells).

Genetic Inheritance

You inherited one set of chromosomes from each of your parents and thus have two copies of each gene (excluding genes on the sex chromosome). The position of each gene is in a corresponding location on the same chromosome of every human. However, your two copies may be slightly different because every so often changes occur in a gene; such a change is called a **mutation**. The change may be that a letter is left out (for example, a series A-T-G becomes A-G); an incorrect letter is inserted (a series A-T-G becomes A-A-G); or an entire series of letters is left out, duplicated, or reversed. The location of the mutation governs the effect. Going back to the analogy of the alphabet, consider the following sentence:

"When my brother came home, he lied."

If we change one letter to a "d," it can turn the sentence into nonsense:

"When my drother came home, he lied."

Or it can change the meaning entirely:

"When my brother came home, he died."

Something similar happens with a mutation in a gene. The change can cause different "meanings" or instructions to be sent to cells. Many mutations are neither harmful nor beneficial (such as changes that lead to blue eyes or brown eyes). Other mutations may be harmful

and cause disease. For example, in sickle cell disease, an adenine (A) is replaced by a thymine (T) in the gene for hemoglobin (a protein that carries oxygen in red blood cells). This single change at a crucial spot changes the gene's instructions and causes it to produce an altered form of hemoglobin that makes red blood cells stiff and misshapen. That in turn leads to an increased risk of red cells blocking arteries and causing pain, infection, and damage to organs. Two important facts about mutations are that (1) they are passed on from generation to generation and (2) they allow for human diversity.

Most characteristics (such as height or skin color) are determined by the interaction of multiple genes at multiple sites on different chromosomes. However, some traits are determined by a single gene, such as whether earlobes are attached or detached (Figure 1.5). To explain the relationship between genes and appearance, we will use this trait. An individual inherits two **alleles** (alternative forms) of the gene for earlobe structure (one copy from each parent). The two alleles can be the same version of the gene or they may be different versions, and one version is likely to be dominant over the other. In our example, the detached-earlobe allele is the *dominant allele,* and it will be expressed and will determine appearance. The other version, the attached-earlobe allele, is a *recessive*

differentiation
The process by which an unspecialized cell divides and gives rise to a specialized cell.

stem cell
An undifferentiated cell that is capable of giving rise to different types of specialized cells.

mutation
An alteration in the DNA sequence of a gene.

allele
Alternative forms of a gene.

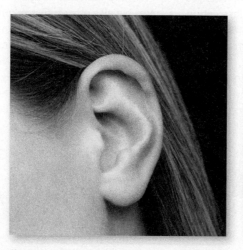

figure 1.5 **Dominant and recessive alleles.**
A single gene determines whether earlobes are detached (left) or attached (right). We all have two copies (alleles) of the "earlobe" gene. The detached allele is dominant, meaning a single copy will make the earlobes appear detached (remember, if a dominant allele is present, it determines appearance). The attached allele is recessive, meaning two copies are required for the earlobes to appear attached. Think about your parents and siblings; can you figure out which alleles you have? Consider other single-gene dominant traits—do you have the ability to roll your tongue, a widow's peak, or freckles? Or single-gene recessive traits—do you have a hitchhiker's thumb, inability to roll your tongue, or blue eyes?
((left): Bernd Eberle/Getty Images; (right): Ken Karp/McGraw-Hill Education)

allele–it will be hidden by the dominant allele and will not be expressed. A recessive allele is expressed only if both copies of the gene are the recessive version. Other relationships are possible between alleles as well: some alleles have incomplete dominance or codominance, meaning that both alleles affect appearance in varying degrees.

multifactorial disorder
A disorder caused by the interaction of genetic and environmental factors.

How does genetic inheritance affect your health? A genetic mutation in just one gene can cause a disease or disorder (as in the example of sickle cell disease). However, the majority of health conditions are caused by interactions among one or more genes, the environment, and health behaviors; these are called **multifactorial disorders**. Examples of multifactorial disorders include heart disease, cancer, diabetes, obesity, and schizophrenia. Many personal characteristics, predispositions, and behaviors are also the results of interactions among genes and multiple environmental factors.

To further complicate this story, the sequence of DNA nucleotides (the building blocks A, T, G, and C shown in Figure 1.5) is not the only way information is passed along. The environment can interact with our genome, and these interactions can actually be passed on from generation to generation. In a new area of study called *epigenetics,* researchers are identifying how health risks such as stress or poor nutrition can be passed from generation to generation independent of DNA sequence changes. What they have found is that the environment can modify the structure of DNA without changing the sequencing of nucleotides, through a process called methylation in which small methyl (carbon and hydrogen) particles attach to the DNA. Methylation changes the way DNA is used within cells. To use the instruction book analogy again, methylation acts like glue between some of the pages, making it more difficult to read sections, as illustrated in Figure 1.6.[44]

Because so many diseases with a genetic component are multifactorial, paying attention to the lifestyle and

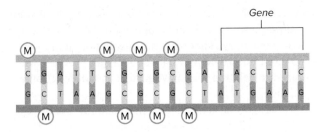

figure 1.6   Methylation of genes.
Methyl particles, a type of chemical modification that alters DNA without changing the nucleotide sequence, can activate or repress gene expression. In this way, the environment interacts with DNA to create changes that are passed along from generation to generation and do not involve changes in DNA sequencing.
Sources: Roth, T. (n.d.). Epigenetic and behavioral outcomes associated with caregiver experiences. Retrieved from http://www.delawareneuroscience.org/Pages/Roth.htm; Conching, A. and Thayer, Z. (2019) Biological pathways for historical trauma to affect health: a conceptual model focusing on epigenetic modifications. Social Science Medicine Jun; 230:74-82.

environmental factors that contribute to them is crucial. Figure 1.7 shows the continuum of genetic and environmental contributions for some common diseases and incidents. Notice that there is no clear distinguishing line between environment and genetics because the precise roles of each are not always clear. For instance, poisoning may seem to have purely environmental causes, but some children may be genetically more predisposed to take risks and thus more prone to eat or drink unknown substances.

You have probably already noticed within your own family that some traits are passed from one generation to the next (see the box "Starting the Conversation: Genetic Testing Online"). You have inherited not only the color of your skin, hair, and eyes but also other traits and predispositions. Your grandmother's history of colon cancer may mean you have inherited an increased risk for colon cancer. Your uncle's heart attack at age 40 may mean you have received an increased risk of heart disease from his side of the family. A family health tree, which we discuss next, is a useful way to organize this information.

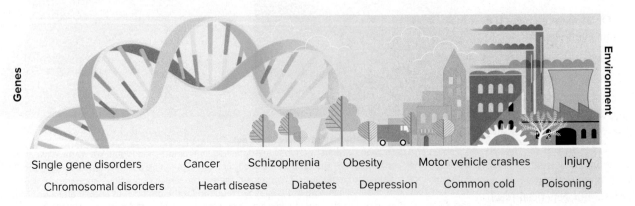

figure 1.7   Relative contribution of environment and genetics.
Source: Adapted from Kingston, H. (2002). Figure 12.1: Relative contribution of environment and genetic factors in some common disorders. *ABC of clinical genetics* (3rd ed.). London: BMJ Publishing Group.

Starting the Conversation
Genetic Testing Online

Q: If you could find out by ordering a home test kit on the Internet whether you have a gene that increases your risk for breast cancer or depression, would you do it?

For most of the 20th century, genetic disorders were diagnosed primarily by noting the presence of the disorder in a family tree across multiple generations. In the past 20 years, however, advances in genetic research have allowed scientists to identify the genes responsible for many inherited single-gene diseases, such as sickle cell disease, Tay-Sachs disease, Huntington's disease, and cystic fibrosis. Historically, genetic testing was used to determine whether someone who showed symptoms of a genetic disease was a carrier of a genetic disorder, to predict the adult onset of a genetic disorder in families with a strong history of certain diseases, or to screen newborns for genetic defects. Testing was done in a clinical laboratory by order of a physician, and genetic counseling was available to help the patient understand the results.

Now, with the rapid expansion of expertise and technology, genetic testing has moved into the realm of for-profit business. Direct-to-consumer marketing bypasses physicians, clinics, and insurance companies to appeal directly to healthy people who may or may not have a family history of a genetic disorder.

A growing number of companies are advertising genetic testing directly to the public over the Internet. Whether your interest is tracing your ancestry or adding to your health information, for a few hundred dollars or less, you can order a testing kit, submit a sample of saliva or blood, and receive information about your individual genome within a few weeks. In 2017, the U.S. Food and Drug Administration (FDA) approved the company 23andMe to report on specific genetic health risks, such as for Parkinson's disease and Alzheimer's disease, and on carrier status for some recessive single-gene diseases, such as cystic fibrosis and sickle cell disease. Since then, more than 23 million people have chosen to have their DNA analyzed. Genetic testing companies assert that the tests assess your genetic risk for a wide range of multifactorial health conditions, including heart disease, stroke, various types of cancer, Type-2 diabetes, allergies, migraine, and weight status. Some companies offer advice about diet and nutritional supplements based on your results.

The advantages of personal genetic testing appear evident at first glance—convenience, time savings, cost savings, privacy. You may also feel a sense of empowerment by gathering your own health information, and you may be motivated by this information to make healthy lifestyle choices or follow screening recommendations if you know you have a genetic risk for a condition.

There are also disadvantages. Often, the claims made about how much information the testing can provide are not adequately backed by evidence and thus may be misleading. At present, 23andMe is the only company with the FDA approval to assess for genetic health risk information. However, the FDA will likely be monitoring and approving other home-testing companies in the future. Home testing may also provide

less quality control over the collection, transport, and testing of your DNA sample than is afforded in a medical setting.

But most important, interpreting the results of genetic testing is complicated, and most consumers report they want guidance from a professional. Except in rare circumstances, genetic profiling can only suggest a *risk of disease*; it does not diagnose disease or predict it with certainty. And because most diseases with a genetic component are multifactorial—that is, several or many genes interact with each other and/or the environment to affect risk—information about genetic risk factors may not be any more meaningful than information about environmental risk factors such as poor diet or smoking. Under former president Barack Obama, research into the role of genetic testing expanded, calling for new research initiatives into precision medicine—the use of more personal test information to guide treatments. However, in 2018 President Donald Trump decreased National Institutes of Health funding, leading to decreased funds available for research in this field.

Another factor in direct-to-consumer (DTC) testing is the risk of sharing data with private companies. Though companies such as 23andMe vow to keep your genetic information confidential, they give consumers the option to share their information with academic, non-profit, and industry organizations for research purposes. They also give the option to share information with for-profit companies such as Pfizer and Genentech for pharmaceutical research. In addition, by sharing information with a private company, you run the risk of data breaches. In 2018, MyHeritage, a non–FDA-approved DTC company, exposed over 92 million users' personal emails and passwords, though they reported that no genetic information was specifically accessed. Companies such as 23andMe stress that data security is a top priority, but during a time when data breaches have become more common, consumers run the risk of exposing genetic information when choosing to share it with a company. Currently, the Genetic Information Nondiscrimination Act (GINA) prevents insurers from using your genetic information for coverage and rate determinations. It also prevents employers from discriminating based on genetic information. However, GINA does not extend to life, disability, or long-term care insurance.

If you are thinking about ordering your genetic profile, consider how the results could affect you and how you would use them. If you already know from your family health tree that you are at risk for heart disease, cancer, or other multifactorial diseases, would genetic testing provide any additional information or encourage you to pursue the lifestyle behaviors that would reduce your risk?

Q: Under what circumstances do you think you would consider ordering a genetic testing kit? What would you hope to find out?

Continued...

Concluded...

Q: Genetic testing is available for diseases that as yet have no cures, such as some degenerative neurological disorders. If your family history suggested you might have a gene for such a disease, would you want to know? Why or why not?

Q: Direct-to-consumer companies such as 23andMe offer the opportunity to share personal genetic information with companies to further medical research. Consider the benefits and risks of sharing personal information online. Would you choose to make your genetic information accessible to companies for research purposes?

Sources: U.S. Federal Food & Drug Administration. (2017). FDA allows marketing of first direct-to-consumer tests that provide genetic risk information for certain conditions. *FDA News Release.* Retrieved from http://www.fda.gov/NewsEvents/Newsroom/PressAnnouncements/ucm551185. htm; Centers for Disease Control and Prevention. (2018). *Consumer genetic testing is booming: But what are the benefits and harms to individuals and populations?* Retrieved from https://blogs.cdc.gov/genomics/2018/06/12/consumer-genetic-testing/; American Medical Association. (2018). *What your patients must know about direct-to-consumer lab tests.* Retrieved from http://www.ama-assn.org/delivering-care/precision-medicine/what-your-patients-must-know-about-direct-consumer-lab-tests; Science Policy. (n.d.) *Trumps' budget sows doubt about the future of precision medicine, major research efforts.* Retrieved from https://scipol.duke.edu/content/trump's-budget-sows-doubt-about-future-precision-medicine-major-research-efforts; CNBC. (2018). *5 biggest risks of sharing DNA with consumer genetic testing companies.* Retrieved from http://www.cnbc.com/2018-06/16/5-biggest-risks-of-sharing-dna-with-consumer-genetic-testing-companies.html

Creating a Family Health Tree

family health tree
A diagram illustrating the patterns of health and illness within a family; also called a genogram or genetic pedigree.

A **family health tree**, also called a *genogram* or *genetic pedigree,* is a visual representation of your family's genetic history. Creating a health tree can help you see your family's patterns of health and illness and pinpoint any areas of special concern or risk for you.

To construct your family health tree, you need to assemble information concerning as many family members as you can. (A sample tree is shown in Figure 1.8.) The more detailed and extensive the tree, the easier it will be for you to see patterns. Your tree should include parents, siblings, grandparents, cousins, aunts, and uncles. Basic information for each family member should include date of birth, major diseases and injuries, and, for deceased relatives, age and cause of

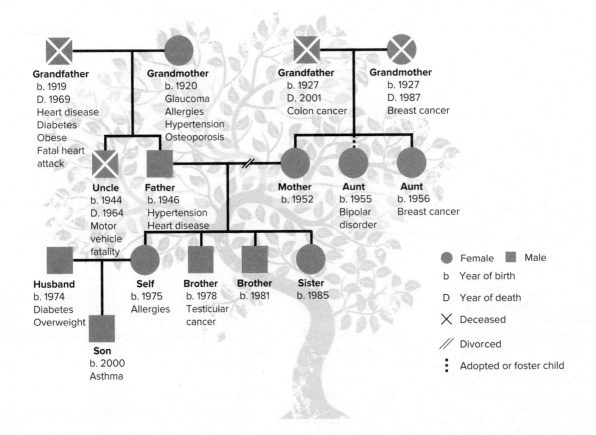

figure 1.8   A family health tree.
What conclusions can you draw from this tree? Perhaps the grandfather's obesity played a role in his heart attack at age 50. Perhaps the uncle would have survived the motor vehicle crash if seat belt laws had been in place in 1964.

death. You might include additional data such as the age of family members when their diseases were diagnosed as well as disabilities, major operations, allergies, reproductive problems, mental health disorders, and behavioral problems. Because we are learning more about genetic responses to medications, you may want to include information about what medications worked well to treat your uncle's depression or your father's high cholesterol. The Personal Health Portfolio at the end of the chapter contains an activity that provides detailed instructions on how to put together your own family health tree. As the tree reveals patterns in your family's health, you can think about the roles that lifestyle habits, community factors, and even public policies may play.

Gathering family health information to construct a tree may not be easy. In some cultures, it is taboo to discuss the dead or certain diseases, such as cancer, depression, or HIV. Such cultural views may influence the information you are able to collect. In addition, if you were adopted, you may not have the same access to your biological family's health history. Only one-third of U.S. adults report that they have tried to gather information for a family health tree. In recognition of the importance of the task, the U.S. surgeon general launched a national public health campaign called the U.S. Surgeon General's Family History Initiative. The initiative encourages families to use opportunities when they are gathered together to discuss and record health problems that seem to run in the family.[45]

What Can You Learn From Your Health Tree?

Certain patterns of illness or disease suggest a genetic link, as in the following instances:

* An early onset of disease is more likely to have a genetic component.

* The appearance of a disease in multiple individuals on the same side of the family is more likely to have a genetic correlation.

* A family member with multiple cancers represents a greater likelihood of a genetic association.

* The presence of disease in family members who have good health habits is more suggestive of a genetic cause than is disease in family members with poor health habits.

If you discover a pattern of illness or disease in your health tree, you may want to consult with your physician or a genetic counselor about its meaning and implications (see the box "Life Stories: Janet: A Family History of Breast Cancer"). You may want to implement lifestyle changes, have particular screening tests, or watch for early warning signs. Again, a pattern of illness in your family does not automatically mean that you will be affected. The main use of a health tree is to highlight your personal health risks and strengths so that you can make informed lifestyle choices.

Life Stories

Janet: A Family History of Breast Cancer

Janet, a college sophomore, lost her mother to breast cancer when she was 10 years old and her mother was just 34. Since then, Janet had felt sure that she, too, was destined to get breast cancer. In high school, she struggled with decisions about whether to go to college and pursue a career or to start a family as early as she could so that she would have at least some time with her children. She chose to go to college, but her ambivalence about that decision was reflected in her often risky approach to contraception. On those occasions when she had sex with her boyfriend without using birth control, she knew that on some level, she hoped she would get pregnant.

A turning point came when Janet learned in one of her classes that some cases of breast cancer are associated with specific genes, referred to as *BRCA1* and *BRCA2*. Genetic tests can be performed to determine whether a person has a mutated copy of either of these genes. Learning this empowered Janet to find out more. Using her college library and online sources, she learned about options available to high-risk people like herself. They included starting mammograms (breast screenings) at an earlier age than recommended for the

general population, taking certain medications, and even considering mastectomy (breast removal) to prevent cancer.

For the first time since her mom died, Janet felt she had some control over her future. She couldn't change her genes, but there were actions she could take to reduce her risk. She had never really talked to her dad about her mom's health history because she didn't want to upset him by stirring up sad memories. Now she realized it was important to her own health to get as much information as possible about her mom's cancer. She decided to talk to him about it the next time she was home. She also decided to make an appointment with a genetic counselor to find out more about testing for the *BRCA1* and *BRCA2* genes.

* What obstacles—psychological as well as logistical—do you think make it hard for people to find out more about their family health histories?

* What conditions or diseases seem to run in your family? What behavioral choices or environmental factors might increase or decrease the likelihood that these conditions will actually occur?

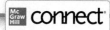

LOOKING AHEAD

When compared with other high-income countries, the United States spends more on health care but has a population with a shorter average life span and worse health outcomes. The United States has higher rates of infant mortality, injury and homicide, sexually transmitted infections and pregnancy among youth, chronic disease, obesity, and drug- and alcohol-related mortality.[15] Clearly, we have many challenges on both the personal level and the community/societal level. Throughout this book, we will ask you to consider your personal health and health choices within the context of your environment. As you read each chapter, reflect on your current level of health in that area. What are your predispositions based on family history? Which of your behaviors is affecting your health in that area? If there is a behavior you would like to change, assess your readiness to change; then develop a behavior change plan based on the guidelines in this chapter and throughout the rest of the book.

At the same time, think about the influences that shape your decisions. What factors restrict your choices or support them? Consider your family and friends, your classmates and peers, your school and instructors, the community you live in, government policies, and the prevailing socioeconomic and political climate. For example, consider how U.S. policies allow you to access health care in the box "You Make the Call: Is It Time for a Single-Payer System for Health Care in the United States?" What do you have to take into account to be successful at behavior change? To help you think more deeply about these issues, we have provided a Personal Health Portfolio at the end of each chapter. It includes self-assessment and critical thinking activities.

Even if you decide not to make a personal change right now, perhaps you can share health information with a family member or encourage a friend to change a worrisome habit. Maybe you can do something to make a difference in your community, such as participating in a community garden or a recycling drive or advocating for schools. Or perhaps you will become engaged in the nation's health care debate, or in activities aimed at improving quality of life for underserved segments of the population. The socioecological model of health is not just about how your environment influences you—it's also about how your efforts shape your environment.

You Make the Call

Is It Time for a Single-Payer System for Health Care in the United States?

If you need to go to a doctor, do you know where you can go or how much it will cost? Living in the United States, you are part of a complex health insurance system that makes it difficult to answer these questions. And yet, it is very clear that access to health care is critical to the health of a community. The United States is the only wealthy country in the world that does not provide universal health care—defined by the World Health Organization as a system in which "all people and communities can use the promotive, preventive, curative, rehabilitative and palliative health services they need, of sufficient quality to be effective, while also ensuring that the use of these services does not expose the user to financial hardship." Let's look at how our current health care insurance system works and consider whether it is time to move to a single-payer system.

Our current system:

- Forty-nine percent of the U.S. population receives health insurance through an employer or through a family member's employer with a private, group health insurance plan. Employer-sponsored plans usually have the advantage of ease of enrollment, reduced cost, and often a wide range of plan choices. However, they are linked to employment, and thus people who are temporarily or permanently out of work (sometimes due to health-related issues) lose employment-based coverage.
- Fourteen percent of the U.S. population gets insurance through Medicare, a federal program that covers people who are 65 years of age or older and meet other criteria for work history and citizenship status. When on Medicare, a

person can choose to add a supplement for additional prescription medication coverage (for a fee).
- Twenty percent of the U.S. population gets insurance through Medicaid or CHIP, a federal-state program that covers people of low socioeconomic status, up to certain percentages of the poverty line depending on state rules and on whether the state expanded Medicaid with passage of the Affordable Care Act.
- Seven percent of the U.S. population purchases insurance through the Individual Market, a system set up with passage of the Affordable Care Act to assist people who are self-employed or who work for small companies that don't provide employer-based insurance to access affordable and comprehensive health plans.
- Two percent of the U.S. population receives care through the U.S. Veterans Administration (VA) or other military plan. In the VA system, the federal government provides the insurance coverage and the medical providers and hospitals are federally owned and managed. There is a movement for veterans to be able to use private hospitals and clinics, due to high demand for services and limited access within the VA system.
- Just under 1 percent of the U.S. population receives services through the Indian Health System—established as part of treaty obligations between the U.S. government and federally recognized tribes.
- Nine percent of the U.S. population, an estimated 30 million people, remains uninsured.

Continued...

Concluded...

In a single-payer system, a single entity, usually the federal government, collects all the health care fees and pays all the health care costs. In such a system, all residents can be covered and it is possible to simplify the administration of the system. In fact, we already have several potential examples within the United States—at present, however, none of them covers everybody. Here is how two of them work:

The U.S. Veterans Administration system structure is similar to the British National Health Service (NHS). Both are single-payer systems in which the government collects fees (taxes) and pays all health care costs. In both these systems, the government actually owns the hospitals and facilities and hires the providers to perform services. In the United States, veterans meeting specific requirements are eligible for coverage in the VA, whereas in England, all the nation's residents are covered by the NHS.

U.S. Medicare is a single-payer system similar to the Canadian single-payer system. In both, the federal government collects fees (taxes) and provides an insurance plan that pays providers and hospitals a negotiated rate for services. The federal government makes payments, but the providers and hospitals remain independent—either for-profit or non-profit. In the United States, Medicare is available to people over the age of 65 who meet specific criteria or people with specific disabilities, whereas in Canada, all residents are eligible for Canadian health care.

The single-payer principle does not dictate *how* a country should or might ensure that all residents have access to necessary medical care without financial hardship; that is left to the population to decide. However, problems and dissatisfaction with our current piecemeal system suggest it is time for change. Despite our high overall spending on health care, we don't visit the doctor or go to the hospital more than people in other countries. In fact, the major differences between us and people in other rich countries are that (1) more of our health care dollars go toward administrative costs for all the different insurance companies, and (2) we pay enormous costs for prescription medications.

In summary, we spend more per person than other high-income countries but we do not ensure residents can get the health care they need, when they need it, without financial hardship. We are alone among high-income countries in not providing universal health coverage. Is it time to simplify the system, reduce cost, and ensure people have access to health care through a change to a single-payer system?

Pros

- A single-payer system would reduce the complexity and administrative costs of the U.S. current system.
- A single-payer system establishes insurance for all residents, which increases access and allows health care to focus on preventing disease, promoting health, and reducing costs.
- A single, governmental payer has a stronger negotiating position with pharmaceutical companies to address the high costs of prescription medications in the United States.
- A single-payer system does not require health providers and hospitals to become government employees—it can be structured so the government is the payer but providers remain independent.
- A single-payer system moves the burden of health insurance coverage away from employers; it allows them to focus on business and employees to make employment decisions independent of concerns about losing their health insurance.

Cons

- The health insurance industry operates in the private realm, driven by market forces; government involvement increases bureaucracy, costs, and regulation that stifles competition and job creation.
- With the passage of the Affordable Care Act, the number of uninsured people has decreased so a single-payer system is less necessary.
- Health providers and hospitals want independence in decision making and would see loss of income with a single-payer system.
- Federal policy changes could allow for prescription drug price negotiations without implementation of a single-payer system.

Sources: World Health Organization. (n.d.). *Universal health coverage and health financing.* Retrieved from http://www.who.int/health_financing/universal_coverage_definition/en/; U.S. Department of Health and Human Services, Centers for Disease Control and Prevention, National Center for Health Statistics. (2019). *Health insurance coverage: Early release of estimates from the National Health Interview Survey, 2018.* Retrieved from http://www.cdc.gov/nchs/data/nhis/earlyrelease/insur201905.pdf; Health Insurance.org. (n.d.). *ACAs effect on health care coverage in the U.S.* Retrieved from http://www.healthinsurance.org/acas-effects-on-coverage-in-the-u-s/

In Review

How are *health* and *well-being* defined?

Health is defined by the World Health Organization as a state of complete physical, mental, social, and spiritual well-being, not just the absence of disease. *Well-being* is a sense of how you think and feel your life is going. Well-being is a relative state in which ideally you maximize your physical and emotional functioning to live a full and satisfying life.

What factors influence a person's health?

Individual health-related behavior choices play a key role in health, and personal genetic makeup is an important starting point. However, economic, social, cultural, and physical conditions—the social determinants of health—are critical for creating the opportunities for people to achieve health and well-being. Population health actions are needed to ensure the personal health of individuals.

What health-related trends are occurring in our society?

As the United States becomes more multiethnic and multicultural, advances in medicine and health care have not reached many minority and low socioeconomic communities. Eliminating health disparities among different segments of the population is one of the broad goals of the national health initiative *Healthy People*.

What is health-related behavior change?

The process of changing a health behavior (e.g., quitting smoking, changing your diet) has been conceptualized in the Health Belief Model, a framework that shows how people's perceptions affect their health choices, and the Stages of Change Model, which suggests that change has six stages, from precontemplation to maintenance of new behavior or termination of old behavior.

What challenges do we face in changing our health behavior?

Health challenges for individuals include learning to be more informed consumers of health information and making lifestyle decisions that enhance rather than endanger their health. Health challenges for society include finding a balance between the freedom of individuals to make their own choices and the responsibility of society to protect individuals from poor choices and to offer increasing access to affordable health care.

How do genes affect your health?

Although some diseases and disorders are caused by a single gene, most genetic disorders are multifactorial; that is, they are associated with interactions among several genes and interactions of genes with environmental factors, such as tobacco smoke, diet, and air pollution. Even if you have a genetic predisposition for a disease, you may never get that disease if the contributing environmental factors are not present.

Personal Health Portfolio

Chapter 1 Physical and Mental Health Assessment

Are you wondering how you are doing in regard to your overall health and well-being? This is the first of a series of self-assessment activities that are included in this text. Your Personal Health Portfolio, the final product of all activities, will be a collection of documents that explore your strengths and challenges. It will represent a snapshot of your health and self-reflections throughout the course.

This first portfolio activity is centered on an adaptation of a well-studied assessment tool (the Rand Corporation's Short Form 36) that will help you take a general look at components of your physical and mental health.

Read each question carefully and circle the point value corresponding to your answer.

PHYSICAL FUNCTIONING

The following items are about activities you might do during a typical day. Does your health now limit you in these activities? If so, how much?

	Yes, limited a lot	Yes, limited a little	No, not limited at all
1. Vigorous activities, such as running, lifting heavy objects, participating in strenuous sports	0	50	100
2. Moderate activities, such as moving a table, pushing a vacuum cleaner, bowling, or playing golf	0	50	100
3. Lifting or carrying groceries	0	50	100
4. Climbing several flights of stairs	0	50	100
5. Climbing one flight of stairs	0	50	100
6. Bending, kneeling, or stooping	0	50	100
7. Walking more than a mile	0	50	100
8. Walking several blocks	0	50	100
9. Walking one block	0	50	100

LIMITATIONS DUE TO PHYSICAL HEALTH

During the past month, have you had any of the following problems with your work or other regular daily activities as a result of your physical health?

	Yes	No
1. Cut down the amount of time you spent on work or other activities	0	100
2. Accomplished less than you would like	0	100
3. Were limited in the kind of work or other activities you did	0	100
4. Had difficulty performing work or other activities (e.g., it took extra effort)	0	100

LIMITATIONS DUE TO EMOTIONAL PROBLEMS

During the past month, have you had any of the following problems with your work or other regular daily activities as a result of any emotional problems (such as feeling depressed or anxious)?

	Yes	No
1. Cut down the amount of time you spent on work or other activities	0	100
2. Accomplished less than you would like	0	100
3. Didn't do work or other activities as carefully as usual	0	100

ENERGY/FATIGUE

These questions are about how you feel and how things have been going for you during the past month. For each question, give the one answer that comes closest to the way you have been feeling. How much of the time during the past month . . .

	All of the time	Most of the time	A good bit of the time	Some of the time	A little of the time	None of the time
1. Did you feel full of pep?	100	80	60	40	20	0
2. Did you have a lot of energy?	100	80	60	40	20	0
3. Did you feel worn out?	0	20	40	60	80	100
4. Did you feel tired?	0	20	40	60	80	100

EMOTIONAL WELL-BEING

These questions are about how you feel and how things have been going for you during the past month. For each question, give the one answer that comes closest to the way you have been feeling. How much of the time during the past month . . .

	All of the time	Most of the time	A good bit of the time	Some of the time	A little of the time	None of the time
1. Have you been a very nervous person?	0	20	40	60	80	100
2. Have you felt so down in the dumps that nothing could cheer you up?	0	20	40	60	80	100
3. Have you felt calm and peaceful?	100	80	60	40	20	0
4. Have you felt downhearted and blue?	0	20	40	60	80	100
5. Have you been a happy person?	100	80	60	40	20	0

SOCIAL FUNCTIONING

1. During the past month, to what extent has your physical health or emotional problems interfered with your normal social activities with family, friends, neighbors, or groups? (Circle one number.)

Not at all	100
Slightly	75
Moderately	50
Quite a bit	25
Extremely	0

2. During the past month, how much of the time has your physical health or emotional problems interfered with your social activities (such as visiting with friends, relatives, etc.)? (Circle one number.)

All of the time	0
Most of the time	25
Some of the time	50
A little of the time	75
None of the time	100

PAIN

1. How much bodily pain have you had during the past month? (Circle one number.)

None	100
Very mild	80
Mild	60
Moderate	40
Severe	20
Very severe	0

2. During the past month, how much did pain interfere with your normal work (including both work outside the home and housework)? (Circle one number.)

Not at all	100
A little bit	75
Moderately	50
Quite a bit	25
Extremely	0

GENERAL HEALTH

1. In general, you would say your health is

Excellent	100
Very good	75
Good	50
Fair	25
Poor	0

How TRUE or FALSE is *each* of the following statements for you?

	Definitely true	Mostly true	Don't know	Mostly false	Definitely false
2. I seem to get sick a little easier than other people.	0	25	50	75	100
3. I am as healthy as anybody I know.	100	75	50	25	0
4. I expect my health to get worse.	0	25	50	75	100
5. My health is excellent.	100	75	50	25	0

SCORING

Add up your scores from each section and divide by the number of questions in the section to obtain an average score. The highest possible score in each section is 100.

PHYSICAL FUNCTIONING

___ + ___ + ___ + ___ + ___ + ___ + ___ + ___ + ___ = ___ ÷ 9 = ___
 1   2   3   4   5   6   7   8   9   raw score   average

LIMITATIONS DUE TO PHYSICAL HEALTH

___ + ___ + ___ + ___ = ___ ÷ 4 = ___
 1   2   3   4   raw score   average

LIMITATIONS DUE TO EMOTIONAL PROBLEMS

___ + ___ + ___ = ___ ÷ 3 = ___
 1   2   3   raw score   average

ENERGY/FATIGUE

___ + ___ + ___ + ___ = ___ ÷ 4 = ___
 1   2   3   4   raw score   average

EMOTIONAL WELL-BEING

___ + ___ + ___ + ___ + ___ = ___ ÷ 5 = ___
 1   2   3   4   5   raw score   average

SOCIAL FUNCTIONING

___ + ___ = ___ ÷ 2 = ___
 1   2   raw score   average

PAIN

___ + ___ = ___ ÷ 2 = ___
 1   2   raw score   average

GENERAL HEALTH

___ + ___ + ___ + ___ + ___ = ___ ÷ 5 = ___
 1   2   3   4   5   raw score   average

Your scores can be interpreted in the following manner. Mark an X where your score falls on the continuum for each section. Recognize that the behaviors exist on a continuum with low scores indicating areas of concern and higher scores indicating healthier behaviors/feelings.

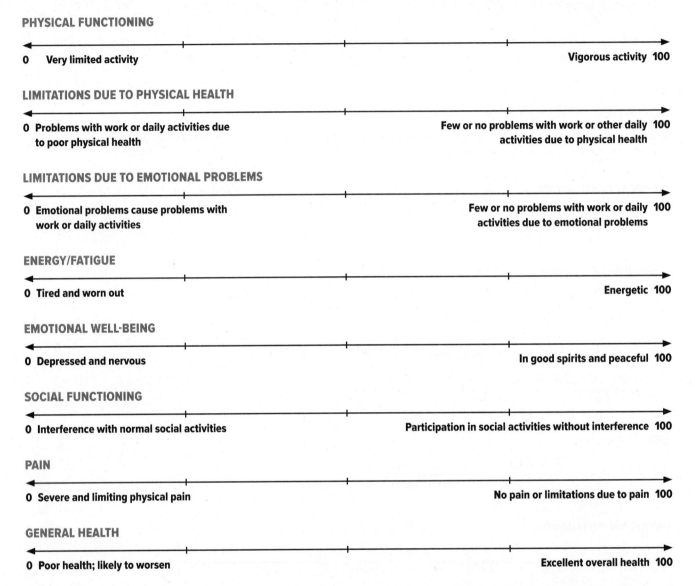

PHYSICAL FUNCTIONING

0   Very limited activity   Vigorous activity 100

LIMITATIONS DUE TO PHYSICAL HEALTH

0   Problems with work or daily activities due   Few or no problems with work or other daily 100
     to poor physical health   activities due to physical health

LIMITATIONS DUE TO EMOTIONAL PROBLEMS

0   Emotional problems cause problems with   Few or no problems with work or daily 100
     work or daily activities   activities due to emotional problems

ENERGY/FATIGUE

0   Tired and worn out   Energetic 100

EMOTIONAL WELL-BEING

0   Depressed and nervous   In good spirits and peaceful 100

SOCIAL FUNCTIONING

0   Interference with normal social activities   Participation in social activities without interference 100

PAIN

0   Severe and limiting physical pain   No pain or limitations due to pain 100

GENERAL HEALTH

0   Poor health; likely to worsen   Excellent overall health 100

Source: Adapted from the 36-Item Short Form Health Survey developed from the Medical Outcomes Study. Santa Monica, CA: RAND Corporation.

CRITICAL THINKING QUESTIONS

1. Look over your total scores. In what areas do you have high scores—reflecting healthier behaviors and feeling? In what areas do you have lower scores—reflecting possible areas of concern?

2. In areas of higher scores, what helps you maintain healthy behaviors? Consider your personal knowledge about what it means to be healthy and your attitudes and beliefs. Then consider the other levels of the socioecological model—consider how you are supported by friends and family, your school community and living situation, institutions to which you belong, and local or national policies.

3. In areas of lower scores, what are some of the barriers that make improvement difficult for you? As with your strengths, consider each level in the socioecological model of health.

4. Finally, consider whether there are areas in which you would like to make changes. What would these changes look like? How ready are you to make changes? What steps would you take to start the change process? If you are ready, complete a behavior change contract (see next activity).

This general quality-of-life assessment is a starting point for exploring your health and the role of the context in which you live your life. In areas where your scores are at the lower or higher end of the continuum, you may already have a sense of what factors contribute to your concerns or strengths. As you continue through each chapter, you will be asked to complete portfolio activities that will help you explore in greater detail factors that influence your general health and well-being. Keep this portfolio activity in mind. Come back and revisit it throughout the term. See whether you think differently about various factors in your life as you learn more.

Personal Health Portfolio

Chapter 1 Behavior Change Contract

Behavior I want to change: _____

My goal: _____

_____

Remember that your goal should be SMART: specific, measurable, attainable, realistic, and time-bound.

I will achieve my goal by _____.
　　　　　　　　　　　　　　　　date

Along the way, I will create a series of smaller, incremental goals to help me reach my overall goal:

　　Incremental goal 1: _____　Target date: _____

　　Incremental goal 2: _____　Target date: _____

　　Incremental goal 3: _____　Target date: _____

Benefits associated with this behavior change:

* _____

* _____

* _____

Barriers I expect to encounter:

* _____

* _____

* _____

Strategies for overcoming these barriers:

* _____

* _____

* _____

Signature: _____　Date: _____

Witness signature: _____　Date: _____

1. How important is this change to you?

　not very important　　　　　　　　　　　　　　　　　　　　　　**very important**

2. How confident are you that you can make this change?

　not confident　　　　　　　　　　　　　　　　　　　　　　　　**very confident**

Personal Health Portfolio

Chapter 1 Creating a Family Health Tree

A family health tree is a diagram of your family's health history over several generations. As such, it can provide important clues to the genes you have inherited from your parents, grandparents, and ancestors. It can also give you an opportunity to think about the context in which your family members lived and how that may have affected their health. Constructing a family health tree has three broad steps: (1) mapping the family structure, (2) recording family information, and (3) exploring family relationships. Refer to the model provided in Figure 1.8 for a sample tree. An online tool is available at https://phgkb.cdc.gov/FHH/html/index.html. You can complete the tree online or create a family health tree on paper.

Once you have gathered all the information, analyze your family health tree by completing the Critical Thinking Questions. You may want to share your family health tree with your siblings and other family members. Depending on what you find, you may want to review your family health tree with your health providers. They may recommend that you modify certain lifestyle behaviors (such as diet or exercise), have particular screening tests (such as an early test for cancer), or visit a genetic counselor. You may want your family health tree to become part of your medical file for future reference.

CRITICAL THINKING QUESTIONS

1. What are your family's strengths? Consider such things as longevity, fitness, mental well-being, etc. What individual, interpersonal, community, or policy factors may have contributed to the strengths? Consider where, when, and how different generations of your family lived. How might this have influenced their health?

2. Are there patterns of disease or illness in your family? Do certain diseases appear frequently? Does the pattern suggest a possible genetic link? What lifestyle factors may have contributed to illness in your family? Again consider how the environment in which your relatives lived might have contributed to illness.

Design Icons: ©McGraw-Hill Education

2 Mental Health and Stress

Wong yu liang/123RF

Ever Wonder...

what it means to be "mentally healthy," as opposed to "mentally ill"?

how to tell whether you are seriously depressed or just feeling down?

what you can do to reduce the effects of stress in your life?

ental health encompasses several aspects of health and wellness—emotional, psychological, cognitive, interpersonal, and spiritual aspects of a person's life. It includes the capacity to respond to challenges in ways that allow continued growth and forward movement in life. The key to mental health and happiness is not freedom from adversity, but the ability to respond to adversity in adaptive, effective ways. A mentally healthy person is able to deal with life's inevitable challenges without becoming impaired or overwhelmed by them.

The majority of people are mentally healthy, but many experience emotional or psychological difficulties at some point in their lives, and mental disorders are fairly common. In 2017, 13.1 percent of young adults aged 18 to 25 had a major depressive episode during the past year. This number represented 4.4 million young adults. Almost 19 percent of the adult U.S. population was affected by a diagnosable mental disorder in 2017, with 4.5 percent identified as having a serious mental illness.[1] An estimated 50 percent of U.S. adults experience some symptoms of depression during their lifetime. Many mental health problems—as well as many general health problems—are triggered or worsened by stress.

Which virtues and character strengths listed in Table 2.1 seem to be expressed in the actions of these young people? *(Steve Debenport/Getty Images)*

WHAT IS MENTAL HEALTH?

Like physical health, mental health is not just the absence of illness; it is also the presence of many positive characteristics.

Positive Psychology and Character Strengths

Psychologists have long been interested in such positive human characteristics as optimism, attachment, love, and emotional intelligence. In recent years, this interest has coalesced in the **positive psychology** movement. Rather than focusing on mental illness and problems, positive psychologists focus on positive emotions, character strengths, and conditions that create happiness—in short, "what makes life worth living." The focus for much of their research has been on examining happiness as a potential cause of desirable outcomes rather then a consequence of them.[2] Others have focused on "grit," or an individual's perseverance and passion for achieving long-term goals, as a predictor of life success.[3]

One outcome of this research has been the identification of character strengths and virtues that "enable human thriving" and that are endorsed by nearly all cultures across the world.[4] The six broad virtues are wisdom, courage, humanity, justice, temperance, and transcendence. Related to each virtue are particular strengths that meet various criteria.

Character is a combination of thoughts, feelings and behaviors, and increased self-awareness that can provide the basis for self-confidence (see Positivity Project, posproject.org). For example, strengths contribute to individual fulfillment and satisfaction, they are valued in their own right and not as a means to an end, they do not diminish others, and they are deliberately cultivated by individuals and societies. The most commonly endorsed strengths are kindness, fairness, authenticity, gratitude, and open-mindedness. The character strengths and virtues are described in Table 2.1. Which ones are your top strengths? How can you use them more often?

positive psychology
The area within the field of psychology that focuses on positive emotions, character strengths, and conditions that create happiness.

self-esteem
A sense of positive regard and valuation for oneself.

altruistic
Unselfishly concerned for the welfare of others.

Characteristics of Mentally Healthy People

People who are described as mentally healthy have certain characteristics in common (often expressions of the character strengths and virtues in Table 2.1):

- They have high **self-esteem** and feel good about themselves.

- They are realistic and accept imperfections in themselves and others.

- They are **altruistic**; they help others.

- They have a sense of control over their lives and feel capable of meeting challenges and solving problems.

Table 2.1   Classification of 6 Virtues and 24 Character Strengths

Virtue and Strengths	Definition
1. Wisdom and knowledge	**Cognitive strengths that entail the acquisition and use of knowledge**
Creativity	Thinking of novel and productive ways to do things
Curiosity	Taking an interest in ongoing experience, openness to experience
Open-mindedness	Thinking things through and examining them from all sides
Love of learning	Mastering new skills, topics, and bodies of knowledge
Perspective	Being able to provide wise counsel to others
2. Courage	**Emotional strengths that involve the exercise of will to accomplish goals in the face of opposition, external or internal**
Authenticity	Speaking the truth and presenting oneself in a genuine way
Bravery	Not shrinking from threat, challenge, difficulty, or pain
Persistence	Finishing what one starts
Zest	Approaching life with excitement and energy
3. Humanity	**Interpersonal strengths that involve "tending and befriending" others**
Kindness	Doing favors and good deeds for others
Love	Valuing close relations with others
Social intelligence	Being aware of the motives and feelings of self and others
4. Justice	**Civic strengths that underlie healthy community life**
Fairness	Treating all people the same, according to notions of fairness and justice
Leadership	Organizing group activities and seeing that they happen
Teamwork	Working well as a member of a group or team
5. Temperance	**Strengths that protect against excess**
Forgiveness	Forgiving those who have done wrong
Modesty	Letting one's accomplishments speak for themselves
Prudence	Being careful about one's choices; not saying or doing things that might later be regretted
Self-regulation	Regulating what one feels and does
6. Transcendence	**Strengths that forge connections to the larger universe and provide meaning**
Appreciation of beauty and excellence	Noticing and appreciating beauty, excellence, and/or skilled performance in all domains of life
Gratitude	Being aware of and thankful for the good things that happen
Hope	Expecting the best and working to achieve it
Humor	Liking to laugh and tease; bringing smiles to other people
Religiousness	Having coherent beliefs about the higher purpose and meaning of life

Source: Peterson, C. & Seligman, M. (2004). *Character strengths and virtues: A handbook and classification.* Washington, DC: American Psychological Association.

- They demonstrate social competence in their relationships with others, and they are comfortable with other people and believe they can rely on them.

- They are not overwhelmed by fear, love, or anger; they try to control irrational thoughts and levels of stress.

- They are optimistic; they maintain a positive outlook.

- They have a capacity for intimacy; they do not fear commitment.

- They are creative and appreciate creativity in others.

- They persevere and take on challenges.

- They take reasonable risks in order to grow.

- They bounce back from adversity.

The Self-Actualized Person

Many of these healthy characteristics are found in the self-actualized person. The concept of **self-actualization** was developed by Abraham Maslow in the 1960s as a model of human personality development in his "hierarchy of needs" theory (Figure 2.1). Maslow proposed that once people meet their needs for survival, safety and security, love and belonging, and achievement and self-esteem, they have opportunities for self-exploration and expression that can lead them to reach their fullest human potential. According to Maslow, a self-actualized person is realistic, self-accepting, self-motivated, creative, and capable of intimacy, among

other traits. Those who reach this level achieve a state of transcendence, a sense of well-being that comes from finding purpose and meaning in life.

Optimism, Self-Efficacy, and Resilience

A key characteristic of mentally healthy people is *optimism*—the general expectation that things will turn out well. People with an "optimistic explanatory style"—the tendency to see problems as temporary and specific rather than permanent and general—seem to have better physical and mental health than pessimistic people do.[5,6] Optimistic people react to failures as things they can do something about, as challenges and opportunities for learning and growth. Pessimistic people tend to attribute failure to personal defects and react with discouragement and a sense of defeat. A recent examination of the relationship between dispositional optimism and physical health suggests that optimism is associated with a variety of health outcomes. While not definitive, these findings are described as being "impressive and extensive."[7] Compared with pessimists, optimists appear to have better physical functioning, report less pain, have better outcomes after surgery, experience lower levels of depression, and live longer. Of course, we also need to be realistic and recognize our limitations; people who disregard the information provided by their successes and failures will end up with only disappointment.[8] For more about balance, see the box "Starting the Conversation: Is Optimism Overrated?"

Related to optimism is *self-efficacy*, a general sense that we have some control over what happens in our lives. Mentally healthy people have a basic belief that they can guide their own lives; they take unexpected events in stride, adapt, and move on.

This ability to bounce back from adverse events is known as **resilience**, and it is another characteristic of mentally healthy individuals. People who can respond flexibly to life's challenges and redirect their energies toward positive actions tend to be more successful in life. Our lives will always have moments of adversity and be filled with challenging situations. Individuals who are resilient learn ways to respond to these events and situations. Resilience involves patterns of thinking, feeling, and behaving that contribute to a balanced life based on self-esteem, satisfying relationships, and a belief that life is meaningful. There are practical tips in the literature that can help you when adversity occurs. For example, Sandberg and Grant suggest that building resilience is a lifelong activity that helps us all get through difficult situations.[9] More specifically, to help children develop resilience, it is important to support a "growth" mindset, enhancing their belief that they have the ability if they work hard enough to solve any problem. Encouraging individuals to take thoughtful risks and leaving an opportunity to learn from failure can also help individuals develop the skills needed to respond to

self-actualization
In Maslow's work, the state attained when a person has reached his or her full potential.

resilience
The ability to bounce back from adversity.

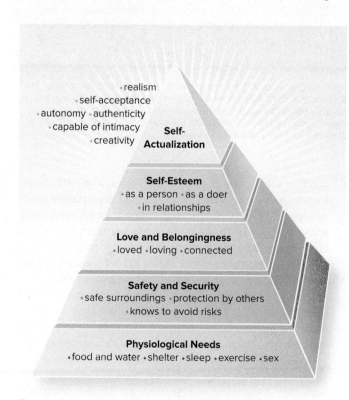

- realism
- self-acceptance
- autonomy • authenticity
- capable of intimacy
- creativity

Self-Actualization

Self-Esteem
• as a person • as a doer
• in relationships

Love and Belongingness
• loved • loving • connected

Safety and Security
• safe surroundings • protection by others
• knows to avoid risks

Physiological Needs
• food and water • shelter • sleep • exercise • sex

figure 2.1 **Maslow's hierarchy of needs.**
Source: Maslow, A. H., Frager, R. D., & Fadiman, J. (Eds.) (1987). *Motivation and personality* (3rd ed.). New York: Harper & Row.

Starting the Conversation
Is Optimism Overrated?

Q: Do you wonder whether you are optimistic enough to reap the supposed benefits of optimism, such as better health outcomes?

Research has consistently found associations between optimism and good health, both physical and mental. The reasons for these associations aren't entirely clear, but one possibility is that optimists have better coping skills in stressful situations, so they avoid some of the damaging effects of stress on their bodies. Another possibility is that optimistic people have healthier lifestyles and take better care of themselves, behaviors linked to the belief that we have some control over future outcomes. It may be that optimism is adaptive in the evolutionary scheme of things, or even hard-wired into our brains, helping people feel confident enough to plan, explore, and pursue goals. The literature also indicates that positive affect, or the experience of pleasurable emotions such as happiness, excitement, and enthusiasm, can have a positive impact on health outcomes.

But is it possible to be *too* optimistic? Critics warn against the "optimism bias," the tendency to be overly optimistic about expected outcomes, often as a result of self-delusion, an "illusion of control," or "magical thinking." They point to events like the 2008 financial crisis that swept Wall Street and the 2010 Deepwater Horizon oil spill as cases where optimistic thinking was so extreme that there were no contingency plans, resulting in disasters.

On a personal level, the optimism bias leads individuals to harbor such beliefs as "I can write this paper in one night" (despite previous experience), or "I will not get cancer from smoking" (despite health statistics). One study of undergraduates found that a positive outlook on life was correlated with self-rated abilities and predictions of success but not with GPA, suggesting that many were overestimating their talents.

Being *over*optimistic and *over*confident can bring problems. Overoptimistic people are likely to take more risks (such as with alcohol, drugs, cars, or thrill-seeking behaviors) and to practice less preventive care than others. They may neglect dangers that give others pause, and they may be more gullible. They may avoid confronting problems and fail to plan ahead because of their belief that things will somehow work out, and they may be more disappointed by failures than someone with lower expectations. Some research indicates that people experiencing positive emotions are more likely to rely on their beliefs, expectations, and stereotypes to evaluate a person or situation rather than systematically processing relevant information.

The solution is not to trade in your rose-colored glasses for a more pessimistic outlook. Pessimism—the expectation that things will work out badly—is associated with poorer health outcomes, including depression. Although pessimists have been found to have a more accurate view of reality, they may experience unnecessary suffering and miss out on opportunities for positive feelings like excitement and joy. A better choice is to temper your optimism with a healthy dash of realism—to use your critical thinking skills to weigh the likelihood of different outcomes. Although you may never achieve a truly objective assessment of a situation, your awareness of the optimism bias may help you come to more balanced decisions.

Q: Do you see yourself as an optimist or a pessimist? Do you think you were born that way? Could you change?

Q: Do you believe that some people overvalue optimism and positive thinking? Can you describe people from some countries as being more optimistic?

Sources: Sharot, T. (2011). *The optimism bias.* New York: Pantheon; Nickerson, C., Diener, E., & Schwartz, N. (2011). Positive affect and college success. *Journal of Happiness Studies, 12*(4), 717–746; Gruber, J., Mauss, I., & Tamir, M. (2012). A dark side of happiness? How, when, and why happiness is not always good. *Perspectives on Psychological Science, 6*(3), 222–233; Mayo Clinic. (2011). *Positive thinking: Reduce stress by eliminating negative self-talk.* Retrieved from http://www.mayoclinic.com/health/positive-thinking/SR00009; Pressman, S.D., Jenkins, B.N., & Moskowitz, J.T. (2019). Positive affect and health: What do we know and where should we go? *Annual Review of Psychology, 70,* 627–650.

adversity and discover more about their own resilience.[9] To assess your own resilience, complete the Personal Health Portfolio activity for this chapter.

Happiness and Positive Psychology

The study of happiness is part of the positive psychology movement, which focuses on what makes life worth living. In general, people who are in good romantic relationships, are physically healthier, and attend some form of religious institution seem to be the happiest. Other sources of happiness include time spent with friends and family and sufficient income, as Figure 2.2 shows. Most Americans describe themselves as either very happy (31 percent) or pretty happy (56 percent); only 13 percent describe themselves as not too happy. Clergy, firefighters, and special education teachers describe themselves as most happy; gas station attendants, roofers, molding machine operators, and construction workers describe themselves as least happy.[10] In addition, compared to adulthood, youth is a time of less happiness. Overall, however, few experiences seem to affect us for more than three months; we seem to celebrate or feel bad for a while and then recover and move on. Most individuals seem to be resilient.[11]

Positive psychologists have found that happiness has three components: positive emotion and pleasure (savoring sensory experiences), engagement (being deeply involved with family, work, romance, and hobbies), and meaning (using personal strengths to serve some larger end).[12] The happiest people are those who orient their lives toward all three, but the latter two—engagement and meaning—are the most important in giving people satisfaction and happiness. Accordingly, positive psychologists suggest "happiness exercises," described in

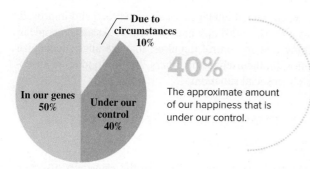

Due to circumstances 10%

In our genes 50%

Under our control 40%

40%
The approximate amount of our happiness that is under our control.

$75,000*
The annual income that makes people happiest; more doesn't make people happier; less can make life difficult.

10 friends
The number of regular contacts that leads to the most happiness.

6 to 7 hours
The amount of time each day spent socializing with friends and family that leads to the most happiness.

5 interactions
The happiest couples have 5 good interactions for every bad one.

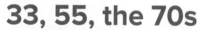

33, 55, the 70s
Different studies call these the happiest ages.

figure 2.2   Happiness by the numbers.
((currency): RealVector/Shutterstock; (clock): Robuart/123RF; (three women): Blendevo/123RF; (group of people): hobbit/Shutterstock; (couple walking): Grmarc/Shutterstock)
Source: Cassity, J. (2016). *Happiness by the numbers: 8 stats that could change your life.* Retrieved from http://my.happify.com/hd/happiness-by-the-numbers/.
*More recent information uses $83,000 as a new benchmark; in data by state, Mississippi is the low at $65,850 and Hawaii the high at $122,175. (*Business Insider,* January 22, 2015).

the box "Action Skill-Builder: Increase Your Happiness," to help people feel more connected to others.

However, people may have a happiness "set point," determined largely by genetics, as the pie chart in Figure 2.2 shows. That is, no matter what happens in life, people may have a tendency to return to their norm. The notion that people can increase their happiness reinforces Western cultural biases about how individual initiative and a positive attitude can solve complex problems.[13] In addition, because happiness research focuses on internal processes, it pays little attention to

the very real sources of unhappiness that are connected to social and economic circumstances.

Emotional Intelligence

Another aspect of mental health is the concept of **emotional intelligence**. Goleman argued that such qualities as self-awareness, self-discipline, persistence, and empathy are much more important to success in life than IQ.

emotional intelligence
The kind of intelligence that includes an understanding of emotional experience, self-awareness, and sensitivity to others.

Action Skill-Builder

Increase Your Happiness

Happiness research has found that people can increase their level of happiness by practicing "happiness exercises." Here are three that you can try:

☐ *Three good things in life.* Every night for a week, write down three things that went well that day and their causes. Research suggests that this can increase happiness and decrease depressive symptoms for up to six months.

☐ *Using signature strengths in a new way.* Using the classification of character strengths and virtues (see Table 2.1), take inventory of your character strengths and identify the top five, your "signature strengths." Use one of these top strengths in a new and different way every day for a week.

☐ *Gratitude visit.* Write a letter of gratitude and then deliver it in person to someone who has been especially kind to you but whom you have never thanked properly. Research suggests that this exercise can significantly increase happiness for one month.

Related research has identified other ways to increase happiness and life satisfaction, including performing acts of kindness, savoring life's joys, and learning to forgive. Positive psychologists say that happiness exercises give meaning to life by helping people feel more connected to others. Almost everyone feels happier when they are with other people, even those who think they want to be alone.

Source: Seligman, M., Steen, T., Park, N., & Peterson, C. (2005). Positive psychology progress: Empirical validation of interventions. *American Psychologist, 60*(5), 410–421.

People who are emotionally intelligent are able to do the following:

• Recognize, name, and understand their emotions

• Manage their emotions and control their moods

• Motivate themselves

• Recognize and respond to emotions in others

• Be socially competent[14]

Social competence calls upon our skills in understanding relationships, cooperating, solving problems, resolving conflicts, communicating assertively, and being considerate and compassionate.[15]

People with more emotional intelligence have more positive relationships, perform better academically, have more adaptive decision-making skills, and tend to be mentally healthy.[16] In addition, it seems that emotional intelligence can reduce the likelihood of participating in risky behaviors. Like many of the other characteristics of mentally healthy people, emotional intelligence can be learned and improved. Many groups, workshops, and self-help books assist people in learning how to control impulses, manage anger, recognize emotions in themselves and others, and respond more appropriately in social situations.

THE GRIEVING PROCESS: PART OF LIFE

Mental health is determined not by the challenges a person faces, but by the way the person responds to those challenges. The challenges come in a range of intensities—from being turned down for a date to experiencing the death of a loved one—and people's responses also vary in how well they work in allowing the person to maintain an overall sense of balance and well-being. The COVID-19 epidemic has resulted in more illness and death than many have ever faced. The intensity of the loss and the possibility of dying alone have brought on a new set of end-of-life challenges for those dying and their loved ones.

Coping with the loss of a loved one or acknowledging your own mortality may represent the biggest challenge to mental health you will experience in life. Grief can occur following the death of a family member, the death of a pet, a miscarriage, and many other life circumstances. Grieving is an extremely personal experience, yet it is one you have in common with everyone in your community and culture. Life and death are part of the cycle of existence and the natural order of things, and therefore grieving is also a universal process. Understanding more about this process can help you prepare for a situation in which you or someone you know experiences a loss.

Bereavement and Healthy Grieving

Grief is a natural reaction to loss; in fact, many of the familiar rituals that surround death and dying are actually for the living, to help people cope with their reactions to loss. Rituals help mourners move through the emotional work of grieving. When a person has been important to us, we never forget that person or lose the relationship. Instead, we find ways of "emotionally relocating" the deceased person in our lives, keeping our bonds with him or her while moving on. Cultural rituals can facilitate this process.

Cultural rituals aside, grieving is also a very personal process, often expressed by feelings of sadness, loneliness, anger, and guilt. These feelings are part of the process of healing because we do not begin to feel better until we have acknowledged and felt sorrow over our loss.[17]

Physical symptoms of grief may include crying and sighing, aches and pains, sleep disturbances, headaches, lethargy, reduced appetite, and stomach upset. The intense emotions you feel at the time of a loss can have a negative impact on immune system functioning, reducing your ability to fight off illness. Studies have shown that surviving spouses may have increased risk for heart disease, cancer, depression, alcoholism, and suicide.[18,19]

Everyone has higher risk for disease after the loss of a loved one, but those who are more resilient may cope with the loss better. Resilient people seem to be more likely to find comfort in talking and thinking about the deceased and are flexible enough to either suppress or express emotions about a death.[20] It is critical to remember that flexibility is the key: being able to choose when to talk and when it might be more helpful not to share. For example, suppressing an emotion might be useful when it allows you to concentrate on the current task.

Bereavement after the loss of a loved one typically occurs in four phases:

1. *Numbness and shock.* This phase occurs immediately after the loss and lasts for a brief period. The numbness protects you from acute pain.

2. *Separation.* As the shock wears off, you start to feel the pain of loss, and you experience acute yearning and longing to be reunited with your loved one.

3. *Disorganization.* You are preoccupied and distracted; you have trouble concentrating and thinking clearly. You may feel lethargic and indifferent. This phase can last much longer than you anticipate.

4. *Reorganization.* You begin to adjust to the loss. Your life will never be the same without your loved one, but your feelings have less intensity and you can reinvest in life.

When you experience the death of a loved one, it is important to take care of yourself while you are grieving. Eat a balanced diet, exercise regularly, drink plenty of fluids, and get enough rest. Keeping a journal and talking about the person who has died can also be part of the healing process.[21] Finally, you should not hesitate to ask friends for support because having a nurturing social network is particularly helpful in coping with loss.

There is no right or wrong way to grieve and no specific timetable. Friends who suggest it's time to move on need to understand that you are on your own journey and cannot be rushed. You need to give yourself permission to feel the loss and take time to heal. Some people cope better if they talk about the death rather than internalize their feelings.

Approximately 10 to 15 percent of those in grief will experience persistent and intense symptoms related to the loss. If you are in that group, it is important to seek professional help. The American Psychiatric Association's *Diagnostic and Statistical Manual* (*DSM-5*) allows a diagnosis of depression during the first two months following the death of a loved one; some observers worry that this change may result in overdiagnosis and overmedication.[22] However, if intense grief persists, or if you find yourself losing or gaining weight or not sleeping, consult a health professional to get a treatment referral. Treatment options include support groups, family therapy, individual counseling, or a psychiatric evaluation.

Facing Death

In 1969, Elisabeth Kübler-Ross published *On Death and Dying,* one of the first books to propose stages that people go through when they believe they are in the process of dying.[23] The five stages are (1) denial and isolation, (2) anger, (3) bargaining, (4) depression, and (5) acceptance. Over time, further study has shown that these stages are not linear—individuals may experience them in a different order or may return to stages they have already gone through, nor are they necessarily universal—individuals may not experience some stages at all.

Although the Kübler-Ross model serves as a good baseline for understanding the stages that a dying person might go through, attitudes about mental health have changed drastically since 1969. Health care professionals and patients can now talk more openly about the emotional toll of illness and death, and this can help shift the focus on ways to *live* with an illness rather than simply looking at the diagnosis as the

■ Spiritual beliefs and rituals can help people deal with grief and pain when a loved one dies. *(Rubberball/Brand X Pictures/Getty Images)*

frontal cortex
The part of the brain where the executive functions of planning, organizing, and rational thinking are controlled.

point at which someone begins to prepare for death. The dying person may find comfort and strength in talking through the process with family and friends or with a doctor or counselor. Also, there is often time to repair relationships, to build memories, and to review your life.

Spiritual and religious beliefs can also help terminally ill people through the final stages of their lives. Many people report that because of their personal faith, they do not fear death because they know their lives have had meaning within the context of a larger plan. In fact, studies suggest that, unrelated to belief in an afterlife, religiously involved people at the end of life are more accepting of death and less anxious about it than are those who are less religiously involved.[24]

THE BRAIN'S ROLE IN MENTAL HEALTH AND ILLNESS

The human brain has been called the most complex structure in the universe.[25] This unimpressive-looking organ is the central control station for human intelligence, feeling, and creativity. All behavior, both normal and abnormal, is mediated in some way by the brain and the nervous system.

Since the 1980s, knowledge of the structure and function of the brain has increased dramatically. In fact, the 1990s were called the "decade of the brain" because of the advances made in understanding how the brain works. Most of these discoveries were made possible by advances in imaging technologies, such as computed axial tomography (CAT scans), positron emission tomography (PET scans), magnetic resonance imaging (MRIs), and functional MRIs (fMRIs).

The Developing Brain

One surprise that recent brain research produced is that the brain continues to change and grow through adolescence into the early 20s (Figure 2.3). Previously, scientists thought that brain development was completed in childhood, and in fact, 95 percent of the structure of the brain is formed by the age of 6. Scientists discovered, however, that a growth spurt occurs in the **frontal cortex**—the part of the brain where "executive functions" such as planning, organizing, and rational thinking are controlled—just before puberty. During adolescence, these new brain cells are pruned and consolidated, resulting in a more mature, adult brain by the early to mid-20s.

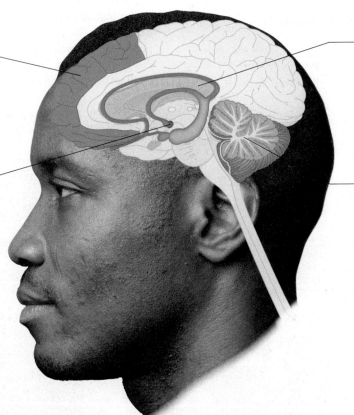

Frontal cortex
Controls planning, organizing, rational thinking, working memory, judgment, mood modulation. Undergoes rapid growth just before puberty, followed by pruning and consolidation during adolescence.

Amygdala
Controls emotional responses and instinctual, "gut" reactions. Adolescents appear to rely more heavily on this part of the brain to interpret situations than adults do. As they mature, the center of brain activity shifts to the frontal cortex.

Corpus callosum
Relays information between the two hemispheres of the brain and is believed to play a role in creativity and problem solving. Grows and changes significantly during adolescence.

Cerebellum
Long known to be involved in motor activity and physical coordination; now understood to coordinate thinking processes, including decision making and social skills. Undergoes dynamic growth and change during adolescence.

figure 2.3   The teenage brain.
(Mklrnt/123RF)

Sources: Spinks, S. (2005). Adolescent brains are works in progress. *Frontline.* Retrieved from www.pbs.org; National Institute of Mental Health. (2001). Teenage brain: A work in progress. NIH Publication No. 01-4929. Retrieved from www.nimh.nih.gov; Giedd, J.N. (2015). The amazing teen brain. *Scientific American, 312*(6), 33–37.

It also appears that the limbic system, which is related to emotion, becomes more powerful at puberty, whereas the prefrontal cortex, which controls impulses, does not mature until the 20s. This evolutionary process may leave teens and young adults prone to take risks while also allowing them to respond to their environment.[26,27]

Because structural changes are taking place in the brain into early adulthood, the activities that teenagers engage in can have lifelong effects. The brain cells and connections used for academics, music, sports, language learning, and other productive activities—or, alternatively, for watching television, using a smartphone,[28] and playing video games—are the ones that are more likely to be hardwired into the brain and survive.[29]

Some experts have disputed these conclusions about the brain. They argue that the differences seen in brain images are not necessarily the *cause* of erratic or impulsive behaviors, and they point out that young adults in other cultures are often fully ready to regulate and be responsible for their behavior. In addition, some research has indicated a relationship between impulsive, risk-taking behavior and exposure to movies, television, and video games. More research is needed to sort out the effects of biological versus cultural influences on behavior.[30]

Mental Illness and the Brain

Human beings have always experienced mental disturbances: descriptions of conditions called "mania," "melancholia," "hysteria," and "insanity" can be found in the literature of many ancient societies. It wasn't until the 18th and 19th centuries, however, that advances in anatomy, physiology, and medicine allowed scientists to identify the brain as the organ afflicted in cases of mental disturbance and to propose biological causes, especially damage to the brain, for mental disorders.

Since then, other explanations have been proposed, including psychological factors, sociocultural and environmental factors, and faulty learning. Debate over the roles of these various categories of causal factors continues, but the central role of the brain in mental health and mental illness is beyond doubt. Mental illnesses are diseases that affect the brain.[31]

Mental disorders are caused by complex interactions of biological factors, psychological processes, social influences, and cultural factors, especially those affecting a person during early childhood. In addition, some mental disorders, including depression, bipolar disorder, and schizophrenia, have a genetic component.

Cognitive mental disorders, which affect learning, memory, and problem-solving abilities, can be caused by tumors, brain trauma, or stroke. Alzheimer's disease, dementia, and amnesia are examples of cognitive disorders.

In recent decades, research has expanded on the physiology of the brain and the function of **neurotransmitters**. These brain chemicals are responsible for the transmission of signals from one brain cell to the next. There are dozens of neurotransmitters, but four seem to be particularly important in mental disorders: norepinephrine (active during the stress response; see later in this chapter), dopamine (implicated in schizophrenia), serotonin (implicated in mood disorders), and gamma-aminobutyric acid (GABA; implicated in anxiety).[32]

Neurotransmitter imbalances are believed to be involved in a variety of mental disorders (Table 2.2). For example, dopamine gives us the positive feelings we experience when

neurotransmitters
Brain chemicals that conduct signals from one brain cell to the next.

Table 2.2 Common Neurotransmitters Involved in Mental Disorders

Neurotransmitter	Normal Effects	Effects of Imbalance	Related Mental Disorders	Neurotransmitter-Related Medications
Norepinephrine	Stress response	Prolonged or severe stress, weakening nearly all body systems	Chronic stress	Antidepressants (e.g., Cymbalta, Pristiq)
Dopamine	Feelings of pleasure (all addictive drugs trigger dopamine)	Erratic behavior, increased sexual desire, aggressiveness, risk taking	Schizophrenia, including delusions and hallucinations	Antipsychotics
Serotonin	Regulates emotion and mood	Low levels: Depression, problems with anger control and concentration High levels: Serotonin syndrome (nausea, changes in blood pressure, agitation)	Mood disorders, depression	Antidepressants (e.g., Cymbalta, Pristiq, Viibryd)
GABA	Promotes relaxation and regulates anxiety	Low levels: Restlessness, short temper, night sweats, acid reflux, poor verbal memory	Anxiety	Anxiolytics (antianxiety drugs; e.g., benzodiazepines such as Valium, Xanax, Ativan)

eating and participating in sexual activity, and all addictive drugs appear to trigger a dopamine release. However, under consistently high levels of dopamine, a person will behave erratically, with increases in sexual desire, aggressiveness, and risk taking. Serotonin is associated with emotion and mood. Low levels of serotonin have been shown to be related to depression, problems with anger control and concentration, and a variety of other disorders. High levels of serotonin, which can be an unintended side effect of some migraine medicines and some antidepressants, can result in serotonin syndrome. Its symptoms include nausea, vomiting, changes in blood pressure, and agitation. GABA is a chemical messenger that promotes relaxation and inhibits excitation. It is typically found in high concentrations in the hypothalamus and hippocampus. Symptoms of GABA deficiency include night sweats, reflux, poor verbal memory, restlessness, and a short temper. Many drugs have been developed to correct neurotransmitter imbalances, such as the class of antidepressants that affect levels of serotonin.

MENTAL DISORDERS AND TREATMENT

Although evidence of mental disorders like depression or schizophrenia can be found in the brain, and many disorders can be treated with drugs that act on the brain, neither of these facts means that all mental disorders originate in the brain. In general, a mental disorder is diagnosed on the basis of the amount of distress and impairment a person is experiencing. According to the *DSM-5*, a **mental disorder** is a pattern of behavior in an individual that is associated with distress (pain) or disability (impairment in an important area of functioning, such as school or work) or with significantly increased risk of suffering, death, pain, disability, or loss of freedom.[25]

Deciding when a psychological problem becomes a mental disorder is not easy. Nevertheless, a basic premise of the DSM-5 is that a mental disorder is qualitatively different from a psychological problem that can be considered normal, and it can be diagnosed from a set of symptoms. For example, feelings of sadness and discouragement are common, especially during the college years. These feelings can occur in response to disappointment, loss, failure, or other negative events, or they can occur for no apparent reason. Usually, such experiences don't last too long; people recover and go on with their lives. If the feelings *do* go on for a long time and are painful and intense, however, the person may be experiencing depression.

Similarly, worries, fears, and anxieties are common during the college years. Individuals have stresses to deal with, such as grades, relationships, and learning how to live on their own without parental guidance

mental disorder
A pattern of behavior associated with distress (pain); disability (impairment in an important area of functioning, such as school or work); or significantly increased risk of suffering, death, pain, disability, or loss of freedom.

or support. They may be feeling homesick and lonely, or they may be having problems sleeping. Most people gradually make their way, learning who they are and how they want to relate to other people. Some people, however, may develop anxiety disorders or stress-related disorders, experience panic attacks, or be overwhelmed with fears and worries.

People experience many emotional difficulties in the course of daily living that are not a cause for alarm. At the same time, it is important to be able to recognize when a person needs professional help. Far too often, people struggle with mental disorders without knowing that something is wrong or that treatments are available. They don't realize that their problems may be causing them unnecessary distress and that professional treatment can help.

In 2013, after a more than 11-year effort and not without controversy,[33,34] the American Psychiatric Association revised the *DSM*, the text that is used to diagnose those with a mental disorder. Among the changes were the inclusion of hoarding as an official mental disorder, the introduction of gambling disorder, and modifications in the diagnosis of those with autism.[22] Here, we discuss the *DSM*'s major categories of mental disorders.

Neurodevelopmental Disorders

Neurodevelopmental disorders, according to the *DSM-5*, are groups of conditions that often start before a child enters grade school and include limitations of learning and difficulty with behavior control and social skills. Examples of neurodevelopmental disorders include autism spectrum disorder (ASD) and attention-deficit/hyperactivity disorder (ADHD).

ADHD is one of the most common childhood disorders and can continue into adulthood. It is not clear what causes ADHD, but many believe genetics plays a large role. Currently, researchers are looking at the relationship between environmental causes and ADHD; these include cigarette smoking and alcohol drinking during pregnancy, exposure to environmental toxins during pregnancy or when the child is young, childhood brain injuries, and certain food additives.[35]

Children who have attentional issues are easily distracted, have difficulty focusing, often daydream, and have difficulty following instructions. Those who are hyperactive may fidget, talk a great deal, and seem to be constantly in motion. Impulsivity seems to also be a potential symptom; it is expressed by impatience, the showing of intense emotions, and a tendency to interrupt conversations. The median age at onset is 6 years, and ADHD affects about 9 percent of children aged 13 to 18 and 4 percent of adults over age 18. Boys are three times more likely than girls to be diagnosed with ADHD. Finally, there has been a 42 percent increase in ADHD diagnoses between 2003 and 2011.[36]

Autism spectrum disorder is a group of developmental brain disorders that can cause social, communication, and behavioral difficulties. About 1 in 68 children has been identified with ASD, and it is five times more common in boys.

Children and adults with ASD range in the severity of their challenges, with some individuals having acute problems relating to the world. Symptoms of ASD include avoiding eye contact, having trouble understanding others' feelings, being uncomfortable with cuddling, and displaying repetitive actions. Diagnosis of ASD can be difficult, and although there is no cure, early interventions can improve a child's chances of developing at a normal pace, particularly those who do not have severe symptoms.[37]

Mood Disorders

Also called depressive disorders or affective disorders, mood disorders include major depressive disorder and bipolar disorder (formerly called manic depression). They are among the most common mental disorders worldwide.

People of all ages can get depressed, including children and adolescents, but the average age at onset for major depressive disorders is the mid-20s. In 2017, an estimated 17.3 million adults in the United States had at least one major depressive episode—about 7.1 percent of the adult population.[38] Women experience depressive episodes twice as frequently as men. It also appears that increased use of social media is related to increases in depression.[39] Some even suggest that adolescents' social media and television viewing should be regulated to prevent depression.[40]

Often, the illness goes undiagnosed, and people struggle for long periods of time. About two-thirds of depressed individuals seek help, but many are undertreated, meaning that they don't get enough medication or they don't see a therapist regularly. Many medications for depression take up to four weeks to begin to have an effect, so some people conclude they aren't working and stop taking them prematurely.

The *DSM-5* contains a number of new depressive disorders, including disruptive mood dysregulation disorder and premenstrual dysphoric disorder. In addition, dysthymia (neurotic or chronic depression) and chronic major depressive disorder are now included in the *DSM-5* as persistent depressive disorders. This change was made because of the difficulty in differentiating between these two conditions.

Major Depressive Disorder Symptoms of **depression** include depressed mood, as indicated by feelings of sadness or emptiness or by behaviors such as crying; a loss of interest or pleasure in activities that previously provided pleasure; fatigue; feelings of worthlessness; and a reduced ability to concentrate. If a person experiences one or more episodes of depression lasting at least two weeks, he or she may be diagnosed with **major depressive disorder**.

Bipolar Disorder A person with **bipolar disorder** experiences one or more manic episodes, often but not always alternating with depressive episodes. A **manic episode** is a distinct period during which the person has an abnormally elevated mood. Individuals experiencing manic episodes may be euphoric and full of energy or, alternatively, highly irritable.

US swimmer Michael Phelps, winner of 28 olympic medals, 23 of them gold, is a spokesperson for Talkspace and has struggles with depression. *(Leonard Zhukovsky/Shutterstock)*

They may have an inflated sense of their own importance and power; they may have racing thoughts and accelerated and pressured speech. They may stay awake for days without getting tired or wake from a few hours of sleep feeling refreshed and full of energy. People experiencing a manic episode typically are not aware they are ill.

Bipolar disorder occurs equally in men and women, with an average age at onset of about 20. Family and twin studies offer strong evidence of a genetic component in this disorder.

Anxiety Disorders

Along with depression, anxiety disorders are the most common mental disorders affecting U.S. adults. Almost 12.9 million have had at least one anxiety disorder.[41]

depression
A mental state characterized by a depressed mood, loss of interest or pleasure in activities, and other related symptoms.

major depressive disorder
A mood disorder characterized by one or more episodes of depression lasting at least two weeks.

bipolar disorder
Mood disorder characterized by one or more manic episodes that may alternate with depressive episodes.

manic episode
An abnormally elevated or irritable mood during a specific period of time.

Many of these disorders are characterized by a **panic attack**, a physiological and psychological experience of apprehension or intense fear in the absence of real danger. Symptoms include heart palpitations, sweating, shortness of breath, chest pain, and a feeling of "going crazy." There is a sense of impending doom or danger and a strong urge to escape. Panic attacks usually occur suddenly and last for a discrete period of time, reaching a peak within 10 minutes, but some can last longer. Many people may have only one or two panic attacks in a lifetime.[42]

Panic disorder is characterized by recurrent, unexpected panic attacks along with concern about having another attack. The attacks may be triggered by a situation, or they may "come out of nowhere." Twin studies and family studies indicate that there is a genetic contribution to panic disorder.

A **specific phobia** is an intense fear of a specific activity, situation, or object, exposure to which evokes immediate anxiety. Examples of common phobias are fears of flying, heights, specific animals or insects (dogs, spiders), and blood. Individuals with phobias realize their fear is unreasonable, but they cannot control it. Usually, they try to avoid the phobic situation or object, and if they can't avoid it, they endure it with great distress. Often, the phobia interferes with their lives in some way.

A **social phobia** is an intense fear of certain kinds of social or performance situations, again leading the individual to try to avoid such situations. If the phobic situation is public speaking, individuals may be able to structure their lives so as to avoid all public speaking. However, some social phobias cause fear of simply conversing with other people. This is different from shyness; individuals with this disorder experience tremors, sweating, confusion, blushing, and other distressing symptoms when they are in the feared situation.

Excessive and uncontrollable worrying, usually far out of proportion to the likelihood of the feared event, is known as **generalized anxiety disorder**. Adults with this disorder worry about routine matters such as health, work, and money;

■ Fear of flying is a common anxiety-producing phobia. *(Peter Dazeley/Iconica/Getty Images)*

children with the disorder worry about their competence in school or sports, being evaluated by others, or even natural disasters.

Obsessive-compulsive disorder is now included in the *DSM-5* as a separate chapter. It is characterized by persistent and intrusive thoughts, impulses, or images that cause intense anxiety or distress. For example, the person may have repeated thoughts about contamination, persistent doubts about having done something, or a need to have things done in a particular order. To control the obsessive thoughts and images, the person develops compulsions—repetitive behaviors performed to reduce the anxiety associated with the obsession.

Addiction

Addiction—dependence on a substance or a behavior—is classified as a mental disorder. All addictions in the *DSM-5* are classified as substance-related and addictive disorders. The key characteristic of addiction is continued, compulsive use of the substance or involvement in the behavior despite serious negative consequences. Individuals with a substance addiction may spend a great deal of time trying to obtain the substance; give up important parts of their lives to use it; and make repeated, unsuccessful attempts to cut down or control their use.

A person with **physiological dependence** on a substance experiences *tolerance,* reduced sensitivity to its effects such that increased doses are needed to give the same high, and *withdrawal,* uncomfortable symptoms that occur when substance use stops. Tolerance and withdrawal are indicators that the brain and body have adapted to the substance. Even without physiological dependence, the person can experience *psychological dependence.*

Typically, a person begins by using a substance to reduce pain or anxiety or to produce feelings of pleasure, excitement, confidence, or connection with others. With repeated use, users can come to depend on being in this altered state, and

Alcohol   AA has more than 2 million members—only a small proportion of those who are dependent on alcohol.

Drugs   More than 9 percent of the population currently use illicit drugs, with marijuana by far the most commonly used.

Tobacco   Smoking rates have declined dramatically since their peak in the 1960s, but one in five Americans still smokes.

Caffeine   The most widely used psychoactive drug in the United States, caffeine is consumed in coffee, soda, and, most recently, energy drinks with names like Red Bull and Full Throttle.

Food   Some people who are addicted to food have binge-eating disorder—a psychological disorder like anorexia or bulimia—and are likely to be overweight or obese.

Gambling   About 1–2 percent of those who gamble are believed to do so compulsively.

Shopping   A cultural emphasis on material goods, fueled by advertising, contributes to compulsive shopping.

Sex   Sex addicts are preoccupied with sexual thoughts and activities much of the time. The vast majority grew up in abusive family environments.

Internet   Internet addicts spend hours online every day instead of spending time on real-life activities and relationships.

figure 2.4 What we're addicted to: substances and behaviors.
The common feature in all addictions is loss of control.
((alcohol): Burke/Triolo Productions/Getty Images; (drugs): Artgray/Shutterstock; (tobacco): Photodisc Collection/EyeWire/Getty Images; (caffeine): Fotosearch/Ingram Publishing; (food): Comstock/PunchStock/Getty Images; (gambling): Steve Allen/Stockbyte/Getty Images; (shopping): Janis Christie/Photodisc/Getty Images; (sex): Terraxplorer/Getty Images; (internet): nd3000/Shutterstock)

without the drug, they may feel worse than they did before they ever took it. Although most people don't think they will

become addicted when they start, gradually the substance takes over their lives. Research has established that drugs cause addiction by operating on the "pleasure pathway" in the brain and changing brain chemistry (see Chapter 10 for details of this process).

Although addiction is usually associated with drug use, many experts now extend the concept of addiction to other areas in which behavior can become compulsive and out of control, such as gambling. In fact, there appear to be similarities between changes in a gambler's brain when viewing a videotape on gambling and changes in a cocaine user's brain when viewing a video focused on cocaine use.

In the *DSM-5*, gambling disorder was included as an addictive disorder because recent evidence suggests that the brains of those addicted to substances and to gambling appear to have similar changes. The results in both cases include feelings of euphoria along with a strong desire to repeat the behavior and a craving for the behavior when it stops. Internet use gaming disorder has also been included in the *DSM-5*, although it is in a section reserved for conditions that require further study rather than being treated as a mental disorder. Recently the World Health Organization identified gaming disorder in the 11th Revision of the International Classification of Diseases (ICD-11).

People can also be addicted to sex, shopping, eating, exercising, social media, or other activities (Figure 2.4), but at this time they are not listed in the *DSM-5* as addictive disorders. The common characteristic is that the person feels out of control and powerless over the behavior. Both psychotherapy and self-help groups are available to assist individuals struggling with these troubling behavior patterns.

Schizophrenia and Other Psychotic Disorders

Psychotic disorders are characterized by delusions, hallucinations, disorganized speech or behavior, and other signs that the individual has lost touch with reality. The most common psychotic disorder is **schizophrenia**. A person with schizophrenia typically has disorganized and disordered thinking and perceptions, bizarre ideas, hallucinations (often voices), and impaired functioning.[43] The symptoms are sometimes so severe that the person becomes socially, interpersonally, and occupationally dysfunctional. Signs and symptoms of schizophrenia usually appear between the ages of 16 and 30, with men usually getting diagnosed in their late teens and 20s and women in their late 20s to early 30s.

Schizophrenia has a strong genetic component. First-degree relatives of individuals with schizophrenia have a risk for the disorder

psychotic disorders Mental disorders characterized by signs that the individual has lost touch with reality.

schizophrenia A psychotic disorder characterized by disorganized and disordered thinking and perceptions, bizarre ideas, hallucinations (often voices), and impaired functioning.

10 times higher than that of the general population.[44] Brain scanning and visualizing technologies reveal abnormalities in the brains of people with schizophrenia. Studies indicate that these abnormalities are present before the onset of symptoms, suggesting that this illness is the result of problems in brain development, perhaps even occurring prenatally. In most cases, symptoms of the disease can be controlled with medication.

Mental Disorders and Suicide

A major public health concern, particularly among young people, suicide is the second leading cause of death among college students. According to the Fall 2018 National College Health Assessment, approximately 53.1 percent of those questioned felt things were hopeless in the past 12 months, 67.9 percent felt very sad at some point in the past year, and 62.3 percent had periods of overwhelming anxiety. In addition, 41.4 percent felt so depressed that it was difficult to function, about 11.3 percent of students had seriously considered suicide, and 1.9 percent had attempted to kill themselves in the past year.[45]

In the United States, women are more likely than men to attempt suicide, but men are four times more likely to succeed, probably because they choose more violent methods, usually a firearm. Firearms are used in approximately 50 percent of all suicides. Women tend to use less violent methods for suicide, but in recent years they have begun to use firearms more frequently.

What Leads a Person to Suicide? Suicide is a leading cause of death in the United Stares and rates have increased in almost every state since 1999. It has also been reported that 54 percent of people who died from suicide did not have a known mental condition.[46] Individuals contemplating suicide are most likely experiencing unbearable emotional pain, anguish, or despair. Studies indicate that the symptom linking depression and suicide is a feeling of hopelessness. Depression and alcoholism may be involved in two-thirds of all suicides. Abuse of substances other than alcohol is another factor; the combination of drugs and depression can be lethal. People experiencing psychosis are also at risk.

Major risk factors associated with suicide are relationship problems, substance use, a crisis in the past or upcoming two weeks, family history of suicide, serious medical problems, and access to the means, such as a gun or pills.[46] A tolerance for physical pain and a reduced fear of death might also be related to suicidality.[47] The most significant risk factor, however, is a previous suicide attempt or a history of such attempts.

Sometimes, vulnerable individuals turn to suicide in response to a specific event, such as the loss of a relationship or job, an experience of failure, or worry that a secret will be revealed. Other times there is no apparent precipitating event, and the suicide seems to come out of nowhere. However, suicide is always a process, and certain behavioral signs indicate that a person may be thinking about suicide:

- Comments about death and suicide threats
- Increasing social withdrawal and isolation
- Intensified moodiness
- Increase in risk-taking behaviors
- Sudden improvement in mood accompanied by such behaviors as giving away possessions (which may indicate a decision to attempt suicide)

How to Help If you know someone who seems to be suicidal, it is critical to get the person help. All mentions of suicide should be taken seriously. It is a myth that asking a person whether he or she is thinking about suicide will plant the seed in the person's mind. Ignoring someone's sadness and depressed mood only increases the risk. Encourage the person to talk, and ask direct questions:

- Are you thinking about killing yourself?
- Do you have a plan?
- Do you have the means?
- Have you attempted suicide in the past?

Encourage the person to get help by calling a suicide hotline or seeking counseling. Do not agree to keep the person's mental state or intentions a secret. If he or she refuses to get help or resists your advice, you may need to contact a parent or relative or, if you are a student, share your concern with a professional at the student health center. Do not leave a suicidal person alone. Call for help or take the person to an emergency room.

The JED Foundation (https://www.jedfoundation.org) can be a useful resource to help young adults learn how to help themselves and others and how best to respond when someone is contemplating suicide.

If you have thought about suicide yourself, we encourage you to seek counseling. Therapy can help you resolve problems, develop better coping skills, and diminish the feelings that are causing you pain. It can also help you see things in a broader perspective and understand that you will not always feel this way. Remember the saying, "Suicide is a permanent solution to a temporary problem."

Self-Injury

Self-injury, sometimes known as self-harm, self-mutilation, or self-injurious behavior, is defined as any intentional injury to your own body. Specific behaviors include cutting, burning, scratching, branding, and head banging. Self-injurious behaviors are sometimes mistaken for suicide attempts. Individuals who self-injure often have a history of physical and/or sexual abuse as well as coexisting problems such as substance abuse and eating disorders.

Public Health Is Personal

Emergency Rooms: Overused and Overwhelmed

In any economic crisis, the most vulnerable tend to be at greatest risk for cutbacks in services. In the past few years, many states have cut back their mental health budgets and closed programs to save money. Emergency rooms are overwhelmed by mentally ill individuals, who often have coexisting chronic physical illnesses. Almost 70 percent of emergency rooms indicate that they keep mentally ill individuals for 24 hours, and in some cases, mentally ill individuals linger in emergency rooms for several days waiting for care or specific placement. At times they are simply warehoused in general medical units where their psychiatric conditions go untreated. At the same time, the overall number of ER patients has risen because many people are using emergency rooms for non-emergency issues, and even those who are newly insured because of health care reform may be high utilizers of emergency rooms.

Continued overuse of the ER will only result in bankrupting medical facilities. What can be done to reduce the use of emergency rooms by mentally ill individuals and ensure that they receive appropriate care? Here are some proposals:

- *Develop patient navigator positions.* When mentally ill individuals are admitted into a hospital setting, they would be assigned a patient navigator who would help them arrange for follow-up services once they leave the hospital.

- *Improve primary care access.* All mentally ill individuals would have primary care providers who can help them with their nonurgent medical situations. This would reduce the use of the ER as a primary care clinic.

- *Increase funds for Assertive Community Treatment (ACT) teams.* ACT teams provide multidisciplinary care for the mentally ill, including home visits and follow-up care.

- *Increase funding.* More funding could help provide a variety of outpatient day treatment, job training, and housing programs for people with mental illnesses.

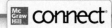

Sources: Gold, J. (2013). Emergency rooms provide care of last resort for mentally ill. *Kaiser Health News.* Retrieved from http://khn.org/news/er-psychiatric-patients/; Creswell, J. (2013). E.R. costs for mentally ill soar, and hospitals seeks better way. *New York Times.* Retrieved from www.nytimes.com/2013/12/26/health/er-costs-for-mentally-ill-soar-and-hospitals-seek-better-way.html; Taubman, S. L., Allen, H., Wright, B.J., et al. (2014). Medicaid increases emergency-department use: Evidence from Oregon's health insurance experiment. *Science, 343,* 263–268.

It has been estimated that approximately 7.4 percent of college students have intentionally cut, burned, bruised, or otherwise injured themselves within the past 12 months.[45] Many of the college students reporting self-injurious behaviors had never been in therapy, and few had disclosed their behaviors to anyone.[48] Self-injury seems to be equally prevalent among men and women, and the behavior does not appear to be correlated to race, ethnicity, education, sexual orientation, socioeconomic status, or religion. A variety of treatments can help people who injure themselves, including family therapy and medications. The *DSM-5* does not list either nonsuicidal self-injury or personal history of self-harm as a mental illness.

Treatments for Mental Disorders

More than 250 different models of psychotherapy exist for the treatment of mental disorders, and many different drugs can be prescribed. Most of the mild and moderate mental disorders are readily treatable with therapy and, if needed, medications. Currently, hospital emergency rooms are the primary source of treatment for many mentally ill people; see the box "Public Health Is Personal: Emergency Rooms: Overused and Overwhelmed."

Psychotherapy The key feature of most forms of **psychotherapy** (or *counseling*) is the development of a positive interpersonal relationship between a person seeking help (the client or patient) and a therapist—a trained and licensed professional who can provide that help. Most therapy models agree on the central importance of this interpersonal relationship.

Most therapists espouse a particular theoretical orientation, but many fuse ideas from a variety of different theories and approaches. A number of evidence-based psychotherapies and factors that are part of all effective treatments have been well researched and appear to have a positive impact on those who participate.[49,50] The most researched behavioral intervention has been cognitive-behavioral therapy (CBT).

What should you expect if you decide to try therapy? You can expect to be treated with warmth, respect, and an open, accepting attitude. The therapist will try to provide you with a safe place to explore your feelings and thoughts. At the end of the first session, the therapist will probably propose a plan for treatment, such as a series of 10 sessions or a referral to another professional. (See the box "Consumer Clipboard: Choosing a Mental Health Care Provider.")

Medications Until the 1950s, few effective medications for the symptoms

> **psychotherapy**
> Treatment for psychological problems usually based on the development of a positive interpersonal relationship between a client and a therapist.

of mental illness existed. Since that time, discoveries and break-throughs in drug research have revolutionized the treatment of mental disorders. Today, the symptoms of many serious disorders can be treated successfully with drugs.

The symptoms of schizophrenia and other psychotic disorders, especially delusions and hallucinations, can be treated with *antipsychotics.* Symptoms of mood disorders can be relieved with any of several different types of *antidepressants,* most of which act on the neurotransmitters serotonin and norepinephrine. Cymbalta, Pristiq, and Viibryd are used to treat depression and are among the most frequently prescribed drugs in the United States today.[51] The U.S. Food and Drug Administration (FDA) recently approved Ketamine as an option for individuals who have not responded well to at least two antidepressants. Antidepressant use has increased 65 percent from 1999 to 2014. Approximately 12.7 percent of individuals in the United States now take antidepressants; one-fourth of those who took an antidepressant in the past month have a 10-year history of use.[52] Symptoms of anxiety disorders can be reduced with anti-anxiety drugs (or *anxiolytics*). Benzodiazepines, the most widely used of these, are believed to act on the neurotransmitter GABA, which has a role in the inhibition of anxiety in the brain during stressful situations. Common anti-anxiety medications include Valium, Xanax, and Ativan.

The use of medications for mental disorders for children and adolescents has increased dramatically in recent years. The controversy over this practice was highlighted in 2004 when a study showed that certain antidepressants increased the risk of suicidal thinking and behavior in adolescents.[57] The FDA directed manufacturers of all antidepressants to include on their labels "black box" warnings to physicians and parents.

More recent studies indicate that antidepressants also significantly increase the risk of suicidal thoughts and behaviors in young adults aged 18 to 24, usually during the first one to two months of treatment. The FDA has proposed that warnings on antidepressants include information for young adults.[58]

The increase in the use of drug treatments is due not just to improvements in the drugs themselves, but also to the growing use of managed health care in the United States. Insurance companies often prefer to pay for medications, which tend to produce faster, more visible, and more verifiable results, than for psychotherapy, which may last for months or years and produce results that are less objectively verifiable.

(Photodisc Collection/ Stockbyte/Getty Images)

Drugs treat only the symptoms of mental disorders, however, and although they often remain the treatment of choice, research has been mixed about their overall effectiveness.[59] For example, some antidepressants are not recommended for individuals diagnosed with minor depression and should be used only by people who are suicidal or have a family history of mood disorders.[60] Psychotherapy is usually necessary as a supplement to drug treatment, because it helps the person understand the root causes of problems and change maladaptive patterns of thinking, feeling, and behaving.

WHAT IS STRESS?

Although stress can sometimes trigger a mental disorder, for most people, stress is a fact of life. It has been linked to 7 of the 10 leading causes of death in the United States, including heart disease, cancer, stroke, injuries, and suicide/homicide.[61] Although stress is described as a "creatively ambiguous word without a universally agreed upon definition," it has usually been understood to be an individual's perception and subsequent reaction to a harmful, challenging, and possibly threatening event that tests the person's ability to cope.[61] You experience varying levels of stress throughout the day as your body and mind continually adjust to the demands of living. We often think of stress in negative terms, as an uncomfortable or unpleasant pressure—for example, the need to complete a project on time or to deal with a traffic ticket. However, stress can also be positive. When you get a promotion at work or when someone throws you a surprise birthday party, you also experience stress.

Stress produces symptoms such as headaches and feelings of being overwhelmed, sad, or depressed.[62] In the 2017 *Stress in America Survey,* for the first time in 10 years, individuals reported a significant increase in their stress levels. This additional stress also appears to be affecting our health, with 80 percent of respondents describing themselves as experiencing at least one stress-related symptom; 34 percent reported headaches, 33 percent described themselves as feeling overwhelmed, and 32 percent said they felt depressed or sad.[62] The political climate and overall safety appear to be among the issues Americans are stressed about, with 57% describing the current political climate as a significant stressor. Some of these trends continued in the 2018 *Stress in America Survey,* focused on Generation Z (those born between 1995 and 2004). As the Who's At Risk box shows, individuals in Generation Z are perceiving greater stress when compared to all adults. The 2018 survey indicated that Gen Z individuals were the most likely to report poor mental health and more likely to seek professional help. There is also continued concern about sexual harassment and gun violence among Gen Z.[63] Over the past years, money, work, health care, and the economy have typically been described as sources of stress.

It also appears that attachment to electronic devices and the constant checking of technology have resulted in increased stress levels. Surveys indicate that more than 8 in 10 people in the United States say they are connected to electronic devices

Consumer Clipboard

Choosing a Mental Health Care Provider

Think you might like to talk to a therapist? Wonder if you could benefit from medication? Use these guidelines to get the right care.

Would it be helpful to see a mental health care provider?

- Am I feeling sad (homesick, lonely) a lot of the time?
- Am I having trouble studying for exams?
- Am I having difficulty concentrating?
- Do I feel inadequate, guilty, or worthless?
- Am I feeling overwhelmed?
- Have I lost interest in doing the things I usually like to do?
- Is this problem interfering with my everyday life?
- Have my friends and family asked if there's a problem?
- Am I avoiding friends because of the problem?

These are the kinds of problems a counselor can help you with. Many colleges provide free psychological assessments, short-term counseling, and referrals.

What's the difference among kinds of providers?

- Psychiatrists are medical doctors (M.D.s) who have completed medical school and at least a three-year residency in psychiatry. They can independently prescribe medication but often do not have a great deal of training in psychotherapy. If you see a psychiatrist, you will probably be prescribed a medication but will not meet for therapy sessions.

- Psychiatric nurse practitioners (PNPs) have completed training in nursing and have additional qualifications in psychiatry. PNPs can prescribe medications but often have to be supervised by an M.D. Like psychiatrists, they focus on psychiatric diagnosis and medication treatment.

- Licensed psychologists most often have a Ph.D. or Psy.D. (doctor of psychology) and receive four to five years of training following their bachelor's degree. They have to fulfill a specific number of supervised hours before they can be licensed. They cannot prescribe medication but are trained in providing psychotherapy.

- Licensed clinical social workers, counselors, and marriage and family therapists typically have at least a master's degree and have to fulfill a specific number of supervised hours before they can be licensed. Like psychologists, they cannot prescribe medication but are trained in providing psychotherapy.

No matter what type of provider you see, you should feel comfortable and emotionally safe sharing your concerns.

Are there other options?

- Support groups provide the opportunity to share your problems with peers, which may help you put them in perspective. This may be all the help you need.

- Pastoral counseling may be available in your religious community. Pastoral counselors have a professional degree from a seminary, a master's degree or doctorate in the mental health field, and clinical training.

Does insurance cover mental health care?

- Your college tuition fees or health insurance may cover some mental health services. If you choose to go off campus for counseling, those services may not be covered by your college benefits. If your insurance is through your parents, you will need to check with that insurance company about coverage.

Are parents informed about mental health care?

- If you're over 18, most schools leave this decision up to you. Communication between a mental health care provider and a client is considered confidential, with a few exceptions. If you're considered to be at risk for suicide, most counselors will encourage you to inform your parents about the counseling.

---

on a typical day, and 63 percent of Millennials and 47 percent of Gen Xers report they feel attached to their phones. In addition, there appear to be generational differences in the negative effects social media have on physical and emotional health. For example, 48 percent of U.S. Millennials report the negative impact of social media, whereas only 22 percent of baby boomers and 15 percent of mature respondents agree that social media is having an impact on their physical and mental health.[62] The Who's at Risk box describes the comparison between Gen Zers and all adults on a number of key issues.

Many people have developed strategies to better manage their use of technology and keep it from overwhelming their lives. These include not allowing cell phones at the dinner table or during family time and limiting the amount of time spent watching TV.[64] It's important to manage the stress in our lives and reduce its negative impact on our well-being. When excessive stress is unavoidable, having a repertoire of stress management techniques to fall back on is invaluable.

Events or agents in the environment that cause us stress are called **stressors**. They can range from being late for class to having a close friend die, from finding a rare parking space to winning the lottery. Your reaction to these events is called the *stress response;* we discuss this concept at length in the next section. Stressors disrupt the body's balance and require adjustments to return systems to normal.

stressors
Events or agents in the environment that cause stress.

49

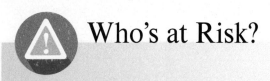

Who's at Risk?

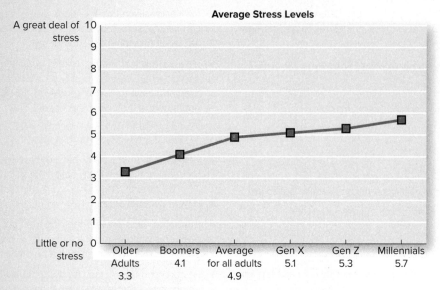

Average Stress Levels

A great deal of stress — 10

Little or no stress — 0

| Older Adults 3.3 | Boomers 4.1 | Average for all adults 4.9 | Gen X 5.1 | Gen Z 5.3 | Millennials 5.7 |

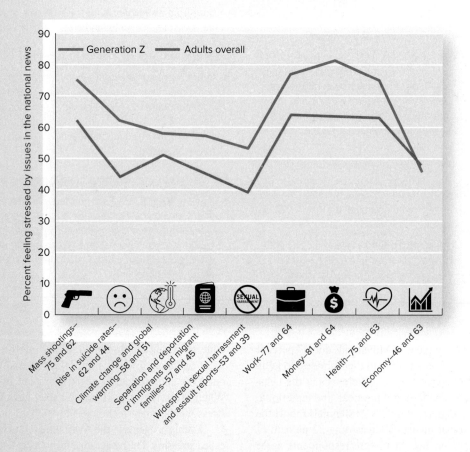

Percent feeling stressed by issues in the national news

Generation Z   Adults overall

Mass shootings—75 and 62
Rise in suicide rates—62 and 44
Climate change and global warming—58 and 51
Separation and deportation of immigrants and migrant families—57 and 45
Widespread sexual harrassment and assault reports—53 and 39
Work—77 and 64
Money—81 and 64
Health—75 and 63
Economy—46 and 63

Sources of stress, Gen Z and Adults Overall

Source: American Psychological Association. (2018). *Stress in America: Generation Z. Stress in America™ Survey*, 7. Retrieved from https://www.apa.org/news/press/releases/stress/2018/stress-gen-z.pdf

Not all stress is bad. Under certain circumstances, stress might even improve recall and performance.[65] Because there is so much variation in individual responses to stressors, stress can be thought of as a *transaction* between an individual and a stressor in the environment, mediated by personal variables that include the person's perceptions and appraisal of the event.[66] When faced with a stressor, you evaluate it without necessarily realizing you are doing so: Is it positive or negative? How threatening is it to my well-being, my self-esteem, my identity? Can I cope with it or not? When you appraise an event as positive, you experience **eustress**, or positive stress. When you appraise it as negative, you experience *distress.* Often, it is not the stressor itself that is debilitating, but the feeling that stress is constant and unrelieved by the opportunity to relax.

Regardless of your situation, stressors can make it more difficult for you to achieve your goals. For example, college students report to researchers that stress is the top impediment to academic performance.[48] However, there are tools that anyone can use to reduce stress before it becomes chronic.

The Stress Response

Whether the individual's appraisal of the stressor is negative or positive, all stressors elicit the **stress response** (also known as the **fight-or-flight response**), a series of physiological changes that occur in the body in the face of a threat. All animals, it appears—humans included—need sudden bursts of energy to fight or flee from situations they perceive as dangerous.

The stress response is carried out by the *autonomic nervous system,* which controls involuntary, unconscious functions such as breathing, heart rate, and digestion. The autonomic nervous system has two branches: the *sympathetic branch* initiates the stress response, and the *parasympathetic branch* turns off the stress response and returns the body to normal.

The stress response begins when the cerebral cortex (in the front of the brain) sends a chemical signal to the hypothalamus, which sends a signal to the pituitary gland. The pituitary gland sends adrenocorticotropic hormone (ACTH) to the adrenal glands, which release the hormones cortisol, epinephrine (adrenaline), and norepinephrine (noradrenaline) into the bloodstream. Glucose and fats are released from the liver and other storage sites to provide energy. As stress hormones surge through your body, your heart rate, breathing rate, muscle tension, metabolism, and blood pressure all increase, and other changes occur to prepare you for fight or flight (Figure 2.5). All this happens in an instant.

The Relaxation Response

When a stressful event is over—you decide the situation is no longer dangerous, or you complete your task—the parasympathetic branch of the autonomic nervous system takes over, turning off the stress response.[67] Heart rate, breathing, muscle tension, and blood pressure all decrease. The body returns to

eustress
Good stress or a positive form of stress.

stress response or fight-or-flight response
A series of physiological changes that activate body systems, providing a burst of energy to deal with a perceived threat or danger.

figure 2.5   **The stress response will include changes in the body triggered by a particular threat.**
(MPH Photos/Shutterstock)

homeostasis
A state of stability and balance in which body functions are maintained within a normal range.

relaxation response
A series of physiological changes that calm body systems and return them to normal functioning.

acute stress
Short-term stress, produced by the stress response.

chronic stress
Long-term, low-level stress in which the stress response continues without resolution.

General Adaptation Syndrome (GAS)
Selye's classic model describing the physiological changes associated with the stress response. The three phases are alarm, resistance, and exhaustion.

homeostasis, a state of stability and balance in which functions are maintained within a normal range. This process is called the **relaxation response**, which we will discuss in more detail in the section "Relaxation Techniques."

Acute Stress and Chronic Stress

According to evolutionary biology, the fight-or-flight response served an important function for our ancestors. Today, most of us do not live in such dangerous environments, but this innate response to threat is still essential to our survival, warning us when it is time to fight or flee. Although the fight-or-flight response requires a great deal of energy—which is why you often feel so tired after a stressful event—your body is equipped to deal with short-term **acute stress** as long as it does not happen too often and as long as you can relax and recover afterward.

A frequent or persistent stress response, however, can lead to problems. In these instances, the stress response itself becomes damaging. Many people live in a state of **chronic stress**, particularly those in marginalized groups in which stressful conditions are ongoing and the stress response often continues without resolution. Chronic stress increases the likelihood that the person will become ill or, if already ill, that her or his defense system will be overwhelmed by the disease. Prolonged or severe stress has been found to weaken nearly every system in the body.

STRESS AND YOUR HEALTH

Researchers have been looking at the relationship between stress and disease since the 1950s. Chronic stress can weaken body systems, and mediators such as personality traits and attitudes can intensify or diminish the physical effects of stress.

The General Adaptation Syndrome

One of the first scientists to develop a broad theory of stress and disease was Hans Selye.[67] Selye introduced the **General Adaptation Syndrome (GAS)** to describe and explain the physiological changes that he observed and that he believed to be predictable responses to stressors by all organisms. The syndrome has three stages—alarm, resistance, and exhaustion (Figure 2.6):

1. In the *alarm stage,* the body's fight-or-flight response is activated, accompanied by reduced immune system functioning.

2. In the *resistance stage,* the body uses energy to cope with the continued stress and stay at peak level.

3. After prolonged exposure to stress, the body may either recover or enter the *exhaustion stage* and become totally depleted, leading to illness and even death.

Physical Effects of Chronic Stress

Stress plays a role in illness and disease in a variety of ways. For example, stress-triggered changes in the lungs increase the symptoms of asthma and other respiratory conditions.[68] Stress also appears to inhibit tissue repair, which increases the likelihood of bone fractures and is related to the development of osteoporosis (porous, weak bones).[69] Stress can lead to sexual problems, including failure to ovulate and amenorrhea (absence of menstrual periods) in women and sexual dysfunction and loss of sexual desire in both men and women.[70] Some researchers suggest that high levels of stress can even speed up the aging process.[71] Overall, ongoing stress

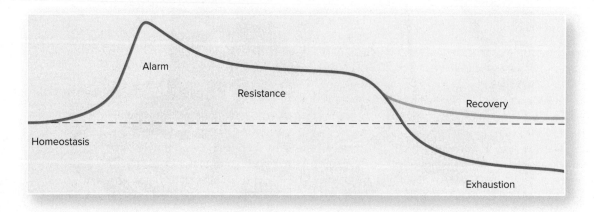

figure 2.6   **General Adaptation Syndrome.**
Source: Benson, H. (1993). The relaxation response. In D.P. Goleman & J. Gurin (Eds.), *Mind-body medicine: How to use your mind for better health* (pp. 233–257). Yonkers, NY: Consumer Reports Books.

appears to be related to an increase in chronic conditions that might have an impact 10 years later.[72]

Stress and the Immune System Since Selye's time, research has definitively shown that stress decreases immune function. One study demonstrated a strong relationship between levels of psychological stress and the possibility of infection by a common cold virus. Other studies have found that both brief and long-term stressors have an impact on the function of the immune system.[73,74,75] Stressors as diverse as taking exams, experiencing major life events, and providing long-term care for someone with Alzheimer's disease affect the immune system. Scientists do not yet fully understand why the stress response suppresses immune function or whether there is an evolutionary explanation for this result.

Stress and the Cardiovascular System The stress response causes heart rate to accelerate and blood pressure to increase. Chronic stress causes heart rate and blood pressure to remain elevated for long periods of time. Chronic hypertension (high blood pressure) makes blood vessels more susceptible to the development of atherosclerosis, a disease in which arteries are damaged and clogged with fatty deposits. Both hypertension and atherosclerosis increase the risk of heart attack and stroke. Overall stress levels are typically higher for individuals who have suffered heart attacks.

Stress and the Gastrointestinal System Although not conclusive, evidence suggests that gastrointestinal problems might be stress related. More specifically, conditions such as acid reflux, indigestion, and stomach pain all seem to be more common in people who have higher levels or more frequent occurrences of stress. Irritable bowel syndrome (IBS) may be an example of individual response differences to stress by the gastrointestinal tract. When IBS patients are under stress, food seems to move more slowly through the small intestine in those individuals who are constipated; the opposite is true for those who suffer from diarrhea.

For a long time, stress was commonly believed to cause stomach ulcers. Research suggests, however, that ulcers may be caused or exacerbated by a bacterial infection that irritates the stomach lining. Although not causing ulcers, stress may contribute to their development.

Stress and Mental Health Both acute and chronic stress can contribute to psychological problems and the development of psychological illnesses, including anxiety disorders and depression.[76] Overall, chronic stress appears to take a toll on an individual's mental health.[77] In *acute stress disorder,* for example, a person develops symptoms after experiencing severe trauma, such as assault, rape, domestic violence, child physical or sexual abuse, terrorist attacks, or natural disasters. Symptoms can include a feeling of numbness, a sense of being in a daze, amnesia, flashbacks, increased arousal and anxiety, and impaired functioning.

If such symptoms appear six months or more after the traumatic event, the person may have *post-traumatic stress disorder (PTSD),* a condition characterized by a sense of

■ The stress and trauma of combat can lead to post-traumatic stress disorder in some individuals. *(Peter Parks/AFP/Getty Images)*

numbness or emotional detachment from people, repeated reliving of the event through flashbacks and/or nightmares, and avoidance of things that might be associated with the trauma. In some cases, years may pass after the trauma before PTSD symptoms appear.[78]

Low-level, unresolved chronic stress can also be a factor in psychological problems. An example is *adjustment disorder,* in which a response to a stressor (such as anxiety, worry, and social withdrawal) continues for a longer period than would normally be expected. Stress can diminish wellness and reduce the ability to function at the highest level even without an identifiable disorder. Symptoms such as irritability, impatience, difficulty concentrating, excessive worrying, insomnia, and forgetfulness can be addressed, like physical symptoms, with stress management techniques.

Mediators of the Stress Response

Different people respond differently to stressors. Among the reasons are differences in their past experiences and overall levels of wellness. Also critical are personality traits, habitual ways of thinking, and inborn or acquired attitudes toward the demands of life.

Personality Factors In the 1970s two cardiologists, Meyer Friedman and Ray Rosenman, described and named the **Type A behavior pattern**.[79] Type A individuals tend to be impulsive, need to get things done quickly, and live their lives on a time schedule. They are hard-driving, achievement-oriented, and highly competitive individuals. Some estimates are that more than 40 percent of the U.S. population—and possibly half of all men—might be Type As.

Individuals who fit this description are prime candidates for

Type A behavior pattern
A set of personality traits originally thought to be associated with risk for heart disease. Type A individuals are hard driving, competitive, achievement oriented, and quick to anger; further research has identified hostility as the key risk factor in the pattern.

stress-related illnesses. The relationship between Type A personality traits and heart disease has been known for some time. More recently, there have been indications that a Type A personality can mean increased risk for a number of other diseases, including peptic ulcers, asthma, headaches, and thyroid problems.

However, not all the characteristics of this personality seem to be harmful. Many Type As are achievement-oriented and successful and yet remain healthy. According to recent research, a key culprit is **hostility**, defined as an ongoing accumulation of irritation and anger. Research has indicated that hostility, by itself, is related to coronary heart disease, and it may also contribute to premature death.[80]

Friedman and Rosenman also described a constellation of personality traits they labeled Type B. In contrast to the Type A personality, the Type B personality is less driven and more relaxed. Type Bs are more easygoing and less readily frustrated. All other things being equal, Type Bs are less susceptible to coronary heart disease.

Other experts have expanded on Friedman and Rosenman's research and have described two additional personality types. Type C personalities are introverted, detail-oriented people who may have trouble communicating and appear to be very cautious and reserved. These individuals might be at greater risk for autoimmune disorders and demonstrate a tendency to please others. Type D individuals appear to hold in negative emotions and are not very expressive. They experience negative emotions such as anger, anxiety, and sadness while fearing negative judgments from others. Type Ds are at risk for arterial disease, heart failure, and poor health ratings.[81,82,83]

Cognitive Factors   Until you decide that an event is a threat and beyond your ability to cope, it remains merely a potential stressor. For example, a person may think she has to get straight As in order to be a worthy human being. If she gets a B, she will experience much more stress than if she had more realistic expectations about herself and was more self-forgiving. Her ideas can transform a relatively neutral event into a stressor.

Other common illogical ideas and unrealistic expectations are "life should be fair," "friends should be there when you need them," "everyone I care about has to love and approve of me," and "everything has to go my way." When everyday experiences don't live up to these ideas, people who hold them end up feeling angry, frustrated, disappointed, or demoralized. Common patterns of distorted thinking include focusing on the negative and filtering out the positive, catastrophizing (expecting the worst), thinking in polarities (using black-and-white reasoning), and personalizing (thinking everything's about you).

hostility
An ongoing accumulation of irritation and anger.

hardiness
Effective style of coping with stress, characterized by a tendency to view life events as challenges rather than threats, a commitment to meaningful activities, and a sense of being in control.

With a more realistic attitude, people can take things in stride and reduce the frequency and intensity of the stress response. This doesn't mean they should have unrealistically low expectations. When expectations are too low, people may experience underachievement, depression, resignation, and lowered self-esteem. The goal is a realistic balance.

Resilience and Hardiness   Just as resilience is a factor in mental health, it is also a factor in the ability to handle stress. Stress-resistant people also seem to focus on immediate issues and explain their struggle in positive and helpful ways. They are able to adapt successfully to a wide range of life challenges.[84] For example, a poor grade on one exam might motivate the stress-resilient person to study harder, using the grade as motivation. A person who is not so resilient might react to a poor grade by feeling like a failure and giving up. More intense examples might include an individual's responses to threats such as disasters, war, poverty, and pandemics.

Another line of research has developed the concept of **hardiness**, an effective style of coping with stress. The researchers suggest that positive ways of coping with stress may buffer the body from its effects.[85,86,87] They have suggested that people high in hardiness are more resistant to illness. These researchers found that hardy people (1) perceive the demands of living as a challenge rather than a threat, (2) are committed to meaningful activities, and (3) have a sense of control over their lives. Having a sense of control may be especially critical in avoiding illness and responding to stressful situations.

SOURCES OF STRESS

Contemporary life presents us with nearly limitless sources of stress, ranging from major life events to our interpersonal relationships to some of our own feelings. In this section, we describe some of these stressors; in the next section, we present a variety of tips for handling them.

Life Events

Can stressful life events make people more vulnerable to illness? Thomas Holmes and Richard Rahe, medical researchers at the University of Washington, observed that individuals frequently experienced major life events before the onset of an illness. They proposed that life events—major changes and transitions that force the individual to adjust and adapt—may precipitate illness, especially if several such events occur at the same time.[88] Holmes and Rahe examined medical records to determine if there was such a relationship. From this work, they developed the Holmes-Rahe Social Readjustment Scale, a ranking of life events that require the individual to adjust and adapt to change. The higher a person's score on the scale, the more likely that person is to experience symptoms of illness.

The most stressful event on this scale is the death of a spouse, followed by such events as divorce, separation, a personal injury, and being fired from a job. Less stressful events on the scale include moving, going on vacation, experiencing a change in sleeping habits, and dealing with a minor violation of the law.

Daily Hassles

Surprisingly, everyday hassles can also cause health problems. In fact, daily hassles are related to subsequent illness and disease to a greater degree than are major life events.[89] Examples of daily hassles are arguments, car problems, deadlines, traffic jams, long lines, and money worries. All these events can lead to a state of chronic, low-level stress, especially if they pile up and you don't have a period of recovery.

College Stress College students experience a great deal of life change, and some studies even suggest that the college years may be the most stressful time in people's lives.[90] It has been reported that distress among young student adults has continued to rise with growing numbers self-reporting poor emotional health. The range of stressors for these young adults includes academic pressures, financial concerns, and making career decisions.[91] Considering the health effects of stress, it should not be surprising that colds, mononucleosis, and sexually transmitted infections are familiar on college campuses. It also appears that there is a deterioration of an individual's quality of life illustrated by poor sleep patterns and depression.[92]

Besides the effect of this major life transition, common sources of stress for college students include academic work, exams and grades, sleep deprivation, worries about money, relationship concerns, and uncertainty about the future. The stress of college may be growing even more intense, particularly for young women.[48] Nontraditional college students, including those who have returned to school after a hiatus, face additional stressors. These can include having to adapt to new technologies on campus, remembering how to study, trying to retrain for a new career, and balancing coursework with the demands of a job or family. Rising tuition costs also appear to increase stress levels of many students. A record number of students say they have to work to afford college. Concern about the economy and being successful also have an impact on students. (See the box "Life Stories: Jason: A New Financial Reality.")

College officials indicate that although more young people are going to college, they might also be less prepared to deal with college stressors and expectations.

■ Starting college is a major life transition with unique stressors. Individuals with the qualities of resilience and hardiness are able to take the challenges in stride and respond with energy and excitement. *(Cathy Yeulet/123RF)*

Almost all college students describe themselves as being depressed during their college experience, although the depression is often moderate and of a short duration. These episodes are often related to specific stressors, such as difficulties in a relationship, poor grades, and general adjustment concerns. When the intensity of the situation increases or the student is unable to find support, symptoms such as changes in appetite or increases in risk-taking behaviors, self-injurious behaviors, and smoking may appear.

Job Pressure Sixty-nine percent of U.S. adults say that work is a significant source of stress, and stress has been

■ Work overload and time pressure are major sources of stress and stress-related illnesses, including headaches, stomachaches, and depression. *(Paul Bradbury/ Caiaimage/Glow Images)*

Life Stories

Jason: A New Financial Reality

Jason, a first-year college student, was an athlete with a passion for everything having to do with sports, from exercise physiology to sport psychology. He planned to major in exercise science and hoped to eventually become a college professor and football coach.

Jason's parents had been saving money for their children's education for years, and with the help of his scholarship, they had been able to pay nearly all Jason's first-year expenses. Unfortunately, Jason's dad was laid off from his management position at a manufacturing company and was still looking for a comparable job. His mom worked part-time at a county office and had asked to increase her hours, but she was told there was a freeze on government spending.

With one son in college and two younger children at home, Jason's parents were struggling to make ends meet. They cut back on expenses in every way they could, from canceling gym memberships, magazine subscriptions, and cable to reducing spending on groceries, clothes, and auto maintenance. There was no longer any extra for the kids' guitar lessons, soccer registration, or class trips, and it wasn't clear where more college money was going to come from.

While at school, Jason video-chatted with his parents, and he could see they were under a great deal of stress. When he came home for spring break, he was startled to hear that they were worried about keeping up with the mortgage payments. The idea that his family could lose their home was shocking to Jason. He knew his dad hadn't been able to find another job, but he didn't know his parents had been living off their savings and had started dipping into their retirement funds.

Jason and his family sat around the kitchen table talking about options. Jason offered to reduce his course load and get a part-time job at school, though it would take him longer to get his degree. He also had the idea of transferring to a community college to reduce costs and then transferring back to his four-year college after he had his two-year degree. His parents said they didn't want him to do that yet and asked him to talk to someone in the financial aid office about grants, loans, and work-study programs.

When Jason returned to campus, he realized how shaken he was. He felt selfish for "living in a bubble" at school while his family was struggling, and he found himself avoiding friends, especially some whose families were well off. For a few weeks, he found it hard to focus on his schoolwork or his practices, and he had trouble sleeping. He felt that his whole view of the world was shifting, from one in which anything was possible to one in which his dreams might have to be tempered with a dose of reality.

- What would you do if you were in Jason's position? What options would you consider?

- How do you think Jason handled his reaction? What could he have done to help himself handle the stress he was experiencing?

found to affect productivity.[62] Half of all employees stated that they lost productivity at work due to stress, and 60 percent of young people report being less productive because of work stress.[93] Satisfaction with employers remains low, and about one in three workers reports an intention to seek employment elsewhere.[62,93]

Job pressure contributes to many stress-related illnesses, including cardiovascular disease, and may be related to the incidence of back pain, fatigue, muscular pain, and headaches. The costs are high in terms of dollars and worker performance, seen in accidents, absenteeism, turnover, reduced levels of productivity, and insurance costs.

Over the past century, many jobs have become physically easier, but expectations have grown that people will work more. Managers and professionals seem to work the longest days and are subject to associated stresses.[94] They bring work home and thus never really leave the job. Sixty-three percent of Americans have not taken a vacation in the past six months, with 28 percent of those individuals waiting more than a year without taking a vacation. Vacation deprivation is also a global issue, with 58 percent of workers describing themselves as being either very or somewhat vacation deprived. Almost a quarter of all Americans "check in" while on vacation although younger workers appear to be the least likely to stay in touch with their workplace.[95] Many people who want to be successful become *workaholics,* never taking a break from work and setting up themselves for burnout.

Burnout is an adverse, work-related stress reaction with physical, psychological, and behavioral components.[96] The symptoms of burnout include increasing discouragement and pessimism about work; a decline in motivation and job performance; irritability, anger, and apathy on the job; and physical complaints.[97]

Money and Financial Worries Seventy-two percent of U.S. adults say that money is a source of stress.[62] Financial worries take a particular toll on young people, with 75 percent of Millennials and 76 percent of Gen Xers saying money is a somewhat or very significant source of stress.[98]

Many people experience financial stress because their income is not equal to their expenditures. Familiar sources of financial stress are fear of running short of money before the end of the month, too much debt, reduced employment or unemployment, no savings to cover medical emergencies, and unexpected home or car repairs.

burnout
An adverse work-related stress reaction with physical, psychological, and behavioral components.

One of the best ways to relieve financial stress is to plan ahead. Being willing to follow a budget and make the lifestyle changes necessary to live within available funds may be the key to relief from financial stress. Simplifying your life, shedding those items and events that you can live without, can be liberating. Finding ways to ensure financial peace of mind is an excellent stress-reduction technique.

Family and Interpersonal Stress Families have to continuously adapt to a series of life changes and transitions. The birth of a baby places new demands on parents and siblings, and families must adapt as a teenager moves through adolescence to adulthood and leaves home. A family may be disrupted by death or divorce, and in fact, a growing number of children spend part of their lives in single-parent households, blended family units, or stepfamily systems. Families may become weakened by these experiences, or they may become stronger and more resilient.

Relationships of all kinds have the potential to be stressful, including intimate partnerships. Many experts agree that the key to a successful relationship is not finding the perfect partner but being able to communicate effectively with the partner you have. Whereas poor communication skills can cause interactions to escalate into arguments and fights (or deteriorate into cold silences), thoughtful communication and conflict resolution techniques can resolve issues before they become problems.

Time Pressure, Overload, and Technology Most of us experience some degree of time pressure in our lives. Many people find that they have more and more to do, despite time-saving devices, and want to compress more activity into less time. Multitasking is common—people talk on the phone while driving and answer e-mail while eating lunch. Although many people think they are more productive when they multitask, multitasking actually distracts people and causes them to perform poorly on a variety of tasks.[99] The rush to do things quickly and simultaneously ends up increasing levels of stress.

Many people do not see their overstuffed schedules as a problem. Instead, they go to time management classes to learn how to squeeze more activities into the time they have. Although planning and good use of time are effective stress management techniques, there are limits to how much a person can do. Many times the solution is not to use time more effectively but to do less. Stressed-out people are not poor stress managers; they are simply overloaded with responsibilities. Sometimes, learning to say no to others' requests is the best way to handle time management issues.

Technology makes us constantly available and never fully alone. Friends can reach us anytime with a text message or an e-mail, and work colleagues know how to contact us outside the office. With communication happening so quickly, we feel we must respond right away—even if we are doing something else or trying to relax. We may find that we have more "friends" on social networking sites than we can have meaningful contact with, but we continue to widen our social circles, simply adding stress to our lives. The idea of spending high-quality time with children has even been compromised. On a typical visit to a playground, you are likely to find parents checking their e-mail and reviewing their fantasy football teams on a smartphone while their children play. About 43 percent of U.S. adults are "constant checkers." This focus on devices increases stress, particularly among Millennials, who report the highest level of stress related to technology.[64] See the box "You Make the Call: How 'Connected' Should We Be?" for some thoughts about the effect of technology on communication.

Anger Sometimes, the source of stress is within the individual. Unresolved feelings of anger can be extremely stressful. The idea that blowing off steam, or venting, is a positive way to deal with anger is generally not valid. Releasing anger in an uncontrolled way often reinforces the feeling and may cause it to escalate into rage.[67] Venting can create anger in the person on the receiving end and hurts relationships. Suppressing anger or turning it against oneself is also unhealthy, lowering self-esteem and possibly fostering depression.

If you find yourself in a situation in which you are getting angry, take a time-out, remove yourself from the situation physically, and take some deep breaths. Examine the situation and think about whether your reaction is logical or illogical, and whether you could see it another way. Look for absurdity or humor in the situation. Put it in perspective. If you cannot avoid the situation or reduce your reaction, try some of the stress management strategies and relaxation techniques described later in this chapter.

Trauma The effect of traumatic experiences has received a great deal of study. The events of September 11, 2001, and military service in Iraq and Afghanistan are frequently cited as traumatic events of the highest order. The deadly COVID-19 pandemic of 2020 is another example of an extremely stressful event having a profound impact on many people, including health care professionals, and resulting in an increase in those who are depressed, anxious, or struggling with PTSD. Events of this magnitude overwhelm our ability to cope and destroy any sense of control, connection, or meaning. They shake the foundations of our beliefs about the safety and trustworthiness of the world.

Some people develop post-traumatic stress disorder in response to trauma, as mentioned earlier in this chapter. For example, approximately 13 percent of those with operational infantry war zone experience in Afghanistan and Iraq developed PTSD.[100] In 2012, almost half a million veterans asked for medical treatment for the disorder.[101] While many veterans do not develop symptoms of PTSD, they do experience a great deal of stress as they transition home. This often-overlooked need results in many veterans never receiving needed services.[102]

Although the triggering event may be overwhelming, often it alone is not sufficient to explain the occurrence of PTSD. Again, this is evidence of the role of mediating factors in the individual experience of stress. It appears that early life

You Make the Call

How "Connected" Should We Be?

Are there times when we would be better off turning off our electronic devices? Can we really multitask and walk and text or sit in a meeting and text, tweet, or e-mail our friends? What do you do when you are socializing with friends and your smartphone tells you that you have a message? Do you respond? Have we forgotten how to have conversations and develop relationships, since so much of our lives are handled in 280-character communications?

We have created a culture in which technology organizes much of what we do and at times can even dominate our lives. But is all this bad? Our level of connectivity allows us to stay in touch more easily. We can see pictures of grandchildren instantly and have more face-to-face meetings across states and continents.

Evidence suggests, however, that when students multitask while doing schoolwork, they are not as focused on the learning activity and actually learn less. Evidence is also mounting about the dangers of using an electronic device when driving or walking, yet automobiles now come equipped with a GPS, phone system, and other electronic ways to stay connected. To have uninterrupted face-to-face time, some people have turned to cell phone stacking while socializing. They place all cell phones in the middle of the table, and the first person to check his or her phone is required to buy the next round of drinks or even pay for everyone's dinner.

As a culture, we seem to be providing mixed messages. On one hand, we are telling people that technology can distract them and make them less efficient, yet on the other hand, we are demanding that people stay connected. Where is the balance? Will we hurt a relationship if we don't stay connected to our friends and lovers? Will our work dominate our lives because we are expected to respond to electronic messages at any time of day or night? Are we less likely to get promoted if we do not respond?

What are the pros and cons of constant connectivity?

Pros

- Being available by smartphone allows us to stay more connected to friends and family.
- Geography does not have to be a barrier for either the development or the maintenance of social relationships.
- More information is available, and more easily accessible, than ever before.

Cons

- We are always expected to be on call and available.
- We are often distracted, anticipating the next interruption.
- In-person relationships have to compete with online friends.

Sources: Stavrinos, D., Pope, C.N., Shen, J., & Schwebel, D.C. (2017). Distracted walking, bicycling and driving: Systemic review and meta-analysis of mobile technology and youth crash risk. *Child Development.* doi:10.1111/cdev.12827; Patterson, M. (2017). A naturalistic investigation of media multitasking while studying and effects on exam performance. *Teaching of Psychology, 44*(1), 51–57; Lau, W. F. (2017). Effects of social media usage and social media multitasking on the academic performance of university students. *Computers in Human Behavior, 68,* 286–291.

adversity is a predictor of PTSD, and those who report childhood adversity are at far greater risk. In addition, people with more resources, including cultural capital, social support, and life advantages, are less likely to be affected by psychological distress.[103]

Societal Pressures Intolerance, prejudice, discrimination, injustice, poverty, pressure to conform to mainstream culture—all are common sources of stress for members of modern society. Exposure to racism and homophobia, for example, can cause distrust, frustration, resentment, negative emotions such as anger and fear, and a sense of helplessness and hopelessness. Experiencing racism has been associated with both physical and mental health-related symptoms, including hypertension, cardiovascular reactivity, depression, eating disorders, substance abuse, and violence.[104,105,106,107]

In May 2020, the killings of George Floyd, Ahmaud Arbery, and Breonna Taylor triggered international protests focused on changing structural racism and the historical mistreatment of communities of color. These traumatic events affected entire communities and in time may also result in more cases of people struggle with PTSD stress-related health issues. The pain and suffering of living with long-standing systemic structural racism affects both individual and population mortality, as evidenced by the number of stress-related disorders and lower age of mortality among African Americans. While the consequences of racism, health disparities, and differences in access to services have been known for years, recent events continue to illustrate that we do not have an equal or equitable society. Will we be able to finally examine these structural barriers and decide to take actionable steps that can end in change?

Similarly, lesbians, gay males, bisexuals, and transgender (LGBT) individuals experience symptoms of stress when they are the targets of prejudice and homophobia.[108,109,110] These individuals often have higher rates of school-related problems, substance abuse, criminal activity, prostitution, running away from home, and suicide than do their non-LGBT peers.

MANAGING STRESS

The effects of unrelieved stress on the body and mind can range from muscle tension to a pervasive sense of hopelessness about the future, yet aiming for life without stress is unrealistic, if not impossible. The solution is to find effective ways to manage stress.

Healthy and Unhealthy Ways to Manage Stress

There are many ways to manage stress, but some are ineffective, counterproductive, and unhealthy, such as the following:

- *Use of tobacco.* The chemicals in tobacco can make a smoker feel both more relaxed and more alert. However, nicotine is highly addictive, and smoking causes a host of health problems. Tobacco use is the leading preventable cause of death in the United States.

- *Use and abuse of alcohol.* Moderate use of alcohol can lower inhibitions and create a sense of social ease and relaxation, but drinking provides only temporary relief without addressing the sources of stress. Heavy drinking and binge drinking carry risks of their own, including the risk of addiction. All too often, what began as a solution becomes a new problem.

- *Use and abuse of other drugs.* Like alcohol, illicit drugs alter mood and mind without solving problems, and they often cause additional problems. For example, stimulants such as methamphetamine and cocaine increase mental alertness and energy, but they can induce the stress response and disrupt sleep. Opiates such as oxycodone (OxyContin) and hydrocodone (Vicodin) can relieve pain and anxiety, but tolerance develops quickly, making dependence likely. Marijuana can cause panic attacks, and even caffeine raises blood pressure and levels of stress hormones.

- *Use of food.* Many people overeat or eat unhealthy foods when they feel stressed. According to one survey, the top "comfort foods" are candy, ice cream, chips, cookies and cakes, fast food, and pizza, in that order.[111] Other people eat less or skip meals in response to stress. For most of us, eating is a pleasurable, relaxing experience, but using food to manage feelings and stress can lead to disordered eating patterns as well as overweight and obesity.

Other approaches to stress management that are especially popular with college students are listening to music, socializing with friends, going to movies, and reading. Though not unhealthy, these sedentary activities need to be balanced with more active stress-management techniques, such as walking or exercising. Colleges usually offer resources to help students deal with stress, and at some major universities, 40 percent of all undergraduates visit the counseling center. However, a sign that not enough students are getting the help they need is the fact that suicide is the second leading cause of death on college campuses. More effort must be made to reach and educate students about stress reduction and stress management techniques, including time management, relaxation techniques, exercise, and good nutrition.

No single stress-management technique is helpful or comfortable for everyone. For example, some individuals feel comfortable with meditation, while others who need a more active stress-reduction method might choose exercise. Some methods are very simple, such as scheduling "worry time"[112] by basically setting aside a time to focus on your worries. Others, such as yoga, take a great deal more time and practice. As you review the methods described in the following pages, consider how they might fit with your personality and lifestyle. Experiment with a few methods—and try something new—before you settle on something you think will work for you. Whatever methods you choose, we recommend practicing them on a regular basis. They will become second nature to you and part of your everyday life, available during stressful moments and possibly even activated naturally.

Sometimes, stressful events and situations are overwhelming, and your resources and coping abilities are insufficient to support you. These times call for professional help. Don't hesitate to visit your college counseling center or avail yourself of other resources if you find you need more support.

Stress-Reduction Strategies

Any activity that decreases the number or lessens the effect of stressors is a stress-reduction technique. Although you might not think of avoidance as an effective coping strategy, sometimes protecting yourself from unnecessary stressors makes sense. For example, try not listening to the news for a few days. You'll find that world events continue as always without your participation. If certain people in your life consistently trigger negative feelings in you, try not seeing them for a while. When you do see them, you may have a better perspective on your interpersonal dynamics. If you have too many activities going on in your life, assert your right to say no to the next request for your time. Downscaling and simplifying your life are effective ways of alleviating stress.

Time Management Time management is the topic of seminars and books, and some experts have devoted their entire careers to helping people learn how to manage their time. Here, we focus on just two key points: planning and prioritizing.

To improve planning, ask yourself whether you are focusing on the things that are most important to you. You may be focusing on the right tasks if:

- You're engaged in activities that advance your overall purpose in life.

- You're doing things you have always wanted to do or that make you feel good about yourself.

- You're working on tasks you don't like, but you're doing them knowing they relate to the bigger picture.[113]

To make sure you focus on the things that matter to you, ask whether each task is worthy of your time. Obviously, you need time for sleeping, working, and studying, but remember to allow yourself time for maintaining wellness through such activities as relaxing, playing, and spending time with family and friends. A global picture of your goals and priorities provides a perspective that can give you a sense of control and reduce stress.

To manage your time on the everyday level, keep a daily "to do" list and prioritize the items on it. Write down the items because it's stressful to just keep them in your head! As you look at the list, assign each task a priority:

- Is it something you must get done today, such as turning in a paper?

- Is it something you would like to get done, such as catching up on the week's reading?

- Is it something that can wait until tomorrow, such as buying a new pair of jeans?

Then organize the items into these three categories. Complete the tasks in the first category first, before moving on to tasks in the other two categories. This approach will help you be more purposeful, organized, and efficient about the use of your time, giving you more of a sense of control in your life.

In the course of evaluating your goals and prioritizing your daily tasks, you may find that you have too many commitments. Trying to do more than you have time for and doing the wrong things in the time you have are stressful. Managing your time well is a key to reducing stress.

Social Support   Another key to reducing stress, just as it is a key to maintaining mental health and achieving a meaningful spiritual life, is social support.[114] Numerous studies show that social support decreases the stress response hormones in the body. Dean Ornish points out that people who have close relationships and a strong sense of connection and community enjoy better health and live longer than do those who live in isolation. People who suffer alone suffer a lot.[115]

Many people lack the sense of belonging and community that was provided by the extended family and closer-knit society of our grandparents' day. You may have to consciously create a social support system to overcome isolation and loneliness and buffer yourself from stress.[116,117,118] With the outbreak of COVID-19 many individuals have felt even more isolated and lonely and more stress. Use of virtual communication methods may help alleviate some of those feelings. The benefits make the effort worthwhile. They include having a shoulder to lean on and an ear to listen when you need support. Communicating about your feelings reduces stress and helps you to work through problems and feel better about yourself.

The best way to develop a support system is to give support to others, establishing relationships and building trust, in the following manner:

- Cultivate a variety of types of relationships.

- Stay in touch with your friends, especially when you know they're going through a hard time, and keep your family ties strong.

- Find people who share your interests and pursue activities together, whether it's hiking, dancing, or seeing classic movies.

■ Having a strong social support system is an important ingredient in both the maintenance of psychological health and the reduction of stress.
(Brand X Pictures/Stockbyte/Getty Images)

You may want to join a group with a goal that interests you, such as a church group, a study group, or a book club.

- Try to get involved with your community and participate in activities that benefit others.

- Maintain and improve your communication skills—both listening to other people's feelings and sharing your own.

A Healthy Lifestyle   A healthy lifestyle is an essential component of any stress management program. A nutritious diet helps you care for your body and keeps you at your best. Experts recommend emphasizing whole grains, vegetables, and fruits in the diet and avoiding excessive amounts of caffeine (see Chapter 5). Getting enough sleep is also essential for wellness (see Chapter 4), as are opportunities for relaxation and fun.

Exercise is probably the most popular and most effective stress buster available (see Chapter 6). It has a positive effect on both physical and mental functioning and helps people withstand stress. Regular exercisers are also less likely to use smoking, drinking, or overeating as methods for reducing their levels of stress.[119,120] A growing body of evidence suggests that getting regular exercise is the best thing you can do to protect yourself from the effects of stress. While many people say they "just don't have enough time," all you really need is a jump rope and 15 to 20 minutes each day.

Relaxation Techniques

If you are in a state of chronic stress and the relaxation response does not happen naturally, it is in your best interest to learn how to induce it. Relaxation techniques seem to have an effect on a number of physiological functions, including blood pressure, heart rate, and muscle tension.[121] Here, we describe a few of the many techniques that have been developed.

Deep Breathing   One relaxation tool that is simple and always available is breathing. When you feel yourself starting to experience the stress response, you can simply remember to breathe deeply. As you learn to be aware of breathing patterns and practice slowing that process, your mind and body will begin to relax. Breathing exercises have been found to be effective in reducing panic attacks, muscle tension, headaches, and fatigue.

To practice deep breathing, inhale through your nose slowly and deeply through the count of 10. Don't just raise your shoulders and chest; allow your abdomen to expand as well. Exhale very slowly through your nose or through gently pursed lips and concentrate fully on your breath as you let it out. Try to repeat this exercise a number of times during the day even when you're not feeling stressed. Once it becomes routine, use it to help yourself relax before an exam or in any stressful situation.

Progressive Relaxation

Progressive muscle relaxation is based on the premise that deliberate muscle relaxation will block the muscle tension that is part of the stress response, thus reducing overall levels of stress. Progressive relaxation may help with sleep and has provided relief of such stress-related symptoms as neck and back pain and high blood pressure.[121]

To practice progressive muscle relaxation, find a quiet place and lie down in a comfortable position without crossing your arms or legs. Maintain a slow breathing pattern while you tense each muscle or muscle group as tightly as possible for 10 seconds before releasing it. Begin by making a fist with one hand, holding it, and then releasing it. Notice the difference between the tensed state and the relaxed state, and allow your muscles to remain relaxed. Continue with your other hand, your arms, shoulders, neck, and so on, moving around your entire body. Don't forget your ears, forehead, mouth, and all the muscles of your face.

If you take the time to relax your body this way, the technique will provide significant relief from stress. You will also find that once your body learns the process, you will be able to relax your muscles quickly on command during moments of stress.

Visualization

Also called *guided imagery,* visualization is the mental creation of visual images and scenes. Because our thoughts have such a powerful influence on our reactions, simply imagining a relaxing scene can bring about the relaxation response.[67,76,121] Visualization can be used alone or in combination with other techniques such as deep breathing and meditation to help reduce stress, tension, and anxiety.

To try visualization, sit or lie in a quiet place. Imagine yourself in a soothing, peaceful scene, one that you find particularly relaxing—a quiet beach, a garden, a spot in the woods. Try to visualize all you would see there as vividly as you can, scanning the scene. Bring in your other senses; what sounds do you hear, what scents do you smell? Is the sun warm, the breeze gentle? If you can imagine the scene fully, your body will respond as if you were really there. Commercial tapes are also available that use guided imagery to promote relaxation, but because imagery is personal and subjective, you may need to be selective in finding a tape that works for you.

Mindfulness-Based Meditation

Mindfulness meditation[121] is a form of meditation that asks you to pay attention to the present moment and let thoughts and feelings come and go without judging them. Other mindfulness-based practices include yoga and focused breathing. Research on mindfulness meditation indicates that it can lower blood pressure, improve immune system functioning, and alleviate a variety of mental and physical conditions. It may also improve psychological well-being, enhance cognitive functioning, and increase momentary positive emotions.[122,123,124] The specific components that contribute to positive outcomes include attention regulation, emotional regulation, body awareness, and changes in self-perspective.[124]

Yoga

The ancient practice of yoga is rooted in Hindu philosophy, with physical, mental, and spiritual components. It is a consciously performed activity that includes posture, breath, and body and mind awareness. In the path and practice of yoga, the aim is to calm the mind, cleanse the body, and raise awareness. The outcomes of this practice include a release of mental and physical tension and the attainment of a relaxed state.

The most widely practiced form of yoga in the Western world is hatha yoga. The practitioner assumes a number of different postures, or poses, holding them while stretching, breathing, and balancing. The poses are performed slowly and gently, with focused attention. Yoga stretching improves flexibility as well as muscular strength and endurance. For yoga to be effective, the poses have to be performed correctly. If you are interested in trying yoga, we recommend that you begin by taking a class with a certified instructor. There are also commercial videos that can get you started.

T'ai Chi

T'ai chi is a form of Chinese martial arts that dates back to the 14th century. Central to this method is the concept of qi, or life energy, and practicing t'ai chi is said to increase and promote the flow of qi throughout the body.

■ T'ai chi is a calming and energizing practice that can be used to elicit relaxation and manage stress.
(Dougal Waters/Digital Vision/Getty Images)

T'ai chi combines 13 postures with elements of other stress-relieving techniques, such as exercise, meditation, and deep breathing. Research has shown that t'ai chi is beneficial in combating stress, although exactly how it works is unclear. You can take t'ai chi classes, although these are not as widely available as yoga classes. Using instructional videos to learn t'ai chi is another option.

Biofeedback   Biofeedback is a kind of relaxation training that involves the use of special equipment to provide feedback on the body's physiological functions. You receive information about your heart rate, breathing, skin temperature, and other autonomic nervous system activities and thus become more aware of exactly what is happening in your body during both the relaxation response and the stress response. Once you have this heightened awareness, you can use relaxation techniques at the first sign of the stress response in daily life. Biofeedback can be used to reduce tension headaches, chronic muscle pain, hypertension, and anxiety.[121,125] If you are interested in trying biofeedback, check with your school to see whether the special equipment and training are available.

Affirmations   Researchers have found that when people have an optimistic attitude and a positive view of themselves, they are less likely to suffer the negative effects of stress. **Affirmations** are positive thoughts that you can write down or say to yourself to balance the negative thoughts you may have internalized over the course of your life. Repeatedly reciting such negative, distorted thoughts can increase stress levels. Although they may seem silly to some people, affirmations can help you shift from a negative view of yourself to a more positive one. The more often you repeat an affirmation, the more likely you are to believe it.

To create affirmations for yourself, think about areas of your life in which you would like to see improvements, such as health, self-esteem, or happiness, and then imagine what that change would look like. Here are some examples:

- I make healthy choices for myself.
- I am the right weight for me.
- The more grateful I am, the more reasons I find to be grateful.
- I love and accept myself.
- I attract only healthy relationships.
- I have abundant energy, vitality, and well-being.
- I can open my heart and let wonderful things flow into my life.

We have provided a sampling of stress-reducing techniques; there are many others such as listening to soothing music, going for walks in a beautiful setting, or enjoying the company of a pet. Whatever your preferences, learn to incorporate peaceful moments into your day, every day. You will experience improved quality of life today and a better chance of avoiding stress-related illness in the future.

Web-Based Mobile Health and Virtual Reality Interventions

It is clear that technology has changed our world, including our physical and mental health care. For example, there are many apps for relaxation, meditation, cognitive-behavioral therapy, and the treatment of depression. The entire telehealth area has expanded accessibility for many, for everything from keeping track of our heart rates and sleep patterns to monitoring exercise and diet. The evidence supporting the effectiveness of these interventions is currently sparse, but be prepared to see continued growth in the application of web-based and mobile interventions to health and mental health issues.[121] Recently, mental health professionals have begun to use virtual reality to treat individuals challenged by anxiety and other disorders. Early studies have supported the use of virtual reality to treat PTSD, fear of flying, and the aftermath of sexual trauma.[126]

In Review

What is mental health?
Mental health is usually conceptualized as the presence of many positive qualities, such as optimism, a sense of self-efficacy, and resilience (the ability to bounce back from adversity). Some specific approaches include positive psychology's focus on "character strengths and virtues," Maslow's self-actualization model, and Goleman's concept of emotional intelligence.

How do we respond to a loss?
Having someone close to you die is part of life, but it is also one of the most difficult life transitions you will face. Grieving is an extremely personal experience, yet it is one that others in your community and culture share. Give yourself the time to recover from the loss of a loved one, and seek out support from friends. If you feel sad or at a loss after many months, consider seeking out professional help.

What is the brain's role in mental health and illness?
Structural changes in the brain until early adulthood affect both learning and behavior. A few mental disorders are caused by some pathology in the brain, but research in recent decades has found that neurotransmitter imbalances lead to a variety of mental disorders, from stress and anxiety to mood disorders and schizophrenia. Typically, mental illness is caused by a

complex interaction of biological, genetic, psychological, social, and cultural factors.

What are common mental disorders, and how are they treated?

A mental disorder is a pattern of behavior associated with excessive distress or impaired functioning, and it is not always easy to discern when a common psychological problem becomes a mental disorder. Major categories of mental disorders according to the *Diagnostic and Statistical Manual of Mental Disorders* (*DSM-5*) include mood disorders, such as depression and bipolar disorder; anxiety disorders, such as panic attacks, phobias, and obsessive-compulsive disorder; addiction; and psychotic disorders, such as schizophrenia. Most people who commit suicide have a mental disorder. The two broad approaches to treatment to mental disorders are medications and psychotherapy. Although some drugs have serious side effects, both treatments can be effective, especially in combination.

What is stress?

Stress is a general state of the body, mind, and emotions when an environmental stressor has triggered the stress response. It is mediated by personal variables that include the person's perceptions and appraisal of the event; stress can be positive (eustress) or negative (distress). The stress response, also known as the fight-or-flight response, is the set of physiological changes that occur in the face of a threat. When the stressful event is over, the body returns to homeostasis in the relaxation response. The human body can handle short-term acute stress, but chronic stress often leads to illness.

How does stress affect health?

Selye's General Adaptation Syndrome (GAS) describes three stages of the physiological response to stress: alarm, resistance, and exhaustion. Stress can decrease immune function, increase the heart rate and blood pressure, cause gastrointestinal problems, and contribute to mental disorders such as post-traumatic stress disorder. Mediators, including personality traits, self-perceptions and expectations, and resilience and hardiness, affect how the body responds to stress.

What are the main sources of stress and the main approaches to managing stress?

Common stressors are life events, both bad and good, daily hassles at school and work, money problems, family and interpersonal problems, time pressures, anger, trauma, and societal pressures.

Healthy alternatives to self-medicating with alcohol, drugs, and tobacco are reducing stress through time management, social support, maintaining a healthy lifestyle, and practicing relaxation techniques, such as deep breathing, progressive relaxation, visualization, mindfulness-based meditation, yoga, t'ai chi, biofeedback, and affirmations. New advances in technology may also lead to new methods for treating mental health issues.

Personal Health Portfolio

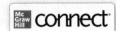

Chapter 2   How Resilient Are You?

Resilience is described as the ability to regain equilibrium or recover when faced with adversity. Individuals who are resilient are often more self-confident, recognizing their strengths and abilities. For those people whose resilience is low, failures and setbacks are a drain on their energy and motivation, and they are more prone to depression and other mental disorders. Resilience is also important in dealing with stress. Resilient people have the perseverance to deal with stressors in positive ways and rebound more quickly after stressful events.

Take some time and complete the Resilience Scale to gain a better understanding of your ability to respond during times of adversity.

Resilience: The ability to bounce back after or recover following a difficult situation.

Directions: Complete the following by circling the number corresponding to the most appropriate choice for each statement; then add up your total score and divide by the total number of questions.

	Very Infrequently or Never	Less Than 50% of the Time	More Than 50% of the Time	Usually or Always
1. I believe I can control difficult situations.	1	2	3	4
2. I feel like I typically bounce back after not being successful.	1	2	3	4
3. I learn from my mistakes and don't repeat them.	1	2	3	4
4. I try to create innovative solutions when I feel stuck.	1	2	3	4
5. I take care of most things by myself.	1	2	3	4
6. I enjoy being part of a team and relying on others for help.	1	2	3	4
7. I easily ask for help.	1	2	3	4
8. When others ask me for help I say yes.	1	2	3	4
9. I have a set of clear life goals.	1	2	3	4
10. When I feel defeated I have a hard time getting back on track.	1	2	3	4

Total Score _____

Divided by 10 _____

A high score suggests that you are more resilient. Also take a moment and look at your responses to individual questions. Then determine if an increase in self-awareness resulting from your responses indicates that there are changes you would like to make.

Sources: Scale created based on information provided in Smith, B.W., Dalen, J., Wiggins, K., Tooley, E., Christopher, P., & Bernard, J. (2008). The brief resilience scale: Assessing the ability to bounce back. *International Journal of Behavioral Medicine*, *15*(3), 194–200; Sinclair, V.G., & Wallston, K.A. (2004). The development and psychometric evaluation of the Brief Resilient Coping Scale. *Assessment*, *11*(1), 94–101.

CRITICAL THINKING QUESTIONS

1. Analyze your score. Was it higher or lower than you expected? What areas of strength or weakness do you see?

2. It has been suggested that when you face adversity and find a way to recover, you actually gain confidence for the next time you face a difficult situation. Think back to your own adolescence. Was it easy? Or did you face issues related to building friendships, becoming comfortable with your body, or participating in sexual activity? How have your past experiences contributed to your resilience today?

3. What people or circumstances have influenced your resilience? Consider your parents, other family members, and friends and the community in which you were raised. Describe your social support network and other factors that might contribute to your bouncing back (being resilient) when facing adversity.

3 Social Connections

Tyler Olson/123RF

Ever Wonder...

how you can find a partner?

how you can be better at forming more satisfying relationships and communicating with other people?

what is important about community?

Relationships are a vital part of wellness. For many of us, close social ties give meaning and significance to our lives. It must also be recognized that relationships exist on a continuum from acquaintances to those we are romantically involved with. Evidence indicates that an individual's social relationships are important predictors of health and well-being.[1,2,3] It also appears that loneliness is closely related to premature mortality.[4] People with strong social support systems have better mental and physical health, and they are more capable of handling stress and adverse life events. In fact, people with strong social support may even live longer than those without it. Some researchers believe that some of our personal behaviors, such as food choices and degree of life satisfaction, can spread throughout social networks and greatly influence the behaviors of larger groups of people.[5] Other researchers have found that "extreme giving" individuals who say yes to others without an expectation of immediate gain, share credit easily, are willing to mentor others, and are genuinely concerned about others have more satisfying and successful lives.[6]

This chapter addresses the social aspects of health, particularly interpersonal relationships and community involvement.

HEALTHY PERSONAL RELATIONSHIPS

Relationships are at the heart of human experience. We are born into a family; grow up in a community; have classmates, teammates, and colleagues; find a partner from among our acquaintances and friends; and establish our own family. Yet for all their importance in our lives, relationships are fraught with difficulties and challenges.

There have been many changes in the structure of relationships over the past years. For example, 69 percent of people were living in marital relationships in 1970, whereas only about half of adults 18 and over in the United States were married in 2017, a number that has remained stable in recent years.[7] It also seems as though more people are getting married to someone of a different race or ethnicity, with 17 percent meeting that description in 2015, compared to 3 percent in 1967.[8] With the increase in divorce there is also an increase in remarriage, with 4 in 10 new marriages involving at least one spouse who had previously been married.[7] Many people in the United States now live alone, either by choice or by chance, and the number of cohabiting adults has increased, particularly among those over age 50.[9] Since the legalization of same-sex marriage in 2015, about 1 in 10 LGBT people in the United States have married a same-sex spouse; 61 percent of cohabiting same-sex couples are married.[7] Finally, in today's electronically connected world, college students seem to have less of an opportunity to experience real relationships on campus, where electronic meetings and dating have often become the norm.

Three kinds of important relationships are the one you have with yourself, the ones you have with friends, and the ones you have with intimate partners. In each, certain qualities serve to enhance the relationship's positive effects.

A Healthy Sense of Self

All your relationships begin with who you are as an individual. A healthy sense of self, reasonably high self-esteem, a capacity for empathy, and the ability both to be alone and to be with others are attributes that make successful relationships possible. Many people develop these assets growing up in their families, but people who experience deficits in childhood can still make up for them later in life.

Friendships and Other Kinds of Relationships

Friendship is a reciprocal relationship based on mutual liking and caring, respect and trust, interest and companionship. We often share a big part of our personal history with our friends. Compared with romantic partnerships, friendships are usually more stable and longer lasting. In fact, the bonds created among friends can be so powerful that the mood of one person spreads to the other people in a friendship network. That is, if you are happy and healthy, it is possible that the factors in your happiness might be determined by a friend of a friend of a friend.[10]

There is a great deal of evidence suggesting the importance of social support. Social support means having family and friends to turn to when you simply want to share positives as well as during times of crisis. Most of us have between one and six close social contacts; the average is four.[11] Generally, we find and keep friends who are geographically close to us,[12] and we are much more likely to be happy if we have a close friend who lives within a mile.[10] However, social media forums such as TikTok and Twitter and communication devices such as smartphones may be changing that.

Like family ties and engagement in social activities, friendships offer a psychological and emotional buffer against stress, anxiety, and depression. People who are surrounded by happy people and those who have high status in any network are most likely to be happy. Overall, friendships and networks can help protect you against illness and help you cope with problems if you do become ill. Friendships and other kinds of social support may also increase your sense of belonging, purpose, and self-worth.[13]

It also appears that the benefit of having close relationships during middle adolescence can carry over into adulthood and result in increased self-worth and the formation of a positive identity.[14]

(Susanne Walstrom/Getty Images)

Social isolation and loneliness can have a profound impact. More than 60 percent of high school students[15] and 40 percent of middle-aged and older adults[16] describe themselves as lonely. Research has indicated that those who are isolated have more health issues and report more difficulties with basic life activities.[17]

The impact of isolation on all generations may be greater now with the need to socially isolate due to COVID-19. It is unclear, at this time, what the long-term strategy will be to reduce the impact of this pandemic.

Strengths of Successful Partnerships

An intimate relationship with a partner has many similarities to friendship, but it has other qualities as well. Compared with friendships, partnerships are more exclusive, include deeper levels of connection and caring, and have a sexual component. The following are some characteristics of successful partnerships:

- The more mature and independent individuals are, the more likely they are to establish intimacy in the relationship. Independence and maturity often increase with age; in fact, one of the best predictors of a successful marriage is the age of the partners when they get married. The current median age for marriage is 30 for men and 28 for women,[7] and marriage at a younger age (under 23) is associated with higher rates of divorce.[18]

- The partners have both self-esteem and mutual respect.

- The partners understand the importance of good communication and are willing to work at their communication skills. They know that listening to the other's feelings and trying to see things from the other's perspective are key in communication, even if they do not ultimately agree.

- The partners have a good sexual relationship, one that includes the open expression of affection and respect for the other's needs and boundaries.

- The partners enjoy spending time together in leisure activities, but they also value the time they spend alone pursuing their own interests.

- The partners are able to acknowledge their strengths and failings and take responsibility for both.

- The partners are assertive about what they want and need in the relationship, and flexible about accommodating the other's wants and needs. They can maintain a sense of self in the face of pressure to agree or conform.

- The partners know that disagreement is normal in relationships, that when conflict is handled constructively it can strengthen the relationship, and that the best relationships will have many more positive moments than those considered negative.[19]

- The partners are friends as well as lovers, able to focus unselfish caring on each other.

- The couple has good relationships with family and friends, including in-laws, members of their extended family, and other couples.

- The partners have shared spiritual values.

Intimate close relationships, whether they include marriage or not, take work and effort. If for some reason the relationship does not appear to be going as well as you might hope, it might be useful to seek out a trained couples counselor who can help you through the tough times. Remember that ignoring or avoiding the troubling issues that threaten the relationship over time will typically not make things better.

LOOKING FOR A PARTNER

How do we go about finding the right person for a successful intimate partnership, and how do we know when we have found that person? Is it all about magic and chemistry, or is there something more deliberate and purposeful about it?

Attraction

People appear to use a systematic screening process when deciding whether someone could be a potential partner. It seems that romantic love progresses through a pattern, beginning with a nonstop focus on the person you are in love with.[20] According to one scholar, love may allow us to overlook our partner's flaws, and we fall in love for a variety of reasons, not necessarily accidentally. Some of the conscious and unconscious factors that affect this process include odor, physical attractiveness, and similarity.[20]

Proximity is an often overlooked but significant factor in our discovery of romantic partners.[20] Simply being physically close to people makes it more likely that we will establish a relationship with them. Sometimes attraction is a function of

(Ronnarong/123RF)

familiarity, and proximity determines how often two people are exposed to one another.

Of the people in proximity to us, we are most interested in those we find physically attractive. If we find a person attractive we are willing to consider other traits, although "signaling" devices, such as coy looks and other flirtatious moves, are also effective at garnering attention.[20] In general, people who are perceived as attractive in our society have an advantage. They are evaluated more positively by parents, teachers, and potential employers; make more money; and report having better sex with more attractive partners. Online choices might be made a bit differently, however, with individuals sending out many more messages in an effort to attract someone "out of their league" and also rejecting those they perceive to be undesirable.[21]

We are also drawn to people who are similar to ourselves, usually in characteristics such as age; physical traits such as height, weight, and attractiveness; educational attainment; family, ethnic, and cultural background; religion; political views; and values, beliefs, and interests. We are attracted to people who agree with us, validate our opinions, and share our attitudes. For example, when it comes to politics, 77 percent of both Republicans and Democrats said their partner was in the same party.[7] There is even an online dating app called "righter" that focuses on meeting like-minded conservatives. Even though opposites may initially attract, partners who are like each other tend to have more successful relationships. The more differences partners have, the more important communication skills become.

The Process of Finding a Partner: Dating and More

Both in and out of college, many people prefer a flexible approach to finding a life partner rather than traditional dating. For example, some women take the lead in asking men out and play a more assertive role in the development of the relationship. Other people take an indirect approach—they play hard to get or convey interest with a flippant pickup line. However, research generally suggests that indirectness is not an effective strategy, and people who are straightforward and respectful are more likely to get a positive response.[20]

One of the oldest ways in which people have found potential partners is through their social connections. For example, you may be introduced to someone by your family members, or a friend you know from the community center might invite you out for a double date. However, the Internet has expanded these networks, and physical proximity may soon be a less significant factor than it has been in the past.[22,23] Almost a third of people now use texting to arrange a first date. Currently, more than one-third of U.S. marriages get their start online, and at least one study has described these relationships as more satisfying and less likely to end in divorce.[24] Others have found that online couples were less likely to get married and that breakup rates were higher for those who met online.[25]

It also appears that attitudes toward online dating are growing more positive; almost 60 percent of U.S. adults say online dating is a good way to meet people, and 27 percent of those aged 18 to 24 have used dating sites or apps.[26] Couples who meet online also tend to be younger and more likely to meet people who are different from them. It also appears that same-sex partners are more likely to meet online than opposite-sex couples.[27] There is also research that focuses on online dating and mate choice. For example, when focusing on attributes such as physical attractiveness and income, people using dating apps tend to respond to the most attractive profiles, while in considering other attributes they tend to look for similarities. The tone of your online dating "pitch" profile might not make a difference; it seems that even a happy message might not result in more responses.[28] Online daters send longer messages to those they perceive to be more desirable, as though extra words will make a difference. Some have also suggested that both men and women pursue partners online who are about 25 percent more desirable than themselves.[21]

The COVID-19 epidemic may be changing how we meet now and possibly permanently. With the emphasis on social distancing many individuals are faced with meeting people on line as the only option.

It makes sense to cast a wide net in the search for a partner. Even participation in social groups, volunteering, sports, and church may not bring you into contact with a broad range of people. Furthermore, most people lead busy lives, and online approaches to dating readily enlarge the pool of potential partners.

It is always a good idea to do some research about different dating sites before deciding where to put your profile and what to include. Many people stopped using online dating sites because they did not like the quality of their matches, and that could also be why 28 percent had tried four or more such sites. Online dating has also created an entire new vocabulary that describes potential responses to another person. For example, "breadcrumbing" is stringing a potential partner along without committing, "ghosting" is disappearing without warning, "rebating" is what happens when a rejected person submits a Venmo request for half the cost of the date, and "cloaking" is when a person not only stands you up on a date but also blocks you on any app you have previously communicated on. "Cookie jarring" describes when one person is pursuing a relationship while holding on to others as a backup. Finally, "paper-clipping" refers to an ex who continues to stay in contact after a breakup. According to a survey of 9,600 people when asked which dating services they had joined, 48 percent said Match.com, with Plenty of Fish and eHarmony tied for second at 23 percent.[29]

Still, if you decide to pursue a relationship with someone you meet over the Internet, be cautious (see the box "Consumer Clipboard: Know Your Online Dating Site OR App") because there can be much you do not know about the person, and scams are possible.[30] Incidents of "catfishing," in which people pretend to be someone else and "hook" a person into an online relationship with exploitative intentions, are all too common.

Consumer Clipboard
Know Your Online Dating Site or App

Since the original online dating site, Match.com, went live in 1995, the number and variety of sites have expanded exponentially, as have the types of technology employed. Only 14 percent of U.S. adults were even Internet users then. Now, almost 90 percent of people in the United States are online, and website dating has increased dramatically. At many sites, you can narrow your search by age, religion, ethnicity and race, sexual orientation, parental status, occupation, type of encounter you're seeking, and more. Some controversial dating sites, such as carrotdating.com and WhatsYourPrice.com, require paying for a date. Most apps charge subscription fees, but some are free. Social networking sites like Facebook, Twitter, TikTok, Snapchat, and Instagram also account for a large proportion of the time people spend connecting online with others.

Regardless of the type of site you use, follow these basic guidelines to stay safe *(Continued on next page)*:

- Online dating sites provide access to a much larger pool of potential partners than most people would otherwise encounter. Be prepared to meet a lot of people, and don't take it personally if the chemistry isn't there with most of them.

- Never share personal or financial information online.

- Guard your identity. Remain anonymous until you feel safe enough to share it.

- Protect your online access information if you share a computer.

- Remember that people may lie about themselves and alter their photos.

- When meeting offline, meet in public, tell a friend where you'll be, stay sober, don't leave personal items unattended, and use your own transportation.

(Box images: Nd3000/123RF; Eric Audras/Onoky/SuperStock; Image Source/Getty Images; Image Source/Getty Images; Chihiro Ishino/Image Source; George Doyle/Stockbyte/Getty Images; Stockbyte/SuperStock)

Continued...

WHAT IS LOVE?

Passionate love has been defined as "a state of intense longing for union with another."[31] A more biological view of romantic love portrays it as a basic human drive, and natural chemicals, including dopamine, direct how you feel.[32] Of all the people we are attracted to and all the potential mates we screen, what makes us fall in love with one or a few in a lifetime?

Some theorists propose that we fall in love with people who are similar to us in important ways (*similarity theory*). Couples with more similarities seem to have not only greater marital harmony but also higher fertility rates. Other theorists suggest that falling in love and choosing a partner are based on the exchange of "commodities" such as love, status, property, and services (*social exchange theory*). According to this view, we are looking for someone who fills not only our

70

Concluded...

- It is wise to transition to face-to-face interactions quickly because that's where two people can get a real sense of their romantic potential.

The following are some of the types of online dating sites available:

- **General:** User browses profiles of a wide range of potential partners. *Examples:* Match.com, PlentyofFish (POF.com)

- **Niche:** User browses profiles of potential partners from specific populations. *Examples:* JDate.com, ChristianMingle.com, BlackPeopleMeet.com, SeniorPeopleMeet.com

- **Self-report algorithm:** User reports data about self, and site uses algorithms to create matches. *Examples:* eHarmony.com, OKCupid.com

- **Non-self-report algorithm:** Site uses non-self-reported data and algorithm to create matches. *Example:* GenePartner.com

- **Video dating sites:** User interacts with potential partners via webcam. *Example:* SpeedDate.com

- **Virtual dating sites:** User creates avatar and goes on virtual date in online setting. *Example:* Weopia.com

- **Smartphone and Facebook apps:** User connects with people via social networks. *Example:* Zoosk.com

A number of other apps create opportunities for people to meet. Lulu is a female-only app with more than 1 million registered users where women share opinions and create reviews of men. Tinder is an app for both men and women that facilitates conversations between people who have an online attraction. It is one of the fastest-growing free dating apps and had more than 13 billion swipe rates one year after it was launched. Bumble is a female-initiated app and Farmers Only is a dating app for those who want to meet farmers or who live in more rural areas.

After signing up and providing information about gender, location, and sexual orientation, users simply swipe through profile pictures based on attraction. Once there is a mutual attraction, a private chat box appears so that interested people can get together only minutes after a match. The average Tinder user checks the site 11 times each day, 7 minutes per visit. Grindr is an app for gay, bisexual, and bi-curious men who want to meet potential partners.

Sources: Smith, A., & Anderson, M. (2015). 5 facts about online dating. *Pew Research Center.* Retrieved from http://www.pewresearch.org/fact-tank/2015/04/20/5-facts-about-online-dating/; Finkel, E. L., et al. (2012). Online dating: Critical analysis from the perspective of psychological science. *Psychological Science in the Public Interest, 20*(10): 1–64; Summers, N. (2013). Dating app Tinder catches fire. *Bloomberg Business Technology.* Retrieved from www.businessweek.com/articles/2013-09-05/dating-app-tinder-catches-fire; eBizMBA. (2015). *Top 15 most popular dating websites.* Retrieved from http://www.ebizmba.com/articles/dating-websites; Meltzer, M. (2017). Online dating: Match me if you can. *Consumer Reports.* Retrieved from https://www.consumerreports.org/dating-relationships/online-dating-guide-match-me-if-you-can/; 5 tips for staying safe when online dating. (2018). Safedate. Retrieved from https://www.yoursafedate.com/5-tips-for-staying-safe-online-dating/; 10 tips for staying safe with online dating. (2019). Safety.com. Retrieved from https://www.safety.com/10-online-dating-safety-tips/

emotional needs but also our needs for security, money, goods, and more.

The Course of Love

The beginning stages of falling in love can feel like a roller-coaster ride, taking the lovers from the heights of euphoria to the depths of despair. They may actually become "lovesick" and find themselves unable to eat, sleep, or think of anything but the object of their desire. These early stages of a love relationship are typically romantic, idealistic, and passionate. The lovers are absorbed in each other and want to spend all their time together, sometimes to the exclusion of other people and everyday responsibilities.

Researchers think this experience of love relies on increased levels of the neurotransmitter dopamine in the brain.[32] Dopamine is associated with the experience of pleasure. On the physiological level, this kind of love also causes arousal of the sympathetic nervous system, as evidenced by such physiological signs as increased heart rate, respiration, and perspiration. These responses gradually decrease as the relationship develops and progresses. Intense passion may subside as lovers become habituated to each other. In some cases, passion continues at a more bearable level and intimacy deepens; the relationship becomes more fulfilling and comes to include affection, empathy, tolerance, caring, and attachment. The partners are able to become involved in the world again, while maintaining their connection with each other. In other cases, the lessening of passion signals the ending of the relationship; the lovers drift apart, seeking newer, more satisfying partnerships. It also appears that romantic love may be gender neutral, meaning individuals can fall in love with anyone.[33]

Sternberg's Love Triangle

Psychologist Robert Sternberg has proposed a view of love that can give us insight into its various aspects. In this view, love has three dimensions: intimacy, passion, and commitment. **Intimacy** is the emotional component of love and includes feelings of closeness, warmth, openness, and affection. **Passion** is the sexual component of love; it includes attraction, romance, excitement, and physical

intimacy
The emotional component of love, including feelings of closeness, warmth, openness, and affection.

passion
The sexual component of love, including attraction, romance, excitement, and physical intensity.

intensity. **Commitment** is the decision aspect of a relationship, the pledge that you will stay with your partner through good times and bad, despite the possibility of disappointment and disillusionment.[34]

Different combinations of these three components, represented metaphorically as a triangle, produce different kinds of love (Figure 3.1). When there is only intimacy, the relationship is likely to be a friendship. Passion alone is infatuation, the high-intensity early stage of a love relationship. Commitment alone is characteristic of a dutiful, obligatory relationship, one that many people would consider empty. When there is both intimacy and passion, the relationship is considered "romantic love"; commitment may develop in time. When there is passion and commitment, the relationship has probably developed rapidly, without the partners getting to know each other very well; when passion fades, there may not be much substance to this type of relationship. When there is intimacy and commitment but no passion, the relationship may have evolved into more of a long-term friendship; Sternberg calls this relationship "companionate love." Finally, when all three components are present, the couple has "consummate love."[35] This type of relationship is what many dream of, but it's difficult to find and even harder to sustain. No matter how we conceptualize love, however, it is something that enhances happiness and satisfaction in life.

commitment
The decision aspect of a relationship; the pledge to stay with a partner through good times and bad.

nonverbal communication
Communication that takes place without words, mainly through body language.

metamessage
The unspoken message in a communication; the meaning behind the message, conveyed by nonverbal behavior and by situational factors such as how, when, and where the message is delivered.

COMMUNICATION SKILLS AND STYLES

We establish, maintain, and nourish our relationships—or, alternatively, damage and destroy them—through communication. Clear, positive communication is a key to successful intimate relationships.

Nonverbal Behavior and Metamessages

A good deal of communication takes place as **nonverbal communication** through facial expressions, eye contact, gestures, body position and movement, and spatial behavior (how far apart people sit or stand). People tend to monitor their verbal behavior—what they say—much more carefully than their nonverbal behavior, yet nonverbal communication may convey their real message.

Nonverbal behavior is part of the **metamessage**—the unspoken message you send or get when you are communicating. The metamessage encompasses all the conscious and unconscious aspects of a message, including the way something is said, who says it, when and where it is said, or even that it is said at all. It includes the meaning and intent behind a message, rather than just the words someone says. Often, the metamessage is what triggers an emotional response.

Building Communication Skills

To be an effective communicator when you speak, know what you want to say. Examine your feelings, motives, and intentions before you speak. When you do speak, use "I" statements to state what you feel or want in a clear, direct way without blaming or accusing the other person. Using "I" statements helps you take responsibility for your own emotions and reactions rather than trying to place responsibility on someone else. For example, it is more productive to say, "I feel . . . when you . . . " than to say, "You make me feel . . . Saying what you would like to have happen is also more productive than complaining about what isn't happening. Other keys to positive, effective communication are avoiding generalizations, making specific requests, and remaining calm. If you feel yourself starting to get angry, take a time-out and come back to the conversation after you cool off.

When you are the listener, do just that—listen. Don't interrupt, give advice, explain, judge, analyze, defend yourself, or offer solutions. Give the other person the time and space to say fully what is on his or her mind, just as you would like when you are speaking. Attentive listening shows that you respect and care about the other person. It is the cornerstone of good communication.

Forgiveness is also valuable in relationship communication. Strategies that include making more opportunities for discussion and explicitly stating you forgive the other person can be important when trying to sustain a relationship.[36]

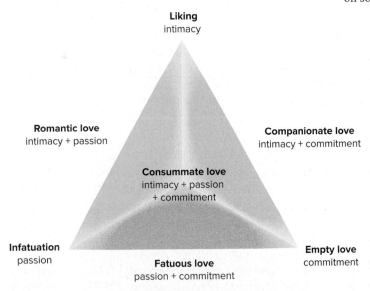

figure 3.1   Sternberg's triangular theory of love.
Source: Sternberg, R. J. (1986). A triangular theory of love. *Psychological Review, 93*(2), 119–135.

If you and your partner are experiencing conflict, good communication skills can help you resolve it constructively. Conflict is a normal part of healthy relationships. Often, it is a sign that partners are maintaining their right to be different people and to have different points of view; it can also indicate that the relationship is changing or growing.

When you are trying to resolve a conflict with your partner, keep the topic narrow. Try not to generalize to other topics, incidents, or issues. Avoid being either passive or aggressive; **assertiveness** means speaking up for yourself without violating someone else's rights. Be prepared to negotiate and compromise, but don't give up something that is really important to you (such as time to keep up your other friendships). If you feel that demands are being made on you that you cannot or do not want to meet, this may not be the right relationship for you. For example, see the box "You Make the Call: Will Sending Nude Pictures Bring You Closer?" at the end of the chapter. Communicating clearly about any relationship demands/requests is important and critical to the long-term health of that relationship.

Gender Differences in Communication Styles

According to linguistics scholar Deborah Tannen, gender differences in communication patterns have a significant impact on relationships (see Table 3.1). Tannen suggests that men are more likely to use communication to compete, and women are more likely to use communication to connect.[37]

Although these patterns are broad and general, they are sometimes at the root of misunderstandings between men and women. If you find yourself experiencing confusion or conflict in your communications with another person, consider whether gender differences may be involved. Neither style is right or wrong, better or worse—they are just different.

Table 3.1   Gender Differences in Communication

Men	Women
Feel oppressed by lengthy discussions	Expect a decision to be discussed first and made by consensus
Do not want to have long discussions, particularly about what they consider to be minor decisions	Appreciate the discussion itself as evidence of involvement
Are inclined to resist what they perceive as someone telling them what to do; do not want to take orders	Are inclined to do what is asked of them
Think every question needs to be answered	Believe a question is not simply a question but the opening for a negotiation
Believe they are showing independence by not asking probing questions	Believe that when men change the subject they are showing a lack of interest and sympathy
Goal is to "fix" the problem	Goal is to share, develop relationships, and listen

Source: Tannen, D. (1990). *You just don't understand: Women and men in conversation.* New York: William Morrow.

SEX AND GENDER

Most adult partnerships and intimate relationships include not only sexual behavior but also biological, psychological, sociological, and cultural aspects of sexual identity. In this section, we consider two such dimensions—gender roles and sexual orientation.

Although they are often used interchangeably, the terms *sex* and *gender* have different meanings. **Sex** refers to a person's biological status as male or female; it is usually established at birth by the appearance of the external genitals. A person with female genitals usually has XX chromosomes, and a person with male genitals usually has XY chromosomes.

Sex is not always clear-cut, however. For example, chromosomes are sometimes added, lost, or rearranged during the production of sperm and ova, causing such conditions as Klinefelter syndrome (XXY) and Turner syndrome (XO). Sometimes, as a result of genetic factors or prenatal hormonal influences, a baby is born with

assertiveness
The ability to stand up for oneself without violating other people's rights.

When words fail, body language speaks volumes. *(stockbroker/123RF)*

ambiguous genitals—a condition referred to as **intersex**. Other times, a person experiences a sense of inappropriateness about his or her sex and identifies psychologically or emotionally with the other sex.

Gender refers to the behaviors and characteristics considered appropriate for a male or a female in a particular culture. The term **cisgender** is used to refer to an individual whose gender matches an assigned gender.

We are assigned a gender when we are born, which gets reinforced through language and expectations over the first years of our life. For most people, gender identity is permanent, but some individuals make a nonbinary choice and identify as *bigender, genderfluid,* or *pangender.*

Gender Roles and Gender Identities

A **gender role** is the set of behaviors and activities a person engages in to conform to society's expectations. Gender role stereotypes suggest that a masculine man is competitive, aggressive, ambitious, power-oriented, and logical, and that a feminine woman is cooperative, passive, nurturing, supportive, and emotional.

Today, we commonly assume that both genders are capable and can be successful in a variety of roles at home and at work. However, gender roles and gender stereotypes are learned in childhood and may be hard to change, even when we are aware of them. Some individuals may be attracted to those who are more like themselves, and others desire a partner who is very different. For example, those who are very expressive might be more interested in those who are equally curious and novelty-seeking, whereas someone who is sweet, nurturing, and good with words might be more likely to choose someone who is high-powered and tough-minded.[32]

The term *androgynous* is applied to a person who displays characteristics or performs tasks traditionally associated with both sexes; sometimes, it is also applied to a person who does not display overt characteristics associated with either sex.

Individuals who experience discomfort or a sense of inappropriateness about their sex, called *gender dysphoria,* and who identify strongly with the other sex are referred to as cross-gender identified, transsexual, or **transgender**. The term *transgender* can describe anyone whose **gender identity** differs from the sex of his or her birth. Many transgender individuals dress in the clothes of the other gender (*cross-dressing*) and live in society as the other gender. Some

undergo surgery and hormone treatments to experience a more complete transformation into the other sex. Transgender individuals have typically experienced gender dysphoria since earliest childhood.

Most children who do not fit the cultural stereotype of masculinity or femininity do not grow up to be transgender. According to the National Center for Transgender Equality, less than 1 percent of the population in the United States (between 750,000 and 3,000,000 people) is transgender.[38] Transgender individuals often face discrimination and limitations on opportunities. Look at the box "Action Skill Builder: Learning to Be Supportive of Nonbinary Individuals"

intersex
Having ambiguous reproductive or sexual anatomy.

gender
Masculine or feminine behaviors and characteristics considered appropriate for a male or a female in a particular culture.

cisgender
sometimes abbreviated as cis and is the term for people whose gender identity corresponds to the sex they are assigned at birth

gender role
The set of behaviors and activities a person engages in to conform to society's expectations of his or her sex.

transgender
Having a sense of identity as a male or female that conflicts with one's biological sex.

gender identity
The internal sense of being male or female.

Action Skill-Builder

Learning to Be Supportive of Nonbinary Individuals

You don't have to understand what it means for someone to be nonbinary to respect them. Some people haven't heard a lot about nonbinary genders or have trouble understanding them, and that's okay. But identities that some people don't understand still deserve respect.

Use the name a person asks you to use. This is one of the most critical aspects of being respectful of a nonbinary person, as the name you may have been using may not reflect the person's gender identity. Don't ask nonbinary persons what their old name was.

Try not to make any assumptions about people's gender. You can't tell if someone is nonbinary simply by appearance, just like how you can't tell if someone is transgender by doing the same.

If you're not sure what pronouns someone uses, ask. Different nonbinary people may use different pronouns. Many nonbinary people use "they" while others use "he" or "she," and still others use other pronouns. Asking whether someone should be referred to as "he," "she," "they," or another pronoun may feel awkward at first, but is one of the simplest and most important ways to show respect for someone's identity.

Advocate for nonbinary-friendly policies. It's important for nonbinary people to be able to live, dress, and have their gender respected at work, at school, and in public spaces.

Understand that, for many nonbinary people, figuring out which bathroom to use can be challenging. For many nonbinary people, using either the women's or the men's room might feel unsafe, because others may verbally harass them or even physically attack them. Nonbinary people should be supported by being able to use the restroom that they believe they will be safest in.

Talk to nonbinary people to learn more about who they are. There's no one way to be nonbinary. The best way to understand what it's like to be nonbinary is to talk with nonbinary people and listen to their stories.

National Center for Transgender Equality. (2018). Understanding non-binary people: How to be respectful and supportive. National Center for Transgender Equality. Retrieved from https://transequality.org/issues/resources/understanding-non-binary-people-how-to-be-respectful-and-supportive to learn how to be supportive and respectful of nonbinary people.

Sexual Orientation

Sexual orientation refers to a person's emotional, romantic, and sexual attraction to a member of the same sex, the other sex, or both. It exists along a continuum that ranges from exclusive heterosexuality through bisexuality to exclusive homosexuality. Although the role of genes in sexual orientation is not clearly understood, sexual orientation is known to be influenced by a complex interaction of biological, psychological, and societal factors, and these factors may be different for different people.

Sexual orientation is a basic and enduring emotional, romantic, or sexual attraction to other people.[39] Most experts believe it is not a choice and does not change (perhaps especially in men). Sexual orientation may or may not be evidenced in a person's appearance or behavior, and the person may choose not to act on that sexual orientation.

Heterosexuality is emotional and sexual attraction to members of the other sex. Heterosexuals are often referred to as "straight." Throughout the world, laws related to marriage, child rearing, health benefits, financial matters, sexual behavior, and inheritance generally support heterosexual relationships. **Homosexuality** is emotional and sexual attraction to members of one's own sex. In today's usage, homosexual men are typically referred to as "gay," and homosexual women are referred to either as "gay" or "lesbian."

Homosexuality occurs in all cultures, but researchers have generally had difficulty determining exactly what proportions of the population are straight and gay. Sex researcher Alfred Kinsey estimated that about 4 percent of U.S. males and 2 percent of U.S. females were exclusively homosexual.[40,41] More recently it has been estimated that almost 5 percent of the U.S. population is LGBT.[42]

Emotional and sexual attraction to both sexes is referred to as **bisexuality**. Bisexuals may date members of both sexes, or they may have a relationship with a member of one sex for a period of time and then a relationship with a member of the other sex for a period of time. After having relationships with members of both sexes, a bisexual may move toward a more exclusive orientation, either heterosexual or homosexual.

sexual orientation
A person's emotional, romantic, and sexual attraction to a member of the same sex, the other sex, or both.

heterosexuality
Emotional and sexual attraction to members of the other sex.

homosexuality
Emotional and sexual attraction to members of the same sex.

bisexuality
Emotional and sexual attraction to members of both sexes.

COMMITTED RELATIONSHIPS AND LIFESTYLE CHOICES

In this section, we consider marriage—one of the most important social and legal institutions in societies throughout the world—along with other relationship and lifestyle choices that many people make today.

Marriage

Marriage is not only the legal union of two people but also a contract between the couple and the state. In the United States, each state specifies the rights and responsibilities of the partners in a marriage. Although marriage has traditionally meant the union of a man and a woman, many same-sex couples are interested in marriage, and since 2015 same-sex marriage has been legal in all 50 states.

One of the most noticeable changes in marital patterns since the mid-1980s is the rise in age at first marriage. Since the 1950s, the median age at first marriage has risen from 23 for men and 20 for women to 30 for men and 28 for women.[7] The delay in marriage, along with the increase in the number of cohabiting couples, has contributed to an overall decline in the number of people who are married.

Most people state that love is a very important reason for getting married. Desire for a lifelong commitment, companionship, children, financial stability, and legal rights and benefits are also reasons people list for getting married.[7] Marriage confers benefits in many domains. Partnerships and family relationships provide emotional connection for individuals and stability for society. Married people live

Kirstin Beck is a former U.S. Navy Seal who came out as a trans woman following her retirement. During her military career, she earned multiple awards and decorations. She published her memoir, *Warrior Princess: A U.S. Navy SEAL's Journey to Coming Out Transgender,* in June 2013. *(Jim Urquhart/REUTERS/Newscom)*

■ Relationships are more likely to be strong and lasting when partners share important values, including spiritual values. (*westend61/123RF*)

longer than single or divorced people, partly because they lead a healthier lifestyle. On average, married people have better mental and physical health and fewer health concerns related to threats from cancer, heart attacks, and surgery.[43] Satisfied marital partners are also able to manage conflict constructively, develop trusting relationships, and build commitment.[19]

What makes a marriage successful? One predictor of a successful marriage is having positive reasons for getting married. Positive motivations include the desire for companionship; the presence of love, intimacy, and a supportive partnership; sexual compatibility; and interest in sharing parenthood. Poorer reasons, associated with a reduced chance of having a successful marriage, include premarital pregnancy, desire to rebel against parents, quest for independence, desire for economic security, family or social pressures, and a rebounding reaction from another relationship.

Love alone is not enough to make a marriage successful. Research has found that among the best predictors of a happy marriage are realistic attitudes about the relationship and the challenges of marriage, satisfaction with the personality of the partner, enjoyment of communicating with the partner, ability to resolve conflicts together, agreement on religious and ethical values, egalitarian roles, and a balance of individual and joint leisure activities. The characteristics associated with successful and unsuccessful marriages are typically present in a couple's relationship before they are married.[19,44]

Infidelity mars some marriages, and although it does not necessarily end them, it is the reason most often reported for divorce. While 90 percent of U.S. adults consider marital infidelity to be morally wrong, researchers estimate that 20 to 25 percent of married men and 10 to 15 percent of married women have participated in extramarital sex.[45] Men in heterosexual married relationships feel more threatened if their partner has a sexual affair than if she falls in love with someone else, whereas women in these relationships are more distressed if their partner falls in love with someone else.[46]

Gay and Lesbian Partnerships

Like heterosexual couples, same-sex couples desire intimacy, companionship, passion, and commitment in their relationships. The reasons for getting married described by same-sex couples are very similar to those held by heterosexuals; most cite love as a very important reason. However, **LGBTQ** people in the United States were twice as likely to cite gaining spousal legal rights and benefits as being important and having children as far less important.[47]

The social context for same-sex couples has changed dramatically over the past 10 years. With the legalization of same-sex marriage there has been a growing interest in the study of same-sex relationships. Among the strengths of same-sex couples described in the literature are appreciation and respect for differences, positive interactions, feelings of deep connection, and effective communication.[48] The literature also indicates that children brought up in same-sex families appear to be as well adjusted as those with heterosexual parents.[49]

Unfortunately, gays and lesbians often have to deal with discrimination and **homophobia**—an irrational fear of homosexuality and homosexuals. Same-sex relationships do not

LGBTQ
An abbreviated adjective that stands for "lesbian, gay, bisexual, transgender, or questioning."

homophobia
An irrational fear of homosexuality and homosexuals..

■ Gay and lesbian partnerships are very similar to heterosexual partnerships, but same-sex couples and families often have to deal with bias and discrimination. (*Juanmonino/E+/Getty Images*)

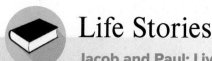

Life Stories

Jacob and Paul: Living Together . . . Happily Ever After?

Jacob and Paul were both 24 and had just graduated college. They had been in an exclusive relationship for the past two years but hadn't talked about their long-term plans or the future of their relationship. Paul was interviewing for jobs in New York City and hoping to move there. He asked Jacob to come live with him. They could save money by living together, Paul said, and besides, they cared about each other.

Jacob hesitated. Paul said it would be easier for him to find a job there, and Jacob wasn't sure what would happen to their relationship if he didn't move with Paul. He did love Paul, and the prospect of living in New York was exciting, so he said yes. They agreed to split rent and utilities in proportion to their earnings once they both found jobs.

Jacob turned out to really enjoy living in New York—and with Paul. They bought furniture together and developed a social circle of old friends from school and new friends from work. A year passed quickly, and Jacob found himself thinking about their future together. He was ready to make a commitment to Paul. But when he brought up the subject of marriage or the future, Paul always seemed to deflect the conversation. He said he didn't know what the rush was and didn't know why they needed to get married. Why change a good thing? He was happy just living together.

Jacob felt hurt by Paul's responses. He knew he wanted to be married—but perhaps Paul merely found living together convenient until something better came along. Jacob didn't want to push Paul away, and because he didn't bring it up again, Paul thought everything was fine between them.

Finally, Jacob felt he had to talk to someone about the growing distance he felt in the relationship. When he told Paul he was going to see a therapist, Paul was surprised and concerned. He said he had no idea Jacob had so many doubts about their relationship and their future. He apologized for giving the appearance that he didn't want to talk about their plans—he could see now that it was important to Jacob. He told Jacob he knew he had some fears about marriage based on his parents' relationship and that he wasn't sure he felt ready to get married yet. Still, he said, he would be happy to go to counseling with Jacob so they could talk more about the issue in a healthy way.

- Do you think Paul and Jacob made the right decision when they decided to live together? Why or why not?

- What problem occurred in their communication? How could they have prevented this problem from occurring?

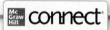

---

receive the same level of societal support and acceptance as heterosexual relationships. There has, however, been a cultural attitude shift, with more than 60 percent of the U.S. population supporting same-sex marriage[7,50] and the Supreme Court deciding in June 2015 that it is legal.

A great deal of research has examined the relationship between health outcomes and marriage. Most of it has looked exclusively at heterosexual couples, however, leaving us unaware of the impact of marriage and cohabitation on the health of LGBT adults.[51] There are a few studies that indicate however that married same-sex couples benefit from the relationship and have better health outcomes than those who don't marry.[52] It is hoped that future research on health-related issues will also focus on LGBT couples and families.

Cohabitation

The U.S. government defines **cohabitation** as a relationship in which two people of the opposite sex live together as unmarried partners. Since the 1960s, cohabitation has become one of the most rapidly growing social phenomena in the history of our society. The rate of cohabitation has increased more than 10-fold since the 1960s; almost 50 percent of women enter a cohabiting relationship at some point, and more than 60 percent of marriages are preceded by a cohabiting relationship. Approximately half of cohabiters are younger than 35, but an increasing number are people over

50. Many younger cohabiters have never been married, whereas most of those over 50 have been divorced.[9]

For many couples, cohabitation is an accepted part of the process of finding a mate (see the box "Life Stories: Jacob and Paul: Living Together . . . Happily Ever After?"). Most couples today believe it is a good idea to live together in order to decide whether they should get married, though cohabiting couples report higher levels of conflict and less commitment than couples who do not live together. While some studies have shown that cohabitation decreases the likelihood of success in marriage, recent studies suggest that cohabiting couples in engaged, fast-moving relationships are more successful than other types of couples.[53] Some observers might suggest that the differences in divorce rates between those who cohabit and those who do not might be attributable to the age at which they choose to cohabit. Those who cohabit in their late 20s were less likely to get divorced than those who cohabited in their late teens or early 20s.[54] Others have found that cohabitation improves psychological well-being and, on a range of outcomes, might be very similar to marriage.[55] Overall, it seems that cohabitation is a form of social attachment that many individuals are now choosing as either a path to marriage or an end in itself.[9]

cohabitation
A living arrangement in which two people of the opposite sex live together as unmarried partners

Who's at Risk?

Divorce Rates by Gender, Race/Ethnicity, and Education

What is the likelihood that a marriage in the United States will last? Individual circumstances exist for every married couple, but some factors are statistically linked to higher divorce rates. Couples are more likely to divorce if the partners are poor, are uneducated, have had premarital births, are victims or perpetrators of domestic violence, or are unfaithful to each other. What does the following graph indicate about gender, race, educational attainment, and the likelihood of divorce?

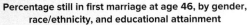

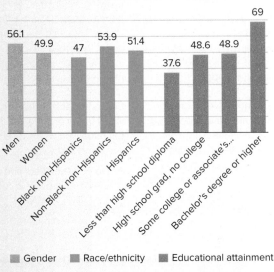

Percentage still in first marriage at age 46, by gender, race/ethnicity, and educational attainment

Source: U.S. Department of Labor: Bureau of Labor Statistics. (2013). Marriage and divorce: Patterns by gender, race, and educational attainment. *Monthly Labor Review,* Table 3. Retrieved from http://www.bls.gov/opub/mlr/2013/article/marriage-and-divorce-patterns-by-gender-race-and-educational-attainment.htm

Divorce

For a large percentage of couples, the demands of marriage prove too difficult and the parties choose to divorce. The current divorce rate is nearly twice what it was in 1960, although it has declined since reaching its highest point in the 1980s. The lifetime probability that a couple in their first marriage will divorce is between 40 and 50 percent.[56] With more individuals delaying marriage until they get older, we may see a continued decline in divorce rates among those getting married for the first time. For a closer look at divorce rates during the first 20 years of marriage, see the box "Who's at Risk: Divorce Rates by Gender, Race/Ethnicity, and Education."

Why do so many couples divorce in our society? Many couples may not have the necessary problem-solving skills, or they may not be sufficiently committed to the relationship. Many people enter marriage with unrealistic expectations, and some choose an unsuitable mate.

The termination of a marriage is almost always a traumatic process lasting months or years. Divorce is a leading cause of poverty, leaving many children in impoverished homes headed by a single mother, often the parent with the lower income.[57] Most single-parent families cannot maintain the lifestyle they had before the divorce.

Divorce is especially hard on children, leading to different kinds of problems for children of different ages. For many children, however, the impact of divorce can be reduced with time if the parents work to keep stress at a minimum and provide their children with a secure environment. In these situations, the children will not display any negative impact from the divorce as they get older.[58] Counseling can help both children and adults deal with the stress of divorce and adjust to a new life. Children are often best served by having continued contact with both parents as long as the adults can get along.

Blended Families

Many divorced people eventually remarry, and **blended families**, in which one or both partners bring children from a previous marriage, are becoming a common form of family. It can take two years or more for stepparents and stepchildren to build relationships. Adults should allow time for trust and attachment to develop before they take on a parenting role with their stepchildren. When children regularly see their noncustodial parent, they are better able to adjust to their new family. Children also adjust better if the

blended families
Families in which one or both partners bring a child or children from a previous marriage.

78

parents in the blended family have a low-intensity relationship and if the relationships between ex-spouses are civil.

Singlehood

Although marriage continues to be a popular institution, many young adults are delaying marriage to pursue educational and career goals or are choosing to cohabit. Since 1920, more people have been choosing not to get married; only half of U.S. adults 18 and over were married in 2015.[7] An increasing number also view singlehood as a legitimate, healthy, and satisfying alternative to marriage. They find in it the freedom to pursue their own interests, spend their money as they wish, invest time in their careers, develop a broad network of friends, have a variety of sexual relationships, and enjoy opportunities for solitude. For them, being single is a positive choice.

Keeping Your Relationships Strong and Vital

A characteristic of relationships—both partnerships and families—is that they change over time. For example, changes in sexual desire occur in long-term partner relationships, and the way couples move through these changes can be directly related to their satisfaction in that relationship.[59] Many individuals need to recognize that building and sustaining a long-term marriage is hard, and there will be challenges through the relationship. The critical thing to remember is that there are things you can do.[60] No matter what specific challenges come up, three basic qualities seem to make partnerships and families strong: cohesion, flexibility, and communication.[61]

Cohesion is the dynamic balance between separateness and togetherness in both couple and family relationships. Relationships are strongest when there is a balance between intimacy and autonomy. There are times when partners and family members spend more time together and other times when they spend more time apart, but they come back to a comfortably cohesive point.

■ Some couples discover the secrets to a long and happy marriage. *(Syda Productions/Shutterstock)*

Flexibility is the dynamic balance between stability and change. Again, relationships are strongest when there is a balance. Too much stability can cause rigidity; too much change can cause chaos. Communication is the tool that partners and families use to adjust levels of cohesion or flexibility when change is needed. It is important that communication with a partner include expressions of appreciation, healthy complaining, and recognition of both partners' levels of sensitivity.[19]

When relationship problems persist for two or three months and the partners are not able to resolve them, the couple should probably seek help. Couples who receive help with difficulties before they become too severe have a better chance of overcoming them and developing a stronger relationship than do those who delay.

Marriage and family therapists are specifically trained to help couples and families with relationship problems. If you are having relationship issues, look for a therapist who is licensed by your state or who is a certified member of the American Association for Marriage and Family Therapists. Your physician or clergyperson may be able to recommend a qualified professional. A couples therapist can help you develop the strengths and resources you need to nourish and enhance this vital part of your life.

COMMUNITIES

Connection with others within a community, as well as with a partner, family, and friends, promotes personal health and growth. Healthy relationships in all cases include a balance between closeness and separateness and are characterized by mutual support, respect, good communication, and caring actions. Having strong personal relationships improves health and self-esteem and gives greater meaning to life.[62] Some believe that increased use of the Internet will reduce loneliness and social isolation for many individuals. While social networking might enhance existing connections for some, it might insulate others from in-person interactions and increase their feelings of loneliness.[63]

A **community** is a group of people connected in a way that transcends casual attachment. Although a physical neighborhood can be a community, we are using the term here in a larger sense, as an association of like-minded people or people with a common goal.[64] Participating in a spiritual practice, volunteer service, political campaign, intramural sports, or any type of hobby-focused club is a form of community involvement and fosters social connectedness.

Being active in a community usually has a positive impact on health. Several studies have demonstrated links between social connectedness and individual health

cohesion
The degree to which couples come together, feel close to or distant from each other.

flexibilty
The degree to which a couple is open to change.

community
A group of people connected by values, purpose, and goals.

Public Health Is Personal

Individual Freedom Versus the Common Good

By definition, public health includes areas in which individual health is connected to the health of others. In these cases, for example, the government makes decisions that can sometimes be seen as restricting individual freedom but that are justified as supporting community health and promoting the common good. For example, should we all be wearing masks as COVID-19 spreads? These cases represent what might be our strongest social connection—our dependence on one another for good health, longer life, and a better quality of life.

The following examples are just a few of the many public health issues that affect all of us:

- *Child abuse.* Should families be allowed to discipline their children in whatever way they see fit, or should society set standards and limits on these actions? In all states, child abuse and neglect are crimes and must be reported by those identified as mandatory reporters, including therapists, teachers, and physicians. In 2017 a national estimate of 674,000 children were the victims of abuse and neglect. The highest number of those abused and/or neglected were in their first year of life. There was also an estimated 1,720 fatalities during that year.[67]

- *Smoking.* Should people be allowed to smoke wherever and whenever they want? Research clearly indicates that smoking is bad for your health, and it also shows that secondhand smoke damages the health of children and others who live or work with smokers. The U.S. surgeon general has determined that there is no safe level of exposure to secondhand smoke. Across the United States, a growing number of states and localities ban smoking in workplaces, restaurants, or bars, or some combination of these places.

- *Syringe exchange.* Should communities provide drug users with clean syringes so that they can inject drugs with less risk of disease? Research suggests that syringe exchange programs reduce HIV and hepatitis C transmission and are cost-effective without resulting in any increase in drug abuse. Although the positive impact of syringe exchange programs has been supported by the literature, they are not legal in all localities, and the federal government provides support only indirectly. For instance, it might pay for counseling services, case management, and administrative costs but not for syringes. Under discussion currently are supervised injecting facilities where drug users can get clean syringes and inject in a safe environment, reducing, it is hoped, the likelihood of overdose and disease transmission.

- *Vaccinations.* Should parents be required to have their children vaccinated against infectious diseases? Many school districts require specific vaccinations before a child can enter school. Colleges also often require proof of vaccination against specific contagious diseases, such as measles, mumps, and hepatitis B. Some parents refuse to have their children vaccinated because of fears of complications, relying instead on the "herd immunity" secured by others. During the first six months of 2019 there were cases of measles confirmed in 30 states, the largest number since 1992. It appears that, although vaccines are available, many parents are choosing not to get their children vaccinated, thus impacting many communities.

- *"Presenteeism."* Should people stay home when they are sick with a cold or other contagious illness or when they have a sick child? Many people avoid "absenteeism"—staying home from work—because they fear losing a day's pay or even their job. By going to work sick or sending a sick child to school, however, they expose others to contagious diseases and even risk contributing to epidemics. The government encourages people with the flu to stay home and avoid contact with others, but many people still go to work, and many employers have not adjusted their sick leave policies to accommodate necessary absences.

To participate in the conversation about public health issues like these, become educated about the facts, support programs that make sense to you, and vote from an informed perspective.

Source: National Statistics on Child Abuse, National Children's Alliance, 2015.

and well-being.[17,65,66] In general, the size of a person's social network and his or her sense of connectedness are inversely related to risk-related behaviors such as alcohol and tobacco consumption and physical inactivity, and behaviors leading to obesity.[11,62] Evidence also shows that social participation and engagement are related to the maintenance of cognitive function in older adulthood and to lowered mortality rates.

A sense of trust among individuals who belong to communities can promote social stability and strong collaborative networks. For example, unpaid work by a group of people results in an improved environment for all, whether that means organizing a block party, producing a community newsletter, or working with friends to repaint the local library. People with a strong sense of their community also have more social capital than those who do not—that is, they are more likely to share and exchange resources with others whom they trust in their communities.

Public health is an arena in which the connections between individuals and community become concrete, and decisions about regulating personal behaviors for the good of the community sometimes lead to debate and controversy. For some examples, see the box "Public Health Is Personal: Individual Freedom Versus the Common Good."

Community Starts Within

In the act of joining a community, you bring your deepest beliefs and intentions into the world. Participation in a

■ Participating in community activities can reinforce feelings of connectedness with others and enhance a person's sense of well-being. *(Blend Images/Ariel Skelley/Getty Images)*

Action Skill-Builder

Live Your Values

Many of us fail to think through our values and guiding principles until we are faced with a difficult choice, and then we may make a "gut decision" without knowing why. For inspiration, we often look to people who stood up for their values despite enormous pressure or who took action even if it put their lives at risk. They may be whistle-blowers, social activists, or people who started foundations in support of particular causes. We see them as courageous because they spoke up while others remained silent or did nothing. If you observed something that contradicted your values, would you speak up?

Living your values doesn't always require taking action on a grand scale. In fact, you live your values every day, when you actively listen to a friend, speak up about a bigoted comment, or treat the environment with respect. How would you articulate your own core values? How do you express them in your daily life? What guiding principles do you derive from them? Do your values influence decisions you make? The way you vote?

Consider the following list of values and identify those that are important to you. If some of your values aren't on the list, add them. Take some time to consider how you can embody them in your life and what kinds of communities share them. What steps can you take to bring your behaviors into line with your values? What opportunities arise each day for you to put your values into action?

☐ Achievement	☐ Health
☐ Autonomy	☐ Home
☐ Care for the environment	☐ Honesty
	☐ Integrity
☐ Compassion	☐ Learning
☐ Connectedness	☐ Love
☐ Creativity	☐ Personal growth
☐ Determination	☐ Prestige
☐ Education	☐ Relationships
☐ Fairness	☐ Respect
☐ Family	☐ Service
☐ Financial well-being	☐ Social justice
☐ Freedom	☐ Spirituality
☐ Hard work	☐ Status

community requires that you understand your beliefs and how you fit into a particular community. Figuring out what your values are, what gives meaning to your life, and what you want to accomplish will help you identify the communities whose members share your values and in which you will feel most personally fulfilled.

Values   Your personal value system is a set of guidelines for how you want to live your life. **Values**, the criteria for judging what is good and bad, underlie moral principles and behavior. Your value system shapes who you are as a person, how you make decisions, and what goals you set for yourself. When you develop a way of life that makes sense and enables you to navigate the world effectively, the many choices you face each day become much less complex and easier to handle. Your value system becomes your map, providing a structure for decision making that allows flexibility and the possibility of change (see the box "Action Skill-Builder: Live Your Values").

Purpose   Why am I here? What gives my life meaning? These questions have been asked by people all over the world, in all eras, and at all stages of life. Searching for the answers is part of life's journey. For some people, the answers are developing relationships and connections. For others, they are caring for others or working for a healthier planet. Positive psychology (discussed in Chapter 2) contributes the idea that meaning in life comes from using our personal strengths to serve some larger end. To examine your own sense of meaning and purpose, complete the Personal Health Portfolio activity at the end of this chapter.

Goals   When you identify and pursue your personal goals, you are taking responsibility for yourself and taking charge of your life. Personal growth and achievement of goals involve an incremental process through which you develop a reservoir of inner strengths, self-esteem, and fulfillment. A community can help you reach your goals. For example, if you

want to learn to play chess, you can join a chess club and learn from people who are passionate about the game—and probably happy to share their knowledge. In addition, the mere process of participating in a

values
The set of criteria for judging what is good and bad that underlies moral decisions and behavior.

community can help you achieve broader goals for personal improvement, such as becoming more compassionate, being a better listener, developing a more optimistic attitude, or simply becoming less self-absorbed.

What is most important to you in life? If you were to write a personal statement of purpose, what would it say? It could be as simple as "to live and learn" or "to know my higher being and teach and express love."

Finding a Community That Works for You

Community involvement provides a feeling of participation in something greater than yourself and a sense of unity with your surroundings and neighbors. No matter what your values and purpose in life are, you can be confident that there is a community out there for you. Having a purpose in life moves us forward and makes life worth living.[68]

People who have strong ties to a religious or community group are more likely to have a network of people who can support and help them in time of need. *(Brand X Pictures/Getty Images)*

Religious and Spiritual Communities For thousands of years, humans have found personal and social connectedness in religious or spiritual communities. Spirituality means different paths for different people, so it has been defined in many ways. In health promotion literature, **spirituality** is commonly defined as a person's connection to self, significant others, and the community at large. Many experts also agree that spirituality includes a personal belief system or value system that gives meaning and purpose to life.[69]

For some individuals, this personal value system may include a belief in and reverence for a higher power, which may be expressed through an organized religion. Worldwide, there are more than 20 major religions and thousands of other forms of spiritual expression. Many individuals count religion or spirituality as an important part of their lives. According to recent surveys, 90 percent of Americans believe in some type of higher power, with almost half of U.S. adults believing that God determines what happens to them most or all of the time. Adults under 50 are less inclined to describe themselves as believing in a biblical God or higher power.[70] Worldwide, the number of religiously unaffiliated people is expected to fall because the number of births in regions where people are more religiously affiliated will increase, while deaths will outnumber births in unaffiliated regions.[71]

spirituality
The experience of connection to self, others, and the community at large, providing a sense of purpose and meaning.

Although there is no definitive scientific proof that religious involvement has positive health benefits, there are many scientific articles focused on the relationship between spirituality and health,[72,73] and more than half the nation's medical schools now offer courses on spirituality and medicine, whereas 25 years ago only three did. Many believe that religion and/or spirituality may have a positive impact on health and well-being.[74] Others argue that attendance at religious activities, social support, and individual psychosocial resources may be the real reasons for reduced mortality among religious people.[75,76]

Another possible explanation for better health among people who are spiritually engaged is that they react more effectively to health crises. They seem more willing than others to alter their health habits, to be proactive in seeking medical treatment, and to accept the support of others. People who have strong ties to a religious group or another community segment may also receive help and encouragement from that community in times of crisis.[77] Friends may transport them to the doctor and to church, shop for them, prepare meals, arrange child care, and encourage them to get appropriate medical treatment. Overall, according to a recent survey, actively religious people around the world are more likely to describe themselves as very happy than are those who are less religious.[78] The pursuit of conclusions in this area is not without skeptics, however, and the connection between spirituality and health remains an area of controversy and debate.

In addition, spiritual practices such as meditation, prayer, and worship seem to promote positive emotions such as hope, love, contentment, and forgiveness, which can result in lower levels of anxiety. Studies have also

Starting the Conversation
Can You Influence Public Policy?

Q: Does voting matter?

Only 53 to 57 percent of the voting-age public in the United States has voted in presidential elections since 1996. Compared to 35 other developed countries, the United States ranks 27th in voter turnout. U.S. citizens aged 18 to 29 are least likely to vote; in the 2016 presidential election, African American voting declined and approximately half of Asians and Hispanics turned out to vote. In the 2018 midterm election, more than 47 percent of the voting-eligible population voted, a number far higher than the 37 and 41 percent who voted in the midterms in 2014 and 2010. Some countries require voting, and others make registration automatic or aggressively seek out and register eligible voters. The United States has a history of restricting voting rights, and recent requirements for voter IDs as well as other requirements and restrictions may make it even more difficult for some people to vote. But voting determines who makes public policy.

For example, consider that tobacco, poor diet, physical inactivity, alcohol, toxic agents, motor vehicles, and firearms are the top causes of death in the United States. Some researchers also suggest that many premature deaths are attributable to social factors such as low education, racial segregation, low social support, and income inequality. All these causes of death have one thing in common: They can be affected by public policy. If you want to change public policy, you have to vote and become active in your community.

Ferguson, Missouri, provided a recent example of how people can affect public policy. On August 9, 2014, white police officer Darren Wilson fatally shot Michael Brown, an unarmed 18-year-old African American suspected of having stolen cigarillos from a convenience store in Ferguson. The shooting sparked a series of riots and peaceful protests, expanded the Black Lives Matter movement, and prompted a U.S. Department of Justice (DOJ) investigation into the practices of the Ferguson Police Department.

Two-thirds of Ferguson's population is Black, but in 2014, the overwhelming majority of city officials and 50 of the police

department's 54 officers were white. The DOJ investigators found that more than 90 percent of those cited for the most common offenses—"peace disturbance," "failure to comply," and "manner of walking" (jaywalking)—were African American. They also discovered that Ferguson's city budget depended on increasing municipal-court fines, most of which were paid by Black people. The report concluded that Garner's shooting was the spark that ignited deep distrust and fear of the police among Ferguson's Black residents.

After the DOJ report was issued in March 2015, the city officials and police supervisors who had been most responsible for the discriminatory policies and behaviors resigned. In April 2015, the citizens of Ferguson elected two African Americans to the city council, marking the first time that half its members were Black. More than twice as many people had voted as the year before.

An examination of social movements and shifting attitudes in the United States suggests that change is possible when the public becomes active and provides visibility for those who are marginalized and often invisible. When we look, for example, at the shift in attitudes about gay marriage over the past 20 years, it is easy to see that developing connections between people of different backgrounds can make a difference and spawn social movements that bring about change. One of the most recent examples is Black Lives Matter and current efforts to advocate for anti-racism. Other examples of changes due to citizen action and legislative action include smoking bans, availability of guns, school testing, and the minimum wage. All these public policy issues are related to public health concerns.

Q: Do you believe that participation by voting can promote social change?

Q: What public policy issues are most important to you?

McGraw Hill connect

Sources: Taylor, P., & Lopez, M. H. (2013). Six take-aways from the Census Bureau's voting report. Pew Research Center. Retrieved from http://www.pewresearch.org/fact-tank/2013/05/08/six-take-aways-from-the-census-bureaus-voting-report/; U.S. Department of Justice, Civil Rights Division. (2015, Mar. 4). Investigation of the Ferguson Police Department; Alcindor, Y. (2015, Apr. 8). Ferguson voters make history and increase turnout. *USA Today*.

shown that prayer and relaxation techniques such as meditation, yoga, and hypnotherapy reduce the secretion of stress hormones and their harmful side effects. This in turn may help to minimize the stress response, which suppresses immune functioning.[79,80,81]

Social Activism and the Global Community

Some people connect with their communities—local, national, and global—through social activism. A social cause, such as overcoming poverty or fighting illiteracy, can unite people from diverse backgrounds for a common good. Getting involved can take many forms. (See the box "Starting the Conversation: Can

You Influence Public Policy?") In its simplest form, social activism can mean becoming an informed voter and making sure you vote at all levels: local, state, and national. In this process, you can become part of social networks active in your communities.

On a larger scale, many people find it meaningful to participate in global citizenship by joining organizations through which they can put their values into practice in the world. Here are a few:

- The Peace Corps was inspired by President John F. Kennedy's call to college students to give two years of their lives to help people in developing nations. Today, it is still sending people to developing nations from Ecuador to Ghana to the Ukraine with the goal of promoting world peace and friendship. The services its volunteers provide include helping teachers develop their teaching methodologies, raising awareness about health issues such as HIV/AIDS, teaching environmental conservation strategies, and teaching computer skills.

- Habitat for Humanity is widely known for its work providing housing for needy people in the United States, but it also works to eliminate poverty and homelessness on a global level. So far, the organization has built more than 350,000 houses in more than 90 countries.

- Greenpeace focuses on the most crucial worldwide threats to the planet's biodiversity and environment. Greenpeace has been campaigning against environmental degradation since 1971, bearing witness in a nonviolent manner.

- Clowns Without Borders offers laughter to relieve the suffering of all people, especially children, who live in areas of crisis including refugee camps, conflict zones, and territories in crisis situations.

Aaker and Smith coined the term "the dragonfly effect" to describe how social media has been used to facilitate social change.[82] The reach of the Internet has dramatically changed how social change can occur. From facilitating governmental reform to providing funding for nonprofits to getting a friend a bone marrow transplant donor, the possibilities of social media are limitless. Blogs, Twitter, and crowdsourcing sites reach people quickly, tell your story, and get an electronic audience to become "team members" devoted to your cause.

If you are interested in social activism, look for ways to participate through your school, your religious community, or groups you locate on the Internet or through social media. When you volunteer for such an organization, you commit yourself to building a foundation for a better world, making a contribution through service to others, and creating opportunities for mutual understanding.

service learning
A form of education that combines coursework with community service.

Volunteering Volunteering is another way to find social connectedness and personal fulfillment. It seems that most students who volunteer do it because they have compassion for those in need.

Volunteers benefit others and themselves when they serve their communities. Regular and enjoyable volunteer work can have significant health benefits and even add years to life. *(track5/Getty Images)*

Volunteers may also gain health benefits from participation and experience a "helper's high."[83,84]

Not all kinds of volunteering have the same effect, however. One-on-one contact and direct involvement significantly increase the effects of volunteering on the volunteer. Working closely with strangers appears to confer potential health benefits. Liking the volunteer work, performing it consistently, and having unselfish motives increase the helper's high and the health benefits associated with it.[85,86] Simply donating money or doing volunteer work in isolation does not seem to have the same positive effect.

Those who volunteer only to pad their résumé invest fewer hours in the activity and may not get the maximum benefit of participation.[87]

Service Learning One way that people can connect classroom activities to community service and community building is through **service learning**. The main purpose behind service learning is to integrate meaningful community service with specific activities such as verbal classroom sharing and reflective writing. Integrating community service with academic study is meant to enrich learning, teach civic responsibility, and strengthen communities. Students are encouraged to take a positive role in their community, such as by tutoring, caring for the environment, or conducting oral histories with senior citizens. All these activities are meant to teach students how to extend themselves beyond their enclosed world, taking the risk of getting involved in the lives of others. In this way they learn about caring and taking care of—two particularly important concepts for personal growth.

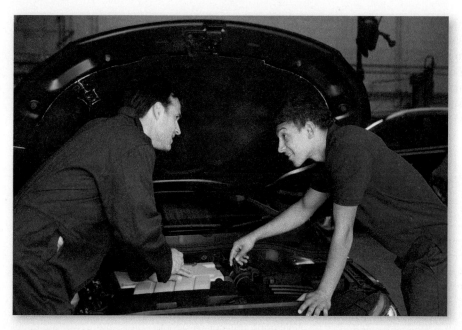

The Arts Experiencing the arts—whether sculpture, painting, music, poetry, literature, theater, storytelling, dance, or some other form—is another way to build connections with your community. Experiencing great art can inspire you, through felt experience, to think about the purpose of life and the nature of reality.[88] By engaging your heart, mind, and spirit, art can give you fresh insights, challenge preconceptions, and trigger inner growth. Scholar Joseph Campbell once asserted, "The goal of life is rapture. Art is the way we experience it. Art is the transforming experience."[89]

When you enjoy and appreciate the arts, you embrace diverse cultures past and present and frequently discover in them the universal themes of human existence—love,

■ Engagement in meaningful activities—such as sharing your expertise and passion with a younger person—is a major source of happiness and satisfaction for most people. (*MBI/Alamy Stock Photo*)

You Make the Call

Will Sending Nude Pictures Bring You Closer?

The increased use of technology has had a dramatic impact on social connections. Many more people are meeting online and expanding their circles far beyond the people they might meet in their communities, schools, or workplaces.

One consequence is that the number of individuals posting nude pictures online has been increasing over the past few years. In one study, 21 percent of participants reported sending and 28 percent reported receiving sexually explicit text messages. Twenty-three percent reported receiving sexy photos and 16 percent reported sending sexy photos of themselves. For many people under age 30, sexting is seen as part of a modern relationship, a replacement for the love letters people wrote before the Internet. Many people believe that posting nude pictures of themselves is just a new way to flirt or enhance a long-distance relationship. Many young people also believe, mistakenly, that the Internet is a safe place to share intimate information.

An uncomfortable consequence of sharing nude pictures online while people are in intimate relationships is the rise of "revenge porn" or nonconsensual image sharing. If a relationship has not ended well, it may increase the likelihood that the person holding your pictures will share them with others, resulting in embarrassment and possibly affecting your career and potential new relationships.

Approximately 25 percent of U.S. adults who use the Internet have either been threatened or had sensitive images posted without their permission. In the past few years, many states have passed legislation making "revenge porn" illegal.

Should you provide intimate information, sext, or share nude images online?

Pros

- It is no big deal if others see my images even without my permission.
- I am in a long-distance relationship, and these pictures will keep our relationship alive.
- "Cool" and famous people are sharing, and I want to be popular.

Cons

- Once I share an image, I will lose control of it forever.
- Some people will not hire me if they see I have posted sexts or nude pictures online.
- I will be humiliated and embarrassed if anyone but my significant other sees these pictures.

McGraw Hill **connect**

Sources: Lenhart, A., Ybarra, M., & Price-Feeney, M. (2016). Nonconsenual image sharing: One in 25 Americans has been a victim of revenge porn. Data Memo. Retrieved from https://datasociety.net/pubs/oh/Nonconsensual_Image_Sharing_2016.pdf; Alter, C. (2017, July 10-17). The new scarlett letter. *Time*; American Psychological Association. (2017). Stress in America. *Technology and Social Media*. Retrieved from https://www.apa.org/news/press/releases/stress/2017/technology-social-media.PDF; Garcia, J. R., Geselman, A. N., Siliman, S. A., Perry, B. L., Coe, K., & Fisher, H. E. (2016). Sexting among singles in the USA: Prevalence of sending, receiving, and sharing sexual messages and images, *Sexual Health, 13,* 428-435.

loss, birth, death, isolation, community, continuity, and change. When you express yourself creatively, you may be able to experience a spiritual connection between your inner core and the natural world beyond yourself. Both experiences—art appreciation and artistic expression—can be transforming. If the visual or performing arts are not part of your life right now, try to schedule time to visit a museum or attend a concert. Make notes or sketches in a journal reflecting on your experiences. Doing so may stimulate a new sense of fulfillment in your life.

Internet Communities In addition to blogs and communities like Facebook, Instagram, LinkedIn, and Twitter, websites like Meetup help you find and form groups around your interests—from Android developers to Zen meditation centers—based on your ZIP code. Sites like idealist.org help you find volunteer opportunities, start an organization or business, and connect with like-minded people interested in social and environmental problems. The social connections that begin at your doorstep now extend around the world.

In Review

What kinds of relationships are important for health?
People are social beings and need connections with friends and intimate partners to live fully functioning lives. People with strong social support networks tend to enjoy better health than do those with fewer connections. Healthy relationships allow people to be themselves and to grow.

Two important kinds of relationships are friendships and intimate partnerships. Friendships are reciprocal relationships based on mutual liking. Intimate partnerships have additional qualities, usually including exclusivity, commitment, and sexuality.

How do people attract and find intimate partners?
Proximity, physical attractiveness, and similarity are key factors in attraction, although today proximity may be electronic rather than physical. Finding a potential life partner is more likely to be successful with a direct, respectful approach and a social connection. The Internet has had a powerful impact on the way people meet, but meeting online might not be a remedy for loneliness.

What makes people fall in love and out of love?
According to the similarity theory, we fall in love with people who are similar to us in important ways. According to the social exchange theory, we fall in love with people who can fulfill emotional and other needs, such as security, money, and status. The early stage of a love relationship is romantic, idealistic, and passionate. Physiological changes, such as increased dopamine, gradually decrease. Sometimes intimacy increases as passion lessens; for other couples, the end of passion is the end of the relationship. According to Sternberg's love triangle, different kinds of love have different combinations of intimacy, passion, and commitment.

What are different communication skills and styles?
Clear, positive communication is key to successful intimate relationships. Communication is both conscious and unconscious, verbal and nonverbal—together they constitute the metamessage. Effective communicators use "I" statements, make specific requests, remain calm, and listen thoughtfully to the other person.

What are the differences between *sex* and *gender*?
Sex is a person's biological status as female or male. *Gender* refers to the qualities a particular culture considers appropriate for males and females. A *gender role* is the set of attributes and activities defined by a society as masculine or feminine. Individuals who integrate masculine and feminine traits are androgynous; individuals who feel their gender identity does not match their biological sex are transsexual. *Sexual orientation* depends on the sex of those to whom a person is emotionally, romantically, and sexually attracted; people can be heterosexual, homosexual, or bisexual.

What are different types of relationship choices?
The most common type of committed relationship is marriage. Research has found that successful marriages are based on positive reasons for getting married and realistic, shared expectations of marriage. Cohabitation is an option for couples; for two-thirds of cohabiting couples, it leads to marriage. Research findings have been varied about the effect of cohabitation on the relationship. About 40 to 50 percent of first marriages now end in divorce, and many single-parent families struggle with poverty. Many people who remarry bring their children to the new relationship, creating a blended family. A growing number of young adults are postponing marriage, and older adults are choosing to remain single. Cohesion, flexibility, and communication are key to maintaining any kind of partnership or family.

What are the benefits of connecting with a community?
Community involvement provides a feeling of participation in something greater than yourself and a sense of unity with your surroundings and neighbors. Recognizing your values and goals in life is key to finding a community that works for you. Communities can be based on religion, social activism, volunteering, service learning, or the arts. Increasingly, the Internet is a way to locate others of like mind.

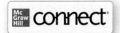
One important aspect of well-being is your perceived meaning in life. Do you believe you have a meaningful life? Are you interested in personal growth and developing your own values?

Researchers believe that there is a relationship between finding meaning in life and a person's well-being. As you search to uncover the meaning in your life, the first step in the process is increasing your self-awareness about your sense of meaning and purpose.

There are two subscales in the questionnaire. The first, Presence of Meaning, measures how meaningful people perceive their life to be. The second, Search for Meaning, measures how actively people are seeking to discover or augment the level of meaningfulness they experience in life.

PRESENCE OF MEANING

	Absolutely untrue		Can't say true or false			Absolutely true	
1. I understand my life's meaning.	1	2	3	4	5	6	7
2. My life has a clear sense of purpose.	1	2	3	4	5	6	7
3. I have a good sense of what makes my life meaningful.	1	2	3	4	5	6	7
4. I have discovered a satisfying life purpose.	1	2	3	4	5	6	7
5. My life has no clear purpose.	7	6	5	4	3	2	1

SEARCH FOR MEANING

	Absolutely untrue		Can't say true or false			Absolutely true	
1. I am looking for something that makes my life feel meaningful.	1	2	3	4	5	6	7
2. I am always looking to find my life's purpose.	1	2	3	4	5	6	7
3. I am always searching for something that makes my life feel significant.	1	2	3	4	5	6	7
4. I am seeking a purpose or mission for my life.	1	2	3	4	5	6	7
5. I am searching for meaning in my life.	1	2	3	4	5	6	7

SCORING

Add up your numbers for each section. Scores will range from 5 to 35.

Presence of Meaning score: _____

Search for Meaning score: _____

If you scored **above** 24 on Presence and also **above** 24 on Search, you feel your life has a valued meaning and purpose, yet you are still openly exploring that meaning or purpose. You likely are satisfied with your life, are somewhat optimistic, experience feelings of love frequently, and rarely feel depressed. You are probably somewhat active in spiritual activities, and you tend not to value pursuing sensory stimulation as much as others. You are generally certain of, and occasionally forceful regarding, your views and supportive of having an overall structure in society and life. People who know you would probably describe you as conscientious, thoughtful, easy to get along with, somewhat open to new experiences, and generally easygoing and emotionally stable.

If you scored **above** 24 on Presence and **below** 24 on Search, you feel your life has a valued meaning and purpose, and you are not actively exploring that meaning or seeking meaning in your life. One might say that you are satisfied that you've grasped what makes your life meaningful, why you're here, and what you want to do with your life. You probably are satisfied with your life, are optimistic, and have healthy self-esteem. You frequently experience feelings of love and joy and rarely feel afraid, angry, ashamed, or sad. You probably hold traditional values. You are usually certain of, and often forceful regarding, your views and likely support structure and rules for society and living. You are probably active in and committed to spiritual pursuits. People who know you would probably describe you as conscientious, organized, friendly, easy to get along with, and socially outgoing.

If you scored **below** 24 on Presence and **above** 24 on Search, you probably do not feel your life has a valued meaning and purpose, and you are actively searching for something or someone that will give your life meaning or purpose. You are probably not always satisfied with your life. You may not experience emotions like love and joy that often. You may occasionally, or even often, feel anxious, nervous, or sad and depressed. You are probably questioning the role of spirituality in your life, and you may be working hard to figure out whether there is a God, what life on Earth is really about, and which, if any, religion is right for you. People who know you would probably describe you as liking to play things by ear or "go with the flow" when it comes to plans, occasionally worried, and not particularly socially active.

If you scored **below** 24 on Presence and also **below** 24 on Search, you probably do not feel your life has a valued meaning and purpose and are not actively exploring that meaning or seeking meaning in your life. You may not always be satisfied with your life, or yourself, and you might not be particularly optimistic about the future. You may not experience emotions like love and joy that often. You may occasionally, or even often, feel anxious, nervous, or sad and depressed. You probably do not hold traditional values and may be more likely to value stimulating, exciting experiences, although you are not necessarily open-minded about everything. People who know you would probably describe you as sometimes disorganized, occasionally nervous or tense, and not particularly socially active or especially warm toward everyone.

Sources: Adapted from Steger, M. F., Frazier, P., Oishi, S., & Kaler, M. (2006). The meaning in life questionnaire: Assessing the presence of and search for meaning in life. *Journal of Counseling Psychology, 53,* 80–93; Steger, M. F., Kashdan, T. B., Sullivan, B. A., & Lorentz, D. (2008). Understanding the search for meaning in life: Personality, cognitive style, and the dynamic between seeking and experiencing meaning. *Journal of Personality, 76,* 197–227.

CRITICAL THINKING QUESTIONS

1. Analyze your scores for each scale. Were they higher or lower than you expected? What areas of strength do you see? Where is there room for growth?

2. Think about the environmental factors in your life, such as your friends, family, school, and community. How do they affect your pursuit of meaning in life?

3. After having taken this assessment and considered the results, do you want to be able to find more meaning in your life? If so, what are some actions you can take to begin this process?

Sleep

4

Wavebreakmediamicro/123RF

Ever Wonder...

why alcohol interferes with deep sleep?

whether some college students can be so addicted to their smartphones that they sleep-text?

why caffeine from late-night energy drinks interferes with sleep?

College students have a reputation for missing early-morning classes or falling asleep in class. The typical college student's bedtime is 11:40 p.m. on weekdays and 1:17 a.m. on weekends. Wakeup time is 7:42 a.m. on weekdays and 9:45 a.m. on weekends.[1,2] Although sleep scientists often refer to students' tendency to go to bed two hours later on weekends as "social jet lag," it doesn't necessarily mean students have been out partying. Most young adults have a **circadian rhythm**—an internal daily cycle of waking and sleeping—that tells them to fall asleep later in the evening and to wake up later in the morning than older adults. These circadian rhythms in a demanding college environment make college students vulnerable to chronic sleep deprivation.

Most adults need about eight to nine hours of sleep each night, but the typical college student sleeps only six to seven hours on weeknights.[3] Lack of sufficient sleep impairs academic performance.[4] About 44 percent of college students (40.7 percent of men, 46.3 percent of women) are tired, exhausted, or sleepy three to five days a week. About 12 percent (9.8 percent of men, 13.0 percent of women) report sleepiness as a big problem, and for about 5 percent (3.9 percent of men, 5.3 percent of women) it's a very big problem.[3] To help the sleep-deprived, some colleges and universities include programs on sleep and health in summer orientation for incoming students. However, only 27 percent say their college or university provides information about sleep difficulties.[3]

The National Sleep Foundation (NSF) has developed the Sleep Health Index (SHI) as a measure of sleep duration, sleep quality, and disordered sleep. The SHI was used with the NSF's 2018 Sleep in America poll, which concluded that sleep health is strongly associated with a consistent regular sleep schedule. Fifty-eight percent of survey respondents had gone to bed at least 30 to 60 minutes earlier or later than usual on at least one workday/weekday in the previous seven days. Almost 50 percent had different bedtimes and awake times on weekdays than on weekends/nonwork days. The nature of college life makes it very difficult for college students to maintain a consistent sleep schedule. Those reporting regular and consistent weekday sleep schedules were 1.5 times more likely than others to feel well rested. Overall, U.S. adults had a score of 77 on the 0 to 100 SHI scale. But those with consistent sleep schedules scored 11 points higher than those with inconsistent sleep schedules. The higher the variability in bedtime and awake time, the greater the disparity in emotional effects, physical effects, and productivity effects.[5]

The conclusion from the 2018 NSF poll and the SHI stressed the importance of maintaining consistent sleep schedules on weekdays and weekends/nonwork days. Adults with excellent SHI scores were two times more likely to maintain consistent sleep schedules than those with poor SHI scores. Those with excellent SHI scores were 3.5 times more likely to say they felt well rested on a typical weekday than those with poor SHI scores (from 76 percent to 22 percent). Women and non-whites reported higher levels of physical effects and emotional effects from inconsistent sleep schedules than white men.[5]

The United States, like some other Western industrialized nations, has been described as a "sleepless society." Sleep debt for U.S. adults is very common. To calculate sleep debt, compare actual sleep to preferred sleep hours. U.S. adults on average have a sleep debt of 26 minutes per night on workdays and averaged 17 minutes more sleep on nonwork days.[1] The general rule is that for every hour you are awake, you need 20 to 30 minutes of sleep.[6]

U.S. adults place priority on fitness/nutrition (35 percent), work (17 percent), habits/personal interests (17 percent), and sleep (10 percent). Only social life (9 percent) has a lower priority score than sleep.[7] Prioritizing sleep means establishing a consistent sleep schedule for going to bed and waking up that attains a sleep duration in which you awaken refreshed. Twelve percent of adults are not motivated to make sleep a priority. Those who are motivated average 7.1 hours of sleep on workdays and 7.7 hours on nonwork days. Those who do not prioritize sleep average 6.5 hours of sleep on workdays and 7.3 hours on nonwork days.[8] It is not surprising that people who prioritize sleep report good or very good sleep quality. See box "Public Health Is Personal: *Healthy People 2020* Sleep Goals." Many people are unaware of the vital role that adequate sleep plays in good health.[9]

SLEEP AND YOUR HEALTH

Sleep is commonly understood as a period of rest and recovery from the demands of wakefulness. It can also be described as a state of unconsciousness or partial consciousness from which a person can be roused by stimulation (unlike a coma, for instance). We spend about one-third of our lives sleeping; that fact alone indicates how important sleep is.

Health Effects of Sleep

Sleep is strongly associated with overall health and quality of life. During the deepest stages of sleep, restoration and growth take place. Growth hormone stimulates the growth and repair of the body's tissues and helps to prevent certain types of cancer. Natural immune system moderators increase during deep sleep to promote resistance to viral infections. When sleep time is deficient, a breakdown in the body's health-promoting processes can occur.

Sleeping less than seven hours—sometimes called *short sleep*—increases the risk for negative health outcomes in both men and women. Sleeping 10 hours or more—*long sleep*—has not been found to have negative health outcomes.[6] However, sleep scientists subscribe to the U-curve view of sleep and longevity. People who sleep fewer than 5 hours or more than 12 hours a night have a higher mortality rate

---

circadian rhythm
A daily 24-hour cycle of physiological and behavioral functioning.

sleep
A period of rest and recovery from the demands of wakefulness; a state of unconsciousness or partial consciousness from which a person can be roused by stimulation.

Public Health Is Personal

Healthy People 2020 Sleep Goals

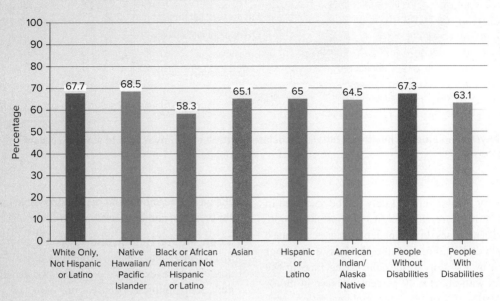

In its 10-year "Healthy People 2020" agenda, the U.S. Department of Health and Human Services (HHS) now includes sleep health as a target goal for the first time. The target goal is for 70.8 percent of U.S. adults age 18 or older to attain sufficient sleep per night. Sufficient sleep is defined as eight or more hours a night for ages 18 to 21, and seven or more hours for ages 22 and older. In 2018 about 69 percent of adults met the goal (67.9 of females and 67.8 of males). Disparities by race, ethnicity, and disability are shown in the accompanying bar graph.

The core goal of *Healthy People 2020* is to increase knowledge and awareness of the importance of sufficient sleep for improving health, productivity, wellness, quality of life, and safety on the roads and at work. Its specific objectives are to:

- Increase the proportion of persons with symptoms of sleep apnea who seek medical care (from 25.5 to 28 percent).

- Reduce the rate of vehicular crashes per 100 million miles traveled that are due to drowsy driving (from 2.7 to 0.1).

- Increase the proportion of students in grades 9 to 12 who get sufficient sleep, defined as eight hours or more on an average school night (from 30.9 to 33.2 percent).

- Increase the proportion of adults who get sufficient sleep, defined as eight or more hours for those aged 18 to 21 years and seven or more hours for those aged 22 years and older (from 69.6 to 70.9 percent).

Healthy People 2020 emphasizes the three pillars of good health as sleep, exercise, and balanced diet. The HHS reports that the public health burden of insufficient sleep is substantial. The 10-year *Healthy People 2020* is a call for a well-formed and coordinated effort to improve the sleep-related health of all Americans.

Sources: Department of Health and Human Services. (2019). *Sleep health is one of the new goals of Healthy People 2020*. Retrieved from www.sleepscholar.com/sleep-health-is-one-of-the-new-goals-of-healthy-people-2020/; Healthy People 2020. (2019). *2020 Topics and Objectives*. Retrieved from https:www.healthypeople.gov/2020/topics-objectives/topic/sleep-health

than people who sleep 7 to 8 hours.[10] A genetic mutation may enable some people to function effectively on 20 to 25 percent less sleep than average, but scientists estimate only 1 percent of people have this mutation. Sleep deprivation and other sleep behavior disruptions are often associated with serious physical and mental health conditions (see Figure 4.1).[6,9,11,12,13,14,15,16]

Sleep and Metabolism Adults who sleep less than seven hours a night are at a higher risk for obesity than adults who sleep seven to eight hours. Scientists believe the association between weight and sleep is caused by five factors: (1) alteration of glucose metabolism so that the body does not

metabolize food effectively; (2) hormone imbalance involving ghrelin (increases appetite) and leptin (suppresses appetite); (3) less time spent in rapid eye movement (REM) sleep (more calories are burned in REM sleep); (4) increased production of cortisol, which encourages food binges on high-calorie, high-fat foods; and (5) raised level of a lipid called endocannabinoid, which acts similarly to marijuana in the brain by making eating more enjoyable and increasing cravings for foods such as cookies, candy, and chips. People who are sleep deprived eat two times as much fat and 300 more calories the next day than people who are not sleep deprived.[17] Obesity is worrisome because, among other effects, it is a primary risk factor associated with diabetes.

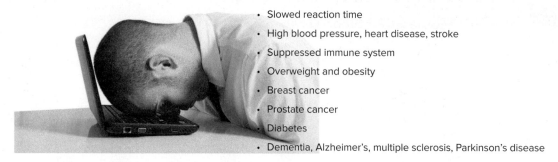

- Slowed reaction time
- High blood pressure, heart disease, stroke
- Suppressed immune system
- Overweight and obesity
- Breast cancer
- Prostate cancer
- Diabetes
- Dementia, Alzheimer's, multiple sclerosis, Parkinson's disease

figure 4.1   Physical and mental health conditions associated with sleep deprivation and sleep disorders.
(Alphaspirit/Shutterstock)

Sleep and Safety Motor vehicle safety will be discussed in detail in Chapter 16. Here, however, it is important to note that even small increases in sleep deprivation can cause drowsiness while driving. For example, the loss of one hour of sleep caused by the shift to daylight saving time in the spring coincides with about a 20 percent increase in motor vehicle accidents the day or two after implementation. African Americans and Hispanics have twice the risk for drowsy driving compared to whites.[18] The end-of-chapter feature "You Make the Call: Snooze You Lose: Criminalizing Drowsy Driving" focuses on the emerging public health issue of whether sleep deprivation causing fatalities to others should be prosecuted as a criminal offense.

Sleep and Heart Disease People who chronically sleep less than six hours a night are at higher risk for heart disease, stroke, and high blood pressure than are people who sleep more than six hours a night. For example, a person's risk for a heart attack increases by 5 percent during the three weeks after the start of daylight saving time in the spring.[19] The metabolic causes associated with heart disease include increased fat in the blood and pro-inflammatory processes, which are discussed in Chapter 14.

Sleep and Immune Function Inadequate sleep reduces the effectiveness of the immune system in a number of ways. It suppresses the production of cells that help fight infections, so if you are sleep deprived, you are more likely to catch an infection such as a cold or the flu, and it will take your body longer to recover. In addition, inadequate sleep causes an increase in cells associated with inflammation, including C-reactive protein, which is described in more detail in Chapter 14. Inflammation is a healthy response to an acute infection or injury, but over the long term, chronic, low-level inflammation can damage tissues and organs and increase risk for a variety of chronic diseases. Adequate sleep is needed for effective functioning of the immune system.[20]

Sleep and Cancer Research on sleep and cancer has focused primarily on shift workers. Shift workers experiencing extreme sleep disruption disorders have a 50 percent increase in risk for breast cancer in women and prostate cancer in men. The causes for this increased risk are thought to include

changes in hormonal and metabolic systems, immune system suppression, and decreased melatonin levels.[21]

Sleep, Mental Health, and Neurodegenerative Diseases Sleep complaints are also symptoms of various mental disorders. They are regularly reported by people with bipolar disorder, schizophrenia, depression, and substance abuse.[21] Abnormal sleep is also associated with such neurodegenerative diseases as dementia, Alzheimer's, Huntington's, Parkinson's, and multiple sclerosis. The specific mechanisms causing abnormal sleep for people with mental health disorders and neurodegenerative diseases are not known.[22]

Sleep and Your Brain Your brain is very active when you are sleeping. Neurons send electronic signals to process information that flooded the brain during the day. Levels of hormones, enzymes, and proteins are checked for proper balance, and toxic wastes are removed. Free radicals build up if brain debris is not removed.[23,24]

Sleep and Your Thyroid

Your thyroid helps regulate core body temperature and maintains proper organ functions. Sleep can be disturbed by hyperthyroidism or hypothyroidism. Hyperthyroidism is the presence of too much thyroid hormone, which can cause some body functions to speed up. Significant weight loss not due to exercise or nutrition changes, and jittery or anxious feelings, may be symptoms of hyperthyroidism. A racing heart rate and elevated metabolism may interfere with a relaxed state and disturb sleep.

Hypothyroidism is underproduction of the thyroid hormone, which causes your body to slow down and feel chronically fatigued. The bottom line is, if you are experiencing sleep problems, you may want to visit your provider to see whether your thyroid is functioning properly.

Sleep and Menstruation

Many U.S. women report their sleep is affected by the menstrual cycle. This change is due to the luteinizing hormone, follicle-stimulating hormone, estrogen, and progesterone. Twenty-three percent of women report sleep difficulty one week before the onset of menstruation, and 30 percent during menstruation. Feelings of sleepiness can also occur during ovulation as progesterone levels increase.

Causes of poor sleep include bloating (51 percent), cramps or pain (69 percent), and constipation (8 percent). Almost half of women say poor sleep from menstruation leads to feelings of anger or sadness. It is recommended that women maintain a sleep diary for a few months to determine whether their menstrual cycle is affecting sleep quality.[25] If it is, a visit with a health provider is recommended.

Health Effects of Sleep Deprivation

Sleep deprivation is a condition caused by the achievement of less sleep than a person actually needs to feel vibrant. Most of us know what it feels like when we don't get enough sleep—we feel drowsy, our eyes burn, we find it hard to pay attention. The effects of sleep deprivation can be much more serious than this, however. Studies have shown that individuals with severe sleep deprivation (say, from staying awake for 19 to 24 hours) score worse on performance tests and alertness scales than do people with a blood alcohol concentration (BAC) of 0.1 percent—legally too drunk to drive.[6,26]

Sleep deprivation has effects in all domains of functioning. Heightened irritability, lowered anger threshold, frustration, nervousness, and difficulty handling stress are some of the emotional effects. Reduced motivation may affect school and job performance, and lack of interest in socializing with others may cause relationships to suffer. Performance of daily activities is affected, as is the brain's ability to learn new material. Reaction time, coordination, and judgment are all impaired. Individuals who are sleep deprived may experience microsleep—brief episodes of sleep lasting a few seconds at a time—which increases their risk of being involved in accidents.[27]

The impact of sleep deprivation on memory is well documented. Sleep scientists believe sleep is the time when the hippocampus and neocortex (two brain memory systems) communicate with each other. Initial memories are formed in the hippocampus. To be retained, they must then be transmitted from the hippocampus to the neocortex, where they are stored as long-term memories.[28,29] The strengthening of neuron links between the two areas is called "sleep-dependent memory processing." Sleep provides the optimal time for this transmission. Some sleep experts believe that for every two hours a person stays awake, the brain will need an hour of sleep to support communication between the hippocampus and the neocortex.[27]

Chronic sleep deprivation damages brain cells and impairs debris removal. When you sleep, glial cells act like master pumps, removing the brain's garbage. Brain cells shrink, allowing more room for brain and spinal cord fluid, which helps flush out brain garbage. Glial cell effectiveness in removing brain garbage is reduced by about 15 percent if a person is sleep deprived. This is why sleep deprivation causes a buildup of brain garbage such as amyloid protein. In effect, chronic sleep deprivation accelerates brain aging and may contribute to degenerative brain disorders.[23,27]

According to scientific research, if you sleep after learning a finger-tapping sequence, the memory of this motor task will be imprinted in your brain so that you become better at the task. Deep sleep is needed for this imprint to occur. If you do not attain deep sleep, your brain does not have the opportunity to solidify what you have learned. This is why pulling an all-nighter for an exam results in short-term memory but not long-term memory.

Sleeping less than you need causes a **sleep debt**. Your sleep debt accumulates over time. For example, sleeping one hour less than you need every night for a week makes your body feel as if you have been staying up all night, and sleeping less than six hours each day for two weeks is equivalent to going for 24 hours with no sleep. If you sleep less than four hours a night for one week, this is equivalent to going 48 to 72 hours without sleep.[6,12,13,14,15,16,21]

Many college students and others who build up a sleep debt during the week—night-shift workers, for example—try to cancel the debt by sleeping more on the weekends. This "solution," however, can actually worsen sleep deprivation during the week by disrupting sleep structure. Consistently getting a sufficient amount of sleep strengthens sleep structure (described in the section "The Structure of Sleep").

Prescription stimulants—which are used to treat a variety of ailments, including asthma and attention-deficit/

sleep deprivation
Lack of sufficient time asleep, a condition that impairs physical, emotional, and cognitive functioning.

sleep debt
The difference between the amount of sleep attained and the amount needed to maintain alert wakefulness during the daytime, when the amount attained is less than the amount needed.

■ Train derailment caused by an engineer's sleep deprivation.
(JOHN ANGELILLO/ UPI/Alamy Stock Photo)

melatonin
A hormone that in-creases relaxation and sleepiness, re-leased by the pineal gland during sleep.

hyperactivity disorder (ADHD), are not a healthy solution to sleep depri-vation. They work by increasing the amount of norepinephrine and dopa-mine in the brain. These chemicals in turn increase blood pressure and heart rate, constrict blood vessels, increase respiration rate, and increase blood glucose. The result is heightened alertness, attention, and energy and a sense of euphoria. However, side effects include cardiovascular fail-ure and deadly seizures. High doses can cause feelings of hostility or paranoia, dangerously high body temperature, ir-regular heart beat, and addiction.[30,31] Nonmedical use of pre-scription stimulants (that is, their use other than as prescribed), or what is also referred to as off-label use, is as-sociated with excessive drinking and other drug use, lower grade point average, attention difficulties, psychiatric distress or depressed mood, and class absenteeism.[32] College stu-dents typically perceive little harm in using prescription stim-ulants.[32] Today, many are using prescription stimulants such as Adderall, Ritalin, and Vyvanse as study aids, party aids, and weight-loss aids.

How can you tell whether you are getting enough sleep? A prime symptom of sleep deprivation is daytime drowsiness. If you feel alert during the day, you are probably getting enough sleep. If you are sleepy in sedentary situations such as reading, sitting in class, or watching television, you may be sleep deprived. Another measure of sleep deprivation is the length of time you need to fall asleep at night. A well-rested person will need 15 to 20 minutes to fall asleep.[27] If you fall asleep the instant your head hits the pillow, there is a good chance you are sleep deprived.

WHAT MAKES YOU SLEEP?

Over the course of the day, your body undergoes rhythmic changes that help you move from waking to sleep and back to waking. These *circadian rhythms* are maintained primarily by two tiny structures in the brain, the *suprachiasmic nuclei* (SCN), which are located in the hypothalamus directly be-hind the optic nerve (Figure 4.2). These structures form an internal "biological clock" that controls body temperature and levels of alertness and activity. The SCN are active in the daytime, increasing wakefulness; less active in the early after-noon; and inactive at night, allowing the body to relax and sleep. In addition, the SCN control the release of certain hormones. They signal the pineal gland to release **melatonin**, a hormone that increases relaxation and sleepiness, and they signal the pituitary gland to release growth hormone during sleep, to help repair damaged body tissues.[27]

Also important in maintaining circadian rhythms are ex-ternal environmental cues, especially light. Neurons in the SCN monitor the amount of light entering the eyes, so that as daylight increases, the SCN slow down the secretion of mela-tonin and begin to be more active.[27] This process keeps your sleep/wake cycles generally synchronized with the changing lengths of day and night. The process is sensitive to artificial light as well as natural light, so even relatively dim lights in the evening (such as from a lamp or a computer screen) may delay the moment your biological clock induces sleepiness.

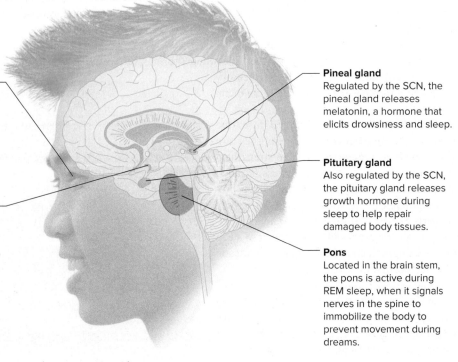

figure 4.2   Brain structures involved in sleep and waking.
(PhotoAlto/PunchStock)

The retina contains melanopsin cells, which make the SCN especially sensitive to blue light.[33] The SCN thus work as a master sleep cycle clock, coordinating the functions of organ systems—brain, cardiovascular, metabolic, reproductive, endocrine, renal, immune, and muscle.

The biological clock operates even without the cues of daylight or darkness, though not in perfect synchrony with a 24-hour day. Without the stimulation of light and dark, human beings would have a daily cycle several minutes longer than 24 hours. Every morning your body resets your biological clock to adjust to the next 24-hour period. Your body may tolerate a one-hour adjustment. However, when bedtimes and awakening times differ greatly from their established norms, the adjustment is more difficult. Working the night shift or flying across several time zones, for example, can wreak havoc with your biological clock.[33]

Because shift workers don't receive the powerful sleep-regulating cues given by sunlight, they are at increased risk for heart disease, digestive disorders, cancers, and mood problems. Similarly, many blind people experience a misalignment of the circadian clock called "non-24-hour sleep/wake disorder" because their retinas are not able to sense light. Their circadian clock is dysfunctional, so it is as if they have permanent jet lag and periodic insomnia.

THE STRUCTURE OF SLEEP

Studies have revealed that sleep consists of distinct stages in which muscle relaxation and nervous system arousal vary, as do types of brain waves and levels of neural activity. The brain cycles into two main states of sleep: non–rapid eye movement (NREM) sleep, which has four stages, and rapid eye movement (REM) sleep.

NREM Sleep

You spend about 75 percent of your sleep time in **non–rapid eye movement (NREM) sleep**, a time of reduced brain activity with four stages.

Stage 1 of NREM sleep is a transitional, light sleep—a relaxed or half-awake state. Your heart rate slows and your breathing becomes shallow and rhythmic. This stage may last from 10 seconds to 10 minutes and is sometimes accompanied by visual imagery. People awakened in stage 1 often deny that they were asleep.[9,27]

In stage 2, your brain's activity slows further, and you stop moving. Ventrolateral preoptic nucleus cells in the hypothalamus and parafacial zone cells in the brain stem switch on in stage 2 to cause a loss of consciousness. This lack of movement decreases muscle tension and brain stem stimulation so that sleep is induced. Stage 2 lasts about 10 to 20 minutes and represents the beginning of actual sleep. You are no longer consciously aware of your external environment. People awakened in stage 2 readily admit that they were asleep.[27,34]

During stages 3 and 4, your blood pressure drops, your heart rate and respiration slow, and the blood supply to your brain is minimized. If you were suddenly awakened during stage 4, referred to as *deep sleep,* you would feel momentarily groggy. You usually spend about 20 to 40 minutes at a time in deep sleep, and most of your deep sleep takes place in the first third of the night.[6] Brain neurons become more silent and the oscillation of brain waves slows in deep sleep. Overall, 20 to 25 percent of sleep after the full sleep cycles will be restorative deep sleep. Slow wave sleep brain activity is homeostatically regulated.[35]

REM Sleep

Rapid eye movement (REM) sleep begins about 70 to 90 minutes after you have fallen asleep. As you enter this stage, your breathing and heart rate increase, and brain wave activity becomes more like that of a waking state. REM sleep is characterized by noticeable eye movements, usually lasting between 1 and 10 minutes. During this period, you are most likely to experience your first dream of the night. Although dreams may occur in all stages of sleep, they generally happen in REM sleep.[36]

When you dream, there are periods when you have no muscle tone and your body cannot move, except for your eyes, diaphragm, nasal membranes, and erectile tissue (such as penis or clitoris).[27] This state is referred to as *REM sleep paralysis.* If you were not immobilized, there is a danger that you would act on—or act out—your dreams. REM sleep is sometimes called *paradoxical sleep* because the sleeper appears peaceful and still, but is in a state of physiological arousal.

Many people believe that dreams have some meaning and relevance to daily life, often reflecting changes or shifts in emotions. By examining your dreams, according to this view, you may gain insight into the mental and emotional processes you are applying to problems or events in your life. Most dreams involve people who are familiar to the dreamer. Dreams are visual and rarely involve taste or smell. However, the dreams of people who have been blind since birth are dominated by sound and emotional feelings. If people lose sight at age 7 or later, their dreams tend to be visually dominated.[27]

Besides giving us time to dream, REM sleep also appears to give the brain the opportunity to "file" important ideas and thoughts into long-term storage, that is, into memory. This reorganization and consolidation may account for the fact that we are sometimes able to solve problems in our dreams. Scientists further believe that creative and novel ideas are more likely to flourish during REM sleep because in this stage we have easier access to memories and emotions.

non–rapid eye movement (NREM) sleep
Sleep characterized by slower brain waves than are seen during wakefulness as well as other physiological markers; divided into four stages of increasingly deep sleep.

rapid eye movement (REM) sleep
Sleep characterized by brain waves and other physiological signs characteristic of a waking state but also characterized by reduced muscle tone, or sleep paralysis; most dreaming occurs during REM sleep.

Because ideas are filed in long-term storage during REM sleep, memory may be impaired if sleep time is insufficient. As a result of such memory impairment, the ability to learn new skills is also impaired. Performance in learning a new skill does not improve until an individual has had six hours of sleep; performance improves even more after eight hours of sleep.[23]

The importance of REM sleep to the brain is demonstrated by what is called the **REM rebound effect**. If you get inadequate sleep for several nights, you will experience longer and more frequent periods of REM sleep when you have a night in which you can sleep longer.[37]

(Andriy Popov/123RF)

Sleep Cycles

After your first REM period, you cycle back and forth between REM and NREM sleep stages. These cycles repeat themselves about every 90 to 110 minutes until you wake up. Typically, you experience four or five sleep cycles each night. After the second cycle, however, you spend little or no time in NREM stages 3 and 4 and most of your time in NREM stage 2 and REM sleep (Figure 4.3). After each successive cycle, the time spent in REM sleep doubles, lasting from 10 to 60 minutes at a time.[27,37]

The sleep cycle pattern changes across the lifespan, with children and young adolescents experiencing large quantities of NREM stages 3 and 4 sleep (deep sleep). Sleep needs are constant across adulthood, but as people get older, high-quality sleep may become more elusive, and older adults may experience less deep sleep and REM sleep and more NREM stage 1 sleep and wakefulness. The production of melatonin and growth hormone declines with age, and the body temperature cycle may also become irregular. All these changes decrease total nighttime sleep.[27]

Although the structure of sleep is essentially the same for men and women, women tend to have more slow wave sleep (NREM stages 3 and 4) than men do and to experience more insomnia. Men have more REM periods. Men and women also tend to have some differences in habits and behaviors related to sleep. For example, women tend to get less sleep than they need during the week, and men tend to get more sleep than they need. A majority of women say they do not get enough sleep

most nights of the week. However, men and women get about the same amount of sleep on the weekends.[38]

REM sleep is controlled by subcoeruleus nucleus cells, which are located in the brain stem. If you experience an injury or disease that damages these cells, you will not experience the general muscle paralysis associated with REM sleep. Sleep disorders that disrupt the paralysis in REM (such as REM sleep behavior disorder) can cause a serious condition in which dreams are acted out in violent movements.[35]

If you decrease your sleep time by 90 minutes or more, you essentially lose one sleep cycle, which can disrupt your circadian rhythm. You tend to get your highest quality of sleep in the first four hours after falling asleep, since these hours play a pivotal role in paying back sleep debt and actually help neutralize the feelings of tiredness you felt before going to bed. This is why you may find it more difficult to fall asleep again if awakening in the first four hours. The remaining hours of sleep are critical for nurturing the brain and aiding the body in repair and rejuvenation.

REM rebound effect Increase in the length and frequency of REM sleep episodes that are experienced when a person sleeps for a longer time after a period of sleep deprivation.

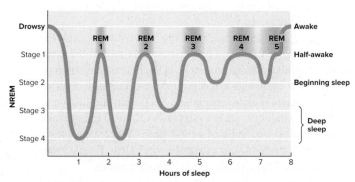

figure 4.3   **One night's sleep cycles.**

SLEEP DISORDERS

The National Sleep Foundation estimates that at least 40 million U.S. adults suffer from long-term sleep disorders each year; another 20 million experience occasional sleep problems.[5] Because many sleep disorders are undiagnosed or are not reported to physicians, many people who are chronically exhausted may not know why. Common sleep disorders affecting college students include insomnia, sleep apnea, sleep walking, and nocturnal eating disorders. For a helpful tip, see the Action Skill Builder box.

Insomnia

The National Sleep Foundation found that many adults suffer from **insomnia**—defined as difficulty falling or staying asleep—at least a few nights a week.[38] Clinical symptoms of insomnia include (1) taking longer than 30 minutes to fall asleep, (2) experiencing five or more awakenings per night, (3) sleeping less than a total of 6.5 hours as a result of these awakenings, and/or (4) experiencing less than 15 minutes of deep/slow wave sleep. Cognitive-behavioral therapy may be more effective for treating insomnia than relying on sleep medicine.[6,39]

Insomnia can be caused by stress, anxiety, medical problems, poor sleep environment, noisy or restless partners, and schedule changes (due to travel across time zones or shift work, for example).[39] For adult women, more than half of whom report symptoms of insomnia during any given month, additional causes may include depression, headaches, effects of pregnancy, premenstrual syndrome, menopausal hot flashes, and overactive bladder. Menstruation itself has been shown to be a cause of sleep disturbances. Insomnia causes for men include depression, headaches, and overactive bladder. Often, people with insomnia become distressed by their inability to fall asleep, which increases arousal and makes it even harder to fall asleep. In time, the bedroom, bedtime, or sleep itself becomes associated with frustration instead of relaxation, and a vicious cycle sets in.

Chronic insomnia is difficult to treat, but individuals may be able to break the cycle and experience relief by improving their sleep habits and sleeping environment, and by using relaxation techniques such as deep breathing and massage. Exercise has also been shown to significantly improve sleep quality for chronic insomnia. The exact mechanism for this benefit is not known. Scientists conjecture that an increase in core body temperature post-exercise is the likely reason that exercise is beneficial. But avoid intense exercise for at least two hours before bedtime.

Sleep Apnea

Also known as breathing-related sleep disorder, **sleep apnea** is a condition characterized by periods of nonbreathing during sleep. Some health experts estimate that almost 40 percent of the U.S. population has some form of sleep apnea, and that half of those afflicted may have a severe condition. Some 80 to 90 percent of these cases are undiagnosed. The condition occurs in all ethnic, age, and socioeconomic groups, although men are more at risk for developing sleep apnea than women are.[40]

Scientists have distinguished two main types of sleep apnea: central sleep apnea and obstructive sleep apnea. In *central sleep apnea,* a rare condition, the brain fails to regulate the diaphragm and other breathing mechanisms correctly. In *obstructive sleep apnea,* by far the more common type, the upper airway is obstructed during sleep.[6,12,13,14,15,16,21] Individuals with obstructive sleep apnea are frequently overweight and have an excess of bulky soft tissue in the neck and throat. When the muscles relax during sleep, the tissue can block the airway (Figure 4.4).

insomnia
A sleep disorder characterized by difficulty falling or staying asleep.

sleep apnea
A sleep disorder characterized by periods of nonbreathing during sleep; also known as breathing-related sleep disorder.

Women are more likely than men to get insufficient sleep. New mothers are particularly at risk for sleep deprivation. *(Jamie Marcial/Purestock/ SuperStock)*

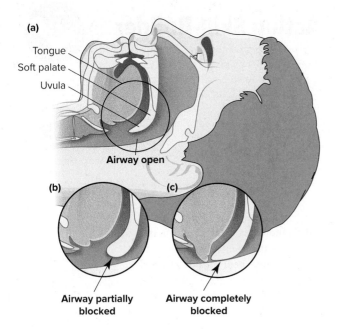

figure 4.4   Obstructive sleep apnea.
(a) Normally, the airway is open during sleep. (b) When the muscles of the soft palate, tongue, and uvula relax, they narrow the airway and cause snoring. (c) If these structures collapse on the back wall of the airway, they close the airway, preventing breathing. The efforts of the diaphragm and chest cause the blocked airway to become even more tightly sealed. For breathing to resume, the sleeper must rouse enough to cause tension in the tongue, which opens the airway.

Obstructive sleep apnea is a potentially dangerous condition; occasionally, it is even fatal. It is frequently seen in association with high blood pressure, and it can increase the risk of heart disease and stroke. Oxygen saturation of the blood decreases and levels of carbon dioxide rise when a person stops breathing, increasing the likelihood that heart and blood vessel abnormalities may occur. If sufficient oxygen is not delivered to the brain, death may occur during sleep.

If sleep apnea is not severe, it can be addressed with a variety of behavioral strategies. They include losing weight, forgoing alcoholic nightcaps and sedatives, avoiding allergens, not smoking, using a nasal decongestant spray, using a firm pillow and mattress, and not sleeping on the back. In addition, adjustable mouthpieces are available that extend the lower jaw, adding room to the airway. They are expensive, however, and may not be covered by health insurance.

In cases of severe sleep apnea, one treatment option is a continuous positive airway pressure (CPAP) machine. Through a comfortable mask, a CPAP machine gently blows slightly pressurized air into the patient's nose. Other treatment options include surgery to cut away excess tissue at the back of the throat and a newer technique called *somnoplasty* that involves shrinking tissue in the back of the throat with radio-frequency energy.[41]

Sleepwalking Disorder

People with **sleepwalking disorder** rise out of an apparently deep sleep and act as if they are awake. They do not respond to other people while in this state, or if they do, it is with reduced alertness. Sleepwalking takes place during the first third of the night's sleep. Episodes typically last less than 10 minutes.[6] If sleepwalkers are awakened, they are often confused for several minutes; if they are not awakened, they may return to bed and have little or no memory of the episode the next day.[37]

Although there may be a genetic link to sleepwalking, most sufferers do not have a family history of this disorder. Episodes may be brought on by excessive sleep deprivation, fatigue, stress, illness, excessive alcohol consumption, and the use of sedatives.[21]

Sleep-Related Eating Disorders

A person with **sleep-related eating disorder (SRED)** rises from bed during the night and eats and drinks while asleep. Distinct from sleep-related eating disorder is a newly identified sleep disorder, **night eating syndrome**, in which affected persons binge eat late at night, have difficulty falling asleep, repeatedly awaken during the night and eat again, and then eat very little the next day. Some people with night eating syndrome consume more than 50 percent of their daily calories at night. Sleep experts estimate that the syndrome affects about 1.5 percent of the general population and up to 10 percent among obese people seeking treatment for their weight. Treatments include medications and behavior management techniques.[37]

Evaluating Your Sleep

How can you tell whether you have a sleep problem? First, get a sense of your general level of daytime sleepiness by taking the **sleep latency** test (a measure of how long it takes you to fall asleep) in Part 1 of the Personal Health Portfolio activity at the end of the chapter. Next, check to see whether you have any symptoms of a sleep disorder by completing Part 2 of the activity. Then take a look at the various behavior-change strategies in the "Getting a Good Night's Sleep" section of the chapter and make any appropriate improvements. Part 3 addresses time-restricted eating (TRE), which has been shown to have a significant effect on the circadian clock. Of course, the most basic recommendation is to make sure you are getting enough hours of sleep every night. If you still experience a sleep problem after following these recommendations, you may want to consult your physician. If the problem is serious enough, your physician may refer you to a sleep clinic or lab or a sleep disorder specialist.

sleepwalking disorder
A sleep disorder in which a person rises out of an apparently deep sleep and acts as if awake.

sleep-related eating disorder (SRED)
A sleep disorder in which a person rises from bed during the night and eats and drinks while asleep.

night eating syndrome
A sleep disorder in which a person eats excessively during the night while awake.

sleep latency
The amount of time it takes a person to fall asleep.

GETTING A GOOD NIGHT'S SLEEP

Although sleep is very important, sleep scientists use the term *orthosomnia* to describe obsessing over sleep causing anxiety and inducing insomnia. Most people occasionally experience what is called *disordered sleep*. Disordered sleep includes the symptoms of sleep disorders, but they are less frequent and much less severe. What is the best way to avoid disordered sleep and ensure healthy sleep patterns over the course of your lifespan? In this section, we provide several strategies and tips that will help you get a good night's sleep.

Take a Break From Technology

A 2015 survey on the bedroom environment found that 62 percent of adults have a television in their bedroom, 26 percent a computer, 45 percent a tablet or smartphone, 13 percent a video game player, and 36 percent a music player or radio.[8] Many of these devices were left on during the night, even though electronic devices can interfere with sleep.

The artificial blue light from computers, televisions, and phones blocks the production of melatonin, the hormone produced by the pineal gland that induces sleep. Light-emitting diode (LED) screens can block the rise of melatonin. As a result, those who watch TV or surf the Web too close to bedtime may have a hard time drifting off unless their computer or TV screen can filter out blue light. Scientists also believe melanopsin, a light-sensitive protein in the retina and the cerebral cortex, is a primary regulator of the circadian clock and melatonin. Melanopsin reacts most strongly to blue light.[42] See the box "Action Skill-Builder: Blue Light Filtering."

Some college students are so addicted to their smartphones that they text and update their social media while they're half-asleep. This behavior not only interrupts sleep architecture, but it can lead to awkward and embarrassing texts. It takes about 30 seconds for people who are awakened from sleep to realize they are awake. This means that sleeping students who text in response to the beep of their smartphone are likely to send a garbled message and have no memory of sleep-texting the next morning.[43]

Communicating during sleep is not a new activity: texting has simply replaced the phone. People have long answered phone calls in the middle of the night with no memory of the conversation in the morning. This has been referred to as the "on-call" effect because doctors are especially prone to this behavior.[43] In other words, sleep-texting is an arousal disorder; the person is awakened by an outside stimulus and responds while half-conscious.[43] For a good night's sleep, turn off the phone.

Artificial light can also disturb sleep. A small bedside lamp can emit 20 to 80 lux (or units of brightness). In perspective, 1 lux is the measure of light received by the eye when standing 1 foot away from a burning candle. Full-sun daytime light is about 200,000 lux; it is less (1,000 lux) on a cloudy day. Blue LEDs offer significant energy savings over yellow incandescent lights, but have significant suppression

Action Skill-Builder

Blue Light Filtering

The amount of light emitted from your computer or iPad over one to two hours can disturb your sleep by suppressing melatonin levels. Reading on an iPad late at night instead of from a printed book can suppress melatonin by more than 50 percent and delay melatonin increase by three hours. Dimming your computer or smartphone screen's brightness level as it becomes dark outside can help maintain your normal melatonin levels. Another strategy is to turn off the blue in your screen's color palette, which will give the screen a red hue. Red does not interfere with melatonin production. Or you may want to eliminate the blue wavelengths emanating from your laptop or smartphone by downloading software such as f.lux or Redshift. Apple uses a function called Night Shift for its iPhone and iPad that mimics f.lux, changing the screen's emitted light around sunset to the warm end of the light spectrum. Wearing glasses with orange-tinted lenses at night can also effectively filter out blue light. Despite these strategies, even orange-tinted screens can interfere with sleep. The best method is to shut off electronic devices that use bright screens at least 30 minutes before going to sleep.

Source: Jabr, F. (2016). Blue LEDs light up your brain. *Scientific American*. Retrieved from https://www.scientificamerican.com/article/blue-leds-light-up-your-brain/; Walker, M. (2017). *Why we sleep*. New York, NY: Simon & Schuster, Inc.

effect on melatonin. The typical living room incandescent light is 20 to 80 lux and can suppress melatonin by 50 percent. LEDs suppress melatonin more than incandescent lights even when their lux power is the same.[44]

Your body depends on bright, natural daylight, not just soft, filtered blue light, to synchronize your circadian clock, which is important for regulating sleep and wellness. Insufficient daylight and high nighttime blue light can be a lighting purgatory. To optimize your circadian clock, it is essential to manage both indoor and outdoor light. See the box "Life Stories: Sam: Managing Indoor and Outdoor Light."

(Ocusfocus/123RF)

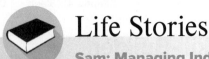

Life Stories

Sam: Managing Indoor and Outdoor Light

Sam learned in his Science of Sleep course about the importance of managing indoor light at night and daytime outdoor light for optimizing his circadian clock, which affects sleep and health. To monitor his light exposure, Sam installed MyLux on his smartphone.

This meter helped him discover that late-night visits to convenience marts and mall stores were exposing him to 500 blue-light lux luminance. Luminance is defined as the amount of light emitted from a surface, which can delay melatonin and interfere with sleep. Sam's exposure was well over the recommended under-5 lux exposure during the 30 to 60 minutes before bedtime.

Sam also used Apple's Nightshift on his Apple computer, and he connected the Drift TV box to his Samsung TV HDMI input, which filtered up to 50 percent of blue light from his TV at night. The filtering of blue light from his electronic devices helped relieve his chronic migraines.

Sam's daylight exposure was very revealing. Sunlight provides physical and mental health benefits, increases resilience to blue-light sensitivity at night, and is especially important for regulating the circadian clock and facilitating sleep quality. Health experts recommend getting at least 10,000 lux daylight exposure for 30 to 90 minutes, especially in the morning hours. A sunny day on the beach provides about 100,000 lux light (wearing sunglasses can safely decrease the sunlight reaching the eyes by 7- to 15-fold). Using his MyLux recorder, Sam discovered that sitting next to a large window in the classroom provided 2,000 to 5,000 lux light exposure on a sunny day. If he sat 6 feet from the window, his lux light exposure was only 500. Sam elected to choose classroom seats close to the window, and to get 30 minutes of daylight exposure every morning.

Source: Sunlight Inside. (2019). How much natural light do we need (for our health)? https://www.sunlightinside.com/light-and-health/how-much=natural-light=do-we-need-for-our-health/

Establish Good Sleep Habits

Several habits and behaviors affecting when and where you sleep and what you do before can help you sleep better and solve sleep problems. The box "Who's at Risk? Activities Done Almost Every Night Within the Hour Before Sleep" shows that although there is some variation in different countries, most of us could improve our sleep habits.

Maintain a Regular Sleep Schedule Try to get about eight hours of sleep every night, seven days a week. With a regular sleep schedule, you fall asleep faster and awaken more easily because you are psychologically and physiologically conditioned for sleep and waking. Most college students have an irregular sleep schedule.[45] As noted earlier, such a schedule throws off your internal biological clock and disrupts the structure of sleep. People setting a regular sleep schedule pattern average 7.2 hours of sleep each night, compared to 6.9 hours for those who do not establish a regular sleep schedule. Sixty percent of people with regular sleep schedules report their sleep quality as good or very good. Only 45 percent of people without a regular sleep schedule report sleep quality as good or very good. The typical U.S. adult's bedtime is 11:02 p.m. on workdays with wake-up at 7:05 a.m, and 11:24 p.m. on nonwork days with wake-up at 8:13 a.m.[8] The factor that makes the biggest difference in sleep debt, however, is bedtime, not wake time.[8]

(Collage Best/Getty Images)

Be Smart About Napping Thirty-one percent of U.S. adults take one or two naps a week.[46] If you are a napper, sleep experts recommend naps of only 15 to 45 minutes, which can be refreshing and restorative. If you nap longer than 45 minutes, your body can enter stage 4 deep sleep. It is more difficult to awaken from this stage, and you are likely to feel groggy when you do.[46] Just 10 to 20 minutes of napping can produce alertness, increase productivity, and improve mood. The optimal time for a nap is between 2 p.m. and 4 p.m., since biological mechanisms make it easier to fall asleep during this time frame.

If you know you will be going to bed later than usual, you may want to take a "preventive nap" of two to three hours. You can take one long nap or nap 15 minutes every four hours until you attain two hours of preventive napping. Research suggests that people who take preventive naps increase their alertness by about 30 percent over that of people who do not nap. This short-nap strategy has been used effectively by physicians and law enforcement officers, who must be able to perform in emergency situations while working very long shifts.[46]

Create a Sleep-Friendly Environment Your bedroom should be a comfortable, secure, quiet, cool, and dark place for inducing sleep.

• *Mattress.* Ninety-three percent of U.S. adults consider a comfortable mattress important for sleep.[46] Your mattress should be hard enough to allow you to get into a comfortable

Who's at Risk?

Activities Done Almost Every Night Within the Hour Before Sleep

As the section "Taking a Break from Technology" points out, watching a screen just before bedtime is not conducive to falling asleep. Yet many people in North America, Mexico, Europe, and Asia are likely to be looking at a TV, computer, or cell phone screen shortly before they go to bed. More relaxing activities include meditating or praying, taking a warm bath or shower, reading a print book or magazine, and having a soothing beverage that does not contain caffeine or other stimulant ingredients.

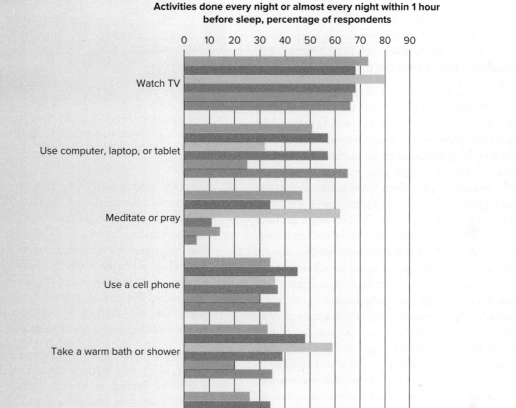

Activities done every night or almost every night within 1 hour before sleep, percentage of respondents

Legend: USA, Canada, Mexico, United Kingdom, Germany, Japan

Source: National Sleep Foundation. (2013). *International bedroom poll: Summary of findings.* Retrieved from https://sleepfoundation.org/sites/default/files/RPT495a.pdf

sleep position. If it is too hard, however, it may not provide an adequate cushion to prevent painful pressure on your body. Your body and the condition of your mattress both change over time. Bed mattresses should be replaced every seven to eight years.

- *Sheets.* Eighty-six percent of U.S. adults feel comfortable sheets and bedding are important for sleeping.[46] You should use mattress pads that can protect against liquid spills, urine, blood, and allergens such as dust mites. Dust mites are microscopic insects that feed on dead skin cells, and their droppings can become airborne. Inhaling the droppings can cause allergic reactions and asthma in sensitive individuals. If you experience itchy or watery eyes, sneezing, wheezing, congestion, or difficulty breathing in your bedroom, the culprit may be dust mites. Wash your bed linens regularly.

- *Pillow.* Ninety-one percent of U.S. adults view a comfortable pillow as important for sleep.[46] When picking the ideal pillow, ensure that it is properly aligned with your cervical spine. Proper cervical alignment will help prevent tightness in your neck muscles. Pillow thickness should be based on your preferred sleep position. Side sleepers need a pillow that fills the space between the ears and shoulders (5 to 6 inches). Back sleepers need a pillow thin enough so that the chin points straight ahead (1 to 2 inches). And stomach sleepers should use pillows that do not put pressure on the head, neck, or lower back (1 to 2 inches). Pillows should be replaced every two to three years.

- *Quiet.* Twenty-eight percent of U.S. adults report inside noise and 16 percent report outside noise as disrupting sleep. Women are more likely than men to find noise a bedroom factor disturbing sleep.[47] Noise can reduce the odds of getting restful sleep. Research on people who live near airports has found that excessive noise may jog them out of deep sleep and into a lighter sleep. Street noises, such as the sound of a motorcycle revving its engine, have a similar effect.[37] Measurable effects of noise on sleep begin at about 35 decibels (dB); significant health problems from sleep disruption occur at 55 dB and higher with long-term exposure. (A normal conversation is about 60 dB; a vacuum cleaner, about 80.) College residence halls and apartment complexes often have noise levels that exceed 35 decibels.

  Earplugs and earphones can reduce noise levels by as much as 90 percent. Earplugs with a noise reduction rating of 32 dB or below are recommended so that you can still hear a fire alarm or a crying child.[23] If it isn't possible to reduce or eliminate noise, try creating *white noise,* a monotonous and unchanging sound such as that of an air conditioner or a fan. White noise generators that create soothing sounds such as falling rain, wind, and surf have also been proven effective in protecting sleep.[48] If you can't find an inexpensive noise generator, start with a fan.[48] Intelligent sound machines use sensors that determine the audible sounds in a room and then produce the appropriate masking sound. These machines typically have a timer that can turn off the machine after a designated period.

- *Temperature.* Thirty-five percent of U.S. adults report bedroom temperature as a factor disrupting sleep. Women are more likely than men to consider temperature a factor affecting their sleep.[47] Your core body temperature needs to drop by 2 to 3 degrees Fahrenheit to facilitate sleep. Once core body temperature falls below this threshold, thermo-sensitive cells in the hypothalamus signal the suprachiasmatic nucleus to release melatonin.[47] The ideal temperature for a bedroom is usually 62° F to 65° F, but you will sleep best when the temperature is within your specific comfort zone. A temperature below or above that zone often causes fragmented sleep or wakefulness. Generally, temperatures above 75° F and below 54° F cause people to awaken.

  The temperature in a sleeper's hands and feet will increase after the onset of sleep.[49] This rise can disrupt sleep as

Short naps can refresh and restore, but napping longer than 45 minutes can interfere with your regular sleep schedule. *(Lightfieldstudios/123RF)*

the body works to reset its thermostat to a comfortable temperature. In a normal sleeper, blood vessels will dilate to radiate heat as the core body temperature drops.[50] Some people who have insomnia have a thermoregulatory system dysfunction that raises body temperature before they go to bed, however. Thus, if you have trouble sleeping, keep your room temperature at the cool end of your comfort zone. Placing a hot water bottle or a heating pad by your feet, or taking a warm bath, may also help by lowering your core body temperature and increasing blood flow to the extremities.[48]

- *Air quality.* Irritating agents such as allergens in the air disrupt sleep and increase the risk of upper respiratory infections. Typical air irritants include cigarette smoke, pollen, dust mites, and pet dander. Poor ventilation will aggravate the effects of the irritants, so open your bedroom windows at least once a week to allow fresh air to flow through. Replace filters in air conditioners and air purifiers every three months.

- *Body position.* Don't expect to get a good night's sleep if you cannot lie down. Research has shown that people sleeping in an upright position have poorer quality sleep than those sleeping in a horizontal position. The amount of slow-wave sleep a person experiences in a sitting position is almost zero. If you fall asleep while standing up, your body begins to sway so that you quickly awaken. Perhaps the brain operates in a similar fashion when you are sleeping in a seated position. With your body mainly upright, your brain may interpret this position as not sufficiently safe to allow deep sleep. Sleeping on your side is recommended to help prevent stress on joints and connective tissues. It also opens the airway and helps prevent sleep apnea.[51]

- *Pain and sleep.* Pain is a major factor interfering with sleep quality. About 15 percent of the U.S. population suffers from chronic pain. Pain is divided into categories: chronic pain and acute pain. Chronic pain is frequent and long-lasting. Twenty-one percent of U.S. adults have experienced chronic pain. People with chronic pain report a sleep debt of 42 minutes each week. Acute pain is sharp and of short duration. Thirty-six percent of U.S. adults experience acute pain. People with acute pain report a weekly sleep debt of 14 minutes. Moreover, 50 percent of people with chronic or acute pain are more likely to have daily sleep problems that negatively affect mood, relationships, activities, job performance, and quality of life.[52]

People with chronic pain feel they are not in control of their sleep and are worried that disrupted sleep has a significant impact on their health. Both chronic and acute pain sufferers are more likely to report that factors of the bedroom environment such as noise and lighting interfere with sleep quality than are people without pain. Sixty percent do not take any pain medication, 21 percent take pain medication a couple times a week, and 11 percent take pain medication most days of the week. Thirty-two percent of people taking pain medication report their sleep quality as good or very good, in comparison to the 47 percent of people reporting high sleep quality who do not take pain medication.[52]

The bottom line is that chronic or acute pain caused by headache, joint or muscle pain, or back pain makes it difficult to fall asleep at night, causes frequent awakenings, and prevents restorative sleep. Pain also affects sleep position, which can cause sleep-onset insomnia and sleep-maintenance insomnia. Sleep-onset insomnia refers to taking longer to fall asleep. Sleep-maintenance insomnia means you will have more frequent awakenings and shorter sleep duration. Sleep deprivation in turn may increase the production of cytokines. Cytokines are inflammatory chemicals that can make people more sensitive to pain when they are sleep deprived.[53] It is important to consult a health provider to determine whether pain is causing sleep disruption, or sleep disruption is causing pain.

Common pain medications, such as morphine and codeine, complicate the problem by causing fragmented sleep and insomnia. Opioid pain medications place people at higher risk for sleep apnea episodes. Alternatives to treatments with medicine include physical therapy, talk therapy, and meditation.[54] It is especially important to pay attention to the bedroom environment factors discussed in this chapter. If you are consulting a health provider, collect information about your sleep quality. The Personal Health Portfolio activity for this chapter will help you do so.

Avoid Eating Too Close to Bedtime
Try not to eat heavy meals within three hours of bedtime, particularly meals with high fat content. When you are lying down, the force of gravity cannot assist the movement of food from the stomach into the small intestine to complete digestion, and you may experience acid indigestion, often known as heartburn.

Also avoid caffeinated beverages, citrus fruits and juices, and tomato-based products such as pasta sauce, because these foods can temporarily weaken the esophageal sphincter. When weakened, this sphincter allows stomach contents to move back into the esophagus, a condition known as *acid reflux.* If you have acid reflux, try raising the head of your bed 6 to 8 inches, which will allow gravity to help move stomach contents into the small intestine. Tilting the bed is more effective than elevating the upper body with pillows. For those who are overweight, moderate weight loss may reduce discomfort because excessive stomach fat can cause abdominal pressure that contributes to heartburn.[6,33]

Empirical evidence is mixed on whether foods that contain tryptophan, an amino acid, can induce sleepiness. These foods include turkey, eggs, chicken, fish, and nuts.

Avoid Caffeine, Nicotine, and Alcohol
Whether it comes in the form of coffee, tea, chocolate, or soda, caffeine disrupts sleep. Caffeine, a stimulant, enters the bloodstream quickly and reaches peak effectiveness in about 30 to 60 minutes. It may take five to seven hours for half a given caffeine intake to clear the blood system of a young adult. A single cup of coffee may double the amount of time it takes an average adult to fall asleep. It may also reduce the number of slow-wave or deep-sleep episodes by half and quadruple the number of nighttime awakenings.[48] Thus, avoiding caffeine intake six to eight hours before going to bed may improve sleep quality. For late-night studying, you could choose to take a quick walk or eat some fruit instead. Exercise stimulates acetylcholine, which improves memory, and fruit contains sugar, which can provide an energy boost.

Energy drinks are especially high in caffeine. The Food and Drug Administration (FDA) limits caffeine content in soft drinks to 71 milligrams per 12 fluid ounces, but caffeine levels in energy drinks can be much higher, and they often contain additional stimulants such as taurine. For more about the effects of high levels of caffeine, see the box "Starting the Conversation: Caffeinated Energy Drinks and Sleep."

People who consume large amounts of cola tend to sleep five or fewer hours a night, and not just because of caffeine. Caffeine is the primary cola ingredient blocking brain chemicals that induce sleep. But carbonation can also cause you to feel bloated and make you vulnerable to heartburn and acid reflux. If you have a cola with your early evening meal, the caffeine can remain in your body systems for almost six hours.[55]

Like caffeine, nicotine is a stimulant that can disrupt sleep. People who smoke a pack of cigarettes a day have been shown to have sleep problems. Brain-wave-pattern analysis indicates that they do not sleep as deeply as nonsmokers. Smoking also affects the respiratory system by causing congestion in the nose and swelling of the mucous membranes lining the throat and upper airway passages. These physiological factors increase the likelihood of snoring and aggravate the symptoms of sleep apnea. They also decrease oxygen uptake, which leads to more frequent awakenings.[9,16]

About 20 percent of U.S. adults consume alcohol to help induce sleep.[47] Alcohol is linked to both delta and alpha brain activity. Delta activity is slow-wave brain patterns. Alpha activity, however, is also activated by alcohol and is more associated with stage 1 sleep, not stages 2 to 4. Alpha brain waves are fast

Starting the Conversation
Caffeinated Energy Drinks and Sleep

Q: Do you consume energy drinks for late-night studying? Partying? Do these drinks impede your ability to attain deep, reenergizing sleep every night?

Energy drinks are a popular form of stimulant used by college students for late-night studying and partying. They contain 50 to 500 milligrams (mg) of caffeine, their primary ingredient. Doctors generally recommend a maximum intake of 200 to 250 mg per day.

How does caffeine work? Caffeine looks like adenosine to nerve cells, so they let caffeine bind to their adenosine receptors. Adenosine causes drowsiness by slowing down nerve cell activity and dilating blood vessels to deliver oxygen to the brain during sleep. In contrast, caffeine speeds up nerve cell activity and constricts blood vessels to the brain. Caffeine causes the release of the "fight or flight" stress hormones cortisol and adrenaline (see Chapter 2). The result is a boost in energy and mental alertness.

Caffeine affects people differently, depending in part on dosage level and genetics. Caffeine is metabolized by a liver enzyme, and some people have a fast-acting liver enzyme for degrading caffeine but others have a slow-acting enzyme. People with the slow-acting enzyme are very sensitive to caffeine effects. For many people, consuming as little as 200 mg per day (the amount in two cups of coffee) increases stress levels. Too much caffeine in a short period of time causes a "caffeine crash": loss of focus, irritability, anxiety, racing heart rate, elevated blood pressure, headache, nausea, and jittery feelings. Some people even experience panic attacks and ringing in the ears.

Many college students do not understand a caffeine crash. It takes about 30 minutes for levels of caffeine to peak. Caffeine's half-life drug efficacy is about five to seven hours. This means it takes about five to seven hours before your body can remove 50 percent of caffeine concentration. If you consumed one cup of brewed caffeinated coffee, about 75 to 140 mg caffeine (average 95 mg) caffeine, at 7 p.m., your body would still be circulating 50 percent of this caffeine to your brain between 12 a.m. and 2 a.m. Keep in mind that one cup of decaffeinated coffee has about 10 to 15 percent of the caffeine in a regular cup of coffee. A caffeine crash occurs when your body has successfully removed caffeine from your body.

Caffeine's effects can make relaxation difficult and impede the ability to enter stage 2 in NREM (light sleep). Caffeine is also a diuretic, causing more frequent trips to the bathroom during the night. A study of soldiers in war zones found that those who consumed three or more energy drinks daily reported significantly more disrupted sleep than soldiers who consumed fewer or no energy drinks.

Q: Should the FDA mandate that energy drinks not contain more than 50 mg of caffeine?

Q: Energy drinks can be addictive due to high caffeine levels. What steps can you take to reduce your dependence on energy drinks?

McGraw Hill connect

Sources: Reissig, C. J., Strain, E. C., & Griffiths, R. R. (2009). Caffeinated energy drinks: A growing problem. *Drug and Alcohol Dependence, 99*(1-3), 1–10; Walker, M. (2017). *Why we sleep.* New York: NY: Simon and Schuster; Panda, S. (2018). *The circadian clock.* New York, NY: Rodale Books.

brain waves associated with being awake. The combination of delta and alpha brain wave activity inhibits restorative sleep.

Alcohol also makes it more likely that you will awaken in the middle of the night.[56] It affects the normal production of sleep chemicals associated with sleepiness, particularly adenosine. Adenosine, the sleep-inducing chemical, increases as you move from stage 1 to stage 2 NREM sleep, which enables a fast onset from stage 1 to stage 2. But alcohol also causes adenosine to subside quickly and can cause you to awaken before attaining needed restorative sleep.[56]

Alcohol is a depressant that prevents REM sleep from occurring until most of it has been absorbed. Even moderate amounts of alcohol consumed in the afternoon or early evening can interfere with REM sleep. Remember, REM is critical for memory consolidation. Memory remains vulnerable to alcohol's effect on REM sleep even up to three nights later when REM sleep is naturally restored.[49] After absorption, vivid dreams are more likely. Sleep experts call this an "alcohol rebound effect," in which the body seems to be trying to recover REM sleep that was lost earlier. This is why you awaken feeling groggy and unfocused the morning after an alcohol binge.

Alcohol can also aggravate sleep disorders such as obstructive sleep apnea and trigger episodes of sleepwalking and sleep-related eating disorders. The impact of alcohol on sleep apnea is of particular concern; it can even be deadly. Alcohol consumption makes throat muscles more relaxed than during normal sleep; it also interferes with the ability to awaken.[56]

Exercise Regularly, but Not Close to Bedtime Regular exercise during the day or early evening hours may be beneficial for sleep. Exercising within three hours of going to bed, however, is not recommended, because exercise stimulates the release of adrenaline and elevates core body temperature. It takes at least three hours after vigorous exercise for body temperature to drop enough for drowsiness to occur and deeper sleep to take place.[48]

Manage Stress and Establish Relaxing Bedtime Rituals Twelve percent of U.S. adults have severe or very severe stress levels, and 31 percent have moderate stress levels. People with severe or very severe stress average 49 minutes less sleep each night than do people who are not stressed. Eighty-three percent of those with severe or very severe stress report having poor or very poor sleep quality, compared to 35 percent who are not stressed.[52] Women are more likely than men to report stress as a problem.[52] Stress increases physiological arousal and can adversely affect sleep patterns.

Stress management and stress reduction techniques, such as those described in Chapter 2, can be used to help induce sleepiness. For example, keep a worry book by your bedside and record bothersome thoughts and problems that keep you awake at night. Once you've written them down, tell yourself you'll work on them during daylight hours, and then let go of them. Use your notes to focus energy and attention on these problems over the next few days.

It can also be helpful to develop a bedtime ritual, such as reading, listening to soothing music, or taking a warm (but not too hot) bath; your mind and body will come to associate bedtime with relaxation and peacefulness. Avoid stressful or stimulating activities before bedtime, such as working or paying bills, and dim the lights to let your internal clock know that drowsiness is appropriate. Experiment until you find a method of calming down and relaxing at bedtime that works for you.

If you do have a hard time falling asleep, don't stay in bed longer than 30 minutes. Get up, leave the room, and listen to soothing music or read until you feel sleepy. Listening to classical music 45 minutes before bedtime has been found to help people get to sleep faster and to experience fewer sleep disturbances during the night.[48]

Research suggests that smell can have an effect on sleep. Lavender has been shown to facilitate a relaxed state by decreasing heart rate and blood pressure. One study found that sniffing lavender before sleeping produced more restorative sleep.[47] Ideas for using smell to induce sleep are presented at the end of the chapter.

Weighted blankets for easing anxiety and facilitating sleep have become popular. These blankets, weighing 2 to 24 pounds, were designed to emulate feelings of being hugged, called deep-pressure therapy (DPT). DPT may stimulate the parasympathetic nervous system to reduce high arousal levels and help children with autism sleep better. Evidence of its effectiveness for resolving sleep problems for insomnia and neurological disorders is sparse and inconsistent, however. If you are interested in using a weighted blanket, the recommendation is for a blanket that is about 10 percent of your body weight spread evenly across the entire blanket. The blanket should not be shared with others because it is designed to mold to the user's body. Weighted blankets are considered safe but should not cover your face or neck while sleeping, and they should be kept away from children under 50 pounds since they could cause suffocation.[57]

Consider Your Bed Partner Thirty-seven percent of U.S. adults snore regularly. More men snore than women. However, after menopause women snore as much as men.[51] Snoring is a major disruption of partners' sleep, and body movement during sleep can also be a problem for partners. Avoiding alcohol before bedtime, using nasal sprays, sleeping on your side, and using a humidifier may help reduce snoring.

Men tend to thrash around in bed more than women do, and older couples tend to move in less compatible ways than do younger couples.[49] A firm mattress with low motion transfer may help prevent sleep disruption caused by a partner's movement. Sleep can also be disrupted if a partner has a different sleep schedule or a sleep disorder. If your partner's sleep habits create a problem for you, encourage your partner to improve his or her sleep habits or to see a sleep disorder specialist. As a last resort, you or your partner may have to sleep in different beds or rooms.

Be Wise If Sleeping With a Fan Some scientists view sleeping with a fan as toxic and unsafe because it may circulate dust and allergens and dry out nasal passages. However, circulating air can certainly be invaluable in lowering the bedroom temperature. If you opt to use a fan when sleeping, keep it far enough from your bed so the air does not blow directly on you. A well-functioning bedroom air filter is also recommended.[58]

Sleeping in Unfamiliar Environments

Did you know that birds and aquatic mammals experience unihemispheric sleep? Unihemispheric sleep, technically called the cross-cortical default mode, occurs when one brain hemisphere is awake during sleep and the other is in deep sleep. Birds, for example, sleep with one eye open in case they need to quickly fly away after sensing an environmental threat. Although humans do not sleep with one eye open, they may experience unihemispheric sleep on their first night in an unfamiliar bed, or at home in a familiar bed on the first day when a significant sleeping partner is absent. Sleep scientists conjecture that unihemispheric sleep is an evolutionary mechanism in which your brain knows something is not right in your bedroom environment.[35] Frequent travelers may find it helpful to bring along an item from their home bedroom environment, such as a favorite pillow.

Prescription Medications Popular prescription sleep medications include Lunesta, Sonata, and Ambien. The safest and most effective sleep medications

- Can be taken at various doses
- Are not addictive
- Do not produce serious side effects
- Wear off quickly so that you are not drowsy the next day

Sleep experts disagree about whether today's sleep medications meet these criteria.[59] No sleep medication should be used for longer than two weeks without consulting a physician.

The most frequently prescribed longer-acting sleep medications are the benzodiazepines Restoril and Doral. These drugs induce sleep but suppress both deep sleep and REM sleep. Their effects can last from 3 to 24 hours, and daytime side effects include decreased memory and intellectual functioning. People quickly build tolerance to long-lasting benzodiazepines, which are addictive and lose their effectiveness after 30 nights of consecutive use. There are some shorter-acting benzodiazepines on the market that do not suppress deep sleep and REM sleep.

Consumer Clipboard
Sleep-Tracking Apps

As you learned in this chapter, it is best to disconnect from electronics at least 30 minutes before going to sleep. It may seem contradictory, but smart sleep technology has popularized connecting with electronics for collecting quantifiable sleep data. There are numerous sleep-tracking devices in various shapes, sizes, and styles, most designed to track the sleeper's movement and sound. They use white noise to block unwanted sounds, guided imagery to calm stressed minds, and sensors to monitor sleep patterns and snoring, detect restless limb movements, and help fix bad sleep habits.

The initial wave of sleep trackers focused on the number of hours slept. Today's devices track sleep brain waves, core body temperature, respiration rate, and heart rate. They include wearable rings, wrist bands, headbands, smartphones, bedside trackers that use ultralow radio waves, and thin between-the-sheets bands to collect sleep data without touching the body. For example, the Apple Sleep Cycle App uses its smartphone microphone placed 10 inches away to listen to body movements during sleep, and to awaken the sleeper in the morning only during the light sleep stage. Nokia Sleep is connected to smart homes to turn off or dim room lights, mute the phone, adjust room temperature, and transfer sleep data to Google Docs. Wearable sleep devices will continue to boom as they are interfaced with smart-home features using sonar technology.

Many consumers using sleep technology devices are sharing the collected data with their health providers. The American Academy of Sleep Medicine (AASM) views consumer sleep technology, or CST, as a nonprescriptive means of monitoring sleep quality. According to the AASM position statement, sparse empirical evidence validates CST use as a diagnostic or treatment tool. Instead, CST monitors are classified as "lifestyle/entertainment devices" that are not subject to regulation by the FDA.

Despite the AASM's reservations, consumer sharing of data from CST devices has blurred the lines between lifestyle/entertainment and medical functions. If you are interested in CST, there are some general consumer recommendations to consider. Try out wearable CST for comfort before purchasing and understand the return policies, terms, and exclusions. Check the permissions in Settings to see whether the device collects personal information you do not need or do not want to share with a third party. Remember, CSTs are not subject to the same privacy-protection laws that govern health providers.

Sources: Walker, M. (2017). *Why we sleep.* New York, NY: Simon & Schuster, Inc; L'Amie, L. (2018). Plug in, drift off: The world of hyperconnected smart sleep devices. *New York Magazine.* Retrieved from http://numag.com/selectall/smartphone/do-smart-sleep-monitors-and-trackers-actually-work.html; Khosla, S., Deak, M., Gault, D., et al. (2018). Consumer sleep technology: An American Academy of Sleep Medicine position statement. *Journal of Clinical Sleep Medicine, 14*(5), 877–880; Landau, M. (2019). Do sleep apps really work? *Consumer Reports.* Retrieved from https://www.consumerreports.org/sleeping/do-sleep-apps-really-work/

rebound insomnia Insomnia that occurs after a person stops taking sleep medication and that is worse than it was before the medication was started.

A new category of sleep medications is the imidazopyridines. The National Sleep Foundation considers these drugs the best prescription sleeping aids. One drug in this category, zolpidem, sold under the trade name Ambien, has become the best-selling prescription sleep aid in the United States, but it has been associated with some disturbing side effects, such as sleep driving and sleep-related binge eating disorder. Although the National Sleep Foundation endorses imidazopyridines as the best category of sleep medications, it has major concerns about Ambien, and the manufacturer has been required to more specifically identify cognitive distortion side effects on its label.

Orexins, chemicals produced by the hypothalamus, are a new class of prescriptive sleep medications considered "orexin receptor antagonists." Orexin is a chemical that plays a pivotal role in keeping people awake and alert. Blocking the alert state theoretically helps people sleep. Orexin targets a localized area of the brain, possibly causing fewer side effects than other sleep medications. Its brand name is Belsomra.[60]

Many over-the-counter (OTC) sleep products contain antihistamine, a type of drug developed to treat allergies. The effects of antihistamines occur throughout the body; besides drowsiness, they are dehydration, agitation, and constipation.

You can also quickly develop tolerance to antihistamines, and when you stop taking them, you may experience **rebound insomnia**—insomnia that is worse than what you experienced before you started taking the medication.[61]

You can avoid rebound insomnia by gradually reducing the dose. If you use OTC sleep aids, be sure to read and follow the label instructions, which advise that these drugs not be taken for longer than two weeks. If sleep problems persist, consult your health provider. Cognitive-behavioral therapy is widely recognized as the first line of treatment before using drugs to resolve sleep problems.[49]

Using Sleep Aids and Sleep Apps

About 10 percent of U.S. adults use sleep-tracking devices.[62] The more sophisticated sleep apps are sleep trackers, which you use by putting your smartphone under your pillow or sheet rather than beside your bed. These apps use your phone's microphone and accelerometer to record noise and movement and then apply algorithms to evaluate the quality of your sleep. Most can wake you with an alarm (or a playlist from your music library) when you are in light sleep, so you will wake up refreshed rather than groggy. They all try to give you an idea of how well you are sleeping.

A number of wristband fitness devices can also be programmed to measure and record the wearer's sleep pattern, though the data they provide is limited. See the box "Consumer Clipboard: Sleep-Tracking Apps."

Complementary and Alternative Products and Approaches Complementary and alternative products and approaches to sleep problems include herbal products, dietary supplements, aromatherapy, and relaxation drinks. The herbal product most commonly used for insomnia is valerian, which has a tranquilizing or sedative effect. Hops is another product currently receiving attention as a possible sleep aid. Both are widely available in health food stores. Herbal products can interact with other medications and drugs, including caffeine and alcohol; it is strongly recommended that you consult your physician before trying any herbal remedies.[48]

The dietary supplement melatonin has been marketed as a sleep aid, but health experts are divided on its effectiveness. As noted earlier in this chapter, melatonin is a hormone naturally secreted by the pineal gland in response to darkness. It lowers body temperature and causes drowsiness. Most experts agree that the 3-mg dose of synthetically produced melatonin available in health food stores is too high and that a dose of 0.1 mg is as effective.[48] Potential side effects, interactions with drugs, and long-term health effects of melatonin supplements have not been studied extensively. Use caution, because some studies have reported increased risk of heart attack, infertility, fatigue, and depression with melatonin use.

It takes 90 minutes for melatonin to effectively induce sleepiness, and it has a half-life of six hours. This means taking melatonin in the second half of sleep will increase the likelihood of waking up groggy.

Melatonin is considered safe to take for up to three months. After that, you should consult your health provider for continued use. The recommendation is to try sleep behavior changes before relying on melatonin.[49]

Cannabis (CBD, the chemical found in marijuana) is also being used as an insomnia supplement due to its anti-inflammatory ingredients; it interacts with serotonin to regulate mood and anxiety. Research on the effectiveness of CBD for treating insomnia is in its infancy,[63] but early research suggests it may increase total sleeping time but delay the time for falling asleep. Anecdotal evidence supports CBD for resolving sleep problems in people with underlying anxiety.

In aromatherapy, certain essential oils, such as jasmine and lavender, are used to induce relaxation and sleepiness. Aromatherapists believe these oils relieve insomnia by reducing stress, enhancing moods, and easing respiratory or muscular problems, but no strong scientific evidence supports these claims.[48] Aromatherapy oils may be applied to the skin by full-body massage, or a drop may be placed on the wrist or at the base of the throat so that the scent is inhaled during sleep. Scented sprays can be used on bed linens, but aromatherapy candles should not be burning while you are sleeping. Aromatherapy products are generally available in health food stores. If you are interested in trying this approach, however, it is recommended that you consult a trained aromatherapist before making any purchases.

You Make the Call

Snooze You Lose: Criminalizing Drowsy Driving

Eye-catching phrases such as "You Snooze, You Lose" are being used in new public health roadside campaigns warning people not to drive if drowsy. State campaigns have now moved into the judicial system as law enforcement officials and public health professionals have begun advocating holding sleep-deprived drivers criminally accountable for fatalities and injuries they cause in accidents. Ophadell Williams has become the nation's poster child for the criminal consequences that are possible under new laws targeting sleep-deprived driving. Williams had only 5 hours of sleep in the preceding 24 hours when the bus he was driving crashed, killing 15 passengers. The Bronx district attorney charged Williams with manslaughter, which carries a 15-year sentence. Williams was found not guilty of manslaughter and negligent homicide, illustrating the difficulty in criminal prosecution of drowsy driving.

Other states are also cracking down on sleep-deprived drivers. A bus driver in Virginia was convicted of manslaughter after killing four people and injuring dozens. New Jersey passed a "Death by Auto" law, which is in effect when a sleep-deprived driver causes an accident resulting in fatalities. Conviction under the New Jersey law carries a sentence of up to 30 years, a $250,000 fine, and a mandate that 85 percent of the sentence be served before the driver becomes eligible for parole.

The Bureau of Labor Statistics estimates that 35 percent of U.S. adults usually sleep less than seven hours, 12 percent less than five hours, and 2 percent less than four hours. Moreover, the AAA Foundation for Traffic Safety reports that 16 to 21 percent of all fatal vehicle crashes involve a sleep-deprived driver. Consider the following risk rates, comparing drivers who have slept at least 7 of the preceding 24 hours with drivers who had not:

- Those who slept two to three hours less than usual had 3.0 times the crash rate.
- Those who slept four or more hours less than usual had 10.2 times the crash rate.[64]

Traffic safety and public health advocates argue that education and safety campaigns about wearing seat belts and not texting while driving have proven insufficient to change risky behaviors. The threat of criminal prosecution may increase driver awareness of the consequences of driving when sleep deprived. Although it will be difficult to prove conclusively that driver fatigue caused an accident, law enforcement officials are now using traffic cameras, vehicle black boxes, GPS tracking, and cell phone records to support their cases.

Some people, however, view laws like New Jersey's Death by Auto law as too draconian and an encroachment on

Continued...

Concluded...

people's daily lives. Many also consider sleep deprivation a product of a sleepless American culture, even a badge of honor driven by the need to make personal sacrifices in order to keep up with peers at work and school. But testimony by victims of drowsy drivers has led an increasing number of states to criminalize sleep-deprived driving.

What do you think? Should sleep-deprived drivers who cause injuries and fatalities be subject to criminal prosecution?

Pro Arguments

- Educational campaigns have not been effective in preventing drowsy-driving accidents. Criminalizing this offense will be an effective deterrent.
- Criminalizing drowsy-driving accidents that inflict death or injury will educate the public about the problem and ignite a cultural change.

- Driving when drowsy is the same as being intoxicated or distracted behind the wheel and should be treated the same way.

Con Arguments

- Criminalizing drowsy driving is too severe a response. Rest areas, highway rumble strips, and smart car technology provide a more effective prevention strategy.
- Laws against drowsy driving will be virtually unenforceable. There are intoxication meters for alcohol, but no meter exists for detecting drowsiness.
- People with sleep disorders (for example, apnea) are more at risk for driving when drowsy. Criminalizing drowsy driving may have the unintended consequence of discouraging people with sleep problems from seeking help from health providers.

Sources: AAA Foundation for Traffic Safety. (2017). *Fact sheet: Acute sleep deprivation and risk of motor vehicle crash involvement.* Retrieved from www.AAAFoundation.org; CBS News Staff. (2017). Why sleep deprivation can kill. *CBS News.* Retrieved from http://www.cbsnews.com/news/why-sleep-deprivation-can-kill/; Harvard Medicine. (2017). Push to prosecute drowsy driving may hinge on definition. *The New York Times.* Retrieved from https://nyti.ms/VbsuBh/; Pewtrusts. (2017). Why it's hard to crack down on drowsy driving. https://www.pewtrusts.org/en/research-and-analysis/blogs/stateline/2017/10/31/why-its-hard-to-crack-down-on-drowsy-driving

In Review

How does sleep affect your health?
Quantity and quality of sleep are strongly associated with overall health and quality of life. Adequate sleep gives the body time for repair, recovery, and renewal. Sleep deprivation is associated with a wide range of health problems, ranging from cardiovascular disease to depression to overweight and obesity. The National Sleep Foundation is using the Sleep Health Index to evaluate sleep quality. The *Healthy People 2020* goals now stress the importance of sleep for health, productivity, and well-being for the first time.

What makes you sleep?
Sleep is induced by the activity of a specific set of structures in the brain, in combination with environmental cues such as darkness. Humans have a circadian rhythm slightly longer than 24 hours; every morning the body resets this biological clock to adjust to the next 24-hour cycle.

What is the structure of sleep?
Every night people cycle through several stages of sleep, characterized by different brain waves, different states of muscle relaxation, and different nervous system activity. NREM sleep includes stages of deep sleep, whereas REM sleep includes dreaming and brain activity related to the consolidation of learning and memory.

What are common sleep disorders?
Insomnia, or difficulty falling or staying asleep, is experienced by 30 to 40 percent of adults. Sleep apnea, or periods during sleep when breathing stops, is almost as common, but men are more at risk for it than women. Nighttime eating disorders are somewhat less common.

How can you enhance the quality of your sleep?
The key to getting a good night's sleep is cultivating good sleep habits, such as keeping a regular sleep schedule, creating a sleep-friendly environment, avoiding stimulants late in the day, exercising regularly, managing stress, avoiding heavy meals close to bedtime, turning off electronics or dimming the screen at least 30 minutes before you plan to go to sleep, and being considerate of your sleep partner. Sleep aids, whether prescription, OTC, or alternative, can help with situational sleep problems but shouldn't be used long term. Alternative approaches to sleep include herbal products, dietary supplements, and aromatherapy. Evidence supporting CBD to facilitate sleep is sparse. Managing both indoor and outdoor light is important for sleep quality.

Sleep Apps and Consumer Sleep Technology
Sleep apps are very popular and have diverse types and functions. Many consumers are using consumer sleep technology (CST) devices to share sleep data with their health providers. CST tools are classified as "lifestyle/entertainment" devices and are not regulated by the FDA.

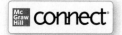
Part 1 Sleep Diary

A sleep diary can help identify habits that interfere with quality sleep. The diary can also be a source of valuable information if you need to consult a medical professional about sleep. Use the accompanying sleep diary to track your sleep for seven days. It is most accurate when you complete it each day. Keep it close to your bed so that you will remember to fill it out before you go to sleep and when you awaken.

Part 2 Do You Have Symptoms of a Sleep Disorder?

Ask yourself the following questions:

- Do you have trouble falling asleep three nights a week or more?

- Do you wake up frequently during the night?

- Do you wake up too early and find it difficult to get back to sleep?

- Do you wake up unrefreshed?

- Do you snore loudly?

- Are you aware of gasping for breath or not breathing while you are sleeping, or has anyone ever told you that you do this?

- Do you feel sleepy during the day or doze off watching TV, reading, driving, or engaging in daily activities, even though you get eight hours of sleep a night?

- Do you have nightmares?

- Do you feel unpleasant, tingling, creeping sensations in your legs while trying to sleep?

- Does chronic or acute pain interfere with your sleep? If so, how do you manage this pain?

If you answer yes to any of these questions, it is possible that you are suffering from a sleep disorder. The first step is to make sure you have good sleep habits and practices as described in this chapter. If you are doing everything you can to ensure a good night's sleep, consult your health provider, who may refer you to a sleep disorder specialist.

Part 3 Eating and Circadian Rhythm

Satchin Panda, in his book *The Circadian Clock,* stresses the importance of time-restricted eating (TRE) for maintaining a healthy circadian clock. Panda estimates 50 percent of U.S. adults eat food over a 15-hour period. This lengthy span disrupts the circadian clock and not only interferes with sleep quality but also causes weight gain and acid reflux. Panda recommends the window should not be more than 10 hours. Track your eating window for one week in your weekly diary by recording the following: day, time of first bite, time of last bite, hours slept, and changes in mood and energy.

Sources: Part 1: Weekly Sleep Diary. (n.d.). Helpguide. Retrieved from www.helpguide.org; Part 2: Adapted from National Sleep Foundation. (2004). www.sleepfoundation.org; Part 3: Panda, S. (2018). *The circadian clock.* New York, NY: Rodale Books.

SLEEP DIARY

	Day 1 Date:	Day 2 Date:	Day 3 Date:	Day 4 Date:	Day 5 Date:	Day 6 Date:	Day 7 Date:
Daytime Activities & Pre-Sleep Ritual (Fill in each night before going to bed)							
Exercise What did you do? When? Total time?							
Naps When? Where? How long?							
Alcohol & Caffeine Types, amount and when							
Feelings Happiness, sadness, stress, anxiety, major cause							
Food & Drink (Dinner/snacks) What and when?							
Medications or Sleep Aids Types, amount and when							
Bedtime Routine Meditation/Relaxation? How long?							
Bed Time							
Sleeping & Getting Back to Sleep (Fill in each morning)							
Wake-up Time							
Sleep Breaks Did you get up during the night? If so, what did you do?							
Quality of Sleep & Other Comments							
Total Sleep Hours							

Source: "Weekly Sleep Diary," Helpguide, www.helpguide.org

CRITICAL THINKING QUESTIONS

1. Analyze your sleep. What was the average number of hours you slept for the five weekday nights? What was the average number of hours you slept on the weekend? Discuss the factors (individual and environmental) that affected the duration or quality of your sleep. For example, perhaps you slept worse on the days you drank Pepsi after dinner, or perhaps you slept worse on the weekend because your neighbors had a noisy party. Conversely, perhaps you slept well because you didn't play video games before going to sleep or because your partner goes to sleep and wakes up at the same time you do.

2. In Part 2, did you answer yes to any of the questions? If so, do you think you need to see your doctor about your sleep quality?

   In Part 3, does your TRE correspond to a healthy circadian rhythm?

3. Overall, do you think you are meeting your sleep needs? Why or why not? If you are not meeting your sleep needs, what are some things you can do to change this? Use the material included in the section "Establishing Good Sleep Habits" in your discussion.

4. Do you leave your cell phone on at night? If so, do your respond to texts or send emails after you have gone to sleep?

5. The United States has been described as "Sleepless America." What can be done to change a sleepless culture?

Design Icons: ©McGraw-Hill Education

5 Nutrition

Marctran/123RF

Ever Wonder...

why food insecurity is a public health problem on college campuses?

whether sugar is toxic?

whether you should avoid gluten?

Your day begins with a bagel spread with cream cheese and a jolt of caffeine from freshly brewed coffee. Mid-morning hunger pangs are relieved by an energy bar and an energy drink. Lunch at the local fast-food place includes a cheeseburger, fries, and a soda. Another energy bar in mid-afternoon, accompanied by a bottle of water, tides you over to dinner. Still, you're so hungry when you get to the campus food court that you overindulge, downing several soft tacos with salsa, shredded lettuce, and sour cream. Late-night studying is supported by the consumption of popcorn, cookies, and another energy bar. Welcome to college dining!

Unfortunately, healthy dining can be a challenge in a culture that promotes the consumption of fast foods and convenience foods in shopping malls, sports arenas, airports, and college dining halls. Many people have acquired a taste for the high-calorie, full-fat, heavily salted foods so plentiful in our environment. It *is* possible to choose a healthy diet, however, and this chapter will help you see how, starting with research-based guidelines for healthy eating.

UNDERSTANDING NUTRITIONAL GUIDELINES

In 1997, the National Academies' Food and Nutrition Board introduced the **Dietary Reference Intakes (DRIs)**, a set of recommendations designed to promote optimal health and prevent both nutritional deficiencies and chronic diseases such as cancer and cardiovascular disease. The DRIs, developed by American and Canadian scientists, encompass four kinds of recommendations. The **Estimated Average Requirement (EAR)** is the amount of nutrients needed by half of the people in any one age group, for example, teenage boys. Nutritionists use the EARs to assess whether an entire population's normal diet provides sufficient nutrients. The EARs are used in nutrition research and as a basis for Recommended Dietary Allowances.[1,2,3]

The **Recommended Dietary Allowance (RDA)** represents the average daily amount of any one nutrient an individual needs to protect against nutritional deficiency. If there is not enough information about a nutrient to set an RDA, the Food and Nutrition Board provides an *Adequate Intake (AI)*. The *Tolerable Upper Intake Level (UL)* is the highest amount of a nutrient a person can take in without risking toxicity.

The Food and Nutrition Board also provides the **Acceptable Macronutrient Distribution Range (AMDR)**. AMDRs represent intake levels of essential nutrients associated with reduced risk of chronic disease while providing adequate nutrition. If your intake exceeds the AMDR, you increase your risk of chronic disease. For example, the AMDR for dietary fat for adult men is 20 to 35 percent of the calories consumed in a day. A man who consumes more than 35 percent of his daily calories as fat increases his risk for chronic diseases.[1,2,3]

Whereas the DRIs are recommended intake levels for individual nutrients, the *Dietary Guidelines for Americans* provides scientifically based diet and exercise recommendations designed to promote health and reduce the risk of chronic disease. The *Dietary Guidelines,* first published in 1980 and revised every five years by the U.S. Department of Agriculture (USDA) and the U.S. Department of Health and Human Services, is the cornerstone of U.S. nutrition policy. The most recent version is 2015–2020, which is discussed in detail later in the chapter.

To translate DRIs and the *Dietary Guidelines* into healthy food choices, the USDA publishes **MyPlate**, a graphic nutritional tool that can be customized for different calorie needs (see Figure 5.3). The Food and Drug Administration (FDA) developed the **Daily Values** used on food labels to indicate how a particular food contributes to the recommended daily intake of major nutrients in a 2,000-calorie diet (see Figure 5.4).[1,2,3]

Before we explore how you can use these tools to choose a healthy diet, we take a look at the major nutrients that make up our diet. For each nutrient, we include general recommendations for intake based on either the DRIs or the AMDRs.

TYPES OF NUTRIENTS

As you engage in daily activities, your body is powered by energy produced from the food you eat. Your body needs the **essential nutrients**—water, carbohydrates, proteins, fats, vitamins, and minerals—contained in these foods, but not only to provide fuel. Nutrients also build, maintain, and repair

---

Dietary Reference Intakes (DRIs)
An umbrella term for four sets of dietary recommendations: Estimated Average Requirement, Recommended Dietary Allowance, Adequate Intake, and Tolerable Upper Intake Level; designed to promote optimal health and prevent both nutritional deficiencies and chronic diseases.

Estimated Average Requirement (EAR)
The amount of nutrients needed by half of the people in any one age group.

Recommended Dietary Allowance (RDA)
The average daily amount of any one nutrient an individual needs to protect against nutritional deficiency.

Acceptable Macronutrient Distribution Range (AMDR)
Intake ranges that provide adequate nutrition and that are associated with reduced risk of chronic disease.

Dietary Guidelines for Americans
Scientifically based recommendations designed to promote health and reduce the risk for many chronic diseases through diet and physical activity.

MyPlate
A graphic nutritional tool developed by the USDA that can be customized depending on your calorie needs.

Daily Values
Dietary standards used on food labels to indicate how a particular food contributes to the recommended daily intake of major nutrients in a 2,000-calorie diet.

essential nutrients
Chemical substances used by the body to build, maintain, and repair tissues and regulate body functions. They cannot be manufactured by the body and must be obtained from foods or supplements.

electrolytes
Mineral components that carry electrical charges and conduct nerve impulses.

tissues; regulate body functions; and support the communication among cells that allows you to be a living, sensing human being.

We need large quantities of *macronutrients*—water, carbohydrates, protein, and fat—for energy and important functions like building new cells and facilitating chemical reactions. We need only small amounts of *micronutrients*—vitamins and minerals—for regulating body functions. People who fail to consume adequate amounts of an essential nutrient are likely to develop a nutritional deficiency disease, such as kwashiorkor from inadequate protein or scurvy from lack of vitamin C. Nutritional deficiency diseases are seldom seen in developed countries because most people consume an adequate diet.

Water—The Unappreciated Nutrient

You can live without the other nutrients for weeks, but you can survive only a few days without water. We need water to digest, absorb, and transport nutrients. Water helps regulate body temperature, carries waste products out of the body, and lubricates our moving parts.[1,2]

The right *fluid balance*—the right amount of fluid inside and outside each cell—is maintained through the action of substances called **electrolytes**, minerals that carry electrical charges and conduct nerve impulses. Electrolytes include sodium, potassium, and chloride. Water and a balanced diet replace electrolytes lost daily through sweat.[3]

Many people assume bottled water is purer and safer than tap water, but for the most part the water supply in the United States is well regulated and very safe. The Environmental Protection Agency (EPA) sets standards for water quality and inspects water supplies for bacteria and toxic chemicals. (Some bottled water is drawn from municipal water supplies, including Coca-Cola's Dasani and Pepsi's Aquafina, despite ads and labels showing pristine springs and snowy mountain peaks.) You can check the quality of your community's water supply at the National Drinking Water Database (www.ewg.org/tap-water/whats-in-yourwater.php).

In contrast, the FDA regulates bottled water only if it is shipped across state lines. About 70 percent is bottled and sold within the same state, so it is exempt from FDA inspection.

Federal regulations do not require bottled water companies to list how their water was purified, the results of any contaminant tests, or any other safety information. Bottled water has been found to contain contaminants, and health experts warn that it lacks fluoride, which is added to most water supplies and prevents tooth decay.[4] Another disadvantage is that most U.S. consumers discard plastic water bottles and do not recycle them.

What about water that's been enhanced with vitamins, minerals, and other nutrients? Although such products offer a colorful and flavorful alternative to plain water, they add little nutritional value to the typical U.S. diet because the average U.S. adult already consumes 100 percent of the DRI for most vitamins. Enhanced water does pack a wallop when it comes to added sugars, however. A 20-ounce bottle of Vitaminwater, for example, has 31 to 32 grams of sugar (two heaping tablespoons) and 120 calories, about the same as a soft drink.

Adults generally need 1 to 1.5 milliliters of water for each calorie spent in the day. If you expend 2,000 calories a day, you require 2 to 3 liters—8 to 12 cups—of fluids.[5] Heavy sweating also increases your need for fluids. You obtain fluids not only from the water you drink, but also from the water in foods, particularly fruits such as oranges and apples. Caffeinated beverages and alcohol are not good sources of daily fluid intake because of their dehydrating effects, although some recent research suggests that the water in such beverages may offset these effects to some extent.[5]

The Beverage Guidance Panel provides beverage recommendations based on their health benefits. Beverages are ranked in tiers ranging from 1 (best) to 6 (worst). Not

■ Water is an essential nutrient. In most communities in the United States, the quality and safety of tap water are equal or superior to the quality and safety of bottled water. *(Ron Chapple/ Thinkstock Images/Jupiter Images)*

Tier 6. Calorie-rich beverages without nutrients
(up to one 8-oz serving, and less if trying to lose weight) such as carbonated and non-carbonated sodas, lemonade, and any other "ade"drinks. Flavored coffees and teas, smoothies, and energy drinks also fall into tier 6. The Beverage Council gives its "least recommended" rating to beverages sweetened with high-fructose corn syrup and other high-calorie sweeteners that contain little nutrients. The primary concerns with tier 6 drinks are weight gain and increased risk for type 2 diabetes.

Tier 5. 100 percent fruit and vegetable juices, whole milk, sports drinks, alcohol beverages, vitamin-enhanced waters
(up to one 8-oz serving). Each of these drinks has pluses and minuses for nutrition, depending on its sodium, chloride, potassium, calorie, and sugar content.

Tier 4. Diet beverages with sugar substitutes
(up to two 8-oz servings). Diet drinks contain artificial sweeteners that are discussed later in this section. Diet beverages should be consumed only as an occasional drink and not as a regular drink.

Tier 3. Nonfat or low-fat milk, and fortified soy beverages
(up to two 8-oz servings). Skim milk or low-fat milk at 1 or 1/12 percent are the preferred choice since they contain less saturated fat than whole milk. Adults should limit limit milk to one or two glasses per day. Recommendations for growing children are less clear, but health scientists believe two glasses per day are sufficient to meet calcium needs.

Tier 2. Unsweetened coffee and tea—iced or hot
(up to four 8-oz servings of tea or four 8-oz servings of coffee). Whipped cream and flavorings used in coffee or tea can turn it into a tier 6 beverage.

Tier 1. Water--The Institute of Medicine recommends 125 ounces (about 15 cups) per day for men and 91 ounces for women (about 11 cups). Fluids from other tier levels can be used to meet this recommendation.

Tier 6.
Calorie-rich beverages without nutrients

Tier 5.
100 percent fruit and vegetable juices, whole milk, sports drinks, alcohol beverages, vitamin-enhanced waters

Tier 4.
Diet beverages with sugar substitutes

Tier 3.
Nonfat or low-fat milk, and fortified soy beverages

Tier 2.
Unsweetened coffee and tea

Tier 1.
Water

Source: U.S. Beverage Guidance Panel. (2017). Beverage panel recommendations and analysis. Global Beverage Guidelines. Retrieved from: http://www.epc.unc.edu/project/beverage/us-beverage-panel/

surprisingly, water is in tier 1 and soda fits in tier 6. Here are the beverage ratings.[6,7]

Tier 1. Water: The Institute of Medicine recommends 125 ounces (about 15 cups) per day for men and 91 ounces for women (about 11 cups). Fluids from other tier levels can be used to meet this recommendation.[6]

Tier 2. Unsweetened coffee and tea: iced or hot (up to four 8-oz servings of tea, or four 8-oz servings of coffee). Whipped cream and flavorings used in coffee or tea can turn it into a tier 6 beverage.

Tier 3. Nonfat or low-fat milk, and fortified soy beverages: up to two 8-oz servings. Skim milk or low-fat milk at 1 or 2 percent are the preferred choice since they contain less saturated fat than whole milk. Adults should limit milk to one or two glasses per day. Recommendations for growing children are less clear, but health scientists believe two glasses per day are sufficient to meet calcium needs.

Tier 4. Diet beverages with sugar substitutes: up to two 8-oz servings. Diet drinks contain artificial sweeteners that are discussed later in this section. Diet beverages should be consumed only as an occasional drink, not as a regular drink.

Tier 5. 100 percent fruit and vegetable juices, whole milk, sports drinks, alcohol beverages, vitamin-enhanced waters: up to one 8-oz serving. Each of these drinks has pluses and minuses for nutrition, depending on its sodium, chloride, potassium, calorie, and sugar content.

Tier 6. Calorie-rich beverages without nutrients: up to one 8-oz serving, and less if trying to lose weight, such as carbonated and noncarbonated soda, lemonade, and any other "ade" drinks. Flavored coffees and teas, smoothies, and energy drinks also fall into tier 6. The Beverage Council gives its "least recommended" rating to beverages sweetened with high-fructose corn syrup and other high-calorie sweeteners that contain little nutrients. The primary concerns with tier 6 drinks are weight gain and increased risk for type 2 diabetes.

The importance of water to health is well established. Most people, however, are not aware of how the temperature of water affects the body. Room-temperature water, between 50 and 72 degrees Fahrenheit, is more effective at hydrating the body than cold water. Cold water causes the blood vessels around the stomach to constrict, which decreases absorption. Room-temperature water helps relax the stomach, which increases absorption. As cold water is consumed, it tends to solidify fat from food you have eaten and makes it more difficult to digest food and eliminate unwanted fats. Room-temperature water does not solidify fat, which keeps it more liquid and easier to digest and can also reduce the risk of clogged arteries. If your body is feverish, cold water is more beneficial as long as it does not cause shivers or a chilled feeling. Drinking room-temperature water is more effective for such ailments as headaches, pain, injuries, constipation, and cramps. There is no difference between cold and room-temperature water in weight loss effectiveness, however. The bottom line is to drink the daily recommendation for water and to remember that room-temperature water is often preferred for health benefits.[8]

An interesting question is whether drinking water improves cognitive function. The brain is 75 percent water, and dehydration decreases alertness, increases fatigue and sleepiness, and causes confusion. So, staying properly hydrated is important for maintaining optimal cognitive function. However, water is absorbed from the mouth and into the blood within five minutes and absorption peaks (reaches the highest absorption level rate) within 20 minutes.[9]

Carbohydrates—Your Body's Fuel

Carbohydrates are the body's main source of energy.[5] They fuel most of the body's cells during daily activities; they are used by muscle cells during high-intensity exercise; and they are the only source of energy for brain cells, red blood cells, and some other types of cells. Athletes in particular need to consume a high-carbohydrate diet to fuel their high-energy activities.

Carbohydrates are the foods we think of as sugars and starches. They come almost exclusively from plants (the exception is lactose, the sugar in milk). Most of the carbohydrates and other nutrients we need come from grains, seeds, fruits, and vegetables. Carbohydrates are divided into simple carbohydrates and complex carbohydrates.[3]

Simple Carbohydrates   **Simple carbohydrates** are easily digestible carbohydrates composed of one or two units of sugar. Six simple carbohydrates (sugars) are important in nutrition: glucose, fructose, galactose, lactose, maltose, and sucrose. Sugars are absorbed into the bloodstream and travel to body cells, where they can be used for energy. Glucose is the main source of energy for the brain and nervous system. Glucose also travels to the liver and muscles, where it can be stored as **glycogen** (a complex carbohydrate) for future energy needs.

simple carbohydrates
Easily digestible carbohydrates composed of one or two units of sugar.

glycogen
The complex carbohydrate form in which glucose is stored in the liver and muscles.

Action Skill Builder
Are Smoothies Healthy?

Smoothies have become very popular. Proponents claim they contain valuable nutrients (e.g., vitamins B12, C, and D), use whole food sources for macronutrients, and are tasty, convenient, and healthy. Opponents claim they have high levels of sugar and unhealthy fats, cause tooth enamel erosion, lead to weight gain, and are associated with fatty liver. For example, a 20-ounce Hulk Strawberry smoothie at Smoothie King contains 910 calories, 27 grams of fat (13 saturated), and 127 grams of sugar.[11] Remember that the recommended grams of sugar is 25 g for women and 36 g for men. If you are ordering a smoothie, the Centers for Disease Control and Prevention (CDC) recommends asking for the child-size portion and having it prepared without sugar.

If you make your own smoothies, consider these tips:

☐ Use in-season and organic fruits and vegetables.

☐ Use herb powders as the base instead of water, milk, or juice to create a creamy and healthy texture.

☐ Juice your own fruits and vegetables as a base.

☐ Enhance flavor by using cinnamon, ginger, nutmeg, or cayenne pepper.

☐ Use healthy fats (e.g., coconut, flax, hemp oil, avocado).

☐ Use super foods (e.g., Maco, cacao, goji berries, bee pollen, acai).

Source: Healthy Smoothies Headquarters. (2019). 20 tips for making the healthiest smoothies ever. Retrieved from https://www. com/20-tips-for-making-the-healthiest smoothies-ever/

The types of sugar are measured on a sweetness scale. The higher the score, the sweeter the sugar. Sucrose (most commonly in the form of table sugar) is used as the benchmark, with a score of 1.0. Sugars with scores of 1.0 or higher are more likely to contribute to obesity and inflammatory diseases, diabetes, and high blood pressure. See the box "Action Skill Builder: Are Smoothies Healthy?" The scores for other sugars are:

- Fructose (found in fruits and vegetables): 1.4
- Glucose: 0.7
- High-fructose corn syrup: 1.0
- Lactose (found in milk): 0.2
- Maltose (found in beer, cereal, malt, pasta, and potatoes): 0.3
- Stevia (a naturally occurring, no-calorie sugar substitute): 300[10]

High-fructose corn syrup (HFCS) is a common sugar used in soft drinks and in hundreds of foods, ranging from candy bars to breads to lunch meats, since it is cheap and has a high sweetness score. U.S. adults consume 22.5 teaspoons of sugar per day, most of it from highly sweetened beverages.[10] Fatty liver disease is linked to fructose consumption. About 20 percent of U.S. adults have fatty liver disease; 10 to 20 percent of them have liver inflammation and liver cell damage that can lead to cirrhosis or liver failure. Your liver makes fat in response to fructose. If the liver is overwhelmed, less fat is shipped to the blood and more fat is stored in the liver. When the liver retains too much fat, it can become insulin resistant, which causes even more fat to be stored in the liver.[9]

When you eat food containing large amounts of simple carbohydrates, sugar enters your bloodstream quickly, giving you a burst of energy or a "sugar high." Sugar is also absorbed into your cells quickly, leaving you feeling depleted and craving more sugar. Consumption of **added sugars** has been linked to the epidemic of overweight and obesity in the United States and to the parallel increase in the incidence of diabetes, a disorder in which body cells cannot use the sugar circulating in the blood.[1,2,3]

The USDA's 2015–2020 *Dietary Guidelines* recommends that less than 10 percent of calories come from added sugars. Currently, 70 percent of the U.S. population exceeds that goal, and added sugars account for an average of 270 calories a day in the U.S. diet.[12] According to the American Heart Association, women should consume no more than 100 calories per day of sugar (about 6 teaspoons) and men no more than 150 calories per day (9 teaspoons).

To cut back on sugar, check food labels for ingredients to avoid, like sugar, corn syrup, fructose, dextrose, molasses, and evaporated cane juice. You may be surprised at the relatively high sugar content of many foods. For example, two servings of spaghetti sauce can contain almost 5.5 teaspoons of sugars.[2,12,13]

Because of the negative health effects of sugar, particularly weight gain and tooth decay, sugar substitutes have been developed as alternative low-calorie sweeteners. Some are naturally occurring (stevia, sorbitol, xylitol), but most are synthetic and are usually referred to as artificial sweeteners (saccharin, aspartame, sucralose). Many artificial sweeteners are intensely sweet—hundreds of times sweeter than sugar—so very small amounts can be added to foods or beverages without adding calories. Aspartame (Nutrasweet, Equal) is 180 times sweeter than sugar, and sucralose (Splenda) is 600 times sweeter than sugar.[10]

Concerns have been raised about the safety of artificial sweeteners, but the FDA has determined that they are safe if used in recommended amounts. Still under investigation is the possibility that alternative sweeteners actually result in weight gain due to their effect on appetite and insulin response, a factor in feelings of hunger and fullness. The Center for Science in the Public Interest recommends avoiding the alternative sweeteners acesulfame, aspartame, and saccharin (Sweet'n Low).

Sugar alcohols (such as xylitol) are nutritive sweeteners that contain fewer calories than sugar. They are especially useful for people with diabetes who want to enjoy the flavor of sweeteners but limit sugars in their diet. Sugar alcohols are safe when used in moderation. The alternative sweeteners advantame, neotame, and stevia leaf extract were rated safe because they are so sweet they can be used in minuscule amounts.[1,2,14]

Complex Carbohydrates The type of carbohydrates called **complex carbohydrates** is composed of multiple sugar units and includes starches and dietary fiber. **Starches** occur in grains, vegetables, and some fruits. Most starchy foods also contain ample portions of vitamins, minerals, proteins, and water. Starches must be broken down into single sugars in the digestive system before they can be absorbed into the bloodstream to be used for energy or stored for future use.

Whole grains are often refined to make them easier to digest and more appealing to the consumer, but the refining process removes many of the vitamins, minerals, and other nutritious components. **Refined carbohydrates** include white rice; white bread, pasta, pastries, and other products made from white flour; and sweet desserts. About 90 percent of the grains U.S. consumers eat are refined.[1,2] Like sugar, refined carbohydrates can enter the bloodstream quickly and just as quickly leave you feeling hungry again. **Whole grains** (such as whole wheat, brown rice, oatmeal, and corn) are preferred because they provide more nutrients, slow the digestive process, and make you feel full longer. The consumption of whole grains lowers the risk of diabetes, obesity, heart disease, and some forms of cancer.[2,13,14]

The RDA for carbohydrates is 130 g for males and females aged 1 to 70 years. The AMDR for carbohydrates is 45 to 65 percent of daily energy intake, which amounts to 225 to 325 g in a 2,000-calorie diet (even though only about 130 g per day is enough to meet the body's needs). In the typical U.S. diet, carbohydrates contribute about half of all calories, and most are in the form of simple sugars or highly refined grains. Instead, carbohydrates should come from a diverse spectrum of whole grains and other starches, vegetables, and fruits.[15]

Fiber **Dietary fiber**, a complex carbohydrate found in plants, cannot be broken down in the digestive tract. A diet rich in dietary fiber makes stools soft and bulky. They pass through

added sugars
Sugars that are added to foods when they are processed; they are listed as ingredients on food packages.

complex carbohydrates
Carbohydrates that are composed of multiple sugar units and that must be broken down further before they can be used by the body.

starches
Complex carbohydrates found in many plant foods.

refined carbohydrates
Foods made from plant sources, such as grain or sugar cane, whose fiber has been processed away and that have been ground into small particles.

whole grains
Grains, such as wheat, rice, and corn, whose outer coating is intact.

dietary fiber
A complex carbohydrate found in plants that cannot be broken down in the digestive tract.

■ The smaller the particles and the lighter in color, the more the grain has been refined. *(Elena Schweitzer/Shutterstock)*

functional fiber
Natural or synthetic fiber that has been added to food.

total fiber
The combined amount of dietary fiber and functional fiber in a food.

protein
An essential nutrient made up of amino acids; needed to build and maintain muscles, bones, and other body tissues.

essential amino acids
Amino acids that the body cannot produce on its own.

complete proteins
Proteins composed of ample amounts of all the essential amino acids.

incomplete proteins
Proteins that contain small amounts of essential amino acids or some, but not all, of the essential amino acids.

the intestines rapidly and are expelled easily, helping to prevent hemorrhoids and constipation.[1,2,15] Some foods contain **functional fiber**, natural or synthetic fiber that has been added to increase the healthful effects of the food. **Total fiber** refers to the combined amount of dietary fiber and functional fiber in a food.

Dietary fiber that dissolves in water, referred to as *soluble fiber*, is known to lower blood cholesterol levels and can slow the process of digestion so that blood sugar levels remain more even. Dietary fiber that does not dissolve in water, called *insoluble fiber*, passes through the digestive tract essentially unchanged. Because it absorbs water, insoluble fiber helps you feel full after eating and stimulates your intestinal wall to contract and relax, serving as a natural laxative.[16]

The RDAs for fiber are 25 g for women aged 19 to 50 and 38 g for men aged 14 to 50 (or 14 g of fiber for every 1,000 calories consumed). For people over 50, the RDAs are 21 g for women and 30 g for men.[1,2] The typical U.S. diet provides only about 14 or 15 g of fiber a day. If you want to increase the fiber in your diet, it is important to do so gradually. A sudden increase in daily fiber may cause bloating, gas, abdominal cramping, or even a bowel obstruction, particularly if you fail to drink enough liquids to easily carry the fiber through the body.[3]

Fiber is best obtained through diet. Pills and other fiber supplements do not contain the nutrients found in high-fiber foods.[3] Excessive amounts of fiber (generally 60 g or more per day) can decrease the absorption of important vitamins and minerals such as calcium, zinc, magnesium, and iron.[17] Fruits, vegetables, dried beans, peas and other legumes, cereals, grains, nuts, and seeds are the best sources of dietary fiber.

Fewer than 3 percent of U.S. adults meet the daily recommendation for fiber.[9] If you do not meet the recommendation for fiber, consider that adding only 7 ounces of fiber (one serving of baked beans) to your daily diet decreases your risk of stroke by 7 percent. Insufficient fiber intake can stiffen or harden brain arteries. Some health experts recommend 25 g of soluble fiber and 47 g of insoluble fiber each day to minimize the risk of stroke.[9] This is well above the USDA recommendation for fiber.

Protein—Nutritional Muscle

Your body uses **protein** to build and maintain muscles, bones, and other body tissues. Proteins also form enzymes that in turn facilitate chemical reactions. Proteins are constructed from 20 different amino acids. There are nine amino acids that your body cannot produce on its own. These are called **essential amino acids**, and they must be supplied by foods. Those that can be produced by your body are called nonessential amino acids.

Food sources of protein include both animals and plants. Animal proteins (meat, fish, poultry, milk, cheese, and eggs) are usually a good source of **complete proteins**, meaning they contain ample amounts of all the essential amino acids. Vegetable proteins (grains, legumes, nuts, seeds, and vegetables) provide **incomplete proteins**, meaning they contain small amounts of essential amino acids or some, but not all, of the essential amino acids. If you do not consume sufficient amounts of the essential amino acids, body organ functions may be compromised.

People who eat little or no animal protein may not be getting all the essential amino acids they need. One remedy is to eat plant foods with different amounts of incomplete proteins. For example, beans are low in the essential amino acid methionine but high in lysine, and rice is high in methionine and low in lysine. In combination, beans and rice form *complementary proteins*. Eating the two over the course of a day provides all the essential amino acids.[3] The matching of such foods is called *mutual supplementation*.

The AMDR for protein is 10 to 35 percent of daily calories consumed.[5] The need for protein is based on body weight: the larger your body, the more protein you need to consume. A healthy adult typically needs 0.8 g of protein for every kilogram (2.2 pounds) of body weight, or about 0.36 g for every pound.[5] At the upper end of the AMDR range, the percentages provide a more than ample amount of protein in the diet. Studies do not support a relationship between protein and cancer. However, they do show that large amounts of animal protein in the diet increases the risk of permanent loss of kidney function. People with kidney disease, cardiovascular disease, diabetes, and other chronic disease are advised to eat less protein.[18]

Fats—A Necessary Nutrient

Fats are a concentrated energy source and the principal form of stored energy in the body. The fats in food provide essential fatty acids, play a role in the production of other fatty acids and vitamin D, and provide the major material for cell membranes and the myelin sheaths that surround nerve fibers. They assist in the absorption of the fat-soluble vitamins (A, D, E, and K) and affect the texture, taste, and smell of foods. Fats provide an emergency reserve when we are sick or our food intake is diminished.

Types of Fat Fats, or lipids, are composed of fatty acids. Nutritionists divide these acids into three groups—saturated, monounsaturated, and polyunsaturated—on the basis of their chemical composition. **Saturated fats** remain stable (solid) at room temperature; **monounsaturated fats** are liquid at room temperature but solidify somewhat when refrigerated; **polyunsaturated fats** are liquid both at room temperature and in the refrigerator. Liquid fats are commonly referred to as oils.

Saturated fatty acids are found in animal sources, such as beef, pork, poultry, and whole-milk dairy products. They are also found in certain tropical oils and nuts, including coconut and palm oil and macadamia nuts. The *2015–2020 Dietary Guidelines* recommend that less than 10 percent of daily calories should come from saturated fats; 70 percent of U.S. adults consume more than this. Food sources of saturated fat include butter, cream, cheese, and fatty beef.[12] Monounsaturated and polyunsaturated fatty acids are found primarily in plant sources. Olive, safflower, peanut, and canola oils, as well as avocados and many nuts, contain mostly monounsaturated fat. Corn and soybean oils contain mostly polyunsaturated fat, as do many kinds of fish, including salmon, trout, and anchovies.

Cholesterol Saturated fats pose a risk to health because they tend to raise blood levels of **cholesterol**, a waxy substance that can clog arteries, leading to cardiovascular disease. More specifically, saturated fats raise blood levels of low-density lipoproteins (LDLs), known as "bad cholesterol," and triglycerides, another kind of blood fat. Unsaturated fats, in contrast, tend to lower blood levels of LDLs, and some unsaturated fats (monounsaturated fats) may also raise levels of high-density lipoproteins (HDLs), known as "good cholesterol."[19,20,21]

Cholesterol is needed for several important body functions, but too much of it circulating in the bloodstream can be a problem. The body produces it in the liver and also obtains it from animal food sources, such as meat, cheese, eggs, and milk. It is recommended that no more than 300 milligrams of dietary cholesterol be consumed per day. The *2015–2020 Dietary Guidelines* removed cholesterol as a "nutrient of concern for over consumption" (although it still recommends consuming as little dietary cholesterol as possible), but the Physicians Committee for Responsible Medicine and the American College of Cardiology strongly oppose this change. The effects of cholesterol on cardiovascular health are discussed in detail in Chapter 14.

A much debated question is whether eggs are bad for your heart because of their cholesterol content. One large egg has 185 mg of cholesterol in its yolk. Studies suggest that each additional one-half egg eaten per day increases risk of cardiovascular disease by 6 percent and premature death by 8 percent. It is important to know that these are observational and not cause-and-effect studies. Still, the circumstantial evidence associated increased egg consumption with greater risk for cardiovascular disease, coronary artery disease, stroke, and premature death. Also note that people are generally affected by cholesterol in different ways, depending on both genetic and metabolic factors. Although eggs provide important amino acids and minerals, the level of cholesterol in egg yolk is such that the general health recommendation is to limit egg consumption, or to eat only egg whites.[22]

Trans Fats Another kind of fatty acid, **trans fatty acid**, is produced through **hydrogenation**, a process whereby liquid vegetable oils are turned into more solid fats. Food manufacturers use hydrogenation to prolong a food's shelf life and change its texture. Peanut butter is frequently hydrogenated, as is margarine.

Trans fatty acids (or trans fats) are believed to pose a risk to cardiovascular health similar to or even greater than that of saturated fats because they tend to raise LDLs and lower HDLs. Foods high in trans fatty acids include baked and snack foods such as crackers, cookies, chips, cakes, pies, and doughnuts, as well as deep-fried fast foods such as french fries.[20] In packaged foods, the phrase "partially hydrogenated vegetable oil" in the list of ingredients indicates the presence of trans fats. In 2006, the FDA began requiring that trans fat be listed on nutrition labels if a food contains more than 0.5 g, and many food manufacturers and restaurants have stopped using trans fats in their products. The FDA banned trans fats from the U.S. food supply in 2018.[24]

Omega-3 and Omega-6 Fatty Acids Unlike trans fats, two kinds of polyunsaturated fatty acids—omega-3 and omega-6 fatty acids—provide health benefits. **Omega-3 fatty acids**, which contain the essential nutrient alpha-linolenic acid, help slow the clotting of blood, decrease triglyceride levels, improve arterial health,

fats
Also known as lipids, fats are an essential nutrient composed of fatty acids and used for energy and other body functions.

saturated fats
Lipids that are the predominant fat in animal products and other fats that remain solid at room temperature.

monounsaturated fats
Lipids that are liquid at room temperature and semisolid or solid when refrigerated.

polyunsaturated fats
Lipids that are liquid at room temperature and in the refrigerator.

cholesterol
A waxy, fatlike substance that is essential in small amounts for certain body functions.

trans fatty acids
Lipids that have been chemically modified through the process of hydrogenation so that they remain solid at room temperature.

hydrogenation
The process whereby liquid vegetable oils are turned into more solid fats.

omega-3 fatty acids
Polyunsaturated fatty acids that contain the essential nutrient alpha-linolenic acid and that have beneficial effects on cardiovascular health.

You can reduce your risk of chronic diseases by building your diet around colorful meals that include whole grains, legumes, two or more vegetables, and small quantities of chicken or fish. (*Nelea33/Shutterstock*)

omega-6 fatty acids
Polyunsaturated fatty acids that contain linoleic acid and that have beneficial health effects.

minerals
Naturally occurring inorganic micronutrients, such as magnesium, calcium, and iron, that contribute to proper functioning of the body.

the EPA fish advisory site at https://www.epa.gov/choose-fish-and-shellfish-wisely/fish-and-shellfish-advisories-and-safe-eating-guidelines.)

Dietary Recommendations for Fat How much of your daily caloric intake should come from fat? The AMDR is 20 to 35 percent.[3] The American Heart Association recommends that less than one-third of that (7 to 10 percent) come from saturated fats and trans fats; in a 2,000-calorie diet, that's about 22 g. The *2015–2020 Dietary Guidelines* recommend less than 10 percent of calories per day from saturated fat.[12] Most adults need only 15 percent of their daily calorie intake in the form of fat, whereas young children should get 30 to 40 percent of their calories from fat to ensure proper growth and brain development, according to the American Academy of Pediatrics. A tablespoon of vegetable oil per day is recommended for both adults and children.[1,2]

These recommendations are designed to help improve cardiovascular health and prevent heart disease. On average, fat intake in the United States is about 34 percent of daily calorie intake.[1,2] You can limit your intake of saturated fat by selecting vegetable oils instead of animal fats, reducing the amount of fat you use in cooking, removing all visible fat from meat, and choosing lean cuts of meat over fatty ones and poultry or fish over beef. Limit your consumption of fast-food burgers and fries because these foods are loaded with saturated fats.

and lower blood pressure. They may also help protect against autoimmune diseases such as rheumatoid arthritis.[20,21] **Omega-6 fatty acids,** which contain the essential nutrient linoleic acid, are also important to health, but nutritionists believe that people in the United States consume too much omega-6 in proportion to omega-3.[1,2] They recommend increasing consumption of omega-3 sources—fatty fish such as salmon, trout, and anchovies; vegetable oils such as soybean, walnut, and flaxseed; and dark green leafy vegetables—and decreasing consumption of omega-6 sources, mainly corn and cottonseed oils.

Although the USDA recommends two servings of fish per week, there are concerns about contamination with mercury and other industrial pollutants, which can accumulate in the tissue of certain types of fish. Mercury may cause fetal brain damage, and high levels of mercury may damage the adult heart. Polychlorinated biphenyls (PCBs) and dioxin may be associated with cancer. The FDA and the EPA regularly update joint recommendations for pregnant women, women planning to become pregnant, nursing mothers, and young children, stating they should consume no more than 12 ounces of fish and shellfish per week, they should avoid certain types of fish (king mackerel, golden bass, shark, and swordfish), and they should vary the kinds of fish they eat. (For more information, see

Minerals—A Need for Balance

Minerals are naturally occurring inorganic substances that are needed by the body in relatively small amounts. Minerals are important in building strong bones and teeth, helping vitamins and enzymes carry out many metabolic processes, and maintaining proper functioning of most body systems.

Our bodies need 20 essential minerals. We need more than 100 milligrams (mg) daily of each of the six *macrominerals*—calcium, chloride, magnesium, phosphorus, potassium, and sodium. We need less than 100 mg daily of each of the *microminerals,* or *trace minerals*—chromium, cobalt, copper, fluorine, iodine, iron, manganese, molybdenum, nickel, selenium, silicon, tin, vanadium, and zinc. Other minerals are present in foods and the body, but no requirement has been found for them.[1,2] Table 5.1 provides an overview of food sources and DRIs for the most important vitamins and minerals.

Table 5.1   Key Vitamins and Minerals for Adults Aged 19 to 50

Vitamins/ Minerals	Food Sources	Adult Daily DRI	
		Men	Women
Vitamin A	Liver, dairy products, fish, dark green vegetables, yellow and orange fruits and vegetables	900 µg	700 µg
Vitamin C	Citrus fruits, strawberries, broccoli, tomatoes, green leafy vegetables, bell peppers	90 mg	75 mg
Vitamin D	Vitamin-fortified milk and cereals; fish, eggs	15 µg	15 µg
Vitamin E	Plant oils, seeds, avocados, green leafy vegetables	15 mg	15 mg
Vitamin K	Dark green leafy vegetables, broccoli, cheese	120 µg	90 µg
Vitamin B$_1$ (thiamine)	Enriched and whole-grain cereals	1.2 mg	1.1 mg
Vitamin B$_2$ (riboflavin)	Milk, mushrooms, spinach, liver, fortified cereals	1.3 mg	1.1 mg
Vitamin B$_6$	Vitamin-fortified cereals; meat, poultry, fish, bananas, potatoes, nuts	1.3 mg	1.3 mg
Vitamin B$_{12}$	Vitamin-fortified cereals; meat, poultry, fish, dairy products	2.4 µg	2.4 µg
Niacin	Meat, fish, poultry, peanuts, beans, enriched and whole-grain cereals	16 mg	14 mg
Folate	Dark green leafy vegetables, legumes, oranges, bananas, fortified cereals	400 µg	400 µg
Calcium	Dairy products, canned fish, dark green leafy vegetables	1,000 mg	1,000 mg
Iron	Meat, poultry, legumes, dark green leafy vegetables	8 mg	18 mg
Magnesium	Wheat bran, green leafy vegetables, nuts, legumes, fish	420 mg	320 mg
Potassium	Spinach, squash, bananas, milk, potatoes, oranges, legumes, tomatoes, green leafy vegetables	4,700 mg	4,700 mg
Sodium	Table salt, soy sauce, processed foods	1,500 mg	1,500 mg
Zinc	Vitamin-fortified cereals, meat, poultry, dairy products, legumes, nuts, seeds	11 mg	8 mg

Source: Food and Nutrition Board, Institute of Medicine, National Academy of Sciences. (2011, Updated). *Dietary reference intakes (DRIs): Estimated average requirements and recommended intakes (including the 2011 updated recommendations for calcium and vitamin D).* Retrieved from nationalacademies.org/hmd/~/media/Files/Report%20Files/2019/DRI-Tables-2019/2_RDAAIVVE.pdf?la=en

A varied and balanced diet provides all the essential minerals your body needs, so mineral supplements are not recommended for most people. (Exceptions are listed in the next section.) These insoluble elements can build up in the body and become toxic if consumed in excessive amounts.

Vitamins—Small but Potent Nutrients

Like minerals, **vitamins** occur in nature and are needed in the body in only small amounts. Unlike minerals, vitamins are organic; that is, they have a biological origin. They are catalysts, aiding chemical reactions that release energy from carbohydrates, proteins, and fats in foods you have eaten. By doing this, they help maintain your immune system, nervous system, and bones.

Our bodies need at least 11 specific vitamins: A, C, D, E, K, and the B-complex vitamins—thiamine (B1), riboflavin (B2), niacin, B6, folic acid, and B12. Biotin and pantothenic acid are part of the vitamin B complex and are also considered important for health. Choline, another B vitamin, is not regarded as essential.

Four of the vitamins—A, D, E, and K—are fat soluble (they dissolve in fat), and the rest are water soluble (they dissolve in water). The fat-soluble vitamins can be stored in the liver or body fat, and if you consume larger amounts than you need, you can reach toxic levels over time. Excess water-soluble vitamins are excreted in the urine and must be consumed more often than fat-soluble vitamins. Most water-soluble vitamins do not cause toxicity, but vitamins B6 and C can build to toxic levels if taken in excess. Toxicity usually occurs only when these substances are taken as supplements.

Nearly half the people in the United States take vitamin and mineral supplements. The 2015 *Dietary*

vitamins
Naturally occurring organic micronutrients that aid chemical reactions in the body and help maintain healthy body systems.

Guidelines for Americans recommends that people get all their nutrients from food, although there are some population groups for whom vitamin and mineral supplements may be needed, including

- People with nutrient deficiencies

- People with low energy intake (less than 1,200 calories per day)

- Individuals who eat only foods from plant sources

- Women who bleed excessively during menstruation

- Individuals whose calcium intake is too small to preserve strength

- People in certain life stages (infants, older adults, women of childbearing age, and pregnant women)

Taking supplements to enhance your energy level or athletic performance or to make up for perceived inadequacies in your diet is not generally recommended.[1,2] Many foods provide, in one serving, the same amounts of nutrients found in a vitamin supplement pill. However, there is some debate about multivitamins. Because many people in the United States have diets deficient in certain nutrients, some public health experts do advocate taking a daily multivitamin as a kind of nutritional insurance policy.[5] The dietary supplement industry promotes this practice as well, to sell more vitamin pills. There is little evidence that taking a daily multivitamin makes people healthier,[23] but it probably does no harm and may provide some benefits. If you decide to take a multivitamin, follow the guidelines shown in the box "Consumer Clipboard: What Your Multivitamin Should Contain" and refer to Table 5.1. For a concise summary of recommended daily intakes of all the categories of macronutrients and micronutrients, see Table 5.2.

phytochemicals
Substances that are naturally produced by plants to protect themselves and that provide health benefits in the human body.

free radicals
Unstable molecules that are produced when oxygen is metabolized and that damage cell structures and DNA.

antioxidants
Substances in foods that neutralize the effects of free radicals.

Other Substances in Food: Phytochemicals

One promising area of nutrition research is **phytochemicals**, substances that are naturally produced by plants. In the human body, phytochemicals may keep body cells healthy, slow tissue degeneration, prevent the formation of carcinogens, reduce cholesterol levels, protect the heart, maintain hormone balance, and keep bones strong.[25,26] A large European study found that people who ate eight or more servings of fruits and vegetables per day were 22 percent less likely to die from heart disease than those who ate three servings or less. Eight servings is about 23 ounces, which can sound like a lot until you realize that a large orange or apple weighs about 8 ounces.[27]

Table 5.2 Overview of Recommended Daily Intakes of Macronutrients and Micronutrients

Water	1–1.5 ml per calorie spent; 8–12 cups of fluid

Carbohydrates
  Added sugars
 	
  Fiber
	AMDR: 45–65% of calories consumed
	No more than 10–25% of calories consumed
	14 g for every 1,000 calories consumed; 21–25 g for women, 30–38 g for men

Protein	AMDR: 10–35% of calories consumed; 0.36 g per pound of body weight

Fat
  Saturated fat
  Trans fat
	AMDR: 20–35% of calories consumed
	Less than 10% of calories consumed
	As little as possible

Minerals
  6 macrominerals
  14 trace minerals
	
	More than 100 mg
	Less than 100 mg

Vitamins 11 essential vitamins	 Varies

Source: Institute of Medicine of the National Academies. (2002, Sept.). *Macronutrients table, dietary reference intakes for energy, carbohydrate, fiber, fat, fatty acids, cholesterol, protein, and amino acids, by the food and nutrition board.* Retrieved from http://iom. nationalacademies.org/Reports/2002/Dietary-Reference-Intakes-for-Energy-Carbohydrate-Fiber-Fat-Fatty-Acids-Cholesterol-Protein-and-Amino-Acids.aspx.

Antioxidants Every time you take a breath, you inhale a potentially toxic chemical that could damage your cell DNA: oxygen. If you breathed 100 percent oxygen over a period of days, you would go blind and suffer irreparable damage to your lungs. Oxygen is essential for cell metabolism, however. Oxygen toxicity can occur if the process of oxygen metabolism in the body (metabolic processes used by cells to produce energy as food molecules react with oxygen) produces unstable molecules, called **free radicals**, which can damage cell structures and DNA. The production of free radicals can also be increased by exposure to certain environmental elements, such as cigarette smoke and sunlight, and even by stress. Free radicals are believed to be a contributing factor in aging, cancer, heart disease, macular degeneration, and other degenerative diseases, although some of the research supporting these claims may be questionable.[1,2]

Antioxidants are phytochemicals in foods that neutralize the effects of free radicals. Antioxidants are found primarily in fruits and vegetables, especially brightly colored ones (yellow, orange, and dark green), and in green tea. Vitamins E

Consumer Clipboard
What Your Multivitamin Should Contain: Adults Aged 19 to 50

Multivitamin labels tell you the amount per dose, and the current Daily Value established by the FDA. Daily Values can vary by age and sex. The FDA recently updated the Daily Values. They were implemented on new labels on January 1, 2020. Small companies with less than $10 million in sales per year have until January 1, 2021, to comply with the food label mandate. When you choose a multivitamin, look for one that contains amounts similar to those shown here in the sample Supplement Facts label.

Refer to the Tolerable Upper Intake Level (UL) column to the right of the Supplement Facts label to make sure the product does not exceed the maximum daily amounts that you can take without risking toxicity.

Supplement manufacturers load their multivitamins with excessive levels of metals that may be linked to brain damage. Copper and iron are of particular concern. Excessive amounts can damage the brain, particularly for people at higher risk for dementia and Alzheimer's disease. Because meats and vegetables contain copper and iron, you can easily get as much as you need from your diet. Some vitamins have been associated with increased risk of kidney stones and cancer. Health scientists generally recommend avoiding excessive intake of calcium and vitamin A. There is essentially no evidence supporting vitamin C, vitamin B3, and vitamin E. Vitamin E has been associated with cancer and calcium with kidney stones. Folic acid if pregnant, and vitamin D3, vitamin B12, or zinc to prevent or shorten the duration of colds, are recommended.

Choose brands from nationally recognized pharmacies or supermarkets.
Don't be fooled by a brand name that suggests the ingredients are "natural"—vitamins from whole foods are no better than synthetic vitamins.

Check the price.
Multivitamins should cost no more than 10 cents per pill.

Look for a U.S. Pharmacopeia (USP) seal, which means the manufacturer has paid an independent lab to test the product and affirm that it contains what the label says it does and that it will disintegrate or dissolve for GI absorption.

Ignore health claims—the FDA doesn't recognize them. They usually have an asterisk referring to a disclaimer somewhere else on the label.

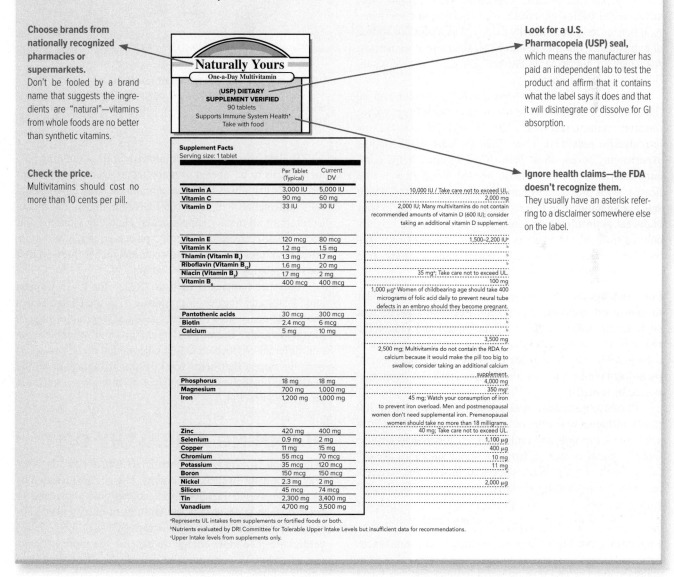

Naturally Yours
One-a-Day Multivitamin

(USP) DIETARY SUPPLEMENT VERIFIED
90 tablets
Supports Immune System Health*
Take with food

Supplement Facts
Serving size: 1 tablet

	Per Tablet (Typical)	Current DV	Notes
Vitamin A	3,000 IU	5,000 IU	10,000 IU / Take care not to exceed UL.
Vitamin C	90 mg	60 mg	2,000 mg
Vitamin D	33 IU	30 IU	2,000 IU; Many multivitamins do not contain recommended amounts of vitamin D (600 IU); consider taking an additional vitamin D supplement.
Vitamin E	120 mcg	80 mcg	1,500–2,200 IU[a]
Vitamin K	1.2 mg	1.5 mg	[b]
Thiamin (Vitamin B₁)	1.3 mg	1.7 mg	[b]
Riboflavin (Vitamin B₁₂)	1.6 mg	20 mg	[b]
Niacin (Vitamin B₃)	1.7 mg	2 mg	35 mg[a]; Take care not to exceed UL.
Vitamin B₆	400 mcg	400 mcg	100 mg
Pantothenic acids	30 mcg	300 mcg	1,000 μg[a] Women of childbearing age should take 400 micrograms of folic acid daily to prevent neural tube defects in an embryo should they become pregnant.
Biotin	2.4 mcg	6 mcg	[b]
Calcium	5 mg	10 mg	[b]
Phosphorus	18 mg	18 mg	3,500 mg
Magnesium	700 mg	1,000 mg	2,500 mg; Multivitamins do not contain the RDA for calcium because it would make the pill too big to swallow; consider taking an additional calcium supplement.
Iron	1,200 mg	1,000 mg	4,000 mg
			350 mg[c]
Zinc	420 mg	400 mg	45 mg; Watch your consumption of iron to prevent iron overload. Men and postmenopausal women don't need supplemental iron. Premenopausal women should take no more than 18 milligrams.
Selenium	0.9 mg	2 mg	40 mg; Take care not to exceed UL.
Copper	11 mg	15 mg	1,100 μg
Chromium	55 mcg	70 mcg	400 μg
Potassium	35 mcg	120 mcg	10 mg
Boron	150 mcg	150 mcg	11 mg
Nickel	2.3 mg	2 mg	[a]
Silicon	45 mcg	74 mcg	2,000 μg
Tin	2,300 mg	3,400 mg	
Vanadium	4,700 mg	3,500 mg	

[a]Represents UL intakes from supplements or fortified foods or both.
[b]Nutrients evaluated by DRI Committee for Tolerable Upper Intake Levels but insufficient data for recommendations.
[c]Upper Intake levels from supplements only.

Sources: Brodwin, E. (2019). Most vitamin pills are useless, but here are the ones you should take. Science alert. Retrieved from https://www.sciencealert.com/are-vitamin-pills-goof-or-bad-some-you-should-take-folicacid-zinc; Center for Science in the Public Interest. (2013, Nov.). Multi-dilemma: Should you take one. *Nutrition Action Healthletter:* 2–7; Silicon, N., & Vanadium. T. (2016, Nov.). How to read a multivitamin label. *Nutrition Health Letter,* 6–7.

kilocalorie
The amount of energy needed to raise the temperature of 1 kilogram of water by 1 degree centigrade; commonly shortened to *calorie*.

and C are antioxidants, as are some of the precursors to vitamins, such as beta carotene.

Fifty-two percent of U.S. adults take large doses of antioxidant supplements daily. The American Heart Association and the American Diabetes Association advise that antioxidants should not be taken, however, except to treat a vitamin deficiency.[5] Most nutritionists do not recommend supplements as a source of antioxidants because vitamin megadoses have the potential to cause fertility problems, reduce the benefits of exercise, and aggravate illnesses.[1,2] The best source of antioxidants is whole foods. The top antioxidant-containing foods and beverages are blackberries, walnuts, strawberries, artichokes, cranberries, brewed coffee, raspberries, pecans, blueberries, cloves, grape juice, unsweetened baking chocolate, sour cherries, and red wine. Açai berries have been heavily marketed as a superior source of antioxidants, but they are no better than any other berries. Also high in antioxidants are brussels sprouts, kale, cauliflower, and pomegranates.

Nitric oxide (NO) can prevent artery stiffening and inflammation by using artery linings to cue muscle fibers within the artery walls to relax and dilate. (This is similar to the way nitroglycerin pills work when given to heart attack victims experiencing severe chest pain. Nitroglycerine helps coronary arteries dilate to increase needed blood flow to the heart.) NO is produced by an enzyme called synthase, which acts like an antidote to free radicals. To increase NOs in your body, eat antioxidant-rich foods such as grains and brightly colored fruits like blueberries and vegetables like beets, rhubarb, and arugula. These foods contain natural nitrates that enable your body to produce NOs.[9]

Phytoestrogens *Phytoestrogens* are plant hormones similar to human estrogens but less potent. Research suggests that some phytoestrogens may lower cholesterol and reduce the risk of heart disease. Other claims—that they lower the risk of osteoporosis and some types of cancer and reduce menopausal symptoms such as hot flashes—have not been supported by research.

Phytoestrogens have been identified in more than 300 plants, including vegetables of the cabbage family such as brussels sprouts, broccoli, and cauliflower. Phytoestrogens are also found in plants containing lignin (a woody substance like cellulose), such as rye, wheat, sesame seed, linseed, and flaxseed, and in soybeans and soy products. Foods containing phytoestrogens are safe, but, as with all phytochemicals, research has not established the safety of phytoestrogen supplements.[1,2]

Phytonutraceuticals *Phytonutraceuticals* are substances extracted from vegetables and other plant foods and used in supplements. For example, lycopene is an antioxidant found in tomatoes that may inhibit the reproduction of cancer cells in the esophagus, prostate, and stomach.[27] A group of phytochemicals known as *bioflavonoids* are believed to have a beneficial effect on the cardiovascular system.[28]

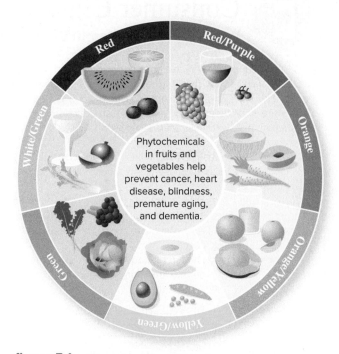

figure 5.1   **The color wheel of foods.**
An optimal diet contains fruits and vegetables from all seven groups. Source: Heber, D. (2001). *What color is your diet?* New York, NY: HarperCollins.

To date, the FDA has not allowed foods containing phytochemicals to be labeled or marketed as agents that prevent disease. Nutritionists do not recommend taking phytochemical supplements.[1,2] In 2007, the FDA announced that manufacturers of all dietary supplements, including vitamins and herbs, must evaluate the identity, purity, strength, and composition of their products and accurately label them so that consumers know what they are buying.[1,2,5,29]

National campaigns such as "Reach for It" in Canada and "Fruits and Veggies—More Matters" in the United States encourage consumers to select fruits and vegetables high in phytochemicals.[3] Because different fruits and vegetables contain different phytochemicals, a color-coded dietary plan has been developed that helps you take full advantage of all the beneficial phytochemicals available by eating from all seven groups (Figure 5.1).

PLANNING A HEALTHY DIET

When food is *metabolized*—chemically transformed into energy and wastes—it fuels our bodies. The energy provided by food is measured in kilocalories, commonly shortened to *calories*. One **kilocalorie** is the amount of energy needed to raise the temperature of 1 kilogram of water by 1 degree centigrade. The more energy we expend, the more kilocalories we need to consume. We get the most energy from fats—9 calories per gram of fat. Carbohydrates and protein provide 4 calories per gram. In other words, fats provide more calories than do carbohydrates or proteins, a factor to consider when planning a balanced diet that does not lead to weight gain.

To build a healthy eating pattern, combine healthy choices from all food groups based on an appropriate calorie level. A healthy eating pattern includes these food groups and subgroups:	A healthy eating pattern limits these components:

 A variety of vegetables from all of the subgroups, including dark green (e.g.,broccoli, spinach, romaine, kale, collard greens) and red and orange (e.g., tomatoes, carrots, sweet potatoes, winter squash); legumes (beans and peas, e.g., kidney beans, lentils, split peas, edamame); starchy vegetables (e.g., white potatoes, corn, green peas, plantains, cassava); and other (e.g., lettuce, cucumbers, zucchini, green beans, onions, mushrooms).

Fruits, especially whole fruits (e.g., oranges, apples, grapes, raisins, bananas, melons).

 Grains (e.g., cereals, bread, crackers, rice, pasta), at least half of which are whole grains (e.g., whole wheat bread, whole-grain cereals, oatmeal, popcorn, brown rice, quinoa).

Fat-free or low-fat dairy, including milk, yogurt, cheese, and fortified soy milk, yogurt, and other dairy replacements.

A variety of protein foods, including seafood, lean meats and poultry, eggs, legumes (beans and peas), and unsalted nuts, seeds, and soy products.

Oils (e.g., canola, corn, olive, peanut, safflower, soybean, and sunflower oils) instead of solid fats (e.g., butter, stick margarine). However, tropical oils (e.g., coconut and palm oils) are as high in saturated fats as solid fats are and are not part of a healthy eating pattern.

  Saturated fats and trans fats: less than 10 percent of calories per day.

Added sugars: less than 10 percent of calories per day.

 Sodium: less than 2,300 mg (about 1 teaspoon) per day.

Alcohol: if it is consumed, no more than one drink per day for women and two drinks per day for men.

In addition, Americans of all ages should meet the *Physical Activity Guidelines for Americans* to promote health and reduce the risk of chronic disease. (These guidelines are discussed in Chapter 6.)

figure 5.2 *2015–2020 Dietary Guidelines for Americans:* **Basics of a Healthy Eating Pattern.**
((Tomato): Floortje/iStock/Getty Images; (Red apple and a green apple): Visage/Getty Images; (Loaf of bread) : Ingram Publishing/SuperStock; (Glass of milk): McGraw-Hill; (Slice of salmon): Stockbyte/Getty Images; (Olive oil): Iconotec/Glow Images; (Stick of Butter): D. Hurst/Alamy; (Pile of sugar with wooden scoop): mistac/123RF; (Salt shaker [XL]): Suzannah Skelton/E+/Getty Images; (Red wine XL): PLAINVIEW/E+/Getty Images)
Source: U.S. Department of Agriculture. (2015). *Dietary guidelines for Americans: 2015–2020.* Retrieved from www.dietaryguidelines.gov/

Knowing your daily nutritional requirements in grams and percentages is not enough to ensure a healthy diet; you also need to know how to translate DRIs, RDAs, and AMDRs into healthy food choices and appealing meals. In this section we look at several tools that have been created to help you do that.

2015–2020 Dietary Guidelines for Americans

The *2015–2020 Dietary Guidelines for Americans* focuses on building healthy eating patterns. Eating patterns can be adapted to cultural and personal preferences so that U.S. consumers can select a healthy diet they will be able to follow throughout their lives. This revision of the guidelines emphasizes that healthy eating is not a rigid prescription.

The *2015–2020 Dietary Guidelines* are based on five overarching concepts:

- Follow a healthy eating pattern across the lifespan.
- Focus on variety, nutrient density, and amount.
- Limit calories from added sugars and saturated fats and reduce sodium intake.
- Shift to healthier food and beverage choices.
- Support healthy eating patterns for all.

The guidelines describe three food patterns:

- A healthy U.S.-style eating pattern
- A healthy Mediterranean-style eating pattern
- A healthy vegetarian-style eating pattern

The healthy U.S.-style eating pattern is based on the types of foods people in the United States typically consume, but in nutrient-dense forms and appropriate amounts. Figure 5.2 describes the basics of a healthy eating pattern. A healthy Mediterranean-style pattern contains more fruits and seafood and less dairy than the U.S.-style pattern; in addition, olive oil, a monounsaturated fat, provides more than half the fat calories in

Table 5.3   Estimated Calorie Requirements at Three Levels, by Age and Gender

| Gender | Age (years) | Activity Level | | |
		Sedentary	Moderately Active	Active
Female	14–18	1,800	2,000	2,400
	19–25	2,000	2,200	2,400
	26–50	1,800	2,000	2,200
	51+	1,600	1,800	2,000–2,200
Male	14–18	2,000–2,400	2,400–2,800	2,800–3,200
	19–35	2,400–2,600	2,600–2,800	3,000
	36–50	2,200–2,400	2,400–2,600	2,800
	51+	2,000–2,200	2,200–2,400	2,400–2,800

Source: U.S. Department of Agriculture. (2015). *Dietary guidelines for Americans: 2015–2020.* Retrieved from www.dietaryguidelines.gov/

nutrient density
The proportion of nutrients to total calories in a food.

the diet. A healthy vegetarian-style pattern includes more legumes (beans and peas), soy products, nuts and seeds, and whole grains than the U.S.-style pattern. And, of course, it contains no meats, poultry, or seafood.

The Personal Health Portfolio activity at the end of this chapter will help you assess your food intake. Estimate the appropriate number of calories based on your gender, age, and activity level, as shown in Table 5.3. The three activity levels are defined as

- *Sedentary.* Only light physical activity associated with typical day-to-day life.

- *Moderately active.* Physical activity equivalent to walking about 1.5 miles per day at 3 to 4 miles per hour.

- *Active.* Physical activity equivalent to walking more than 3 miles per day at 3 to 4 miles per hour.

For the *2015-2020 Dietary Guidelines* recommendations for various calorie levels, see its Appendix 3, at http://health.gov/dietaryguidelines/2015/guidelines/appendix-3. Figure 5.3, The USDA MyPlate, shows the recommended amounts from each food group for 2,000 calories a day.

Choose MyPlate

In 2010, the USDA introduced Choose MyPlate, a visual icon that illustrates the five food groups (fruits, vegetables, grains,

protein, and dairy) and is intended as a reminder about maintaining a healthy diet (Figure 5.3). Visit the USDA Choose MyPlate website and use the interactive tools to calculate your calorie needs, develop a customized food plan, and learn strategies for achieving a healthy weight.

The *Dietary Guidelines* and MyPlate differ significantly from current eating patterns in the United States. Specifically, they encourage more consumption of whole grains, vegetables, legumes, fruits, and low-fat milk products and less consumption of refined grain products, total fats, added sugars, and calories. They emphasize foods high in **nutrient density**—the proportion of vitamins and minerals to total calories. Especially in a lower calorie diet, the goal is for all calories consumed to provide nutrients (as opposed to the "empty calories" in sodas, sweets, and alcoholic beverages). Otherwise, you reach your maximum calorie intake without having consumed the nutrients you need.

If you choose nutrient-dense foods from each food group, you may have some calories left over—your discretionary calorie allowance—that can be consumed as added fats or sugars, alcohol, or other foods. At the 2,000-calorie level, your discretionary calorie allowance is 270 calories. For comparison, that is about the number of calories in two beers, two glasses of wine, two cans of regular cola, 30 potato chips, or half a brownie.

The DASH Eating Plan

Based on clinical trials, the National Heart, Lung, and Blood Institute developed the DASH (Dietary Approaches to Stop Hypertension) Eating Plan to reduce high blood pressure. The DASH plan is similar to the *2015-2020 Dietary Guidelines,* except it puts more emphasis on sodium reduction.[30] It is also similar to Choose MyPlate, but it has a nuts, seeds, and legumes group. For more information, visit http://www.nhlbi.nih.gov/files/docs/public/heart/dash_brief.pdf.

Limiting Red Meats

Research strongly supports a link between red meat consumption and heart disease, cancer, and diabetes.[31] (The USDA classifies meats as red if they are red before they are cooked; it considers pork as well as beef, lamb, and veal red meats.) The Nurses Health Study found that people who eat two servings a day (3-ounce servings of cooked steak, hamburger, or other unprocessed meats or 1-ounce servings of processed meat such as bacon, ham, and sausage) have a higher risk of heart disease than people who average a half-serving a day. About 8 percent of deaths in women and 10 percent of deaths in men could be prevented if people ate no more than a half-serving of red meat a day.[31] The primary components of concern in red meats are heme iron, nitrites,

Find Your
Healthy Eating Style
& Maintain It for a Lifetime
Start with small changes to make healthier choices you can enjoy.

Follow the MyPlate building blocks below to create your own healthy eating solutions—"MyWins." Choose foods and beverages from each food group—*making sure that your choices are limited in sodium, saturated fat, and added sugars.*

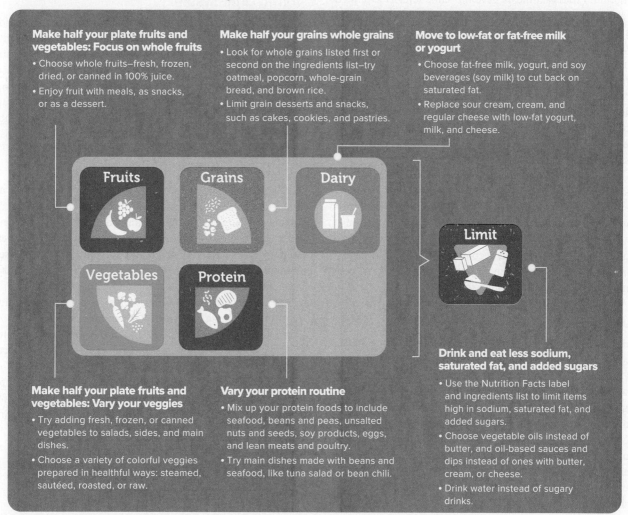

Make half your plate fruits and vegetables: Focus on whole fruits
- Choose whole fruits—fresh, frozen, dried, or canned in 100% juice.
- Enjoy fruit with meals, as snacks, or as a dessert.

Make half your grains whole grains
- Look for whole grains listed first or second on the ingredients list—try oatmeal, popcorn, whole-grain bread, and brown rice.
- Limit grain desserts and snacks, such as cakes, cookies, and pastries.

Move to low-fat or fat-free milk or yogurt
- Choose fat-free milk, yogurt, and soy beverages (soy milk) to cut back on saturated fat.
- Replace sour cream, cream, and regular cheese with low-fat yogurt, milk, and cheese.

Make half your plate fruits and vegetables: Vary your veggies
- Try adding fresh, frozen, or canned vegetables to salads, sides, and main dishes.
- Choose a variety of colorful veggies prepared in healthful ways: steamed, sautéed, roasted, or raw.

Vary your protein routine
- Mix up your protein foods to include seafood, beans and peas, unsalted nuts and seeds, soy products, eggs, and lean meats and poultry.
- Try main dishes made with beans and seafood, like tuna salad or bean chili.

Drink and eat less sodium, saturated fat, and added sugars
- Use the Nutrition Facts label and ingredients list to limit items high in sodium, saturated fat, and added sugars.
- Choose vegetable oils instead of butter, and oil-based sauces and dips instead of ones with butter, cream, or cheese.
- Drink water instead of sugary drinks.

figure 5.3   The USDA MyPlate.
Introduced in 2010, MyPlate promotes a dietary balance of five basic food groups: fruits, grains, vegetables, protein, and dairy. The MyPlate website, choosemyplate.gov, contains resources and interactive tools.
Source: U.S. Department of Agriculture, Center for Nutrition Policy, and Promotion. (2016, May.) *MyPlate, my wins tipsheet.* Retrieved from https://choosemyplate-prod.azureedge.net/sites/default/files/printablematerials/mini_poster.pdf

and compounds that cluster when red meats are cooked at high temperatures. Some consumers are also cutting back on meat consumption because of the high ecological cost of raising animals for food. For more on these costs, please see Chapter 18 (online).

The Harvard Health Newsletter calls cooking red meat a "preparation paradox." Cooking red meat thoroughly is critical for preventing food infections, discussed later in this chapter. The color and texture of cooked meat is not reliable for determining whether it is undercooked; instead, a meat thermometer is an essential kitchen tool for safely preparing meat. However, cooking red meat longer and/or at high temperatures increases the presence of heterocyclic amines (HCAs).[9] Women who eat bacon, beefsteak, and hamburgers well done, for instance, increase their risk for brain cancer fivefold compared to women who prefer these meats cooked rare or medium. PhIP is a chemical abundant in HCAs when muscle meats (beef, pork, poultry, fish) are cooked at high temperature. It is called a complete carcinogen, since it can damage cell DNA and initiate cancer, promote tumor growth, and facilitate the spread of cancer throughout the body.[9]

The American Cancer Society (ACS) recommends eating no more than 18 ounces (cooked weight) of red meats per week and avoiding or strictly limiting processed meat consumption. Processed meats have the same level of saturated fat as unprocessed meat but contain more calories, four times the sodium, 50 percent more preservatives that have nitrates and nitrites, and less protein. Nitrates and nitrites stiffen arteries and cause metabolic changes that mimic diabetes and cancer.[32] ACS research indicates that the risk for colon and rectal cancers increases when people eat more than that amount. Studies also suggest an increased risk for pancreatic, prostate, and esophagus cancers. Processed meats have long been linked to diabetes, and recent research is linking unprocessed red meats to diabetes as well.[9]

The *2015–2020 Dietary Guidelines* notes that most processed meats are high in sodium and saturated fat, so eating them makes it hard to stay within the recommended 10 percent limits for sodium and saturated fat. The guidelines also note that U.S. males between ages 19 and 50 are getting more protein than they need and recommend that they consume less meat (particularly red meat), poultry, and eggs and consume more vegetables and other foods.[12]

Cultured Meat

The FDA in 2019 approved cell-cultured meat that is lab-grown, using a live animal's adult muscle stem cells that are set in a nutrient-rich liquid. The generated product looks and tastes like meat, since it is made from animal cells and not from plant-based products that do not contain animal tissue. Since this process uses few natural resources, it has been well received by environmental and animal welfare advocacy groups. FDA regulators debated calling culture meat "clean meat," "alt meat," "in vitro meat," or "artificial meat." However, less than 50 percent of consumers say they would purchase cultured meat.[33]

Vegetarian Diets

Vegetarian diets may offer protection against obesity, heart disease, high blood pressure, diabetes, digestive disorders, and some forms of cancer, particularly colon cancer,[1,2] depending on the type of vegetarian diet followed. Some research suggests that vegetarians live longer than non-vegetarians.[34] Despite the potential benefits of vegetarian diets, however, vegetarians need to make sure that their diets provide the energy intake and food diversity needed to meet dietary

% Daily Value (DV) The percentage of your daily need for a given nutrient that is contained in a serving of food.

guidelines.[1,2] Vegetarians should visit the food plan for vegetarians available on MyPlate and the *2015–2020 Dietary Guidelines*, especially Appendix 5 (https://health.gov/dietaryguidelines/2015/guidelines/appendix-5/).

Many people follow a vegetarian diet due to the ecological cost of eating meat. Environmental impacts from production and air pollution of meat occurs from fuel usage, animal methane gas, water waste, and land use. This topic is addressed in Chapter 18 (online).

Traffic-Light System

Although health-choice indicators on food labels provide helpful information, some college cafeterias have adopted a traffic-light labeling system to provide visible and easy-to-understand nutrition information at the point of purchase. Foods and beverages are classified by color; green is most healthy and red least healthy. Unfortunately, evidence supporting the traffic-light system in improving college students' selection of healthier diet choices is mixed.[35]

Diet for a Healthy Brain

The latest scientific studies support the idea that diet plays an important role in maintaining a healthy brain. Diets in Mediterranean countries, Scandinavian countries, and Japan have been shown to protect brain mass, for example. These diets contain lower levels of sugar and sodium, fewer processed foods, vast amounts of antioxidants from fruits and vegetables, moderate amounts of meat, and plenty of whole grains. The Mediterranean diet is more plant based than the traditional Western diet. Seafood often replaces meats.

Docosahexaenoic acid (DHA) may be the primary nutrient contributing to brain health. This omega-3 comes primarily from seafood. Scientists believe DHA increases levels of brain-derived neurotrophic factor, which supports and protects brain cells. Nutrition intervention diets that promote brain health will be important for reversing the increasing rates of mental illnesses and cognitive disorders.[36]

GETTING HELP FROM FOOD LABELS

Once you have figured out a healthy eating pattern that fits you, you can use the labels on packaged foods and the information on restaurant menus to stick with that pattern.

The Nutrition Facts Label

Food labels on packaged foods are regulated by the FDA to inform consumers about the nutritional values of different products. The top of the label lists serving size and number of servings in the container. The second part of the label gives the total calories per serving. The next part of the label shows the % **Daily Value (DV)** percentage of nutrients, as well as cholesterol and sodium, contained in the food. DVs are based on a variety of dietary guidelines and recommendations. A

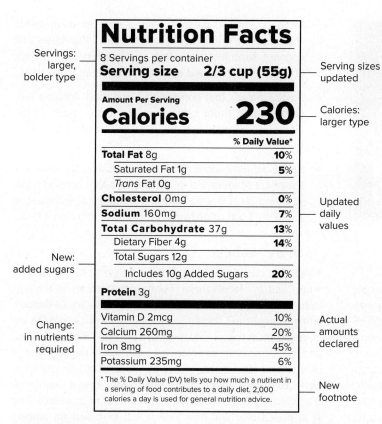

Nutrition Facts

8 Servings per container
Serving size   2/3 cup (55g)

Amount Per Serving
Calories   230

	% Daily Value*
Total Fat 8g	**10%**
Saturated Fat 1g	**5%**
Trans Fat 0g	
Cholesterol 0mg	**0%**
Sodium 160mg	**7%**
Total Carbohydrate 37g	**13%**
Dietary Fiber 4g	**14%**
Total Sugars 12g	
Includes 10g Added Sugars	**20%**
Protein 3g	
Vitamin D 2mcg	10%
Calcium 260mg	20%
Iron 8mg	45%
Potassium 235mg	6%

* The % Daily Value (DV) tells you how much a nutrient in a serving of food contributes to a daily diet. 2,000 calories a day is used for general nutrition advice.

Labels: Servings: larger, bolder type; Serving sizes updated; Calories: larger type; Updated daily values; New: added sugars; Change: in nutrients required; Actual amounts declared; New footnote

figure 5.4   Nutrition Facts panel on an original (left) and new food label (right).
Source: U.S. Food and Drug Administration. "What's New with the Nutrition Facts Label." https://www.fda.gov/food/new-nutrition-facts-label/whats-new-nutrition-facts-label

quick calculation will tell you whether a product is relatively high or low in the major nutrients. (*A tip:* Look for foods with no more than 30 percent of their calories from fats and no more than 10 percent from added sugar.) The bottom part of the label shows the DV for key vitamins and minerals.[37,38]

In 2016, the FDA finalized updates of the Nutrition Facts label. The changes draw from new scientific evidence that establishes a link between diet and chronic diseases, particularly obesity and heart disease. Key changes include information about added sugars (sugars added during processing and preparation), more realistic serving sizes, and calorie and nutrition information for the whole package for certain products (such as soft drinks). Calories from fat no longer appear, and the total number of calories is emphasized instead. DVs of potassium and vitamin D are now included on the label, but showing DVs of vitamins A and C is no longer provided since deficiency for these vitamins is unlikely. Sugar in grams and percent of daily value were added. The bottom panel better explains % DV. The label has been redesigned to emphasize calories, serving size, and DV percentages DV indicates how much in a given food contributes to a daily diet. calories are for general nutrition advice. (Figure 5.4). The purpose of these changes is to make it easier for consumers to choose healthy packaged food products. The Nutrition

Facts label appears on all packaged foods, but not on meat, poultry, and processed egg products, which are regulated by the USDA.[38] Most food producers with more than $10 million annual sales will be required to use the new label by January 2020. Small companies have an additional year to make the change.

Claims on Food and Dietary Supplement Packaging

Packaged foods frequently display food descriptors and health claims, some of which are also regulated by the FDA. For example, the term *light* can be used if the product has one-third fewer calories or half the fat of the regular product. Other claims are not yet well regulated, as discussed in the next section, "Current Consumer Concerns." To find out more about common nutritional claims on food packages, visit the FDA website.

Because dietary supplements are subject to less regulation than foods, their manufacturers have been able to include a wide variety of health claims on supplement labels, asserting everything from support of heart health to promotion of muscle growth without steroids. Food and beverage manufacturers have pressured Congress to allow similar health claims on their labels.[37] Because the FDA's authority to regulate such claims is limited, health claims on food and beverage products have proliferated without much oversight. Examples of such meaningless claims are "gluten-free," "lightly sweetened," and "all natural."

Today, more than 12 different symbols, logos, and icons appear on the front of food product packaging to communicate nutrition information to consumers—none of which has yet been officially designed or endorsed by the FDA. Some of these front-of-package (FOP) labels provide straightforward facts about nutrient content, but others can be misleading and confusing.[39] Studies have found that well-constructed, uniform FOP labels can lead to healthier food choices.[37,38]

Restaurant Menu Labels

People in the United States consume about one-third of their calories away from home.[40] Can menu labeling make us healthier? The 2010 Affordable Care Act includes a requirement that all chain restaurants (restaurants with more than 20 locations) provide calorie counts on their menus.[39] The FDA finalized regulations about menu labels in December 2014 but extended compliance to a later date. In 2015, New York City became the first city to require chain-restaurant menus to warn about high-sodium dishes; its board of health mandated a salt-shaker symbol for foods prepared with a teaspoon or more of salt per serving.[41] See Figure 5.5 for an example of restaurant menu labeling.

figure 5.5   Restaurant menu with calories.
(EMMANUEL DUNAND/AFP/Getty Images)

Proponents of menu labeling believe it will help people make healthier decisions and manage their weight more successfully.[39,41,42] Information about the health and weight effects of specific ingredients in menu items could help people choose healthier food options. But studies that support menu labeling show only a marginal change in calorie consumption.[39,41,42] Opponents argue that people choose unhealthy foods because they lack self-control, not because they lack information.[39,42] In addition, it is difficult to provide precise nutrition information about fast food because most people add condiments such as mustard, mayonnaise, and ketchup, as well as salt and butter. One recommendation is that restaurants provide a range of potential calories counts for menu items.[39,41,42] See the box "You Make the Call: Does Menu Labeling Change Consumer Behavior?" at the end of the chapter for more on this debate.

Other methods of guiding consumers may prove to be more effective than providing nutrition information alone. For example, menus could be designed to encourage healthier eating by listing healthy choices first.[39,43] A Healthy Choice symbol indicating that a food product is low in fats, saturated fats, sodium, and sugar and high in dietary fiber can lead people to make healthier food choices. Researchers have found that symbols are more likely than numbers to affect food choices. The Center for Science in the Public Interest recommends five facts for consumers to look for before ordering from a menu[44]:

- *Calorie ranges.* A single food item can be listed with a range of calories (for example, chicken sandwich, 960 to 1,250 cals) that depends on sides, sauces, toppings, beverages, and so on.

- *Unit foods.* Companies get to define what a "unit" means when foods come in slices or pieces, for example, one slice of pizza or four buffalo wings or bread bites. To find calories in your serving, you will need to divide or multiply the calories in your serving.

- *Slashes.* Slashes are used when consumers are provided two food choices; for example, shrimp combination may be

listed as 370/580 calories. This means the main grilled shrimp entree would be 370 calories, and 580 calories with coconut shrimp. Other slash designations may include grilled versus fried food option, or half versus full serving.

- *Salads.* Salads that come with a standard dressing typically include those calories in the menu count. If you choose a different dressing, you will need to add additional calories.

- *Additional information.* Menus may include, on request, a statement of additional information for such items as sugar, salt, and fat. Or a statement for additional information based on 2,000 calories a day for general nutrition advice.

"Sell By" Labels

Most U.S. consumers do not have a clear understanding of what "Sell by" labels mean. Food manufacturers in the past used 10 different kinds of "Sell by" labels to try to indicate when unused food should be discarded. Now the USDA encourages them to use only two, "Use by" and "Best if used by," and most have done so voluntarily to forestall the adoption of new federal regulations.[45] "Use by" notifies consumers when perishable foods are no longer safe to eat. "Best if used by" is a subjective guess by the food manufacturer as to when a food is at peak flavor and how long it will look best on grocery shelves. Foods are typically safe to eat well beyond their "Best by" date. Ninety-one percent of U.S. consumers mistakenly throw out food that has passed the "Best if used by" date, even though the date refers only to when food is at peak quality.[45]

The Grocery Manufacturers Association (GMA) launched the "less-waste campaign" in 2018. It uses the social media hashtag #10ItemsLess to encourage consumers to follow the "Best by" and "Use by" labels to prevent throwing out good food prematurely. The goal of the campaign is for every consumer to throw out 10 fewer good food items in 2019, and to do the same for each year that follows. The GMA assumes each food item weighs 8 ounces, so the campaign could result in at least 638 million pounds less food waste each year.

As of 2019, only 44 percent of consumers were using the "Sell by" labels to avoid throwing out good food. An increasing number, however, support the use of the more transparent two food date labels. The new food label was required to be used by food manufacturers that had $10 million or more in annual sales. Manufacturers with less than $10 million in annual sales were required to use the new two-label system by January 1, 2021.[46]

CURRENT CONSUMER CONCERNS

The most common food-related topics that you are likely to hear about in the media are related to obesity and poor health because of our overconsumption of soft drinks, high-sodium diets, and fast foods. These topics are important because obese young adults and middle-aged adults are likely to live almost a decade less, on average, than those who maintain a healthy weight. This section also addresses several other current issues of concern to consumers. For a discussion of probiotics, see Chapters 7 and 17 (online).

Overconsumption of Soft Drinks

One in every four beverages consumed in the United States is a soft drink. One 12-ounce can of soda contains about 10 teaspoons of sugar.[1,2] The American Heart Association recommends no more than 6 teaspoons of sugar a day for women and 9 teaspoons for men. Sugar is believed to promote and maintain obesity[1,2,32,43,47]; cause and aggravate diabetes; increase the risk of heart disease; and cause dental decay, gum disease, osteoporosis, and kidney stones. One study estimated that sugary drinks cause 25,000 deaths per year in the United States from Type 2 diabetes, heart disease, and cancer.[47] Note, however, that scientific evidence suggests moderate levels of sugar (no more than 10 percent of total calories) pose no health risk.[1,2]

Diet Sodas What about diet sodas? Diet soft drinks don't contain sugar, but like regular soft drinks, they fill you up without providing any nutrients. In addition, artificial sweeteners disrupt the body's ability to regulate calorie intake based on food sweetness. The body is tricked into thinking sugar is being consumed, which leads to sugar craving. People who regularly consume diet sodas may experience cravings for sugar. The theory is that habitual consumption of artificial sugars may prevent the release of hormones needed to process sugar (Figure 5.6).

Diet soda drinkers have the same health concerns as regular soda drinkers: weight, Type 2 diabetes, and heart disease.[48,49] After 10 to 20 years, diet soda drinkers actually have worse health outcomes due to changes in their metabolic system.[47,48] A study found that even one diet soda a day may increase the risk for metabolic syndrome (high blood pressure, high LDL, low HDL, belly fat), which places a person at risk for heart disease. Diet fizzy drinks are especially troublesome. The average consumer of fizzy drinks has three diet sodas per day.[50] Another study found that drinking two or more diet sodas a day may be associated with a twofold risk of kidney disease. Because this decline is not associated with sugar-sweetened sodas, scientists believe the cause is likely artificial sweeteners.[51]

In addition, many diet sodas also contain preservatives called mold inhibitors (sodium benzoate, potassium benzoate) that are not found in regular sodas. Mold inhibitors can damage DNA and have been linked to allergic reactions such as hives and asthma as well as mild irritations to the skin, eyes, and mucous membranes. Finally, diet soda has a pH of 3.2, which is very acidic. Acid dissolves tooth enamel. Not surprisingly, researchers have found that people who drink three or more diet sodas a day are at higher risk of tooth decay.[49]

Caramel is an artificial coloring used in soft drinks and some food products. It contains 4-Methylimidazole (4-Mel), which is considered a carcinogenic chemical. Caramel is not regulated by the FDA, and food and beverage manufacturers do not have to list it on product labels. The state of California, however, requires beverage labels to carry a cancer warning if the product exposes consumers to more than 29 micrograms (μg) of 4-Mel.

Consumer Reports tested 4-Mel levels in California. Pepsi contained 43 μg of 4-Mel in a 12-ounce can, and Diet Pepsi

What Happens One Hour
After Drinking A Diet Soda

1 First 10 Minutes

Tricks Your Taste Buds & Attacks Your Teeth
Sugar and artificial sweeteners trick taste buds into believing they just processed sugar. Phosphoric enamels begin to erode teeth enamel.

2 20 Minutes

Can Switch On Fat Storage Mode
Artificial sugars and sugar alcohol may trigger insulin release, which causes the body to go into fat storage mode. Interference with natural gut bacteria occurs, disrupting the immune and digestive systems.

40 Minutes 3

Can Cause Addiction
The combination of caffeine and artificial sugars such as aspartame causes excitotoxins to be released that can overstimulate neuroreceptors and release dopamine and glutamate (brain neurotransmitters).

60 Minutes 4

Can Deplete Nutrients, Make You Hungry & Thirsty For More
Diet sodas are empty calories that result in nutrient depletion and sensations of hunger and thirst. Artificial sweeteners can cause an increase in ghrelin, a hormone that increases appetite, and a reduction in leptin, a hormone that decreases appetite. Your body is encouraged to gain and store weight as fat.

(Gaby Campo/Shutterstock)

figure 5.6

Source: The Renegade Pharamacist. (2019). What happens one hour after drinking diet coke, coke zero, or any other similar diet soda? Retrieved from https://therenegadepharmacist.com/diet-coke-exposed-happens-one-hour-drinking-diet-coke-coke-zero-similar-diet-soda/

30 µg. Coke Zero had 4 µg and Diet Coke 3 µg of 4-Mel. PepsiCo, the maker of Pepsi, disputes the need for a cancer warning, claiming the average consumer drinks only one-third of a 12-ounce can per day. Data from *Consumer Reports* suggest consumption of diet soda each day is much higher than one-third of a 12-ounce can. So what should consumers do? The best advice is to limit consumption of foods and beverages that contain caramel coloring.[52]

Caffeine Nearly all soft drinks contain relatively high levels of caffeine, which is mildly addictive and can lead to nervousness, irritability, insomnia, and bone demineralization. Although soft drink manufacturers claim that caffeine is added for flavoring, its primary effect is to stimulate the central nervous system.[49] Nutritionists recommend limiting soft drinks and to drink water and low-fat milk instead. Figure 5.7 shows the amount of caffeine in a variety of beverages.

Decreased Consumption of Milk As serious as the overconsumption of soft drinks is the decreased consumption of milk, which is a major source of calcium, protein, and vitamins A and D. Decreased consumption of orange juice and other fruit juices is also a health concern.[53] Soft drinks contain about the same number of calories as milk and juice, but none of the nutrients.

Fat-free and low-fat milk are more nutrient-dense choices than heavily sweetened beverages, and many varieties of milk are available to fit people's needs[1,2]:

- Omega-3 fortified milk, which contains small amounts of healthy omega-3 fatty acids.

- Ultra-pasteurized milk, which is treated to have an especially long shelf life when unopened, beneficial for those who shop ahead or buy in bulk.

- Lactose-free milk, which contains no lactose (milk sugar). Lactose is hard for about 6 percent of adults to digest.

- "Plus" or "deluxe" milk, which is fortified with milk powder, stabilizers, and/or fiber to increase the nutrient content and produce a creamier consistency that some people find closer to that of whole milk.

- Nondairy milk, which is made from soy, rice, almonds, or another nondairy source; it is appropriate for anyone but particularly for vegans and those who are lactose intolerant.

Overconsumption of Salt

U.S. adults consume an average of 3,400 milligrams (mg) of salt per day,[54] men more and women less. Sodium is an essential nutrient, but we need only about 500 mg per day—about 1/10 of a teaspoon. Although many foods contain sodium, we get most of our sodium—about 90 percent—from salt (which is made up of sodium and chloride). The *2015-2020 Dietary Guidelines* recommends no more than 2,300 mg of sodium per day for the general population and no more than 1,500 mg per day for African Americans, people who are 51 or older, and people who have hypertension, diabetes, or chronic kidney disease. The American Heart Association recommends no more than 1,500 mg per day for *all* adults. If U.S. consumers adopted the American Heart Association's sodium recommendation, about 92,000 deaths per year could be prevented.[9]

Many packaged foods, convenience foods, fast foods, and restaurant foods are heavily salted, primarily to enhance flavor. Some contain more than 5,000 mg of sodium in a serving. Canned soups, lunch meats, pickles, soy sauce, teriyaki sauce, ketchup, mustard, salad dressing, and barbecue sauce are especially high in sodium.[55]

You can reduce the amount of salt in your diet by emphasizing whole foods, such as grains, vegetables, and fruits, which are naturally low in sodium. Remove the salt shaker from your table, and don't use salt in cooking. When buying packaged foods, read the labels to check for sodium content and look for descriptors such as "reduced sodium" or "low sodium." Highly salted food is an acquired taste; if you use less salt, you will gradually rediscover the natural taste of the food. Although scientists have found substitutes for sugar, substitutes for salt are much more elusive.

Is Black Pepper Healthy for You? Although salt has received significant attention by health experts, black pepper has been mostly ignored. There is increasing evidence that black pepper marinades may help eliminate heterocyclic amines (HCAs), which are cancer-causing chemicals that form in charred meat or meat cooked at high temperatures. Adding about a

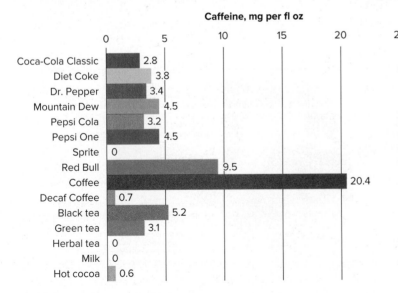

Caffeine, mg per fl oz

Coca-Cola Classic	2.8
Diet Coke	3.8
Dr. Pepper	3.4
Mountain Dew	4.5
Pepsi Cola	3.2
Pepsi One	4.5
Sprite	0
Red Bull	9.5
Coffee	20.4
Decaf Coffee	0.7
Black tea	5.2
Green tea	3.1
Herbal tea	0
Milk	0
Hot cocoa	0.6

figure 5.7   **Caffeine in selected sodas and other beverages.**
Source: Caffeine Informer. (2015). Caffeine content of drinks. Retrieved from www.caffeineinformer.com/-caffeine-database.

teaspoon of fine black pepper per half pound of meat may be effective in preventing the formation of HCAs during cooking, especially grilling. Black pepper may also aid in food digestion by stimulating the secretion of digestive enzymes. Piperline, an organic compound in black pepper, may increase absorption of curcumin and resveratrol. Curcumin is an antioxidant that has anti-inflammatory effects. Resveratrol has been associated with reducing brain disorder risks, heart disease, and Type 2 diabetes.[56]

Health scientists, however, caution that almost all studies on spices have been conducted on animals and cell cultures. There are very few human studies. Experts also warn that piperline may interfere with medications, particularly antihistamines. The bottom line: Black pepper sprinkled onto food likely poses no health risks and may provide some digestive anti-inflammatory effects, prevent diarrhea, and provide nutrient-absorption benefits. Still, avoid large doses of black pepper to prevent burning sensations in your mouth or stomach.[57]

Food Allergies and Food Intolerances

Food allergies occur when the immune system overreacts to specific proteins in food; they affect about 7 percent of children and 2 percent of adults. More than 200 food ingredients can cause an allergic reaction, but eight foods are responsible for 90 percent of food allergies—milk, eggs, peanuts, tree nuts, fish, shellfish, soy, and wheat. Allergic reactions to these foods cause 30,000 emergency room visits each year and 150 to 200 deaths.[58] The Food Allergen Labeling and Consumer Protection Act of 2004 requires that these allergens be clearly identified below the list of ingredients on all packaged foods.

People with food allergies rely on cautionary food labels. However, the words "may contain" cause confusion. Manufacturers use the "may contain" label when food is manufactured on shared equipment, since there is a risk that a trace of some allergen may still be contained in a food product that does not use it as an ingredient. The use of the word "may" falsely suggests to consumers that foods with this label are not as dangerous as foods actively containing a particular allergen. In other words, "may" should be considered food containing the allergen.[59]

Typical symptoms of allergic reactions include skin rash, nasal congestion, hives, nausea, and wheezing. Most children eventually outgrow food allergies, except for allergies to peanuts, nuts, and seafood.[1,2] Food allergies that develop during adulthood are typically lifelong. Many food allergies are associated with other diseases, such as asthma, eczema, and esophagitis.

Generally, people suffer temporary discomfort from allergic reactions, but approximately 30,000 people each year in the United States have an *anaphylactic shock* reaction to a food they have eaten—in which the throat swells enough to cut off breathing.[3] A person experiencing this type of allergic reaction needs immediate medical attention because symptoms can worsen rapidly and sometimes result in death.

Therefore, the National Institute of Allergy and Infectious Diseases stresses the importance of having an emergency plan in case of an anaphylactic allergic reaction.[5,10] You can attain an example of an emergency plan from the American Academy of Allergy, Asthma, and Immunology.

Most food reactions are not caused by allergies, however; most are caused by food intolerances.[5] Intolerances are less severe than allergies and can be triggered by almost any food. As we saw earlier, lactose intolerance, a condition that results from an inability to digest the milk sugar lactose, is especially prevalent.

There is no treatment or cure for food allergies or intolerances. If you experience these reactions, the best you can do is try to avoid the offending food.[1,2] Recently, however, Learning Early About Peanut Allergy (LEAP) studied the effects on the immune system of introducing peanuts to infants who were at high risk for peanut allergy, one of the most dangerous food allergies. The study's results cast doubt on the age-old physician advice to avoid feeding allergenic foods to infants. LEAP also suggests using food allergen products early when introducing solid foods to infants who are not at high risk for food allergies.[60]

It can be especially hard to avoid allergenic foods when eating out because restaurants are not required to reveal what menu items may contain them. Peanut butter, for example, can be used to flavor everything from salad dressing to cakes and cookies. Many health experts are now calling for menu labeling by restaurants, not only for health reasons but also for personal, cultural, and religious reasons. For example, vegetarian groups and Muslim associations have brought class-action suits against McDonald's for flavoring french fries with small amounts of meat, milk, and wheat products without informing customers.

Celiac Disease and Gluten

Celiac disease, an immune reaction in people who eat gluten, has been getting increasing attention in recent years. About 1.8 percent of the U.S. population has celiac disease, but 83 percent of them do not know it.[61] Gluten is a form of protein found in wheat, barley, rye, and triticale (a cross between wheat and rye). Over time, the immune system's reaction to gluten causes inflammatory damage to the small intestine lining. As the box "Life Stories: Ricardo: Celiac Disease" indicates, this damage can result in many symptoms, including weight loss, bloating, and occasionally diarrhea. If damage persists, there is an increased risk for osteoporosis, intestinal cancers, infertility, and other diseases and disorders. People with celiac disease are at higher risk for other autoimmune diseases.

If you are diagnosed with celiac disease, there are a few important questions you should ask your health care professional: How bad is the intestinal damage? Do I need to take a nutritional supplement? Can I eat dairy products? What follow-up tests are needed? Should my family be tested for celiac disease?[62]

Life Stories

Ricardo: Celiac Disease

Ricardo started noticing frequent rumbling in his stomach at age 17. By his sophomore year in college, the rumblings had graduated to severe stomach pain. He felt tired and cranky, and his body hurt all over. Ricardo also noticed that he was often experiencing tingling and numbness in his hands and legs, especially after he had eaten. An itchy skin rash had also appeared. Ricardo felt bloated and frequently felt an urge to go to the bathroom. He lost his appetite for food and lost 10 pounds in six weeks. He found it increasingly difficult to sleep. His roommate advised Ricardo that he most likely had a stomach bug and should see a doctor.

Ricardo decided to visit a walk-in health clinic, where he was given a blood test that revealed he was severely deficient in iron and was anemic. Iron supplementation was prescribed, but after several months of treatment, the level of iron in Ricardo's blood had not increased. Ricardo decided to consult a gastrointestinal (GI) specialist. The GI specialist suspected celiac disease, which has no cure. A strict gluten-free diet is the treatment of choice.

This was a very difficult diagnosis for Ricardo and would mean a huge lifestyle change. After all, he had grown up able to eat any type of food. Now even a minor slip, such as eating a biscuit, would trigger a severe immune system reaction. If the condition were left untreated, Ricardo's brain, nervous system, bones, liver, and other organs could be deprived of needed nourishment.

Because celiac disease can be inherited, Ricardo advised his other family members to be tested. A family history of thyroid problems, arthritis, and diabetes may be an indicator of possible celiac disease. Surgery, pregnancy, childbirth, a viral infection, or traumatic stress may trigger the onset of celiac disease in people who are prone to it.

- Are you or a friend on a gluten-free diet?
- What types of food must be avoided in a gluten-free diet?
- Do your local grocery stores sell gluten-free foods?
- Should restaurants be required to label gluten-free items on their menus?

In 2013, the FDA released a new labeling law that makes it much easier for people with celiac disease to avoid gluten. Foods labeled "gluten-free" must contain less than 20 parts per million of the gluten protein. This is about an eighth of a teaspoon of flour, a small enough amount for people with mild to severe gluten allergies to avoid an immune reaction. If you are just starting a gluten-free diet, it is recommended that you consult a registered dietitian.[61]

Gluten Sensitivity

There has been a significant increase in the number of people on gluten-free diets. Empirical evidence does not support any special benefits for gluten-free diets for people who do not have celiac disease, except for a decrease in processed foods in the diet. Those who are sensitive to gluten tend to be sensitive to other foods, for example, eggs and cow's milk. Some empirical evidence suggests that gluten-free diets may damage the gut of those who do not have celiac disease or wheat sensitivity. If you are concerned that you may be sensitive to gluten, you should consult your health provider before adopting a gluten-free diet. Your health provider will likely suggest a healthier diet that includes fruits, vegetables, whole grains, and beans and limited processed foods.[9]

Is gluten affecting your thyroid? The autoimmune umbrella of thyroid health problems includes an immune response by people who are sensitive to gluten. This response can cause some unpleasant symptoms such as chronic fatigue, weight gain, hair loss, brittle nails, and constipation. If you are experiencing these symptoms, your health provider may use a blood test to diagnose and treat thyroid problems. Thyroid-stimulating hormone (TSH) is the standard thyroid test that evaluates the signal from your brain to produce more thyroid hormones. Still, whether gluten is influencing thyroid function is a different question. Most research in this area has focused on people with celiac disease. People with celiac disease have about three times the risk of thyroid disease as do those without celiac disease.

The relationship between gluten sensitivity and thyroid disease is clouded. If you suspect gluten is triggering thyroid dysfunction, there are three recommended actions.[63] First, completely eliminate gluten from your diet for three months to see whether symptoms of a thyroid problem disappear. Second, if symptoms persist, have your health provider conduct the ALCAT food sensitivity test. (Some health providers use an alternative test that addresses immunoglobulin G [IgG] antibodies. The IgG test is not as accurate as the ALCAT test.) Third, have your health provider conduct a celiac disease test.

Energy Bars and Energy Drinks

Energy bars are a convenient source of calories and nutrients for people with busy schedules or intense exercise regimens. Luna Bars, Power Bars, and Balance Bars are examples of such products. Most are low in saturated and trans fats and contain up to 5 grams of fiber. They are better for you than candy bars and other snack foods high in saturated fat, but they can also be high in calories and sugar. Healthier alternatives are whole foods such as fruits and vegetables, with their abundant vitamins, minerals, and phytochemicals. If you do buy energy bars, check the labels for calories, total fat, saturated fat, protein, fiber, and sugar and choose the healthiest ones.[1,2,3] See the box "Action Skill-Builder: Five Tips for Enhanced-Protein Bars and Shakes."

Action Skill-Builder

Five Tips for Enhanced-Protein Bars and Shakes

Enhanced-protein bars and shakes usually contain fruit mixed with powdered protein supplements such as whey, soy, or eggs. Although these bars and shakes are healthier snack foods than chips or candy bars, there are some health concerns. Adding protein changes the natural composition of food and reduces nutrients. Monosodium glutamate (MSG), a flavor-enhancing salt, and artificial sweeteners and flavorings are typically added to mask the taste of the added protein. This mix is acidic and causes the kidneys to work harder to filter and remove excess acid from the body. Many bars and shakes contain gluten, which can cause GI distress for some people. In sum, excessive consumption of enhanced-protein bars and shakes can cause digestive problems, weight gain, and heart and kidney health issues.

Enhanced-protein bars and shakes are marketed as beneficial for weight loss, weight gain, and convenient meal replacements. Check labels to reap these benefits:

☐ Enhanced-protein foods should contain no more than 20 grams of protein. More than that does not provide additional benefit for protein synthesis.

☐ Higher quality enhanced-protein foods use whey protein or a whey-casein blend; if you see soy on the label, the ingredients are probably lower quality.

☐ The bar or shake should have fewer net grams of carbohydrates than grams of protein. Net grams of carbohydrate is the total carbohydrate grams minus grams of fiber.

☐ Bars and shakes should contain sufficient fat to match your calorie goal. For example, bars and shakes used as a meal replacement should contain fewer than 10 grams of fat.

☐ Bars and shakes should not have more than 20 ingredients; more ingredients than that are likely to be unnecessary and possibly unhealthy.

Sources: Cook, M. S. (2013). The shocking truth about protein bars, shakes, & enhanced foods. Care2. Retrieved from www.care2.com/greenliving/the-shocking-truth-about-protein-bars-shakes-and-enhanced-foods.html; Lagakos, W. (2013). How to choose a healthy protein bar that isn't candy. Builtlean. Retrieved from www.builtlean.com/2013/05/08/healthy-protein-bar/

U.S. adults consume about 4 quarts of energy drinks per person per year. With names like Red Bull, 5-Hour, Full Throttle, and Monster, these products are marketed as a source of instant energy, improved concentration and memory, and enhanced physical performance. They are not considered a health risk if consumed in recommended amounts, but there are no long-term studies on their effectiveness or their possible side effects.[1,2,3] The FDA does not monitor energy drinks because they are dietary supplements. Recently, however, deaths that may have been associated with energy drinks have drawn the attention of the FDA.[64,65]

All energy drinks contain water, sodium, and glucose. Glucose is converted into acid by bacteria. One study found that consuming energy drinks consistently over five days can produce enough acid to destroy teeth. The acid in energy drinks caused twice the enamel damage that sports drinks did. The American Beverage Association challenged the study's findings by arguing that tooth erosion is more likely associated with personal hygiene, lifestyle, diet, and family history of dental disease.[66]

Many energy drinks also contain caffeine and a variety of dietary supplements, such as ginseng, guarana, and B vitamins. Caffeine can stimulate mental activity and may increase cardiovascular performance, but more than 400 milligrams a day can produce negative effects, including loss of focus, racing heart beat, nausea, and anxiety. A severe overdose of caffeine can even cause death. Recently, Internet vendors have started selling pure powdered caffeine for increased energy. A teaspoon is equivalent to the caffeine in 25 cups of coffee. Common kitchen tools are not precise enough to accurately differentiate between safe and toxic quantities, and at least two young men died of an overdose of powdered caffeine in 2014.[67] The FDA issued warning letters in 2015 to five powdered caffeine manufacturers because these products present an unreasonable risk of injury or illness to consumers.[68]

Mixing hard alcohol and energy drinks has become popular with young adults. Combining a stimulant (caffeine and other herbal ingredients) with a depressant (alcohol) disguises the intoxication effects of alcohol by helping the drinker feel alert and sober. In a recent study, people who had been drinking energy drinks with liquor were three times more likely to be drunk than those who drank only alcohol and were four times more likely to say they planned to drive within the hour.[64] Multiple cocktails of energy drinks and liquor can also pose a danger to heart muscle fibers and cause extreme dehydration. The Centers for Disease Control and Prevention (CDC) estimates that college students who mix alcohol and energy drinks are three times more likely to binge drink, two times more likely to take unwanted sexual advantage, four times more likely to drive while intoxicated, two times more likely to ride with an intoxicated friend, and two or three times more likely to pass out or have a hangover.[69]

If you consume energy drinks, your maximum intake should be two 20-ounce cans a day. Consuming more than 20 ounces in an hour can cause an increase in arterial pressure and in blood sugar levels. Energy drinks should not be consumed immediately after a vigorous workout or in combination with alcohol. They should not be consumed by pregnant women, children, young teens, older adults, or people with cardiovascular disease, glaucoma, or sleep disorders. The bottom line, according to many health experts, is that the risks associated with energy drinks outweigh any perceived benefits.

Fast Foods

People in the United States eat out more than four times a week, and every day, one in four of us eats fast food.[55] Although plenty of people choose to eat fast food over healthier options, people who live in *food deserts* do not have adequate access to healthy, affordable food, and fast food is often their only alternative (food deserts are discussed in detail in the next section). Fast-food meals tend to be high in calories, fat, sodium, and sugar and low in vitamins, minerals, and fiber. A single fast-food meal can approach or exceed the recommended limits on calories, fat, saturated fat, and sodium for a whole day's meals (Figure 5.8).

Even one fast-food meal high in animal fats or animal proteins can cause your arteries to stiffen within hours. Stiffened arteries have difficulty relaxing, and it can take 5 to 6 hours before the artery inflammation caused by stiffening wears off. Endotoxins are believed to be the cause of this inflammation. High cooking temperatures, stomach acids, and digestive enzymes do not destroy endotoxins. This means endotoxins are readily ushered into the small intestine and bloodstream to cause artery inflammation.[70]

The effects of fast food on gut health are greater than you likely realize. Your gut contains a microbiome unique to you, with multiple bacteria to aid digestion that were established within the first few years after your birth. Some of the bacteria used in digestion also help your immune system to fight off unfriendly bacteria, viruses, and diseases. This microbiome can be altered by your gut environment.

Recent research has shown that the high fat and calorie content of fast foods can alter the gut immune system and cause diabetes, obesity, and arteriosclerosis. However, it is never too late to change your diet and restore microbiome balance to increase the presence of "good" bacteria and reduce gut inflammation. If gut inflammation is not resolved, it can lead to the onset of Crohn's disease, irritable bowel syndrome, and possibly acute pancreatitis. Foods that may cause gut inflammation include added processed sugars, trans fatty oils, vegetable and seed oils, refined carbohydrates (with the fiber removed), processed meats, excess alcohol, and diet soda. The underlying point is that an imbalance of microbiota caused by fast food may slow the body's early warning system for chronic infections and diseases.[71]

The USDA dietary guidelines have called for everyone to eat more fruits and vegetables, less red meat, less processed foods, less food additives, and less fast food that is high in calories, salt, and sugar.[1,2,5] Consequently, many fast-food restaurants (and restaurants in general) are offering healthier choices.

The least healthy options are fried fish and fried chicken sandwiches, chicken nuggets, croissants and pastries, onion rings, and large fries. Most fast-food restaurants will give you a nutritional brochure if you ask for it, or the information may be posted; choose the healthiest options.

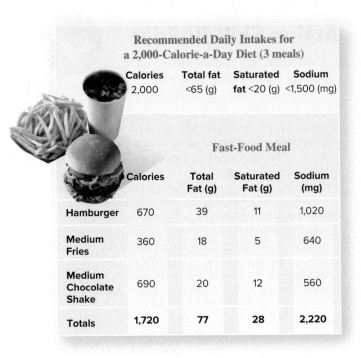

Recommended Daily Intakes for a 2,000-Calorie-a-Day Diet (3 meals)			
Calories	Total fat	Saturated	Sodium
2,000	<65 (g)	fat <20 (g)	<1,500 (mg)

Fast-Food Meal

	Calories	Total Fat (g)	Saturated Fat (g)	Sodium (mg)
Hamburger	670	39	11	1,020
Medium Fries	360	18	5	640
Medium Chocolate Shake	690	20	12	560
Totals	1,720	77	28	2,220

figure 5.8   **A fast-food meal compared with recommended daily intakes.**
(Brand X Pictures/Getty Images)

Microwaving Food

Does microwaving food remove nutrients? Nutrients are best retained by methods that heat food in the shortest amount of time and limit the liquid used in the process. The small amount of water contained in the food is used in a microwave to steam food from the inside out, which effectively retains nutrients.

A common question is whether microwaving food in plastic is safe. Bisphenol (BPA), used to make clear, hard plastic, and phthalates (PHA), used to make plastic soft and pliable, are possible endocrine disrupters that can cause serious health problems such as cancer. Food wrapped in plastic or in plastic containers when microwaved may cause BPA and PHA to leach into food. This leaching is more likely to occur in meats and cheeses than other foods.

Due to leaching concerns, the FDA requires manufacturers to test their containers for microwaved foods. Containers passing this test are labeled with a microwave-safe icon, the words "microwave safe," or similar words to show they are FDA approved for microwave use. Containers without the FDA-safe label only imply that the FDA has not determined whether they are safe. Some styrofoam and polstyrene containers may be safely used, but you should always check the label if you are concerned about the safety of using plastic containers.[72]

Here are some other safety tips for microwaving food:

- Check the container for the FDA safety label.

- Use glass or ceramic containers labeled "safe for microwave use."

- Prevent plastic wrap from touching food to be microwaved.

- Do not use old or scratched containers.

- Vent the container before microwaving the food; for example, lift the edge of the cover.[72]

Food Deserts

For many years, health experts have been looking at lack of access to affordable and nutritious food as a contributing factor in increasing levels of overweight and obesity among low-income people and the related increase in diet-related diseases like diabetes. There are typically many more supermarkets in affluent neighborhoods than in low-income neighborhoods and more convenience stores and fast-food restaurants in low-income neighborhoods than in affluent ones. Wealthy communities have three times as many supermarkets as poor communities. And white neighborhoods have about four times as many supermarkets as predominantly Black neighborhoods.[73] When fresh produce and other healthy foods aren't available, people cannot choose a healthy diet even if they want to.[74,75]

Areas where there are no stores with healthy foods are known as food deserts. The USDA defines **food deserts** as low-income areas where at least 500 people or 33 percent of the population has low access to a supermarket or large grocery store, with "low access" defined as a travel distance of more than 1 mile to a store in urban areas and more than 10 miles in rural areas. Other definitions also take into account whether people in such areas have access to transportation to get to a store. Large supermarket chains like Walmart, Target, and Costco are now opening and expanding their stores in areas designated as food deserts.[74,76]

Food Insecurity on the College Campus

Many people feel that struggling financially as a college student is a rite of passage that builds character. However, for the 45 percent[77] of U.S. college students who experience food insecurity, the struggle can involve deciding whether to buy food or purchase a required textbook. One student described the problem as a need to take "poverty naps" in order to ease hunger pangs.[77] **Food insecurity** is defined as a lack of affordable access to sufficient quality and quantity of healthy food. The Government Accountability Office (GAO) says the most vulnerable college students are first-time students who are raising children, and single parents. The GAO report concludes that food insecurity has become a "college-completion" issue.[78] The increasing challenge of food insecurity on college campuses is driving a collective response by colleges, universities, and state governments to confront a burgeoning problem that is undermining education success for thousands of U.S. college students. See the box "Public Health Is Personal: Hunger on Campus."

FOOD SAFETY AND TECHNOLOGY

Although the FDA is charged with monitoring the safety of the U.S. food supply, consumers, too, need to learn to distinguish between safe and unsafe foods and understand key elements of food safety.

Organic Foods

Plant foods labeled "organic" are grown without synthetic pesticides or fertilizers,[3] and animal foods labeled organic are from animals raised on organic feed without antibiotics or growth hormones. Organic foods appeal to health- and environment-conscious consumers.[1,2] They tend to be about 40 percent more expensive than foods grown using conventional methods, however, and consumers cannot always determine exactly how some foods were grown.[9]

The USDA regulates the use of terms related to organic foods on the labels of meat and poultry products. The label "100% organic" means that all contents are organic; "organic" means that contents are at least 95 percent organic; "made with organic ingredients" means the contents are at least 70 percent organic. Meat and poultry manufacturers that comply with the USDA standards can place the seal "USDA Organic" on their labels.

Although it seems that organic foods ought to be healthier and safer than foods produced conventionally, no research has demonstrated that this is the case. Conventional food products do contain pesticide residues that can be toxic at high doses, but research has not documented ill effects from them at the levels found

food desert
A low-income area where more than 500 people or 33 percent of the population has low access to a supermarket or large grocery store.

food insecurity
A lack of affordable access to sufficient quality and quantity of affordable healthy food.

■ Organic foods aren't necessarily healthier, but organic farming is better for the environment. Many consumers are now choosing organic, locally grown produce and other foods. *(Happycreator/Shutterstock)*

Public Health Is Personal

Hunger on Campus

For some time the perception by many public policy makers that college students are all members of a privileged class has hidden the problem of food insecurity on college campuses. College students facing food insecurity are not just low-income adults. Middle-income students who are too affluent for Pell grants and too poor to afford to afford college costs are also struggling with food insecurity. The seriousness of this problem is no longer being ignored, However, fixing it will take a collaborative effort by state governments, college and university administrations, and local communities. Consider the following:

- 45 percent of college students face food insecurity; about a quarter of those have very high levels of food insecurity.

- 32 percent of college students who are food insecure report that this problem has negatively affected their education; for example, they have missed class, dropped a course, or been unable to buy a required textbook.

- College students who are food insecure are more likely to have difficulty paying rent or utilities.

- Feeding America, a national nonprofit network of food banks, estimates that almost 50 percent of its clients are college students.

The rising cost of college education, decreased state funding, increased enrollments of low-income students, and the growing number of nontraditional students struggling to balance education, family responsibilities, work, and academics have fueled the rise of food insecurity on campus. Some college students have confronted the problem on their own. At Columbia University, for example, students created a phone app called Swipes that enables students on meal plans to forego a meal and swipe in a student not on the meal plan, who then gets a free meal in the dining hall. Share Meals is another program that enables college students to donate extra dining hall meals to students in need. Colleges and universities are also creating campus food pantries in partnership with the College and University Food Bank Alliance, campus community gardens, and food recovery programs. More than 700 colleges and universities are members of the partnership.

Some colleges and universities are exploring meal-plan scholarships for low-income students, redistributing leftover food from college dining halls and catered events, making students eligible for food stamps, and lobbying for national and state student funding to cover living expenses and not just tuition. Sedexo USA, for example, one of the primary college dining hall operators, implemented a pilot program at Northern Arizona University to alert students in need of available food left over from catered events.

The movement to confront college student security originally focused mostly on food banks. Today's efforts are zeroing in on prevention, mostly at community and state colleges since they register more low-income students. Many states, for example, are now using the Supplemental Nutrition Assistance Program (SNAP) to help fight college food insecurity. Advocates want SNAP benefits to be redeemable at campus dining halls and stores. The Debt-Free College Act, reintroduced in 2019, would expand the definition of college costs to include both tuition and living costs. Legislative advocates are also petitioning Congress to expand the National School Lunch program to higher education students.

The profile of college students today is very different from what it was in generations past. Ensuring access to an affordable college education is essential for low-income students. It is also essential that, once enrolled, these students are not forced to sacrifice their academic careers due to an inability to meet their basic nutrition needs. Student hunger on college campuses is a public health problem, and one that is no longer hidden.

McGraw Hill connect

Sources: Laterman, K. (2019). Tuition or dinner? Nearly half of college students surveyed in a new report are going hungry. The New York Times. Retrieved from https://www.nytimes.com/2019/05/02/nyregion/hunger-college-food-insecurity.html; Students Against Hunger. (2017). *Report: Hunger on campus.* Retrieved from https://studentsagainsthunger.org/hunger-on-campus; The Atlantic. (2019). Millions of college students are going hungry. Retrieved from https://ww.theatlantic.com/education/archive/2019/01/college-student-hunger/579877/

in foods, nor is there any evidence that people who consume organic food are healthier than those who don't.[1,2]

What has been documented is that organic farming is beneficial to the environment. It helps maintain biodiversity of crops; it replenishes the earth's resources; and it is less likely to degrade soil, contaminate water, or expose farm workers to toxic chemicals. As multinational food companies get into the organic food business, however, environment-conscious consumers should look for foods that are not only organic but also locally grown. The average food item currently travels at least 1,500 miles to its destination, requiring massive amounts of oil for transportation. In addition, locally grown food tastes fresher, keeps money in the local economy, and cuts down on the consumption of processed food. The burgeoning popularity of farmers' markets is a sign of growing interest in locally grown food.

Foodborne Illnesses

The CDC estimates that 48 million people in the United States, or about one in six, get sick every year from foodborne illness; 128,000 are hospitalized; and 3,000 die.[79] The CDC and state health departments play a critical role in setting food standards and in inspecting, licensing, and regulating food-related businesses. Federal and state budget reductions have made it more difficult for the CDC and state health departments to effectively meet these responsibilities. Foodborne illnesses may be caused by food intoxication or by food infection; both types are commonly referred to as *food poisoning.*

Food poisoning causes flulike symptoms such as diarrhea, abdominal pain, vomiting, fever, and chills. More serious complications can include rheumatoid arthritis, kidney or heart disease, meningitis, *hemolytic uremic syndrome* (HUS), and death. Raw or undercooked sushi and other seafood is of special concern. Anisakiasis, for example, is caused by eating raw or undercooked fish infected by a parasitic worm that attaches to the esophagus, stomach, or intestine causing GI pain, nausea, and vomiting. *Vibrio vulnificus* is also a bacterium of concern commonly found in seafood from coastal ocean waters. The CDC estimates that 15 to 30 percent of infections caused by *V. vulnificus*, sometimes referred to as flesh-eating bacteria, are fatal.[80] Shellfish and oysters are common culprits for *V. vulnificus*. These general symptoms are cause for seeking immediate medical attention:

- Bloody diarrhea or pus in the stool
- Fever that lasts more than 48 hours
- Faintness, rapid heart rate, or nausea when standing up suddenly
- Significant drop in the frequency of urination[5]

Food intoxication occurs when a food is contaminated by natural toxins or by microbes that produce toxins. Botulism is an example of food intoxication. When food has been contaminated with the botulism bacterium and then improperly prepared or stored, the bacterium releases a dangerous and potentially fatal toxin. Warning signs of botulism poisoning are double vision, weak muscles, difficulty swallowing, and difficulty breathing.[1,2] Immediate medical treatment is needed.

Food infection is caused by disease-causing microorganisms, or pathogens, that have contaminated the food. Some commonly contaminated foods are ground beef, chicken, turkey, salami, hot dogs, ice cream, lettuce and other greens, sprouts, cantaloupe, and apple cider. Leafy green vegetables are the top source for food infection, causing about one in five cases. Half of food infections are attributed to fruits and vegetables. Most vegetable-related food infections come from norovirus, which is most often spread by cooks and food handlers. This means food infection is usually caused by unsanitary food production or preparation and not by the food itself. Although vegetable-related food infections are the most common, most deaths (one in five) are caused by poultry consumption.[81]

In addition to norovirus, three other common pathogens that cause food infection are *Escherichia coli*, salmonella, and campylobacter. *E. coli* occurs naturally in the intestines of humans and animals. Raw beef, raw fruits and vegetables, leafy greens, sprouts, and unpasteurized juices and cider are the foods most commonly contaminated by it. One strain, *E. coli* 0157:H7, is especially dangerous because it can cause hemolytic urea syndrom (HUS), which can lead to kidney failure, a potentially fatal condition. The CDC estimates that *E. coli* 0157:H7 causes nearly 73,000 illnesses each year in the United States and kills 250 to 500 people.[79,82] Young children and older adults are particularly at risk. *E. coli* is a hearty microbe, thriving in moist environments for weeks and on kitchen countertops for days. One study found that 72 percent of grocery carts tested had fecal matter on them, and 50 percent had *E. coli*. After multiple trips to the grocery store, reusable shopping bags can become a "bacterial swamp"; they should be cleaned after each use.[79,81]

Salmonella enteritis can contaminate raw eggs, poultry and meat, fruits and vegetables, and other foods. Eggs containing salmonella enteritis are the number-one cause of food poisoning outbreaks in the nation. The best way to prevent salmonella infection is to thoroughly cook eggs, chicken, and other foods to kill the bacterium. Avoid eating raw or undercooked eggs, such as in raw cake batter or cookie dough, salad dressings, and eggnog.[83,84] Federal safeguards implemented in 2012 were expected to reduce salmonella infections by 80,000 per year and deaths by 30 per year. The safeguards mandate rodent control programs on egg-producing farms and require eggs to be refrigerated during storage. The CDC reported a 9 percent drop of salmonella infections in 2018.[85]

Many people do not realize that pet food can contain salmonella. Anyone with an impaired immune system is very vulnerable to salmonella infections and should use extra caution when handling pet foods. This includes young children, whose immune systems are still developing, and older adults, whose immune systems become compromised with age. To protect against potential salmonella infection, make sure that canned or bagged dry pet food product has no visible signs of damage to packaging, such as dents, tears, or discoloration. After handling pet food, wash your hands thoroughly before preparing, serving, or eating other food. Children under the age of 5 years should not be allowed to touch dry pet foods and should be kept away from pet feeding areas.[83,84]

Campylobacter occurs in raw or undercooked poultry, meat, and shellfish, in unpasteurized milk, and in contaminated water. Campylobacter from contaminated poultry can spread when juices from packages spill onto kitchen surfaces and other foods; it can also be spread by hand.[79] Campylobacter and salmonella together cause

food intoxication
A kind of food poisoning in which a food is contaminated by natural toxins or by microbes that produce toxins.

food infection
A kind of food poisoning in which a food is contaminated by disease-causing microorganisms, or pathogens.

Clean

- Before you handle food, wash your hands for 20 seconds with soap and running water.
- Wash cutting boards, countertops, and cooking utensils after each use. Clean sponges and dish towels regularly with a bleach solution.
- Wash fruits and vegetables, but not meat, poultry, or eggs.

Separate

- Use separate cutting boards and plates for produce and for meat, poultry, seafood, and eggs.
- Keep meat, poultry, seafood, and eggs separate from all other foods at the grocery.
- Keep meat, poultry, seafood, and eggs separate from all other foods in the refrigerator.

Cook

- Because the bacteria that cause food poisoning multiply quickest between 40° and 140° F, use a food thermometer to be sure food cooked in the oven or on top of the stove is done.
- Microwave food to 165° F or above. Let the food sit for a few minutes if the directions call for it. The extra time lets heat reach the colder areas of the food.
- Never thaw or marinate foods on the counter. Thaw meat in the refrigerator, in cold water, or in the microwave. Marinate food in the refrigerator.

Chill

- Refrigerate perishable food, including leftovers, within 2 hours, or within 1 hour if temperature is above 90° F. Store leftovers in shallow containers to facilitate cooling.
- The refrigerator temperature should be 40° F or below, and the freezer at 0° F. Don't pack your refrigerator too full because cool air must flow freely to keep food safe.
- Throw food out before it goes bad; harmful bacteria start multiplying before food starts getting moldy or sour smelling. Consult the Storage Times chart at www.foodsafety.gov/keep/charts/storagetimes.html.
- In a power outage, food in the refrigerator is usually safe (under 40°) for 4 hours; food in a full freezer will stay frozen for 48 hours, and in a half full freezer for 24 hours. To maintain the cold temperatures, keep refrigerator and freezer doors closed as much as possible. For the length of time specific foods are safe above 40° F, see USDA Food Safety and Inspection Service's chart at www.fsis.usda.gov/wps/portal/fsis/topics/food-safety-education/get-answers/food-safety-fact-sheets/emergency-preparedness/keeping-food-safe-during-an-emergency/CT_Index.

figure 5.9   Food safety in the kitchen.
((Close up handwashing): Dave & Les Jacobs/Getty Images; (Diced peppers on cutting board): Tarek El Sombati/Getty Images; (Meat thermometer): Alex Cao/Photodisc/Getty Images; (Refrigerator interior): New Africa/Shutterstock)
Sources: FoodSafety.gov, U.S. Department of Health and Human Services. (n.d.). Check your steps. *FoodSafety.gov.* Retrieved from www.foodsafety.gov/keep/basics/index.html; USDA FSIS. (2013). *Keeping food safe during an emergency.* Retrieved from www.fsis.usda.gov/wps/portal/fsis/topics/food-safety-education/get-answers/food-safety-fact-sheets/emergency-preparedness/keeping-food-safe-during-an-emergency/CT_Index.

80 percent of the illnesses and 75 percent of the deaths associated with meat and poultry practices.[79,83,84]

Clostridium difficile has become a serious bacterial threat. *C. difficile* is a hypervirulent bacteria strain that is becoming more resistant to medical management, particularly penicillin treatment. Until recently, it was viewed as mainly a hospital-acquired infection, but today meat is seen as another potential culprit. The bacteria have been found in chicken, turkey, beef, and pork. In fact, the United States has the highest rate of *C. difficile* meat contamination in the world. The general recommendation is to cook meat to an internal temperature of at least 71° C (175° F). But the *C. difficile* bacteria can survive two hours at that temperature. Moreover, alcohol-based hand sanitizers kill only 0.01 percent of the *C. difficile* bacteria.[9] Why should we be concerned? *C. difficile* can cause toxic megacolon, which has a 50 percent survival rate.

Medical treatment may require removal of the colon to prevent death.[86]

Although only about 20 percent of food poisoning cases originate at home, the best defense against foodborne illness is the use of safe food preparation and storage practices in your own kitchen (Figure 5.9).

Recent foodborne illness and salmonella outbreaks, including those implicating tainted chicken from California, cucumbers from Mexico, tuna from multiple states, and *Clostridium perfringens* in Ohio, have also prompted continued food safety concerns. Until passage of the Country-of-Origin Law (COOL) in 2009, consumers had little idea where everyday foods originated. COOL requires retailers to notify consumers of the country of origin of common unprocessed foods such as raw beef, veal, lamb, vegetables, frozen fruits, and many other foods. However, processed foods are not included under COOL; for example, raw pork chops have to be labeled, but ham and bacon do not. Butcher shops selling meat and/or seafood are also exempt.[87]

Are food trucks and food vendors safe? Food trucks and food vendors are required to be licensed so that local health departments can track them for inspections. Most operators are required to post their licenses on the window so that they can be easily seen by customers. Some states require operators to post their inspection grade on the window as well.

Illegal operators are less likely to follow food safety laws, so here are some other red flags you need to check: Food handlers should be wearing gloves and changing them frequently to prevent bacteria cross-contamination. In cities that do not require food handlers to wear gloves, they are required to wash their hands frequently. You can get a good idea of hand cleanliness by looking at someone's fingernails. Dangling hair is another red flag. Hot food should be served hot and not lukewarm. Cold foods such as salads should feel like they were just taken out of the refrigerator.

The safety of food served at professional sports stadiums is also a concern. Rat infestations, ice machines with mold, undercooked meat, food stored at unsafe temperatures, and food workers not wearing sanitary gloves when handling food have all been reported. ESPN's Outside the Lines inspection of 107 North American arenas and stadiums found 28 percent of concessions had at least one critical or major health violation. The pressure to serve high volumes of food quickly has made arenas and stadiums places of high risk to consumers for foodborne diseases such as *E. coli*, salmonella, and listeria. Inspection standards vary by state in scrutinizing food operations, defining violations, and penalties for violations.

Food service operators at arenas and stadiums may use professional vendors such as Aramark, or use nonprofit organizations. College stadiums often rely on food service volunteers, whose training is often lacking. Although there have been no reported epidemics of foodborne outbreaks at professional or college arenas or stadiums, there have been numerous anecdotal complaints. Consumers should have access to information about violations, and one suggestion is to post a letter grade on concession stands based on inspection reports. This is done at professional arenas and stadiums in Toronto. Consumers are likely to frequent high-grade food concessions and bypass those with low grades.[88]

Genetically Modified Foods

Farmers, scientists, and breeders have long been tinkering with the genetic makeup of plants and animals to breed organisms with desirable traits, a process known as *selective breeding*. Compared with modern techniques, however, selective breeding is slow and imprecise. Using biotechnology to produce **genetically modified (GM) organisms** is a faster and more refined process. Genetic modification uses the addition, deletion, or reorganization of an organism's genes to change that organism's protein production. Many crops have already been genetically modified, and 60 percent of processed foods currently sold in supermarkets contain one or more GM ingredients.[5]

Proponents of GM crops and animals say we must develop new agricultural technologies that increase crop and animal productivity and support food growers and producers economically while not harming the environment. They see genetic modification as a promising agricultural technology that may meet these needs, and many in the food and biotechnology industries have hailed the benefits of GM organisms.[5]

On the other hand, a growing number of consumers, animal rights supporters, national consumer watchdog organizations, and environmentalists have expressed concerns about GM foods. They fear that agriculture driven by biotechnology without restraint will destroy natural ecosystems, create new viruses, increase cruelty to animals, and reduce biodiversity.[5] They have called for all foods containing GM ingredients to be so labeled. Connecticut and Maine have legislated mandatory GM labeling, and about 30 other states are also considering it. An extensive investigation of GM crops by *The New York Times* found they did not increase food yield per acre in the United States and Canada or result in less overall use of chemical pesticides. This investigation also established that empirical evidence does not support the existence of harmful effects from eating GM foods.[89]

The safety of food products produced by biotechnology is assessed by the FDA's Center for Food Safety and Applied Nutrition. To date, the center has held that GM foods do not require any special safety testing—nor do they have to be labeled as GM foods—unless they differ significantly from foods already in use.[1,2]

North Americans enjoy the safest and most nutritious food supply in the world. We also enjoy immense choice in what we eat. With choice comes responsibility—the responsibility to be informed, to make wise decisions, and to consume foods that promote health and prevent disease. After reading this chapter, you have sufficient information to make nutrition choices that support your own lifelong health and, by extension, the well-being of society at large. We encourage you to make those healthy choices!

The Future of Food

Frozen cream deserts were introduced into the U.S. diet in the late 1930s. Foods continue to evolve and new tastes developed. What can we expect for the future of food by 2028? See the box "Starting the Conversation: The Future of Food."

genetically modified (GM) organisms Organisms whose genetic makeup has been changed to produce desirable traits.

Starting the Conversation
The Future of Food

Fruits and vegetables in the past have been subject to selective breeding and intensive farming that often comes at a nutrient cost measured in lost minerals such as calcium and iron. Food scientists now predict, however, that by 2028 genetics and bio-molecular science will have mastered the art of inserting DNA from one plant organism into another to acquire certain food traits. The more controversial technique of transplanting DNA from totally different organisms will create new botanical edibles that contain more protein or healthy omega fats. Plant-based meat and animal-free milk are likely new products.

By 2028, neurogastronomy will merge our understandings of neurology and of food. Restaurants will use aromatic mists, subtle sound effects, and controlled lighting to enhance our perception of the taste of food. Augmented reality head-sets to superimpose digital imagery at home could transfer the feeling of being by the ocean when eating fish, or camping outdoors when eating steak. Nanotechnology may be used to develop foods that provide delayed bursts of flavor in the mouth. We can expect ice cream and chocolate products that do not easily melt in the summer sun. Robotic kitchens will not be pie-in-the-sky advancements, either. You may have a robot chef that prepares, cooks, and serves your food. Exotic dishes might even be created with 3-D printers.

Q: Although these advances may be exciting, will you be accepting of a system that depends on genetically engineered foods, patenting, and corporatization of the U. S. food system?

Q: Will technology advances in food production serve to enrich agrochemical corporations at the expense of family farmers, community brick-and-mortar grocery stores, and the environment?

Q: Family farmers have already been hit hard by corporate domination of agriculture. Are Black farmers being hurt more than white farmers? If so, will technology advances in food production aggravate this problem?

Q: Rather than investing in unregulated genetic engineering of food, should we invest in the more transparent and organic production of real food?

Source: Farrimond, S. (2018). The future of food: What we'll eat in 2028. Retrieved from https://www.sciencefocus.com/future-technology/the-future-of-food-what-well-eat-in-2028/

You Make the Call
Does Menu Labeling Change Consumer Behavior?

Many people consume as many as four meals per week outside the home. To reduce rates of obesity and chronic diseases associated with unhealthy diets, the Affordable Care Act required that chain restaurants provide calorie counts on their menus and inform customers that detailed nutrition information is available upon request. The American Heart Association and the American Public Health Association believe that menu labeling will encourage restaurants to serve smaller portions and healthier ingredients. The National Restaurant Association supports the law but opposes adding information beyond calorie content.

Nutrition experts are studying whether menu information influences consumer food choices. Preliminary research suggests that consumers are not more likely to choose healthier menu items when presented with calorie information, because many of them do not know how many calories they should be eating or what constitutes a healthy meal. Although there is considerable public support for menu labeling, empirical evidence suggests that it affects different types of customers differently.

What do you think? Does menu labeling lead consumers to choose healthier food items?

Pros

- Seventy-six percent of U.S. adults claim calorie and nutrient information about restaurant food choices would be at least somewhat useful.
- Nutrition information at point of purchase, whether on food packages in grocery stores or on restaurant menus, provides a convenient and proactive way to enhance nutrition awareness. Currently, most consumers do not seek out nutrition information about food they buy in restaurants.
- Some evidence suggests that menu labeling has little negative revenue impact for restaurants. Many restaurants have actually seen customer satisfaction improve with the provision of healthier food choices.

Cons

- The impact of menu labeling is not uniform. Women are more likely to be influenced by menu labeling than men, and wealthier individuals are more likely to be influenced than poor individuals.

Continued...

Concluded...

- Surveys of menu use suggest that only 15 to 20 percent of customers use point-of-purchase information to make food choice decisions. Taste, price, and convenience are more likely to influence food choices than menu labeling.

- Research on menu labeling suggests it has more influence on what restaurants offer than on what patrons order.

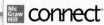

Sources: Robert Wood Johnson Foundation. (2013, June). Impact of menu labeling on consumer behavior: A 2008-2012 updated. *Healthy Eating Research Review:* 1–23; Kriger, J. C., et al. (2013). Menu labeling regulation and calories purchased at chain restaurant. *American Journal of Preventive Medicine, 44*(6): 595–604; NBC News. (2017). Studies show impact of menu calorie counts sometimes in small. Retrieved from http://www.nbcnews.com

In Review

What kinds of nutritional guidelines are established by the federal government?

Used by nutritionists, researchers, and the food industry, the Dietary Reference Intakes (DRIs) encompass four kinds of recommendations: the Estimated Average Requirement (EAR) of nutrients needed by different age groups; the Recommended Dietary Allowance (RDA), which is the average daily amount needed of a particular nutrient; the Tolerable Upper Intake Level (UL), which is the largest amount that can be ingested without risking toxicity; and the Acceptable Macronutrient Distribution Range (AMDR), or the range between the amount of an essential nutrient needed for adequate nutrition and the amount associated with the risk of some kind of chronic disease.

What are the categories of nutrients?

The macronutrients are water, carbohydrates, proteins, and fats. The micronutrients are vitamins and minerals. A balanced diet includes adequate intake of all the nutrients, primarily from nutrient-rich foods (as opposed to dietary supplements). Whole foods and especially plant foods contain additional important substances, such as antioxidants. Room temperature water offers more health benefits than cold water.

How do you plan a healthy diet?

The U.S. diet tends to include too many calories; too much sugar, salt, and fat; and too few vegetables, fruits, and whole foods. The *Dietary Guidelines for Americans* translates the findings of nutritional research into recommendations for healthy eating patterns, and Choose MyPlate customizes these recommendations, based on activity levels and calorie needs. Food labels and restaurant menu information can help people stay within these recommendations. The sell-by labels provide the transparency consumers need to make sure their food is safe, and that good food is not prematurely thrown out.

What are the main nutrition-related concerns currently affecting our society?

Most people in the United States do not eat a very healthy diet compared to what is recommended, and overweight and obesity are significant problems. Current concerns include the overconsumption of soft drinks and salt, food allergies and intolerances, overuse of energy bars and energy drinks, the prevalence of fast food, and the tendency for low-income neighborhoods to be food deserts. Gluten foods are of particular interest to many. Gluten sensitivity may be associated with thyroid health problems. Microwaving food is safe but you should always read the safe for microwave label. Campus food insecurity has become a major public health issue.

What are the main food safety issues?

Although organic foods are sometimes preferable because pesticides can cause health problems, the main safety issue is food poisoning typically caused by pathogens such as *E. coli,* salmonella, and campylobacter. The U.S. food supply is safe overall, but increasing centralization of food production and distribution creates the conditions for widespread outbreaks of foodborne illness from a single source of contamination. A growing concern is the common use of antibiotics in food-producing animals and the spread of antibiotic-resistant bacteria. Another issue of interest to consumers is genetically modified foods. Sports stadium and arena food has been indicated for major food violations causing foodborne disease and food poisoning.

Personal Health Portfolio

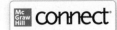

Chapter 5   Assessing Your Diet

For this activity, you will use the diet analysis tool NutritionCalc Plus, available in Connect. Launch NutritionCalc Plus from the Resources list on your Connect course home page, and complete the Profile section. If you are not using Connect, you can google free dietary assessment tools. The USDA discontinued its food tracker tool in 2018. But, you can still track your food in My Food Record and Choose MyPlate Plan to analyze your diet. Your course instructor may also assign an online diet analysis tool.

Part 1 Food Log

Complete the food log provided, recording all the food you eat and drink in one full day. Make sure to include everything you drink—water, soft drinks (even diet), coffee, alcohol, and so on. List the foods you eat and drink and the serving size (1/2 apple, 2 cups of pasta, 24 oz. Diet Mountain Dew, etc.).

Day/Date: _____

Food/Drink item	Serving size/Amount

Part 2 Diet Analysis

Enter the information from your log into the "Intakes" section of NutritionCalc Plus. Once your food intake record is complete, click on the "Reports" section to assess your diet and identify areas where you do and do not meet the recommendations. Use these reports as part of your portfolio to see where you are meeting your goals and to identify diet areas that need improvement. You can also use NutritionCalc Plus to track your diet over time and follow any changes.

CRITICAL THINKING QUESTIONS

1. Analyze how well your food intake for the day matches up to your Choose MyPlate recommendations (use the Choose MyPlate Report). Did you meet your recommendations for milk, meat and beans, vegetables, fruits, and grains?

2. Now analyze your food intake in terms of calories, fat, fiber, sugar, sodium, and cholesterol (use the Bar Graph Report). How did you do in nutrient intake? What nutrients did you get enough of? What nutrients do you need more of?

3. Consider how the socioecological model of health and wellness (see Chapter 1, Figure 1.2) relates to your own life. Describe the specific behavioral and environmental factors that make it easier or more difficult for you to reach your goals of eating healthfully.

4. Based on your analysis, do you think you need to make any dietary changes? Why or why not? If you do need to make changes, what specific dietary modifications do you need to make and how can you realistically achieve them? Consider both behavioral and environmental strategies.

You may want to analyze your diet for a few more days—or even longer—to get a better idea of how well your diet is meeting your nutritional needs.

6 Fitness

Erik Isakson/Blend Images LLC

Ever Wonder...

- how much exercise you should be getting?
- whether shoe insoles sold in drug and grocery stores are effective in preventing stress fractures?
- why icing soft tissue injuries may cause more harm than good?
- how long it takes to burn off the calories gained from a burger and fries?

You're jogging through the airport to catch a connecting flight on your way home for winter break. Your smartphone is blaring your favorite song into your earbuds when a voice from your fitness app suddenly interrupts the music: "5 minutes completed. 0.42 mile. Pace, 5 miles per hour. Calories burned, 45." Smartphone apps are just one of many new devices designed to motivate people to exercise, particularly young adults.

Unfortunately, U.S. adults need a lot of motivation. Although many public health campaigns are aimed at our sedentary habits, the fact is that most people don't exercise. Thirty-four percent of U.S. adults do not participate in any leisure-time physical activity, and only 48 percent get the recommended amount of exercise each week.[1] Less than 20 percent meet the physical activity recommendations for both aerobic and muscle-strengthening activity.[2] Among college students, about 20 percent (males 22.7, females 18.6) meet the recommendations for moderate-intensity cardio or aerobic exercise at least 30 minutes 5 or more days per week, and 27 percent (men 32, women 26) meet vigorous-intensity cardio or aerobic exercise at least 20 minutes 3 days per week. About 46 percent (men 51, women 45) meet the recommendation for a combination of moderate-intensity and vigorous exercise (2 moderate exercise periods = 1 vigorous-intensity exercise period). Recommendations are from the American College of Sports Medicine and the American Heart Association.[3] For details, see the box "Who's at Risk? College Students Meeting Physical Activity Guidelines for Aerobic Activity."

The good news is that there are simple and enjoyable ways to build physical activity into your lifestyle and to increase the amount of exercise you get. This chapter will show you how.

Who's at Risk?

College Students Meeting Physical Activity Guidelines for Aerobic Activity

Why do you think only half of college students meet the 2008 physical activity guidelines (for details, see the section "General Guidelines for Physical Activity")? What does your college do to promote physical activity?

Moderate-intensity cardio or aerobic exercise for at least 30 minutes:

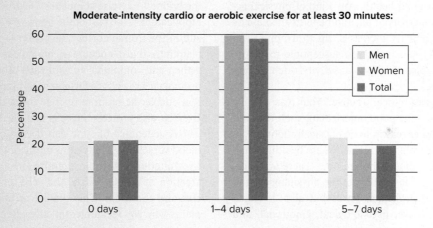

Vigorous-intensity cardio or aerobic exercise for at least 20 minutes:

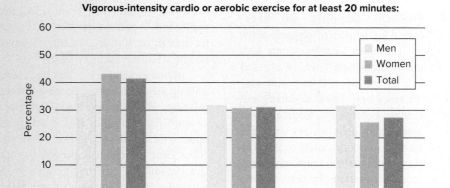

Source: American College Health Association, National College Health Assessment. (2018, Spring). *Reference group executive summary*. Hanover, MD: American College Health Association. Recommendations from the American College of Sports Medicine and the American Heart Association: Moderate-intensity cardio or aerobic exercise for at least 30 minutes on 5 or more days per week, or vigorous-intensity cardio or aerobic exercise for at least 20 minutes on 3 or more days per week.

WHAT IS FITNESS?

Physical fitness, in general, is the ability of the body to respond to the physical demands placed upon it. It is closely related to good health, which is the state of having sufficient energy and vitality to accomplish daily living tasks and leisure-time physical activities without undue fatigue. When we talk about fitness, we are really talking about two different concepts: skill-related fitness and health-related fitness.[4]

Skill-related fitness is the ability to perform specific skills associated with various sports and leisure activities. Components of skill-related fitness include agility, speed, power, balance, coordination, and reaction time. **Health-related fitness** is the ability to perform daily living activities (e.g., shopping for groceries) and other activities with vigor.[5] Components of health-related fitness are cardiorespiratory fitness, musculoskeletal fitness, and body composition. Musculoskeletal fitness, in turn, includes muscular strength, muscular endurance, and flexibility. Shortly, the chapter will look at each of these fitness components in turn.

Benefits of Physical Activity and Exercise

Physical activity—activity that requires any type of movement—is necessary for good health. Any kind of physical activity is better than no activity at all, and benefits increase as the level of physical activity increases, up to a point. Too much physical activity can make you susceptible to injury. **Exercise** is structured, planned physical activity, often carried out to improve fitness.

Why should you be physically active? Your reasons may include having fun, looking good, and feeling good. Beyond these, however, is another reason to be physically active: People who are active are healthier than those who are not.[5] There are benefits not only at the physiological and molecular levels but also in cognitive, psychological, emotional, and economic terms.

physical fitness
The ability of the body to respond to the physical demands placed upon it.

skill-related fitness
The ability to perform specific skills associated with various sports and leisure activities.

health-related fitness
The ability to perform daily living activities with vigor.

physical activity
Activity that requires any type of movement.

exercise
Structured, planned physical activity, often carried out to improve fitness.

Physical Benefits of Exercise
One benefit of physical activity is a longer lifespan: people with moderate to high levels of physical activity live longer than people who are sedentary.[6] Physical activity and exercise improve functioning in just about every body system, from the cardiorespiratory system to the skeletal system to the immune system. A sedentary lifestyle, by contrast, has been associated with 28 percent of deaths from the leading chronic diseases, including cancer, heart disease, osteoporosis, and diabetes, as well as high blood pressure and obesity.[7]

Bones   Bones are living tissue. Young adults expel about 10 percent of bone matter due to bone demineralization after age 30. Exercise makes new developing bone denser and stronger than the bone tissue expelled. But peak bone mass occurs between 25 and 30 years of age. You can gain net bone mass up to about age 30 by working with weights two to three times your body weight. Standard exercise routines after age 30 are not likely to generate increased bone mass.

Weight-bearing exercises such as walking and weight training are essential for bone growth. Non-weight-bearing exercises such as swimming and bike riding do not create sufficient weight load to stimulate bone growth. A 1 to 2 percent increase in bone mass density (BMD) from weight-bearing exercise may seem insignificant, but this increase can offset the decrease in BMD that typically occurs over a 4-year period in postmenopausal women and elderly men. Bottom line: Use weight-bearing exercise to increase your peak bone mass before age 30, then continue these exercises to slow the loss of bone mass after age 30.[6]

Cognitive Benefits of Exercise
Although there is no conclusive evidence to suggest that short-term exercise significantly improves cognitive functioning, some studies on animals and humans suggest that physical activity can be beneficial to the brain.[7,8] Exercise stimulates the growth of new cells in the hippocampus (the part of the brain where learning is centered) and in the frontal cortex (the center for decision making and planning). It also encourages brain cells to branch out, join together, and communicate with each other in new ways, and it prompts nerve cells to form denser, more interconnected webs that enable the brain to operate more quickly and efficiently. Exercise also protects the cells that line blood vessels.

A sedentary lifestyle can decrease blood flow to small blood vessels in deep regions of the brain that promote executive functions. Aerobic exercise, in contrast, increases the creation of mitochondria, the cells' energy furnace, in muscles and the brain. This impact on mitochondria likely explains why you feel a mental edge after aerobic exercise. The increased heart rate we experience from exercise facilitates the ability to grow new brain cells.[7] More physically active people are 20 percent less likely to be diagnosed with dementia than those who are inactive. Cognitive function in active people also declines more slowly.[9]

Running, aerobic cycling, yoga, and even nonstrenuous walking may also improve learning, concentration, and abstract reasoning. Basically, any type of exercise is good for cognitive health.[10] Exercising just after a study session can help you to retain information you learned. There are two reasons for this effect. First, exercise can increase the neurotransmitter acetylcholine, which is important for memory. Second, the effects of physical arousal on the brain are similar to those of strong emotion, and emotional memories tend to be long-lasting.[10]

Psychological and Emotional Benefits of Exercise
Moderate to intense levels of physical activity have been shown to influence mood, decrease the risk of depression and anxiety, relieve stress, and improve overall quality of life.[11] (In contrast,

Life Stories

Colleen: Obsessed with Running

Colleen is an intense, high-achieving perfectionist and a running devotee. She began running in high school, and by the time she was a college sophomore, Colleen tried to run at least 5 miles every day, usually alone. Colleen tried to get to bed no later than 9 p.m. so that she could get her run in before her early morning classes. She ran even when the temperature was below freezing and the roads were covered in black ice. She ran when she had a cold and when her back and legs ached from fatigue. On days she didn't run, she felt irritable and anxious.

Colleen's family and friends were supportive of her running at first and impressed with her determination, though they weren't surprised, because Colleen did everything all-out. But by the middle of her sophomore year, people were becoming concerned about her preoccupation with daily runs. She would miss family and social events if they interfered with her running schedule or her early-to-bed routine. She didn't have time to date or to socialize with her friends. When she wasn't running she was planning her next run, reading running blogs, or checking out running gear online.

When confronted about her preoccupation with running, Colleen responded, "Running is my life. It gives me my sense of identity. I'm proud of having goals and being committed to a healthy activity. A lot of people don't get any exercise at all. What's wrong with trying to be healthy?"

In April, Colleen was diagnosed with stress fractures in both feet. She had no choice but to stop running for a few months. In the first week after the diagnosis, she was anxious and on edge, beset by worries and feelings of dread and hopelessness. She started having crying spells and felt reluctant to leave her room. She realized that the only time she really felt in control of her life was when she was running.

Concerned about her feelings, Colleen made an appointment with a counselor at the campus health clinic. The counselor told her that if running was interfering significantly with her personal and school life, it had become a mental health issue. He told her about recent research suggesting that running can become an addiction. Like cocaine or opium, running can cause a spike in levels of the neurotransmitter dopamine, stimulating reward centers in the brain and giving the runner a sensation of pleasure. What Colleen was going through was like experiencing withdrawal from a drug.

The first step in overcoming any addiction is acknowledging the problem. This was hard for Colleen to do, and it was only in her third session that she was able to admit to herself that running had become a problem for her. With more counseling, she was able to develop a more balanced approach to her physical, emotional, and psychological health.

- What do you think could cause healthy activities to become unhealthy addictions?

- What do you think are the signs that an activity has become an addiction?

- If you had to speculate, what needs do you think Colleen was trying to meet by running so much? What do you think she was trying to avoid?

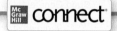

excessive exercise has the potential to become addictive; see the box "Life Stories: Colleen: Obsessed with Running.") Although biological explanations have been proposed for the improved sense of well-being associated with physical activity, other explanations are improved self-esteem, improved quality of sleep, and more opportunities for social interaction.

The helpful effects of exercise on mood have been well publicized; however, the beneficial impact on mental illness is not as well accepted by researchers, health care providers, or health insurance companies. Empirical evidence supports the idea that exercise is as effective in treating mild or moderate depression as are medication and counseling.[11] Some health experts conjecture that depression is a stress management disorder. Regular exercise may rewire both the brain and the immune system to better manage physical and mental stress. Research also supports exercise as mimicking the chemical effects of drugs used to treat depression. Severe depression is associated with atrophy of brain cells in the amygdala, hippocampus, and prefrontal cortex. Exercise may increase levels of brain-derived neurotrophic factor (BDNF), a protein that offsets atrophy of brain cells.

Scientists are currently looking at the benefits of "green exercise"—exercising outdoors in natural settings. Research findings suggest that if you walk, run, or hike in a green space area, in the city or countryside, you are more likely to feel better all around than if you exercise indoors. Green exercise replaces the multitasking of everyday life with the sounds, smells, and colors of the natural landscape. Benefits of green exercise may include improved mood and overall well-being, as well as reduced feelings of anger, tension, confusion, and depression. In one study, green exercisers performed better on tests requiring memory and attention, had lower blood pressure, and felt more spiritually connected than people who did not exercise outdoors. "Blue exercising" by the ocean or large bodies of water has also been shown to be especially beneficial for emotional and spiritual health.[12]

Benefits of Exercise at the Molecular Level Research is challenging what scientists believed were the reasons exercise is beneficial in preventing heart disease—decreasing blood pressure, lowering LDL levels, increasing HDL levels, and creating collateral blood vessel branches to the heart. It has been found that the impact of exercise on blood pressure is marginal. However, moderate or vigorous aerobic exercise has been shown to increase the size of LDL particles and decrease the number of small LDLs.[13,14]

149

Exercise also lowers blood glucose (blood sugar). Your liver, pancreas, and skeletal muscles work in concert so that each part of your body receives glucose as needed while you are at rest or active. The demands that exercise makes on skeletal muscles increase their demand for glucose, and prolonged exercise enables muscle fibers to use glucose more efficiently. This efficiency helps your body keep blood glucose levels between 70 and 140 milligrams/deciliter (mg/dL). Blood glucose needs to be above 70 mg/dL to provide your brain with sufficient energy, but levels above 140 mg/dL, if sustained, can clog your arteries and cause cells to die prematurely.

Stable blood glucose levels are especially important for people with type 2 diabetes. Exercise makes muscle cells more sensitive to insulin, which helps reduce the workload on your pancreas in maintaining stable blood glucose levels. Current research also suggests that exercise removes glucose from the blood by stimulating muscle cells to make a protein called PGC-1a. This finding may provide a valuable new pathway for treating people with diabetes.[13]

An overview of the health benefits associated with physical activity is presented in Figure 6.1.

General Guidelines for Physical Activity

In 2018 the Department of Health and Human Services (HHS) issued its second edition of the widely accepted set of physical activity guidelines aimed at promoting and maintaining health and preventing chronic diseases and premature mortality. These guidelines recommend that adults should accumulate one of the following:

- 150 minutes (2 hours 30 minutes) of moderate-intensity exercise each week. For additional health benefits, increase moderate-intensity aerobic physical activity to 300 minutes (5 hours) each week.

- 75 minutes (1 hour 15 minutes) of vigorous-intensity exercise. For additional health benefits, increase vigorous-intensity aerobic physical activity to 150 minutes (2 hours, and 30 minutes) each week.

- An equivalent amount of both moderate-intensity and vigorous-intensity exercise.

- Moving more and sitting less throughout the day.

- Muscle-strengthening activities of moderate or greater intensity for all major muscle groups at least 2 or more days a week.[14,15]

People who meet these guidelines have a lower risk of heart disease, type 2 diabetes, breast cancer, and colon cancer.[16] These are minimum recommendations; exercise levels beyond the minimum can confer additional health benefits, such as preventing unwanted weight gain.[17] In general, people with disabilities should follow the same recommendations as people without disabilities.

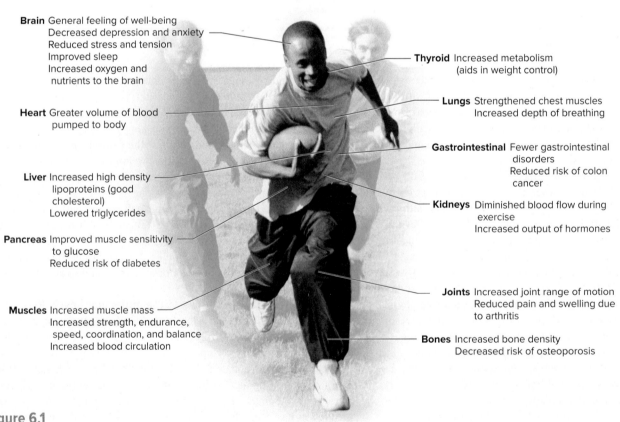

figure 6.1
(Photodisc/Getty Images)

Table 6.1 **Examples of Light-, Moderate-, and Vigorous-Intensity Activities**

Light	Moderate	Vigorous
Slow walking	Walking 3.0 mph	Walking 4.5 mph
Canoeing	Cycling leisurely	Cycling moderately
Golf with cart	Golf, no cart	Jogging 7 mph
Croquet	Table tennis	Tennis singles
Fishing—sitting	Slow swimming	Moderate swimming
Billiards	Boat sailing	Volleyball
Darts	Housework/gardening	Basketball
Playing cards	Calisthenics	Competitive soccer
Walking the dog	Tennis doubles	Rope skipping
Grocery shopping	Yoga	Martial arts
Laundry	Playing with children	Snowboarding

Source: American College of Sports Medicine. (2017). *Quantity and quality of exercise for developing and maintaining cardiorespiratory, musculoskeletal, and neuromotor fitness in apparently healthy adults: Guidance for prescribing exercise.* Retrieved from http://journals.lww.com/ acsm-msse/pages/default.asps.

The American College of Sports Medicine (ACSM) released its own guidelines in 2011, which are similar to the HHS guidelines. The ACSM recommends that adults do moderate-intensity exercise for at least 30 to 60 minutes on 5 or more days a week (for a minimum of 150 minutes of moderate-intensity exercise a week), or vigorous-intensity exercise for 20 to 60 minutes on 3 or more days a week (for a minimum of 75 minutes of vigorous-intensity exercise a week). One continuous session or multiple sessions of at least 10 minutes can be used to meet the accumulated minute objective.[18]

Moderate-intensity activity is defined as activity that noticeably accelerates the heart rate and causes you to break a sweat; an example is a brisk walk (see Table 6.1 for more examples). Vigorous-intensity activity causes rapid breathing and a substantial increase in heart rate, as exemplified by jogging. A broad indicator of vigorous intensity is being able to say only a few words without taking a breath while exercising. Moderate- and vigorous-intensity activities are recommended in addition to the light-intensity activities associated with daily living.[17]

The HHS and ACSM guidelines also include recommendations for improving muscular strength and endurance; we describe these recommendations later in the chapter. The Physical Activity Guidelines Advisory committee met in 2017–2018 to investigate the relationship between sedentary behavior and all-cause mortality. Physical activity guidelines will be reevaluated based on this investigation. The Personal Health Portfolio activity for this chapter will help you assess your current level of physical activity.

COMPONENTS OF HEALTH-RELATED FITNESS

Fitness training programs can improve each of the components of health-related fitness—cardiorespiratory fitness, musculoskeletal fitness (muscular strength, muscular endurance, and flexibility), and body composition. In this section, we discuss each component separately.

The key to fitness training is the body's ability to adapt to increasing demands by becoming more fit—that is, as a general rule, the more you exercise, the fitter you become. The amount of exercise, called *overload,* is significant, however. If you exercise too little, your fitness level won't improve. If you exercise too much, you may be susceptible to injury. When you are designing an exercise program, you need to think about four dimensions of your exercise sessions that affect overload:

- Frequency (number of sessions per week)
- Intensity (level of difficulty of each exercise session)
- Time (duration of each exercise session)
- Type (type of exercise in each exercise session)

You can remember these dimensions with the acronym FITT.

Cardiorespiratory Fitness

Cardiorespiratory fitness is the ability of the heart and lungs to efficiently deliver oxygen and nutrients to the body's muscles and cells via the bloodstream. Cardio fitness should be at the center of any fitness program. It is developed by activities that use the large muscles of the body in continuous movement, such as jogging, running, cycling, swimming, cross-country skiing, and aerobic dance.

Cardiorespiratory Training Benefits of cardiorespiratory training are an increase in the oxygen-carrying capacity of the blood, improved extraction of oxygen from the bloodstream by muscle cells, an increase in the amount of blood the heart pumps with each heartbeat, and increased speed of recovery back to a resting level after exercise. Cardiorespiratory training improves muscle and liver functioning and decreases resting heart rate, resting blood pressure, and heart rate at any work level.

How do you develop a cardiorespiratory training program to improve your level of fitness? Start with the FITT acronym (frequency, intensity, time, and type of activity).

Frequency In general, you must exercise at least twice a week to experience improvements in cardiorespiratory functioning. The ideal frequency is three times a week. Exercising five or six times a week is appropriate if weight control is a primary concern. However, there are potential negative consequences if you do the same cardio training every day of the week. First, you may experience overtraining syndrome, which exercise experts refer to as your body running on "empty." Overtraining can cause fatigue, mood swings, immune system dysfunction, and overuse muscle injuries. Second, skipping an exercise recovery period increases your risk of cardiovascular problems. Third, you may be causing muscle imbalance by doing the same cardio exercise every day. It is advisable to build a rest day into your exercise routine, and, at the very least, diversify the type of cardio activity or decrease the cardio intensity.[19,20]

The physical activity guidelines of the American Heart Association (AHA) advise that the health benefits of exercise can be attained in small doses of at least 10 minutes. According to the AHA, the total accumulation of exercise minutes is associated with health benefits, not the duration of a single session. The underlying premise is that you should sit less and move more. For example, desk-bound college students should get up and move at least 2 minutes every 30 minutes. The implementation of the AHA physical activity guidelines is supported by the Office of Disease Prevention and Health Promotion's Move Your Way campaign, which you can find at https://health.gov/PAGuidelines/.[21]

Intensity The point at which you are stressing your cardiorespiratory system for optimal benefit but not overdoing it is called your **target heart rate (THR) zone**. The ACSM recommends that people set their THR at 55 to 80 percent of their maximum heart rate (MHR)—that is, that they exercise at 55 to 80 percent of their maximum heart rate. The most accurate way to find your THR zone is to calculate your **heart rate reserve (HRR)**, or the difference between your MHR and your resting heart rate (RHR):

1. To find your RHR, take your pulse at the carotid (neck) or radial (wrist) artery while you are at rest. Use your middle finger or forefinger or both when taking your pulse; do not use your thumb because it has a pulse of its own. Take your pulse for 15 seconds and multiply by 4.

2. To find your MHR, subtract your age from 220.

3. To calculate your THR objective, use the maximal HRR formula. The THR is usually 60 to 80 percent for young adults and 55 to 70 percent for older adults. Here is the HRR formula:

$$THR = X\% \, (MHR - RHR) + RHR$$

Example: Serena is 20 years old and just starting a cardiorespiratory training program. Her THR goal is 60 to 80 percent, and she has an RHR of 70. For a 60 percent threshold, her THR is calculated as follows:

$$0.6(200 - 70) + 70 = 0.6(130) + 70 = 78 + 70 = 148$$

For an 80 percent threshold, the THR is calculated as follows:

$$0.8(200 - 70) + 70 = 0.8(130) + 70 = 104 + 70 = 174$$

Thus, Serena's THR zone is between 148 and 174.

A quicker way to determine your target heart rate is to use the maximum heart rate formula: MHR (220 minus your age) times your desired intensity. For example, if you are 20 years old and want to work out at 60 to 80 percent intensity, subtract 20 from 220 and multiply by 0.60 and 0.80. Your target heart rate zone is 120 to 160.

Heart rate alone should not determine your workout intensity: To ensure that intensity is not too low or too high, use the breathing test and perceived exertion test. The breathing test is simply to see whether you can speak in complete sentences without breathing hard as you exercise. The perceived exertion test is a subjective measure of how you feel when you are exercising. Moderate intensity would be perceived as "somewhat hard." The feeling test may also be of value. This test assesses pleasantness/unpleasantness for self-regulating exercise intensity.

cardiorespiratory fitness
The ability of the heart and lungs to efficiently deliver oxygen and nutrients to the body's muscles and cells via the bloodstream.

target heart rate (THR) zone
The range of exercise intensity that allows you to stress your cardiorespiratory system for optimal benefit without overloading the system.

heart rate reserve (HRR)
The difference between maximum heart rate and resting heart rate.

Time (Duration) Generally, exercise sessions should last from 15 to 60 minutes; 30 minutes is a good goal. Duration and intensity of exercise have an inverse relation with each other so that a shorter, higher intensity session can give your cardiorespiratory system the same workout as a longer, lower intensity session.

Type of Activity *Aerobic exercise* is brisk physical activity that increases the circulation of oxygen through the blood vessels and is associated with increased respiration. There are two types of aerobic exercises: (1) activities that require sustained intensity with little variability in heart rate response, such as running and rowing, and (2) stop-and-go activities that do not require continuous intensity, such as basketball, soccer, and tennis. Stop-and-go activities usually have to be done for a longer period of time than do sustained-intensity activities before they confer cardiorespiratory benefits. Both types of activity can be part of a cardiorespiratory training program.

Training Progression To continue to receive benefit from exercise, you need to adjust your level of activity by altering duration and intensity every so often. After you have obtained a satisfactory level of cardiorespiratory fitness, you can maintain your fitness level by continuing the same level of workout.[22]

High-Intensity Interval Training (HIT) The primary reason people give for not exercising is lack of time. HIT is a cardio program that provides a way to receive fitness benefits in less time by alternating high- and low-intensity exercise. Research has shown that 20 minutes of HIT and 40 minutes of continuous aerobic training have similar benefits. In HIT your body is never given the chance to plateau; getting used to one setting is common in most forms of cardio activity.[23]

The typical HIT workout uses 30 seconds of "hard" exercise followed by a 30-, 60-, or 90-second "easy" interval and repeats the combination 10 times. *Hard* (high intensity) is defined as exercise that gets your heart rate up to 80 to 90 percent of MHR, or 8 to 9 on the perceived exertion scale. *Easy* (low-intensity) activity achieves 40 to 50 percent MHR, or 5 on the perceived exertion scale. Another definition of *hard* is simply getting out of your comfort zone. For example, when walking across campus, go at a very fast rate (4.2 to 4.4 mph) for a block, and then slow down to 3.5 mph for a block. If it is hard for you to talk when walking, then you are out of your comfort zone.[24]

Developing Your Own Program To develop your own regular cardiorespiratory training program, start out slowly to avoid injury and gradually build up your endurance. If you have any medical conditions, or if you have been sedentary and are over the age of 40, see your physician for a checkup before starting. To ensure that you will stick with your program, select activities you enjoy and that are compatible with the constraints of your schedule, budget, and lifestyle. Whether you choose running, swimming, cycling, a team sport, or another aerobic activity, try to build sessions of at least 30 minutes' duration into your schedule three times a week. If you make these sessions part of your life, they can be the foundation of a lasting fitness program.

Muscular Fitness

Muscular fitness has two main components: muscular strength and muscular endurance. **Muscular strength** is the capacity of a muscle to exert force against resistance. It is primarily dependent on how much muscle mass you have. Your muscular strength is measured by how much you can lift, push, or pull in a single, all-out effort. **Muscular endurance** is the capacity of a muscle to exert force repeatedly over a period of time, or to apply and sustain strength for a period lasting from a few seconds to a few minutes.

muscular strength The capacity of a muscle to exert force against resistance.

muscular endurance The capacity of a muscle to exert force repeatedly over a period of time.

Strength Training Muscular strength and endurance are developed by strength training, also known as weight training or resistance training. In this type of exercise, the muscles exert force against resistance, such as free weights (dumbbells, barbells) or exercise resistance machines. Your major muscle groups (legs, back, abdomen, shoulders, chest, and arms) should all be part of your strength training program.

Frequency and Type of Activity Two to three resistance training sessions a week are sufficient for building muscle strength and endurance. The primary muscle groups targeted in resistance training are the deltoids (shoulders), pectorals (chest), triceps (back of upper arms), biceps (front of upper arms), quadriceps (front of thighs), hamstrings (back of thighs), gluteus maximus (buttocks), and abdomen. Other areas to exercise are the upper back, the lower back, and the calves. Whether you choose free weights or weight machines, try to exercise every muscle group during your strength training sessions.

Intensity and Duration: The Strength-Endurance Continuum The same exercises develop both strength and endurance, but their intensity and duration vary. To develop strength, you need to exercise at a higher intensity (greater resistance or more weight) for a shorter duration; to develop endurance, you need to exercise at a lower intensity for a longer duration. Duration is measured in terms of repetitions—the number of times you perform the exercise (say, lift a barbell). If you lift a heavy weight a few times (one to five repetitions), you are developing strength. If you lift a lighter weight more times (20 repetitions), you are developing endurance.

Gender Differences in Muscle Development Muscle mass growth is influenced by the male sex hormone testosterone, and although women produce this hormone, they do so at only about 10 percent of the level of men. Thus the amount of muscle the body can develop differs by gender. Women can increase muscle mass through strength training programs, but the increase will be less than that achieved by men.[25]

There is also a wide range of individual variability in both men and women. Regardless of gender, some people can develop significantly more muscle than others can. Body type (*somatotype*) plays a role in these differences. People with a *mesomorphic* (stocky, muscular) body type gain muscle more easily than those with an *ectomorphic* (tall, thin) or

■ Muscular strength and endurance, important components of a fitness program, are developed by weight training, using weight machines, free weights, or the weight of the body (as in calisthenics). *(Holbox/Shutterstock)*

endomorphic (short, fat) body type. Both men and women with mesomorphic bodies have higher levels of testosterone, and thus a greater ability to build muscle, than do those with the other two body types.

Other Types of Muscular Fitness Training and Equipment
In addition to strength training, there are many other ways of developing the physical capabilities of the body. The amount of work that can be performed in a given period of time is known as **muscular power**. Power is determined by the amount and quality of muscle; it requires great strength and the ability to produce that strength quickly. You can train for muscular power by performing any exercise faster. But speed of execution is important not only to sports performance but also to health. The sitting-rising test has been used to illustrate the importance of power. This test was used to predict premature death in a group of people 50 to 80 years old. People with the lowest scores were five times more likely to die within a 6-year period than those with higher scores. The reason may be that the test measured power, flexibility, balance, and body composition and not just muscle strength. The underlying point is to include power in your fitness regimen by

muscular power
The amount of work performed by muscles in a given period of time.

core-strength training
Strength training that conditions the body torso from the neck to the lower back.

selecting weights difficult to lift but with which you can complete six to eight repetitions, and then rest 20 seconds between sets.[26]

One type of exercise program developed specifically for muscular power is *plyometrics,* a program that trains muscles to reach maximum force in the shortest possible time. A muscle that is stretched before contracting will contract more forcefully and rapidly. For example, you can jump higher if you initiate the jump from a crouched position.[25]

Another type of training is **core-strength training**, also called *functional strength training,* which conditions the body torso from the neck to the lower back. The objectives of core-strength training are to lengthen the spine, develop balance, reduce the waistline, prevent back injury, and sculpt the body without bulking it up. Scientific evidence in support of these claims is sparse. Exercise experts argue, however, that training programs increase muscle mass and that metabolic expenditure provides health benefits.[25]

Probably the most popular core-strength training program today is *Pilates* (pi-*lah*-teez), an exercise system developed in the 1920s by physical trainer Joseph Pilates. The exercises, performed on special apparatus and a floor mat, are based on the premise that the body's "powerhouse" is in the torso, particularly the abdomen. Exercises are taught by trained instructors and are tailored to the individual.

Resistance cords are convenient devices for strength training and flexibility. These cords are designed for different age groups and with different strength levels. Cords can be used with other equipment, such as exercise bars and medicine balls. The most important benefit of resistance cords is that they allow you to proceed gradually through your exercise.

Stability balls help the user develop balance, strength, and postural awareness. In particular, stability balls help to develop core muscles (abdomen, lower back, gluteals, and thighs). They are versatile, inexpensive, and portable. Stability balls come in four sizes: 45 cm, 55 cm, 65 cm, and 75 cm. To find the optimal size for you, sit on it with your feet on the floor. Your legs need to be at a 90-degree angle, with your hips even with your knees and thighs parallel to the floor.[27]

Posterior Chain
The posterior chain consists of the muscles on your backside from head to feet. They consist of erector spinae, gluteus maximums, hamstrings, trapezius, posterior deltoids, and gastroc/soleus complex muscles. These muscles propel you forward and are essential for everyday activities such as picking something up from the floor, jumping, and standing up from a sitting position.

The sedentary nature of today's U.S. culture has made the anterior muscles (muscles in front of your body such as

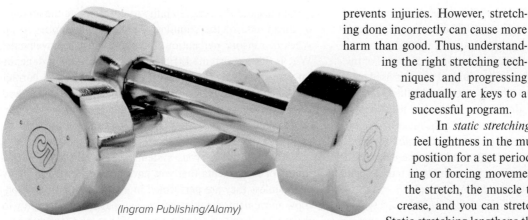

(Ingram Publishing/Alamy)

trapezius, pectoris, deltoids, and front thigh) dominant. Exercises such as running, walking, and yoga strengthen the anterior muscles and not the posterior muscles. The imbalance between anterior and posterior muscles increases the risk for injury of the ankle, knee, and hip joints; neck and low back pain; and poor posture (slouching). To determine whether you have a weak posterior muscle chain, look at your side profile in a mirror. Are your shoulders rounded forward? Is your butt flat? Do your front thigh muscles (quadriceps) appear popped out and hamstrings flat? If so, you need to focus on strengthening your posterior chain muscles by doing back squats, dead lifts, lunges, kettleball swings, glute bridges, calf raises, and pullups.[28]

Breathing and Safety Oxygen flow is vital for preventing muscle fatigue and injury during resistance training. Inhale when your muscles are relaxed, and exhale when you initiate the lifting or push-off action. Never hold your breath while performing resistance exercises.

Flexibility

Another important component of musculoskeletal fitness is **flexibility**, the ability of joints to move through their full range of motion. Good flexibility helps you maintain posture and balance, makes movement easier and more fluid, and lowers your risk of injury. It is a key factor in preventing low back pain and injury.

Your flexibility is affected by factors you cannot change, such as genetic endowment, gender, and age, and by factors you can change, such as physical activity patterns. A common misconception is that flexibility declines steadily once a person reaches adulthood. Flexibility does seem to be highest in the teenage years, and aging is accompanied by a shortening of tendons and an increased rigidity in muscles and joints. However, there is also strong evidence that much of the loss of flexibility experienced in aging can be reduced by stretching programs.[29]

Types of Stretching Programs Medical and fitness experts agree that stretching the muscles attached to the joints is the single most important part of an exercise program because it promotes flexibility, reduces muscle tension, and

prevents injuries. However, stretching done incorrectly can cause more harm than good. Thus, understanding the right stretching techniques and progressing gradually are keys to a successful program.

In *static stretching,* you stretch until you feel tightness in the muscle and then hold that position for a set period of time without bouncing or forcing movement. After you have held the stretch, the muscle tension will seem to decrease, and you can stretch farther without pain. Static stretching lengthens the muscle and surrounding tissue, reducing the risk of injury. Static stretching is the kind of stretching done in Hatha yoga and is the type recommended for general fitness purposes.

In *passive stretching,* a partner applies pressure to your muscles, typically producing a stretch beyond what you can do on your own. Passive stretching is often used by physical therapists. If you can totally relax your muscle fibers, the use of

Developing flexibility through stretching exercises should be part of a regular fitness program. Stretching is most beneficial and effective when the muscles are warm, as they are after a workout. *(Oleksiy Rezin/Shutterstock)*

pressure by another person can help prevent the problem of partial contraction of muscle fibers. There is a danger, however, of forcing a stretch beyond the point of normal relaxation of the muscles and tendons, causing tearing and injury. For this reason, passive stretching should be limited to supervised medical situations and persons who cannot move by themselves.[29]

In *ballistic stretching,* the muscle is stretched in a series of bouncing movements designed to increase the range of motion. As you bounce, receptors in the muscles, called *muscle spindles,* are stretched. Ballistic stretching is used by experienced athletes, but because it can increase vulnerability to muscle pulls and tears, it is not recommended for most people.

Proprioceptive neuromuscular facilitation (PNF), a type of hold/relax stretching, is a therapeutic exercise that causes a stretch reflex in muscles. It is used primarily in the rehabilitation of injured muscles.[29]

Developing Your Own Flexibility Program The ACSM recommends that stretching exercise be done for all the major joints, including the neck, shoulders, upper back and trunk, hips, knees, and ankles. Stretching should be done 2 to 3 days a week or more. Stretch to a point of mild discomfort (not pain) and hold the stretch for 10 to 30 seconds. Do two to four repetitions of each stretch, to accumulate 60 seconds per stretch.

Stretching can be part of your warm-up for your cardiorespiratory or resistance training program as long as these stretches are gentle, slow, and steady. To prevent injury, warm up first with 5 to 10 minutes of brisk walking, marching in place, or calisthenics. This warm-up will increase your heart rate, raise your core body temperature, and lubricate your joints. You will experience the greatest improvement in flexibility, however, from doing stretching exercises after your other exercise, when your muscles are warm and less likely to be injured by stretching.

Neuromotor Fitness

Neuromotor fitness, also called functional fitness, uses motor skills to improve balance, coordination, gait, agility, and proprioceptive training, which trains your body to know where all your body parts are at any given time during movement. T'ai chi, qigong, and yoga are examples of functional fitness training that combine motor skills with resistance exercise, and flexibility exercise. Functional fitness trains your upper body, lower body, and core muscles to work together in a way that simulates movements used at home, work, and recreation. In addition to specialized fitness classes, fitness balls, kettle balls, and weights are tools commonly used in functional fitness training.[30]

Consider one of your favorite professional athletes, perhaps Dustin Johnson. You would like to emulate Dustin's golf swing, which would require extensive practice and patience, perhaps more than 10,000 hours of practice. Many people are now using the concepts of slow mindful movement to develop motor skills. The Weber Fechner principle that guides this strategy is based on the relationship between a stimulus and the brain's ability to differentiate the amount or magnitude of the stimulus. The principle applies to all types of sensory perception, including muscle movements. Why is this important? Efficient muscle movement depends on your brain's ability to sense muscular effort and correct inefficient effort. This capacity is best achieved by slow and easy movements. Slow movements help the brain to develop motor skill maps that stimulate body awareness through the central nervous system when executing new movements.

Your central nervous system rebels against new movements or movements that you have not performed in many years unless they are performed in a slow, rhythmic fashion. Slow movements enable you to pay particular attention to movement details. Coordination is wiring and rewiring neural circuits in the brain's motor cortex, which controls movement. It is based on neuroplasticty, the brain's ability to change.[31] Many elite athletes, musicians, and dancers are turning to neuroscience that uses brain stimulation to build motor skill coordination.[32] See the box, "Action Skill-Builder: Neuroplasticity Training."

Action Skill-Builder
Neuroplasticity Training

You may have seen professional golfers or tennis players mimicking their practice swings in very slow motion. They are likely using the concept of neuroplasticity, the art of brain training, to access and retain the motor skills used in that precise movement. Neuroplasticity is based on functional neural pathways, which are a driving force for learning and memory behind motor skills. To learn new skills, the brain prunes neural synapses, deletes neural connections that are no longer needed, and strengthens essential neural connections.

Multiple training sessions are usually required to master motor skills, often by combining a fast-training phase and a slow-training phase. The fast phase consists of quick motor skill acquisition developed by a single training session, while slow phase training consists of small and consistent acquisitions over multiple training sessions. For example, if you have never played golf before, your first fast-learning practice session will focus on the entire swing to demonstrate all the coordinated muscle movements needed to execute it. Then slow learning may be used to break the swing into components so that the vision in the motor cortex of your brain matches the movements in your body. Through fast and slow learning, the motor cortex can supply conscious initiation of voluntary muscle movements. Once the motor skills have been developed, the motor cortex defers to lower brain processing centers such as the cerebellum, which stores subconscious memories. Less and less thinking is required until eventually the movement can be executed with no conscious effort.

Source: Halo Neuroscience. (2016). The athlete's guide to the brain: Motor skill learning. https://blog.haloneuro.com/the-athlete-s-guide-to-the-brain-motor-skill-learning-43b4de7bd71d.

Conscious Movement

Conscious movement has become a popular exercise trend. This technique draws from mindful exercise and t'ai chi, focusing on how the whole body moves, using minimal effort for precise movements that maintain proper postural structure and a calm mind. Used as a warm-up before intense exercise or as a cool-down routine, it decreases the risk of injury. The steps in conscious movement are twofold: (1) take slow, deep breaths that stimulate the parasympathetic nervous system and slow the heart rate, and (2) remain present in your thoughts as a mindfulness practice.

Self-awareness nourishes spiritual, emotional, and physical health. Your brain plays a core role in regulating muscle movement by sending strong neurological signals to working muscles. Conscious movement is often used when walking, and in yoga and Pilates. Niche yoga classes (e.g., yoga for climbers and yoga for cyclists) are becoming as or more popular than HIT.[33]

Body Composition

We discuss body composition in more detail in Chapter 7. Here, the basic message is that you can control body weight, trim body fat, and build muscle tissue by incorporating more physical activity into your daily life. Use the stairs rather than taking the elevator, walk or ride your bike rather than driving, and if you drive, park your car at the far end of the parking lot and walk the rest of the way.

According to the *Healthy People 2020 Physical Activity Guidelines for Americans,* maintaining weight stability requires 150 to 300 minutes of moderate- to vigorous-intensity exercise per week. Strength-training activities are helpful in maintaining weight stability but are not as effective as aerobic exercise. Losing a substantial amount of weight or maintaining a substantial weight loss requires a high amount of physical activity to burn calories. People who want to lose weight or prevent weight regain may need to do more than 300 minutes a week of moderate- to- vigorous-intensity exercise.[34] If you work toward these goals, you will see improvements not only in your body composition but also in your overall well-being.

Is the fat-burning heart rate zone a myth? Fitness clubs and personal trainers often claim that maintaining a heart rate zone of 60 percent of your MHR duration is the secret of using exercise to lose weight. The argument is that you will thus burn more fat than glycogen as an energy source, which results in greater weight loss than high-intensity exercise. Glycogen is stored carbohydrates (converted sugar). A gram of fat has 9 calories and a gram a carbohydrates has 4 calories. Thus, the arguments is burning more fat than glycogen from carbohydrates is more effective for losing weight.

Although there are elements of truth in this claim, it is very misleading. Exercise is fueled (calories are burned) by energy drawn from a mixture of stored fats and glycogen. The less active you are, the greater the percentage of energy from stored fats you use as fuel. For example, at rest your body may use 85 percent of its fuel from fats. If you are walking, fats as an energy source may decrease to 70 percent. If you increase your pace to moderate running, your energy source may be 50 percent fat and 50 percent carbohydrates.

So, higher workout intensity is associated with burning more fat than glycogen. But burning calories is the secret to weight loss, not just burning fat. Weight management (discussed in Chapter 7) is a function of balancing calories in and calories out, and exercising at lower intensity burns fewer calories than exercising at higher intensity. A person of average weight walking 2 miles in an hour will burn about 200 calories an hour, 40 percent fueled by fat. By cycling at moderate intensity for 1 hour, that same person may burn close to 500 calories. There is nothing wrong with using low-intensity exercise to lose weight, though mixing exercise intensities is ideal. But the so-called fat heart rate zone is misleading at best.[35]

Micro Workouts Highly focused micro-workout facilities have arisen to create a new niche in the saturated fitness market, differentiating themselves from the "sweat and burn" exercises of major fitness clubs. For example, because high-intensity spinning classes and strength-training fitness classes may cause quad muscles to become more developed than glute muscles, low-impact glute training classes emerged solely to correct the imbalance and tighten butt appearance. FaceGym opened to provide micro-workouts addressing the 40 facial muscles, using microcurrent sculpting and skin-tightening radio frequency to heat facial muscle tissue for more effective manipulation of cheekbones and jaw lines.

This type of singular training quickly evolved to focus on pelvic floor muscles, inner thigh muscles, and even the mouth, toes, and ears. "Pump and Kegel" routines for pregnant women aim to develop a

Stretching before cardiovascular exercise is very important to provide sufficient warm-up and prevent exertion injuries. *(Wavebreak Media Ltd/123RF)*

strong pelvic floor before birth to support the bladder, bowel, and uterus and to address postbirth back pain and incontinence. P.volve workouts focus on the smaller inner thigh muscles. Face and body clubs use lip pursing, jaw clenching, and contorted facial expressions to remove smile lines, forehead wrinkles, and droopy skin below the eyes. Buccal massage is said to increase facial blood circulation and reduce lymph gland damage. Stretch*d uses toe-webbing and toe-flexing to support foot health and decrease arthritic pain. Some clubs focus on the ears, which contain a network of nerves that stimulate the central nervous system.[36]

Combining Fitness Activities

When you participate in one activity or sport to improve your performance in another, or when you use several different types of training for a specific fitness goal, you are **cross training**. For example, you might lift weights, run, and cycle on different days of the week. Two key advantages of cross training are that you avoid the boredom of participating in the same exercise every day and you reduce the risk of overuse injuries.

For a summary of physical activity recommendations for adults related to the various components of fitness, see Table 6.2.

cross training
Participation in one sport to improve performance in another, or use of several different types of training for a specific fitness goal.

Falling Out of Shape

If you stop exercising, how long will it take for your body to become less fit? One week is not likely to have an impact. Two weeks, however, can lead to reduced cardiovascular fitness, loss of lean muscle mass, and lower muscle insulin sensitivity. Two months or longer can cause total loss of fitness gains. Strength training is more likely to be more affected by skipping workouts for a long time than is endurance exercise. The muscle fibers associated with strength tend to atrophy more quickly than those associated with endurance activities.[37]

IMPROVING YOUR HEALTH THROUGH MODERATE PHYSICAL ACTIVITY

As noted earlier, exercise does not have to be vigorous to provide health benefits. There are many simple, easy, and enjoyable ways to use physical activity to obtain health benefits.

Making Daily Activities More Active

How much time do you spend in sedentary activities during your day? How can you make these minutes more active? Try going for a walk instead of watching television or videos. Ride your bike to class instead of taking the bus, take the stairs instead of the elevator, or walk around in your room instead of sitting while checking your cell phone messages. These kinds of unstructured physical activities can actually make a difference. In one study, researchers found that obese people sat for an average of 2 hours longer a day than people who were not obese, and that if the obese people were to mirror the

Table 6.2 Summary of Physical Activity Recommendations for Adults

Aerobic (endurance) activity	150 minutes of moderate-intensity aerobic activity per week. OR 75 minutes of vigorous-intensity aerobic activity per week. OR A combination of moderate- and vigorous-intensity physical activity that meets the recommendation.
Muscle-strengthening activity	8 to 10 exercises that stress the major muscle groups on 2 or more nonconsecutive days per week. Do two to four sets of 8 to 12 repetitions for each exercise using sufficient resistance to fatigue the muscles.
Flexibility	Stretching exercise for all major joints, at least 2 or 3 days per week. Stretch to the point of tension, hold for 10 to 30 seconds, repeating two to four times, to accumulate 60 seconds per stretch.
Weight management	To prevent unhealthy weight gain, 150 to 300 minutes of moderate- to vigorous-intensity physical activity per week. For substantial weight loss or to sustain weight loss, 300 minutes or more of moderate- to vigorous-intensity exercise per week.

Sources: Department of Health and Human Services. (2009). *2008 Physical activity guidelines for Americans.* Retrieved from www.health.gov/paguidelines; American College of Sports Medicine. (2009). Position stand: Progression models in resistance training for healthy adults. *Medicine & Science in Sports & Exercise, 41*(3): 687–708; Bushman, B. (2017). *ACSM's complete guide to fitness & health.* Champaign, IL: McGraw-Hill Education.

unstructured physical activities of those who were not obese, they would burn an extra 350 calories a day.[38]

How helpful can it be to make your daily activities more active? Consider that an order of french fries contains about 400 calories. If you are sitting and watching television, it will take you 308 minutes, or more than 5 hours, to use up that many calories. If you are walking briskly or jogging slowly, it will take you about 1 hour. For more on the negative effects of inactivity, see the box "Starting the Conversation: Could You Spend Less Time Sitting?"

The U.S. Department of Health and Human Services has added a section on the health risks of a sedentary lifestyle in its Physical Activity Guidelines. Since 2018, the percentage of people spending at least 1 hour a day using the computer has increased across all age groups; among adults it

increased from 29 percent to 50 percent. Men spend more time sitting than women, and Black Americans spend more time sitting than other racial groups.[39] The tendency to spend increased sitting time begins in early childhood.

Walking for Fitness

Walking is the most popular physical activity in North America,[40] and it has many health benefits. As with other activities, increasing the pace and/or duration of walking results in greater health benefits.

People of normal weight can control their weight if they walk 10,000 steps each day.[41] Walking 10,000 steps (about 5 miles) expends between 300 and 400 calories, depending on body size and walking speed. Walking 10,000

Starting the Conversation
Could You Spend Less Time Sitting?

Q: What differences do you notice in the way your body feels after 4 hours of watching television and after 30 minutes of vigorous exercise?

How much time do you spend sitting? Between classes, computer time, television, movies, video games, and hanging out, your sitting time probably adds up to a significant portion of your day. Your sitting profile after graduation could look even worse if you take a desk job. The average sitting time of U.S. adults increased by 1 hour per day from 2007 to 2016 to more than 6.4 hours. Some sit far longer. Obese people, for example, sit over 2.5 hours a day more than lean people. Agricultural workers sit only 3 hours a day, whereas office hours average 15 hours of sitting each day.

Research shows that prolonged sitting is bad for your health even if you exercise regularly. Prolonged sitting sends the body into a kind of shutdown in which metabolism slows, electrical activity in the muscles drops, fat-burning enzymes turn off, and almost no energy is expended. People who sit for long periods have less healthy cholesterol and blood sugar profiles, as well as bigger waists and stiffer muscles. The "physiology of inactivity" puts people at higher risk of heart disease, obesity, diabetes, some cancers, chronic pain, and premature death. One study found that sitting for more than 6 hours a day for 10 to 20 years can shave off 7 chronological years of high-quality life—life free of major illnesses or disabilities that limit instrumental living skills.

Experts recommend regularly interrupting sitting with a few minutes of physical activity—standing up, stretching, walking, or running in place. These short bouts of activity, along with smaller movements like fidgeting and bigger activities like doing daily tasks, all contribute to *nonexercise activity thermogenesis*

(NEAT)—the expenditure of energy in activities other than exercise. Studies have found that burning calories in NEAT each day—standing, cooking, folding the laundry, and so on—can help counteract the effects of sitting. The more short bouts of low-intensity activity you can accumulate throughout the day, the better.

Some researchers have begun designing indoor environments that promote physical activity and NEAT. Dr. James Levine, the force behind the movement, created an "office of the future" with walking workstations, or "walkstations"—vertical desks that let people walk at a slow pace on a treadmill while working on their computers. Levine sees offices becoming dynamic environments in the near future, with people using treadmill desks, bike desks, balance ball chairs, and more.

The bottom line is that getting regular exercise is not enough to keep you healthy if you spend most of your day sitting. In fact, the association between prolonged sitting and premature death likely occurs regardless of physical activity level. Until every classroom, library, and office has options that promote physical activity, it's up to you to build movement into your day—the more the better!

Q: What changes can you make in your life right now to decrease your sitting time?

Q: As you think ahead to your working life, how will you build NEAT into your day? What will your work environment look like? What equipment helps motivate you to move?

Sources: Levine, J. A. (2015). What are the risks for sitting too much? Retrieved from www.mayoclinic.org.Healthy-lifestyle/faq-20058005; Levine, J. (2017). Killer chairs: How desk jobs ruin your health. *Scientific American.* Retrieved from https://www.scientificamerican.com/article/killer-chairs-how-desk-jobs-ruin-your-health; Abbott, B. (2019). Americans are sitting more and we have computers to blame. *The Wall Street Journal.* Retrieved from https://www.wsj.com/articles/americans-are-sitting-more-and-we-have-computers-to-blame-11556031601

Counting steps with a pedometer is one way to move toward fitness. Walking 10,000 steps a day confers health benefits and helps people control their weight. The typical U.S. adult walks only 5,117 steps a day. *(Michael Simons/123RF)*

steps a day 5 days a week expends the optimal 2,000 calories per week recommended for preventing premature death. This is good news for anyone who spends time on college campuses, which are usually designed to be pedestrian friendly. At a traditional university, many college students walk more than 10,000 steps a day. Although 10,000 steps may be a goal, a lower number also brings health benefits. Walking 100 steps per minute is an approximation of moderate-intensity walking. The best advice is to combine both steps per minute and the recommended duration in setting your walking goal.

To set a walking goal for yourself, first find out how many steps you typically take each day. You can count your steps with a pedometer, a pager-sized device worn on the belt or waistband centered over the hipbone or an app built into your smartphone. Record the number of steps you take every day for 7 days. Most inactive people take between 2,000 and 4,000 steps a day. Then increase this number by about 500 steps at a time. If you typically take 5,000 steps a day, set a goal of 5,500 steps. Once you have achieved 5,500 steps, raise your goal by

500 steps and continue until you reach 10,000 steps. This is an easy and painless way to add physical activity to your day and to move from a light to a moderate activity level.

If you have access to stair-climbing machines at your fitness center, they can provide a good workout. Dual-action climbers exercise your legs, arms, and heart. These machines—as well as treadmills, ellipticals, and stationary bikes—provide a moderate- to high-intensity workout with low impact on your joints.

Getting the Most from Cardio Exercise Equipment

The biomechanics of walking or running on a treadmill are slightly different from those of road walking or running. Because you do not need to produce the same amount of power on a treadmill, you will have more forward trunk lean and more hip and knee flexion.[42] This difference in body alignment burns minimally fewer calories than walking or running outside unless your speed on the treadmill is 8.5 mph or higher. If you want to simulate outside walking or running, increase the treadmill incline to 2 degrees.

Is an elliptical trainer or a treadmill better for fitness and health? Elliptical machines use an uninterrupted circular motion that develops an impact-free workout. People who have ankle, knee, or lower-back injuries find elliptical machines preferable due to this low impact. The two long handles that extend from the machine base also allow the user to burn more calories per hour than the treadmill, since they require use of the upper body. A drawback to elliptical exercise machines is that they offer limited opportunity for increasing range of motion. People using short strides on elliptical equipment also hyperextend their knees, which can cause chronic knee inflammation and soreness. The pace is more difficult to control on elliptical equipment than on treadmills.

A major benefit of treadmills is a running or walking motion that is more familiar to the user and requires little time to get used to. The surface of a treadmill is also designed to cushion compression force, but the device is still an injury risk for people with joint disorders since it facilitates a weight-bearing exercise. They—and people who want to lose weight more quickly—are generally advised to use elliptical equipment rather than treadmills.

Are the calorie counts on cardio exercise machines accurate? Those with display features that enable the user to input age, body weight, and gender are the most accurate. The machines typically calculate not only duration but also workload, based on the relationship between exercise heart rate and oxygen consumption. This association is not precise, however, because such factors as body position, body size, fitness level, body temperature, and muscle groups exercised influence calories burned. Treadmills and stair-climbing machines are likely more accurate than ellipticals and stationary bikes that do not factor in the user's weight.[43]

The following guidelines will help you minimize inaccuracies and work out more efficiently:

- Try to use the same model and brand consistently, because models and brands can differ significantly on accuracy. Your estimated calorie expenditure should increase as you become more fit.

- Wearing a heart rate monitor can help you to increase workload more accurately. Equipment that contains a heart rate monitor typically requires a steady grip on a pair of hand electrodes or an ear clip that sends a signal to a wireless sensor.

- Do not lean on the handle bars. Leaning can decrease calories burned by as much as 50 percent.

- Enter your accurate weight. Inaccurate weight input can cause an overestimate or underestimate of calories burned.

- Mix up your exercise workout. If you don't, your body will adapt as it becomes more familiar with the machine and you will burn fewer calories at the same level of effort.

■ Exergaming is a popular consumer-oriented approach to fitness. *(CB2/ZOB/WENN/Newscom)*

Exergaming and Other Replacements for Sedentary Technology

Efforts to reduce sedentary behaviors include replacing technology that encourages inactivity—television, computers, traditional video games—with physical activity environments that are fun and engaging. Exergaming uses video games to enhance physical activity.[44] This new generation of video games involving physical movement is marketed specifically as exercise and fitness games. For example, you can train using EA Sports Active NFL Training or EA Sports Active: More Workouts with your PlayStation4 or get in shape with Your Sport Fitness on your Xbox360. New motion controllers and advanced sensors provide realistic simulations for t'ai chi, beach volleyball, golf, soccer, football, hockey, and many other activities. They track how many calories you burn as you play and can even analyze your body dynamics and track your progress over time.[44,45] Although research on the benefits of virtual reality exercise equipment is in its infancy, outcomes to date are showing both physiological and psychological benefits.[46] Exergames can change people's attitudes about physical movement. Almost 90 percent of people in the United States have mobile phones and 80 percent smartphones. Exercise games on smartphones have become popular.[47]

The drawbacks of exergames are that they can be expensive, they may limit social interaction, and they may send a message that being fit requires technology. In addition, research into the health benefits of these games has been inconclusive.[45] Fitness video games should not be considered a substitute for active outdoor play and physical activity.

Real boxing, for example, uses 200 percent more energy than Wii boxing.[44]

Keeping Track with Fitness Apps

Wristbands such as Fitbit no longer dominate the fitness app market. Cell phone fitness apps can count your steps or keep track of exercise routines from weight lifting to office yoga.[48] Apple, Google, and Samsung market wearable fitness devices, such as exercise clothing and the Apple Smartwatch. Accelerometer chips are used in the new generation of fitness apps. Wearable fitness apps such as smartwatches and wrist bands are portable and do not interfere with everyday activities (e.g., swimming). Smartphone apps are fairly accurate when you carry your smartphone in your pocket. The step count for the day, however, will be less than you will get from a hip pedometer or wristband if you do not consistently carry the smartphone in your pocket throughout the day.[49] Fitness apps provide tracking information that is good for summarizing digital health data, but empirical evidence has not yet shown whether they are effective for making actual lifestyle changes.

SPECIAL CONSIDERATIONS IN EXERCISE AND PHYSICAL ACTIVITY

When you engage in exercise and physical activity, you need to warm up and cool down and pay attention to warning signs from your body. You also need to know how to accommodate the effects of heat and cold. In addition, physical activity is important for people with disabilities and chronic health problems; appropriate exercise opportunities need to be available to them.

Health and Safety Precautions

Injuries and illness associated with exercise and physical activity are usually the result of either excessive exercise or improper techniques. In this section, we look at several considerations related to health and safety.

Warm-Up and Cool-Down

Proper warm-up before exercise helps to maximize the benefits of a workout and minimize the potential for injuries. Muscles contract more efficiently and more safely when they have been properly warmed up. Suggested warm-up activities include light calisthenics, walking or slow jogging, and gentle stretching of the specific muscles to be used in the activity. You can also do a low-intensity version of the activity you are about to engage in, such as hitting tennis balls against a wall before a match. Your warm-up should last from 5 to 10 minutes.

A minimum of 5 to 10 minutes should also be devoted to cool-down, depending on environmental conditions and the intensity of the exercise program. Pooling of blood in the extremities may temporarily disrupt or reduce the return of blood to the heart, momentarily depriving your heart and brain of oxygen. Fainting or even a coronary abnormality may result. However, if you continue the activity at a lower intensity, the blood vessels gradually return to their normal smaller diameter.

Walking, mimicking the exercise at a slower pace, and stretching while walking are all excellent cool-down activities. Never sit down, stand in a stationary position, or take a hot shower or sauna immediately after vigorous exercise.

Fatigue and Overexertion

If you train hard, it is important to take breaks between bouts. Indicators for taking a break include prolonged fatigue and muscle soreness that last longer than 24 hours. Fatigue is generally defined as an inability to continue exercising at a desired level of intensity. The cause of fatigue may be psychological—for example, depression can cause feelings of fatigue—or physiological, as when you work out too long or too hard, do an activity you're not used to, or become overheated or dehydrated. Or fatigue can occur because the body cannot produce enough energy to meet the demands of the activity. In this case, consuming enough complex carbohydrates to replenish the muscle stores of glycogen may solve the problem. Athletes need to eat a high-carbohydrate diet to make sure they have enough reserve energy for their sport.[50]

Overexertion occurs when an exercise session has been too intense. Warning signs of overexertion include (1) pain or pressure in the left or midchest area, jaw, neck, left shoulder, or left arm during or just after exercise; (2) sudden nausea, dizziness, cold sweat, fainting, or pallor (pale, ashen skin); and (3) abnormal heartbeats (such as fluttering), rapid heartbeats, or a rapid pulse rate immediately followed by a very slow pulse rate. These symptoms are similar to signs of a heart attack. If you experience any of these symptoms, consult a physician before exercising again.

Soft-Tissue and Overuse Injuries

Injuries to soft tissue (muscles and joints) include tears, sprains, strains, and bruises; they usually result from a specific incident, such as a bicycle crash. Overuse injuries are caused by the cumulative effects of motions repeated many times. Tendinitis and bursitis are examples of overuse injuries. Tendinitis is the inflammation or irritation of the tendon cord, which attaches muscle to bone. Bursitis is inflammation of the bursa sac, which provides a gliding surface to reduce friction between bones and body tissues. (For tips on choosing the right shoe to prevent walking- and running-related injuries, see the box "Consumer Clipboard: You and Your Shoes.")

Muscle lengthens during contraction against an exercise load, such as when you are running downhill. Exercises using frequent eccentric contractions like this can cause muscle soreness Muscle soreness is the burning sensation felt in the working muscles as a result of the production of lactate and other metabolites. Microscopic muscle damage may also occur, causing an inflammatory response, likely in connective tissue between muscle fibers and at the junction between the muscle and tendon. Your body is designed to prevent permanent damage during extreme exercise exertion. For example, as your intensity decreases, your body will rely more on its aerobic system, which enables oxygen to revert lactate back to pyruvate.

Muscle soreness typically peaks within 24 to 72 hours and is relieved over a few days as your body clears lactate and other metabolites from the working muscles. You can help reduce soreness and inflammation by staying hydrated, using gentle massage, and taking alternating warm and cold baths to open and close blood vessels. If pain persists and is severe after 72 hours, you may need to consult your health provider. Extreme pain may indicate muscle cell death, which can release toxins into the bloodstream and myoglobin into the kidneys. Intense muscle pain, muscle swelling, and red or brown urine is an indicator of rhabdomyolysis, a very serious health condition requiring emergency treatment.

Both overuse injuries and soft tissue injuries have often been treated according to the R-I-C-E principle:

Rest

Ice

Compression

Elevation

This treatment means immediately stopping the activity, applying ice to the affected area to reduce swelling and pain, compressing the area with an elastic bandage to reduce swelling, and elevating it to reduce blood flow to the area. Rest, compression, and elevation are well-accepted treatments. Ice, however, may cause more harm than good, as discussed later in the chapter. Do not apply heat until all swelling has disappeared. When you no longer feel pain in the area, you can gradually begin to exercise again. Don't return to your full exercise program until your injury has completely healed.

Consumer Clipboard

You and Your Shoes

If walking or running is part of your fitness activity, the right shoes are essential. In either case, to prevent injury, you should know the basic differences between walking shoes and running shoes.

In walking, your foot has a natural rolling motion from heel to toe, bending at the ball of the foot with each step. Your foot also rolls from the little toe to the big toe, and your toes bend upward fully. In running, you may strike the ground farther forward on the foot than when you're walking, and with more force. Running can thus create a force more than five times your body weight on every foot strike, whereas walking creates a force about twice your body weight.

For these reasons, running shoes need to provide more cushioning and stability than walking shoes. Both types need to be flexible, but in different places.

Walking shoe:

- **Heel:** Rounded or undercut, no more than 1 inch thicker than the rest of the sole
- **Midsole:** Bends at ball of foot
- **Toes:** Flexible toe area, twists horizontally and bends vertically

Running shoe:

- **Heel:** Flared or built-up heel for stability and cushioning
- **Midsole:** May bend at arch of foot

- **Toes:** More horizontal flex, less vertical flex than walking shoe

Midsole tests:

- Place shoe on level surface and lift heel toward toe. Walking shoe should bend at ball of foot; running shoe may bend at arch. Then poke toe down. Heel of walking shoe should rise off surface; this natural curvature helps you roll through each step. Heel of running shoe should rise very little or not at all.

Toe tests:

- Grasp shoe with both hands and twist toe area from side to side; then bend toes up and down. In a walking shoe, there should be both horizontal flex and vertical flex. In a running shoe, there should be more horizontal and less vertical flex.

(Kai_Wong/Getty Images)

Sources: Trudeau, M. B., Von, Y., Vinzenz, J., et al. (2015). Assessing footwear effects from principal features of plantar loading during running. *Medicine & Science in Sports & Exercise, 27,* 1988-1996; ACSM. (n.d). *Selecting running shoes.* Retrieved from www.acsm.org/does/brochures/running-shoes.pdf; Bumgardner, W. (2011). *Walking shoe guide: Test your shoe flexibility.* Retrieved from http://walking.about.com/cs/shoes/a/shoeflex.htm; Spillner, M. (2011). The great shoe debate. *Prevention.* Retrieved from www.prevention.com/fitness/fitness-tips/differences-between-walking-and-running-sneakers.

Stress fractures are another kind of overuse injury, and they can be very painful for physically active people, especially runners. The metatarsals, the group of five long bones connecting your ankle to your toes, are a common stress fracture site. These bones are stressed whenever you walk or run. If you have had a stress fracture, your risk for another one increases fivefold. Females have more than twice the risk for stress fractures than males due to their lower bone density. There is sparse evidence that the walking/running surface or the intensity of workout affects the risk of stress fractures. Sudden changes in distance or surface conditions are a more likely cause of stress fractures. The best preventive advice is to pay attention to symptoms that accompany overuse injuries.

A common question is whether shock-absorbing insoles sold in shoe stores and drugstores can prevent compression force injuries. The answer is no. Foot orthotics available at medical supply stores and podiatry clinics are much more costly than cushioned insoles, but they are effective for preventing stress fractures, shin pain, and other lower-leg problems.[51]

The Exercise-Recovery Industry

Is the exercise-recovery industry bogus? Ice, cupping, float tanks, sports drinks, power bars, water quotas, compression shorts, and even recovery beer are just a few of the gimmicks marketed to elite athletes and recreational exercisers with promises of improved performance and injury prevention/treatment. Some of the recovery products and treatment may be legitimate, while others may cause more harm than good.

Dehydration and Hydration The American College of Sports Medicine (ACSM) exercise guidelines warn of dangers associated with losing more than 2 percent of body weight through sweat and recommend hydrating well before, during, and after exercise. Pepsi's Gatorade and Coca-Cola's Powerade, to name two products, are marketed as a way to make sure you are replacing both water and electrolytes (essential molecules that create ions when dissolved in water) lost during sweaty exercise. The underlying message of sports drinks like these is that thirst is not a good indicator of whether you are drinking enough during exercise so you should drink them whether you are thirsty or not. But science

hypnatremia
Overhydration or water intoxication caused when healthy adults drink more than 6 gallons of water in a day.

plasma osmolality
The body's concentration of salt and other blood-soluble compounds.

aquaporins
Tiny, strawlike proteins that pull water back into the blood.

supports thirst as a valid indicator of dehydration. Moreover, electrolytes lost through sweating are quickly replaced by a postexercise meal. The bottom line: Sports drinks are not needed unless you are exercising more than 60 minutes, or in very hot and humid conditions.[52]

Exercisers should actually be more concerned about **hyponatremia**, which is overhydration or water intoxication and is usually caused when healthy adults drink 6 gallons of water or more in a day. In the last three decades, at least five marathoners have died from overhydration, as have soldiers in Iraq and Afghanistan, and many more have become critically ill. Although dehydration is associated with exertion heat disorders, the human body is well designed to cope with losing water during exercise by maintaining **plasma osmolality**, the concentration of salt and other blood-soluble compounds. A decrease in plasma osmolality triggers the kidneys to activate **aquaporins**, which are are tiny, strawlike proteins that pull water back into the blood. Aquaporins are recruited by the kidneys before you feel thirsty. In other words, your body is naturally built to make sure that you seek hydration as needed.[52] See the box, "Action Skill-Builder: Urine Charts and Hydration."

Flushing the Blood Cold lasers, massage beds, compression pajamas, and fitness clubs that promote infrared saunas have been marketed as ways to flush the blood of toxins and stimulate blood flow to treat soft-tissue injuries. What is an infrared sauna? The typical sauna heat is set between 150° F and 220° F. An infrared sauna runs at 90° F to 117° F, using heat radiation instead of the convective radiating heat of the typical sauna. Convective saunas create steam to heat the air, and the heat is then absorbed by the skin as energy that transfers to the blood and body. Advocates of infrared saunas claim, in contrast, that radiant heat, produced without steam, penetrates the skin and moves into the soft tissues, heating from inside to help the body remove toxins. Although infrared heat is a new buzzword in the fitness industry, there is sparse empirical evidence that the human body needs special assistance to flush itself of toxins. The liver and kidneys are very effective at performing that function.[52]

Many exercise recovery products claim to boost blood flow. The theory is that these products help rid muscle tissue of metabolic waste and deliver blood and oxygen to injured muscle sites to decrease inflammation. Products include heat, massage, foam rollers, and compression clothes. For example, compression pajamas promoted by Tom Brady supposedly rid the body of lactic acid and other toxins, reduce inflammation, boost the immune system, and increase hormone levels to help in muscle recovery. Empirical evidence does not support this claim.

Massage therapists and foam roller manufacturers claim massage promotes protein synthesis, flushes toxins, and

Action Skill-BUILDER

Urine Charts and Hydration

When it is very hot or very cold, you will need to adjust your physical activity and exercise workload to avoid placing too much stress on your body. The body does not get as hot and sweat evaporates more quickly in cold weather. Warm air and humid air increase core body temperature. Skin blood vessels dilate and the sweat glands work harder to cool the body to maintain ideal core body temperature. Checking the color of your urine is one quick way to determine sufficient hydration, since the color of urine is a measure of the concentration of waste. Light-colored urine that is mostly clear has more water than waste. Urine that is dark has a higher concentration of waste and may suggest you are not sufficiently hydrating, or it could mean that your kidneys are maintaining plasma osmolality by conserving water. The problem with relying on urine charts is that you need to know about the concentration of nutrients, oxygen, and waste products in your blood, too, and urine cannot tell you this.

You should also be cautious of water quota recommendations. For example, Tom Brady, the former New England Patriot's star quarterback, promotes the TB12 Method as a magical hydration formula. TB12 calls for drinking half your body weight in ounces of water every day. This means a 200-pound person would consume 100 ounces of water daily. The TB12 formula is not absurd and likely results in light-colored and clear urine. But, again, this does not tell you what is occurring in the blood. When it comes to hydration, you should listen to your body's thirst signal and not rely on the promises and recommendations of sports drink manufacturers.

Sources: Aschwanden. C. (2019). *Good to go.* New York, NY: W. W. Norton & Company, Inc.

increases blood flow to the muscles to speed recovery. Advocates for massage often target the fascia, or connective layers covering muscle tissue under the skin. Fascia are not passive tissues, which means they can contract and stiffen, and adhesions, or scar tissue, can form on them. Adhesions, inflammation, and stiffness of fascia tissue can cause pain, which massage balls and rollers might loosen by breaking down adhesions. Supporters of massage also claim there may be a neural connection between the muscles and the brain that signals muscles to relax. Although these theories are reasonable, empirical evidence has yet to support them, and research on fascia has only recently begun.[52]

Compression tights, socks, and sleeves have become very popular. Copper Fit and 2XU are popular compression clothing used by athletes in basketball and track. Manufacturers claim compression clothing is a flushing system that helps blood move from the legs and arms back to the heart, resulting in more highly oxygenated blood that promotes improved performance and optimizes recovery by ridding the body of lactic acid and preventing muscle soreness. If you have ever been supine in a hospital bed for an extended time,

(Photodisc/Getty Images)

Hyperhydration is taking in extra fluids shortly before participating in physical activity in a hot environment.[50] This practice is recommended by the ACSM and may improve cardiovascular function and temperature regulation during physical activity when it is very hot.[50]

If you are going to be exercising in very hot or humid conditions, you can hyperhydrate by drinking a pint of water (16 ounces) when you get up in the morning, another pint 1 hour before your activity, and a final pint 15 to 30 minutes before exercising. Plan to consume 4 to 8 ounces of fluid every 15 minutes during your exercise. After exercise, consume 24 ounces of water for every pint you lose.[50] The goal is to prevent excessive changes in electrolyte balance and body water loss of 2 percent or more.

nurses likely placed pneumatic cuffs (Norma Tec System) on your lower legs to prevent fluid from pooling there. The squeezing of the cuffs pushes fluid from your lower legs toward your heart. Pneumatic cuffs have been shown to be effective in preventing deep vein thrombosis (DVT) (discussed in Chapter 14), but the use of compression clothing as an exercise-recovery device has gotten only mixed results. The feel-good effect may promote a psychological benefit, but a cheaper way to increase blood flow and serve as a flushing system is simply to cool down by mimicking your exercise at a much lower intensity.[52]

Cold Therapy Cold therapy for exercise recovery includes the application of ice tubs, ice sleeves, ice cuffs, and the more sophisticated cryosaunas and cryochambers that use refrigerated air or liquid nitrogen to quickly plunge the body into temperatures as low as −250° F. Cryochambers have become a popular cold therapy product used by many professional sports teams. The U.S. Food and Drug Administration (FDA) warned consumers in 2016, however, that cryotherapy is not supported by empirical evidence and may not be safe, and its effectiveness is now being questioned by health experts. The perceived benefits may be more psychological (via the placebo effect) than physical.[52] See the box, "Action Skill-Builder: Cold Therapy."

Effects of Heat and Cold on Exercise and Physical Activity Heat disorders can be caused by impaired regulation of internal core temperature, loss of body fluids, and loss of electrolytes (Table 6.3).[50] Two strategies for preventing excessive increases in body temperature are skin wetting and hyperhydration. Skin wetting involves sponging or spraying the head or body with cold water. This strategy cools the skin but has not been shown to effectively decrease core body temperature.[50] Resting in a cool environment and hyperhydrating are more effective strategies for reducing core body heat.

Action Skill-BUILDER

Cold Therapy

Cold therapy for soft-tissue injuries has been a staple of the recovery industry for decades. The theory is that cold stimulates sympathetic nervous system fibers that then constrict blood vessels in the extremities to send blood to core body organs. The rush of blood away from the injury site in the extremities slows the inflammatory response to reduce swelling in the area. If ice water is used, it provides a compression force against muscles and blood vessels that slows swelling and inflammation. Icing also provides a temporary numbing of pain. Although the pain numbing and compression force of ice water is accepted, an increasing number of sports medicine physicians conclude that the slowing of the inflammatory response actually delays healing by rushing blood away from the soft-tissue injury site.[53]

Sports medicine guru Gabe Mirkin introduced RICE, discussed earlier in this section, in 1978. Since then, RICE has become a standard sports medicine treatment for soft-tissue injuries. However, Mirkin and many exercise scientists are now questioning whether cold therapy causes more harm than good. It may actually delay muscle healing by blocking cytokines from the immune system's inflammation response. Cytokines are small proteins that act as essentially a cleanup crew, removing damaged muscle tissue to rebuild new tissue. Although the American Academy of Orthopedic Surgeons still endorses cold therapy for soft-tissue injuries, the evidence for the effectiveness of this treatment is equivocal. The underlying principle is that the body uses inflammation to heal itself, but cold therapy likely delays the inflammation response and thus slows healing.[52]

Sources: Aschwanden, C. (2019). *Good to go.* New York, NY: W. W. Norton & Company, Inc; Jam, B. (2019). Paradigm shifts: Use of ice & NSAIDs post acute tissue injuries (part 1 of 2). Physical Therapy Web. Retrieved from https://physicaltherapyweb.com.paradigm-shifts-ice-nsaidpost-acute-soft-tissue-injuries-part-1-2/.

Table 6.3   Heat-Related Disorders

Heat Disorder	Cause	Symptoms	Treatment
Heat cramps	Excessive loss of electrolytes in sweat; inadequate salt intake	Muscle cramps	Rest in cool environment; drink fluids; ingest salty food and drinks; get medical treatment if severe.
Heat exhaustion	Excessive loss of electrolytes in sweat; inadequate salt and/or fluid intake	Fatigue; nausea; dizziness; cool, pale skin; sweating; elevated temperature	Rest in cool environment; drink cool fluids; cool body with water; get medical treatment if severe.
Heat stroke	Excessive body temperature	Headache; vomiting; hot, flushed skin (dry or sweaty); elevated temperature; disorientation; unconsciousness	Cool body with ice or cold water; give cool drinks with sugar if conscious; get medical help immediately.

Source: Williams, M. H., Rawson, E. S., & Branch, D. J. (2017). *Nutrition for health, fitness and sport* (7th ed.). New York, NY: McGraw-Hill Education.

---

hypothermia
Low body temperature, a life-threatening condition.

Exercising in excessive cold also puts a strain on the body. Symptoms of **hypothermia** (dangerously low body temperature) include shivering, feelings of false euphoria, and disorientation.[50] Core body temperature influences how severe these symptoms are and whether the hypothermia is considered mild, moderate, or severe. To stay warm, dress in several thin layers of clothes and wear a hat and mittens. If cold air bothers your throat, breathe through a scarf.

Many people do not take in sufficient fluid when exercising outside during the winter. Fluid losses can be very high because cold, dry conditions require the body to humidify and warm the air you breathe, resulting in the loss of significant amounts of water. An effective strategy is to consume needed fluids 1.5 to 2 hours before exercising and to drink more fluids just before exercising.

Some health experts claim exercising in cold weather burns more calories and boosts the immune system. The theory is that exercise in the extreme cold causes vasoconstriction in blood vessels to send more blood to your body core, resulting in more calories burned and improved artery health. The theory also suggests that exercise in extreme cold can generate more brown fat, which is highly metabolic and increases calories burned at rest. Evidence, however, has not yet been generated to support this theory.[54]

Sleep and Recovery   In Chapter 4, we discussed the importance of sleep and health. Sleep is also essential for muscle recovery. Rapid movement is the sleep stage critical for restoring your brain. The slow wave stage of sleep restores your body. Intense physical workouts break down muscle tissue. In slow wave sleep, this damage is repaired and the muscles become stronger. Slow wave sleep is dominant in the childhood years since it induces muscular growth and regeneration in the growth years. In other words, maintaining a regular sleep schedule of 8 to 10 hours serves as a vital radar for muscle recovery.[55]

Exercising in Dirty Air   Sources of dirty air include motor vehicle traffic, plant pollen, wind-blown dust, construction sites, power plants, and many more. Strenuous exercise requires you to inhale about 10 to 20 times more frequently than you do when sitting. Over an extended time, exposure to air pollutants increases the risk of lung inflammation, heart disease, headaches, eye and throat irritations, and premature death from lung cancer and heart disease.[56] When exercising in dirty air conditions, you should follow community air-pollution alerts, time your workouts to avoid peak pollution times such as rush hours, avoid high air-pollution areas (pollution levels are likely to be highest within 1.4 miles of major roads), and opt to exercise indoors.[57]

Is there a "sweet spot" for cyclists and walkers to best achieve the health benefits of physical activity and avoid the health risks associated with dirty air? The faster you move, the faster you breathe in dirty air. But moving faster also means spending less time exposed to dirty air created by traffic. Research on youth and young adult cyclists on flat roads suggests that the sweet spot for female cyclists is a pace of 7.8 mph, and for males 8.3 mph. For people aged 20 to 60, the sweet spot for walking is 2.5 mph.[58]

Face Masks and Exercise During COVID-19

Face masks and coverings have become more widespread in outside environments during the COVID-19 outbreak. Many of these masks provide little or no virus protection, except for the N95 respirator mask. The N95 mask, however, is recommended only for health providers, emergency responders, and people with pulmonary disorders or heart disease. If correctly fitted and worn, it can filter out 95 percent of the solid particles and liquid droplets suspended in the atmosphere that are believed to transport the coronavirus, which causes COVID-19. But these masks make it more difficult to breathe and are generally used only for a short period of time.[59]

Surgical masks do not filter out aerosol particles and allow air leakage from the side during inhalation. Surgical masks should be worn only when the user has COVID-19 and must be around others. Cloth and homemade masks are very porous and provide limited protection from aerosol particles.

In general, exercising outside without a mask is most likely safe when maintaining the recommended social distancing. Still, the CDC recommends, and some cities now require, that everyone wear a face covering or mask of some kind when leaving home. These face coverings provide limited protection and make breathing more difficult when exercising, but they reassure people you may encounter on sidewalks, running paths, and bike paths.[60] COVID-19 will be covered in more depth in Chapter 13.

Exercise for People with Disabilities

Physical activity and exercise are especially beneficial for people with disabilities and chronic health problems. Immobility or inactivity may aggravate the original disability and increase the risk for secondary health problems, such as heart disease, osteoporosis, arthritis, and diabetes. The ACSM stresses the importance of physical activity for people with disabilities for two reasons: (1) to counteract the harmful effects of bed rest and sedentary living patterns and (2) to maintain optimal functioning of body organs or systems.[61]

Not too long ago, regular physical activity was missing in the lives of many people with disabilities.[62] The reasons included lack of knowledge about the importance of physical activity, limited access to recreation sites and difficulty with

■ Having a disability does not mean a person can't exercise or be fit. Exercise counters the effects of immobility and inactivity, improves all body functions, and enhances self-esteem for individuals with disabilities as well as for people in the general population. *(Adam Pretty/Getty Images)*

transportation, a low level of interest, and the lack of exercise facilities and resources designed to accommodate people with disabilities. Dan Cummings, for example, broke his neck and was diagnosed as a quadriplegic. He was told he would never walk again. Through extensive physical therapy that included using a walker, Dan walked again 4 years later and founded a physical rehabilitation center that supports people with spinal cord injuries.[61]

Laws have strengthened the rights of people with disabilities and fostered their inclusion in programs and facilities providing physical activity opportunities. Increased visibility and positive images of people with disabilities engaging in physical activity, such as in the Special Olympics, Paralympics, and wheelchair basketball, have also helped raise awareness.

PHYSICAL ACTIVITY FOR LIFE

The most significant drop in a person's physical activity typically occurs in the last few years of high school and the first year of college.[62] The decline accelerates again after college graduation. However, people can make physical activity a lifetime pursuit. In this section, we consider two helpful factors—commitment to change and social/community support.

Making a Commitment to Change

Assess your physical activity status in terms of the Stages of Change Model (described in Chapter 1). This model proposes five stages: precontemplation, contemplation, preparation, action, and maintenance. In the precontemplation and contemplation stages, the biggest challenges for most people are barriers to exercise.[63] Common barriers to active lifestyles cited by adults are inconvenience, lack of self-motivation, lack of time, fear of injury, the perception that exercise is boring, lack of social support, and lack of confidence in the ability to be physically active.[64]

In the preparation stage, self-assessment is critical. Ask yourself these four questions: (1) What physical activities do I enjoy? (2) What are the best days and times for me to participate in physical activities? (3) Where is the best place to pursue them? (4) Do I have friends or family members who can join me? In preparing to exercise, you also need to take into account your current level of fitness and your previous experiences in various physical activities. All this information will help you develop an exercise program that you can commit to and maintain.

In the action stage, goal setting is key. Your goals should be based on the benefits of physical activity, but they should also be specific and reasonable. Achievable and sustainable goals are essential for exercise compliance. Include both short-term and long-term goals in your plan, and devise ways to measure your progress. Build in rewards along the way.

Once you have been physically active almost every day for at least 6 months, you have reached the maintenance stage. One key to maintaining an active lifestyle is believing that your commitment to physical activity can make a difference in your life. People who establish this personal stake in physical

Public Health Is Personal

Active Lifestyles and the Built Environment

Inactive lifestyles strongly coincide with neighborhoods that were not designed to promote walkability and bikeability. Until recently, however, the health community did not associate the built environment with chronic diseases and mental health. *Healthy People 2020* and the Institute of Medicine are now targeting the built environment in designing urban and suburban communities to promote active lifestyles. The *built environment* refers to human-made space in which people live, work, and recreate on a daily basis.

Ideally, neighborhood design includes four land uses to promote active lifestyles: (1) residential, (2) industrial, (3) green space, and (4) institutional (schools, parks, recreational facilities). Traditional built neighborhoods, with their long distances between homes, schools, and businesses, instead increased residents' reliance on cars for trips to parks, recreational facilities, and stores. Air pollution and heavy auto traffic on major roads were also problems, and the frequent lack of sidewalks and walking or biking trails discouraged physical activity. The redesign of neighborhoods and communities can play a significant role in achieving the physical activity objectives promoted by the Surgeon General and the Centers for Disease Control and Prevention (CDC). Consider the following:

- Walking and biking increase when people are shielded from traffic by sidewalks, well-lit streets, walking paths, and biking paths.

- Neighborhood walkability had been found to increase a person's physical activity by 35 to 49 minutes per week.

- Walking and biking trails that are improved by lighting, good trail conditions, cafes, and restrooms promote use. People who use walking and biking trails on a weekly basis are twice as likely to meet the Surgeon General's and CDC's objectives than those who don't.

- Adults walk for only about 21 percent of trips that are less than 1 mile. Achieving "traffic calming" (by imposing slower driving speeds) and designing neighborhoods to offset the threat of crime (such as by taking advantage of the natural surveillance opportunities created when storefronts face transit facilities) both increase walkability.

Active Living by Design (ALD) was founded to work with communities to improve community health, particularly by encouraging active lifestyles. It is a multidisciplinary organization engaged in public health, public policy, urban planning and design, community development, communications, nutrition, architecture, and social work activities that help rural, suburban, urban, and local and state governments build a culture of active living and healthy nutrition.

McGraw Hill connect

Sources: Sallis, J. F., Floyd, M. F., Rodriguez, A. A., et al. (2012). The role of built environments in physical activity, obesity, and CVD. *Circulation, 125*(5), 729-737; Living by Design. (2017). *Community action model.* Retrieved from http://activelivingbydesign.org/about/community-action-model.

activity are more likely to maintain an active lifestyle. Being a mentor to friends and family members can also help you become or stay motivated to make exercise a lifelong habit. When exercise has become entrenched as a lifelong behavior—when it's as much a part of your day as eating and sleeping—you are in the termination stage. Remember, the more active you are, the more health benefits you will receive.

Do You Have Time to Exercise? As you read in this chapter, most people do not get enough exercise. One of the common reasons they give is that they don't have time. But the American Time Use survey disputes this explanation, noting that U.S. adults on average have 5 hours of free time each day. Rather than being used for exercise, it is dominated by television watching (men, 3 hours 31 minutes; women, 2 hours 55 minutes). About 2 hours is spent in other leisure (mobile phone, computer). Men average 24 minutes of exercise in leisure time and women 14 minutes. Although college graduates have 90 minutes less daily leisure time than people with less than a high school degree, they spend on average 10 minutes more on daily exercise than those with a graduate education diploma (GED)[65].

Although lack of time is not the real reason people do not exercise enough, the energy required and the cost of exercise

are factors. Lower-income adults may be working multiple jobs to meet family financial demands, and limited leisure time is devoted to necessary rest and recuperation. Gym memberships and exercise clothing and equipment cost money and may limit exercise options, Still, the underlying point is that for most people time is not a barrier to getting sufficient exercise.[65]

Using Social and Community Support

A network of friends, coworkers, and family members who understand the benefits of exercise and join you in your activities can make the difference between a sedentary and an active lifestyle. For example, using a fitness app on a smartphone to share exercise data has been shown to be socially contagious. A study found that people run faster, run farther, run longer, and run more often when their exercise data are shared with their peers.[66] Family and friends are not enough, however; activity-friendly communities are also instrumental in promoting physical activity.

Your health is a function of the interaction between your personal competencies and the environmental barriers and supports in your neighborhood (see the box "Public Health Is Personal: Active Lifestyles and the Built Environment"). Many communities have paths, trails, sidewalks, and safe

When communities provide spaces for physical activity and improve access to those spaces, people respond by becoming more active. Thus, public policy and community planning play important roles in the physical fitness of community members. *(Deposit Photos/Glow Images)*

streets that encourage people to become and remain physically active.[67] There are also community programs that encourage parents to walk their children to school, that promote "mall walking" (walking for exercise at nearby shopping malls), and that sponsor biking and walking days. In addition, access ramps and adapted transportation help people with disabilities overcome barriers that discourage physical activity or make it difficult.[68]

Core principles for active communities are shown in the ecological model for designing communities in Figure 6.2. The components of the model are individual, physical activity domains, social/cultural environment, built environment, and policy environment. The model emphasizes that no single factor alone determines the level of a person's physical activity; the individual, the built environment, the social/cultural environment, and the policy environment are all interrelated. As you can see, the individual is

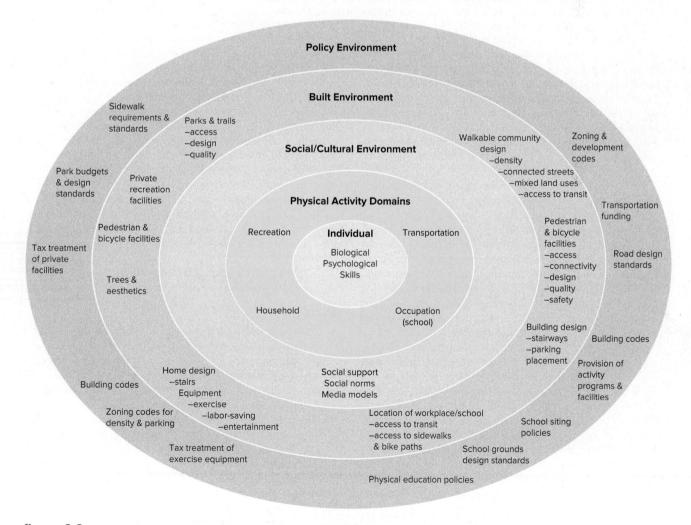

figure 6.2   **Ecological model for designing active communities.**

at the center of the model, which includes personal factors that influence physical activity—knowledge, attitudes, behaviors, motivations, perceived barriers, skills, and disabilities or injuries. The social/cultural environment includes peers, family, partners, work colleagues, support institutions (schools, employers), social support services, cultural norms, and community socioeconomic status. The built environment includes weather, geography, safety, community design, and public transportation. The policy environment refers to legislation, city ordinances, urban planning policies, and local politics that have the potential to affect physical activity.[68,69,70]

When you make personal choices about where to live and work, look at a map of the immediate area and think about how the community you're considering is planned. Are recreational areas nearby? What types of places are within a 10-minute walking distance of home and work? Will living in this community help to make you more active and physically fit? Taking such questions into consideration will give you more opportunities to make physical activity and exercise a natural part of your life.

The key message of this chapter is that physical activity is a natural, enjoyable, sometimes thrilling, frequently challenging part of human life. It is a part of life that children instinctively embrace but that adults may have lost touch with by living in a fast-paced but sedentary culture. We encourage you to get up, get moving, and get back in touch with the lifelong pleasures of physical activity.

Due to the many benefits of active lifestyles, one issue is whether the race to build state-of-the-art campus recreation centers using student fees needs to slow down. See the box "You Make the Call: Should Public Colleges and Universities Continue to Rely on Student Fees to Build Elaborate Campus Recreation Centers?"

You Make the Call

Should Public Colleges and Universities Continue to Rely on Student Fees to Build Elaborate Campus Recreation Centers?

To enhance the student campus life experience and boost enrollments, colleges and universities are building elaborate resident halls, student unions, dining halls, and campus recreation centers. These facilities address the nonacademic side of campus life. But how much is too much when it comes to state-of-the-art campus recreation centers? Many public colleges and universities are finding out that funds from the state, corporate sponsorship, and private donors are drying up. Administrators are relying more and more on student fees to construct campus recreation centers that are placing a financial burden on students.

Campus recreation centers have expanded from the traditional core of gymnasium, weight rooms, basketball courts, and pool to incorporate wellness programs, social functions, and leisure time activities. Students no longer must share the center's recreation space with athletic programs. Many centers now offer wave-park features such as a lazy river and exotic slides. Fitness facilities include modern equipment, functional workout space, spas, and sports-beverage cafes. Some centers have bowling alleys and movie theaters. To lure students, faculty, staff, and even local community members, campus recreation centers must be well located, efficient, and offer health club luxuries.

The financial arms race to compete with other colleges and universities for student enrollment by building palatial campus recreation centers has caused many public colleges and universities to incur significant debt. There are three profound consequences. First, campus life amenities have driven up tuition and thus student debt. Rising student debt and student defaults on college loans creates bad publicity for colleges and universities. Second, increased capital expenditures have led to inadequate budget expenditures for building maintenance and funding of new academic buildings. Many public and colleges and university academic buildings are more than 20 years old, obsolete, or in desperate need of repair. Third, these expenditures on campus amenities reinforce the perception that college students are consumers who must be catered to in order to prevent them from taking their business elsewhere. An intriguing question is whether appealing to their aesthetic tastes will lead students to place less attention on their academics.

Only about 50 percent of public colleges and universities allow student referendums on funding campus recreation projects. Administrators who deny the use of referendums may be concerned that it would establish a precedent in which students have political power over their institutions' financial decisions. The encouraging news is that students are now demanding referendums, and in some cases they are voting down the use of student fees for nonacademic facilities. This message may send a signal to administrators that they need to decelerate the arms race for campus living facilities.

What do you think? Should student fees be used for building luxury-level campus recreation centers?

Pros

- College students are demanding luxury-quality campus life experiences. Colleges and universities are simply meeting that demand by building state-of-the-art recreation centers.
- Declining state support has forced public colleges and universities to rely more on student fees to meet student demand for campus amenities.
- The only thing worse than being part of the campus recreation center arms race is not being part of it. Campus recreation centers are used as a campus life feature to attract enrollments. Failure to build these facilities places public college and universities at a disadvantage in student recruitment.

Continued...

Concluded...

Cons

- Studies estimate that up to 50 percent of college students do not use student recreation centers.
- Student fees should be used to support only academic programs and not campus-life experiences.

- Per-student recreation fees now exceed $200 at many public universities. Many college students are already in significant debt to fund their education. Colleges and universities should pursue corporate funding in place of student fees to build state-of-the-art campus recreation centers.

Sources: Bady, S. (2013). Trends report: New facilities enhance the quality of campus life. BDC Network. Retrieved from https://www.bdcnetowrk.com/trends-report-new-facilities-enhance-quality-campus-life; Nietzel, M. (2018). Students begin to tap the brakes on the campus amenities arms race. Forbes. Retrieved from htttps://www.forbes.com/sites/michaelnietzel/2018/11/05/students-beging-to-tap-the-brakes-the-campus-amenities-arms-race/#5b88a6321bcc; Atwood, E. (2017). The evolution of campus recreation facilities and programs. Athletic Business. Retrieved from http://athleticbusiness.com/rec-center/the-evolution-of-campus-recreation-facilities-and-programs.html.

In Review

What is fitness?

Physical fitness is generally defined as the ability of the body to respond to the demands placed upon it, and good health depends on physical fitness. Skill-related fitness is the ability to perform specific skills associated with recreational activities and sports; health-related fitness is the ability to perform daily living activities with vigor.

What are the benefits of physical activity and exercise?

Physical activity is activity that requires any kind of movement; exercise is structured, planned physical activity. Physical activity and exercise confer benefits in every domain of wellness, including physical benefits to the cardiorespiratory, skeletal, and immune systems; improved cognitive functioning; relief from depression, anxiety, and stress; and benefits to LDL cholesterol and blood glucose levels. Inactivity is a leading preventable cause of premature death from such causes as cardiovascular disease and cancer. Of all the positive health-related behavior choices you can make, exercising may be the easiest, most effective, and most important. Strength training for bone mass density is especially important before age 30.

How much should you exercise?

A widely accepted set of guidelines aimed at promoting and maintaining health and preventing chronic disease, issued by the U.S. Department of Health and Human Services, calls for 150 minutes of moderate-intensity aerobic activity or 75 minutes of vigorous-intensity aerobic activity each week. Activity should also be included each week for cardiorespiratory fitness, muscle strengthening, flexibility, and weight management.

What are the components of health-related fitness?

The components of health-related fitness are cardiorespiratory fitness, musculoskeletal fitness (muscular strength, muscular endurance, and flexibility) and body composition. When you are designing an exercise program, consider the FIT dimensions of your sessions: frequency, intensity, time, and type. Cardio fitness, the center of any fitness program, is developed by activities that use the large muscles of the body in continuous movement. Muscular strength and endurance are developed by weight, or resistance, training. To gain muscle tissue, exercise is preferable to drugs and dietary supplements. Flexibility is developed by stretching. Body composition can be controlled by the amount of physical activity you engage in. It is important to strengthen the posterior muscle chain and not just the anterior muscle chain. Conscious movement and slow movement are receiving attention for neuromotor fitness. Micro-workouts are a new trend in fitness clubs.

How can you improve your health through moderate physical activity?

To make your daily activities more active, try to lessen the time you spend sitting, walk 10,000 steps a day, take the stairs instead of the elevator, and try exergaming.

What special exercise-related considerations and precautions are important for health and safety?

It's important to warm up and cool down before and after exercise, to avoid fatigue and overexertion, to take proper care of injuries, to wear shoes designed for your activity, and to take the outdoor temperature into account. Everyone, including people with disabilities, can benefit from exercise, as long as they follow any relevant special guidelines. The exercise recovery industry is promoting products said to flush the blood, increase blood flow, boost the immune system, and facilitate hydration. Cold and heat therapy and compression forces are especially marketed. Although some of their products may be effective, many such marketers make false claims.

What strategies can help you be physically active throughout your life?

Assess your commitment to physical activity, and overcome obstacles to beginning and maintaining it, by using the Stages of Change Model. Join friends, coworkers, and family members in regular physical activity, and advocate for community planning that encourages physical activity.

Personal Health Portfolio

Chapter 6   Assess Your Physical Activity

Part 1 Daily Physical Activity Log

Complete the following activity log, noting all your activity over a period of 24 hours, including time spent sleeping, watching television, and so on. This log will help you evaluate your overall activity pattern and how much time you spend in sedentary activities.

Day/Date: _____

Activity	Duration

Part 2 Physical Activity for Fitness: Weekly Log

Next, evaluate the activities you engage in that count toward meeting the physical activity recommendations for adults. Enter the activity name (e.g., walking or stretching) and activity category (aerobic, muscle-strengthening, or flexibility), and note which days you engage in the activity. For aerobic activities, enter the intensity level and how long you were active; only count activity sessions of 10 or more minutes. Log activities for a week; then total your time for moderate- and vigorous-intensity aerobic activities.

Activity Name	Activity Category	Intensity Level*	Mon	Tue	Wed	Thu	Fri	Sat	Sun
Sample: Brisk walking	Aerobic	Moderate		30 min			45 min		
Sample: Stretching	Flexibility		X		X		X		

*Aerobic activities only

Weekly total moderate-intensity activity: _____ min   **Weekly total vigorous-intensity activity:** _____ min

CRITICAL THINKING QUESTIONS

1. What is your weekly total for moderate-intensity equivalent minutes? Note that every minute of vigorous exercise counts as 2 minutes of moderate activity. Light activity and activity of less than 10 minutes in duration do not count toward your weekly total.

2. Did you meet your weekly goal number of days for muscle-strengthening and flexibility activities?

3. As mentioned in the text, walking is an excellent lifestyle physical activity for health. Walking to public transportation, such as the bus or the subway, can be an easy way to accumulate the weekly recommended amount of physical activity. How do you get to and from campus (and around your campus itself) and to your job if you have one? What factors affect how much you are or aren't able to incorporate walking into your daily activity? For example, perhaps you are taking this class online and thus don't have to leave the house to attend class. Or perhaps your part-time job as a dog walker means you walk for 2 hours on 5 days of the week. If you use Fitbit to track steps walked in a day, you can use this information to help you with your activity analysis.

4. If you did not meet the Physical Activity Guidelines for Americans, what are some things you can do to increase your daily physical activity?

5. Think about your neighborhood or community. Does it facilitate physical activity, or does it present barriers to physical activity? For example, can you and your neighbors walk to the local grocery store? Is there a park nearby where you can walk or play sports? If your community does not encourage physical activities, what needs to change?

6 Choose either walking or biking. Is your campus and local community walkable or bikeable? To help with your assessment, you may want to consult the Delaware checklist for walkability, at http://www.ipa.udel.edu/healthyDEtoolkit/walkability/checklist.html. For bikeability, use this checklist: http://www.pedbikeinfo.org/cms/downloads/bikeability_checklist.pdf.

7 Body Weight and Body Composition

Deklofenak/123RF

Ever Wonder...

how to maintain a healthy weight?

whether being overweight can run in families?

what normal portion sizes look like?

verweight and obesity are increasingly worrisome problems in the United States and around the world. Among U.S. adults, 31.8 percent meet the criteria for overweight and 39.8 percent meet the criteria for obesity.[1] **Overweight** is defined as body weight that exceeds the recommended guidelines for good health; **obesity** is body weight that greatly exceeds the recommended guidelines.

In 1990, 10 states and territories reported a rate of obesity under 10 percent, and no states or territories reported rates greater than 15 percent. Twenty-six years later, in 2017, no state or territory had an obesity rate under 20 percent, 23 states and territories had rates between 30 and 35 percent, and 7 states and territories had rates of more than 35 percent (see the box "Who's at Risk? Variation in Prevalence of Obesity Among Adults in the United States").[2] There appears to be a slowing in the rate of increase in obesity since 2011, which is critical because otherwise all U.S. adults could be overweight within a few generations.[3] Worldwide, rates of obesity have more than tripled since 1975. An estimated 650 million people (13 percent of the world's population) are obese; rates vary tremendously within and between countries, but at this time overweight and obesity are a greater risk to health than underweight for most of the world's populations.[4]

No sex, age, state, ethnic or racial group, or educational level is spared the problem of overweight, although the young and the poor are most affected. In the United States, rates of obesity for youth have almost tripled since 1980, and today an estimated 17 percent of those aged 2 to 19 years are obese. Youth from low-income families have significantly higher rates of obesity than their peers from high-income families. The connection between poverty and obesity is also seen at a country level, with the majority of the worlds' overweight and obese children living in developing countries. Childhood rates of overweight and obesity are particularly worrisome because, without intervention, overweight children tend to become overweight adults.[5,6]

WHAT IS A HEALTHY BODY WEIGHT?

How much should you weigh? The question is tricky because there is no right answer given that at the individual level it is more important to consider body composition and the way your body functions. Yet people often ask this question, and for a variety of reasons. Consider the following scenarios. A 16-year-old varsity wrestler may feel pressure from a coach as a competition weigh-in approaches or may desire to compete in a particular weight class. An 18-year-old woman comparing herself with the fashion models in magazines may have an unhealthy (and unrealistic) weight goal influenced by a media-generated cosmetic ideal. A 25-year-old man with a new diagnosis of diabetes may wonder whether the 10 pounds he gained over the summer will worsen his health.

Overweight
Body weight that exceeds the recommended guidelines for good health.

obesity
Body weight that greatly exceeds the recommended guidelines for good health, as indicated by a body mass index of 30 or more.

Who's at Risk?
Variation in Prevalence of Obesity Among Adults in the United States

Rates of obesity have soared since 1990. Multiple factors—some known, some still to be identified—account for this trend. While no area is spared, rates of obesity vary significantly by state and region, and by race and ethnicity as well. Consider how the factors in the socioecological model introduced in Chapter 1 might account for these variations.

Prevalence of Self-Reported Obesity Among U.S. Adults by State and Territory, 2017

Source: "Adult Obesity Prevalence Maps," from Behavioral Risk Factor Surveillance System, Centers for Disease Control and Prevention, 2017, https://www.cdc.gov/obesity/data/prevalence-maps.html

Table 7.1 Body Mass Index (BMI)

Find your height in the left-hand column and look across the row until you find the number that is closest to your weight. The number at the top of that column identifies your BMI. The darkest shaded area represents healthy weight ranges.

BMI	18	19	20	21	22	23	24	25	26	27	28	29	30	31	32	33	34
Height																	
4'10"	86	91	96	100	105	110	115	119	124	129	134	138	143	148	153	158	162
4'11"	89	94	99	104	109	114	119	124	128	133	138	143	148	153	158	163	168
5'0"	92	97	102	107	112	118	123	128	133	138	143	148	153	158	163	168	174
5'1"	95	100	106	111	116	122	127	132	137	143	148	153	158	164	169	174	180
5'2"	98	104	109	115	120	126	131	136	142	147	153	158	164	169	175	180	186
5'3"	102	107	113	118	124	130	135	141	146	152	158	163	169	175	180	186	191
5'4"	105	110	116	122	128	134	140	145	151	157	163	169	174	180	186	192	197
5'5"	108	114	120	126	132	138	144	150	156	162	168	174	180	186	192	198	204
5'6"	112	118	124	130	136	142	148	155	161	167	173	179	186	192	198	204	210
5'7"	115	121	127	134	140	146	153	159	166	172	178	185	191	198	204	211	217
5'8"	118	125	131	138	144	151	158	164	171	177	184	190	197	203	210	216	223
5'9"	122	128	135	142	149	155	162	169	176	182	189	196	203	209	216	223	230
5'10"	126	132	139	146	153	160	167	174	181	188	195	202	209	216	222	229	236
5'11"	129	136	143	150	157	165	172	179	186	193	200	208	215	222	229	236	243
6'0"	132	140	147	154	162	169	177	184	191	199	206	213	221	228	235	242	250
6'1"	136	144	151	159	166	174	182	189	197	204	212	219	227	235	242	250	257
6'2"	141	148	155	163	171	179	186	194	202	210	218	225	233	241	249	256	264
6'3"	144	152	160	168	176	184	192	200	208	216	224	232	240	248	256	264	272
6'4"	148	156	164	172	180	189	197	205	213	221	230	239	246	254	263	271	279
6'5"	151	160	168	176	185	193	202	210	218	227	235	244	252	261	269	277	286
6'6"	155	164	172	181	190	198	207	216	224	233	241	250	259	267	276	284	293

Underweight (≤18.5)	Healthy Weight (18.5–24.9)	Overweight (25–29.9)	Obese (≥30)

Source: National Heart, Lung, and Blood Institute. (n.d.). *Body mass index table.* Retrieved from www.nhlbi.nih.gov/guidelines/obesity/bmi_tbl.htm.

There is no "ideal" body weight for any of us because body composition and function are more important than weight measures. A healthy body weight is defined as one that achieves (1) a healthy body mass index (BMI), (2) body composition with an acceptable amount of body fat, (3) fat distribution that is not a risk factor for illness, and (4) the absence of any medical conditions (such as diabetes or hypertension) that suggest a potential benefit from weight loss. If you currently meet these criteria, you will want to focus on maintaining your current weight and composition. If you don't meet them, you may need to lose or gain weight or work on body composition. Let's start by examining BMI, then look at body composition and body fat distribution.

Body Mass Index

Body mass index (BMI) is a measure of your weight relative to your height. It is important to take height into account when looking at weight. You can use a table to find your BMI (see Table 7.1) or calculate it using the following formula:

$$BMI = \frac{\text{weight in kg}}{(\text{height in meters})^2} \quad OR \quad \frac{\text{weight in pounds}}{(\text{height in inches})^2} \times 703 (\text{conversion factor})$$

BMI is used to *estimate* the health significance of body weight. BMI correlates with increased risk of death. People with BMIs at the high end (greater than 30) or at the low end

body mass index (BMI)
A measure of body weight in relation to height.

Starting the Conversation
What's the Problem with the BMI?

Q: How would you react if your parents received a report card "grading" you on your BMI?

Over half the states across the country now have legislation requiring primary and secondary schools to screen students for BMI. Many schools will then send the results home to parents as part of a BMI report card. The screening is in response to the rapidly rising rates of overweight and obesity in children and youth across the country (and the world). The goal of screening is to identify youth at high risk of negative health outcomes and to educate and inform parents to increase the likelihood that they will help change children's diet and physical activity levels.

However, parents, as well as some organizations, are concerned that there may be some unintended negative consequences. They worry that weight screening may increase weight-based stigma and lead to embarrassment and lower self-esteem, which may then lead to unhealthy weight-control practices and make matters worse.

Given a lack of evidence about what the results of school-based screening actually are, the Centers for Disease Control and Prevention (CDC) does not make a recommendation about whether schools should conduct it. The agency does, however, recommend that safeguards be put in place before schools start screening to ensure confidentiality and educational opportunities for follow-up.

Another criticism is that BMI is not an accurate measure of the problem. Health risks are associated with body composition—in particular, with high levels of body fat. BMI levels are strongly correlated with body fat levels, but individuals can have healthy or unhealthy body composition at different BMI levels.

Distinctions among healthy weight, overweight, and obesity are arbitrary, and there is no scientific reason to set the BMI thresholds for overweight and obesity at 25 and 30, respectively. Over the past several decades, the threshold for overweight set by different health organizations has varied from 24.9 to 27.8. The risk of mortality in the overweight category (BMI = 25 to 29.9) is not significantly higher than that in the healthy weight category.

Thus, although research shows that the incidence of cardiovascular disease (CVD) and other diseases increases with overweight and obesity, BMI may not be the best indicator of risk. Body composition assessment (waist-to-height ratio, waist circumference, and waist-to-hip ratio or actual measures of body fat) or nutrition and fitness assessments may be more accurate. A person who is sedentary and eats a high-fat, high-calorie diet could be in the healthy weight range and have health problems.

Given all these criticisms, why does use of the BMI persist? The CDC recommends the use of BMI because it is a convenient measure and the test is easy to administer. In addition, there is simplicity in using a single number to make medical diagnoses and give weight-loss advice. Some critics assert that it's good business for the pharmaceutical and diet industries if millions of people think they are overweight and should lose weight. Despite concerns, BMI remains a popular tool for individual and population measures.

Q: Given current public health efforts to combat childhood obesity, do you think schools have a role in educating parents about their children's weight-related health risks? If so, do you think measuring BMI is a way to do this?

Q: How might schools reduce potential stigma for students in the overweight and obese categories?

Q: Why is the 25 to 29.9 BMI category labeled "overweight" when the risk of mortality is not significantly different from that in the 20 to 25 "healthy" range?

Sources: Thompson, H. R. & Madsen, K. A. (2017). The report card on BMI report cards. *Current Obesity Reports,* 6(2), 163-167; Madsen, K. A., Linchey, J., Ritchie, L., & Thompson, H. R. (2017). The fit study: Design and rationale for a cluster randomized trial of school-based BMI screening and reporting. *Contemporary Clinical Trials,* 58, 40-46; Centers for Disease Control and Prevention. (2017). *Body mass index (BMI) measurement in schools.* Retrieved from https://www.cdc.gov/healthyschools/obesity/bmi/BMI_measurement_schools.htm

(less than 18.5) have an increased risk of health problems and death, as we will discuss later. Consequently, the National Institutes of Health and the World Health Organization use the following guidelines for adult BMI categories:[4,7]

	BMI
Underweight	Less than 18.5
Healthy weight	18.5 to 24.9
Overweight	25 to 29.9
Obese	30 and above

We use a comparative calculation to define overweight in children and adolescents. For these age groups, BMI is plotted using growth charts, and a percentile ranking is identified (the percentile indicates the individual's BMI compared to that of other children of the same sex and age).

There are limitations to using BMI to calculate risk of disease at the individual level, because it is only an estimate of body composition. For example, even if you and your friend have the same BMI, you may have different body compositions. In athletes or others with a muscular build, BMI may overestimate body fat (and risk). In the elderly or others who have lost muscle mass, BMI may underestimate body fat (and risk). For more on the limitations of the BMI, see the box "Starting the Conversation: What's the Problem with the BMI?"

Body Composition

Body composition is an important measure in assessing and improving health. There are many ways to think about

Fat mass (FM)		Fat-free mass (FFM) or lean mass		
Essential lipids	Non-essential lipids	Total body water	Protein	Bone mineral

figure 7.1 **Body composition: Fat mass and fat-free mass are the most commonly measured components. FM consists of essential and nonessential lipids. FFM or lean mass consists of total body water, protein, and bone minerals.**

composition, from the atomic level to the cellular level to the tissue-organ level. The most common methods for body composition assessment assess the ratio of fat mass (FM) to fat-free (or lean) mass (FFM), as illustrated in Figure 7.1. This measure is based on the assumption that the FFM components of total body water, protein, and bone mineral components have a fairly constant relationship.[8]

Body fat is essential for vital hormone function. As with body weight, there are ranges for healthy body fat. For men, 8 to 24 percent is considered a healthy range, although 5 to 10 percent may be appropriate for athletes. For women, 21 to 35 percent is considered the general-health range, and 15 to 20 percent for athletes. Below these ranges, hormone production decreases and health problems can occur, such as infertility, loss of sex drive, hair loss, bone loss, lack of menstruation, and depression.[9]

Excess body fat is what appears to be the cause of increased health risk. A BMI in the overweight or obese category suggests an increased likelihood of excess body fat and lower lean mass. However, someone in the "healthy" BMI category can have excess body fat and low lean mass, and someone in the overweight or obese BMI category can have high lean mass and low excess body fat. That is why BMI is only a screening test and why body composition can help you determine individual health needs.

So, how do you know your body composition? It can be measured during a physical or fitness assessment. The most accurate methods are expensive and require special equipment, so they are used less frequently. They include weighing a person underwater (immersion) and using a special type of X-ray (DXA). Two simpler but slightly less reliable methods are measuring thickness of skin and fat in several locations of the body (skinfold measurement or caliper testing) and sending a weak electrical current through parts of the body to measure the electrical resistance of tissue (bioelectrical impedance) and calculate body fat.[8] New technologies being used in research include total body MRI or CT scans, which can visualize and measure muscle, fat, and organ tissues. In addition, smartphone apps are making bioelectrical impedance analysis more accessible by collecting information about the user's activity level, energy expenditure, heart rate, and other physiological processes.[10]

Body composition is critical to pay attention to if you decide you want to make changes to improve your health. Some dietary approaches (which we'll discuss later) are more effective at maintaining or improving body composition, whereas others may promote loss of protein mass rather than loss of nonessential body fat.

Body Fat Distribution

It is not only the amount of fat you carry that's important in assessing your disease risk, but also where you carry it. Fat carried around and above the waist is abdominal fat and is considered more "active" than fat carried on the hips and thighs. Abdominal fat (also called visceral fat or *central obesity*) is a disadvantage because it breaks down more easily and enters the bloodstream more readily.

A large abdominal or waist circumference is associated with high cholesterol levels and higher risk for heart disease, stroke, diabetes, hypertension, and some types of cancer. If your BMI is in the healthy range, a large waist circumference may signify an independent risk for disease. If your BMI is in the overweight or obese range, measuring your waist circumference can be an additional tool to determine your health risk. If your BMI is above 35, your health risk is already high.

To measure your waist circumference, use a tape measure. Measure your waist right above your hip bones, with the tape crossing your navel. Keep the tape level. It should be snug, but not tight. A waist circumference associated with increased health risk is:

Greater than 40 inches (102 cm) for men.
Greater than 35 inches (88 cm) for women.[11]

Hormones influence fat distribution. Obese men tend to accumulate abdominal fat, whereas obese women tend to accumulate fat on the hips and thighs. However, in women fat shifts to the abdomen with the drop in estrogen that occurs at the onset of menopause. This shift coincides with an increased risk of heart disease for women.

Issues Related to Obesity

A weight and body composition in the healthy range reduces your risk of health problems. In contrast, elevated body fat levels (associated with obesity)

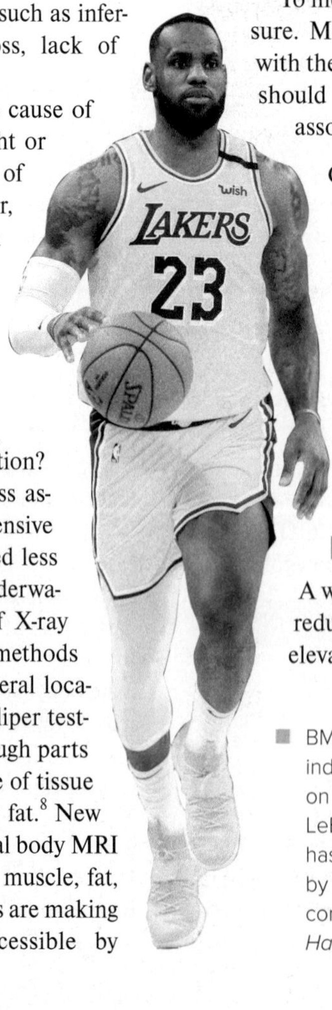

■ BMI is a screening tool that can be an inaccurate indicator of healthy body weight and fat percentage on an individual level. For example, basketball player LeBron James, at 6 feet 8 inches tall and 250 pounds, has a BMI of 27 and would be classified as overweight by his BMI category. But as an individual he is considered fit based on body composition. *(Sean M. Haffey/Getty Images Sport/Getty Images)*

increase your risk. Obese people are four times more likely than people with a healthy weight to die before reaching their expected lifespan. They have an increased risk of high blood pressure, diabetes, elevated cholesterol levels, coronary heart disease, stroke, gallbladder disease, osteoarthritis (a type of arthritis caused by excessive wear and tear on the joints), sleep apnea (interrupted breathing during sleep), lung problems, and certain cancers, such as uterine, prostate, and colorectal.[12,13] Women who are obese may also have more difficulty becoming pregnant, and once pregnant they have an increased risk of diabetes, high blood pressure, and birth complications, and of having a child with a disability.[14,15]

To quantify the impact of obesity on health, studies try to measure the percent of annual deaths from all causes that can be attributed to obesity. Estimates range from 5 to 15 percent.[12] These estimates take into account the role obesity plays in increasing risks primarily for diabetes, cancer, and heart disease.[16] Of great concern, given the high rates of childhood obesity, is the fact that the earlier people become obese and thus the longer they live with obesity, the greater their risk of poor health outcomes.[12,17]

Diabetes and Obesity Rates of obesity and diabetes in the United States have risen in parallel. Diabetes is a disease in which the levels of glucose circulating in the bloodstream are too high, setting the stage for heart disease, kidney failure, blindness, and sexual dysfunction. (A detailed discussion of diabetes is in Chapter 14.) There are several types of diabetes, but 90 to 95 percent of people with diabetes have Type 2 diabetes, the form strongly associated with obesity. Not everyone who is obese will get diabetes, but obesity is the major risk factor (again because it is a marker for high levels of nonessential fat mass). As more children and adolescents become overweight, Type 2 diabetes, previously rare in this age group, has become more common among them. Approximately 80 percent of U.S. youths with Type 2 diabetes are obese. For people in any age group who are overweight or obese, small reductions in weight through diet and exercise reduce the risk of developing diabetes and are the first step in treating Type 2 diabetes.[18]

Discrimination and Obesity People who have been overweight or obese for most of their lives are likely to have suffered from childhood bullying or teasing. Weight-related bullying does not stop with adulthood; people who are overweight or obese face discrimination in educational opportunities, hiring practices, and wages, as well as social stigma. Health-promotion activities that focus on weight and individual responsibility further increase stigma and discrimination against people who are overweight or obese.[19] This response has real impacts: a study reported a significant wage difference between people of normal weight and those who are obese. The overall cost of obesity for a woman was $4,879 per year and $2,646 for a man.[20] Unfortunately, evidence shows that the experience of weight discrimination increases the likelihood of engaging in behaviors that contribute to further

weight gain—avoidance of physical activity, binge eating, low self-esteem—thus creating a vicious cycle.[21]

The Problem of Underweight

Although obesity receives more attention, the problem of underweight can be as serious. A sudden, unintentional weight loss without a change in diet or exercise level may signify an underlying illness and should prompt a visit to a physician. Depression, substance abuse, eating disorders (see Chapter 8), thyroid disease, infections, and cancer can all be associated with unexpected weight loss.

However, some people just have difficulty keeping on weight. For them, calorie intake is inadequate for energy output. To gain weight, they need to change the energy balance. Calories can be increased by eating more frequent meals (every 3 hours or so) and choosing more energy-dense foods, such as nuts, fish, and yogurt. Adding protein powders or nutritional supplements to the diet is another option. The pattern of physical activity can also be changed to reduce aerobic exercise and increase weight training.

WHAT FACTORS INFLUENCE YOUR WEIGHT AND BODY COMPOSITION?

There is no simple answer to the question of why people in the United States (and around the world) are gaining weight. The complex factors that contribute to this trend include individual, social, and environmental components. Where you live, the foods and resources you have access to, and the norms of your community strongly influence your body composition. You may look to other family members, for example, and think it is your genes that make you overweight. Unless you are adopted, however, the people who gave you your genes also taught you how to eat, chose your neighborhood, and influenced your educational status and perhaps your occupation. It appears that for most people, obesity is a multifactorial condition; that is, your susceptibility to obesity is due to a complex interaction among multiple genes and your environment.[22]

Genetic and Hormonal Influences

If neither of your parents is obese, you have a 10 percent chance of becoming obese. The risk increases to 80 percent if both your parents are obese. Adopted children also tend to be similar in weight to their biological parents, and twin studies support the idea that there is a genetic tendency toward obesity. These findings have led to the search for genes associated with obesity.

Hundreds of genes have been associated with BMI and obesity. In rare cases, a single gene may account for weight gain. In most cases, however, obesity is a multifactorial disorder in which multiple genes may predispose toward obesity, but interactions with the environment influence outcomes, and diets high in fruits and vegetables can reduce the impact of genetic susceptibility.[23,24] In addition to specific gene changes, there is strong evidence that epigenetic changes can occur in utero and contribute to obesity. These alterations in the structure of DNA change the way genes are transcribed into RNA and proteins. As an example, maternal undernutrition or overnutrition influences the risk of obesity in offspring through epigenetic changes.[25] ("Genetic Inheritance" in Chapter 1 discusses epigenetics.)

Genetic mutations that influence obesity predominantly act by increasing or decreasing the levels of nearly two dozen hormones. Adjustments in the hormone levels (or the function of receptors to which they bind) result in alterations in appetite or energy expenditure. The hormones act in the brain to influence our desire to start or finish eating; to monitor external cues for food such as smells, sights, texture, conditioned responses, and advertising; to monitor internal cues such as body fat stores, glucose level, free fatty acids, and stomach fullness; and to adjust metabolic rate.

Most of human history has occurred during times when food was scarce. Thus, our bodies have adapted systems that conserve energy if our energy intake (the food we eat) is decreased. When we decrease calorie intake, hormonal signals increase hunger and decrease nonresting energy expenditure. In times of food scarcity, these hormonal adaptive changes are life-saving. However, in times of increased access to high-calorie foods, the same adaptive changes make intentional weight loss challenging.[8]

The food-brain pathways have some overlap with drug-brain pathways in that foods can trigger the release of dopamine and opioids in the brain. This release then contributes to our wanting and liking food (similar to addiction) and complicates our relationship with food, making it more than an energy source. It is not yet fully understood how our bodies regulate energy intake and output, but it is certainly complicated. If you are maintaining your current weight, the interaction of hormones controls your daily calorie intake to within 10 calories (a single potato chip) of balanced food intake and energy expenditure.[8,26]

Thyroid disorders can be associated with weight gain or loss. The thyroid gland, located in the neck, produces a hormone that is involved in metabolism. If the gland becomes less active, metabolism slows and weight is gained. If the gland is overactive, metabolism speeds up and weight can be inappropriately lost.

gut microbiome
The millions of bacteria, viruses, and other microorganisms that reside in your stomach and small and large intestines and play an active role in digestion and metabolism.

The rapid rise in obesity since the 1980s is too sudden to be explained by genetics. Genes require generations and hundreds of years to change. Epigenetic changes can occur more quickly—within a generation. Environmental influences such as abundant food, and behaviors such as a sedentary lifestyle, are much more likely to produce such effects in a much shorter period.[8,22]

Stress Stress is linked with body composition and weight gain. There are multiple ways this link occurs. The stress response affects physiology. In response to it, our bodies release several hormones, including adrenaline and cortisol. Fat cells release fatty acids and triglycerides in response to these hormones and increase the amount of circulating glucose. These responses are vital in enabling the body to handle acute stress, especially physical stress. The release of glucose provides energy for your muscles so you can fight or flee. But when stress is chronic, the constant presence of these hormones can influence fat deposits, increasing the amount of fat stored in the abdomen. Stress also affects behaviors and can alter eating patterns. Adrenaline is an appetite suppressant, whereas cortisol stimulates the appetite. You may find that in high-stress situations, such as the transition to college or final exams week, you eat more for comfort or increase your intake of high-fat or high-sugar foods.[27]

Chronic stress can also lead to decreases in physical activity and increases in sedentary behavior. You may find it harder to stick with an exercise plan or to get away from your computer and meet up with friends. Chronic stress also alters sleep patterns, which can exacerbate changes in food behavior and physical activity. And interestingly, while stress can affect you, new research shows that it is also influencing the bacteria in your gut, which may increase our concerns about body weight and composition.[27]

Gut Microbiome An increasing amount of research is looking at the role of the **gut microbiome**—the millions of bacteria, viruses, and other microorganisms that reside in your stomach and small and large intestines and play a role in food digestion, absorption of nutrients, and metabolism. At birth, your intestinal tract becomes colonized and many factors influence the type and diversity of microorganisms that live within you. The way you were born (vaginal birth versus cesarean section), whether you were breast or formula fed, your diet and physical activity throughout life, and medications you take all influence the diversity and function of your microbiome. Your microorganisms are even influenced by stress you may experience.[28,29]

Studies are starting to show a relationship between obesity and the gut microbiome. Gut microorganisms are necessary for humans to digest carbohydrates. Certain types of bacteria digest monosaccharides, oligosaccharides, and polysaccharides and convert them into short-chain fatty acids, which we can then absorb. In addition, gut bacteria appear to act on the release of hormones that influence eating behaviors, thus affecting appetite and energy storage and expenditure. Further exploration of the complex role our microorganisms play may allow for new interventions to improve body composition and weight (discussed later).[28,29]

Age and Gender

It's helpful to take a life-course approach with regard to health and obesity, since there are life stages when it is easier or harder to maintain a healthy body composition. The first 1,000 days of life (from periconception through pregnancy, infancy, and early childhood up to 24 months) are critically important and set health patterns and trends for life. At birth, your susceptibility to obesity has already been partially programmed. Not only did you inherit half your genes from your biological mother, she gave you your first environment—in utero. If she experienced obesity, rapid weight gain, or starvation during pregnancy, your cells will maintain a memory of that through epigenetic changes, and it will increase your risk for future obesity. In addition, your first exposure to gut microorganisms occurs during birth, and whether you are breast or formula fed influences the way the microorganisms develop.[29,30]

Early-childhood physical activity and feeding patterns establish biological programming and lifestyle habits. Breast-feeding, avoidance of sugar-sweetened beverages, maintenance of regular sleep patterns, and promotion of physical activity all improve body composition and reduce the risk of obesity later in life. In early childhood, you learn eating patterns from your family. Your lifelong food choices are shaped by these social, cultural, and traditional influences. Because of the powerful impact of the first 1,000 days on long-term health, there is increasing emphasis on the returns from investing in support for women during pregnancy, for families with young children, and for young children themselves. Communities that develop social policies such as paid leave, flexible work hours, and support for breastfeeding increase the likelihood of healthy starts.[31,32]

During adolescences, rapid growth occurs, and lean body mass increases and generally reaches its peak. Gender-specific patterns of fat mass distribution occur as a part of healthy puberty. Testosterone increases muscle development and results in greater increases in lean mass and a decrease in fat mass for males, whereas estrogen increases healthy fat deposition in females. As a result, postpuberty, men and women have a difference in body fat of about 10 percent of body weight. This difference remains fairly stable throughout life.[33] Transgender or gender-fluid youth can find puberty especially distressing because the development of secondary sex characteristics may be discongruent with their identified gender and can lead to disordered eating patterns. Gender-affirming hormone therapy can reduce psychological distress.[34,35,36]

Physical activity during adolescence influences body composition and increases fat-free mass. However, adolescence is a time for changing patterns in physical activity. Adolescent girls are on average less physically active than their male peers. By high school, only 6 percent of females and 18 percent of males meet the adolescent physical activity guidelines of 60 minutes of aerobic activity a day and strength training three times per week. Participation in organized sports appears to decrease most during the late teens, whereas youth do appear to have a stable or increasing amount of physical activity relating to work or chores in later adolescence.[37,38]

Between the ages of 20 and 40, further changes usually affect body composition. With completion of high school comes a further decline in physical activity, and the transition to college is associated with weight gain.[39,40] Pregnancy can be a factor in changing body composition for women during this time. Weight gain is common during pregnancy, and an estimated 40 percent of women gain excessive weight, which increases their risk of obesity later in life.[41]

For most people, changes in body composition continue with aging. There is an ongoing gradual decrease in lean mass and an increase in body fat mass and a redistribution of body fat for both males and females toward the central or abdominal location. In women, the hormonal changes of menopause lead to more rapid changes in body composition and fat distribution. Without active intervention, muscle mass peaks at around age 30 and gradually decreases by about 20 to 40 percent by age 70. With this composition change comes a decrease in energy requirements and a risk of further increases in body fat and weight gain even if calorie and physical activity levels remain constant. During these years, weight-bearing exercise, such as walking, becomes critical to maintain body mass and bone strength. Increasing resistance training can help slow the loss of muscle mass.[42]

■ Family, social, cultural, and other environmental factors, as well as genes and hormones, play a role in weight. These can include favorite family and ethnic foods, mealtime rules and traditions, and the kinds of restaurants and grocery stores available in the community. *(Stockbroker/123RF)*

Life Stories

Lisa: Trying to Make Healthy Changes

Lisa, a biology major at a state college, is the first member of her family to attend college. Her parents and two younger siblings live in a small industrial town about 200 miles from campus. Her father has worked in an automotive parts plant for the past two decades, and her mother works part-time as the office administrator at the high school. Both Lisa's parents are overweight, and her maternal grandmother has diabetes. Because her parents get home late, the family tends to eat a lot of pre-packaged and processed foods. When her mom cooks, she tends to make "comfort meals" like meatloaf and mashed potatoes, fried chicken with biscuits and gravy, and pot roast. No one in the family has time for exercise; they are too busy working and running the household.

When Lisa got to college she was overweight and not physically fit; even walking the quarter-mile from the residence hall to her classes left her out of breath. She was worried about her health. However, she did so much walking on campus that she actually started to get stronger and have more endurance. She even started to slowly lose weight. She became friends with two women in her residence hall who were much more conscious about food choices than she was, and they often ate dinner together. Following their lead, Lisa found herself frequenting the salad bar more often than the taco bar. One of the women was a vegetarian, and Lisa started enjoying some vegetarian dishes as well, though she still ate fast food when she was rushed during exam weeks.

Lisa spent the summer after freshman year at home, working a summer job. In the evenings, her mom served the same high-fat, high-calorie meals she always had. At first, Lisa talked up her new eating patterns, trying to interest her parents in a healthier diet, but her mom seemed hurt by Lisa's suggestions, and her dad was angry that her mom was hurt. Lisa even offered to do the grocery shopping one week, thinking she would get some good fruits and veggies, at least for herself if not for the whole family. She was disappointed to see there was not much choice in produce at the local supermarket, and what was there looked wilted and unappetizing. When she brought home strawberries for dessert, her younger brother and sister ignored them and went for the ice cream.

Lisa slipped back into her old eating and activity patterns and spent more and more time watching television with her family in the evenings. She had hoped to continue walking, but her neighborhood wasn't very safe and there wasn't a fitness center or gym in town. She was unhappy with herself but she also felt guilty trying to be different from her family, and there was a certain comfort in doing familiar things.

When the summer was over, Lisa felt both sad and relieved to be leaving her family and going back to school. She would be living in a campus apartment with her two friends, and she knew it would not be such a struggle to eat well and add physical activity back into her day. She worried about her family and wished they had the same resources she did.

- How did social or cultural factors influence Lisa's food patterns at home and at school?

- Can you think of things Lisa could have done differently with her family?

- How has college changed your patterns of eating and activity? What happens when you go home for breaks?

Obesogenic Environments and Lifestyle

The term *obesogenic environment* highlights the fact that components of our environment can make it harder for us to establish health dietary and physical activity patterns, thus increasing the likelihood of unhealthy body composition and obesity. You have learned about the recommended physical activity levels and nutrients required for healthy body function, but knowledge is obviously not enough. You are living in a world in which populations are consistently overfed but undernourished.

The automobile, television, and computer have improved our lives in many ways, but they have also led to unhealthy habits. Before the mid-1900s, most people's daily lives included regular physical activity. Our current lifestyle has become so mechanized and sedentary, however, that many of us can go through a day spending almost no energy on physical activity. With decreases in activities of daily living has come an emphasis on the need for focused exercise, yet meeting activity recommendations is hard for most people. For example, only 43.9 percent of college students, who typically have access to recreational facilities and intramural sports, meet the recommended aerobic physical activity guidelines for adults.[43] As you read about each of the following factors, recall the socioecological model (see Chapter 1) and think about how you might influence your family or community to create healthier environments.

Food Choices We all have a diet, the sum total of food and beverages that we eat. Many factors influence it, including health, culture, economics, and philosophical beliefs. Your choice in foods is driven by availability—cost and convenience—as well as by your upbringing. As a college student, you are probably on a limited budget and have limited time to prepare food. Chapter 5 discussed the rising rates of food insecurity on college campuses. This scenario will likely remain relevant after you leave college and enter the workforce. Maintaining a healthy diet depends on having knowledge about healthy food choices, the money to buy healthy foods, and the time to prepare a healthy meal[44,45] (see the box "Life Stories: Lisa: Trying to Make Healthy Changes").

In general, unhealthy foods are more available, more convenient, more heavily advertised, and less expensive than healthy foods. The least expensive sources of food are highly

Action Skill-Builder

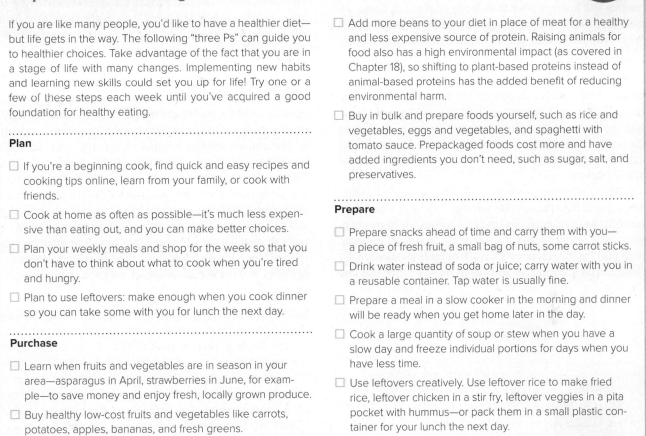

Steps to Healthier Eating

If you are like many people, you'd like to have a healthier diet—but life gets in the way. The following "three Ps" can guide you to healthier choices. Take advantage of the fact that you are in a stage of life with many changes. Implementing new habits and learning new skills could set you up for life! Try one or a few of these steps each week until you've acquired a good foundation for healthy eating.

Plan

☐ If you're a beginning cook, find quick and easy recipes and cooking tips online, learn from your family, or cook with friends.

☐ Cook at home as often as possible—it's much less expensive than eating out, and you can make better choices.

☐ Plan your weekly meals and shop for the week so that you don't have to think about what to cook when you're tired and hungry.

☐ Plan to use leftovers: make enough when you cook dinner so you can take some with you for lunch the next day.

Purchase

☐ Learn when fruits and vegetables are in season in your area—asparagus in April, strawberries in June, for example—to save money and enjoy fresh, locally grown produce.

☐ Buy healthy low-cost fruits and vegetables like carrots, potatoes, apples, bananas, and fresh greens.

☐ Add more beans to your diet in place of meat for a healthy and less expensive source of protein. Raising animals for food also has a high environmental impact (as covered in Chapter 18), so shifting to plant-based proteins instead of animal-based proteins has the added benefit of reducing environmental harm.

☐ Buy in bulk and prepare foods yourself, such as rice and vegetables, eggs and vegetables, and spaghetti with tomato sauce. Prepackaged foods cost more and have added ingredients you don't need, such as sugar, salt, and preservatives.

Prepare

☐ Prepare snacks ahead of time and carry them with you— a piece of fresh fruit, a small bag of nuts, some carrot sticks.

☐ Drink water instead of soda or juice; carry water with you in a reusable container. Tap water is usually fine.

☐ Prepare a meal in a slow cooker in the morning and dinner will be ready when you get home later in the day.

☐ Cook a large quantity of soup or stew when you have a slow day and freeze individual portions for days when you have less time.

☐ Use leftovers creatively. Use leftover rice to make fried rice, leftover chicken in a stir fry, leftover veggies in a pita pocket with hummus—or pack them in a small plastic container for your lunch the next day.

Source: U.S. Department of Agriculture. (2017). *10 tips: Eating better on a budget.* Retrieved from https://www.choosemyplate.gov/ten-tips-eating-better-on-a-budget; U.S. Department of Agriculture. (2017). Plan your weekly meals. Retrieved from https://www.choosemyplate.gov/budget-weekly-meals

processed refined grains, foods with high added-sugar content, and foods with high oil content. These calorie-dense foods have low nutritional value. In contrast, the foods recommended in the Dietary Guidelines are nutrient dense—fresh fruits, vegetables, poultry, fish, whole grains, and meat. They cost substantially more per serving than calorie-dense foods, however, and the cost disparity has increased significantly over the past 20 years. When you are hungry and have limited time and budget, our societal structures make inexpensive, highly processed, calorie-dense and nutrient-poor foods more accessible, and they become the easier choice.[44]

The impact of these choices is exaggerated in low-income communities where fast-food outlets and small food markets dominate the retail food landscape, providing easier access to foods with high fat and sugar content (see "Food Deserts" in Chapter 5). In affluent neighborhoods, supermarkets predominate, providing easier access to low-fat, whole-grain foods and diverse fresh fruit and vegetable choices. In addition, with higher incomes comes the ability to purchase healthier prepackaged foods or to eat at higher-end restaurants offering

healthier food choices when time is an issue.[45] These factors contribute to the strong association between poverty and obesity and nutritional deficiency. Obesity rates are highest among the poorest and least-educated segments of the population.[44] College campuses are not immune to this effect. The rising rates of food insecurity on campuses mean students are struggling to meet healthy nutrition guidelines, with only 4.2 percent eating five or more fruits and vegetables per day.[43]

Being aware of the factors influencing your food choices can help you achieve and maintain a healthier diet. A little planning can go a long way toward supporting healthy food choices (see the box "Action Skill-Builder: Steps to Healthier Eating"). In addition, recognizing the role of community and policy can help you advocate for changes on a larger scale.

Eating Out   Today, eating out has become a part of daily life. In the United States, an estimated 50 percent of total food money is spent on foods eaten away from home.[45] The increase to this level is likely related to the increased number of dual-career households and single-parent households and the convenience and accessibility of fast foods, prepared foods, and restaurants. The concern is that foods served in restaurants and fast-food outlets tend to be higher in fat and total calories and lower in fiber than foods prepared at home. Increased reliance on eating out is associated with weight gain.[46] What options for eating out are available in your community?

Larger Portions People consistently eat and drink more when offered larger servings. Serving size has increased steadily both inside and outside the home. The largest increases in serving size have occurred in fast-food restaurants and may be due to "supersized" pricing strategies. The larger the portion of food, the worse we become at estimating how much we are eating. (See Figure 7.2 for some visual images of portion sizes.)

Paying attention to serving sizes on food labels, dividing prepackaged food into smaller servings, and using visual cues can help you eat more appropriate portions. At home, consider using smaller plates and glasses.[47] New federal regulations now require restaurants with 20 or more locations to list calorie counts on menus and menu boards.[48] See the box

figure 7.2   **Visual images of portion sizes.**
Half a cup of fruit, vegetables, pasta, or rice is about the size of a small fist. One cup of milk, yogurt, or chopped fresh greens is about the size of a small hand holding a tennis ball. Three ounces of meat, poultry, or fish is about the size of a computer mouse or a deck of cards. Two tablespoons of salad dressing, oil, or butter is about the size of a ping pong ball. One ounce of cheese is about the size of a pair of dice.
((Closeup of right male hand): dinga/123RF; (Hand holding tennis ball): Pixtal/SuperStock; (Deck of cards): Hutchings Photography/ Digital Light Source; (Golf ball): Photobvious/Getty Images; (Die): C Squared Studios/Getty Images)

"Consumer Clipboard: Get the Most Out of Your Menu" for more tips on healthy eating when you're eating out.

The Built Environment People are increasingly living in urban centers around the world, raising the role of the built environment, which includes the way neighborhoods are designed and transportation systems interact, and the level of environmental outputs such as air quality and pollution and physical activity. Design of individual buildings, neighborhoods, and entire communities alter our physical activity. Inside a building, visible and well-lit stairs increase the likelihood people will use them. Housing built in close proximity to destinations such as schools, shops, and work sites will increase the likelihood that people walk or bike for transportation rather than drive. Well-lit roads with low traffic speeds and designated bike lanes and sidewalks further encourage active forms of transportation. Green space, good air quality, and safe neighborhoods encourage and increase physical activity throughout the life span. They are all beyond the control of individuals, however; they require community planning and the consideration of health in urban planning policies.[49,50]

Sedentary Lifestyle Sedentary behavior—sitting or lying down while awake—has become increasingly recognized as important for its impact on health. With the increasing use of electronic devices for work and leisure, people are engaging in more sedentary behavior than ever before. Whether you are at work, home, or play, sitting too long in front of a screen or in a car is bad for your health. (For more on this topic, see the box "Could You Spend Less Time Sitting?" in Chapter 6.) If you sit or lie down for 23.5 hours a day, your 30 minutes of physical exercise is not going to reverse the negative effects.[51,52]

Sleep The amount of sleep you get may also put you at risk for gaining weight. Energy expenditure is lower when you are sleeping, so it would seem logical that the less you sleep, the less likely you are to gain weight. However, studies have consistently shown the opposite: reduced sleep is associated with weight gain. People are more likely to increase food intake, particularly of energy-dense foods, when sleep deprived, in part due to hormonal changes. Attempts to lose weight and improve body composition can become more challenging, too. The impact of sleep deprivation on health appears to be strongest in children, adolescents, and young adults. With only 10 percent of college students reporting getting enough sleep to feel rested on a daily basis, paying attention to your sleep patterns may be important.[43,53]

Social Networks Friends and social networks also appear to influence weight. If your friends gain weight, you are more likely to gain weight. The more strongly you identify a person as a friend, the more likely you are to match his or her weight gain. This effect may relate to social norms and how comfortable you are with overweight and obesity. The good news is that recruiting friends in your efforts to maintain a healthy weight or lose weight may make those efforts more successful.[54,55]

Consumer Clipboard

Get the Most Out of Your Menu

Effective May 2018, restaurants with more than 20 outlets are required to list calories on their menus.
Many restaurants have nutrition brochures available on request, and many post complete nutritional information on their websites.

Popular restaurant chains load up their menus with fat and salt.
An order of 8 chicken nachos can have more than 1,000 calories and nearly 2,000 mg of sodium. Buffalo wings with blue cheese can have nearly 1,500 calories and more than 4,500 mg of sodium (twice the recommended daily limit).

If you can't tell from the menu, ask if a soup is cream based or broth based.
Cream-based soups have more calories, fat, and saturated fat. Soups can also be laden with salt, so avoid them if you're trying to reduce sodium in your diet.

Calories and fat soar when you add a creamy or ranch dressing; most restaurants have a low-fat option, such as low-fat Italian or vinaigrette.
Ask for dressing on the side so you can control the amount you consume.

If you need a sweet taste after a meal, order one dessert for the table with spoons for everyone.
Instead of pie (300 to 500 calories per slice) or ice cream (270 calories per half-cup scoop), try a yogurt parfait (300 calories) at Starbucks, a fruit and yogurt parfait (130 calories) at McDonald's, or a cup of fresh berries (about 50 calories).

Regular soda is loaded with sugar and calories.
A large (32-ounce) cola drink has 86 grams of sugar, the equivalent of about 21 teaspoons, and 310 calories, virtually all from sugar (4 grams of sugar = 1 teaspoon = 16 calories). Water is free and has 0 calories.

Calculate calories from fat by multiplying grams of fat by 9 (fat supplies 9 calories per gram).
Calories from fat should not exceed 30 percent of total calories. For example, if an item has 300 calories and 15 grams of fat, it has 135 calories from fat (15 × 9), which equals 45 percent of the total calories (135/300). Calculate calories from saturated fat the same way. Calories from saturated fat should not exceed 10 percent of total calories.

Portion and plate sizes can be three or more times the amount considered a serving.
- Consider splitting an entrée or taking half home for lunch the next day. Notice when you feel full and stop eating!
- Grilled chicken and grilled fish are likely to be the healthiest items on the menu.
- Ask for any sauce on the side.

One fast-food meal can provide your entire recommended daily allowance of calories, fat, saturated fat, cholesterol, and sodium.
A burger and fries from a restaurant can have 2,000 calories.

A large order of french fries from a fast-food restaurant can have 500 calories, with 200 or more of those calories from fat.
Consider a side salad instead.

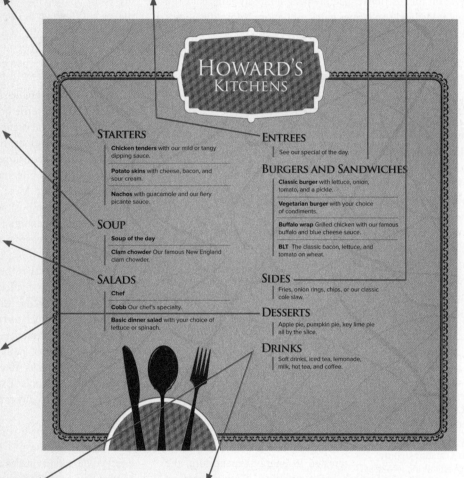

Coffee drinks can be very high in calories, especially if they include whipped cream or ice cream.
- A 16-ounce Starbucks Mocha Frappuccino with whipped cream has 400 calories, 15 grams of fat, and 60 grams of sugar (15 teaspoons). Ask for nonfat milk and skip the whipped cream—that reduces calories to 260 and fat to 1 gram, but sugar stays high (58 grams).
- Starbucks "Trente" size for iced drinks is 31 ounces, a volume of 916 milliliters. The capacity of the average adult stomach is about 900 milliliters. Ask for a smaller size.
- Coffee and tea have 0 calories (but not if you add milk and sugar!).
- A medium smoothie has about 250 calories, whether at McDonald's or at Jamba Juice. A medium vanilla shake at McDonald's has 680 calories.
- A glass of wine has about 100 calories; a 12-ounce beer has between about 150 and 180 calories; a light beer usually has fewer than 100 calories. Because of added sugar and other ingredients, a mixed drink can soar to hundreds of calories. Alcohol itself supplies 7 calories per gram.

Dieting and Obesity Contributing to the obesity trend is "yo-yo dieting," or **weight cycling**. People frustrated with their weight often turn to cycles of diets in hopes of finding a solution. Fad diets do not consist of realistic food plans that can be maintained for a lifetime. People may lose weight initially, but most find it difficult to maintain the harsh restrictions, returning to their previous patterns. Rapid weight loss is usually associated with a loss in lean mass, not fat mass. With rapid weight loss on a highly restrictive diet, the body can enter starvation mode, with decreased basal metabolism. Once off the restrictive diet, the person rapidly gains back the weight lost and sometimes gains even more before the body's metabolism readjusts.

THE KEY TO HEALTHY BODY COMPOSITION: ENERGY BALANCE

The relationship between the calories you take in and the calories you expend is known as your **energy balance**. If you take in more calories than you use through metabolism and movement (giving you a positive energy balance), you store these extra calories in the form of body fat. If you take in fewer calories than you need (so you have a negative energy balance), you draw on body fat stores to provide energy. Energy in must equal energy out to maintain your current weight. In simple terms, if you adjust one or the other side of the equation, you will gain or lose weight. In reality, however, the human body adapts, and metabolism can change in complex ways in response to adjustments in calories in and calories out.

weight cycling
Repeated cycles of weight loss and weight gain as a result of dieting; sometimes called yo-yo dieting.

energy balance
The relationship between caloric intake (in the form of food) and caloric output (in the form of metabolism and activity).

thermic effect of food
An estimate of the energy required to process the food you eat.

basal metabolic rate (BMR)
The rate at which your body uses energy for basic life functions, such as breathing, circulation, and temperature regulation.

Estimating Your Daily Energy Requirements

In Chapter 5, we discussed energy intake, the calories-in side of the energy equation. Here, we are more interested in energy expenditure, the calories-out side. Components of energy expenditure include the energy required to process food and respond to environmental and physiological changes, the basal metabolic rate, and physical activity. These components are influenced by genetics, age, sex, body size, fat-free mass, and intensity and duration of activity.

The **thermic effect of food** is an estimate of the energy required to process the food you eat—to chew, digest, metabolize it, and so on. The thermic effect is generally estimated at 10 percent of energy intake. If, for example, you ingested 2,500 calories of food during a day, you would burn approximately 250 calories processing what you ate. However, protein has a higher thermic effect than simple carbohydrates and fats, meaning it takes more energy to digest a high-protein meal than a high-fat meal. In addition, the more processed foods are, the less energy your body uses digesting them. Thus, what you eat makes a difference in the amount of energy required to digest it. The thermic effect of food accounts for approximately 8 to 15 percent of daily energy expenditure.[8]

The **basal metabolic rate (BMR)** is the rate at which the body at rest uses energy to maintain the function of vital organs such as the heart, lungs, nervous system, liver, intestines, muscles, and skin. About 60 to 70 percent of energy consumed is used for these basic metabolic functions. BMR is affected by several factors, including age, gender, and weight. Most important to our discussion is the fact that body composition influences BMR. Lean muscle mass burns more energy (calories) than fat mass. Increasing muscle mass increases your BMR; losing muscle mass decreases it.

Physical activity is the other component of energy expenditure. It is usually divided into nonexercise activity (such as the activity of working, daily living, and even fidgeting) and exercise activity (such as running, biking, and hiking). **Nonexercise activity thermogenesis (NEAT)** varies tremendously, from 15 percent of daily energy expenditure in sedentary people to as much as 50 percent of daily energy expenditure in highly active people. **Exercise activity thermogenesis (EAT)** also can vary—typically ranging from 15 to 30 percent of daily energy.[8]

You can estimate your daily energy expenditure by considering (1) the thermic effect of the food you eat, (2) the energy you spend on basal metabolic functions, and (3) the energy you spend on physical activities. Severe injury, prolonged illness, and extreme environmental conditions can affect BMR, but these factors are not usually taken into account unless their influence is pronounced. Keep in mind, however, that dietary composition, body composition, and activity levels vary and have meaningful impact on these estimates. To estimate your daily energy expenditure, complete the Personal Health Portfolio activity at the end of the chapter.

nonexercise activity thermogenesis (NEAT)
The energy expenditure associated with all physical activity that is not specifically exercise related—such as the activity of work, daily living, or fidgeting.

exercise activity thermogenesis (EAT)
The energy expenditure associated with exercise activity—such as running, biking, or hiking.

Adjusting Your Caloric Intake

In simple terms, if you are trying to lose weight, 1 to 2 pounds per week is a healthy goal. Because a pound of body fat stores about 3,500 calories, you need to decrease your total calorie intake for the week by about 3,500 calories to lose 1 pound per week. If you lose weight at a faster rate, you are likely to lose lean tissue such as muscle, which decreases your BMR. Diets too low in calories may not provide enough nutrients and may trigger a further drop in BMR if the body perceives a need to "hold on" to calories. The body also adapts to a calorie-restricted environment by reducing NEAT; people move less and even fidget less when they are calorie restricted.

If you are trying to increase your weight, you will need to increase your total calorie intake for the week by 3,500 calories to gain 1 pound per week. However, the body can adapt in a calorie-rich environment by increasing NEAT in an attempt at weight stabilization. (Note that these figures are estimates.)

Focusing on nutrient-rich foods and reducing calorie-dense, low-nutrient foods is important. Watch your intake of high-fat foods because they are energy dense, meaning they have high numbers of calories per ounce and low nutrient quality. Eating high-fat foods usually leads to higher total caloric intake and is linked with obesity. Foods high in complex carbohydrates, such as whole grains, have a greater thermic effect than do high-fat foods, such as whipped cream. Thus, it takes more energy to process a high-carbohydrate diet (when the carbohydrates are complex carbohydrates), and less of the food's energy is available for storage as fat.

Pay attention to the calories you drink, too. Juices, sodas, protein drinks, and alcoholic beverages are all high in calories, and most of those are considered empty calories because they offer little nutritional value. Shifting your beverage intake to water can significantly reduce non-nutritional calories and improve diet quality.

ARE THERE QUICK FIXES FOR A HEALTHY BODY COMPOSITION AND HEALTHY WEIGHT?

Most of us would love a quick and easy way to achieve and maintain a healthy body composition for life. However, there are no quick fixes to our current obesity trend. People are beginning to recognize that holistic approaches are important. If you want to make a change and are assessing the best approach for you, be skeptical of unrealistic promises and use your critical thinking skills when considering a dietary or weight loss program. Some programs have been around for years, while others seem to come and go. If you determine weight loss is necessary, you will need to change the balance between energy in and energy out. We discussed some diets, including DASH and a vegetarian diet, in Chapter 5. Here we will explore some approaches to weight-loss diets.

Weight-Loss Diets

Every year, "new and improved" fad diets seduce consumers despite the fact that their safety and effectiveness are often unproven. These diets follow a pattern of altering the balance

Any diet plan that requires you to eat only certain foods or to stop eating entire food groups is not a recipe for long-term success. *(Photoroyalty/Shutterstock)*

of carbohydrates, protein, and fat with the goal of promoting weight loss. Many will label certain foods as "good" or "bad," require the elimination of one of the five food groups, or prescribe certain "fat-burning foods." Popular diets frequently promote rapid change, and even if some do lead to short-term weight loss, they are not associated with long-term loss. In addition, recall that rapid change is usually due to loss in lean mass, which can be associated with detrimental effects.

If you are exploring a promoted weight-loss diet, it will likely fall into one of a few major groups. *Low-carbohydrate diets* (sometimes called "ketogenic" diets) restrict how many carbohydrates you eat. Without carbohydrates to use for energy, your body breaks down fats, creating ketones, which it can use for fuel in place of glucose. Another option is a *high-fiber diet,* which recognizes that not all carbohydrates are treated similarly by the body. Increasing fiber can promote a full feeling sooner, and fiber can bind to fats in the gastrointestinal (GI) tract and decrease calorie absorption. *High-protein diets* emphasize increasing protein intake above 10 to 35 percent of total calorie recommendations. The concept is that with higher protein intake you will reduce total calorie intake, due to feeling full earlier. A *low-fat diet* acknowledges the fact that fat is calorie dense and lower in nutrients, and thus decreasing overall fat intake can reduce energy intake. When body composition is evaluated alongside weight loss with the different variations in dietary approaches, the high-protein diet appears to be associated with the least loss of lean body mass.[8,56]

Most dietitians and physicians continue to encourage people to monitor energy balance and eat a diet that emphasizes complex carbohydrates rather than trying fad diets. When evaluating a diet, consider whether the food plan is something you can live with for the long haul. (How to evaluate diets is discussed in the section "Tasks for Individuals" later in this chapter.) The factors that influence our food choices most are taste, cost, and convenience. You are unlikely to stick with a diet if it is too drastically different from your current eating patterns, if it calls for complete elimination of certain foods (especially ones you really like), if it requires hours of preparation, or if it requires the purchase of expensive prepackaged foods.[11]

Weight-Management Organizations

Weight-management organizations offer group support, nutrition education, dietary advice, exercise counseling, and other services including online options. Weight Watchers, Jenny Craig, Take Off Pounds Sensibly (TOPS), and Overeaters Anonymous are well-known weight-management organizations. TOPS and Overeaters Anonymous are free and provide group support. Weight Watchers and Jenny Craig are commercial programs. TOPS focuses on teaching. Overeaters Anonymous may be more suitable for people who binge eat or others with emotional issues related to weight.[57] With any behavior change, clearly stating a plan for change and seeking support enhance success.

The Medical Approach

Because obesity and the associated high-fat mass body composition is a major risk factor for many health conditions, health centers try to help people find solutions. We consider here four medical strategies used to treat obesity: very-low-calorie diets (VLCDs), prescription drugs, surgical procedures, and nonprescription diet drugs.

Very-Low-Calorie Diets An aggressive option for patients with high health risks because of obesity, VLCDs require a physician's supervision. These diets provide a daily intake of 800 calories or less, need to be fortified, and *must* be monitored closely to ensure provision of essential nutrients. VLCDs are used for moderately to severely obese patients (people with BMIs of 30 or greater) who are highly motivated but have not had success with more conservative plans. These diets are short term only (8 to 12 weeks), and then patients transition to a less restrictive program. Weight loss is difficult to maintain, and these diets have little applicability for most healthy people.[8]

Prescription Drugs Because of the expense, potential for side effects, and need for medical supervision, the use of weight-loss drugs is not recommended for everyone. However, medications can be an adjunct to diet, exercise, and behavior changes, and they can support modest weight-loss goals. Per guidelines, the addition of medication can be considered for someone with a BMI of 27 or greater and health conditions that benefit from weight loss (such as diabetes, hypertension, or high lipid levels) or a BMI of 30 or greater.[58,59]

The Food and Drug Administration (FDA) has approved five medications: lorcaserin, phentermine-topiramate, naltrexone-bupropion, liraglutide, and orlistat. The first four work by reducing appetite and increasing the likelihood of success in behavior change. None works independently of behavior change, because the body's biological response to calorie restriction is to adjust hormones to increase hunger signals and slow metabolism. Orlistat works in a different way. It prevents the absorption of 25 to 30 percent of fat calories. Thus it decreases calorie intake. In addition, its main side effect is diarrhea if a person eats a high-fat diet—thus reinforcing the desire to maintain a low-fat intake.[58,59,60,61]

Other drugs and medications are sometimes used in an attempt to help with weight loss, but they are not currently approved for such use by the FDA. The antidepressant fluoxetine (Prozac) has been shown to have some potential weight-loss benefits.

Surgical Options Like medications, surgery should be viewed as an adjunct to supporting dietary and exercise behavior changes. The National Institutes of Health's formal guidelines state that surgical therapy should be considered for patients with a BMI of 40 or greater or for patients with a BMI of 35 or greater with illnesses or risk factors. However, there is increasing research to suggest that surgery may be beneficial for others. A less invasive form of surgery has been recommended for people with a BMI of 30 or higher and poorly controlled diabetes. At present, surgery is not recommended for anyone with a BMI less than 30.

Typical weight loss after gastric surgery is greater than weight loss with medication or lifestyle change approaches and ranges from 20 to 30 percent of weight. Most people have significant improvement in or resolution of diabetes, hypertension, and other obesity-related conditions. As with any surgical procedure, side effects can occur at the time of surgery or after.[62,63]

Nonprescription Diet Drugs and Dietary Supplements Popular over-the-counter diet drugs and dietary supplements include diet teas, bulking products, starch blockers, diet candies, sugar blockers, and benzocaine. A range of herbal supplements—including turmeric, mulberry leaf, ginseng, CQ (*Cissus quadrangularis*), bittermelon, and zingiber—may have modest benefits for weight loss.[64,65] Green tea and chromium picolinate may help conserve lean body mass in the setting of weight loss due to calorie restriction. Caffeine, a stimulant available in many over-the-counter forms, is sometimes used to increase basal metabolic rate and produce weight loss. Caffeine can also cause side effects such as shakiness, dizziness, and sleep problems.[56]

Probiotic supplements are receiving interest as a way to assist in weight management. Given the increasing understanding of the role of our gut microbiome in energy and nutrient absorption and weight management, studies are looking at whether intentional supplementation with healthy gut bacteria (such as lactobacillus and streptococcus) can lead to improvements in metabolism and enhance health weight loss.[29]

Safety concerns continue to be raised about the use of supplements for weight management. A study of emergency room visits for dietary supplements found weight-loss or energy products caused 71 percent of visits and usually involved young adults experiencing chest pain, palpitations, or fast heart rate.[66]

Manufacturers of dietary supplements do not have to submit proof of their efficacy or safety to the FDA prior to sale. Use your critical thinking skills when considering the use of any product, including herbal and dietary supplements, to help in weight loss. All medications, supplements, and herbal treatments have the potential for side effects and risks. Ask yourself the following questions prior to use:

- Is there evidence to support the claims that this product works? Look for peer-reviewed research in mainstream publications and be wary of small, unpublished studies conducted by the product's manufacturer.

- What are the potential risks and side effects of the product? Do the proven benefits (if any) outweigh the risk and side effects?

If you cannot find the answers to these questions, it is best to avoid the product!

The Size-Acceptance Movement

The size-acceptance movement started in response to the frustration felt by many people attempting to lose weight and in response to the discrimination faced by those who are overweight or obese. The approach seeks to decrease negative body image, encourage self-acceptance, and end discrimination. The focus is on how people can be healthy at any size and is in line with research showing that body composition is the most important aspect of health. The movement also aims to draw attention to the fact that good health is a state of physical, mental, and social well-being. Self-esteem and body image are strongly linked, and helping people respect themselves improves their overall health. Size acceptance also emphasizes that people of any size can become more fit and benefit from healthier food choices.[67,68]

The size-acceptance movement has made strides in changing health approaches from weight loss to weight management and in improving fitness at any size, sometimes referred to as the "fit and fat movement." However, pleas by the movement should not obscure the fact that obesity is associated with serious medical problems. The goal is to find a balanced approach that combines personal acceptance with promotion of a healthy body composition.

ACHIEVING A HEALTHY BODY COMPOSITION FOR LIFE

Overweight and obesity are long-term issues that require long-term solutions. Both individuals and society have roles to play in reversing this trend.

Tasks for Individuals

If your genetics or behavioral history predisposes you toward an unhealthy body composition, you can improve your overall health through moderate lifestyle changes. The emphasis should be on a healthier lifestyle, with these components:

- A balanced diet emphasizing fruits, vegetables, and whole grains in appropriate portion sizes.

- A goal of 150 minutes of moderate-intensity or 75 minutes of vigorous-intensity physical activity every week.

This should be divided into smaller sections of time throughout the week (more physical activity may be necessary if you are aiming to lose weight, less if you are aiming to gain weight).

- Reduced time spent in sedentary activities, such as watching television, working or playing on a computer or smartphone, and riding in a car. Try to incorporate movement and consider using a standing or treadmill desk or exercise ball instead of a chair.

- A goal of overall health improvement through targeted improvement in selected areas, such as blood pressure, cholesterol level, and blood sugar level.

- Peer support for your health goals.

- Self-acceptance of body size.

- Follow-up evaluation by a health professional, as needed.

Set SMART Goals Drastic diet changes and quick-fix solutions are unlikely to last for long. The key to long-term weight management is making reasonable, moderate changes that fit in with your life, culture, and tastes. Let's revisit SMART goals, which were presented in Chapter 1, and apply them to weight management:

- *Is the goal specific?* Deciding to eat fresh fruit instead of candy as a late-night snack is a specific goal. So is deciding to go to the gym to run on the treadmill for 30 minutes on Monday, Wednesday, and Friday after chemistry class. Specific goals are easier to accomplish than more general ones.

- *Is the goal measurable?* You can track how often you actually eat fresh fruit as a snack instead of candy or how often you make it to the gym after chemistry class. A measurable goal allows you to track your progress and see how close you are to reaching it.

- *Is the goal attainable?* Your goal should be something that you are able to do rather than something that happens to you. There should be an action on your part.

- *Is the goal realistic?* Small, gradual changes, such as deciding to change from regular soda to diet soda or from whole milk to low-fat milk, are realistic. Once you accomplish the first change, you can then add another small change. With small steps, you are more likely to be successful.

- *Is the goal timely?* When you make a decision to change behavior, set a timeline for when you will reach your goal. You might, for example, give yourself an entire semester to reach your goal of getting 150 minutes of exercise a week.

Choose an Appropriate Dietary Approach Which of the following goals are you hoping to accomplish?

- Lose or gain a small amount of weight? Increase lean muscle mass?

- Maintain weight long-term?

- Replace unhealthy eating and exercise behaviors with more healthy behaviors?

• Reduce risk or control symptoms of diabetes (including maintainable short-term weight loss)?

• Improve heart health?

Which of the approaches in Table 7.2 have you tried? What do you see as its pros and cons based on this chapter?

Evaluate the Support and Obstacles in Your Environment Try to identify supports and barriers to achieving your health goals in the past. Recall the socioecological model in Chapter 1 and then think about how the components of that model might influence your eating and physical activity patterns. With those supports and obstacles in mind, evaluate each of the following characteristics in terms of a change in diet:

• *Realistic.* Are the dietary changes drastically different from the way you currently eat? Although making change is likely part of your goal, if the new foods are too different from your usual patterns or if the change requires you to do a lot of tracking and monitoring, it may not be realistic.

• *Moderate and flexible.* Sudden, drastic changes are hard to implement and to maintain. Balanced diets based on moderation and flexibility are easier to maintain over the long haul.

• *Safe.* Does the diet provide a balanced intake of the major food groups and the necessary vitamins and minerals?

Diets that are too restrictive or that cut out major food groups can endanger your health. For health reasons, some people need to avoid certain foods such as nuts, seafood, or gluten if they are allergic, and some people avoid certain foods for social or cultural reasons. Otherwise, there are no health reasons to completely avoid specific foods.

• *Holistic.* Healthy behavior change for weight loss or gain incorporates regular exercise. Avoiding loss of muscle mass is important. Does your plan incorporate walking, resistance training, or strenuous exercise in addition to dietary changes?

• *Informative.* Are you learning how to choose healthy foods and portions, how to get adequate exercise, and how to eat only when you are hungry and not when you are upset?

• *Compatible.* Food is a strong part of our interpersonal relationships. Will your changes prevent you from eating with friends and family? A diet will be hard to maintain if you do not have a social support system.

• *Affordable.* Money is a major factor influencing food choices. How much can you afford to spend? Commercial plans are likely to charge for membership and for counseling, prepared meals, and other services. Following a raw-food diet is hard without a juicer, blender, and dehydrator.

Table 7.2   Strategies for Changing Body Composition

Type	Theory	Examples
Balanced diets (for diabetes and heart health as well as weight loss)	Encourage some restriction of total calorie intake and focus on complex carbohydrates and lower fats. They tend toward balance among food groups.	DASH, Dr. Weil's Anti-inflammatory, flexitarian, Jenny Craig, Mediterranean, Mayo Clinic, traditional Asian, Volumetrics, Weight Watchers, Zone
Commercial diet programs	Typically based on changing food patterns and increasing exercise, with the help of behavioral counseling and support systems.	Jenny Craig, Nutrisystem, Weight Watchers
Low-calorie diets (includes most weight management organizations)	Specifically incorporate reduction in overall calorie intake.	Body Reset, HMR, Jenny Craig, Nutrisystem, raw food, Weight Watchers
Food-group-restrictive diets	Certain types of food classified as "bad" are eliminated; other foods are "good" metabolic promoters.	• Low fat: macrobiotic, Ornish, TLC, vegetarian, vegan • Low carb/high protein: Atkins, Paleo, South Beach • Detox: Master Cleanse (aka Lemonade Diet)
Meal replacements (shakes and bars)	Prepackaged bars and drinks are used to control calorie intake.	Body Reset, HMR, Medifast, Slim-Fast
Prepackaged meals	Purchased meals are used to control calorie intake.	HMR, Jenny Craig, Nutrisystem, Weight Watchers

Building physical activity into your routine in small ways every day is one key to weight management and weight-loss maintenance. *(Sam Edwards/Caia Image/Glow Images)*

- *Research based.* Is the diet created by a nutrition expert and backed up by objective research? Or is a fad diet intended to give its creator publicity?

Use Tools to Help Change Your Patterns Many behavior management tools are available to help you learn new eating and activity patterns. The following strategies may help get you started:

- *Stimulus control.* Identify environmental cues associated with unhealthy eating habits. Become conscious of when, where, and why you are eating. For example, if you eat a pastry for breakfast because you stop at a coffee shop on the way to class, consider changing your routine—brew coffee at home and make your own fruit-and-yogurt parfait to take with you.

- *Self-supervision.* Keep a log of the foods you eat and the physical activity you do. Schedule time for exercise and plan meals to preempt urges and cravings.

- *Social support and positive reinforcement.* Recruit others to join you in your healthier eating and exercising habits. Exercise together, encourage each other, and plan non-food rewards for reaching goals.

- *Stress management.* Use relaxation techniques, exercise, and problem-solving strategies to handle stresses in your life, instead of overeating or skipping meals.

- *Cognitive restructuring.* Moderate self-defeating thoughts and emotions, redefine your body image by thinking about what your body can do (rather than how it looks), and be realistic about weight loss or gain.

Tasks for Society

Changes in social policies and community design are also needed to combat the obesity epidemic.

Promote Healthy Foods The U.S. Surgeon General has asked that all schools reduce junk food and promote healthy,

balanced meals. Schools can limit access to candy and soda, and municipalities can provide better access to healthy foods through community gardens and equitable supermarket distribution. Federal, state, and local governments can provide financial incentives, such as loan guarantees and reduced property taxes, for supermarkets and small stores that provide healthy foods.

Food subsidies and pricing strategies are a broad-based intervention that can alter eating patterns. Lowering the price of low-fat, nutritious food would increase the rates at which people buy them. However, current food and agricultural policies have supported subsidies for foods that are not always aligned with health-related goals. Adoption of local, state, or federal policies to reduce the cost of fresh fruits, vegetables, and whole foods would increase access.

Look around your campus to see what is being done to promote healthy foods. Do dining halls and food courts offer nutritious choices? Is food labeling available to tell you what meals contain, or which are healthier choices? Do healthy food choices such as fresh fruits, vegetables, and salads cost more than the fried foods or sweets? Is there a community garden or a campus farm where you can grow your own food?

Support Active Lifestyles Through Community Planning Suburbanization and a cultural focus on cars play a major role in our decreased physical activity. As a society, we need to consider ways to encourage a more active lifestyle (see the box "Public Health Is Personal: Walkable Communities"). Community planning can incorporate ideas to encourage physical activity, such as walking areas and parks in all communities, increased public transportation, showering and changing-room facilities in workplaces to encourage biking or walking to work, and flexible work hours to reduce stress and encourage activity.

Support Consumer Awareness about Healthy Eating Choices In a free society, we avoid restricting the media and advertising, but consumers can become more conscious of their effects on eating patterns. Advertising is a supply-and-

Are food choices on your campus healthy ones? Or is there room for improvement? *(Andrew Francis Wallace/Getty Images)*

Public Health Is Personal

Walkable Communities

- Does your campus have well-lit sidewalks?
- Are there curb cut-outs to enable those who roll to do so with ease?
- Are there shared green spaces to gather and play?

"Step It Up! Make Our Communities Walkable" was the U.S. Surgeon General's 2015 Call to Action. Recognizing that individuals, communities, and governments all play roles in increasing rates of physical activity, the Surgeon General is emphasizing the role of walking. People walk for lots of reasons—transportation, socializing, exercise, and health. However, communities differ in their walkability.

Communities with strong public transportation systems encourage people to walk to the bus or train instead of driving. Communities with neighborhood grocery stores, libraries, schools, and parks encourage people to go outside and walk for errands and exercise. Malls with prolonged hours encourage people to walk in regions where cold weather or rain limits their ability to be outside. Campuses that are closed to cars increase walking by students, staff, and faculty. Sidewalks with ramps encourage and enable people in wheelchairs to roll more readily. Well-lit sidewalks reduce risk of falls and increase safety for walkers in the mornings and evenings.

High-income communities tend to have more lights, sidewalks, and parks. Lower-income communities tend to have fewer safe walking areas, fewer parks, and fewer community resources. The difference in access to safe spaces increases disparities in health outcomes between populations.

The first step toward improving walkability is identifying what would make walking safer, easier, and more fun. All community members, especially people who walk in their communities, can identify changes that would enhance equitable access to safe walking. If sidewalks on your campus or in your community are cracked, unlit, too close to busy roads, or even nonexistent, whom can you contact about creating change? Zoning and land-use policies can determine how development occurs and can be influenced by your school administrators or elected officials. Encourage policy makers on your campus and in your community to get out and walk so they can see what barriers exist.

You have to decide to walk, but conditions in your community make it easier or harder, safer or more dangerous, inviting or daunting. What can you do to help your community "step it up"?

Source: U.S. Department of Health and Human Services, Office of the Surgeon General. (2015). *Step it up! The Surgeon General's call to action to promote walking and walkable communities.*

demand industry. If consumers don't buy the products depicted in ads, or if they complain about the content of ads, food manufacturers will eventually respond.

What types of food advertising are present on your campus? How does the campus encourage or limit exposure to media? If a promotional event is occurring on campus, is it clear to students who the sponsor is and what, if anything, is being marketed?

Encourage Health Insurers to Cover Weight-Related-Prevention Programs If individuals, insurers, and health care providers accepted the definition of obesity as a chronic degenerative condition, they might move away from the quick-fix mentality. As with any chronic condition, the focus has to be on sustainable changes. Compared to unrealistic diets, programs that combine nutritional education, exercise education, and lifestyle modification are more likely to promote healthier, more sustainable body composition.

Although conclusive evidence shows that obesity is associated with risks of multiple medical conditions, few insurance plans cover health visits for nutrition, fitness evaluation, body composition testing, or obesity education and treatment. The Affordable Care Act requires health insurance companies to expand coverage for preventive health care, and with concern about health care costs rising, we may see other changes in the future. Employers and educational institutions can push legislators to make preventive medicine a priority for insurance companies.

You Make the Call

Should Employers Encourage Individual Employee Weight Loss and Fitness or Focus on Changing the Environment to Be More Healthy?

Work-based health-promotion activities have gained popularity across the country. Employers are interested in healthy workers because healthy workers increase productivity and reduce health insurance costs to the employer. Workplace health promotion can focus on individual education and behavior change or organizational structures to improve employee health. Given that research shows that people who are overweight or obese face discrimination in the workplace with bias

Continued...

Concluded...

in hiring, lower starting wages, and fewer opportunities for promotion than people in the 18-to-25 BMI category, the impact of these practices is worth considering.

When promotion activities include individual education about lifestyle decisions affecting nutrition, healthy choices, and the importance of physical activity, employers and employees increase their beliefs that the individual is responsible for being overweight or obese. In this setting, stigma and discrimination toward people who are overweight increases.

When employers focus on the job and working conditions and make changes to the organizational environment, including work schedules, pay structures, and food offerings on site, employees and employers recognize the role of structural factors and the way these contribute to health concerns. Weight-associated stigma and discrimination do not increase.

With increasing evidence of the role of environment in healthy body composition, employers can play an important role in improving the health of the workforce by creating healthier environments for workers rather than focusing on employees' behavior. What do you think? How do work-based health-promotion activities affect your perceptions of weight, body composition, and healthy living? Does your work experience create an environment that encourages healthy living or push you to change individual behavior?

Should employers focus more on the context in which you work?

Pros

- The focus on individual behavior change with minimal acknowledgment of the role of the environment, the workplace, and circumstances beyond an individual's control leads employees to assign personal responsibility to weight management and increases anti-fat attitudes and stigma against obese people.
- Employers have control over time schedules and wages. Given that time and cost are major drivers of eating decisions, employers have the ability to support healthy lifestyles with structural changes.
- Your employer shouldn't be telling you how to make your individual lifestyle decisions.

Cons

- Individuals do have responsibility for decisions they make about their lifestyle, and education can be important in improving those decisions.
- Employers bear a cost when employees are unhealthy and thus should try to influence individual lifestyle behaviors.

Sources: Tauber, S., Mulder, L. B., & Flint, S. W. (2018). The impact of workplace health promotion programs emphasis on individual responsibility on weight stigma and discrimination. *Frontiers Psychology, 19*(9), 2206; Dor, A., Ferguson, C., et al. (2011). Gender and race wage gaps attributable to obesity. George Washington University and School of Public Health. Retrieved from www.gwumc.edu/sphhs/departments/healthpolicy/dhp_publications/pub_uploads/dhpPublication_FA85CB82-5056-9D20-3DBD361E605324F2.pdf; Jackson S. E., Beeken, R. J., & Wardle, J. (2015). Perceived weight discrimination and changes in weight, waist circumference and weight status. *Obesity, 22*(12), 2485-2488.

In Review

How is healthy body composition defined?
Overweight and obesity rates, defined respectively as body weight that exceeds or greatly exceeds the guidelines for good health, have been increasing in the United States. Healthy body composition can be defined as an acceptable body mass index (a measure of weight relative to height), an acceptable percentage of body fat, a pattern of body fat distribution that is not a risk factor for illness, or the absence of a medical condition that suggests a need for weight loss (such as diabetes or hypertension). People who don't meet these criteria could improve their health by potentially losing weight and increasing lean body mass. Unexpected weight loss can be the sign of an illness.

What factors influence weight?
Influences on weight include genetic and hormonal factors (including the stress response), gender, age, stress, the gut microbiome, and obesogenic environments and lifestyle (eating out, sedentary living, inadequate sleep, "yo-yo dieting").

What is the best way to manage body weight?
The key to weight control is balancing energy intake (calories) with energy output (physical activity and exercise). This is a

complex relationship, though, due to the body's ability to adapt to changes on both sides of the equation.

Are there quick fixes for overweight and obesity?
Quick fixes such as fad diets usually don't work—they are difficult to sustain and often lead to loss of lean body mass. Realistic goal setting and developing support systems for dietary and activity change are necessary. Medical approaches, including surgery and prescription drugs, are available but don't work on their own—they support dietary, physical activity, and other lifestyle changes. The size-acceptance movement is an alternative that focuses on self-esteem.

How can individuals and society promote healthy weight and body composition throughout life?
The best approach for individuals is long-term, moderate lifestyle changes that include a balanced diet, daily physical activity, specific health-related goals, social support, and self-acceptance. Goals that are specific, measurable, attainable, realistic, and timely are key to long-term weight management. Behavior management strategies can also help. Communities can support healthy weight by promoting healthy foods, planning activity-friendly environments, supporting consumer awareness, and encouraging insurance coverage of obesity-prevention programs.

Personal Health Portfolio

Chapter 7   What Are Your Daily Energy Needs?

You can *estimate* your daily energy needs by (1) measuring your basal metabolic rate (BMR) and (2) calculating your energy expenditure above BMR from your physical activity. Combining the two numbers gives you an estimate of your total energy requirement. This will require fine-tuning based on your body composition, metabolism, and activity and is intended as a start.

1. First, estimate your BMR, the minimum energy required to maintain your body's functions at rest. Begin by converting your weight in pounds to weight in kilograms. Then multiply by the BMR factor, which is estimated at 1.0 calorie/kg/hour for men and 0.9 for women. Then multiply by 24 hours to get your daily energy needs from BMR.

    - Let's look at Gary, a 30-year-old, 180-pound man.

    $$\frac{180\ lb}{2.2\ lb/kg} = 82\ kg$$

    82 kg × 1 calorie/kg/hour = 82 calories/hour

    82 calories/hour × 24 hours/day = 1,968 calories/day

    Gary's BMR—the energy he uses every day just to stay alive—is 1,968 calories.

    - Now let's look at Lisa, a 24-year-old, 115-pound woman.

    $$\frac{115\ lb}{2.2\ lb/kg} = 52\ kg$$

    52 kg × 0.9 calorie/kg/hour = 47 calories/hour

    47 calories/hour × 24 hours/day = 1,128 calories/day

    Lisa's BMR is 1,128 calories per day.

    - Now calculate your own BMR.

    Your weight in lbs _____ /2.2 lb/kg = _____ kg

    _____ kg 1 (men) = _____ calories/hour

    _____ kg 0.9 (women) = _____ calories/hour

    _____ calories/hour 24 hours/day = _____ calories/day

2. Next, estimate your voluntary muscle activity level. The following table gives approximations according to the amount of muscular work you typically perform in a day. To select the category appropriate for you, think in terms of muscle use, not just activity.

Lifestyle	BMR factor
Sedentary (mostly sitting)	0.4–0.5
Lightly active (such as a student)	0.55–0.65
Moderately active (such as a nurse)	0.65–0.7
Highly active (such as a bicycle messenger or an athlete)	0.75–1

A certain amount of honest guesswork is necessary. If you have a sedentary job but walk or bicycle to work every day, you could change your classification to lightly active (or even higher, depending on distance). If you have a moderately active job but spend all your leisure time on the couch, consider downgrading your classification to lightly active. Competitive athletes in training may actually need to increase the factor to above 1.

- Let's assume Gary works in an office. He does walk around to talk to coworkers, go to the cafeteria for lunch, and do other everyday activities. We'll assess his lifestyle as sedentary but on the high side of activity for that category, say 0.5. To estimate Gary's energy expenditure above BMR, we multiply his BMR by this factor:

    1,968 calories/day × 0.50 = 984 calories/day

- Let's assume that Lisa works as a stock clerk in a computer store. She spends a lot of time walking around and sometimes lifts fairly heavy merchandise. She doesn't own a car and rides her bike several miles to and from work each day and also for many errands, so she's at the high end of moderately active, say 0.7. To estimate Lisa's energy expenditure above BMR, we multiply her BMR by this factor:

    1,128 calories/day × 0.70 = 790 calories/day

Note that although Lisa is much more active than Gary, she uses less energy because of her lower body weight.

- Now calculate your own estimated energy expenditure from physical activity.

    _____ calories/day × BMR factor _____ = _____ calories/day

3. To find your total daily energy needs, add your BMR and your estimated energy expenditure.

    - For Gary, this is

        1,968 calories/day + 984 calories/day = 2,952 calories/day

    - For Lisa, it is

        1,128 calories/day + 790 calories/day = 1,918 calories/day

Because several estimates are used in this method, total daily energy needs should be expressed as a 100-calorie range roughly centered on the final calculated value, which would be about 2,900–3,000 calories/day for Gary and about 1,870–1,970 calories/day for Lisa.

- Now calculate your total daily energy needs.

    BMR calories/day _____
       + physical activity calories/day _____
         = _____ total calories/day

Finally, compare your daily energy needs with your daily calorie intake. You may want to refer to the Chapter 5 Personal Health Portfolio activity, where you recorded your calorie intake for one day.

Your daily energy needs: _____

Your daily calorie intake: _____

Remember, if you want to lose weight, you need to take in less energy than you use up. You can shift the balance by increasing your activity level or decreasing your food intake. Moderate changes in both intake and activity level are the safest way to lose weight.

CRITICAL THINKING QUESTIONS

1. How do your calorie needs and calorie intake match up? Are you balancing your needs with your intake, or is one higher than the other? Do you need to make any changes to your calorie intake and/or your energy expenditure?

2. What factors influence how well you are able to balance your food intake and energy expenditure? Consider your taste in food and its cost and convenience. Also consider the factors that influence your ability to get daily physical activity, such as your available leisure time, your community's walkability and safety, availability of recreation areas, affordability of the campus gym or local gyms, etc.

8 Body Image

Massonforstock/123RF

Ever Wonder...

- about the role of gender and body image?
- how to know whether your diet crosses the line to disordered eating or an eating disorder?
- whether you're ever going to change your mind about your tattoo, and what you can do about it?

Do you admire your body and celebrate differences in appearance? The way you evaluate your appearance usually reflects the societal and cultural values and ideals conveyed by family, peers, language, advertising, and the media. Very often, cultural "ideals" are far removed from people's natural appearance. Developing a positive body image, strong self-esteem, and a sense of satisfaction in the face of these discrepancies is important for mental and physical well-being.

Chapter 7 focused on the rising rates of overweight and obesity and ways to achieve and maintain a healthy body composition. This chapter considers body image, self-esteem, and psychological well-being. Attaining a healthy body composition includes developing a positive body image, setting realistic goals, and maintaining emotional well-being.

WHAT SHAPES BODY IMAGE?

Like all beliefs, **body image**—the mental representation we have of own own body, including perceptions, attitudes, thoughts, emotions, and actions about it—is strongly influenced by sociocultural factors. People self-evaluate by comparing themselves to others—whether those are family, peers, or media images. Body image is on a continuum, from strongly positive with a healthy appreciation and enjoyment of our body to strongly negative with unhealthy distress and dissatisfaction with our body. Negative body image and body dissatisfaction can lead to low self-esteem, depression, and increased risk for unhealthy behaviors such as smoking and sexual risk-taking. When they focus on weight and shape concerns, negative body image and body dissatisfaction are strongly associated with disordered eating and eating disorders.[1]

Mainstream U.S. culture places a premium on appearance, especially for women and increasingly for men. Every day we see hundreds of images and messages about how we "should" look. Pressure to conform to social ideals can become an internalized goal and create a sense of inadequacy and distress. (See the box, "Consumer Clipboard: Social Media Literacy.") Let's explore these influences and our responses to them in more depth.

body image
The mental representation that a person has of his or her own body, including perceptions, attitudes, thoughts, emotions, and actions.

Consumer Clipboard
Social Media Literacy

Social media are becoming increasingly important as an influence on body image and body satisfaction. Young adults use social media more than any other demographic group, with 90 percent reporting use on a regular basis. Social media websites and apps differ from more traditional forms of media, such as advertising and movies, in that users themselves create and share the content, actively choosing the images and content to be viewed.

The ability to both present images of ourselves and compare them to images of peers may actually increase social media's impact on how we internalize those images. Women have been shown to feel anxious, less attractive, and less self-confident after posting selfies, even when they are allowed to alter the photos. Time spent viewing and sharing on social media may have such a strong impact because it is among peers, and peer competition is strongly linked to greater body dissatisfaction and body image concerns.

However, there are some ways in which social media use appears to improve mood and increase body satisfaction and self-perception. A #bodypositive movement on Instagram encourages people to post a wide range of body types, sizes, and colors, broadening the concept of what is beautiful. In addition, instead of images that present people as objects, there is more intentional focus on acceptance and appreciation of the body. Exposure to body positive content has been shown to be beneficial.

Once you become conscious of all the images you post and view, you can gain control over how you participate and contribute to the messages. To protect your self-esteem and body image, consider the following:

- How do you feel after spending time on social media? Which images or content leaves you feeling good about yourself? Which content leaves you feeling inadequate?

- Do the images you view present diverse body types or a narrowly defined representation of beauty? Consider how images might be seen by people of a different age, race, sexual identity, gender identity, ethnicity, or religion?

- Do images and content celebrate body function or present the body as an object to be viewed? Do you think images have been altered or enhanced? How has content been selected prior to the images being posted?

- Do you post content that shows appreciation for your body and what your body is able to do? What values are being promoted in the messages your post? How might they mean something different to people of different age, race, sexual identity, gender identity, ethnicity, or religion?

- Do you highlight and celebrate inner characteristics and relationships or only how you look? Do you feel differently about yourself after different types of postings?

Sources: Bennett, B. L., Whisenhunt, B. L., Hudson, D. L., Wagner, A. F., Latner, J. D., et al. (2019). Examining the impact of social media on mood and body dissatisfaction using ecological momentary assessment. *Journal of American College Health.* doi:10.1080/07448481.2019.1583236; Hogue, J. V., & Mills, J. S. (2019). The effects of active social media engagement with peers on body image in young women. *Body Image, 28,* 1-5; Mills, J. S., Musto, S. M., Williams, L., & Tiggemann, M. (2018). "Selfie" harm: Effects on mood and body image in young women. *Body Image, 27,* 86-92; Cohen, R., Irwin, L., Newton-John, T., & Slater, A. (2019). #bodypositivity: A content analysis of body positive accounts on Instagram. *Body Image, 29,* 47-57.

Positive Body Image

A positive body image is associated with enhanced well-being, body satisfaction, and healthy eating behaviors. Having a positive body image includes developing body appreciation and acceptance, adopting a broad concept of beauty, investing in self-care, and learning to interpret information in a body-protective manner.[2,3,4,5]

By focusing on the features and functions of your body that you see as assets, you develop body appreciation. Considering your body for what it is able to do—physically, socially, spiritually, and intellectually—enhances your opportunities to find assets and appreciate your body. In addition, thinking about how your body functions encourages you to consider your body as part of you, not an object to be observed or manipulated. Becoming attentive to and allowing a pleasurable connection to desires, experiences, and physical activities allows you to accept your body. When you are able to identify and focus on the aspects of your body that you see as assets, you may feel a stronger sense of uniqueness and pride and lower self-criticism. You will likely still see imperfections, but shifting your focus to body appreciation and acceptance will provide perspective.

A broad concept of beauty is linked to a positive body image. We cannot define beauty as belonging only to a limited range of body types. Beauty includes a wide range of appearances and is strongly influenced by inner characteristics and actions. Having a broad concept of beauty frees us from appearance stereotypes and helps us appreciate uniqueness over conformity.[4]

A positive body image allows for self-care, too, because you see your body as part of you and not an abstract object. You are attuned to the way your body functions (not just focused on the way it appears) and can listen to and attend to your needs. People with positive body images report higher rates of intuitive eating—eating in response to the body's physiological needs—instead of eating for other reasons, such as emotional need, habit, or social occasions. In addition, people with positive body images report higher rates of emotional self-care—they recognize stressful environments and take time out to take care of themselves. Finally, healthy self-care includes taking care of your physical appearance—from being well groomed to taking pride in or having fun with aspects of your appearance—but it does not allow appearance to become the sole focus or measure of self-care.[3,4]

Essential to maintaining a positive body image is the ability to interpret information in a body-protective manner. You will receive messages from the media, social networks, friends, and family that may challenge your positive body image. Being aware of these challenges can help you recognize and be mindful of them without allowing them to overwhelm you or prevent you from being active. Developing self-compassion, composed of kindness towards self, a belief in being part of a common humanity, and mindfulness, appears to be supportive of healthy body image and body satisfaction. Developing a sense of belonging, as can be found in social, religious, or identity groups, can help you feel part of a common humanity.[5,6] Social media is becoming an increasingly important influence on body image, so being an informed consumer and active creator of social media content is critical.[7]

Gender and Body Image

Western social constructs for females and males have long been presented in binary, stereotyped ways. In the female stereotyped construct, beauty has long been held as a desirable trait. Pioneering English feminist Mary Wollstonecraft pointed out back in 1792 that societal pressures encouraged women to submit to anything to reach the ideal of beauty, even giving up the right to think for themselves. Repeated cycles of feminist thinking and activism since that time have attempted to change the message society sends to women and to free them from the obsession and objectification of the female body.

Today, women have more educational and occupational opportunities than ever before, and they fill a broad range of valued roles in society. Despite progress, however, our culture still strongly values its objectification of women. The female body is portrayed by the media as an object of desire, with a heavy emphasis placed on women's physical attributes rather than on their abilities, performance, or accomplishments.[5,8]

Since the 1970s the dominant female body type presented in the media has been unrealistically thin. Even the recent shift toward a more athletic body type as "ideal" continues to focus on appearance. Analysis of #fitspo and #fitspirational postings shows a focus on thin or athletic women and an emphasis on looks rather than on achievement or performance.[9] In addition, "ideal" images continue to be thinner than the majority of the population. After women view media images of thin or athletic women, they are less satisfied with their own bodies than after viewing images of average-sized women.[10] Unrealistic images can leave women feeling inadequate, preoccupied with a desire to be thin, unhappy with their own bodies, and afraid of becoming fat. The more women internalize narrow media presentations, the less accepting they are of their bodies.[8,11,12]

Comedian Amy Schumer has spoken openly about her struggles with body image—especially in the entertainment industry. She wants to be a role model for women to feel empowered and encouraged to speak about important issues, not just what dress they are wearing. *(WENN Ltd/Alamy Stock Photo)*

In contrast, the male stereotyped construct is one of power and muscularity. Historically, masculine imagery has emphasized body function and achievement rather than appearance. However, this is changing. The marketing of the male body image has started to make a man's physique as important as his possessions and accomplishments. Men's magazines publish more advertisements and articles about how to change body shape than stories about weight loss. Men are increasingly displayed as sexual objects.

As it has for women, society's "ideal" male body shape has become more unrealistic, distorted, and extreme. The evolution of G.I. Joe action figures mirrors society's changing male image. In 1964, G.I. Joe had the physique of an average man in reasonably good shape. By 1992, he had a build most men could not attain without the use of anabolic steroids, and that unrealistic imagery has endured. The exposure to muscular male images leads men to feel worse about their bodies and to have increased feelings of depression. Eighteen percent of U.S. adolescent boys report being highly concerned about their appearance, with most wanting to be more muscular.[10,13,14,15]

As men buy into the cultural stereotypes for physical perfection and pursue unrealistic goals, they are more likely to have feelings of inadequacy and body dissatisfaction. Like women, the more they are exposed to and internalize media messaging, the worse they feel about their bodies. However, men's body talk and reasons for dissatisfaction are more shape oriented than weight oriented; they focus on the upper body rather than the lower body; and they usually diet for a specific reason, such as sports performance.[15,16] In addition, men appear to make fewer social comparisons than women, which may reflect the fact that representations in the media show a wider range of "ideals" for men than for women.[10]

The binary female and male stereotyped ideals are themselves in contrast to reality. Gender identification occurs across a spectrum from male to female. Early research evaluating body image and body satisfaction among transgender and gender nonconforming youth and adults suggests that dissatisfaction with body may be more related to undesired sex features than to body composition or weight, with disordered eating serving as a way to delay or reduce the appearance of secondary sex characteristics. This suggests a need for body image research to expand its gender definitions, since prevention approaches may differ when gender is not seen as a rigidly binary construct, and when media representation of gender is more fluid.[6]

■ Action figures with unrealistic physiques increase the risk men will feel worse about their bodies and increase their desire to be more muscular. *(JG Photography/Alamy Stock Photo)*

Race, Ethnicity, and Body Image

In the same way that they focus on gender differences, media messages create and exaggerate stereotyped and narrow definitions for racial and ethnic body image ideals. Internalization of stereotyped messages appears to be a critical factor in body acceptance or disturbance. The more we are invested in appearance, the more likely we are to compare ourselves to media representations, and to feel dissatisfaction with our own body if the media representations are narrowly and unrealistically defined. This situation creates an additional conflict for people of color. They are underrepresented in the media, a factor that further marginalizes them because they do not see themselves in the images. Media could show the true diversity in shapes and colors of society. Links to family and peers and participation in cultural traditions that create pride in different body types and appearances appear to be strong protective factors in forming a healthy body image.[3,4,5,17,18]

White women have historically experienced greater body dissatisfaction and eating disturbances than women in other racial and ethnic groups. However, this is slowly changing, and at present there are more similarities than differences between racial and ethnic groups in this regard. Research is showing that healthy body image and body satisfaction correlate with healthy identity formation. Someone who is struggling with identity is increasingly vulnerable to focusing on body image or weight for self-definition.[19] What appears most likely is that intersecting identity roles (gender, race, ethnicity) are critical to the way people from all racial and ethnic groups internalize messaging from media, family, and peers. A stronger attachment to our cultural (or multicultural) identity reduces our risk of body dissatisfaction. African American men and women appear to have less strongly internalized the "thin ideal," and thus they fairly consistently report less body image dissatisfaction. Black women appear to internalize appearance-focused messaging less and describe beauty more holistically, encompassing personality traits and not just physical attributes. Asian women appear to have higher levels of attachment to the thin ideal than do African American or white women. Research evaluating Latinas is inconsistent. Some studies show rates of body dissatisfaction and disordered eating similar to or higher than rates in whites. However, other studies have not found this and have highlighted the importance of identity formation and the relationships to assimilation, acculturation, and duration in the United States.[18,19,20,21,22]

Life Stages and Body Image

Adolescence is a time of significant transition and change—physically, emotionally, and socially. During this critical phase in identity formation, teens expand and explore new relationships and new friends, sexual experiences, and peer dynamics.

Peer conversations regarding appearance and comparisons to others and media images become increasingly influential. In addition, beliefs and concerns about what is attractive to partners start to develop and gain importance. Explorations around gender identity and sexual identity heighten during adolescence and occur along a spectrum from male to female, in contrast to the dominant societal presentation of binary genders and a predominant social and media focus on heterosexual attraction.[6,22,23]

As noted in Chapter 7, pubertal hormonal changes cause changes in body shape and composition. These physical changes occur alongside sexual identity formation and an increased focus on the processing of societal body- and gender-related messages. The majority of research on body image, disordered eating, and eating disorders has focused on cisgender youth (who identify with the gender assigned at birth). In healthy girls, body fat increases during puberty, moving them away from the socially constructed "ideal" female image. For boys, puberty increases muscle mass and definition, moving them toward the socially constructed male image "ideal." Timing of puberty appears to play a role in the development of body appreciation. Girls who go through puberty before their peers and boys who go through puberty after their peers experience more body-related teasing and express more body dissatisfaction.[22]

For trans or gender-conflicted youth, the physiological changes of puberty present an increased risk of body dissatisfaction. The development of features of biological gender that conflict with features of desired gender can be tremendously stressful. Disordered eating patterns and other forms of self-harm can develop in attempts to control pubertal changes.[6,23,24]

Adolescence and young adulthood also bring changes in physical activity level, such as decreased physical activity and decreased participation in sports. This shift influences body image and body satisfaction, in particular as they relate to body appreciation. Participation in sports confers many health benefits, including higher levels of self-esteem and a focus on performance rather than appearance. However, high-intensity activities in which leanness is a competitive advantage, such as wrestling, dance, gymnastics, swimming, cycling, distance running, and horse racing, can increase the focus on body appearance. The risk of eating disorders appears to be greatest for athletes competing at elite levels, such as on college teams. Athletes who compete in nonelite sports that do not emphasize leanness have the least risk of developing eating disorders. Lifelong participation in pleasurable, noncompetitive physical activities in nonstress environments (such as yoga and walking or hiking in nature) supports a consistent focus on what the body can do physically and may be protective in developing body satisfaction and acceptance and self-esteem.[25,26,27,28]

disordered eating behaviors
Abnormal eating patterns (e.g., restrictive dieting, skipping meals, binge eating and purging, laxative abuse) that may not fit the diagnostic rules for anorexia or bulimia but affect quality of life.

African American women are more likely than white, Asian American, and Latina women to be satisfied with their bodies. They are more likely to describe beauty in more holistic ways, encompassing personality, not just appearance. *(Jonathan Kantor Studio/Photodisc/Getty Images)*

Transitions are a time of stress and adjustment, and midlife is becoming an increasingly recognized time of risk for the onset (or re-onset) of disordered eating and eating disorders in women. Perimenopause and menopause bring physical and hormonal changes to the body. These changes are associated with increased body dissatisfaction and disordered eating.[29]

DISORDERED EATING AND EATING DISORDERS

A disturbance in body image, with a preoccupation on appearance, can interfere with daily life and cause significant distress. Body dissatisfaction and a sociocultural focus on unrealistically thin and muscular ideals can lead to unhealthy eating and exercise patterns in attempts to control emotional distress. For some people, the emotional distress and attempts to reach an unrealistic ideal become more severe and can lead to disordered eating behaviors and eating disorders. These occur on a spectrum, and guidelines for diagnosis and treatment have been developed.

Disordered eating behaviors include restrictive dieting, skipped meals, occasional binge eating and purging, laxative abuse, and other unhealthy behaviors. They may occur in response to emotional stress, an upcoming athletic event, concern about personal appearance, a new diet recommendation, or any one of innumerable other stressors. Disordered eating behaviors are more common when people are dissatisfied with their bodies and among college populations, with studies showing that 50 to 60 percent of college women and 10 to 50 percent of college men report disordered eating.[30]

The line between healthy and disordered eating can sometimes be unclear. For example, in a new movement toward "clean eating," people become so focused on eating only healthy, "pure" foods that they severely restrict and eliminate entire categories of food from their diets. This preoccupation becomes a problem, called orthorexia nervosa, when it impairs social functioning or causes calorie or nutritional deficiencies.[31,32] In other situations, there is a clearer line and medical definitions to indicate when extreme, disordered eating has become a full-blown eating disorder.

Eating disorders are chronic illnesses that jeopardize physical and mental health; they can be life threatening. The key characteristic of eating disorders is a severe disturbance in eating behavior associated with a distorted body image or body dissatisfaction, and often with low self-esteem. Such patterns can turn into self-induced starvation or repeated cycles of binge eating and purging, which in turn can interfere with the person's ability to lead a healthy, functional life. Rates of eating disorders appear to be directly related to rates of weight-loss dieting in a population.

Anorexia nervosa, bulimia nervosa, and binge-eating disorder are classified as psychiatric disorders in the American Psychiatric Association's *Diagnostic and Statistical Manual of Mental Disorders (DSM-5)*. Using the strict criteria proposed by the *DSM-5*, about 0.4 percent of women have anorexia and 1.0 to 1.5 percent of women have bulimia; the rate in men is about 10 percent that of women. There is less gender difference in binge eating disorder, with an estimated 1.6 percent of women and 0.8 percent of men suffering from it.[33]

Eating disorders occur primarily among people in Western industrialized countries, where they are found in every ethnic, cultural, and socioeconomic group. They appear to become more prevalent when food is abundant and has taken on symbolic meanings, such as comfort, love, belonging, fun, and control. They are also more common where being attractive is socially promoted as related to being thin.

Contributing Factors

Many factors contribute to the development of disordered eating and eating disorders, and much about the process remains unknown. Why the widespread cultural ideals and beliefs promoting thinness and dieting for women and extreme muscularity for men become an overvalued, ruling passion for some is not totally clear. As discussed, exposure to a narrowly defined thin "ideal," social pressure to conform, and recognition of a discrepancy between the ideal and the person's own body can lead to body dissatisfaction, which is clearly associated with an increased risk for eating disorders. However, this isn't the entire story, because the social pressures to be thin (or muscular) are pervasive and spreading globally, and yet only a fraction of people go on to develop eating disorders.[8,34]

Gender is a risk factor for eating disorders; identifying as female increases risk. Sexual orientation may also affect risk. Men who identify as gay or bisexual report placing greater importance on physical appearance and leanness than men who identify as heterosexual. In addition, they report higher rates of body dissatisfaction and disordered eating and are overrepresented among males diagnosed with eating disorders. Their desire to attract men may increase their identification with the pressures faced by women who identify as heterosexual—the emphasis on appearance and sexual objectification in the media. Women who identify as lesbian or bisexual report higher rates of unhealthy dieting behaviors than their heterosexual peers, but the reasons are less clear.[6,15,35,36]

Other factors also play a role. For example, a family history of eating disorders, depression, substance abuse, anxiety, obsessive-compulsive disorder, or obesity increases the risk for anorexia and bulimia. Most likely, multiple genes predispose an individual, and then certain experiences or characteristics further contribute to the development of eating disorders.[26,37] For additional factors, see the box "Who's at Risk? Eating Disorders."

The connection between eating disorders and depression and anxiety disorders is complicated. People with anorexia and bulimia frequently report symptoms of depression and anxiety. A history of depression appears to increase risk for eating disorders, but it can be difficult to diagnose depression in a person with anorexia because the starvation process produces similar symptoms, including changes in sleep patterns, a decline in energy level, and decreased interest in activities.

Diagnosing Eating Disorders

As recently as the 1980s, the terms *anorexia nervosa* and *bulimia nervosa* were unknown to the general public. Today, many people are familiar with the concept of disturbed eating patterns. Detecting when someone with disordered eating makes the transition to having an eating disorder is difficult, however. In this section, we review the most common eating disorders and their diagnostic criteria.

Anorexia Nervosa The word *anorexia* is of Greek origin; it comes from *an,* which means "lack of," and *orexis,* which means "appetite." However, most people with **anorexia nervosa** do not have a lack of appetite; they are more likely to be obsessed with food. At the same time, they are starving themselves and appear ultra-thin or emaciated.

Criteria for anorexia nervosa are as follows[33,38]:

- Limited calorie intake so weight is significantly lower than recommendations (a BMI less than 18.5)

- Fear of weight gain or becoming fat despite being below healthy weight recommendations

- Distorted view of self and lack of recognition of seriousness of health issues with low body weight

eating disorders Conditions characterized by severely disturbed eating behaviors and distorted body image; eating disorders jeopardize physical and psychological health.

anorexia nervosa An eating disorder marked by distortion of body image and refusal to maintain a minimally normal body weight.

Who's at Risk?

Eating Disorders

No one seems to be immune to eating disorders. They affect all genders; they affect people of all different ages, races, ethnicities, and backgrounds; they affect people who grew up with loving families and those who had difficult childhoods. Still, a few trends have been observed:

- Eating disorders are most common during the teens and early 20s.

- Eating disorders are more likely to occur during life transitions, which can trigger emotional stress and a sense of loss of control.

- Although the incidence is increasing among men, especially gay and trans men, eating disorders remain more common in heterosexual women, trans women, and lesbians.

- Substance abuse, depression, anxiety, obsessive-compulsive disorder, and obesity are associated with an increased risk of eating disorders.

- Frequent dieting is associated with the onset of eating disorders.

- Overly controlling or critical family relationships can increase the risk of eating disorders.

- Frequent exposure to media messages promoting stereotyped ideals—thin or muscular body types, whiteness, and sexual objectification—can increase the risk of eating disorders.

- Stress, including the chronic stress of identifying with a racial, sexual, or gender minority status, can increase the risk of disordered eating.

- Sports that emphasize thin body type or weight restrictions may increase the risk of eating disorders.

- Social connection, religious or spiritual affiliation, and strong identity formation appear to be protective and reduce risk.

- Certain individual characteristics or thought patterns are associated with an increased risk and include low self-esteem, self-critical attitude, belief in the importance of thinness, black-and-white thinking, feelings of emptiness, need for power and control, difficulty expressing feelings, lack of coping skills, lack of trust in self or others, and perfectionism.

Sources: Rieger, E., & Hirsch, J. (2018). Eating disorder symptoms and proneness in gay men, lesbian women, and transgender and gender non-conforming adults: Comparative levels and a proposed mediational model. *Frontiers in Psychology, 9,* 2692; Bulik, C. M., Blake, L., & Austin, J. (2019). Genetics of eating disorders: What the clinician needs to know. *Psychiatric Clinics of North America, 42,* 59-73; Piran, N. (2015). New possibilities in the prevention of eating disorders: The introduction of positive body image measures. *Body Image, 14,* 146-157.

bulimia nervosa
An eating disorder marked by distortion of body image and repeated episodes of binge eating, usually followed by purging in the form of self-induced vomiting, misuse of diuretics or laxatives, excessive exercising, or fasting.

binge eating disorder
An eating disorder marked by binge eating behavior without the vomiting or purging of bulimia.

People with anorexia attempt to control their emotional distress and body dissatisfaction by severely restricting calories or excessively exercising. To get a sense of how anorexia plays out in a person's life, see the box "Life Stories: Alexis: The Gradual Onset of an Eating Disorder."

Bulimia Nervosa The word *bulimia* is of Latin origin and means "hunger of an ox." People with **bulimia nervosa** eat a huge amount of food at one sitting and then use an inappropriate method to get rid of the calories they have consumed, either purging or excessive exercise. They are usually neither underweight nor overweight, but they have a disturbed perception of body size and image. Binge-eating and purging behaviors are usually socially isolating.

Criteria for bulimia nervosa are as follows[33,38]:

- A recurring pattern of eating more than most people would in a set period of time, and a sense of loss of control over how much is eaten

- Unhealthy behaviors to compensate for the excessive food intake, such as self-induced vomiting, use of laxatives or diuretics, fasting, or exercise

- Disordered eating that occurs at least weekly and has lasted at least 3 months

- Sense of self that is influenced by body shape and weight to a degree that causes distress

Binge Eating Disorder Disordered eating patterns can also cause obesity. **Binge eating disorder** has increasingly been recognized as a psychological disturbance that is associated with weight fluctuation and obesity. This disorder includes binge-eating behaviors without vomiting or purging.[33]

People with binge eating disorder can be normal weight or overweight, but if the disorder goes unrecognized, they often eventually become obese. They have body weight and shape concerns, emotional distress (possibly including depression), and disordered eating patterns similar to those of people with anorexia or bulimia. Binge eating disorder is the most common eating disorder, occurring in 2 to 3.5 percent of the population. It is more common in women, but there is less gender difference than with anorexia and bulimia.[33,38,39]

Criteria for binge eating disorder are as follows[33,38]:

- A recurring pattern of eating more than most people would in a set period of time, and a sense of loss of control over how much is eaten

- Rapid eating, regular eating to the point of feeling uncomfortable, and eating when not hungry

- Eating alone due to feelings of embarrassment, disgust, or guilt over eating patterns

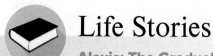

Life Stories

Alexis: The Gradual Onset of an Eating Disorder

Alexis was a first-year student at a university in a large city, though she had grown up in a small town in the same state. When she first arrived on campus, she was assigned to a dorm room with Leah, a student from out of state. Leah was tall and athletic and made friends easily, and she quickly became popular in the residence hall. Alexis was introverted and not used to making friends quickly. Most of the people she knew at school were friends from her hometown, people she had known her entire life. She began to avoid the room because she felt self-conscious about her lack of new college friends.

Classes were harder than Alexis had expected, and she began to question her ability to succeed. She wanted to talk to her parents, but they had always told her how much fun college was going to be, and she feared they would not understand why she was struggling.

Alexis had never been overweight, but she had never really been happy with her body either. Leah and her friends frequently engaged in "fat talk"—commenting on how people looked in the residence halls or in classes. Alexis often compared herself to Leah and became self-conscious about her body. She concluded that if she lost weight, it might be easier to fit in. She decided she would start eating a healthier diet by cutting out fat, which meant most meat and dairy products. This made it hard to eat in the dining hall, so she started eating foods she didn't need to prepare and could keep in her room. To avoid Leah, she also tried to be in her room as little as possible, so she ended up eating only twice a day, in the morning and at night. She also started walking a lot around campus. She found that she felt better if she could keep moving, and pretty

soon she was walking several hours a day. When she tried to sit and study, she was usually too tired to concentrate. During lectures, her mind would wander to how much she had eaten the day before and when she could eat that day. She was finding it more difficult to focus on course work because she began thinking about food and her appearance all the time.

Alexis did not think she had lost much weight, but when she went home for winter break, her parents were shocked to see her. When they asked her about it, she denied intentionally trying to lose weight and said she was just trying to be healthier. They took her to see the family doctor, who observed that Alexis's weight and BMI had plummeted. The doctor was concerned by her weight loss as well as by her lack of insight into her condition and appearance. Alexis wanted to return to school, but her parents were reluctant to allow it. Her doctor and parents finally agreed to let her go back on the condition that she see a nutritionist at the student health center who could monitor her weight while she worked to get it back into a healthy range. They also wanted her to see a counselor to address the emotional and interpersonal issues that were affecting her self-esteem and body image. Reluctantly, Alexis agreed.

- How is your transition to college going? Do you find it easy to fit into new social groups, or do you find it challenging? What do you think about different styles of interacting with others?

- Are there any foods you have eliminated from your diet? If so, why? Are these changes in your diet truly making you healthier, or do they limit your calorie intake or nutrient intake to an unhealthy degree?

- Disordered eating that occurs at least weekly and has lasted at least 3 months

- Lack of associated purging behaviors

Health Effects of Eating Disorders

Eating disorders have serious health implications. Some short-term problems, such as heart rate abnormalities, can lead to death. Long-term problems can cause significant disability. Eating disorders are associated with different medical problems.

Health Effects of Anorexia Anorexia nervosa carries the highest death rate of all psychiatric diagnoses and all eating disorders.[40,41] Death is usually due to cardiac arrest, electrolyte imbalance, or suicide.[42] The signs and symptoms of anorexia are due to starvation and are shown in Figure 8.1. Most of the physical complications are reversible if the person receives enough calorie and nutritional replacement. However, some complications—most notably, bone loss—do not appear to be reversible. Decreased bone calcium (osteoporosis) is one of the most serious long-term effects of severe calorie restriction. Peak bone density is reached during the adolescent years. After that it remains relatively stable until the mid-30s,

when it starts a slow decline. People with anorexia do not reach the same peak bone density as those without the disease and thus have a lifelong increased risk of bone fracture.[43]

Suicide accounts for 20 to 40 percent of deaths in people with anorexia nervosa. This highlights the importance of addressing the emotional well-being aspects of eating disorders.[40] As discussed in Chapter 2, being alert to warning signs for suicide and getting help for yourself or a friend if warning signs are present is critical.

Health Effects of Bulimia Bulimia is associated more with electrolyte imbalance than with starvation. Electrolytes, such as sodium, potassium, calcium, phosphate, and magnesium, are essential components of body fluids and required for cell function. Repetitive vomiting causes the loss of certain electrolytes—in particular, potassium—and makes it difficult for the body to maintain electrolyte balance. Bulimia can also be deadly due to low potassium, because heart cells and the cardiac electrical conduction system can malfunction and lead to cardiac arrest. The signs and symptoms of bulimia are shown in Figure 8.2.[43] Like anorexia, bulimia is associated with an increased risk of suicidal ideation and suicide attempts.[42]

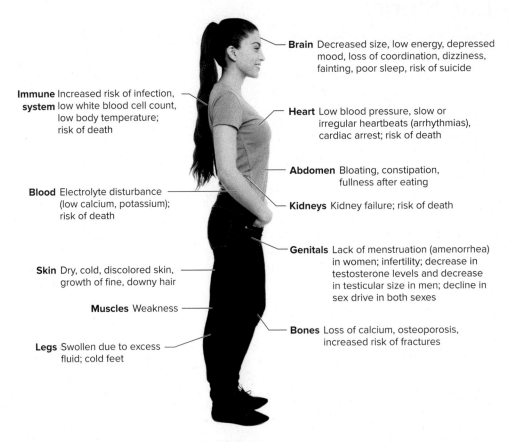

Brain Decreased size, low energy, depressed mood, loss of coordination, dizziness, fainting, poor sleep, risk of suicide

Immune system Increased risk of infection, low white blood cell count, low body temperature; risk of death

Heart Low blood pressure, slow or irregular heartbeats (arrhythmias), cardiac arrest; risk of death

Abdomen Bloating, constipation, fullness after eating

Blood Electrolyte disturbance (low calcium, potassium); risk of death

Kidneys Kidney failure; risk of death

Genitals Lack of menstruation (amenorrhea) in women; infertility; decrease in testosterone levels and decrease in testicular size in men; decline in sex drive in both sexes

Skin Dry, cold, discolored skin, growth of fine, downy hair

Muscles Weakness

Bones Loss of calcium, osteoporosis, increased risk of fractures

Legs Swollen due to excess fluid; cold feet

figure 8.1 **Anorexia can cause changes throughout the body.**
Not all of these signs and symptoms will be present in all people with the disease. *(Stockyimages/123Rf)*

- **Face** Swollen parotid and salivary glands, puffy cheeks, broken blood vessels under the eyes, sore throat

- **Teeth** Erosion of tooth enamel, pain, sensitivity

- **Esophagus** Heartburn, inflammation; tears can cause severe, life-threatening bleeding

- **Hands** Calluses from self-induced vomiting

- **Large intestine** Bloating, diarrhea, abdominal pain caused by laxatives

- **Stomach** Can enlarge dramatically with binge eating and even burst; risk of death

- **Heart** Irregular heart rhythms due to low potassium; risk of death

- **Blood** Electrolyte imbalances (low potassium, sodium); risk of death

- **Kidneys** Low blood pressure, dehydration caused by diuretics

figure 8.2 **Bulimia can cause changes throughout the body.**
Not all of these signs and symptoms will be present in all people with the disease. *(TUBIRY.PHOTOGRAPHY/Shutterstock)*

■ Actor and activist Karla Mosley is a National Eating Disorder Association (NEDA) ambassador who regularly raises awareness about the dangers of eating disorders. *(Kathy Hutchins/Shutterstock)*

Health Effects of Binge Eating Disorder The health consequences of binge eating disorder are related primarily to obesity.[39] As discussed in Chapter 7, obesity is a chronic health condition that increases risk for health problems such as cardiorespiratory disease, diabetes, high blood pressure, gallbladder disease, osteoarthritis, sleep apnea, and certain cancers.

Treating Disordered Eating and Eating Disorders

Aside from osteoporosis and suicide, most medical conditions associated with anorexia, bulimia, and binge eating disorder are reversible. Keys to recovery appear to be early intervention, lower incidence of purging behavior, the support and participation of family members and loved ones, and treatment of other psychological problems. The earlier you recognize disordered eating and body dissatisfaction, the more successful treatment will be.

Recognizing the Problem People with eating disorders often do not recognize they are ill and refuse treatment. The disease itself distorts perception, and this creates a dilemma. If a person denies having a potentially life-threatening disease, it can be difficult to provide effective treatment. In fact, disordered eating patterns can develop in response to a person's sense of lack of control over aspects of her or his life. If treatment then requires a health care provider to take control of refeeding, power struggles can worsen.

Friends, roommates, parents, and others who are close to those with disordered eating or eating disorders may also deny there is a problem or fail to recognize it because dieting, exercise, and preoccupation with food are so much an accepted part of our culture. The box "Starting the Conversation: Social Media and Health Apps" looks at the fine line between monitoring your diet and exercise regimen and obsessing about them. Treatment is most effective when the patient and family members all recognize the problem and are active in making treatment decisions.

Components of Treatment Ideally, a pattern of food obsession or body image preoccupation can be detected by the individual or by friends and family at an early point. When identified early, restricted or binge-purge patterns of eating are not as firmly established. This is key because, as with any habit, the more firmly entrenched disordered eating patterns become, the more difficult it is to reestablish healthy eating patterns.

Local campus resources may be sufficient to address unhealthy thought patterns, identify sources of stress, and teach healthier coping mechanisms. Help should be focused on the whole you—your social, physical, and emotional well-being. For some suggestions, see the box "Action Skill-Builder: Take Action to Prevent Eating Disorders." Many campuses have a health center, counseling facilities, food and nutritional services, recreational facilities, and student groups that can help in early phases of the disordered body image and eating continuum.

However, if an individual has progressed farther along the continuum to a more severe eating disorder, treatment often requires a multidisciplinary team. Members of this group of health care providers with different expertise—physician, psychiatrist, psychologist, social worker, nutritionist, nurse—work together to address all areas of a patient's health. Sometimes this requires referral from campus services to a center that specializes in the treatment of eating disorders. If severe weight loss or another medical abnormality has occurred, hospitalization may be necessary while adequate nutrition is restored. While patients are in a physical crisis, they may find it hard to work on long-term change.

Once weight has been stabilized, the second phase of treatment—including psychotherapy, behavioral relearning and modification, and nutritional rehabilitation and education—can be initiated. Because eating disorders are psychiatric illnesses, the most important part of treatment (aside

Starting the Conversation
Social Media and Health Apps

Q: Have you downloaded an app to assist you in monitoring calories, daily weight, and physical activity? Is it helpful or harmful?

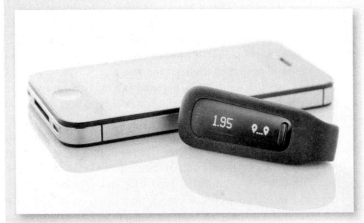

(Simon Lees/Tap Magazine/Getty Images)

Your new health app gives you points for entering daily weights, keeps accurate calorie counts for each meal, and monitors your physical activity level. Or an article pops up in your Facebook newsfeed called "Five Foods Never to Eat." Social media is the new advertising front, focusing on raising awareness about health and energy balance. However, much of the language may promote unhealthy thinking about food and body image. When does calorie counting cross the line between a healthy focus on energy equations to an obsession or an unhealthy task? We are in conflict as a society. We have rising rates of obesity and an increasing need for people to maintain energy balance, and yet we have unhealthy relationships with food and the potential for disordered eating. The constant messaging about and positive reinforcement of weight loss and calorie counting may be harmful to some members of the population.

FitBit, MyFitnessPal, Fooducate, and DailyBurn are just a few of the applications available for download. Each is designed to assist in daily monitoring of activity, calorie intake, and weight to motivate behavior change. However, meticulous daily calorie counting can become an obsession and move people farther away from "intuitive eating"—listening to the body's cues and learning to recognize when we are hungry. Intuitive eating counters the primary triggers for disordered eating—such as boredom, stress, sadness, celebration, and other sources of emotional eating. Social media and apps that focus on counting calories, measuring activity level, weight, and forbidden categories of food may create added stress and distraction. How do these factors influence your life?

Q: How do you use social media tools to track nutrition and physical activity?

Q: When is tracking calories unhealthy? How do you decide?

Action Skill-Builder

Take Action to Prevent Eating Disorders

Disordered eating and eating disorders are associated with the internalization of society's idealizations of thinness. Low self-esteem and a distorted self-image can start you down the road to unhealthy habits. Treating yourself as if you were your own best friend can help build resilience and healthier patterns. Do you or your friends talk negatively about yourselves or others? Do your recognize when you are going through tough times and give yourself a break? If you are concerned about slipping into disordered eating, or just trying to build a positive perspective on your body, try taking these actions as early steps.

☐ Avoid skipping meals or restricting types of foods. Regular meals facilitate healthier nutrition. Your body needs fuel to function. Notice if you are starting to alter your eating patterns, and think about why.

☐ Exercise for fitness, not to compensate for eating too much or to punish yourself. Exercise is good for you, but if you sense that it is becoming a compulsion, it may no longer be healthy. Find ways to exercise that you enjoy.

☐ Avoid sudden weight loss or gain. Healthy weight loss or gain is gradual—1 to 2 pounds per week. Sudden change may be a sign that you are not using healthy methods to manage your weight.

☐ Use positive language about your body. Do you find yourself or friends talking about "being fat" or not liking the look of a body part? Try to be aware of the language you use. Try going a week without making any critical remarks about your body—or anyone else's.

☐ If you make a mistake or do poorly on a test, do you criticize yourself or label yourself a failure? Instead, be kind. Recognize mistakes and experience as part of growth. Don't ignore your feelings, but keep them in perspective and forgive yourself.

☐ Give yourself a break! Keep a balance when thinking about strengths and areas for growth. Distinguish between what is within your control and what isn't. For things within your control, think about small steps you can take. For things not in your control, keep a sense of perspective or try to let go of them as best you can. Remember that no one is perfect and that differences among people are what make life interesting.

from weight gain for severely anorexic patients) is psychotherapy. A goal of treatment is to teach the person to recognize self-destructive patterns of behavior and to develop better coping skills. Therapy focuses on learning how to maintain a positive body image, high self-esteem, and healthy eating patterns for life. Nutritional education includes information about healthy eating patterns, normal weight, and nutritional needs. Treatment for eating disorders often includes the entire family.

In some cases, medications, particularly antidepressants, are a component of treatment. During the weight-gain phases of anorexia treatment, antidepressants do not appear to be beneficial, but they may be helpful in reducing relapses during the weight-maintenance phase. In the treatment of bulimia, the use of antidepressants leads to a rapid decrease in the binge-purge cycle. Treatment for binge eating disorder may differ from other obesity treatment programs; emphasizing patterns of eating and putting less emphasis on dieting can be important.[44]

BODY DYSMORPHIC DISORDER

Many of us look at our body, compare it to those of others, and see things we'd like to change. For an estimated 2 percent of the general population, however, the pattern of seeing faults becomes intrusive and unwanted and significantly interferes with their lives.[33,45] A key feature of **body dysmorphic disorder** is a preoccupation with a defect in appearance. The preoccupation can be about a wholly imagined defect or a slight defect.

Criteria for body dysmorphic disorder are as follows[33]:

- Focus on a "flaw or flaws" in appearance that is not evident to others

- An overwhelming need to keep looking at the flawed area or to mentally compare appearance to that of others

- Impaired daily functioning due to distress caused by the self-perceived flaw

- Lack of other eating disorder that would better explain the distress

The perceived fault can be in any part of the body. For men, the preoccupation tends to be about the genitals or hair; for women, concern centers on the breasts, thighs, or legs. Concern about the perceived defect can lead to low self-esteem, social isolation, and impairment of daily life.[45,46]

Muscle Dysmorphia

Muscle dysmorphia is a subcategory of body dysmorphic disorder. This condition occurs predominantly in males, and the preoccupation focuses on muscularity and low body fat.[33,47,48] People with muscle dysmorphia may diet, exercise, and lift weights, often to extremes that cause injury or illness. In addition, they can turn to use of supplements

Like eating disorders, muscle dysmorphia involves a distorted body image and compulsive behaviors. People with this disorder exercise to feel in control and to manage uncomfortable emotions rather than to improve their fitness and health. *(Halfpoint/Shutterstock)*

or anabolic steroids to increase muscle size. Side effects associated with steroid use include extreme mood swings, aggression, impaired judgement, acne, high blood pressure, and liver damage.

The concerns and preoccupation with their body can lead people with muscle dysmorphia to feel shame and avoid social contact. They may also become isolated because of the time demands of maintaining a meticulous diet and excessive workout schedule. The disorder may originate in experiences that undermine self-esteem, such as taunting by peers, domestic violence, or sexual assault. It may be aggravated by media images that glorify bulging muscles and present them as a realistic goal. Still, most people who are exposed to these experiences and images do not develop muscle dysmorphia.[48]

Cosmetic Surgery

Some people with body dysmorphic disorder turn to cosmetic surgery to correct the supposed flaw in their appearance. However, not everyone who turns to cosmetic surgery has this disorder. In fact, cosmetic surgery and makeovers of every kind have become commonplace in the past few decades. The increase is most likely related to the ever-growing emphasis on appearance. By definition, cosmetic surgery is elective; it is not done to treat a medical condition.

In the United States, an estimated 18.1 million cosmetic procedures were performed in 2019, at a cost of nearly $16.7 billion. The rate at which women undergo these procedures is high and continues to increase. Rates for men are much lower and have slightly decreased. The most common cosmetic surgical procedures in 2019 were breast augmentation, liposuction, nose reshaping, eyelid surgery, and

body dysmorphic disorder Preoccupation with an imagined or exaggerated defect in appearance.

tummy tuck. The most commonly performed minimally invasive procedures were Botox injections, soft-tissue fillers, chemical peels (for wrinkles), hair removal, and skin resurfacing.[46]

As with any surgery or medical procedure, there are risks. A key risk is psychological: People who are unhappy with their appearance because they have a distorted body image or are comparing themselves to an unrealistic ideal are unlikely to be made significantly happier with a single operation. There are also physical risks, both at the time of surgery (reactions to anesthesia, blood loss, infection) and later (such as reactions to the silicone in breast implants).

However, cosmetic surgery can also have psychological and physical benefits. Some people are happy with the results of cosmetic surgery. Some become more confident about their appearance and more successful socially or professionally. Surgeries such as otoplasty (cosmetic ear surgery) and rhinoplasty (nose reshaping) can change a physical characteristic that has caused a person emotional distress for years; breast reduction can enable a woman to feel less self-conscious about her appearance or engage in sports or activities that were previously uncomfortable. Careful consideration of why the procedure is being sought and the benefits and risks is critical.

Body Art

With an increasing frequency, people choose to use body art to express themselves, recognize important life transitions, celebrate family and friends, and present a certain image. Like other forms of self-expression, body art is closely tied to an individual's sense of self. Tattoos, permanent makeup, eyebrow rings, and nose piercings may seem like a recent trend, but their roots go far back in history. Many cultures have used piercings or tattoos to mark tribal origin or status. Ancient Egyptians used navel piercing as a sign of royalty. Crusaders in the Middle Ages were tattooed with crosses so their bodies would be given a Christian burial.

An estimated 30 percent of adults report having a tattoo; nearly 70 percent of them have more than one. Among college students, body art is no longer seen as a form of rebellion or a sign of membership in a marginalized group. No political party, class, gender, age, or occupation is excluded from the trend. Despite their increasing frequency, prejudice remains against people with tattoos and piercings—especially when these are on the face, neck, or other areas that cannot be concealed. Body art choices can affect future employment opportunities—especially in customer-facing careers.[49,50,51,52]

College students usually consider obtaining a piercing or tattoo for an extended period of time; it is not often an impulsive act. Their satisfaction is greatest when the tattoo has life significance, such as marking a life transition, and when the work is of high quality. Tattooing should be considered a permanent process. It involves making a puncture wound in the skin and injecting ink deep into the second layer of skin (called the dermis). There is some pain, minor bleeding, and possible risk of bacterial, viral, or fungal infection. Some

people may develop an allergic reaction to the dye. There is a possibility that some tattoo inks will increase the risk of cancer, but this is still under investigation. Tattoo removal can be done with laser treatment, but the process is painful, time-consuming, and expensive and it can leave scars. The most common reasons for wanting a tattoo removed are embarrassment, negative comments from others, and difficulty covering the tattoo with clothing.[51,52]

Body piercing carries some of the same risks as tattooing and is even more common, with estimates that 50 percent of young adults have a piercing in a site other than their ear lobe. There is increasing regulation and training for professional piercers and licensing of facilities to reduce risk of infection. General risks include bleeding or damage at the piercing site and potential for allergic reaction to the material. Certain body sites are more likely than others to result in problems. Piercing of the mouth or nose often results in infection, and tongue piercing can damage teeth. Piercing of the ear cartilage can lead to cartilage growth and "cauliflower ear." The longer a piercing is left in place, the more likely it is that scarring or a residual opening will occur should the jewelry be removed.[52,53]

Tattoos and piercing should be approached with caution and considered permanent alterations to the body. If

■ Tattoos and piercings are a popular form of self-expression and can mark key life transitions. Social norms around body art are shifting, but there still is some associated stigma.
(Jose Manuel Gelpi Diaz/123RF)

you decide to proceed with either, give yourself a waiting period to make sure the location, design, and type of the tattoo or piercing are what you really want. Consider how it will look 5, 10, or 20 years from now and how you might feel about it at a different phase of your life. If you decide to proceed, ensure that the facility where you will be receiving the tattoo or piercing follows proper infection-control procedures.[54]

EXERCISE DISORDERS

Energy balance is critical for maintaining a healthy body composition and body function. A new syndrome, **relative energy deficiency in sport (RED-S)**, has been defined by the International Olympic Committee and is drawing attention to the health and performance problems that arise when dietary intake does not meet the body's needs for energy. Such patterns may exist in conjunction with disordered eating and eating disorders or be related to lack of awareness, competition demands, and lack of access to sufficient food.[33,55,56]

In women, this syndrome has been called the **female athlete triad**, meaning a set of three interrelated conditions: insufficient energy intake for level of exercise (which may or may not be associated with an eating disorder), amenorrhea (cessation of menstruation), and premature osteoporosis (reduced bone density). However, increasing evidence shows relative energy deficiency is not limited to women. Male athletes face similar health implications when exercise levels exceed energy intake. In addition, the "triad" does not acknowledge the much broader health implications, including increased risk of stress fractures, overuse injuries, and decreased concentration. [55,56]

The energy imbalance may begin when an athlete engages in unhealthy eating patterns (restrictive eating or purging) and excessive exercise to lose weight, to attain a lean body appearance that fits a specific athletic image, or to improve performance. RED-S can have features similar to those of eating disorders, and the condition is noted most in sports that focus on weight loss or lean body appearance, such as wrestling, distance running, biking, and horse racing. The low calorie intake can also be unintentional due to lack of nutritional education or insufficient access to foods.

Often, a first sign of a problem is a decrease in performance, a muscle injury, or an exercise-related stress fracture.[57,58] Physical symptoms include fatigue, decreased focus, increased compulsion to exercise, decreased heart-rate response to exercise, and muscle degeneration. Cycles of repetitive overuse injuries are common.[55,56]

Treatment for energy imbalance disorders can be as simple as education and food access, or it can be similar to that for eating disorders if there is associated body dissatisfaction and disordered eating. The focus needs to be on increasing caloric intake or decreasing activity level until a balance has been reached.

PROMOTING A HEALTHY BODY IMAGE AND HEALTHY EATING

Promotion of a healthy body image, body satisfaction, and health eating includes many components and requires coordinated efforts by individuals and institutions.

Individual Attitudes and Actions

As an individual, you can begin to challenge the way you interact with the world. Value yourself based on your goals, talents, and strengths rather than on your body shape, appearance, or weight. Start to look critically at the images and messages you receive from people and the media. Develop skills to handle stress in a healthy way, and avoid judging yourself or others. Challenge the people in your life to speak positively about their bodies instead of participating in "fat talk." Complete the Personal Health Portfolio activity at the end of this chapter to take a closer look at your self-esteem and body image.

College Initiatives

Ideally, efforts to promote positive body image among young people will include both individual measures and campus-wide activities. Colleges have a role in ensuring that students learn how to transition successfully to new environments, new relationships, and different sociocultural pressures. These are skills that will translate well into future environments and relationships. Campus life typically affords many opportunities for people to recognize individuals who are at increased risk for disordered eating patterns and psychological distress. Residence advisors, professors, coaches, trainers, and other college staff can be trained to watch for signs that students are having challenges with the transition to college life. Health and counseling services can be made visible and accessible so students feel comfortable accessing help early if they are feeling distressed.

Public Health Approaches

Public health approaches focus on raising awareness about positive body image, disordered eating, and eating disorders by changing widely accepted social norms. The "Love Your Body Day" campaign is one example of a public health campaign aimed at promoting positive body images. Its goal is to challenge narrow cultural body "ideals" and promote diverse body-ideal messages to encourage acceptance of physical differences, including various body shapes and sizes and the normal changes of healthy aging (see the box "Public Health Is Personal: Love Your Body Day").

relative energy deficiency in sport (RED-S)
A condition in which an athlete's energy intake is not enough to support the level of exercise being performed. The imbalance leads to health problems.

female athlete triad
Interrelated conditions of insufficient food intake, amenorrhea, and osteoporosis.

Public Health Is Personal

Love Your Body Day

A healthy lifestyle, regardless of body type, should be the ideal, *ideally*. Every body is built differently. Too big for one person may be too small for another; one size typically never fits all. The narrow beauty standards to which people have been subconsciously primed by television, movies, social media, music videos, magazines, toys, clothing, and advertisements are unrealistic and can lead to body dissatisfaction.

Since 1998, the National Organization for Women (NOW) has sponsored a public health intervention against negative media influence, "Love Your Body Day." The day is a fun but serious way to help people fight back against unrealistic body images promoted by Hollywood and the fashion, cosmetics, and diet industries. NOW encourages colleges and schools across the country to host events that draw attention to body image issues and highlight the importance of healthy diversity in body shape, size, and function.

Events have included picketing the headquarters of publications that promote offensive images of women and girls, creating T-shirts with slogans that initiate discussions (such as "This is what Barbie OUGHT to look like"), and hosting forums to discuss and highlight body image issues. Every year there is a "Love Your Body" poster contest to highlight a healthy body image; the winner receives a monetary prize and the poster becomes the official announcement of the upcoming year's event.

(iStock/Getty Images)

On the Love Your Body website, NOW provides other resources to help the public become active in confronting the media. For example, it posts "Offensive Ads" and "Positive Ads" with explanations of how ads affect body image, thus enhancing media literacy. It also promotes advocacy by asking visitors to nominate ads for posting. For further information and to find out when the next annual Love Your Body Day is scheduled, visit the website at https://now.org/now-foundation/love-your-body/.

McGraw Hill connect®

Source: NOW Foundation. (2019). *Love your body*. Retrieved from http://now.org/now-foundation/love-your-body/.

College campuses can provide opportunities to support students in developing self-compassion and body-positive approaches. "The Body Positive" is a national organization that runs campus leadership programs and online courses and supports campuses in creating environments that support self-compassion, healthy eating, and healthy body image.[59] In addition, creating opportunities for students to access and develop skills in yoga, meditation, or mindfulness supports body appreciation and awareness.

In short, to promote healthy attitudes, we can begin by resisting current cultural messages and becoming active in changing them. The media and advertising industry spends millions of dollars every year finding out what consumers want and selling products. It conducts research on consumer attitudes, holds focus groups, monitors sales, and pays attention to consumer reactions. By supporting healthy body images and buying products that reflect diversity, we can move our society in the direction of realistic, accepting, and healthy attitudes toward the body.

You Make the Call

Should Digital Enhancement of Photos in the Media Be Banned?

Magazine cover and ad photos are routinely altered to create idealized versions of models and celebrities. Standard graphics software (such as Adobe Photoshop) is all a skilled photo editor needs to enlarge busts, reduce waists, remove cellulite, whiten teeth, lighten dark skin, darken light skin, erase lines and wrinkles, increase biceps, and modify a host of other human "flaws." The alterations are often hard to recognize, but sometimes they are hard to miss.

In June 2013, for example, Beyoncé released a digitally enhanced promotional photo for her upcoming tour. Her body proportions were not physically possible, and her designers said the photo was intended as an artistic vision. When *Men's Fitness* enlarged his biceps next to the headline "How to Build Big Arms in 5 Easy Steps," tennis star Andy Roddick joked on his blog about his "22-inch guns." Supermodel Cindy Crawford, commenting on digitally altered images of herself, remarked, "I wish I

Continued...

Concluded...

looked like Cindy Crawford." Actor Kate Winslet publicly objected to the slimmed-down version of herself on the cover of *British GQ,* saying, "I don't look like that and I don't desire to look like that." In October 2015, Winslet negotiated into her contract with L'Oréal a clause that prevents retouching of photographs. Saying "I do feel we have a responsibility to the younger generation of women," she argues that advertising needs to tell the truth.

What difference does enhancement make? It is not exactly clear, but we do know that all genders experience feelings of inadequacy, lower self-esteem, and increased dissatisfaction with their bodies after viewing fashion magazines. Models and actors already represent a look shared by only 2 percent of the population, and photo enhancement sometimes gives them body proportions that are physically unattainable. The images of models and celebrities are often taken at face value, and people aspire to achieve the same look or compare themselves unfavorably to them, or both. False representation also raises questions about media responsibility and transparency.

Truth-in-Advertising acts have twice been proposed in Congress; these would direct the Federal Trade Commission (FTC) to assess the prevalence and impact of altered images used in advertising and the media. Neither bill has even moved to a vote. Some argue that the FTC already prohibits "unfair or deceptive acts or practices in or affecting commerce" and thus is already responsible for oversight of digital enhancements.

Members of the fashion and advertising industries assert that photo enhancement and "post-production corrections" are well-known standard practices of their industries. Cover photos aren't meant to convey reality, they say; rather, they demonstrate artistry and creativity and are meant to inspire and please. Photographers have manipulated their images since the invention of the technology in the 19th century, and digital enhancement is commonplace today among the general population. With photo enhancement part of everyday life, only the very naive would take a magazine cover or ad at face value, according to fashion and advertising spokespeople.

In response to concerns about the effects of false and unattainable images, advocates for change have begun to promote the attachment of health warnings ("Warning: Trying to look as thin as this model may be dangerous to your health") or disclaimers ("These images have been digitally altered") to digitally enhanced photos. The assumption is that identification of enhancements will allow consumers to be more informed—and thus less likely to internalize unrealistic (and unreal) representations as a cultural ideal. Studies about the effectiveness of such warnings, however, suggest that they actually lead viewers to look longer at enhanced areas and have increased body dissatisfaction.

Media literacy encourages consumers to think critically and to assess sociocultural ideals portrayed in the media. Should federal policies explicitly cover truth in advertising? Should digitally enhanced photos be forbidden? Could policies require more appearance diversity in the media?

Pros

- Models and actors are public role models and should not be in the position of individually arguing to be authentic representations of themselves.
- The FTC act addresses other deceptive practices and should specifically regulate misrepresentation and deception in advertising and media.
- Digital enhancement is becoming so widespread and normalized that we need more action assessing the impacts of these practices.

Cons

- A change isn't necessary because the FTC act covers deceptive actions already.
- Photo enhancement is common practice in everyday life, and companies should be able to use it in advertising.
- Influences on body image come from many areas of society, and restricting advertising and media puts an unfair emphasis on their role.

Sources: USA Today Staff. (2015). Kate Winslet won't let her ads be airbrushed. USA Today. Retrieved from www.usatoday.com/story/life/entertainthis/2015/10/22/kate-winslet-wont-allow-airbrushing-her-beauty-ads/74378740/?AID=10709313&PID=6151680&SID=igco8ybscw00mzb200dth; Bury, B., Tiggemann, M., & Slater, A. (2016). Disclaimer labels on fashion magazine advertisements: Impact on visual attention and relationship with body dissatisfaction. *Body Image, 16,* 1-9; *Four and Six.* (2012). Photo tampering throughout history. Retrieved from www.fourandsix.com/photo-tampering-history/?currentPage=2; Paraskeva, N., Lewis-Smith, H., & Diedrichs, P. C. (2017). Consumer opinion on social policy approaches to promoting positive body image: Airbrushed media images and disclaimer labels. *Journal of Health Psychology, 22*(2), 164-175; H.R. 4445 – Truth in Advertising Act of 2016. Retrieved from https://www.congress.gov/bill/114th-congress/house-bill/4445; Federal Trade Commission. (n.d.). Truth in advertising. Retrieved from https://www.ftc.gov/news-events/media-resources/truth-advertising

In Review

What is body image, and how is it determined?

Body image is our mental representation of our body—our perceptions, attitudes, thoughts, and emotions about it. Via advertising, fashion, and language, our culture sends strong messages about appearance, beauty, and acceptable body size and shape. The media typically promote narrowly defined, binary-gender ideals of unrealistic thinness for women and excessive muscularity for men.

What is disordered eating, and what are eating disorders?

To meet narrowly defined standards of appearance, many people practice unhealthy disordered eating behaviors, such as dieting or binging and purging on occasion, but some people develop full-blown eating disorders. These disorders are characterized by distortions in body image, body dissatisfaction, and consistent unhealthy eating behaviors. They are serious, chronic illnesses and are classified as mental disorders. Anorexia nervosa, characterized by self-starvation, is the most severe eating disorder. Bulimia nervosa, characterized by binge eating and purging, is more difficult to identify because people with bulimia are of normal weight. Binge eating disorder leads to obesity, but only a small percentage of obese people have this disorder. All eating disorders have serious health consequences.

Why do people develop eating disorders?

Aside from social pressures and cultural messages, which affect everyone to greater or lesser extent, some people may be vulnerable to eating disorders because of a genetic predisposition, family factors, or other underlying emotional problems and characteristics, such as low self-esteem, a sense of powerlessness, perfectionism, and lack of coping skills. Eating disorders are most commonly present during the teens and early 20s, but there is an increased risk during life transitions at any age. Frequent dieting, obesity, substance abuse, depression, anxiety, and obsessive-compulsive disorder are all associated with an increased risk of eating disorders.

How are eating disorders treated?

The first step is recognition of the problem, and early recognition makes successful treatment more likely. Because they are mental disorders, eating disorders are usually treated with psychotherapy to address psychological issues, along with weight stabilization, behavior modification, nutritional rehabilitation and education, and, in some cases, medication, especially antidepressants. For anorexia, hospitalization may be required at first to prevent starvation. Treatment usually involves the whole family.

What is body dysmorphic disorder?

Body dysmorphic disorder is an acute preoccupation with a perceived flaw in the person's physical appearance. A subcategory, which affects mainly men, is muscle dysphoria, an obsessive need to bulk up the body regardless of physique. People with body dysmorphic disorder who undergo cosmetic surgery are likely not to be satisfied with the results, but opting to alter bodily appearance with cosmetic surgery or body art does not indicate a body dysmorphic disorder. Dissatisfaction with a tattoo or other body art is usually a result of changing life circumstances that make it less desirable.

What are exercise disorders?

Exercise disorders, or abnormal exercise patterns, can disrupt health. Relative energy deficiency is a broad category in which the energy consumed is insufficient to support the energy needed due to exercise levels. A subcategory includes the female athlete triad (disordered eating patterns, amenorrhea, and premature osteoporosis); however, the health impacts of insufficient calories are much broader and are not restricted to females. Exercise disorders share some symptoms with eating disorders, and treatments are also similar.

What are individual and public ways to promote healthy eating and healthy body images?

Individuals can learn to think critically about social pressures that promote particular body shapes or weights. They can be conscious of language used with peers to support positive body talk. Supporting campaigns to promote more diverse representations in the media increases body satisfaction. Colleges can evaluate the campus environment and ensure inclusive representation of people with diverse body shapes, sizes, and colors across campus. In addition, faculty, staff, and students can be trained to look for signs of eating disorders. Organizations can mount campaigns supporting acceptance of diversity.

Personal Health Portfolio

Chapter 8   Self-Esteem and Body Image

The goal of this activity is to help you think about your self-esteem and body image. Consider the following statements and then circle the response indicating how strongly you agree or disagree with each.

1. On the whole I am satisfied with myself.	Strongly agree	Agree	Neutral	Disagree	Strongly disagree
2. I have a number of good qualities.	Strongly agree	Agree	Neutral	Disagree	Strongly disagree
3. I am able to do things as well as most other people.	Strongly agree	Agree	Neutral	Disagree	Strongly disagree
4. I have done things I am proud of.	Strongly agree	Agree	Neutral	Disagree	Strongly disagree
5. I wish I had more respect for myself.	Strongly agree	Agree	Neutral	Disagree	Strongly disagree
6. I feel more in control when I restrict the food I eat.	Strongly agree	Agree	Neutral	Disagree	Strongly disagree
7. I consistently compare myself to others.	Strongly agree	Agree	Neutral	Disagree	Strongly disagree
8. I make sure to exercise if I have eaten too much.	Strongly agree	Agree	Neutral	Disagree	Strongly disagree
9. I would agree to cosmetic surgery if it were free.	Strongly agree	Agree	Neutral	Disagree	Strongly disagree
10. I am anxious about how people perceive or judge me.	Strongly agree	Agree	Neutral	Disagree	Strongly disagree
11. I eat to make myself feel better when I am sad, upset, or lonely.	Strongly agree	Agree	Neutral	Disagree	Strongly disagree
12. I often skip meals to lose weight.	Strongly agree	Agree	Neutral	Disagree	Strongly disagree

CRITICAL THINKING QUESTIONS

Consider your responses and answer the following questions.

1. Statements 1 through 5 relate to self-esteem. How do you think you do in regard to your self-esteem? What areas do you feel are your strengths? How are you supported in maintaining high self-esteem? Are you supported by family, friends, and colleagues? What about community factors—academics, sports, or student organizations? How about larger policies, such as institutions or social policies?

2. In areas of lower self-esteem, what are some of the factors that make it difficult or contribute to feelings of self-doubt? Are there areas that you could strengthen or change? Are there ways that family, friends, or community could help you? What role does social media play?

3. Statements 6 through 12 relate to body image. Your responses here are probably linked to your responses to the self-esteem statements. What areas appear to be your strengths? What factors support them?

4. Are there areas of concern for you in your body image responses? How might factors in your environment be contributing to these concerns? Is there anything you would like to change or could change in your environment to reduce the impact of these factors?

Note: This activity is not intended to diagnose eating disorders. The intent is to help you think about the factors discussed in the chapter and apply them to your life.

Alcohol and Tobacco

9

Serts/E+/Getty images

Ever Wonder... | what counts as having "too much" to drink?

what to do for someone who has passed out from drinking?

whether campus tobacco-free policies should include e-cigarettes and vaping?

lcohol and tobacco are the most common—and the most problematic—addictive substances in our society. Both can have profound effects on individuals, families, communities, and society in general. The use of both also illustrates the tension between personal choice and the common good. For these reasons, making responsible choices about alcohol and tobacco is particularly important.

UNDERSTANDING ALCOHOL USE

The alcohol culture permeates many college campuses, celebrated in tailgate parties, bar crawls, 21-shot birthday celebrations, and an endless variety of rituals marking the end of classes, the first snowfall, or spring break. For decades, college administrators ignored or condoned this culture. But recently, chilling statistics have brought alcohol-related problems to the forefront. Death, sexual assaults, physical violence, vandalism, and academic casualties are problems associated with the campus alcohol culture.[1,2,3]

Because alcohol is a **psychoactive drug**—it causes changes in brain chemistry and alters consciousness, inducing a state referred to as **intoxication**—it can have wide-ranging effects on all aspects of our thinking, emotions, and behavior. It is in society's interest to regulate the use of such a powerful substance, but it is up to individuals to determine what role they want alcohol to play in their lives.[4]

Patterns of Alcohol Use

The National Institute on Alcohol Abuse and Alcoholism (NIAAA) has set parameters for low-risk and high-risk drinking. For men, **low-risk drinking** means no more than 14 drinks per week and no more than 4 drinks on any one day. For women, it means no more than 7 drinks per week and no more than 3 drinks on any one day. Alcohol consumption above these levels is considered heavy or at-risk drinking. The USDA's *2015–2020 Dietary Guidelines for Americans* (see Chapter 5) advises alcohol only in moderation for adults of legal drinking age who choose to drink: 1 drink a day for women and up to 2 drinks a day for men. The risk level for women is set at a lower standard because men typically weigh more than women, and women have less body water than men (alcohol disperses in water). Compared with men, women are exposed to higher risks associated with blood alcohol concentration as a result of these weight and body water differences (see the section "Blood Alcohol Concentration" later in this chapter).[5]

psychoactive drug
A substance that causes changes in brain chemistry and alters consciousness.

intoxication
An altered state of consciousness as a result of drinking alcohol or ingesting other substances.

low-risk drinking
Fourteen drinks a week for men and no more than four on one day; seven drinks a week for women and no more than three on one day.

| Beer 12 oz. | Wine 5 oz. | Shot 1.5 oz. | Mixed drink 1.5 oz. |

figure 9.1   What is "one drink"?
Each drink contains about 0.5 ounce of alcohol.
((Beer): Bjorn Heller/Getty Images; (Wine): Clarke Robertson/iStockphoto; (Shot): C Squared Studios/Getty Images; (Mixed Drink): Comstock Images/Alamy Stock Photo)

"One drink" is defined by the NIAAA as 0.5 ounce (or 15 grams) of alcohol, the amount contained in about 12 ounces of beer, 5 ounces of wine, a 1.5-ounce shot of 80-proof distilled liquor, or 1.5 ounces of liquor in a mixed drink (Figure 9.1). The term *proof* refers to the alcohol content of hard liquor, defined as twice the actual percentage of alcohol in the beverage; for example, 80-proof liquor is 40 percent alcohol by volume.

Regardless of the guidelines about levels of drinking, you should not consume alcohol if doing so will put you or others at risk.[5] The Personal Health Portfolio activity at the end of this chapter will help you assess whether you are a low-risk or at-risk drinker.

Who Drinks?

Drinking patterns are established by the adolescent years. In general, people are more likely to drink at certain stages in the lifespan, such as in adolescence and early adulthood, at the threshold of middle age, and following retirement. Older adults drink significantly less than younger adults do. Women of all ages drink less than men do and start later. Among adults who have had at least one heavy drinking day in the past year, 5.7 percent are Hispanic/Latino, 7.4 percent are non-Hispanic whites, 2.1 percent are Asian, and 5.2 are Black. See the box, "Who's at Risk? Heavy Drinkers Are at Risk for Alcohol-Related Diseases."[6]

Differences in the rates of alcohol consumption among ethnic groups are strongly influenced by sociocultural or environmental factors, including poverty, discrimination, feelings of powerlessness, immigration status, and degree of acculturation.[7,8] Economic factors, such as the heavy marketing of alcoholic beverages in minority neighborhoods, play a considerable role. For example, the number of liquor stores located in African American communities is proportionately much higher than the number in white communities.[7,8] Given these pressures, it is notable that alcohol consumption is generally lower among African Americans than among other groups.

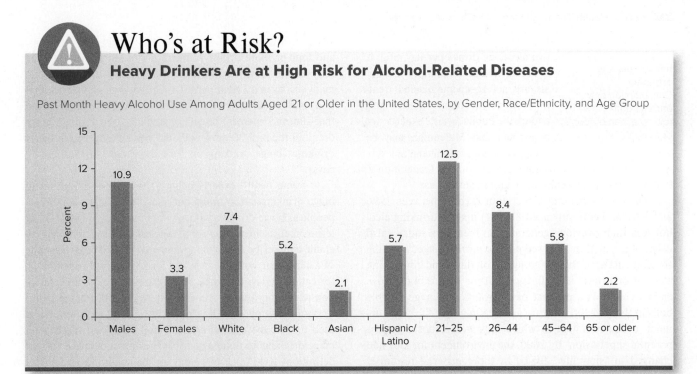

Who's at Risk?

Heavy Drinkers Are at High Risk for Alcohol-Related Diseases

Past Month Heavy Alcohol Use Among Adults Aged 21 or Older in the United States, by Gender, Race/Ethnicity, and Age Group

Source: U.S. Substance Abuse and Mental Health Services Administration. (2016). *Behavioral health barometer*. HHS Publication No. SMA-16-Bar2015. Rockville, MD: Substance Abuse and Mental Health Services Administration.

Among Native Americans, alcoholism is recognized as the number-one health problem.[7] The death rate from alcoholism for Native Americans is more than five times greater than that for other groups.[8] Numerous factors contribute to these disparities, most notably sociocultural factors such as poverty and discrimination. Scientists have also suggested that genetic factors may contribute to patterns of alcohol use by Native Americans.

Among Asian Americans, alcohol consumption overall is lower than that among white Americans. Approximately half of all Asian Americans have a gene that impairs the metabolism of alcohol, causing a set of unpleasant reactions (facial flushing, sweating, nausea) referred to as the *flushing effect.*[9]

Are Millennials and Generation Z Drinking Less Alcohol Than Previous Generations? Millennials (born between 1981 and 1995) are drinking less alcohol than baby boomers (born between 1943 and 1964) and members of Generation X (born between 1965 and 1980). Finances and potential health effects certainly influence attitudes toward alcohol consumption. However, Millennials may also be less inclined to drink excessively. This does not mean they do not have alcohol problems. Seventy-two percent view regular alcohol drinking as a problem. Alcohol consumption peaked at age 19 for the baby boom generation and Generation X, but peaks at age 22 for Millennials. Millennials report a stress rating of about 5.5, in contrast to the average U.S. stress rate of 4.9, and 25 percent of them drink alcohol to cope with financial stress. Millennials also binge drink more, but they are more likely than baby boomers and Gen Xers to disapprove of the regular drinking of

An oversupply of liquor stores in poor and minority neighborhoods plays a role in both the availability of alcohol and the social acceptability of alcohol use. *(Walter Cicchetti/Shutterstock)*

217

heavy episodic drinking
Consumption of five or more drinks in a row by a man or four or more drinks in a row by a woman.

two alcoholic drinks per day. Still, it is estimated that 10 million Millennials are not receiving needed treatment for substance abuse and addiction. Public health experts are concerned that Millennials may be using recreational marijuana as a substitute for alcohol. It is Generation Z that may be forcing a cultural change in alcohol use.[10]

There are signs that Generation Z (born between 1996 and 2012 and currently aged 8 to 24) may be drinking alcohol less than previous generations. Teenagers today (also called iGen or Gen Wii) seem to be more engaged in using social media apps than in going out on dates and consuming alcohol or drugs. Jean Twenge, author of the book *iGen,* claims Gen Z is a product of environment change. People born in the mid-20th century grew up in a "fast-life" environment, an environment in which kids were exposed to less parental supervision. By 2000, the environment for kids had changed to "slow life," fueled by more material resources and encouragement by parents to stay kids longer.[11]

The suicide rate for today's Gen Z is higher than the homicide rate for this group and the highest it has been since 1999. Twenge believes its members are more likely to be inside, tethered to their social media devices, than outside socializing. This environmental change has led them to have less sex and to avoid alcohol, tobacco, and illegal drugs. It is estimated that Gen Zers are drinking 25 percent less per person than their Millennial peers at the same age. Most have not yet been influenced by alcohol industry promotions. Still, unlike Millennials, Gen Zers are displaying less interest in intoxicants from alcohol to tobacco. Although baby boomers and Gen Xers drink alcohol mostly for fun and social reasons, both Millennials and Gen Zers are drinking to cope with mood disorder symptoms (that is, stress and anxiety). Many are also choosing marijuana over alcohol, since it does not leave them feeling sick and hung over. Sober bars are opening nationwide in response to Millennials and Gen Zer adults who want a socializing barlike atmosphere but without alcohol. Alcohol distributors are also responding by developing low-alcohol and nonalcoholic beverages.[11,12]

Drinking on the College Campus

Drinking rates at most colleges are very high; surveys indicate that up to 79 percent of college students drink alcoholic beverages.[2,13] College students under the age of 21 drink less frequently than older students do, but they are more likely to binge drink during these episodes and to drink simply to get drunk.[14] They are also more likely to be injured or encounter trouble with law enforcement than are older students who binge drink.[13] Although college students binge drink, 70 percent of binge drinking episodes involve adults aged 26 years or older.[15]

Binge Drinking and Extreme Drinking Binge drinking, also called **heavy episodic drinking**, is generally defined as the consumption of five or more drinks within 2 hours for men

and four or more drinks within 2 hours for women, at least once in the previous 2-week period. When people have that many drinks in a 2-hour period, their blood alcohol concentration rises to 0.08 percent or more. A NIAAA survey reported that almost 57 percent of college students aged 18 to 22 binge drank in the past 30 days, and 10.5 percent engaged in heavy drinking (binge drinking on 5 or more days in the past 30 days).[16]

Some health experts believe the current definition of binge drinking is too broad and classifies a large number of people as binge drinkers who may not have a problem.[17] Other terms, such as *heavy drinking* or *high-risk drinking,* may be preferable to describe the drinking currently labeled *binge drinking.* The latter term could be reserved for a prolonged period of intoxication (2 days or more). This definition would direct attention to the minority of students who have real problems with alcohol consumption. The term *extreme drinking* is now being used to describe alcohol consumption that goes well beyond binge drinking, to double or triple the amounts in the current definition—10 to 15 drinks a day for men and 8 to 12 drinks a day for women. Many colleges and universities are now targeting such extreme drinking on campus.

Consequences of Binge Drinking in College Binge drinking can have serious physical, academic, social, and legal consequences. Individuals who have been drinking heavily are more likely to be injured, commit a crime or fall victim to violence, drive while intoxicated, and experience unintended and unprotected sexual activity.[18] According to the College Alcohol Survey, about one in four students reported that their drinking caused them to miss class, turn in mediocre work, fail exams, or earn failing grades.[19] Frequent binge drinkers are more likely to experience these consequences than are occasional binge drinkers or those who do not binge drink. Frequent binge drinking is defined as three or more binges in the previous 2 weeks or more than one a week.

Binge drinkers also cause problems for other students. These "secondhand effects" of binge drinking include serious arguments, physical assault, damaged property, interrupted sleep or studying, unwanted sexual advances, sexual assault, and the need to care for a drunk student. NIAAA estimates that drinking alcohol by students aged 18 to 24 contributes to 1,825 student deaths each year, as well as 96,000 assaults and 97,000 sexual assaults and date rapes.[16]

Binge drinkers are more likely to meet the *Diagnostic and Statistical Manual of Mental Disorders* criteria for alcohol abuse and alcohol dependence 10 years after college and are less likely to work in prestigious occupations, compared with those who do not binge drink. Alcohol-related convictions for crimes such as driving under the influence, vandalism, assaults, and providing alcohol to a minor may jeopardize ambitions in many careers, especially engineering, medicine, law enforcement, and teaching.

Why Do College Students Binge Drink? Students may drink to ease social inhibitions, fit in with peers, imitate role models, reduce stress, soothe negative emotions, or cope with

Alcohol consumption among college students is influenced by the social norms around drinking on their campus. In some cases, there is a gap between student-perceived levels of alcohol consumption and actual consumption by most students. Students perceiving other college students are drinking more leads them to thinking that it is accepted for them to drink more. *(milkos/123RF)*

academic pressure—or for a variety of other reasons. The mistaken belief that alcohol increases sexual arousal and performance may also account for some binge drinking (heavy drinking actually suppresses sexual arousal).[15]

Binge drinking is also promoted by easy access to alcohol and cheap prices. Thus, social norms and the campus culture contribute to patterns of drinking.[17] Students are more likely to binge drink on campuses where heavy drinking is the norm and less likely to do so where drinking is discouraged.[17]

Pregaming Drinking *Pregaming* is the excessive consumption of alcohol prior to attending an event or activity at which more alcohol will be consumed. It is also referred to as prepartying, prebar, and front-loading. Pregaming is considered high risk because it usually consists of heavy consumption of alcoholic drinks in a short period of time. One study found that students who pregame consumed more than three drinks in about an hour and usually consumed hard alcohol. Although college men and women consume similar levels of alcohol in pregaming, men typically drink more during events following pregaming.

One study found that about 40 percent of underage college students pregamed on multiple days per month and had more drinks on pregaming days. First-year students were more likely to pregame than other students. The first weeks of college appear to be the highest-risk period for pregaming. Negative consequences associated with pregaming include low class attendance, declining grade point average, vandalism, driving under alcohol influence, and fatal alcohol poisoning.[20]

Pregaming can quickly move a college student from low-risk drinking to at-risk drinking. The typical U.S. adult averages 1.3 pregame drinks before an event. College fraternity men average 1.7 pregame drinks. Twenty-five percent of men and 21 percent of women pregame drink. Almost 75 percent of adults who pregame drink before going out say it helps them have more fun, and 40 percent report it has a calming effect.[21,22]

Heavy consumption of alcohol in a relative short period of time is a college football tailgating ritual for many college students. *Bleacher Report* even ranks the top 25 football tailgating colleges. As discussed later in this chapter, consuming large amounts of alcohol for a regular period of time can damage your heart by causing scar tissue formation, a condition called alcohol cardiomyopathy. Congestive heart failure and ventricular arrhythmias are complications associated with alcohol cardiomyopathy. A primary symptom is a racing heart.

A more common condition for college students is the "holiday heart syndrome" that may occur from binge drinking. Large amounts of alcohol in a short period of time can cause abrupt alterations in the heart's electrical system and abrupt changes in the blood's adrenaline levels that lead to cardio arrhythmias such as atrial flutter and atrial fibrillation. Diuretic effects of alcohol can also cause dehydration. The racing heart is a response to dehydration that attempts to keep the heart's electrical system stable. The holiday heart syndrome may resolve on its own or require a visit to the hospital emergency room. Many colleges and universities are introducing new policies to limit the pregaming experience of football tailgating, for example, by offering alcohol-free tailgating zones.[23]

Spring-Break Drinking Thousands of college students descend on spring-break locales every year to celebrate. Beaches, bikinis, bands, and free or cheap alcoholic beverages marketed by the alcohol industry and bars create an environment conducive to excessive drinking. Males average 18 drinks per day and females 10 drinks per day. Seventy-five percent of college men and 44 percent of women reported being drunk daily during spring break. Many of these students will pass out from heavy alcohol consumption.[24] Collapse, sexual assaults, and unprotected sex are common. One study found that more than 50 percent of all men and 40 percent of all women drank until they became sick or passed out. Another study of frequent binge drinkers at spring break reported that 50 percent engaged in unplanned sex, 52 percent engaged in unprotected sex, 58 percent had trouble with law enforcement, and 59 percent were injured. Some colleges and universities have responded by banning spring-break marketing and promotion on campus.[25]

Many popular spring break destination cities are promoting safety campaigns. Miami Beach, for example, is promoting "Come on vacation, don't leave on probation." The U.S. State Department is issuing safety travel warnings about popular spring break destinations in foreign countries, for example, Mexico, Jamaica, Bahamas, and the Dominican Republic. These urge people to travel with caution due to kidnappings, drug violence, and other local violence. Student City, a popular spring break travel service, monitors State Department travel warning levels but does not announce lower-level warnings to its spring break patrons.

Most campuses are flooded with spring break ads and posters. Promotional messages by spring break travel countries encourage students to tell their parents spring break is

central nervous system depressant A chemical substance that slows down the activity of the brain and spinal cord.

an educational opportunity, or not to worry about the water in Mexico because they will be drinking beer. Some college women may be getting fed up with spring break marketing, however. In an American Medical Association poll of college women and graduates aged 17 to 35, 59 percent favor restricting the content of spring break promotions on campus, 61 percent support prohibiting alcohol drinking specials as part of tour packages, and 81 percent want colleges to offer alternative spring break community service packages.[26]

Powdered Alcohol Powdered alcohol (palcohol) was approved by the U.S. Alcohol and Tobacco Tax and Trade Bureau in 2015 to be sold in pouches. It is available in diverse flavors such as vodka, rum, and mixed drinks. One pouch mixed with 6 ounces of liquid creates an alcoholic beverage equivalent to one standard drink. Powdered alcohol is marketed as convenient for people enjoying outdoor activities or wanting to travel light with their favorite alcoholic beverages. Despite federal approval, more than half the states have banned powdered alcohol due to its potential to increase underage drinking. There are also concerns that users may snort powdered alcohol, but this is unlikely since it would create a burning sensation.[27]

Flavored Alcohol Flavored alcoholic beverages have increased in popularity for young adults and underage drinkers. These brands come in three categories that also designate serving sizes: malt-based has alcohol content of 7.8 percent, ready-to-drink cocktails have 14.2 percent, and supersized alcopops have 10.8 percent. The popularity of flavored alcohol and its high alcohol volume content are of concern since these drinks disproportionately contribute to alcohol-related emergencies.[28]

Pot-Infused Alcohol Beer companies are lacing beer with tetrahydrocannabinol (THC), the primary ingredient in cannabis that produces the "high" experience. Presently, pot-infused beer is sold at marijuana dispensaries, but beer manufacturers are projecting that THC beer will soon be legally available in bar operations.

Cannabidiol (CBD) is already being legally served as cocktail drinks. The mixing of alcohol and CBD, however, may have negative effects. CBD is not a psychoactive ingredient that produces a high like THC, but it does have a relaxant effect like alcohol's. CBD and alcohol in combination can exponentially lower inhibitions, increase levels of intoxication, and reduce motor coordination. People who do not drink or smoke marijuana regularly are likely to be more vulnerable to the effects of CBD-infused alcohol drinks, Still, there is more concern about mixing alcohol with THC than with CBD. Mixing alcohol with THC increases THC levels in the blood eightfold.[29,30]

Addressing the Problem The transition from high school to college presents colleges with a critical opportunity to implement integrated prevention measures for at-risk drinking at several levels. Many colleges are now targeting at-risk drinking by first-year students by offering alcohol-free options, limiting alcohol availability, restricting marketing and promotion of alcohol beverages on campus and off, promoting social norms to counteract the belief that heavy drinking is an expected student behavior, and strengthening policy development and enforcement.[2,15,31] The NIAAA developed a 3-in-1 framework, based on the socioecological model described in Chapter 1, to confront at-risk drinking on college campuses; see Figure 9.2.

EFFECTS OF ALCOHOL ON THE BODY

Within minutes of ingestion, alcohol is distributed to all the cells of the body (Figure 9.3). In the brain, alcohol alters brain chemistry and changes neurotransmitter functions. It particularly affects the cerebellum—the center for balance and motor functions—and the prefrontal cortex—the center for executive functions such as rational thinking and problem solving.[2] Alcohol is a **central nervous system depressant**. While your body is absorbing alcohol and alcohol levels in the blood and brain are rising, you experience feelings of relaxation and well-being and a lowering of social inhibitions. At higher levels, and especially when blood levels are falling, you are more likely to feel depressed and withdrawn and to experience impairments in thinking, balance, and motor coordination. These effects last until all the alcohol is metabolized (broken down into energy and wastes) and excreted from the body.

Alcohol Absorption

Faster absorption of alcohol into the blood results in a quicker increase in blood alcohol concentration than when alcohol is absorbed more slowly. Many factors affect the rate of alcohol absorption.

- *Food in the stomach.* Alcohol consumed on an empty stomach can reach the brain in less than 1 minute. Food slows the movement of alcohol into the small intestine by closing the valve between the stomach and small intestine.

- *Gender.* Women absorb alcohol into the bloodstream more quickly than men do.

- *Age.* Older adults do not tolerate alcohol as well as younger people.

- *Body fat.* The more body fat a person has, the less alcohol is absorbed by body tissues and the more there is to circulate in the bloodstream and reach the brain. In other words, higher body fat results in a quicker intoxication than lower body fat.

- *Drug interaction.* Interactions with many prescription and over-the-counter drugs can intensify a drinker's reaction to alcohol, leading to more rapid intoxication.

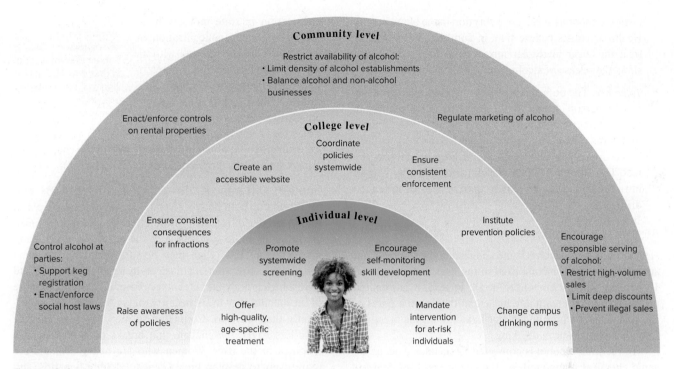

figure 9.2   **3-in-1 framework: Addressing college drinking.**

Sources: National Institute on Alcohol Abuse and Alcoholism. (2015). NIH releases comprehensive resource to help address college drinking. Retrieved from www.niaaa.nih.gov/news-events/news-releases/nih-releases-comprehensive-resource-help-address-college drinking; University of Minnesota Alcohol Epidemiology Program. (2015). College systems model: Addressing student alcohol use and related problems. Retrieved from www.aep.umn.edu/index.php/aep-tools/college/.

(pkchai/Shutterstock)

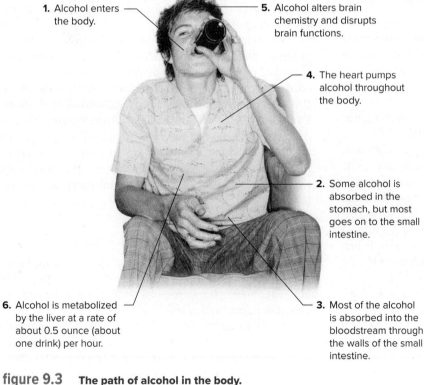

1. Alcohol enters the body.

5. Alcohol alters brain chemistry and disrupts brain functions.

4. The heart pumps alcohol throughout the body.

2. Some alcohol is absorbed in the stomach, but most goes on to the small intestine.

6. Alcohol is metabolized by the liver at a rate of about 0.5 ounce (about one drink) per hour.

3. Most of the alcohol is absorbed into the bloodstream through the walls of the small intestine.

figure 9.3   **The path of alcohol in the body.**

Source: Hart, C.L., Ksir, C., & Ray, O. (2015). *Drugs, society, and human behavior.* New York: McGraw-Hill.

(George Doyle/Stockbyte/Getty Images)

- *Cigarette smoke.* Nicotine extends the time alcohol stays in the stomach, increasing time needed for absorption into the bloodstream. This means smoking slows the increase in blood alcohol concentration.

- *Mood and physical condition.* Fear and anger tend to speed up alcohol absorption. The stomach empties more rapidly than normal, allowing the alcohol to be absorbed more easily. People who are stressed, tired, or ill may also feel the effects of alcohol sooner.

- *Alcohol concentration.* The more concentrated the alcohol, the more quickly it is absorbed. Hard liquor is absorbed faster than are beer and wine.

- *Carbonation.* The carbon dioxide in champagne, cola, and ginger ale speeds the absorption of alcohol. In contrast, drinks that contain water, juice, or milk are absorbed more slowly.

- *Diet soda.* The artificial sugars in diet soda cause alcohol to empty more rapidly from the stomach into the small intestine and thus speed up absorption in the bloodstream. Health scientists believe that, in contrast, the body may treat the sugar in regular mixers as it does food, which slows the release of alcohol into the small intestine.

• *Tolerance.* The body adapts to a given alcohol level. Each time a person drinks to the point of impairment, the body attempts to minimize impairment by adapting to that level. Thereafter, more alcohol is needed to overcome the body's adaptation and achieve the desired effect. This means an experienced drinker absorbs alcohol into the blood more slowly than a less experienced drinker.

Alcohol Metabolism

A small amount of alcohol is metabolized in the stomach, but about 90 percent is metabolized in the liver. Between 2 and 10 percent is not metabolized at all; instead, it is excreted unchanged in the breath and urine and through the pores of the skin. This is why you can smell alcohol on the breath of someone who has been drinking.

In the liver, alcohol is converted to acetaldehyde, an organic chemical compound, by the enzyme *alcohol dehydrogenase (ADH).* The ability to metabolize alcohol depends on the amount and kind of ADH enzymes available in the liver. If more alcohol molecules arrive in the liver cells than the enzymes can process, the extra molecules circulate through the brain, liver, and other organs until enzymes are available to degrade them. Slower degrading of alcohol molecules means a higher blood alcohol concentration until they are metabolized.

Blood Alcohol Concentration **Blood alcohol concentration (BAC)** is a measure of the grams of alcohol in 100 milliliters (ml) of blood, expressed as a percentage. For example, for 100 milligrams of alcohol in 100 ml of blood, the BAC is 0.10 percent.

BAC is influenced by the amount of alcohol consumed and the rate at which the alcohol is metabolized by the body. Because alcohol is soluble in water and somewhat less soluble in fat, it does not distribute to all body tissues equally.[32] The more body water a person has—in body tissues and fluids that contain water, such as muscle tissue and blood—the more the alcohol is diluted and the lower the person's BAC will be. The more body fat a person has, the less alcohol is absorbed by body tissue and the more there is to circulate in the bloodstream and reach the brain. Thus, a person with high body fat will have a higher BAC than will a person of the same weight but with more lean body tissue who drinks the same amount. Body size alone influences BAC as well; a larger, heavier person has more body surface to diffuse the alcohol (as well as a higher body water content to dilute the alcohol). To estimate your blood alcohol content, you can use the calculator at http://bloodalcoholcalculator.org/.

BAC provides a good estimate of the alcohol concentration in the brain, which is why it is used as a measure of intoxication in state motor vehicle laws. The alcohol concentration in the blood corresponds well with alcohol concentration in the breath, so breath samples are accurate indicators of BAC. For this reason, breath analyzers are legal in most states for identifying and prosecuting drunk drivers, which is discussed later in the chapter (see "Harm Reduction: Approach, Policies, and Laws").

blood alcohol concentration (BAC) The amount of alcohol in grams in 100 milliliters of blood, expressed as a percentage.

Gender Differences in Alcohol Absorption and Metabolism Both body size and body fat percentage play a role in gender differences in the effects of alcohol. Women are generally more susceptible to the effects of alcohol and have a higher BAC than men do after drinking the same amount, because women are generally smaller than men and have a higher body fat percentage. Women also absorb more of the alcohol they drink because they metabolize it less efficiently than men do. Compared to men, women generally have less ADH, the enzyme that breaks down alcohol metabolites in the liver. Women who are heavy drinkers are more likely to develop breast cancer, alcohol hepatitis, and heart problems than women who do not drink heavily.[33]

Rates and Effects of Alcohol Metabolism Alcohol is metabolized more slowly than it is absorbed. This means the concentration of alcohol in the blood builds when someone consumes additional drinks before metabolizing earlier drinks. As a rule of thumb, people who have normal liver function metabolize about 0.5 ounce of alcohol (about one drink) per hour.[34]

The behavioral effects of alcohol, based on studies of moderate drinkers, are summarized in Table 9.1. Because of individual differences in sensitivity to alcohol, people experience impairment at different BAC levels, but a person with a BAC of 0.08 percent is considered legally drunk in all states. The National Highway Traffic Safety Administration reports that driving function can be impaired by BAC levels as low as 0.02 to 0.04 percent.[7] For more on the public debate about the legal limit, see the box "Starting the Conversation: Should the Legal Limit for Driving Under the Influence Be Lowered to 0.05 BAC?"

Visible Effects: Weight and Wrinkles

Deeper wrinkles, red cheeks, and weight gain are just a few of the visible effects of regular heavy drinking. To see how alcohol might affect your looks, download a "Drinking Mirror" app from changemyface.com.

Alcohol's empty calories have a tendency to be deposited in the abdomen, giving drinkers a characteristic "beer belly." At the same time, long-term heavy drinkers who substitute the calories in alcohol for those in food are at risk for weight loss and malnutrition. They are also vulnerable to mental disorders caused by vitamin deficiencies.

Table 9.1   Stages of Effects of Alcohol

Blood Alcohol Concentration (grams/100 ml)	Physiological and Psychological Effects	Impaired Functions
0.01–0.05	Relaxation Sense of well-being Loss of inhibition	Decreased alertness Impaired concentration Impaired judgment Impaired coordination (especially fine motor skills)
0.06–0.10	Euphoria Blunted feelings Nausea Sleepiness	Slower reflexes Impaired reasoning Impaired visual tracking Reduced depth perception
0.11–0.20	Emotional arousal Mood swings Anger or sadness Boisterousness	Slowed reaction time Staggering gait Slurred speech Impaired balance
0.21–0.30	Aggression Reduced sensations Depression Stupor	Lethargy Increased pain threshold Severe motor impairment Memory blackout
0.31–0.40	Unconsciousness Coma Death possible	Loss of bladder control Impaired temperature regulation Slowed breathing Slowed heart rate
0.41 and greater	Death	Respiratory arrest

Source: B.R.A.D.21 (n.d.). *Effects at specific B.A.C. levels.* Retrieved from www.brad21.org/effects_at_specific_bac.html.

Acute Alcohol Intoxication

People who drink heavily in a relatively short time are vulnerable to **acute alcohol intoxication** (also called *acute alcohol shock* or *alcohol poisoning*), a potentially life-threatening BAC level of about 0.35 or greater. Acute alcohol intoxication can produce collapse of vital body functions, notably respiration and heart function, leading to coma and/or death (see the box "Action Skill-Builder: Alcohol Poisoning: Know the Signs, Know What to Do"). Vomit can also be inhaled under intoxication, leading to death by asphyxiation. Dehydration caused by vomiting can cause seizures, which can permanently damage the brain.

Slow, steady drinking suppresses the vomiting reflex, and BAC can increase to dangerously high levels. The gag reflex is also slower or nonexistent when a person experiences alcohol poisoning. At very high alcohol concentrations, 0.35 or greater, a person can become comatose, sustain irreversible brain damage, or die. Some colleges have instituted "Good Samaritan" rules that provide amnesty for students who seek help for themselves or others in a medical emergency due to drinking that occurred in a residence hall room or where underage drinkers were present.

Blackouts

A **blackout** is a period of time during which a drinker is conscious but has impaired memory function; later, he or she has amnesia about events that occurred during this time. Alcohol blackouts occur when BAC levels spike too high and too quickly. An *en-bloc blackout* results in the inability to recall anything that happened during the intoxication period. A person who has suffered a *fragmentary blackout* has the ability to recall some but not all events from the intoxicated period.

Anyone with a BAC of 0.14 is vulnerable to blackouts. The impairment is associated with changes in the hippocampus, a brain structure essential for memory and learning.[32,35] These changes may be temporary or permanent. Either way, a blackout is a warning sign that fundamental changes have occurred in the structure of the brain.[32,35,36] Alcohol-induced blackouts are a common experience among nonalcoholics who binge drink. Some people may be genetically predisposed to

acute alcohol intoxication
A life-threatening blood alcohol concentration.

blackout
A period of time during which a drinker is conscious but has partial or complete amnesia for events.

Starting the Conversation

Should the Legal Limit for Driving Under the Influence Be Lowered to 0.05 BAC?

The National Transportation Safety Board (NTSB) in 2013 proposed that the legal driving-under-the-influence (DUI) threshold for BAC should be lowered from 0.08 to 0.05 in the United States. This recommendation was announced on the 25th anniversary of one of the deadliest traffic accidents in the United States: On May 14, 1988, an intoxicated driver drove on the wrong side of the road in Kentucky, crashing into a bus and killing 27 people and injuring more than 30. Twenty-four of the victims were children returning from a church outing at an amusement park.

According to the NTSB, about 10,000 people die each year from alcohol-related crashes, so lowering the legal threshold to 0.05 may save 500 to 800 lives each year. More than 100 countries have legal threshold laws for DUI of 0.05 or lower. The NTSB emphasizes that these countries have experienced a significant decrease in alcohol-related traffic deaths.

However, the NTSB does not have the power to implement its recommendation. Congressional action, as well as federal and state agency action, is needed. Passage of a 0.05 legal threshold for DUI will not be easy. In essence, the lower threshold would make driving after moderate consumption of alcohol illegal for many people. A 170-pound man will usually reach 0.05 BAC after four drinks in 2 hours, but a 135-pound woman reaches this level after three drinks. Because it takes only one standard drink to reach a 0.02 BAC, critics of the NTSB 0.05 proposal have referred to it as the "one-drink limit."

Not surprisingly, the National Restaurant Association (NRA) and the American Beverage Institute (ABI) argue that federal and state efforts should be directed at offenders with higher BAC levels and with multiple convictions. Many states have increased penalties based on exceptionally high BAC, for example, California 0.15, New York 0.18, Pennsylvania 0.1, and Colorado 0.15. Some cities may even have stricter BAC limits than state laws. Both organizations consider the NTSB 0.05 recommendation "ludicrous" and the needless criminalization of a perfectly responsible behavior. Surprisingly, Mothers Against Drunk Driving (MADD) does not support it either. MADD emphasizes that it took years to reduce the legal threshold from 0.10 to 0.08 and argues that a 0.05 BAC threshold would not be as effective as the further use of technologies such as ignition interlock devices.

The NTSB has not been deterred by the torrent of criticism of its 0.05 BAC legal threshold recommendation. The Insurance Institute for Highway Safety, for example, estimates that lowering the BAC from 0.08 to 0.05 would save more than 7,000 lives each year. This estimate is drawn from research on driver behavior at different BAC levels. Utah was the first state to lower the legal BAC from 0.08 to 0.05. According to one study, even a BAC of 0.01 is capable of producing a "buzz" that can increase the odds of a deadly accident. (A BAC of 0.01 for many adults occurs with consumption of about half a beer in an hour.) Drivers who are buzzed are more likely to speed and less likely to use a seat belt. The risk of alcohol-related accidents increases at each 0.01 increase in BAC level, but once the 0.05 BAC threshold has been reached, that risk increases sevenfold. The bottom line is that alcohol in any amount is dangerous for the driver.

States that passed lower BAC laws have experienced reductions in alcohol use and alcohol-related accidents. The use of zero-tolerance laws and administrative driver's license suspension has in effect provided law enforcement with the means to lower the legal BAC below 0.08.

So, what do you think? Should the legal threshold for BAC while driving be lowered to 0.05?

Sources: Alcohol Organization. (2019). Legal BAC limits in different states, counties, and cities. Retrieved from https//www.alcoho.org/dui/bac-limits/; In the Know Zone. (n.d.). Blood alcohol concentration. Retrieved from http://inthe knowzone.com/substance-abuse-topics/alcohol/bac.html; Fell, J.C. (2016). The merits of adopting a 0.05 administrative blood alcohol concentration limit for driving. *American Journal of Public Health Perspectives, 106*(6), 977-978.

experience blackouts. To prevent blackouts, eat food before consuming alcohol, alternate alcoholic drinks with at least 8 ounces of water, do not consume large amounts of alcohol if sleep-deprived, pace your alcohol consumption, and don't mix alcohol with medications, particularly pain killers and sleep drugs.[37]

En bloc blackout is not the same as alcohol-induced anesthetic disorder. En bloc blackout is a temporary effect. Alcohol-induced anesthetic disorder is a long-term effect caused by changes in brain neurotransmitters used for transferring short-term memory from the frontal lobe to the hippocampus for long-term memory storage. Although alcohol blackouts are not a sign of alcoholism, they are a symptom of alcohol abuse.[38] Frequent blackouts indicate the person is causing serious personal damage physically, mentally, and socially.

Effects of Alcohol Ingestion Fads

Up to 28 percent of college students reportedly mix alcohol and energy drinks, despite evidence that doing so is dangerous.[36] Alcohol acts as a depressant, which sedates the body and causes a drinker to become sleepy. The stimulants in energy drinks keep the body awake. When alcohol and stimulants are combined, the alcohol intoxicates the drinker but the stimulants induce wakefulness, tricking the body into believing it is sober. College students who mix alcohol and energy drinks are three times more likely to leave a bar drunk and four times more likely to drive drunk. There is also an increased risk of sexual assaults.[36]

Some college students who are bored with the liquid form of alcohol, want to get drunk faster, or think they can limit alcohol's calories have turned to vaporizing alcohol

Action Skill-Builder

Alcohol Poisoning: Know the Signs, Know What to Do

Do you know the symptoms of alcohol poisoning? Do you know what you should do and when you should seek help? People who have passed out from heavy drinking should be watched closely. All too often they are carried to bed and forgotten. For their safety, follow these measures:

☐ Know and recognize the symptoms of acute alcohol intoxication:

✓ Lack of response when spoken to or shaken

✓ Inability to wake up

✓ Inability to stand up without help

✓ Rapid or irregular pulse (100 beats per minute or more)

✓ Rapid, irregular respiration or difficulty breathing (10 seconds or more between breaths)

✓ Slow breathing (fewer than eight breaths per minute)

✓ Cool, clammy, bluish skin

✓ Bluish fingernails or lips

✓ Hypothermia (low body temperature)

☐ Call 911. An intoxicated person who cannot be roused or wakened or has other symptoms listed here requires emergency medical treatment.

☐ Do not leave the person to "sleep it off." He or she may never wake up. BAC can continue to rise even after a person has passed out.

☐ Roll an unconscious drinker onto his or her side to minimize the chance of airway obstruction from vomit.

☐ If the person vomits, make certain his or her head is positioned lower than the rest of the body. You may need to reach into the person's mouth to clear the airway.

☐ Try to find out whether the person has taken other drugs or medications that might interact with alcohol.

☐ Stay with the person until medical help arrives.

Source: National Institute on Alcohol Abuse and Alcoholism. (2015). Facts about alcohol poisoning. *College Drinking: Changing the Culture.* Retrieved from www.collegedrinkingprevention.gov/OtherAlcoholInformation/factsAboutAlcoholPoisoning.aspx; Addiction Centers. (2019). Symptoms of alcohol poisoning. Retrieved from https://american addictioncenters.org/alcoholism-treatment/overdose

with dry ice, carbon dioxide pills, asthma nebulizers, pressurized air pumps, or a device called a Vaportini and inhaling, or "smoking," the alcohol vapor. A Vaportini is a glass ball containing a small amount of alcohol that is heated over a small candle; the resulting vapors are sucked through a straw. Inhaling alcohol is extremely dangerous because it bypasses the buffering effects of the digestive system and delivers alcohol vapors directly into the lungs, where the chemicals are absorbed into the bloodstream and sent directly to the brain. At a minimum, the inhaled vapors can dry out nasal passages and the mouth, which increases the risk of infections. Of greater concern—because the alcohol is absorbed into the bloodstream so quickly and the gag reflex cannot be triggered—is that inhaling alcohol makes alcohol poisoning more likely. Liver failure, brain damage, and blindness are additional health concerns.[39,40]

Another dangerous fad is the alcohol enema. A beer enema involves inserting a full beer bottle into the anus or pouring beer through a funnel and tube or a drip bag into the anus. Alcohol enemas can make the user very drunk in a very short period of time. They bypass the stomach so the alcohol is absorbed directly into the intestines. Risks include rectal damage and alcohol poisoning.[40]

Some teenagers are now guzzling hand sanitizer, which contains 62 percent ethyl alcohol content. Distilled, it would be a 120-proof alcohol beverage. For comparison purposes, Wild Turkey bourbon comes in 80- to 101-proof forms. Even children as young as 8 have gotten into the hand sanitizer "buzz" fad. The Internet provides people with the information needed to convert it into a potent alcoholic beverage. Of course, users can bypass the extraction process by ingesting hand sanitizer straight from the bottle. Side effects include throat-burning sensations, severe diarrhea, memory impairment, acute alcohol poisoning, and internal organ damage.[41]

Other ingestion fads have included ways to get high without drinking alcohol, such as vodka tampons, vodka eyeballing, and syringe alcohol injection. Tampons drenched in vodka and inserted into the vagina delivers alcohol directly into the bloodstream. Although it can produce a quicker and longer high, this also irritates the vaginal wall. Pouring vodka, 40 percent pure alcohol, directly onto the eyeball sears the eye capillaries. The resulting eye pain likely causes an adrenaline rush from its intensity. Injection of alcohol into the veins by syringe is an especially dangerous fad. It leads to immediate absorption into the bloodstream, but it causes permanent damage to veins and the potential for fatal levels of BAC.[40]

Hangovers

Hangovers are characterized by headache, stomach upset, thirst, and fatigue. Health experts speculate that alcohol disrupts the body's water balance, causing excessive urination and thirst the day after excessive drinking. The stomach lining may be irritated by increased production of hydrochloric acid, resulting in nausea. Alcohol also reduces the water content of brain cells. When the brain cells rehydrate and swell the next day, nerve pain occurs.[42] The only known remedy for a hangover is pain medication, rest, and time.

Acetaldehyde, cystine, and congeners have been identified as sources of alcohol hangovers. Some health experts believe that beef bouillon, toast, bacon, eggs, kimchi and rice, bananas, borscht, herbal teas, honey, and analgesics may help relieve alcohol symptoms. You should be cautious of using

fetal alcohol syndrome (FAS)
The combination of birth defects caused by prenatal exposure to alcohol, characterized by abnormal facial appearance; slow growth; intellectual disabilities; and social, emotional, and behavior problems.

analgesics to treat hangovers, however. Tylenol and Anacin-3 contain acetaminophen, which can damage your liver when alcohol is in your body. Aspirin and buffered aspirin are considered safe, but you should not take aspirin for at least 6 hours before or after consuming alcohol because it may lead to a higher BAC. Aspirin can also cause gastrointestinal (GI) distress. Ibuprofen (Advil or Motrin) may be a better option since it is easier on the GI system and not toxic to the liver. There is no support for caffeine, nicotine, or carbonated sodas offering relief of hangover symptoms. The evidence is mixed on whether the "hair of the dog" (such as a Bloody Mary) can relieve hangover symptoms. The bottom line: Alcohol abstinence for at least a few days is the best course of action.[43]

The Centers for Disease Control and Prevention (CDC) estimates that the cost of hangovers to the economy is $1.90 per drink. The U.S. Food and Drug Administration (FDA), however, now recommends a hangover product called Blowfish that may actually work. You simply drop a couple of Blowfish tablets into a glass of water, wait for the fizzing to stop, and drink it down. Blowfish contains maximum-strength aspirin that enters the blood twice as quickly as regular aspirin. It is more gentle on the stomach than regular aspirin or coffee. It also suppresses vasopressin, a hormone that triggers your body to overproduce urine and causes dehydration.[44]

Is it easy to return to your regular routine after the physical effects of an alcohol hangover dissipate? No. It takes longer to recover from an alcohol binge than many people think. To compensate for dehydration, for example, body organs draw in more fluid than usual, which can make it difficult for

the brain to be sufficiently hydrated. Magnesium, potassium, sodium, and other nutrients essential for stable cognitive functioning are depleted. Replenishing them takes time even after alcohol has left the body. It may take up to a day before the brain returns to normal functioning. This means the cognitive functions of attention, memory, reaction time, and decision making are not fully engaged until the needed brain nutrients are fully replenished.[45]

What Happens in the Body When You Stop Drinking Alcohol

This chapter addresses the many ill effects caused by heavy consumption of alcohol. Fortunately, the human body can quickly bounce back from the negative effects of too much alcohol consumption (see Table 9.2).

HEALTH RISKS OF ALCOHOL USE

Alcohol is toxic and has an effect on virtually all body organs and systems as well as on all aspects of a person's functioning, as was indicated in Table 9.1.

Medical Problems Associated With Alcohol Use

The major organs and systems damaged by alcohol use are the cardiovascular system, the liver, the brain, the immune system, and the reproductive system (Figure 9.4). When pregnant women drink, alcohol can cause a set of fetal birth defects known as **fetal alcohol syndrome (FAS)** (discussed in Chapter 12). Children born with FAS have permanent physical and mental impairments.

Table 9.2   What Happens When You Stop Drinking Alcohol?

Time Line	Body Effects
1 hour	Liver in overdrive to metabolize remaining alcohol. Pancreas releases insulin, which leads to intense carbohydrate craving.
12 to 24 hours	Blood sugar normalizes. Body still dehydrated. Sleep stages still disturbed.
48 Hours	Body completes alcohol detoxification. Minor hangover symptoms may remain.
7 Days	Sleep stages normalized. Skin takes on more even texture. Body no longer dehydrated.
1 Month	Liver fat decreased by 15 percent, which filtering out alcohol improves. Cures fatty liver.
1 Year	On average lose 13 pounds, most of which is belly fat. Decreased risk of mouth, liver, and breast cancers.

Source: Montell, A. (2016). 7 things that happen to your body when you stop drinking alcohol. Retrieved from http://www.byrdie.com/what-does-alcohol-do-to-your-body/.

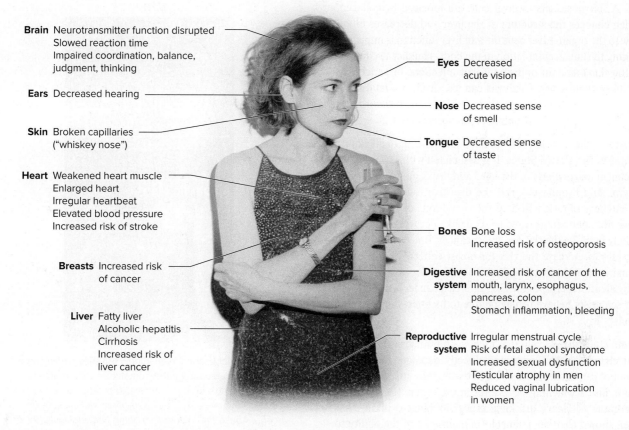

Brain Neurotransmitter function disrupted
Slowed reaction time
Impaired coordination, balance,
judgment, thinking

Ears Decreased hearing

Skin Broken capillaries
("whiskey nose")

Heart Weakened heart muscle
Enlarged heart
Irregular heartbeat
Elevated blood pressure
Increased risk of stroke

Breasts Increased risk
of cancer

Liver Fatty liver
Alcoholic hepatitis
Cirrhosis
Increased risk of
liver cancer

Eyes Decreased
acute vision

Nose Decreased sense
of smell

Tongue Decreased sense
of taste

Bones Bone loss
Increased risk of osteoporosis

Digestive Increased risk of cancer of the
system mouth, larynx, esophagus,
pancreas, colon
Stomach inflammation, bleeding

Reproductive Irregular menstrual cycle
system Risk of fetal alcohol syndrome
Increased sexual dysfunction
Testicular atrophy in men
Reduced vaginal lubrication
in women

figure 9.4   **Effects of alcohol on the body.**
(Andersen Ross/Getty Images)

Heart Disease and Stroke   Chronic heavy drinking is a major cause of degenerative disease of the heart muscle, a condition called alcoholic **cardiomyopathy**, and of heart arrhythmias (irregular heartbeat). Abnormal heart rhythm is a cause of sudden death in alcoholics, whether or not they already had heart disease. The heavy consumption of alcohol has been shown to increase the risk of arrhythmias by 75 percent.[46] Heavy drinking also causes coronary heart disease (disease of the arteries serving the heart). In addition, long-term heavy drinking can elevate blood pressure and increase the severity of high blood pressure, which increases the risk for stroke (an interruption in the blood supply to the brain). One study found that one alcoholic drink a day can increase the risk of stroke. One to two drinks per day increased stroke risk by 15 percent, and four drinks a day increased risk by 35 percent. This study questions previous findings suggesting that moderate alcohol consumption has positive effects in preventing cardiovascular disease.[17,40,47]

Liver Disease   The liver enables the body to digest food, absorb nutrients, control infections, and rid itself of toxins. Excessive alcohol consumption interferes with these functions. Alcohol-related liver disease occurs in three phases. The first, called **fatty liver**, occurs when the liver is flooded with more alcohol than it can metabolize, causing it to swell with fat globules. This condition can literally develop overnight as a result of binge drinking. It makes the liver more vulnerable to inflammation, such as alcoholic hepatitis. Fatty liver can be reversed with abstinence (usually about 30 days or so).[5,17,40]

The second phase of liver disease is called **alcoholic hepatitis**, which includes inflammation of the liver and impaired liver function. This condition can occur in the absence of fatty liver, which suggests that direct toxic effects of alcohol may be the cause.[5,17,40] Inflammation causes fibrous tissue, called collagen, to develop, which interferes with blood flow to liver cells.

The third phase of liver disease is **cirrhosis**, scarring of the liver tissue. Although other diseases can cause cirrhosis (such as viral hepatitis), between 40 and 90 percent of people with cirrhosis have a history of alcohol abuse.[48] The risk rises sharply with higher levels of consumption. It usually takes at least 10 years of steady, heavy drinking for cirrhosis to develop.[5,17,40]

cardiomyopathy
Disease of the heart muscle.

fatty liver
A condition in which the liver swells with fat globules as a result of alcohol consumption.

alcoholic hepatitis
Inflammation of the liver as a result of alcohol consumption.

cirrhosis
Scarring of the liver as a result of alcohol consumption.

As cirrhosis sets in, liver cells are replaced by collagen, which changes the structure of the liver and decreases blood flow to the organ. Liver cells die and liver function is impaired, leading to fluid accumulation in the body, jaundice (yellowing of the skin), and an opportunity for infections or cancers to establish themselves. Cirrhosis can also lead to a fatal brain disorder called hepatic encephalopathy.[5,40] The prognosis for people with alcoholic hepatitis or cirrhosis is poor.

Cancer   Alcohol accounts for about 3.5 percent of all cancer deaths in the United States. It is associated with several types of cancer, particularly of the head and neck (mouth, pharynx, larynx, and esophagus) and the digestive tract.[5,49] In 2011, researchers reported finding that low levels of alcohol consumption, defined as three to six drinks per week, may moderately increase the risk for breast cancer. Binge drinking also appears to increase the risk for breast cancer. These results remain consistent regardless of the type of alcohol consumed. Why alcohol increases the risk for breast cancer is not known, but scientists believe it may be due to its effects on estrogen levels.[5,50]

Brain Damage   Heavy alcohol consumption causes anatomical changes in the brain and directly damages brain cells. Alcohol can cause a loss of brain tissue, inflammation of the brain, and a widening of fissures in the cortex (covering) of the brain.[5,40] Heavy drinking, especially binge drinking, has been shown to disrupt short-term memory and the ability to analyze complex problems.[5,40] Although women are more sensitive to alcohol, research suggests that men and women are equally vulnerable to alcohol-induced brain damage.[5,40]

Because the brain continues to grow and mature until the early 20s, heavy alcohol use during the teen years can be harmful to the developing brain. Studies have revealed that the hippocampus (a center for learning and memory) is 10 percent smaller in teenagers who drink heavily than in those who don't. Research has also found differences in the prefrontal cortex, the center for executive functions (rational thinking, planning).[5,40]

In long-term alcohol abuse, loss of brain tissue results in a mental disorder called alcohol-induced persisting dementia, an overall decline in intellect. Some of this loss may be reversible if the person abstains from alcohol use for a few months, but after age 40, improvement is less likely, even with abstinence.[5,40]

Lung Damage   Recent studies suggest that alcohol abuse causes dysfunction in lung cells that can increase the risk of severe lung injury or impairment following a major trauma, such as a car crash, a gunshot wound, or an acute illness. This disruption in lung function also makes a person more susceptible to lung infections.[5,40]

Social Problems Associated With Alcohol Use

Alcohol can lead to many kinds of social difficulties. Sexual risk problems are of particular concern. Alcohol reduces social inhibitions, and reduced inhibition may lead to

This magnetic resonance imaging (MRI) shows how chronic alcohol use can damage the frontal lobes of the brain, increase the size of the ventricles, and cause an overall reduction in brain size (shrinkage). *(National Institute on Alcohol Abuse and Alcoholism of the National Institutes of Health)*

high-risk sexual activity and a lowered likelihood of practicing safe sex (such as using a condom). Heavy drinkers are more likely to have multiple sex partners and to engage in other risky sexual behaviors. These behaviors are associated with increased risk of sexually transmitted infection and unplanned pregnancy.[1,18]

Violence is another problem associated with alcohol use. The National Crime Victimization Survey has consistently found that alcohol is more likely than any other drug to be associated with all forms of violence, including robbery, assault, rape, domestic violence, and homicide. Women who binge drink or date men who binge drink are at increased risk for sexual exploitation (rape and other forms of nonconsensual sex).[1,18]

The relationship between alcohol and risk of injury has been established for a variety of circumstances, including automobile crashes, falls, and fires. Reduced cognitive function, impaired physical coordination, and increased risk-taking behavior (impulsivity) are the alcohol-related factors that lead to injury.[51]

Alcohol use is also a factor in about one-third of suicides, and it is second only to depression as a predictor of suicide attempts by youth.[52] The relationship between alcohol and depression is very strong. The prevalence of suicide is 120 times higher among adult alcoholics than in the general population.[52] Alcohol-associated suicides tend to be impulsive rather than premeditated acts.[52]

Alcohol Misuse, Abuse, and Dependence

Alcohol misuse refers to the consumption of alcohol to the point where it causes physical, social, and moral harm to the drinker. **Problem drinking** is a pattern of alcohol use that impairs the drinker's life, causing personal difficulties and difficulties for other people. For college students, such difficulties might be missed classes or poor academic performance. **Alcohol abuse** is defined as the continued use of alcohol despite negative consequences. It is a pattern of drinking that not only impairs the person's ability to fulfill major obligations at home, work, or school but also often causes legal or social problems.[5]

Alcohol dependence is characterized by a strong craving for alcohol. People who are dependent on alcohol use it compulsively, and most will eventually experience physiological changes in brain and body chemistry as a result of alcohol use. As described in Chapter 2, one indicator of dependence is the development of *tolerance,* reduced sensitivity to the effects of a drug so that larger and larger amounts are needed to produce the same effects.[5,32] Another indicator is experiencing *withdrawal,* a state of acute physical and psychological discomfort when alcohol consumption stops abruptly.[53]

Alcohol dependence is also known as **alcoholism,** defined as a chronic disease with genetic, psychosocial, and environmental causes. It is often progressive and fatal. About one in four heavy drinkers or at-risk drinkers can be defined as an alcoholic or alcohol abuser. The manifestations of alcoholism include lack of control over drinking, preoccupation with alcohol, use of alcohol despite adverse consequences, and distortions in thinking (most notably denial).

Are you a problem drinker—or are you an alcoholic? It may not matter because the latest edition of the *Diagnostic and Statistical Manual of Mental Disorders* (*DSM-5*) eliminated the medical distinction between problem drinking and alcoholism. Many health experts are critical of this change. They are concerned that college binge drinkers could be wrongly labeled as lifelong alcoholics. Previous editions of the *DSM* included the less severe "alcohol abuse" classification for people with less entrenched problems, such as college binge drinkers. The *DSM-5* combines abuse and dependence into a single condition with varying levels of severity. College binge drinkers are likely to be diagnosed as "mild alcoholics." The stigma of this diagnosis could limit employment and insurance opportunities even if the person resolves his or her alcohol problem. The Affordable Care Act increases screening for alcohol problems, so even temporary abuse will be included in the patient's electronic medical record.[5,54]

Another View: Health Benefits

Scientists speculate that moderate alcohol consumption can have some health benefits. Alcohol has an anticlotting effect on the blood, and it enhances the body's sensitivity to insulin, which may lower the risk of developing Type 2 diabetes. Because alcohol is a depressant, it may help reduce stress. The high water content in beer and its diuretic effect may also help prevent the formation of kidney stones.[32]

Moderate alcohol consumption also appears to be associated with a lowered risk of heart disease because it increases high-density lipoproteins (HDLs, also called "good cholesterol"). The beneficial effects of alcohol on HDL levels and blood clotting may be only temporary, lasting perhaps 24 hours, so that optimal protection against heart disease requires drinking moderately every day. Not all health experts agree on the benefits of moderate alcohol consumption. A meta-analysis of cohort studies found no mortality benefit of moderate alcohol consumption compared to abstinence or infrequent consumption. This finding has significant implications for public policy focusing on risky-drinking guidelines. The bottom line from the

problem drinking
A pattern of alcohol use that impairs the drinker's life, causing difficulties for the drinker and for others.

alcohol abuse
A pattern of alcohol use that leads to distress or impairment, increases the risk of health and/or social problems, and continues despite awareness of these effects.

alcohol dependence
A disorder characterized by a strong craving for alcohol, the development of tolerance for alcohol, and symptoms of withdrawal if alcohol consumption stops abruptly.

alcoholism
A primary chronic disease characterized by excessive, compulsive drinking.

■ Brief intervention programs for high-risk young adult drinkers include counseling sessions that help individuals to see the consequences of alcohol use and develop strategies for change. *(Pixel-Shot/Shutterstock)*

U.S. Department of Agriculture (USDA) recommendations is that no one should begin drinking alcohol on the belief that it provides health benefits.[55]

It is apparently the pattern of drinking, not the type of alcoholic beverage, that confers benefits. People who drink wine, for example, tend to do so in small amounts every day rather than in large amounts. Binge drinking does not serve as a protective factor and can actually increase the risk for heart disease.[56]

TREATMENT OPTIONS

Treatment options for alcohol-related disorders include brief interventions, inpatient treatment programs, outpatient treatment programs, self-help, and harm-reduction approaches.

Brief Interventions

Many colleges and universities focus their intervention efforts on high-risk groups such as freshmen, athletes, fraternity members, and, more recently, gay men, lesbians, and transgender individuals. Programs are also directed at high-risk times and events such as spring break, fraternity rushing, homecoming, and pre-graduation events for seniors.[57,58]

The Alcohol Skills Training Program is a model brief intervention program adapted by many colleges and community-based organizations around the country. It is designed for college students and other young adults considered at risk for alcohol-related problems, such as poor class attendance and grades, accidents, sexual assault, and violence. It consists of a series of group sessions (usually six to eight) focusing on skills and knowledge development through lectures, discussion, and role-plays.

Some colleges have introduced Internet-based programs that educate students about alcohol use on and around campus. For example, AlcoholEdu is a 2- to 3-hour online course that[59] provides students with personalized information and feedback about alcohol. It offers information about the physical, social, and behavioral effects of alcohol abuse, as well as strategies for finding alcohol-free activities and drinking responsibly. Alcohol.edu for College is the largest online education course in higher education. Sites such as e-CHUG Up To Go (online alcohol self-assessment used by university wellness programs) and MyStudentBody.com target students who have recently engaged in heavy drinking. These sites engage students with personalized interactive exercises and normative feedback, which help them to correct misperceptions about heavy drinking on campus and equip them with skills needed to avoid situations that will put them at risk of drinking heavily. Unfortunately, there is little empirical evidence showing that online alcohol education programs are effective. The CDC has developed an alcohol screening and brief intervention (SBI) for primary care settings directed at people who

controlled drinking
An approach to drinking that emphasizes moderation rather than abstinence.

abuse alcohol. It is administered as part of a patient's wellness visit. The SBI is now being used in other settings such as student health services.[58,59]

Inpatient and Outpatient Treatment

When alcohol-related problems are severe, individuals benefit from placement in a residential facility specializing in alcohol recovery. The first stage of treatment is detoxification, the gradual withdrawal of alcohol from the body. During this time, the patient usually experiences withdrawal symptoms. This phase may include medications, such as antidepressants and anti-anxiety drugs. Treatment programs typically also include group and individual counseling, education, and skills training. Because recovery from alcoholism is a lifelong process, relapse-prevention strategies are emphasized. In outpatient programs, patients participate in treatment programs during the day and return home in the evening. In both types of programs, family members are encouraged to participate in the recovery process.

Self-Help Programs

The best-known self-help program is Alcoholics Anonymous (AA), the goal of which is total abstinence from alcohol. A basic premise of AA is that alcoholics are biologically different from nonalcoholics and consequently can never safely drink any alcohol at all. Key components of AA are progression through a 12-step path to recovery and group support.[60]

Other self-help programs include Rational Recovery and Women for Sobriety. Programs for family members of alcoholics include Al-Anon and Alateen. Adult Children of Alcoholics is a program that provides support for people recovering from the effects of growing up in an alcoholic household.

Harm Reduction: Approach, Policies, and Laws

The Harm Reduction Abstinence, and Moderation Support (HAMS) approach to treatment focuses on reducing the harm associated with drinking, both to the individual and to society. Rather than forcing abstinence on people, HAMS encourages people to set their own goals and then provides strategies to help them attain those goals. For alcohol intervention, HAMS follows Kenneth Anderson's book, *How to Change Your Drinking: A Harm Reduction Guide to Alcohol*. An example of harm reduction is **controlled drinking**, which emphasizes moderation rather than abstinence.[17] Controlled drinking is considered appropriate for early-stage problem drinkers.[61] Most mental health experts agree that total abstinence is the most effective approach for recovery from alcoholism.[17]

A variety of public policies and laws are aimed at reducing the harm caused by alcohol consumption. A prime example is the minimum drinking age. Since 1984, all states have had laws prohibiting the purchase and public possession of alcohol by people under the age of 21. Despite inconsistent compliance with these laws, research suggests that they result in less underage drinking than occurred when the drinking age was 18.[17] Evidence also suggests that these laws result in less drinking after age 21.[60,62,63,64,65]

Drunk-driving laws are another form of harm reduction, and sobriety checkpoints are a tool that substantially increases compliance with these laws. Law enforcement agents check drivers for intoxication with alcohol sensors and breath analyzer tests. Widespread use of sobriety checkpoints may reduce drunk driving fatalities by 8 percent. However, only 12 states employ weekly sobriety checkpoints, and a few states prohibit their use. Alcohol sensors are noninvasive tests that can detect the presence of alcohol on the breath when held in the vicinity of a driver. Passive alcohol sensors at sobriety checkpoints increase detection of alcohol-impaired

■ Breath analysis and sobriety checkpoints are public health measures designed to reduce the harm to self and others associated with alcohol use. *(Olena Kachmar/123RF)*

drivers by 50 percent.[66] Breath analyzer tests measure the amount of alcohol exhaled in the breath. The box presented earlier in the chapter, "Starting the Conversation: Should the Legal Limit for Driving Under the Influence Be Lowered to 0.05 BAC?" addresses a proposed policy change for BAC and laws related to driving under the influence.

People convicted of alcohol-related offenses might be required to wear ankle bracelet breath analyzers as part of their sentences. The ankle bracelet monitors whether the person has been consuming alcohol by periodically sampling the perspiration on the skin. If the device's reading indicates that alcohol is detected at a BAC of 0.02 or higher, then the court or probation officer is notified.

The National Highway Traffic Safety Administration collaborated with the automobile manufacturers on a 5-year research project to develop in-vehicle technology that can be used to prevent alcohol-impaired driving in the United States. The Driver Alcohol Detection System for Safety project is researching accurate technologies that measure a driver's BAC in a noninvasive manner. If the driver's BAC is at or above 0.08, the legal limit in all states, then the vehicle will be disabled and cannot be driven. Many states already mandate installation of an ignition interlock device (IID) for drivers with a DUI conviction, especially repeat offenders and first-time offenders with a BAC above 0.20; however, the IIDs used today rely on an ethanol-specific fuel cell sensor that is not as accurate or reliable as the infrared spectroscopy technology used in breathalyzers by law enforcement officers.[67]

Another harm-reduction approach for alcohol use is restrictions on liquor sales and outlets. These restrictions include minimum-age restrictions on sales, limits on the number and locations of liquor outlets, and high taxes to limit alcohol availability. The more places there are to purchase alcohol within a certain geographical area, the higher the rates of alcohol consumption and alcohol-related harm.[5,17] Some communities have worked for a more even distribution of alcohol outlets throughout their area to curb this problem. Although underage drinkers usually get their alcohol from parents and other adults, they also buy alcoholic beverages at convenience stores, liquor stores, and bars.[5,17,60] Most states have passed laws holding such establishments liable for harm caused by intoxicated patrons (referred to as "dram shop liability"). Recently, the Internet has become a source for underage purchase of alcoholic beverages, although regulations are being put in place to curb this practice.

Another way to control alcohol consumption is by increasing the tax on alcohol. Research suggests that an increase in the price of alcohol reduces consumption by underage and moderate drinkers but not by heavy drinkers. College students tend to be price-sensitive, and increased taxes have been shown to decrease student drinking, making abstainers less likely to become moderate drinkers and moderate drinkers less likely to become heavy drinkers. However, raising prices too high has the potential to create a black market for alcoholic beverages.[17,62,68]

Fake IDs

It is not unusual for underage college students to use fake IDs for purchasing alcohol and tobacco products or to get into

21-and-up clubs. However, the prevalence of fraudulent identification documents has led federal and state governments to classify their use as a crime that ranges from a serious misdemeanor to a felony. Fines, loss of a driver's license, and community service hours are typical penalties after conviction.[69] Some states view the use of fake IDs as forgery or criminal impersonation, which are felonies and eligible for up to 18 months in state prison. If a fake ID is used to purchase a firearm, the prison time may be 7 years. A felony shows up on background checks and can affect future employment and graduate school acceptance.

State governments have cracked down by using holograms and magnetic strips to make it more difficult and more costly to create a fake driver's license. These technological hurdles have not reduced demand. Although college students do not need to provide legitimate personal information for such documents, many do in order to create a more valid-looking fake. Some college students use "chalking," use of colored pencils to modify driver's license information. Chalking is considered tampering with official government documents and can be viewed as a felony. The state of New York imposes a penalty of up to 7 years in state prison for chalking. Identity-protection companies warn that people who provide legitimate personal information to companies that create fake IDs are placing themselves at increased risk of identity theft. State law enforcement is using new technology, such as the Law ID app, to catch underage people using fake IDs to purchase alcohol. The Law ID app on police officer smartphones matches the ID information with state driving records.[70]

TAKING ACTION

Is alcohol a problem in your life? Do you wonder what you can do to reduce or prevent harm from alcohol-related activities? In this section, we provide some suggestions for individual actions.

Are You at Risk?

Physicians sometimes use the CAGE questionnaire to identify individuals at risk for alcohol problems:

> **C:** Have you ever tried to *cut down* on your drinking?
>
> **A:** Have you ever been *annoyed* by criticism of your drinking?
>
> **G:** Have you ever felt *guilty* about your drinking?
>
> **E:** Have you ever had a morning *"eye-opener"*?

A "yes" answer to one or more of these questions suggests that you may be at risk for alcohol dependence.

Developing a Behavior Change Plan

If you decide you would like to change your behavior around alcohol, you can develop a behavior change plan to do so. First, for 2 weeks keep track of when, how much, and with whom you drink, and then analyze your record to discover your drinking patterns. Do you drink mostly on weekends, or do you drink every day? Do you drink mostly with certain people, or alone? Do you drink when you're under stress? Information like this can help you get a sense of the role alcohol plays in your life.

If you decide you want to change your drinking behavior, set goals for yourself. Goals should be specific, motivating, achievable, and rewarding and have a time line. "I'm going to drink less" is too vague a goal. "I'm going to drink only once a week and have no more than four drinks" is a more specific, measurable goal.

Then develop specific strategies to attain your goals. For example, if you drink in social situations or with certain people, learn to say no to some drinks. Tell people you feel better when you don't drink, and avoid people who can't accept that. Plan ahead what you will do when you're tempted to have a drink. Ask family and friends for their support. After a few weeks, evaluate the outcome of your behavior change plan. Did you achieve your goals? If not, what obstacles prevented you from succeeding? How can you overcome these obstacles? Periodically assessing your progress allows you to devise alternative strategies for reaching your goals.

Be an Advocate

Boost Alcohol Consciousness Concerning the Health of University Students (BACCHUS Network) is a nonprofit organization with hundreds of chapters across North America. It is run by student volunteers and promotes both abstinence and responsible drinking. Some BACCHUS chapters have joined with Greeks Advocating the Mature Management of Alcohol (GAMMA) to provide a peer education network. This network program may be called BACCHUS or GAMMA on your college campus. The merging of BACCHUS and GAMMA has led to a broadening of approaches to health issues that affect college students.

UNDERSTANDING TOBACCO USE

Like alcohol, tobacco poses a problem of individual rights versus social good. Adults are free to use it, but such use causes an array of health problems, both for users and for those around them. Tobacco use is the leading preventable cause of death in the United States, implicated in a host of diseases and debilitating conditions. The health hazards of tobacco use are well known, yet almost one in seven U.S. adults currently smokes, and nearly 4,000 young people under the age of 18 start smoking every day.[71]

Who Smokes? Patterns of Tobacco Use

About 14 percent of people 18 years old or over in the United States are smokers. That percentage is down from a high of nearly 42 percent in 1965. The decline has occurred largely as a result of public health campaigns about the hazards of

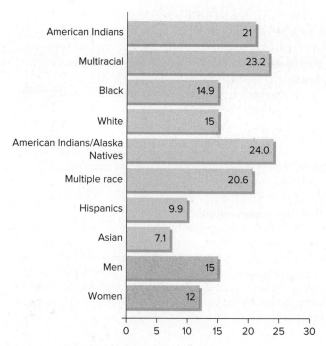

figure 9.5 data:
- American Indians: 21
- Multiracial: 23.2
- Black: 14.9
- White: 15
- American Indians/Alaska Natives: 24.0
- Multiple race: 20.6
- Hispanics: 9.9
- Asian: 7.1
- Men: 15
- Women: 12

figure 9.5 **Percentages of U.S. adults who were smokers in 2015.**
Sources: Centers for Disease Control and Prevention. "Adult cigarette smoking in the United States current estimate." https://www.cdc.gov/tobacco/data_statistics/fact_sheets/adult_data/cig_smking.index.htm; National Center for Health Statistics. "2018 National Health Interview Survey." https://publictableu.com/views/Figure8_4?:embed=y&:showVisHome=no&:embed=true.

■ Tobacco originated in the Americas, where it was used ceremonially and medicinally by native populations. By 1600, it was being exported to Europe and Asia. Today, tobacco is still an important crop in Virginia, Kentucky, North and South Carolina, and other southeastern states. *(Jonanderswiken/ Shutterstock)*

smoking. Although the prevalence of smoking in the United States continues to decline, the rate of decline has slowed since 1990.[71]

Overall, however, cigarette smoking is negatively correlated with educational attainment. Adults with less than a high school education are three times more likely to smoke as those who graduate from college.[32,71]

Smoking is more prevalent among the white population than among African Americans and Hispanics. Figure 9.5 shows the highest rates of smoking occur among American Indians and Alaska Natives.[72]

Tobacco Products and E-cigarettes

Tobacco is a broad-leafed plant that grows in tropical and temperate climates. Tobacco leaves are harvested, dried, and processed in different ways for the variety of tobacco products—rolled into cigars, shredded for cigarettes, ground into a fine powder for inhalation as snuff, or ground into a chewable form and used as smokeless tobacco.

Substances in Tobacco When tobacco leaves are burned, thousands of substances are produced, and nearly 70 of them have been identified as carcinogenic (cancer causing). The most harmful substances are tar, carbon monoxide, and nicotine.

Tar is a thick, sticky residue that contains many of the carcinogenic substances in tobacco smoke. Tar coats

the smoker's lungs and creates an environment conducive to the growth of cancerous cells. Tar is responsible for many of the changes in the respiratory system that cause the hacking "smoker's cough."

One of the most hazardous gaseous compounds in burning tobacco is carbon monoxide, the same toxic gas emitted from the exhaust pipe of a car. Carbon monoxide interferes with the ability of red blood cells to carry oxygen, so that vital body organs, such as the heart, are deprived of oxygen. Many of the other gases produced when tobacco burns are carcinogens, irritants, and toxic chemicals that damage the lungs.

Nicotine is the primary addictive ingredient in tobacco. It is carried into the body in the form of thousands of droplets suspended in solid particles of partially burned tobacco. These droplets are so tiny that they penetrate the alveoli (small air sacs in the lungs) and enter the bloodstream, reaching body cells within seconds.

Nicotine is both a poison (it is used as a pesticide) and a powerful psychoactive drug. The first time it is used, it usually produces dizziness, light-headedness, and nausea, signs of mild nicotine poisoning. These effects diminish as tolerance grows. Nicotine causes a cascade of stimulant effects throughout the body by triggering the release of adrenaline, which increases arousal, alertness, and concentration. Nicotine also stimulates the release of endorphins, the body's "natural opiates" that block pain and produce mild sensations of pleasure. (The effects of nicotine are discussed in greater detail later in the chapter.)

tar
The thick, sticky residue formed when tobacco leaves burn, containing hundreds of chemical compounds and carcinogenic substances.

nicotine
The primary addictive ingredient in tobacco; a poison and a psychoactive drug.

Consumer Clipboard

Are E-Cigarettes Safer Than Regular Cigarettes?

If the claim made by a product sounds too good to be true, it probably is. The following is a list of some questions you can ask when you want to evaluate the validity of claims related to a given product. Here, the questions are applied to e-cigarettes.

How does the product work in comparison to other products on the market?

A battery-powered device provides inhaled doses of nicotine by heating a nicotine chemical solution into a vapor. The vapor provides flavor and a physical sensation similar to that of inhaled smoke.

What claims does the manufacturer make about the product in ads and on product packaging?

E-cigarettes are marketed as a safer alternative to regular cigarettes because they produce no tar or smoke, do not pollute the air, and are odorless. Target markets include young people and people who have never smoked, and e-cigarettes come in flavors that may especially appeal to young people.

What doubts might a reasonable person have about these claims?

E-cigarettes contain tobacco-specific organic compounds and other potentially carcinogenic chemicals, so they can't really be safe. They deliver nicotine, so they must be addictive. They replicate the rituals, actions, and flavor of lighting up a real cigarette, which reinforces their addictive potential. E-cigarettes appear to be another way to recruit new customers for the tobacco industry.

How is the product regulated?

Initially, the FDA sought to regulate e-cigarettes as a drug delivery device. This would have required manufacturers to prove their products are safe. The courts struck down the FDA's request, so there are no legal age restrictions on e-cigarette sales and no health warnings on the packages. Several states have banned the use of e-cigarettes in public places, however.

Does independent research suggest that the product is safe to use?

Clinical studies have not been submitted to the FDA, so consumers have no way of knowing whether e-cigarettes are safe or exactly what an e-cigarette contains. The FDA discourages the use of these products and warns parents to caution their children about them.

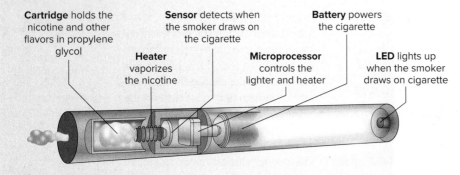

Cartridge holds the nicotine and other flavors in propylene glycol

Sensor detects when the smoker draws on the cigarette

Battery powers the cigarette

Heater vaporizes the nicotine

Microprocessor controls the lighter and heater

LED lights up when the smoker draws on cigarette

Sources: Kaplan, S. (2018). E-cigarettes' risks and benefits: Highlights from the report to the FDA. *New York Times*. Retrieved from https://www.nytimes.com/2018/01/23/health/e-cigarettes-health-evidence.html

Cigarettes By far the most popular tobacco product is cigarettes, followed by cigars and chewing tobacco. Cigarettes account for nearly 95 percent of the tobacco market in the United States. About 14 percent of college students smoked cigarettes in the past 30 days; 79 percent report they have never used cigarettes.[71,73] Nicotine from a cigarette reaches peak concentration in the blood in about 10 minutes and is reduced by half within about 20 minutes as the drug is distributed to body tissues. Rapid absorption and distribution of nicotine enable the smoker to control the peaks and valleys of nicotine absorption and effect. This process of control—absorption, distribution, elimination—makes cigarettes an effective drug-delivery system for nicotine.

In 2009, the U.S. Congress passed the Family Smoking Prevention and Tobacco Control Act (also known as the Tobacco Control Act), which gave the FDA the power to regulate tobacco and ban a variety of once-legal cigarettes. Fruit- and candy-flavored cigarettes are now prohibited due to concerns that they appealed particularly to children. Also banned are clove cigarettes, which contain higher levels of tar

and nicotine than regular cigarettes, and bidis, small cigarettes made from unprocessed tobacco that also contain higher levels of tar and nicotine than regular cigarettes.

E-cigarettes About 10 percent of college students have used electronic cigarettes (ECs). Only 2.0 percent use e-cigarettes daily.[73] The EC, also called the electronic nicotine delivery system (ENDS), was introduced in the U.S. market in 2007. Sales of ECs[2] may surpass those of regular cigarettes by 2025.[74] Because ECs contain no tobacco, they can be purchased without proof of age. Although they are marketed as safe, they still contain nicotine and are associated with other health risks. (To evaluate the advertising claims, see the box "Consumer Clipboard: Are E-cigarettes Safer Than Regular Cigarettes?")

E-cigarettes contain three major ingredients: nicotine, flavoring, and propylene glycol. Smoking them with drags longer than 3 to 5 seconds can cause liquid nicotine to be released in the mouth. Propylene glycol is an ingredient in some foods and body soaps and is considered safe. However, scientists do not know the potential toxic effects when *vaping* (inhaling and exhaling the vapor produced by the electronic cigarette) exposes the user to propylene glycol taken in from the air. Propylene glycol may damage bronchial epithelial cells, making these cells more vulnerable to allergens and bacteria. Epithelial cells provide a protective layer in the airway and lungs.[75] Flavorings used in ECs include pina colada, cookies and cream, menthol, strawberry, and Captain Crunch Berries. These flavorings increase vapor toxicity as their chemicals are heated. Strawberry flavoring is especially of concern for vapor toxicity. Some users increase the voltage, which increases the EC temperature and delivers an increased nicotine hit and increased toxicity.[76,77]

Accidental breakage of the e-cigarette may expose users to diethylene glycol, a component in antifreeze, and cancer-causing compounds such as nitrosamines. In addition to disease risks, there have been anecdotal reports of ECs exploding, particularly during recharging. There are also concerns that refillable EC cartridges contain flavored nicotine fluids that can be used for vaping experiences. Young children may confuse flavored EC fluid containers for soft drinks and juices, putting them at risk for dangerous unintentional overdoses of nicotine. EC brands that use sealed refilled cartridges are recommended to prevent spillage and accidental poisoning. Overdoses from vaping and accidental use can cause harmful vascular and neurological damage.[78] More than 50 percent of adults using ECs do not know that EC use exposes children to nicotine and propylene glycol.[79]

There is little research on the health effects of flavored EC toxicants. Secondhand health effects on children are of particular concern. Many flavored ECs contain diacetyl and propionyl chemicals, which are approved for food use but have adverse effects on the respiratory system. However, the concentration of these chemicals in ECs is 10 to 100 times lower than levels in regular cigarettes. Still, cartridges may contain 14 milligrams of nicotine, which is high enough to cause significant harm to children. Symptoms of harmful secondhand effects in children include hyperactivity, flushing, headache, rapid heart rate, dizziness, sweating, vomiting, and diarrhea.[74,78]

If the potential health effects of e-cigarettes are not enough to alarm you, consider "smart packs," a new type of e-cigarette that can alert the user (by means of a light flash or vibration) if anyone else is using the same device within 50 feet. Smart-pack devices can connect to each other and share information about their respective owner's social networking profiles.[80]

Should e-cigarettes be banned in public places? Manufacturers claim the water vapor emitted does not harm people who are exposed to it. This claim has not been verified by the FDA. Nicotine reacts with oxidizing chemicals in the air. This reaction can form secondary pollutants such as carcinogenic nitrosamines.[81] Research is also needed on whether this smoke leaves deposits on various surfaces, called third-hand smoke. Meanwhile, can ECs help smokers quit? Do ECs lead to youths becoming addicted to nicotine? Are ECs a safer form of tobacco? These questions are hotly debated. Sparse research on them has led to opinions that are not based on

evidence. The box "You Make the Call: Should E-cigarettes Be Included in Tobacco-Free Campus Policies?" at the end of the chapter addresses the pros and cons of the issue.

Vaping A vape is an electronic device that simulates tobacco smoking by heating a liquid to produce an aerosol called vapor. The user then inhales the vapor into the lungs ("vaping") and exhales it. The vapor is a water vapor, but it is chemically similar to cigarette smoke because it contains nicotine, propylene glycol, glycerin, and flavorings from the heated liquid. It does not smell like cigarette smoke and evaporates into the air in 3 to 4 seconds.

Vapes include vapor cigarettes, vaping pens, and e-cigarettes, and vaping devices can be portable and handheld, or desktop models the size of a toaster. They typically include a mouthpiece, battery, e-liquid cartridge, and heating component. When these components are in place, vapers push a button to activate the heat component and inhale the aerosol vapor through the mouthpiece. JUUL is the most popular vaping device on the market; the Volcano Vaporizer is the most popular desktop model. Some people vape THC or synthetic drugs such as flakka in place of nicotine to produce mind-altering effects. Active compounds in cannabis, such as THC, are heated at low temperatures.[81]

Manufacturers of vaping products claim they are a safer alternative to smoking cigarettes and a more enjoyable way of smoking electronic cigarettes. Vaping provides a nicotine hit, allows the user the familiar feeling of having something in the mouth or held between the fingers, and maintains smoking as a social habit but does not contain many of the cancer-causing ingredients found in cigarettes. The FDA has not yet ruled on whether vaping e-cigarettes is a safer alternative to smoking cigarettes, and there is growing empirical evidence that vaping is dangerous.

The FDA is investigating the occurrence of nicotine-induced seizures as a side effect of vaping e-cigarettes. Although the agency has not yet validated the seizure effect of vaping, it is known that nicotine can cause seizures. Tobacco products with high levels of nicotine (for example, JUUL) are thus of concern. Vaping causes lung illnesses, called EVALI, and deaths from vaping significantly increased in 2019. Vaping can also inflame lung tissue, leading to the presence of harmful germs and chronic infection.

The CDC identified vitamin E acetate as a key agent in vaping illnesses and deaths. Health experts recommend that people who vape cigarettes and e-cigarettes not use THC (tetrahydrocannabinol oil)-containing vaping products, particularly from black market international sources. Vaping has also been linked to popcorn lung, a disease called *bronchiolitis obliterans* that causes damage to the smallest parts of lung cells and is presently not curable. Popcorn lung derives its name from the circumstances in which early victims developed the disease by inhaling vapors heated by flavoring agents (for example, diacetyl) in microwave popcorn industrial plants. Scar tissue builds up in the small lung cells and eventually makes it difficult to inhale and exhale.[82,83]

The science behind vaping additives is not yet understood. In 2016, the FDA extended its regulatory authority to all tobacco products, including e-cigarettes, cigars, hookahs, and pipe tobacco. Vaping could be affected by FDA regulations to be imposed in 2022 on premarket tobacco application, limiting the amount of nicotine contained in tobacco products, and flavor bans on e-liquid. The underlying goal is to make tobacco products less appealing, less toxic, and less addictive. Vaping inspectors will be hired to enforce the 2022 FDA policy.[84,85]

Vaping in enclosed public places is not legal in many states. Although vaping does not produce secondhand smoke, it does create secondhand aerosols that may be toxic. As of 2019, more states are imposing bans on e-cigarettes and vaping by prohibiting their use in venues that already ban cigarette smoking. The prohibition on e-cigarettes and vaping on college campuses is a controversial issue. Many colleges enacting campus-free tobacco policies are banning cigarettes, cigars, smokeless tobacco, snuff, water pipes, and e-cigarettes. The American College Health Association has called for banning e-cigarettes and vaping on college campuses.

Hookahs   About 17 percent of college students have smoked a hookah or water pipe.[13] Among these, African Americans have higher rates of hookah-only and dual hookah and cigarette smoking. The location of hookah bars and cafes close to college and university campuses has increased the prevalence of hookah smoking by college students.[86] Groups of smokers pass the mouthpiece around, inhaling *shisha,* a mixture of tobacco, molasses, and fruit flavors (also known as narghile and arghile). The aromatic flavors of hookah tobacco and the smooth smoke produced by the water pipe, which is less irritating to the throat than cigarette smoke, have driven the perception that hookah use is safe.

The World Health Organization and the CDC warn, however, that hookah use can pose even greater dangers than cigarette smoking. The average cigarette provides 20 puffs, whereas a 1-hour session of hookah results in about 200 puffs. The depth of inhalation and frequency of puffs may cause hookah smokers to absorb high concentrations of carbon monoxide, heavy metals, and cancer-causing chemicals. Risks for lung, bladder, and oral cancers are of particular concern. The smoke from the tobacco and heat source also poses a secondhand smoke risk for nonsmokers.[87,88]

Steam stones and hookah pens are new forms of hookah smoking. They are battery-powered devices that convert liquid nicotine, flavorings, and other chemicals into a vapor that is inhaled.

Cigars   Cigars have more tobacco and nicotine per unit than cigarettes do, take longer to smoke, and generate more smoke and more harmful combustion products than cigarettes do.

(Simon de Glanville/Alamy Stock Photo)

The tobacco mix used in cigars makes it easier for cigar smoke to be absorbed through the mucous membranes of the oral cavity than is the case with cigarettes. Nicotine absorbed via this route takes longer to reach the brain than nicotine absorbed in the lungs and has a less intense but longer-lasting effect.

Cigar smokers who do not inhale have lower mortality rates than cigar smokers who do.[89,90] Inhalation substantially increases the cigar smoker's exposure to carcinogenic chemicals and increases the risk of lung cancer and chronic respiratory disease.[89] Whether or not smoke is inhaled, cigar smoking exposes the oral mucosa to large amounts of carcinogenic chemicals; consequently, cigar smokers have a higher risk than cigarette smokers for oral cancers.[90]

Black & Mild cigarillos, or "little cigars," are popular among teens and young adults. Black & Milds are long and thin like a cigarette but wrapped in tobacco leaf rather than paper, like a cigar. The difference in wrapping means they are not subject to certain cigarette regulations and taxes. They contain more tobacco and more nicotine than cigarettes and are addictive if inhaled. Use of Black & Mild cigarillos is much higher among African Americans (54 percent) than among any other ethnic group.[90]

Pipes   Pipe smoke has more toxins than cigarette smoke and is more irritating to the respiratory system. Pipe smokers who do not inhale are at less risk for lung cancer and heart disease than are cigarette smokers. Like cigar smokers, however, pipe smokers are exposed to more toxins than cigarette smokers. Pipe smokers are just as likely as cigarette smokers to develop cancer of the mouth, larynx, throat, and esophagus.[90]

Smokeless Tobacco   *Snuff* is a powdered form of tobacco that can be inhaled through the nose or placed between the bottom teeth and lower lip. *Chewing tobacco* is available as loose leaf or as a plug (a compressed, flavored bar of processed tobacco); a cud or pinch is lodged between the cheek and gum. Smokeless tobacco is sometimes called *spit tobacco* because users spit out the tobacco juices and saliva that accumulate in the mouth.

Spit tobacco is believed to cause about 10 to 15 percent of oral cancers, leading to about 6,000 deaths each year. When spit tobacco is kept in contact with the oral mucosa, it can cause *dysplasia,* an abnormal change in cells, and *oral lesions,* whitish patches on the tongue or inside the mouth that may become cancerous. Spit tobacco also causes gum disease, tooth decay and discoloration, and bad breath.[91] The amount of nicotine absorbed from smokeless tobacco is two to three times greater than that delivered by cigarettes.

Snus is a smokeless tobacco marketed as a safer alternative to cigarettes since it usually contains few carcinogenic ingredients. It is made from tobacco mixed with water, salt, sodium carbonate, and aroma and is often packaged in small bags resembling teabags. Snus contains more nicotine than

Life Stories

Ramiro: An Occasional Smoker

Ramiro tried a cigarette when he was 15 and a sophomore in high school. A group of friends he was hanging out with after a basketball game were smoking, and out of curiosity he asked to take a hit of his friend's cigarette. He was embarrassed that he started coughing as he inhaled the first drag, but he tried a few more puffs and felt dizzy and a little bit high—kind of good. However, Ramiro's parents were vehemently opposed to smoking. Ramiro respected them and knew that it would be impossible to get away with smoking behind their backs, so he didn't try cigarettes again.

About 2 months into his first year at a college in another state, Ramiro was at a party and started talking to a friend from one of his classes. His friend pulled out a pack of cigarettes and lit up. The smell of the smoke distracted Ramiro and reminded him of his first time smoking. His friend noticed him staring at her cigarette and offered him one. He hesitated, but he was opening up to a lot of new experiences, and his parents' rules seemed part of his distant past. He didn't see the harm of having just one, so he accepted the cigarette and lit up. He felt the same dizzy and high feelings he had with his first cigarette. Later in the evening he had a second cigarette, and the following Saturday he bummed a few cigarettes from someone at another party.

Over the next 2 months, Ramiro gradually started smoking more. He allowed himself a cigarette to celebrate a good grade on a paper or to get over a disagreement with a roommate. He no longer felt high when he smoked, but he still enjoyed it. He knew he was smoking more, but he knew several other people with smoking patterns similar to his. None of them really considered themselves smokers—they just smoked occasionally and could quit at any time.

When he went home for winter vacation, Ramiro thought it would be a good idea to take a break from cigarettes, and he didn't want his parents to know he was smoking. After being at home for 2 days, he felt unusually irritable and unfocused. He wanted a cigarette to calm down and clear his mind, and the more he tried not to think about it, the more he wanted one. That night after everyone had gone to bed, he pulled out his cigarettes from where he had hidden them in his backpack, sneaked out of the house, and lit up. He instantly felt better. At the same time, he realized that what he had just gone through was an indication that he had gotten hooked. Although he enjoyed smoking, he didn't want to be addicted. He decided that he had to quit and find better ways to reward himself, deal with stress, and socialize.

- What has your experience with smoking been so far in your life? Do any of Ramiro's experiences ring true for you?

- Why do you think some people seem to be able to smoke only on occasion and others become regular smokers?

- What are some healthy ways that Ramiro could relieve stress without smoking?

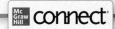

---

cigarettes but lower levels of other dangerous compounds, and because it isn't burned, there is no secondhand smoke. The risk of certain cancers is lower with snus than with other types of smokeless tobacco, but snus may cause oral lesions, hypertension, and complications in pregnancy.[91]

Dissolvable Tobacco Products Dissolvable tobacco products are small pellets, sticks, or strips that consist of finely ground and pressed tobacco; they dissolve on the tongue like a breath mint. They are marketed as forms of tobacco to use when you can't smoke. These products can contain a potent level of nicotine, and the health risks are similar to those associated with other oral tobacco products, particularly oral cancer. The FDA regulates dissolvable tobacco products.

WHY DO PEOPLE SMOKE?

Tobacco use and its relationship to health are complex issues that involve nicotine addiction, behavioral dependence, and aggressive marketing by tobacco companies, among other factors.

Nicotine Addiction

Nicotine is a highly addictive psychoactive drug—some health experts believe it is the most addictive of all the psychoactive

drugs—and tobacco products are very efficient delivery devices for this drug. Once in the brain, nicotine follows the same pleasure and reward pathway that other psychoactive drugs follow (see Chapter 10). Increases in release of the neurotransmitter dopamine produce feelings of pleasure and a desire to repeat the experience. As noted earlier, nicotine also affects alertness, energy, and mood by increasing levels of endorphins and other neurotransmitters, including serotonin and norepinephrine.

With continued smoking, neurons first become more sensitive and responsive to nicotine, causing *addiction,* or dependence on a steady supply of the drug; over time, they become less responsive to nicotine, developing *tolerance.* Smokers experience *withdrawal* symptoms if nicotine is not present (see the box "Life Stories: Ramiro: An Occasional Smoker"). Nicotine withdrawal symptoms include irritability, anxiety, depressed mood, difficulty concentrating, restlessness, decreased heart rate, increased appetite, and increased craving for nicotine.[90]

More than two-thirds of cigarette smokers who attempt to quit relapse within 2 days, unable to tolerate the period when withdrawal symptoms are at their peak. It takes about 2 weeks for a person's brain chemistry to return to normal. Withdrawal symptoms decrease and become more subtle with prolonged abstinence, but some smokers continue to

■ Many young smokers don't realize they are addicted to nicotine until they try to quit. *(David J. Green/Lifestyle/Alamy Stock Photo)*

experience intermittent cravings for years. Smoking tobacco may cause permanent changes in the nervous system, which may explain why some people who haven't smoked in years can become addicted again after smoking a single cigarette.[90]

Behavioral Dependence

People who smoke are not just physiologically dependent on a substance; they also become psychologically dependent on the habit of smoking. Through repeated paired associations, the effects of nicotine on the brain are linked to places, people, and events. Tobacco companies design their advertising to take advantage of these associations. Many smokers have a harder time imagining their future life without cigarettes than they do dealing with the physiological symptoms of withdrawal.[90]

Weight Control

Nicotine suppresses appetite and slightly increases basal metabolic rate (rate of metabolic activity at rest). People who start smoking often lose weight, and continuing smokers gain weight less rapidly than nonsmokers. Weight control is one of the major reasons young women give for smoking, and weight gain can be a deterrent to quitting. People who quit smoking initially consume about 300 to 400 additional calories a day but expend only an additional 100 to 150 calories a day. Gaining 7 to 10 pounds is typical before the body adjusts to the absence of nicotine.[90] Once a person has successfully quit, this small amount of weight can be lost through exercise and sensible eating.

Tobacco Marketing and Advertising

Every day, the tobacco industry loses 4,600 smokers, either to quitting or to death.[93] These users have to be replaced if tobacco companies are to stay in business. Because most smokers get hooked in adolescence, children and teenagers are prime targets of tobacco advertising. Tobacco advertising aimed at children associates smoking with cartoon characters, and advertising aimed at teenagers associates smoking with alcohol, sex, and independence. Judging by the number of people who take up tobacco use every year, tobacco advertising and marketing are extremely effective. Although the industry continues to claim that it does not market its products to children, research suggests otherwise.[94]

EFFECTS OF TOBACCO USE ON HEALTH

Besides its role in cancer, tobacco use is also a causal factor in heart disease, respiratory diseases, and numerous other debilitating conditions. Overwhelming evidence confirms that smoking is the single greatest preventable cause of illness and premature death in North America. The CDC reports that more than 480,000 people in the United States die from smoking per year, and 41,000 die from exposure to secondhand smoke each year. For every smoking death, another 30 people suffer from smoking-related illnesses (cancer, heart disease).[95] Even people who are only occasional smokers, or "chippers," face health risks.[90]

Short-Term Effects

Smoking affects virtually every system in the body (Figure 9.6). When a smoker lights up, nicotine reaches the brain within 7 to 10 seconds, producing both sedating and stimulating effects. Adrenaline causes heart rate to increase by 10 to 20 beats per minute, blood pressure to rise by 5 to 10 points, and body temperature in the fingertips to decrease by a few degrees.[90,96] The tar and toxins in tobacco smoke damage cilia, the hairlike structures in the bronchial passages that prevent toxins and debris from reaching delicate lung tissue. Researchers believe that chemicals in tar, such as benzopyrene, switch on a gene in lung cells that causes cell mutations that can lead to cancerous growth.[90,96] These chemicals may also damage a gene that plays a role in killing cancer cells.[90,96]

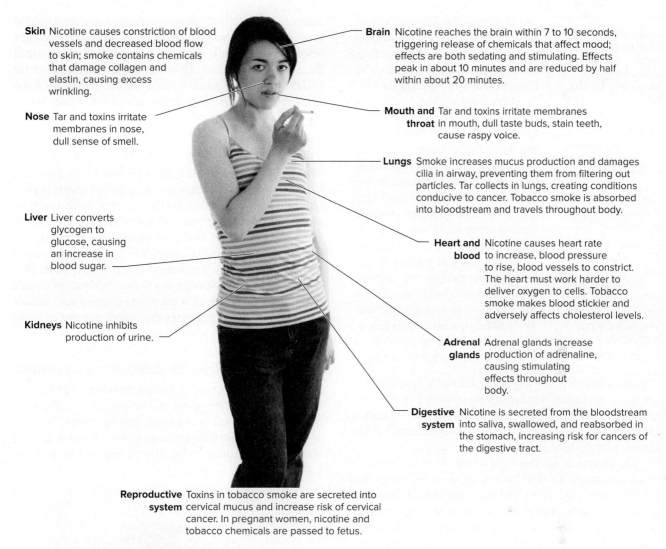

Skin Nicotine causes constriction of blood vessels and decreased blood flow to skin; smoke contains chemicals that damage collagen and elastin, causing excess wrinkling.

Nose Tar and toxins irritate membranes in nose, dull sense of smell.

Liver Liver converts glycogen to glucose, causing an increase in blood sugar.

Kidneys Nicotine inhibits production of urine.

Brain Nicotine reaches the brain within 7 to 10 seconds, triggering release of chemicals that affect mood; effects are both sedating and stimulating. Effects peak in about 10 minutes and are reduced by half within about 20 minutes.

Mouth and throat Tar and toxins irritate membranes in mouth, dull taste buds, stain teeth, cause raspy voice.

Lungs Smoke increases mucus production and damages cilia in airway, preventing them from filtering out particles. Tar collects in lungs, creating conditions conducive to cancer. Tobacco smoke is absorbed into bloodstream and travels throughout body.

Heart and blood Nicotine causes heart rate to increase, blood pressure to rise, blood vessels to constrict. The heart must work harder to deliver oxygen to cells. Tobacco smoke makes blood stickier and adversely affects cholesterol levels.

Adrenal glands Adrenal glands increase production of adrenaline, causing stimulating effects throughout body.

Digestive system Nicotine is secreted from the bloodstream into saliva, swallowed, and reabsorbed in the stomach, increasing risk for cancers of the digestive tract.

Reproductive system Toxins in tobacco smoke are secreted into cervical mucus and increase risk of cervical cancer. In pregnant women, nicotine and tobacco chemicals are passed to fetus.

figure 9.6 **Short-term effects of smoking on the body.**
(Tim Large - Youth Social Issues/Alamy Stock Photo)

Carbon monoxide in tobacco smoke affects the way smokers process the air they breathe. Normally, oxygen is carried through the bloodstream by hemoglobin, a protein in red blood cells. When carbon monoxide is present, it binds with hemoglobin and prevents red blood cells from carrying a full load of oxygen. Heavy smokers quickly become winded during physical activity because the cardiovascular system cannot effectively deliver oxygen to muscle cells.[96] Respiration is immediately affected by smoking because of the increased carbon monoxide in the blood and decreased oxygen absorption. Nicotine constricts bronchial tubes, and lung function is compromised further by phlegm production. The smoker has less oxygen available for exercise as well as for recovery.

Long-Term Effects

The greatest health concerns associated with smoking are cardiovascular disease, cancer, and chronic lower respiratory diseases.

Cardiovascular Disease The increased heart rate, increased tension in the heart muscle, and constricted blood vessels caused by nicotine lead to hypertension (high blood pressure), which is both a disease in itself and a risk factor for other forms of heart disease, including coronary artery disease, heart attack, stroke, and peripheral vascular disease. Nicotine also makes blood platelets stickier, increasing the tendency of blood clots to form. It raises blood levels of low-density lipoproteins ("bad cholesterol") and decreases levels of high-density lipoproteins ("good cholesterol").[97,98,99] People who smoke more than one pack of cigarettes per day have three times the risk of nonsmokers for heart disease and congestive heart failure.[90] People who smoke only one to four cigarettes a day still double their risk of heart disease.[90]

Cancer Smoking is implicated in about 30 percent of all cancer deaths. It is the cause of 87 percent of deaths from lung cancer, and it is associated with cancers of the pancreas, kidney, bladder, breast, and cervix. Smoking and using smokeless tobacco play a major role in cancers of the mouth, throat,

emphysema
An abnormal condition of the lungs characterized by decreased respiratory function and increased shortness of breath.

chronic bronchitis
A respiratory disorder characterized by mucous secretion, cough, and increasing difficulty in breathing.

asthma
A respiratory disorder characterized by recurrent episodes of difficulty in breathing, wheezing, coughing, and thick mucous production.

and esophagus. Oral cancers caused by smokeless tobacco tend to occur early in adulthood. The use of alcohol in combination with tobacco increases the risk of oral cancers.[100]

Why does smoking cause cancer? Tobacco poisons at the cellular level damage cells' DNA, which changes the cells' metabolism. Some body tissues are more vulnerable to tobacco poisons, particularly the lungs and gastrointestinal tract. Usually, the immune system sends tumor-fighting white blood cells to attack and kill cancer cells. However, research suggests that poisons in cigarette smoke weaken the immune system's tumor-fighting cells, so cancer cells are able to multiply. Therefore, smoking not only causes cancer, but it can also block the immune system from effectively battling cancer.[90]

Chronic Obstructive Pulmonary Disease Smoking is a key factor in causing the diseases encompassed by the category *chronic obstructive pulmonary disease* (COPD, also called chronic lower respiratory disease). These are emphysema, chronic bronchitis, and asthma.

Emphysema is an abnormal condition of the lungs in which the alveoli (air sacs) become enlarged and their walls lose elasticity. Late in the disease, it becomes increasingly difficult to breathe. Bronchitis is irritation and inflammation of the bronchi, the airway passages leading to the lungs. **Chronic bronchitis** is characterized by mucous secretion, cough, and increasing difficulty in breathing. **Asthma** is a respiratory disorder characterized by recurrent episodes of difficulty in breathing, wheezing, coughing, and thick mucous production.[90]

People with COPD who smoke are at much higher risk for lung cancer than those people with COPD who do not smoke.[90] Thousands more live with COPD complications and discomfort that seriously compromise their quality of life.[90]

Other Health Effects Tobacco is associated with a variety of physical and health risks, including changes in the skin (wrinkling), increased risk of complications during surgery, infertility and sexual dysfunction, periodontal disease, duodenal ulcers, osteoporosis, and cataracts. Smoking also reduces the effectiveness of some medications, particularly anti-anxiety drugs and penicillin.

Special Health Risks for Women

Smoking is associated with fertility problems in women, menstrual disorders, early menopause, problems in pregnancy, lung cancer, heart disease, and respiratory diseases. Women who smoke during pregnancy are at increased risk for

miscarriage, stillbirths, preterm delivery, low birth weight in their infants, and perinatal death (infant death a few months before or after birth). Research indicates that infants are at three times higher risk for sudden infant death syndrome (SIDS) if their mother smoked during pregnancy.[90] Infants' risk continues to be higher after birth if they are exposed to environmental tobacco smoke.[99]

Special Health Risks for Men

The overall drop in smoking rates for men in the past three decades has led to a reduction of lung cancer deaths in men, but the greater use by men of other forms of tobacco—cigars, pipes, and smokeless tobacco—places them at higher risk for cancers of the mouth, throat, esophagus, and stomach. Like women, men who smoke experience problems with sexual function and fertility. Smoking adversely affects blood flow to the erectile tissue, leading to a higher incidence of erectile dysfunction (impotence); it also alters sperm shape, reduces sperm motility, and decreases the overall number of viable sperm.[90]

Special Health Risks for Ethnic Minority Groups

Mortality rates from several diseases associated with tobacco use, including cardiovascular disease, cancer, and SIDS, are higher for ethnic minority groups than for whites.[90] For example, African American men and women are more likely to die from lung cancer, heart disease, and stroke than are

■ Sexual dysfunction is one of the lesser-known health effects of tobacco use for both men and women. This billboard is part of an antismoking campaign warning that "Smoking causes impotence." *(Dpa picture alliance/Alamy Stock Photo)*

members of other ethnic groups, despite lower rates of tobacco use. The reasons for these disparities are conjectured to include genetics, limited access to health care, workplace exposures, smoking behaviors, and stress. Reductions in smoking among African Americans since the mid-1980s have led to a decline in lung cancer in African American men and a leveling off in African American women. Reduced smoking rates have also led to a decrease in lung cancer deaths in Hispanic men.[101]

Benefits of Quitting

Smokers greatly reduce their risk of many health problems when they quit. Health benefits begin immediately and become more significant the longer the individual stays smoke-free. Respiratory symptoms associated with COPD, such as smoker's cough and excess mucous production, decrease quickly after quitting. Recovery from illnesses such as colds and flu is more rapid, taste and smell return, and circulation improves; see Table 9.3.

Effects of Environmental Tobacco Smoke

Abundant evidence shows that inhaling the smoke from other people's tobacco products—called **environmental tobacco smoke (ETS)**, secondhand smoke, or passive smoking—has serious health consequences. Even 30 minutes of daily secondhand smoke exposure causes heart damage similar to that experienced by a habitual smoker. People who are exposed daily to secondhand smoke have a 30 percent higher rate of death and disease than nonsmokers.[98,99] About 4 in 10 nonsmokers are exposed to secondhand smoke. This exposure is higher for children than adults and higher for African Americans than for other groups. Nonsmoking Mexican Americans have the lowest secondhand exposure.[98,99] Nonsmokers are exposed to about 1 percent of the smoke that active smokers inhale.[98,99]

Because of their smaller body size, infants and children are especially vulnerable to the effects of ETS. Children exposed to ETS experience 10 percent more colds, flu, and other acute respiratory infections than do those not exposed. ETS aggravates asthma symptoms and increases the risk of SIDS.[98,99] Some city governments have enacted local laws to protect children from secondhand smoke by banning smoking in apartment buildings and public housing projects, where rates of smoking tend to be much higher than they are among

environmental tobacco smoke (ETS) Smoke from other people's tobacco products; also called secondhand smoke or passive smoking.

Table 9.3   When You Quit Smoking: Health Benefits Timeline

Immediately	You stop polluting the air with secondhand smoke; the air around you is no longer dangerous to children and adults.
20 minutes	Blood pressure decreases; pulse rate decreases; temperature of hands and feet increases.
12 hours	Carbon monoxide level in blood drops; oxygen level in blood increases to normal.
24 hours	Chance of heart attack decreases.
48 hours	Nerve endings start to regrow; exercise gets easier; senses of smell and taste improve.
72 hours	Bronchial tubes relax, making breathing easier; lung capacity increases.
2–12 weeks	Circulation improves; lung functioning increases up to 30 percent.
1–9 months	Fewer coughs, colds, and flu episodes; fatigue and shortness of breath decrease; lung function continues to improve.
1 year	Risk of smoking-related heart attack is cut by half.
5 years	Risk of dying from heart disease and stroke approaches that of a nonsmoker; risk of oral and esophageal cancers is cut by half.
10 years	Risk of dying from lung cancer is cut by half.
10–15 years	Life expectancy reaches that of a person who never smoked.

Source: Health Canada. (2008). Health Canada: On the road to quitting. Retrieved from www.hc-sc.gc.ca.

nicotine replacement therapy (NRT) Treatment for nicotine addiction in which a controlled amount of nicotine is administered to gradually reduce daily nicotine use with minimal withdrawal symptoms.

the general population. Some states, including California, Arkansas, and Louisiana, have moved to ban smoking in cars when children under the age of 6 are present.

ETS residue on clothes, carpets, furniture, and other household items poses a risk for pets. Pets ingest ETS residue by licking their owner's face, hair, and clothes. They also swallow ETS residue when grooming themselves or other pets. Dogs are particularly at risk, since the size of a dog's nose increases the animal's risk of breathing in more residue and can lead to nose cancer and lung cancer. Cats are at triple the risk for lymphoma if their owner smokes a pack of cigarettes or more per day. Even birds and fish are at risk.[102]

QUITTING AND TREATMENT OPTIONS

Once a person becomes an established smoker, quitting is exceptionally difficult. Nearly 7 of every 10 smokers want to quit smoking. Most smokers who quit are not successfully abstaining a year later. Even among smokers who have lost a lung or undergone major heart surgery, only about one-half stop smoking for more than a few weeks.[103]

The good news is that smokers who quit for 1 year have a high success chance of maintaining their abstinence. Those who make it to 5 years have a better chance of continued success. Most people don't succeed the first time they try to quit—in fact, it usually takes several attempts, but many succeed on subsequent attempts.[104]

Treatment Programs to Quit Smoking

Treatment programs can be quite effective; many smokers who enter good ones are able to quit smoking for at least a year.[103] In some cases, smokers choose an intensive residential program; such a program might include daily group and individual therapy, stress reduction techniques, nutrition information, exercise, and a 12-step program similar to Alcoholics Anonymous.

Many programs encourage smokers to limit or eliminate their consumption of alcohol while they are quitting because alcohol interacts with nicotine in complex ways and can make quitting more difficult. Dieting is not recommended while trying to quit. Combining exercise with smoking cessation appears to be the most effective approach to managing the potential for weight gain. Another element is social support and encouragement from important people in the smoker's life.

Medications to Quit Smoking

Smokers who are deprived of nicotine often experience anhedonia, or reduced pleasure, in the first week of cessation due to being deprived of tobacco chemicals that stimulate the brain's pleasure centers. The anhedonia effect is a primary reason smokers relapse in their cessation attempts. This reduced pleasure is temporary, however. Nicotine replacement therapy can help smokers succeed in countering the effect.

In **nicotine replacement therapy (NRT)**, a controlled amount of nicotine is administered to gradually reduce daily nicotine use with minimal withdrawal symptoms. Over-the-counter nicotine replacement products include the transdermal patch, lozenges, nicotine hand gel, and nicotine gum. Prescription-only products are sold under the brand name Nicotrol and include a nasal spray and an oral inhaler. The nicotine gel, sold under the name Nicogel, is marketed as a product for tobacco users who find themselves in situations where they can't smoke. A quick-evaporating hand gel made from tobacco extracts, it can reduce nicotine cravings for up to 4 hours.[105]

Although nicotine is addictive no matter how it is administered, NRT products contain none of the carcinogens or toxic gases found in cigarette smoke, so they are a safer form of nicotine delivery.[105] Using one or more NRT products doubles a person's chances of success in quitting. NRT is beneficial when used as part of a comprehensive physician-promoted cessation program. It can help control withdrawal symptoms and cravings while the individual is learning new behavioral patterns.[105] Before taking a NRT product, you should consult your health care professional.

Other smoking cessation aids work not by replacing nicotine but by acting on the neurotransmitter receptors in the brain that are affected by nicotine. Bupropion is a prescription smoking-cessation drug that acts in this way. It was approved in 2001 by the FDA, and a low-dose version is marketed under the trade name Zyban. Bupropion is also prescribed at a higher dose as an antidepressant under the name Wellbutrin; Zyban and Wellbutrin should not be taken together. Bupropion is not approved by the FDA for use by people under the age of 18.

Varenicline (marketed in the United States as Chantix) is another smoking cessation drug that acts on neurotransmitter receptors. Clinical studies found that more than one in five people using varenicline quit smoking for at least 1 year, a significant improvement over rates for other smoking-cessation drugs. This medication is not recommended for people under the age of 18.

Beginning in 2009 both Chantix and Zyban carried black-box warnings (the strictest warning issued by the FDA) due to the potential risks of psychiatric problems associated with their use, particularly depression and suicidal thinking. The warning was removed by the FDA in 2016, based on a large patient study of smokers that concluded there was no increased risk of psychiatric problems among Chantix users.[106] The FDA also mandated that these drugs include more prescription information on the drug label and new information for patients that explains the potential mental health risks and their symptoms.[107]

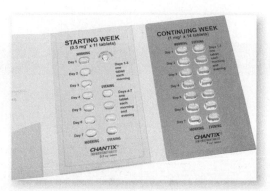

■ Chantix and Zyban belong to a category of smoking-cessation aids that work by acting on neurotransmitter receptors in the brain rather than by replacing nicotine. However, both carry warnings about potential side effects, such as depression and suicidal thinking. *(GIPhotoStock/Science Source)*

NicVAX is an experimental nicotine vaccine that blocks the pleasurable effects of smoking. It works by eliciting the production of antibodies that bind with nicotine molecules in the bloodstream, preventing them from entering nicotine receptors in the brain. NicVAX is still in the FDA clinical trial process. As of now, the FDA has not approved smoking vaccines on the market.[108]

Quitting on Your Own: Developing a Behavior Change Plan

Despite the hardships of withdrawal and the challenges of behavior change, quitting smoking is worth it, and the majority of people who quit do so on their own.

One approach is to develop a behavior change plan similar to the one described for cutting back on alcohol consumption. The first step is determining your readiness to quit. As discussed in Chapter 1, trying to change a behavior when you are not ready to change is pointless and counterproductive. It will only lead to failure and discouragement. Refer to the box "Action Skill-Builder: Change to a New Behavior" in Chapter 1 for a quick evaluation of your own stage of change in regard to quitting smoking. If you are in the contemplation or action stage, you can develop a behavior change plan by following the steps described next.

Record and Analyze Your Smoking Patterns First, keep track of your smoking for 2 weeks, noting when, where, and with whom you smoke. Record the triggers or cues for smoking and your thoughts and feelings at the time. Then analyze your record to get a sense of your smoking patterns. Understanding these patterns can help you develop strategies for avoiding or dealing with the most challenging times and situations.

Establish Goals Set a specific date to quit. Choose a time when you will be relatively stress-free—not during exams, for example—so that you will have the needed energy, attention,

■ Once an advocate for legalizing marijuana, Miley Cyrus recently gave up smoking after undergoing surgery on her vocal cords. *(DFree/Shutterstock)*

and focus. Experts recommend aiming for some time within 2 weeks of when you begin to plan. Plan to quit completely on that date; tapering off rarely works because it only prolongs withdrawal.

Prepare to Quit Your most important asset in quitting is your firm commitment to do so. At the same time, you can take specific, concrete steps to increase your chances of success. Consider these questions:

- Why do you want to quit? Make a list of your reasons and post them in a prominent place.

- If you tried to quit in the past, what helped and what didn't? Learn from your mistakes.

- What situations are going to be the most difficult? How can you plan ahead to handle them? To the extent you can, reorganize your life to avoid situations in which you were accustomed to smoking.

- What pleasures do you get from smoking? How can you get those pleasures from life-enhancing activities instead of smoking?

- Who can help you? Tell your family and friends you are planning to quit and ask for their support. Find out the number of your state's telephone quitline.

Table 9.4   What to Expect When You Quit

Symptom	Reason	Duration	Relief
Irritability	Body craves nicotine.	2–4 weeks	Take walks, hot baths; use relaxation techniques.
Fatigue	Nicotine is a stimulant.	2–4 weeks	Take naps; don't push yourself.
Insomnia	Nicotine affects brain waves.	2–4 weeks	Avoid caffeine after 6:00 p.m.; use relaxation techniques.
Coughing, dry throat, nasal drip	Body is getting rid of excess mucus.	A few days	Drink fluids; try cough drops.
Poor concentration	Nicotine is a stimulant, boosts concentration.	1–2 weeks	Get enough sleep; exercise; eat well.
Tightness in chest	Muscles are tense from nicotine craving or sore from coughing.	A few days	Use relaxation techniques, especially deep breathing; take hot baths.
Constipation, gas, stomach pain	Intestinal movement decreases for brief time.	1–2 weeks	Drink fluids; add fiber to diet (fruits, vegetables, whole grains).
Hunger	Nicotine craving can feel like hunger.	Up to several weeks	Drink water or low-calorie drinks; have low-calorie snacks on hand.
Headaches	Brain is getting more oxygen.	1–2 weeks	Drink water; use relaxation techniques.
Craving for a cigarette	Withdrawal from nicotine.	Most acute first few days; can recur for months	Wait it out; distract yourself; exercise; use relaxation techniques.

Source: Quitnet. (n.d.). *Quitnet by MeYouHealth.* Retrieved from www.quitnet.com.

Implement Your Plan Be prepared to experience symptoms of withdrawal and have a plan for handling them, even if it's just "toughing it out." Exercise will help ease cravings for nicotine and elevate your mood, so make sure you exercise daily. Exercise will also improve sleep and help limit weight gain. Drink plenty of fluids; they help flush nicotine from your body.[109]

Prevent Relapse Symptoms of nicotine withdrawal last from 2 to 4 weeks, although the most acute symptoms may last only a few days. See Table 9.4 for a summary of symptoms, their causes, and suggested relief strategies.

Abstinence becomes easier with time, although it can still be difficult. Most relapses occur within the first 3 months.[110] There are two main lines of defense for maintaining prolonged abstinence. First, avoid high-risk situations, and second, develop coping mechanisms. Relapses are prompted by stress, anger, frustration, and depression.[110] Make sure you have strategies to deal with these feelings, whether relaxation techniques, exercise, social support, or cognitive techniques. Examples of cognitive techniques are reminding yourself why you quit, thinking about the people you know who have quit, adjusting your self-image so that you think of yourself as an ex-smoker or a nonsmoker rather than a smoker, and congratulating yourself every time you beat an urge to smoke.

CONFRONTING THE TOBACCO CHALLENGE

Tobacco has been part of the economy of the United States since colonial times, and today it is a multibillion-dollar industry with tremendous lobbying power and a huge impact on the nation's economic health. Many state economies depend on tobacco, and elected representatives from those states make sure tobacco interests are protected at the federal level. Because smoking is viewed as a personal decision, there are many constraints on the government's ability to protect citizens and consumers from the hazards of tobacco use. Still, significant inroads have been made in confronting the challenge posed by tobacco, and the tobacco industry is facing tremendous pressure on many fronts.

Lawsuits and Court Settlements

In the 1990s, tobacco companies began to face class action suits, cases representing claims of injury by hundreds or thousands of smokers. In addition, states began suing tobacco companies for losses incurred by state health insurance funds used to pay for tobacco-related diseases.

These pressures led to the 1998 Master Settlement Agreement (MSA), in which the tobacco industry agreed to pay $206 billion to 46 states over a 25-year period in exchange for protection from future lawsuits by the states and other public entities. Other provisions of the MSA included a ban on billboard advertising and restrictions on advertising aimed at children. The settlement money from the MSA was to be used by the states primarily to fund tobacco education and prevention programs.[111]

Limiting Access to Tobacco

Access to tobacco can be limited by increasing cost, reducing physical availability, and regulating tobacco-marketing campaigns. When taxes on tobacco products are increased, raising their price, sales and use decline. Cigarette tax increases have been particularly effective in discouraging people from starting smoking.[112,113]

Physical availability of tobacco products is reduced when the laws restricting sales to minors are enforced. States are required to conduct random, unannounced inspections of places where tobacco is sold, and reports detailing results of these inspections must be submitted to the federal government each year.

FDA Regulation of Tobacco

The Tobacco Control Act of 2009 granted authority to the FDA to regulate tobacco products specifically for the protection of the public. Congress's goal was to decrease the number of Americans who die or who are harmed by tobacco products. Cigarette manufacturers have so far successfully challenged its requirement for larger and stronger warning labels on cigarette packs. Other key provisions include the following[113,114]:

- The advertising descriptors "light," "low," or "mild" can no longer be placed on tobacco packaging.

- Reinforcing state laws that already existed, federal law now officially prohibits the sale of cigarettes and smokeless tobacco products to anyone under 18 years of age.

- Cigarettes and smokeless tobacco can be sold in vending machines only in venues that prohibit entry to persons under age 18.

- Retailers may not sell single cigarettes or packages containing fewer than 20 cigarettes, except in vending machines in venues that prohibit entry to persons under age 18.

- Free samples of tobacco products are no longer permitted. Free samples of smokeless tobacco products are allowed only in adult-only facilities in certain restricted situations.

- Branded sponsorship of athletic or cultural events and free branded product tie-ins such as T-shirts are prohibited.

Tobacco products marketed for therapeutic purposes are regulated as medical products under the Food, Drug, and Cosmetic Act. Cigarettes, cigarette tobacco, roll-your-own tobacco, and smokeless tobacco are also regulated by the FDA. In 2016, the FDA used the "deeming rule" to add e-cigarettes, hookah tobacco, pipe tobacco, and cigars to its regulation authority. The deeming rule restricts sales of tobacco products to minors, requires health warnings, and requires manufacturers to attain FDA marketing authorization before selling new tobacco products. The Supreme Court upheld the deeming rule in 2018. A bill was introduced in 2016 to exempt e-cigarettes and premium cigars from the deeming rule. Congress did not approve the bill but may consider exemption at a later date in the 2020s.

The Tobacco Control Act directed the FDA to review the public health implications of raising the minimum legal age (MLA) to access tobacco products. The panel convened for this purpose predicted public health impacts for raising the MLA to 19 years, 21 years, and 25 years (see the box "Public Health Is Personal: Raising the Minimum Legal Age to Buy Tobacco Products").

Public Health Warnings

In June 2011, the FDA released nine proposed graphic images for public health warnings on tobacco products, selected from a field of 36 through public comment and feedback. The images have been described as disturbing, if not gruesome, and deliberately so, because upsetting images have been shown to be more likely to cause behavior change.

In response, four of the top five U.S. tobacco manufacturers successfully sued the federal government, claiming the labels violated their First Amendment rights to free speech. They asserted that as manufacturers of a lawful product, they should not have to use their own packaging to convey a message urging consumers to avoid their product. They said the images go beyond providing information to unfairly appeal to buyers' emotions, and they claimed the law would cost them millions in new equipment to print and rotate the messages.

A federal judge hearing the case in August 2011 upheld the labeling requirements, but in November 2011 and August 2012, appellate courts ruled that the images unconstitutionally compel speech and that there was little evidence they would reduce smoking rates. The Supreme Court refused to hear tobacco company claims as to the legal validity of the labeling requirements. The FDA in 2013 decided not to pursue further review of the judicial decision. More than 100 countries/jurisdictions use graphic smoking warning images. The United States, however, stands alone in denying graphic smoking warning images on grounds they violate free speech protected by the First Amendment.[115]

Public Health Is Personal

Raising the Minimum Legal Age to Buy Tobacco Products

The FDA convened an Institute of Medicine (IOM) panel to review effects on children and young adults of raising the minimum legal age (MLA) to 19 years, 21 years, and 25 years. The estimated decrease in rates of those who would be likely to start smoking at various ages is shown in the graph.

The IOM panel reached three principal conclusions: (1) Raising the MLA will prevent or delay initiation of tobacco use by adolescents and young adults; (2) raising the MLA to 21 years will have a substantially greater impact on tobacco initiation than raising it to 19 years; and (3) raising the MLA to 25 years will have considerably less added impact on tobacco initiation than raising it to 21 years.

Public health benefits of raising the MLA to 21 years would include the prevention of 250,000 premature deaths and 50,000 deaths from lung cancer among people born between 2000 and 2019. Raising the MLA to 25 years would decrease the prevalence of adolescent smokers continuing to smoke in their young-adult years by 16 percent. Prevalence would decrease by 12 percent if the MLA were set at 21 years and by 3 percent if set at 19 years. The decrease in smoking prevalence is important because more than 50 percent of dependent smokers and "chipper" smokers started smoking before the age of 18. People aged 15 to 17 are very vulnerable to addiction because their brains are still developing.

Bottom line: Raising the MLA reduces smoking prevalence, reduces premature deaths, reduces lung cancer deaths, improves health across the lifespan, and significantly reduces health care costs. The Trump administration raised the legal age in late-Fall 2019 to 21 for purchase of nicotine and vaping products.

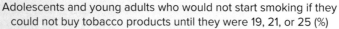

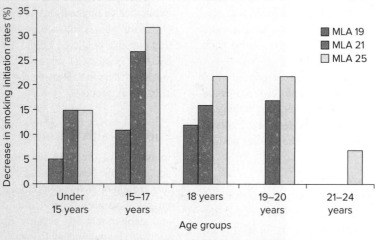

Source: Institute of Medicine. (2015). Public health implications of raising the minimum age of legal access to tobacco products. Retrieved from http://www.nationalacademies.org/hmd/~/media/Files/Report%20Files/2015/TobaccoMinAge/tobacco_minimum_age_report_brief.pdf; Tobacco 21. (2019). Critical issues: The toll of tobacco. Retrieved from https://tobacco21.org/critical-issues/

Tobacco-Free College Campuses

An important cultural issue is whether college campuses should become tobacco-free without a way to enforce the change. Of the more than 6,000 college campuses in the United States, more than 2,270 were smoke-free or tobacco-free in 2019, and 1,880 included e-cigarettes in their ban, according to Americans for Nonsmokers' Rights. Vaping is included in the tobacco-free policy.[116] In many cases, however, the policy is not enforced. Backlash from faculty, staff, and students, especially against e-cigarette bans, has been a significant barrier to smoke-free campuses.[117] (See the box "You Make the Call: Should E-cigarettes Be Included in Tobacco-Free Campus Policies?") Policy that cannot be enforced has minimal impact.

The identification of campus hot spots where smoke-free policies are being violated has had mixed success in improving compliance rates. A growing number of colleges are considering issuing warnings and then fining repeat violators; money from fines would be used to support smoking-cessation initiatives. Vaping devices like JUUL can be as small as a USB drive and do not smell like tobacco, which makes them easy to conceal in public and in residence halls. The debate about whether to include vaping in campus bans will heat up. Higher-education institutions are inheriting nearly 3.6 million middle and high schools students who smoke e-cigarettes and vape.[116] The tobacco addiction of these students will make it very challenging for colleges and universities to wean them away from e-cigarettes and vaping.[118]

You Make the Call

Should E-Cigarettes Be Included in Tobacco-Free Campus Policies?

Some students, faculty, and staff claim that having a tobacco-free campus that also bans e-cigarettes infringes on their personal rights. Other students, faculty, and staff support including ECs in their tobacco-free campus policies. Is banning ECs a knee-jerk reaction to a misunderstood nicotine delivery system technology? Or does the ban contribute to the health of everyone on campus?

The primary argument for lumping ECs with other tobacco products in tobacco-free campus policies is the danger of exposure to environmental tobacco smoke (ETS). Empirical evidence shows that chronic exposure to ETS is associated with increased risk of lung cancer, heart disease, and exacerbation of asthma.

This research, however, is about indoor ETS exposure. Outdoor ETS exposure is very different since smoke dissipates quickly outdoors. Moreover, there is a lack of consensus among health scientists and public health experts as to whether long-term use of ECs is associated with health effects on nonsmokers.

Despite the lack of high-quality research on ECs, the American College Health Association recommends the inclusion of ECs in tobacco-free campus policies. It bases this recommendation on three public health concerns: (1) ECs have the potential to renormalize cigarette smoking in restaurants and bars that ban it; (2) ECs can appeal to nonsmokers to become smokers; and (3) potential health effects of ECs on the smoker and the nonsmoker are not known.

What do you think? Should ECs be included in tobacco-free campus policies? Are ECs a threat to public health? Is the banning of ECs on college campuses discriminatory?

Pros

- ECs produce tiny particles that can lodge in the lungs and cause disease in both smokers and nonsmokers.
- Early research on ECs shows effects on the lungs that are similar to those of regular smoking.
- Although ECs pollute the air less than regular cigarettes, they still release potentially dangerous toxins.
- If not included in a tobacco ban, ECs can undermine the effectiveness of tobacco-free campus policies by making enforcement difficult.

Cons

- Banning the use of ECs on campus without solid evidence of negative health effects to nonsmokers is a violation of smokers' individual rights. In fact, switching from cigarettes to ECs reduces the risk of tobacco-related death by 99 percent.
- Colleges are better served by focusing on smoking-cessation programs than by implementing and enforcing EC bans.
- The risk of secondhand smoke and the threat of ETS are significantly less when outdoors. It is plausible that ECs smoked outdoors do not present a serious ETS concern.
- The banning of ECs would be difficult to enforce with visitors to campus for academic, sport, and entertainment events.

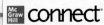

Sources: Donoghue, B. (2014). *Banning E-cigarettes on college campuses is a questionable policy.* Retrieved from http://lawstreetmedia.com/news/banning-e-cigarettes-on-college-campuses-is-a-questionable-policy/; Kentucky Center for Smoke-free Policy. (2014). *Reasons to include E-cigarettes in your tobacco-free campus policy.* Retrieved from www.kcsp.uky.edu.

In Review

Why do people drink, and why do some people develop problems with alcohol?

People ingest psychoactive substances such as alcohol for a wide range of reasons, from wanting to enhance positive feelings to wanting to numb negative feelings. A complex interplay of individual and environmental factors leads some people who drink to develop problems with alcohol, including alcohol dependence. Binge drinking, or heavy episodic drinking, is common on college campuses because of easy access to alcohol and social norms.

Millennials and Gen Zers are drinking less alcohol than previous generations.

However, they are motivated to drink alcohol primarily to relieve stress and anxiety than for fun and social reasons.

What are the effects of alcohol on the body?

After alcohol has been consumed, it goes to the stomach, where a small amount is absorbed. The rest goes into the small intestine, where it is absorbed into the bloodstream. The heart pumps the alcohol in the blood throughout the body. In the liver, it is metabolized at the rate of about one drink an hour. In the brain, it impairs cognitive and motor functioning. Acute alcohol intoxication can lead to death. Pot-infused beer with THC and CBD can cause health consequences.

What are the health risks of alcohol consumption?

Over the long term, alcohol consumption can cause cardiovascular disease, liver disease, cancer, brain damage, and unhealthy changes in body weight and food absorption. Alcohol use is also associated with high-risk sexual activity, violence, injury, and suicide. By contrast, scientists have found some health benefits from moderate alcohol consumption for middle-aged and older adults. Alcohol blackouts are a symptom of alcohol abuse.

What are treatment approaches for problem drinking?

Treatment options for alcohol-related disorders include brief interventions, inpatient and outpatient treatment programs, self-help programs such as AA, and harm-reduction approaches, which range from controlled drinking to laws regulating the drinking age and driving while drunk.

What kinds of actions can you take to reduce harm caused by alcohol?

You can assess your personal risk for alcohol dependence and develop a behavior change plan if you are at risk. You can also be an advocate for abstinence and responsible drinking on your campus.

Who smokes, and why is it a problem?

About 14 percent of the U.S. adult population are smokers, with higher rates of smoking among men than women and among college students than the general population. Tobacco use is the leading preventable cause of death in the United States.

What are the main tobacco products?

Cigarettes are by far the most commonly used tobacco products, trailed by cigars and cigarillos, pipes, and smokeless (chewing) tobacco. Other products such as tobacco for water pipes and e-cigarettes are marketed as safer alternatives, but nearly all contain nicotine and, when burned, produce thousands of toxic substances. Electronic cigarettes deliver nicotine through inhaled vapor but still contain potentially harmful chemicals.

What are the effects of tobacco use on health?

Smoking affects every system in the body from the brain to the reproductive system. Tobacco is a causal factor in cancer, heart disease, respiratory diseases, and numerous other debilitating conditions. Smoking is the single greatest preventable cause of illness and premature death in the United States. Secondhand smoke, or environmental tobacco smoke, has serious health consequences for the people around the smoker. Smokers greatly reduce their risk of many health problems when they quit.

What treatment options are available for quitting tobacco?

Quitting smoking is very difficult, and smokers try an average of seven times before they succeed. Aids for quitting include treatment programs, medications, and behavior-change plans. Some withdrawal symptoms last for only a day or two; others can last for a month.

What are various governmental and public health approaches to the tobacco challenge?

Over the past four decades, the nonsmokers' rights movement has encouraged the passage of laws to limit the use of tobacco in public places. Lawsuits have been won against tobacco companies. Cigarette taxes have been increased, and bans on selling cigarettes to minors have become stricter. State governments are cracking down on fake IDs by making use of them a misdemeanor or felony.

The FDA deeming rule includes regulation of e-cigarettes, premium cigars, hookkah, and vaping.

Many colleges' tobacco-free campus policies also include bans on e-cigarettes and vaping.

Personal Health Portfolio

Chapter 9   Assessing Your Drinking

Drinking alcohol is not necessarily bad for you. What does matter is how much you drink and how it affects your life. This activity will help you explore the place of alcohol in your life.

Part 1 Track Your Consumption

Recall as best as you can your alcohol consumption during the past week (do not include today).

Date	Situation (people, place) or trigger (incident, feelings)	Type of drink(s)	Amount	Consequence (what happened?)

Now track your alcohol consumption for the next week, starting with today.

Date	Situation (people, place) or trigger (incident, feelings)	Type of drink(s)	Amount	Consequence (what happened?)

Part 2 Assess Your Consumption

Using the drink sizes from Figure 9.1 in your text or from www.rethinkingdrinking.niaaa.nih.gov, answer the following questions:

1. On any one day in the past 2 weeks, have you ever had

   Men: more than 4 drinks? Yes _____   No _____

   Women: more than 3 drinks? Yes _____   No _____

2. On average, how many days a week did you drink alcohol?

_____ Days

3. On average, how many drinks did you have over the past 2 weeks?

_____ Drinks

Source: Rethinking Drinking, National Institute on Alcohol Abuse and Alcoholism, 2009, NIH Publication No. 09-3770.

CRITICAL THINKING QUESTIONS

1. If you consume alcohol, are you a low-risk drinker or an at-risk drinker? Recall that low-risk drinking means no more than 14 drinks per week and no more than 4 drinks on any one day for men. For women, it means no more than 7 drinks per week and no more than 3 drinks on any one day. Drinking above these levels is considered at risk.

2. What were the situations and triggers that affected your decision to drink or not to drink on various days? For example, if you ended up drinking more on one day than you had intended to, what led you to overindulge? If you did not drink at all during the 2 weeks, were you ever tempted to, or does your environment make the decision not to drink an easy one?

3. What are some reasons why you may want to make a change in your alcohol consumption? What are some of the barriers to making this change? How will you overcome these barriers?

4. Use Figure 9.2 to discuss efforts by your college or university to address at-risk drinking at the college level and community level.

Drugs

Photobyphm/Shutterstock

Ever Wonder...

which drugs have the highest potential for physical and psychological dependence?

why some people can't seem to stop using drugs?

how to know whether someone is starting to have a problem with drugs?

ike alcohol, drugs have a pervasive presence in U.S. life. We use them for headaches, insomnia, anxiety, stress—and some of us use them for fun. In 2017, an estimated 11.2 percent of the U.S. population aged 12 or older, or about 30.5 million people, had used an illicit (illegal) drug in the past 30 days (Figure 10.1).[1] Illicit drugs include marijuana, hashish, cocaine, heroin, hallucinogens, and prescription medications used for nonmedical reasons.

Drugs are used by different people for different reasons. Many people take drugs as a recreational activity—to alter their state of consciousness, to relax and feel more sociable, to experience euphoria, and to get high. Some people take drugs to rebel, and others take them to fit in. For some people, drug use is a way to cope with stress, pain, or adversity; for others, it is a way of life, a behavior they can no longer control.

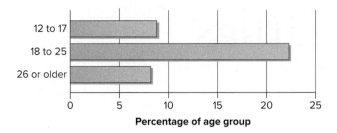

figure 10.2   **Illicit drug use in the past month, by percentage of age group, 2014.**
These statistics represent people aged 12 or older in the United States who reported using drugs within the last month at the time of being surveyed.
Source: Center for Behavioral Health Statistics and Quality. (2016). 2015 National Survey on Drug Use and Health: Detailed Tables. Substance Abuse and Mental Health Services Administration, Rockville, MD.

WHO USES? PATTERNS OF ILLICIT DRUG USE

Rates of illicit drug use in the United States vary by age, gender, race and ethnicity, education, employment status, and geographical region (see Figure 10.2). In 2017 an estimated 1 in 9 individuals age 12 and older had used illicit drugs in the past month. This represented almost 8 percent of adolescents, 24.2 percent of young adults, and 9.5 percent of those older than 26.[1]

In the United States, the most commonly used drug is marijuana. There are more than 43.5 million current users among people aged 12 or older,[1] up from 14.5 million in 2007. The number of people using marijuana daily or almost daily increased from 5.1 million in 2007 to 7.6 million in 2012. Almost 10 percent of those age 12 or older report having used marijuana in the past month.

In 2017 an estimated 6 million people had used psychotherapeutic drugs in the past month, including pain relievers, tranquilizers, stimulants, and sedatives. About 3.2 million

people age 12 or older (1.2 percent of the population) were misusing pain medications. While it appears that illicit drug use may often start with marijuana, pain relievers may be the drug of first use for a substantial number of individuals. Some observers suggest that nonmedical prescription drug use, particularly use of opioids, may be the fastest-growing drug problem in the United States.[2]

The most commonly used illicit drugs by people age 12 and older are marijuana, prescription pain relievers, prescription tranquilizers and sedatives, hallucinogens, and cocaine.[1] Although prescription drug use or abuse stands out as a relatively recent phenomenon among college students, there appears to be a decline in use among secondary and college students in recent years. Overall, approximately 6 percent of those age 12 or older report misusing prescriptions drugs at least once in the past month.[3]

Even under proper supervision, prescription drug use has become a national issue; more than 80 percent of those between age 57 and 85 use at least one medication on a daily basis. The use of narcotics other than heroin without medical supervision was greater for non-college groups (6.5 percent) than for those attending college (3.8 percent). The same finding applies to drugs such as Vicodin and OxyContin, but levels of amphetamine use without medical supervision (e.g., Adderall and Ritalin) were higher for those in college.[4]

The year 2018 has seen a reduction in the percentage of individuals age 12 and older who used pain relievers and stimulants when compared to the

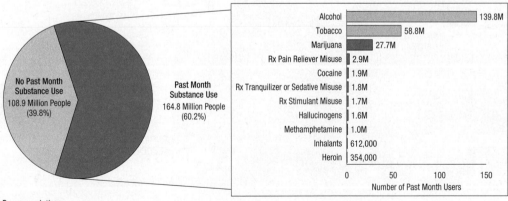

Rx = prescription.

Note: The estimated numbers of current users of different substances are not mutually exclusive because people could have used more than one type of substance in the past month.

figure 10.1   **Past Month Illicit Drug Use among People Aged 12 or Older, by Age Group: 2017**
Substance Abuse and Mental Health Services Administration. (2019). Key substance use and mental health indicators in the United States: Results from the 2018 National Survey on Drug Use and Health (HHS Publication No. PEP19-5068, NSDUH Series H-54). Rockville, MD: Center for Behavioral Health Statistics and Quality, Substance Abuse and Mental Health Services Administration. Retrieved from https://www.samhsa.gov/data/

Who's at Risk?

Illicit Drug Use in the Past Month among Individuals Aged 12 or Older, by State: Percentages, Annual Averages Based on 2016 and 2017 NSDUHs

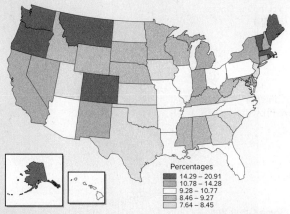

Percentages
- 14.29 – 20.91
- 10.78 – 14.28
- 9.28 – 10.77
- 8.46 – 9.27
- 7.64 – 8.45

Source: SAMHSA, Center for Behavioral Health Statistics and Quality, NSDUH, 2016 and 2017. https://www.samhsa.gov/data/report/2016-2017-nsduh-national-maps-prevalence-estimates-state

Age-adjusted drug overdose death rates, by sex: United States, 1999–2018

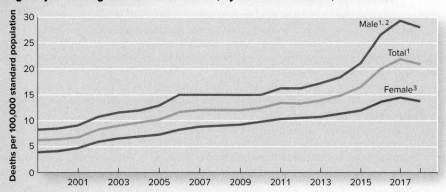

NCHS Data Brief ■ No. 356 ■ January 2020 U.S. DEPARTMENT OF HEALTH AND HUMAN SERVICES Centers for Disease Control and Prevention National Center for Health Statistics Drug Overdose Deaths in the United States, 1999–2018 Holly Hedegaard, M.D., Arialdi M. Miniño, M.P.H., and Margaret Warner, Ph.D.

Drug Overdose Mortality by State

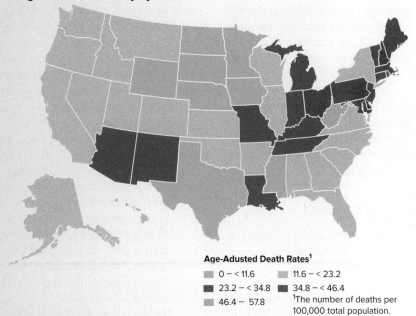

Age-Adusted Death Rates[1]
- 0 – < 11.6
- 11.6 – < 23.2
- 23.2 – < 34.8
- 34.8 – < 46.4
- 46.4 – 57.8

[1]The number of deaths per 100,000 total population.

Source: https://www.cdc.gov/nchs/pressroom/sosmap/drug_poisoning_mortality/drug_poisoning.htm

Last reviewed April 29, 2020.

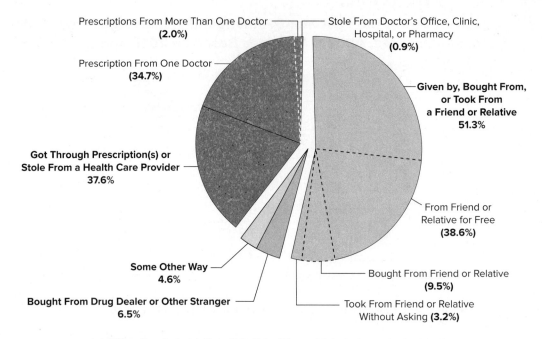

Prescriptions From More Than One Doctor **(2.0%)**

Prescription From One Doctor **(34.7%)**

Stole From Doctor's Office, Clinic, Hospital, or Pharmacy **(0.9%)**

Given by, Bought From, or Took From a Friend or Relative 51.3%

Got Through Prescription(s) or Stole From a Health Care Provider 37.6%

From Friend or Relative for Free **(38.6%)**

Some Other Way 4.6%

Bought From Drug Dealer or Other Stranger 6.5%

Bought From Friend or Relative **(9.5%)**

Took From Friend or Relative Without Asking **(3.2%)**

9.9 Million People Aged 12 or Older Who Misused Pain Relievers in the Past Year

Note: Respondents with unknown data for the Source for Most Recent Misuse or who reported Some Other Way but did not Specify a valid way were excluded

figure 10.3 **Source Where Pain Relievers Were Obtained for Most Recent Misuse among People Aged 12 or Older Who Misused Pain Relievers in the Past Year: 2018**
Source: Substance Abuse and Mental Health Services Administration. (2019). Key substance use and mental health indicators in the united States: Results from the 2018 National Survey on Drug Use and Health (HHS Publication No. SMA 18-5068, NSDUH Series H-53). Rockville, MD: Center for Behavioral Health Statistics and Quality, Substance Abuse and Mental Health Services Administration. Retrieved from https://www.samhsa.gov/data/report/2019-nsduh-annual-national-report

drug
A substance other than food that affects the structure or function of the body through its chemical action.

substance
A drug of abuse, a medication, or a toxin; the term is used interchangeably with drug.

percentages of those using in 2015–2017. The use of medications for the relief of anxiety or as sedatives to aid sleep (e.g., benzodiazepines) did not appear to change much over the same period. Finally, the use of hallucinogens in 2018 was higher than that in 2015.[1]

It appears that most individuals who are misusing prescription drugs get them from a friend or relative. More specifically, almost 40 percent of those who misused pain relievers in the past year got them from a friend or relative for free[1] (Figure 10.3).[5]

WHAT IS A DRUG?

A **drug** is a substance other than food that affects the structure or the function of the body through its chemical action. Alcohol, caffeine, aspirin, and nicotine are all drugs, as are amphetamines, cocaine, hallucinogens, sedatives, and inhalants. The drugs discussed here are *psychoactive drugs*—substances that cause changes in brain chemistry and alter consciousness, perception, mood, and thought. This state is known as *intoxication.*

Psychoactive drugs are used for both medical and nonmedical (recreational) purposes. For example, Ritalin, a central nervous system (CNS) stimulant with effects similar to those of amphetamine, is prescribed to treat hyperactivity in children—a medical use. Cocaine, another CNS stimulant, can be used recreationally to cause a burst of pleasurable sensations and to increase energy and endurance—a nonmedical use. When a medical drug is used for nonmedical (recreational) purposes, or when a drug has no medical uses, it is referred to as a *drug of abuse.*

All drugs have the potential to be toxic, that is, poisonous, dangerous, or deadly. Central nervous system depressants such as alcohol, barbiturates, tranquilizers, and opium-derived drugs, including morphine and heroin, can cause death if used in sufficient amounts to suppress vital functions such as respiration. At the other extreme, CNS stimulants such as cocaine can cause sudden death by speeding up heart rate, elevating blood pressure, and accelerating other body functions to the point that systems are overwhelmed and collapse. See the box "Consumer Clipboard: Understanding Drug Side Effects and Interactions."

The American Psychiatric Association (APA) uses the term **substance** to refer to a drug of abuse, a medication, or a

Consumer Clipboard
Understanding Drug Side Effects and Interactions

A side effect is an undesirable or unexpected secondary effect of a particular drug, whether prescription or over the counter (OTC). Some side effects are common and mild (such as constipation or an upset stomach), and others are severe and require immediate medical attention (such as chest pain or blurred vision). If you aren't expecting a side effect, or if a side effect is unpleasant, it may cause you to stop taking the medication before it has had a chance to work, so it is important to be aware of side effects at the outset. Medications can also have unwanted interactions with foods or other medications, amplifying the effects of another drug or interfering with them.

Prescription drugs include a required patient insert that includes information about side effects, and OTC drugs carry a "Drug Facts" label. The U.S. Food and Drug Administration (FDA) sets the format for OTC labels. You can get information about potential side effects and drug interactions from several parts of the label.

Drug Facts

Active ingredient (in each tablet) .... **Purpose**
Chlorpheniramine maleate 2 mg ....Antihistamine

Uses temporarily relieves these symptoms due to hay fever or other upper respiratory allergies:
■ sneezing ■ runny nose ■ itchy, watery eyes ■ itchy throat

Warnings
Ask a doctor before use if you have
■ glaucoma ■ a breathing problem such as emphysema or chronic bronchitis
■ trouble urinating due to an enlarged prostate gland

Ask a doctor or pharmacist before use if you are taking tranquilizers or sedatives

When using this product
■ You may get drowsy ■ avoid alcoholic drinks
■ alcohol, sedatives, and tranquilizers may increase drowsiness
■ be careful when driving a motor vehicle or operating machinery
■ excitability may occur, especially in children

If pregnant or breast-feeding, ask a health professional before use.
Keep out of reach of children. In case of overdose, get medical help or contact a Poison Control Center right away.

Directions

adults and children 12 years and over	take 2 tablets every 4 to 6 hours; not more than 12 tablets in 24 hours
children 6 years to under 12 years	take 1 tablet every 4 to 6 hours; not more than 6 tablets in 24 hours
children under 6 years	ask a doctor

Other information store at 20–25°C (68–77°F) ■ protect from excessive moisture

Inactive ingredients D&C yellow no. 10, lactose, magnesium stearate, microcrystalline cellulose, pregelatinized starch

Source: U.S. Food and Drug Administration. (2015). OTC drug facts label. Retrieved from www.fda.gov/Drugs/ResourcesForYou/Consumers/ucm143551.htm.

---

toxin.[6] In this chapter, we use the terms *drug* and *substance* interchangeably.

Types of Drugs

Drugs are classified in several different ways. A basic distinction is between legal drugs and illicit (illegal) drugs. *Legal drugs* include medications prescribed by physicians, OTC medications, and herbal remedies.

Legal drugs developed for medical purposes, whether available OTC or by prescription, are referred to as **pharmaceutical drugs**. Prescription drugs have undergone a rigorous testing and approval process by the FDA and can be ordered for patients only by a specific health care provider. Today, the pharmaceutical industry is one of the largest and most profitable industries in the United States, with annual sales expected to be over $350 billion.[7]

OTC medications include common remedies for headache, pain, colds, coughs, allergies, stomach upset, and other mild symptoms and complaints. Herbal remedies are usually botanical in origin; there are hundreds of substances in this group. At this time, the FDA does not regulate herbal remedies the way it regulates the development and approval of pharmaceutical drugs. The FDA does have the power to remove an herbal remedy from the market if it has proven harmful. This was the case with the dietary supplement ephedra, a stimulant used for weight loss and body building, which the FDA banned after it was linked to more than 100 deaths from heart attack and stroke. If you have questions about the interactions between herbal remedies and prescribed medications, or about the effectiveness of a particular herbal remedy, ask your pharmacist.

Illicit drugs are generally viewed as harmful, and it is illegal to possess, manufacture, sell, or use them. Many prescription drugs are legal when obtained through a physician but illicit when manufactured or sold outside the regulated medical system. Tobacco and alcohol are illegal drugs in the hands of minors, but they are usually not considered illicit because of their widespread availability to adults.

Drug Misuse and Abuse

There are different ways to define problematic use of drugs. The term **drug misuse** generally refers to the use of prescription drugs for other purposes or in greater amounts than as prescribed. The term can also

pharmaceutical drugs
Drugs developed for medical purposes, whether over the counter or by prescription.

illicit drugs
Drugs that are unlawful to possess, manufacture, sell, or use.

drug misuse
Use of prescription drugs for purposes other than those for which they were prescribed or in greater amounts than prescribed, or the use of nonprescription drugs or chemicals for purposes other than those intended by the manufacturer.

drug abuse
Use of a substance in amounts, situations, or a manner such that it causes problems, or greatly increases the risk of problems, for the user or for others.

refer to the use of nonprescription drugs such as Tylenol, or chemicals such as glues, paints, or solvents, for any purpose other than that intended by the manufacturer.

The term **drug abuse** generally means the use of a substance in an amount, situation, or manner that causes problems, or greatly increases the risk of problems, for the user or for others. The Americana Psychiatric Association's most recent version of the *Diagnostic and Statistical Manual of Mental Disorders* (*DSM-5*)[6] defines *substance use disorders* as cognitive, behavioral, and physiological symptoms that persist even as the individual experiences a number of significant life-changing substance-related problems. These symptoms include changes in brain circuitry that may continue after detoxification and can cause repeated relapses and drug cravings. Drug cravings are defined as the substance users' need to get their next drug fix. It is an all-encompassing focus driven by the feeling of being high as well as the physiological response by the person's body to reduce the impact of drug withdrawal.

The National Institute of Drug Abuse (NIDA) defines any use of an illicit drug as *drug abuse* and defines *addiction* as a chronic, relapsing brain disease characterized by compulsive drug seeking and use, despite harmful consequences.[8] Significant adverse consequences are a key component of many definitions of abuse, addiction, and substance use disorders.

As described in Chapter 2, the main two indicators of physiological dependence are the development of *tolerance,* or reduced sensitivity to the effects of the drug, and *withdrawal,* or uncomfortable feelings when drug use stops. Withdrawal symptoms are different for different drugs. For example, withdrawal from amphetamines is marked by intense feelings of fatigue and depression, increased appetite and weight gain, and sometimes suicidal thinking. Withdrawal from heroin causes nausea, vomiting, sweating, diarrhea, yawning, and insomnia.

EFFECTS OF DRUGS ON THE BODY

All psychoactive drugs have an effect on the brain, and they reach the brain by way of the bloodstream. Like alcohol, some psychoactive drugs are consumed by mouth, but other routes of administration are used as well.

Routes of Administration

Psychoactive drugs can be taken by several methods: orally (by mouth), injection, inhalation, application to the mucous membranes, or application to the skin. The speed and efficiency with which a drug acts are strongly influenced by the route of administration. Table 10.1 shows these routes in the order of their speed.

Oral Most drugs are taken orally. Although this is the simplest way to take a drug, it is the most complicated way for the drug to enter the bloodstream. A drug in the digestive tract must be able to withstand stomach acid and digestive enzymes and not be deactivated by food before it is absorbed. Drugs taken orally are absorbed into the bloodstream in the small intestine.

Injection The injection route uses a hypodermic syringe to deliver the drug directly into the bloodstream (intravenous injection), to deposit it in a muscle mass (intramuscular injection), or to deposit it under the upper layer of skin

Table 10.1   Routes of Administration

Route	Time to Reach Brain	Drug Example	Potential Adverse Effects

Inhalation
    Smoking
    Huffing
	7–10 seconds	Marijuana
		Crack cocaine
		Tobacco
		Inhalants
			Irritation of lungs
			Liver and kidney damage
			Hearing loss
			Vomiting

Injection
    Intravenous
    Intramuscular
    Subcutaneous
	15–30 seconds
	3–5 minutes
	5–7 minutes
		Heroin
		Cocaine
		Methamphetamine
			Danger of overdose
			Collapsed veins
			Infection at injection site
			Blood infection
			Transmission of HIV, hepatitis C,
			    and other pathogens

Mucous membranes Snorting	3–15 minutes	Cocaine Methamphetamine Heroin	Irritation or destruction of tissue Difficulty controlling dose
Oral ingestion Eating, drinking	20–30 minutes	Alcohol Pills	Vomiting

(subcutaneous injection). With an intravenous (IV) injection ("mainlining"), the drug enters the bloodstream directly; onset of action is more rapid than with oral administration or other means of injection.

Inhalation The inhalation route is used for smoking tobacco, marijuana, and crack cocaine and for "huffing" gasoline, paints, and other inhalants. An inhaled drug enters the bloodstream quickly because capillary walls are very accessible in the lungs.

Application to Mucous Membranes Application of a drug to the mucous membranes results in rapid absorption because the mucous membranes are moist and have a rich blood supply. People who snort cocaine absorb the drug quickly into the bloodstream through the mucous membranes of the nose. People who chew tobacco absorb nicotine through the mucous membranes lining the mouth. Rectal and vaginal suppositories are also absorbed quickly, although these methods are less commonly used.

Factors Influencing the Effects of Drugs

The effect a drug has on a person depends on a number of variables, including the characteristics of the drug, the person, and the situation.

The drug's chemical composition may speed up body processes or slow them down, produce a mild high or acute anxiety, or cause disorientation or hallucinations. These effects also depend on how much of the drug is taken, how often it is taken, and how recently it was taken. In addition, if a person has taken other drugs, the interactions of the chemicals can influence outcomes, such as when one CNS depressant intensifies the effect of another.

Characteristics of the person include age, gender, body weight and mass, physical condition, mood, experience with the drug, and expectations. Generally speaking, the same dose of a drug has less effect on a 180-pound man than on a 120-pound woman.

The effects of drugs are also influenced by the characteristics of the situation or the environment. Taking a drug at home while relaxing with friends may produce a different experience than taking it at a crowded, noisy bar or club, surrounded by strangers.

Effects of Drugs on the Brain

What accounts for the phenomenon of drug dependence? Scientists studying the effects of drugs on the brain have found that many addictive drugs, including cocaine, marijuana, opioids, alcohol, and nicotine, act on neurons in three brain structures—the ventral tegmental area (VTA) in the midbrain, the nucleus accumbens, and the prefrontal cortex.[9] Neurons in these three structures form a pathway referred to as the **pleasure and reward circuit** (Figure 10.4).

Under normal circumstances, this network of neurons is responsible for the feelings of satisfaction and pleasure when

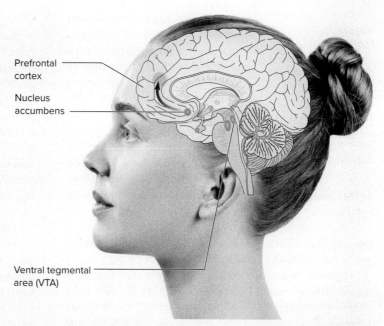

Prefrontal cortex

Nucleus accumbens

Ventral tegmental area (VTA)

figure 10.4   **The pleasure and reward circuit in the brain.** (123RF)

a physical, emotional, or survival need—such as hunger, thirst, bonding, or sexual desire—is met. When it is activated, the circuit powerfully reinforces the behavior that satisfied the need (say, eating), sending the message to "do it again." Neurons in the VTA increase production of dopamine, a neurotransmitter associated with feelings of pleasure. The VTA neurons pass messages to clusters of neurons in the nucleus accumbens, where the release of dopamine produces intense pleasure, and to the prefrontal cortex, where thinking, motivation, and behavior are affected.

Addictive psychoactive drugs activate this same pathway, causing an enormous surge in levels of dopamine and the associated feelings of pleasure. The nucleus accumbens sends the message to repeat the behavior that produced these feelings, and using an addictive drug begins to take on as much importance as normal survival behaviors. Because the drug produces such huge surges of dopamine, the brain responds by reducing normal dopamine production. Eventually, the person is unable to experience any pleasure, even from the drug, due to the disrupted dopamine system. Parts of the brain involved in rational thought and judgment are also disrupted, leading to loss of control and powerlessness over drug use. The very parts of the brain needed to make good life decisions are "hijacked" by addiction. Nonaddictive drugs do not cause these changes.

All or nearly all addictive drugs operate via the pleasure and reward circuit, but some also operate via additional mechanisms. For example, the brain has neurons with receptors

pleasure and reward circuit
A pathway in the brain involving three structures associated with drug dependence: the ventral tegmental area, the nucleus accumbens, and the prefrontal cortex.

endorphins
Natural chemicals in the brain that block pain during stressful or painful experiences.

stimulants
Drugs that speed up activity in the brain and the sympathetic nervous system.

for **endorphins**—brain chemicals that block pain when the body undergoes stress, such as during extreme exercise or childbirth. The structure of drugs in the opium family (opium and its derivatives, morphine, codeine, and heroin) is similar to the structure of endorphins, so opioids readily bind to endorphin receptors, reducing pain and increasing pleasure. These effects occur in addition to the dopamine-related changes in the pleasure and reward circuit.

Individuals trying to recover from addiction are disadvantaged by their altered brain chemistry, drug-related memories, and impaired impulse control. Recovery is not simply a matter of willpower, nor does it require only abstinence from substances. Rather, multiple areas of the person's life have to be addressed—emotional, psychological, social, occupational. More specifically, treatment can help people resolve family concerns, develop new social support systems, and simply learn to deal with boredom. As a chronic, recurring disease, addiction typically consists of repeated relapses and treatments before the person achieves recovery and returns to a healthy life.

DRUGS OF ABUSE

Drugs of abuse are usually classified as:

- Stimulants
- Depressants
- Opioids
- Hallucinogens
- Inhalants
- Cannabinoids

For an overview of commonly abused drugs, their trade and street names, and their long- and short-term health consequences, see Table 10.2 later in this section.

Central Nervous System Stimulants

Drugs that speed up activity in the brain and sympathetic nervous system are known as **stimulants**. Their effects are similar to the response evoked during the fight-or-flight reaction (see Chapter 2). Heart rate accelerates, breathing deepens, muscle tension increases, the senses are heightened, and attention and alertness increase. These drugs can keep people going, mentally and physically, when they would otherwise be fatigued. The drugs may stimulate movement, fidgeting, and talking, and they may produce intense feelings of euphoria and create a sense of energy and well-being. Although stimulants do not meet the strict definition for physical dependence, users can develop tolerance and experience serious withdrawal effects.

Cocaine A powerful CNS stimulant, cocaine heightens alertness, inhibits appetite and the need for sleep, and provides intense feelings of pleasure. Pure cocaine was first extracted from the leaves of the coca plant in the mid-19th century; it was introduced as a remedy for a number of ailments and used medically as an anesthetic. Cocaine has high potential for abuse.

The most common form of pure cocaine is cocaine hydrochloride powder, made from coca paste. The intensity and duration of cocaine's effects depend on the route of administration. Injecting or smoking produces a quicker, stronger high than snorting. Snorting produces a relatively quick effect that lasts from 15 to 30 minutes, but the high from smoking may last only 5 to 10 minutes.[10]

Crack is a form of cocaine that has been processed to make a rock crystal. It can be freebased or smoked. Freebasing is heating cocaine hydrochloride with a volatile solvent such as ether or ammonia and smoking it. This practice is dangerous because the solvent can ignite and burn the user. Crack appeared in the mid-1980s and led to an epidemic of cocaine use in the United States. When smoked, crack cocaine produces the highest rate of dependence. Cocaine mixed with heroin produces a drug called a "speedball."

Cocaine is still used as a local anesthetic, often for nose and throat surgeries. Most uses, however, are recreational. See Table 10.2 for lists of the short-term and long-term effects. When the effects wear off, the user typically wants to repeat the experience. Dependence can occur after only a few uses. Withdrawal after prolonged use is characterized by a depressed mood, fatigue, sleep disturbances, unpleasant dreams, and increased appetite.

At higher doses, cocaine use can lead to cardiac arrhythmias, respiratory distress, bizarre or violent behavior, psychosis, convulsions, seizures, coma, and even death. Regular snorting can irritate the nasal passage and result in a chronic runny nose.

Amphetamines For centuries, practitioners of Chinese medicine have made a medicinal tea from herbs called Ma Huang. In the 1920s, a chemist working for the Eli Lilly Company identified the active ingredient in Ma Huang as the compound ephedrine. The actions of this compound include opening the nasal and bronchial passages. The drug quickly became an important treatment for asthma, allergies, and stuffy noses. A few years later, a synthetic form, amphetamine, was developed. Nasal amphetamine inhalers quickly grew in popularity; consumers found that they not only cleared the bronchioles but also produced elation.

In the 1930s, amphetamines were put to additional uses: helping patients with narcolepsy stay awake, suppressing appetite in people who wanted to lose weight, and treating depression. In the 1940s, soldiers fighting in World War II took amphetamines to combat drowsiness. By the 1960s, amphetamines were widely available and were quickly swept up into the drug culture.

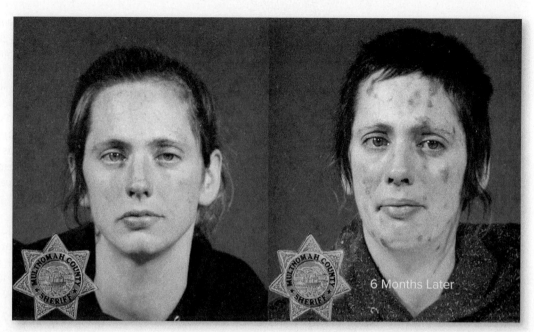

■ Faces of Meth is a project initiated by an Oregon sheriff to combat methamphetamine addiction in his county. The before-and-after photographs he compiled of methamphetamine users are shown in presentations to high school students. To see more photographs, go to www.facesofmeth.us. *(Multnomah County Sheriff's Office/Barcroft USA/Getty Images)*

Amphetamines are no longer recommended for treatment of depression or weight control, but they are still used to treat *attention-deficit/hyperactivity disorder* (*ADHD*) in children and adults. Although they are stimulants, they have a paradoxical effect in individuals with ADHD, helping them gain control of their behavior. In 2016, almost 3.5 million children were reported to be taking medications for ADHD.[11]

Concerns about the use of amphetamines include their effects on the heart, lungs, and many other organs. At low levels, amphetamines may cause loss of appetite, rapid breathing, high blood pressure, and dilated pupils. Decision making can be impaired even at moderate dosage levels. At higher levels, deaths due to heart failure and burst blood vessels in the brain have also been reported. (See Table 10.2 for lists of short-term and long-term effects of amphetamines and other prescription stimulants.) Withdrawal symptoms after continued amphetamine use include a drop in energy, feelings of helplessness, and thoughts of suicide. The person may "crash" into depression or sleep for 24 hours. Some symptoms can continue for days or weeks.

Methamphetamine ("speed") has a chemical structure similar to that of amphetamine and produces similar but more intense effects. It is usually snorted, but it can also be inhaled, smoked, or injected. A very pure form of methamphetamine, called "ice" or "crystal meth," can be smoked, producing an intense rush of pleasure lasting a few minutes. Because the high starts and fades quickly, many people take repeated doses. Meth is highly addictive, and short-term effects include increased wakefulness and physical activity and decreased appetite. Long-term effects include extreme weight loss, violent behavior, and severe dental and sleeping problems. In 2017 about 15 percent of all fatal overdoses involved meth-category drugs, and 50 percent of those deaths also included an opiate.[12]

Meth is more addictive and dangerous than most other forms of amphetamine because it contains so many toxic chemicals. Although methamphetamine can be prescribed by a physician, its medical uses are limited. There is a high potential for abuse, and repeated use can lead to addiction.[12] The popular body-building supplement called Craze contains a chemical similar to methamphetamine. Its effectiveness and dangers are not clearly known.

Meth can be manufactured from relatively inexpensive and commonly available drugs and chemicals. One such drug is pseudoephedrine, a nasal decongestant used in some cold and allergy medications. In 2005, Congress passed the Combat Methamphetamine Epidemic Act requiring that medications like pseudoephedrine be sold from behind the counter and be subject to additional regulations.

MDMA Also known as Ecstasy, MDMA has chemical similarities to both stimulants (such as methamphetamine) and hallucinogens (such as mescaline).[13] Thus it produces both types of effects. MDMA appears to elevate levels of the neurotransmitter serotonin, the body's primary regulator of mood, perhaps in a manner similar to the action of antidepressants. Effects last 3 to 6 hours; users experience increased energy, feelings of euphoria, and a heightened sense of empathy with and closeness to those around them. Some users report enhanced hearing, vision, and sense of touch, but only a few report actual visual hallucinations.[13] See Table 10.2 for lists of MDMA's short-term and long-term health effects.

Molly is the powder or crystal form of MDMA and is especially popular at music festivals. Short for *molecule,* Molly is pure MDMA and is a Schedule I controlled substance. Between 2005 and 2011, there was a 128 percent increase in emergency room visits due to MDMA and Molly.[14]

■ The synthetic stimulants called "bath salts" are sold in some headshops and convenience stores. *(Kitch Bain/Alamy Stock Photo)*

Bath Salts A relatively recent development is the use of "bath salts" (synthetic cathinones) to get high. The term *bath salts* refers to an emerging group of drugs containing an amphetamine-like stimulant found in the khat plant, which has been chewed for centuries by people living in the Horn of Africa and the Arabian Peninsula. Bath salts appear to have effects on the brain similar to those produced by amphetamines, although they are chemically different. They come in powder form and can be taken by mouth, snorted, or injected. Because of the risk of serious side effects and the potential for overdose, the U.S. Drug Enforcement Agency and some local governments have banned these products.[15] See Table 10.2 for a list of their short-term and long-term health effects.

Central Nervous System Depressants

Central nervous system **depressants** slow down activity in the brain and sympathetic nervous system. This category of drugs includes sedatives (barbiturates), hypnotics (sleep medications), and most anti-anxiety drugs. (See Table 10.2 for specific examples of CNS depressants.) They can be deadly if misused, especially when mixed with one another or with alcohol (another CNS depressant). CNS depressants carry a high risk for dependence.

depressants
Drugs that slow down activity in the brain and sympathetic nervous system.

rebound effect
The phenomenon that occurs when a person stops using a drug and experiences symptoms that are worse than those experienced before taking the drug.

Barbiturates and Hypnotics Barbiturates ("downers") are powerful sedatives that produce pleasant feelings of relaxation when first ingested, usually followed by lethargy, drowsiness, and sleep. Users experience impairments in judgment, decision making, and problem solving, as well as slow, slurred speech and lack of coordination. Dependence is common among middle-aged and older adults who use barbiturates as sleep aids. Withdrawal is difficult, and symptoms, including insomnia, anxiety, tremors, and nausea, can last for weeks; they can be mitigated by gradually tapering off the drug.

Hypnotics are prescribed for people with insomnia and other sleep disorders. They are also used to control epilepsy and to calm people before surgery or dental procedures.

Anti-anxiety Drugs The most widely prescribed CNS depressants fall into the group of anti-anxiety drugs known as the *benzodiazepines;* examples are Xanax, Valium, and Ativan. Also known as *tranquilizers,* the benzodiazepines are used to control panic attacks and anxiety disorders. Users are at risk for dependence and for increasing dose levels as they become tolerant of the drug.

Another concern is the **rebound effect**, which occurs when a person stops using a drug and experiences symptoms worse than those exhibited before taking the drug. The rebound effect can make it difficult to stop taking a particular medication.

Rohypnol A relatively new CNS depressant is flunitrazepam, also called Rohypnol; it started appearing in the United States in the 1990s. This powerful sedative has depressive effects and causes relaxation, lowered inhibitions, confusion, loss of memory, and sometimes loss of consciousness. It is especially dangerous when mixed with alcohol. (See Table 10.2 for a list of short-term health effects and effects in combination with alcohol.) Rohypnol is known as a date rape drug because men have slipped it into women's drinks in order to sexually assault them later.[16] It is no longer sold by the manufacturer as a white tablet but is now easier to detect and will turn blue or cloudy in a liquid. Although recent formulations are also made to dissolve more slowly, generics can still be bought that remain hard to notice when slipped into someone's drink.

GHB Another so-called date rape drug is gamma hydroxybutyrate (GHB). This CNS depressant produces feelings of pleasure along with sedation. It can be made in several forms, including a clear, tasteless, odorless liquid and a powder that readily dissolves in liquid. Like Rohypnol, it has been slipped into the drinks of women who later did not remember being sexually assaulted. It usually takes effect within 15 to 30 minutes and lasts from 3 to 6 hours. (See

Table 10.2 for a list of short-term health effects and effects in combination with alcohol.) Sustained use can lead to dependence.[16]

GHB, Rohypnol, and MDMA are sometimes referred to as *club drugs* because of their widespread use at clubs and parties. When GHB and Rohypnol are consumed with alcohol, the combined sedative effects can lead to life-threatening conditions. All three drugs are typically produced in unregulated labs, so dose and purity are uncertain.[17]

Opioids

Natural and synthetic derivatives of opium, a product harvested from a gummy substance in the seed pod of the opium poppy, are known as **opioids**. Opium originated in the Middle East and has a long history of medical use for pain relief and treatment of diarrhea and dehydration.

■ Opium poppies are an important cash crop for subsistence farmers in developing countries around the world. Although there are legal medical uses for opium, virtually all opium poppy harvest is sold on the international market as heroin. (*Associated Press/AP Images*)

Drugs in this category include morphine, heroin, codeine, and oxycodone. Also known as *narcotics,* opioids are commonly misused and abused. They produce a pleasant, drowsy state in which cares are forgotten, the senses are dulled, and pain is reduced. They act by altering the neurotransmitters that control movement, moods, and a number of body functions, including body temperature regulation, digestion, and breathing.

With low doses, opioid users experience euphoria, followed by drowsiness. With higher doses, users can experience depressed respiration, loss of consciousness, coma, and death. When first used, opioids often cause nausea, vomiting, and a negative mood rather than euphoria. Chronic users usually experience dry mouth, constipation, vision problems, and dry, itchy skin. Opioids have a high potential to create dependence.

Drug overdoses killed more than 70,000 people in the United States in 2017.[18] Synthetic opioids, such as fentanyl, appear to be responsible for the increase in overdose deaths. Some sources are now describing an "opiate epidemic"; opioids have become the leading cause of death for people under age 50.[19] In 2017 there were 70,237 overdose deaths in the United States[20]; however, the 2018 data suggest the first decline in years, to 68,500 deaths.[21] Although naloxone, an opiate antagonist, has been made more widely available in many states to counteract overdoses, it does not appear that naloxone alone will be sufficient to reduce the number of deaths related to drug overdose. Other potential interventions include the setting up of safe consumption sites and increasing drug treatment programs and public health programs focusing on responsible physician prescribing.

Morphine The primary active chemical in opium, morphine is a powerful pain reliever. Its first widespread use, facilitated by the development of the hypodermic syringe in the 1850s, occurred during the Civil War. So many soldiers became addicted that, after the war, morphine addiction was called "the soldier's disease."[17] Because of the high risk of dependence, physicians prescribing morphine today do so conservatively. See Table 10.2 for a list of prescription opioids and their health effects.

opioids
Natural and synthetic derivatives of opium.

Heroin Heroin is three times more potent than morphine. It was developed in the late 19th century as a supposedly non-addictive substitute for codeine (another derivative of morphine, useful for suppressing coughs). Although morphine has medical uses, heroin is almost exclusively a drug of abuse. Just as Civil War veterans suffered from morphine addiction, many soldiers came home from the war in Vietnam addicted to heroin.

Heroin use is associated with unemployment, divorce, and drug-related crimes, and with a variety of adverse health conditions, particularly among those who inject it and do not use clean syringes. Among these health problems are infectious diseases (including hepatitis, tuberculosis, and HIV/AIDS), various types of pneumonia, collapsed veins, liver and kidney disease, and permanent damage to various vital organs. Among individuals who use heroin, about 23 percent become dependent on it. Babies born to women who used heroin during pregnancy are often drug-dependent at birth. See Table 10.2 for lists of heroin's short-term and long-term health effects.

Life Stories

Diana: Pain, Stress, and Painkillers

Diana was a junior with dreams of becoming an athletic trainer after college. She had run two half-marathons and was training for a third. One day while she and her friend Ravi were out running, Diana twisted her ankle and needed Ravi's help to limp back to her car. She called the health clinic and made an appointment for the next morning. Ravi returned after class and brought her a bottle of Percocet he had been prescribed last year with a few pills left in it. Diana's pain was intense, so she took one right away. Soon the pain vanished, and Diana began to feel blissful.

The next day she woke up in pain and took another Percocet. With crutches borrowed from a friend, she hobbled to her health clinic appointment. After an x-ray showed she hadn't fractured any bones, the nurse practitioner wrapped her ankle in an Ace bandage and told her to keep her weight off the foot, ice and elevate it, and take ibuprofen for the pain. Diana lied that she had taken ibuprofen yesterday and it hadn't helped. She asked for something stronger, and the nurse practitioner agreed to write a 5-day prescription for Vicodin. After a few days her pain should subside, he said.

Diana went through the Vicodin in 3 days. She was stressed about gaining weight now that she wouldn't be able to run for a while, and the high from the Vicodin helped her not think about it. On the fourth day, she had to take ibuprofen, but it didn't help as much with the pain and it didn't give her the same buzz. She returned to the health clinic the day after and told the nurse practitioner she needed more Vicodin because she was still in a lot of pain. He examined her ankle and said she was on the path to recovery, explaining that Vicodin was not necessary and the school had specific guidelines for when synthetic opioids could be prescribed. He told her prescription-strength ibuprofen should be sufficient.

Diana was a little panicked as she left the appointment. She called Ravi and asked whether he could get a refill on his Percocet prescription. Ravi was surprised and concerned. He couldn't get a refill on a prescription that had expired a year earlier. Was she okay? Diana said she was and apologized for having asked him. After she hung up, Diana felt embarrassed about the call. She realized that she was not acting like herself and was becoming someone she didn't want to be.

- Based on Diana's experience, how would you describe the process of becoming dependent on prescription painkillers? What role do you think is played by psychological mechanisms like denial, wishful thinking, and rationalization?

- What steps do you think Diana needs to take at this point to overcome her growing dependence on painkillers?

- What are some cautions you would give about the best ways to educate teens and young adults about the possibilities of dependence on prescription drugs?

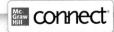

Synthetic Opioids Some of the most widely prescribed drugs in the United States are synthetic opioids, made from oxycodone hydrochloride. Brand names include OxyContin, Vicodin, Demerol, Dilaudid, Percocet, and Percodan. (See Table 10.2 for more brand names and health effects in combination with alcohol.) Fentanyl is 50 to 100 times more potent than morphine and has lately been mixed with heroin or cocaine and sold on the street. An unaware user is at great risk of overdose, and high doses of fentanyl can cause breathing to stop.[22] Fentanyl and its analogs were responsible for 28,400 overdose deaths in 2017. Some people who start using these drugs for pain become addicted and misuse or abuse them (see the box "Life Stories: Diana: Pain, Stress, and Painkillers").

OxyContin, for example, provides long-lasting, timed-release relief for moderate to severe chronic pain when taken in tablet form. If the tablets are chewed, crushed and snorted, or dissolved in water and injected, they provide an immediate, intense rush similar to that of heroin. A person high on OxyContin may be energetic and talkative at first, before becoming relaxed and drowsy. Medical workers with access to controlled substances are particularly susceptible to opioid misuse.

The nonmedical use and abuse of prescription drugs, particularly opioids and benzodiazepines (drugs used to treat anxiety), is a serious public health problem. Medications for pain are among the most common reason people see a medical provider.[1] Abuse of these drugs has resulted in an increase in emergency room visits and fatal drug overdoses.[23]

Hallucinogens and Dissociative Drugs

LSD, psilocybin, and peyote are a few of the so-called **hallucinogens** (also called *psychedelics*). They differ chemically but their effects are similar: They alter perceptions and thinking in characteristic ways, producing intensification and distortion of visual and auditory perceptions as well as hallucinations. Some hallucinogens and dissociative drugs are synthetic (LSD, ketamine, PCP); others are derived from plants (mescaline, from peyote, and psilocybin, from psilocybin mushrooms).[24]

LSD Lysergic acid diethylamide (LSD) is a synthetic hallucinogen that alters perceptual processes, producing visual

hallucinogens
Drugs that alter perceptions and thinking, intensifying and distorting visual and auditory perceptions and producing hallucinations, also called psychedelics.

■ Abuse of prescription painkillers has soared in the past 10 to 15 years, especially among teenagers and young adults. *(Artemfurman/123RF)*

its use was discontinued. Since the 1960s, it has been manufactured illegally and sold on the street, often under the name "angel dust." It causes fewer hallucinogenic effects than LSD and more disturbances in body perception. The drug is particularly associated with aggressive behavior, probably as a result of impaired judgment and disorganized thinking. Combined with insensitivity to pain, these effects can produce dangerous or deadly results.

Another dissociative drug is ketamine, which was originally developed as a veterinary anesthetic. Ketamine has recently been approved by the FDA for the treatment of depression in those who have tried other medications. See Table 10.2 for lists of short-term and long-term health effects of PCP and ketamine.

distortions and fantastic imagery. Use of LSD peaked in the late 1960s and then declined, as reports circulated of "bad trips," prolonged psychotic reactions, "flashbacks," self-injurious behavior, and possible chromosomal damage.

LSD is one of the most potent psychoactive drugs known. It is odorless, colorless, and tasteless, and a dose as small as a single grain of salt (about 0.01 mg) can produce mild effects. At higher doses (0.05 to 0.10 mg), hallucinogenic effects are common. Most users take LSD orally; absorption is rapid and effects last for several hours, depending on the user's mood and expectations, the setting, and the dose and potency of the drug. It usually takes hours or days to recover from an LSD trip. Although LSD is thought to stimulate serotonin receptors in the brain, its exact neural pathway is not completely understood.

Besides visual distortion, LSD can produce auditory changes, a distorted sense of time, changes in users' perception of their own body, and *synesthesia*—a "mixing of senses" in which sounds may appear as visual images or a visual image changes in rhythm to music. Feelings of euphoria may alternate with waves of anxiety. A person on LSD may be disoriented or delusional. (See Table 10.2 for lists of short-term and long-term health effects.) In a bad trip, the user may experience acute anxiety or panic. LSD does not produce compulsive drug-seeking behaviors, and physiological withdrawal symptoms do not occur when use is stopped. LSD and other hallucinogenics are being studied as potential treatments for PTSD, depression, and anxiety at the end of life.[25]

Phencyclidine (PCP) and Ketamine First developed in the 1950s as an anesthetic, PCP was found to produce such serious side effects—agitation, delusions, irrational behavior—that

Inhalants

The drugs called **inhalants** are breathable chemical vapors that alter consciousness, typically producing a state of intoxication that resembles drunkenness. The vapors come from substances such as paint thinners, gasoline, glue, and spray can propellant. (See Table 10.2 for a list of substances as well as health effects.) The active ingredients in these products are chemicals such as toluene, benzene, acetone, and tetrachloroethylene—all dangerously powerful toxins and carcinogens.[26]

At low doses, inhalants cause light-headedness, dizziness, and feelings of euphoria. At higher doses, they can cause muscle weakness, confusion, and stupor. An overdose can result in a loss of consciousness, coma, or death. Perhaps the most significant negative effect for chronic users is widespread and long-lasting brain damage,[27] which can cause behavioral and psychological changes and impair social and occupational functioning. In 2018 approximately 2 million individuals older than 12 had used inhalants in the past year with a majority of these users being older than 26.[1]

Cannabinoids

The most widely used illicit drug in the United States is marijuana. In 2018, almost 10 percent of 8th graders reported marijuana use in the past year; that proportion increased to almost 36 percent among 12th graders.[28] Among 12th graders, 5.8 percent reported daily use,[29] while among college-aged young adults, daily or near-daily use of marijuana

inhalants
Breathable chemical vapors that alter consciousness, producing a state resembling drunkenness.

■ The *Cannabis* plant has a variety of uses, including as fiber (hemp), food, and medicine, and for its psychedelic effects. From its probable origin in China or central Asia, the plant spread to India, ancient Rome, Africa, Europe, and the Americas. *(Yarygin/Shutterstock)*

and nausea associated with cancer and chemotherapy, and for the involuntary weight loss associated with AIDS. Research suggests that smoking marijuana is as effective as taking THC in pill form for these purposes, but the use of marijuana for medical reasons has become a matter of political debate. Proponents assert that it makes life livable for many people with painful and debilitating medical conditions and that there is no reason not to legalize it. They suggest that cannabidiol (CBD) may stop the spread of many aggressive cancers. (Cannabidiol can be found in cannabis plants and may offer medical benefits without giving a high.) Critics say that legalizing marijuana will result in an increased use in young people and also increase the likelihood of an increase of other drugs. In addition, like alcohol, marijuana affects the skills required to drive a car safely, including concentration, attention, coordination, reaction time, and the ability to judge distance. Because it also clouds judgment, people who are high may not realize their driving skills are impaired.

was reported by almost 5 percent of those surveyed, with 38 percent having used the drug in the past 12 months.[30] Over the past few years many states have changed their marijuana laws. Eleven states and the District of Columbia enacted laws permitting nonmedical adult use, and another 23 states allow the use of medical marijuana[31] (discussed later).

Marijuana is derived from the hemp plant, *Cannabis sativa,* thus the name *cannabinoids.* Hashish is a resin that seeps from the leaves of the plant. The active ingredient in marijuana is delta-9-tetrahydrocannabinol (THC). The potency of the drug is determined by the amount of THC in the plant, which in turn is affected by the growing conditions. Over the past two decades, the potency of cannabinoids appears to have been increasing.[32]

Marijuana's effects (see Table 10.2) typically begin within a few minutes and last 3 to 4 hours. The impact of chronic marijuana use on the developing brain is currently being studied with some suggesting that heavy use may result in cognitive impairments. In addition marijuana use disorders may be associated with physiological symptoms of withdrawal such as irritability, sleep difficulties, and physical discomfort, which can last for up to 2 weeks after quitting.[33]

Researchers have found that THC has a variety of effects on the brain. One is the suppression of activity in the information-processing system of the hippocampus, perhaps accounting for some impairment in problem solving and decision making associated with being high on the drug. Marijuana smoke has negative effects on the respiratory system and is highly irritating to the lining of the bronchioles and lungs. Thus marijuana use can increase the likelihood of breathing problems and can result in more outpatient visits for respiratory problems.[34]

Many people claim that marijuana does have medical uses, especially as a treatment for glaucoma, for the pain

Emerging Drugs of Abuse

New drugs of abuse appear quickly and are often accompanied by rumor, inaccurate information about effects, and minimization of toxicity. Many are compounded more quickly than law enforcement can call them illegal, yet they are highly dangerous. Some can cause strokes, heart attacks, and kidney damage as well as psychosis. The newest drugs being experimented with include the following:

- Anabolic steroids are synthetic variants of the male sex hormone testosterone and are either taken orally or injected. Their use by men can result in the shrinkage of testicles, reduced sperm count, and the development of breasts. Side effects for female users include the growth of facial hair, changes in the menstrual cycle, and a deepened voice. See Table 10.2 for other health effects. Also known as performance-enhancing drugs, anabolic steroids and human growth hormone can increase muscle mass and strength.[35]

- Synthetic cannabinoids such as K2 and Spice are among the number of person-made, mind-altering chemicals that can be sprayed on plant material and smoked or sold as liquids to be used in e-cigarettes. They seem to be more powerful than marijuana, and their effects can be unpredictable, severe, and potentially life threatening. See Table 10.2 for a list of health effects. For many years, these types of drugs have been easy to buy at gas stations and online.[36]

- Syrup, Purple Drank, Sizzurp, and Lean are all names for prescription-strength cough syrup containing codeine and promethazine mixed with soda. Overdose of this combination of an opioid and an antihistamine presents a risk of death because it can slow or stop the heart and lungs.

Table 10.2   **Commonly Abused Drugs**

Category and Name	*Trade Names*/Street Names	Short-Term Health Effects	Long-Term Health Effects/Effects in Combination with Alcohol
Stimulants			
Cocaine	*Cocaine hydrochloride topical solution* (rarely used local anesthetic). Blow, Bump, C, Candy, Charlie, Coke, Crack, Flake, Rock, Snow, Toot	Narrowed blood vessels; enlarged pupils; increased temperature, heart rate, and blood pressure; headache; abdominal pain and nausea; euphoria; increased energy, alertness; insomnia, restlessness; anxiety; erratic and violent behavior, panic attacks, paranoia, psychosis; heart rhythm problems, heart attack; stroke, seizure, coma.	Loss of sense of smell, nosebleeds, nasal damage, and trouble swallowing from snorting; infection and death of bowel tissue from decreased blood flow; poor nutrition and weight loss from decreased appetite. *With alcohol:* Greater risk of overdose and sudden death than from either drug alone.
Prescription stimulants	*Amphetamine (Adderall, Benzedrine).* Bennies, Black Beauties, Crosses, Hearts, LA Turnaround, Speed, Truck Drivers, Uppers *Methylphenidate (Concerta, Ritalin).* JIF, MPH, R-ball, Skippy, The Smart Drug, Vitamin R	Increased alertness, attention, energy; increased blood pressure and heart rate; narrowed blood vessels; increased blood sugar; opened-up breathing passages. *High doses:* dangerously high temperature and irregular heartbeat; heart failure; seizures.	Heart problems, psychosis, anger, paranoia. *With alcohol:* Masks depressant action of alcohol, increasing risk of alcohol overdose; may increase blood pressure and jitters.
Methamphetamine	*Desoxyn.* Chalk, Crank, Crystal, Fire, Glass, Go Fast, Ice, Meth, Speed	Increased wakefulness and physical activity; decreased appetite; increased breathing, heart rate, blood pressure, temperature; irregular heartbeat.	Anxiety, confusion, insomnia, mood problems, violent behavior, paranoia, hallucinations, delusions, weight loss, severe dental problems ("meth mouth"), intense itching leading to skin sores from scratching. *With alcohol:* Masks depressant effect of alcohol, increasing risk of alcohol overdose; may increase blood pressure and jitters.
Khat	*No commercial uses.* Abyssinian Tea, African Salad, Catha, Chat, Kat, Oat	Euphoria, increased alertness and arousal, increased blood pressure and heart rate, depression, inability to concentrate, irritability, loss of appetite, insomnia.	Tooth decay and gum disease; gastrointestinal disorders such as constipation, ulcers, stomach inflammation, and increased risk of upper gastrointestinal tumors; cardiovascular disorders such as irregular heartbeat, decreased blood flow, and heart attack. In rare cases associated with heavy use: psychotic reactions such as fear, anxiety, grandiose delusions, hallucinations, and paranoia. *With alcohol:* Unknown.
Synthetic cathinones ("bath salts")	*No commercial uses.* Bloom, Cloud Nine, Cosmic Blast, Flakka, Ivory Wave, Lunar Wave, Scarface, Vanilla Sky, White Lightning	Increased heart rate and blood pressure; euphoria; increased sociability and sex drive; paranoia, agitation, and hallucinations; psychotic and violent behavior; nosebleeds; sweating; nausea, vomiting; insomnia; irritability; dizziness; depression; suicidal thoughts; panic attacks; reduced motor control; cloudy thinking.	Breakdown of skeletal muscle tissue; kidney failure; death. *With alcohol:* Unknown.
Club Drugs			
MDMA (Ecstasy, Molly)	*No commercial uses.* Adam, Clarity, Eve, Lover's Speed, Peace, Uppers	Lowered inhibition; enhanced sensory perception; confusion; depression; sleep problems; anxiety; increased heart rate and blood pressure; muscle tension; teeth clenching; nausea; blurred vision; faintness; chills or sweating; sharp rise in temperature leading to liver, kidney, or heart failure and death.	Long-lasting confusion, depression, problems with attention, memory, and sleep; increased anxiety, impulsiveness, aggression; loss of appetite; less interest in sex. *With alcohol:* May increase risk of cell and organ damage.

Continued...

Table 10.2 **Commonly Abused Drugs** *(Continued)*

Category and Name	*Trade Names*/Street Names	Short-Term Health Effects	Long-Term Health Effects/Effects in Combination with Alcohol
Rohypnol	*Flunitrazepam, Rohypnol.* Circles, Date Rape Drug, Forget Pill, Forget-Me Pill, La Rocha, Lunch Money, Mexican Valium, Mind Eraser, Pingus, R2, Reynolds, Rib, Roach, Roach 2, Roaches, Roachies, Roapies, Rochas Dos, Roofies, Rope, Rophies, Row-Shay, Ruffies, Trip-and-Fall, Wolfies	Drowsiness, sedation, sleep; amnesia, blackout; decreased anxiety; muscle relaxation, impaired reaction time and motor coordination; impaired mental functioning and judgment; confusion; aggression; excitability; slurred speech; headache; slowed breathing and heart rate.	Long-term effects unknown. *With alcohol:* Severe sedation, unconsciousness, and slowed heart rate and breathing, which can lead to death.
GHB	*Gamma-hydroxybutyrate or sodium oxybate (Xyrem).* G, Georgia Home Boy, Goop, Grievous Bodily Harm, Liquid Ecstasy, Liquid X, Soap, Scoop	Euphoria, drowsiness, decreased anxiety, confusion, memory loss, hallucinations, excited and aggressive behavior, nausea, vomiting, unconsciousness, seizures, slowed heart rate and breathing, lower temperature, coma, death.	Long-term effects unknown. *With alcohol:* Nausea, problems with breathing, greatly increased depressant effects.
CNS Depressants			
Prescription sedatives, anti-anxiety drugs, and sleep medications	*Barbiturates: pentobarbital (Nembutal), phenobarbital (Luminal).* Barbs, Phennies, Red Birds, Reds, Tooies, Yellow Jackets, Yellows *Benzodiazepines (anti-anxiety drugs): alprazolam (Xanax), chlorodiazepoxide (Limbitrol), diazepam (Valium), lorazepam (Ativan), triazolam (Halicon).* Candy, Downers, Sleeping Pills, Tranks *Sleep medications (hypnotics): eszopiclone (Lunesta), zaleplon (Sonata), zolpidem (Ambien).* Forget-me Pill, Mexican Valium, R2, Roche, Roofies, Roofinol, Rope, Rophies	Drowsiness, slurred speech, poor concentration, confusion, dizziness, problems with movement and memory, lowered blood pressure, slowed breathing.	Long-term effects unknown. *With alcohol:* Further slows heart rate and breathing, which can lead to death.
Opioids (Narcotics)			
Prescription opioids	*Codeine (various brand names of prescription cough syrup).* Captain Cody, Cody, Lean, Schoolboy, Sizzurp, Purple Drank *With glutethimide:* Doors & Fours, Loads, Pancakes and Syrup *Fentanyl (Actiq, Duragesic, Sublimaze).* Apache, China Girl, China White, Dance Fever, Friend, Goodfella, Jackpot, Murder 8, Tango and Cash, TNT *Hydrocodone or dihydrocodeinone (Vicodin, Lortab, Lorcet, and others).* Vike, Watson-387 *Hydromorphone (Dilaudid).* D, Dillies, Footballs, Juice, Smack *Meperidine (Demerol).* Demmies, Pain Killer *Methadone (Dolophine, Methadose).* Amidone, Fizzies *With MDMA:* Chocolate Chip Cookies *Morphine (Duramorph, Roxanol).* M, Miss Emma, Monkey, White Stuff *Oxycodone (OxyContin, Percodan, Percocet, and others).* O.C., Oxycet, Oxycotton, Oxy, Hillbilly Heroin, Percs *Oxymorphone (Opana).* Biscuits, Blue Heaven, Blues, Mrs. O, O Bomb, Octagons, Stop Signs	Pain relief, drowsiness, nausea, constipation, euphoria, confusion, slowed breathing, death.	Long-term effects unknown. *With alcohol:* Dangerous slowing of heart rate and breathing leading to coma or death.

Continued...

Table 10.2   Commonly Abused Drugs *(Continued)*

Category and Name	*Trade Names*/Street Names	Short-Term Health Effects	Long-Term Health Effects/Effects in Combination with Alcohol
Heroin	*No commercial uses.* Brown sugar, China White, Dope, H, Horse, Junk, Skag, Skunk, Smack, White Horse. *With OTC cold medicine and antihistamine:* Cheese	Euphoria; warm flushing of skin; dry mouth; heavy feeling in the hands and feet; clouded thinking; alternate wakeful and drowsy states; itching; nausea; vomiting; slowed breathing and heart rate.	Collapsed veins; abscesses (swollen tissue with pus); infection of the lining and valves in the heart; constipation and stomach cramps; liver or kidney disease; pneumonia. *With alcohol:* Dangerous slowdown of heart rate and breathing, coma, death.
Hallucinogens			
LSD (lysergic acid diethyamide)	*No commercial uses.* Acid, Blotter, Blue Heaven, Cubes, Microdot, Yellow Sunshine	Rapid emotional swings; distortion of ability to recognize reality, think rationally, or communicate with others; raised blood pressure, heart rate, temperature; dizziness and insomnia; loss of appetite; dry mouth; sweating; numbness; weakness; tremors; enlarged pupils.	Frightening flashbacks (hallucinogen persisting perception disorder [HPPD]); ongoing visual disturbances, disorganized thinking, paranoia, and mood swings. *With alcohol:* May decrease perceived effects of alcohol.
Ketamine	*Ketalar (veterinary anesthetic).* Cat Valium, K, Special K, Vitamin K	Problems with attention, learning, and memory; dreamlike states, hallucinations; sedation; confusion and problems speaking; loss of memory; problems moving; raised blood pressure; unconsciousness; slowed breathing that can lead to death.	Ulcers and pain in bladder; kidney problems; stomach pain; depression; poor memory. *With alcohol:* Increased risk of adverse effects.
PCP	*No commercial uses.* Angel Dust, Boat, Hog, Love Boat, Peace Pill	Delusions, hallucinations, paranoia, problems thinking, a sense of distance from one's environment, anxiety. *Low doses:* slight increase in breathing rate; increased blood pressure and heart rate; shallow breathing; face redness and sweating; numbness of the hands or feet; problems with movement. *High doses:* lowered blood pressure, pulse rate, breathing rate; nausea; vomiting; blurred vision; flicking up and down of the eyes; drooling; loss of balance; dizziness; violence; suicidal thoughts; seizures, coma, and death.	Memory loss, problems with speech and thinking, depression, weight loss, anxiety. *With alcohol:* Increased risk of coma.
Inhalants			
Inhalants	*Paint thinner or remover, degreaser, dry-cleaning fluid, gasoline, lighter fluid, correction fluid, permanent marker, electronics cleaner and freeze spray, glue, spray paint, hair or deodorant spray, fabric protector spray, vegetable oil spray, butane lighter, propane tank, whipped cream aerosol container, refrigerant gases, ether, chloroform, halothane, nitrous oxide. Also nitrites, which are prescription medications for chest pain.* Poppers, snappers, whippets, laughing gas	Confusion; nausea; slurred speech; lack of coordination; euphoria; dizziness; drowsiness; disinhibition, lightheadedness, hallucinations/delusions; headaches; sudden sniffing death due to heart failure (from butane, propane, and other chemicals in aerosols); death from asphyxiation, suffocation, convulsions or seizures, coma, or choking. Nitrites: enlarged blood vessels, enhanced sexual pleasure, increased heart rate, brief sensation of heat and excitement, dizziness, headache.	Liver and kidney damage; bone marrow damage; limb spasms due to nerve damage; brain damage from lack of oxygen that can cause problems with thinking, movement, vision, and hearing. Nitrites: increased risk of pneumonia. *With alcohol:* Nitrites: dangerously low blood pressure.
Cannabinoids			
Marijuana	*Various brand names where sale is legal.* Blunt, Bud, Dope, Ganja, Grass, Green, Herb, Joint, Mary Jane, Pot, Reefer, Sinsemilla, Skunk, Smoke, Trees, Weed *Hashish:* Boom, Gangster, Hash, Hemp	Enhanced sensory perception and euphoria followed by drowsiness/relaxation; slowed reaction time; problems with balance and coordination; increased heart rate and appetite; problems with learning and memory; hallucinations; anxiety; panic attacks; psychosis.	Mental health problems, chronic cough, frequent respiratory infections. *With alcohol:* Increased heart rate, blood pressure; further slowing of mental processing and reaction time.

Continued...

Table 10.2   Commonly Abused Drugs (Concluded)

Category and Name	Trade Names/Street Names	Short-Term Health Effects	Long-Term Health Effects/Effects in Combination with Alcohol
Synthetic cannabinoids (K2, Spice)	No commercial uses. Black Mamba, Bliss, Bombay Blue, Fake Weed, Fire, Genie, Moon Rocks, Skunk, Smacked, Yucatan, Zohai	Increased heart rate; vomiting; agitation; confusion; hallucinations, anxiety, paranoia; increased blood pressure and reduced blood supply to the heart; heart attack.	Long-term effects unknown. With alcohol: Effects unknown.
Steroids			
Steroids (anabolic)	Nandrolone (Oxandrin), oxandrolone (Anadrol), oxymetholone (Winstrol), stanozolol (Durabolin), testosterone cypionate (Depo-testosterone). Juice, Gym Candy, Pumpers, Roids	Headache, acne, fluid retention (especially in the hands and feet), oily skin, yellowing of the skin and whites of the eyes, infection at the injection site.	Kidney damage or failure; liver damage; high blood pressure, enlarged heart, or changes in cholesterol increasing risk of stroke or heart attack; extreme mood swings; anger ("roid rage"); paranoid jealousy; delusions; impaired judgment. Males: shrunken testicles, lowered sperm count, infertility, baldness, development of breasts, increased risk for prostate cancer. Females: facial hair, male-pattern baldness, menstrual cycle changes, enlargement of the clitoris, deepened voice. Adolescents: stunted growth. With alcohol: Increased risk of violent behavior.

Source: https://www.drugabuse.gov/drugs-abuse/commonly-abused-drugs-charts revised July 2019

APPROACHES TO THE DRUG PROBLEM

Drug abuse and dependence have negative consequences affecting individuals, communities, and society. In addition to the human costs, illicit drug use and addiction cause considerable economic damage. In the United States, the abuse of tobacco, alcohol, and illicit drugs costs more than $740 billion annually when expenses related to crime, lost work productivity, and health care are taken into consideration.[37] Of the $500 billion spent by federal and state governments, only 2 cents of every dollar are spent on prevention and treatment.[38]

An estimated 2.5 million emergency room visits each year are a result of medical emergencies involving drug misuse or abuse.[39] Between 2004 and 2009, the total number of drug-related ER visits increased by 81 percent, and the number of ER visits related to the nonmedical use of prescription drugs increased by more than 98 percent. The largest increases were associated with oxycodone products, hydrocodone products, and alprazolam (Xanax, an anti-anxiety drug).[40] There has also been an increase in emergency room visits for narcotic pain relievers accounting for 366,181 visits in 2011.[41] For more about the misuse of prescription drugs, see the box "Starting the Conversation: Should We Hold Doctors Responsible When Their Patients Overdose on Prescription Drugs?"

Other economic costs of illicit drug use include social welfare costs, workplace accidents, property damage, incarceration of otherwise productive individuals, goods and services lost to crime, work hours missed by victims of drug-related crime, and costs of law enforcement.

Government approaches to the drug problem have traditionally fallen into two broad categories: supply reduction and demand reduction. A newer approach is harm reduction, a remedy used in alcohol treatment programs as well.

Supply-Reduction Strategies

Strategies to reduce the supply of drugs are aimed at controlling the quantity of illicit substances that enter or are produced in the United States. An example is interdiction, the interception of drugs before they enter the country, as when customs officials use dogs to sniff out drugs at airports or when the Coast Guard boards ships to search for drugs as they enter U.S. waters.

The U.S. government also puts pressure on governments in other countries to suppress the production and exportation of drugs. Unfortunately, the plants that yield drugs are important and profitable cash crops for farmers in many countries, and the drug smuggling business is controlled by criminal interests that are often beyond the control of the government. Efforts to reduce the drug supply at the international level have led to human rights abuses, an expansion of oppressive regimes, and increased corruption among police, government, and military workers.

Starting the Conversation
Should We Hold Doctors Responsible When Their Patients Overdose on Prescription Drugs?

Q: What has your experience been with prescription painkillers, if any?

In 2012, a physician in southern California was arrested and charged with murder in three fatal overdoses by patients taking drugs she prescribed. Prosecutors accused the doctor of recklessly prescribing narcotic painkillers and other addictive drugs to her patients—including OxyContin, Vicodin, Xanax, and Valium—"without a legitimate purpose." Previously, she had settled several wrongful-death lawsuits with families of people who overdosed on the drugs she prescribed.

In November 2011, Dr. Conrad Murray was convicted of involuntary manslaughter in the death of pop star Michael Jackson. Murray had administered the powerful anesthetic propofol to the star to help him sleep. His actions were found to "be recklessly outside the bounds of accepted medical practice." Jackson was said to be taking numerous prescription drugs at the time of his death, including anti-anxiety medications and painkillers.

These criminal cases are unusual. Negative medical outcomes are usually not criminalized, and prescribing physicians have generally not been held responsible when someone dies as a result of their actions. Although several physicians have been prosecuted on drug-dealing charges, it's rare for a physician to be charged with criminal gross negligence, much less manslaughter or murder.

Deaths from prescription drug overdoses have soared in the past several years; since 2003, more overdose deaths have resulted from opioid analgesics (painkillers) than from heroin and cocaine combined. Drug overdoses are the leading cause of accidental death in the United States, accounting for over 60,000 deaths[42] per year. In many large cities, overdose deaths are more common than homicides. Overdoses often result from the combined effects of several drugs, often in conjunction with alcohol. Actor Heath Ledger, for example, died from a lethal combination of OxyContin, Valium, Xanax, Ritalin, Vicodin, and sleep aids.

Numerous factors have contributed to this trend. More drugs have been developed, and pharmaceutical companies use aggressive sales campaigns to market them, including direct-to-consumer campaigns. Doctors prescribe these drugs in well-meaning efforts to relieve suffering, particularly among the growing number of older and overweight patients with chronic pain and musculoskeletal problems. The number of prescriptions doctors write has increased greatly over the past two decades. On an average day, more than 650,000 opioid prescriptions are written; 3,900 people initiate opiate use; and 580 start using heroin. This means that there are more drugs around, and they are easier to get.

In addition, attitudes toward prescription drugs are different from attitudes toward illicit drugs. While many heroin users start by using prescription opioids like hydrocodone and oxycodone, many people assume that anything prescribed by a doctor is safe.

All this has left some physicians unsure of how to respond to their patients in pain. They have effective medications at hand, but they also have concerns about patients' taking the drugs correctly, sharing their medications, protecting the medication from others, and becoming addicted. Their concerns extend to fear of losing their license or being charged with a crime.

One method for responding to the prescription drug abuse epidemic is physician education, focusing on raising awareness of the dangers of prescription drug use and the possibility of addiction, overdose, and death. These efforts would include training requirements for doctors. In the absence of such requirements, physicians continue to write prescriptions for narcotics and other addictive drugs for their patients, in most cases without being held responsible for negative outcomes. President Barack Obama proposed that an additional $1.1 billion be budgeted to address the increased use of opioids and heroin, as well as the increasing death rate due to narcotics overdose. More recently, Congress has proposed setting aside millions to treat those addicted to drugs. President Donald Trump has appointed a commission to review the drug epidemic, and longer prison terms were suggested for those who deal drugs. Up to now, however, no new policies have been implemented.

Q: Do you think physicians are responsible when their patients become addicted to prescription painkillers or overdose on them? If so, are they also responsible for people who borrowed or stole the drugs from the patient?

Q: What are the disadvantages of holding physicians criminally responsible for the outcomes of their medical actions?

Q: What responsibility, if any, do you think pharmaceutical companies have in this situation?

McGraw Hill connect

Sources: Girion, L., Glove, S., & Branson-Potts, H. (2012). Doctor charged in fatal prescription overdose. *Los Angeles Times.* http://articles.latimes.com/2012/mar/01/local/la-me-drug-doctor-20120302; The White House. (2011). Epidemic: Responding to America's prescription drug abuse crisis. www.whitehouse.gov/sites/default/files/ondcp/issues-content/prescription-drugs/rx_abuse_plan.pdf; National Institute on Drug Abuse. (2011). Topics in Brief: Prescription drug abuse. www.drugabuse.gov/publications/topics-in-brief/prescription-drug-abuse; Martins, S., Sarvet, A., Santaella-Tenorio, J., Saha, T., Grant, B., & Hasin, D. (2017). Changes in US lifetime heroin use and heroin use disorder. *JAMA Psychiatry,* 445–455; Fox, M. (2017, March 29), Heroin use & spikes fivefold in US. *NBCNEWS.*

The government also attempts to prevent domestic production of drugs by raiding suspected underground drug labs or stamping out enterprises that grow marijuana on a large scale. Another domestic supply-side strategy is to obstruct the distribution of drugs, such as when a massive police presence is used in an area where drugs are sold.

Demand-Reduction Strategies

Demand-side strategies include penalizing users through incarceration, preventing drug use primarily through education, and treating individuals once they have become dependent on drugs.

Incarceration for Drug-Related Crimes
Penalizing users means enforcing the laws against drug possession, arresting offenders, and putting people in prison. An estimated 300,000 people are currently held in federal and state prisons for drug-law violations.[43] The assumptions behind this approach are that incarceration will reduce drug-related crime by getting users off the streets and that the threat of punishment will deter others from using drugs. Most states mandate harsh prison terms for the possession or sale of relatively small quantities of drugs, regardless of whether the person is a first-time or repeat offender. It now appears that incarceration for nonviolent drug crimes has disproportionally affected communities of color, particularly African American males. African Americans are sent to prison in far greater numbers than white individuals and serve as much time in prison for drug offenses as whites do for violent crimes.[44]

Overall, however, evidence indicates that imprisonment is not an effective drug reduction strategy.[45] Incarceration as a drug use reduction strategy also does little to address the larger problem of drug use in our society.[46,47] Because prisoners are a captive audience, it would make sense to provide treatment while they are in jail, but only a small percentage of prisoners who need drug treatment—between 7 and 17 percent—receive it. Interventions with drug users who become involved with the criminal justice system, such as alternative-to-incarceration programs, drug courts, and cooperative social service programs that include partnerships between parole officers and family members, are seen as prevention methods for reducing arrests and recidivism.

Prevention Strategies
A second demand-side strategy is prevention through education. Prevention strategies focus on reducing the demand for drugs by increasing an individual's ability to decline drug use when confronted with an opportunity to experiment. Programs rely on primary, secondary, or tertiary prevention, depending on their targeted audience. *Primary, or universal, prevention programs* are designed to reach the entire population without regard to individual risk factors. Public service commercials on television asking us to imagine a world without cigarettes or billboards referring to crystal meth as "crystal mess" are examples of primary prevention strategies.

Secondary, or selective, strategies focus on those subgroups that are at greatest risk for use or abuse, with the aim of increasing protective factors and decreasing potential risk factors. An example is a class that teaches problem-solving skills to adolescents.

Tertiary, or indicated, strategies target at-risk individuals rather than groups, again focusing on protective factors such as academic, interpersonal, social, or job skills. An example is a program that tutors individual students in ways to manage emotions and maintain self-esteem without drugs.

A prevention strategy used in the workplace is drug testing, usually random urine screening. The goal of drug testing is not to catch drug users and fire them but to create an environment in which it is clear that drug use is not condoned. Companies also want to limit their liability by reducing the likelihood that an employee using drugs will make a mistake that causes someone harm. Federal law requires that people in jobs involving transportation, such as air traffic controllers, train engineers, and truck drivers, undergo regular testing to ensure public safety. Members of the U.S. military also undergo regular drug testing. Although some observers see the practice as an infringement of privacy rights, so far it has withstood judicial challenges.

On college campuses, a number of steps can be taken to prevent drug use and to reduce harm to those students who do use (see the box "Action Skill-Builder: Recognize Signs of a Drug Problem"). A comprehensive approach, known as *environmental management,* attempts to modify an environment that often benignly accepts or overlooks drug use and experimentation during college. The most effective approaches seem to have a number of common factors:

- Sending clear messages that drug use is not acceptable

- Changing the climate of drug tolerance on campus, if it exists

- Engaging parents

- Identifying and intervening with at-risk students

- Providing alternative activities

- Engaging students in the planning of prevention programs

For those individuals who will experiment regardless of changes made on campus, harm-reduction strategies are important. Implementing such strategies should not be seen as "giving permission" to students to use; rather, it reduces the likelihood that they will harm themselves or others. The following are some harm-reduction strategies that have been implemented on college campuses:

- Providing containers in college buildings for the safe disposal of needles and syringes

- Providing condoms so that students will not transmit infectious diseases if drug use leads to sexual activity

- Making naloxone (Narcan) available in case of opioid overdose. Naloxone is an opiate antagonist that can counteract life-threatening depression of the respiratory system.

Action Skill-Builder

Recognize Signs of a Drug Problem

As a college student, you are in an environment where one in five people uses illicit drugs—mostly marijuana, but also cocaine, ecstasy, and LSD. A smaller number misuse prescription drugs ranging from Adderall to Vicodin. Some people can use drugs recreationally without experiencing problems, but others cannot—they find themselves continuing to use a drug even though it is causing problems at school, at work, or in relationships. Because of the changes drugs cause in the brain, most people don't realize they are slipping into dependence, and what began as a choice becomes a need.

Most colleges focus on alcohol abuse and have fewer programs aimed specifically at helping students recognize early signs of drug dependence. If you have a friend, roommate, or classmate who is beginning to have a problem with drugs, you may notice some of these signs:

☐ A noticeable change in behavior, such as withdrawal or agitation

☐ Mood swings, irritability, or angry outbursts

☐ A change in sleep habits, needing either more or less

☐ Nodding off during conversations or in class on a regular basis

☐ Lack of interest in activities that used to be a source of enjoyment

☐ Decline in academic performance

☐ An increase in physical complaints or pain

☐ Preoccupation with a drug or sense of urgency around its use; activities scheduled around drug use

☐ Financial problems or unexplained need for money; an increase in requests to borrow money

☐ Physical signs such as vomiting, constricted pupils, slurred speech

If you notice these behaviors in a friend, here are a few things you can do:

☐ Speak up. Express your concerns; ask questions; give your friend a reality check. Keeping silent does nothing to help your friend acknowledge and address the problem.

☐ Be prepared for excuses and denial by listing specific examples of your friend's behavior that worry you.

☐ Know where help is available on campus or in the community so that you can suggest resources.

☐ Don't enable your friend. Don't make excuses or help him or her avoid consequences. Continue to be supportive and look out for your friend's best interest.

☐ Take care of yourself. Make sure you have someone to talk to or someplace you can go for support.

Source: Helpguide.org. (2012), Drug abuse and addiction. Retrieved from www.helpguide.org/mental/drug_substance_abuse_addiction_signs_effects_treatment.htm.

One of the best ways to understand and control your drug use is to first do a self-assessment to see what part drugs play in your life. To measure their impact and find out whether you are in need of treatment by a professional, complete the self-assessment and questions in this chapter's Personal Health Portfolio activity.

Drug Treatment Programs The third type of demand-side strategy is helping people to stop using drugs after they have started—that is, providing treatment. As with alcohol, treatment is available in a variety of formats, ranging from hospital-based inpatient programs to self-help/mutual-help groups such as Narcotics Anonymous (NA).

Most experts agree that treatment is a long-term process, often marked by relapses and requiring multiple treatment episodes. The first step is acknowledging that there is a problem and getting into a program. No single treatment is appropriate for everyone; matching services to individual needs is important.[48]

Treatment is more successful when the program lasts at least 3 months, includes individual counseling, and addresses all aspects of the client's life, including with medical treatment, family therapy, living skills, and occupational skills. In counseling, clients work to increase motivation, build relapse-prevention skills, improve problem-solving and interpersonal skills, and develop life-enhancing behaviors. Participating in self-help support programs during and following treatment often helps maintain abstinence.[49] Many also believe that medication-assisted treatment can be an effective method for helping people with opioid-use disorders. This includes giving drug users methadone or buprenorphine as a way to suppress withdrawal symptoms and relieve cravings.[48]

Harm-Reduction Strategies

Harm-reduction strategies are based on the idea that attempting to completely eliminate substance use is futile and that efforts should be focused on helping addicts reduce the harm associated with their substance use.[50,51,52] Advocates of the harm-reduction approach assert that drug users are in need of treatment rather than punishment. Strategies

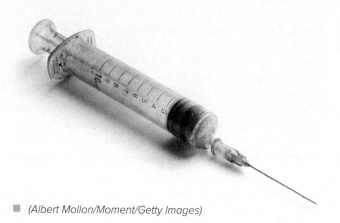

(Albert Mollon/Moment/Getty Images)

Public Health Is Personal

Needle Exchange Programs: Public Health Policy or Political Football?

Needle exchange programs began informally in the 1970s and were widely adopted in the 1980s and 1990s by many U.S. states and by countries around the world in response to the HIV/AIDS epidemic. However, the U.S. Congress made sure no federal funds would be used to support these programs by passing a ban on such funding in 1998. After years of advocacy by public health and harm-reduction activists, the ban was repealed in 2009, but it was reinstated by a differently configured Congress in 2011. In 2016 the ban on funding syringe exchange programs was essentially ended when Congress agreed to fund programs but not pay for needles. With the increase in drug overdoses, there has also been some discussion about starting safe injection sites in the United States. Why is there so much political action around this public health issue?

Needle exchange (or syringe exchange) programs allow injection-drug users to obtain clean hypodermic needles and related injection equipment at little or no cost; many programs require them to turn in used needles for the same number of new needles. Advocates of needle exchange programs assert that the programs reduce the spread of HIV and hepatitis C, remove used needles from the environment, and bring drug users into contact with health care providers who can guide them toward treatment if they are interested. Opponents of needle exchange programs argue that this type of harm-reduction approach only enables and encourages individuals to practice harmful behaviors by giving them "permission" to use; they assert that the programs attract drug sellers to neighborhoods and have a negative impact on living conditions and commerce.

Overall, the evidence indicates that needle exchange programs do reduce the sharing of needles and the spread of HIV and hepatitis C. The programs have not been shown to increase drug use or cause harm. Implementation of syringe exchanges is supported by the CDC, the American Medical Association, the National Academy of Science, the American Public Health Association, the World Health Organization, and numerous other scientific bodies.

Despite the scientific support, there is intense resistance to implementing these programs, primarily for political reasons. Advisors have cautioned U.S. presidents that supporting the programs might "send the wrong message" and open them to charges of being "soft on drugs." Some members of Congress oppose needle exchange programs on moral and religious grounds. U.S. cities and states continue to run these programs as one part of their HIV/AIDS prevention strategies, but in Washington the debate continues: Should social policy be based on scientific evidence, or should it be shaped by partisan politics?

Mc Graw Hill connect

Sources: Smith, D. (2011). Congress votes to restore needle exchange funding ban. http://stopthedrugwar.org/chronicle/2011/dec/19/congress_votes_restore_needle_ex; Mazzotta, M. (2012). Expert panel strategizes to repeal the federal ban on funding for syringe exchange. http://sciencespeaksblog.org/2012/02/09/expert-panel-strategizes-to-repeal-the-federal-ban-on-funding-for-syringe-exchange; Almendrala, A. (2005, September 3). Washington DC is proof that needle exchange saves lives. *Huffington Post.*

include needle exchange programs, in which addicts are provided with sterile needles in exchange for their used ones, and drug substitute programs, in which individuals are maintained on addictive but less debilitating drugs, such as methadone for heroin addicts (see the box "Public Health Is Personal: Needle Exchange Programs: Public Health Policy or Political Football?").

Some groups are beginning to advocate for safer consumption in safe injecting spaces. First established in Berne, Switzerland, these organizations provide a safe and healthy place to use drugs while also offering other services to active drug users. These services might include warm meals, medical care, and referral services for drug treatment and employment. Although many people consider development of safe consumption sites in the United States controversial, there is evidence they can reduce deaths from overdose and lead to an increase in referrals for treatment.[53,54]

Other harm-reduction strategies include controlled availability (which makes certain drugs available through a government monopoly), medicalization (which makes drugs available by prescription but only to individuals who are already addicted to them), and decriminalization (which reduces or eliminates the penalty for possession of certain drugs if the quantity held is below a certain limit).

Proponents of harm-reduction strategies claim that they represent a more realistic approach to the drug problem and would allow resources to be directed away from punishment, which is ineffective, and toward treatment, which is effective. Opponents argue that harm-reduction strategies are thinly disguised forms of drug legalization and that any softening of a zero-tolerance position would result in an epidemic of drug use. Although effective harm-reduction programs are in place in England and Canada, they have been rejected as an official policy by the U.S. government.

You Make the Call

As of September 2019, 33 states and the District of Columbia had laws legalizing marijuana in some form. Colorado, Oregon, Washington, California, Massachusetts, Maine, Vermont, Alaska, and Nevada have all legalized marijuana for recreational use. In other states, marijuana use has been decriminalized. Opponents argue that legalizing marijuana would imply approval of its use for recreational purposes and open the floodgates to abuse of all drugs. Although marijuana has become legal in many states, its use still remains a federal crime that creates an ambiguous situation for users, depending on how aggressively the federal government enforces those laws. Ohio rejected a legalization bill in 2015; more recently, others in that state are arguing for legalization.

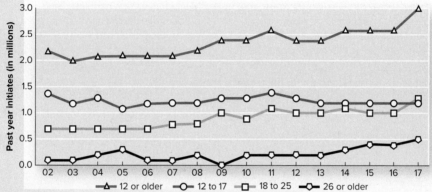

†Difference between this estimate and the 2017 estimate is statistically significant at the .05 level.

Past Year Marijuana Initiates among People Aged 12 or Older, by Age Group (in Millions): 2002-2017.
Substance Abuse and Mental Health Services Administration. (2018). Key substance use and mental health indicators in the United States: Results from the 2017 National Survey on Drug Use and Health (HHS Publication No. SMA 18-5068, NSDUH Series H-53). Rockville, MD: Center for Behavioral Health Statistics and Quality, Substance Abuse and Mental Health Services Administration. Retrieved from https://www.samhsa.gov/data/

Allocation of research funds for studying the harms of marijuana has also far outpaced that of money for research that focuses on its benefits. Although some people believe it has therapeutic possibilities, others argue that making marijuana more available even for medical reasons would be a mistake.

A somewhat different debate is also taking place—about whether marijuana should be legalized for nonmedical use. This debate grew louder in 2010, when California became the first state to consider legalization of marijuana for adult recreational use. In national surveys, 60 percent of U.S. adults think marijuana should be legalized, 52 percent of those over age 18 have smoked at some point in their lives, and 8.4 million smoke daily or near daily.

Proponents of legalization contend that marijuana is safer than alcohol and tobacco. An estimated 88,000 people die each year due to excessive alcohol consumption,[55] and more than 480,000 die each year from the effects of smoking.[56] Proponents of legalized marijuana cite statistics connecting alcohol with violence and point out that marijuana does not make people belligerent. There also appears to be clear relationship between alcohol and violent and aggressive behavior. Opponents respond that we should not legalize another substance that will cause harm, even if it is relatively less harmful than alcohol or tobacco. They point to the negative health consequences of smoking marijuana, which include heart and respiratory problems, as evidence that marijuana is not a benign drug.

Continued...

Proponents also argue that the legalization of marijuana would result in financial benefits for the government, which would gain revenue from income taxes on profits made by marijuana businesses. States would no longer have to use money and resources to enforce current marijuana laws and would also gain revenue from taxes on the sale of marijuana. The California Legislative Analyst's Office estimates that the legalization of marijuana would result in substantial additional tax revenue for the state each year. Some of these tax monies could even be used to bolster underfunded prevention and treatment programs, proponents say.

Opponents respond that the additional revenue would not result in a financial boon because states would have to spend more money on treatment programs, and individuals and society would have to bear the costs of marijuana-related health problems. They say legalization would increase the number of young people using marijuana and likely lead to higher rates of use of more addictive drugs. The federal government currently classifies marijuana itself as a Schedule I drug, meaning that it has a high potential for abuse. More teens are in treatment for marijuana use than for any other drug, and increasing the availability of marijuana to adults would increase the opportunities for children and teens to obtain it for themselves, opponents say.

As the accompanying graph of the results of a 2016 Pew Research poll shows, the percentage of people in the United States who favor legalization is increasing steadily. Should marijuana be legalized for recreational or medical use?

Pros

- The number of states that have legalized medical marijuana and the most recent poll numbers show that public opinion is shifting favorably toward legalizing the drug.
- Marijuana is a relatively safe drug when compared with legal drugs like alcohol and tobacco.
- Legalizing marijuana will save money on law enforcement and generate tax revenue.

Cons

- Marijuana is not a harmless drug. It can cause many health problems, including heart, respiratory, and short-term memory problems.
- Legalization would make the drug more available to children and teens.
- Taxing the sale of marijuana would not result in a net increase in federal and state revenues because health care costs from marijuana-related problems would outweigh any gains.

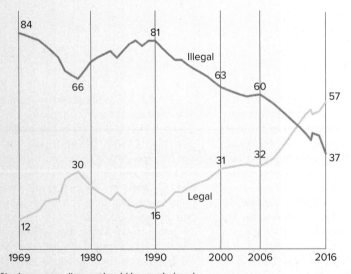

Opinion on legalizing marijuana, 1969–2016
*Do you think the use of marijuana should
be made legal, or not? (%)*

% who say marijuana should be made legal

Continued...

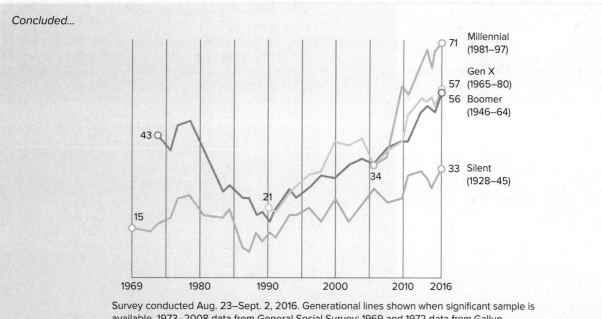

Concluded...

71 Millennial (1981–97)

57 Gen X (1965–80)

56 Boomer (1946–64)

33 Silent (1928–45)

Survey conducted Aug. 23–Sept. 2, 2016. Generational lines shown when significant sample is available. 1973–2008 data from General Social Survey; 1969 and 1972 data from Gallup.

Sources: Motel, S. (2015). 6 facts about marijuana. Pew Research Center, *Fact Tank: News in the Numbers*, www.pewresearch.org/fact-tank/2015/04/14/6-facts-about-marijuana/; Gallup Politics. (2012). Record-high 50% of Americans favor legalizing marijuana use. www.gallup.com/poll/150149/record-high-americans-favor-legalizing-marijuana.aspx; ProCon.org. (2009). Deaths from marijuana v. 17 FDA-approved drugs. http://medicalmarijuana.procon.org/view.resource.php?resourceID=000145; Miller, S. (2010). Don't legalize marijuana. *Los Angeles Times.* http://articles.latimes.com/2010/jan/28/opinion/la-oe-miller28-2010jan28; Khamsi, R. (2013). How safe is recreational marijuana? *Scientific American*, 308(6). www.scientificamerican.com/article/how-safe-recreational-marijuana; graph from Swift, A. (2013). For the first time, Americans favor legalizing marijuana. *Gallup Politics online.* www.gallup.com/poll/165539/first-time-americans-favor-legalizing-marijuana.aspx; Pew Research Center. (2016). Opinion on legalizing marijuana, 1969-2016.

In Review

Why do people use drugs, and what are current patterns of drug use?

As with alcohol, people use drugs to feel better, often as a recreational activity; however, some people become addicted and lose control of their drug use. The most commonly used illicit drug is marijuana, but the nonmedical use of prescription-type drugs has increased dramatically in recent years.

What are the different categories of drugs, and what are the differences between drug misuse and abuse?

Drugs can be categorized as legal or illicit. Drugs developed for medical purposes are pharmaceutical drugs; some are available

only by prescription, whereas others are available over the counter. Drug misuse is the use of prescription drugs for purposes other than those for which they were prescribed, or the use of any drug or chemical for any purpose other than its intended one. Drug abuse is the use of a substance in an amount, situation, or manner that causes problems for the user or for others.

How do drugs affect the body?

As psychoactive substances, drugs affect the brain and the central nervous system (CNS). Effects vary depending on the route of administration, the chemical properties of the drug, the characteristics of the person, and the environment. Drug addiction causes changes in the brain, particularly the brain structures that make up the pleasure and reward circuit and those parts of the brain involved in rational thought and judgment.

What are the different categories of drugs?
Drugs are classified as CNS stimulants (e.g., cocaine, methamphetamine), CNS depressants (barbiturates, benzodiazepines), opioids (heroin, oxycodone), hallucinogens (LSD), inhalants (paint thinner, glue), and cannabinoids (marijuana).

What are the main approaches to the drug problem?
The main approaches are supply-reduction strategies (e.g., interdiction), demand-reduction strategies (incarceration, prevention through education, treatment), and harm-reduction strategies (e.g., needle exchange programs). Because college administrations are often focused more on alcohol-related problems than on drug-related problems, students may have to be more proactive in identifying and helping friends who are developing a drug problem.

The following questions concern information about your possible involvement with drugs (not including alcoholic beverages) during the past 12 months.

"Drug abuse" refers to (1) the use of prescribed or over the counter drugs in excess of the directions, and (2) any nonmedical use of drugs.

The various classes of drugs may include cannabis (marijuana, hashish), solvents (e.g., paint thinner), tranquilizers (e.g., Valium), barbiturates, cocaine, stimulants (e.g., speed), hallucinogens (e.g., LSD), and narcotics (e.g., heroin). Remember that the questions do not include alcoholic beverages.

Please answer every question. If you have difficulty with a statement, then choose the response that is mostly right.

	In the past 12 months...	Circle
1.	Have you used drugs other than those required for medical reasons?	Yes No
2.	Do you abuse more than one drug at a time?	Yes No
3.	Are you always able to stop abusing drugs when you want to? (If you never use drugs, answer yes.)	Yes No
4.	Have you ever had blackouts or flashbacks as a result of drug use?	Yes No
5.	Do you ever feel bad or guilty about your drug use?	Yes No
6.	Does your spouse (or parents) ever complain about your involvement with drugs?	Yes No
7.	Have you neglected your family because of your use of drugs?	Yes No
8.	Have you engaged in illegal activities in order to obtain drugs?	Yes No
9.	Have you ever experienced withdrawal symptoms (felt sick) when you stopped taking drugs?	Yes No
10.	Have you had medical problems as a result of your drug use (e.g., memory loss, hepatitis, convulsions, bleeding)?	Yes No

Scoring: Score 1 point for each question answered "Yes," except for question 3 for which a "No" receives 1 point.

Interpretation of Score		
Score	Degree of Problems Related to Drug Abuse	Suggested Action
0	No problems reported	None at this time
1–2	Low level	Monitor, reassess at a later date
3–5	Moderate level	Further investigation
6–8	Substantial level	Intensive assessment
9–10	Severe level	Intensive assessment

Source: National Institute on Drug Abuse. (n.d.). Drug abuse screening test (DAST-10). Retrieved from https://www.drugabuse.gov/sites/default/files/dast-10.pdf

CRITICAL THINKING QUESTIONS

1. Reflect on your score. What do your responses indicate about your drug use?

2. Is there anything in your environment that makes it easy or difficult to control or limit your drug use? Think about your relationships, your community, and local policies.

3. In what direction are you moving on the continuum—toward increased dependence, toward decreased dependence, or holding steady? Do you need to make any changes to your substance use? If so, what?

Sexual Health

Getty Images/Cavan Images/Getty Images

Ever Wonder...

whether condom stealthing should be criminalized as a form of sexual assault?

how often most college students have sex, and how often they use condoms?

whether digisexuality technology is promoting healthy or unhealthy sexual behaviors?

exuality is a vital aspect of physical and psychological wellness. In the context of intimate relationships, sexuality plays a role in some of life's most meaningful experiences. Sexual activity is a source of pleasure, excitement, and connection with other people, and it is even good for your health. Studies show that an active sex life reduces the risk of heart disease, decreases risk of depression, provides temporary relief from chronic pain, boosts the immune system, and lowers the risk of death.[1,2] But sexuality is a complex human behavior, and it can be associated with negative experiences, such as worries and anxieties, relationship discord, health issues, and societal problems.

Sexual health includes satisfying intimate relationships based on mutual respect and trust and the ability and resources to procreate if so desired. It involves acceptance of our own sexual feelings and tolerance for those of others. It also includes knowledge about sexuality and access to the information needed to make responsible decisions.

Although sexual anatomy and physiology are similar in all human beings, sexual behavior and expression vary tremendously across societies, cultures, and eras. There are even differences in what is considered sexually pleasurable from one culture and time to another. Sexual pleasure has been defined as positively valued feelings induced by sexual stimuli.[3] Sensory signals arriving in the brain are not inherently pleasurable; rather, the brain interprets them as pleasurable. This interpretation and evaluation of stimuli by the brain as sexually pleasurable is influenced by everything the individual has learned about sex in his or her society and culture, including expectations, attitudes, and values.

In the United States, sexual attitudes are marked by an ongoing tension between the two poles of sexual restrictiveness and sexual freedom. The so-called sexual revolution of the 1960s gave way to a more conservative climate in the 1980s and 1990s. Prevailing attitudes toward sex and sexual pleasure in the early 21st century will be determined, in part, by the decisions of college students and other young adults.

SEXUAL ANATOMY AND FUNCTIONING

Although sexuality serves many purposes in human experience—for example, sexual pleasure—the biological purpose of sexuality is reproduction. In this section, we explore some of the biological aspects of sexuality.

The male and female sex organs arise from the same undifferentiated tissue during the prenatal period, becoming male or female under the influence of hormones (discussed later in this section). In this sense, the sexual organs of males and females are very similar, and their purpose and functions are complementary. The female sex organs are responsible for the production of ova and, if pregnancy occurs, the development of the fetus. The male sex organs are responsible for producing sperm and delivering them into the female reproductive system to fertilize the ovum.

Female Sex Organs and Reproductive Anatomy

The external genitalia of the female are called the vulva and include the mons pubis, the labia majora and labia minora, the clitoris, and the vaginal and urethral openings (Figure 11.1). The mons pubis is a mound or layer of fatty tissue that pads and protects the pubic bone. The labia majora (major lips) and labia minora (minor lips) are folds of tissue that wrap around the entrance to the vagina. The labia minora form a protective hood, or prepuce, over the clitoris. The clitoris is a highly sensitive, cylindrical body about 3 centimeters in length that fills with blood during sexual excitement. Consisting of a glans, corpus, and crura, the clitoris is located at the top of the vulva between the lips of the labia minora.

The urethral opening, the passageway for urine from the urinary bladder, is located immediately below the clitoris. The hymen is a thin membranous fold, highly variable in appearance, which may partially cover the opening of the vagina. The hymen has no known biological function and is frequently absent. The perineum is the area between the

■ What we find sexually exciting, attractive, and acceptable is largely determined by the messages we get from our culture. *(Phil Rees/Alamy Stock Photo)*

(a) External Organs (Vulva)

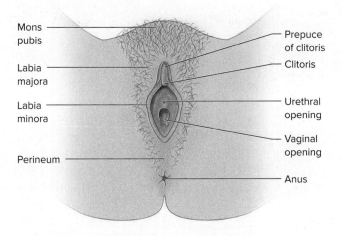

Mons pubis

Labia majora

Labia minora

Perineum

Prepuce of clitoris

Clitoris

Urethral opening

Vaginal opening

Anus

(b) Internal Organs

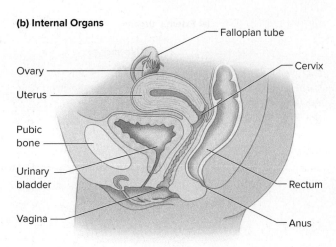

Ovary

Uterus

Pubic bone

Urinary bladder

Vagina

Fallopian tube

Cervix

Rectum

Anus

figure 11.1 **Female sexual and reproductive anatomy**

bottom of the vulva and the anus. It contains many nerve endings. Bartholin glands secrete mucus to facilitate vaginal lubrication, which moistens the labial opening of the vagina.[4]

The internal sex organs of the female include the vagina, cervix, uterus, Fallopian tubes, and ovaries. The vagina is a hollow, muscular tube extending from the external vaginal opening to the cervix. The walls of the vagina are soft and flexible and have several layers. The existence of an area called the G-spot on the lower front wall of the vagina is a subject of debate; if it is present, it may feel like an elevated bump.[5] Located on either side of the vagina under the labia are the crura, extensions of the clitoris.

The cervix is the lower part of the uterus; it extends into the vagina and contains the opening to the uterus. The cervix produces a mucus that changes with different stages of the menstrual cycle (described later in this chapter). The uterus is the organ in which a fertilized egg develops into an embryo and then a fetus. Approximately the size of a pear, the uterus is made up of several layers of muscle and tissue. The endometrium is the layer that is shed during menstruation.

The ovaries are the female reproductive glands that store and release the ova (eggs) every month, usually one at a time—the process of ovulation. They also produce the female sex hormones estrogen and progesterone. The ovaries are located on either side of the uterus. Extending from the upper sides of the uterus are the Fallopian tubes, or oviducts, the passageways through which ova move from the ovaries into the uterus. Their openings are lined with fimbria, appendages with beating cilia that sweep the surface of the ovaries during ovulation and guide the ovum down into the tubes.

The mammary glands, or breasts, are also part of female sexual and reproductive anatomy. They consist of 15 to 25 lobes that are padded by connective tissue and fat. Within the lobes are glands that produce milk when the woman is lactating following the birth of a baby. At the center of each breast is a nipple, surrounded by a ring of darker-colored skin called

the areola. The nipple becomes erect when stimulated by cold, touch, or sexual stimuli.

Male Sex Organs and Reproductive Anatomy

The external genitalia of the male include the penis and the scrotum, which contains the testes (Figure 11.2). The penis, when erect, is designed to deliver sperm into the female reproductive tract. The shaft of the penis is formed of three columns of spongelike erectile tissue that fill with blood during sexual excitement. The glans, or head of the penis, is an expansion of the corpus spongiosum (one of the three columns of erectile tissue in the penis shaft). The glans contains a higher concentration of nerve endings than the shaft and is highly sensitive.

The corona is a crownlike structure that protrudes slightly and forms a border between the glans and the shaft; it is also highly sensitive. The frenulum is a fold of skin extending from the corona to the foreskin. The foreskin, or prepuce, covers the glans, more or less completely. **Circumcision** removes this skin and leaves the head of the penis permanently exposed. The urethral opening, through which both urine and semen pass at different times, is located at the tip of the penis in the glans. The urethra runs the length of the penis from the urinary bladder to the exterior of the body.

The scrotum, a thin sac composed of skin and muscle fibers, contains the testes. The scrotum is separated from the body to keep the testes at the lower temperature that is needed for sperm production. The area between the scrotum and the anus is the perineum; as in females, it contains many nerve endings.

The male internal reproductive organs include the testes, a series of

circumcision
Removal of the foreskin of the penis; a procedure often routinely performed on newborn male infants in the United States.

(a) External Organs

Circumcised   Uncircumcised

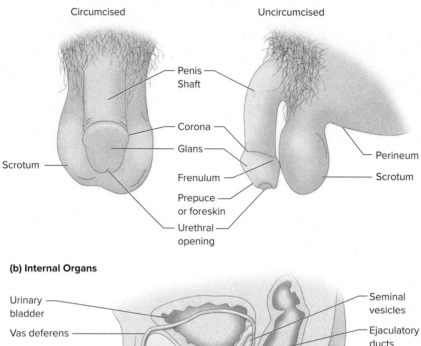

Penis
Shaft

Corona

Glans

Frenulum

Prepuce
or foreskin

Urethral
opening

Scrotum

Perineum

Scrotum

(b) Internal Organs

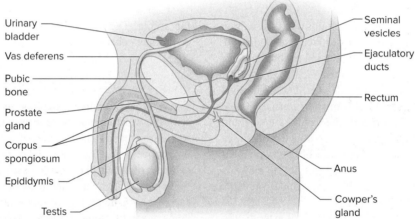

Urinary
bladder

Vas deferens

Pubic
bone

Prostate
gland

Corpus
spongiosum

Epididymis

Testis

Seminal
vesicles

Ejaculatory
ducts

Rectum

Anus

Cowper's
gland

figure 11.2   **Male sexual and reproductive anatomy**

ducts that transport sperm (the epididymis, vas deferens, ejaculatory ducts, and urethra), and a set of glands that produce semen and other fluids (the seminal vesicles, prostate gland, and Cowper's glands). The two testes, located in the scrotum, are the male reproductive glands; they produce both sperm and male sex hormones such as testosterone. Once sperm are produced in the testes, they enter the epididymis, a highly coiled duct lying on the surface of each testis. As they move along the length of the epididymis, immature sperm mature and develop the ability to swim.

When the male ejaculates, sperm are propelled from the epididymis into the vas deferens (Latin for "carrying-away duct"), which joins the seminal vesicles to form the short ejaculatory ducts. The two seminal vesicles, located at the back of the bladder, produce about 60 percent of the volume of semen, the milky fluid that carries sperm and contains nutrients to fuel them. The sperm and semen travel through the ejaculatory ducts to the prostate gland, a doughnut-shaped structure that encircles the urethra and contributes the remaining volume of semen. The semen is then ejaculated

through the urethra. The two Cowper's glands, located below the prostate gland, produce a clear mucus that is secreted into the urethra just before ejaculation. The pre-ejaculation fluid neutralizes acidity in the uterus, helping sperm to travel in a more receptive environment.[6] The volume of semen in one ejaculation is about 2 to 5 milliliters, containing between 100 and 600 million sperm.

A slight majority of U.S. males are circumcised. Rates of male circumcision are decreasing. The practice, however, varies by ethnicity and religious affiliation, and circumcision is increasingly controversial. The arguments for it include prevention of pain to return the foreskin to its original location, decreased incidence of urinary tract infections, lower incidence of sexually transmitted infections (STIs), decreased risk of cancer of the penis, and decreased risk of cancer of the cervix in sexual partners. Arguments against circumcision include increased risk of inflammation of the penis and the lack of any medical reason to circumcise newborns. The American Academy of Pediatrics (AAP) and the American College of Obstetricians and Gynecologists (ACOG) maintain a neutral position and neither condone nor condemn circumcision. Recent studies support a much lower rate of HIV transmission in circumcised males than in noncircumcised males. These studies may lead the AAP and ACOG to reconsider their neutral position.[7]

Many men wonder about "summer penis." Summer heat is capable of causing the penis to expand as blood vessels dilate to allow temperature regulation. There is actually no increase in the size of the penis, but the skin may appear thicker. In winter, the penis slightly contracts as the body conserves internal heat. Health scientists believe the penis's reaction to ambient temperature is associated with the need to maintain a specific temperature in the testes to produce sperm. The scrotum skin expands in warm ambient temperatures and contracts in cold temperatures.[8] Still, the reality is that there is no enlargement of the man's penis in summer heat.

Intersex Anatomy A person born with a sex or reproductive anatomy that does not fit the standard definition of male or female is categorized as **intersex**. For example, a child may be born with the sexual organs of a male outside and primary female sex organs on the inside. Although often described as a born condition, intersex anatomy may not show up until puberty or even later in life. It is even possible for some people to die late in life and never realize they have an intersex anatomy.

Intersex is a socially constructed category that reflects biological variation and is classified as a disorder of sexual development. Physicians typically make the diagnosis, but their opinions vary. Some physicians do not diagnose intersex anatomy unless the brain has also developed atypically. Others believe both ovarian and testicular tissues need to be present for an intersex diagnosis. Thus it is difficult to estimate the prevalence of intersex anatomy. The standard figure is 1 in 1,500 to 1 in 2,000 people.[9] To learn more about intersex anatomy, consult the Intersex Society of North America (ISNA). The ISNA's mission is to help end the stigma, secrecy, and unwarranted surgeries associated with intersex anatomy.

Sexual Response

For reproduction to occur, ova and sperm have to be brought into close association with each other. The psychological and motivational mechanism for this is the human sexual response, which includes sex drive, sexual arousal, and orgasm.

Sex Drive Sex drive—sexual desire, or libido—is defined as a biological urge for sexual activity. The principal hormone responsible for the sex drive in both males and females is testosterone, produced by the testes in males and by the adrenal glands in both sexes. Testosterone stimulates increased release of the neurotransmitters dopamine and serotonin in the brain; they are thought to be involved in making external stimuli arousing. Dopamine and serotonin levels peak at orgasm and then decline.[10] Serotonin is thought to have an effect on feelings of sexual satisfaction and orgasm. The hormones epinephrine (adrenaline) and norepinephrine

(noradrenaline), released by the adrenal glands, stimulate arousal and increase heart rate, blood pressure, respiration, and other autonomic nervous system functions.

People usually seek to satisfy the sex drive through physical stimulation and release, either with a partner or through masturbation. Besides hormones, sex drive is influenced by sexual imagery and sexual fantasies, which in turn are influenced by the person's culture. Sex drive can also be stimulated by sights, sounds, smells, tastes, and myriad other external stimuli, thoughts, and fantasies. The goal of arousal varies by culture. Western cultures typically focus on attaining orgasm. Some cultures encourage the suppression of the sex drive; other cultures emphasize spiritual and sensual outcomes as the goals of sexual activity.[2,10]

The frequency of sex between committed couples is associated with relationship satisfaction and life satisfaction. Frequency of sex for single adults is not tied to life satisfaction. For committed couples, sex once a week meets the relationship satisfaction benchmark. Sex more than once a week does not appear to influence relationship satisfaction or life satisfaction. The leveling off of satisfaction after once a week may be due to couples' accepting once a week as the norm in their peer group. Sex frequency is likely affected by external stressors (work, commutes, parenting) that drain energy that make people feel too tired for sex. There is also sex satiation with the same person that causes boredom. Aging, chronic illness, weight gain, and physical injury can affect sex frequency and sex satisfaction.[11]

Sexual Arousal Sexual arousal on the physiological level causes vasocongestion and myotonia. **Vasocongestion** is the inflow of blood to tissues in erogenous areas. In men, the arterioles supplying blood to the erectile tissue of the penis are normally constricted. Sexual arousal causes nerves in the penis to release nitric oxide, which in turn activates an enzyme that relaxes the arterioles and allows the penis to fill with blood. Engorgement compresses the veins in the penis and prevents blood from flowing out. In women, a similar process causes engorgement of the clitoris, labia, vagina, and nipples; vaginal lubrication also increases. **Myotonia** is a voluntary or involuntary muscle tension occurring in response to sexual stimuli. Both vasocongestion and myotonia build up during sexual excitement and decrease afterward.[12,13]

The Human Sexual Response Model In the 1960s, sex researchers William Masters and Virginia Johnson conducted detailed studies of sexual activity and developed a four-phase model of the human sexual response (Figure 11.3). The four phases are excitement, plateau, orgasm, and resolution.[12,14]

intersex.
Having ambiguous reproductive or sexual anatomy.

sex drive
The biological urge for sexual activity; also called sexual desire or libido.

vasocongestion
Inflow of blood to tissues in erogenous areas.

myotonia
Voluntary or involuntary muscle tension occurring in response to sexual stimuli.

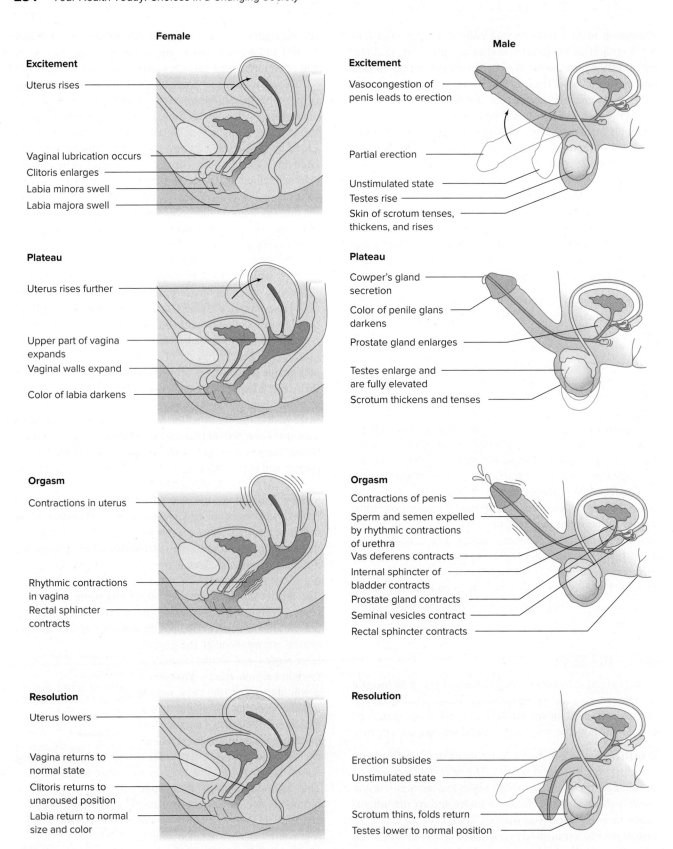

figure 11.3   The human sexual response model

The excitement stage begins with stimulation that initiates vasocongestion and myotonia. The first sign of excitement in men is penis erection. In women, signs include vaginal lubrication and, frequently, nipple and clitoral erection. Heart rate and respiratory rate generally increase in both men and women.

The plateau phase is a leveling-off period just before orgasm. Increased muscle tension continues during the plateau phase. The heart rate remains elevated and breathing is deep. The penis increases in size and length, and the upper two-thirds of the vagina widens and expands.

A more complex view of sexual response is the dual control model, which is based on brain function. Sexual excitement and sexual inhibition are viewed as separate systems. People with low propensity for sexual excitement or high sex inhibition are more likely to experience difficulty in sexual response to sexual stimuli. High-risk sexual activity, such as not practicing safe sex, is a more likely outcome for people with high sexual excitement and low sexual inhibition. Most people score in the middle for excitation and inhibition, but there is great variability from one person to the next. For example, men tend to score higher on sexual excitement and lower on sexual inhibition than women, and gay men score higher on excitation and lower on inhibition than straight men.[10]

Another model suggests that many women, especially those in long-term relationships, may not experience sexual desire (conscious sexual urges) moving to sexual arousal. Instead, sexual arousal more commonly precedes sexual desire. Sexual desire occurs only after a sufficient period of sexual arousal and is more of a responsive event than a spontaneous event.[14] The choice to initiate sexual arousal is more likely due to intimacy needs (needs for emotional closeness, bonding, love, affection) than to a need for physical sexual arousal or release. Intimacy benefits and appreciation for the sexual well-being of the partner are the motivations to move from sexual neutrality to sexual arousal.[12] This model may also apply to some men in long-term relationships.

Sexual Arousal Noncordance As you have read, penile erection is the most apparent sexual response in males. Female sexual arousal includes vaginal lubrication and swelling and engorgement of external genitals, and internal enlargement of the vagina. It is a myth that females take longer than males to experience sexual arousal. The average time for both females and males is 10 minutes. **Sexual concordance** is defined as the degree to which a person's physiological sexual arousal matches the mental response (self-assessment as to whether a sexual stimulus is pleasing and triggers a genital response).[15] There are times when genital sexual arousal does not match the mental experience. While female brains are more sensitive to the mental experience than male brains, some men are more sensitized and some women less.

The mismatch of physical and mental sexual arousal is called **sexual noncordance**. In other words, the body may react to sexual arousal, but the mind does not correlate with this genital response. Males generally experience complete sexual concordance 50 percent of the time, and females 10 percent.

Sexual noncordance is a normal part of human sexuality, and there can be different reasons for it. For example, traumatic experiences such as sexual assault may cause sexual response noncordance. If you are experiencing feelings of anxiety or fear during sex, you may want to consult a sex therapist. If experiencing physical pain, you should consult a physician.

The practical application of sexual response noncordance is that females more than males may need to communicate more with their sexual partners what they like and do not like in the sexual experience. More boldly stated, vagina wetness is not a green light indicating that females are ready for and enjoying the sexual-arousal experience.[15]

Orgasm Orgasm is a physiological reflex in which a massive discharge of nerve impulses occurs in the nerves serving the genitals, usually in response to tactile stimulation, causing rhythmic muscle contractions in the genital area and a sensation of intense pleasure. In men, contractions occur in the penis, ducts, glands, and muscles in the pelvic and anal regions; orgasm is accompanied by the ejaculation of semen. In women, contractions occur in the uterus, vagina, and pelvic and anal regions.

Most people experience a feeling of deep warmth or pressure when orgasm is imminent or inevitable. Orgasm is usually felt as waves of intense pleasure accompanied by contractions in the penis, vagina, or uterus. The sensations may be localized to the genitals, or they may be generalized over the whole body.

Although orgasm is physically experienced in the genitals, it is also a mental and emotional event. The subjective experience of orgasm can be influenced by an infinite variety of physical, emotional, psychological, interpersonal, and environmental factors.

After orgasm, men enter a **refractory period**, lasting from minutes to hours, during which vasoconstriction of the arterioles supplying the erectile tissue causes the penis to become flaccid (soft) again. During the refractory period, the man is not able to have another orgasm. Most young men can have one to three orgasms in an hour, as can some older men.

Women do not have a refractory period and can experience multiple orgasms during a single sexual experience. Multiple orgasms may be experienced as part of the general climactic wave or as a series of orgasms as much as 5 minutes apart.

About 50 percent of women reach orgasm from the sensations produced in the vagina by the thrusting of the penis, but many women need direct stimulation of the clitoris to reach

sexual concordance The degree to which a person's physiological sexual arousal matches the mental response.

sexual noncordance The mismatch of physical and mental sexual arousal.

orgasm A physiological reflex characterized by rhythmic muscle contractions in the genital area and a sensation of intense pleasure.

refractory period The time following orgasm when a man cannot have another orgasm.

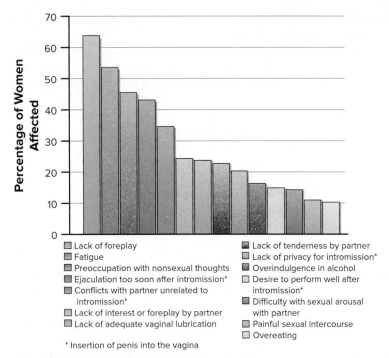

- ☐ Lack of foreplay
- ☐ Fatigue
- ☐ Preoccupation with nonsexual thoughts
- ☐ Ejaculation too soon after intromission*
- ☐ Conflicts with partner unrelated to intromission*
- ☐ Lack of interest or foreplay by partner
- ☐ Lack of adequate vaginal lubrication
- ☐ Lack of tenderness by partner
- ☐ Lack of privacy for intromission*
- ☐ Overindulgence in alcohol
- ☐ Desire to perform well after intromission*
- ☐ Difficulty with sexual arousal with partner
- ☐ Painful sexual intercourse
- ☐ Overeating

* Insertion of penis into the vagina

figure 11.4 **Factors inhibiting women's orgasm during intercourse**
Source: Yarber, W., Sayad, B., & Strong, B. (2018). *Human sexuality: Diversity in contemporary America.* New York, NY: McGraw-Hill.

orgasm.[10,12] Most intercourse positions do not include such direct pressure or stimulation, so intercourse alone may not be completely satisfying for a woman. Women reach orgasm only about 50 to 70 percent of the time. Active stimulation of the clitoris with fingers or a vibrator can help women reach orgasm. When a woman is unable to reach orgasm, it is usually due to inhibition or lack of needed stimulation (see Figure 11.4). Women are more likely to experience orgasm if the sexual encounter includes oral sex or anal sex. About 95 percent of men experience orgasm in sexual encounters that include vaginal intercourse.[10,12]

androgens
Male sex hormones, secreted primarily by the testes.

estrogens
Female sex hormones; secreted by the ovaries.

progestins
Female sex hormones; secreted by the ovaries.

ejaculation
The emission of semen during orgasm.

menarche
The onset of menstruation.

menses
Flow of menstrual blood; the menstrual period.

Orgasm Gap There is considerable research on the heterosexual orgasm gap. Heterosexual men tend to have a 30 percentage point higher rate of orgasm than heterosexual women (men, 95%; women, 65%). The orgasm gap by sexual orientation is 22 percent for bisexuals (88 percent bisexual men, 66 percent bisexual women) and 3 percent for gay men and women (gay men, 89%; gay women, 86%).[16]

Some people pretend to have reached orgasm during sex when they haven't. One study found that about 60 percent of heterosexual college women and 71 percent of lesbian or bisexual women had faked an orgasm. In contrast, 28 percent of heterosexual men and 27 percent of gay or bisexual men had faked an orgasm.[10] The primary reason women fake orgasms is to protect the feelings of their sexual partner, but other reasons include the desire to expedite boring or painful intercourse and fear of their own sexual inadequacy. Faking an orgasm can undermine a relationship. A satisfying relationship includes honest discussions about what helps both partners enjoy sex the most.

Sexual Development and Health Across the Lifespan

The biology of sexual development is directed by hormones throughout the lifespan. Male sex hormones, called **androgens**, are secreted primarily by the testes, and female sex hormones, called **estrogens** and **progestins**, are secreted by the ovaries. Hormones play a role in the prenatal development of sex organs and again at puberty, when secondary sex characteristics appear and the reproductive system matures: the sex organs become larger, and pubic and underarm hair appears. In boys, the voice deepens, facial hair begins to grow, and the onset of **ejaculation** occurs. Boys begin to experience nocturnal emissions (orgasm and ejaculation during sleep), and the testes start to produce sperm. In girls, breasts develop, body fat increases, and **menarche**, the onset of menstruation, occurs.

Every month between the ages of about 12 and about 50, except during pregnancy, women experience monthly menstrual periods. During the first half of the cycle, the lining of the uterus thickens with blood vessels in preparation for the possibility of pregnancy, and an ovum matures in one of the ovaries. About halfway through the cycle, the ovum is released (ovulation) and is carried into the uterus. If sperm are present, the ovum may be fertilized and begin to develop into an embryo. If an ovum isn't fertilized, the uterine lining is shed, causing **menses**, and the cycle begins again.

Some girls and women experience uncomfortable physical symptoms during their periods, such as cramps and backache, and some experience physical and emotional symptoms before their periods, such as headache, irritability, and mood swings, referred to as premenstrual tension or premenstrual syndrome (PMS). If symptoms are severe and interfere with usual work, family, or social activities, the woman may be diagnosed with premenstrual dysphoric disorder (PMDD). The exact causes of PMS and PMDD are not known, but lifestyle changes—such as exercising, eating well, and avoiding alcohol—may help relieve symptoms. A physician may prescribe medications for more severe symptoms. Endometriosis is also a concern. This painful gynecological disorder, which affects more than 5 million women, occurs when the endometrial lining grows outside the uterus. Lesions form that can bleed or break down each month, resulting in scar-tissue adhesions that bind endometrial tissue together.

In middle age, hormonal changes cause a gradual reduction in ovarian functioning that culminates in menopause, the cessation of menstruation. During the time leading up to menopause, a period of 3 to 7 years called perimenopause, many women experience symptoms caused by hormonal fluctuations, such as hot flashes, night sweats, irritability, and insomnia. A decrease in estrogen production can cause less visible symptoms as well, such as a reduction in bone density and changes in blood levels of cholesterol. These changes contribute to women's increased risk of osteoporosis and heart disease later in life. Uncomfortable symptoms of perimenopause and menopause can be relieved in many cases by increased physical activity, stress management, and other lifestyle changes.[10]

Men do not experience as dramatic a change in reproductive capacity in midlife as women do; the testes continue to produce sperm throughout life. Some researchers believe, however, that middle-aged men experience a period during which testosterone levels fluctuate, and there may be changes in sexual functioning, irritability, mild to moderate mood swings, and other symptoms. For both men and women, however, biological changes in the sexual response phases have only a marginal effect on sexual interest and activity. The more sexually active a person is, the less effect these biological changes have.[17]

Sexuality and Disability

Although individuals with disabilities may experience limitations in their sexuality or may have to develop new or alternative forms of sexual activity, most people with disabilities can have a rewarding sex life. For people with physical limitations, different forms of sexual expression may be possible. A person with spinal cord injury may not be able to have an orgasm, but he or she may be able to have intercourse, experience sensuous feelings in other parts of the body, or have a child. As in any relationship, the key is nurturing emotional as well as sexual intimacy. Information and education can help individuals with disabilities, as can counseling that focuses on building self-esteem and overcoming shame, guilt, fear, anger, and unrealistic expectations.

Changes in sexual functioning and desire can also be caused by chronic disease, such as diabetes, arthritis, cancer, and cardiovascular disease, as well as by the medications used to treat them. For example, diabetes can cause nerve damage and circulatory problems that affect erectile functioning in men. Individuals and couples may have to make significant adjustments in their forms of sexual expression to accommodate such disabling conditions.[10]

Information and education are also important for members of the general public, who too often fail to acknowledge the full humanity of individuals with disabilities, including their sexuality. The Developmental Disabilities Assistance and Bill of Rights Act of 2000 clearly states that sexual rights for people with disabilities should be the same as for people without disabilities, including the right to sexual expression, the right to have or not have children, and the right to privacy.

VARIETIES OF SEXUAL BEHAVIOR AND EXPRESSION

Rather than thinking in terms of "normalcy," social scientists think in terms of behavior that is typical and behavior that is less typical.

Common Forms of Sexual Expression

Typical forms of sexual behavior and expression in U.S. society include celibacy, erotic touch, kissing, self-stimulation, oral-genital stimulation, anal intercourse, and sexual intercourse.

Celibacy Continuous abstention from sexual activities with others is called **celibacy**. People may be completely celibate (do not engage in masturbation) or partially celibate (engage in masturbation). Moral and religious beliefs lead some people to choose celibacy. Lack of a suitable sexual partner or sexual relationship may be another reason for celibacy.[2,10]

Some people use the term *abstinence* interchangeably with *celibacy,* but **abstinence** usually means abstention only from sexual intercourse. As such, abstinence is promoted as a way to avoid STIs and unintended pregnancy.

Abstinence Abstinence from sexual intercourse is an option for many people. For some, abstaining from sexual intercourse for periods of time between relationships is an effective choice. This can include abstaining from intercourse in a new relationship until partners are in agreement about their goals and expectations for the relationship. For others, total abstinence from sexual intercourse until in a long-term committed relationship (or until marriage) is an option. There are religious organizations that promote this option. While it can be a goal based on values and beliefs, some entities are pushing strongly for this to become the norm.

A growing number of groups of conservative college students believe in abstinence until marriage. The Anscombe Society at Princeton University, for example, drew extensive media attention with its call for members to commit to chastity until marriage. Harvard's True Love Revolution is based on a similar platform.[10] The Love and Fidelity Network is dedicated to educating, training, and equipping college students with resources that uphold traditional marriage, family, and sexual values. It wants to ignite a movement on college campuses that values committed relationships and fidelity as opposed to the hook-up culture of casual sex.

Erotic Touch Touch is a sensual form of communication that can elicit feelings of tenderness and affection as well as sexual feelings. It is an important part of **foreplay**, touching that increases sexual arousal and

celibacy Continuous abstention from sexual activities with others.

abstinence Abstention from sexual intercourse, usually as a way to avoid conception or sexually transmitted infections.

foreplay Touching that increases sexual arousal before sexual intercourse.

autoerotic behaviors
Self-stimulating sexual activities, primarily sexual fantasies and masturbation.

masturbation
Self-stimulation of the genitals for sexual pleasure.

precedes sexual intercourse. Some areas of the body are more sensitive to touch than others. Skin in the non-specific erogenous zones of the body (the inner thighs, armpits, shoulders, feet, ears, and sides of the back and neck) contains more nerve endings than do many other areas; these areas are capable of being aroused by touch. Skin in the specific *erogenous zones* (penis, clitoris, vulva, perineum, lips, breasts, and buttocks) has an even higher density of nerve endings, and nerve endings are closer to the skin surface.[18,19] The landscape of erotic touch includes holding hands, kissing, stroking, caressing, squeezing, tickling, scratching, and massaging.

A popular metaphor for pleasure-oriented touching is the five "gears of connection." First gear (affective touching) includes such interactions as holding hands, hugging, and kissing. Second gear (sensual touching) involves touching the body but not the genitals. Third gear (playful touching) includes playful nongenital and genital touching. Fourth gear (erotic touching) includes manual and oral genital touching, rubbing, and vibrator stimulation. The fifth gear is intercourse. The model emphasizes savoring each of the five touching dimensions rather than rushing through the first four gears to reach the final gear.[2,10]

Kissing Typically, kissing is a person's earliest interpersonal sexual experience. Kissing is the most accepted of all sexual activities because it represents a romantic expression of affection as well as sexual desire. The lips and mouth are erotic parts of the human body. Touching, tasting, and smelling with the lips, mouth, and nose activate our unconscious memories and associations. Scientists conjecture that the testosterone in a male's saliva can stimulate female sex hormones.[10]

Both emotionally and practically, women and men tend to think about kissing differently. Women typically place more importance than men on kissing for beginning and sustaining a relationship. They are less likely than men to believe it is acceptable to kiss on the first date or that a woman should make the first move for a kiss. Women are more likely to say no to sex with someone whose kissing they don't like. In contrast, men may view kissing as a means to advance to oral sex or intercourse.[10] For some people, regardless of gender, kissing can make or break a relationship: 66 percent of women and 59 percent of men consider being a "bad kisser" as a new-relationship breaker.[10]

Self-Stimulation The two most common self-stimulation sexual activities, called **autoerotic behaviors**, are sexual fantasies and masturbation. Sexual fantasies are mental images, scenarios, and daydreams imagined to initiate sexual arousal. They range from simple images to complicated erotic stories. The fact that the body can become aroused when a person thinks about sex highlights the fact that the brain is a major player in sexual functioning. Fantasies are effective and harmless ways of exploring sexual fulfillment.

Masturbation is self-stimulation of the genitals for sexual pleasure. It is usually done manually or with a vibrator or other sex toy. The stigma attached to masturbation is left over from a previous era, when it was considered sinful and dangerous to one's health, probably because its purpose was pleasure rather than procreation. Today, masturbation is better understood and more widely accepted as a natural and healthy sexual behavior. One study found that the proportion of college students who say they masturbate has increased from 60 percent in 1990 to 98 percent for college men and 64 percent for college women today.[10] This increase is associated with the popularity of sex toy parties on college campuses.[20] Masturbation is a part of sex therapy programs designed to help people overcome sexual problems, and mutual masturbation is promoted as a way to practice safer sex.[21]

Mutual masturbation and other ways people use their fingers and hands are less risky for STI transmission than sex involving the exchange of body fluids. There are, however, still STI risks. The use of latex or nitrite gloves or finger cots reduce the transmission of bacteria and other pathogens that can be found on the skin or under the nails. Cutting nails or

■ The lips are a highly sensitive part of the body, making kissing an intimate act.
(Arlene Sandler/Purestock/SuperStock)

padding nails with cotton before putting on a glove can prevent making a hole in the glove. It is also a good idea to lubricate hands or gloves to prevent chafing or skin damage.[21]

Oral-Genital Stimulation **Cunnilingus** is oral stimulation of the female genitals with the tongue and lips. **Fellatio** is oral stimulation of the male genitals with the tongue, lips, and mouth. Oral stimulation can be part of foreplay, or it can be a sexual activity leading to orgasm. Some people find oral-genital stimulation very pleasurable; in fact, many women find that it is easier for them to reach orgasm through cunnilingus than through vaginal intercourse. Other people refrain from oral-genital stimulation because of religious or moral beliefs or simply because it makes them uncomfortable. Some women hesitate about cunnilingus because they are concerned about possible vaginal odors or their partner's enjoyment. A common concern with fellatio is whether to ejaculate into the partner's mouth. This is a matter of personal preference; the person receiving fellatio should respect the partner's feelings. Some men try autofellatio, oral stimulation to their own penis. This practice rarely leads to orgasm.[10]

Oral sex is not an entirely safe form of sex because infections can be transmitted via the mouth. Unprotected oral sex can transmit HIV, herpes, human papillomavirus (HPV), gonorrhea, chlamydia, syphilis, and hepatitis B. These STIs are discussed in depth in Chapter 13. Using some form of protection during oral sex is recommended. Dental dams and condoms are effective forms of protection; they are discussed later in the chapter. Condoms lubricated with nonoxynol-9 (N-9) are not safe for vaginal or oral sex. Semen should not be swallowed. HIV can be transmitted through small fissures in the throat. It is also recommended that the person giving oral stimulation rinse the mouth with hydrogen peroxide afterward.[22,23]

Anal Intercourse About 33 percent of college men and 24 percent of college women view anal sex, penetration of the rectum with the penis, as acceptable, though many college women report it to be uncomfortable and painful.[20] The anal area has a high density of nerve endings and is sensitive to stimulation. Because the skin and tissue of the anus and rectum are delicate and can be easily torn, anal intercourse is one of the riskiest sexual behaviors for the transmission of STIs, particularly HIV. Condom use is strongly recommended during anal intercourse. One study estimated the probability of HIV infection in a single unprotected act of receptive anal intercourse at 3.4 percent. The risk of contracting HIV through vaginal intercourse is much lower, less than 0.01 percent per act.[10]

A small percentage of heterosexual couples and a larger percentage of gay male couples practice anal intercourse. About 40 percent of people aged 15 to 44 have practiced anal intercourse, with higher rates among whites than among Hispanics or Blacks. It is also more prevalent among people with more education. In heterosexual anal penetration, the male is seen as masculine and the female as feminine. But in gay anal intercourse, both partners are seen as masculine.[2,10]

Anal eroticism also includes analingus, licking of the anal region. It is also called "rimming" or "tossing salad." The skin around the anus is very sensitive and stimulates sexual arousal. It is very important to keep the anal region clean since the intestine carries diverse microorganisms.

Penile-Vaginal Intercourse Penile-vaginal sexual intercourse, also known as coitus, is by far the most common form of adult sexual expression. It is a source of sexual pleasure for most couples. In sexual intercourse, a man typically inserts his erect penis into a woman's vagina and thrusts with his hips and pelvis until he ejaculates. A woman who is aroused responds with matching hip and pelvic thrusts, but she may or may not reach orgasm solely from penetration and thrusting, as mentioned earlier.

Sexual intercourse can be performed in a variety of positions. The most common is the so-called missionary position, in which the man lies on top of the woman. In this position, the penis can penetrate deeply into the vagina. When the woman lies on top of the man, penetration may not be as deep, but the woman has more control, an important psychological factor for some women. When the woman sits or kneels on top of the man, penetration is deeper and the woman can increase clitoral stimulation by rocking back and forth.[19]

In the rear-entry position, the woman lies face down and the man lies on top of her, or both lie on their sides. Although penetration is not as deep in this position, there is more opportunity for clitoral stimulation by either the woman or the man. Side-by-side positions are often preferred by sexual partners with significant weight differences, pregnant women, partners with chronic pain disorders like arthritis, and partners who do not enjoy deep thrusting.[12]

Atypical Sexual Behaviors and Paraphilias

The *DSM* view of atypical sexual behavior has changed over time. *DSM-1* classified sexual disorders as psychopathic personality disorder with engagement in unlawful (criminal) acts. *DSM-2* broadly defined sexual deviations as personality disorders or nonpsychotic mental disorders. Paraphilias were introduced in *DSM-3* as psychosexual disorders that included gender identity disorder, psychosexual dysfunctions, and ego-dystonic homosexuality. *DSM-4* maintained the diagnostic classification for paraphilia but changed transvestism from a gender identity disorder to a paraphilia condition called transvestic fetishism.

DSM-5 redefined paraphilia as "any intense and persistent sexual interest other than sexual interest in genital stimulation or preparatory fondling with phenotypically normal, physiologically mature consenting human partners."[24] *DSM-5* adds that paraphilia may be a preferential sexual interest. The classification of paraphilia as a disorder is new in *DSM-5,* which also changed the nomenclature to paraphilic disorder. "Disorder" was used to symbolize a condition causing significant distress or impairment that may lead to risk of personal

cunnilingus
Oral stimulation of the female genitals with the tongue and lips.

fellatio
Oral stimulation of the male genitals with the tongue, lips, and mouth.

harm or harm to others.[24] Hypersexuality and paraphilic coercive personality were new disorders included in *DSM-5*. For more details about paraphilia, consult *DSM-5,* https://www.psychiatry.org.

Whereas atypical sexual behaviors are practiced by consenting partners, paraphilias are practiced by an individual and often cause harm to others. Most paraphilias have victims and are illegal, and many are classified as mental disorders. For example, sexting with a partner is an atypical sexual behavior, but making obscene phone calls is a paraphilia. Other examples of atypical sexual behaviors are sex games in which partners enact sexual fantasies, use sex toys (vibrators, dildos), or engage in phone sex (talk about sex, describe erotic scenarios). Another kind of sex game is bondage and discipline, in which restriction of movement (such as by using handcuffs or ropes) or sensory deprivation (using blindfolds or masks) is used for sexual enjoyment. Most sex games are safe and harmless, but partners need to openly discuss and agree beforehand on what they are comfortable doing.[2,10]

Examples of paraphilias include exhibitionism (exposing the genitals to strangers), voyeurism (observing others' sexual activity without their knowledge), telephone scatologia (making obscene phone calls), sexual sadism/masochism (inflicting psychological or physical suffering), and pedophilia (sexual attraction to and activity with children). Treatment of individuals with these disorders typically focuses first on reducing the danger to them and their potential victims and then on strategies to suppress the behavior. Relapse prevention is essential because these behaviors are usually longstanding.[12] People who practice paraphilias may have personality disorders and substance abuse disorders.[10]

The high desire for frequency of sexual activity has sometimes been labeled sex addiction. **Nymphomania** is **hypersexuality** in women, and **satyriasis** refers to hypersexuality in men. Whether nymphomania and satyriasis should be classified as sex addiction is debated by mental health professionals. Although hypersexuality is sometimes labeled sex addiction, this classification is not accepted by the American Psychiatric Association. The challenging question is when excessive sexual behavior crosses into sex addiction.

Sex addiction is defined as compulsive, out-of-control sexual behavior that results in severe negative consequences. Sex addicts lose time every day to the isolating activities of fantasy and masturbation. They may spend so much time in sexual activities that it interferes with their job and other important parts of their lives. Other negative outcomes may include erectile difficulties and difficulty regulating sexual feelings. Although health care professionals frequently use the statistic that 6 percent of the U.S. population is sexually addicted, national representative samples report 0.8 percent of men and 0.6 percent of women have sexual behaviors that interfere with their daily lives. There is some controversy over whether sex addiction is a real phenomenon, but some addiction experts believe that sex addicts, like other types of addicts, experience changes in brain chemistry that affect what is found motivating and rewarding. The current version of the American Psychiatric Association's *Diagnostic and Statistical Manual of Mental Disorders* (*DSM-5*) does not include sex addiction, but it does list it as requiring more research.[25]

Some health care providers conceptualize addiction as having an impact in five domains: causing problems in everyday life functions, having a sense of lack of control, feeling bad about sexual use on the Internet, subjective feeling that lack of control has reached a point of porn addiction, and the sense that this addiction requires intervention by a health care professional.[25] If you think you might be at risk for sex addiction, talk to a mental health professional at your campus counseling center. You can also learn more about sex addiction at Elements Behavioral Health (www.sexualrecovery.com).

A related phenomenon is the compulsive avoidance of sex, dubbed *sexual anorexia* and described as the flip side of sex addiction. Named for its parallels with the eating disorder anorexia nervosa, sexual anorexia is characterized by an intense fear of sexual contact or intimacy, a preoccupation with sexual matters, rigid and judgmental attitudes toward sex, and shame and self-hatred over sex.[25] Those at risk for this disorder include people who have experienced past sexual abuse, sexual assault, or other sexual trauma; people who were raised in sexually repressive families; and people who are fearful of underlying homosexual tendencies. People who watch pornography compulsively may also be at risk for sexual anorexia because they are no longer able to respond sexually to a real partner. Sexual anorexia is not just a low sex drive; it is a physical, mental, and emotional condition that can benefit from professional help.[26]

SEXUAL DYSFUNCTIONS

At some point in their lives, many people experience some kind of **sexual dysfunction**—a disturbance in sexual drive, performance, or satisfaction. Up to 50 percent of couples report having experienced sexual dissatisfaction or dysfunction.[27] Sexual difficulties may occur at any point in the sexual response, although lack of sexual desire is cited as the most frequent problem in marital and long-term relationships.[28,29] Most forms of sexual dysfunction are treatable.

Female Sexual Dysfunctions

Common sexual dysfunctions in women include pain during intercourse, sexual desire disorder, female sexual interest/arousal disorder, and orgasmic dysfunction.

Pain During Intercourse Some women experience pain during intercourse as a result of **vaginismus**, intense

---

nymphomania
Hypersexuality in women.

hypersexuality
The act of displaying excessive sexual behavior.

satyriasis
Hypersexuality in men.

sexual dysfunction
A disturbance in sexual drive, performance, or satisfaction.

vaginismus
Intense involuntary contractions of the outer third of the muscles of the vagina that prevent penetration or make it uncomfortable.

involuntary contractions of the outer third of the muscles of the vagina that tighten the vaginal opening when penetration is attempted. The muscle spasm may range from mild (causing discomfort during intercourse) to severe (preventing intercourse altogether). Vaginismus may be caused by the physiological effects of a medical condition, such as a pelvic or vaginal infection; by psychological factors, such as fear of intercourse; or by lack of vaginal lubrication.

A physician may recommend **Kegel exercises**, the alternating contraction and relaxation of pelvic floor muscles, to relieve vaginismus. Vaginal infections include bacterial vaginosis and yeast infections. Vaginal infections are treated with antibiotics. These infections can be prevented by practicing good genital hygiene, avoiding douching and vaginal deodorants, wearing cotton rather than nylon underpants, wiping the anus from front to back (away from the vagina) after bowel movements, and using water-soluble vaginal lubricants instead of oil-based types (such as Vaseline) that facilitate bacterial growth.[10,29]

The *DSM-5* does not include dyspareunia, genital pain with sexual intercourse, as a urinary disorder or as a sexual dysfunction. In *DSM-IV-RE*, dyspareunia was collapsed with vaginismus into a single category called genitopelvic pain/penetration disorder. Four diagnostic criteria are applied: vaginal intercourse penetration, vaginal or pelvic intercourse pain or penetration attempt, anxiety about vaginal or pelvic pain, and tensing or tightening of the pelvic floor muscles during attempted vaginal penetration.[10]

Thirty percent of women report experiencing pain the last time they had vaginal intercourse, and 72 percent reported pain from anal intercourse. Most women do not inform their partner of experienced sexual pain. Some sexual psychologists believe women internalize pain or discomfort as simply due to being female. Digital porn serving as sex education for young men may lead them to pursue sexual acts like anal intercourse that are mainstream in digital porn but painful to their sexual partner. This behavior is referred to as "spectatoring," which is modeling sexual behaviors seen on the digital porn screen. Some men believe they can stimulate any partner to orgasm simply by pounding away even if it causes discomfort to their sexual partner. Erotic asphyxiation (choking) is another example. Getting sex education from hooking up perpetuates the problem.[30]

Nausea after sex is not normal and can be a symptom of potential health issues that deserve special attention. Cervical stimulation from sex can cause a vasovagal response that occurs when blood pressure and pulse rate drop. This response can result in nausea and even cause the woman to pass out. A woman's cervix changes throughout the menstrual cycle, dropping lower during a period, which makes it more vulnerable to a vasovagal response during penetration. Women with endometriosis or pelvic inflammatory disease may experience painful intercourse due to cervical infections and fibroids (benign tumors in the uterus's connective tissue). The bottom line: pain or nausea during or after sex is not normal and is a signal to contact your family health provider or gynecologist.[31]

■ Sexuality has physical, psychological, emotional, and interpersonal dimensions. Although sexual problems can have medical or physical causes, they often occur because of relationship problems.
(Radius Images/Alamy Stock Photo)

Sexual Desire Disorder Sexual desire disorder is characterized by lack of sexual fantasies and desire for sexual activity. Because individuals have different normal levels of sexual desire, this is considered a disorder only if a person is dissatisfied with his or her own or a partner's level of sexual desire. Low sexual desire can have physical causes, such as medications or hormonal changes, or it can be caused by psychological, emotional, and relationship problems.

Kegel exercises
Alternating contraction and relaxation of pelvic floor muscles, which can help relieve vaginismus, among other effects.

In contrast to sexual desire disorder, *sexual discrepancy* is a mismatch between the partners' levels of sexual desire, that is, between the desired and the actual frequency of sexual intercourse. Sexual discrepancy is associated with relationship dissatisfaction, poor quality of sexual experiences, and emotional discomfort and is more pronounced in long-term relationships. Most research on sexual discrepancy has been conducted on heterosexual individuals and heterosexual white couples. Limited research has addressed sexual discrepancy for same-sex couples and minority couples.[32]

Female Sexual Interest/Arousal Disorder The *DSM-5* combines hyposexual desire disorder and female sexual arousal disorder into one category called "female sexual interest/arousal disorder." This is the most common sexual dysfunction for women. It is characterized by an inability to attain or maintain the lubrication-swelling response of sexual arousal to the completion of sexual activity. The symptoms occur not because of insufficient or misplaced sexual stimulation, but because, as in sexual desire disorder, female sexual interest/arousal disorder is considered a problem only if the individual experiencing it considers it a problem. Most often female sexual interest/arousal disorder is associated with psychological stressors such as depression, interpersonal relationship problems, and stressful daily life events. Fatigue, chronic illness, substance abuse, and pain during intercourse are also factors.

The DSM uses six diagnostic symptoms for females sexual interest/arousal disorder. At least half of them must persist for at least 6 months and cause significant distress. Although lack of sexual pleasure is a common complaint, ignoring female sexual interest/arousal disorder can create significant strain in committed relationships.[10]

Orgasmic Dysfunction   Orgasmic dysfunction is defined as the persistent inability to have an orgasm following normal sexual arousal. Eighty-six percent of lesbian women, 66 percent bisexual women, and 65 percent of heterosexual women report they usually reach orgasm during intimate sexual activity. Between 25 and 35 percent of women report having had difficulty with orgasm on one or more occasions, and 10 to 15 percent of women report that they have never had an orgasm.[10,18] Some women can achieve orgasm through masturbation or oral sex but not with penile penetration. Although orgasm is not necessary for conception or enjoyment of sex, difficulty achieving it can become a frustrating experience.

Orgasmic dysfunction may be influenced by psychological and emotional factors, by lack of knowledge and experience, or by the person's beliefs and attitudes about sex.[10,18] Certain medications, including some antidepressants, also reduce the ability to reach orgasm. Therapy for orgasmic dysfunction focuses on encouraging women to experiment with their own bodies to discover what stimulates them to orgasm. They are then encouraged to transfer this learning to their sexual relationships.

Treatment of Female Sexual Dysfunctions   Much of what is known about the neurophysiology of sexual arousal, desire, and orgasm has come from research on men that has been applied to women.[18] But women's sexuality is different from men's and is much more complex than previously thought. Currently, there is a new interest in female sexuality on the part of scientists, sex therapists, and pharmaceutical companies, partly as a result of the success of Viagra in relieving men's sexual problems (described in the next section).[18]

One approach to treatment of sexual problems in women is testosterone replacement therapy. As noted earlier, testosterone is responsible for sex drive in both men and women. Sensibly prescribed, medically necessary testosterone can increase a woman's sex drive, but possible side effects include increased risk of heart disease and liver damage.[18] Viagra has been tried in women to treat low sexual desire, but results have been disappointing. A few studies suggest that Viagra combined with low doses of testosterone replacement may have good results. Despite setbacks, the drug market for treating female sexual dysfunction is likely to grow.[29]

The U.S. Food and Drug Administration (FDA) approved the prescription drug Addyi (flibanserin) in 2015 for treating low sexual desire in women. Whereas Viagra treats testosterone deficiencies and erection problems, Addyi changes the balance of neurotransmitters such as dopamine, norepinephrine, and serotonin to increase sexual desire. However, critics argue that Addyi is effective in only about 13 percent of women and has side effects such as low blood pressure, fainting, nausea, dizziness, and sleepiness, and the risk of these effects is increased by the use of alcohol. Unlike Viagra, Addyi is a long-term drug taken daily; peak effects occur after about 8 weeks of use.[33] Common sense suggests exploring other potential causes of low sexual arousal such as stress, physical and mental health, and use of other medications before taking FDA-approved Addyi. In 2019, the FDA approved Vyleesi as a second medication to treat hypoactive sexual desire disorder (HSDD). Vyleesi is injected into the thigh or abdomen 45 minutes before sex. The theory is Vyleesi stimulates the release of dopamine, which triggers a feeling of excitement. Although Addyi and Vyleesi were introduced as the female Viagra, they only work on a small percentage of women experiencing HSDD.[34,35]

Male Sexual Dysfunctions

Male sexual dysfunctions include pain during intercourse, sexual desire disorder, erectile dysfunction, and ejaculation dysfunction.

Pain During Intercourse   Penile pain usually results from infections from STIs. Herpes can cause painful lesions on the penis, and gonorrhea and chlamydia cause a penile discharge and pain with urination or ejaculation for most men. Peyronie's disease, an abnormal curvature of the penis, can also make intercourse painful. Infections of the prostate and epididymis also cause pain and should be treated.

Anodyspareunia is pain experienced by the recipient of anal penetration. Depth of penetration, lack of sufficient lubrication, and rate of thrusting are common causes. One study reported anodyspareunia and low sexual desire are the most common sexual dysfunction problems reported by gay men. Ten percent of heterosexual women who have two or more anal intercourse experiences in the past year reported severe pain. The inability to relax anal muscles is also a major cause of recipient pain during anal intercourse.[10]

Sexual Desire Disorder   Sexual desire disorders are frequently caused by emotional problems, including relationship difficulties, depression, guilt over infidelity, worry, stress, and overwork. Reduced sexual desire also can have some physical causes, such as changes in testosterone level.

Erectile Dysfunction   The inability to have or maintain an erection is classified as erectile disorder by the *DSM-5*. About 18 percent of men report erectile disorder problems.[10] In men with **erectile dysfunction (ED)**, smooth-muscle cells constrict the local arteries and reduce blood flow into the penis to a trickle, preventing a buildup of blood. The penis remains flaccid if the smooth-muscle cells are contracted.

anodyspareunia
Pain experienced by the recipient of anal penetration.

erectile dysfunction (ED)
A condition in which the penis does not become erect before sex or stay erect during sex.

The causes of ED (formerly called impotence) can be psychological, physical, or both. Fewer than 20 percent of ED cases have psychological causes.[21] Examples of such causes are anxiety about sexual performance, fatigue, stress, and problems in the relationship.[10]

Some of the physical causes of ED are low testosterone levels, medications (blood pressure medications, some antidepressants), drugs (alcohol, tobacco), injury, and nerve damage, such as from diabetes, multiple sclerosis, atherosclerosis, spinal cord injury, or prostate surgery. Obesity can also cause hormone changes associated with ED. Losing weight, avoiding alcohol, quitting smoking, and adopting a low-fat diet are recommended lifestyle changes to treat the disorder.[36]

Ejaculation Dysfunction

Premature ejaculation, defined as ejaculation less than 2 minutes after the beginning of intercourse, is probably the most common type of ejaculation dysfunction.[21] (Men typically average 2 to 7 minutes before ejaculation.) About one-third of sexually active men experience premature ejaculation; gay men have lower rates of premature ejaculation.[21,37] Like ED, premature ejaculation often results from anxiety about sexual performance or unreasonable expectations. For example, a man might be worried about maintaining an erection and rush to a climax.[18]

An effective technique for preventing premature ejaculation is to stop before orgasm, slow down, and then start again. The stop-start method trains the body to lengthen the duration of the sexual arousal state and can increase enjoyment.

A delay in ejaculation or inability to ejaculate when stimulated is classified by *DSM-5* as delayed ejaculation. Delayed ejaculation must occur 75 to 100 percent of the time to be classified as a sexual disorder. Age-related changes in the peripheral nervous system, chronic diseases, medications, and stress are primary causes of delayed ejaculation.[10] Delayed ejaculation and orgasm are distinct events. A man who has delayed or no ejaculation may still experience a whole-body orgasm.

Treatment of Male Sexual Dysfunction

Treatment of sexual dysfunction in men often relies on testosterone. Men with a low testosterone level may benefit from testosterone replacement therapy. It is not prescribed for men with normal testosterone levels because it can increase blood pressure, affect blood cholesterol levels, and possibly increase the risk of prostate cancer.[21,37]

Several drugs are now on the market for the treatment of ED. They work by increasing the concentration of the chemical that allows smooth-muscle cells in the erectile tissue to stay relaxed so that the spongy chambers of the penis can remain filled with blood. Viagra (sildenafil) is taken an hour before sex and lasts about 4 hours. Use of Viagra is dangerous for men with health conditions such as heart disease, high blood pressure, and diabetes; fatalities have been reported in connection with its use. Sildenafil can interact with nitrates found in some prescription drugs, especially nitroglycerin drugs, which are commonly prescribed for diabetes, high blood pressure, or high cholesterol. The interaction of sildenafil with nitrates can lower blood pressure to dangerous levels. Levitra (vardenafil) and Cialis

(tadalafil) are chemically similar to Viagra, but they work more quickly, last longer, and have fewer side effects. The FDA advises consumers not to use a product known as Herb Viagra because it contains sildenafil.[38]

Trimix is a new drug injected on either side of the penis (but not the base) to treat erectile dysfunction. It is a potent medication. Papaverine is an ingredient in Trimix that acts to relax and dilate penile blood vessels. Prostaglandin is also an ingredient; this increases blood flow into the penis and provides resistance to venous blood outflow so that blood remains in the penis. The initial injection is a low dose in order to avoid a prolonged erection and is taken a few minutes before foreplay. The erection typically lasts 5 to 20 minutes. Two to four pseudoephedrine pills are administered if the erection lasts more than 2 hours. If an erection continues for another hour after taking the pills, the man should seek immediate medical attention. Not all patients have an erection outcome from Trimix.[38,39]

Drug approaches to sexual dysfunctions do not take into account the importance of relationships. ED drugs may offer a temporary confidence-builder, but they do not provide a long-term solution to issues that may lie behind sexual problems. Correcting unhealthy lifestyles, working on relationships, and cultivating a more realistic expectation of aging can improve mid- and late-life sexuality.

Homeopathic products advertised as natural sexual enhancers that promise long-lasting, "rock hard" erections do not work. These products are not regulated by the FDA.

A new product is a condom containing a gel that helps men maintain a firmer erection.[40] The gel is a vasodilator absorbed through the skin to increase blood flow. This condom is intended for men who struggle to maintain an erection specifically while wearing a condom; it is not being marketed for treatment of ED.

PROTECTING YOUR SEXUAL HEALTH

Safer sex practices prevent the exchange of body fluids during sex. Two safer sex practices are using condoms and "outercourse," or sex acts such as kissing and rubbing or stroking that do not involve genital contact or penetration. (However, herpes and HPV can be transmitted by any skin-to-skin contact.) Another key to safeguarding your sexual health is communicating with your partner or prospective partner about sex. The only 100 percent protection against pregnancy and STIs is abstinence; the abstinence movement on campuses is discussed in the next section of this chapter.

Using Condoms

The **condom** (or *male condom*) is a thin sheath, usually made of latex, that fits over the erect penis during sexual intercourse. It

safer sex
Sexual activities that do not include exchange of body fluids.

condom
A thin sheath, usually made of latex, that fits over the erect penis during sexual intercourse to prevent conception and protect against sexually transmitted infections.

Action Skill-Builder

Learn How to Use a Condom

It's possible to put on a male condom or insert a female condom in 10 seconds or less if you are prepared. (Consider practicing so that you can do it with ease in the heat of the moment and possibly in the dark.) Remember, to reduce risk of pregnancy and STI transmission, a condom must be in place prior to any contact between genital areas.

Male Condom

1. Open the condom package, being careful not to tear the condom.

2. Place the rolled condom over the head of the erect penis (or you can use a banana to practice). If you or your partner have foreskin, gently retract it prior to putting on the condom.

3. Pinch the reservoir tip to remove air and leave 0.5 inch of the condom as a space for semen.

4. Unroll the condom in a downward direction, smoothing out any air bubbles.

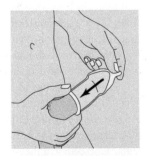

5. Once the condom is unrolled and secure at the base of the penis, you may apply a water-based lubricant, if desired, at any time. K-Y Jelly and Astroglide are two popular options.

6. After ejaculation, hold the condom around the base of the penis until the penis has been completely withdrawn to avoid any leakage of semen.

7. Gently pull the condom off while still holding at the bottom edge to reduce the risk of spilling semen.

Female Condom

1. Open the condom package, being careful not to tear the condom.

2. If desired, apply a water-based lubricant at the closed end of the condom.

3. Find a position that is comfortable for you (squatting, on your back, sitting).

4. Pinch the smaller ring at the closed end of the condom and flex it gently to fit into the vaginal canal and push it as far up as you can. When the condom is in place, the smaller ring covers the cervix and the larger ring remains outside the vagina.

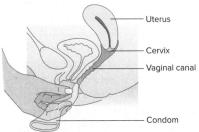

5. After ejaculation, remove the condom by squeezing and twisting the outer ring so that it stays closed and the semen is contained.

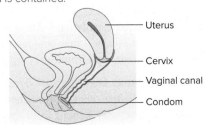

6. Pull the condom out of your vagina.

Disposing of a Used Condom

Wrap it in toilet paper or tissue and discard it in a trash bin. Do not flush it down the toilet; this will clog the sewage system.

---

female condom
A soft pouch of thin polyurethane that is inserted into the vagina before intercourse to prevent conception and protect against sexually transmitted infections.

provides a barrier against penile, vaginal, or anal discharges and genital lesions or sores. Although condoms do not provide complete protection against all STIs or unplanned pregnancies, they greatly reduce the risk when used correctly (see the box "Action Skill-Builder: Learn How to Use a Condom"). The slippage and breakage

rate during intercourse ranges from 1.6 to 3.6 percent,[41] and STIs can occur in skin areas not covered by the condom. The risk for breakage is much higher during anal sex.

Protection against STIs is also offered by the **female condom**, a soft pouch of thin polyurethane that is inserted into the vagina before intercourse. Since polyurethane is somewhat expensive, a newer female condom called FC2 is made of nitrile. Female condoms made of latex are also being developed (such as Reddy and Cupid). Polyurethane and nitrile are stronger than latex and

Consumer Clipboard
Purchasing Condoms

Condoms are an accessible, inexpensive, easy-to-carry, over-the-counter method of contraception, but the choices can be overwhelming. Here are some things to consider before you buy.

Check the expiration date.
If stored properly, condoms may last four to five years. To protect them from deterioration, store in a cool, dark place.

Choose a shape.
Most condoms have a reservoir tip, which helps contain semen. Beyond that, different shapes are designed to meet different personal preferences. For simple protection, a traditional condom with straight sides does the trick. Form-fitted models hug the tip of the penis so that they stay in place. Contours, flares, or bulbs around the head of the condom leave extra room and can feel more natural for the wearer, especially if he is uncircumcised. Ribs or studs along the shaft of the condom are generally intended to create pleasurable friction for women, but they can enhance both partners' pleasure.

Decide about spermicide.
Nonoxynol-9 is the most commonly used spermicide in condoms. As noted, spermicides degrade latex, increasing the risk of transmission of HIV and other STIs.

Consider the country of origin.
Condoms made in the United States require the FDA approval. Those manufactured anywhere else should contain approval marks from the country in which they were made.

Think about thickness.
Condoms made of thinner material are less noticeable during sex and, if used correctly, are just as effective as standard thickness condoms. Anal intercourse puts extra strain on a condom; standard condoms are effective for preventing STIs during anal sex if used properly, but use thicker ones for extra peace of mind.

(Mark Dierker/McGraw-Hill)

Find the right size.
Too small, and a condom is uncomfortable. Too big, and it slips off during sex. There are no standard condom sizes, and brands vary in length and width. Try a few different brands to find the right fit. Manufacturers' websites may offer some specific guidelines to get you started.

Want lubrication, or not?
Either is safe, but a little extra moisture might be a lot more comfortable for you or your partner. Condoms lubricated with a spermicide such as nonoxynol-9 (N-9) are not recommended because it can irritate tissues and increase the risk of HIV transmission.

Pick a material.
Latex is the most common material and the only one proven to reduce risk of sexually transmitted infections. Polyurethane condoms reduce risk of pregnancy for those with latex allergies, but their effectiveness in reducing the risk of STIs is still unproven. Natural membrane condoms reduce only the risk of pregnancy but not the risk of STIs.

---

are less likely than the male condom to break. They can also be used with both water- and oil-based lubricants.[10]

The female condom has a soft flexible ring at both ends. The ring at the closed end is fitted against the cervix, and the ring at the open end remains outside the body. The female condom covers more of the genital area, so it may provide more protection against an STI lesion or sore than the male condom does. It is not known whether the female condom used for anal sex effectively prevents STIs and HIV. Spermicidal foam can be used with both male and female condoms to kill some infectious agents, including HIV, herpes, gonorrhea, and chlamydia.

Most spermicides contain nonoxynol-9 (N-9) or octoxynol-9 (O-9). High doses or frequent use of spermicides can damage the vagina's skin cells and inflame the vagina and cervix. This damage makes a woman more vulnerable to STIs and makes it easier for her to transmit STIs to her sexual partner. To avoid these problems, use nonlubricated condoms with a water-based or silicone-based lubricant, or use nonspermicide condoms. Do not use oil-based lubes (petroleum jelly, mineral oil, body lotions, massage oil). You should

put the condom on first and then administer the water-based or silicone-based lube. The lube should continue to be applied as needed.[42] For oral sex, do not use N-9 or O-9 condoms. They have an unpleasant taste and will cause your tongue to go numb if kept in the mouth for a long time.

There are many types of novelty condoms on the market. They include glow-in-the-dark condoms, flavored condoms, studded condoms, warming condoms, edible condoms, colored condoms, QuikStrip condoms, French ticklers, tingling condoms, and "green" condoms for the environmentally savvy. It is important to read the label of novelty condoms to see whether they are approved by the FDA for preventing STIs and pregnancy; condoms manufactured outside the United States should contain approval marks from the country in which they were made. Some flavored condoms contain lubricants with sugar that disrupt normal yeast levels in the vagina, which increases the risk for infection.[43] Avoid oil-based food products as oral sex aids when using a latex condom because oil will quickly degrade the latex (see the box "Consumer Clipboard: Purchasing Condoms").

⚠ Who's at Risk?

Sexual Activity and Condom Use Among College Students

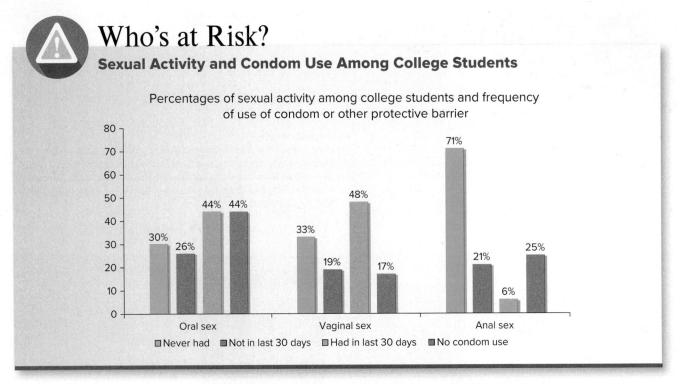

Percentages of sexual activity among college students and frequency of use of condom or other protective barrier

Source: American College Health Association. (2018). *National college health assessment survey, 2018*. Retrieved from www.acha-ncha.org/docs/ACHA-NCHA-II_ReferenceGroup_ExecutiveSummary_Spring2018.pdf

dental dams
Small latex squares placed over the vulva during oral sex.

Pre-exposure prophylaxis (PrEP) has been receiving attention as an effective way to reduce HIV infection in men and women. PrEP pills are used for HIV-negative people who are at high risk of HIV infection and are willing to take a pill every day. The most effective prevention, however, is the use of PrEP in combination with condoms and a reduced number of sexual partners.[32]

Many people believe only males resist using condoms. However, women may be reluctant to have their sexual partner use a condom because they have an allergy to latex (a rubber made from plant protein) or sensitivity to N-9, or because there is not enough lubricant. If more lubricant would make sex more comfortable, use a nonlubricated condom and apply a water-based or silicone-based lubricant that does not contain N-9. If latex allergy is a problem, try condoms made of nonlatex materials or even different brands of latex condoms.

One alternative is polyurethane condoms, which are made from a type of latex-free plastic and can be used with oil-based lubricants. However, polyurethane condoms are more expensive than latex condoms and may more easily slip off. The effectiveness of these condoms for preventing STIs is still being studied. They should be considered only as a substitute for individuals with latex allergies. A third choice is polyisoprene condoms, called SKYN; these are made from synthetic rubber and have no plant proteins. They are as strong and safe as conventional latex condoms. They are more stretchy than polyurethane condoms and thus have lower breakage and slippage rates. The FDA has approved polyisoprene condoms for preventing pregnancy and STIs. Lambskin condoms are a fourth alternative, and people like the feel of them. These condoms are effective for preventing pregnancy but not STIs.[10,43,44,45]

Condoms and **dental dams** (small latex squares placed over the vulva) should be used during oral sex because bacteria and viruses can be transmitted in semen and vaginal fluids. Plastic wrap placed over the vulva, or a piece of latex cut from a latex glove, is an alternative to a dental dam. Protection is especially important if there are any cuts or sores in the mouth; even bleeding gums can increase the risk of getting an STI.

A New Generation of Condoms

The fight against STIs began in the 16th century with the development of the male condom. The primary advances in condom technology have been the change from linen and lamb intestine to latex and the inclusion of a reservoir tip. Novelty condoms have tinkered with colors, textures, flavorings, and anti-ejaculation chemicals.[44] But still many people do not like to use condoms.

Fifty percent of men who have sex with men do not use condoms. The nonuse of condoms is a major contributor to increased HIV infections among gay men. College students' low use of condoms is also troublesome. Studies indicate that students are more likely to have unprotected sex as they progress from freshmen to seniors. In fact, seniors are 2.5 times more likely to have unprotected casual sex than freshmen.[45] Condom use drops most sharply between freshman and sophomore years. College students from affluent communities are less likely to use condoms than those from poor communities. The American College Heath Association surveyed college students in 2018 and found that the use of condoms and other barrier devices varied by type of sexual contact. For details, see the box "Who's at Risk? Sexual Activity and Condom Use Among College Students."

The i.Con Smart condom is not a condom. A ring worn at the base of the penis, it is actually a smart device that collects performance data and is connected to your smartphone. Performance data collected include calories burned during sexual intercourse, thrust speed, total number of thrusts, total sexual session duration, average thrust velocity, girth measurement, and average skin temperature. The i.Con will eventually include different sexual positions used. Sensors include LED lighting, Bluetooth, and a USB port for charging. The i.Con was designed to fit over the condom to prevent slippage. It is waterproof, and its purple light can be used to detect chlamydia and gonorrhea. The i.Con is a wearable accessory and not a prophylactic. There is concern that it may be inappropriately used for rough sex in an attempt to set thrust records. Although some sex experts consider the i.Con to be of dubious value, it has generated discussion of sexual pleasure and safe sex. The analytic device is expensive, costing about $100.[46]

Condom Accessibility on College Campuses

Eighty-seven percent of college students report having had intercourse. Women lose their virginity by age 16 on average and men by age 17.[20] As the box "Who's at Risk? Sexual Activity and Condom Use Among College Students" shows, only about half of college students engaging in vaginal sex use a condom. Condom dispensers provide a low-cost, high-impact way to distribute free condoms on college campuses as well as in bars, restaurants, and health clinics. Large dispensers can hold about 800 condoms. The condoms are made of high-quality thermoplastic material.[45,47] Organizations providing condom dispensers often attach safer-sex messages, such as information about how to get tested for STIs. The use of free condom dispensers has not been met with enthusiasm on all college campuses, however.

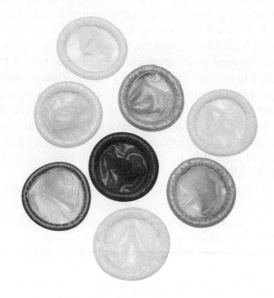

(Photodisc Collection/Getty Images)

Communicating About Sex

Sixty-seven percent of college men and women say they have not changed their sexual behaviors in response to the risk of HIV/AIDS. Some view the HIV/AIDS epidemic as a distant memory and no longer a major threat. Other college students claim they have long practiced safe sex and do not need to worry about HIV/AIDS. These attitudes affect whether college students actively communicate with their sexual partners about past sexual activity. Consider the following: 81 percent of college students ask their partners how many sexual partners they have had in the past, and college students are less likely today to guess whether their sexual partner might be HIV positive than in 1990, but they are also less likely to take safer sex precautions if they feel their partner is "not the type" to be infected by HIV/AIDS.[20]

Conversations about sexual topics are important to your health, your partner's health, and the success of your relationship. If you are about to begin a sexual relationship, take the time to tell your partner your sexual health history and find out about his or hers. Here are some questions to guide your conversation:

- Are you having sex with anyone else? Are you willing to be monogamous with me?

- Have you ever had an STI? If so, how long ago, and what treatment did you get? Do you now have a clean bill of health?

- How many sexual partners have you had? As far as you know, did any of them ever have an STI?

- When was the last time you were tested for STIs? Would you be willing to get tested along with me?

- Are you willing to use condoms every time we have sex?

The last question implies no sexual activity unless the partner agrees to use a condom. If you are not satisfied with the answers you get, take care of yourself by insisting on further conversations and behavioral changes before you begin a sexual relationship.

SEX AND CULTURE: ISSUES FOR THE 21ST CENTURY

Many societal issues involving sex are as old as civilization itself, such as prostitution. We also face new issues such as hooking up, sexting, stealthing, revenge porn, and digital pornography.

Hooking Up

A major trend on college campuses is the decline of traditional dating and the rise of the "hook-up" culture that is devoid of emotional intimacy and romance. A *hook-up* is defined as a casual sexual contact between nondating partners without expectation of forming a committed relationship.[48] About one-third of college students abstain from hooking up, one-third are described as dabblers who occasionally hook up, and one-third engage in *serial hook-ups* by hooking up with the same person multiple times over several months, even years.[30] In a hook-up culture, students rarely go on formal dates. Instead, they frequent parties or bars in large groups, consume alcohol and/or drugs, and hook up with casual friends or strangers. It is estimated that between 66 and 80 percent of college students hook up at some point during their college careers. Hookups are most likely to occur between the second semester of freshman year and the fall semester of the sophomore year.[10,48]

Men like hook-ups more than women do. One study found that 26 percent of women reported a positive reaction after hooking up, 49 percent had a negative reaction, and 25 percent were ambivalent. In contrast, 50 percent of men reported a positive reaction, 26 percent a negative reaction, and 24 percent an ambivalent reaction.[49,50] Black college students are less likely than white students to participate in hook-ups. As the statistics also show, many college women and men do not enjoy the hook-up experience and view hook-ups as emotionless sex, perfunctory, and promoting nonpleasurable sex, drunken sex, and coercive sex.[10]

Role-playing on the college party circuit has fueled the hook-up culture. Many party themes center on pornography and prostitution, starting with "Pimps and Hos"; variations have included "Politicians and Prostitutes," "Santa and His Reindeer Ho, Ho, Hos," and "Superheroes and Supersluts." Party scenarios generally call for women to show up in skimpy dress and "wasted" from alcohol. Among college students, 31 percent of women and 28 percent of men say they would not have hooked up if they had not been drinking alcohol. Obtaining sexual benefits from hook-ups appears to be one of the primary benefits to getting drunk.[51] In the "porn party" scenarios, men have roles of power and women have submissive ones. Theme parties give participants an excuse not to feel responsible for the outcomes of their sexual behavior.[2,10]

Student entrepreneurs have also created hook-up websites where students can post anonymously. Those who frequent such sites often say they do not have time for relationship commitments. They think of college as a temporary place for fun and career preparation. The lack of relationships generated by a hook-up culture has been described as "social stunting." This is a self-cyclical process; hook-ups occur because of poor social skills, and social skills go undeveloped because of the hook-up culture.[52]

The downside of the hook-up culture has been significant increases in STIs and emotional and mental health issues, including sexual regret, negative or ambivalent emotional reactions, psychological distress, depression, and anxiety.[52] Women tend to suffer from these consequences more than men do. Perhaps the costliest consequence of hook-up culture is failure to develop the qualities essential for healthy long-term relationships—trust, respect, admiration, honesty, caring, and communication.[48,53] The Personal Health Portfolio activity at the end of this chapter addresses key issues in communication. Many college students prefer sexual pleasure hook-ups that are not entangled by romantic relationships.

Dating Apps

Examples of dating apps include Bumble, Match, OK Cupid, Tinder, Match.com, Friendsy, Zoosk, Coffee Meets Bagel, and Grindr. Grindr is a dating site for gays. College Singles Club uses a connection website for college student singles to find other singles and socialize at diverse college events.

Are these apps useful? The average user of dating apps logs in 11 times each day. Men spend about 7.2 minutes logged in per session and women about 8.5 minutes. One dating app company reported 1.6 billion swipes every day but only 26 million matches. Some dating apps use assortative matching algorithms to match users by desirability characteristics (e.g., physical attractiveness, leisure interests). Companies' claims that they lead to more successful outcomes than traditional ways of finding relationship partners have not been supported by empirical evidence. The vast majority of matches do not result in a two-way text exchange and date. Physically attractive users, especially women, are much more likely to be swiped and messaged. In other words, dating apps appear to be a waste of time for most users. They may also be dangerous. See box, "Action Skill-Builder: Dangers of Online Dating and Ways to Protect Yourself."[30]

If dating apps are a waste of time and potentially dangerous, why do young adults continue to use them? Perhaps the dating landscape has changed. Young adults are less likely to engage other adults in public. Today's romantic relationships may be more segregated from daily life activities. This segregation may be accelerating as public attention is captivated by the problems of sexual assault and sexual harassment. One national poll found that 17 percent of U.S. adults aged 18 to 29 believe a man asking a new acquaintance out for a drink is a form of sexual harassment. The #Me Too movement has made college students, especially men, much more aware of social and legal issues involving affirmative consent. (Affirmative consent is discussed in Chapter 16.) College men are reexamining their past sexual experiences and actions, and as a result some are avoiding romantic overtures for fear they may be considered unwelcome advances. The bottom line is that online dating apps may make it more difficult to make romantic advances in person without being viewed as inappropriate.[30]

Dating apps have also become a diversion that some college students see as "gamified" interactions. They likely have very low expectations of actually meeting up with an app contact in person. The multiple choices to swipe on dating apps have caused choice overload and option paralysis (fear of a better option).

Despite these problems, online dating apps remain popular. The underlying belief is that they are less stressful since

Action Skill-Builder

Dangers of Online Dating and Ways to Protect Yourself

Usage of dating apps by 18- to 24-year-olds has tripled in the past few years. Dating app sites are likely more dangerous than the traditional way of meeting people and establishing relationships. The risks in meeting strangers include rape, sex trafficking, and attempted murder. Consider the following statistics:

☐ 10 percent of sex offenders use online dating sites.

☐ 10 percent of online dating profiles are false.

☐ Every year, 16,000 abductions, 100 murders, and thousands of sexual assault are committed by online predators.

☐ 53 percent of online dating profiles contain exaggerated data (age, income, weight, height).

☐ 62 percent of users lie about their current relationships (11 percent are already married).

☐ 33 percent of women report having sex on their first date with someone they met online, and 80 percent do not use safe-sex protection.

There are thousands of dating app sites. Choose trusted sites by consulting your friends and family members, and look for sites that provide evidence of their success and have positive ratings in media outlets such as *Forbes*. Read reviews by past and present users. Research your matches by running their names through your state's sex offender registry, and Google-search them. Video chat with a potential date before meeting in person.

You should never provide your personal information such as home address, phone number, and place of work until you have established a comfortable relationship. Be aware of financial scams. Requests for money, social security number, and credit card information are red flags. Use the dating apps feature that blocks abusive users if you are being harassed. Report suspicious activity to the site's customer service staff. Finally, consult Rape Abuse & Incest National Network's (RAINN) dating app safety tips, https://www.rainn.org/new-graphics-online-dating-and-dating-app-safety.

Source: Mayer, B. (2017). The dangers of online dating (7 statistics & 5 ways to protect yourself). Dating Advice. https://www.datingadvice.com/online-dating/dangers-of-online-dating.

they do not entail the potential embarrassment of face-to-face interactions. They are especially popular in what economists call "thin markets," markets with a low number of participants. For example, unpartnered gay men and unpartnered lesbians use dating apps at much higher rates than unpartnered heterosexuals. They also have more active dating lives than heterosexuals. This differentce may result from successful use of online dating app services.[30]

The Sex Recession

Jean Twenge, in his book *iGen*, claims that in the period from 1991 to 2017 teenagers and young adults have been having less sex. The percent of high school students who regularly have sex has dropped from 54 to 40 percent. Although there has been a significant drop in teenage pregnancy, this change may be signalling a more general withdrawal in physical intimacy that extends into the young adulthood years. Young adults are likely to have fewer sexual partners than the two preceding generations.[54]

Some sex researchers disagree with Twenge's assessment. Every generation is influenced by the social, economic, and political events that shape culture. Generation Z is no different and is the first generation to be saturated with social media technology. Labeling a generation tends to establish stereotypes, but members of Generation Z will continue to be shaped by the cultural events they experience as they move from early to late adulthood. Sex educators who agree with Twenge about the "sex recession" fault the hook-up culture, economic pressure, surges in emotional and psychological problems, declining testosterone levels, streaming television, leaked environmental estrogen from plastic, dating apps, digital porn, sleep deprivation, obesity trends, careerism, and even smartphones. The sex recession is not unique to the United States; many Western industrialized nations are experiencing the same trend.[30,54]

Although there are legitimate reasons for changes in sex frequency and satisfaction, physical intimacy is important in a long-term relationship. Orgasm releases the "feel good" hormone oxytocin that maintains overall relationship bonding. So, what is maintenance sex? Maintenance sex is making sex a priority by engaging in it even when not in the mood. Most couples do not have the same sex drives. Compatible couples find a way to meet each other's sex drive.[55]

Stealthing: Is It a Criminal Act?

Although the prevalence of *stealthing* is not known, health professionals claim it has become a disturbing trend. It is defined as the intentional removal of the condom during sex without the consent of the sexual partner. Stealthing is an increasing trend in both heterosexual and gay male relationships. Underlying it is often misogyny and one partner's feeling of being superior to the sexual partner. The law has been largely silent on stealthing, but law enforcement and state legislatures are exploring potential criminal and civil remedies for its victims. New York, Wisconsin, and California introduced state bills to criminalize stealthing as sexual assault even if the victim did not get pregnant or contract an STI; see the box "Life Stories: Sophia: A Victim of Stealthing." Stealthing was added to the Title IX handbook. College students who are victims of stealthing should consult "Know Your Title IX Rights," which is provided by the U.S. Department of Education, https://www.knowyourix.org/college-resources/title-ix/.[56]

Life Stories

Sophia: A Victim of Stealthing

Sophia was aware of stealthing but never thought she would be one of its victims. She was in a 3-month-old relationship with Aaron when he requested that their relationship become more intimate by including sexual activity. Sophia consented to include intercourse in their relationship but insisted that Aaron always wear a condom. She was very concerned about becoming pregnant or acquiring an STI. Sophia and Aaron also had a thorough discussion of their sexual histories and STIs. In this frank conversation, Sophia explained she was sexually inexperienced, did not use illicit drugs, and had no STIs. Aaron revealed he had had many sexual partners, used cocaine and marijuana, had chlamydia a year earlier, and currently had genital herpes in an inactive stage. Aaron agreed to Sophia's demand that a condom always be worn during intercourse.

Aaron used a condom the first time he had intercourse with Sophia. However, the second time, he slipped it off during the middle of sex. Sophia was not aware that Aaron was not using a condom until he ejaculated inside her. She was shocked and told Aaron that he had disrespected her and broken their agreement on condom use. Aaron tried to explain that the condom had likely broken during sex. Sophia knew he was lying and broke off their relationship. Traumatized at having been a stealthing victim, she went to her university's student health center the next day to receive post-exposure prophylaxis to protect against pregnancy and HIV. She knew the prophylaxis had to be taken within 72 hours of exposure, preferably sooner rather than later. The prophylaxis is effective but not a 100 percent guarantee.

Sophia googled *stealthing* to learn more about this phenomenon. She was shocked by what she read. Websites and blogs were filled with suggestions for how men could trick women into not realizing they had slipped a condom off during sex. Posters commented that women who became pregnant or acquired an STI during condom-less sex got what they deserved, since that is the "price" of having pleasurable sex. Some men claimed it was their natural right to spread their "seed" in this way.

Sophia wondered whether stealthing is sexual assault. After all, she never gave consent for sex without a condom. Through her research, she learned that law enforcement, state legislatures, and the judicial system had essentially marginalized stealthing. Even where a judicial system had criminalized it, stealthing was seen as a misdemeanor and not a felony. Civil courts were reluctant to hear stealthing cases because it was generally seen as a clouded issue in which it was difficult to determine whether consent was given or not.

There is no question that victims of stealthing are traumatized and suffer physically, emotionally, and financially. What do you think?

- Should stealthing be seen as criminal and civil sexual assault? If it is criminalized, will it have a chilling effect on sexual relationships?

- Should colleges and universities suspend students who commit stealthing sexual acts? Is stealthing a problem on your campus?

Sexting

About 80 percent of college students engage in *sexting*—sending nude, sexually explicit text, photo, or video messages electronically, mostly by cell phone.[10] More than 50 percent of college students have received graphic sexual text messages. About 10 percent of such texts are forwarded to friends without the consent of the original sender.[57] Although sexting between adults is legal, distributing images without the subject's knowledge can cause embarrassment, humiliation, and may be seen as harassment.[58,59] Anthony Weiner's infamous sexting tweets destroyed his campaign for mayor of New York City and resulted in a criminal conviction carrying a 17-month jail sentence for texting a "dick pic" to a teenager. Jilted exes have been known to release explicit photos and videos in what is called "revenge porn," a phenomenon discussed later in this chapter. Some college students are making money by creating sexting websites and serving as "chat hosts" for sexting activity.[60]

College students who engage in sexting may think they are more tech savvy than older people. But this belief gives them a false sense of security if they do not fully consider the real-life consequences if their phones are misplaced, stolen, or hacked. Nor do they consider that images leave a digital footprint that can last for years, potentially damaging prospects for future relationships and careers.

Using a smartphone to text unsolicited "dick pics" may be seen as exhibitionism and illegal. Most states have enacted indecent exposure laws that make displaying the genitals in public a crime. Moreover, sending unsolicited "dick pics" is increasingly viewed as virtual sexual assault (sexual harassment). Ex-Olympic star Shaun White was sued for alleged graphic sexual harassment. If the recipient is underage, the sender may be in violation of state child pornography laws. #stopthedicks is a social media campaign that educates perpetrators and victims that "dick pics" are now subject to state laws governing sexual assault. Any unsolicited sexual pictures sent to another person may be seen as a form of virtual sexual harassment.[61]

Internet Pornography

Although pornography has always existed, the Internet has vastly increased its availability. According to one report, one in four Internet users looks at a pornography website in any given month, and 66 percent of men aged 18 to 34 do so every month. Among college-age students, 87 percent of men and 31 percent of women reported using pornography sites in the last year.[10] So-called femme porn, for women, usually has more of a story line and includes erotic fantasies and emotional intimacy.[10] In contrast, however, the vast majority of Internet pornography has become increasingly explicit and violent.

Many people defend the right of adults to choose what they want to view on the Internet without restriction or censorship, and the courts have upheld their constitutional right to do so. Some sexual health experts argue that Internet pornography reduces health-risk behaviors by managing sex drive effectively and safely.[62] However, there are concerns about possible harmful consequences of Internet pornography. The compulsive Internet pornography user has high frequency of use, more secret usage, and more serious negative health outcomes.[63,64,65]

Viewing pornography also seems to have negative effects on relationships (see box, "Public Health Is Personal: Cybersex: A Hidden Public Health Issue"). *Internet infidelity* occurs when someone forms an emotional or physical relationship on the Internet that a partner views as a breach of their relationship intimacy contract. One anti-porn activist cites "procrasturbation," the act of putting off something important by engaging in masturbation, as a behavior that leads young men to fail sexually, academically, and socially. Anti-porn activists also claim that masturbating to digital porn is addictive because it causes structural changes in the brain that lead to erectile dysfunction. Empirical evidence does not support this claim, but the mental health community is divided on the addictive nature of digital porn.[30]

There is also debate about whether pornography promotes violence against women and sexual exploitation of children. Some social scientists have suggested that exposure to depictions of sexual violence and exploitation can increase criminal behavior, especially in men with psychological problems or other vulnerabilities. Although a direct relationship has not been established between pornography and sexual violence, studies do show that viewing pornography negatively affects viewers' attitudes, feelings, and behaviors as well as their sense of sexual norms.[62,63,64]

Some heterosexual women believe digital porn encourages disturbing fictional sexual habits. Hentai, rated the second-most popular digital porn site in 2018-2019, is an animated porn site that teases out erotic human shapes by supersizing breasts and penises. These shapes represent hallucinatory sex pictures that are not real. It is no wonder some women are disturbed by the possibility of fictional sex habits generated from digital porn.[30]

The gap between men's and women's use of cybersex is quickly eroding, and women are now engaging in cybersex at almost the same rate as men. Gay and bisexual men use cybersex more than heterosexual men. Male-centered digital pornography tends not to focus on relationships, emotional intimacy, or a woman's sexual satisfaction. As women have increased their consumption of digital pornography, there has been more attention on *femme porn,* where story lines focus on sexual equality, emotional intimacy, and consent,

with less or no aggression or violence and more attention to erotic fantasies. Moreover, femme porn focuses more on diversity of age, ethnicity, sexual orientation, and body types.[10]

The compulsive use of cybersex by college students has raised the question whether it is a form of sex addiction. Sex addiction is a broad term that generally refers to a dependence on sex that persists even when it harmful to the individual, the family, and other core aspects of life. Compulsion, in contrast, is an intense urge that may or may not lead to a particular behavior. Pleasure and reality are the criteria that differentiate addiction and compulsion. Compulsion does not include the experience of pleasure but addiction does. In other words, compulsion is reinforced by feelings of relief, and addiction is dependent on expectations of pleasure despite the discomforts from the addiction.

Revenge Porn

Revenge porn websites differ from other pornography sites because the culprit uploading the explicit photos is usually a jilted ex-lover/partner or someone seeking to humiliate or expose the victim. The most common form of revenge porn is a sext from one former lover to another accompanied by a screen shot of the victim's Facebook profile. The consequences can be devastating for the victim.[65]

Most states do not view the posting of a person's personal information and photos without consent as a crime. Revenge porn, however, is defined as nonconsensual dissemination of private sexual images with the intent to cause harm.[66] Advocates for victims of revenge porn argue that it should be criminalized because it is a form of sexual harassment and an invasion of privacy. Forty states and the District of Columbia passed legislation criminalizing revenge porn. Facebook, Messenger, and Instagram have also taken action by using artificial intelligence tools to prevent and remove revenge porn posts. Civil remedies are sometimes available, and people may succeed in removing their private images from revenge porn websites, although this is a very challenging task. College students can file civil suits under a Title IX complaint at their academic institution.[65] If you are a victim of revenge porn, endrevengeporn.org's Online Removal Guide may help you.

Misuse of Erectile Dysfunction Drugs by Young Men

The misuse of Viagra and other ED drugs on college campuses has recently come to the attention of health experts. Viagra has been tagged the "thrill pill" on many campuses, where young men are taking it as a party drug at clubs, raves, and private parties. They mistakenly believe they will quickly and easily attain an erection that will allow them to have sex for hours. Erection drugs do not work unless nitric oxide is present in the penis, and nitric oxide is produced only in response to physical and mental stimulation. Any effect these drugs seem to have is more likely a placebo effect in healthy young men.

Public Health Is Personal

Cybersex: A Hidden Public Health Issue

Cybersex—virtual sexual encounters on the Internet—includes the viewing of online porn (pictures, audio, video, or text), real-time interactions (chat rooms posts, exchanges of images and files), and the use of multimedia software (X-rated movies, sexual games, online erotic media). About one-third of adults in the United States visit Internet sex sites.

Some observers argue that cybersex impairs real relationships and robs people of the ability to experience sexual pleasure through interpersonal communication and intimacy. Partners of people who participate in these activities say they feel as betrayed as they would by actual infidelity. Compulsive use of pornographic websites is now a significant factor in many divorces.[47] Other risks include arrest for trying to make a connection with a person under the age of 18, assault after agreeing to meet a stranger first encountered in a chat room, and public embarrassment. But cybersex is viewed as a hidden public health problem because few see it as a serious issue.

States passing resolutions identifying porn as a public health epidemic are primarily basing their resolutions on the model promoted by the National Center on Sexual Exploitation. Utah, Montana, and Tennessee have passed anti-porn resolutions. Resolutions acknowledge the need for education about pornography dangers, prevention, and a platform for research on potential pornography harmful effects. But these resolutions will receive a lot of criticism if they focus on censorship. A public health concern is defined as a situation that has widespread effects that negatively impact the health of the community and people who live in these communities. Does pornography rise to a public health concerns level? Proponents for saying it does claim pornography can change the user's brain, rewire sexual tastes, and is associated with aggression and violence. Critics claim this is fear mongering based on exaggeration and no or little empirical evidence. Moreover, censoring porn is a violation of the First Amendment.

Suppression of pornography through censorship has been blocked on the national level by the free speech criteria of the First Amendment. State and local governments, however, have passed obscenity laws to make sexually explicit material illegal. The criteria used to define obscenity are three-fold: (1) dominant theme appeals to prurient sexual interest and displays sexual content in a patently offensive manner; (2) the work as a whole does not demonstrate accepted literary, artistic, political, or scientific value; and (3) a reasonable person would view the whole work not to be of social value.

The subjective nature of the reasonable person standard has created legal challenges. The possession of obscene material in the home is not illegal unless it is child pornography. Human sexual intercourse with animals has also been viewed as obscene and can be censored. The 1998 Child Protection Act was intended to prevent children from accessing Internet adult sexual content, but the Supreme Court overturned this act in 2009. Millions of children today access sexually explicit material on the Internet. The difficult debate about how to legally define obscenity under free speech continues to make censorship challenging.[10]

Mc Graw Hill connect

Sources: Yarber, W., & Sayad, B. (2018). *Human sexuality: Diversity in contemporary society.* New York, NY: McGraw-Hill; Taylor, E. (2018). Pornography as a public health issue: Promoting violence and exploitation of children, youth, and adults. *Dignity, 3*(2). Retrieved from https://digitalcommons.uri.edu/dignity/vol3/iss2/8/; Gill, B. (2019). Why America's porn problem is a public health crisis. CBS News. Retrieved from https://https://www1.cbn.com/cbsnews/us/2019/may/why-americas-porn-problem-is-a-public-health-crisis

More important, the combination of ED drugs with alcohol or illicit drugs such as cocaine, amphetamines, or Ecstasy can be life threatening. Even more dangerous is combining them with amyl nitrate (poppers). The combination of ED drugs with any stimulant drug dilates blood vessels, which can result in a sudden drop in blood pressure.[18,21]

Aphrodisiacs

Aphrodisiacs include drugs, perfumes, and some foods resembling male and female anatomy (such as bananas and oysters) used as a magic potion for enhancing sexual pleasure. Although both men and women use aphrodisiacs, most are targeted for male testosterone.[67]

The use of drugs for sexual pleasure has long been a part of U.S. culture. These drugs have included poppers, cocaine, Ecstasy, marijuana, cantharides (Spanish Fly), and, recently, methamphetamine. Some scientists believe the placebo effect is behind any reported sexual pleasure derived after taking the drugs. Other scientists believe that changes in brain chemistry do have an effect on sexual pleasure. Long-term use of recreational drugs has been proven to cause low sexual desire, infertility, organ damage, heart damage, and many other health problems.

The Future of Sex

Sex technology has been evolving with the help of five innovations: virtual reality, teledildonics, augmented reality, direct neurostimulation, affective technology, and sex robots. The first wave of this technology, introducing dating apps, hook-up sites, and social media platforms, has been embraced by U.S. society as offering ways of interacting with current or potential relationship partners. The second wave, introducing sexual experiences without a human partner, is generally seen as amoral, devoid of real-life interactions, and a violation of sexual taboos.

Teledildonics is the remote use of sex toys via the Internet to pleasure a sexual partner. It is also known as cyberdildonics. The teledildonics virtual sex worlds offer multiplayer online sex games such as Red Light Center and 3DXChate in which players can actually feel the action through synchronized sex toys as their avatars have sex. By 2027, teledildonics may combine remote sex devices and holograms of lovers. One of the most difficult aspects of a long-term relationship is the lack of physical connection. Flex-N-Feel, adding touch from a distance, will use interactive gloves so the long-distance couples can feel each other.[68] Advances in neuroscience and biotech will someday let users share personal feelings through brain-to-brain interactions. If you think these sex technology advances sound far-fetched, consider that Real Touch is a male masturbation device already on the market that is synchronized in real-time with online porn. It works by warming itself, lubricating, pulsing, and providing grip touch sensations.[69,70,71]

Augmented reality devices advance virtual reality by enabling the user to learn, understand, and share experiences with others, including erotic interests, gender preference, and availability. Viewers can integrate their body parts into an adult entertainment scene and customize their experiences with 3-D avatars. Immersive entertainment with avatars is predicted to be widely available by 2020.[72] The positions and appearance of the avatar will be controlled by the user.

Direct neurostimulation removes the barrier between lifelike and real-life events. Skin sensors enable users to see, hear, taste, smell, and feel sexual pleasure. For example, you may put on a tactile cybersuit and then use virtual-reality goggles to simulate sex with another person. Direct neurostimulation has already been used to help deaf people hear, blind people see, and people with disabilities operate prosthetic limbs.

Sensors using affective technology may enable online users to share their degree of sexual arousal with each other. Brain-to-brain interfaces for sexually stimulating partners from remote distances are predicted to be available by 2027.[73] Remote sex using electronic toys operated by computers or devices that rely on personal data to enhance sexual pleasure is already possible. Smart vibrators and male sex sleeves can interact with each other through desktop and mobile devices to mimic the sensations of physical sex over long distances. OhMiBod's BlueMotion vibrator was designed for women and is controlled by mobile apps. Connected pillows enable users to hear their partner's heart beat and breathing from long distances. By 2020, the abilities of remote sex devices will expand from transmitting sensations of touch to providing haptic body prototype suits that allow a more fulfilling physical feeling during long-distance sex. By 2025, 3-D printing will enable people to create tailor-made sex toys and molds that replicate a lover's body parts.

Figure 11.5 displays some predicted technologies for the future of sex. Examples include 3-D printing of customized sex toys at home, hyperrealistic sex dolls, a high-tech bra that flies off with a clap of your hands, an all-in-one alarm clock and vibrator, dating apps that enable date selection based on whether genetic makeup is compatible, robotic prostitution that is STI-free and provides longer and more intense orgasms, Google Glass Glance apps that allow you to watch yourself and your partner having sex, and built-in Bluetooth panties placed in Durex's Fundawear so that a partner can click a phone app thousands of miles away to stimulate an orgasm. Bluetooth Sex Toy connects sex toys to any Bluetooth-enabled device that can be remotely controlled via a device app. An Internet connection and app permissions enable a remote partner to communicate with the sex toy device and adjust settings. For example, long-distance partners can use their smartphones to pair the Lovesense Nora sex vibrator for women and Lovesense Max men vibrator to sexually pleasure each other remotely.[74,75]

In this book, we have talked about wearable fitness apps, nutrition apps, and sleep apps. Now manufacturers are exploring sex app wearables. The average adult in the United States has sex about once to twice a week. Men have an average of about 6.4 sexual partners and women 7 sex partners in a lifetime. Earlier in the chapter we discussed the smart condom that provides personal sex analytics (e.g., skin temperature, thrust speed, heart rate, and calories burned). Self-improvement sex analytics has been called the "quantified self." To accompany this trend, companies have developed "smart" sex toys. SexFit and Lovely are sexual fitness apps worn around the penis. Recorded data are connected to the smartphone by Bluetooth. Sex

(Marco Fine/Shutterstock)

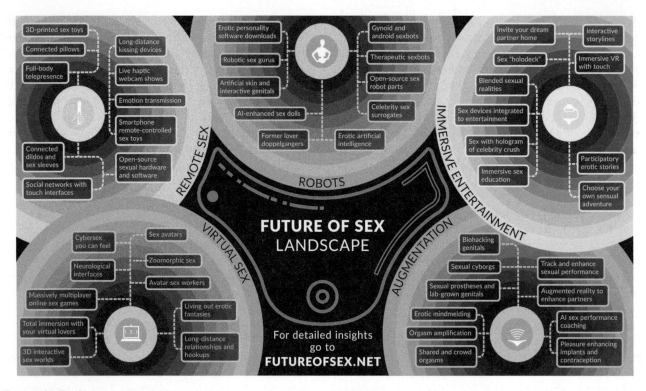

figure 11.5   The future of sex
Future of Sex Landscape, futureofsex.net. Copyright ©2017 Future of Sex. All rights reserved. Used with permission.

toys for the quantified self have received mixed reactions. Some see them as playful fun while others call quantified-self sex toys junk technology and, possibly, dangerous.[76] What do you think? Can sex analytics for the quantified self improve sex lives?

Sex dolls two decades ago were inflatable sex toys. Today, silicone/latex sex dolls have taken on real-life features and come in male and female versions. Artificial intelligence is adding brains so sex dolls can use biometric data to learn the preferences of their users. AI dolls can tell dirty jokes, simulate orgasm, and even flirt with or reject the user. Users can choose hair color, breast size, penis size, and facial expression; heaters inside the doll project humanlike warmth. Today, sex dolls for men are often viewed as erotic sex toys for men but are taboo for women. As they become more innovative and higher quality, developers project they will become more popular and accepted for women. See the box "Starting the Conversation: What Are Sex Doll Brothels?"

These innovations pale in comparison to the potential of sex robot technology. By 2050, sex technology entrepreneurs envision sophisticated, lifelike sex robots that can pleasure men and women. No matter what your opinion is about digisexuality, the sex technology revolution is exploding. It is driven by a society in which more and more people find it difficult to establish a relationship with a real-life partner.[77] Humanoid sex robots are not yet in the market. But their depiction in movies has stimulated erotic imagination and curiosity about potential robot lovers. The question is whether sex technology provides opportunities for people to sexually connect with others in healthy ways or whether it

dehumanizes sexual interactions. For example, some people actually fall in love with their synthetic sex dolls. A Michigan man describes himself as technosexual, someone who is sexually attracted to robots. He is hopeful that the Supreme Court will one day hear his case and approve marriage to his sex doll.[78] A bottom-line question is whether we need to be tolerant and accepting of another person's sexual preferences for a sex robot or sex doll.[79,80,81] For more on this question, see the box "You Make the Call: Will Sex Technology Help or Harm Human Sexual Interactions?" at the end of this chapter. For a full review of the future of sex, consult *The 2017 Future of Sex Report*, published by futureofsex.net.

Public health officials are particularly concerned about the use of crystal Meth in "party-and-play" sex marathons (also known as "slamming"), particularly among gay men.[82] Crystal meth increases the urgent need to have sex, provides the ability to have sex for hours and even days, and leads to an inability to ejaculate or reach orgasm. It lowers sexual inhibitions and may cause users to behave recklessly or become forgetful. Sex marathons often result in vaginal and anal tearing and trauma to sex organs that increase the risk for STIs and HIV. Crystal Meth can also cause erectile dysfunction, called "crystal dick," which leads users to engage in more receptive anal sex and fisting (shoving a fist into a partner's anal cavity). A recent trend is to combine crystal Meth with poppers, Ecstasy, and Viagra. Although party-and-play sexual marathons have been more visible in the gay community, the health dangers posed to heterosexual couples participating in sexual marathons have also become a concern.[83]

Starting the Conversation

What Are Sex Doll Brothels?

Sex doll brothels are opening all over the world, including in Spain, France, Canada, Germany, and Japan. In fact, a proposed sex doll brothel in Houston, to be run by a Canadian company, has run into opposition from the mayor who claims it is a violation of city ordinances.

What is a sex doll brothel? A sex brothel is a place where it is legal for people to engage in sex with professional sex workers. Sex doll brothels are places where sex dolls, available in different ethnicities and nationalities, replace professional sex workers. Most sex doll brothels cost about $100 per hour. If you want a multisexual experience, two dolls will cost you about $160. Sex dolls do not provide the complete sexual experiences (humanlike interactions) offered by a sex robot. If you frequent a sex doll brothel, it is still important to use a condom. It is not 100 percent guaranteed that a sex doll has been sanitized to prevent STIs.

Professional sex workers are fighting the proliferation of sex doll brothels. They argue that only they can provide authentic human interaction in the form of two-way affection, while sex dolls provide an unhealthy view of sex that inhibits customers' response to genuine sexual and emotional interactions. And, of course, sex dolls make it more difficult for professional sex workers to earn a living.

- Should sex doll brothels be legal?
- Should prison inmates be provided with sex dolls as a way to prevent prison rape?
- Should child pedophiles be give childlike sex dolls to curb their craving for child molestation?
- Sex dolls can be programmed to reject sex intercourse in order to allow the user to simulate rape. Does this type of behavior encourage sexual violent behavior?

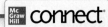

Sources: Neuwave, R. (2018). Legal prostitutes take stand against sex doll brothel 'epidemic'. AVN. Retrieved from https://avn.com/business/articles/legal/legal-prostitutes-take-stand-against-sex-doll-brothels/; Lifesite News. (2018). https://www.lifenews.com/blogs/sex-doll-brothels-are-coming-to-america-why-women-should-be-terrified.

You Make the Call

Will Sex Technology Help or Harm Human Sexual Interactions?

Human-computer sexual interactions (HCSI) include the following categories:

1. *Sexual communications media* include e-mail, video, and sexting. Communication may be with a specific person or with the general public.
2. *Social network services* let users find sexual partners or negotiate sexual interactions (such as hook-up websites).
3. *Real-life sexual activities*. Computer sex-play roles are used to enhance sexual pleasure in solo and partner sex play.
4. *Explorations of sexual orientation*. Anonymity enables users to develop alternate personas online to experience different sexual interactions (such as by using avatars in virtual space).
5. *Sexual education websites* are being developed to offer sex education for youth and adults.
6. *Sexual entertainment* includes pornographic videos, sex video games, and virtual strip clubs on the Internet.
7. *Teledildonics*. Computer-mediated software and hardware facilitate remote sex between two or more people, as discussed in the chapter.

There is certainly educational value in sex technology. But HCSI innovations have generated a fundamental moral question: Is HCSI healthy or unhealthy, or both? For example, using virtual reality to explore a bordello may provide temporary amusement and escape. One sex partner e-mailing a series of instructions for the other partner to download into a programmable vibrator may help sustain a long-distance relationship. Several versions of robotic sex dolls are already on the market—attractive, lifelike robots programmed with artificial intelligence that can be used for a one-night stand, cuddling up for comfort, or trying something sexually that your partner is not willing to try. These sex dolls present a much more divisive moral issue, although the idea has already taken hold in popular culture with films like *Lars and the Real Girl*.

So, what do you think? How much HCSI is too much? Could HCSI become addictive? Will HCSI make sex with humans less enjoyable or even obsolete?

Pros

- Millions of people are in unsatisfactory sexual relationships. Sex robots could provide a healthy alternative for satisfactory sexual relationships.
- Sex robots provide an option for people to engage in physical intimacy who are unable to engage in physical contact

Continued...

Concluded...

with real humans because of past trauma but still crave intimacy in a controlled and safe environment.
- Availability of sex robots might reduce sex trafficking.

Cons

- HCSI may eventually eliminate human touching, which is essential for meaningful, long-term relationships.

- Sex entrepreneurs should focus on technologies that reflect ethical principles of dignity, respect, and mutuality.
- Chronic use of sex robots could erode the empathy of users over time.

Sources: Jauregui, A. (2016). 6 NSFW reasons why robots are the future of sex. *Huffington Post.* Retrieved from www.huffingtonpost.com/entry/robot-sex-is-the-future_55c2016de4b0d928r04cf76; Gray, H. (2015). *The campaign against sex robots: Is banning them the answer?* Retrieved from http://futureofsex.net/robots/the-campaign-against-sex-robots-is-banning-them-the-answer/; New York Post Staff. (2015). Sex robots are definitely coming in the future. *New York Post.* Retrieved from http://nypost.com/2015/09/29/sex-robots-are-definitely-coming-in-the-future/; Silverberg, C. (2009). What are examples of sex tech? *About.com.* Retrieved from http://sexuality.about.com/od/sex_tech_faq_f_tech_examples.htm.

In Review

How do the sex organs function, and what are the components of sexual response?

The male and female sex organs arise from the same undifferentiated tissue during the prenatal period, becoming male or female under the influence of hormones. In this sense, the sexual organs of males and females are very similar, and their purpose and functions are complementary. For reproduction to occur, ova and sperm have to be brought into close association with each other. The psychological and motivational mechanism for this is the human sexual response, which includes sex drive, sexual arousal, and orgasm. The degree to which the genitalia response matches the mental sexual response is categorized as sexual response concordance or sexual response nonconcordance. Individuals with a sex or reproductive anatomy that does not fit the standard definition of male or female is categorized as intersex anatomy.

What are common varieties of sexual behavior?

Common forms of sexual expression include celibacy, abstinence, erotic touch, kissing, self-stimulation, oral-genital stimulation, anal intercourse, and sexual intercourse. Less common forms are atypical sexual practices, such as sex toys and sex games, which are consensual and cause no harm, and paraphilias, which are not consensual and are classified as mental disorders and crimes. The *DSM-5* changed the nomenclature of paraphilia to paraphilic disorder. Compulsive sexual behaviors, notably sex addiction and sexual anorexia, are conditions that can benefit from professional help.

What are sexual dysfunctions in males and in females?

Sexual dysfunctions can have physical, psychological, emotional, or relationship causes. Some are deemed problems only if one of the partners considers it a problem. Female sexual dysfunctions include pain during intercourse, sexual desire disorder, female sexual interest/arousal disorder, and orgasmic dysfunction. Male sexual dysfunctions include pain during intercourse, sexual desire disorder, erectile dysfunction, and ejaculation dysfunction. Testosterone and drugs are common therapies. Pain and nausea for women during or after sex is not normal and should be checked for a possible underlying health condition.

What are the best ways to protect your sexual health?

Using condoms, practicing abstinence, avoiding alcohol in sexual situations, and practicing good communication skills are the best ways to protect your sexual health. The i.Con smart condom uses performance analytical data that may be misused.

What are important sex-related issues in the 21st century?

Hooking is a common issue on college campuses, and condom dispensers have become the subject of debate. Venues for cybersex, sexting, and revenge porn are constantly changing. Stealthing, nonconsensual removal of the condom during intercourse, may be a criminal act. Claims that dating apps are more effective than traditional relationship methods are not supported by empirical evidence.

What is the future of sex?

Sex technologies are pushing the envelope on what may turn out to be healthy or unhealthy innovations. The misuse of ED drugs and the use of methamphetamines in sex marathons are recent concerns.

Personal Health Portfolio

Chapter 11   Are You a Good Communicator?*

Good communication is vital to keeping your relationships healthy. However, bad communication habits—like avoiding discussing difficult subjects—are easy to fall into. This assessment will help you determine how well you are communicating with your partner. If you aren't currently in an intimate relationship, take this assessment with a close friendship in mind. Communication is important in all relationships—intimate or not.

Read each question and choose the response that reflects how you think or respond the majority of the time. Think about what you actually do or believe as opposed to what you "know" you should do or believe.

1. Do you believe that disagreements or arguments are
   a. harmful and negative for a relationship?
   b. helpful and positive for a relationship?

2. Do you believe that your partner should
   a. know what you are thinking and feeling?
   b. hear what you are thinking and feeling?

3. Do you
   a. drop hints about your concerns in the relationship?
   b. get right to the point when discussing a concern in the relationship?

4. Do you tell your partner
   a. what you don't like about him or her and your relationship?
   b. what you like about him or her and your relationship?

5. Do you
   a. withdraw from a conflict or conversation with your partner?
   b. stay around until there is a resolution of the conflict or conversation?

6. Do you
   a. hint at what you want or don't want from your partner?
   b. state clearly what you want and don't want?

7. Do you
   a. interrupt your partner's conversation?
   b. wait until your partner has finished stating his or her thoughts and ideas?

8. Do you
   a. blame your partner or others for your relationship problems?
   b. acknowledge and accept your part in your relationship problems?

9. Were your parents
   a. poor communicators?
   b. good communicators?

Martin, S., & Martin, C. (2017). Communication assessment. How well do you communicate? Nine questions and analysis. Copyright ©2017 by The Positive Way, from www.positive-way.com/communication.htm. All rights reserved. Used with permission.

SCORING

The answer "b" to all questions indicates more effective communication. The more "b's" you have, the better you're doing. The "a's" indicate an opportunity to improve.

Here is why "b" is the better answer for each question:

1. Intimacy and conflict go hand in hand. If you want real intimacy with your mate, then there will be real conflict. People just don't agree on everything at all times. How you handle the resulting disagreements is more important than whether or not you have them. The most successful couples work through their disagreements and conflicts together and develop a stronger relationship as a result of that teamwork.

2. No one is a mind reader, and it is really impossible for your partner to know what you are thinking and feeling no matter how long you have known each other. It is

important that you agree to *say* what is important and to *talk* until you both agree that you *understand*.

3. Dropping hints wastes your time and your partner's time, and it usually leads to misunderstanding and disappointment. Get right to the point so that your partner won't have to guess what your concerns are in the relationship. State how you feel by using "I" statements instead of "you" statements.

4. Concentrating on what you like about your mate and your relationship will lead to a more positive relationship.

If you concentrate on the things you don't like, it's easy to overlook the good things. Negativity breeds negativity, which then makes communication and problem solving more difficult. Use positive elements of the relationship as a foundation upon which to learn and grow.

5. Communication requires two people. Issues will remain unsettled unless you and your partner agree to communicate. We recommend that you agree to communicate with the guidelines of *understanding, kindness, honesty,* and *respect* as ground rules. These guidelines will serve to reduce tension and remind you both that you are on the same team. As a couple, agree to your own discussion rules, which can include such things as *time-outs* for cooling off or thinking.

6. Most of us don't pick up on hints, so don't expect your partner to guess what you do or don't want. Make clear and direct statements. Follow the guidelines of *understanding, kindness, honesty,* and *respect.* These guidelines make it easier to state your desires in a positive way and are more likely to be understood and well received.

7. Successful communication requires good listening. No one wants to be interrupted while speaking. We all want our feelings and thoughts to be heard, valued, and understood. Listen for understanding. Rephrase what you have heard your partner say, and then ask if this is correct. Save your side of the discussion until you have validated your partner's feelings. Validating your partner's feelings and thoughts is the key to success.

8. Blame fuels the fire of disagreement. Most of the time we believe that our position is acceptable and tend to blame the other person for any misunderstanding rather than seeing our own flaws in communicating. Analyze your part in fueling a problem, and avoid blaming others. Be responsible for your role in the relationship.

9. We tend to learn by example. If your parents were poor communicators, more than likely you have learned and now act out some ineffective ways of communicating. These habits may seem quite comfortable to you even if they are not working. It is up to you to learn new positive ways to communicate. Be persistent and practice until they become habit.

CRITICAL THINKING QUESTIONS

1. How did you do on the assessment? Discuss your strengths and any areas for improvement.

2. Think more about your parents' communication. Why did you respond the way you did to question 9? How did they handle conflict? Do you see yourself following any of their habits, good or bad?

Design Icons: ©McGraw-Hill Education

Reproductive Choices

12

Georgeclerk/E+Getty Images

Ever Wonder...

- what the best form of contraception is?
- how to have the "contraception talk" with your partner?
- how much it costs to raise a child?

Are you ready to be a parent? If your answer is no, many safe and effective methods of contraception are available that you and your partner can use to avoid an unintended pregnancy. If your answer is yes, a wealth of knowledge is available that you can use to increase the likelihood that pregnancy is a positive experience. If you want to have children sometime in the future, planning for it now—by using contraception and choosing healthy lifestyle behaviors—can give you peace of mind and the knowledge that you are doing everything you can to protect the health of your future family. Reproductive health considerations are important regardless of your gender and sexual identity. This chapter builds on the topics discussed in Chapters 3 and 11—relationships and sexual health—to discuss reproductive choices and issues in building a family.

CHOOSING A CONTRACEPTIVE METHOD

Choosing and using a contraceptive method that is right for you is important for one very significant reason: it lowers your risk of unintended pregnancy. About 45 percent of all pregnancies in the United States are unintended, and many are unwanted, either because the couple do not want a child at the time or because they don't want a child at all. High rates of unintended pregnancy are preventable. Modern contraceptives work! Women who consistently use effective contraceptives account for only 5 percent of unintended pregnancies. Women who use contraceptives inconsistently or not at all account for 95 percent of unplanned pregnancies.[1,2]

Women in the United States have higher unintended pregnancy rates than women in other developed countries.[3]

Who's at Risk?
Unintentional Pregnancy in the United States

If access to effective contraception is believed to explain decreasing rates of unintended pregnancy, what factors might help explain ongoing differences in rates of unintentional pregnancy? Consider the socioecological model of health and wellness presented in Chapter 1 (see Figure 1.2).

Pregnancies by intention status
Nearly half of pregnancies are unintended.

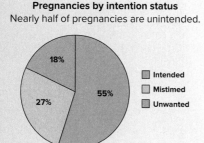

- Intended
- Mistimed
- Unwanted

Unintended pregnancies
(3.4 Million)

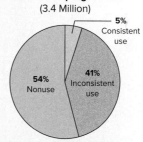

By consistency of method used during month of conception

Rates of unintended pregnancy per 1,000 women ages 14–44

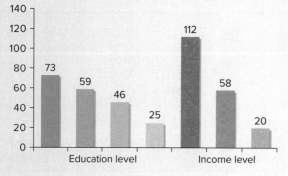

■ Not high school graduate   ■ High school graduate or GED   ■ Some college or AA
■ College graduate   ■ Below federal povertylevel   ■ 100–199% federal poverty level
■ Above 200% federal poverty level

Sources: Guttmacher Institute Fact Sheet (2018) Contraceptive use in the United States. Retrieved August 17, 2019 at https://www.guttmacher.org/fact-sheet/contraceptive-use-united-states Guttmacher Report (2019). Unintended Pregnancy in the United States. Retrieved August 13, 2019 from https://www.guttmacher.org/fact-sheet/unintended-pregnancy-united-states

Action Skill-Builder

Discussing Contraception

It is estimated that nearly three in four college students will engage in a hookup (i.e., a casual sexual encounter ranging from kissing to sexual intercourse) during college. People have different expectations about the hookup itself regarding what behaviors are acceptable and desired. And post-hookup emotional responses vary tremendously, from higher self-esteem and positive emotion to anxiety and conflict in identity development and/or faith beliefs. In any sexual relationship, lack of planning is associated with a higher risk of unprotected sex. Being prepared to talk about expectations can save you future regrets and worries. In addition, an open conversation about birth control is a sign of respect for yourself and your partner.

Before you have the conversation:

☐ *Consider which method of contraception you think is best for you and your type of relationship.* It will be easier to discuss if you are honest with yourself and feel educated and confident about what you want to use.

☐ *Prepare yourself for the conversation.* Consider how you will start the conversation, and think about your partner's potential responses. If you are comfortable doing so, role-play the discussion with a friend.

☐ *Don't make assumptions about whether your partner is on birth control or ready to use a condom.* Plan to

ask specifically about that. Contraception is everyone's responsibility. Ninety percent of college women feel contraceptive responsibility should be shared, yet only half report it actually is shared.

When you have the conversation:

☐ *Talk about the relationship.* Do you both have the same expectations about your relationship status—are you going to be monogamous, or does either of you plan to be sexually involved with other people?

☐ *Discuss what you would want to do if your birth control fails.* Can you agree on a contingency plan in the event of a pregnancy?

☐ *Have this conversation prior to the initiation of any sexual contact.* This requires being honest with yourself as well as your partner(s) about what you expect from the relationship.

☐ *Be prepared to take more time before starting a sexual relationship.* You and your partner may not agree on a method to use, or you may have very different beliefs regarding what you would do if you or your partner became pregnant.

The consequences of unprotected sex affect both partners, and thus the responsibility should be shared.

Sources: Black, S. W., Kaminsky, G., Hudson, A., Owen, J. & Fincham, F. (2019). A short-term longitudinal investigation of hookups and holistic outcomes among college students. *Archives of Sexual Behavior,* 48(6), 1829–1845; Olmstead, S. B., Norona, J. C., & Anders, K. M. (2019). How do college experience and gender differentiate the enactment of hookup scripts among emerging adults? *Archives of Sexual Behavior,* 48(6), 1769–1783; How to talk to your partner about birth control and sex. Retrieved from https://www.verywellhealth.com/how-to-talk-to-your-partner-about-birth-control-and-sex-906910

Unintended pregnancies occur among women of all ages and ethnic groups, but rates are highest among low-income, racial/ethnic minority (Black, American Indian, Alaska Native, and Hispanic) women, and sexually active women in the 15- to 24-year-old age group. See the box "Who's at Risk? Unintentional Pregnancy in the United States" to compare the rates among different educational, and income groups. In addition, sexual minority women (lesbian, bisexual, or heterosexual with same-sex attraction) have an increased risk of unintentional pregnancy than do heterosexual women and are more likely to have used less effective or no contraception with last vaginal intercourse.[4]

Overall, rates of unintended pregnancy have decreased, a result believed to be due to increased use of contraceptives, especially highly effective forms.[5] Access to sexual health education and contraceptive options is considered a human right and the most effective way to reduce unintended pregnancy.[6]

Empowering women (and their partners) to have the pregnancies they want improves the lives of women, their children, and their communities. In addition, when women (and their partners) control the timing and number of pregnancies, abortion rates decrease, since 40 percent of unintended pregnancies end in abortion. The availability of safe, effective, and affordable family planning services is consistently associated with decreased abortion rates.[7,8] Compared with women having unintended pregnancies, women with

planned pregnancies are more likely to receive adequate **prenatal care**; are less likely to drink alcohol and smoke before and during pregnancy, which can harm their babies; and are more likely to have babies with a healthy birth weight.[5]

Acceptable and reliable contraceptive methods are available. In this section, we take a look at several of these methods. Complete the Personal Health Portfolio activity at the end of this chapter to decide which contraceptive method may best suit your needs.

prenatal care
Regular medical care during pregnancy, designed to promote the health of the mother and the fetus.

Communicating About Contraception

Whether intentional or unintentional, pregnancy requires an egg, a sperm, and a uterus. If you have sex and these components are present, you and your partner need to discuss pregnancy. All sexual discussions are more difficult if you are not comfortable with your gender or sexual identity and if you do not know your partner well. You may want to consider abstinence from penetration intercourse until you are more comfortable with your identity and in a relationship where open conversation is possible.

How do you have the conversation? See the box "Action Skill-Builder: Discussing Contraception" for some steps you can take.

Which Contraceptive Method Is Right for You?

Choosing a method of contraception can be difficult given the number of variables to consider: effectiveness, cost, convenience, permanence, safety, protection against sexually transmitted infections (STIs), and consistency with personal values. As the box "Choosing a Reversible Contraceptive" shows later in this section, the most effective methods to prevent pregnancy are long-acting contraceptives—intrauterine devices (IUDs), sterilization, and hormonal implants. Injection and oral and vaginal hormonal contraceptives come next. Less expensive but also less effective as contraception are barrier methods such as condoms and diaphragms. However, barrier methods protect against STIs, whereas hormonal methods, IUDs, and implants do not.

Inconsistent or incorrect use contributes to half of all unintended pregnancies. The long-acting methods are so effective because, once in place, they require no action for years. Pills must be taken every day. Condoms and diaphragms must be put in place for each act of intercourse. Fertility awareness methods require daily monitoring, and abstinence requires control in all situations.[9]

Here are some questions to consider when choosing a contraceptive method:

Having a talk about contraception may be uncomfortable at first, but you and your partner will both be glad you had it. Think about what you want to say ahead of time and use good communication skills. *(Aleksandr Davydov/123RF)*

- *How challenging would it be if you or your partner became pregnant now?* If the answer to this question is "very challenging," then consider the most effective forms of reversible contraceptives—long-acting contraceptives. If pregnancy would not be desirable but would not be a problem, you might consider slightly less effective methods. The male and female condoms, the diaphragm, the cervical cap, and the contraceptive sponge are all safe, nonpermanent methods with slightly lower efficacy because they require action at the time of intercourse and thus afford more opportunity for error.

- *Do you sometimes have sex under the influence of alcohol or drugs or have partners whose sexual history you do not know?* In these situations, you are at risk for both STIs and pregnancy. The best option is dual contraception—a barrier method plus a hormonal method or IUD. Condoms are the best way to reduce risk for STIs. A long-acting contraceptive such as an IUD or implant is important because its efficacy does not rely on your decision-making abilities at the time of intercourse.

- *Do you already have the children you want or know you do not want children at all?* Surgical sterilization is a highly effective method with no hassles after the initial procedure. It is considered permanent, though.

- *How much can you afford to pay for contraception?* There are several factors to consider here. For example, how often do you need contraception? If you have sex daily, the cost of buying condoms can quickly add up, whereas the one-time cost of an IUD or sterilization may be lower. If you have sex once a month or less, the opposite may be true. State and federal policies regulate insurance coverage for family planning services, including setting rules for contraception coverage and providing funding for family planning services for low-income populations. The most effective forms of contraception require access to a health care provider, and making these services available without a fee can significantly reduce unplanned pregnancy (see the box "Starting the Conversation: Should Contraception Be Available to All?"). Don't forget to take into account the financial and emotional cost if you or your partner gets pregnant while using the form of contraception you select. It might be the cost of raising a child or the cost of having an abortion.

- *Are you worried about the safety and health consequences of contraception?* Contraceptive options available today are relatively safe. To put the risks in perspective, the chance of being killed in a car crash in a given year is 1 in 5,900; the risk of dying from a pregnancy carried past 20 weeks is 1 in 10,000; and for a nonsmoking woman aged 15 to 44 the risk of dying from the use of birth control pills is 1 in 66,700. Some health conditions increase risks and should be discussed with a health care provider.[10]

- *Is your choice influenced by your religious, spiritual, or ethical beliefs?* Sexually active women of all denominations who do not want to become pregnant use contraception. Among sexually active women, 89 percent of Catholics, 90 percent of Protestants, and 80 percent of Muslims report the use of contraceptives. And 70 percent of these women use highly effective forms, such as sterilization, hormonal methods, or IUDs. Levels of nonuse do not vary by religious affiliation.[1,11]

Starting the Conversation
Should Contraception Be Available to All?

Q: The most effective contraceptive methods require access to health care providers and prescriptions. Should these services be available to all?

Access to safe and effective contraception has long been an issue within the United States. The federal Title X family planning program has been in place since the 1970s with the goal of reducing inequities in access to contraception. Funding under the program supports clinics that serve low-income patients and those facing other barriers to reproductive care. Title X regulations affirm individuals' right to choose contraceptive methods that best meet their needs and ensure informed consent, including factual, unbiased, and comprehensive information about all options.

Before the 1990s, birth control medications were rarely covered by insurance. However, when the FDA approved and insurance companies began to cover the costs of Viagra—an erectile dysfunction medication—women argued that this was an inequity. Many states then enacted laws requiring insurance plans to provide coverage for contraceptive options, but passage of the Affordable Care Act (ACA) made this a federal mandate because the law includes a provision for all employer-sponsored plans to cover FDA-approved contraception and to do so without charging a copay.

However, the right of women to have unfettered access to contraception continues to be challenged. Proposed changes to the Title X program, if implemented, would prevent federal funds from going to reproductive care facilities that provide comprehensive pregnancy counseling and care, including abortion and referral to abortion. These changes would most directly affect Planned Parenthood, which provides contraceptive care for 41 percent of women who rely on Title X for

contraceptive care. The ACA federal mandate has also been challenged by employers. Some religious owners of family businesses say it violates their religious beliefs. In 2014, the Supreme Court ruled in favor of family-owned businesses and said they could not be forced to cover contraception. The Trump administration has proposed changes that would allow private companies and religious nonprofits the ability to opt out of providing contraception at no cost to employees. At present, federal courts have blocked the proposed changes.

With calls for the repeal of the ACA mandate and restrictions on Title X funding, the right of women to maintain access to the most effective forms of contraceptives is certainly unclear. Yet, the evidence is clear—reducing barriers to effective contraception, such as cost, increases its use and reduces unintentional pregnancy. Pregnancy planning improves long-term health outcomes for women and their babies. Cancer screening, vaccinations, and cholesterol screening, other evidence-based preventive methods, are covered by insurance and federal programs providing low-income safety nets. Yet reproductive health coverage is frequently under discussion. What do you think?

Q: Should reproductive health care be treated differently than other forms of health care? Why or why not?

Q: Should your employer's or political representative's religious beliefs determine whether you have access to affordable contraception? Why or why not?

Sources: Hasstedt, K. (2018). A domestic gag rule and more: the administrations proposed changes to Title X. Guttmacher Institute. Retrieved from https://www.guttmacher.org/article/2018/06/domestic-gag-rule-and-more-administrations-proposed-changes-title-x; Scott, D. (2019). Two federal judges just blocked Trump's rollback of Obamacare's birth control mandate. Retrieved from https://www.vox.com/2019/1/14/18181966/trump-birth-control-mandate-lawsuit-court-ruling; Durante, J. C., & Woodhams, E. J. (2017). Patient education about the Affordable Care Act contraception coverage requirement increases interest in using long-acting reversible contraception. *Women's Health Issues, 27*(2), 152–157.

Abstinence

The only guaranteed method of preventing pregnancy and STIs is *abstinence*. As noted in Chapter 11, abstinence is usually defined as abstention from sexual intercourse; in regard to pregnancy, this means there is no penile penetration of the vagina. Among heterosexual couples who have vaginal intercourse and use no contraceptive method, 85 percent of the women will become pregnant in 1 year.[10]

Abstinence requires that both partners feel empowered and free of sexual coercion. It requires control and commitment—that is, the ability or the determination not to change your mind in the heat of the moment, especially in situations where one or both partners are intoxicated.

Long-Acting Reversible Contraceptive Methods

Long-acting reversible contraceptives (LARCs), which include the **intrauterine device (IUD)** and the **contraceptive**

implant, are the most effective nonpermanent contraceptive options. Women prefer these methods; 86 percent of those who start an LARC continue use after 1 year, versus 53 percent who continue with non-LARC contraceptive methods.[12] LARCs are recommended as the first option for all sexually active women, regardless of age or prior pregnancy status. The percentage of women aged 15 to 44 using LARCs is 7.2 percent.[1] The main advantage is that once these methods are in place, users don't have to do anything else for years. But they can be removed with a rapid return to fertility at any time.

long-acting reversible contraceptives (LARCs) A collective term used to describe IUDs and implants—the most effective, reversible forms of contraception.

intrauterine device (IUD) A small T-shaped device that, when inserted in the uterus, prevents conception.

contraceptive Implant A small flexible plastic rod that contains progesterone and is inserted under the skin and provides effective contraception for years.

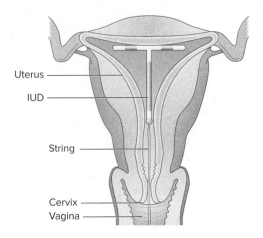

figure 12.1   T-shaped IUD correctly positioned in the uterus

hormonal contraceptives
Contraceptive methods that deliver hormones via a pill, an injection, a patch, a vaginal ring, or an implant to prevent ovulation and discourage implantation of fertilized ova.

Intrauterine Devices Four IUDs are available in the United States: the copper IUD ParaGard and the progesterone IUDs Mirena, Skyla, and Liletta. All are small, T-shaped devices that a health care provider inserts through the cervix into the uterus. A correctly placed IUD is shown in Figure 12.1. IUDs work by altering the uterine and cervical fluids to reduce the chance that sperm will move up into the Fallopian tubes, where they can fertilize an ovum. In addition, some women using the progesterone-containing IUD do not ovulate.

IUDs are highly effective and safe for the majority of women. They do require a pelvic exam and placement by a provider. Because it is possible for an IUD to shift its position in or to be expelled from the uterus, women are taught to check each month that the device is still properly located. Women may experience a change in menstrual patterns with IUDs. The copper IUD may cause slightly heavier periods and cramping; the progesterone IUDs may cause irregular spotting initially and then the cessation of periods at 1 year for 20 percent of women. Neither appears to

■ The development of "the pill" and its approval by the FDA in 1960 ushered in an era in which women could more reliably take control of their reproductive planning. Today, birth control pills remain the most popular form of reversible contraception. *(Photodisc/Getty Images)*

increase the risk of pelvic inflammatory disease unless a woman is infected with gonorrhea or chlamydia at the time of insertion. IUDs have few contraindications and can be used by almost all women who need to prevent pregnancy.[10,13]

Contraceptive Implant The only implant currently available in the United States is Nexplanon. It is a small, flexible plastic rod that contains progesterone. After insertion under the skin on the inner side of the upper arm, it slowly releases hormone and can be left in place for 3 years, eliminating user error. The implant prevents ovulation, alters cervical mucus, and thins the lining of the uterus. The most common side effect is irregular menstruation, especially during the first few months, but many women will then stop having periods altogether. Nexplanon may be less effective for women with a body mass greater than 30 percent of ideal, but otherwise it has very few contraindications.[10]

Hormonal Contraceptive Methods

Hormonal contraceptives come in a variety of forms—pills, injections, patches, vaginal rings, and implants (discussed with LARCs)—and work by preventing ovulation. They also alter cervical mucus, making it harder for sperm to reach ova, and they affect the uterine lining so that a fertilized egg is less likely to be implanted. They must be prescribed or administered by a health care provider. The advantages of hormonal methods include their effectiveness, ease of use, limited side effects, and the fact that they do not permanently affect fertility. They require daily, weekly, or monthly action but do not require action at the time of intercourse and thus are more effective than barrier methods. In addition, they offer some general health benefits. They reduce menstrual cramping and blood loss, premenstrual symptoms, ovarian cysts, risk of and symptoms associated with endometriosis (a condition in which endometrial tissue moves outside the uterus and causes pain), and the risk of endometrial and ovarian cancers. They can also improve symptoms of acne.

Hormonal contraceptives, like LARCs, offer no protection against STIs. In some women, they can also cause some minor side effects, including symptoms of early pregnancy (nausea, bloating, weight gain, and breast tenderness), mood changes, lowered libido, and headaches. Serious side effects are rare and more common in women who are older, who smoke, or who have a family history of early heart disease, stroke, or clotting disorders (Figure 12.2). Hormonal contraceptives require a visit to a health care provider to determine which method is best for you and to ensure you do not have a contraindication for use.

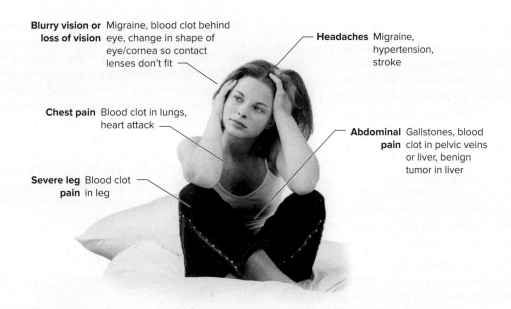

Blurry vision or Migraine, blood clot behind
loss of vision eye, change in shape of
eye/cornea so contact
lenses don't fit

Headaches Migraine,
hypertension,
stroke

Chest pain Blood clot in lungs,
heart attack

Abdominal Gallstones, blood
pain clot in pelvic veins
or liver, benign
tumor in liver

Severe leg Blood clot
pain in leg

figure 12.2   **Rare but serious potential side effects of hormonal contraceptives**
(LeLu/MediaBakery)

Birth control pills (oral contraceptives), usually provided as a 1-month supply, are the most popular reversible form of contraception, used by 16 percent of women aged 15 to 44 and 25 percent of all contraceptive users.[1] They usually contain a combination of estrogen and progesterone. Some formulations contain only progesterone; they are slightly less effective but can be used by women who can't take estrogen (for instance, because they are breastfeeding or have a family history of blood clots).

When birth control pills were introduced, they were designed to mimic the chemistry of a woman's typical menstrual cycle. Thus, placebo pills with no hormones, taken for 7 days each month, cause the uterine lining to shed and menstruation to take place. As the use of hormonal contraceptives has become more accepted, however, so too has the idea that it may be nice *not* to menstruate each month. Sixty percent of women report they would be interested in skipping their monthly period. When a woman is taking hormonal contraceptives, it is safe to eliminate periods by taking the medication continuously. This regimen may lead to a slight increase in irregular spotting or bleeding but is otherwise well tolerated. If a woman who is not taking hormonal contraceptives misses a period, it can signify a hormone imbalance that may be due to weight gain or loss, stress, some other health conditions, too much exercise, or pregnancy.[10]

Some newer ways of delivering hormones are becoming popular, especially among college women who find it difficult to take a daily pill due to irregular sleep, a hectic schedule, or daily stress. The *transdermal patch* works by slowly releasing estrogen and progesterone into the bloodstream through the skin. A woman places a new patch on her skin every week for 3 weeks; during the fourth week, she does not use a patch and has a light period. Potential side effects are similar to those of the pill, except that the patch results in higher levels of estrogen in the blood (about 60 percent higher than with a typical birth control pill) and may be associated with an increased risk of blood clots compared to pills.[10]

The *vaginal contraceptive ring* is a soft, flexible plastic ring that is placed in the vagina and slowly releases estrogen and progesterone. It is generally left in place for 21 days and then removed. After 7 more days, a new ring is inserted. However, the ring can also be left in place for the entire month to avoid menstruation. Women and their partners report that they rarely feel the ring during intercourse. The advantage of the ring is the once-a-month application; side effects are similar to those of birth control pills.

At this time, there are no hormonal contraceptive methods available for men, and none are likely in the near future. Differences between men's and women's reproductive physiology, the lack of research success, the reluctance of pharmaceutical companies to invest in more research, and the lengthy process of securing FDA approval for new drugs all pose seemingly insurmountable obstacles. A primary problem for researchers is that suppressing the production of 10,000 sperm per second is more challenging than suppressing the production of one egg per month. Although a majority of men believe contraception is the responsibility of both partners and report that a male hormonal contraceptive would be acceptable, the technology of male contraception has lagged far behind that of female contraception.[14]

Barrier Methods

Contraceptive methods known as **barrier methods** physically separate the sperm from the female reproductive tract. These methods include the male condom, the female condom, the diaphragm, the cervical cap, and the contraceptive sponge. To increase their effectiveness, the diaphragm and cervical cap should be used with **spermicide**, chemical agents that kill sperm. Spermicide usually comes in a foam or jelly and can be purchased at a grocery store or drugstore. The contraceptive sponge already has spermicide in it.

The chance of becoming pregnant while using a barrier method is low if the method is used consistently and correctly—that is, if the barrier is used 100 percent of the time and spermicide is applied correctly. However, this is often not the case.

Condoms—Male and Female Neither male nor female condoms provide 100 percent protection from STIs, but they are the only form of contraception proven to reduce the risk of transmission. The *male condom* is a thin sheath, usually made of latex, that is rolled down over the erect penis before any contact occurs between the penis and the partner's genitals. The *female condom* is a pouch of thin polyurethane that is inserted into the vagina before intercourse. Newer male, female, and anal condoms are under development.[15] Male and female condoms should not be used together. For more information about condoms, including how to use them, see Chapter 11.

Female Barrier Methods The vaginal **diaphragm** is a circular rubber or silicone dome inserted in the vagina before intercourse; correct placement is shown in Figure 12.3. The diaphragm fits between the pubic bone and the back of the vagina and covers the cervix. Spermicidal jelly or foam is placed in the dome, or cup, of the diaphragm before it is inserted; thus, the spermicide covers the cervix, where it provides the best protection. Nonoxynol-9 is the most common spermicide available in the United States. Spermicide can cause irritation for some people and, due to the irritation, may increase risk of HIV transmission. Spermicide must be reapplied into the vagina if a second act of sex occurs. The diaphragm is removed 6 to 12 hours after sex. Diaphragm use has been associated with an increased risk of urinary tract infections.

barrier methods
Contraceptive methods based on physically separating sperm from the female reproductive tract.

spermicide
Chemical agents that kill sperm.

diaphragm
A circular rubber dome that is inserted in the vagina before intercourse to prevent conception.

■ The advantages of condoms include that they are portable, inexpensive, and available over the counter. Condoms provide some protection against STIs, including HIV. The disadvantage is that they must be used with every sexual act. *(Jill Braaten/McGraw-Hill)*

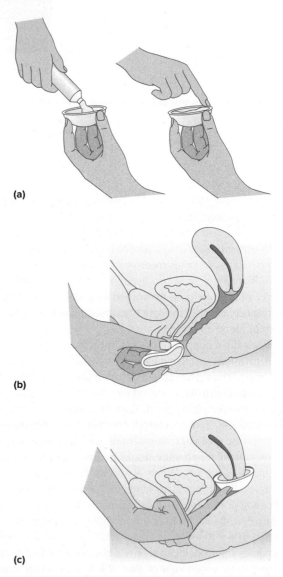

figure 12.3 **Use of the diaphragm**
(a) With clean hands, place about 1 tablespoon of spermicide (jelly or cream) in the diaphragm, spreading it around inside the diaphragm and on its rim. (b) Using the thumb and forefinger, compress the diaphragm. Insert it into the vagina, guiding it toward the back wall and up into the vagina as far as possible. (c) With the index finger, check the position of the diaphragm to make sure that the cervix is covered completely and the front of the rim is behind the pubic bone.

■ The FemCap cervical cap (left) and the diaphragm (right) work by creating a physical barrier at the cervical opening, preventing sperm from entering the uterus. Both are used with spermicidal cream or jelly. *(Jill Braaten/McGraw-Hill)*

The rubber diaphragm comes in multiple sizes and requires fitting, but a new silicone diaphragm is available in one size and fits most women. Both require prescription by a health care provider.[16]

The **cervical cap** is a small, cuplike device that covers the cervix and prevents sperm from entering the uterus. Like a diaphragm, the cervical cap requires a fitting by a health care provider; it is replaced annually. Currently, the FemCap is the only model available in the United States. It is made of nonallergenic silicone and comes in three sizes. A small amount of spermicide is placed in a groove on the vaginal side of the cap prior to insertion. The cap should be left in place for 6 to 48 hours after intercourse.[10]

The **contraceptive sponge** is a small, polyurethane foam device presaturated with 1 gram of the spermicide nonoxynol-9. The sponge is moistened with water and inserted into the vagina. It fits snugly over the cervix, becomes effective immediately, and remains effective for 24 hours. It should be left in place for at least 6 hours after intercourse. The sponge is available over the counter without prescription; one size fits all. The sponge should not be used during menstruation or if the user or her partner is allergic to sulfa medicines or polyurethane. It may be less effective in women who have had a pregnancy.

Toxic shock syndrome (TSS) is a very rare, potentially life-threatening bacterial infection that has been associated with the use of contraceptive sponges and diaphragms. In the 1980s, there was a sudden increase in the number of cases of TSS, most affecting young women who were using superabsorbent tampons. The infection is caused by an overgrowth in the vagina of the bacterium *Staphylococcus aureus* (or more rarely with *Streptococcal* infection). The risk is very low, but to reduce it further, women should change tampons frequently (at least every 4 to 8 hours) and should not leave female barrier methods of contraception in place beyond the recommended time. Symptoms of TSS include sudden high fever, vomiting or diarrhea, muscle aches, headache, seizures, and a rash that looks like a sunburn and eventually leads to peeling of the skin on the hands and feet.

Fertility Awareness–Based Methods

Women become pregnant in a window of time around ovulation (release of an ovum). **Fertility awareness–based methods** of contraception rely on identification of the fertile days in the menstrual cycle and abstinence from sex (or use of a barrier contraceptive) during the fertile time. Identification of the fertile time is based on the fact that an egg is most likely to be fertilized within 24 hours of release from the ovary. In addition, sperm can survive up to 6 days inside a woman's body. As a result, a woman is most likely to become pregnant if she has unprotected sex during the 6 days before ovulation, on the day of ovulation, or a few days after ovulation. All fertility awareness–based methods are ways of calculating when a woman will ovulate and avoiding unprotected intercourse during that time.[17]

• *Standard days method.* The standard days method is a calendar-tracking method that can be used only by women who consistently have a regular menstrual cycle 26 to 32 days long, because abstinence or barrier methods must be used for 7 days before ovulation. The method relies on the fact that ovulation usually occurs 14 days *before* the menstrual period begins (Figure 12.4). For a woman with a 28-day cycle, ovulation usually occurs on day 14. However, for a woman with a shorter or longer cycle, the time difference is in the first part of the cycle (from menstruation to ovulation), not in the second part of the cycle (from ovulation to menstruation). For example, if a woman has a 21-day cycle, ovulation will usually occur on day 7. If a woman has a 32-day cycle, ovulation will usually occur on day 18. To avoid pregnancy, the couple would need to avoid intercourse or use another method of contraception between day 8 and day 19. Cycle beads (as well as a Cycle Beads app) have been developed as a tool to help women track their cycles and fertile times.

• *Temperature method.* A woman's basal body temperature (BBT) rises slightly with ovulation. To use the temperature method, a woman must record her temperature when her body is at rest—typically first thing in the morning before getting out of bed. A 0.1- to 0.5-degree rise in basal body temperature occurs with ovulation, and BBT stays slightly elevated until menstruation begins. The

cervical cap
Small, cuplike rubber device that covers only the cervix and is inserted in the vagina before intercourse to prevent conception.

contraceptive sponge
A small polyurethane foam device presaturated with spermicide that is inserted in the vagina before intercourse to prevent pregnancy.

toxic shock syndrome (TSS)
A rare, life-threatening bacterial infection in the vagina associated with the use of tampons and female barrier contraceptive methods.

fertility awareness-based methods
Contraceptive methods based on abstinence during the window of time around ovulation when a woman is most likely to conceive.

figure 12.4   **Fertility awareness–based methods**
Fertility awareness–based methods use the menstrual cycle to determine when fertilization is likely to occur and when unprotected sexual intercourse should be avoided. If a woman does not have a 28-day cycle, the variability in her cycle will be in the part of the cycle from menstruation to ovulation.

temperature spike means ovulation *has* occurred, but it cannot predict when ovulation *will* occur. Using the temperature method, it is safe to have unprotected sex beginning with the fourth day *after* the temperature spike until BBT drops with onset of menses.

- *Cervical mucus method.* The cervical mucus method identifies when ovulation has occurred based on changes in cervical mucus. Cervical mucus becomes thinner and stretchier, resembling egg white, and increases in quantity just before ovulation, so the vagina feels wetter. Unsafe days begin 2 days before onset of the increase in cervical mucus and end 4 days after the peak of slippery mucus. Menses can mask the quality of cervical mucus; as a result, the days of menstruation are not considered safe days. In the 2-day method, a woman asks herself, "Did I

withdrawal
A contraceptive method in which the man removes his penis from the vagina before ejaculating.

emergency contraception (EC)
A contraceptive method used after unprotected sex to prevent pregnancy.

have cervical mucus today? Did I have cervical mucus yesterday?" If the answer to either question is yes, it is an unsafe day for unprotected intercourse. If the answer to both is no, it is considered a safer day.

- *Symptothermal method.* The symptothermal method uses a combination of calendar, temperature, and cervical mucus to predict fertile and infertile times. The combination of methods provides the most reliable confirmation of ovulation. In addition, ovulation testing kits can confirm ovulation.

Withdrawal

Withdrawal, or *coitus interruptus,* is the removal of the penis from the vagina prior to ejaculation. As a method of contraception, it is controversial; however, 30 percent of college students who used contraception at last vaginal intercourse report using withdrawal.[18] Withdrawal is significantly less effective than hormonal methods, but with perfect use, it can be similar to barrier methods in effectiveness. If used, withdrawal is recommended as a dual method, in combination with hormonal, barrier, or LARC methods.[19]

Withdrawal is highly dependent on the characteristics of the users. Success depends on a man's ability to know when he is about to ejaculate and to have the self-control to withdraw with impending orgasm. However, sperm can be present in pre-ejaculation, so this method can fail even if a man withdraws prior to ejaculation. Both partners need to be committed to interruption of intercourse at the time of the man's orgasm. Failure rates appear to be higher in unmarried couples. Withdrawal does not protect from STIs.

Emergency Contraception

Also referred to as the *morning-after pill, post-sex contraception,* or *backup birth control,* **emergency contraception (EC)** can prevent pregnancy after unprotected vaginal intercourse. It is most effective if taken within 72 hours but must be taken within 5 days of unprotected intercourse. EC reduces the chance of pregnancy by preventing ovulation and fertilization. It may reduce the likelihood of implantation, but this is not proven. EC will not cause the termination of an existing pregnancy and so is not an *abortogenic* (abortion-causing) agent. Emergency contraception comes in different forms, including one-time progesterone-only pills (Plan B, Take Action, and others), progesterone-blocking pills (Ella), and copper IUDs. Progesterone-blocking pills and the copper IUD are more effective in the 3- to 5-day window than the progesterone-only pill.[20]

Emergency contraception may be used when another method fails, such as when a condom breaks or a diaphragm or cervical cap slips out of position. It is also useful in cases of forced sex, including rape and incest. The FDA approved over-the-counter sales of progesterone-only EC without prescription to all women, regardless of age.

Consumer Clipboard

Choosing a Reversible Contraceptive

When it comes to reducing the risk of STIs, condoms are key. But if your main concern is avoiding pregnancy, you have a myriad of methods of contraception to choose from. All have benefits and drawbacks. Some are more effective than others. In making your choice, consider all the factors—effectiveness, the medical and practical pros and cons of each method, and the cost. Considered here are the most commonly used reversible contraceptives:

Failure Rate by Average Users*	Method of Birth Control	Factors to Consider	STI Risk Reduction	Cost**
1%	Long-acting reversible contraceptives: Implants and IUDs	Once placed, no further action required for 3-10 years. Reversible. Minor procedure required to place and remove. Some contain hormones	No	$$
4%	Injection (Depo-Provera): *hormonal method*	A provider visit is required every 3 months. Side effects include weight gain and decreased bone density over time. Contains no estrogen.	No	$$
7%	Oral contraceptives (birth control pills): hormonal method	Must be taken daily. Requires a prescription. Safe for most women, but serious health problems can occur. Noncontraceptive benefits include improvement in acne, reduction in menstrual cramps and blood loss, and reduction in risk of ovarian and endometrial cancers.	No	$$
13%	Male condom: *barrier method*	Must be used with every act of intercourse. Accessible, easily carried, and available over the counter. Requires placement on penis prior to insertion of penis.	Best method for reducing risk of STI transmission.	$
18%	Withdrawal	Must be practiced with every act of intercourse. An exercise in self-control. No drugs or devices to buy, and no side effects. Interrupts sexual expression.	No	None
24%*	Fertility awareness-based methods	Requires both partners to learn about the fertility cycle and refrain from intercourse on certain days of the month. No drugs or devices to buy and no side effects. Variations in cycle may make method difficult for some women.	no	None
85%	No method	No protection against pregnancy or STIs.	No	†

*Average use takes into account user variability, whereas "perfect use" would be effectiveness in preventing pregnancy if a user never missed a pill or always used a condom; average use and "perfect use" can vary greatly when action is required at time of intercourse.

**This is initial upfront cost but varies by amount of sexual activity and length of time using method; longer-acting methods become less expensive when averaged over time used. In addition, the ACA requires all new insurance plans to cover costs of contraceptive prescriptions and devices.

†"No method" has no initial cost but carries a high risk of pregnancy and associated costs.

Sources: Adapted from Sundaram, A., Vaughan, B., Kost, K., Bankole, A., Finer, L., et al. (2017). Contraceptive failure in the United States: Estimates from the 2006-2010 National Survey of Family Growth. *Perspectives on Sexual and Reproductive Health, 49*(1), 7-16; Trussell, J. (2011). Contraceptive failure in the United Sates. *Contraception, 83*(5), 397–404; Contraceptive procedures. *Obstetrics and Gynecology Clinics*, 40(4), 697–729; Guttmacher Institute Fact Sheet. (2015). Contraceptive use in the United States. Retrieved from www.guttmacher.org/pubs/fb_contr_use.html#table2; Guttmacher Institute State Policies in Brief. (2015). Insurance coverage of contraceptives. Retrieved from www.guttmacher.org/statecenter/spibs/spib_ICC.pdf.

Emergency contraception can be taken to prevent pregnancy after unprotected sex or used as a backup when another form of contraception fails, as when a condom breaks. Emergency contraception does not cause an abortion.
(Justin Sullivan/Getty Images)

Emergency contraception is an important tool in preventing unintended pregnancy. It has been shown to be extremely safe in almost all women. Its over-the-counter status has increased accessibility, but many college women still remain uninformed about how to access it and when to use it if they have an unprotected sexual encounter. Colleges have tried to increase student education about its safety and availability. Women using EC regularly should evaluate their contraceptive use, because it is not a long-term solution and can cause disruption of menstrual cycles, nausea, and headaches.

The progesterone pill forms of EC (available over the counter) may be less effective in women who are overweight or obese (body mass index greater than 25). In these women, the copper IUD would be the emergency contraceptive of choice. This can be inserted within 5 days of unprotected sex and has the advantage of providing ongoing contraception.[20,21]

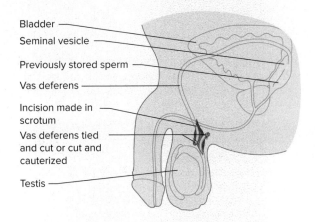

Bladder
Seminal vesicle
Previously stored sperm
Vas deferens
Incision made in scrotum
Vas deferens tied and cut or cut and cauterized
Testis

figure 12.5   Vasectomy
With only local anesthesia needed, this surgical procedure offers permanent sterilization.

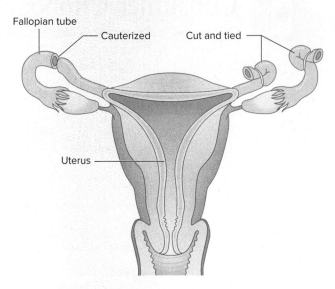

Fallopian tube
Cauterized
Cut and tied
Uterus

figure 12.6   Tubal ligation
This surgical procedure is often performed via laparoscopy, which involves creating two small incisions, one for the scope device and the other for the surgical instruments. It usually requires only local anesthesia.

Permanent Contraception

Permanent contraception is available for men and women through surgical procedures. Worldwide, it is the most commonly used form of contraception and is especially popular among men and women who do not want to have any more children. Although reversal can be performed, the likelihood of pregnancy after a surgical reversal varies widely, from 10 to 92 percent, and cannot be guaranteed. These methods should thus not be considered reversible forms of contraception.[22,23]

The permanent contraceptive procedure for men is **vasectomy**. Besides condoms, vasectomy is currently the only form of contraception available to men. In this procedure, a health care professional makes a small incision or puncture in the scrotum, then ties off and severs the vas deferens, the duct that carries sperm from the testes to the seminal vesicle, where sperm would mix with semen (Figure 12.5). Vasectomy is usually a relatively quick procedure performed with a local anesthetic.

The most common permanent contraceptive procedure for women is **tubal ligation or occlusion**. In this procedure, a physician makes an incision in the abdomen, then severs and ties or seals the Fallopian tubes, the ducts through which ova pass from the ovaries to the uterus (Figure 12.6). The procedure can be done via a surgical method called *laparoscopy*. A laparoscope, a tube that the surgeon can look through with a tiny light on the end, is inserted through a small incision, and the surgical instruments are inserted through another small incision. Recovery usually takes somewhat longer than recovery from a vasectomy. Tubal ligation is also associated with more risk of complications than vasectomy.

Tubal ligation does not alter a woman's menstrual cycle or hormone levels. The ovaries continue to function, but ova are prevented from traveling through the Fallopian tubes to the uterus and so cannot be fertilized. Another former option for permanent contraception in women, called Essure, is no longer available for sale in the United States. Essure consists of the placement of a micro-rod in each of the Fallopian tubes by a hysteroscope inserted through the uterus. Tissue begins to develop around the micro-rods, and after 3 months, this tissue barrier prevents sperm from reaching the egg. Due to reports of complications (including abdominal pain, bleeding), use has stopped; the FDA continues monitoring for complications in women who have received Essure in the past.[24,25]

UNINTENDED PREGNANCY

If you or your partner becomes pregnant unexpectedly, you have to make a monumental decision in a very short period of time. The options are to (1) carry the pregnancy to term and raise the child, (2) carry the pregnancy to term and place the child in an adoptive family, or (3) terminate the pregnancy. Read about the concerns raised for one couple in the box "Life Stories: Jack and Michelle: Unexpected Pregnancy."

Signs of Pregnancy

Some signs of pregnancy are common early on, even before a missed period, as a result of hormonal changes. They can include breast tenderness and swelling, fatigue, nausea and vomiting, light-headedness, and mood swings. Some women have

permanent contraception
Surgical procedures considered permanent in preventing future pregnancies.

vasectomy
A permanent contraceptive procedure for men, involving tying off and severing the vas deferens to prevent sperm from reaching the semen.

tubal ligation or occlusion
A permanent contraceptive procedure for women, involving severing and tying off or obstructing the fallopian tubes to prevent ova from reaching the uterus.

Jack was a senior in college and looking forward to graduation. He had applied to medical school and was confident he would get in, but he did not yet know where he would be going. He wanted to move to a new part of the country and meet new people, but a call from his ex-girlfriend Michelle meant they needed to discuss plans for the future.

Michelle was a junior in college and also on the pre-medicine path when she told him that she was pregnant. The two had seen each other for a few months but had broken up about 3 weeks earlier. When they started dating, Michelle was taking birth control pills and they had agreed to use condoms as an extra precaution. However, a couple of times, after they had been out late at parties and drinking, they had had sex without a condom. Jack hadn't thought much about it, because he considered the condoms a backup method. He didn't realize Michelle had stopped taking the pill.

Jack was glad Michelle had called him, and when they met to talk about options, it was pretty clear to him that she did not want to consider an abortion. She had talked to her sister and parents, and they were ready to support and help her if she needed it. They were encouraging her to move home, but home was in a different state several hundred miles away and meant she would have trouble finishing her degree. Neither Michelle nor Jack felt ready to become a parent, but both wanted to take responsibility. Jack was very close to his father and could imagine being close to his child if he had one. However, the pregnancy complicated the plans of both.

Neither Jack nor Michelle wanted to get back together—they both knew their relationship would not last and a child would not solve that. But when Michelle talked about going home, Jack got scared that he might never see the child. He wondered about his rights as a father and whether they could find a way to be parents together.

- Do you have ongoing discussions about contraception with partners, or do you make assumptions about what method a partner is using?

- Do you have discussions with your partner about what you would do in the event of an unintended pregnancy? If not, why not?

- Do you know what your legal rights and responsibilities are in your state in the event of an unintended pregnancy?

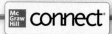

light vaginal bleeding or spotting 10 to 14 days after conception—at about the time of a normal period but shorter in duration. If you experience any of these symptoms after unprotected sex or a missed period, you may want to take a pregnancy test.

A rare complication in early pregnancy is **ectopic pregnancy**, in which the fertilized egg implants or attaches outside the uterus, usually in the Fallopian tube. Signs of this potentially life-threatening condition are severe lower abdominal pain or cramping on one or both sides; vaginal spotting or bleeding with abdominal pain; and light-headedness, dizziness, or fainting (a possible sign of internal bleeding). If you experience any of these signs, contact your physician or go to the emergency room immediately.

Deciding to Become a Parent

Are you ready to become a parent? Here are some questions to consider:

- What are your long-term educational, career, and life plans? How would having a child at this time fit in with those plans?

- What is the status of your relationship with your partner? Is he or she someone you want to commit to and share parenthood with? If you are the mother, the greater part of the pregnancy experience will fall on you, but parenting will require making decisions with your partner about childrearing. Do you have similar goals for a child? Can you communicate well with each other?

- Do you feel emotionally mature enough to take on the responsibility of raising a child? Parenthood requires patience, sacrifice, and the ability to put aside your own needs to meet the needs of another person.

- What are your financial resources at this point? Having a child is expensive. Factoring in inflation, a middle-income family of a child born in 2015 could expect to spend $304,480 (not including college tuition) to raise the child until age 18.[26]

- Do you plan to be financially, emotionally, or physically involved with the child? Historically, unmarried fathers have had fewer rights to interact with their children than unmarried mothers. However, fathers have challenged this, and most states now have statutes establishing how to define fatherhood, paternity, and the rights of fathers.[27]

- How large is your social support system? Do you have family members and friends who will help you? Does your community have resources and support services? Social support has been found to be one of the most important factors in helping couples make a successful adjustment to parenthood.

- What is your health status and age? Do you smoke, drink, or use recreational drugs? Do you have an STI or other medical condition

ectopic pregnancy
A pregnancy in which a fertilized egg implants or attaches outside of the uterus, usually in a Fallopian tube.

■ Adoption offers the possibility of parenthood to people who are not able to conceive a child or who choose not to. Shown here is Viola Davis with her adopted daughter. *(Eugene Powers/Shutterstock)*

that needs to be treated? Are you under 18 or over 35? Babies born to teenagers and women over 35 have a higher incidence of health problems.

Adoption

Adoption can be a positive solution for an unintended pregnancy if you and your partner are not able or willing to become parents at this time in your lives. All forms of adoption require that both biological parents of the adopted child relinquish their parental rights.

In an *open adoption,* the biological parents help to choose the adoptive parents and can maintain a relationship with them and the child. The degree of involvement can range from the exchange of information through a third party to a close and continuous personal relationship among all parties throughout the child's life. Open adoption can make it easier for parents to give up a baby, and it allows the child to know his or her biological parents, siblings, and relatives. Many adoption agencies offer this option.

In a *closed adoption,* the more traditional form of adoption, the biological parents do not help choose the adoptive parents, and the adoption records are sealed so that the adoptive and biological parents remain unknown to each other. Closed adoption provides more privacy and confidentiality than open adoption does. In some states, the child in a

elective abortion
Voluntary termination of a pregnancy.

spontaneous abortion
Involuntary termination of a pregnancy, or miscarriage.

closed adoption may be granted access to the sealed records at the age of 18. In many states, new legislation would allow this even for adoptions that occurred decades ago, when the biological parents thought the records would remain sealed. One reason for the proposed change is the realization that knowledge about their biological parents can be important to adopted persons for both psychological and health reasons.

International adoptions have become less common in recent years. Legislative changes have eased the path to citizenship for children of international adoptions who are under the age of 18.[28]

Elective Abortion

Terminating the pregnancy through **elective abortion** is the third option for a woman with an unintended pregnancy. (This type of abortion is called *elective* to distinguish it from **spontaneous abortion**, or miscarriage.) Since 1973, elective abortion has been legal in the United States. In the case of *Roe v. Wade,* the U.S. Supreme Court ruled that the decision to terminate a pregnancy must be left up to the woman, with some restrictions applying as the pregnancy advances through three *trimesters* (segments of the pregnancy that are each about 3 months long). Women of all ages, races, religious affiliations, and socioeconomic statuses have elective abortions; in the United States, 89 percent occur in the first 12 weeks of pregnancy.[29]

Since the 1973 passage of *Roe v. Wade,* many attempts have been made at state and national levels to limit access to legal abortion. The resulting debate is one of the most highly charged political issues of our time. States continue to enact what are called TRAP (targeted regulation of abortion providers) laws in attempts to restrict access. As of 2019, eight states had only a single location within their borders where women could access abortion services.[30] Yet a majority (54 percent) of U.S. adults believe abortion should be legal in all or most cases; only a very small minority (15 percent) believe abortion should be illegal in all cases.[31]

There are significant differences of opinion by political party affiliation, with 70 percent of Democrats, 55 percent of Independents, and 34 percent of Republicans believing abortion should be legal in all or most cases. However, only 22 percent of Republicans believe abortion should be illegal in all cases.[31] International studies show that women around the world seek abortion regardless of the legality of the procedure. Legality thus does not appear to alter the rates of women seeking abortion, but it does alter the safety of the procedure. In countries where access to abortion is restricted, abortion is less safe and is associated with higher rates of complication and death for women. The only factors that appear to correlate with reduced rates of abortion are knowledge about and access to reliable methods of contraception.[32]

Unintended pregnancy raises complex emotions. Fifty-nine percent of women who have an abortion have one or more children already; they report that their concern for or responsibility to others, and their inability to afford the cost of raising a child, are the major factors in their choice. This may help explain why the majority of women who have an abortion report a feeling of relief after the procedure.[29,33]

Women who are pregnant and considering abortion should seek health care counseling as soon as possible to discuss their options, the risks associated, and the technique to be used. The most common technique currently in use is surgical abortion, but the use of medical abortion is increasing.

Surgical Abortion In **surgical abortion**, the embryo or fetus and other contents of the uterus are removed through a surgical procedure. (Between 2 and 8 weeks of gestation, the term *embryo* is used; after the eighth week, the term *fetus* is used.) The most common method of surgical abortion performed between the 6th and 12th weeks is vacuum aspiration; it is used for the majority of abortions (64 percent) performed in the United States. A provider performs this procedure in a clinical setting, such as a medical office or hospital. The cervix is numbed with a local anesthetic and opened with an instrument called a dilator. After the cervix has been opened, a catheter, a tubelike instrument, is inserted into the uterus. The catheter is attached to a suction machine, and the contents of the uterus are removed.[33,34]

The procedure takes about 10 minutes and requires a few hours' recovery before the woman can return home. An IUD can be placed at the time of procedure for ongoing contraception. When performed in a legal and safe setting, elective abortion does not increase the risk of infertility or of complications in future pregnancies. For later-stage pregnancies, usually when the mother's life is at risk, induction of labor or a surgical procedure called dilation and extraction is sometimes used.[34]

Medical Abortion An alternative to surgical abortion is **medical abortion**, in which a medication is used to induce an abortion. Medical abortions can be performed early in pregnancy (up to 8 weeks of gestation); they now account for about 30 percent of early abortions in the United States.[35]

After an ultrasound to confirm the woman is less than 8 weeks past gestation, she is given the medication mifepristone (RU-486), which blocks progesterone. Progesterone is necessary to maintain a pregnancy. Between 24 and 72 hours later, a second medication, misoprostol, is administered, which causes the uterus to contract and expel the pregnancy. Most women have cramping and bleeding and abort the pregnancy within 1 to 14 days. The success rate is 92 percent and serious complications are rare, but women will experience bleeding and cramping that is heavier than normal menstruation. If abortion does not occur with medication, a surgical abortion becomes necessary.[36]

In the United States, the FDA has imposed restrictions on access to mifepristone, and many states have implemented further restrictions limiting woman's access to the health care system for abortion needs. This has led women to utilize online pharmaceutical sources to obtain medications for a medical abortion.[37,38]

FERTILITY CARE

For many reasons, some individuals and couples require interventions to assist with fertility. Recall the requirement of an egg, a sperm, and a uterus for pregnancy. In some situations, we can predict that a component may be missing at present or in the future. For example, if someone is undergoing chemotherapy or surgery, counseling about the impact of medications and options for preserving eggs or sperm for future use should be considered. A similar discussion should occur prior to the onset of transition in transgender care; transgender people and cisgender people (those whose gender identity corresponds with the gender assigned at birth) have similar desires for biological children. The transition process affects sperm and egg production for trans women and trans men, respectively.[39] People in same-sex relationships may need to consider the use of a surrogate or an egg or sperm donor to replace the missing components.

An estimated 6 percent of married heterosexual couples attempting pregnancy are unable to conceive within a year and are considered to have **infertility**. An estimated 12 percent of women, regardless of marital status, have difficulty getting pregnant or carrying a pregnancy to term. Genetics, infections, and environmental and occupational exposures to water, food, or airborne contaminants can all play a role in infertility. In about 8 percent of couples, infertility is attributable to male factors such as low sperm count or lack of sperm movement. In about 37 percent of couples, infertility is attributable to female factors such as scarring of the Fallopian tubes, endometriosis, or irregular ovulation. In about 35 percent of couples, infertility is attributable to male and female factors combined. In the rest, the cause is unknown.[40]

With delays in childbearing becoming more common, the influence of age on fertility is increasingly clear. Among women aged 15 to 34 years who have not had children previously, 7 to 9 percent will experience infertility; among 40- to 44-year-olds, 30 percent will experience infertility. As women age, the quality of their eggs decreases, and the regularity of egg release also changes. Men experience decline in sperm quality and quantity with aging. And a nearly 60 percent decrease in sperm concentration for men around the world has been noted over the past 35 years. The cause is unclear but is believed to be likely due to environmental exposures.[41] The longer childbearing is delayed, the greater the chance that conception will be difficult and pregnancy complicated.[40]

Reproductive technology options for individuals and couples include counseling and advice, surgery

surgical abortion Surgical removal of the contents of the uterus to terminate a pregnancy.

medical abortion Use of a medication to terminate a pregnancy.

infertility The inability to become pregnant after not using any form of contraception during sexual intercourse for 12 months.

to open blocked Fallopian tubes or correct anatomical problems, fertility (hormonal) drugs to promote ovulation and regulate hormones, and more advanced reproductive techniques. Intrauterine (artificial) insemination is a process whereby sperm are collected and placed directly into a woman's uterus by syringe. This procedure can be helpful if a man has a low sperm count or low sperm movement. Donor sperm can be used if a man has absent sperm or a genetic abnormality, or if no biological male is involved. In vitro fertilization is a technique by which hormones are used to stimulate egg production in the ovaries, multiple eggs are collected through a surgical procedure, the eggs are fertilized in the clinic, and the fertilized eggs are transferred to the uterus.[40]

PREGNANCY AND PRENATAL CARE

The first 1,000 days of life—from conception through the 9 months of pregnancy and up to a child's second birthday—are potentially the most critical phase in life for influencing health and development. Exposure to undernutrition, stress, poverty, violence, and environmental toxins during pregnancy and early childhood disrupt brain development with impacts that last a lifetime. The best approach to ensuring lifelong good health is to give every child the best possible start.[42,43]

Pregnancy Planning

When is the best time to have a child? Although this is a highly personal decision influenced by many factors—educational and career plans, relationship status, health issues, and others—evidence indicates that the least physical health risk for mother and baby occurs when women have pregnancies between the ages of 18 and 35, and when they space births 18 to 24 months apart. Before age 18, a woman's body is still growing and developing. The additional demands of pregnancy and nursing at this time can impair her health, and the baby is more likely to be born early and have a low birth weight. Too short or too long an interval between births also appears to increase the risk of preterm birth and low birth weight.[44,45,46]

With increased economic and educational opportunities, women around the world are delaying having children. In the past 50 years, the average age of first pregnancy in the United States has increased from 22 to 28. While there are advantages to delay, women are more likely to have difficulty getting pregnant as they get older because fertility gradually declines with age. Women over 35 are also more

likely to have medical problems during pregnancy, including miscarriage, and to have a baby who is born prematurely, has low birth weight, or has a genetic abnormality like Down syndrome. As women get older, they are also more likely to have underlying medical conditions, such as diabetes and hypertension, that can further complicate pregnancy.[44,46,47]

Male fertility also declines with age. Men over 40 are twice as likely to be infertile as men in their early 20s, and they have an increased risk of fathering a child with certain health conditions including autism, schizophrenia, and Down syndrome. Health behaviors can affect male fertility at all ages. Tobacco use, alcohol consumption, and obesity can decrease sperm count and sperm mobility.[48,49,50]

Prepregnancy Counseling

People who use effective contraception can reduce the risk of unplanned pregnancy and take advantage of **prepregnancy counseling** when they are ready to attempt pregnancy. Prepregnancy counseling typically includes an evaluation of current health status, health behaviors, and family health history. If you smoke, use drugs, or drink alcohol, you should try to quit *before* becoming pregnant. If you have existing health conditions, pregnancy is an added incentive to make sure you are in the best health and taking medications for your condition that are the safest options for pregnancy. This can be especially important if you take medications for high blood pressure, a seizure disorder, and some psychiatric disorders. If you and your partner are at increased risk for a genetic disease on the basis of your ethnic background or family history, you may want to seek genetic counseling and testing prior to pregnancy.[46]

Nutrition and Exercise

Because so many women become pregnant unintentionally, every sexually active woman who might become pregnant should be aware of the importance of healthy lifestyle factors. A balanced, nutritious diet before and during pregnancy helps ensure that mother and child get required nutrients. A baby needs calcium for its growing bones, and the baby's ability to meet this need is linked to the mother's calcium intake. Iron is critical for a baby's brain development, and women of childbearing years have a high risk of iron deficiency. Getting folic acid in food or in a folate supplement is also recommended, to reduce the risk of neural tube defects (problems in the development of the brain and spinal cord) in the baby. Ideally, women should increase their folic acid intake 1 month *before* getting pregnant so they have a high level of folic acid in their bodies at the time of conception. Given the high rates of unplanned pregnancy in the United States, however, many women will not be able to do so; thus, it is recommended that all women of childbearing age who may become pregnant consume at least 400 micrograms of folic acid a day, usually in the form of a supplement.[46,51,52]

Foodborne infections can have more serious effects in pregnant women than in the general population. Pregnant women are advised to avoid unpasteurized foods, soft cheese (for instance, Brie, Camembert, and feta), and raw or smoked seafood. Monitoring of fish and shellfish intake is advised for pregnant women, women who might become pregnant, nursing mothers, and young children because of possible contamination with mercury.[53] For guidelines on safe fish consumption, see the "Fats—A Necessary Nutrient" section in Chapter 5.

Weight-gain goals during pregnancy vary based on the woman's prepregnancy weight. A woman in the healthy weight range needs to increase calorie intake by only 300 calories a day to achieve a total goal weight gain for her pregnancy of 25 to 35 pounds. An underweight woman should gain more, and an overweight woman should gain less.[53] Regular exercise during pregnancy is recommended to help maintain muscle strength, circulation, and general well-being. Women can usually maintain their prepregnancy level of activity throughout the pregnancy, and women who have not been active can start an exercise program during pregnancy. In the second and third trimesters, women should be cautious about exercise that might cause injury or trauma (such as contact sports and sports with an increased risk of falling such as downhill skiing) and favor safer forms of exercise like walking, swimming, yoga, and low-impact aerobics.[54]

Infection and Pregnancy

Because some infections *during* pregnancy increase the risk of complications for a developing fetus, women should be up to date on their routine vaccinations *before* pregnancy. Especially important are vaccinations for rubella (German measles) and hepatitis B. Rubella can cause spontaneous abortion or serious birth defects, including deafness and blindness. Hepatitis B is a highly infectious disease that causes liver damage and can be transmitted from mother to child during pregnancy and delivery in a process called **vertical transmission**. Pregnant women are also at higher risk of complications from influenza and should get a flu shot during the flu season. They should receive a booster of Tdap (tetanus, diphtheria, and acellular pertussis vaccination) prior to delivery, because pertussis is the bacterium that causes whooping

■ Prenatal care includes regular, moderate physical activity.
(LWA/The Image Bank/Getty Images)

cough in infants, which can result in serious illness or death. Maternal antibodies from vaccines pass to the fetus and infant through the placenta and breast milk, providing early protection for the baby.[55]

If vaccines are not available, women should try to reduce their risk of exposure to infection. Examples of dietary changes to reduce risk of infection were mentioned earlier. Toxoplasmosis is another infection that, in pregnancy, can cause problems like blindness or brain damage in the newborn; it is primarily transmitted through cat feces. Thus, pregnant women are advised to have someone else change the cat litter box.[53] Zika virus infection during pregnancy is associated with microcephaly (small head and brain) in the infant. The virus is transmitted by the *Aedes* mosquito and by sexual transmission. There is no current vaccine or treatment, so women who are pregnant should not travel to affected areas. Women who may become pregnant and their partners are advised to know the risks about such travel. If travel is unavoidable (or if you live in an affected area), use protective clothing, screens, and insect repellents to prevent mosquito bites, and use condoms with a partner who might have been exposed to Zika.[56]

Chronic Health Conditions

Chronic health conditions can complicate pregnancy. About half the adult U.S. population is living with a chronic disease such as diabetes, asthma, or a mental health condition. Women at risk of pregnancy or planning pregnancy can reduce the risk of complications to themselves and their fetus by improving control of their condition. In addition, adjusting medications to the safest treatment option before conceiving reduces risk of damage to the fetus.[57]

More than 80 percent of women report taking over-the-counter or prescription medications while pregnant. The uterus is a highly protected place, but most substances that enter the mother's bloodstream eventually reach the fetus, including medications, drugs, and other substances. When the medication, drug, or substance is known to cause physical damage or abnormality in the fetus, it is called a **teratogen**. Risk of harm is often greatest during the first trimester, when rapid development of body organs is occurring. Examples of common

vertical transmission
The transmission of an infection or disease from mother to child during pregnancy and delivery.

teratogen
A substance that can cause physical damage or abnormality in the fetus, especially if they are present during the first trimester, when rapid development of body organs is occurring.

sudden infant death syndrome (SIDS)
Unexpected death of a healthy baby during sleep.

fetal alcohol syndrome (FAS)
The combination of birth defects caused by prenatal exposure to alcohol, characterized by abnormal facial appearance; slow growth; intellectual disabilities; and social, emotional, and behavior problems.

teratogens include alcohol, tetracycline, cocaine, and isotretinoin (a medication commonly used to treat acne). Exposure to environmental and occupational toxins, including lead, mercury, and pesticides, can increase risk of birth abnormality. Assessing the mother's exposure to intimate partner violence and the availability of social support systems is also important in decreasing the risk of trauma and improving the mother's mental and physical well-being.[57,58]

Tobacco and alcohol are the drugs most commonly used during pregnancy. Tobacco use is associated with increased risk of spontaneous abortion, low birth weight, early separation of the placenta from the uterine wall, and infant death. Babies living in homes where adults smoke have a higher incidence of respiratory infections and **sudden infant death syndrome (SIDS)**.

Consuming 3 or more ounces of alcohol daily (about six drinks) during pregnancy is associated with **fetal alcohol syndrome (FAS)** in the child. This condition is characterized by abnormal facial appearance, slow growth, intellectual disabilities, and social, emotional, and behavior problems. A safe level of alcohol consumption during pregnancy has not been established, and binge drinking, even occasionally, may carry significant risk.

Illicit drugs have a variety of effects on a fetus, depending on the chemical action of the drug. Cocaine causes blood vessels to constrict in the placenta and fetus, increasing the risk of early separation of the placenta from the uterine wall, low birth weight, and possible birth defects. Heroin, OxyContin, and other narcotics can cause retarded growth or fetal

■ Exposure to environmental toxins, including lead, mercury, and pesticides, during pregnancy can increase risk for premature birth, low birth weight, and birth defects. *(Sergey Rogovets/123RF)*

death as well as behavior problems in a child exposed to them in the womb. Illicit drugs are also dangerous because they are often contaminated with harmful substances, such as glass, poisons, and other drugs.[57]

Prenatal Care and Delivery Choices

Every pregnant woman should visit her health care provider regularly for *prenatal care*. The health care provider screens for infections and health conditions and monitors the fetus's growth and development. In the United States, pregnant women have a number of options for health care providers, ranging from midwives to obstetricians, and for delivery; they can give birth at home, in a birthing center, or in a hospital. A woman's choice depends on her personal preferences, her medical and health history, and the likelihood of complications during pregnancy.

Midwives and family doctors usually accept patients who are at lower risk for medical or pregnancy complications. If complications develop during prenatal care or delivery, they will consult with or refer the patient to an obstetrician. Midwives and family doctors tend to view pregnancy and birth as a family event. They are usually trained in support methods (such as breathing and relaxation techniques) so the woman can have a delivery without anesthetic medications, and they usually stay with the woman throughout labor.

Obstetricians are trained to handle all kinds of pregnancies, from low risk to high risk. Perinatologists are obstetricians with additional training in the management of high-risk pregnancy. These specialists are usually found at major medical centers. Most women see a perinatologist only if serious complications arise in the pregnancy.

Complications of Pregnancy for the Mother Despite improvements in health, every day around the world 830 pregnant or postpartum women and 11,233 infants in their first year of life die. The majority of these deaths (99 percent) occur in developing countries, but in the United States, approximately two women and 60 infants die daily.[59,60,61,62] U.S. rates of maternal and infant death are higher than the rates in 16 peer countries (Australia, Austria, Canada, Denmark, Finland, France, Germany, Italy, Japan, Netherlands, Norway, Portugal, Spain, Sweden, Switzerland, and the United Kingdom). Mortality is highest in low socioeconomic groups and among racial minority groups. The disparity in health outcomes is shocking; Black women and American Indian/Alaska Native women have 3.3 and 2.5 times higher rates of maternal mortality than white women. The inequities highlight the role of socioeconomic factors such as racism, lack of prenatal care, lack of access to health information, dietary differences, environmental exposures, and underlying stress. But even U.S. women at the highest socioeconomic levels experience worse health outcomes than equivalent groups in other developed countries.[63,64]

Different health risks are more common at different stages of pregnancy. Early complications include the diagnosis of an STI, usually treated with antibiotics or antiviral medications, and miscarriage. Approximately 15 to 50 percent of all pregnancies end in miscarriage, most during the first trimester.

Pregnancy predisposes some women to develop diabetes, called *gestational diabetes.* Most women are screened between 24 and 28 weeks because the condition occurs midway through pregnancy. Women with gestational diabetes are advised to exercise, control their diet, and monitor glucose levels, but some need to start taking insulin.

Toward the end of pregnancy, the risk for several complications increases. An especially dangerous condition is **preeclampsia**, characterized by high blood pressure, fluid retention, possible kidney and liver damage, and potential fetal death. Signs include facial swelling, headaches, blurred vision, nausea, and vomiting. If not treated, the condition can progress to **eclampsia**, a potentially life-threatening disease for the mother marked by seizures and coma.

Preterm or early labor is another complication of pregnancy. If a woman experiences contractions, cramping, pelvic pressure, or vaginal bleeding before 37 weeks, she should be evaluated to prevent preterm labor.

Complications of Pregnancy for the Child The death of a fetus or infant is a devastating event. Fetal death, the involuntary loss of a fetus during pregnancy, is reported by most states if it occurs after 20 weeks of pregnancy. In a third of cases, no cause is clearly identified; in the other cases, the loss is most commonly related to abnormalities in the placenta, the effect on the fetus of complications in the mother's health, or congenital abnormalities in the fetus.[65] After birth, the leading causes of infant death are preterm birth, low birth weight, and sudden infant death syndrome (SIDS). Despite years of improvement, there has been a recent increase in Black infant mortality, such that the rate of death from both preterm birth and low birth weight is four times higher for Black infants than for white infants.[64,66]

Fetal Development

Within 30 minutes of fertilization in the Fallopian tube, the single-celled fertilized ovum, called a *zygote,* starts to divide. After 5 days, the resulting cluster of cells has made its way down the tube into the uterus. By the end of 1 week, it has attached to the uterus and begun to send small rootlike attachments into the uterine wall to draw nourishment. By the end of the second week, it is fully embedded in the lining of the uterus.

The period from week 2 to week 8, called the embryonic period, is a time of rapid growth and differentiation. By 4 weeks, the cluster of cells has divided into cells of different types, forming an embryo, a **placenta**, and an **amniotic sac**. By 8 weeks, all body systems and organs are present in rudimentary form, and some, including the heart, brain, liver, and sex organs, have started to function.

The period from the end of the eighth week after conception to birth is called the fetal period. By 16 weeks, the sex of the fetus can be readily determined, and the mother can feel fetal movements. By 24 weeks, the fetus makes sucking movements with its mouth.

By week 26, the eyes are open, and by week 30, a layer of fat is forming under the skin. At 36 weeks, the fetus has an excellent chance of survival outside the uterus. A baby is considered to be full term at 38 weeks of gestation, 40 weeks after the mother's last menstrual period. Full-term babies usually weigh about 7 pounds and are about 20 inches long. An overview of fetal development is shown in Figure 12.7.

Diagnosing Problems in a Fetus

About 5 percent of babies born in the United States have a disability. Several tests have been developed to detect

preeclampsia
A dangerous condition that can occur during pregnancy, characterized by high blood pressure, fluid retention, possible kidney and liver damage, and potential fetal death.

eclampsia
A potentially life-threatening disease that can develop during pregnancy, marked by seizures and coma.

placenta
The structure that develops in the uterus during pregnancy and links the circulatory system of the fetus with that of the mother.

amniotic sac
The membrane that surrounds the fetus in the uterus and contains amniotic fluid.

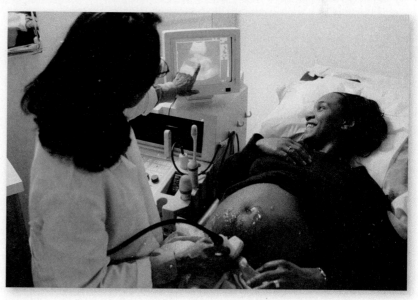

■ Ultrasound is a commonly used prenatal screening tool that can reveal the sex of the fetus, along with other information. Sonograms give expectant parents their first view of their child. *(Kevin Brofsky/Getty Images)*

Time (weeks from gestation)	Changes/milestones
9 weeks (2 months)	Head is nearly as large as the body Limbs are present but legs are short Cardiovascular system is functioning Eyelids are fused closed External genitalia are not distinguishable as male or female Crown-to-rump length: 50 mm (2 inches) Weight: 8 grams (0.3 ounces)
12 weeks (3 months)	Head is still large but body lengthening Facial features begin to appear Arms near relative full length and legs still relatively short Skin is apparent Fingernails starting to form Sex can be determined from genitalia Crown-to-rump length: 87 mm (3.4 inches) Weight: 45 grams (1.6 ounces)
16 weeks (4 months)	Head and body come into greater balance Legs lengthening Ears stand out from head Bones visible on ultrasound Lungs remain immature Crown-to-rump length: 140 mm (5.5 inches) Weight: 200 grams (7 ounces)
20 weeks (5 months)	Fatty secretions (vernix caseosa) covers skin Lanugo (silky hair) covers body Limbs are reaching final proportions Mother feels "quickening"—movement of fetus (usually by 18 weeks) Crown-to-rump length: 190 mm (7.5 inches) Weight: 460 grams (1.0 pounds)
24 weeks (6 months)	Lungs developing but remain immature Fingernails developed Skin wrinkled and red Lean body Crown-to-rump length: 230 mm (9 inches) Weight: 820 grams (1.8 pounds)
28 weeks (7 months)	Brain can control rhythmic breathing and body temperature (if born early) Eyes open, eyelashes present Scalp hair developing Skin less wrinkled as body fat increasing Crown-to-rump length: 270 mm (10.6 inches) Weight: 1300 grams (2.9 pounds)
32 weeks (8 months)	Substantial weight gain Skin smooth Testes descending to scrotum in males Toenails present Crown-to-rump length: 300 mm (12 inches) Weight: 2100 grams (4.6 pounds)
36-38 weeks (9 months)	Plump body Lanugo (silky hair) absent Firm grasp Breasts begin to protrude Crown-to-rump length: 360 mm (14 inches) Weight: 3400 grams (7.5 pounds)

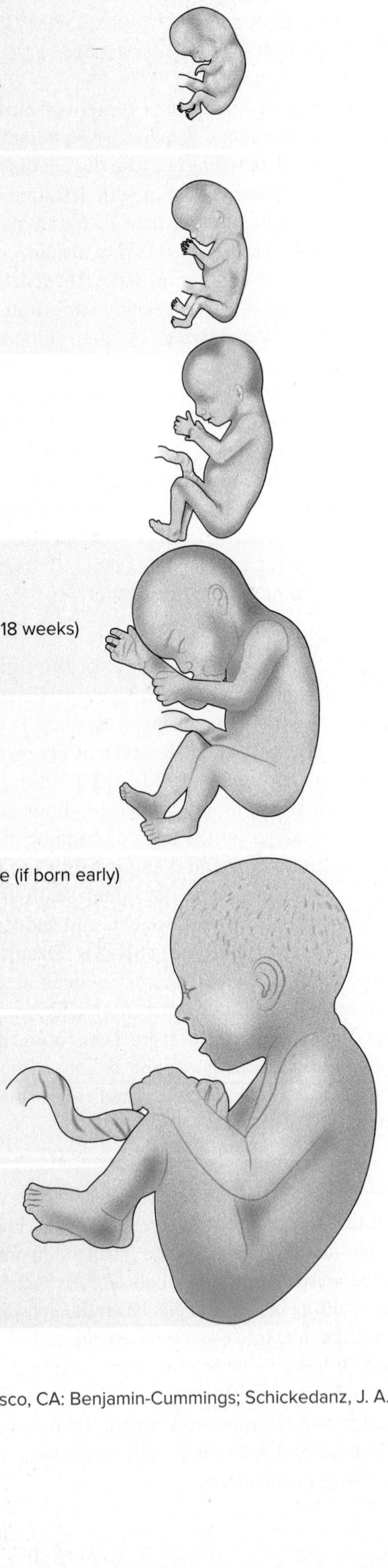

figure 12.7   **Fetal development**

Sources: Data from Marieb, E. N. (2004). *Human anatomy and physiology* (6th ed.). San Francisco, CA: Benjamin-Cummings; Schickedanz, J. A., et al. (2001). *Understanding children and adolescents* (4th ed.). Boston, MA: Allyn & Bacon.

abnormalities in a fetus before birth. In the first trimester, all women are offered screening tests for chromosomal abnormalities, including for Down syndrome, the most common chromosomal abnormality, which occurs in 1 in 800 births in the general population but in 1 in 35 births to women over age 45. All women are offered a combination of a maternal blood test, which can identify fetal DNA, and an **ultrasound**, the use of high-frequency sound waves to produce a visual image of the fetus in the womb.[67,68] Ultrasound is commonly used to establish the size and gestational age of the fetus, its location in the uterus, and any major anatomical abnormalities. It can also reveal the sex of the fetus.

For women at increased risk (due to maternal age or abnormal findings on other screenings), **amniocentesis** and **chorionic villus sampling (CVS)** are offered. Both allow sampling of fetal cells that can then be analyzed. CVS can be performed between 10 and 13 weeks and amniocentesis between 15 and 20 weeks. Because they are invasive procedures, both tests have a slight risk of miscarriage, fetal loss, or infection.

CHILDBIRTH AND THE POSTPARTUM PERIOD

By the ninth month, the pregnant woman is usually feeling uncomfortable and eager to have the baby, despite any apprehension she may harbor about the process of giving birth.

Labor and Delivery

Labor begins when hormonal changes in both the fetus and the mother cause strong uterine contractions to begin. The pattern of labor and delivery can be different for every woman, but early contractions are often irregular.

When labor begins in earnest, the contractions will become regularly spaced and begin to get stronger and more painful. The contractions cause the cervix to gradually pull back and open (dilate), and they put pressure on the fetus, forcing it down into the mother's pelvis. This first stage of labor can last from a few to many hours.

When the cervix is completely open, the second stage of labor begins. The baby slowly moves into the birth canal, which stretches open to allow passage. The soft bones of the baby's head move together and overlap as it squeezes through the pelvis. When the top of the head appears at the opening of the birth canal, the baby is said to be *crowning*. After the head emerges, the rest of the body usually slips out easily.

The third stage of labor is the delivery of the placenta, which usually takes another 10 to 30 minutes. An overview of the process of labor and delivery is shown in Figure 12.8.

Many techniques have been developed to help women with the discomfort of the labor and delivery process. Childbirth preparation classes help women and their partners learn breathing and relaxation techniques to use during contractions. Several medication options are available in hospitals to further help with the discomfort.

Occasionally, the birthing process does not go smoothly. Sometimes, the infant is too big to pass through the mother's pelvis or is in the wrong position, either sideways, buttocks first, or face first. Occasionally, the placenta covers the cervix so the baby cannot move into the birth canal. And sometimes the infant just does not tolerate the stress of the process well.

In these situations, the health care provider usually recommends **cesarean section (C-section)**, the surgical delivery of the infant through the abdominal wall. Although many women are not enthusiastic about this option, it has saved many infants' and mothers' lives.

Newborn Screening

Babies are evaluated at birth to determine whether they require any medical attention or will need developmental support later. The Apgar scale is used as a quick measure of the baby's physical condition: A score of 0 to 2 is given for heart rate, respiratory effort, muscle tone, reflexes, and color. The scores are added for a total score of 0 to 10. The baby's neurological condition may also be assessed, and various screening tests may be given, such as tests for hearing and for phenylketonuria, a genetic disorder that requires a special diet. Most babies are pronounced healthy and taken home within 24 to 48 hours of birth.

The Postpartum Period

The first few months of parenthood, known as the postpartum period, are a time of profound adjustment, as parents learn how to care for their newborn or **neonate** and the newborn takes his or her place in the family. Early childhood development is critical to long-term health (see the box "Public Health Is Personal: The Importance of Early Childhood Education"). A few issues that deserve attention are growth and nutrition, illness and vaccinations, and attachment.

Growth and Nutrition Babies have very high calorie requirements. One reason is their rapid rate of growth—they triple their birth weight by their first birthday—and another

ultrasound
A technique for producing a visual image of the fetus using high-frequency sound waves.

amniocentesis
A technique for testing fetal cells for chromosomal abnormalities by removing a sample of amniotic fluid from the amniotic sac.

chorionic villus sampling (CVS)
A technique for testing fetal cells for chromosomal abnormalities by removing cells from the chorionic villus, part of the placenta in the uterus.

labor
The physiological process by which the mother's body expels the baby during birth.

cesarean section (C-section)
Surgical delivery of the infant through the abdominal wall.

neonate
Newborn.

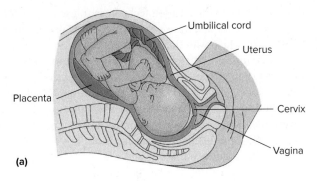

(a)

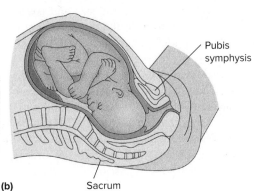

(b)

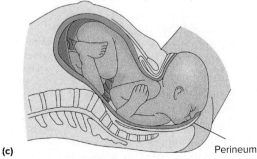

(c)

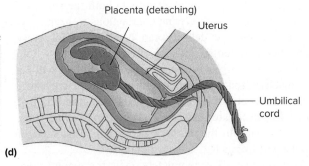

(d)

Early first stage

The cervix thins (*effacement*) and begins to open (*dilation*). Short contractions (30 seconds) occur in 15- to 20-minute cycles. If the mucus plug that blocked the opening of the cervix during pregnancy gives way, light bleeding may occur (*bloody show*). The amniotic sac may also rupture (*water breaking*).

Late first stage

In the transition phase, contractions become stronger and more frequent. These contractions may last from 60 to 90 seconds and occur every 1 to 3 minutes. When the cervix is completely open, with a diameter of about 10 centimeters, it is ready for passage of the baby's head.

Second stage

With strong and frequent contractions, the baby moves downward through the pelvic area, past the cervix, and into the vagina. The mother is instructed to "bear down" with the contractions to aid in the baby's passage through the birth canal. The baby's head emerges first, followed by the shoulders and rest of the body.

Third stage

Contractions of the uterus continue, and the placenta (*afterbirth*) is expelled. If the placenta is not expelled naturally, the health care provider puts pressure on the mother's abdomen to make this happen. The entire placenta must be expelled from the uterus or bleeding and infection may result.

figure 12.8   Labor and delivery
(a) In the first stage of labor, the cervix thins and dilates, ending with (b) the transition phase. (c) Delivery of the baby occurs in the second stage. (d) In the third stage, the placenta is expelled.

reason is the great relative mass of the infant's organs, especially the brain and liver, compared with muscle. Organs have much higher metabolic and energy requirements than muscle does.

The American Academy of Pediatrics recommends that infants be exclusively breastfed until 6 months of age, and that breastfeeding be continued until 1 year of age with the introduction of other foods. Breast milk is perfectly suited to

babies' nutritional needs and digestion; it also contains antibodies that reduce the risk of infections, allergies, asthma, and SIDS. For mothers, breastfeeding enhances bonding with the baby, contributes to weight loss after pregnancy, and may decrease the risk of ovarian cancer and breast cancer after menopause.

Breastfeeding rates are increasing, with 84 percent of U.S. women starting to breastfeed, 57 percent continuing at

Public Health Is Personal

The Importance of Early Childhood Education

As an infant, you are born into a family and environment that provides you with either tremendous opportunity or potential disadvantage. Research is increasingly showing that fetal and early childhood experiences are critical for lifelong health. Development of the brain is most intense from gestation until age 3 (the first 1,000 days of life). Early experiences can even influence which genes are turned on or off and thus shape a child's developing brain structure.

Children exposed to positive early environments activate their brain's learning and memory circuits and experience epigenetic changes that have the potential for lifelong positive health outcomes and resiliency. For example, the number of words a child has by age 3 directly correlates with his or her ability to read by third grade, which directly correlates with the likelihood of graduating from high school. Positive early childhood environments are linked to improved educational outcomes, increased earning potential, and reduced crime rates.

In contrast, children born into stressful environments—such as the experience of poverty, food insecurity, racism, or family or neighborhood violence—are more likely to have negative health outcomes. Adverse childhood events cause brain changes that influence the stress-response cycle of a child and affect lifelong responses to adversity. Racism and racial discrimination at the individual, institutional, and cultural levels significantly contribute to early childhood stress and cumulative stress. Poverty is another particularly relevant early childhood stressor, given that the United States has more children living in poverty than any of its peer developed countries. Chronic stress and lack of academic preparedness in early childhood reduce the foundation children have when they enter kindergarten and increase the likelihood of poor school performance. This, in turn, increases the lack of preparedness for work or college, and ongoing cycles of poverty.

Young children need stimulating learning opportunities and positive relationships with adults. High-quality early care and education programs can provide these for children, yet such programs are limited. Passage of the Federal Every Student Succeeds Act in 2015 created an opportunity for states and school districts to increase resources for early childhood education, and 47 states received funding to plan comprehensive approaches for early childhood education.

Early childhood education has wide support from a broad cross section of the country, including the military (because young adults will be better prepared to serve), law enforcement (because early education may reduce crime), and business and industry (because workers will be better qualified). After all, who can argue with the value of providing infants with high-quality, safe, and stimulating environments?

McGraw Hill connect

Sources: ACE Study. (2014). Injury prevention and control: Division of Violence Prevention. Centers for Disease Control and Prevention. Retrieved from www.cdc.gov/violenceprevention/acestudy/index.html; National Scientific Council on the Developing Child. (2010). Early experiences can alter gene expression and affect long-term development: Working Paper No. 10. Retrieved from www.developingchild.net; New America. (n.d.). ESSA and early learning: A look at state and local implementation. Retrieved from https://www.newamerica.org/education-policy/edcentral/essa-and-early-learning-look-state-and-local-implementation/; Woolf, S.H., & Aron, L. (2013). U.S. health in international perspective: Shorter lives, poorer health. Washington, DC: National Academies Press; Bernard, D.L., Calhoun, C.D. et al. (2020) Making the "C-ACE" for a culturally-informed Adverse Childhood Experiences framwork to understand the pervasive mental health impact of racism on Black youth. Journal of Child & Adolescent Traum. https://doi.org/10.1007/s40653-020-00319-9

6 months, and 36 percent continuing at 1 year.[69] New mothers need advice and support to start and continue breastfeeding. Health providers, lactation consultants, and breastfeeding support groups improve success by encouraging mothers to room with their infants, not give pacifiers, and initiate nursing within an hour of birth. Partners and family can also provide support by encouraging the nursing mother. Workplaces and childcare centers can support breastfeeding by providing lactation rooms and offering flexible scheduling. Paid-leave policies also support breastfeeding by allowing women more time with a child prior to returning to work. Breast milk can be pumped and fed by bottle if necessary or desired. At times there are medical reasons why a women is unable to breastfeed, or in cases of adoption or surrogate parenting, breastfeeding may not be an option. In these cases, it is important to support parents and recognize that bottle-feeding provides adequate nutrition.[69]

Illness and Vaccinations Birth and early childhood are times of increased risk of infection for an infant. Starting at 2 months, children receive vaccinations against several childhood diseases that, in the past, caused serious illness and death. They include diphtheria, pertussis (whooping cough), tetanus, measles, rubella (German measles), mumps, and polio, among others. The vaccinations are inexpensive and safe, especially when compared with the physical, emotional, and social costs of childhood diseases. Most states require that children be vaccinated before they start public school (see Chapter 13 for a more in-depth discussion about vaccinations).

Adjustment and Attachment Although babies are tiny, they quickly become the center of attention in the household. They spend their time in recurring states of crying, alertness, drowsiness, and sleep. Parents spend much of their time feeding their newborn (at first, every 2 hours or so), changing diapers, and trying to soothe the crying infant. A strong emotional bond between parents and infant, known as **attachment**, develops during this period, and the infant begins to have feelings of trust and confidence as a result of a

attachment
The deep emotional bond that develops between an infant and its primary caregivers.

331

comforting, satisfying relationship with parental figures. This sense of trust is crucial for future interpersonal relationships and social and emotional development. Thus, a healthy infancy lays the foundation for a healthy life. Spending high-quality time with an infant is important for establishing healthy attachment, but many factors, including paid leave from work, contribute to a parent's ability to be present (see You Make the Call: Should the United States Provide Paid Family Leave After the Birth or Adoption of a Child?).

About 13 percent of women experience depression in the first year after giving birth, referred to as *postpartum depression*. Rapid hormone changes after delivery, broken sleep patterns, self-doubt about her ability to provide for the infant, a sense of loss of control, and changes in her support system can all contribute to a mother's feelings of sadness, restlessness, loss of interest, and guilt. Postpartum depression can also have significant effects on a woman's relationships with her partner and baby. Effective treatments exist, and women and their partners should be aware of the signs and symptoms of the condition.

◼ Attachment between parent and infant—a strong emotional bond—develops in response to an engaged parent's interaction with and comforting of the child. An infant's development of trust is crucial for future relationships and emotional development.
(Francisco Cruz/Purestock/SuperStock)

You Make the Call

Should the United States Provide Paid Family Leave After the Birth or Adoption of a Child?

What do the United States, Suriname, and Papua New Guinea have in common? None consistently offer some form of paid parental leave. The United States is the only industrialized country in the world that does not have guaranteed paid parental leave. In 1993, the Family Medical Leave Act (FMLA) was signed into law and allowed U.S. workers to take up to 3 months of paid or unpaid leave when seriously ill or when needed to care for a baby, spouse, or family member. A revision in February 2015 amended the definition of spouse to include eligible employees in legal same-sex marriages. The assumption at that time was that employers would make the choice to provide paid family leave, but in reality only 17 percent of U.S. civilian workers have access to any paid leave for childbirth (or the adoption of an infant). The employees who have access to paid leave tend to be higher-income earners (managers and professionals), while those who have no paid leave are employees with lower incomes (those in transportation, construction,

service, and retail industries). These minimum-wage and hourly workers are the least likely to be able to afford to take unpaid time off work.

Some states have established requirements for paid leave; California, New Jersey, Rhode Island, and New York offer 4 to 8 weeks. Some companies are taking the lead and offering paid family leave as a perk of the job. Netflix offers employees up to 1 year of paid parental leave following childbirth. Microsoft and Airbnb offer 22 weeks of paid leave for employees. Amazon offers *all* employees working at least 26 hours per week—from its hourly warehouse workers to its top executives—20 weeks of paid leave, and an additional 8 weeks with a flexible work schedule to ease the transition back to work.

What do other countries offer? Paid leave ranges from 12 weeks in Pakistan, South Africa, and Mexico to 44 weeks in the United Kingdom, Italy, and Norway. Canada offers the highest level: 50 weeks of paid family leave.

Continued...

Concluded...

Advocates give a number of reasons for supporting paid leave. From a business perspective, it makes sense financially because it acknowledges the reality that workers will have children and sick family members. Planning for paid leaves helps workers make smoother transitions to the new role of parent (or caregiver for a sick family member), and they will be better prepared to return to work smoothly. They will feel more valued as a worker and, in turn, have more loyalty and work harder. This will reduce employee turnover and the resulting loss in production.

There are also health arguments for paid time off. Women who feel a financial strain because they have no paid time off are more likely to return to work within 12 weeks of delivery. However, those who return to work 13 weeks or more after the birth of a child are more likely to breastfeed and bond more closely with their infant. Breastfeeding improves the newborn's immunity and helps the mother lose pregnancy-related weight. Paid leave decreases financial stress and supports parent-infant relationships that promote positive early childhood development.

Another argument is that paid leave is a social justice issue for women. Women make up 47 percent of the workforce, and 40 percent of households with children under the age of 18 are headed by a mother who is the primary breadwinner, so women need paid leave to care for newborn or sick children. Women should not have to choose between providing financially for their family and taking time to be with a new child or sick family member.

Opponents argue that time off work will be disruptive to the workforce and place undue financial burden on employers. Employee leave reduces production levels and places a burden on individuals who do not have children, and hiring temporary workers to replace workers on leave increases expenses. In addition, some observers argue that requiring companies to pay for maternity leave might motivate them to discriminate against women of childbearing age when hiring, making it more difficult for women to find work.

What do you think? Is it time for the United States to mandate paid family leave?

Pros

- It makes business sense to plan for and support employees taking time off for their families.
- Paid leave benefits parent-child bonding and children's health.
- It is unjust to ask parents to choose between achieving financial stability and caring for a newborn or sick family member.

Cons

- Paid leave is a burden on employers that will reduce their ability to compete on a global scale.
- Paid time off will encourage employees to take longer leaves, which will be more disruptive to the workforce.
- Worksites will discriminate more against women if they are required to contribute to family leave.

Sources: U.S. Department of Labor. (2015). Final rule to revise the definition of "spouse" under the FMLA. Retrieved from www.dol.gov/whd/fmla/spouse/index.htm; Molla, R. (2018). Netflix parents get a paid year off and Amazon pays for spouses' parental leave. Vox. Retrieved from https://www.vox.com/2018/1/31/16944976/new-parents-tech-companies-google-hp-facebook-twitter-netflix; Bureau of Labor Statistics, U.S. Department of Labor. (n.d.). *The Economics Daily*, Access to paid and unpaid family leave in 2018 on the Internet. Retrieved from https://www.bls.gov/opub/ted/2019/access-to-paid-and-unpaid-family-leave-in-2018.htm.

In Review

What are the commonly available contraceptive methods?
The most reliable method, if practiced perfectly, is abstinence. The most reliable method of reversible contraception is long-acting contraception with an IUD or implant. Other methods include hormonal methods (birth control pills, the transdermal patch, the contraceptive ring, and injectable contraceptive), barrier methods (male and female condoms, the diaphragm, the cervical cap, and the contraceptive sponge), fertility awareness–based methods, and emergency contraception. Male and female sterilization are effective permanent contraceptive options. Methods vary in their effectiveness, cost, convenience, permanence, safety, protection against STIs, and consistency with personal values.

What are the options in the event of unintended pregnancy?
The three options are having and keeping the baby, placing the baby for adoption, and having an abortion. The vast majority of elective abortions, nearly 90 percent, are performed during the first 12 weeks of pregnancy. Abortions can be performed surgically or medically (with medication).

What are the options when fertility is a problem?
Treatments are increasingly available for fertility care and include proactively preserving eggs or sperm, surgery, fertility drugs, intrauterine fertilization, in vitro fertilization, and other advanced technologies.

What are the basics of prenatal care?
Prepregnancy care can include improving chronic health conditions, adjusting medications, ensuring healthy nutrition, and maintaining or modifying physical activity levels. In addition, genetic counseling and vaccinations against common infectious diseases, especially pertussis, rubella, and hepatitis B, may be necessary. Once a woman is pregnant, prenatal care includes good nutrition and exercise, avoidance of substances that could harm the fetus, and regularly scheduled health care visits. Problems in the fetus can be diagnosed prenatally by advanced technologies.

What happens during prenatal development?

The fertilized egg (zygote) implants in the uterine wall and begins a period of rapid growth and differentiation. During the first trimester, all the body systems form and start functioning (e.g., the heart starts beating), the limbs are molded, and the sex of the fetus can be recognized. During the second trimester, the fetus continues to develop, and the proportion of the body to head becomes more balanced. The third trimester is a period of rapid weight gain. At birth, the typical baby weighs about 7 pounds and is about 20 inches long.

What happens during labor and delivery?

During the first stage of labor, strong uterine contractions cause the cervix to shorten and open and push the baby down into the mother's pelvis. During the second stage of labor, the baby moves into the birth canal and emerges from the mother's body, usually head first. During the third stage of labor, the placenta is delivered.

What concerns arise during the postpartum period?

The first 1,000 days are important for setting patterns for lifelong health. Breast milk is the ideal food for a baby, either directly from the breast or via a bottle. If unable to breastfeed or in certain medical conditions, formula is an acceptable alternative. Newborns are especially vulnerable to infections; they start receiving routine vaccinations at about 2 months. The newborn period is one of profound adjustment for all family members.

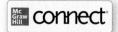

Personal Health Portfolio

Chapter 12 Which Contraceptive Method Is Right for You?

As you learned in the text, many contraception options are available to you. This activity will help you determine which contraceptive method best fits your needs. You may also want to discuss your options and decisions with your health provider, especially since the most effective methods require a visit.

Part 1 Your Partner's and Your Preferences

	Yes	No
1. I am sure I do not want children at this time.		
2. My partner and I are in a monogamous relationship with no concerns about sexually transmitted infections.		
3. I want a method that I can control myself.		
4. My partner or I am good at remembering to take medication daily.		
5. My partner or I am willing to visit a health provider or clinic to get birth control.		
6. My partner or I like sexual spontaneity and don't want to have to worry about contraception right before sex.		
7. Using birth control is not acceptable within my moral and/or religious belief system.		

Part 2 Your Sexual Behavior

	Yes	No
1. I sometimes have sex after using alcohol or drugs.		
2. I sometimes hook up with people I don't know well.		
3. I am in a relatively new relationship or have more than one partner.		
4. I have not discussed with my partner his or her prior sexual history or history of sexually transmitted infections.		

Part 3 Risk Factors

Do any of the following apply to you or your partner?	Yes	No
1. Over age 35 and a smoker		
2. Liver disease, blood clots, breast cancer		
3. Personal history of migraine headaches		
4. Family history of blood clots, stroke, heart attack		

Interpretation

Part 1

Question 1. Yes responses: If you do not want children at any time in the future, permanent sterilization may be the best option. However, if your goal is to delay children for several years, you may want a reliable long-acting reversible contraceptive, such as an IUD or implant.

Question 2. Yes responses: You may not need to use condoms or other barrier methods to provide STI protection. Hormonal methods are an option for you.

Question 3. Yes responses: If you are male, the male condom and vasectomy will allow you to take full responsibility for contraception. If you are female, tubal ligation, hormonal contraception, and barrier methods (excluding the male condom) will allow you to take full responsibility for contraception.

Question 4. Yes responses: Birth control pills would be an effective option for you since they need to be taken daily. The vaginal ring and the transdermal patch, which must be changed every month, are other options.

Question 5. No responses: Contraceptive methods that can be purchased over the counter include male and female condoms and the contraceptive sponge.

Question 6. Yes responses: You may benefit from hormonal contraception such as an IUD or a contraceptive implant that does not require any action at the time of sex. However, if you are at risk for STIs, you will still need to use a barrier method like a condom, even if you would prefer not to.

Question 7. Yes responses: Your options are fertility awareness-based methods if you are sexually active or abstinence. Withdrawal may be another option, but it is less effective at preventing pregnancy.

Part 2

If you answered yes to the majority of questions in this section, condom use is an important part of your contraceptive needs. Hooking up, alcohol use, and drug use all increase the risk for sexually transmitted infections. However, these behaviors also make it less likely that you will actually use a condom or other barrier method at the time of intercourse, so it is also recommended that women use a reliable contraceptive to prevent pregnancy that does not require action at the time of intercourse (like birth control pills or the vaginal ring).

Part 3

These factors increase the risk of side effects from hormonal contraceptives. If you answered yes to any of these questions, you and your partner may want to consider a barrier contraceptive or permanent contraception, depending on your future plans.

See the "Consumer Clipboard" box in this chapter for an overview of specific contraceptive methods.

CRITICAL THINKING QUESTIONS

1. What personal factors influence your sexual decision making and contraception use? Consider your partner pattern and your social network.

2. What factors in your environment influence your sexual decision making and contraception use? Consider the socioecological model and how community and policies have impacted your beliefs, values, access to sexual health education, and sexual health care.

3. Is there anything you would like to change in this area of your life? If so, consider making a behavior change plan and decide what your first steps would be.

Infectious Diseases

13

princessdlaf/Getty Images

Ever Wonder...

whether you are up to date on your vaccines?

how SARS-CoV-2 (COVID-19) might affect you?

which STIs can be cured and which can't?

Before 1900, infectious diseases were the leading cause of death in the United States, with 30 percent of all deaths occurring among young children. Antibiotics and public health measures, including vaccinations, are responsible for reducing the death rate from infectious diseases in the United States to about 2 percent of all deaths by the end of the 20th century. The rate has remained relatively stable since that time. The greatest reductions in infectious diseases have come from improved sanitation and hygiene practices, especially sewage treatment and the wide availability of clean water supplies. In recent years, the causes of deaths from infectious diseases have changed, as a result of newer diseases such as SARS-CoV-2 (COVID-19) and AIDS the reemergence of existing diseases once thought vanquished, and new challenges such as drug resistance.[1,2] This chapter provides an overview of infectious diseases, including sexually transmitted infections (STIs), and offers guidelines for protecting yourself and your community from infections.

THE PROCESS OF INFECTION

Microorganisms, the tiniest living organisms on earth, do what all living organisms do: eat, reproduce, and die. An **infection** occurs when part of a microorganism's life cycle involves you. An infection is considered an illness or disease if it interferes with your usual lifestyle or shortens your life.

The process of infection often follows a typical course, with the length of each stage depending on the **pathogen** (Figure 13.1). Infections can also result in different outcomes. Some cause a sudden illness with a high risk of death, such as infection with the Ebola virus or SARS-CoV-2 (the virus that causes COVID-19).

Some stimulate your body's immune response, causing the death of the microorganism, as occurs with common cold viruses. Still others may persist without signs of illness for years and yet be passed on to other people, as is the case with the human immunodeficiency virus (HIV). Finally, some infections are dormant or walled off by the immune system, such as tuberculosis, and are held at bay in a latent phase for as long as the immune system is healthy. Latent infections may activate at a later point. Other infections are incompletely cleared by the body and continue at a low level indefinitely.

The Chain of Infection

The **chain of infection** is the process by which an infectious agent, or pathogen, passes from one organism to another. Pathogens often live in large communities, called *reservoirs,* in soil or water or within organisms. Many pathogens cannot survive in the environment and require a living *host.* To cause infection, pathogens must have a *portal of exit* from the reservoir or host and a *portal of entry* into a new host (Figure 13.2).

A pathogen can exit a host (portal of exit) via respiratory secretions (coughing, sneezing), feces, genital secretions, blood or blood products, open sores, nasal or eye discharge, or an insect or animal bite. The pathogen enters the new host (portal of entry) in similar ways: through cuts or open sores on the skin or mucous membranes (the lining of the mouth and genital tract), inhalation of respiratory droplets, swallowing of pathogens, or insect or animal bites. If the transfer from host to host or from reservoir to host is carried out by an insect or animal, that organism is called a **vector**.

Altering or breaking the chain of infection at any point can increase or decrease the risk of infection. For example, urban development that encroaches on deer populations increases the chance of humans coming into closer contact with deer and deer ticks and increasing their risk of contracting tickborne disease; raising chickens close to the house can increase risk of novel influenza viruses because chickens can also be infected and serve as a reservoir; and contracting genital herpes affects the portal of exit or the portal of entry for HIV by creating open sores on the skin and increasing the

infection
A disease or condition caused by a microorganism.

pathogen
An infectious agent capable of causing disease.

chain of infection
Process by which an infectious agent passes from one organism to another.

vector
An animal or insect that transmits a pathogen from a reservoir or an infected host to a new host.

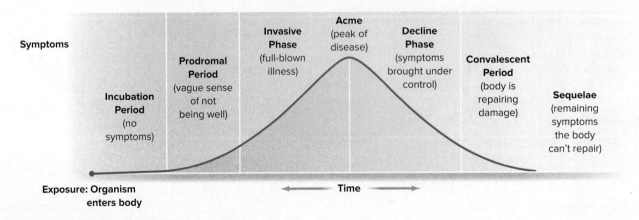

figure 13.1   Stages of infection
At the peak of the disease, either the immune system gains control, medical treatment occurs, or death ensues.

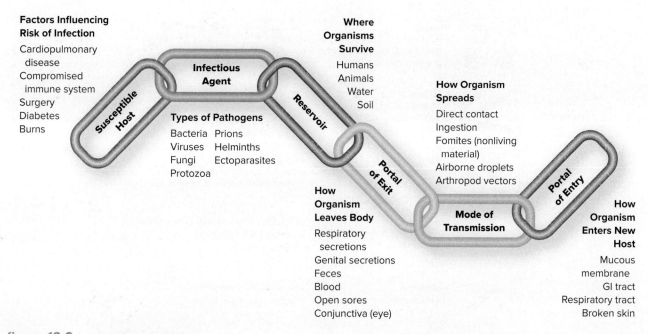

figure 13.2   The chain of infection
Breaking the chain at any point decreases the risk of infection.

risk of HIV transmission. Chronic health conditions and poor nutritional status affect the host and increase the risk of becoming infected if exposed to a pathogen. Meanwhile, chlorinating drinking water reduces the number of pathogens and the size of reservoirs for waterborne infections; using condoms disrupts both the portal of exit and the portal of entry for infectious agents that may be present in semen or vaginal secretions; wearing masks disrupts both the portal of exit and the portal of entry for respiratory diseases; and controlling mosquito populations eradicates vectors and disrupts many pathogens' mode of transmission.

The extent or spread of an infection depends on several factors, including the **virulence** of the pathogen—that is, its speed and intensity—the mode of transmission (the way an infection spreads from person to person), the ease of transmission, the duration of infectivity (the length of time during which a person with infection can spread it to other people), and the number of people an infected person has contact with while infectious. If an infected person does not transmit the infection to anyone else, that person's disease dies out. If the person transmits it to at least one other person, the infection continues. If the infection is transmitted to many people, an **epidemic** may occur.

Pathogens

Millions of different pathogens cause human infections, but they fall into several broad categories, as shown in Figure 13.3 and discussed next.

Viruses Viruses are some of the smallest pathogens. They are also among the most numerous; it is estimated that there are more different types of viruses than of all other living organisms combined.

Viruses consist of a genome (a genetic package of either DNA or RNA), a capsid (protein coat), and, in some cases, an outer covering or envelope. They are unable to reproduce on their own; they can replicate only inside another organism's cells and do not usually survive long outside humans or other hosts. A virus infects a host cell by binding to its receptors and injecting its genetic material into the cell. Once inside, the virus can have a number of different effects. It can make many copies of itself, burst the cell, and release the copies to infect more cells. It can persist within the cell, slowly continuing to cause damage or becoming inactive and reactivating at a later time. Some viruses integrate themselves into a cell's DNA and alter the growth pattern of the cells. This process can lead to the development of a tumor or cancer; viruses cause an estimated 12 to 20 percent of cancers (see Chapter 15).[3,4]

Bacteria Bacteria are single-celled organisms that can be found in almost all environments. They are classified based on shape (spherical, rodlike, spiral), the presence or absence of a cell wall, and growth requirements. Speed of replication varies from 20 minutes to 2 weeks. Some bacteria can enter a dormant or spore state in which they can survive for years.

Bacteria are an important part of the human **microbiome**, the collection of microorganisms that live in or on a host in a mutually beneficial way. Bacteria play vital roles in food processing, vitamin

virulence
The speed and intensity with which a pathogen is likely to cause an infection.

epidemic
A widespread outbreak of a disease that affects many people.

microbiome
The collection of microorganisms that live in or on a host and play a vital role in human life.

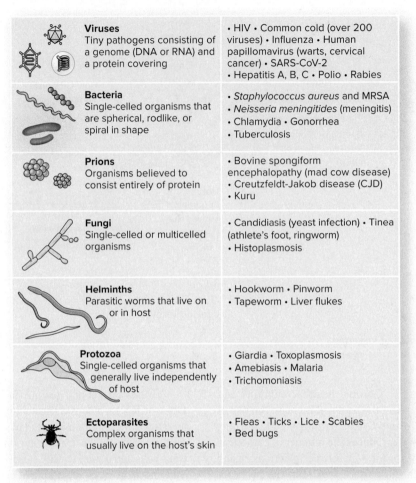

	Viruses Tiny pathogens consisting of a genome (DNA or RNA) and a protein covering	• HIV • Common cold (over 200 viruses) • Influenza • Human papillomavirus (warts, cervical cancer) • SARS-CoV-2 • Hepatitis A, B, C • Polio • Rabies
	Bacteria Single-celled organisms that are spherical, rodlike, or spiral in shape	• *Staphylococcus aureus* and MRSA • *Neisseria meningitides* (meningitis) • Chlamydia • Gonorrhea • Tuberculosis
	Prions Organisms believed to consist entirely of protein	• Bovine spongiform encephalopathy (mad cow disease) • Creutzfeldt-Jakob disease (CJD) • Kuru
	Fungi Single-celled or multicelled organisms	• Candidiasis (yeast infection) • Tinea (athlete's foot, ringworm) • Histoplasmosis
	Helminths Parasitic worms that live on or in host	• Hookworm • Pinworm • Tapeworm • Liver flukes
	Protozoa Single-celled organisms that generally live independently of host	• Giardia • Toxoplasmosis • Amebiasis • Malaria • Trichomoniasis
	Ectoparasites Complex organisms that usually live on the host's skin	• Fleas • Ticks • Lice • Scabies • Bed bugs

figure 13.3   **Main types of pathogens and common examples. Fungi, helminths, and protozoa are part of a larger grouping called eukaryotes.**

production, and colonizing of areas to reduce the risk of harmful pathogens causing disease. Sometimes bacteria that are helpful in one location can be pathogens (or cause disease) in another location, as when *Escherichia coli,* a bacterium that inhabits the large intestine and aids in digestion, enters the bladder, where it causes a bladder or urinary tract infection.[3]

Prions   Prions, the least understood infectious agents, are pathogens known to be responsible for the neurodegenerative disease bovine spongiform encephalopathy (BSE), or mad cow disease. The term *prion* was coined as a shortened form of *proteinaceous infectious particle.* Prions are believed to be made entirely of protein. They are found in brain tissue and appear to alter the function or shape of other proteins when they infect a cell, initiating a degeneration of brain function. Prions appear to spread by the ingestion of infected brain or nerve tissue.[3]

Fungi   A fungus is a single-celled or multicelled organism. There are many types of fungi, including yeasts and molds, and they are found everywhere, including in and on human hosts as part of a healthy microbiome. Fungi tend to cause serious infections when the host immune system is not

■ Skin is an excellent physical barrier, but the female mosquito is able to penetrate it with her proboscis. Mosquitoes serve as vectors for several diseases caused by bloodborne pathogens, including Zika virus, encephalitis, West Nile virus, and malaria. *(James Gathany/CDC)*

working well. Fungi reproduce by budding or by making spores; many fungal infections result from exposure to spores in the environment, such as in the soil or in food. Fungal infections rarely spread from person to person.

Dermatophytes are a group of fungi that commonly infect the skin, hair, or nails. They are sometimes called "ringworm" or "tinea" infections. Many different species can infect humans, and they are usually described by the location they infect rather than by their specific species; we know them as athlete's foot, nail fungus, and jock itch, among others. Another type of fungus, the yeast *Candida,* may be part of a person's normal microbiome but can overgrow and cause an infection in the vagina (vaginal candidiasis), the mouth (thrush), or throughout the body (systemic candidiasis). All the fungi can become serious infections in a person with a compromised immune system (such as someone with HIV infection or AIDS, someone undergoing chemotherapy for cancer, or someone taking immunosuppressant drugs following an organ transplant).[3]

Helminths Helminths, or parasitic worms, include roundworms, flukes, and tapeworms. They are large compared with other infectious agents, ranging in length from 0.4 inch to several feet for adult worms. People usually become infected with parasites by accidentally ingesting worm eggs in food or water, by being exposed to contaminated soil with penetration through the skin, or by being bitten by an insect vector such as a fly or mosquito. Worldwide, especially in developing countries, parasitic worms cause a huge disease burden. For example, hookworm, which attaches to the human intestine and causes blood loss, can lead to anemia and malnutrition, particularly in children.[3,5]

Protozoa Protozoa are single-celled organisms; most can live independently of host organisms. Protozoal infections are a leading cause of disease and death in Africa, Asia, and Central and South America. They may be transmitted by contaminated water, feces, or food, as is the case in giardia, toxoplasmosis, and amebiasis; by air, as is the case in *Pneumocystis carinii* pneumonia; by sexual contact, as is the case in trichomoniasis; or by a vector, such as the mosquito in the case of malaria.[3,5]

Ectoparasites Ectoparasites are complex organisms that usually live on or in the skin, where they feed on the host's tissue or blood. They cause local irritation and are frequently vectors for serious infectious diseases. Examples are fleas, ticks, lice, mosquitoes, bed bugs, and scabies.[3,5]

THE BODY'S DEFENSES

A single square inch of skin on your arm is home to thousands of bacteria. A sneeze projects hundreds of thousands of viral particles into the air. Bacteria can double in number every 20 minutes, and a virus can replicate thousands of times within a single human cell. Although you are substantially larger than microorganisms, you feel the power of their numbers each time you catch a cold. Considering these facts, our ability to overcome invasion and survive infectious diseases is remarkable.

External Barriers

Externally, the body defends itself against pathogens in two ways: by keeping them out physically and by destroying them chemically.

Physical Barriers The skin is the first line of defense against infection. Most organisms cannot get through skin unless it is damaged, such as by a cut, burn, or existing infection, or if passage is aided by an insect bite or needlestick. Most portals of entry into the body, such as the mouth, lungs, nasal passages, and vagina, are lined with mucous membranes. Although these linings are delicate, mucus traps many organisms and prevents them from entering the body. Nasal passages and ear canals have hair that helps trap particles. The lungs are protected by the cough reflex and by cilia, tiny hairlike structures that rhythmically push foreign particles up and out. Damage to these physical barriers increases risk of infection. In addition, millions of healthy bacteria reside on your skin and on the mucous membranes as part of your microbiome. These healthy bacteria take up space and reduce the chance that unhealthy or harmful bacteria can grow.[3]

Chemical Barriers If pathogens get past the physical barriers, they often encounter chemical defenses. Saliva contains special proteins that break down bacteria, and stomach acids make it difficult for most organisms to survive. The small intestine contains bile and enzymes that break down pathogens. The vagina normally has a slightly acidic environment, which favors the growth of normal flora and discourages the growth of other bacteria. The body protects pores and hair follicles in the skin by excreting fatty acids and lysozyme, an enzyme that breaks down bacteria and reduces the likelihood of infection. The physical and chemical barriers to infection are illustrated in Figure 13.4.

The Immune System

The **immune system** is a complex set of cells, chemicals, and processes that protects the body against pathogens when they succeed in entering the body. It has two subdivisions: the **innate immune system**, a rapid response designed to catch and dispose of foreign particles or pathogens in a nonspecific manner, and the **acquired immune system**, a highly specialized response that recognizes specific targets.

The Innate Immune System The body's initial reaction to tissue damage, whether it is due to trauma or infection, is an **acute inflammatory response**, a

immune system
A complex set of cells, chemicals, and processes that protects the body against pathogens when they succeed in entering the body.

innate immune system
Part of the immune system designed to rapidly dispose of pathogens in a nonspecific manner.

acquired immune system
Part of the immune system that recognizes specific targets.

acute inflammatory response
A series of cellular changes that bring blood to the site of an injury or infection.

Nasal passages Mucous membrane lining, hair, sneeze reflex

Ears Hair, ear wax

Whole body Skin

Small intestine Bile, enzymes

Eyes Eyelids, eyelashes, tears

Mouth Mucous membrane lining, saliva

Lungs Mucous membranes, cilia, cough reflex

Stomach Stomach acid

Large intestine Normal flora

Genitals Mucous membrane lining, normal flora; vagina has slightly acidic environment

figure 13.4 **Physical and chemical barriers to infection.**
(Michael Krinke/Getty Images)

series of changes that increase the flow of blood to the site. A complicated series of molecular and cellular events occurs when the innate immune system has been activated. Signs of the inflammatory response are redness, warmth, pain, and swelling.

The cells of the innate immune system are neutrophils, macrophages, and natural killer cells. Neutrophils and macrophages are white blood cells that travel in the bloodstream to areas of infection or tissue damage. These phagocytes ("cell eaters") digest damaged cells, foreign particles, and bacteria. Natural killer cells are white blood cells that recognize and destroy virus-infected cells or cells that have become cancerous.

The Acquired Immune System
Your acquired (or adaptive) immunity

lymphocytes
White blood cells that circulate in the bloodstream and lymphatic system and play a key role in the acquired immune system.

antigen
A marker on the surface of a substance foreign to the body that identifies the substance to immune cells as "nonself."

antibodies
Proteins that bind to specific antigens and trigger events that destroy them.

develops as you are exposed to potential infections and vaccinations. Each time the cells of the acquired immune system are exposed to a pathogen, they form a kind of memory of it and can mount a response the next time they encounter it.

The important white blood cells of the acquired immune system are **lymphocytes**, which circulate in the bloodstream and lymphatic system. If the lymphocytes encounter an **antigen** (a marker on the surface of a substance that is foreign to the body), they rapidly duplicate and "turn on" their specific function. The two main types of lymphocytes are *T cells* and *B cells.*

T cells monitor events that may be occurring inside cells. If a cell is infected, alterations to molecules on its surface indicate it is now "nonself." Helper T cells "read" this message and trigger the production of killer T cells and B cells; helper T cells also enhance the activity of the cells of the innate immune system and of B cells once they have been activated. Killer T cells attack and kill foreign cells and body cells that have been infected by a virus or have become cancerous. Suppressor T cells slow down and halt the immune response once the threat has been handled.

B cells monitor the blood and tissue fluids. When they encounter a specific antigen, they mature to become cells that produce **antibodies**—proteins that circulate in the blood and bind to specific antigens, triggering events that destroy them.

Immunity Once you have survived infection by a pathogen, you often acquire **immunity** to future infection by the same pathogen. The reason is that some B and T cells become *memory cells* when exposed to an infectious agent; if they encounter the same antigen in the future, they can respond rapidly, destroying the invader before it can cause illness. Immunization is based on the principle that the immune system is exposed to enough of an infectious agent to trigger an immune response. On subsequent exposures, the immune system mounts a rapid response, preventing disease.

The concept of immunization was introduced in 1796 by English physician Edward Jenner. Jenner realized that people who had been infected with cowpox (a disease that

immunity
Reduced susceptibility to a disease based on the ability of the immune system to remember, recognize, and mount a rapid defense against a pathogen it has previously encountered.

causes mild illness in humans) seldom became ill or died when exposed to smallpox (a related but often fatal disease). Jenner's observation led to the development of **vaccines**, preparations of weakened or killed microorganisms or parts of microorganisms that are administered to confer immunity to various diseases. Since 1900, vaccines have been developed for many infectious diseases, and significant reductions in death rates

from these diseases have occurred (Figure 13.5).[6]

Vaccination serves two functions. The first is to protect an individual by stimulating an immune response. The second is to protect the community and, in particular,

vaccines
Preparations of weakened or killed microorganisms or parts of microorganisms that are administered to confer immunity to various diseases.

Vaccine ▼ Age group ▶	19–26 years	27–49 years	50–64 years	≥65 years
Influenza inactivated (IIV) or Influenza recombinant (RIV)	1 dose annually			
or Influenza live attenuated (LAIV)	1 dose annually	**or**		
Tetanus, diphtheria, pertussis (Tdap or Td)	1 dose Tdap, then Td or Tdap booster every 10 yrs			
Measles, mumps, rubella (MMR)	1 or 2 doses depending on indication (if born in 1957 or later)			
Varicella (VAR)	2 doses (if born in 1980 or later)		2 doses	
Zoster recombinant (RZV) (preferred)				2 doses
or Zoster live (ZVL)				**or** 1 dose
Human papillomavirus (HPV)	2 or 3 doses depending on age at initial vaccination or condition	27 through 45 years		
Pneumococcal conjugate (PCV13)	1 dose			65 years and older
Pneumococcal polysaccharide (PPSV23)	1 or 2 doses depending on indication			1 dose
Hepatitis A (HepA)	2 or 3 doses depending on vaccine			
Hepatitis B (HepB)	2 or 3 doses depending on vaccine			
Meningococcal A, C, W, Y (MenACWY)	1 or 2 doses depending on indication; at times, additional booster indicated			
Meningococcal B (MenB)	19 through 23 years	2 or 3 doses depending on vaccine and indication; at times, additional booster indicated		
Haemophilus influenzae type b (Hib)	1 or 3 doses depending on indication			

☐ Recommended for all persons who meet the age requirement, lack documentation of vaccination, or lack evidence of past infection

☐ Recommended vaccination based on shared clinical decision-making

☐ Recommended vaccination for adults with additional risk factors (medical, occupational, lifestyle or other indication

figure 13.5   Recommended adult immunizations, 2019.
Additional information about specific recommendations and vaccines can be found at www.cdc.gov/vaccines.
Source: Centers for Disease Control and Prevention. (2019). Recommended adult immunization schedule for adults aged 19 years and older, by vaccine and age group, United States, 2019. https://www.cdc.gov/vaccines/schedules/hcp/imz/adult.html.

those who cannot receive vaccines such as newborns and people with some medical conditions. Widespread vaccination shrinks the reservoir of infectious agents, protecting the community through "herd" immunity. In other words, if someone with a disease enters a community where most people are vaccinated against it, the disease cannot spread because few people are susceptible. The widespread use of the smallpox vaccine, for example, led to the elimination of naturally occurring smallpox worldwide. All future generations benefit from the earlier smallpox vaccination campaigns because they no longer require vaccination themselves.

Deaths from vaccine-preventable diseases are at an all-time low, but high vaccination levels are necessary to maintain this effect. In the case of measles, an estimated 93 to 95 percent of people in the community must be vaccinated for herd or community immunity to be effective. If overall community vaccination levels drop, these diseases will spread more easily because there will be more susceptible people. Outbreaks of vaccine-preventable diseases do occur on college campuses. Visit the "You Make the Call: Should Colleges Tighten Vaccination Requirements?" at the end of this chapter for an in-depth exploration.

Risk Factors for Infection

Your risk of infections depends on numerous factors, some within your control and others beyond it.

Controllable Risk Factors   You can reduce your risk of infection by adopting behaviors that support and improve the health of your immune system. One such behavior is eating a balanced diet; poor nutrition is associated with a higher risk of infectious disease. Other behaviors that support a healthy immune system are exercising, getting enough sleep, and managing stress. Vaccination, when available, can boost your immune system and facilitate a quicker response to specific pathogens. Good hygiene practices like hand washing and not touching your eyes, mouth, and nose reduce the risk of many infections (see the box "Action Skill-Builder: How to Keep Your Hands Clean"), and protecting your skin from damage keeps many pathogens out of your body. Avoiding tobacco and environmental tobacco smoke improves your defenses against respiratory illness.

Uncontrollable Risk Factors   Age plays a role in vulnerability to infection, with higher risks at both ends of the lifespan. Newborns and young children are at increased risk because they have not been exposed to many infections; however, pregnancy and breastfeeding confer **passive immunity**—a health benefit in which a mother's antibodies can pass to the fetus or child to provide temporary immune protection. Older people are at increased risk of infection due to the gradual decline in the immune system that can occur with

passive immunity
Temporary immunity provided by antibodies from an external source—such as passed from mother to child in breast milk.

Action Skill-Builder
How to Keep Your Hands Clean

Your hands go everywhere. They touch the public bathroom doorknob; they rummage through your backpack as it sits on the classroom floor; they grasp the sweaty handles of the elliptical at the gym; they touch the screen of your phone to answer a call; and they grasp your friends' hands when you meet. Then they grip your sandwich or the spoon you use to eat your lunch. They touch your mouth, nose, and eyes repeatedly during the day. Because our hands are there no matter how dirty the job, it's no surprise that hand washing is one of the first lessons we learn as children. It is an easy and effective way to protect yourself and others from germs. Here are some steps to help you brush up on this time-honored practice:

☐ Use warm water and enough soap to produce a bubbly lather. Any type of soap will do. Soaps containing antibiotics are not necessary; in fact, because they increase bacterial resistance to antibiotics, they are not recommended.

☐ Scrub the backs and fronts of your hands with the lather, from your fingertips all the way up to your wrists. Don't forget to scrub between your fingers and under your nails.

☐ Wash for a minimum of 20 seconds to ensure that even the toughest microorganisms get scrubbed off your skin.

☐ Rinse the soap from your hands with warm water, starting with the wrists. Point your fingers down so the dirty soap and water go directly into the sink rather than dribbling up your forearms.

☐ Dry your hands with a clean towel or allow them to air dry.

☐ Do not touch the faucet, the area around the sink, or the bathroom door; doing so will recontaminate your hands. You can use a paper towel to turn off the faucet and open the door.

☐ Avoid touching your mouth, nose, and eyes unless you have recently washed your hands!

If your hands are not visibly soiled, or if no soap and water is available, use a hand sanitizer that contains at least 60 percent alcohol. Apply enough to cover all surfaces of your hands. Rub hands together until all the moisture has been absorbed.

aging. Other factors that increase vulnerability include undergoing surgery, having a chronic disease such as heart disease, diabetes or lung disease, and being bedbound.

Genetic predisposition may play a role in our susceptibility to infectious disease. It is unclear why certain people develop an overwhelming, life-threatening illness when exposed to some pathogens while others develop only a mild fever. Certain sociocultural factors are associated with higher risk

Antibodies for some diseases are passed from mothers to babies in breast milk. Breastfeeding has been shown to reduce the incidence of infections, allergies, and diarrhea in infants and to reduce the risk of breast cancer, enhance bonding, and contribute to postpregnancy weight loss for the mother. *(FatCamera/Getty Images)*

of infectious disease; in many situations, these are not controllable risk factors. Overcrowded living environments (including residence halls, fraternities, and sororities) increase the risk for any infectious disease that is spread from person to person, such as influenza, coronavirus, meningitis, and tuberculosis. Certain occupations (being an essential worker during the COVID-19 pandemic) carry an increased risk of exposure to diseases. Poverty is associated with increased risk for many illnesses, probably owing to poor nutrition, stress, and lack of access to health care, among other factors.

Disruption of Immunity

Because the immune system is so complex, it occasionally malfunctions. Two such disruptions are autoimmune diseases and allergies.

Autoimmune Diseases Sometimes a part of the body is similar enough to a part of a foreign agent that the immune system mistakenly identifies it as "nonself." An **autoimmune**

disease occurs when the immune system does this and makes antibodies against the body in error. For example, in autoimmune thyroid disease, the immune system mistakenly makes antibodies against cells in the thyroid, which stimulates overproduction of thyroid hormone. The development of autoimmune diseases is linked to genetic and environmental factors. There is a also complex relationship between autoimmune diseases and infectious diseases. Certain infections, such as infection with the Epstein-Barr virus, have been associated with autoimmune diseases such as rheumatoid arthritis and multiple sclerosis. However, cumulative exposure to infections, especially in early childhood, appears to be protective, leading to the *hygiene hypothesis,* a theory developed when it was noticed that rates of autoimmune disease and allergies increase in higher-income countries as rates of infectious disease decrease.[7]

Regardless of the cause, the autoimmune disease process is one of self-destruction, because the immune system can damage components of the body's cells and tissues. Autoimmune diseases vary in their effects, depending on which part of the body is seen as foreign. For example, in rheumatoid arthritis, the immune system primarily attacks the joints, and in psoriasis, it primarily attacks the skin. Other autoimmune diseases include hyperthyroidism, multiple sclerosis, scleroderma, and lupus erythematosus. Genetics is known to play a role in some autoimmune diseases.[7] For unknown reasons, most autoimmune diseases are more common in women than in men.

Allergies Allergic reactions occur when the immune system identifies a harmless foreign substance as an infectious agent and mounts a full-blown immune response. Allergic responses to substances like pollen or animal dander, for example, include a runny nose, watery eyes, nasal congestion, and an itchy throat. The poison ivy or poison oak rash is a skin allergic reaction to an oily resin excreted by the plant. In extreme cases of allergic response, the body goes into **anaphylactic shock**, a life-threatening systemic allergic response requiring immediate medical attention.

Asthma, a condition characterized by wheezing and shortness of breath, is caused by inflammation of the bronchial tubes and spasm of the muscles around the airways in response to an allergen or other trigger. Because viruses can trigger an asthma attack, it's especially important for people with asthma to get flu shots annually. Asthma is covered in greater detail in Chapter 14.

Immunity and Stress As described in Chapter 2, stress can weaken the immune system. College students report high levels of stress as they juggle competing demands, and they frequently have more colds and other infections than they did in high school. Short-term stress, such as a single exam or exercise, can actually enhance the immune system's functioning by activating the body's

autoimmune disease when the immune system identifies a part of the body as "foreign" and makes antibodies against itself

anaphylactic shock A hypersensitive reaction in which an antigen causes an immediate and severe reaction that can include itching, rash, swelling, shock, and respiratory distress.

College students report high levels of stress as they juggle competing demands. Stress, both acute and chronic, can weaken the immune system and lead to more frequent colds and other infections.
(9nong/123RF)

responses. However, stress that lasts for more than a few days or for months—such as a difficult housing situation, a heavy course load, financial concerns, discrimination, disruption of sleep, or final exams—suppresses the immune system's functioning and can increase risk for infections in the short term and chronic conditions in the long term.[8]

CHANGING PATTERNS IN INFECTIOUS DISEASE

In 1969, the U.S. surgeon general declared before Congress that it was time to close the book on infectious diseases. Dramatic declines in the death rate from infectious diseases during the 20th century (Figure 13.6) inspired this bold statement. Within a little more than 10 years, however, the first cases of what would soon be identified as human immunodeficiency virus (HIV) infection were causing perplexity and alarm in hospitals in several U.S. cities. Since then, the appearance of the SARS-CoV-2 pandemic, other new infections, changes in patterns of infection, and the development of antibiotic resistance in many strains of bacteria have demonstrated that infectious diseases remain an important health concern.

We will explore some specific areas that warrant focus. We all must eat, and the way food is grown, stored, distributed, and prepared has major implications on health. Behavioral patterns continue to influence disease spread, including global travel, sexual behavior, and illicit drug use. Climate change has major implications for infectious disease and changing patterns of infection. Finally, increasing antibiotic resistance raises concerns that we may no longer be able to treat some infections, making prevention, such as with vaccinations, increasingly critical.

Food-Related Pathogen Transmission

More than 250 organisms are associated with food-related illnesses. They include viruses, bacteria, prions, and parasites.

For example, in April 2019, Grand Park Packing in Franklin, Illinois, and K2D Foods in Carollton, Georgia, recalled a total of 166,624 pounds of raw ground-beef products after investigation of a multistate outbreak of a toxin-producing *E. coli*. An *outbreak* is defined as an event in which two or more people become sick from the same foodborne pathogen after having eaten the same food or eaten at the same location. Local public health agencies first noted clusters of people becoming ill in January and triggered the investigation. PulseNet, a national laboratory tracking system, was used to identify 209 people from 10 states who were ill with genetically identical strains of *E. coli*. Investigators interviewed the sick or their family members and found that many had eaten ground beef in the week prior to becoming ill. Although the investigation could not clearly determine exactly when or where the contamination occurred, ground beef was felt to be the source, and the two large suppliers mentioned earlier conducted recalls because of concerns their products may have been contaminated.[9] For guidelines on food safety, see the tips provided in Chapter 5.

The complexity of the U.S. food system—the process by which food gets from farm to table—makes monitoring and investigating foodborne outbreaks an important public health function. Most of the foods we eat travel a thousand miles or more before reaching our plates. They are grown in one part of the country (or in a foreign country), shipped to a central processing plant, packaged, and then distributed to locations from coast to coast. This widespread distribution lowers some costs, makes production more convenient, and increases the diversity of food choices available, but it increases the risk that contaminated food will cause infectious disease in large numbers of people. Eating locally grown food is not inherently safer, but if an outbreak occurs, it can make it easier to track the pathogen back to the source, and a contaminated item may not reach as many people.

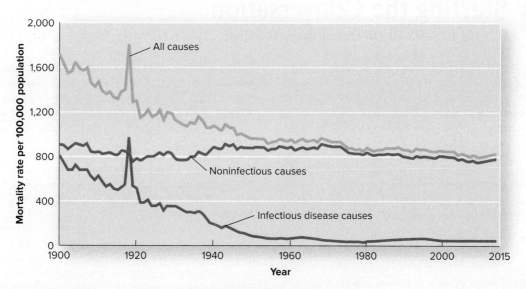

figure 13.6 **Death rate from infectious diseases, United States, 20th century.**
Sources: Adapted from Achievements in Public Health, 1990–1999: Control of Infectious Disease. *Morbidity and Mortality Weekly Report, 48*(29), 621, www.edc.gov/mmwr; Armstrong, G. L., Conn, L. A., & Pinner, R. W. (1999). Trends in infectious disease mortality in the United States during the 20th century. *Journal of the American Medical Association, 281,* 61–66; American Water Works Association. (1973). *Water chlorination principles and practices: AWWA manual M20.* Denver, CO: AWWA; Hansen, V., Oren, E., Dennis, L. K. et al. (2016). Infectious disease mortality in the United States, 1980–2015. *Journal of the American Medical Association, 316*(20), 2149–2151.

Behavior-Related Pathogen Transmission

Disease transmission is affected not just by food but also by changes in behavior, including travel, sexual behavior, and illicit drug use.

Travel and Infectious Diseases When it took weeks to cross the ocean on a ship—a passenger who became sick en route could be isolated and any exposed passengers quarantined (separated from the others so that, if they became sick, officials could prevent further transmission of disease). Today we travel immense distances in hours, potentially carrying incubating pathogens with us and arriving in new places before we have any indication we are ill. The reality of this was felt around the world in 2020. A novel coronavirus infection was detected in Wuhan, China, in December 2019 when hospitals in the area began to see an increase in cases of respiratory distress from unknown cause.[1]

Coronaviruses are a large family of viruses that can cause human disease ranging from a mild cold to severe respiratory distress and death. They often circulate in animal hosts and, when animals are in close contact with humans, there is a risk of animal-to-human transmission. This is believed to be the source of SARS-CoV-2, the name for the novel coronavirus causing the new respiratory disease COVID-19.

The global population has seen novel coronavirus infections in humans before. An outbreak of severe acute respiratory syndrome (SARS) was first noted in southern China at the end of 2002, and by February 2003 it had spread to Hong Kong, Vietnam, Singapore, Germany, and Canada. By the time the disease was contained, there had been 8,098 probable cases and 774 deaths in 26 countries.[10] Another novel coronavirus, MERS-CoV, was identified in Saudi Arabia in

2012 and caused a disease labeled Middle Eastern respiratory syndrome (MERS). With MERS-CoV, the virus did not pass easily from human to human and the primary reservoir host for the virus is dromedary camels. Most human infections have occurred in people with close contact with camels or close contact with an infected person such as family members or health care workers. Since 2012, there have been 2,494 confirmed cases and 858 deaths reported in 27 countries primarily in the Middle East or in people who have traveled from the Middle East to other areas of the world.[11]

International surveillance and preparedness significantly improved as a result of these experiences. WHO's Global Alert and Response Network is an international collaboration of institutions and organizations that pool data and resources to rapidly identify, confirm, and respond to infectious diseases of international importance. The network's coordinated approach is critical, given potential for rapid international disease transmission. Global alerts regarding disease outbreaks have included new strains of avian influenza, Ebola, and the Zika virus. The CDC Travel Health website is also an important resource that posts up-to-date travel alerts, recommendations, and warnings.[12,13]

The former outbreaks primarily caused clusters of disease within countries and were rapidly contained, and pandemic level spread was prevented. SARS-CoV-2 is different. It appears to be more easily transmitted from person to person by coughing, sneezing, or contact with contaminated surfaces. As with all novel viruses, no one has immunity and thus everyone, globally, is at risk of infection. (See the box "Starting the Conversation: How Is COVID-19 Different from the Flu?"). With no vaccine or treatment available,

Starting the Conversation
How Is COVID-19 Different from the Flu?

On March 11, 2020, the World Health Organization declared COVID-19 a global pandemic. At that time, there were 118,000 cases in 110 countries and territories. Since then, COVID-19 cases and deaths have increased and countries around the world have implemented measures to control the pandemic. As of mid-May 2020, there were over 4.6 million cases globally and over 300,000 deaths. Yet, each year between 9 million and 45 million people develop seasonal flu and 12,000 and 61,000 people die from flu, prompting many to question whether we are overreacting to COVID-19. A common question being asked is, "How are COVID-19 and seasonal flu similar and different?"

The Viruses

SARS-CoV-2 is the name for the novel coronavirus that causes COVID-19. As a coronavirus, it is in the family of viruses called *Coronaviridae*. These viruses commonly cause disease in mammals and birds. Some strains are regularly found in humans and cause common cold symptoms. SARS-CoV-2 likely made the jump from a mammal species to humans and is considered novel because humans have not been exposed to this particular virus before and thus have no immunity.

Influenza A and influenza B are the viruses that cause seasonal flu. As influenza viruses, they are in the *Orthomyxoviridae* family of viruses. There are four types of influenza virus (A, B, C, and D), although only influenza A and B cause seasonal flu in humans. They both have small changes in their RNA each season, and thus people can be repeatedly infected, but they will have some level of immunity from prior seasonal strains. Influenza A has caused flu pandemics in the past when major shifts in the genomic material occurs—often when a human influenza strain combines with an animal influenza strain (because influenza A can also infect mammals and birds).

Exposure, Incubation, and Contagiousness

SARS-CoV-2 and influenza are spread from person to person via respiratory droplets, such as when an infected person coughs or sneezes within 3 feet of another person. Direct droplet transmission can also be due to fomites, inanimate objects on which respiratory droplets land, thus making the object infectious when someone touches it.

With SARS-CoV-2, symptom onset occurs within 2 to 14 days after exposure. However, some who are infected, especially young people, do not develop symptoms. With influenza, symptom onset occurs within 1 to 4 days after exposure. With both viruses, people are believed to be contagious (they can spread infection) prior to symptom onset, making it difficult to control spread. Coronavirus is believed to be more contagious than seasonal influenza. On average, a person infected with coronavirus will infect 2.2 other people, whereas a person with the flu will infect 1.3 people.

Risk of Serious Disease and Death

The greatest risk of complications and death from both diseases is in people over the age of 60, people with weakened immune systems, and people with chronic illnesses (such as heart disease, lung disease, or diabetes). Thus far, seasonal influenza appears to pose a greater risk to young children, whereas SARS-CoV-2 appears to cause mild or no symptoms for most children. However, a new multisystem inflammatory syndrome in children (MIS-C) has been identified, associated with SARS-CoV-2, and is causing illness and deaths in children. Pregnant women are known to have greater risk of complications from seasonal influenza, and this is assumed to be true for SARS-CoV-2 as well, but as yet it has not been confirmed.

The fatality rate—deaths from disease/total cases of disease—appears to be higher for SARS-CoV-2 (at somewhere between 0.1 and 1.4) than with seasonal influenza (at 0.1). However, fatality rate numbers are very dependent on testing, and widespread lack of testing for COVID-19 means we don't have an accurate estimate of the total number of cases.

Prevention and Treatment

The biggest difference between COVID-19 and seasonal flu, and the greatest concern, is the fact that no humans have immunity to COVID-19, and thus everyone is at risk for infection. For seasonal flu, people have some natural immunity from influenza A and B from prior years. In addition, each year a seasonal flu vaccine is developed that reduces risk of infection and complications by 40 to 60 percent. At this time, it remains unclear whether and for how long immunity to SARS-CoV-2 will last after infection and recovery. Scientists are working to develop a vaccine for SARS-CoV-2 in hopes of reducing disease spread in the future, and in March 2020, initial vaccine trials began.

Four antiviral medications are used in the treatment of seasonal flu, which can reduce the length and severity of symptoms. At present, there are no known treatments for COVID-19, but multiple different antiviral medication trials are underway.

At present, five steps are known to reduce the spread of both diseases: Wash your hands regularly; cover your nose and mouth with your elbow or a tissue when you sneeze or cough; avoid touching your eyes, nose, and mouth; keep 3 to 6 feet of distance between you and others; and stay home when you feel unwell. Because everyone is susceptible to COVID-19, local, state, and national measures have been implemented to keep people apart, encourage use of masks, and try to slow the spread of disease.

Q: Do you think people are overreacting in adopting the measures implemented to control the spread of COVID-19? Why or why not?

Q: Do you get a seasonal flu vaccine? Will you get a COVID-19 vaccine when it is available?

Sources: World Health Organization. (2020). Coronavirus (COVID-19) pandemic. Retrieved from https://www.who.int/emergencies/diseases/novel-coronavirus-2019; Centers for Disease Control and Prevention. (2020). Influenza (flu). Retrieved from https://www.cdc.gov/flu/index.htm; Centers for Disease Control and Prevention. (2020). Multisystem inflammatory syndrome in children (MIS-C) associated with coronavirus disease 2019 (COVID-19). https://www.cdc.gov/mis-c/

isolation and quarantine of potentially infected people was the key to stopping the spread of infection. Initial delays in communication about the virus in China slowed an initial response. People traveling across borders resulted in a spread to Hong Kong and then the rest of the world. Later efforts at isolation and quarantine did not contain the virus. Community spread occurred in affected countries necessitating further public health measures of restricting movement within and between countries in efforts to contain spread. Health care systems quickly became overwhelmed with severely ill individuals and deaths increased.[1]

Cities, states, and countries around the world enacted emergency public health measures—restricting travel; closing restaurants, bars, and businesses; and preventing gatherings of larger than 10 people—to physically distance people and slow the spread. In some areas, people were ordered to "stay at home" for extended periods—meaning everyone other than "essential" workers were to stay at home and limit movement. Activities that could move online did—online learning occurred throughout the United States at most institutions of higher education and K-12 programs. Many businesses that could not move online, closed. Overall, the world was not prepared to either contain the virus or provide adequate care for those who were sick. The health, economic, and social impacts from this global pandemic will be felt for years to come. Much remains unclear as the situation is rapidly evolving, and it is challenging to write a conclusion to this section as we are living history in the moment. But it does appear that campus life will look very different for the near future (for an example, see the box "Public Health Is Personal: Campus Life in the Time of COVID-19).[1,14]

Sexual Behavior and Infectious Diseases Sexual behavior also affects the transmission of disease. Three factors

■ In 2020, the World Health Organization declared a global pandemic in response to the spread of SARS-CoV-2 around the world. *(Andrew Angelov/Shutterstock)*

influence the likelihood that a person will be exposed to a sexually transmitted infection: partner variables, personal susceptibility variables, and sex act variables.

Partner variables that increase the risk of being exposed to an STI include the total number of sex partners a person has, the frequency with which someone acquires new sex partners, and the number of sexual partners in the same period of time. Adolescents and young adults typically have higher rates of STIs because they are more likely to have concurrent partners (overlapping relationships within a period of time) or sequential relationships of short duration. Certain partner factors are associated with an increased risk of infection; the highest-risk factors are transactional sex (the exchange of money or goods for sex) and partners whose past is unknown. In both cases partners are likely to have had more and/or recent sex partners.[15]

Variables associated with increased susceptibility to infection include gender, age at first intercourse, and general health. Women are at greater risk than men due to anatomy (the mucosal surface of the vagina and the cervix is larger than that of the penis). Young women are at particular risk because the cervix is physiologically more susceptible to infection in the first few years after puberty. Overall health is important because it affects the strength of the immune response and the integrity of the mucosal surfaces. For instance, people who have one STI may be more likely to contract a second infection, and people who use methamphetamine and intravenous drugs have rapidly increasing rates of sexually transmitted infections, suggesting intersecting epidemics of STI and drug use, as discussed later in this chapter.[15,16]

Different types of sexual acts also affect disease transmission. Nonpenetrative sex (fondling, mutual masturbation) has the lowest risk, followed in increasing order of risk by oral sex, penile-vaginal intercourse, and penile-anal intercourse. Penile-anal intercourse carries the highest risk of disease transmission because the rectal lining is highly susceptible to micro tears, creating portals of entry for infection. Other factors can also increase or decrease the risk of transmission. The risk of exposure increases with the number of sexual acts. The amount of lubrication, either natural from foreplay or applied, affects risk because abrasions to the mucosa make it easier for the STI to be transmitted. Forced or violent sex increases the risk of abrasions and of STI transmission.[15,17]

The most effective way to avoid contracting STIs is to abstain from intimate sexual activities until you are ready to be in a mutually monogamous, long-term relationship with an uninfected partner. If you do not abstain, limit the number of partners and be sure to use condoms. Correct and consistent condom use can reduce transmission of some—but not all—STIs.

Public Health Is Personal

Campus Life in the Time of COVID-19

In the spring of 2020, colleges and universities across the United States and the world closed campuses to slow the spread of COVID-19. Courses rapidly moved online. Students were forced to decide if they remained near campus and friends or if they returned home to families in response to widespread shelter-in-place orders. The reopening of campuses is challenging in a pandemic where the more individuals interact, the greater the risk of COVID-19 spread. College and campus life are designed around exploring new relationships, sharing ideas, and developing new social networks. The Centers for Disease Control and Prevention has developed considerations for institutions of higher education and the students, staff, and faculty who utilize them. No institution or community will be able to eliminate risk for COVID-19 spread, but individual behaviors and institutional policies can adjust the risk. Here are some aspects to consider from a public health perspective:

Learning Environment

Large classes and in-person packed lecture halls provide the greatest risk for disease transmission. Virtual classes, activities, and events provide the lowest risk. Individuals and institutions need to find a balance somewhere in between. Institutions need to examine policies, procedures, and classroom spaces taking into consideration that in-person instruction and events should allow for 6-foot spacing between participants. Students should not share supplies in laboratory or active learning settings. Faculty, staff, and students who are at increased risk of complications and death from COVID-19 need the option to be able to participate remotely through virtual learning and/or telework.

Campus Housing

For many students, moving into residence halls or shared housing with age peers is part of the college experience. Yet, these housing options present the greatest risk for spread of COVID-19. Campus housing options should take into consideration that group housing, if allowed, should operate at reduced capacity. Common spaces, such as shared kitchens and bathrooms, recreation rooms, should be closed or tightly regulated. Campus group housing should take into consideration that practices such as shared sleeping rooms increase risk of transmission. Students should discuss with housemates approaches to cleaning, disinfection, and personal behavior given their shared risk when living together.

Individual behaviors to reduce COVID-19 spread:

- Physical distancing

    Stay at least 6 feet away from others.

- Hand hygiene

    Wash hands frequently with soap and water for 20 seconds and use hand sanitizer (60% alcohol or greater) when hand washing is not available.

- Respiratory etiquette

    Cover your cough or sneeze with a tissue or use the inside of your elbow.

- Cloth face coverings

    Wear a cloth face covering when around other people. This is most important when physical distancing is difficult. Wash your hands before putting on your face covering. It should cover your nose and mouth with a snug fit against the sides of your face. When removing, handle the ear ties and place in washing machine. Wash hands after removing.

- Stay home or self-isolate

    Establish a habit of doing a daily temperature check and self-check for signs and symptoms of COVID-19. Self-isolate if you have a temperature above 100.4 and/or symptoms consistent with COVID-19. If you have tested positive for COVID-19, self-isolate for 10 days and until you have at least 24 hours with no fever and your other symptoms are improving. If you have been exposed to someone with COVID-19, stay home for 14 days, which is the incubation period for COVID-19.

- Transportation

    If possible, use forms of transportation that minimize the risk of close contact with other people. Consider walking or biking. If you drive, drive alone or carpool with the same individuals. If you use public transportation, commute during less busy times, wear a mask, and wash your hands as soon as possible after arrival.

Community Engagement and Systems

COVID-19 has disproportionately affected Black and Brown communities. Institutions of higher education should engage their Black and Brown communities to ensure that institutional policies and procedures are examined and adjusted so they do not contribute to ongoing disproportionate impact of COVID-19 on campus. Implementing flexible sick leave, telework, and virtual learning policies are just a few policy measures that can support individuals. Campus life will probably never look the same after the pandemic; however, with public health measures, we can reduce the risk.

Source: Centers for Disease Control and Prevention. (2020). Considerations for Institutes of Higher Education. Retrieved from https://www.cdc.gov/coronavirus/2019-ncov/community/colleges-universities/considerations.html

Finally, get tested if you are at risk of sexually transmitted infections; most STIs have no symptoms. STI testing recommendations are discussed later in the chapter.

Illicit Drug Use: The Case of Hepatitis C When users of illicit drugs share needles and syringes, some blood from the first user is injected into the bloodstream of the next user, creating an effective means of transmitting bloodborne infections. Several viral infections, specifically HIV, hepatitis B, and hepatitis C, are easily transmitted through shared needles. We discuss HIV and hepatitis B later in the chapter; here, we consider hepatitis C.

All hepatitis viruses cause inflammation of the liver, with symptoms such as fatigue, weakness, loss of appetite, and jaundice (a yellow discoloring of the skin and eyes). The hepatitis C virus was discovered in 1989. Before 1990, approximately 10 percent of blood transfusion recipients developed hepatitis, nearly always from hepatitis C. After blood banks started screening for hepatitis C, transfusion-related infection dropped.

Hepatitis C is not a highly infectious virus—meaning it is not easily passed from person to person—and yet it is the most common form of bloodborne infection, with 2.4 million people having chronic infection in the United States. There are different viral types of hepatitis C; genotypes 1 through 6 are most common. The virus requires introduction directly into the bloodstream for transmission, so risk factors include intravenous drug use and sharing of other drug paraphernalia that may have infected blood on it, receipt of blood or blood products prior to 1992, sex with a person infected with hepatitis C (although sexual transmission is rare except among men who have sex with men), and other exposures to blood from a person who has hepatitis C. The virus can also be transmitted through contaminated tattoo ink or equipment.[18,19,20]

The incubation period for hepatitis C infection is about 4 to 6 weeks, but only about 20 percent of infected people will develop symptoms. However, the virus causes a chronic, low-level infection in 75 to 85 percent of people, and after about 20 years, 1 in 10 infected people will develop liver failure, scarring of the liver (cirrhosis), or liver cancer. Hepatitis C is a leading cause of liver failure requiring liver transplantation. Since 2011, new antiviral medications have changed the treatment of hepatitis C. They are well tolerated and more effective than prior regimens but remain very expensive. In addition, an estimated 75 percent of people with hepatitis C do not know they are infected.[18,21]

Individuals reduce their risk for hepatitis C by not using injection drugs and by maintaining mutually monogamous sexual relationships with noninfected partners. Those who do use drugs should reduce risk by not sharing needles or syringes or, at the very least, cleaning them with bleach after every use. A one-time screening is recommended for anyone born between 1945 and 1965 and for others at high risk, defined as those with past or present injection drug use, those who have had sex with an injection drug user, and those who had a blood transfusion before 1992. People with hepatitis C can reduce the risk of disease progression by avoiding alcohol, limiting the use of medications that affect the liver (such as acetaminophen), and getting vaccinated for hepatitis A and B.[18,21]

Climate Change and Infectious Diseases
The geographic distribution of many infectious diseases depends on the environment. With climate change increasing average temperatures and precipitation and bringing more extreme weather events, patterns of infectious disease are likely to change. This is especially true for waterborne and vectorborne diseases. Increased rainfall, hurricanes, and flooding cause the immediate spread of bacterial and parasitic diseases due to runoff from farms, breaches in septic systems, and damage to sewage plants. In addition, there are immediate risks associated with displaced persons being in crowded housing and having insufficient sanitation and clean drinking water.

Severe storms, such as 2018's Hurricanes Florence and Michael and 2019's Hurricane Dorian, are likely to increase in number and lead to more immediate infectious disease concerns, given the breakdown of community infrastructure and sewage treatment that such storms can bring. In addition, changes in precipitation and an increase in average temperatures will affect diseases transmitted by ticks and mosquitoes, such as Lyme disease, malaria, and West Nile virus, because the number of vectors will increase and the geographic area in which they can survive will increase. The health impacts of climate change will most affect already disadvantaged and vulnerable communities because the infrastructures and safety nets in those areas are less robust.[22,23]

Human behavior and nutrition are also likely to be affected by climate change. Changes in access to food, housing, and migration in response to weather and environmental events can increase susceptibility to infectious diseases. Climate change is likely to make access to clean water, sanitation, and food more challenging. Societal response will be important in minimizing the spread of infectious disease and its impact on vulnerable populations.[24,25]

Antibiotic Resistance

When penicillin, the first **antibiotic**, was discovered in 1928, it was declared a miracle drug. It was widely used during World War II and saved the lives of many wounded soldiers. Since that time, antibiotics have saved millions and millions of people. However, microorganisms respond to their environment and develop mechanisms to resist being killed. By the 1950s, bacteria were already showing signs of resistance to penicillin. A new antibiotic, methicillin, was introduced in 1960 and proved effective, but resistance began developing by 1961. Methicillin-resistant *Staphylococcus aureus* (MRSA) is becoming common on college campuses and will be discussed in detail in the section "Infectious Diseases Worldwide and on Campus." In the United States, 2 million people a year are infected with antibiotic-resistant organisms, and 23,000 people die as a result of these resistant infections. Thus started the race to develop new antibiotics faster than microorganisms developed resistance. Since the discovery of penicillin, hundreds of new antibiotics have been developed.[26,27]

The 21st century may mark the beginning of a post-antibiotic era as **antibiotic resistance** grows (as well as antiviral and antifungal

antibiotic
A drug that works by killing or preventing the growth of bacteria.

antibiotic resistance
The ability of bacteria to adapt and grow in the presence of antibiotics.

Climate change increases the risk of extreme weather events. Severe storms can cause flooding of communities and increasing risk of infectious diseases.
(Roschetzky Photography/Shutterstock)

resistance). Antibiotic resistance is the ability of bacteria to adapt and grow in the presence of antibiotics. *Antimicrobial resistance* is a broader term to address any microorganism (bacteria, virus, fungus) that has developed the ability to adapt and grow in the presence of a medication intended to prevent its growth. Sharp increases in antibiotic (and antimicrobial) resistance have been noted, whether infections are acquired in hospitals, nursing homes, or the community. Some bacteria are becoming resistant to all known antibiotics.[26,28,29] Two factors are believed to account for bacterial resistance: the frequency with which resistant genes arise naturally among bacteria through mutation, and the overuse of antibiotics.

Resistant genes arise naturally because bacteria (and other microorganisms) reproduce quickly, and mutations in their DNA occur frequently. This kind of mutation is amplified when a population of bacteria is exposed to an antibiotic. The most sensitive bacteria die quickly, while those with some resistance survive. Once the nonresistant bacteria are out of the way, the resistant bacteria have more space and food, and they quickly produce more resistant bacteria. They can also share resistant genes with other bacteria. Inappropriate use of antibiotics in health care, home care, and food production increase the risk of resistance. Measures to cut down on inappropriate use are critical.

Even if every person used appropriate antimicrobials only when necessary, resistance would still occur. Antibiotics not only have improved human life, but they also have significantly improved animal well-being and food production. An estimated 70 percent of the antibiotics produced in the United States are given to cattle, poultry, hogs, and other food animals. Some are used to treat animals for diseases; however, a significant amount is mixed into animal feed or

drinking water in low doses to promote growth and weight gain. Long-term use of low doses of antibiotics is much more likely to promote bacterial resistance than are short courses of high-dose treatments. When the dose of an antibiotic is not enough to kill a bacteria, it can cause damage and accelerate mutations. Bacteria with random mutations that promote survival in an environment with antibiotics survive longer and reproduce more than bacteria without resistant genes. Antibiotic-resistant bacteria in food animals can also cause human disease or pass resistant genes on to other bacteria that, in turn, cause human disease.[26,28]

Resistance affects everybody, regardless of where they live, their economic status, and their lifestyle and behavior. It affects human health, animal health, food security and production, and economic development. Consequently, individual action alone cannot solve the problem of antibiotic resistance. Public health actions are necessary to ensure that available antibiotics will be successful in treating human and animal disease when and where it occurs. Given the global implications, calls for action at a worldwide level include raising awareness about resistance; increasing surveillance for resistant organisms; reducing infections through sanitation, hygiene, and vaccination; optimizing antimicrobial use in human and animal health; and continuing investment in new medication development and research.[26,28,30]

Vaccination Controversies

You may never have seen a case of measles, mumps, polio, diphtheria, or rubella. The incidence of vaccine-preventable childhood diseases that devastated previous generations is at an all-time low. And vaccines are hailed as one of the greatest public health achievements of the age.[6] The past 30 years have seen rapid expansion in vaccine development, and with increasing concerns about the development of antibiotic resistance, vaccines will remain a critical tool for fighting infectious diseases. However, since the earliest introduction of vaccination in the 18th century, some people have been skeptical about the necessity and safety of the vaccines.

The controversy was exacerbated in 1998 when Andrew Wakefield, a British medical researcher, published a study supposedly confirming a link between the measles, mumps, and rubella (MMR) vaccine and autism. After 10 years, no other researchers had been able to reproduce his findings, and in 2010 his work was declared fraudulent. Wakefield was found guilty of ethical, medical, and scientific misconduct and banned from practicing medicine in the United Kingdom. However, his work contributed to the rise in an anti-vaccination movement. Since that time, vaccination rates have dropped steeply, and cases of measles and other diseases have increased.[31]

Maintaining high levels of vaccination within communities is critical. Even if cases of vaccine-preventable diseases are few, the diseases can rapidly return if less than 90 percent of people in a community are vaccinated. Other than smallpox (which was eradicated by worldwide vaccination efforts), the viruses and bacteria that cause these diseases still exist. As rates of vaccination drop, the likelihood of a disease recurrence increases. For example, if you or a classmate travel to a part of the world where a vaccine-preventable childhood disease still regularly occurs, you could bring the pathogen back to your local community, and the disease could spread quickly if local vaccination rates are low.

Although some minor, temporary side effects may occur after vaccination—such as a local reaction, fever, discomfort, irritability, or, more rarely, an allergic response—serious reactions to currently recommended vaccinations are very rare. The risk of the vaccine must be weighed against the risk of the disease. For example, the risk of developing encephalitis (brain inflammation) after a dose of the MMR vaccine is lower than 1 in 3 million doses, whereas the risk of developing encephalitis from measles is 1 in 1,000 cases, and the risk of death from measles is 2 in 1,000 cases.[32,33]

As new vaccines are developed and introduced, they are monitored constantly in an effort to improve vaccine safety. The CDC and the FDA jointly run the Vaccine Adverse Event Reporting System, which collects and analyzes information about possible adverse events that occur after vaccinations.[33]

INFECTIOUS DISEASES WORLDWIDE AND ON CAMPUS

Of the hundreds of thousands of infectious diseases that occur throughout the world, a handful, relatively speaking, are responsible for most cases of illness and death on a global scale. However, most of the infectious diseases common on college campuses are more easily prevented and treated.

Global Infectious Diseases

From an infectious disease perspective, the world has become a small community. Diseases do not respect borders or boundaries. New diseases and pathogens arise, such as H1N1 flu and SARS-CoV-2, and other diseases reemerge as public health concerns, such as tuberculosis. In this section, we consider the four leading causes of infectious disease mortality around the world: pneumonia, diarrhea, tuberculosis, and malaria.

Pneumonia Pneumonia—infection of the lungs or lower respiratory tract—is the leading cause of death in children after the first month of life, the leading cause of death in low-income countries, and the fourth most common cause of death (behind cardiovascular disease, cancer, and respiratory disease) for all ages worldwide.[34,35,36] Young children and older adults are at greatest risk for pneumonia; besides age, factors that increase risk include exposure to environmental pollutants and use of tobacco, alcohol, or drugs, all of which reduce the lungs' ability to clear infection. Poor nutrition is a risk factor because it reduces overall immune function. Close living situations, such as college dormitories or military barracks, can also increase risk.

Pneumonia can be viral or bacterial (it can also be caused by other organisms). The pathogens are usually inhaled in infected air droplets transmitted from an infected person who is coughing or sneezing nearby. Symptoms of pneumonia include fever, cough, chest pain, shortness of breath, and chills. Viral pneumonia tends to come on more gradually and is often milder than bacterial pneumonia, but both types can be serious and deadly. SARS-CoV-2 is a virus that causes severe respiratory disease and pneumonia.[1]

Vaccines are available to reduce the risk of contracting some forms of pneumonia (see Figure 13.5), and some antiviral and antibacterial medications can shorten the course of the illness and reduce complications. Discovering whether the cause is a virus or a bacteria is important for determining best treatment. Prevention strategies include avoiding tobacco smoke and crowded living conditions, practicing good hygiene, ensuring adequate nutrition, improving air quality, and following vaccination recommendations.

Antibiotic resistance is a problem in treating pneumonia. Up to 30 percent of the *Streptococcus* bacterium that causes pneumonia is resistant to penicillin, and the majority of influenza A, one of the viruses that causes pneumonia, is resistant to one of the four antiviral drugs used for treatment. Both these causes are vaccine preventable (see the box "Consumer Clipboard: Preventing Influenza with Annual Flu Vaccinations").[37,38]

Diarrhea Worldwide, diarrhea is the eighth leading cause of death among people of all ages and the fourth leading cause among children under age 5. The majority of diarrhea deaths occur in low- and middle-income countries.[34,35] Severe diarrhea leads to dehydration and electrolyte imbalances, and repeated episodes lead to malnutrition and growth delay. Multiple organisms cause diarrhea, including viruses and bacteria; rotavirus is the most common cause of diarrhea deaths in young children. Rates of death from diarrhea have decreased in many areas of the world thanks to efforts to improve sanitation, hygiene, and access to clean water. Efforts to improve the nutritional status of children can further reduce the risk of death from diarrhea. A vaccine against rotavirus is available and has been recommended for all infants

Consumer Clipboard
Preventing Influenza With Annual Flu Vaccinations

Ever wonder why every October you start to see advertisements promoting this year's flu vaccine? None of the other vaccinations require annual updates. So why does influenza? Influenza is an RNA virus and has several different strains. The major types that infect humans are called A and B. Influenza A has several different subtypes based on two types of proteins on the outer surface of the virus—a hemagglutinin (H) protein and a neuraminidase (N) protein, such that human influenza A will be identified as influenza A, subtype H1N1 or subtype H3N2. During the annual flu season, several types of influenza A or B and subtypes H1N1 or H2N2 will circulate and cause illness.

Influenza has an amazing propensity to change genetically. Thus, frequent minor changes occur in the viral genome of both influenza A and B—called *genetic drift*. If you contract the flu one year (or get a flu shot), you develop immunity to one particular subtype. Genetic drift may make next year's virus slightly different such that your immune system doesn't quite recognize it. Because the genetic drift changes are small, you will be susceptible to flu the next year, but you are unlikely to get really sick or die from it because the viral strains (or vaccine) to which you were already exposed usually provide minor protection.

Abrupt and major changes in the influenza A viral genome are infrequent; they are called *genetic shift*. These changes create a new H or N subtype, and the virus becomes so different that most people have no immunity to it. Such major genetic shifts were responsible for influenza pandemics that have altered history. In 1918, Spanish influenza swept across the globe and led to the deaths of 20 million to 40 million people, the most devastating epidemic in world history. This virus was an influenza A H1N1 subtype. In 1947 and 1978, pandemics were caused by a similar H1N1 subtype. In 1957, an H2N2 pandemic swept the globe, and in 1968, an H3N2 subtype did so.

How can influenza A make such major changes? Influenza A can infect birds, pigs, horses, humans, whales, and bats. Each species has its primary influenza subtypes. Wild bird populations are the major reservoir for influenza A, and all subtypes have been identified in wild birds. Pigs can be infected with their own subtypes (called swine influenza strains) and with human or avian (bird) influenza strains. If a pig is infected with two subtypes of influenza at the same time, major genetic

recombination can occur, creating totally novel viral subtypes. If the new virus spreads to humans—and if it can spread from human to human and cause disease—a new pandemic may occur.

Predicting the upcoming year's influenza strains for inclusion in vaccines is a global effort. Each year, scientists look at patterns of influenza circulation and spread in over 100 countries. The results of this surveillance are sent to five World Health Organization centers, located in Atlanta, Georgia; London, England; Melbourne, Australia; Tokyo, Japan; and Beijing, China. Twice a year, WHO brings together the directors of these centers and recommends viral strains to be included for the upcoming year. Each country has the final decision about which vaccines from the list to include. In the United States, the FDA chooses three or four subtypes—typically two influenza A subtypes and one or two influenza B subtypes—to be used in U.S. flu vaccinations. Because it takes about 6 months to produce sufficient vaccine, the decisions for the United States are made in February of the preceding year. In a good year, the predictions will be accurate and the vaccine will work well. In "mismatched" years, the vaccine is less effective but often still provides some coverage.

Influenza can be a serious illness and lead to hospitalization and even death. In the past 5 years, the number of annual U.S. flu-associated deaths has ranged from 4,000 to 20,000. The flu vaccine is now recommended for all people aged 6 months or older. Each year there are multiple options for types of flu vaccine and, in general, the CDC does not recommend one version over another. Options include a standard trivalent shot (two influenza A subtypes and one influenza B subtype), a quadrivalent shot (two influenza A and two influenza B subtypes), and a high-dose vaccine (for people aged 65 or older). The vaccine shots are all inactivated vaccines and cannot cause influenza disease; they can sometimes cause soreness at the injection site, low-grade fever, and muscle aches as the immune system is boosted to develop immunity. A quadrivalent nasal spray vaccine is also available for people 2 to 49. The nasal spray contains a live attenuated virus (meaning it has been altered so it can't cause full-blown disease), and thus it is not recommended for pregnant women or people with medical conditions that compromise the function of the immune system.

Source: Centers for Disease Control and Prevention. (2019). Influenza (flu). Retrieved from https://www.cdc.gov/flu/index.htm

starting at age 2 months. Even in the United States, before the vaccine was available, 20 to 60 infants would die each year from rotavirus infection. The vaccine has significantly reduced rates of rotavirus illness and death.[33,39]

latent infection
An infection that is not currently active but could reactivate at a later time.

Tuberculosis Worldwide, tuberculosis (TB) is the most common infectious disease. Approximately 25 percent of the world's population is infected, although rates have been

decreasing since 2002. The disease is caused by *Mycobacterium tuberculosis,* a member of a subset of bacteria, and is spread primarily through aerosolized droplets coughed out of the lungs of an infected person and breathed in by another person. Once the mycobacterium has been inhaled, a healthy immune system creates a wall around it and prevents it from growing or spreading. In this **latent infection**, the bacterium is in the body but is not causing any signs of disease or infection.[40]

About 5 to 10 percent of infected people develop the active disease at some point in their lives, meaning the

Worldwide, diarrhea remains a leading cause of death, especially for children under the age of 5 years. Improving overall nutritional status reduces the risk of death from diarrhea illness. *(ZUMA Press,Inc./Alamy Stock Photo)*

People with latent infection are treated to reduce the risk that they will develop active tuberculosis. Researchers are trying to develop simpler treatments, new medications, and new vaccines to reduce the world burden of TB.

Malaria Malaria is a mosquito-borne disease transmitted by any of four species of the *Plasmodium* parasite. Approximately 228 million people were infected in 2018, with 405,000 deaths, mostly among young children. Currently, 93 percent of malaria cases and 94 percent of malaria deaths occur in Africa, predominantly in sub-Saharan Africa.[43]

Malaria symptoms, which include high fever, chills, sweats, headache, nausea, vomiting, and body aches, develop 7 to 30 days after a bite from an infected *Anopheles* mosquito. Symptoms are often cyclic, recurring every few days. Severe malaria can lead to confusion, seizures, coma, heart failure, kidney failure, and death.

Prevention strategies include eliminating mosquito breeding grounds (such as standing water), applying insecticides, using screens and mosquito netting, and staying inside during peak mosquito-activity hours (dawn and dusk). People who travel to malaria-endemic areas should use mosquito repellent and take chemoprophylaxis—a medication given before, during, and for a period of time after travel. Malaria used to be endemic in parts of the southeastern United States, but the CDC, working with local health agencies, undertook a program that targeted mosquito-breeding grounds and included other anti-mosquito measures. Efforts to eradicate malaria worldwide are underway, with researchers attempting to develop a vaccine, new treatments, and new preventive measures. These efforts are especially important with the development of resistance to antimalarial medications and concerns that climate change may expand and shift the locations where the mosquito that transmits malaria is found.[43,44]

bacterium is no longer controlled and can replicate, spread, and be transmitted to other people. Symptoms of active tuberculosis include fatigue, weight loss, night sweats, fever, and coughing that may bring up blood. The active disease is more likely to develop if the immune system is impaired, as in people with HIV infection, poor nutrition, or diabetes.[40]

Tuberculosis has reemerged as a major health problem in part because of the rapid spread of HIV. Tuberculosis is the leading cause of death for people with HIV.[41] Anyone with a new case of active TB should be screened for possible co-infection with HIV. Changes in population patterns have also influenced the spread of TB. Poverty and crowded living situations enhance the spread of disease. In the United States, the people at highest risk for tuberculosis are recent immigrants (particularly from Asia, Africa, Mexico, and South and Central America), homeless people, prison populations, and people infected with HIV.

Active tuberculosis is treated with a combination of four anti-tuberculosis drugs taken for 6 months (making it a difficult treatment to complete, although most cases are successfully treated). Drug-resistant TB is a major concern. Globally, 3.4 percent of new TB cases have multiple drug resistance (MDR-TB). Over 50 percent of MDR-TB cases are in India, China, and the Russian Federation. Of graver concern is that an even more resistant strain, called extensively drug-resistant tuberculosis (XDR-TB), has recently developed in 123 countries (there were two cases in the United States in 2017). In these cases, treatment options are extremely limited.[41,42]

International public health efforts are essential for the control of TB. Screening of people at risk for tuberculosis, access to appropriate medications, and tracking systems to ensure successful completion of treatment are essential.

Infectious Diseases on Campus

Infectious diseases also cause illness on college campuses, and the most common non–sexually transmitted infectious diseases you are likely to encounter are reviewed in Table 13.1. The SARS-CoV-2 pandemic will significantly alter how campuses operate for potentially years to come. College students consistently list colds, flu, and sore throat among the top 10 impediments to academic performance. Assess your risk of infectious disease by completing the immunizations table and answering the questions in this chapter's Personal Health Portfolio activity.

Table 13.1   Infectious Diseases on Campus

Illness	Cause (Pathogen)	Incubation	Symptoms	Home Treatment	When to Seek Medical Care	Prevention
Common cold	More than 200 different viruses, including rhinovirus, adenovirus, coronavirus	1–4 days	Runny nose (mucus often clear initially, then thicker, darker), nasal congestion, mild cough, sore throat, low-grade fever (<101° F), sneezing.	Usually ends on its own; fluids, rest, over-the-counter decongestants, antihistamines, cough suppressants, antipyretics, analgesics; avoid alcohol and tobacco.	Inability to swallow, worsening symptoms after 3rd day, difficulty breathing, stiff neck.	Wash hands thoroughly and frequently, avoid sharing personal items, cover you cough/sneeze; avoid touching face, stay home when ill; eat a balanced diet, exercise, get adequate sleep.
Influenza ("the flu")	Influenza A or B virus	1–5 days	Sudden-onset fever (usually >101° F), headache, tiredness (can be extreme), body aches, cough, sore throat, runny or stuffy nose.	Usually ends on its own; same home treatments as for common cold; in addition, antiviral medications can be used by prescription.	Immediately if at risk for complications (e.g., pregnant women, people with chronic lung or heart disease, asthma). Otherwise, if difficulty breathing, severe headache or stiff neck, confusion, fever for more than 3 days, new pain in one area (ear, chest, sinuses).	Annual flu shot in October or November, frequent hand washing; avoid close contact with sick people.
SARS-CoV-2 (COVID-19)	Novel coronavirus	2–14 days	Ranges from no symptoms to fever, cough, fatigue, shortness of breath.	Usually resolves on its own; same home treatment as for common cold.	Immediately if developing shortness of breath.	Same as for common cold.
Strep throat	*Streptococcus* bacteria	2–5 days	Sudden-onset sore throat and fever (often >101° F); mild headache, stomachache, nausea; red and white pus on tonsils, sore lymph nodes in neck; absence of cough, stuffy nose, other cold symptoms.	Salt water gargles, analgesics, antipyretics, throat lozenges.	If symptoms are consistent with strep, visit health care provider, who can prescribe antibiotics to reduce duration of symptoms and reduce risk of complications.	Same as for common cold.
Acute sinus infection	Virus: cold virus most common cause Bacteria: *Streptococcus, Haemophilus influenza*; less common cause, often as complication of cold or allergies	Varies	Pain or pressure in the face, stuffy or runny nose, upper teeth pain, fever; may have headache, bad breath, yellow or green nasal discharge.	Same as for common cold: decongestants or antihistamines; nasal irrigation; most sinus infections resolve on their own with opening and drainage of the sinuses.	Fever >101° F after 3 days; no improvement in facial pain or pressure after 2 days of home treatment with decongestant; cold symptoms continue beyond 10 days or worsen after 7 days.	Same as for common cold. Early treatment of nasal congestion with decongestant or antihistamine.

Continued...

Table 13.1   Infectious Diseases on Campus *(Concluded)*

Illness	Cause (Pathogen)	Incubation	Symptoms	Home Treatment	When to Seek Medical Care	Prevention
Mononucle-osis ("mono")	Epstein-Barr virus (EBV)	4–6 weeks	High fever (>101° F), severe sore throat, swollen glands, weakness and fatigue; loss of appetite; nausea and vomiting possible.	Usually resolves on its own; rest, fluids; avoid contact sports until symptoms resolve due to risk of spleen rupture.	Fever >101° F after 3 days, unable to maintain fluids; low energy, body aches, swollen glands for more than 7–10 days. Severe pain in belly can indicate spleen rupture, which is a medical emergency.	Do not kiss or share utensils or foods with someone who has mono; EBV is spread from saliva.
Bronchitis or cough	Virus: same as common cold Bacteria: rare Other lung irritants: tobacco smoke	Varies	Initial dry, hacking cough; in a few days, may produce mucus; maybe low fever and fatigue; often develops 3–4 days after start of a cold; may last 2–3 weeks.	Rest, fluids, cough drops, and avoid-ance of lung irritants such as tobacco; over-the-counter cold medications may help.	Shortness of breath; history of asthma or chronic lung disease; signs of pneumonia: high fever, shaking chills, shortness of breath; also, if symptoms last more than 4 weeks.	Avoid tobacco smoke; get annual flu shot; wash hands thoroughly and frequently.
Meningitis and encephalitis	Virus: usually not as serious as bacterial; some forms can be spread by mosquitoes Bacteria: rare, must be treated immediately to avoid brain damage and death	Varies	Stiff and painful neck, fever, headache, vomiting, difficulty staying awake, confusion, seizures.	Home treatment is not appropriate until a health care provider deter-mines if cause is virus or bacteria. If viral cause, home treatment to relieve fever and pain symptoms is appropriate.	Immediately if signs of meningitis are present.	Immunization against some pathogens, including mea-sles, mumps, rubella; chicken-pox; *Neisseria meningitides* (meningococcal vaccine). Special immunizations for certain areas of the world; insect repellent. Bacterial: Antibiotics after coming in close contact with infected person.
Cellulitis	Bacteria: Most common are *Streptococcus* and *Staphylo-coccus aureus*	Varies	Infected area will be warm, red, swol-len, and painful. If infection spreads, may have fever, chills, swollen glands.	Warm com-presses; keep area clean and dry; topical antibiotics if only small area of skin involved.	Usually treated with antibiotics; any symptoms should be evaluated by a health care provider.	Healthy skin protects against infection; keep cuts, burns, in-sect bites clean and dry; treat chronic skin con-ditions (e.g., eczema, ulcers, psoriasis); avoid skin-to-skin con-tact with infected people; avoid intravenous drug use, piercing, and tattoos.

Next we will review pertussis, staph skin infections, and urinary tract infections (UTIs) in more detail, due to their prevalence and/or changing patterns.

Pertussis (Whooping Cough) *Whooping cough* is the common name for an infection of the respiratory tract caused by the pertussis bacterium. It is highly contagious and transmitted by the inhalation of respiratory droplets from an infected person's cough or sneeze. Initial infection may seem similar to a common cold, with nasal congestion, runny nose, mild fever, and a dry cough, but after 1 to 2 weeks, the cough becomes the most significant ongoing feature and may occur in spells lasting a few minutes and ending in a "whooping" sound as the person gasps for air. The cough can persist for months. Pertussis is treated with antibiotics if diagnosed early.

Most infants and young children are vaccinated against pertussis, but immunity begins to wear off after 5 to 10 years, leaving adolescents and young adults susceptible to infection. Studies on college campuses show that among students with a prolonged cough, approximately 30 percent may have pertussis. This is annoying but not typically dangerous to teens and adults. However, infected people serve as a reservoir and can transmit to young children and infants, in whom the disease can be life-threatening. For this reason, it is now recommended that all adolescents and adults receive a booster Tdap vaccination (tetanus, diphtheria, and acellular pertussis) to enhance their immunity against this infection and reduce the risk of transmission.

Reported cases of pertussis have increased 20-fold in the past 30 years. Because of the high risk the disease poses to newborns, pregnant women should receive a booster during pregnancy regardless of when they last had a booster, as should anyone who spends time around newborns.[45]

Staphylococcus Aureus Skin Infections *Staphylococcus aureus* (often called "staph"), a common bacterium carried on the skin or in the noses of healthy people, is one of the most frequent causes of skin infection. Some strains of staph are becoming increasingly resistant to antibiotics. Initially seen in hospitals, methicillin-resistant *Staphylococcus aureus* (MRSA) is becoming common in community settings. MRSA is transmitted from person to person by skin-to-skin contact, through the sharing of personal items, and through contact with contaminated surfaces. Outbreaks of infection have been reported among athletes and people in shared living situations (such as on college campuses).

Usually staph infections are mild, taking the form of a pimple or small boil (sometimes mistaken for a spider bite). Sometimes these infections can spread, creating a large abscess (pocket of infection), which can require incision, drainage, and treatment with antibiotics. Less often, staph can cause infection of the blood, lungs, or muscle. These cases usually require hospitalization and intravenous antibiotic treatment.

Good hygiene practices can reduce the risk of staph infection. Keep your hands clean by washing frequently with soap and water, or use an alcohol-based (not an antibiotic-based)

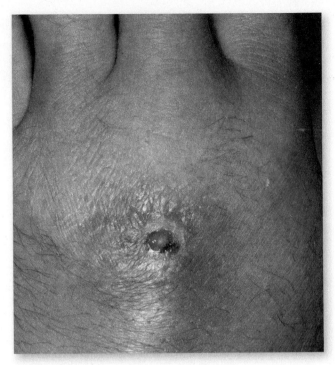

A skin infection caused by MRSA is easy to get and hard to treat. *(Scott Camazine/Alamy Stock Photo)*

hand sanitizer (refer to the box "Action Skill-Builder: How to Keep Your Hands Clean" earlier in the chapter). Shower after exercising, and avoid sharing personal items such as towels, razors, clothing, and uniforms. Keep cuts and scrapes clean and covered until healed. If you have been diagnosed with a staph infection, avoid skin-to-skin contact with others (including contact sports) until the area has healed.[46]

Urinary Tract Infections Urinary tract infections (UTIs) are the most common bacterial infection in women, and one-third of all women will have one in their lifetime. They occur in men, too, but less frequently. The vast majority of UTIs are caused by the bacterium *E. coli,* although they can be caused by other bacteria. Symptoms include pain or burning with urination, pain in the lower abdomen, urgency and frequency of urination, and, if the kidneys become involved, fever and back pain. Recent sexual activity and a history of UTI are risk factors for infection. If a woman is at risk for STIs or has vaginal symptoms, such as discharge or irritation, she should be tested to rule out STIs. Treatment includes fluids and antibiotics, although *E. coli* is becoming increasingly resistant to commonly used antibiotics.

Given how common UTIs are and the growing concerns regarding antibiotic resistance, studies have sought to find effective ways for women to prevent recurrent infections. Increasing fluid intake, urinating after intercourse, and taking daily cranberry juice or cranberry supplements have all been looked at, but the evidence remains inconclusive. Researchers are working to develop a vaccine as another option, but there is nothing likely in the near future.[47,48]

SEXUALLY TRANSMITTED INFECTIONS

Sexually transmitted infections are infections that spread from one person to another predominantly through sexual contact. Most health experts prefer the term *sexually transmitted infection (STI)* because often there are no symptoms, and by definition, a disease is an infection that causes symptoms. However, the CDC continues to use the term *sexually transmitted disease (STD)*.

The primary pathogens responsible for STIs are viruses and bacteria. We begin this section with HIV infection, one of the most serious threats to public health worldwide, and then we discuss the other STIs by type of pathogen. See Table 13.2 for information relating to the incubation period, signs and symptoms, complications, screening and diagnosis, treatment, and prevention of some infections.[49]

HIV/AIDS

Acquired immunodeficiency syndrome (AIDS) is caused by the human immunodeficiency virus (HIV). Since the first case was diagnosed in 1981, more than 20 million people worldwide have died from HIV/AIDS. The pandemic remains a serious infectious disease challenge in public health today.

Progress in the global fight against HIV is measured by declines in the numbers of AIDS-related deaths and new HIV cases. Reductions in mortality are due to early diagnosis and treatment of HIV infection, and steady progress has been made worldwide in reducing deaths from a peak of 1.7 million in 2004 to 770,000 in 2018. Slowing the rate of new infections has been a more gradual process, with the number declining from a peak of 2.9 million in 1997 to 1.7 million in 2018. North America, Western and Central Europe have seen decreases in new cases; this is not yet true in Eastern Europe, Central Asia, the Middle East, North Africa, and Latin America. At the end of 2018, an estimated 37.9 million people worldwide were infected, more than half of them in sub-Saharan Africa (Figure 13.7).[50,51]

Of the 5,000 new HIV infections per day in 2018, 61 percent were in sub-Saharan Africa, 47 percent were in women, and 32 percent were in people age 15 to 24 years. Outside eastern and southern Africa (where transmission occurs in the general population), HIV's spread is predominately

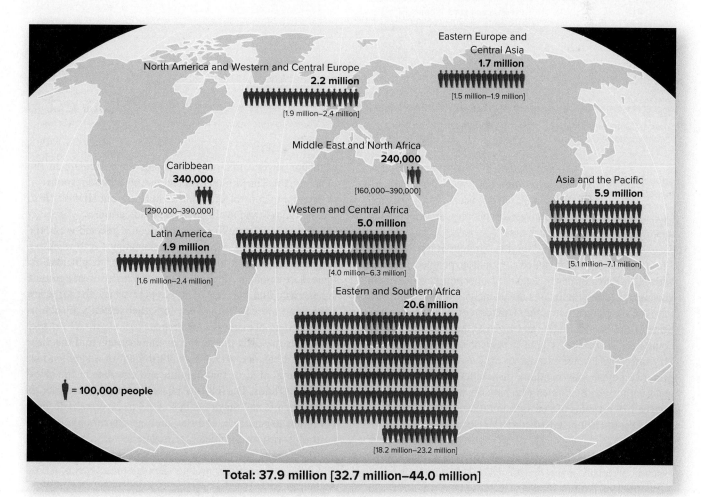

Total: 37.9 million [32.7 million–44.0 million]

figure 13.7 **Adults and children estimated to be living with HIV in 2018.**

Source: Joint United Nations Programme on HIV/AIDS. (2019). UNAIDS data 2019. Retrieved from https://www.aidsdatahub.org/sites/default/files/publication/UNAIDS_data_2019.pdf

Who's at Risk?

Disproportionate Risk for HIV Infections

Certain groups are at disproportionate risk for sexual transmission of HIV infection. The following graph shows the subpopulations that reported the most new HIV cases in the United States. Men who have sex with men account for the majority of new infections. In addition, there are differences by race and ethnicity within sexual behavior categories.

Given that HIV transmission is preventable through condom use and pre-exposure prophylaxis (PrEP) for high-risk groups, how might stigma, access to health care, economics, and other factors in the socioecological model of health and wellness contribute to the differences in new infection rates?

Estimated new HIV infections in the United States, 2017, for the most affected subpopulations.

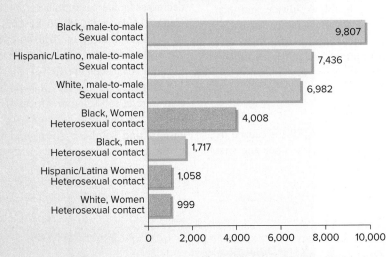

New HIV diagnoses in the US and dependent areas for the most-affected subpopulations, 2018

Subpopulation	New HIV diagnoses
Black, male-to-male Sexual contact	9,807
Hispanic/Latino, male-to-male Sexual contact	7,436
White, male-to-male Sexual contact	6,982
Black, Women Heterosexual contact	4,008
Black, men Heterosexual contact	1,717
Hispanic/Latina Women Heterosexual contact	1,058
White, Women Heterosexual contact	999

Source: Centers for Disease Control and Prevention. (2019). HIV basic statistics. Retrieved from https://www.cdc.gov/hiv/basics/statistics.html

opportunistic infections
Infections that occur when the immune system is weakened.

concentrated in key populations—men who have sex with men, injection drug users, sex workers, transgender people—and their sexual partners.

In the United States, an estimated 1.1 million people are living with HIV. Rates of newly diagnosed infection have declined; however, certain populations are at increased risk. Men who have sex with men account for 66 percent of all new HIV infections in the United States, and high-risk heterosexual sex accounts for 24 percent. About 6 percent of newly diagnosed HIV infections involve intravenous drug use. Racial and ethnic minority populations continue to be affected disproportionately, with young Black men who have sex with men experiencing the highest rates of new infection (see the box "Who's at RIsk? Disproportionate Risk for HIV Infections").[50]

Course of the Disease HIV targets the cells of the immune system, especially macrophages and CD4 cells (a subcategory of helper T cells). Once inside these host cells, the virus uses the cell's DNA to replicate itself and disable the host cell. During the initial infection with HIV, known as *primary infection,* the virus replicates rapidly. Within 4 to 11 days of

exposure, several million viral copies may circulate in the bloodstream. The immune system mounts a rapid response in an attempt to control and remove the virus, but HIV is able to mutate quickly and avoid complete eradication.

Between 50 and 90 percent of people infected with HIV experience an acute infection approximately 4 to 6 weeks after exposure, with symptoms such as fever, weight loss, fatigue, sore throat, swollen lymph nodes, night sweats, muscle aches, rash, and diarrhea. The symptoms may last for a few weeks and are easily mistaken for other infections, such as influenza, mononucleosis, or herpes.

After the early phase, the immune system and the virus come to a balance with the establishment of a *viral load set point,* a level of virus that continues to circulate in the blood and body fluids. During this phase, an untreated person is asymptomatic and may remain so for 2 to 20 years. The virus continues to replicate, and the immune system continues to control it without completely removing it.

Eventually, the immune system is weakened significantly and can no longer function fully, signaling the onset of AIDS. Symptoms of AIDS include rapid weight loss, cough, night sweats, diarrhea, rashes or skin blemishes, and memory loss. These symptoms are due to **opportunistic infections—**infections that occur when the immune system is no longer able to fight them off. Common opportunistic infections include *Pneumocystis carinii* pneumonia, Kaposi's sarcoma (a rare cancer), and tuberculosis. These infections do not usually occur in a person with a healthy immune system.

A note of caution: The symptoms associated with acute HIV infection and AIDS are also associated with many other illnesses. A person experiencing such symptoms should not automatically assume they are signs of HIV infection or AIDS. However, a person who is at risk should get tested for HIV infection.

Methods of Transmission HIV cannot survive long outside a human host; thus, transmission requires intimate contact. The virus can be found in varying concentrations in an infected person's blood, saliva, semen, genital secretions, and breast milk. It usually enters a new host either at a mucosal surface or by direct inoculation into the blood. HIV is not transmitted through casual contact, such as shaking hands, hugging, or sharing a casual kiss, nor is it spread by day-to-day contact in the workplace, school, or home. Although HIV has been found in saliva and tears, it is present in very low quantities. It has not been found in sweat.

Risk of HIV transmission is influenced by factors associated with the host (the already infected person), the recipient (the currently uninfected person), and the type of interaction that occurs between them. An important host factor is the level of virus circulating in the blood. High levels of circulating virus, such as during the initial infection stage, increase the risk of transmission. In addition, some people may have a higher viral load set point during the equilibrium period. Antiviral treatment (see the section "Management of HIV/AIDS") lowers the level of circulating virus and reduces the risk of transmission. Thus ensuring access to treatment for all people infected with HIV is a goal that will help reduce mortality from AIDS and reduce transmission of HIV from person to person, moving the world move toward ending the HIV epidemic.[51]

Sexual Conduct The primary exposure risk for 94 percent of new HIV infections in the United States is sexual contact.[50] HIV can enter the body through the mucosa or lining of the vagina, penis, rectum, or mouth. If the mucosa is cut, torn, or irritated (as can happen with intercourse or if there is another STI, especially genital herpes), the risk increases. The sexual behaviors associated with transmission are, in order of decreasing risk, receptive anal sex, insertive anal sex, penile-vaginal sex, and oral sex.

Although discussing HIV risk and status with a potential sexual partner may be awkward, its importance cannot be overemphasized. As noted, the highest levels of circulating virus occur shortly after initial infection, a time when people may not have any symptoms and may not know they are infected. In fact, 14 percent of HIV-positive people in the United States do not know they are infected. Unless you have a conversation about whether your potential partner has been tested for HIV, what recent behaviors they have engaged in, and what other sexual partners they are or have been involved with, you do not know what your risk is in starting a

sexual relationship. Pre-exposure prophylaxis (PrEP) is recommended for people without HIV who are at very high risk of contracting it (to be discussed later).[50,52]

Injection Drug Use The second most common method of HIV transmission is injection drug use, reported by 6 percent of people with AIDS in the United States. Another 3 percent report both injection drug use and being a man who has sex with other men. Individuals can reduce their risk of HIV infection by avoiding injection drug use. People who are already using drugs can reduce their risk by using sterile needles and not sharing needles with others. In addition, PrEP is recommended for people who are HIV negative but have injected drugs in the past 6 months and have shared needles. Communities can play a role in decreasing the spread of HIV by implementing needle exchange programs and ensuring adequate access to drug treatment programs.[50]

Contact With Infected Blood or Body Fluids HIV can be transmitted by direct contact with the blood or body fluids of an infected person. The risk of transmission depends on how much virus is in the body fluid, how much fluid gets onto the other person, and where the fluid contacts the other person. A small amount of infected blood on the intact skin of another person carries essentially no risk. A larger amount of blood on cut or broken skin or mucosal membranes has a greater risk. The accidental injection of infected blood through a needlestick has an even greater risk.

These types of exposure are most likely to occur in health care settings, and to reduce the risk of transmission of HIV, hepatitis B and C, and other bloodborne infections, these places take a **universal precautions** approach. Universal precautions include the use of gloves, gown, mask, and other protective wear (such as eyewear or face shields) by anyone who is likely to be exposed to the blood or body fluids of another person. In addition, if someone is exposed to bodily fluids or a needlestick, health care settings have protocols for testing and access to medications to reduce risk of infection postexposure (discussed later under prevention). These precautions should be taken with every patient.[53]

Mother-to-Child Transmission Mother-to-child, or vertical, transmission of HIV can occur during pregnancy, during delivery, or during breastfeeding. The risk of transmission from a mother to her child has been reduced by 90 percent through the use of antiretroviral medications in HIV-infected women. Globally, the push to identify HIV-positive women and treat them during pregnancy has been a major focus to eliminate new infections in children.[54]

In the United States, women are routinely offered HIV testing as part of prenatal care. Women who test positive are offered antiretroviral medications to reduce their child's

universal precautions A set of precautions by health care personnel designed to prevent transmission of bloodborne infections such as HIV and hepatitis B and C. They are "universal" because they should be used with all patients.

risk. In untreated pregnant women with HIV, approximately 30 percent of infants are infected; in treated women, less than 1 percent are infected. In addition, in the United States, where women have access to safe water supplies and formula, HIV-infected women are encouraged to feed formula to their baby instead of breast feeding.[55]

HIV Testing   A new CDC campaign called *Let's Stop HIV Together* highlights the fact that we have the tools and resources to eliminate HIV infection. A critical component in stopping transmission is for everyone to know their HIV status. The sooner you know, the better you can take care of yourself and reduce the risk of spreading HIV to others. The only way you know whether you are infected is by getting tested. The CDC recommends that everyone between the ages of 13 and 64 be tested for HIV infection at least once. People with increased risk should be tested annually or even more often. If you have more than one sex partner, are a man who has sex with men, are getting tested for other STIs, or use intravenous drugs, regular testing is recommended. Transgender people are a population with increased risk of HIV infection, and risk assessment should take into account anatomy and sexual behavior.[52,56]

Tests can look for the actual HIV RNA, protein components of HIV (antigens), or antibody reaction to HIV. Each type of test varies in the period of time after an HIV exposure before it can detect infection, ranging from 10 days to 8 weeks. The HIV RNA and antigen tests can detect infection in the shortest time period since exposure. If you think you have been exposed in the last 72 hours, see a health provider about postexposure prophylaxis (PEP).

drug cocktails
Drug combinations used to reduce drug resistance in different strains of HIV.

Testing is fast, easy, and confidential. To increase testing rates, many cities are now offering nonclinical sites for testing—such as mobile units, churches, bathhouses, shelters, and bars. In addition, tests are available that you can use at home. Tests can be done on blood, saliva, or urine, and some can deliver results in about 20 minutes. Currently the Ora-Quick In-Home HIV Test is the only FDA-licensed and approved home test kit available in the United States. (Consumers are warned to use only FDA-approved test kits because others may not be as accurate.) In the privacy of your home, you use a swab in your mouth to collect a small amount of oral fluid and use the kit to test it. If the result is positive, you will be referred to a health clinic for a confirmatory test. If you are HIV-negative, consider how recently you may have been exposed to decide whether you will need to repeat testing. Then consider your risk of exposure to assess whether you can further reduce your risk for infection.[57,58]

Management of HIV/AIDS   The development of new medications and improved understanding of the HIV disease process have prolonged survival for people infected with HIV. Global efforts to increase access to and education about HIV treatment have contributed to these encouraging results.[59]

Antiretroviral Agents   The most important medications in HIV treatment are antiviral drugs—or, more accurately, antiretroviral drugs—because HIV is a type of virus called a *retrovirus.* Antiretroviral medications do not cure the infection, but they slow the rate at which the virus replicates and destroys the immune system, thus prolonging life and improving the quality of life for people who are HIV-positive. In addition, early treatment significantly reduces the risk of transmission. Medications can also be used for prophylaxis in people who are at high risk but currently not infected.

HIV is a rapidly mutating virus and is able to develop resistance to single medications very quickly. Thus, all treatment and prevention regimens rely on multiple drug combinations, called **drug cocktails**. The virus is less likely to develop several mutations that could allow it to evade the combination of drugs. New combinations of multiple medications in a single pill have reduced the complexity and cost of treatment and the risk of side effects, making it easier for people with HIV to successfully stay on treatment.

Prevention   Since the identification of HIV, researchers have been attempting to develop safe and effective measures to reduce risk of infection. An HIV vaccine would be ideal but is challenging. The immune system does not seem to be able to clear HIV and produce immunity; instead, in most people, the virus produces lifelong infection. Furthermore,

The CDC recommends that people aged 13 to 64 get tested for HIV at least once. Over-the-counter home tests make this easier than ever.
(Kristoffer Tripplaar/Alamy Stock Photo)

the virus is a moving target; it mutates frequently and develops new strains rapidly. However, vaccine trials are underway. Adult male circumcision is recognized as an intervention to reduce risk of HIV infection from penile-vaginal sex, possibly because removing the foreskin results in a toughening of the skin covering the penis. The benefits are not seen in men who have sex with men, most likely because the risk of contracting HIV is greatest during receptive anal sex. Other global measures to reduce HIV transmission include empowering women through education and creating opportunities for them to become financially independent, so that they are less at risk of forced early marriage, sexual coercion, exchange of sex for money, and intimate partner violence. At present, the use of antiretroviral medications appears to be the most effective prevention, as we will see next.

People with HIV manage the disease with antiretroviral medications. Multiple drugs are used because the virus can quickly become resistant to individual drugs. Early treatment reduces the risk of HIV transmission. *(Gideon Mendel/Corbis Historical/ Getty Images)*

Treatment as Prevention Early identification of HIV infection allows for antiviral medications to be started immediately. Medications can suppress replication of HIV to the point where there is no detectable virus circulating in a person's bloodstream. This does not mean the infection has been cured, because HIV is still present in lymph tissue and other areas, so antiviral medications must be maintained. However, with an undetectable viral load, health is improved and the risk of spreading infection is very low—possibly even zero.

Postexposure Prophylaxis In an emergency situation when you have had possible exposure to HIV through unprotected sex or intravenous drug use, seeking care and starting a three-drug antiretroviral medication cocktail can reduce your risk of becoming infected. To be effective, medication must be started within 72 hours of exposure and taken for 28 days.[60]

Pre-exposure Prophylaxis If you are HIV-negative but are frequently in high-risk situations—such as by having a partner with HIV infection, a recent diagnosis of a bacterial STI, a high number of sexual partners, or a history of exchanging sex for drugs or money or using intravenous drugs and shared needles—taking a daily cocktail of two medications can significantly reduce your risk of acquiring HIV infection.[50] Daily medication use reduces the risk of sexual transmission by 99 percent and the risk from intravenous drug use by 74 percent. Given that PrEP does not eliminate risk and some people have side effects with medication, steps should still be taken to reduce risk of transmission, such as using condoms, limiting partners, and not sharing needles.[50]

Bacterial STIs

Bacterial STIs are generally curable infections if identified early. Undiagnosed, they can cause serious consequences, including pelvic inflammatory disease (PID), reduced fertility, ectopic pregnancy, and increased risk of HIV transmission.[61]

Chlamydia The most commonly reported bacterial STI is chlamydia. Rates of infection are increasing in the United States, with an estimated 1.7 million cases diagnosed annually. Young women are at greatest risk, with infection rates twice those of young men. Although all racial and ethnic groups are affected, rates among Black women are 5.6 times higher and among American Indian/Alaska Natives 3.7 times higher than among white women.[15]

All sexually active women under age 25 should be screened annually for chlamydia, as should women who are pregnant, women over 25 who have a new sexual partner or multiple sexual partners, and women who are infected with another STI. Early identification and treatment of infection reduces the risk of complications such as PID and infertility.[61]

Men who have sex with men should be tested at least annually (or more frequently if they have multiple or anonymous partners) for rectal, penile, or throat infection (depending on their sexual practice and what site is potentially exposed). There is debate about the cost-effectiveness of screening other sexually active men. Men have fewer long-term after-effects from chlamydial infection; thus, routine screening efforts are targeted at women. However, lower rates in men reflect lower rates of testing, *not* lower rates of infection. Men should be tested if they have symptoms or have a new sexual partner, or if their sexual partner has been diagnosed with chlamydia. Rates of chlamydia are increasing among men due to increased screening of asymptomatic men. Sexual partners need to be referred and treated prior to resuming sexual intercourse.[61]

Table 13.2   Common Sexually Transmitted Infections

Infection	Incubation	Signs and Symptoms	Complications	Screening and Diagnosis*	Treatment	Prevention
Bacterial						
Chlamydia (*Chlamydia trachomatis*)	1–3 weeks	No symptoms for 75% of women and 50% of men. **If symptoms:** watery discharge, burning with urination.	Women: PID, chronic pelvic pain, infertility, ectopic pregnancy. Men: epididymitis (red, swollen testicles) and, rarely, sterility. **If untreated in pregnant women:** premature birth; eye and lung infections in newborns.	Urine or sample collected from penis, cervix, rectum, or throat (site based on sexual practice). Women < age 26: annually. Men who have sex with men (MSM): annually (or more often). Men < age 26: consider annually if new partners.	Antibiotics; sex partners need testing and treatment prior to resuming sexual intercourse.	Condoms.
Gonorrhea (*Neisseria gonorrhoeae*)	2–5 days	No symptoms in most women and some men. **If symptoms:** Men: pain or burning with urination; discharge from penis; itching inside penis. Women: pain or burning with urination; vaginal discharge, bleeding between periods; pain during sex. Rectal infection: discharge, soreness, bleeding, or pain. Throat infection: sore throat.	Women: PID, chronic pelvic pain, infertility, and ectopic pregnancy. Men: epididymitis (red, swollen testicles) and infertility; can spread to blood and joints. **If untreated in pregnant women:** risk of newborn eye, joint, and blood infection.	Urine or sample collected from cervix, penis, rectum, or throat (site based on sexual practice). Women < age 26: annually. MSM: annually (or more frequently). Men < age 26: consider annually if new partners.	Antibiotics; sex partners need testing and treatment prior to resuming sexual intercourse.	Condoms.
Syphilis (*Treponema pallidum*)	**Primary stage:** 10–90 days **Secondary stage:** 3–6 weeks after primary stage **Late stage:** years after initial untreated infection	No symptoms for most people. **If symptoms: Primary stage:** single round, firm, and painless sore (chancre) at exposure site; sore resolves without treatment in 3–6 weeks. **Secondary stage:** skin rash with non-itchy, rough, reddish brown spots on palms and soles; may have fever, swollen lymph nodes, headache, fatigue; resolves without treatment.	**Late stage:** without treatment, infection remains in body and 15% of people will develop deterioration of the brain, arteries, bones, heart, and other organs; death possible. **If untreated in pregnant women:** risk of fetal death or infant developmental delay, seizures, or other complications.	Blood test for antibodies to syphilis. MSM: annually (or more often). Heterosexuals and women who have sex with women (WSW): test if positive for another STI. All pregnant women.	Antibiotics will cure if diagnosed within the first year of infection.	Avoidance of high-risk behaviors; condoms.

Continued...

Table 13.2   Common Sexually Transmitted Infections (Continued)

Infection	Incubation	Signs and Symptoms	Complications	Screening and Diagnosis*	Treatment	Prevention
Viral						
HIV (human immunodeficiency virus)	4–6 weeks	No symptoms for 10–60% of people. **If symptoms:** fever, fatigue, sore throat, lymph node swelling, muscle aches; may include weight loss, rash, night sweats, and diarrhea; often mistaken for other illnesses.	Acquired immunodeficiency syndrome (AIDS) 2–20 years after initial infection if untreated; symptoms include opportunistic infections, weight loss, rashes, and skin changes. **Pregnant women:** can be transmitted to fetus; reduced risk with treatment of mother.	Blood, saliva, or urine test. Annually if intravenous drug user, new sexual partners, or diagnosed with another STI. MSM with multiple or anonymous partners: consider every 3–6 months. All pregnant women.	No cure; management with antiretroviral medications that reduce rate of viral replication and slow rate of immune system decline.	Condoms; treatment as prevention (TasP), post-exposure prophylaxis (PEP), and pre-exposure prophylaxis (PrEP).
HPV (human papillomavirus; more than 40 strains)	Weeks to months	No symptoms for most people. **If symptoms:** Genital warts: small bumps or clusters of bumps in genital area. Cervical cancer: irregular bleeding.	Cancers of cervix, vulva, vagina, anus, and penis. **Pregnant women:** very rarely, newborn can develop throat infection during vaginal birth.	Genital warts: visual identification. Cervical cancer: routine Pap testing starting at age 21 for all women.	In 90% of cases, immune system clears infection within 2 years. Warts: topical medications or cryotherapy (freezing). Cervical cancer: see Chapter 15.	Vaccination for women and men; Pap test for women reduces risk of cervical cancer; condoms reduce risk, but virus can infect areas of genitalia not covered by male and female condoms.
Genital herpes (herpes simplex virus type 1 or type 2)	2–7 days	No symptoms for most people. **If symptoms:** one or more blisters on or around the mouth, genitals, or rectum, which break open, leaving a painful sore that resolves after 2–4 weeks (for first infection); may have associated fever and lymph node swelling.	Recurrent outbreaks, usually less severe than initial one and decrease in severity with time. **Pregnant women:** potential life-threatening infection in newborn if infection during pregnancy or outbreak at time of vaginal birth.	Culture of ulcer or blood test. Routine screening controversial if no symptoms.	No cure; antiviral medications can shorten and prevent outbreaks.	Antiviral medications reduces risk of transmission, which can occur even when lesions are not present. Condoms reduce risk, but virus can infect areas of genitalia not covered by male and female condoms.

Continued...

Table 13.2   Common Sexually Transmitted Infections *(Concluded)*

Infection	Incubation	Signs and Symptoms	Complications	Screening and Diagnosis*	Treatment	Prevention
Hepatitis B	6 weeks–6 months	No symptoms for 30% of people. **If symptoms:** fever, loss of appetite, nausea, vomiting, abdominal pain, dark urine, yellow color of skin or eyes.	Chronic hepatitis B: increased risk of liver failure due to scarring of liver and liver cancer. **Pregnant women:** can transmit infection to newborn.	Blood tests can look for virus and evidence of immune response. All pregnant women.	No treatment for acute infection; several medications for chronic infection but not suitable for all people.	Vaccination recommended routinely for most people, and can be effective if given within 24 hours after exposure. Condoms.
Protozoan						
Trichomoniasis (*Trichomonas vaginalis*)	5–28 days	No symptoms in most men. **If symptoms:** Men: slight burning of penis or mild discharge. Women: frothy, yellow-green vaginal discharge with strong odor; vaginal soreness or itching.	**If untreated in pregnant women:** increased risk of premature delivery.	Identification under a microscope. Test if symptoms.	Antibiotics; treatment of both partners prior to resuming sexual activity.	Condoms.

*Heterosexual women and women who have sex with women (WSW) follow the same recommendations for screening guidelines; men who have sex with men (MSM) should consider increased frequency of screening at 3- to 6-month intervals if multiple or anonymous partners.

Sources: Centers for Disease Control and Prevention. (2016). *Sexually transmitted disease surveillance, 2015*. Atlanta, GA: U.S. Department of Health and Human Services; Centers for Disease Control and Prevention. (n.d.). Sexually transmitted diseases treatment guidelines 2015. Retrieved from www.cdc.gov/STI/treatment/default.htm.

Gonorrhea The second most commonly reported bacterial STI is gonorrhea. The rates of gonorrhea infection are rapidly increasing among men such that rates are now higher among men than among women. People of color are again affected more, with the rate among Blacks 8.3 times higher and among American Indian/Alaska Natives 4.5 times higher than among whites. An estimated 556,000 cases were diagnosed in 2017.[15]

All sexually active women under age 25 should be screened annually for gonorrhea, as should women who are pregnant or at increased risk because they have a new sexual partner or multiple sexual partners or are infected with another STI.

Men who have sex with men should be tested at least annually (or more frequently if they have multiple or anonymous partners) for rectal, penile, or throat infection (depending on their sexual practice and what site is potentially exposed). It is less clear whether other sexually active, asymptomatic men should be screened, because most infected men eventually develop symptoms.[61]

Gonorrhea is treated with antibiotics, but drug resistance is becoming a major concern. Cephalosporins are the only class of antibiotics now available to treat gonorrhea infection, and there are increasing reports of strains resistant to all antibiotics. Gonorrhea infections *must* be treated with two antibiotics instead of one to reduce the risk of further

resistance. Sexual partners need to be referred for evaluation and treatment. Sexual intercourse should not be resumed until all symptoms have resolved and for 7 days after treatment to reduce risk of transmission.[61]

Attempts to develop a vaccine against gonorrhea have been unsuccessful to date. However, early findings suggest that people who have received vaccination against a specific strain of group B meningococcus have a 30 percent reduced risk of contracting a gonorrhea infection. *Neisseria gonorrhea* and *Neisseria meningitidis* cause very different diseases, but the bacteria are in the same genus and are related to each other. These early findings of immunity development from the meningococcal vaccine may lead to development of an even more effective vaccine against gonorrhea, which will be critical given the predictions that gonorrhea may soon be resistant to antibiotic treatment.[62]

Pelvic Inflammatory Disease Pelvic inflammatory disease (PID) is an infection of the uterus, Fallopian tubes, and/or ovaries. The infection occurs when bacteria from the vagina or cervix spread upward into the uterus and Fallopian tubes. These bacteria are usually from STIs, such as chlamydia or gonorrhea, but they can be bacteria that are normally found in the vagina.

Symptoms of PID include fever, abdominal pain, pelvic pain, and vaginal bleeding or discharge. If PID is suspected, a combination of antibiotics is prescribed to cover gonorrhea, chlamydia, and vaginal bacteria. If symptoms are severe, hospitalization may be required. About 18 percent of women with PID develop chronic abdominal or pelvic pain that lasts more than 6 months.

PID can cause severe consequences and can be life-threatening if untreated. Most of the long-term problems arise from scarring in the Fallopian tubes, which increases the risk of ectopic pregnancy and infertility. Screening and treatment of chlamydia and gonorrhea reduce the risk of PID.[61]

Syphilis Rates of syphilis decreased throughout the 20th century but have increased steadily since 2001. Of current syphilis cases, 88 percent are diagnosed in men; 58 percent occur in men who have sex with men. Of concern is an ongoing increase in cases among women and an increase in cases of congenital syphilis (babies born with infection). Racial disparity in syphilis occurrence has decreased, but again people of color bear the greatest burden, with rates among Blacks being 4.5 times greater, among Native Hawaiians/Pacific Islanders 2.6 times greater, among Hispanics 2.2 times greater, and among American Indian/Alaska Natives 2.1 times greater than among whites.[15]

Syphilis progresses through several stages. If left untreated, it can lead to serious complications, including death.[15,61]

Screening is recommended for all pregnant women at their initial prenatal care visit, and for anyone at increased risk for syphilis infection. This includes men who have sex with men, commercial sex workers, and anyone who tests positive for another STI, exchanges sex for drugs, or has sex with partners who have syphilis.[61]

Bacterial Vaginosis Bacterial vaginosis (BV) is an alteration of the normal vaginal flora; *Lactobacillis,* the usually predominant bacteria, is replaced by different bacteria, causing a vaginal discharge and unpleasant odor. It is not clear why women develop bacterial vaginosis. Although it is not considered an STI, women who have never had sex rarely experience the condition. In addition, women who have sex with women have increased rates of BV. Treatment of male partners does not alter the rate of recurrence for women.

Screening for BV is recommended only if a woman has symptoms. BV is diagnosed by an evaluation of the vaginal flora under a microscope. Treatment is recommended not just because the symptoms are unpleasant, but also because BV has been associated with increased risk of PID, complications in pregnancy, and transmission of HIV. The condition is treated with the antibiotic metronidazole, which can be taken orally or vaginally. Treatment of partners is not indicated.[61]

Viral STIs

Viral STIs cannot be cured, making prevention even more important than in cases of bacterial STIs. Antiviral medication treatment can be an option to reduce symptoms and reduce risk of transmission. Vaccination is an option for some viral STIs.

Human Papillomavirus Human papillomavirus (HPV) is the most common STI in the United States. There are more than 100 strains of HPV, 40 of which infect the genital areas. Some are associated with genital warts, and others with cancers of the cervix, vulva, penis, anus, mouth, throat, and other areas. Strains associated with cancer are called high-risk strains; of these, two (HPV-16, HPV-18) are associated with 66 percent of cervical cancer cases. An additional five strains (HPV-31, -33, -45, -52, and -58) account for another 15 percent of cervical cancers. Strains associated with genital warts are called low-risk strains; of these, two (HPV-6, HPV-11) are most commonly associated with 90 percent of genital warts.

HPV is transmitted by skin-to-skin contact, usually through penetrative vaginal or anal sex, but it can be transmitted with oral sex and from woman to woman. Weeks to months after exposure to low-risk strains of HPV, both men and women can develop genital warts—flat or raised, small or large pinkish lesions—on the penis, scrotum, vagina, anus, or skin around the genital area. These warts can be treated with topical medications, but treatment is primarily for cosmetic reasons and may not alter the risk of transmission, because the virus is most likely also present in areas where warts are not visible.

Most women with HPV are diagnosed through screening with the Papanicolaou smear (Pap test), which can detect cervical cancer and precancerous lesions. After infection with HPV, the cells of the cervix undergo specific changes that can be identified under a microscope. A small percentage of exposed women will go on to have persistent infection and increased risk of cervical cancer. Risk appears to be higher in women who smoke and who have impaired immune systems, such as is caused by HIV infection. Pap screening is recommended starting at age 21, and if results are normal, the test should be repeated every 3 years until age 30. From age 30 to 65, Pap screening and HPV testing are recommended every 5 years if both are normal. Transgender men who have not had surgical removal of their cervix should follow similar guidelines. Self-testing with home vaginal swabs may be more acceptable to some women and transgender men.[63,64]

Men and women who have receptive anal intercourse are at high risk for anal HPV infection and anal cancer. The risk of anal cancer is even higher if someone has co-infection with HIV. Rates of anal cancer are increasing, and 95 percent of these cancers are due to HPV. Anal cytology—a test like a Pap test that takes a sample of cells from the rectum—and anal HPV testing can be used as screens for anal cancer and precancers. Currently, testing is not routinely recommended, but some practitioners do provide it, especially for people with HIV or people who have receptive anal sex.[65,66]

Most sexually active people will become infected with at least one strain of HPV in their lifetime. Infection can occur in the genital or oral area.[61] Limiting sexual partners is an

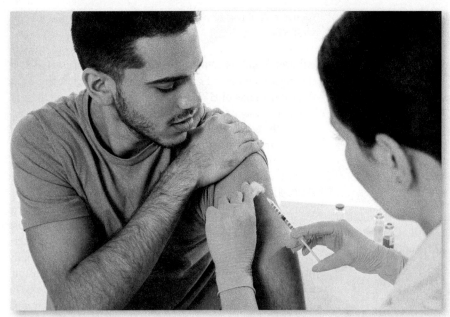

■ HPV vaccination is an important tool in reducing risk of HPV-associated cancers of the cervix, vagina, penis, anus, mouth, and throat. Before age 15, only two doses of the vaccine are necessary, but between ages 15 and 26, three shots are required. *(LightFieldStudios/Getty Images)*

important ways to decrease risk for HPV. Consistent and correct use of condoms may reduce the risk of transmission of HPV, but it may not provide full protection because HPV can infect skin not covered by the condom. Vaccination has become a critical part of HPV-related cancer prevention. Routine vaccination at age 11 or 12 is now recommended for everyone. At that age (and before age 15), only two doses of the vaccine are required. Between ages 15 and 26, three doses are required to generate an adequate immune response.[61,67]

Genital Herpes Genital herpes is caused by the herpes simplex virus (HSV), which has two strains, HSV-1 and HSV-2. Both strains can infect the mouth, genitals, or skin and cause lesions (cold sores) at the site of initial infection. HSV-2 is associated with a higher likelihood of recurrent symptoms than HSV-1. Even when a person does not have symptoms, the virus can be present at the site of infection (mouth, genitals, or skin) and be transmitted to another person. An estimated 15 percent of U.S. adults have genital HSV-2 infection, and many do not know they are infected.[15,61]

Because there is no cure for HSV infection, prevention is particularly important (see the box "Life Stories: Nate: Dealing With a Herpes Diagnosis"). Condoms partially protect people against infection with HSV, but they are not 100 percent effective. They must be used at all times when there is genital-to-genital contact and not just when a lesion is present, because the virus can be spread even without evidence of a sore. Several different vaccines for HSV are currently under study. Antiviral medications are available that shorten the course of outbreaks and reduce their frequency. These medications can also be taken daily to suppress viral shedding and reduce risk of transmission to partners.[61]

Hepatitis

Hepatitis (inflammation of the liver) can be caused by several viruses, but the most common ones are hepatitis A, B, and C. Hepatitis C was discussed earlier in the context of injection drug use, the most common route of acquiring the infection. Hepatitis A and B are both easily transmitted through sexual acts. Hepatitis A is transmitted through fecal-oral contact and can be spread through contact with contaminated food or water. The people at greatest risk for sexual transmission of hepatitis A are those who have oral-anal contact or penile-anal intercourse.

A safe and effective vaccine is available for hepatitis A and is now routinely recommended as part of the childhood vaccine series. Vaccination is recommended for adults who did not receive the vaccine in childhood and who are in a high-risk group, such as men who have sex with men, illicit drug users, people with chronic liver disease, and anyone who lives in a region that has a high rate of hepatitis A or who plans to travel to such areas.[52]

Most hepatitis B infections in the United States are sexually transmitted, although the infection can also be spread by exposure to infected blood. Worldwide, hepatitis B is a major cause of liver disease, liver failure, and liver cancer; unlike hepatitis A, it can cause chronic liver disease. About half of people with a new hepatitis B infection will develop acute symptoms, and 1 percent will develop liver failure and die. The chance of developing chronic disease decreases with age at the time of infection. Chronic infection carries an increased risk of liver failure and liver cancer.

A safe and effective vaccine for hepatitis B is available, and universal vaccination of all children is recommended. Adolescents and adults who were not vaccinated in childhood and are sexually active should be vaccinated; some colleges encourage hepatitis B vaccinations for all entering students. Vaccinations are currently required for all health care workers, and all pregnant women are screened for the virus.[61]

Other STIs

Several other nonbacterial, nonviral infections are transmitted sexually or involve the genital area. Most are treatable infections.

Trichomoniasis Trichomoniasis is caused by a protozoan and is transmitted from person to person by sexual activity. Most people won't have symptoms with infection; however, it can cause a vaginal discharge for women and discomfort with urination for all genders. Sexual partners of the infected

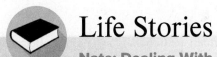

Life Stories

Nate: Dealing With a Herpes Diagnosis

Nate, a second-year student at a community college, had just come home from the student health center after being diagnosed with genital herpes. A week earlier, he had noticed a sore on his penis and went to the doctor to get it checked out, even though he felt embarrassed. The doctor did a culture and gave him the results today. He also gave him a prescription for acyclovir, an antiviral medication that would help reduce the number of future outbreaks, though Nate would carry the virus with him forever.

Nate was still in shock at the results. He couldn't believe he had an STI. He found himself wondering how he had gotten it—he had been with his current girlfriend, Stacy, for more than a year. The doctor explained that Nate may have contracted herpes from a previous partner and just not had any symptoms until now. The doctor also told him he needed to discuss his diagnosis with his girlfriend. That thought filled Nate with dread and embarrassment. He felt confused because he did not know whether he had the virus from a previous relationship or had contracted it from Stacy. What if Stacy had cheated on him and had given him the infection?

To make matters worse, Stacy had just left for a quarter-long internship in a city 3 hours away. They had been arguing a lot before she left, and they hadn't talked much since

then. He worried about how she was going to react. Would she suspect him of cheating and possibly break up with him? His mind raced forward—if they broke up and he started dating again, he would eventually have to tell other women that he had herpes. He couldn't *not* tell them and have sex with them—he would never do something like that—but what if they didn't want to date him or have sex with him after he told them?

Nate brought his thoughts back to the present situation. He felt stuck and alone. He missed Stacy—she was the one to whom he told everything. He didn't want to break up, even though they had been fighting. He knew he needed to talk with her to work through their problems and tell her about his diagnosis. He sent her a text asking whether they could talk later that day and spent the rest of the afternoon planning what to say.

- How do you think you would feel if you were diagnosed with an STI? How hard would it be to tell your current and/or former partners? How about your future partners?

- What are a person's ethical obligations under these circumstances? Are they different in different situations (such as dating vs. a hook-up) or with different people?

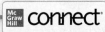

---

person need to be contacted and treated to prevent the further spread and recurrence of the infection.[61]

Candidiasis Candidiasis is usually caused by the yeast *Candida albicans.* Symptoms of yeast infection include vaginal discharge, itching, soreness, and burning with urination. Yeast infections are not usually acquired through sexual intercourse, but they can be mistaken for an STI because the symptoms are similar and they are less common in women who are not sexually active. *C. albicans* can be a normal part of the vaginal flora and may overgrow in response to changes in the vaginal environment, such as those caused by antibiotics or diabetes.

Candidiasis is treated with antifungal medications available over the counter and taken orally as a pill or applied to the vagina as a tablet suppository or a cream. If a woman is unsure of the diagnosis, has recurrences, or is at risk of STIs, she should have the diagnosis confirmed by a health care provider before she treats herself. Treatment of partners is not generally needed.[68]

Pubic Lice and Scabies Pubic lice and scabies are ectoparasites that can be sexually transmitted. Pubic lice (or "crabs") infect the skin in the pubic region and cause intense itching. Scabies can infect the skin on any part of the body and, again, cause intense itching. In adults, both pubic lice and scabies are most often sexually transmitted, but in children, scabies is usually acquired through nonsexual contact. Both infections are treated with a medicated cream or

shampoo containing permethrin. Bedding and clothing must be decontaminated to prevent reinfection.

PREVENTION OF INFECTIOUS DISEASES

There are many steps you can take to protect yourself from infectious diseases. Each will also reduce the risk of spread and the rates of disease in your community.

- *Support your immune system by eating a balanced diet, getting enough exercise and sleep, managing stress, not smoking, and adopting other practices that are part of a healthy lifestyle.*

- *Cover your cough.* If you need to cough or sneeze, cover your mouth with a tissue or cough/sneeze into your upper arm (not your hand!). Put used tissues into a wastebasket. Use masks as appropriate when physical distancing from other people cannot be maintained.

- *Avoid touching your face or mouth.* Every time you touch doorknobs, counters, and other objects, you are potentially picking up germs on your hands. Avoid transmitting these to your nose or mouth by not touching your face unless you have just washed your hands.

- *Get an annual flu shot and booster vaccines as recommended.* Follow government recommendations for vaccinations for both adults and children.

- *Minimize your use of antibiotics.* Antibiotic use increases risk that microorganisms will become resistant to treatment. Antibiotics also alter your health microbiome and increase your risk of unhealthy infections.

- *If you have been exposed to an infectious disease, minimize the chances that you will pass it on to someone else.* For example, if you have a cold or the flu, follow good hygiene practices such as washing your hands frequently, staying home from work, and avoiding crowded public places. If you have been exposed to SARS-CoV-2, follow quarantine and isolation protocols as required. If you have been exposed to an STI, take appropriate action—get tested and seek complete treatment if needed. Do not resume sexual activity until your partner has been treated, and consider safer sex practices.

- *Practice the ABCDs of STI prevention:* **A**bstain from sex until you are ready for a long-term committed relationship, and abstain between relationships; **B**e faithful, and maintain a mutually monogamous relationship with an uninfected partner; use **C**ondoms; and promote **D**etection of any STIs by being tested and following recommended screening guidelines. If you may have been exposed to an STI or have symptoms, get tested! If testing confirms infection, tell any sexual partners that they have been exposed so they can be treated, too. If you are in high-risk relationships, make sure you have the recommended vaccinations, and consider pre-exposure prophylaxis (PrEP) for HIV.

- If you are planning a trip to a new part of the country or a new country, *learn what infectious diseases are common there* and how you can decrease your risk of infection.

- *Reduce the likelihood that new diseases will take hold in your community,* with such actions as following local public health recommendations and getting rid of any standing water in your yard where mosquitoes could breed.

Microorganisms will always be part of human existence. By being vigilant, we can reduce their negative impact and support their positive impact on our lives.

You Make the Call

Should Colleges Tighten Vaccination Requirements?

Each year there are outbreaks of vaccine-preventable diseases across the United States. In April 2019, University of California–Los Angeles reported that 119 students and 8 faculty were under quarantine after potentially being exposed to a case of measles on campus. The students and faculty either had not received the recommended measles vaccine or could not show proof of vaccination. The quarantine orders came during an outbreak of measles in Los Angeles County.

From January to December the same year, 1,282 cases of measles were reported to the CDC, the largest number in the United States since 1992. The outbreaks occurred across 31 states and were predominantly in communities with low vaccination rates; the majority of people infected had not received the recommended two doses of the MMR (measles, mumps, rubella) vaccine. Although no vaccine is 100 percent effective, two doses of the MMR vaccine are 97 percent effective against measles.

College and university campus communities are uniquely vulnerable to infectious disease outbreaks. They are communities of people living in close contact with each other, whether in residence halls, off-campus housing, classrooms, or shared eating facilities. In addition, students, faculty, and staff frequently travel around the world for recreation, academic research, and family opportunities. This gives them an increased likelihood of exposure to infectious diseases, such as measles, which remains common in many parts of the world. Returning travelers can then bring back infections to campus, where illness may spread rapidly.

All 50 states have vaccination requirements for students in the K-12 system. All states allow exemption from vaccination requirements for medical reasons (e.g., severe reaction to vaccine or a medical condition that precludes vaccination). As of 2019, 45 states and Washington, DC, allow exemptions for people who have religious objection to vaccination. In addition, 15 states allow exemption for people who have philosophical objections to vaccination (personal, moral, or other objection). With the significant number of measles outbreaks in 2019, however, several states quickly adopted changes to their vaccination requirements. Washington State removed personal exemptions, Maine eliminated religious and personal exemptions, and New York ended religious exemptions.

College requirements are less consistent. Currently, most colleges require one dose of MMR and recommend—but do not require—immunization for such diseases as meningococcal infection, varicella (chickenpox), pertussis (whooping cough), influenza, and other childhood and adult infectious diseases. To increase herd immunity and reduce the risk of outbreaks, colleges could require immunization against all these diseases.

In response to the episode in the spring of 2019, UCLA will now requires all incoming students to show proof of measles vaccination to be enrolled. Some people think colleges and universities should tighten their restrictions to protect the community and promote the common good. Others see such restrictions as violations of personal freedom, if not of civil rights. Discussions about requiring vaccines often raise a common public health ethical dilemma: Individual freedom is pitted against the collective welfare of the community, or the "common good." Is it time for all college campuses to increase vaccination requirements? How might a COVID-19 vaccine impact campus life and requirements? What do you think?

Continued...

Concluded...

Pros

- Required vaccination reduces the risk of disease for the entire college community. When vaccination levels are high overall, even the few who aren't or can't be vaccinated are protected by herd immunity because widespread vaccination shrinks the reservoir of infectious agents.
- College campuses are unique, tightly linked communities with a high risk of contagion should an infectious agent be introduced.
- Colleges have a responsibility to protect students and other community members from unnecessary risk. Requiring vaccination and taking other restrictive measures helps ensure health and safety for everyone.

Cons

- Individuals should have freedom of choice about health risks and what they do with their bodies. They should not have to take personal risks, such as those associated with vaccination, for the good of the community.
- States set vaccination requirements for the K-12 education system. Colleges should not have the right to enforce a different standard.
- Isolation and quarantine are options to control spread and can be used for people who decline vaccination if an outbreak occurs.

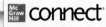

Sources: National Conference of State Legislatures. (2019). States with religious and philosophical exemptions from school immunization requirements. Retrieved from http://www.ncsl.org/research/health/school-immunization-exemption-state-laws.aspx; WebMD. (2019). UCLA, Cal State students under measles quarantine. Retrieved from https://www.webmd.com/children/vaccines/news/20190426/ucla-cal-state-students-under-measles-quarantine; UCLA Newsroom. (2019). Frequently asked questions about measles. Retrieved from https://newsroom.ucla.edu/releases/new-page-2722214; American College Health Association. (2013). Recommendations for institutional prematriculation immunization. Retrieved from www.acha.org/topics/vaccine.cfm

In Review

What causes infection, and how does the body protect itself from infectious diseases?

Several different types of pathogens cause infection and illness in humans, categorized as viruses, bacteria, prions, fungi, helminths, protozoa, and ectoparasites. Infection occurs when one of these microorganisms gains entry to the body and reproduces, sometimes causing symptoms of illness. The body has external barriers to keep pathogens out and a complex immune system to destroy them when they get in.

How are infectious diseases changing?

Changes in food distribution systems, global and local travel, and climate change create new opportunities for widespread disease transmission, as have changes in patterns of sexual behavior and injection drug use. Overuse of antibiotics has led to the appearance of resistant strains of many bacteria and viruses. For new diseases, age-old practices of washing hands, covering cough/sneeze, not touching face, and avoiding people who are ill remain effective tools to reduce disease spread. Vaccinations continue to be an essential preventive approach to infectious disease control.

What are the most common infectious diseases?

Currently the top four infectious diseases worldwide are pneumonia, diarrhea, tuberculosis, and malaria. On college campuses in the United States, common infections include the common cold, pertussis (whooping cough), *Staphylococcus aureus* skin infections, and urinary tract infections.

What are the most serious and most common sexually transmitted infections?

HIV/AIDS is the most serious STI because it is fatal, although it is now possible, with medications, to live with HIV infection as a chronic condition for many years and to prevent transmission of HIV. The virus attacks and eventually overwhelms the immune system, leaving the body vulnerable to opportunistic infections like tuberculosis. The bacterial STIs—which include chlamydia, gonorrhea, pelvic inflammatory disease, syphilis, and bacterial vaginosis—can be treated with antibiotics. The viral STIs—which include human papillomavirus, genital herpes, and hepatitis A and B—can be controlled but not cured. Other STIs include trichomoniasis, candidiasis, and pubic lice and scabies.

How can infectious diseases be prevented?

The best defense is being in good health, so a healthy lifestyle is important. Getting all recommended vaccinations also helps, as do avoiding exposure through physical distancing, hand-washing, and not touching your face. Practicing safer sex, and minimizing unnecessary use of antibiotics also are important. The use of antiretroviral medications for HIV and herpes can decrease risk of transmission. The use of pre-exposure prophylaxis and post-exposure prophylaxis can reduce risk of contracting HIV.

Personal Health Portfolio

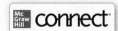

Chapter 13 Evaluate Your Infectious Disease Risk

Vaccination, screening, and good hygiene habits are all ways to prevent the spread of infectious disease. Complete the following activity to see how well you are keeping yourself and others from contracting an infectious disease.

Part 1 Immunizations

Collect your immunization records. If you do not have a copy of your records, start by asking your parents or guardians. If they do not have records, check with your doctor. Your state health department may also have a program to track childhood vaccines. Record your immunizations in the accompanying table.

Vaccine	Type of vaccination	Date	Location (doctor's office and doctor name, health clinic, etc.)
Tetanus, diphtheria, pertussis (TdaP)			
Human papillomavirus (HPV)			
Varicella			
Zoster			
Measles, mumps, rubella (MMR)			
Influenza			
Pneumococcal polysaccharide			
Hepatitis A			
Hepatitis B			
Meningococcal			

Part 2 STD Risk

1. Are you sexually active?

   ☐ Yes   ☐ No

2. If yes, have you ever been tested for sexually transmitted diseases?

   ☐ Yes   ☐ No   ☐ N/A

3. Have you had a new partner since you were last tested?

   ☐ Yes   ☐ No   ☐ N/A

Part 3 Basic Hygiene Practices

1. Do you wash your hands with soap and warm water regularly before preparing food or eating, after using the toilet, and prior to touching your face?

   ☐ Most of the time   ☐ Sometimes   ☐ Rarely

2. Do you shower after exercise?

   ☐ Most of the time   ☐ Sometimes   ☐ Rarely

3. Do you share personal items (clothes, towels, etc.) with others?

   ☐ Often   ☐ Sometimes   ☐ Rarely

4. Do you wear a mask when around other people?

   ☐ Often   ☐ Sometimes   ☐ Rarely

CRITICAL THINKING QUESTIONS

1. Compare your vaccine record to the immunization recommendations in Figure 13.5. Are you current on all your vaccination recommendations? If not, which ones do you need to get? What factors influence your vaccination status? Consider your personal beliefs, family beliefs, and access to health providers.

2. Identify where you can obtain vaccinations in your community. List the name, address, and phone number of two locations. Do you have health insurance, and does it cover care at these locations? If not, is there a local health department or campus resource for vaccines?

3. Based on your responses to Part 2 and based on the recommendations discussed in the "Sexually Transmitted Infections" section of the chapter, is it recommended that you get tested for STIs? Consider factors that influence your ability to receive STI care. What makes you more or less likely to meet the recommendations?

4. Find two sites in your community where you can get tested for STIs. List the name, address, and phone number of each. Do you have health insurance that covers STI testing? If billing goes to your parents, how does this influence your ability to receive care?

5. Based on your responses to Part 3, evaluate your basic hygiene habits. Is there anything in your environment or community that makes it easier or harder to practice good habits? Where is there room for improvement?

14 Cardiovascular Disease, Diabetes, Chronic Lung Diseases, and Dementia

Wavebreak Media Ltd/123RF

Ever Wonder...

- why high blood pressure is harmful?
- how to know whether someone is having a stroke—and what to do?
- whether shortness of breath is normal or concerning?

cardiovascular disease (CVD)
Any disease involving the heart and/or blood vessels.

cardiovascular system
The network of heart and blood vessels that circulate blood throughout the body.

pulmonary (lung) circulation
Pumping of oxygen-poor blood to the lungs and oxygen-rich blood back to the heart by the right side of the heart.

systemic (body) circulation
Pumping of oxygen-rich blood to the body and oxygen-poor blood back to the heart by the left side of the heart.

vena cava
Largest veins in the body; they carry oxygen-poor blood from the body back to the heart.

ot long ago, people believed that heart attacks and strokes were like bolts out of the blue, happening without warning. Today, we know that heart attacks, strokes, and other chronic diseases are the result of processes that begin much earlier, often in childhood. As public health measures have reduced mortality from infectious diseases and lifespans have increased, chronic diseases—including cardiovascular disease (CVD), diabetes, lung diseases, dementia, and cancer—have emerged as the leading causes of death in the United States and the world. This chapter presents an overview of CVD, diabetes, and lung diseases, along with guidelines for living a healthy lifestyle that reduces the risk of these diseases.[1,2,3] Cancer is covered in Chapter 15.

CARDIOVASCULAR DISEASE

The leading cause of death for men and women in the United States, **cardiovascular disease (CVD)** accounts for one in every three deaths. The death rate from CVD has decreased since the 1980s, although there was a slight increase in the 2014 data for men, which appears to have leveled off with the most recent data in 2016

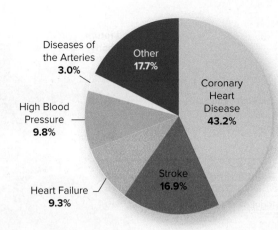

figure 14.2 **Percentage of deaths from types of CVD, United States, 2016.**
Source: American Heart Association. (2019). Heart disease and stroke statistics—2019 update: A report from the American Heart Association. *Circulation, 139,* e56–e528.

(Figure 14.1). The overall drop in the death rate is believed to be the result of lifestyle changes, improved recognition and treatment of risk factors, and improved treatment of the disease itself.[3] *Cardiovascular disease* is a general term that includes heart attack, stroke, peripheral artery disease, congestive heart failure, and other conditions (Figure 14.2).

The Cardiovascular System

The **cardiovascular system** consists of a network of blood vessels (arteries, veins, and capillaries) and a pump (the heart) that circulate blood throughout the body. The heart is a fist-sized muscle with four chambers—the right and left atria and the right and left ventricles—separated by valves.

The right side of the heart regulates **pulmonary (lung) circulation**—pumping oxygen-poor (deoxygenated) blood to the lungs and oxygen-rich blood back to the heart. The left side of the heart regulates **systemic (body) circulation**—pumping oxygen-rich blood to the rest of the body and returning oxygen-poor blood to the heart (Figure 14.3).

During pulmonary circulation, oxygen-poor blood returning from the body to the heart enters the right atrium via large veins called the inferior and superior **vena cava**. After the right atrium has filled, it contracts and moves the blood into the right ventricle. The right ventricle then fills and contracts, moving the blood into the lungs via the right and left pulmonary arteries. The pulmonary artery branches into a network of smaller arteries and arterioles that eventually become the pulmonary capillaries. Capillaries are the

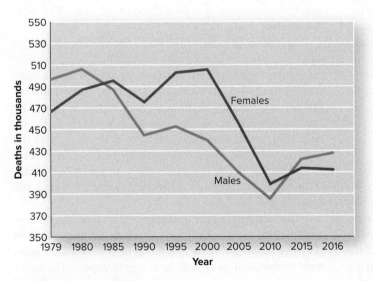

figure 14.1 **Cardiovascular disease mortality trends for males and females, United States, 1979–2016.**
Sources: Centers for Disease Control and Prevention/National Center for Health Statistics, www.cdc.gov/nchs; American Heart Association. (2019). Heart disease and stroke statistics—2019 update: A report from the American Heart Association. *Circulation, 139,* e56–e528.

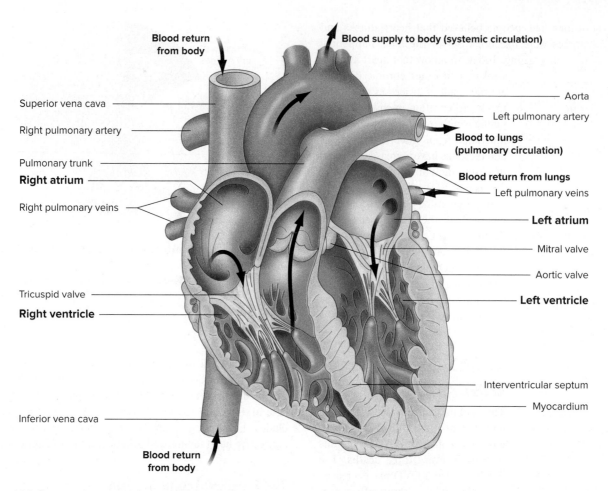

figure 14.3   **The heart, showing interior chambers, valves, and major arteries and veins.**

smallest blood vessels; some capillary walls are only one cell thick, readily allowing the exchange of gases and molecules. In the interweaving network of capillaries, the red blood cells in the blood pick up oxygen and discard carbon dioxide, a waste product from the cells. The capillaries then unite and form venules, and venules join to become pulmonary veins. The pulmonary veins return oxygen-rich blood from the lungs to the left atrium of the heart.

During systemic circulation, the left atrium fills and contracts to move oxygen-rich blood into the left ventricle. The left ventricle fills, contracts, and moves oxygen-rich blood into the body via the **aorta**, the largest artery in the body. The aorta branches into smaller and smaller arteries, and eventually oxygen-rich, nutrient-rich blood enters the capillaries located throughout the body. At these sites, red blood cells release oxygen and nutrients to the tissues and pick up carbon dioxide to be

carried back to the lungs. The capillaries unite to form veins and eventually connect to the inferior and superior vena cava, which returns the oxygen-poor blood to the heart. The cycle then repeats.

Like other muscles of the body, the heart needs oxygen and nutrients provided by blood; the blood being pumped through the heart does not provide nourishment for the heart muscle itself. Two medium-sized arteries, called **coronary arteries**, supply blood to the heart muscle (Figure 14.4). The main vessels are the right coronary artery and the left coronary artery, each distributing blood to different parts of the heart. Good blood flow is important because when a vessel is narrowed, the muscle it supplies does not get enough blood. Without the oxygen and nutrients carried in the blood, the muscle dies.

The four chambers of the heart contract to pump blood in a coordinated fashion. The contraction occurs in response to an electrical signal that starts in a group of cells called the **sinus node or sinoatrial (SA) node** in the right atrium. The signal spreads through a defined course leading first to contraction of the right and left atria, and then to contraction of the right and left ventricles. The contraction and relaxation of the ventricles are what we feel and hear as the heartbeat. The contraction phase is called *systole* and the relaxation phase is called *diastole*.

aorta
Largest artery in the body; it leaves the heart and branches into smaller arteries, arterioles, and capillaries carrying oxygen-rich blood to body tissues.

coronary arteries
Medium-sized arteries that supply blood to the heart muscle.

sinus node or sinoatrial (SA) node
A group of cells in the right atrium where the electrical signal is generated that establishes the heartbeat.

Atherosclerosis

Healthy arteries are strong and flexible. Arteries can harden and become stiff in a process referred to as **atherosclerosis**— the buildup of fats, cholesterol, cellular waste products, calcium, and other substances in artery walls.

Atherosclerosis starts with damage to the inner lining (for example, by tobacco smoke, high blood pressure, or infection), creating a *lesion* where a **fatty streak** can form. Fatty streaks consist of an accumulation of **lipoproteins**, which are a combination of proteins, phospholipids (fat molecules with phosphate groups chemically attached), and **cholesterol** (a waxy, fat-like substance that is essential in small amounts for certain body functions). Lipoproteins can be thought of as packages that carry cholesterol and fats through the bloodstream.

atherosclerosis
A buildup of fats, cholesterol, calcium and other substances in arterial walls that narrow and stiffen arteries and restrict blood flow.

fatty streak
An accumulation of lipoproteins within the walls of an artery.

lipoproteins
Packages of proteins, phospholipids (fat molecules with phosphate groups chemically attached), and cholesterol that transport lipids in the blood.

cholesterol
A waxy, fatlike substance that is essential in small amounts for certain body functions.

plaque
An accumulation of debris in an artery wall, consisting of lipoproteins, white blood cells, collagen, and other substances.

aneurysm
A weak or stretched spot in an artery wall that can tear or rupture, causing sudden death.

coronary heart disease (CHD)
Atherosclerosis of the coronary arteries.

When lipoproteins accumulate within the wall of an artery, they undergo chemical changes that trigger an inflammatory response, attracting white blood cells. Once at the site, white blood cells take up the altered lipoproteins. Some white blood cells leave the site, clearing lipids from the artery wall, but if blood lipoprotein levels are high, more lipoproteins accumulate. Many of the white blood cells die within the lesion, depositing lipid-rich material and forming a fatty streak.

The process may stop at this point, leaving a dynamic lesion that can still undergo repair or can develop further. Together with the white blood cells, smooth muscle cells release collagen and other proteins to form a **plaque**, an accumulation of debris that undergoes continuing damage, bleeding, and calcification. Plaques cause the artery wall to enlarge and bulge into the *lumen,* the channel through which the blood flows, slowing blood flow and reducing the amount of blood that can reach the tissue supplied by the artery (Figure 14.4). Plaques can also break off and completely block the artery, preventing any blood from flowing through.

Heart attacks, strokes, and peripheral vascular disease are all consequences of the narrowing and stiffening of arteries caused by atherosclerosis. A diagnosis of one of these diseases suggests risk for the others. Atherosclerosis may also weaken an artery wall, causing a

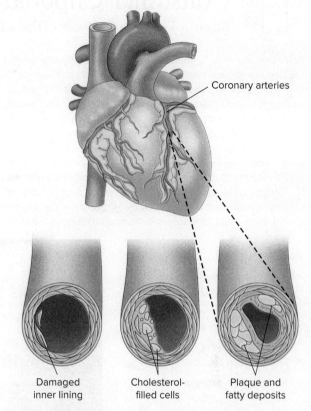

Coronary arteries

Damaged inner lining

Cholesterol-filled cells

Plaque and fatty deposits

figure 14.4   The process of atherosclerosis.
The process begins with damage to the lining of an artery and progresses to narrowing or blockage of the artery by fatty deposits and plaques.

stretching of the artery known as an **aneurysm**. Aneurysms can rupture, tear, and bleed, causing sudden death.

Atherosclerosis is a progressive disease that takes years to develop and starts at a young age. Studies have shown that in early childhood there are measurable differences in the thickness and stiffness of arteries associated with exposure to risk factors that will be discussed in this chapter. The differences become more pronounced in adolescence and adulthood if nothing is done to address the risk factors. This means it is never too early to think about heart health.[4,5]

Coronary Heart Disease and Heart Attack

When atherosclerosis occurs in a coronary artery, the result is **coronary heart disease (CHD)** and, often, a heart attack. Coronary heart disease (also called coronary artery disease [CAD]) is the leading form of CVD, accounting for one in seven U.S. deaths. An estimated 18.2 million people in the United States are living with CHD. Those who survive a heart attack are at increased risk of further heart attacks, heart failure, and stroke (all of which will be discussed later).[3]

When a coronary artery becomes narrowed or blocked, the heart muscle does not get enough oxygen-rich blood,

Consumer Clipboard
Aspirin Therapy for Heart Disease and Heart Attack

Forty percent of U.S. adults over the age of 50 take aspirin regularly to reduce their risk of CVD. Because of its ability to inhibit blood clotting, aspirin is often recommended to reduce recurrent events in anyone who has a history of heart attack, unstable angina, ischemic stroke, or transient ischemic attack. A daily dose of aspirin is usually between 75 and 100 mg per day; a baby aspirin (81 mg) is often recommended for daily aspirin therapy. Someone experiencing the symptoms of a heart attack may be advised to slowly chew a 325-mg aspirin tablet.

What has been controversial is whether taking aspirin to prevent a first event is worth the risk for people without a history of cardiovascular disease. While aspirin reduces risk of MI and ischemic stroke—and in low doses decreases the risk of colorectal cancer—it increases risk of gastrointestinal tract bleeding and hemorrhagic stroke.

Like so many health decisions, taking aspirin requires balancing benefits and risks. Low-dose aspirin may be beneficial for people aged 40 to 70 who have an increased risk of cardiovascular disease and no increased risk of bleeding. For anyone who does not have a history of heart disease and who does have an increased risk of bleeding (which includes people over age 70), it should be avoided. How would you advise your parents or other important people in your life? Consider the benefits and risks:

Benefits

- Inhibits the formation of blood clots, which can clog or block arteries
- Reduces the risk of heart attack
- Reduces the risk of stroke
- Reduces the damage to the heart during a heart attack
- Decreases the pain and inflammation associated with CVD, such as angina or pain in the legs
- Reduces the risk of colorectal cancer

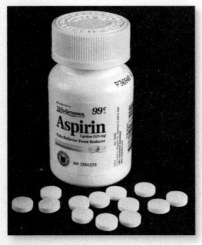

(Jill Braaten/McGraw-Hill)

Risks

- Increases the risk of internal bleeding and stomach ulcers
- Increases the risk of bleeding into the brain during a hemorrhagic stroke
- Should not be taken by pregnant women
- Should not be taken by anyone with an allergy to aspirin
- Should not be taken by people about to undergo surgery
- Should not be taken by children or youth under age 18 who are recovering from a viral infection such as the flu or chickenpox

Source: 2019 ACC/AHA guideline on the primary prevention of cardiovascular disease: a report of the American College of Cardiology/American Heart Association Task Force on Clinical Practice Guidelines. J Am Coll Cardiol; March 17.

---

a condition called **ischemia**. If the artery is completely blocked, the person has a heart attack, or **myocardial infarction (MI)**. The blockage may be caused by an atherosclerotic plaque that has broken loose or a blood clot (a *thrombus*) that has formed in a narrowed or damaged artery. The latter condition is called **coronary thrombosis** and may cause sudden death. During a heart attack, the area of muscle supplied by the blocked coronary artery is completely deprived of oxygen. If blood flow is not restored quickly, that part of the heart muscle will die. For information about restoring the blood flow, see the box "Consumer Clipboard: Aspirin Therapy for Heart Disease and Heart Attack."

ischemia
Insufficient supply of oxygen and nutrients to tissue, caused by narrowed or blocked arteries.

myocardial infarction (MI)
Lack of blood to the heart muscle with resulting death of heart tissue; often called a heart attack.

coronary thrombosis
Blockage of a coronary artery by a blood clot that may cause sudden death.

The severity of a heart attack is determined by the location and duration of the blockage. If the blockage occurs close to the aorta, where the coronary arteries are just starting to branch, a large area of heart muscle is deprived of oxygen. If the blockage is farther out in a smaller coronary artery, the area of muscle supplied is smaller. The duration of the blockage is usually determined by the time between onset of symptoms and initiation of medical or surgical treatment to reopen the artery.

A heart attack may occur when extra work is being demanded of the heart, such as during exercise or emotional stress, but it can also occur during light activity or even rest. A classic symptom of a heart attack is chest pain, often described as a sensation of pressure, fullness, or squeezing in the midportion of the chest. However, symptoms vary, and 37 percent of women and 27 percent of men typically do not have chest pain or discomfort during a heart attack. Both men and women can have a range of symptoms, including pain radiating to the jaw, back, shoulders, or arms. Younger age and female gender are more associated with less-classic symptoms of a heart attack.[6]

Although awareness has increased over the past decade, women continue to be less aware than men that heart disease is a major health concern for them, and thus they are less likely than men to seek help for their symptoms. Even in the 15- to 24-year-old age group, only 10 percent of women are aware that heart disease is the leading cause of death for women. While heart disease may not be an immediate risk, prevention needs to start during this time frame, as will be discussed later.[3,6,7]

When coronary arteries are narrowed but not completely blocked, the person may experience **angina**—pain, pressure, heaviness, or tightness in the center of the chest that may radiate to the neck, arms, or shoulders. Half of all heart attacks are preceded by angina. The difference between a heart attack and angina is that the pain of angina resolves, whereas the pain of a heart attack continues. Angina can be controlled with medical treatment.

Many physical conditions can cause pain in the chest, including irritated esophagus, arthritis of the neck or ribs, gas in the colon, stomach ulcers, and gallbladder disease. Chest pain can also be caused by weight lifting or other heavy lifting or vigorous activity. If you are used to chest pain from any of these causes, you may be inclined to ignore angina or chest pain from a heart attack. Don't let complacency or confusion delay your efforts to seek help if you experience the symptoms of a heart attack.

Arrhythmias The pumping of the heart is usually a well-coordinated event, controlled by an electrical signal emanating from the sinus node in the right atrium, as described earlier. The sinus node establishes a rate of 60 to 100 beats per minute for a normal adult heart. The rate increases in response to increased demand on the heart, such as during exercise, and slows in response to reduced demand, such as during relaxation or sleep. If the signal is disrupted, it can cause an **arrhythmia**, or disorganized beating of the heart. The disorganized beating is usually not as effective at pumping blood.

An arrhythmia is any type of irregular heartbeat. It may be an occasional skipped beat, a rapid or slow rate, or an irregular pattern. Not all arrhythmias are serious or cause for concern. In fact, most people have occasional irregular heartbeats every day; some do not even notice them. However, arrhythmia may cause noticeable symptoms, including palpitations, a sensation of fluttering in the chest, chest pain, light-headedness, shortness of breath, and fatigue.

Arrhythmias occur for a variety of reasons, including damage to the sinus node, chemical imbalances, and the use of caffeine, alcohol, tobacco, cocaine, or medications.

Sudden Cardiac Arrest **Sudden cardiac arrest** describes an abrupt loss of heart function—usually within an hour of symptom onset (although 25 percent of sudden cardiac arrests have no symptoms prior to the cardiac arrest). The sudden loss of function can be due to external causes (such as trauma, drowning, electrocution, or drug overdose) but is most often due to a malfunction in the heart's electrical system due to atherosclerosis or heart abnormality. **Ventricular fibrillation**

■ Automated external defibrillators can be used by the general public and thus decrease the time it takes to provide defibrillation to someone in cardiac arrest. *(Baloncici/123RF)*

(VF) is an arrhythmia common in cases of sudden cardiac death. In VF, the ventricles contract rapidly and erratically, causing the heart to quiver or "tremor" rather than beat. Blood cannot then be pumped by the heart, and death can occur within minutes if attempts to restart the heart are unsuccessful.

In someone under age 35, sudden cardiac arrest is usually due to congenital heart abnormalities, genetic predisposition to arrhythmia, or predisposition to heart muscle abnormality. Although rare, sudden cardiac death is a leading cause of death in competitive athletes. See the box "You Make the Call: Screening for Cardiovascular Disease in Athletes: How Much Is Enough?" at the end of the chapter for an in-depth

angina
Intermittent pain, pressure, heaviness, or tightness in the center of the chest caused by a narrowed coronary artery.

arrhythmia
An irregular or disorganized heartbeat.

sudden cardiac arrest
An abrupt loss of heart function

ventricular fibrillation
A type of arrhythmia in which the ventricles contract rapidly and erratically, causing the heart to quiver or "tremor" rather than beat.

discussion. Over age 35, the cause of sudden cardiac arrest is usually coronary artery disease.[3]

Ventricular fibrillation can be reversed with an electrical shock from a defibrillator, which can restart the heart's normal rhythm. Every second from the onset of fibrillation to the use of an automated external defibrillator (AED) counts in the race for survival. AEDs are designed for use by the general public, ideally by people who have received training at a cardio-pulmonary resuscitation (CPR), first aid, or first-responder class. The installation of AEDs in public places such as gyms, airports, and office buildings makes it more possible for a by-stander to quickly start using one. Increasing the number of people trained in CPR and AED use improves survival (see the box "Action Skill-Builder: What to Do During a Heart Attack or Stroke Emergency").[3]

Stroke

When blood flow to the brain or part of the brain is blocked, the result is a **stroke or cerebrovascular accident (CVA)**. Stroke is the fifth-leading cause of death in the United States, after heart disease, cancer, chronic lung disease, and unintentional injuries, and is a leading cause of severe, long-term disability. Strokes are preventable and treatable.[8]

Ischemic strokes account for 87 percent of all strokes and occur when an artery in the brain becomes blocked (in the same way that a heart attack occurs when a coronary artery is blocked) and prevents the brain from receiving blood flow (Figure 14.5). The blockage can be due to a **thrombus** (a blood clot that develops in a narrowed artery) or an **embolism** (a clot that develops elsewhere, often in the heart, travels to the brain, and lodges in an artery).[9]

Hemorrhagic strokes make up 13 percent of strokes and occur when a brain artery ruptures, bleeds into the surrounding area, and compresses brain tissue. Hemorrhagic strokes may be due to a head injury or a ruptured aneurysm. There are two types of hemorrhagic stroke. *Intracerebral hemorrhagic* strokes account for 10 percent of all strokes and occur when the ruptured artery is within brain tissue. *Subarachnoid hemorrhagic* strokes account for the remaining 3 percent of all strokes and occur when the ruptured artery is on the brain's surface and blood accumulates between the brain and the skull.[8]

In the brain, as in the heart, different arteries supply different areas. The symptoms of a stroke depend on the area of the brain affected. However, they usually include the sudden onset of neurological problems, such as headaches, numbness, weakness, or speech problems.

stroke (cerebrovascular accident [CVA])
Lack of blood flow to the brain with resulting death of brain tissue.

ischemic strokes
Strokes caused by blockage in a blood vessel in the brain.

thrombus
A blood clot that forms in a narrowed or damaged artery.

embolism
A blood clot that travels from elsewhere in the body.

hemorrhagic strokes
Strokes caused by rupture of a blood vessel in the brain, with bleeding into brain tissue.

Action Skill-Builder

What to Do During a Heart Attack or Stroke Emergency

Do you know what to do if a friend, colleague, family member, or stranger has a heart attack or stroke? Recognizing the signs of a heart attack or stroke and responding and getting treatment quickly are critical to survival. Here are steps you can take to be prepared:

1. *Recognize the signs.* People are often embarrassed or in denial when they have a heart attack or stroke. If you know the signs, you can recognize the situation and let the person know how serious it is.

    a. *Heart attack:* chest discomfort that lasts more than a few minutes or that comes and goes, often in the center of the chest (can feel like pressure, squeezing, fullness, or pain); discomfort in other areas of the upper body (can include pain in one or both arms, the back, neck, jaw, or stomach); shortness of breath; nausea; cold sweat; light-headedness, weakness, or faintness; or a sudden loss of consciousness.

    b. *Stroke:* sudden numbness or weakness in the face, arm, or leg, especially on one side of the body; sudden confusion, trouble speaking or understanding; sudden trouble seeing in one or both eyes; sudden trouble walking, dizziness, loss of balance or coordination; or a sudden, severe headache with no known cause.

2. *Don't delay—call 9-1-1.* New treatments can break up the clots that cause heart attacks and strokes, but they must be started as soon as possible (within hours). Paramedics can begin treatments on the way to the hospital and are equipped to administer external defibrillation if needed.

3. *Take a cardiopulmonary resuscitation (CPR) class and learn to use an AED.* If someone suffers from a cardiac arrest, the most critical factor in survival is time. The sooner CPR and an AED are used, the more likely the person is to survive. Most colleges, community centers, and fire stations offer CPR classes on a regular basis. Staying current on guidelines for activation of the emergency medical system, assessment, resuscitation, and use of an automated external defibrillator (AED) will help you stay calm and be ready. Training in "hands-only" CPR is available, and a 9-1-1 operator can even talk you through it in real time if necessary.

Source: American Heart Association. (n.d.). CPR & first aid emergency cardiovascular care. Retrieved from https://cpr.heart.org/en/cpr-courses-and-kits/hands-only-cpr/hands-only-cpr-resources; American Heart Association. (2019). Heart disease and stroke statistics—2019 update: A report from the American Heart Association. *Circulation, 139,* e56-e528.

Hemorrhagic stroke
Caused by ruptured blood vessels; followed by blood leaking into tissue

Ischemic stroke
Caused by blockage in brain blood vessels; potentially treatable with clot-busting drugs; less serious than hemorrhagic stroke

Subarachnoid hemorrhage
A bleed into the space between the brain and the skull

Embolic stroke
Caused by *emboli*, blood clots that travel from elsewhere in the body to the brain blood vessels

Intracerebral hemorrhage
A bleed from a blood vessel inside the brain

Thrombotic stroke
Caused by *thrombi*, blood clots that form where an artery has been narrowed by atherosclerosis

figure 14.5 Types of stroke.
Source: *Harvard Health Letter* (2000, April).

■ Luke Perry was an actor and father of two. He died in 2019 at the age 52 after suffering a an ischemic stroke.
(Joe Seer/Shutterstock)

A small percentage of people have **transient ischemic attacks (TIAs)** before having a stroke. Sometimes called "ministrokes," TIAs are periods of restricted blood supply that produce the same symptoms as a stroke, but in this case the symptoms resolve within 24 hours with little or no tissue death. A TIA should be viewed as a warning sign of stroke. After a TIA, 3 to 10 percent of people will have a stroke within the next 2 days, and 9 to 17 percent will have a stroke within the next 90 days. Early recognition and rapid treatment are as important for TIA and stroke as they are for heart disease. Treatment can improve survival and reduce complications but must be given quickly.[3,9]

Congestive Heart Failure

When the heart is not pumping the blood as well as it should, a condition known as **congestive heart failure** occurs. It can develop after a heart attack or as a result of hypertension (high blood pressure), heart valve abnormality, or disease of the heart muscle. When the heart cannot keep up its regular pumping force or rate, blood backs up into pulmonary veins in the lungs, and then fluid from the backed-up blood leaks into the lungs. A person with congestive heart failure experiences

transient ischemic attacks (TIA)
Periods of ischemia that temporarily produce the same symptoms as a stroke.

congestive heart failure
A condition in which the heart is not pumping the blood as well as it should, allowing blood and fluids to back up in the lungs.

difficulty breathing, shortness of breath, and coughing, especially when lying down. Blood returning to the heart from the body also gets backed up in the veins in the legs, causing fluid to leak out from the veins and leading to swelling of the lower legs. When blood fails to reach the brain efficiently, fatigue and confusion can result.

Other Cardiovascular Diseases

Other conditions can affect the structure of the heart and blood vessels and their ability to function. Some of these conditions are congenital (present from birth), and others result from progressive diseases.

Heart Valve Disorders
Four valves in the heart (see Figure 14.3) keep blood flowing in the correct direction through the heart. A normally functioning valve opens easily to allow blood to flow forward and closes tightly to prevent blood from flowing backward. Sometimes a valve does not open well, preventing the smooth flow of blood, and sometimes a valve does not close tightly, allowing blood to leak backward.

These problems can be caused by congenital abnormalities, rheumatic heart disease (scarring of a heart valve that can follow untreated infection with streptococcus bacteria, usually strep throat), or an aging-related degenerative process. When valves are not functioning normally, the flow of blood is altered and the risks of blood clots and infection increase. Often, the person experiences no symptoms; if symptoms do occur, they can include shortness of breath, dizziness, fatigue, and chest pain.

Congenital Heart Disease
A variety of structural abnormalities that are present at birth can affect the heart valves, major arteries and veins in or near the heart, the heart muscle, or the electrical conduction system. An abnormality can cause the blood to slow down, flow in the wrong direction, or fail to move from one chamber to the next. Congenital heart disease can range from causing no symptoms to being serious enough to cause early death. Undetected cardiac abnormalities are the leading cause of death in competitive athletes. More than 35 types of congenital heart abnormalities have been described, and about 8 of every 1,000 babies are born with a heart problem.[3,10]

peripheral vascular disease (PVD)
Atherosclerosis in the blood vessels of the arms or legs.

cardiomyopathy
Disease of the heart muscle.

dilated cardiomyopathy
Enlargement of the heart in response to weakening of the muscle.

hypertrophic cardiomyopathy
Abnormal thickening of one part of the heart, frequently the left ventricle.

Peripheral Vascular Disease
The result of atherosclerosis in the arteries of the arms or (more commonly) the legs, **peripheral vascular disease (PVD)** causes pain, aches, or cramping in the muscles supplied by a narrowed blood vessel. Although it is usually not fatal, PVD causes a significant amount of disability, limiting the activity levels of many older people because they experience pain when walking. If circulation is severely limited by the ischemia, the affected leg or arm may have to be amputated.

Cardiomyopathy
Cardiomyopathy—disease of the heart muscle—accounts for 1 percent of heart disease deaths in the United States; the highest rates occur among men and Blacks. The most common form of cardiomyopathy is **dilated cardiomyopathy**, an enlargement of the heart in response to weakening of the muscle. The cause is often unknown, although a virus is suspected in some cases. Other factors that can weaken the heart muscle are toxins (alcohol, tobacco, heavy metals, and some medications), drugs, pregnancy, hypertension, and coronary artery disease.

Another form is **hypertrophic cardiomyopathy**, an abnormal thickening of one part of the heart, frequently the left ventricle. The thickened wall makes the heart abnormally stiff, so the heart doesn't fill well. Although most people with hypertrophic cardiomyopathy have no symptoms, warning signs can include dizziness or passing out with exercise. The condition can cause heart failure, arrhythmia, and sudden death. In fact, 36 percent of cases of sudden death in young competitive athletes are due to hypertrophic cardiomyopathy. The cause of the condition is unknown in about 50 percent of cases, but in the rest there is a genetic link. A family history of sudden death prior to age 50 is a risk factor.[3]

PROMOTING CARDIOVASCULAR HEALTH

Cardiovascular disease is a multifactorial disease (see Chapter 1), meaning it is caused by a combination of genetic, environmental, and lifestyle factors interacting over the lifespan. Given that cumulative risk can lead to chronic illness, you are never too young to consider how you can achieve ideal cardiovascular health. The American Heart Association has mounted a campaign—Life's Simple 7—to improve the cardiovascular health of U.S. adults by 20 percent and reduce the number of deaths from CVD by 20 percent by the year 2020.

Life's Simple 7

Life's Simple 7 recognizes that four health behaviors and three health factors make up the majority of risk factors for cardiovascular disease. Addressing these seven areas would mitigate 80 percent of the risk for CVD. The campaign is trying to increase the proportion of people of *all* ages who can say they meet "ideal" status in all seven criteria. The criteria are smoking status, healthy diet, participation in physical activity, healthy body mass index (BMI), and healthy levels of blood pressure, blood glucose, and total cholesterol. Unfortunately, only 5 percent of the U.S. adult population currently meets six of the seven target goals, and even when we look at 12- to 19-year-olds as shown in Figure 14.6, just under 10 percent of youth meet six of the seven target goals. So there is lots of room for improvement![3,11]

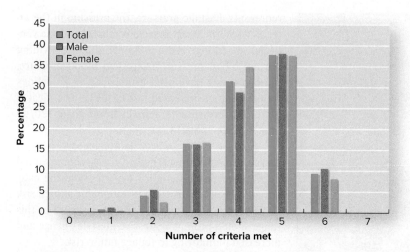

figure 14.6 **Proportion of U.S. children aged 12 to 19 meeting between one and seven of the criteria for ideal cardiovascular health.**
Source: American Heart Association. (2019). Heart disease and stroke statistics—2019 update: A report from the American Heart Association. *Circulation, 139,* e56–e528.

Avoid Tobacco Tobacco use is the leading risk factor for all forms of CVD. The ideal cardiovascular-health behavior is never to have tried a cigarette. If you have started smoking, the ideal is to quit. Cigarette smokers develop coronary artery disease at two to four times the rate of nonsmokers and have twice the risk of sudden cardiac death as nonsmokers. Cigar and pipe smoking also increase the risk of coronary artery disease and perhaps the risk of stroke, although not as much as cigarettes. The relationship between e-cigarettes and CVD remains unclear, but the recent increase in acute lung injury associated with e-cigarettes makes them an inadvisable option, in particular for young adults[12] (see Chapter 9).

Tobacco smoke increases risk in a variety of ways. Components of tobacco smoke damage the inner lining of blood vessels, speeding up the development of atherosclerosis. Toxins in tobacco smoke can stimulate the formation of blood clots in the coronary arteries and trigger spasms that close off the vessels. Smoking raises blood levels of LDL cholesterol ("bad" cholesterol) and decreases blood levels of HDL cholesterol ("good" cholesterol). Exposure to environmental tobacco smoke (secondhand smoke) is also a risk factor for CVD; risk appears to be proportional to the amount of daily exposure.

Eat a Healthy Diet A diet that supports cardiovascular health, such as a Mediterranean-style diet or the DASH (Dietary Approaches to Stop Hypertension) diet, emphasizes fruits, vegetables, whole grains, low-fat dairy products, fish, and lean meat and poultry. Balancing calories in with calories out is important, as is avoiding or limiting saturated fat, trans fat, dietary cholesterol, and added sugars.

Micronutrients (vitamins, minerals, and other substances in food) appear to play a role in cardiovascular health. Many micronutrients, especially antioxidants, are more plentiful in a plant-based diet than in a diet based on foods from animal sources. Foods high in important antioxidants are brightly colored fruits and vegetables and nuts and seeds (see Chapter 5).

Experts recommend that micronutrients be consumed in foods rather than in supplements.

Specific foods have been shown to alter cholesterol levels. Soy products and legumes, such as lentils and chickpeas, have been shown to decrease LDL levels. Garlic appears to have a similar effect on total cholesterol, although fresh garlic (one to two cloves per day) is recommended over synthetic garlic capsules. Foods rich in fiber also help reduce cholesterol levels; they include fruits, vegetables, oats, and barley.

Be Physically Active Regular physical activity reduces the risk of CVD and many cardiovascular risk factors, including high blood pressure, diabetes, and obesity. Physical activity conditions the heart, reduces high blood pressure, improves HDL cholesterol levels, helps maintain a healthy weight, and helps control diabetes. Even low-intensity activities, such as walking, gardening, and climbing stairs, can be helpful. As discussed in Chapter 6, many adults in the United States are not active at levels that can promote health. Exercise is also very important for children because it is associated with lower blood pressure and better weight control, and because active children tend to become active adults.

Maintain a Healthy Body Mass Index Overweight and obesity are associated with increased risk of CVD and greater seriousness of the disease, so it's important to maintain a healthy body weight and body composition. Excess weight puts a strain on the heart and contributes to other risk factors, such as hypertension, high LDL levels, and diabetes. The association among all these risk factors is found across ethnic groups, including Mexican Americans, non-Hispanic Blacks, and non-Hispanic whites.

As discussed in Chapter 7, body fat distribution plays a role in CVD risk. Waist-to-hip ratio may play a greater role than BMI. People with central fat distribution—those who are apple-shaped, as suggested by an abdominal circumference of greater than 40 inches for men and greater than 35 inches for women—have a higher risk of diabetes, high blood pressure, and CVD. Overweight people can improve their cardiovascular risk profile if they lose 10 to 15 percent of their total weight and maintain the loss. Diet and exercise are recommended ways to reduce overweight and obesity.

Maintain Healthy Blood Pressure Levels Blood pressure is the pressure exerted by blood against the walls of arteries, and high blood pressure, or **hypertension**, occurs when the pressure is great enough to damage artery walls. Untreated high blood pressure can weaken the arteries, promote atherosclerosis, and

blood pressure
The force exerted by the blood against artery walls.

hypertension
Blood pressure that is forceful enough to damage artery walls.

Being physically active, avoiding tobacco, eating a balanced diet, and maintaining a healthy weight are four important behaviors to reduce the risk of cardiovascular disease. *(Adam Hester/Getty Images)*

represents **diastolic pressure**, the pressure in the arteries when the heart muscle is relaxed and the ventricles are filling. There is no definite line dividing normal blood pressure from high blood pressure, but categories have been established as guidelines on the basis of increased risk of CVD. The ideal is for blood pressure to remain lower than 120/80 mm/Hg. See Table 14.1.

Elevated blood pressure is a category of blood pressure measurement higher than recommended but not meeting criteria for hypertension; the category has been identified to target people at high risk of developing hypertension. Blood pressure in this range should prompt aggressive lifestyle change and increased monitoring to reduce future risk.[13]

Hypertension is often referred to as the "silent killer" because it usually causes no symptoms. More than 116.4 million people age 20 years and older in the United States (nearly half of U.S. adults) and more than 1 billion people worldwide are estimated to have high blood pressure; rates are similar for men and women. Although people are becoming more aware of this condition, about 20 percent of people with high blood pressure do not know they have it.[14]

In approximately 95 percent of cases, no single cause of hypertension can be identified. In Western societies, aging seems to be a factor, but this is not the case in other cultures. Genetics plays a role in some

force the heart to work harder, weakening it as well. Hypertension increases the risk of heart attack, stroke, congestive heart failure, and kidney disease; the higher the blood pressure, the greater the risk.

Blood pressure is determined by two forces—the pressure produced by the heart as it pumps the blood and the resistance of the arteries as they contain blood flow. When arteries are hardened by atherosclerosis, they are more resistant. Blood pressure is measured in millimeters of mercury (abbreviated as mmHg) and stated in two numbers, such as 120/80 mmHg. The first number represents **systolic pressure**, the pressure produced by the heart muscle contracting and pushing blood out into the arteries; the second number

systolic pressure
Pressure in the arteries when the heart contracts, represented by the upper number in a blood pressure measurement.

diastolic pressure
Pressure in the arteries when the heart relaxes between contractions, represented by the lower number in a blood pressure measurement.

Table 14.1 Blood Pressure Guidelines

Category	Systolic (mmHg) Peak pressure in arteries when heart contracts	Diastolic (mmHg) Resting pressure in arteries when heart is relaxed and refilling
Normal	Less than 120 *and*	Less than 80
Elevated	120–129 *and*	Less than 80
Hypertension Stage 1 Stage 2	130–139 *or* 140 and above *or*	80–89 90 and above
Hypertensive crisis*	180 and above *and/or*	120 and above

*A suddenly elevated blood pressure that exceeds 180/120 should be rechecked in 5 minutes; if remains elevated, seek immediate medical care. If it is associated with symptoms of heart disease or stroke, call 9-1-1.

Source: American Heart Association. (2019). Understanding blood pressure readings. Retrieved from https://www.heart.org/en/health-topics/high-blood-pressure/understanding-blood-pressure-readings

cases. Other factors that contribute to elevated blood pressure include use of alcohol, low potassium levels, physical inactivity, and obesity. Dietary salt intake is associated with elevation in blood pressure, and people with elevated blood pressure or hypertension benefit from lower salt intake.[15] Poor-quality and insufficient sleep can increase blood pressure. Less frequently, medical conditions can cause hypertension. Women can develop hypertension during pregnancy or while taking oral contraceptive pills. Among children and adolescents, rates of hypertension are increasing. The trend appears to be following the rising rates of obesity within these age groups.[3]

There are significant differences in the prevalence of high blood pressure among different racial and ethnic populations. Blacks in the United States have rates of hypertension among the highest in the world. Hypertension affects 59 percent of Black males and 56 percent of Black females, in contrast to 48 percent of non-Hispanic white males and 41 percent of white females, 47 percent of Hispanic males and 41 percent of Hispanic females, and 46 percent of Asian males and 36 percent of Asian females.[3]

In addition, hypertension in Blacks starts earlier, is more severe, and is associated with more complications, such as heart attacks, stroke, and kidney failure. Blacks are on average more sensitive than whites to the dietary effects of salt on blood pressure; thus, dietary difference may contribute to the higher rate of hypertension among Blacks. Given that race and ethnicity are social constructs, there has not been a clear genetic explanation for the differences. Racial segregation, neighborhood poverty, and discrimination have been associated with hypertension, especially among Blacks, and may explain why rates are so high among U.S. Blacks.[3,16]

Regular screening for hypertension is recommended for individuals over age 15. For anyone in the elevated blood pressure or hypertension category, lifestyle changes are recommended, including losing weight, making dietary changes, trying a lower salt intake, increasing physical activity, moderating alcohol intake, and sleeping well (more than 6 hours per night).[17] The DASH diet to reduce elevated blood pressure was developed from research by the National Heart, Lung, and Blood Institute and five medical research centers. If lifestyle changes alone do not reduce blood pressure, medications are recommended.

Maintain Healthy Blood Glucose Levels Elevated levels of glucose circulating in the bloodstream, a sign of diabetes, cause changes throughout the body, including damage to artery walls, changes in some blood components, and damage to peripheral nerves and organs. People with diabetes are twice as likely to develop cardiovascular disease as people without diabetes. Their arteries are particularly susceptible to atherosclerosis, and it occurs at an earlier age and is more extensive. The incidence of Type 2 diabetes has more than doubled since 1990 and is expected to double again by 2050. One-third of people in the United States already have prediabetes, and most of them don't know it. Prevention of diabetes and early treatment if it develops are important to reduce risk

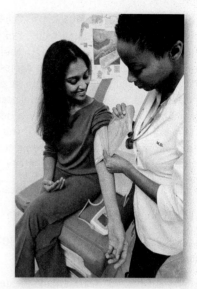

African Americans have higher rates of hypertension than other racial groups. Discrimination, segregation in housing, and other sociocultural factors are associated with increased blood pressure. Regular screening can identify the problem early and help keep blood pressure under control.
(West Coast Surfer/Age Fotostock)

of CVD. Diabetes is not only a risk factor for CVD, but also a disease in and of itself. It is discussed in greater depth later in the chapter.[18]

low-density lipoproteins (LDLs) "Bad" cholesterol; lipoproteins that accumulate in plaque and contribute to atherosclerosis.

Maintain Healthy Cholesterol Levels The amount of cholesterol in your body is affected by what you eat and by how fast your body makes and gets rid of cholesterol. Because cholesterol is a sterol (a type of lipid), it is fatlike and cannot circulate in the blood in a free-floating state; instead, it is combined with proteins and other molecules in packages called *lipoproteins*. Lipoproteins are categorized into five main classes according to density, with each class playing a different role in the body. The categories that have received the most study are total cholesterol and the LDL and HDL subcategories.

Levels of total cholesterol and LDL cholesterol are directly related to frequency of coronary heart disease; that is, as cholesterol levels rise, so does the incidence of heart disease. The good news is that levels of elevated cholesterol in adults have decreased nationally—but primarily due to increased use of medication, not lifestyle changes. A total cholesterol under 200 is one of the health factors in the "Life's Simple 7" ideal cardiovascular health components. Unfortunately, nearly half the adult U.S. population has total cholesterol greater than 200 milligrams per deciliter (mg/dl), and 11 percent have levels greater than 240 mg/dl. Among youths aged 12 to 19 years, one in five has at least one abnormal cholesterol level; the rate is nearly one in two for obese youth.[3,19]

Low-density lipoproteins (LDLs)—"bad" cholesterol—are clearly associated with atherosclerosis. The higher the level of

LDLs, the higher the risk of atherosclerosis. The American Heart Association and the American College of Cardiology guidelines for the treatment of high LDL cholesterol are based on increased evidence showing that cholesterol-lowering statin medications significantly reduce risk of CVD—regardless of the absolute measured level of cholesterol. Instead of focusing on numbers, the new guidelines identify four groups who benefit from statin treatment. If you answer yes to any of the following questions, according to these new guidelines you would benefit from statin therapy:[19,20]

- Do you have a history of cardiovascular disease?

- Is your LDL cholesterol over 190 mg/dl?

- Do you have diabetes *and* are you over age 40 *and* is your LDL cholesterol over 70?

- Is your 10-year risk of heart attack greater than 7.5 percent?[21]

The National Cholesterol Education Program recommends that all adults over age 20 have their cholesterol checked at least once every 5 years. If your LDL cholesterol level, in combination with other risk factors, puts you at risk for CVD, you should develop a plan to reduce your cardiovascular risk. Exercising, maintaining a healthy weight, and making dietary changes—including reducing total and saturated fat intake and increasing dietary fiber—are first-line actions everyone should take. However, if these measures do not sufficiently lower your LDL level, cholesterol-lowering statin medications may be necessary and are now being more widely recommended.

High-density lipoproteins (HDLs)—"good" cholesterol—consist mainly of protein and are the smallest of the lipoprotein particles. HDLs help clear cholesterol from cells and atherosclerotic deposits and transport it back to the liver for recycling. High HDL levels (60 mg/dl or greater) provide protection from CVD.

HDL levels are determined mainly by genetics, but they are influenced by exercise, alcohol, and estrogen. They are higher among Blacks and among women, especially before menopause, and they change little with age. The protective effect of HDL is significant: a 1 percent decrease in HDL level is associated with a 3 to 4 percent increase in heart disease. Cholesterol treatment guidelines are not directly based on HDL level, but HDL level does go into the 10-year risk assessment equation.[3,20]

high-density lipoproteins (HDLs)
"Good" cholesterol; lipoproteins that help clear cholesterol from cells and atherosclerotic deposits and transport it back to the liver for recycling.

triglycerides
Blood fats similar to cholesterol.

Other Contributing Factors in Cardiovascular Health

In addition to the seven major criteria, other factors contribute, or may contribute, to heart health. The effect of some of these may be mediated through the seven major criteria.

Triglyceride Levels **Triglycerides** are another form in which fat exists in the body. They are derived from fats eaten or produced by the body from other energy sources, such as excess carbohydrates. High blood levels of triglycerides are a risk factor for CVD, although they are not linked to CVD as strongly as are high cholesterol levels. Triglyceride levels are reported as part of lipid (cholesterol) screening results.

High triglyceride levels are associated with excess body fat, diets high in saturated fat and cholesterol, alcohol use, and some medical conditions, such as poorly controlled diabetes. The main treatment for high triglycerides is lifestyle modification, but medications, including omega-3 fatty acids, can also be used. Body composition and the distribution of body fat in the abdominal area are associated with elevation in trigylcerides starting in childhood and adolescence.[22,23]

Alcohol Intake The relationship between alcohol and CVD is complicated because different levels of alcohol consumption have different effects. Heavy drinking, defined as more than two drinks per day for men and more than one drink per day for women, can damage the heart, increasing the risk of cardiomyopathy, some arrhythmias, and stroke. Light to moderate alcohol intake, defined as fewer than two drinks per day for men and one drink per day for women, appears to have a protective effect against heart disease and stroke, increasing HDL levels.

The benefit associated with light to moderate alcohol use is seen regardless of the beverage, which suggests that the protective factor is alcohol itself rather than another substance, such as the tannins in red wine. The disadvantages of alcohol consumption are that it may contribute to weight gain, higher blood pressure, and elevated triglycerides, as well as alcoholism in vulnerable individuals. The possible cardiovascular benefits have to be weighed against the disadvantages and potential harm associated with drinking.[24]

Air Pollution Exposure to pollutants in the air has short- and long-term effects on cardiovascular disease. Pollutants in the air include ozone, nitrogen dioxide, sulfur dioxide, and carbon monoxide. When air pollution levels increase, people are at increased risk of dying overall, and from cardiovascular disease in particular. People have different risk levels for exposure to air pollution depending on where they live and what they do for work, with the greatest exposure usually found in the lowest socioeconomic populations. In addition, sudden events such as forest fires can significantly increase air pollution to hazardous levels for entire communities. The Environmental Protection Agency monitors air quality and provides maps showing how safe it is outside based on environmental pollution.[25,26,27]

Mental Well-Being As described in Chapter 2, acute and chronic psychological stress has significant impacts on health. Stress causes the release of stress hormones. When persistent and pervasive, the continuous circulation of these hormones in the blood increases blood pressure and heart rate and triggers the release of cholesterol and triglycerides

Who's at Risk?

Place Matters: Geographical Location and Noncommunicable Disease

When we look within the United States, we see significant differences in deaths from heart disease by area of the country. Why do you think geographical location makes a difference in risk for heart disease? Consider the socioeconomic framework presented in Chapter 1. How might health care, health behaviors, neighborhood environments, education, income, racial discrimination, and public policies play a role?

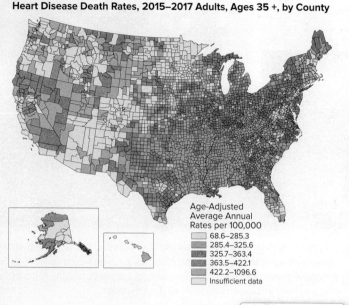

Heart Disease Death Rates, 2015–2017 Adults, Ages 35 +, by County

Age-Adjusted Average Annual Rates per 100,000
- 68.6–285.3
- 285.4–325.6
- 325.7–363.4
- 363.5–422.1
- 422.2–1096.6
- Insufficient data

Mc Graw Hill connect

Source: Centers for Disease Control and Prevention. (2019). Quick maps of heart disease, stroke and socioeconomic conditions. Retrieved from https://www.cdc.gov/dhdsp/maps/quick-maps/index.htm

---

into the blood. All these changes may promote the development of atherosclerosis and, for those with atherosclerosis, increase vulnerability to heart attack or stroke.

The impacts of chronic stress on cardiovascular disease start in early childhood. Children exposed to adverse childhood events (such as chronic poverty, parental abuse, housing instability, and neighborhood violence) have increased rates of CVD in adulthood. Adults with exposure to chronic violence, financial instability, or stress at work (such as job insecurity or a high-demand job with low control over schedule or duties) are at increased risk of CVD. People experiencing and perceiving racism, prejudice, and discrimination have an increased risk of CVD. Depression, anxiety, posttraumatic stress disorder, and certain traits and behavior patterns—specifically anger and hostility—have all been shown to contribute to CVD risk. People who lack social support or live in social isolation are at increased risk of many health conditions, including CVD. Strong social networks have been shown to decrease the risk, and social support, altruism, faith, and optimism are all associated with a reduced risk of CVD.[3,28,29]

If you frequently feel overwhelmed by stress, anger, or depression, try incorporating stress management and relaxation techniques into your daily life. Meditating can lower blood pressure and blood cholesterol levels; biofeedback may help reduce blood pressure; hypnosis may help control hypertension and other chronic health problems. If possibly, try simplifying your schedule and slowing down. In addition, try expanding your connections to family, friends, community, or church. It appears that the strength of people's relationships and their basic attitudes toward life play important roles in maintaining health and protecting against disease.[30]

Sleep Too little sleep (less than 7 hours) and too much (more than 8 hours) are both associated with increased risk of cardiovascular disease. Too little sleep may be a marker for the presence of too many demands on time, lack of time for sleep or relaxation, or increased access to social media and technology. In addition, both insomnia and too much sleep may be related to chronic stress, depression, and anxiety.[31]

Socioeconomic Status Low socioeconomic status is associated with an increased risk of heart attack, stroke, congestive heart failure, hypertension, and other chronic diseases. Income inequality in a country—the gap between the rich and the poor—is directly related to national rates of death from CVD, coronary artery disease, and stroke. Numerous factors may help explain the link between poverty and poor health. For example, poverty limits people's ability to obtain the basic requisites for health, such as food and shelter, as well as their ability to participate in society, which creates psychological stress. Poverty increases exposure to air and water pollutants and limits options for moving away from environmental exposures. Poverty also limits access to health-related information, health care, medications, behavior change options, and physical activity (see the box "Who's at Risk? Place Matters: Geographical Location and Noncommunicable Disease").[3,26,29,32]

Low socioeconomic status is associated with greater risk of cardiovascular disease. Poverty increases chronic stress by causing housing instability, exposure to neighborhood violence, limited access to healthy food, physical inactivity, and increased exposure to discrimination. *(DenisTangneyJr/Getty Images)*

Age Age is probably the most important noncontrollable risk factor in cardiovascular health. Deaths due to heart disease and stroke rise significantly after age 65. Age alone does not cause CVD; there is great variation among older people of the same age. However, as with all chronic noncommunicable diseases, age allows the accumulation of risk factors.[3]

Gender Although heart disease has often been thought of as a man's disease, CVD is the leading cause of death for both men and women. There are some differences between the sexes, however. A 40-year-old man without evidence of heart disease has a one-in-two chance of developing CVD in his lifetime, whereas a 40-year-old woman has a one-in-three chance. Women tend to develop heart disease about 10 years later than men, perhaps because of the protective effect of estrogen before menopause. After age 50 (the average age of menopause), the difference in risk between men and women starts to decrease.

Death rates from CVD are higher in women of all races/ethnicities whether we are looking at heart attack, stroke, hypertension, or congestive heart failure. Three reasons for this difference have been identified. First, women tend to be older and frailer when they develop heart disease, so they are less likely to survive. Second, women are more likely to have either no symptoms before a heart attack or symptoms that make the diagnosis of heart disease more difficult, such as stomach complaints. The third reason women's CVD death rates are higher is that treatment is more likely to be delayed, and thus more damage occurs. Women delay seeking treatment longer than men—they are less likely to think symptoms are serious and less likely to call 9-1-1. In addition, health care providers may delay treatment because of the lack of "classic" symptoms and because they are less likely to suspect heart disease in women.[3]

Postmenopausal Status The hormone estrogen has long been thought to protect premenopausal women from CVD. When levels of estrogen fall during menopause, levels of HDL also decline, and body fat distribution shifts to a more central distribution pattern, similar to the male pattern, which is thought to be less healthy for the heart than the typical female fat distribution around the hips.

For many years, medical practitioners prescribed hormone replacement therapy (HRT) for postmenopausal women to relieve the symptoms of menopause, lower the risk of osteoporosis (bone thinning), and reduce the risk of CVD. Belief in the benefits of estrogen was so strong that, at one point, nearly one in three postmenopausal women was on HRT. However, evidence now shows that HRT does not reduce the risk of CVD and may actually increase it in women over 60. For women under 60 experiencing menopause, HRT may be prescribed as a treatment for the symptoms and for prevention of osteoporosis.[33]

Genetics and Family History Individuals who have a relative with a history of CVD have a higher risk of CVD themselves. High rates of CVD in a family may be related to genetics or lifestyle patterns or both. Early onset of CVD (before the age of 50), especially in a family member with a healthy lifestyle, more strongly suggests a genetic component. A family history of sudden cardiac death at a young age may signify a genetic risk for cardiomyopathy or another congenital cardiac disease.[3,34]

Areas of Interest for Future CVD Research

Given that seven factors (described earlier) explain most of the risk for cardiovascular disease, most people should focus on Life's Simple 7. However, researchers are trying to identify the roles of additional risk factors in order to further prevent disease. Among the promising findings are the following:

- Low levels of vitamin D are associated with heart disease, diabetes, hypertension, and obesity. It remains unclear whether supplementation reduces risk of cardiovascular disease.

- High blood levels of homocysteine, an amino acid that is a product of protein metabolism, have been associated with increased risk of CVD. Blood levels of homocysteine tend to be high in people with diets high in meat and low in fruits and vegetables.

- Metabolic syndrome, a cluster of interrelated risk factors, including abdominal obesity and insulin resistance that can precede the development of Type 2 diabetes, is associated with significantly increased risk of CVD.

- Inflammation is well established as a factor in all stages of atherosclerosis. High levels of C-reactive protein, which can be detected with a blood test that measures inflammation, are associated with increased risk of coronary heart disease. Inflammation may be due to recognized infections, such as influenza, or other still-unidentified sources.

- Lower birth weight is associated with higher risk of CVD later in life.[3,35,36,37,38]

Testing and Treatment

People with no symptoms of CVD are usually not tested for evidence of disease; instead, the focus is on screening for risk factors such as hypertension, cholesterol levels, health behaviors, and family health history. An exception is people in certain occupations, such as airline pilots and truck drivers, whose sudden incapacity would place other people at risk. People may also be screened for signs of CVD before surgery, and the American College of Sports Medicine recommends that an exercise stress test be performed on men older than age 40 and women older than age 50 if they are sedentary and about to begin an exercise program.

For people with a family history of sudden death or symptoms suggestive of CVD—such as shortness of breath, dizziness, chest pain on exertion, weakness, numbness, or neurological problems—physical examination and diagnostic tests can assess whether CVD is present and the extent of the problem. If CVD is found, a variety of steps can be taken, from lifestyle changes to medication to surgery.

Diagnostic Testing for Heart Disease Several tests can evaluate heart function and assess whether underlying disease is present. An **electrocardiogram** (ECG or EKG) uses electrodes taped to the chest, and the results are recorded as a graph of the heart's electrical activity as it beats. An ECG can detect abnormal rhythms, inadequate blood flow (possibly due to ischemia or heart attack), and heart enlargement. An **echocardiogram** (or echo) uses an ultrasound tool like that used to see a fetus (see Chapter 12, "Diagnosing Problems in a Fetus") and shows an image on a screen. An echo can visualize the heart structure and motion and can detect structural abnormalities in the valves, arteries, and heart chambers; the thickness of the muscle walls; and how well the heart pumps. An **exercise stress test** evaluates how well the heart functions with exercise. In a stress test, a person exercises on a treadmill or stationary bicycle while the heart's response is monitored with an ECG or an echo to look for changes in function with activity.

Diagnostic Testing for Stroke At the hospital, a CT scan or an MRI can generate images of the brain and blood flow and establish whether a stroke has occurred. These tests can also show whether a stroke has been caused by a blockage or by a hemorrhage. Further testing may be done to find the source of the blockage. The carotid arteries, the large arteries on the sides of the neck that supply blood to the brain, are examined to see whether they are blocked with atherosclerotic plaques. If so, part of a plaque may have broken off and caused an embolism, blocking a blood vessel in the brain.

Management of Heart Disease Multiple categories of medications can be used in the treatment of heart disease. There are medications that help control heart rhythm (antiarrhythmics), dilate the coronary arteries and reduce angina (antianginals), decrease blood clotting (anticoagulants), and dissolve blood clots during a heart attack (thrombolytics). Other medications, such as antihypertensives, cholesterol-lowering medications, and antiplatelet medications, are used to control risk factors and reduce the chance of developing heart disease or a recurrence of heart disease.

When a heart attack occurs, emergency treatment is critical. The effectiveness of treatment depends on the length of time between the first symptoms and the reestablishment of blood flow to the heart muscle. Thrombolytics are most effective when given within the first hour after a heart attack.

Every day, thousands of people have heart surgery; there are many different types of surgery, depending on the underlying problem. For structural abnormalities, surgeons can repair or replace heart valves, close septal defects (holes) that allow blood to flow abnormally, reposition arteries and veins that are attached incorrectly, and repair aneurysms in the aorta. If the problem is related to abnormal electrical conduction through the heart, a cardiologist can destroy a small amount of heart tissue in an area that is disturbing the flow of electricity or implant a defibrillator into the chest that will automatically shock the heart if a life-threatening arrhythmia develops.

Also, often as a last resort, a surgeon can replace a damaged heart completely with a heart from a donor. If the underlying abnormality is related to coronary artery disease, a surgeon can reopen the vessel with angioplasty, in which a balloon catheter (a thin plastic tube) is threaded into a blocked or narrowed artery and inflated to stretch the vessel open again; a *coronary stent,* a springy framework that supports the vessel walls and keeps the vessel open, is often permanently placed in the artery to prevent it from closing again. Another surgical option is **coronary artery bypass grafting**, usually just called *bypass.* A healthy blood vessel is taken from another part of the body, usually the leg, and grafted to the coronary arteries to allow a bypass of blood flow around a narrowed vessel.

electrocardiogram
A record of the heart's electrical activity as it beats.

echocardiogram
A diagnostic test for a heart attack in which sound waves are used to visualize heart valves, heart wall movement, and overall heart function.

exercise stress test
A procedure that evaluates how well the heart functions with exercise.

coronary artery bypass grafting
A surgical procedure in which a healthy blood vessel is taken from another part of the body and grafted to the coronary arteries to allow a bypass of blood flow around a narrowed vessel.

About two-thirds of people who suffer a stroke survive and require rehabilitation. When a stroke has caused muscle weakness or paralysis, therapy focuses on regaining use of impaired limbs, improving coordination and balance, and developing strategies for bypassing deficits. *(kali9/Getty Images)*

the United States. In the United States alone, 26 million people have been diagnosed with diabetes (10.6 percent of the adult population); an estimated 9.4 million have diabetes but are undiagnosed, and another 91.8 million are at high risk of developing diabetes in the next 10 years. Rates of diabetes have been increasing steadily in past 30 years. Minority and low socioeconomic populations are disproportionately affected, and in these populations rates continue to rise, which further widens health disparities.[3,39]

There are different types of diabetes, but all result in elevated blood glucose levels due to a disruption in the production or use of insulin. Figure 14.7 illustrates the basic relationships among glucose, insulin, and glucose uptake by cells in a healthy person and in people with Type 1 and Type 2 diabetes.

In a healthy person, increased glucose in the blood after a meal triggers the release of insulin from the pancreas. Molecules of insulin bind to cells around the body and facilitate the uptake of

diabetes
A metabolic disorder in which the production or use of insulin is disrupted, so that body cells cannot take up glucose and use it for energy, and high levels of glucose circulate in the blood.

Management of Stroke If a stroke is found to be thrombotic (caused by a blockage) and there is no evidence of bleeding in the brain, thrombolytic medications can be administered to dissolve the clot and restore blood flow to the brain. Thrombolytic medications must not be given if the stroke is hemorrhagic, because they can cause increased bleeding. Aspirin and other anticlotting medications can be used after a thrombotic stroke to reduce the risk of another stroke. Treatment for hemorrhagic stroke depends on the underlying cause of the bleed. Surgery is sometimes necessary to control bleeding and decrease pressure in the brain. Control of blood pressure and other risk factors is important for all people who have had a stroke, whether thrombotic or hemorrhagic.

Rehabilitation is an important component of treatment for stroke. If an area of the brain has been damaged or destroyed, the functions that were controlled by that part of the brain will be impaired. Rehabilitation consists of physical therapy (to strengthen muscles and coordination), speech therapy (to improve communication and eating), and occupational therapy (to improve activities of daily living and job retraining if appropriate). Progress and return of functions vary by individual. Some people recover fully within a few days or weeks, while others experience long-term impairment.

DIABETES

Diabetes is the most common disorder of the endocrine or metabolic system and the seventh leading cause of death in

Normal
Insulin binds to receptors on the surface of a cell and signals special transporters in the cell to transport glucose inside.

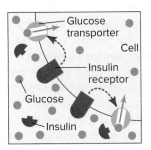

Type 1 diabetes
The pancreas produces little or no insulin. Thus, no signal is sent instructing the cell to transport glucose, and glucose builds up in the bloodstream.

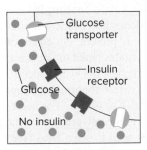

Type 2 diabetes
The body's cells are resistant to insulin. Some insulin binds to receptors on the cell's surface, but the signal to transport glucose is blocked. Glucose builds up in the bloodstream.

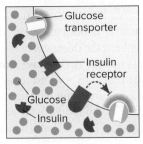

figure 14.7 **Normal insulin and glucose uptake, and with Type 1 and Type 2 diabetes.**
A healthy person's body releases a normal amount of insulin from the pancreas after meals. Type 1 diabetes and Type 2 diabetes disrupt this process, as shown in the second and third diagrams.

Life Stories

Stacy: Living with Type 1 Diabetes

Stacy was diagnosed with Type 1 diabetes during her sophomore year of high school. Her older brother had diabetes, so she wasn't completely surprised when she developed symptoms. With her family's help, she learned how to inject insulin, manage her blood sugar levels, and monitor her meals. When she first got to college, she maintained the same habits she had developed at home. She checked her blood glucose levels in the morning when she woke up, between classes, before she commuted home from campus in the evening, and before bed. She ate well, counted carbohydrates, exercised, and adjusted her insulin as needed. She was able to maintain and monitor her blood glucose levels as well as her diet and activity. This made her diabetes a manageable condition.

During her second quarter, Stacy got a job to help ease the financial burden of college for her family. Her busy schedule meant less time: She grabbed toast and tea for breakfast, was less consistent in the timing of lunch and dinner, and found she was staying up late doing homework and not making time for the gym. She stopped checking her blood sugar as regularly, occasionally neglecting it for days at a time. And because she wasn't sure of her blood sugar levels, she stopped injecting her insulin regularly.

One day when leaving class, Stacy felt so exhausted that she stumbled to a nearby bench, nauseous and light-headed. When a friend asked whether she was okay, she was unable to answer coherently. The friend called 9-1-1, and paramedics took Stacy to the emergency room. There, the nurses immediately recognized the fruity smell on her breath and checked her blood sugar level. It was more than three times higher than normal. Stacy was hospitalized and treated for hyperglycemia and dehydration. She was monitored for 2 days and then allowed to check out.

After this episode, Stacy went home for a week to regain her equilibrium. She saw her endocrinologist and diabetes care team, and they recommended that she start using an insulin pump. The pump would provide a constant low level of insulin and would allow her to give herself extra doses with meals. In addition, when she checked her blood sugar, her pump could calculate and administer the correct amount of insulin. Stacy returned to school feeling more confident about managing her diabetes. The new system allowed her to continue focusing on her academics and job and, with a little additional teaching, improve her glucose control.

- Do you have any health conditions or concerns that affect your daily life? If so, what measures do you have to take to manage them?

- Have you had the experience of sacrificing your health to meet academic deadlines or participate in social activities? If so, how can you balance choices, commitments, and your body's needs to maintain a healthy lifestyle?

glucose into cells, which use it for energy or store it. When levels of blood glucose drop, the pancreas stops releasing insulin, so that blood glucose levels are maintained in a healthy range, typically between 80 and 120 mg/dl, depending on time since the last meal. Problems at any stage of the process can cause blood glucose levels to rise to abnormal levels. Long-term exposure to elevated levels of glucose is toxic, leading to damage to blood vessels and, as a result, kidney failure, blindness, nerve damage, and cardiovascular disease. In addition, people with diabetes are at increased risk of infectious diseases and higher rates of complications from influenza, pneumonia, and skin infections. They also experience more dental problems and more complications in pregnancy.[40]

Type 1 Diabetes

Type 1 diabetes is caused by the destruction of insulin-producing cells in the pancreas by the immune system. When the cells are destroyed, insulin cannot be produced and body cells cannot take up glucose. Levels of glucose circulating in the blood rise rapidly while cells are starving. Insulin must be provided from an external source to keep blood glucose levels under control and to allow the cells to use it. In people with Type 1 diabetes, insulin is necessary for survival and must be supplied every day.

The onset of Type 1 diabetes usually occurs before age 20, though it can occur at any age (see the box "Life Stories: Stacy: Living With Type 1 Diabetes"). Symptoms include dry mouth, frequent urination, extreme thirst, rapid weight loss, fatigue, and blurred vision. Type 1 diabetes is probably caused by a combination of genetic, autoimmune, and environmental factors (such as viruses or dietary triggers). Rates of Type 1 diabetes have increased in the past 20 years, but Type 1 continues to make up only an estimated 5 to 10 percent of all diabetes cases. This type is not associated with obesity, and there are no known ways to prevent it at this time.[40]

Type 1 diabetes must be treated with insulin replacement. Frequent monitoring of blood glucose levels and the use of insulin pumps or self-injected insulin multiple times a day have significantly improved blood glucose control and can prevent or reduce risk of long-term complications. In addition, dietary education is important, because balancing carbohydrate intake with insulin requirements becomes important for stable control of blood sugar. A fine line must be maintained between too-high glucose levels (and increased risk of long-term complications) and too-low glucose levels (and increased risk of loss of consciousness, seizure, or death). Physical activity is an important component of Type 1 diabetes control and reduction of long-term complications.

Type 2 Diabetes

In Type 2 diabetes, the production of insulin by the pancreas is initially normal, but over time the insulin receptors in body cells become insulin-resistant (less able to respond to insulin). Cells cannot take up some of the glucose, and the level of glucose in the blood (blood sugar) rises. The pancreas initially responds by increasing production of insulin, but eventually it cannot keep up.

Normal blood glucose if you have not eaten in the preceding 8 to 10 hours (fasting) is under 100 mg/dl. *Prediabetes* is diagnosed when blood glucose levels are higher than normal but not high enough for the diagnosis of diabetes. In this condition, cells are starting to have a problem with the uptake and utilization of glucose. An estimated 38 percent of U.S. adults (91.8 million people) have prediabetes. Nearly half of them (40 to 50 percent) will go on to develop Type 2 diabetes, which is diagnosed when fasting blood glucose levels are higher than 126 mg/dl. The onset of Type 2 diabetes is usually gradual. Symptoms include excessive thirst, frequent urination, and fatigue; rarely, they include nausea, vomiting, and confusion.

Type 2 diabetes accounts for 90 to 95 percent of all cases of diabetes. It is the type that has been rapidly increasing in parallel with rising rates of overweight and obesity levels.[39,40] Type 2 diabetes was once almost unheard of in people under 20, but in the past 20 years, rates among youth have increased significantly.[3,41]

Risk Factors   Type 2 diabetes is a multifactorial disease with an increased risk if there is a family history of diabetes and factors related to socioeconomic status. Given the strong association with obesity, the risk factors for obesity discussed in Chapter 7 are also those for Type 2 diabetes: higher levels of abdominal fat as indicated by waist circumference, and lack of physical activity. Risk increases with age, and being over 40 is a risk factor. Racial and ethnic minorities and people with low socioeconomic status are disproportionately affected by obesity and diabetes. African Americans, Native Americans, Hispanic Americans, and some Asian Americans have higher rates of diabetes than the general population and are at greater risk for complications.[40]

A cluster of interrelated factors significantly increase the risk of developing diabetes and other health complications. A person who has at least three of the following is diagnosed as having *metabolic syndrome:*

- Fasting glucose (blood sugar) level at or above 100

- HDL cholesterol under 40 in men, or under 50 in women

- Triglycerides at or above 150

- Waist circumference at or above 40 inches (102 cm) for men, or at or above 35 inches (88 cm) for women

- Systolic blood pressure at or above 130 and diastolic blood pressure at or above 85

■ Selma Hayek, shown here attending the 67th Annual Cannes Film Festival, has discussed her family history of diabetes and developed diabetes while pregnant.
(Denis Makarenko/Shutterstock)

An estimated 34 percent of U.S. adults have metabolic syndrome, and overall rates are similar by gender. Rates are highest among American Indians, followed by Hispanics, non-Hispanic whites, Blacks, and Alaska Natives. It is important to identify and address metabolic syndrome because of the high risk of progressing to diabetes and cardiovascular complications. Recommendations for treating metabolic syndrome include increasing physical activity, losing weight, and making dietary changes; medications are often recommended as well.[3,42]

Prevention and Treatment   Screening for diabetes measures glucose levels in the blood to detect early stages of the disease, identify prediabetes, and prevent progression of prediabetes to diabetes. There are four ways to look at blood glucose levels (Table 14.2). The A1c test is a blood test for a form of hemoglobin, and it measures what the average blood level of glucose has been over the preceding 3 months. It can be used both for diagnosis and to monitor treatment. A fasting glucose test measures blood glucose levels after no food has been taken for 8 hours. The 2-hour glucose test requires eating a certain amount of glucose and then having blood drawn 2 hours later. A random glucose test at or above 200 in someone with diabetes symptoms (including frequent urination, extreme thirst, unexplained weight loss) is diagnostic of diabetes.

The U.S. Preventive Services Task Force recommends screening for diabetes in all pregnant women after 24 weeks of gestation and for asymptomatic people between the ages of 40 and 70 if they are overweight or obese. Screening may be indicated at earlier ages and lower weight ranges for people with a first-degree relative with diabetes (mother, father, brother, sister) and people in a racial/ethnic group with increased risk, such as African Americans, Latino Americans, Native Americans, Alaska Natives, Native Hawaiians, or Asian and Pacific Islanders.[43,44]

Public Health Is Personal

Preventing Type 2 Diabetes

The prevention of chronic diseases requires identifying them and understanding their causes, just as the prevention of infectious diseases requires identifying the pathogens that cause them. Identifying the causes of chronic diseases is more difficult, however, because the diseases take years to develop and are multidetermined—that is, they are caused by the interaction of multiple factors.

Public heath efforts typically focus on three levels of prevention, identified as primary, secondary, and tertiary prevention:

- *Primary prevention* efforts are public health interventions that target the underlying causes of a disease—such as an unhealthy diet, hypertension, and tobacco use—and attempt to improve or eliminate them. Primary prevention efforts are intended to stop the development of risk factors. For Type 2 diabetes, an example of primary prevention is a nutrition and exercise program for elementary school children.

- *Secondary prevention* efforts are aimed at people who have developed risk factors but do not yet have symptoms. For Type 2 diabetes, examples of secondary prevention are an educational campaign about the benefits of weight loss and a program to encourage adults to have their blood glucose levels monitored regularly.

- *Tertiary prevention* efforts focus on reducing complications of a disease once it has manifested, or on reversing the effects of the disease to restore function. Tertiary prevention tends to be the most expensive and invasive level of public health intervention; it is more expensive to treat disease and prevent further complications than it is to prevent onset. For Type 2 diabetes, tertiary prevention includes doing regular screenings for nerve damage, kidney function, eye problems, and heart disease. It can also include encouraging lifestyle changes, such as getting a membership at a gym and switching to a healthier diet.

Primary prevention is the most cost-effective approach to decreasing the incidence of chronic diseases. In addition, because many chronic diseases share underlying risk factors, primary prevention can reduce the risk of more than one disease. For example, physical inactivity and obesity are risk factors for CVD, diabetes, and cancer, and smoking is a risk factor for CVD, lung diseases, and cancer. Another advantage of primary prevention is that it starts early, when lifestyle habits are being formed. Behaviors adopted early in life are more likely to continue and become lifelong patterns.

Type 2 diabetes, like other chronic diseases, is a very serious illness—but it is also one of the easiest to prevent and control. Even people with a genetic predisposition can control their risk. In support of prevention efforts, the Centers for Disease Control and Prevention runs the National Diabetes Prevention Program, a research-based lifestyle-change program that reduced the risk of developing Type 2 diabetes by 58 percent in people at high risk for diabetes. If you are at risk or just want to increase your awareness, you can learn more about this program at the CDC website.

Sources: Centers for Disease Control and Prevention. (2019). National diabetes prevention program. Retrieved from https://www.cdc.gov/diabetes/prevention/index.html

Dietary changes, exercise, and weight loss can prevent diabetes, delay its onset, and treat it. The risk of progression to diabetes is significantly reduced with 7 percent weight loss, especially if it occurs through lifestyle modifications (improving diet and increasing physical activity). Increasingly, however, medications are also being used to reduce the risk of progression to full diabetes (see the box "Public Health Is Personal: Preventing Type 2 Diabetes").

Treatment for Type 2 diabetes includes lifestyle modification, oral medications, and eventually for some, insulin replacement. Exercise is especially important because it can improve HDL levels and increase the number of insulin receptors on cells, which enhances the body's ability to use insulin; it also helps prevent prediabetes from progressing to diabetes. Long-term control of both Type 1 and Type 2 diabetes is monitored with the hemoglobin A1c test, and the closer

Table 14.2 Diagnostic Criteria for Diabetes and Prediabetes

	Diabetes	Prediabetes
A1c hemoglobin (%)	At or above 6.5	5.7–6.4
Fasting glucose test (mg/dL)	At or above 126	100–125
2-hour glucose test (mg/dL)	At or above 200	140–199
Random glucose test in patients with classic diabetes symptoms (mg/dL)	At or above 200	Not applicable

the blood glucose is to the normal range, the lower the risk of complications.

Gestational Diabetes

The hormonal changes of pregnancy can affect how well the body responds to insulin. Between 2 and 10 percent of pregnant woman develop gestational diabetes (diabetes of pregnancy). Risk factors for gestational diabetes not only are similar to those for Type 2 diabetes but also include pregnancy after age 35, family history of gestational diabetes, and a personal history of diabetes in a prior pregnancy or delivery of a large infant in a prior pregnancy.

All women should be screened for gestational diabetes after 24 weeks of gestation. Detection and treatment are important to reduce the risk of complications for both mother and child. For most women, glucose levels return to normal after delivery, but for 5 to 10 percent, diabetes becomes an ongoing condition. In addition, a woman with a history of

gestational diabetes is at significant risk of developing diabetes in the next 10 to 20 years.[43]

CHRONIC LUNG DISEASES

Chronic lung diseases, also known as chronic lower respiratory diseases, are the third leading cause of death in the United States. The two most common forms are asthma and chronic obstructive pulmonary disease (COPD), which includes chronic bronchitis and emphysema (Table 14.3). All these diseases impair the ability to breathe.

Although they are all characterized by airway obstruction and shortness of breath, chronic lung diseases have different causes and treatments. Genetic factors play a larger role in asthma than in COPD, although both are triggered by smoking, infection, and pollution. Asthma can have an allergic component and often appears in childhood. COPD is more typical in older adults.

Table 14.3   Comparison of Chronic Lung Diseases

Disease	Characteristics	Common Triggers and Causes	Symptoms	Effects and Risks	Treatment
Asthma	Chronic inflammation of bronchioles; spasm of muscles around bronchioles; excess mucus, blocking airflow. Often appears in childhood.	Smoking; inhaling smoke, air pollution, chemicals, cold air. Viral and bacterial infections. Allergies. Strenuous exercise. Strong emotions, stress. Obesity, heartburn, sleep apnea.	Shortness of breath, prolonged coughing, wheezing. Diagnostic categories range from intermittent to severe.	Death, although rarely, if disease is poorly controlled. Most common chronic lung condition.	Avoid triggers. Use medication, including bronchodilators (quick relief) and inhaled steroids (long-term control). Get an annual flu shot. Self-care is essential.
Chronic bronchitis (component of COPD)	Chronic inflammation and narrowing of bronchioles (airways inside lungs); excess mucus.	Smoking; inhaling smoke, air pollution, chemicals, dust, other lung irritants.	Bronchial congestion, chronic cough.	Increased risk for lung cancer.	Stop smoking.
Emphysema (component of COPD)	Stiffening and destruction of alveoli (clusters of air sacs at end of bronchioles).	Smoking; inhaling smoke, air pollution, chemicals, dust, other lung irritants.	Shortness of breath, gasping for air.	Strain on the heart; increased risk for heart disease.	Stop smoking.
Chronic obstructive pulmonary disease (COPD)	Chronic bronchitis plus emphysema. Usually diagnosed in middle-aged or older adults.	Smoking; inhaling smoke, air pollution, chemicals, dust, other lung irritants.	Ongoing cough, shortness of breath, wheezing, chest tightness.	COPD is third leading cause of death in U.S. and a leading cause of disability.	Stop smoking. To improve symptoms: inhaled bronchodilators and steroids. In late stages: oxygen, lung surgery.

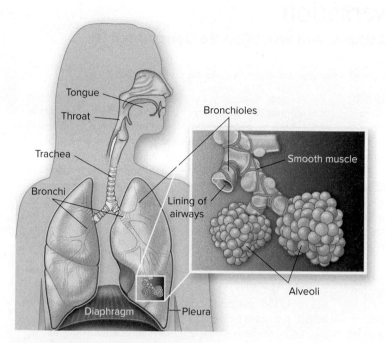

figure 14.8   The respiratory system.

The Respiratory System

When you breathe, air travels down your trachea and enters your lungs through airways called bronchial tubes, or bronchi. The bronchi carry the air through a series of smaller and smaller branching airways (bronchioles) into the alveoli, tiny round air sacs. The alveoli are surrounded by capillaries, which are tiny blood vessels, where gas exchange takes place. Oxygen in the air passes through the walls of the air sacs into the blood in capillaries, and carbon dioxide moves from the capillaries into the air sacs. The carbon dioxide is pushed back through the bronchioles and exhaled, and the oxygen travels through the bloodstream to body cells (Figure 14.8). Healthy lungs are elastic and stretchy; the alveoli work like tiny balloons—they fill when you breathe in and deflate when you breath out.

Asthma

Asthma is the most common chronic lung condition, and rates have been increasing in the past few decades (see the box "Starting the Conversation: Why Do More People Have Asthma, and What Can Be Done About It?"). In the United States more than 19 million adults (7.7 percent of population) and 6.2 million children (8.4 percent of the population) live with this condition. Although asthma cannot be cured, symptoms can usually be controlled by avoiding triggers and using medications, so people can live normal, active lives. Deaths from asthma are rare but do occur; they are usually associated with poor control of the disease.[45]

In asthma, the lining of the airways becomes inflamed and swollen, narrowing the airway passage, and excess mucus is produced, further obstructing the flow of air. In addition, the smooth muscles that encircle the bronchioles become tight or go into spasm, constricting the airways.

The inflammation, obstruction, and constriction cause the symptoms of asthma—wheezing, coughing, chest tightness, and shortness of breath. For a person with asthma, the airways are chronically inflamed; an asthma attack (also called a flare or an exacerbation) occurs when the inflammation increases and airways become further constricted. Some people with asthma have very mild intermittent symptoms, often in response to specific triggers. Other people have persistent, chronic symptoms that affect their daily life.

Risk Factors and Triggers The causes of asthma are not completely understood, but they appear to include both genetic and environmental factors. For people with an underlying genetic predisposition, asthma attacks can occur in response to multiple triggers. Viral infections are associated with 50 to 75 percent of adult wheezing episodes. In particular, the influenza virus can lead to serious worsening of asthma and an increased risk of complications. Bacteria may be the trigger for another 5 to 10 percent of flares. Inhaled irritants—such as smoking or exposure to secondhand smoke, wood smoke, and air pollution—can trigger an attack and exacerbate underlying airway inflammation and muscle spasm. Air pollution can be a major issue, especially in urban areas and poor communities. Other irritants can include perfumes, hair spray, paint fumes, or other chemicals.

Allergies are a common trigger; allergens can include animal dander, dust mites, cockroach droppings, mold, and various foods and food additives. Asthma attacks can also be triggered by strenuous physical exercise, cold air, and strong emotions. Other conditions that have been associated with worsening symptoms include obesity, acid reflux (heartburn), sleep apnea, stress, and chronic sinus infections or nasal congestion. Between 3 and 5 percent of adults can also have an exacerbation triggered by use of aspirin or nonsteroidal anti-inflammatory medications (such as ibuprofen).

Detection and Treatment Asthma is typically diagnosed when a person complains of shortness of breath, prolonged coughing, or coughing with certain activities. A health care provider will listen to the lungs and may hear wheezing as the air moves in and out through narrowed airways. A lung function test can be used to see how quickly and with how much force the person can blow air out of the lungs, which is influenced by how large or small the airways are. Diagnostic categories include the following:

- Intermittent asthma, in which a person has discrete episodes of symptoms but no symptoms in between

- Mild persistent asthma, in which someone has symptoms a few times a week but not daily

- Moderate asthma, in which daily symptoms limit some normal activity

Starting the Conversation
Why Do More People Have Asthma, and What Can Be Done About It?

Q: Do you have asthma, or do you know someone who does? If so, what activity limits does the disease impose?

The prevalence of asthma has been increasing in the United States, and it has been increasing disproportionately among children, women, poor people, and African Americans. These demographic disparities have persisted despite improvements in outdoor air quality and decreases in cigarette smoking and exposure to secondhand smoke.

Among the general U.S. population, 8 percent (1 in 12 people) suffer the symptoms of asthma: shortness of breath, wheezing, coughing, and chronic airway inflammation. The prevalence of asthma strongly correlates with poverty. Incidence rates are 11.7 percent in populations at or below 100 percent of the poverty line, in contrast to 6.8 percent in populations above 450 percent of the poverty level or higher. Black children have significantly higher rates of asthma and are nearly five times more likely than white children to die from asthma.

Reasons for the increase in asthma prevalence, and for the demographic disparities, are not entirely clear. Researchers have identified possible factors, including genetic predisposition, allergies, health factors such as smoking and obesity, and exposure to pollutants, both indoor and outdoor. Black children are born prematurely at higher rates than are children of other racial groups, and premature birth increases asthma risk. But a critical factor is likely to be the neighborhood or ZIP code in which you live.

Exposure to air pollution is strongly linked to acute exacerbation of asthma symptoms. A study in New York City looked at asthma prevalence, which ranged from 3 to 18 percent depending on neighborhood. Researchers evaluated levels of combustion by-products both inside homes and in children's exhalations; they found a correlation between higher rates of asthma and exposure to environmental pollutants, particularly diesel truck exhaust. Where the density of truck routes was higher, so was the prevalence of asthma.

Another study, also conducted in New York City (where asthma rates are among the highest in the nation), looked at differences in environmental conditions between midtown Manhattan and the South Bronx, which are about 4 miles apart. Rates of hospital admissions for asthma in the Bronx were roughly twice those in Manhattan. In the Bronx, researchers noted the presence of 20 waste-transfer facilities where diesel-powered garbage trucks from all over the city congregate; a major wholesale produce market, where 12,000 trucks move in and out daily; and a network of major highways. Schools, playgrounds, and homes are all located within a few blocks of these pollution sources.

Residents in more affluent areas are able to wield the political power necessary to keep highways and waste-transfer facilities out of their neighborhoods. Those in poorer areas bear the burden not just of pollution, but of the diseases caused by it.

Given these realities, are there actions communities can take to ease the burden of air pollution for people with asthma—and everyone else? As described in Chapter 9, one step that many colleges and universities have taken to improve air quality for all is to go smoke-free.

Whatever the underlying causes of asthma, it is certain that air pollution, whether caused by trucks or tobacco, exacerbates asthma's acute symptoms and increases their severity—making life miserable for the growing number of people who suffer from the disease.

Q: Where does your campus stand on the smoke-free movement? Where do you stand on it?

Q: What are your thoughts about the disparities in prevalence of asthma, with children, particularly minority children, being more affected?

Sources: Centers for Disease Control and Prevention. (2018). Most recent national asthma data. Retrieved from https://www.cdc.gov/asthma/most_recent_national_asthma_data.htm; Cornell, A. G., et al. (2012). Domestic airborne black carbon and exhaled nitrous oxide in children in New York City. *Journal of Exposure Science and Environmental Epidemiology, 22,* 258–266; Centers for Disease Control and Prevention. (2012). Asthma in the United States: Growing every year. Retrieved from www.cdc.gov/vitalsigns/Asthma; Thurston, G. D., Spira-Cohen, A., & Chen, L. C. (2007). South Bronx Environmental Policy Study: Final report of NYU School of Medicine Research. Retrieved from http://graphics8.nytimes.com/packages/pdf/nyregion/20081002_SOM.pdf; Alexander, D., & Currie, J. (2017). Is it who you are or where you live? Residential segregation and racial gaps in childhood asthma. *Journal of Health Economics, 55,* 186–200.

- Severe asthma, in which daily symptoms place extreme limits on normal activity

Treatment is based on the diagnostic category and how often someone is having symptoms. Long-term control also includes avoiding common triggers, such as tobacco smoke, allergens, and air pollution. Because of the increased risk of complications associated with the influenza virus, people with asthma are considered a priority group to receive an annual flu shot and a one-time pneumonia shot. When exercise is a trigger, people are encouraged to continue exercising but use medication to control symptoms before or during exercise.

It is recommended that an inhaled steroid be used in the treatment of asthma due to the inflammatory component. If symptoms are mild and intermittent, a low-dose inhaled steroid can be used with a quick-relief bronchodilator medication. Bronchodilator medicines, delivered through an inhaler, cause the smooth muscles lining the bronchioles to relax, opening the airways. They can increase risk of severe asthma attack or even death from asthma when used alone, so they should be used in combination with inhaled steroid.

If symptoms are more persistent, long-term control can be achieved by using a stronger inhaled steroid that works locally within the bronchioles to reduce inflammation, opening the airways and making the smooth muscle less reactive. Inhaled steroid medications reduce the need for quick-relief medicines, reduce the frequency of asthma attacks, and reduce chronic coughing or shortness of breath.[46]

Because asthma is an inherently variable disease with relapses and remissions, management is an active process and self-care is critical. Monitoring and recording of symptoms, such as frequency of coughing or degree of shortness of breath, allow the person to use quick- and long-acting medications to treat and prevent further exacerbation. Understanding what is likely to trigger episodes and attempting to avoid or decrease exposure to triggers is also critical. A personal asthma-control plan allows an individual to take control of care management.

Chronic Obstructive Pulmonary Disease

In contrast to asthma, chronic obstructive pulmonary disease (COPD) tends to develop as people experience cumulative damage to their airways and alveoli over time and is usually diagnosed in middle-aged or older adults. COPD is a leading cause of disability and the third leading cause of death in the United States. There are two components of COPD: chronic bronchitis and emphysema. Most people with COPD have both.

Chronic bronchitis is characterized by persistent inflammation of the bronchioles, which causes the airway walls to thicken and the airway passages to narrow; excess secretion of mucus also occurs, which obstructs airflow. A person with this disorder has bronchial congestion and a chronic cough. Smokers with chronic bronchitis have an increased risk of lung cancer.

In emphysema, the alveoli become less stretchy and elastic, and the walls between alveoli are damaged or destroyed, creating less space for air exchange. It becomes harder for the lungs to take up oxygen and expel carbon dioxide. A person with emphysema is breathless and has to gasp for air. The disease puts a strain on the heart, increasing the risk of heart disease.

The primary cause of COPD is smoking. Exposure to other lung irritants, such as secondhand smoke, air pollution, and inhaled chemicals or dust, can also contribute to these diseases. Symptoms include an ongoing cough, shortness of breath, wheezing, and chest tightness. These often begin gradually, progress slowly, and can eventually hamper activities of daily living, such as cooking or getting dressed. Because the symptoms resemble those of asthma, a health care provider performs lung function testing to correctly identify the cause.

Treatment can improve symptoms and slow the progression, but it cannot cure the disease. Inhaled bronchodilators and inhaled steroids are, again, the mainstay of treatment programs. At later stages, supplemental oxygen may be necessary; sometimes,

lung surgery and even lung transplantation are performed. Influenza and pneumococcal pneumonia vaccinations are strongly recommended, because infections worsen COPD and increase risk of death. The principal way to prevent COPD is not to start smoking and to quit as soon as possible if you have already started.[47]

DEMENTIA

Dementia is not a specific disease but a condition in which brain function significantly declines to a degree that an individual has difficulty participating in work, home, or social functions. Although dementia becomes more common as people age, it is not a normal part of the aging process. Normal aging may include occasionally forgetting a name or where you left the car keys. Dementia-type symptoms that signify abnormal decline include forgetting the name of a close friend or family member, getting lost in a familiar neighborhood, or not remembering a recent event. Dementia, as a broad category, affects an estimated 7 percent of the population over the age of 65. Alzheimer's disease, the most common form of dementia, is the sixth leading cause of death in the United States.[48]

Forms of Dementia

The most common cause of dementia is Alzheimer's disease, which accounts for 60 to 80 percent of cases. Alzheimer's disease is due to a degeneration of nerve cells caused by the formation of plaques, abnormal accumulations of amyloid beta proteins and tau proteins, in areas of the brain. The risk of Alzheimer's increases with age; however, about 5 percent of cases occur prior to age 65 and are called "early onset."[49]

Vascular dementia accounts for another 5 to 10 percent of cases and is caused by cerebrovascular disease (ministrokes), impairing brain nerve cell function. Lewy body dementia is yet another type of dementia in which a different

(Maskot/Getty Images)

type of protein (called Lewy bodies after the physician who discovered the disease) are abnormally deposited in the brain and disrupt function.

Another category of dementia is a group called frontotemporal dementia. In this group of diseases, the frontal and temporal areas of the brain begin to atrophy or shrink. This form is rare but notable because it is the second most common form of dementia in people under 65. The usual age of onset is between 45 and 65 years of age. Frontotemporal dementia symptoms are often associated with socially inappropriate behavior or changes in personality. and thus it is often misdiagnosed as part of a psychiatric illness in early stages.[48,49,50,51]

Risk Factors, Diagnosis, and Treatment

Risk factors for dementia include a family history of dementia, repetitive head trauma, and high blood pressure or other cardiovascular diseases. Multiple genetic mutations have been identified as being associated with Alzheimer's and with frontotemporal dementia. Some of these are autosomal dominant (meaning there is a 50 percent risk of transmission to children), but most identified genetic mutations have a smaller risk of transmission.

Two of every three people incorrectly believe that normal aging causes dementia. This belief can lead to delays in evaluation and support. While it may be normal to occasionally forget someone's name or the details of a story, if someone is having trouble remembering names of close friends and family, struggling to complete accustomed tasks, getting lost or confused in what should be familiar places, or withdrawing from activities, it is good to have a conversation with the person and discuss visiting a health provider for evaluation. Memory and other brain function tests can determine whether cognitive declines are concerning. Laboratory tests and imaging with CT or MRI assist in diagnosis.

Some reversible medical conditions, such as the use or misuse of certain medications, thyroid abnormalities, brain tumors, and vitamin deficiencies, can cause mental confusion and are treatable. If the cause is determined to be vascular, control of cardiovascular risk factors can slow disease progress. While there are no specific treatments yet for Alzheimer's, Lewy body, or frontotemporal dementia, medications and behavior support measures can slow the process of dementia and enable people to live independently and safely for longer periods of time.[49,50,52,53]

PREVENTING CHRONIC DISEASES

As we learn more about the progressive nature of chronic diseases like cardiovascular disease, diabetes, and lung disease, the significance of early prevention becomes clearer. Adopting healthy lifestyle habits now, regardless of your age or current health status, is the best way to reduce your risk of developing chronic disease in the future. To assess your cardiovascular health, complete this chapter's Personal Health Portfolio activity.

Strategies for preventing chronic diseases are included throughout this chapter. Here is a quick review:

- Eat a heart-healthy diet.

- Maintain a healthy body weight.

- Don't smoke, and avoid secondhand smoke.

- Be physically active.

- Limit alcohol consumption.

- Maintain healthy blood pressure levels.

- Maintain healthy lipid levels.

- Maintain healthy blood glucose levels.

- Manage stress, and take care of your mental, emotional, and social health.

You Make the Call

Screening for Cardiovascular Disease in Athletes: How Much Is Enough?

Did you play sports in high school? Are you on a college team, or do you participate in intramural activities? Do you exercise vigorously on your own? If so, you should be aware that sudden cardiac arrest is the most common cause of death in athletes under age 35. Vigorous exercise is a trigger for lethal arrhythmias in those with unrecognized heart disease, typically congenital disease. On average, only 11 percent of athletes will survive a sudden cardiac arrest—a worse outcome than might be expected given their age and fitness level, and the fact that many of these events are witnessed. The low survival rates highlight the critical importance of early recognition and may be due to underlying congenital disease, the exertion at the time of arrest, or slow recognition by bystanders of what has happened.

The American Heart Association (AHA) recommends preparticipation screening of athletes, to include a medical history and a physical exam. However, whether these efforts are enough is a subject of debate.

In 1979, Italy started a national program that added electrocardiograms (ECGs) to the traditional screening. ECGs identified many asymptomatic athletes whose conditions would otherwise have gone unrecognized, and the incidence of sudden cardiac death among athletes in Italy has since dropped

Continued...

Concluded...

by 90 percent. The European Society of Cardiology and the International Olympic Committee thus adopted similar recommendations: screening ECG for athletes prior to participation in competitive sports.

If you played sports in high school, you may or may not have participated in a screening physical first. There is no national mandate in the United States to screen high school athletes, yet 65 percent of sudden deaths among athletes occur in high school students.

On the college level, there are no requirements for intramural sports teams or other school-affiliated teams, such as Ultimate Frisbee teams. The National College Athletic Association (NCAA) does mandate a pre-participation evaluation for all Division I, II, and III athletes. The evaluation includes a physical exam and a standardized 14-point screening by a health care provider to record an athlete's personal and family history. Findings suggestive of heart disease prompt further evaluation. The NCAA allows use of ECG screening but does not require it. This screening has limitations because 60 to 80 percent of athletes have no symptoms, many have no family history of CVD or don't know their family history, and results of physical exams are normal in many people with congenital heart problems.

Some health experts think the United States should add ECG screening as a national pre-participation requirement for high school and college athletes, pointing to the healthy young people whose lives would be saved. A prohibiting factor is cost: If national screening were adopted, an estimated 10 million young athletes would require screening at a theoretical cost of $2 billion a year, or approximately $330,000 for each athlete in whom cardiac disease is detected. Another problem is the estimated 10 percent of results that could be false positives—abnormal ECG findings in athletes who do not have underlying cardiac disease. These athletes would have to go through the stress of an additional workup and temporary disqualification from their sport. Evidence has shown, however, that with careful use of specific criteria, the false-positive rate can be significantly decreased.

Evidence continues to support the idea that ECG screening is more likely to identify cardiac conditions than the recommended history and physical. Additional ECG screening measures would save the lives of otherwise healthy young adults. What do you think? Is it time to require middle school, high school, and college athletes to have a screening ECG to evaluate for heart abnormalities that increase risk of sudden cardiac arrest or death?

Pros

- Because survival rates from sudden cardiac arrest are very low, prevention is critical.
- Although it may be expensive and result in some false positives, the ECG is a straightforward, noninvasive test, and further evaluation is done with another noninvasive test, the echocardiogram.
- Italy demonstrated the will to save lives by adding ECG screening to its other athletic screening requirements. If Italy can institute such screening, the United States should be able to do so, too.
- Cost should not be a factor when the lives of otherwise healthy young adults are at stake.

Cons

- Screening ECGs would yield some false positives, and those athletes may be unnecessarily sidelined from their sports while awaiting further evaluation.
- Because of its larger population and geographical size, the United States cannot do ECG screening with the same ease as Italy or other European countries. The United States does not have the infrastructure (staffing, finances) to support a national program of added ECG screening.
- The United States does not currently require even the traditional screening (personal history, family history, and physical exam). Thus, it is unrealistic to talk about adding an ECG requirement.

McGraw Hill connect

Sources: Maron, B. J., Levine, B. D., Washington, R. L., et al. (2015). Eligibility and disqualification recommendations for competitive athletes with cardiovascular abnormalities: Task Force 2: Preparticipation screening for cardiovascular disease in competitive athletes. A scientific statement from the American Heart Association and American College of Cardiology. *Circulation, 132,* e267–e272; Hainline, B., Drezner, J. A., Baggish, A., et al. (2016). Interassociation consensus statement on cardiovascular care of college student athletes. *Journal of the American College of Cardiology, 67*(25); Drezner, J. A., & Harmon, K. G. (2018). Cardiac arrest during competitive sports. *New England Journal of Medicine, 12;*378(15):1461; Peterson, D., Siebert, D., Kucera, K., Thomas, L., Maleszewski, J., et al. (2018). Etiology of sudden cardiac arrest and death in competitive athletes: A 2 year prospective surveillance study. *Clinical Journal of Sport Medicine.* doi:10.1097/JSM.0000000000000598; Winkelmann, Z. K., & Crossway, A. K. (2017). Optimal screening methods to detect cardiac disorders in athletes: An evidence-based review. *Journal of Athletic Training, 52*(12), 1168–1170.

In Review

What is cardiovascular disease?

The disease process underlying most forms of cardiovascular disease (CVD) is atherosclerosis, a condition in which the arteries become stiffened and narrowed and blood flow is restricted, causing heart attack, stroke, or peripheral vascular disease. A disturbance in the electrical signals controlling the heartbeat can cause an arrhythmia (disorganized beating) and sudden cardiac arrest. Other forms of CVD are hypertension (high blood pressure), congestive heart failure, heart valve disorders, rheumatic heart disease, congenital heart disease, and cardiomyopathy (disease of the heart muscle). A stroke occurs either when a blood vessel serving the brain is blocked or when a blood vessel in the brain ruptures.

What is diabetes?

Diabetes is the most common disorder of the endocrine or metabolic system, resulting in elevated blood glucose levels due to a disruption in the production or use of insulin. Type 1 diabetes typically starts in childhood, and Type 2 diabetes develops later and has genetic and lifestyle causes such as overweight and obesity. Without tight control and treatment, diabetes can lead to blindness, kidney failure, foot and leg amputations, and heart disease.

What is asthma?

Asthma is a condition in the lungs where inflammation and muscle spasm lead to narrowing of the airways and symptoms of difficulty breathing, wheezing, chest tightness, shortness of breath, and coughing. The symptoms any one person experiences with asthma can differ dramatically from the symptoms of another person. Common triggers include viral infections, pollution, tobacco, allergies, and exercise. Medications can control symptoms but do not cure the disease.

What is chronic obstructive pulmonary disease?

Chronic obstructive pulmonary disease (COPD) is a progressive destructive process in the lungs that tends to develop as people get older in response to a lifetime accumulation of exposure to lung irritants that damage the airways and alveoli. There are two main forms of COPD—chronic bronchitis and emphysema. The main risk factor for COPD is tobacco use or exposure to other lung irritants (such as secondhand smoke, air pollution, inhaled chemical or dust exposure). Symptoms often begin gradually and progress slowly. Medications can reduce symptoms but not cure the disease.

What is dementia?

Dementia is not a specific disease but a condition in which brain function significantly declines, to a degree that an individual has difficulty participating in work, home, or social functions. Although dementia becomes more common as people age, it is not a normal part of the aging process. Alzheimer's disease is the most common cause of dementia.

What are the best ways to protect against the diseases discussed in this chapter?

The four health behaviors—smoking status, healthy BMI, healthy diet, participation in physical activity—and three measurable factors—healthy levels of blood pressure, blood glucose, and total cholesterol—identified as being important for ideal cardiovascular health are key factors in reducing risk for *all* chronic diseases. Starting early and trying to maintain ideal cardiovascular health throughout life will protect against heart disease, stroke, chronic lung disease, and diabetes.

Personal Health Portfolio

Chapter 14   How "Heart Healthy" Are You?

Your behaviors, blood pressure, cholesterol levels, and family history are factors that determine your risk for cardio-vascular disease. Complete this assessment of the seven components of ideal cardiovascular health to find out what your risk is in each of these areas.

Part 1 Your Lifestyle

	Yes	No
1. Do you avoid tobacco smoking, or if you have smoked, did you quit at least a year ago?	Yes	No
2. Do you exercise at least 150 minutes at moderate intensity or 75 minutes at vigorous intensity each week?	Yes	No
3. Are you at a healthy body weight (as defined by a BMI between 18.5 and 24.9)?	Yes	No
4. How healthy is your diet?		
a. Are you in energy balance (not gaining or losing weight, unless appropriate based on BMI)?	Yes	No
b. Do you eat at least four to five servings of fruits and vegetables a day?	Yes	No
c. Do you eat at least two 3.5-oz servings of fish a week?	Yes	No
d. Do you eat at least three 1-oz servings of fiber-rich whole grains per day?	Yes	No
e. Is your sodium intake less than 1,500 mg per day?	Yes	No
f. Do you limit sugar-sweetened beverages to less than 450 calories per week?	Yes	No
g. Do you eat at least four servings of nuts, legumes, and seeds per week?	Yes	No
h. Do you limit servings of processed meats to two or fewer servings per week?	Yes	No
i. Do you limit saturated fat to less than 7 percent of total energy intake?	Yes	No

SCORING

Add up your number of "yes" answers and "no" answers. Congratulations for your "yes" answers! These are areas where you have developed strong patterns to promote cardiovascular health. Pay attention to your "no" answers. These are areas you should address now to promote general cardiovascular health.

_____ **"Yes" responses**

_____ **"No" responses**

Part 2 Clinical Parameters

If you do not have this information on hand, you may be able to obtain it by visiting your student health center or your primary care physician. A blood test will be necessary to determine your cholesterol levels.

	Yes	No	Don't know
1. Is your blood pressure < 120/80 mmHg?	Yes	No	Don't know
2. Is your total cholesterol < 200 mg/dl?	Yes	No	Don't know
3. Is your HDL cholesterol > 60 mg/dl?	Yes	No	Don't know
4. Is your fasting blood glucose (sugar) < 100 mg/dl?	Yes	No	Don't know

SCORING

Add up your number of "yes" answers and "no" answers. Congratulations again for any "yes" answers! These additional parameters promote cardiovascular health. "No" answers in this section mean you may have developed risk factors for cardiovascular disease already. It is even more important for you to adopt and maintain the heart-healthy behaviors listed in Part 1. You may also want to seek help from a health professional to explore other options that will help reduce your risk. If you didn't know the responses to these questions, have your blood pressure checked the next time you visit a health provider (and write down the numbers) and ask for a blood test to determine your cholesterol levels.

_____ **"Yes" responses**

_____ **"No" responses**

Part 3 Your Noncontrollable Factors

1. Do any of your first-degree relatives (mother, father, sister, brother, child) have a history of heart disease or stroke?	Yes	No
2. Do any of your first-degree relatives have a history of diabetes?	Yes	No
3. Do any of your first-degree relatives have a history of high blood pressure?	Yes	No
4. Do any of your first-degree relatives have a history of high cholesterol?	Yes	No

Any "yes" answers are red flags for your own health. If you haven't already, talk with your health provider about your family history. Health issues in family members can suggest a genetic predisposition to cardiovascular disease or risk factors. In addition, it can suggest patterns of behavior within your family of origin that increase risk.

CRITICAL THINKING QUESTIONS

1. Reflect on your responses to Part 1. What good lifestyle habits do you have? Where is there room for improvement? Are there ways you could incorporate change into your usual routines?

2. What are your unique characteristics that make it easy or difficult to practice heart-healthy behaviors? Consider such factors as acquired food tastes, cooking skills, money, physical attributes, or tobacco addiction.

3. What characteristics of your environment may be contributing to your behaviors? Consider your access to foods or exercise facilities, family and peer behaviors, campus policies, and other characteristics.

4. How might your family have influenced your own behavior patterns? Think about activity levels and food consumption patterns within your family. Think about where they live and what role their environment plays in their lives. Think about their occupations and hobbies—how do they impact your family members' lifestyle and habits?

5. Overall, how would you rate your cardiovascular health? Why?

6. Consider the relationship between risk factors for cardiovascular health and other chronic diseases. Do you see any risk factors for diabetes or lung disease in the assessment you just completed?

15 Cancer

Chris Parypa Photography/Shutterstock

Ever Wonder... | how where you live influences your cancer risk?

what cancer screening tests you or your parents should be getting?

whether someone who gets cancer can ever be fully cured?

Cancer is the second leading cause of death in the United States. In the past, people with cancer often hid their diagnosis; the word *cancer* was not used even in obituaries. Today, with greater understanding of this complex condition, the stigma has been reduced and cancer patients are diagnosed earlier. They have higher survival rates, better prospects for a cure, and more social support. Although there is still much to learn, there is cause for optimism.

The American Cancer Society (ACS) projected an estimated 1.8 million new cancer cases in 2020 and an estimated 606,520 deaths from cancer, about 1,660 per day. Cancer causes about 25 percent of all deaths in the United States, with lung cancer being the leading killer among both men and women. Combined, the four most common cancers—breast, lung, prostate, and colon—account for nearly half of all cancer deaths (Figure 15.1). In this chapter, we provide an overview of the many forms cancer takes and the steps you can follow to reduce your risk of developing this disease.[1]

WHAT IS CANCER?

Cancer is a condition characterized by the uncontrolled growth of cells. It develops from a single cell that goes awry, but a combination of events must occur before the cell turns into a tumor. The process by which this occurs is called *clonal growth,* the uncontrolled replication of a single cell that produces thousands of copies of itself. With 30 billion cells in a healthy person, the fact that one in three people develops cancer is not surprising; what is surprising is that two in three people do not.

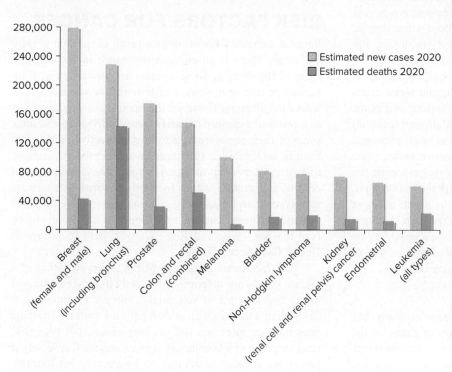

figure 15.1 **The 10 most commonly diagnosed cancers, by estimated new diagnoses and estimated deaths, 2020.**
Sources: American Cancer Society. (2020). *Cancer facts & figures 2020.* Atlanta, GA: American Cancer Society.

Healthy Cell Growth

Healthy cells have a complicated system of checks and balances that control cell growth and division. From the start, beginning with the single-celled fertilized egg, cells develop in contact with other cells, sending and receiving messages about how much space is available for growth. Healthy cells in solid tissues (all tissues except the blood) require the presence of neighboring cells. This tendency to stick together serves as a safety mechanism, discouraging cells from drifting off and starting to grow independently.

Healthy cells divide when needed to replace cells that have died or been sloughed off. Each time a cell divides, there is a possibility that a mutation, an error in DNA replication, will occur. Mutations are always occurring randomly, but the risk of mutations is increased by exposure to certain substances, such as tobacco smoke, radiation, and toxic chemicals. Certain mutations may start the cell on a path toward cancer.

Specific safety mechanisms are designed to correct genetic mutations and destroy cells with mutations. As one safety mechanism, enzymes within the nucleus of each cell scan the DNA as it replicates, looking for errors. If an error is detected, the enzyme repairs it, or the cell destroys itself. As another safety mechanism, cells are programmed to divide a certain number of times, and then they become incapable of further division. The immune system also helps watch for cells that are not growing normally and destroys them.

A special protective mechanism exists for **stem cells**. These are cells that do not differentiate into specific cell types (such as nerve cells, skin cells, bone cells) during prenatal development. Instead, they retain the ability to become different cell types, and they are capable of unlimited division. A small number of stem cells are present within most tissue types, where they are needed to replace lost or damaged cells.

Because stem cells, unlike regular cells, do not have a predetermined number of cell divisions, they pose a risk of cancer. As a safety mechanism, they are located deep within tissues, where they are protected from factors that increase the risk of genetic mutations, such as exposure to the sun, chemicals, and irritation.

Cancer Cell Growth

Cancer starts from a single cell that undergoes a critical genetic mutation, either as a result of an error in duplication or in

cancer
A condition characterized by the uncontrolled growth of cells.

stem cells
Undifferentiated cells capable of unlimited division that can give rise to specialized cells.

carcinogen
A cancer-causing substance or agent in the environment.

oncogene
A gene that drives a cell to grow and divide regardless of signals from surrounding cells.

tumor
A mass of extra tissue.

benign tumor
A tumor that grows slowly and is unlikely to spread.

malignant tumor
A tumor that is capable of invading surrounding tissue and spreading.

metastasis
A cancer that has spread from one part of the body to another.

carcinomas
Cancers that arise from epithelial tissue.

sarcomas
Cancers that originate in connective tissue.

leukemias
Cancers of the blood, originating in the bone marrow or the lymphatic system.

lymphomas
Cancers that originate in the lymph nodes or glands.

carcinogen
A cancer-causing substance or agent in the environment.

response to a **carcinogen** or radiation. This *initiating event* must occur in a location in the cell's DNA that alters the functioning of a growth-controlling safety mechanism and allows a cell to evade one of the restraints placed upon healthy cells. To become a cancer, however, it must escape all the control mechanisms. Usually, this process requires a series of 5 to 10 critical mutations within the cell's genetic material. It may take many years for these changes to progress to cancer, or they may never do so.

In time, perhaps a period of years, another mutation, such as one in an **oncogene**, a gene that drives cell growth regardless of signals from surrounding cells, may allow the cell line to divide forever rather than follow its preprogrammed number of divisions. A condition of cell overgrowth, called *hyperplasia,* develops at the site, and some cells may become abnormal, a condition called *dysplasia.* Eventually, a mass of extra tissue—a **tumor**—may develop.

A **benign tumor** grows slowly and is unlikely to spread. Benign tumors can be dangerous, however, if they grow in locations where they interfere with normal functioning and cannot be completely removed without destroying healthy tissue, as in the brain. A **malignant tumor** is capable of invading surrounding tissue and spreading. Malignant cells do not stick together as much as normal cells, and as the tumor grows, some cancer cells may break off, enter the lymphatic system or the bloodstream, and travel to nearby lymph nodes or to distant sites in the body. At a new site, the cancerous cell can grow and become a secondary tumor, or **metastasis**. When a cancer spreads from one part of the body to another, it is said to have *metastasized.*

Classifying Cancers

Cancers are classified according to the tissue in which they originate, called the *primary site.* If a cancer originates in the cells lining the colon, for example, it is considered colon cancer, even when it metastasizes to other, secondary sites. The most common sites of metastases are the brain, liver, and bone marrow.

When a cancer is still at its primary site, it is said to be *localized.* When it has metastasized, it is referred to as *invasive.* The greater the extent of metastasis, the poorer the *prognosis* (likely outcome).

Cancers are staged at the time of diagnosis—a process that helps guide treatment choices and predict prognosis. The stage of disease is a description of how far the cancer has spread. One common staging system uses five categories (stages 0–IV). Stage 0 is also called cancer in situ, an early cancer that is present only in the layer of cells where it began. Stage I cancers are generally small and localized. Stages II and III are locally advanced and may or may not involve local lymph nodes. Stage IV cancers have metastasized to distant sites.

Types of Cancer

Different tissues of the body have different risks for cancer, due in part to their different rates of cell division. Four broad types of cancer are distinguished, based on the type of tissue in which they originate. **Carcinomas** arise from *epithelial tissue,* which includes the skin, the lining of the intestines and body cavities, the surface of body organs, and the outer portions of the glands. Epithelial tissue is frequently shed and replaced. Eighty to 90 percent of all cancers originate in epithelial tissues—including most lung, colon, breast, and prostate cancers. **Sarcomas** originate in *connective tissue,* such as bone, tendon, cartilage, muscle, or fat tissues. **Leukemias** are cancers of the blood and originate in the bone marrow or the lymphatic system. **Lymphomas** originate in the lymph nodes or glands.

RISK FACTORS FOR CANCER

Because some cancers occur as a result of random genetic mutations, there is an element of chance in the development of the disease. Some cancers are associated with inherited genetic mutations, and thus risk is also associated with family history. However, the majority of cancers occur as a result of exposure to **carcinogens**. Individuals can limit some of their exposure by adopting protective lifestyle behaviors, such as using sunscreen, avoiding tobacco, and getting vaccinations, but other measures are beyond individual control and require action by local authorities, the larger society, or even the global community, as in the case of air pollution, climate change, and access to health insurance (see the box "Who's at Risk? Cancer: Risk in Delays in Health Care Access").

Risk factors are associated with a higher incidence of a disease but do not determine absolutely that the disease will occur. For example, if you smoke, you are 25 times more likely than a nonsmoker to develop lung cancer. Smoking does not guarantee you will get lung cancer, but your risk, relative to that of a nonsmoker, is *much* greater. Conversely, if you do not smoke, you still may get lung cancer, but your risk is much lower than that of a smoker. The most significant risk factor for most cancers is age. Advancing age increases the risk for cancer; 80 percent of all cancers occur in people aged 55 or older.[1]

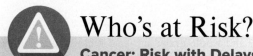

Who's at Risk?

Cancer: Risk with Delays in Health Care Access

Cancer affects people of all identities, but not everyone has the same risk. Differences occur in exposure to risks and in access to screening, diagnosis, and treatment. For cancers in which screening has been shown to improve survival, for example, delays in screening lead to delays in diagnosis and reduced survival with treatment.

Many factors affect who does or does not get cancer screening. Let's consider some characteristics of groups of people and their rates of screening. When you see a difference, you should always ask why some groups would have lower rates.

Take a look at the accompanying graph. Which groups have the lowest rates of screening? Consider the

socioecological model. How might the different levels of the model (individual, interpersonal, community, policy) affect the way people access cancer screening? How does your educational status or sexual identity influence your access to health insurance? What factors might influence new immigrants' access to cancer screening? What is the role of language, culture, stigma, and discrimination in these differences?

Given that delayed screening clearly leads to lower survival from cancer, is it ethical to have such inequity in rates of screening? How might this information help you plan interventions to improve screening for all people?

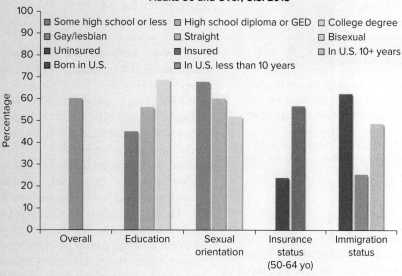

Colorectal Cancer Screening by Flexible Sigmoidoscopy or Colonoscopy (%), Adults 50 and Over, U.S. 2015

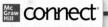

Source: White, A., Thompson, T., White, M., et al. (2017). Cancer screening test use—United States, 2015. *Morbidity and Mortality Weekly Report, 66*(8), 201–206.

Family History

A family history of cancer increases an individual's risk. Examining your family health tree can help you understand whether you have an increased risk for any cancers (see Chapter 1). Family history does alter some cancer screening recommendations, such as when to start screening, how frequently to repeat it, and what types of tests to have performed. However, inherited genes are not the entire story. Only 5 percent of all cancers are due to an inherited genetic alteration. Most result from damage to genes caused by environmental exposures and lifestyle behaviors that accumulate during our lifetime. Social determinants of health—including socioeconomic and cultural factors—are also influential.

Lifestyle Factors

Some environmental agents, called carcinogens, have a direct impact on a cell, causing an initial genetic alteration that can

lead to cancer. Other agents, called *cancer promoters,* have a less direct effect, enhancing the possibility that a cancer will develop if an initiating event has already occurred in a cell.

Tobacco Use Tobacco use is the leading preventable cause of cancer in the United States. It is responsible for 30 percent of all cancer deaths and 80 percent of lung cancer deaths. Second-hand smoke also increases risk of cancers. Risk is directly related to duration and level of exposure to tobacco—the earlier people start smoking, the more tobacco they use; the longer they use it, the greater the risk.[2]

Tobacco use increases the risk of cancers of the mouth, throat, lung, and esophagus by directly exposing them to the chemicals in tobacco smoke. It also increases the risk of other cancers—including bladder, pancreas, stomach, liver, kidney, and bone marrow cancers—because other chemicals from tobacco are absorbed into the bloodstream and travel to distant sites. "Light" and "low tar" cigarettes and cigars have

■ A family history of cancer can indicate that a person may have a genetic predisposition to the disease, especially if the cancer occurred in a first-degree relative (like a parent) at an early age. After Angelina Jolie learned she had inherited a defective *BRCA1* gene, which is linked to breast and ovarian cancer, she had a preventive double mastectomy in 2013. Her mother, grandmother, and aunt had all died of breast or ovarian cancer. *(Joe Seer/Shutterstock)*

the same level of risk as "regular" cigarettes; it is no longer legal to use these misleading terms in cigarette labels. Cigars, pipes, and waterpipes (hookahs) all increase risk for cancers of the mouth, throat, and lungs. Smokeless tobacco products increase risk for oral, esophageal, and pancreatic cancers.

E-cigarette use or vaping has skyrocketed, especially among youth and young adults. Some studies have shown a lower level of exposure to toxic chemicals from e-cigarettes than from regular cigarettes, but the long-term cancer risks are yet to be determined. The trend is concerning given that young adults who use e-cigarettes are much more likely to become addicted to nicotine and use regular cigarettes in the future. In addition, vaping is now associated with a nationwide outbreak of severe lung disease and death in young adults.[2,3,4]

Nutrition and Physical Activity   Nutrition and activity level are also contributors to cancer risk. If population-level tobacco use continues to decrease, they have the potential to become the most important factors. Part of their effect is due to their influence on rates of overweight and obesity (discussed next), but part is due to their direct physiological impacts. Diets rich in foods such as fruits, vegetables, and whole grains are high in antioxidants and other phytochemicals and decrease the risk of many cancers, including lung, colon rectal, breast, stomach, and ovarian cancers. (See Chapter 5 for more on how antioxidants protect against cell damage.) Fruits,

vegetables, and whole grains are also high in dietary fiber, which reduces risk of colon cancer and possibly of breast, rectal, pharyngeal, and stomach cancers. The microbiome appears to play a role in cancer prevention and cancer treatment, and fiber-rich plant foods support a healthy microbiome.[5,6]

To date, there is no clear evidence that taking supplements of individual antioxidants reduces cancer risk as much as simply eating healthy whole foods. In fact, high-dose supplements of beta-carotene (an antioxidant found in fruits and vegetables) and vitamin E (an antioxidant and essential fat-soluble vitamin) have been shown to increase the risk of developing some cancers. Given the fact that only 4.3 percent of college students report eating the recommended five or more servings of fruits and vegetables per day, dietary change is an important opportunity for cancer prevention. To encourage people to eat fruits and vegetables, the National Cancer Institute has partnered with the nonprofit Produce for Better Health Foundation in the "Fruits and Veggies—More Matters" public health initiative.[7,8]

Certain foods and food preparation techniques may also increase the risk of cancer. Cooking meats at high temperatures, such as when grilling, frying, or broiling, may produce chemicals that increase the risk of colon cancer. Processed meats, which are high in nitrites, appear to increase risk for colorectal, prostate, and stomach cancers. However, food irradiation, a practice commonly used with meats and spices to reduce risk of infectious disease contamination, has not been shown to increase cancer risk. Diets low in red meats, processed meats, and animal products reduce risk.[2,9]

Physical activity is directly linked to a reduction in risk of breast, colon, endometrial, and prostate cancers, though its effect on other cancers is less clear. The benefits of exercise on cancer risk go beyond its impact on weight. Exercise improves body functions; for example, it increases the rate at which food travels through the intestines, thus reducing the bowel lining's exposure to potential carcinogens. Physical activity in adolescence is strongly associated with decreased cancer risk. Appropriate exercise after a cancer diagnosis and during treatment can also help people feel better, eat better, and recover faster. Decreasing sedentary activity, such as sitting, is also an important way to reduce cancer risk.[2,9]

Overweight and Obesity   Overweight and obesity increase the risk of developing many types of cancer as well as the risk of dying from cancer once it occurs. Overweight and obesity not only make it harder to detect cancers at an early stage but also delay diagnosis and may make treatment more difficult.

Although it is not clear how fat cells contribute to an increased risk of cancer, several pathways are possible. Fat cells produce hormones, some of which (such as estrogen) are linked to cancer. Fat cells may trigger an immune and inflammatory reaction, alter insulin production, or release proteins that trigger cell growth, all of which may contribute to the development of cancer. Fat cells may also accumulate more environmental toxins. Maintaining a healthy BMI throughout your lifespan is another way to reduce your cancer risk.[2,9]

Alcohol Consumption and Cancer Risk Alcohol consumption, especially in the early 20s, is associated with increased risk of many forms of cancer. Consumption of more than one alcoholic drink a day for women and two drinks a day for men increases the risk of cancers of the mouth, throat, esophagus, liver, breast, and possibly pancreas. Regular intake of just a few drinks per week may increase risk of breast cancer. Alcohol and tobacco used together are associated with a greater risk than either one alone. Total alcohol consumption, not the type of alcohol, is what matters; wine, beer, and hard liquor all increase risk.[2,9]

Social and Economic Factors

Although the number of new cases of cancer and the number of deaths from cancer are reported by gender, age, race, and ethnicity, more complex factors such as income, education, geographical location, housing, and cultural beliefs are believed to be stronger indicators of risk. In addition, researchers are increasingly looking at the role of discrimination in general, and of racism in particular (see the box "Starting the Conversation: Does Racism Increase Cancer Risk?"). These socioeconomic factors, or *social determinants of health,* influence risk behaviors (such as tobacco use), exposure to environmental carcinogens (such as housing proximity to highways or industrial sites), access to health care, and quality of health care.

People who are unemployed, who are poor, who live in rural areas, or who are underinsured or uninsured are at greater risk of developing cancer and of dying from it. They may have less access to safe areas for physical activity and less access to nutritious foods. They may live in areas where transportation is limited by either poor road upkeep or lack of public transportation routes. They may not be able to afford cancer screening tests, or they may not have access to physicians or clinics that provide screening. Getting recommended tests in a timely way increases the likelihood that a cancer will be detected at an earlier and more treatable stage. When cancers are detected at later stages, chances of survival are lower.[2,10,11]

Environmental Factors

Some cancers are caused by exposure to carcinogens in the environment. Some of these environmental factors are more easily avoided than others.

Sunlight and Other Sources of Ultraviolet Radiation Ultraviolet (UV) radiation, the rays of energy that come from the sun (and from sun lamps and tanning beds), can damage DNA, but it doesn't have enough power to penetrate deeply into the body. Two types of UV come from the sun (and sun lamps and tanning beds): ultraviolet B (UVB) and ultraviolet

■ Being poor and living in a rural locale are risk factors for cancer. This low-income family living in the desert has less access to well-paying jobs, health insurance, health information, and health care services, including cancer screening tests, than a more affluent family living in an urban environment.
(MickyWiswedel/Getty Images)

A (UVA). UVB rays are more likely to cause sunburns and have long been associated with skin cancers. UVA rays tend to pass more deeply into the skin and are now believed to cause skin cancer and premature aging of the skin.

The risk of the two milder forms of skin cancer, basal cell and squamous cell carcinomas, is cumulative; the more UV exposure over the years, the higher the risk. The risk of melanoma, the most dangerous form of skin cancer, is related to the timing and number of sunburns. Sunburns that occur during childhood seem to be particularly dangerous, and the more sunburns, the greater the risk. Indoor tanning poses as great a risk of skin cancer as outdoor sunbathing. Every time you get a tan (whether indoors or outdoors), you increase your risk for skin aging, wrinkles, age spots, melanoma, and basal and squamous cell cancer. Many college campuses have indoor tanning facilities or relationships with tanning salons, prompting an initiative for universities to cut such ties and increase education about the risks of indoor tanning.[12,13]

Reducing exposure to UV radiation is important. You can accomplish this by wearing long-sleeved clothing, hats, and sunglasses when outside for prolonged periods. Seeking shade, avoiding sun exposure during peak intensity between 10:00 a.m. and 2:00 p.m., and wearing sunscreen also help. The use of tanning beds should be avoided. Some states have even gone so far as to ban their use by anyone under the age of 18, given the cancer risk.[2]

Other Forms of Radiation Ionizing radiation, radiation with enough energy to interact with an atom and cause it to become charged, is present throughout our environment. Ionizing radiation comes from natural sources, such as radon (a naturally occurring radioactive gas in the ground in certain regions of the world), cosmic rays, and release from soil and

Starting the Conversation

Does Racism Increase Cancer Risk?

Race is a social construct that has played a role throughout the history of the United States. Racism—discrimination against a person or persons based on membership in a particular racial or ethnic group—is known to limit social determinants of health such as economic, educational, housing, and political opportunity. Thus racism influences individuals' health outcomes.

Consider the role racism might play in the fact that Blacks have the highest death rate from cancer of any racial/ethnic group in the United States. Historical structural factors, such as Jim Crow laws, redlining, and discriminatory sentencing laws, have led race to become strongly associated with socioeconomic status in the United States. Twenty-one percent of Blacks live below the poverty line, compared to only 9 percent of non-Hispanic whites. Low socioeconomic status reduces access to healthy foods and physical activity and increases the likelihood of using tobacco-related products, often due to aggressive marketing and the location of less healthy products in low-income communities.

Low socioeconomic status also increases the likelihood of living in environments with greater environmental exposures. Low-income housing is more likely to be located near highways, industrial areas, and other sources of carcinogen exposures.

Finally, the experience of perceived discrimination has a direct physiological impact, reducing immune function (as discussed in Chapter 2) and contributing to lower levels of trust in the health care system, with the potential for delayed health screening or evaluation of symptoms.

Q: Do you think the differences in cancer mortality between Blacks and non-Hispanic whites is due only to disproportionate rates of poverty as a result of historical factors?

Q: What do you think will improve cancer outcomes for racial minority groups in the United States?

Sources: Ramraj, C., Shahidi, F. V., Darity, W., Kawachi, I., Zuberi, D., & Siddiqi, A. (2016). Equally inequitable? A cross-national comparative study of racial health inequalities in the United States and Canada. *Social Science & Medicine, 161,* 19–26; Black, L. L., Johnson, R., & VanHoose, L. (2015). The relationship between perceived racism/discrimination and health among Black American women: A review of the literature from 2003–2013. *J Racial Ethnic Health Disparities, 2*(1), 11–20; Landrine, H., Corral, I., Lee, J. G. L., Efird, J. T., Hall, M. B., & Bess, J. J. (2017). Residential segregation and racial cancer disparities: A systematic review. *Journal of Racial and Ethnic Health Disparities, 4,* 1195–1205; American Cancer Society. (2019). *Cancer facts and figures for African-Americans 2019–2021.* Atlanta, GA: American Cancer Society.

rocks. In addition, there are human-made sources resulting from mining, nuclear energy, medical X-rays, nuclear medicine, tobacco products, building materials, and television and computer screens. We are all constantly exposed to low levels of ionizing radiation from these sources.

Ionizing radiation is known to increase risk for cancers. Residents in some parts of North America are exposed to radon in their homes, particularly homes with basements. In regions known to have high levels of radon in the ground, testing of homes is routinely recommended. A ventilation system can be installed if the level of radon is too high.

At times, humans (and other animals) are exposed to high doses of radiation—such as nuclear fallout in the context of war or nuclear bomb testing, or accidental release from nuclear power plants. Survivors of nuclear bomb explosions and tests have high levels of cancer, particularly of the bone marrow and thyroid. The nuclear reactors used in power plants have not been shown to emit enough ionizing radiation to place surrounding communities at risk. However, accidental releases of radioactive gases from the nuclear power plants in Chernobyl, Ukraine, in 1986 and in Fukushima, Japan, in 2011 contaminated the area for miles around them and are

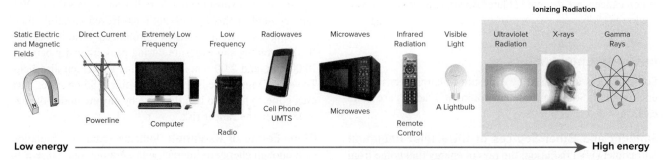

■ The electromagnetic spectrum *(Computer): Ryan McVay/Photodisc/Getty Images; (Radio): Mahantesh C Morabad/Alamy Stock Photo; (Cell Phone): Thomas Northcut/Photodisc/Getty Images; (Microwave): Steve Wisbauer/Photodisc/Getty Images; (Remote Control): Thomas Northcut/Getty Images; (Sun): Dennis McColeman/Getty Images; (X-ray): PASIEKA/Science Photo Library/Getty Images*

responsible for cancers in people exposed to the resulting radiation and radioactive debris.[14]

In medical settings, radiation is used in the treatment of cancers and in diagnostic imaging. High-dose radiation for cancer treatment has been shown to increase the risk of leukemia and thyroid and breast cancers years later. Lower levels of radiation are used in diagnostic X-rays and CT scans, but exposure can accumulate in people who need many tests. To reduce risk, the number of medical procedures using radiation should be minimized as much as possible, especially in children.[14,15]

In contrast, exposure to nonionizing radiation, including visible light, infrared radiation, microwaves, and radio waves, has not been considered a health risk. However, in 2011, the International Agency for Research on Cancer (IARC) listed radio frequency electromagnetic fields (EMF) as a "possible human carcinogen." Cell phone use is the most common exposure to this type of nonionizing radiation.

The question whether cell phones are safe is first a question about whether nonionizing radiation can have harmful effects on humans. We certainly know that the higher frequency, nonionizing radiation used in microwaves generates high-level heat and can damage tissue. The nonionizing radiation of cell phones has a lower frequency, with substantially less intensity than that of microwaves. So the next question is whether long-term exposure to radiation at the radiofrequency level—such as that emitted from cell phones—can cause problems. This is where the data get tricky.

Many studies have investigated whether there is a link between cell phones and human health. An increasing amount of evidence points to a connection. Animal studies and laboratory studies have shown possible mechanisms that produce risk of DNA damage. Brain tumors appear to be slightly more common on the same side of the head on which a cell phone is used, especially after 10 or more years of use. In addition, studies since 2011 increasingly show a higher risk of breast, testis, leukemia, and thyroid cancers associated with increased cell phone use. While the issue is still controversial, it may be wise to keep your cell phone further away from your body when possible.[15,16,17,18]

Chemical and Physical Carcinogens Many substances in the environment have been associated with different forms of cancer. Environmental carcinogens include metals (such as arsenic, mercury, and lead), natural fibers (such as asbestos and silica), combustion by-products (including motor vehicle exhaust, diesel exhaust, and soot), solvents (benzene, toluene), polychlorinated biphenyls (PCBs), and pesticides. Your exposure to environmental carcinogens varies depending on where you live, where you work, what your hobbies and recreational activities are, and what you eat, among other factors. Exposures are higher and rates of cancer are higher in cities, farming states, and industrial areas and near hazardous waste sites. Individuals have less control over environmental exposures, and national and international policies and safety standards are necessary to reduce risk. The U.S. Environmental Protection Agency (EPA) is the federal agency that works with tribal, state, and local agencies to gather and analyze scientific evidence, develop regulations, and ensure compliance and enforcement.[19,20]

Infectious Agents There is strong evidence that infections cause cancer, and more than 15 percent of cancer cases worldwide are attributed to infections. Multiple viruses are known to cause cancer. Human papillomavirus (HPV) is linked to cancers of the cervix, anus, vagina, penis, mouth, and, more recently, lungs and skin. The hepatitis B and C viruses are associated with liver cancer. Certain strains of Epstein-Barr virus, which causes mononucleosis, are associated with Hodgkin's lymphoma, non-Hodgkin's lymphoma, and some stomach cancers. Human immunodeficiency virus (HIV) suppresses the immune system and allows several types of cancer to develop. Data are starting to show, too, that cytomegalovirus, a virus in the herpes family, may be associated with breast cancer.[2,21,22]

The only bacterium definitively linked to cancer thus far is *Helicobacter pylori,* which causes a chronic irritation of the stomach lining and is associated with stomach ulcers and an increased risk of stomach cancer. It is thought to be the cause of one in three cancers of the stomach. Chronic inflammation from other bacteria and the toxins they produce may increase risk for the development of other cancers.[2]

CANCER SCREENING

The earlier a cancer can be identified, the more successful treatment will be. For some cancers, **screening tests** can identify disease in a precancerous stage or early, before someone has symptoms, when it is more treatable. An *ideal* screening test would always detect precursors or cancer at an early, treatable stage and never miss a case (give a false negative) or cause alarm when there is no precancer or cancer (give a false positive).

Unfortunately, no screening test meets the ideal. Thus, recommendations for screening tests are complicated. They have to balance the risk of getting a test (cost, physical complications of tests, and psychological complications from false positives) against the benefits (prevention by removal of precancers or improved prognosis from earlier diagnosis). The first step in cancer screening is to identify your personal risk—are you at higher risk due to patterns in your family history, your behavior, or your age? These factors feed into the recommendations made by health professionals, as you will see when we discuss the screening guidelines for specific cancers in the "Common Cancers" section.

No screening recommendations exist for some cancers, including ovarian cancers, because to date no test has been shown to improve detection and survival without

screening test
A test given to a large group of people who have no symptoms of the disease being tested for to identify a smaller group of people who have cancer, precancer, or a significantly higher risk for a specific disease or condition.

Public Health Is Personal

Changing Screening Test Guidelines

The Pap test, widely used since the 1940s, is credited with a dramatic reduction in the number of deaths from cervical cancer, which was once the leading cause of cancer death for women in the United States. Doctors performing Pap tests look for abnormal cell changes in the cervix, and if any are found, the cells are removed. Although the cause of cervical cancer was not known when screening first began, the Pap test provided a highly effective screening tool for precancerous changes we now know are caused by the human papillomavirus (HPV).

Earlier cervical cancer screening guidelines recommended all people with a cervix have a Pap test starting at age 18 or within 3 years of becoming sexually active, but no later than age 21 (given that exposure to HPV is related to onset of sexual activity). These guidelines recommended that the test, if normal, be repeated every year until age 30, and then every 2 to 3 years.

However, scientists, health care professionals, and public health officials came to the conclusion that Pap tests were being done too often and causing doctors to overdiagnose and overtreat precancerous symptoms. Anxious patients experienced needless emotional, physical, and financial pain after they opted for invasive and costly treatments. It turned out that most HPV precancerous changes at the time of early infection would actually resolve without treatment. The risk was for only a small percentage of women who developed a chronic infection. Thus, most of the treatments were unnecessary and even potentially harmful.

Multiple organizations issued revised guidelines in 2012, delaying the onset of screening until age 21 and decreasing the recommended frequency of Pap testing. In 2020, the American Cancer Society revised again. The new guidelines recommend that women start screening for cervical cancer at age 25 with "primary HPV testing" (an HPV test that screens for the range of cancer-causing HPV types). Women should repeat HPV testing every five years through age 65 as the preferred option. If approved "primary HPV testing" is not available, women should receive a Pap test every three years or co-testing with a Pap test and more limited HPV test every 5 years.

In 2018, screening recommendations for breast and testicular cancers changed. The American Cancer Society (ACS) states that for healthy women without symptoms, there is no clear benefit to regular breast self-examination or breast examination by a health provider. Thus, regular breast exams are no longer recommended. However, women should be familiar with how their breasts look and feel and report any changes to a health provider.

Because of the possibility of unnecessary biopsies and other treatment, there is no consensus about when women at average risk of breast cancer should start getting mammograms (low-dose X-rays of the breast) and how often they should get them. The ACS recommends women have annual mammograms between ages 45 and 55 (and can discuss starting at age 40 with provider) and then, after age 55, women may switch to every other year. The American College of Obstetricians and Gynecologists differs slightly, recommending that women be offered mammograms starting at age 40 and have a screening mammogram every 1 to 2 years between age 50 and 75. After age 75, they may decide to discontinue screening. The U.S. Preventive Services Task Force supports screening every other year between the ages of 50 and 74. All agree that the decision about when to start getting mammograms is up to the woman and her health provider.

For testicular self-exams, the ACS no longer has a recommendation. Self-examination has not been studied enough to know whether it is helpful or harmful. Most testicular cancers are identified when a man notices a lump on the testicle, but it is not clear whether the previously recommended monthly self-checks led to earlier detection and improved survival.

Public policy guidelines like these are intended to promote consistent practices by health providers and educators across the country, based on the latest and best research. Findings from medical research directly affect what happens today when people visit health providers.

Sources: U.S. Preventive Services Task Force. (2019). *Final recommendation statement: Cervical cancer: Screening.* Retrieved from https://www.uspreventiveservicestaskforce.org/Page/Document/RecommendationStatementFinal/cervical-cancer-screening2; American College of Obstetricians and Gynecologists. (2019). Breast cancer risk assessment and screening in average-risk women. Retrieved from https://www.acog.org/Clinical-Guidance-and-Publications/Practice-Bulletins/Committee-on-Practice-Bulletins-Gynecology/Breast-Cancer-Risk-Assessment-and-Screening-in-Average-Risk-Women; American Cancer Society. (2019). *Cancer prevention & early detection facts & figures 2019-2020.* Atlanta, GA: American Cancer Society; U.S. Preventive Services Task Force. (2018). *Final update summary: Breast cancer: Screening.* Retrieved from https://www.uspreventiveservicestaskforce.org/Page/Document/UpdateSummaryFinal/breast-cancer-screening1; American Cancer Society. (n.d.). Can testicular cancer be found early? Retrieved from https://www.cancer.org/cancer/testicular-cancer/detection-diagnosis-staging/detection.html; Fontham, E.T.H., Wolf, A.M.D. et al. (2020) Cervical cancer screening for individuals at average risk: 2020 guideline update from the American Cancer Society. CA: A Cancer Journal for Clinicians. https://doi.org/10.3322/caac.21628.

increasing harm. Similarly, as the box "Public Health Is Personal: Changing Screening Test Guidelines" explains, screening recommendations for some kinds of cancer have changed over the years.

Genetic screening can also be done to assess cancer risk. At this time, it is being reserved for members of high-risk families, that is, families with multiple members with cancer. Complete the Personal Health Portfolio for this chapter to assess your personal risk and protective factors.

CANCER TREATMENTS

Surgery is the oldest treatment for cancer; newer options include chemotherapy, radiation, biological therapies, bone marrow transplantation, and gene therapy.

Surgery

Surgery remains a mainstay in the diagnosis and treatment of cancer. When a cancer is detected early and is small and localized, surgery can cure it, as when an in situ cancer of the breast is removed via a lumpectomy. Sometimes an organ affected by cancer can be removed surgically without threatening life, as in the case of prostate or testicular cancer. Certain cancers are unlikely to spread widely, such as a basal cell carcinoma, and surgery often cures these cancers as well. If a cancer has spread, surgery may still be performed as part of the treatment.

Chemotherapy

Chemotherapy is a drug treatment administered to the entire body to kill cancer cells. The benefit of chemotherapy is that it can both work locally and also kill cancer cells that may have escaped from the local site to the blood, lymph system, or other part of the body. More than 50 chemotherapy medicines have been developed; different combinations are used for different cancers. All chemotherapeutic drugs operate by a similar mechanism—they interfere with rapid cell division. Because cancer cells divide more rapidly than normal cells, they are more vulnerable than healthy cells to destruction by chemotherapy.

Other normal tissues that divide rapidly are also harmed by chemotherapy, including the hair, stomach lining, and white blood cells. Timing and dosage must be carefully adjusted so that the drugs kill cancer cells but do not damage normal cells beyond repair.

Radiation

Radiation causes damage to cells by altering their DNA; when high doses are directed to a specific area, it can destroy cancer cells with minimal damage to surrounding tissues. Radiation is a local treatment that can be used before or after surgery or in conjunction with chemotherapy. It can also be used to control pain in patients with cancer.

Biological Therapies

Biological therapies enhance the immune system's ability to fight cancer—an approach called **immunotherapy**—or reduce the side effects of chemotherapy. One kind of immunotherapy is a vaccine that can be developed after a person has been diagnosed with a cancer. Administering the vaccine can boost the person's immune response to the cancer and may help prevent a recurrence. Vaccines for several types of cancers, including melanoma and cancers of the breast, colon, ovary, and prostate, are in use or development. Vaccines can also be used to prevent cancer, as in the case of the HPV and the hepatitis B vaccines.

Immunotherapy can be used as a way to transport chemotherapy medications directly to the cancer cells. Nanoparticles can be bioengineered to carry and deliver medications directly to the tumor, in theory protecting healthy cells and increasing the dose of medication delivered to the cancer. Medications such as interleukin-2, herceptin, and interferon-alpha all boost a person's immune response and enhance the body's ability to target cancer cells more aggressively. Sometimes these medications can be used alone, or they can be administered along with more traditional chemotherapy regimens.

■ Actress Brittany Daniel, known for roles on *The Game, Sweet Valley High,* and *Joe Dirt,* is a cancer survivor. She was diagnosed with non-Hodgkin's lymphoma at age 38 after experiencing back pain, night sweats, and flulike symptoms. *(DFree/Shutterstock)*

Because both the diagnosis of cancer and cancer treatment can increase baseline stress, immunotherapy also recognizes the roles of stress and the immune response. Stress management in the form of social support, physical activity, and help with anxiety and other mental illness can support the body's immune system. Prolonged cancer survival is associated with good support systems, stress management, and mental well-being.[23,24,25,26]

immunotherapy
Administration of drugs or other substances that enhance the ability of the immune system to fight cancer.

■ Support groups help cancer patients cope with stress. *(SDI Productions/Getty Images)*

Bone Marrow Transplantation

Bone marrow transplantation was initially used for cancer of the white blood cells (leukemia and lymphoma). Now it is sometimes used for other cancers as well, when healthy bone marrow cells have been killed by high doses of chemotherapy. This treatment is controversial for some types of cancer where research has not shown a clear increase in survival after treatment.

Gene Therapy and Genetic Testing

Gene therapy is an innovative treatment that alters the patient's own immune cells to fight tumor cells. It has the potential to improve cancer treatment in several ways. Mutated genes could be replaced with functional genes, decreasing the risk that cancer will occur or stopping a cancer that has started to develop. Or genes could be inserted into immune cells to increase their ability to fight cancer cells. In 2017, the FDA approved the first gene therapy to be used against leukemia when patients have failed to respond to other treatments, and as of 2019 three gene therapies have been approved.[27,28]

Genetic testing may also become important in cancer treatment. *Precision medicine* is a new term to describe the potential future use of genetic testing to identify the specific genetic changes in an individual's cancer, which can then guide treatment. Precision medicine is expected to allow more accurate predictions of how a cancer will behave, which chemotherapy drugs will work best, and which patients will benefit most from chemotherapy. In addition, new drugs are being designed, developed, and tested to target the genetic mutation instead of focusing on the type of cancer as traditional treatment has done.[29]

Clinical Trials

Studies designed by researchers and physicians to test new drugs and treatment regimens are known as *clinical trials.* Patients with cancer enroll in clinical trials both in the hopes of finding a better treatment for their own cancer and in the interest of furthering cancer research in general. Once enrolled in the study, participants are usually randomly assigned to either a group receiving a new drug or a group receiving the standard treatment. In very rare situations, usually when there is no known effective treatment, one group of patients may receive a placebo (a sugar pill that has no effect). If cancer is advancing in a patient who is receiving the placebo, he or she may be switched to the group receiving the drug. For more information about new and ongoing clinical trials, visit the website of the National Cancer Institute.

Complementary and Integrative Medicine

The role of complementary and integrative medicine in cancer treatment is growing (see Chapter 17 for greater detail). People with cancer use complementary and integrative practices at higher rates than the general population, usually with the goal of improving their quality of life by reducing the side effects of cancer or cancer treatment, speeding recovery, improving pain control, and increasing chances of survival. At present, data do not support replacing standard treatments with alternative practices because none have been shown to *cure* cancers. In addition, some of these practices can interfere with chemotherapy; their use should be discussed with the patient's treatment team.[30,31]

Ginger and acupuncture have been shown to reduce treatment-associated nausea and vomiting; acupuncture may reduce cancer pain or surgical pain. Massage, yoga, and mindfulness meditation techniques can help relieve stress, anxiety, depression, and pain; massage and yoga may reduce cancer-related fatigue; meditation and mindfulness practices may boost immune function. Qigong may reduce pain, improve quality of life, and increase physical activity. Hypnosis may reduce pain, nausea, and vomiting.[30,31]

Most herbal, vitamin, and mineral supplements are backed by limited evidence showing benefits, and there is concern they may interact with cancer treatments. They should be used with caution and under the guidance of a cancer treatment doctor. For some cancers, high-dose vitamin C (given intravenously) has been shown to improve quality of life and reduce side effects from chemotherapy, but in other cancers, it has a worsening effect.[32] In particular, vitamin E and beta carotene supplements are associated with increased risk of prostate and lung cancer, respectively. Instead, experts recommend a healthy, balanced diet.

COMMON CANCERS

Since 1930, changes have occurred in the rates of different cancers in the United States. Evaluating the long-term trends highlights the levels of the socioecological model: individual behavior, cultural changes, prevention efforts, and the environment. For example, stomach cancer rates have decreased dramatically since 1930, primarily as a result of improvements in food storage and preparation and advances in sanitation. Lung cancer rates increased dramatically in the 1960s, plateaued in the late 1990s, and have been decreasing ever since. These changes were due to changing rates of smoking and smoking cessation. Rates of smoking increased among women about 20 to 30 years after they increased in men, and there was a corresponding delayed increase in lung cancer among women. Uterine cancer (which includes cervical cancer) went from being the leading cause of cancer-related death in women to the sixth, due in part to screening tests and vaccination. We next review some common cancers.

Breast Cancer

The most commonly diagnosed non-skin cancer in women is breast cancer. It is the second leading cause of cancer death in women. Breast cancer occurs in men as well, but it is much less common. For example, an estimated 276,480 cases were expected in women and 2,620 in men in the United States in 2019.[1]

Risk Factors The strongest risk factors for breast cancer are older age and being female. Other factors associated with an increased risk of breast cancer include early onset of menarche (first menstruation), late onset of menopause, and family history of breast cancer in a first-degree relative (biologic parent or sibling). A mutation in the *BRCA1* or *BRCA2* gene is also associated with a substantial increase in risk. The specific mutations are very rare in the general population, but if you have a strong family history of breast or ovarian cancer, it can be a red flag to consider genetic screening. Although inherited susceptibility accounts for only 5 to 10 percent of all breast cancer cases, having these genes confers a lifetime risk of developing the disease ranging from 45 to 75 percent.[1,33]

Behavioral ways you can reduce your risk for breast cancer include having children before the age of 30 (obviously many other factors go into this decision), avoiding obesity and tobacco, not taking hormone replacements after menopause, and drinking fewer than two alcoholic beverages a day. Breastfeeding, engaging in moderate or vigorous exercise, and maintaining a healthy body weight are all associated with decreased risk.[1]

Signs and Symptoms The earliest stages of breast cancer have no symptoms (something you feel) but may have signs (something that can be seen or detected) that can be identified by a mammogram. In later cancer stages, symptoms may include a persistent lump; swelling, redness, or bumpiness of the skin; and discharge or a change in nipple appearance. Breast pain or tenderness is common in women without cancer and is usually not a cause for concern; more likely explanations are hormonal changes, infection, or breast cysts, which are rarely cancerous.

Screening and Detection Breast cancer can be detected at an early stage by a mammogram. The effectiveness of mammography in detecting cancer depends on several factors, including the size of the cancer, the density of the breasts, and the skills of the radiologist. Although mammograms cannot detect all cancers, they have been shown to decrease the number of women who die from breast cancer due to early detection.

The start date and frequency of mammograms have been a source of confusion and conflicting recommendations. The benefit of a mammogram is early detection. The downside is identification of changes in the breast that are not cancer but require further evaluation and cause distress. These "false positives" are more common in younger women. The ACS's current recommendations for women with average risk are as follows:

- Women aged 40 to 44 have the option to start annual mammograms.

- Women aged 45 to 54 should receive mammograms every year.

- Women aged 55 and older may switch to mammograms every 2 years or continue with yearly screenings.

- Screening should continue for as long as a woman is in good health and is expected to live for 10 years or longer.

The "pink ribbon" is widely used as a symbol to raise awareness about breast cancer. *(Oksana Desiatkina/123RF)*

- For some women at high risk—because of family history or certain other factors—screening with an MRI in addition to mammograms may be started at age 30.[1]

There is insufficient evidence to recommend annual clinical breast examination, and the U.S. Preventive Task Force recommends against health providers teaching breast self-examination. There is no evidence to show clear benefits to either practice, so the ACS no longer recommends them either. However, screening guidelines are only for asymptomatic people with average risk. Women should be familiar with the way their breasts normally look and feel, and if they notice changes, they should report that to a health provider for evaluation.[34]

In younger women, a lump is much more likely to be caused by a cyst or a benign tumor called a fibroadenoma. Pain or redness is more likely due to hormone changes or infection than cancer. Ultrasound and MRI are sometimes used to help determine whether a lump or abnormality is cancerous; they are also used for screening in high-risk women.

Treatment Surgery remains a first line of treatment for breast cancer, either a *lumpectomy* (removal of the tumor and some surrounding breast tissue) or a *mastectomy* (removal of the entire breast). One or more lymph nodes under the arm on the affected side are usually tested to determine whether the cancer has spread from the breast. Radiation, chemotherapy, and hormonal-inhibition therapy are frequently used in the treatment of breast cancer.

The 5-year survival rate for all stages of breast cancer is 90 percent. For cancer that is localized (no lymph node involvement), it is 99 percent; for cancer that has spread regionally (only local lymph node involvement), it is 86 percent; and for cancer that has spread to distant locations, it is 27 percent.[1]

Prostate Cancer

The most commonly diagnosed cancer in men and the second most common cause of cancer death in men is prostate cancer. The incidence of prostate cancer is significantly higher among Black men than among white men, and the death rates for Black men are twice as high as those for white men.[1]

Risk Factors The strongest risk factor for prostate cancer is age. More than 60 percent of prostate cancer cases are diagnosed in men aged 65 and older. Other risk factors include a family history of prostate cancer, African ancestry, smoking, and possibly having a high animal-fat or full-fat dairy diet. The risk of dying from prostate cancer appears to increase with excess body weight. An emphasis on a Mediterranean diet—high in tomatoes and olive oil—appears to reduce risk, likely because it is high in lycopenes, an antioxidant found in red and pink fruits and vegetables.[1,35]

Signs and Symptoms In its early stages, prostate cancer usually has no signs or symptoms. Advanced prostate cancer

bronchoscopy
A procedure in which a fiber-optic device is inserted into the lungs to allow the health care provider to examine lung tissue for signs of cancer.

can be associated with pain or difficulty when urinating, pain in the pelvic region, or blood in the urine. These symptoms can also be caused by more common noncancerous conditions, such as benign enlargement of the prostate gland and bladder infections.

Screening and Detection   Two screening tests are available to detect prostate cancer. One is a *digital rectal exam,* in which a health provider inserts a gloved finger into the rectum and feels for lumps in the prostate gland. The other is the *prostate-specific antigen (PSA) test,* a blood test that detects levels of a substance made by the prostate (prostate-specific antigen). The levels can elevate when certain conditions are present, including benign prostate enlargement, infection, and prostate cancer. If the PSA level is high, a rectal ultrasound and prostate biopsy can be performed to assess and diagnose the cause.

At present, no health organization recommends routine screening for prostate cancer. Instead, the recommendation is for people to discuss screening with their health provider starting at age 50 if at average risk, or at age 45 if at higher risk (or at age 40 if several close family members have prostate cancer). Some fast-growing prostate cancers do not elevate PSA levels, causing false-negative test results. Some prostate cancers give an elevated PSA but grow so slowly that, left untreated, they would not actually lead to an earlier death. However, once these cancers have been identified, treatment can sometimes cause more harm than if they were left untreated (or undiagnosed).[1]

Treatment   Treatment for prostate cancer depends on the stage of the cancer and the man's age and other health conditions. In its early stages, prostate cancer is either monitored with "watchful waiting" or treated with surgery (removal of the prostate gland) and radiation, sometimes in combination with chemotherapy, and hormonal medication, which blocks the effects of testosterone and can cause tumors to shrink. Later stages are treated with chemotherapy, radiation, and hormonal medication. Radiation is sometimes administered by the implantation of radioactive seeds, which destroy cancer tissue and leave normal prostate tissue intact. Hormone blockers and immunotherapy, in the form of a vaccine, can be used in advanced prostate cancer.[1]

The 5-year survival rate for all stages of prostate cancer is 98 percent. Ninety percent of prostate cancer is diagnosed at an early stage when 5-year survival is nearly 100 percent.[1]

Lung Cancer

Lung cancer is the second most commonly diagnosed cancer and the leading cause of cancer death for both men and women in the United States. With an estimated 228,820 new cases and 135,720 deaths in 2020, lung cancer accounts for about 25 percent of all cancer deaths. The incidence of lung cancer and lung cancer death is decreasing for men and women, due

■ Prostate cancer has a high rate of survival. Acclaimed actor Sir Ian McKellen was diagnosed with prostate cancer almost a decade ago and has chosen the course of "watchful waiting" instead of surgery or radiation. He told the press, "When you have got it, you monitor it and you have to be careful it doesn't spread. But if it is contained in the prostate, it's no big deal." *(Charles Norfleet/FilmMagic/Getty Images)*

primarily to declines in smoking rates. However, the rates of decline have been been greater for men than for women.[1]

Risk Factors   The leading risk factor for lung cancer is cigarette smoking. Other tobacco products in any form, including cigars and pipes, also increase risk. Other risk factors include exposures to carcinogenic chemicals, arsenic, radon, asbestos, radiation, air pollution, and environmental (secondhand) tobacco smoke. Many of these factors interact in smokers to compound risk. In addition, dietary supplements containing beta-carotene, a form of vitamin A, further increase the risk in people who smoke. Reducing risk factors, especially exposure to tobacco smoke and environmental tobacco smoke, is the first line of defense against this disease.

Signs and Symptoms   Signs and symptoms of lung cancer include coughing, blood-streaked sputum, chest pain, difficulty breathing, and recurrent lung infections. Unfortunately, symptoms do not appear in most people until the disease is advanced.

Screening and Detection   There is no recommended screening for the general population. Men and women aged 55 to 74 who are in good health and at high risk for lung cancer due to being current or former smokers with a 30-pack/year history should talk to a health provider about low-dose CT screening.[1] If symptoms suggest lung cancer and an abnormality is found on an X-ray or CT scan, the diagnosis is confirmed by a biopsy, performed either by surgery or by **bronchoscopy**.

Treatment   People with small tumors that can be removed surgically have the best prognosis. For more advanced lung cancers or for people who are unable to tolerate surgery, radiation or a combination of radiation and chemotherapy is used. If the cancer has spread to distant sites, radiation and chemotherapy can be used for *palliative care* (care provided to give temporary relief of symptoms but not to cure the cancer). The 5-year survival rate is 19 percent. If cancer is detected early, survival increases to 57 percent, but unfortunately detection at an early stage occurs only 16 percent of the time.[1]

Colon and Rectal Cancer

The third leading cause of cancer diagnosis and cancer death in men and women is colorectal cancer. During the 1990s, the overall incidence of colorectal cancer declined in the United States, along with the number of deaths from the disease. The decrease is believed to be due to improved screening, detection, and removal of **colon polyps** before they become cancer. However, while overall rates of diagnosis of colorectal cancer are decreasing, rates of diagnosis and deaths in people under the age of 55 have actually been increasing since 2004. There is no clear explanation for this.[1,36]

Risk Factors   Despite the concerning trend of increased cases in younger populations, age remains the strongest risk factor for colorectal cancer. The majority of colorectal cancers are diagnosed in people over age 50. A personal or family history of colon polyps or inflammatory bowel disease also increases risk, as does a family history of colorectal cancer, especially in a first-degree relative. Modifiable factors associated with an increased risk of colorectal cancer include smoking, moderate to heavy alcohol use, obesity, physical inactivity, a diet high in fat or red or processed meat, and inadequate amounts of fruits, vegetables, and whole-grain fibers. Regular use of aspirin may reduce colorectal cancer risk but increases the risk for other health issues, discussed in Chapter 14.[1]

Signs and Symptoms   Warning signs of colorectal cancer include a change in bowel movements, change in stool size or shape, pain in the abdomen, and blood in the stool. The signs do not usually occur until the disease is fairly advanced.

Screening and Detection   Screening tests can enhance early detection of polyps or cancer. Four techniques allow "visualization" of the colon. In a **flexible sigmoidoscopy**, a thin, flexible fiber-optic tube is inserted into the rectum and moved through the lower third of the colon. In a **colonoscopy**, a

colon polyps
Growths in the colon that may progress to colon cancer.

flexible sigmoidoscopy
A procedure in which a fiber-optic device is inserted in the colon to allow the health care provider to examine the lower third of the colon for polyps or cancer.

colonoscopy
A procedure in which a fiber-optic device is inserted in the colon to allow the health care provider to examine the entire colon for polyps or cancer.

double-contrast barium enema
A test for colon polyps or cancer in which contrast material is inserted into the colon and X-rays are taken of the abdomen, revealing alterations in the lining of the colon if polyps or cancer is present.

CT colonography
A screening test for colon polyps or cancer using a CT scanner.

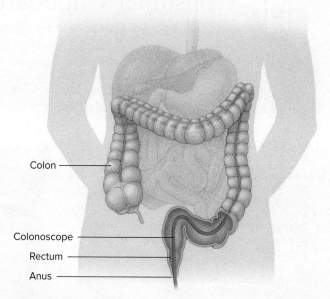

figure 15.2   Colon.
A colonoscopy allows the entire colon to be examined and facilitates the removal of growths, such as polyps, that may become cancerous.
Source: Fahey, T. (2015). *Fit & well: Core concepts and labs in physical fitness and wellness* (11th ed.). New York, NY: McGraw-Hill Education.

longer scope is used, and the entire colon is viewed (Figure 15.2). If a polyp is found, it can be biopsied or removed during the procedure. In a **double-contrast barium enema**, the colon is partially filled with a contrast material and then X-rays are taken. A colon cancer or polyp will alter the lining of the colon and can be seen. In **CT colonography** (or virtual colonoscopy), a CT scanner is used to take multiple pictures of the colon and can detect, but not remove, polyps or cancer.[37,38]

Other tests screen for colon cancer but are not as good at detecting polyps. These include the fecal occult blood test, the stool immunochemical test, and the stool DNA test. The first two screen for trace amounts of blood, which can signal a cancer or a bleeding polyp. The DNA test looks for changes in DNA known to be related to colon cancer.

The ACS recently changed its guideline recommendation and recommends that people of average risk start colorectal cancer screening at age 45. The U.S. Preventive Task Force is currently reviewing its recommendations but continues, at present, to recommend starting at age 50 for people of average risk. For people with higher than average risk (who have a close family member with colon cancer or polyps, for example), earlier and more frequent screening with colonoscopy is usually recommended.[1,39] Per the ACS, beginning at age 45, both men and women at *average risk* should receive screening with one of the following:

- Colonoscopy every 10 years, or

- Flexible sigmoidoscopy *or* CT colonography (virtual colonoscopy) every 5 years, or

- Fecal immunochemical test (FIT) every year or fecal occult blood test (FOBT) every year, or

- Stool DNA test every 3 years

Consumer Clipboard

Sunscreen and Other Sun Protection Products

Sun exposure is the most preventable risk factor for skin cancers. Sunscreens can reduce the damaging effects of UV radiation, but they need to protect you against UVA and UVB exposure, both of which cause skin cancer. UVA penetrates the skin more deeply than UVB and causes the changes associated with aging, such as wrinkles, skin sagging, and age spots. UVB exposure causes sunburns and skin damage. UVA can penetrate through windows, whereas UVB cannot.

Look for the SPF (sun protective factor or sunburn protective factor) number.
SPF indicates the amount of time you can stay in the sun without burning compared to how long you could stay if you weren't wearing the sunscreen. An SPF of 30 means you can stay out in the sun 30 times longer than you could without sunscreen before a sunburn would occur. SPF of 15 or greater can claim to reduce skin cancer and early aging but the American Academy of Dermatology recommends use of SPF 30 or greater.

Look for "broad spectrum" on the label.
A sunscreen may be labeled broad spectrum only if it provides protection against UVA and UVB radiation. Ingredients such as titanium dioxide, zinc oxide, Mexoryl, and Helioplex reduce UVA exposure.

Look for a sunscreen that is "water resistant."
Water resistance labeling tells you how long you can expect to get protection while swimming or sweating; 40 or 80 minutes is standard.

(Ed Endicott/Alamy Stock Photo)

Apply sunscreen liberally to all sun-exposed areas.
Most people do not apply enough sunscreen. An average-sized adult in a swimsuit needs about 1 ounce, or a shot glass, of sunscreen for one application. If applied properly, you could easily use a whole bottle of sunscreen in one day at the beach or pool. Avoid sunscreen powders and sprays.

Avoid combination products unless you really need them.
Combination products, such as sunscreen and insect repellent, reduce the effect of SPF by up to one-third. When using a combination product, use one with a higher SPF and reapply it more frequently.

Reapply early and often, as directed on the bottle.
Sunscreen should be applied at least 20 to 30 minutes before going outside—it takes that long for sunscreen to be absorbed. It should also be reapplied frequently, at least every two hours and after swimming or sweating. Apply even on cloudy days or when behind glass, such as in a car—80 percent of UVA rays still get through.

Don't rely on sunscreen alone.
Consider it your last defense. Decrease UV exposure by limiting time in the sun and wearing protective clothing. The protectiveness of clothing varies. Hats typically offer an SPF between 3 and 6; summer-weight clothing has an SPF of about 6.5; newer sun-protective clothing can have an SPF of up to 30+.

Source: The American Academy of Dermatology (2018). Sunscreen facts. Retrieved from https://www.aad.org/media/stats/prevention-and-care/sunscreen-faqs

---

All positive tests should be followed up with colonoscopy.[1]

Treatment Surgery is the most common treatment for colon and rectal cancer; it can cure the cancer if it has not spread. Chemotherapy and/or radiation is added if the cancer is large or has spread to other areas. The 5-year survival rate is 64 percent, although if colon cancer is detected at a localized stage, the 5-year survival rate is 90 percent.[1]

Skin Cancers

The three forms of skin cancer are basal cell carcinoma, squamous cell carcinoma, and melanoma. Basal cell and squamous cell cancers are common and not always reported in health records, and thus it is difficult to estimate how often they are diagnosed. The most recent estimate suggests at least 5.4 million cases of basal cell and squamous cell cancers occur each year in the United States. Most of these are curable with surgical removal, although both types can be disfiguring and, if ignored, sometimes fatal. Melanoma is a less common form of skin cancer with an estimated 100,350 new cases in 2020, but it is the cause of the majority of the estimated 6,850 skin cancer deaths. Skin cancers occur in all racial and ethnic groups, but they are more common in people with lighter skin color.[1]

All forms of skin cancers are linked directly to ultraviolet light exposure—both UVA and UVB. The most effective way to reduce risk for skin cancer is to limit UV exposure, both from the sun and from UV lights in tanning salons. To limit UV exposure from the sun, in decreasing order of importance, stay out of the sun during midday (10:00 a.m. to 2:00 p.m.), wear protective clothing (including a hat to shade the face and neck, long sleeves, and long pants), use a broad-spectrum sunscreen with a **sun protective factor (SPF)** of 30 or higher (see the box "Consumer Clipboard: Sunscreen and Other Sun Protection Products"), and wear sunglasses that offer UV protection. Be extra careful around snow, sand, and water; they all reflect the sun's rays and increase risk.

sun protective factor (SPF)
A measure of the degree to which a sunscreen protects the skin from damaging UV radiation from the sun.

Life Stories

Maggie: A Case of Skin Cancer

Maggie had just started graduate school when she noticed a mole on the back of her calf that seemed different. She had lots of moles, but this one was darker than the others, and the edges were irregular. She wondered whether she should get it checked, but her classes, teaching assistant responsibilities, new apartment, and new friends all got in the way of her making an appointment at the student health center.

Maggie grew up in southern California and had spent a lot of her childhood outside. As a kid, she was on her school swim team and played tennis. As a teenager, she and her friends went to the beach almost every weekend during the summer. Sometimes they used sunscreen and sometimes they didn't. One time, Maggie got such a bad sunburn on her back that her mother took her to the doctor, who shook his head looking at the open blisters weeping down her back.

In college, Maggie occasionally went to a local tanning salon during the spring when she wanted to start wearing shorts and a bathing suit. Several of her friends went, too, and all of them acquired what they considered a healthy looking tan while other students retained their winter pallor. Maggie heard warnings about tanning, but she liked the look.

A month after she first noticed the mole on her calf, Maggie saw that it had gotten larger and had some red and purple coloring in it. She looked up moles and skin cancer on the Internet and felt alarmed enough by what she read to make an appointment at the health center to get it checked. The doctor agreed that it looked a bit different and said she wanted to remove it and do a biopsy. The mole was removed easily and sent for pathology.

A week later, Maggie received a call from the doctor, saying that the mole was in fact cancerous, a melanoma. Maggie was shocked and could hardly understand what the doctor was saying, but she did hear that the cancer was caught at an early stage and the procedure had completely removed it. The doctor wanted her to come back for a follow-up appointment, to remove extra skin around the area and make sure that there were no remaining cancer cells, and to check her other moles. As she hung up the phone, Maggie felt a mixture of concern and relief, and she resolved to take better care of her skin in the future.

- Why do you think Maggie continued going to the tanning salon even though she had heard warnings about the dangers? Have you done things that you knew could put your health at risk? What was your thought process in making those choices?

- What kinds of information or education would be more effective in deterring people from making unhealthy choices or in encouraging them to make healthy choices?

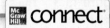

Tanning beds and sun lamps should be avoided. Parents should be particularly vigilant about protecting their children from the sun, and babies under 6 months of age should be kept out of the sun altogether. See "You Make the Call: What Do You Do with Conflicting Health Recommendations?" for a discussion of vitamin D and reduction in sun exposure.[2,40]

Melanoma Because it is capable of spreading quickly to almost any part of the body, melanoma is a particularly dangerous form of cancer. Rates of melanoma have increased rapidly over the past 30 years.

Risk Factors The risk of melanoma is greatest for people with a personal history of melanoma, a large number of moles (especially those that are large or unusual in shape or color), or a family member with melanoma (see the box "Life Stories: Maggie: A Case of Skin Cancer"). The risk is greater in people with fair skin and sun sensitivity (a tendency to burn easily). The rate of melanoma in whites is significantly higher than in people of color, although melanoma does occur in people of color. Although it can occur on any part of the body, melanoma is directly related to sun exposure, especially intermittent, acute UV exposure, as from sunlight (sunburns) or UV light in tanning salons.

Exposure during childhood or adolescence may be particularly dangerous.[1]

Signs and Symptoms Melanomas usually develop in pigmented, or dark, areas on the skin. Signs suggestive of melanoma are changes in a mole: a sudden darkening or change in color, spread of color outward into previously normal skin, an irregular border, pain, itchiness, bleeding, or crusting.

Screening and Detection Early detection of skin cancer is usually the result of individuals' monitoring their own skin and visiting a health care provider for evaluation of any changes or progressive growth (see Figure 15.3). The ACS and U.S. Preventive Task Force do not have a recommendation for routine skin screening by a health provider. Anyone with new or changing growths or itchy or nonhealing changes on the skin should have it evaluated by a health provider.[1]

Treatment Treatment for melanoma begins with surgically excising (cutting out) and doing a biopsy of any suspicious lesions. If melanoma is confirmed, a larger area of surrounding skin is removed, which improves the chance of survival. Chemotherapy and immunotherapy can be added for advanced stages. The overall 5-year survival rate for melanoma is 92 percent; if the melanoma is diagnosed at an early stage, the 5-year survival rate is 99 percent.[1]

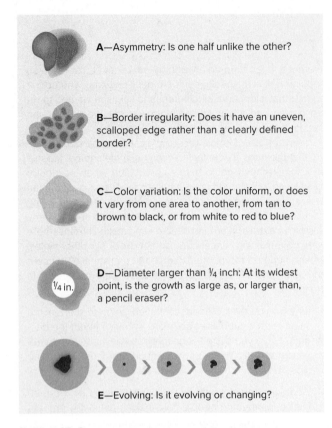

A—Asymmetry: Is one half unlike the other?

B—Border irregularity: Does it have an uneven, scalloped edge rather than a clearly defined border?

C—Color variation: Is the color uniform, or does it vary from one area to another, from tan to brown to black, or from white to red to blue?

D—Diameter larger than ¼ inch: At its widest point, is the growth as large as, or larger than, a pencil eraser?

¼ in.

E—Evolving: Is it evolving or changing?

figure 15.3   **The ABCDE evaluation of moles for melanoma.**
Source: American Academy of Dermatology. (2018). What to look for: The ABCDEs of melanoma. Retrieved from https://www.aad.org/public/spot-skin-cancer/learn-about-skin-cancer/detect/what-to-look-for

Basal Cell and Squamous Cell Carcinomas   Sun-exposed areas of the body are susceptible to basal cell and squamous cell cancers.

Risk   People at high risk include those with fair skin; blonde, red, or light brown hair; blue, green, or hazel eyes; and freckles and moles. Other risk factors are cumulative sun exposure and age, with rates increasing after age 50. However, both basal cell and squamous cell carcinomas are becoming more common among younger people.

Signs and Symptoms   The signs of a basal cell cancer include new skin growth; a raised, domelike lesion with a pearl-like edge or border; or a sore that bleeds and scabs but never heals completely. The signs of a squamous cell cancer include a red, scaly area that does not go away; a sore that bleeds and does not heal; or a raised, crusty sore. Squamous cell cancers often develop from a precancerous spot called an actinic keratosis, a red, rough spot that develops in a sun-exposed area.

Screening and Detection   Early detection of basal and squamous cell cancers relies on monitoring the skin and having any persistent changes evaluated. Again, there are no guidelines for screening examinations but people should monitor for changes in their skin.

Treatment   Treatment usually consists of local removal and destruction of the cancer by surgery, heat, or freezing; radiation therapy is sometimes an option.

Lymphoma

Cancers that originate in the lymph system, part of the body's immune system, are called lymphomas. There are two main types: Hodgkin's lymphoma (about 10 percent of all lymphomas) and non-Hodgkin's lymphoma (about 90 percent). Lymphomas can start almost anywhere because the lymph system exists throughout the body (Figure 15.4). Rates of lymphoma have been slowly declining since the 1970s. Non-Hodgkin's lymphoma is more common in older populations, with an average age at diagnosis in the 60s. Hodgkin's lymphoma has two peaks of occurrence: in the adolescent/young adult years and at older ages.[1]

Risk Factors   Factors that increase risk for lymphoma include infections, medications, and genetic changes that weaken the immune system. Medications to treat autoimmune diseases or to reduce the risk of rejection after an organ transplant can increase risk for lymphoma. HIV infection is associated with an increase in lymphoma risk. Radiation, herbicides, insecticides, and some chemical exposures also increase risk. The bacterium *H. pylori* increases risk for stomach lymphoma, and Epstein-Barr virus increases risk for some lymphoma subtypes.[1]

■ Khloe Kardashian talks openly about having skin cancer on her back. She advocates for the use of sunscreen and other measures to reduce skin cancer risk. *(DFree/Shutterstock)*

Common Cancers in Young Adults

Cancer in young adults is uncommon. However, cancers of the reproductive systems and leukemia, while not among the most frequent kinds of cancers, are reviewed here because they occur at higher frequency in young people. Oral cancers are also included because behaviors that can increase their risk are especially common among young people.

Cervical Cancer The incidence of cervical cancer and the number of related deaths have declined since the 1930s as a result of improved detection and treatment of precursor lesions. Vaccination for HPV is expected to further reduce incidence and mortality.

Risk As described in Chapter 13, most cervical cancer is caused by infection with certain strains of the human papillomavirus. Although HPV infection is common in women, the majority of women never develop cervical cancer. Persistent infection and progression to cancer are influenced by other factors, such as tobacco use, immunosuppression, number of births, early sexual activity, multiple sex partners, socioeconomic status, and nutritional status. Vaccines for HPV are available and reduce the risk of infection, as described in Chapter 13.

Signs and Symptoms In its early stages, cervical cancer usually does not cause any symptoms. Warning signs of more advanced cancer include abnormal vaginal discharge and abnormal vaginal bleeding. Pain in the pelvic region can be a late sign of cervical cancer.

Screening and Detection Early detection through the Pap test has significantly reduced the rates of cervical cancer and mortality. A small sample of cells is collected from the cervix, placed on a slide or into a liquid suspension, processed, and then examined under the microscope to detect cells that may be abnormal. Pap tests are good but not perfect, occasionally giving either a false-negative or false-positive result. HPV tests can identify high-risk HPV strains and can show whether someone has an ongoing HPV infection. New guidelines released in 2020 are as follows:

- Women 25 to 65: Primary HPV testing (with a specifically approved test to detect cancer-causing HPVs) every 5 years
- If "primary HPV testing" is not available: Pap every 3 years, or co-testing (a Pap test and HPV testing) every 5 years.
- Women over 65: if no history of previous abnormal Paps, screening may be stopped.[1,41]

The new guidelines are transitional because not all areas have access to the new "primary HPV tests." When the advanced testing is not available, a Pap test or a combination of Pap and the previous version of HPV test is considered acceptable but should be phased out as possible, leading to the recommendation to delay onset of screening to age 25. Although HPV infection is very common in young sexually active women, most clear the infection within 18 to 24 months. Identification of HPV in these cases increases anxiety but does not alter

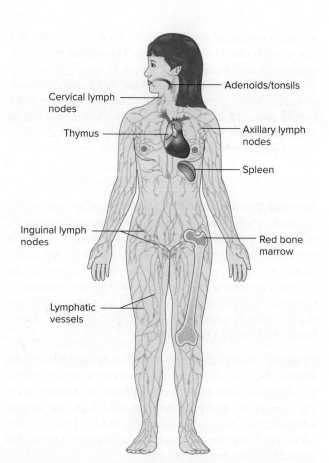

figure 15.4 The lymph system.
Structures include the lymph nodes and lymph vessels, the adenoids/tonsils, the thymus gland, the spleen, and the bone marrow. Clusters of lymph nodes can occur anywhere along the lymphatic vessels. Prominent areas include the neck (cervical lymph nodes), armpits (axillary lymph nodes), and groin (inguinal lymph nodes).

Signs and Symptoms Symptoms of lymphoma depend on where it originates. A swollen lymph node is a common presentation, but the majority of swollen lymph nodes are not due to lymphoma. If the lymphoma originates in the thymus, it can cause a cough or shortness of breath; in the abdomen, it can cause swelling, pain, or loss of appetite; in the tonsils, it can cause a persistent sore throat. Other general symptoms associated with lymphoma include weight loss, fever, drenching night sweats, fatigue, and severe itchiness.

Screening and Detection There is no recommended screening test for people without symptoms. If someone has symptoms as described earlier, diagnosis is made by a biopsy of the swollen lymph node or other tissue. Imaging studies such as chest X-rays, CT scans, and MRIs are important to assessing whether and how far the lymphoma has spread.

Treatment Treatment often consists of a combination of surgery, chemotherapy, and radiation and can sometimes include immunotherapy (to boost the immune system) or stem cell transplant. The 5-year survival rates for Hodgkin's and non-Hodgkin's lymphoma are 87 and 72 percent, respectively.[1]

treatment or monitoring. Screening start time and intervals are different for women with a history of cervical cancer, HIV, or other conditions that weaken the immune system.

Treatment   Treatment for cervical cancer removes or destroys precursor cells. Invasive cervical cancer (cancer that has spread) is treated with a combination of surgery, local radiation, and chemotherapy. The 5-year survival is 66 percent overall, but 92 percent if the cancer is localized at the time of diagnosis, which highlights the importance of screening.[1]

Uterine Cancer

Also called *endometrial cancer,* uterine cancer usually develops in the endometrium, the lining of the uterus. Uterine cancer is diagnosed more often in white women than in Black women, but the death rate among Black women is nearly twice the rate among white women. Black women tend to have more advanced cancer when they are diagnosed, perhaps as a result of having less access to health care and other environmental factors, including discrimination.

Risk Factors   The risk for uterine cancer is related to a woman's exposure to estrogen, so factors that increase estrogen—such as obesity and estrogen replacement therapy without progesterone—increase risk. Other factors associated with increased risk include diabetes, young age at menarche, late-onset menopause, irregular ovulation, and infrequent periods. Pregnancy, intrauterine devices, oral contraceptives, and exercise reduce the risk of uterine cancer.

Signs and Symptoms   Warning signs of uterine cancer include abnormal uterine bleeding (spotting between periods or spotting after menopause), pelvic pain, and low back pain. Pain is usually a late sign of uterine cancer.

Screening and Detection   There is no routine screening test recommended for asymptomatic women. An endometrial biopsy (sampling of the uterine lining) is recommended for women who experience vaginal bleeding or spotting after menopause and usually detects uterine cancer at an early stage.

Treatment   If uterine cancer is diagnosed, a *hysterectomy*—surgical removal of the uterus—is usually performed. Depending on the stage of cancer, other treatment methods may also be used, including radiation, chemotherapy, and hormonal therapy. Overall, the 5-year survival rate is 84 percent for white women and 62 percent for Black women, a significant racial disparity that once more highlights the importance of understanding what drives differences in racial risk exposures and health care access.[1]

Ovarian Cancer

The leading gynecological cause of cancer death and the fifth overall cause of cancer death in women is ovarian cancer. Ovarian cancer has a low rate of survival because most cases are not diagnosed until they have spread beyond the ovaries. In the 15 percent of women diagnosed early, the survival rate is 92 percent. However, the overall 5-year survival rate is 48 percent.[1]

Risk Factors   The strongest risk factor is a family history of breast, ovarian, or colon cancer in a first-degree relative.

About 20 percent of ovarian cancers are familial, with most linked to the *BRCA1* or *BRCA2* gene. The ovarian cancer risk increases from 0.6 percent to between 17 and 39 percent for women with either of these mutations. Risk is also increased in women with a personal history of breast, colon, or endometrial cancer. Tobacco use and overweight increase risk as well. Factors that reduce risk include the use of oral contraceptive pills, pregnancy, and breastfeeding. Women with the *BRCA1* or *BRCA2* may consider more aggressive measures, including removal of the ovaries and Fallopian tubes.[1,33]

Signs and Symptoms   The early stages of ovarian cancer have few signs or symptoms. At later stages, a woman may notice swelling of the abdomen, bloating, or a vague pain in the lower abdomen. No screening test has been shown to decrease mortality, so currently none is recommended for women with average risk. However, several tests continue to be evaluated (a blood test, CA-125, and ultrasound). A screen to increase early detection would be beneficial, given the improved survival with early diagnosis.[42,43]

Treatment   Treatment for ovarian cancer depends on the stage at diagnosis. Typically, all or part of the ovaries, uterus, and Fallopian tubes are surgically removed, and lymph nodes are biopsied to determine whether the cancer has spread. Chemotherapy and radiation usually follow. Treatment options currently under investigation include vaccinations, targeted drugs, and immunotherapy.[1]

Testicular Cancer

Although testicular cancer accounts for only 1 percent of all cancers in men, it is the most common malignancy in men aged 20 to 34. The incidence of testicular cancer has nearly doubled worldwide over the past 40 years, and an estimated 9,610 cases will be diagnosed and an estimated 440 will die from testicular cancer in 2020. Treatment is generally very effective such that, regardless of stage at the time of diagnosis, it is usually curable. In the United States, testicular cancer occurs nearly five times more often in white men than in Black men. Rates for men of Hispanic, Asian, and Native American backgrounds fall between those for white and Black men.[44,45]

Risk Factors   The risk of testicular cancer is significantly higher in men with a history of an undescended testicle (one of the testes fails to descend into the scrotum and is retained in the abdomen or inguinal canal). However, only 7 to 10 percent of men diagnosed with testicular cancer have a history of this condition. Other risk factors include a family history of testicular cancer, a personal history of testicular cancer in the other testicle, abnormal development of the testes, and infertility or abnormal sperm.[44]

Signs and Symptoms   Warning signs of testicular cancer include a painless lump on the testicle and swelling or discomfort in the scrotum. Back pain and difficulty breathing can develop in later stages after the cancer metastasizes.

Screening and Detection   Most testicular cancers are detected by men or their partners. However, self-exam is not routinely recommended because it has not been studied. The recommendation is that men should be familiar with their bodies and feel for changes as part of routine daily living. If a man feels a lump or change in the testicle, he should have further evaluation. An ultrasound and, if necessary, a biopsy confirm the diagnosis.[44,45]

Treatment Testicular cancer is treated with surgery to remove the testicle; depending on the stage of disease, radiation or chemotherapy may be needed as well. Testicular cancer is highly treatable, with 95 percent of cases at all stages being cured. The cure rate approaches 100 percent if the cancer is diagnosed at an early stage. Even with a late-stage diagnosis and extensive metastases, testicular cancer can be cured.[44]

Leukemia Leukemia is a group of cancers that originate in the bone marrow or other parts of the body where white blood cells form. It is the overproduction of one type of white blood cell, which prevents the normal growth and function of other blood cells and can lead to increased risk of infection, anemia, and bleeding. The ACS estimated 60,530 new cases of leukemia in 2020 and 23,100 deaths. Although most leukemia cases occur in older adults, leukemia is the most common childhood cancer.[1]

Risk Factors Risk factors include cigarette smoking and exposure to certain chemicals, particularly benzene, which is found in gasoline products and cigarette smoke. A parent smoking during pregnancy or in the home after birth increases the child's risk of childhood leukemia. Ionizing radiation can increase the risk for several types of leukemia; people who survive other cancers are at risk of developing leukemia as a result of radiation treatment. Infection with human T-cell leukemia/lymphoma virus (HTLV-1) can increase the risk of leukemia and lymphoma, another cancer of the white blood cells.[1]

Signs and Symptoms Symptoms of leukemia include fatigue, increased incidence of infection, weight loss, fevers, and easy bleeding and bruising. These indicators often occur because healthy white blood cells, red blood cells, and platelets are unable to perform their functions. They can appear suddenly in acute leukemia, but in chronic leukemia they may appear gradually.

Screening and Detection Because the symptoms are fairly nonspecific, early detection of leukemia can be challenging. There is no recommended screening test, but a health care provider can diagnose leukemia with a blood test or bone marrow biopsy if symptoms are present.

Treatment The most effective treatment for leukemia is chemotherapy. Therapy can also include blood transfusion, antibiotics, and drugs to boost the function of healthy blood cells. Stem cell transplantation can be effective for certain types of leukemia. Survival rates vary tremendously based on type of leukemia and range from 25 percent for acute myeloid leukemia to 89 percent for acute lymphocytic leukemia at 5 years.[1]

Oral Cancers Cancers that develop in the mouth or the pharynx (the back of the throat) can involve the lips, tongue, gums, or throat and are classified as oral cancers. The rate of new cases had been declining since the 1980s, and death rates have been decreasing. However, rates of a subset of oral cancers linked to HPV infection have increased, particularly in white men. Oral cancers are twice as common in men as in women. Although they are not common in young adults, we include them in this section because risk behaviors strongly linked to oral cancers are common in this age group.[1]

Risk Factors The major risk factor for oral cancers is tobacco use (smoking cigarettes, cigars, or a pipe or using smokeless tobacco); high levels of alcohol consumption further increase the risk. HPV is a newly recognized risk factor and is believed to be associated with oral sexual contact. The HPV vaccine has been primarily shown to reduce risk of genital HPV infection but should reduce oral HPV infection, too.[1,46]

Signs and Symptoms Early signs of oral cancer include a sore in the mouth that bleeds easily or does not heal; a lump or bump that does not go away or that increases in size; or a patch of redness or whiteness along the gums or skin lining the inside of the cheeks. Late signs of oral cancer can include pain or difficulty swallowing or chewing.

Screening and Detection Oral cancers are usually detected by a doctor or dentist as part of routine care, or the individual may notice a sore that does not heal. A biopsy is necessary to confirm the diagnosis.

Treatment Treatment usually starts with surgery to remove as much of the cancer as possible, along with local radiation. If the cancer is advanced, chemotherapy can be added. The 5-year survival rate for all stages of oral cancer is 65 percent, but survival is much lower in Blacks (48 percent) than in whites (67 percent).[1]

LIVING WITH CANCER

As a result of improved screening and treatment, a diagnosis of cancer is no longer seen as a death sentence; rather, many cancers are now curable or controllable, and cancer survivors often return to a healthy life. An estimated 16.9 million people living in the United States have a history of cancer.[1]

As a chronic disease, however, cancer can change the way a person lives. If you or a friend or family member receives a diagnosis of cancer, many issues will arise that you probably have never had to deal with before. Here are some suggestions that may help in this difficult time:

- Participate in decisions about your treatment and care to the greatest extent possible, or ask the person with cancer how much he or she wants to be involved in treatment decisions. Maintaining a sense of control is associated with having better health outcomes.

- Be an informed consumer. Gather information about your cancer (or your family member's cancer). If you have questions, write them down and ask your health care provider at the next appointment. Make sure you are comfortable with the health team's technical expertise and emotional support.

- Consider how you will interact with family members, friends, and acquaintances. With whom will you share the diagnosis and when? Who will provide you with emotional support? If you need assistance, who might help with tasks, such as driving to appointments, cooking meals, or shopping? If you have a friend or family member with cancer, consider your strengths and what you can offer—perhaps a day spent helping in the garden or taking a child on an outing.

- Consider school or work obligations. You may have to take time off for treatment, and you may experience job discrimination. The Rehabilitation Act and the Americans with Disabilities Act are two federal laws that protect cancer patients. Your health insurance provider cannot drop you even if you leave your job (although your rates may go up and you may have to pay for insurance yourself).

- Enlist support. A cancer support group can offer information, teach coping skills, and give you a place to voice your concerns and share your experiences. You can find support groups through your health care team, church, or community, or on the Internet.

- Know what physical changes are likely to occur. Your sense of identity may be affected as you adapt to the changes in your health or appearance. As a support person, remembering the "whole" person and not just focusing on the cancer-related changes can be helpful.

- If you or a partner is about to start a treatment, ask how treatment affects your future fertility. Consider the possibility of sperm or egg donation and freezing.

- If you have spiritual beliefs or practices, they can be an important part of life now. Research suggests that people with a sense of spirituality have a better quality of life while living with cancer than those who are not spiritual.

- Coping with a cancer diagnosis and treatment can be exhausting. Supporting someone with cancer can also lead to burnout. In either situation, it is important not to think about the cancer all the time. Caregivers should try not to feel guilty about enjoying life and activities. They also need to be able to ask for help so that they can remain supportive over the long run.

Important discoveries in the areas of cancer biology, genetics, screening, and treatment have transformed the face of cancer. Greater knowledge of risk factors has led to more effective prevention strategies. Mortality is declining, survival rates are rising, and the quality of life for those with cancer is improving. The future holds great promise for continuing progress.

You Make the Call

What Do You Do with Conflicting Health Recommendations?

In the late 1990s, the Centers for Disease Control and Prevention (CDC) began to report a rise in cases of rickets, a vitamin D deficiency disease not seen for decades. Rickets causes bone softening and deformities in children and bone loss and fractures in adults. The reason for the resurgence of the crippling disease was, in part, avoidance of sun exposure by parents who were protecting their children from the risks of sunburn and future skin cancer, as recommended by health experts. The story of vitamin D deficiency versus risk of skin cancer points to the complexity of current health advisories.

Vitamin D is an essential micronutrient. It is needed for the development and maintenance of bones and teeth and a healthy immune system. Higher levels are associated with lower rates of colon, prostate, breast, esophageal, and pancreatic cancers and improved survival among melanoma patients. Lower levels are associated with multiple health problems, including reduced calcium absorption, osteoporosis (thinning of the bones), autoimmune disorders, and an increased risk of heart disease. Extreme vitamin D deficiency causes rickets.

The body's major source of vitamin D is sunlight. Exposure to sunlight, specifically UVB, triggers synthesis of vitamin D in

skin cells. In some areas of the United States, an estimated 20 to 30 percent of people have moderate to severe vitamin D deficiency, mostly because of lack of sun exposure. Studies have also found that between 40 and 70 percent of adolescents have low levels of vitamin D. Risk is greatest in northern latitudes, in individuals who are homebound, and in people with dark skin. Anything that diminishes sun exposure increases the chance of vitamin D deficiency.

At the same time that sun exposure is needed for vitamin D synthesis, it is also the most dangerous risk factor for skin cancer. To reduce the risk of skin cancer, including melanoma, people are advised to avoid being in the sun between 10:00 a.m. and 2:00 p.m., to stay in the shade, to wear protective hats and clothing, and to use sunscreen. A sunscreen with an SPF of 15 absorbs 99 percent of the UVB radiation in sunlight, reducing the risk for sunburn and skin cancer—but it also decreases the synthesis of vitamin D by 99 percent.

How do we balance these conflicting health recommendations? The Recommended Daily Allowance for vitamin D is 600 International Units (IU). How long do you have to be in the

Continued...

Concluded...

sun to get that amount? Recommendations vary from 10 to 15 minutes of sun exposure without sunscreen twice a week to 30 minutes per day without sunscreen. However, the American Academy of Dermatology recommends that you get vitamin D from foods and supplementation, not from the sun.

Vitamin D can be obtained from only a few foods, including salmon, mackerel, sardines, cod liver oil, and some fortified milks, yogurts, and cereals. Vitamin D is available in the form of a supplement; however, a large review of vitamin D supplementation did not show any change in risk of overall mortality from all causes. Nevertheless, the Institute of Medicine recommends 600 IU of vitamin D a day for people between ages 1 and 70. If you are 71 or older, the recommendation is 800 IU per day. Excess supplementation can result in toxicity, because vitamin D is a fat-soluble vitamin.

At present, there is no routine recommendation to check vitamin D levels in the general public. While others disagree, some experts say a reasonable amount of sun exposure makes sense to ensure obtaining adequate amounts of this micronutrient. What do you think?

Pros

- Sunlight is a natural way to get the vitamin D we need.
- The benefits of a moderate amount of sun exposure might outweigh the risk of skin cancer.
- Even if sun exposure increases the risk of skin cancer, adequate levels of vitamin D reduce the risk of other kinds of cancer and improve survival for people with melanoma—the worst kind of skin cancer.

Cons

- Sun exposure is linked directly to skin cancer—the most common form of cancer—and avoiding time in the sun is recommended by the CDC, the American Cancer Society, and other leading health organizations.
- You can get vitamin D from other, safer sources, including some fish and vitamin supplements.
- Sun exposure causes skin damage and premature aging. It's an irresponsible health behavior choice to spend time in the sun without sunscreen.

Mc Graw Hill **connect**

Sources: National Institutes of Health. (2019). Vitamin D: Fact sheet for health professionals. Retrieved from https://ods.od.nih.gov/factsheets/VitaminD-HealthProfessional/; Papadimitriou, D. T. (2017). The big vitamin D mistake. *Journal of Preventive Medicine and Public Health, 50*(4), 278-281; American Academy of Dermatology. (2017). Vitamin D. Retrieved from https://www.aad.org/media/stats/prevention-and-care/vitamin-d-and-uv-exposure

In Review

What is cancer?
Cancer, the second leading cause of death in the United States, is a condition characterized by an uncontrolled growth of cells, which develop into a tumor and have the potential to spread to other parts of the body.

What causes cancer?
Cancer can be caused by random genetic mutations, a genetic predisposition, or exposure to carcinogens. Usually, a combination of innate and environmental factors is involved. Risk factors include a family history of cancer; lifestyle factors such as tobacco use, poor nutrition, overweight and obesity, physical inactivity, and alcohol consumption; and environmental factors such as exposure to UV radiation, infectious agents, and chemical and physical carcinogens.

How is cancer detected and treated?
Many cancers can be detected early by screening tests such as mammograms and colonoscopies; for other cancers, no test has been shown to improve detection or treatment outcomes. The traditional treatment is surgery to remove the cancer; other treatments include chemotherapy, radiation, immunotherapies, stem cell transplantation, and gene therapy. Some complementary and alternative therapies, such as acupuncture, yoga, and meditation, can give relief from cancer pain or the side effects of cancer treatment. Millions of people have survived cancer and live with it as a chronic condition.

What are the most common cancers?
The leading cause of cancer death for both men and women is lung cancer, and the third leading cause for both men and women is colorectal cancer. The second leading cause of cancer death for women is breast cancer and for men, prostate cancer. Two types of skin cancer, basal cell and squamous cell carcinomas, are highly common and curable, but melanoma is a less common but more aggressive and dangerous form of skin cancer. Cancers of the female reproductive system include cervical, uterine, and ovarian cancer. Testicular cancer, though rare, is the most common cancer among young men. Oral cancer is associated with tobacco use, alcohol use, and, increasingly, HPV infection. HPV vaccination reduces rates of cervical and oral cancers. Leukemia is a cancer of the blood cells, and lymphoma is a cancer that arises in the lymph system.

Personal Health Portfolio

Chapter 15   Assessing Your Risk Factors for Cancer

The more risk factors you have for a particular cancer, the greater the likelihood that you will develop that cancer. In the following lists for six common cancers—lung, colon, breast, prostate, cervical, and melanoma—check any risk factors and protective factors that apply to you. The more risk factors you check, the more important it is that you adopt healthy lifestyle behaviors and have regular screening tests. The final section lists general protective factors against cancer. There is no score.

LUNG CANCER RISK FACTORS

____ Age greater than 40 (median age at diagnosis: 71)

____ Family history of lung cancer

____ Smoking cigarettes

____ Smoking cigars or other nicotine products

____ Exposure to environmental tobacco smoke

____ Exposure to air pollution

____ Exposure to workplace chemicals

____ Fewer than three servings of vegetables per day

____ Fewer than three servings of fruit per day

COLON CANCER RISK FACTORS

____ Age greater than 50 (median age at diagnosis: 71)

____ Family history of colon cancer

____ Overweight

____ More than one serving of red meat per day

____ Fewer than three servings of vegetables per day

____ More than one alcoholic drink per day

____ Less than 30 minutes of physical activity per day

____ Having inflammatory bowel disease for 10 years or more

Lower Risk Associated with:

____ Taking a multivitamin with folate every day

____ Taking birth control pills for at least 5 years

____ Taking postmenopausal hormones for at least 5 years

____ Taking aspirin regularly for more than 15 years

____ Having regular screening tests

BREAST CANCER RISK FACTORS

____ Age greater than 40 (median age at diagnosis: 61)

____ Female sex

____ Family history of breast cancer

____ Jewish ethnicity, especially Ashkenazi descent

____ Overweight

____ Fewer than three servings of vegetables per day

____ More than two alcoholic drinks per day

____ Having had hyperplasia (benign breast disease)

Longer Exposure to Estrogen:

____ Early age at menarche

____ Older age at birth of first child

____ Older age at menopause

____ Fewer than two children

____ Breastfeeding for less than 1 year combined for all pregnancies

____ Currently taking birth control pills

____ Taking postmenopausal hormones for 5 years or more

PROSTATE CANCER RISK FACTORS

____ Age greater than 55 (median age at diagnosis: 68)

____ Family history of prostate cancer

____ Five or more servings per day of foods containing animal fat

____ Having had a vasectomy

____ African American ethnicity

Lower Risk Associated with:

____ Asian ethnicity

____ At least one serving per day of tomato-based food

CERVICAL CANCER RISK FACTORS

____ Older age (median age at diagnosis: 48)

____ Smoking cigarettes

____ Having had sex at an early age

____ Having had many sexual partners

____ Having had an STI, especially HPV

____ Having given birth to two or more children

Lower Risk Associated with:

____ HPV vaccination

____ Using a condom or diaphragm on every occasion of sexual intercourse

____ Having recommended Pap tests

MELANOMA RISK FACTORS

____ Older age (median age at diagnosis: 59)

____ Family history of melanoma

____ Light-colored hair and eyes

____ Having had severe, repeated sunburns in childhood

____ Exposure to ultraviolet radiation

____ Taking immunosuppressive drugs (e.g., after organ transplant)

Lower Risk Associated with:

____ Protecting the skin from the sun

____ Regular self-examination of the skin

GENERAL PROTECTIVE FACTORS

____ Maintaining a healthy weight

____ Living a physically active lifestyle

____ Consuming a balanced diet with at least five servings of fruit and vegetables a day

____ Limiting alcohol consumption (no more than two drinks a day for men and one for women)

____ Avoiding tobacco

____ Having health insurance

Source: Adapted from "Your Disease Risk," Harvard Center for Cancer Prevention, www.yourdiseaserisk.harvard.edu.

CRITICAL THINKING QUESTIONS

1. For which cancers do you have protective factors?

2. For which cancers do you have risk factors?

3. Are there things you can do that would lower your cancer risk? Consider your individual behavior, environmental factors, and recommended screening guidelines.

Design Icons: ©McGraw-Hill Education

16 Injury and Violence

AndreyPopov/Getty *Images*

Ever Wonder...

how to do the Heimlich maneuver?

whether campus tribunals processing sexual assault cases violate due process rights of the accused and the accuser?

whether state law allows your school to decide that concealed weapons can legally be carried on your campus?

Unintentional injuries are injuries that are not purposely inflicted,[1] in contrast to intentional injuries like homicides, assaults, and rapes. Unintentional injuries are the fifth leading cause of death for the U.S. population overall, and the leading cause of death for children and adults between the ages of 1 and 35.[2] Intentional injuries are usually associated with violence; although they account for fewer deaths than unintentional injuries, they also take a toll on individuals every year, physically, psychologically, and materially.

INJURY: CREATING SAFE ENVIRONMENTS

Public health experts avoid the term *accident* when referring to **unintentional injuries**, because *accident* implies that the injury is a chance occurrence or an unpreventable mishap over which individuals have no control.[1] The term *unintentional injuries* implies that injuries are preventable if people adopt behaviors that promote safety and if society does its part in reducing environmental hazards. Examples of safety-promoting behaviors are wearing seat belts in cars, keeping medications in locked cabinets out of the reach of children, and maintaining working smoke detectors in the home.

The leading cause of unintentional-injury death for people of all ages in the United States is motor vehicle crashes, followed by poisoning, falls, choking, and drowning. The leading causes of injury death vary by age and by ethnicity and race. For example, for infants under 1 year of age, the leading cause of injury death is suffocation; for children aged 1 to 4, the leading cause of accidental death is drowning; and for individuals aged 15 to 24,[3] the third leading cause is motor vehicle crashes.

Injury death rates vary by race/ethnicity. Non-Hispanic whites account for 75 percent of preventable deaths, non-Hispanic Blacks account for 12 percent, and Hispanics or Latinos 10 percent.[4]

Motor Vehicle Safety

From 2016 to 2018, about 40,000 people in the United States died each year from injury in motor vehicle accidents. Almost 4.1 million were seriously injured in 2018.[5]

Factors Contributing to Motor Vehicle Crashes About 85 percent of motor vehicle crashes are believed to be caused by **improper driving**, or driving behaviors such as speeding, failing to yield the right of way, disregarding signals and stop signs, making improper turns, passing on a yellow line, and following too closely. Speeding is especially dangerous; it is a major factor in most fatal crashes. Speed-related crashes

decrease with driver age.[6,7] Other factors contributing to motor vehicle crashes include distracted driving, drowsiness, aggressive driving, alcohol-impaired driving, and environmental hazards.

Distracted Driving The National Highway Traffic Safety Administration (NHTSA) estimates that at least nine people are killed and more than 1,060 are injured every day in crashes involving distracted drivers.[8] The three main types of distraction are visual (taking eyes off the road), manual (taking hands off the wheel), and cognitive (taking the mind off the task at hand). Drivers under age 20 are the most likely to be involved in distraction-related crashes.

Electronic devices such as smartphones and iPods visually and cognitively, and sometimes manually, distract drivers from safely operating a vehicle. Talking on a cell phone and sending text messages are major sources of distraction. Texting drivers are eight times more likely to be in a vehicle collision than drivers who do not text.[9] By the time you type "R u home yet" on your smartphone, you have increased your risk for a potential fatal accident by 2,300 percent (see Figure 16.1). Talking on a cell phone increases your risk fourfold; putting on makeup, threefold; and eating or drinking, twofold.[10] Studies have found that it is not using the phone that causes distraction as much as it is the shifting of attention to the conversation and away from driving.[10] As the number of distracting devices inside cars increases, more states are passing legislation to limit the use of electronic devices in motor vehicles.

Although the National Transportation Safety Board has recommended a federal ban on driver use of portable electronic devices when operating a vehicle, research suggests that this will not be a successful response.[10] Education and legislation have failed to decrease the problem of distracted driving due to the difficulty of strictly enforcing such laws. Safety experts believe that technology is the solution. Handheld electronic devices, for example, could be rendered inoperable whenever the vehicle is in motion or the transmission shift lever is engaged. Opponents argue that this technology is a violation of personal freedom and increases the consumer cost for vehicles and electronic devices.

Lawmakers in New York proposed providing law enforcement with an electronic digital roadside test called a Textalyzer. The Textalyzer can tap

unintentional injuries Injuries that are not purposefully inflicted.

improper driving The cause of most motor vehicle crashes, including speeding, failing to yield right-of-way, following too closely, and passing on a yellow line.

(Rick Brady/McGraw-Hill)

figure 16.1 **Typical distance covered while texting.**
The average driver looks away from the road for 5 seconds when texting. At a speed of 55 miles per hour, a vehicle covers about 400 feet—more than the length of a football field, including the end zones—during those 5 seconds. Two seconds is the maximum amount of time a driver can safely look away from the road. *(Nycshooter/Getty Images)*

in to the operating system of smartphones to detect recent texting and email activity. Drivers who refuse to turn over their phones would be subject to suspension of their driver's license. Opponents of the Textalyzer argue that it is an invasion of privacy. Proponents argue that its use is supported by the same legal theory that allows law enforcement's use of a Breathalyzer. Proponents also argue that the "driver mode" on smartphones, which locks out apps and functions, is more effective than a textalyzer.[11] What do you think?

Although navigation systems have been identified as a potential driver safety issue, these devices have also proven to provide safety benefits. Navigation systems help drivers know where they are going without the distraction of trying to read a map, especially at night. To use navigation systems safely, program them before you drive, not while driving, and don't allow the device to block your sight lines. Some states are passing laws to prohibit handheld GPS devices while driving.[12]

Vehicle infotainment systems have come under scrutiny by the U.S. Department of Transportation (DOT). Studies indicate that these systems operate at the high end of the mental-workload scale, which means they shift drivers' attention away from the task of driving. For this reason, the DOT in 2013 released guidelines on vehicle technology that include limiting the time drivers need to

take their eyes off the road to perform a task to 2 seconds at a time and 12 seconds total. Manual text entry, video-based entertainment such as video phoning, and display of text messages, webpages, and social media content should be disabled while the vehicle is moving. The auto industry has responded by making infotainment systems more user friendly, providing features that disable operation, and adding apps to block calls and texts while the vehicle is operated. Unfortunately, many drivers have found ways to disable or bypass the features designed to reduce distraction risk. *Consumer Reports* provides a rating system for vehicle infotainment systems based on their mental-workload requirements.[10]

Drowsiness Drowsiness is another source of driver inattention. Drowsiness reduces awareness of your surroundings, impairs judgment, and slows reaction time. The NHTSA conservatively estimates that 2.5 percent of fatal crashes and 2 percent of injuries are caused by drowsy driving. Cognitive impairment in someone who has been awake for 18 straight hours is equivalent to 0.5 blood alcohol content (BAC) level, and 24 consecutive hours of wakefulness is equivalent to 0.10 BAC level.[13,14] If you start to feel drowsy while driving, it is best to pull over until you are fully rested or change drivers. Opening the window, turning up the radio, and turning down the air conditioner are not effective in preventing drowsy-driving accidents.

Aggressive Driving Driving Tests estimates that 66 percent of all traffic fatalities are associated with overly aggressive driving behavior.[15] An aggressive driver is someone who tailgates, speeds, runs red lights, changes lanes without signaling, and makes illegal turns. Aggressive driving can escalate into *road rage,*[16] an extreme form of aggressive driving. People who experience this kind of uncontrolled anger need to seek help in managing their behavior. If you are in a road rage incident, quickly remove yourself from the situation by taking an exit or, if the road rage driver continues to follow you, pull into a police parking lot or a busy area where other people are around you.

Alcohol-Impaired Driving Alcohol is involved in a large proportion of car crashes, including fatal crashes. Alcohol slows reaction time and impairs perception, judgment, and motor coordination. About 3 in 10 people in the United States are involved in an alcohol-related crash at some point in their lives.[17] Men are responsible for 80 percent of alcohol-impaired driving.[17]

Many drugs other than alcohol impair the ability to drive safely. They include illicit drugs such as marijuana and heroin, prescription drugs, and over-the-counter drugs such as sleep aids.[18] Driving safely requires mental alertness, clear vision, physical coordination, and the ability to react quickly. Any drugs that induce dizziness, light-headedness, nausea, drowsiness, fatigue, nervousness, or fuzzy thinking make driving dangerous.

Environmental Hazards Environmental hazards account for less than 5 percent of vehicle crashes, but when combined with human error, they account for 27 percent. Environmental hazards can be natural, such as snow, ice, wind, poor visibility, or glare, or they can be of human origin, such as construction zones, broken-down cars on the side of the road, or drunk drivers. To reduce the number and lethality of injuries that occur as a result of environmental factors, states and local communities use such measures as ice-melting chemicals, crash cushions, breakaway signs and light poles, and median barriers and guard rails.[19]

Passenger Restraint Safety A major safety approach is designing effective restraint systems and increasing the likelihood that people will use them. Seat belts reduce the risk of fatal injuries by 47 percent for front-seat passengers. People not wearing a seat belt are 30 times more likely to be thrown from a vehicle.[20,21] Still, nearly one in seven adults does not wear a seat belt on every trip. However, 97 percent of college students wear a seat belt all or most of the time.[22]

States have either primary or secondary enforcement laws for seat belt use. Primary laws allow law enforcement officers to pull vehicles over and issue tickets solely because drivers and passengers are not wearing seat belts. Secondary laws allow tickets to be issued only if the vehicle operator has been pulled over for violating another law. States with primary enforcement laws have higher seat belt usage than states with secondary enforcement laws or no laws.[23]

> **passive restraint**
> A safety device that does not require vehicle occupants to engage it.

Air bags—fabric cushions that instantly inflate during a collision—are a kind of **passive restraint** that protects front-seat passengers from impact with the interior of the vehicle in a crash. Generally, sensing devices in the dashboard inflate air bags at impacts of 12 mph or more. The bags deflate seconds after the impact.

Infants and children need to be secured in child seats placed in the backseat and anchored by the vehicle's safety belts. They should not ride in the front seat because air bags can deploy with enough force to cause severe head and neck injuries. Infants should ride in carriers in which they are in a semireclining position facing the rear of the car. The American Academy of Pediatrics recommends that infants and toddlers ride in rear-facing car seats until they are 2 years old or have reached the height and weight limits for their car seat. After age 2, children should ride in a forward-facing car seat with harness straps until they reach height and weight recommendations for the seat. Many convertible car seats and combination car seats set forward-facing weight limits of 65 to 85 pounds when used with harness straps.

The five-point harness, which runs across the child's shoulders and hips and buckles between the legs, should be used until the child weighs more than 85 pounds. Children can be moved to belt-positioning booster seats when they reach the weight and height of harness strap limits. The harness can be used in booster mode until the child exceeds 120 pounds. Children should not be placed in regular seat belts until they are old enough and large enough, usually at least 4 ft 9 inches tall and between ages 8 and 12. Children under age 13 should always sit in the back seat, using the age-recommended restraint.[24]

Pet Restraints The American Society for the Prevention of Cruelty to Animals (ASPCA) recommends that people use restraints for dogs and cats to prevent injury to the pet, driver, or passengers. Only one in six people use animal restraints such as harnesses, pet vehicle seats, or pet carriers. Unrestrained pets can distract a driver and cause serious injury to the driver and passengers in the event of an accident. If thrown during a 30-mph crash, an 80-pound Labrador Retriever will exert 2,400 pounds of force on whatever it strikes. Some states are considering a law that will fine drivers who do not restrain their dogs or cats.[25]

Motorcycle Safety

Motorcyclists are about five times more likely than passenger car occupants to die in a motor vehicle crash and about 26 times more likely to be injured.[1] Contributing factors in these crashes are distraction, alcohol use, lack of proper training, and environmental conditions (weather, road surface, equipment malfunction). Wearing a helmet reduces a motorcyclist's risks of both fatal injury and traumatic brain injury by 37 percent. Despite the safety benefits of a helmet, however, most motorcyclists choose not to wear one unless state law requires it.[26] Only 11 percent of college students report wearing a helmet all the time.[27]

Bicycle Safety

Collisions between bicycles and motor vehicles result in many deaths and nonfatal disabling injuries. A successful bicycle safety program combines the use of safety equipment with injury-reducing behaviors. Three important considerations are making sure your bicycle fits you properly, wearing a helmet, and employing safe cycling practices. Helmets reduce the risk of brain trauma from accidents by 88 percent.[28] Only 14 percent of college students report wearing a bicycle helmet all the time.[27] Although bicycle injuries overall have been reduced by more than 50 percent since 1999, head injuries from bike accidents have increased in cities that have bike-share programs.[1,27] The likely culprits are unfamiliarity with the operation of the bike and failure to wear a safety helmet.

The biggest safety problem for bicyclists is making themselves visible to other vehicle operators. Reflective tape, brightly colored cycling clothes and safety vests, portable leg or arm lights, and headlights are effective for making riders more visible. Air-powered horns can add another dimension to safety. Bicycles are considered vehicles, and riders must follow all traffic laws that apply to cars, including stopping at traffic lights and stop signs and signaling before turning.

Rates of cycling fatalities and serious injuries are much higher in the United States than in most Western European countries. Vision Zero is a collaborative community campaign that works with police, health departments, and traffic engineers to emphasize that traffic crashes should not be considered an inevitable or accepted risk of travel. The campaign's goal is zero traffic fatalities or serious injuries. Cities implementing Vision Zero include New York City, Boston, San Francisco, and San Diego.

Very few large cities have infrastructure designed for cycling safety. If such an infrastructure exists, it is often poorly maintained and not connected to other community transportation networks. Supportive cycling infrastructures include buffers between motor vehicles and cycling paths and intersections designed to reduce cycling crashes. Denmark provides an excellent model that features extensive on-road and off-road bike paths, priority traffic signals, advance stop lines for cyclists at intersections, and cycling "superhighways" parallel to major roads that provide express lanes for commuting to work and minimize road crossings.[29]

E-scooter Safety

The surge in electric or e-scooter injuries led the CDC to investigate the risk of riding them. Although marketed as toys, motorized scooters can reach 30 mph. Forty-five percent of e-scooter accidents cause closed-head injuries (brain bruising or bleeding, and concussions). Arm fractures, leg fractures, and organ damage were also common. Half these injuries were severe. The CDC report found that about 20 of every 100,000 rides resulted in injuries. E-scooter manufacturers claim an injury rate of 32.8 per every 1 million miles, compared to the CDC estimate of 190 injuries for 891,121 miles. The National Highway Traffic Safety Administration found the injury rate of e-scooters to be 2.2 per 10,000 miles traveled, in contrast to 0.5 for motorcycles and 0.1 for cars.[30,31,32]

Avoidable risk factors include not wearing a helmet, but less than 1 percent of e-scooter riders wear a helmet. Speed was another culprit in injuries. Only 10 percent of the injuries involved e-scooter collisions with cars. One-third of injuries occurred in the first scooter ride. The assumed ease of riding an e-scooter lies behind its popularity, but inexperience is a major factor in high injury rates.[30,31,32]

Lime and Bird are companies deploying fleets of e-scooters for rent in cities. Many citizens and municipal governments welcomed them as much-needed transportation alternatives, particularly because they curb the use of gas-guzzling vehicles that contribute to climate change. But ride-share fleets are generally unregulated, and e-scooter injuries have skyrocketed with the arrival of app-based ride-share scooters. Public safety and public clutter have both become community issues. Lime provides free helmets and recommendations for helmet use and requires completion of in-app helmet safety tutorials before first-time users can unlock a scooter. Bird uses a safety operation app for unlocking scooters. Cities, ride-share operators, medical professionals, consumers, and safety experts are working together to curb e-scooter injuries.[32]

Pedestrian Safety

In the next 24 hours in the United States, 12 pedestrians will be killed and about 460 people will be treated in emergency rooms for pedestrian-related injuries.[33] About one of every six pedestrian deaths occurs in a hit-and-run incident. About 45 percent of pedestrian deaths occur when pedestrians enter or cross streets, and 10 percent occur when pedestrians are walking in the roadway. A few times every year, a bicyclist strikes and kills a pedestrian.[33,34]

The pedestrian fatality rate for men is about twice that for women, and the rate of nonfatal pedestrian injuries is also higher for men. The pedestrian fatality rate for Blacks is almost twice that for whites, and for American Indians and Native Alaskans it is nearly three times as high. Safety experts believe this difference can be attributed partly to the fact that members of these groups generally walk more than

(Ken Hurst/Shutterstock)

whites because they own fewer cars. Children and older pedestrians are also especially vulnerable to being injured or killed by a car. The pedestrian annual death rate is 1.5/100,000. In communities with an average per capita income below $36,000, however, the death rate is 2.5/100,000. Low-income communities are more exposed to arterial road systems with high speed, insufficient safety medians, and few pedestrian crossways. Many European nations have adopted Sweden's Vision Zero, which is a systems-based approach to design arterial roads with lower speed limits and more effectively separate pedestrians from road traffic. This system is based on the United Nation's pedestrian safety regulations. The United States has not adopted this approach.[33,34,35]

It is estimated that college students send and receive about 4,000 text messages each month.[36] It's not unusual to see students texting while walking, both on and off campus. Pedestrians who text, e-mail, or talk on their smartphones are vulnerable to inattention blindness. They also walk more slowly, change directions more frequently, and acknowledge others less frequently than those not using their phones while walking. These actions all increase the safety risk for both the walker and other pedestrians.[36]

The term *smartphone zombies* was coined to describe pedestrians wrapped up in electronic distractions. Amsterdam is using LED light strips on sidewalks, synchronized with traffic signals, to alleviate the problem of smartphone zombies who are looking down as they walk. The LED strategy is likely to be more effective than a bill introduced in New Jersey that would have banned walking and texting or using smartphones or other electronic communication devices that are not hands-free. This law would be too difficult to enforce. The NHTSA cites drunk walking as another problem.[37] Research suggests that even listening to music while walking causes cognitive distraction and can increase accident risk by intensifying sensory deprivation called inattentive blindness, for example, by blocking the sound of a car

horn. If using headphones while walking, keep the volume at a reasonable level so you can still hear environmental noise, keep just one earbud in, and avoid noise-cancelling headphones.[38]

Although vehicle manufacturers have introduced pedestrian detection technology, this technology has not proven to be effective at night or when the vehicle is traveling at speeds of 30 mph or higher. In Europe, vehicle manufacturers have designed vehicles with softer bumpers, raised hoods, and repositioned engine components to help prevent pedestrian leg and head injuries from collision impact. To increase your safety as a pedestrian at night, carry a flashlight and wear reflective clothing. Pay attention to the beeping alarm that is activated when some vehicles are backing up. Some newer vehicles have sensor alarms that can detect small children and animals within a few feet behind them. Many safety experts are calling for such alarms to be standard equipment on all vehicles.[39]

personal flotation device (PFD)
A life jacket worn while participating in water sports.

Recreational Safety

Injuries occur in a variety of recreational activities and sports. Water safety, rock climbing, and recreational drones are addressed in this section.

Water Safety Overall, about 10 people drown every day in the United States; 80 percent of them are male.[40] More than one-third of adults are unable to swim the length of a pool 24 yards long.[1] More than half of all drowning victims are white non-Hispanic males, but Black males have the highest drowning rate per 100,000 persons. Drowning rates increase for Blacks through childhood and then peak between ages 15 and 19 years. Drowning rates for Hispanics increase substantially at 15 to 19 years and then peak between the ages of 20 and 24 years.[40]

About half of drownings occur in natural water settings, such as lakes, rivers, and the ocean, or in boating incidents. In boating drownings, more than 80 percent of the victims were not wearing a life jacket.[41,42] Life jackets, or **personal flotation devices (PFDs)**, are essential protection for anyone participating in boating or another recreational activity on the water, including waterskiing and riding personal watercraft (jet skis). PFDs are made of buoyant material; various types have been designed for different watercraft. Check with your local jurisdiction for rules and regulations governing PFDs for your recreational activity.

If you are on a boat that turns over, stay with the boat, where you are more likely to be spotted and rescued, rather than trying to swim to shore. If you are close to shore, however, and immediate rescue is unlikely, attempting to swim to shore may be your best option.[43]

Alcohol is a principal factor in deaths associated with water recreation activities. Many states have laws covering intoxication by people operating boats that are comparable to those covering intoxication by drivers of motor vehicles.

Rock Climbing Safety Indoor rock-climbing walls have become very popular at fitness and campus recreation centers, cruise ships, and public parks. They are marketed as a fun place to celebrate a birthday party, have a bonding experience, socialize, and get healthy exercise. Poor regulation, poor design, poor instruction/supervision, inadequate harness and rope systems, and/or poor maintenance can cause injuries, however. The popularity of climbing walls has resulted in significant increases in emergency room visits due to fractures, dislocations, sprains, strains, and lacerations.

Outdoor climbing is relatively safe, with 72.1 injuries per 100,000 climbing events. Instruction, attention to safety equipment, and environmental protections are needed to lower the risk of injury.[44,45] Analysis by the American Alpine Club suggests that traditional climbing is more dangerous than sport climbing. Traditional outdoor climbing attracts more novice climbers, who are at higher risk for climber error than sport climbers.[46]

Drones Unsafe use of drones, or unmanned aerial vehicles (UAVs), can cause serious injury. Federal Aviation Administration (FAA) laws require private operators to fly UAVs below 400 feet, only during daylight, at speeds less than 100 mph, and to fly the drone within the operator's sight. Drones must not be heavier than 55 pounds and must avoid airline traffic patterns. Commercial operators of UAVs may petition the FAA to receive waivers from the new rules. There have been many incidents of operators violating FAA laws, particularly in airport runway locations. Radar technology is being developed to detect small UAVs and to locate operators who violate FAA laws.[47]

State and local governments are now requiring registration of recreational drones. Campus security forces are expected to increase their reliance on surveillance UAVs to ensure campus safety (an issue we discuss later in the chapter), and some college courses will offer training in the recreational use of UAVs.

Home Safety

Most injuries occur in the home. In fact, nearly 40 percent of all disabling injuries occur there.[48] The primary causes of home injuries and deaths are fires, poisonings, and choking.

Fires On average in the United States, one civilian person dies in a fire every 154 minutes, and someone is injured in a fire every 33 minutes. Most victims die from inhalation of smoke or toxic gases, not burns. Of all fire-related deaths and injuries, 65 to 85 percent occur in homes. About 50 percent of the homes in which a fire fatality occurred did not have smoke detectors or had an inoperable fire alarm.[49,50]

To help prevent injury from fire, your home should have at least one smoke detector on every level, placed on the ceiling or on a wall 6 to 12 inches from the ceiling. Smoke detectors are either battery-operated or powered by household current with a battery backup. Batteries in battery-powered detectors should be replaced every 6 to 12 months. Research indicates that young children are not

PULL THE PIN

AIM AT THE BASE OF FIRE

PUSH

SQUEEZE THE LEVER

SWEEP SIDE TO SIDE

■ To operate an ABC fire extinguisher, remove the locking pin, point the nozzle at the base of the fire, squeeze the handle, and use a sweeping motion as the extinguisher discharges. Although they discharge for less than a minute, even small fire extinguishers can give people time to escape a fire.
(MSSA/Shutterstock)

(Vitalii Nesterchuk/Shutterstock)

easily roused from deep sleep by the sound of a smoke alarm, but they are roused by the sound of their mother's voice calling their names.

Home fire extinguishers are intended to knock down a fire long enough to allow the occupants to escape; most discharge their extinguishing agent for only about 30 seconds.[51] Many contain a multipurpose dry chemical and are labeled ABC, meaning they can be used on any type of fire. Many commercial buildings have sprinkler systems, and most states require them in newly constructed apartments, condominiums, and other multifamily dwellings.[51]

Poisons, Gas, and Carbon Monoxide

A poison is any substance harmful to the body that is ingested, inhaled, injected, or absorbed through the skin.[52] Poisoning can be intentional or unintentional. Intentional poisonings (to commit suicide) account for about 19 percent of poisoning incidents. About half of all unintentional poisoning deaths are from drug overdoses. Prescription drug overdoses now account for as many deaths as cocaine and heroin combined. Alcohol poisoning accounts for a small percentage of poisoning deaths, but some poisoning deaths are caused by alcohol in combination with other drugs. Native Americans have the highest unintentional poisoning death rate, followed by whites and Blacks.[53,54]

Another poisoning hazard in the home is gases and vapors, such as carbon monoxide and natural gas. More than 400 people die and 20,000 go to the emergency room each year in the United States due to carbon monoxide poisoning.[55] Carbon monoxide is a major component of motor vehicle exhaust; other sources are house fires, faulty furnaces and heaters, and gasoline-powered tools used in an enclosed space. Carbon monoxide alarms are recommended for in-home use. An alarm should be installed in the hallway by every bedroom.

Natural gas is used to operate many home appliances, such as furnaces, stoves, and clothes dryers. Because it is normally odorless, producers add a gas with an odor so that leaks can be detected. If you smell gas, check to see whether the gas is turned on but not lit on a stove burner or other appliance. If you cannot find the source of the leak, leave the area and call your utility company.

If you or someone you are with has been poisoned, seek medical advice and treatment immediately.[55] Signs that a person has ingested or inhaled a poisonous substance include difficulty breathing or speaking, dizziness, unconsciousness, foaming or burning of the mouth, cramps, nausea, and vomiting. Prolonged exposure to low levels of carbon monoxide produces flulike symptoms. In all cases of toxic contamination or poisoning, call 911, your local poison control center, or the national poison control hotline (1-800-222-1222).

Many states have passed laws requiring carbon monoxide detectors to be installed in private dwellings. Some states require these detectors in schools, hotels, and motels.

Private landlords are required to have at least one smoke alarm on every floor, and a carbon monoxide alarm in any room containing a solid-fuel burning appliance (e.g., a wood- or coal-burning stove). In 2019, there were several carbon monoxide deaths of U.S. tourists visiting international resorts and at U.S. rented homes. If you are staying in a resort hotel or rented home, it's recommended that you take a mobile carbon monoxide alarm with you.[56]

Heimlich maneuver A technique used to help a person who is choking.

Choking

Rates of death by choking are highest in children under 4 years of age and adults over 65 and especially over 75 years of age. Food accounts for 50 percent of choking deaths for children 4 years and younger; the top three culprits are hot dogs, candy, and whole grapes.[57] Most choking emergencies occur when a piece of food or a swallowed object becomes lodged in the throat, blocking the tracheal opening and cutting the oxygen supply to the lungs. Muscles in the trachea may go into spasm and wrap tightly around the object.[58]

A person whose airway is obstructed may gasp for breath, make choking sounds, clutch the throat, or look flushed and strained. If the airway is only partially blocked, the person may cough forcefully. Do not slap someone on the back if he or she is coughing; usually the coughing alone will clear the obstruction. If the person continues to have difficulty breathing, coughing is shallow, or the person is not coughing or cannot talk or breathe, a rescue technique called the **Heimlich maneuver** is needed (see the box "Action Skill-Builder: The Heimlich Maneuver").

Children and Vehicular Heat Stroke

At least 38 children die each year, one every 9 days, from vehicular heatstroke, more than half of them under 2 years of age.[59] They may have been forgotten or unintentionally left in the vehicle by an adult, or they may have been playing in an unattended vehicle. About 10 percent of these deaths occur in situations involving alcohol, drugs, or neglect.[60] Children can die of hyperthermia (overheating) in vehicles when the ambient temperature outside is as low as 70°F. It takes only 10 minutes for temperatures inside cars to rise by 20°. In less than 15 minutes, the child's body temperature can reach 104°F, at which point internal organs shut down. Death occurs at 107°F. As of 2017, only 20 states have laws specifically addressing the consequences if a child is left unattended in a vehicle on a warm or cold day.

Children should never be left in a vehicle, even if the windows are down, or be allowed to play in an unattended vehicle, and adults should establish a rule to "look back before you leave" every time they vacate a vehicle. A large stuffed animal placed in the front seat can serve as a visual reminder that a child is in the back. Placing needed objects such as a purse or cell phone next to the car seat is another

Action Skill-Builder ✓

The Heimlich Maneuver

The Heimlich maneuver (also referred to as abdominal thrusts) is used to dislodge an object blocking the airway of a person who is choking. To perform the maneuver, follow these four steps:

1. Stand behind the person and put your arms around his or her waist.

2. Make a fist with one hand and place the thumb side of your fist against the victim's upper abdomen, just below the rib cage and above the navel.

3. Grasp your fist with your other hand and thrust upward. Do not squeeze the rib cage. Confine the force of your thrust to your hands.

4. Repeat the upward thrusts until the object is expelled.

(Science Photo Library/Getty Images)

The Heimlich Institute provides special instructions for rescuing infants, adults, and yourself; however, the Heimlich maneuver is not recommended for children under age 1 year. For infants, follow these procedures:

1. Support the infant's face by holding the head with infant facing away from you, with the body on your forearm against your thigh.

2. Using the heel of your hand, give five back slaps between the shoulder blades.

3. If the object is not expelled, role the infant face up, supporting the back of the infant's head with your hand.

4. Place two fingers on the breastbone just below the nipple line.

5. Give five chest thrusts about one per second about 1-1/2 inches deep.

6. Continue the cycle of five back slaps and five chest thrusts until the object has been expelled.

7. If the infant becomes or is found unresponsive, begin CPR.

For details, visit its website at http://www.deaconess-health-care.com/Heimlich_Institute/Heimlich_Maneuver/, or Choking Infants and Children, https://www.nsc.org/home-safety/safety-topics/choking-suffocation

prevention strategy. Call 911 if you see a young child in an unattended vehicle.[61]

Are parents who forget their child in the back seat or leave them unattended in a hot car negligent? State child endangerment laws have been used to prosecute parents for committing these acts. But what may have happened in the brain of the forgetful parent could happen to anyone. Most of us think of memory as retrospective memory (stored memory), in which content remembered is from the past (e.g., names and phone numbers). However, prospective or habitual memory, another type of memory, is remembering to perform a planned action or habitual task at some future point, and it is very vulnerable to forgetting. For example, have you ever driven home or to class and not remembered whether you stopped at all the stop signs or stop lights? In cases of children forgotten in cars, a common cause is a change or disruption in an automatic routine (such as getting an unexpected phone call). Severe sleep deprivation, common for parents with very young children, increases vulnerability for an autopilot memory causing a "forgotten baby syndrome." To avoid this trap, car technology can provide potential preventive measures. In 2017, for example, GMC installed a child reminder system in its Acadia model. Kidsandcars.org calls for child reminder systems, ultrasonic rear-seat sensors, to be standard in all vehicles. In 2019, Congress introduced the Hot Cars Act that would mandate all new vehicles to be installed with rear seat child and pet reminder systems. The reminder system would be both visual and audio. The Alliance of Automobile Manufacturers[62] opposes the Hot Car Act stating only 13 percent of new car buyers have children under the age of 6. It is projected, however, that almost all vehicles by 2025 will have child reminder systems.[63]

Excessive Noise

Loud noise destroys hair cells at the nerve endings in the inner ear that translate sound vibrations into electrical currents going to the brain. Thus exposure to loud noise can damage

(Wasitt Hemwarapornchai/Shutterstock)

Consumer Clipboard
Head Phones and Hearing Loss

(Malgorzata Smigielska/Shutterstock)

About 15 percent of U.S. adults between the ages of 20 and 69 have noise-induced hearing loss. Noise-induced hearing loss is usually a gradual process that can take 10 to 20 years, but people who listen to music at high volume through headphones have been found to have advanced hearing loss beyond their years.

Orchid24/Shutterstock

Manufacturers have developed different kinds of headphones to reduce risk of hearing loss. "Isolator" earphones sit deeper in the ear canal and block out external sound so that volume does not have to be cranked up so high; "supra-aural" headphones sit on top of the ears and deliver sound at lower decibel levels. However, researchers have found that it is not so much the type of earphone that makes a difference in hearing loss as it is the volume. Ultimately it is up to you and not your headphones to protect your hearing.

Noise levels are measured in decibels (dB): the higher the dB level, the louder the noise. Noise levels from portable media players can reach 115 to 125 dB. Exposure to 125 dB for just 1 hour can cause permanent hearing loss, as can repeated exposure to 115 dB for half a minute per day. If you have listened to music at the highest volume for even a few seconds, or if you have felt pain in your ears from loud music, you may already have experienced some hearing damage. The following table classifies noise along a continuum from faint to painful and can help you determine whether your music is too loud.

Protect your hearing by avoiding prolonged exposure to sounds above 85 dB. Here are some ways to listen to music without endangering your hearing:

Classification	dB	Example
Faint	30 to 39	Whisper (30 dB)
Moderate	40 to 60	Clothes dryer (40 dB)
Very loud	61 to 90	Blow-dryer (80 to 90 dB)
Extremely loud	91 to 119	Chainsaw (110 dB)
Painful	120 or higher	Siren (120 dB)

- Follow the 60 percent/60-minute rule, using head phones at volume levels no more than 60 percent of maximum and no more than 1 hour a day.

- Turn the volume down if (1) it's loud enough to prevent normal conversation, (2) it causes ringing in your ears, (3) you have trouble hearing for a few hours after exposure, or (4) the person next to you can hear the music from your headphones.

Sources: American Osteopathic Association. (2019). Headphones & hearing loss. Retrieved from https://osteopathic.org/shat-is-Osteopathic-medicine/headphones-hearing-loss/; Liebman, B. (2016). Can you hear me now? *Nutrition Action Healthletter,* 3-6.

hearing and lead to permanent hearing loss. Some **noise-induced hearing loss (NIHL)** is inevitable and irreversible as we age, so we should protect our hearing from additional, avoidable damage.[64]

Common sources of excessive environmental noise are machinery, power tools, traffic, airplanes, and construction. Loud music is also a hazard (see the box "Consumer Clipboard: Head Phones and Hearing Loss"). When you listen to loud music for a prolonged period, you experience a "temporary threshold shift" that makes you less sensitive to high volumes. In effect, the ears adapt to the environment by anesthetizing themselves. Noise is considered "very loud" if you have to shout to be heard over it from 3 feet away.

Many people do not realize that everyday noise can damage hearing. For example, 63 percent of people exposed to loud or very loud recreational noise never use ear protection, 29 percent sometimes do, and only 8 percent use it all the time. The point is that human ears have not evolved to handle the trauma from today's noise-pollution environment.[65]

Early symptoms of hearing loss include ringing or buzzing in the ears; difficulty understanding speech, especially in noisy settings; and a slight muffling of sounds. More serious symptoms include dizziness, discomfort, and pain in the ears. People who listen to loud music should have their hearing tested periodically, because hearing loss can go unnoticed until damage is extensive. The National Institute on Deafness and Other Communication Disorders provides valuable information about noise-induced hearing loss. If you want to test how

noise-induced hearing loss (NIHL) Damage to the inner ear, causing gradual hearing loss, as a result of exposure to noise over a period of years.

well you hear speech with noise in the background, you can do so for about $5 at https://www.national-hearingtest.org/wordpress/?page_id=2730. This test requires a landline and a quiet room.

Concussions A concussion is a type of traumatic brain injury (TBI) caused by a blow or jolt to the head (a whiplash causing the head to move violently forth and back). Concussion forces twist and break the long, slender axons of brain cells. Broken axons release a cascade of proteins and chemicals that damage nearby brain cells. Blood vessels break on or near the surface of the brain. In recovery, the brain adapts by developing work-around connections and new connections.[66]

Concussions do occur without loss of consciousness. They are graded by level of severity: Grade 1 involves confusion lasting less than 15 minutes; grade 2, confusion and amnesia lasting longer than 15 minutes; and grade 3, brief unconsciousness and more serious amnesia.

It can take weeks, months, or even years for the symptoms of concussion to dissipate. A second-impact concussion (a second blow to the head within hours, days, or weeks of the initial concussion, before the brain has healed fully) can cause life-threatening brain swelling. While concussions kill in 128 of 100,000 concussion incidents each year in the United States, similar data for second-impact concussion deaths has not been confirmed. The reasons behind the severity of second-impact concussions are not fully known, but scientists conjecture that disruption in the brain's balance of sodium and potassium might be a factor. The uptake of sodium and potassium into brain cells that occurs when they are jolted will shut down brain cells and can lead to sensitivity to light or noise. If loss of consciousness occurs, the brain's electrical grid shuts down as well. Brain cells may react by adding more sodium channels along the brain's cell membranes. Although adding new sodium channels effectively turns the electrical grid back on, if you are hit in the head again, the additional access to sodium may have devastating health impacts. This is why it is vital to ensure that you do not expose yourself to head jolts again until fully recovered. You should consult your health provider for prevention guidelines and make sure you follow them.[66,67]

Many TBIs are associated with sports or recreation activities. Seventy percent of sports-recreation TBIs occur between the ages 10 and 19 and are most commonly associated with bicycling and football for males and bicycling, soccer, and basketball for females. There are also concerns about cumulative hits to the head that do not lead to a concussion, especially because youths' brains are still developing. One study found that even one season of youth football causing exposure to head impacts could cause changes in the brain's white matter.[68] Every state has youth-sport concussion safety laws.[69]

Adults with concussions should seek medical help if they have a headache that gets worse and does not go away, or if they experience weakness, numbness, decreased coordination, repeated vomiting or nausea, or slurred speech. If you are checking symptoms in someone else, seek medical assistance if one of the person's pupils is more dilated than the other or if he or she seems very drowsy or cannot be awakened, has convulsions or seizures, cannot recognize places or people, gets more confused or agitated, displays unusual behavior, or loses consciousness.

Moodiness, anxiety, and sleep-disturbance symptoms can be warning signs of postconcussive syndrome. Someone who has had a concussion should get sufficient rest and not return to moderate or vigorous activity until cleared by a health care professional. The idea that you should stay awake after a concussion is a myth; a short sleep may actually help the brain recover. A person who has experienced a concussion should try to go about daily activities after a couple of days of rest. People who rested for 5 days after a concussion had more long-term concussion-related health issues than those who resumed daily activities after only 2 days. However, if concussion symptoms recur, more rest is recommended and then another return to daily activities. This process can be repeated until the brain has fully recovered. Depression and poor mental-health symptoms are warnings of serious postconcussive health issues and require medical attention. Many metropolitan cities and regions with large hospitals have concussion centers that include neurologists, sports medicine physicians, psychiatrists, physical therapists, and occupational therapists who can provide specialized treatment.[66,67]

Providing Emergency Aid

You can help provide care for other people who have been injured or are in life-threatening situations if you learn first aid and emergency rescue techniques. **Cardiopulmonary resuscitation (CPR)** is used when someone is not breathing and a pulse cannot be found. It consists of mouth-to-mouth resuscitation to restore breathing and chest compression to restore heartbeat. Unfortunately, bystanders provide CPR only 20 to 30 percent of the time when needed, largely out of apprehension about placing their mouth on someone else's. In 2008, the American Heart Association (AHA) announced that *hands-only CPR*—with chest compression only—is just as effective for sudden cardiac arrest as standard CPR with mouth-to-mouth breathing. However, mouth-to-mouth resuscitation should still be used for children and for adults who suffer a lack of oxygen caused by near-drowning, carbon monoxide poisoning, or drug overdose.[70] Check the AHA's website (www.americanheart.org) for the latest guidelines.

The AHA recommends training for performing CPR. However, even without training, the AHA states that, on average, any attempt to perform CPR is better than no attempt. Many organizations offer classes, including the AHA and the American Red Cross. Check your community or campus resource center for information about where to take a class in first aid or rescue technique. The AHA offers online certification for CPR and automated external defibrillator (AED) renewal.[71]

Automated external defibrillators increase survival in cardiac arrest events. To be effective, AEDs need to be easily locatable. To find them on your campus, look for signs on the walls of major campus buildings, or use the campus map to find locations, often marked with an AED symbol. AEDs are also likely to be provided in campus police cars.[72]

If you encounter a medical emergency, it will usually take at least 10 minutes before professional first responders arrive. Are you ready to react in these medical emergency situations? If you are interested in proving basic medical emergency care to others by working with emergency medical technicians (EMTs) and paramedics, consider Basic Life Support (BLS) CPR certification. The U.S. Department of Transportation started first-responder training in 1995 to bridge the gap between CPR and EMT programs. First-responder training includes assessing a medical emergency, making sure the injured victim has sufficient airway and ventilation to breathe, monitoring vital signs, and safely moving the injured person from an unsafe environment. Applying a splint, controlling bleeding, blood pathogen training, and emergency administration of oxygen are also part of the certification programs.

There are different types of training for those who reside in rural and urban areas. Training time varies by state, but most programs are between 40 and 60 hours. People living in remote areas are trained as Wilderness First Responders (80 hours). The Red Cross offers a Professional Rescue Responder course in most cities. You may also check with any agency offering CPR and first aid training. If you want national certification, you must first complete a state-approved First Responder/EMR course that has been entered on the National Registry of Emergency Medical Technicians (NREMT) website. Then complete an online application that includes cognitive and psychomotor exams. People convicted of a felony should consult the NREMT felony policy before applying.[73]

Computer Use

Extensive computer use can cause strain not only on the back but also on the neck, arms, hands, and eyes. If your body is not properly aligned while you are using your computer (Figure 16.2), you may end up with irritated or pinched nerves, inflamed tendons, or headaches.

The average human head weighs 10 pounds in a neutral position (ears straight above shoulders). The pressure on

figure 16.2   **Proper workstation setup.**
Your hips should be slightly higher than your knees, and your feet should be flat on the floor or on a footrest slightly in front of your knees. Your monitor should be an arm's length away from you, and your eyes should be level with the top of the screen. When you type, your wrists should be in a neutral position, tilted neither up nor down.

your spine doubles for every inch you tilt your head forward. For example, if you are looking at your smartphone or tablet on your lap, your neck is supporting what feels like 20 or 30 pounds. This forward tilt can cause muscle strain, fatigue, headaches, disc hernias, and pinched nerves. If neck strain continues over time, your cervical spinal column can flatten or reverse the natural curve of your neck.

Bending your neck and hunching your shoulders can also reduce your lung capacity by 30 percent. To experience this decrease, take a deep breath in a slumped position; then straighten up and take a deep breath again. The loss of lung capacity can lead to vascular diseases due to insufficient oxygen delivery to body organs.

To avoid neck strain, keep your feet flat on the floor, roll your shoulders back, and keep your ears directly over your shoulders. If you use a detachable keyboard, it should be 4 to 6 inches away from you on the desk. Position your mouse (if you use one) as close to you as possible, place your feet on the floor (do not cross your legs), and position your screen an arm's length away with top of screen slightly below eye level. Docking stations, headsets, and wrist guards are effective mobile support devices. The Text Neck Institute has a mobile app that provides an electronic warning if your phone is not at a safe viewing angle. In addition to maintaining good posture, take breaks every 20 minutes, stand up, roll your shoulders, and go for a short walk to improve blood flow.[74]

repetitive strain injuries
Injuries to soft tissues that can occur when motions and tasks are repeatedly performed in ergonomically incorrect ways.

carpal tunnel syndrome (CTS)
Compression of the median nerve in the wrist caused by certain repetitive uses of the hands.

When motions and tasks are repeatedly performed in ergonomically incorrect ways, injuries to the soft tissues, known as **repetitive strain injuries**, can occur. A common repetitive strain injury is **carpal tunnel syndrome (CTS)**, the compression of the median nerve in the wrist caused by certain repetitive uses of the hands, including working at the computer, playing video games, and texting. The median nerve is located inside a "tunnel" created by the carpals (wrist bones) and tendons in the hand (Figure 16.3). When the tendons become inflamed through overuse or incorrect use, they compress the median nerve. The symptoms of CTS are numbness, tingling, pain, and weakness in the hand, especially in the thumb and first three fingers. Symptoms are often worse at night, when pain can radiate into the shoulder.

The first steps in addressing this condition are correcting ergonomic problems in the workstation, taking frequent breaks from repetitive tasks, and doing exercises that stretch and flex the wrists and hands. If symptoms persist, a physician should be consulted.

Natural Disasters

A *disaster* is defined as a sudden event resulting in loss of life, severe injury, or property damage. Disasters can be caused by humans, as in the case of terrorist attacks, or by natural forces, such as tornadoes, hurricanes, floods, wildfires, and earthquakes. For example, in March 2011, a magnitude 9.0 earthquake followed by a tsunami with waves reaching 130 feet ravaged Japan and caused a nuclear power plant disaster. The earthquake moved the main island of Japan 8 feet east and shifted the Earth on its axis by several inches. Hurricane Maria struck Puerto Rico in September 2017, devastating the island's electrical grid, leaving people without power for months, and causing an estimated 3,059 fatalities. The 2018 wildfire in Paradise, California, destroyed a town of about 30,000 people.

When natural disasters occur on this scale, governments and international aid organizations have to provide the assistance and relief people need to recover. Individuals can help themselves by preparing as much as they can for the types of disasters that are likely to occur where they live (say, tornadoes in the Midwest or hurricanes on the East Coast). Ninety percent of natural disasters in the United States include flooding. The National Center for

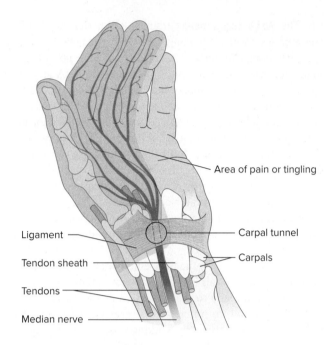

figure 16.3 **Carpal tunnel syndrome (CTS).**
Source: Insel, P., & Roth, W. (2006). *Core concepts in health.* (10th ed.). New York, NY: McGraw-Hill.

Environmental Health (part of the CDC) provides detailed information about preparedness for all types of events, including natural disasters and severe weather emergencies. Visit its website at www.cdc.gov/nceh. The Earthquake Notification Service (ENS) provides a free service that sends automated notification warning emails when earthquakes happen in your area. Earthquake alert apps are also available for iPhone, iPad, or iPod.

■ California Wildfires: The Holy Fire at Lake Elsinore On August 9, 2018
(Kevin Key/Slworking/Getty Images)

VIOLENCE: WORKING TOWARD PREVENTION

Violence is defined as the use of force or the threat of force to inflict intentional injury, physical or psychological, on yourself or another person. Murder, robbery, and **assault** are all violent crimes, but violence also occurs in association with child abuse, sexual harassment, suicide, and several other kinds of conduct. Although violent acts are committed by individuals, the causes of violence are rooted in social and cultural conditions.

This means that taking action to reduce violence is difficult to do as an individual, unlike deciding to improve your diet or get more exercise. What you as an individual can do about violence falls into two categories: knowing how to reduce your own risk of encountering violence, and working to create safer communities and to prevent violence in society. To assess how well you protect yourself from encountering violence, answer the questions in this chapter's Personal Health Portfolio.

Shootings on the College Campus

In 2007, a student at Virginia Polytechnic Institute and State University shot and killed 27 students and 5 faculty members and wounded 16 more. The on-campus killing spree, the worst college shooting incident by a single gunman in U.S. history, stunned the nation. Two students were also killed and four injured in a 2019 campus shooting at University of North Carolina Charlotte. Many people believe college campuses are safe havens and that violence rarely occurs on them.[75] Unfortunately, this is not true. During the first 11 years following the Virginia Tech shooting, from 2007 to 2018, there were 320 people shot on college campuses, almost one-third in mass shootings, and 122 were killed.[76] There have been at least 290 school shootings at technical schools and colleges since 2007. Half these shootings were completed or attempted suicides, accidental gun discharges, or shootings with no injuries. About 64 percent of campus shootings occurred in southern states; the northeastern states experienced the fewest (9 percent).[76,77]

Regardless of whether the campus has distinct boundaries or is an urban campus within a city, colleges confront the same types of societal and violence issues that occur in almost any city in the nation. The U.S. Department of Education provides data about the safety of college campuses. To find out about your campus, visit https://ope.ed.gov/campussafety/#/.

Since the Virginia Tech shooting, college campuses have improved the ways they communicate with students and faculty during an emergency—by e-mail, phone messages, text messages, and siren and/or verbal warnings from communication towers. At some campuses, freshman orientation includes signing up for campus e-mail and phone alerts. Some schools also use social networking sites like Facebook and Twitter to distribute safety alerts. All these measures speed up the distribution of information and the likelihood that students will receive it.

The U.S. Department of Education collaborated with the U.S. Secret Service and the Federal Bureau of Investigation to explore the prevalence of violent incidents on college campuses and to identify perpetrators and potential perpetrators. They looked at data filed under the 1990 Jeanne Clery Disclosure of Campus Security Policy and Crime Statistics Act, which was named for Jeanne Clery, a 19-year-old student at Lehigh University who was raped and murdered in her residence hall in 1986. The act requires all colleges and universities that participate in Title IV federal financial aid programs to collect and disclose information about crimes committed on or near campus. The most commonly reported campus crimes are burglary, motor vehicle theft, and aggravated assault. Other crimes that are tracked include homicides, sex offenses, robbery, and arson.[77,78] Investigators also looked at perpetrators' motivations. They found that current or former relationships between the perpetrator and victim were the predominant trigger for violent acts, followed by retaliation for specific actions.

Hazing

Hazing is defined as "any action taken or situation created intentionally, whether on or off fraternity premises, to produce mental or physical discomfort, embarrassment, or ridicule." According to the National Collegiate Athletic Association (NCAA), four of every five college students are subjected to some form of hazing in their college years, including more than 50 percent of those participating in clubs, sports teams, sororities, and fraternities. Hazing activities have included kidnapping, alcohol chugging, forced swallowing of food and nonfood items, sleep deprivation, beatings, and calisthenics to the point of exhaustion. Deaths have occurred as a result of hazing, most often fraternity hazing; a common cause is alcohol poisoning. Ninety-five percent of hazed students do not report the incident to college officials.[79,80]

Hazing is illegal in most states and may be either a misdemeanor or a felony, depending on the state and the

violence
The use of force or the threat of force to inflict intentional injury, physical or psychological, on oneself or another person.

assault
Attack by one person on another using force or the threat of force to intentionally inflict injury. Aggravated assault is an attack that causes bodily injury, usually with a weapon or other means capable of producing grave bodily harm or death. Simple assault is an attack without a weapon that causes less serious physical harm.

hazing
Actions taken to cause mental or physical discomfort, embarrassment, or ridicule in individuals seeking to join an organization.

hate speech
Verbal, written, or symbolic acts that convey a grossly negative view of particular persons or groups based on their gender, ethnicity, race, religion, sexual orientation, or disability.

severity of the offense. Eighteen fraternity members at Penn State University were arrested in the 2017 alcohol-related hazing death of a first-year pledge.[81] Four of the fraternity members had felony charges dropped. Fourteen stood trial, but the more serious charges of involuntary manslaughter and aggravated assault were dropped. Ten fraternity members pleaded guilty to hazing and alcohol violations and were not sentenced to jail time. Three were convicted of a misdemeanor and sentenced to jail time, and one to house arrest. The judge's message to college students who commit hazing offenses was to "grow up" or face jail time. Parents whose children have died in these senseless incidents have filed wrongful death suits against colleges, fraternities, and fraternity officers. Hazing prevention efforts include zero-tolerance policies, education about hazing dangers, and programs designed to confront the campus hazing culture.[82] Stop-hazing.org and hazingprevention.org are websites providing useful information about hazing prevention.

Hate Speech

Hate speech is defined as verbal, written, or symbolic acts that convey a grossly negative view of particular persons or groups based on their gender, ethnicity, race, religion, sexual orientation, or disability.[83] It is a troublesome phenomenon on many college campuses. Its intent is to humiliate or harm rather than to convey ideas or information, and it has the potential to incite violence. Epithets, slurs, taunts, insults, and intimidation are common modes of hate speech; posters, flyers, letters, phone calls, e-mail,

websites, and even T-shirts are media by which the message is distributed.

Some schools have adopted speech codes that require civility in discourse for all campus community members. Some of these codes have been struck down by the courts as a violation of free speech under the First Amendment. According to court rulings, hate speech must be proven to inflict real, not trivial, harm before it can be regulated.[84] The U.S. Supreme Court has made it clear that colleges and universities cannot suppress speech simply because it is offensive. For this reason, many colleges and universities have adopted conduct codes that regulate certain actions associated with hate speech but not the speech itself. There is an active debate about whether hate speech codes violate free speech and cause more harm than good. Speech codes that are overly broad or vague have been struck down by judicial decisions. See the box "You Make the Call: Free Speech on Campus" later in this chapter.

President Trump signed an executive order to ensure the protection of free speech on college campuses. The order will be enforced by denying or cutting federal research funds to public colleges and universities that do not enact transparent policies that promote free speech on campus.[85] Some state legislatures have enacted measures that prohibit college administrators from intervening to cancel invited controversial speakers. They also require annual reports on the state of free speech on campuses, impose penalties on people who violate the free speech of others, and promote free speech policies in freshman orientation programs. Some state bills prohibit finite areas of college campuses being designated as free-speech zones.

Critics of Trump's executive order argue that it could be unfairly used to enforce "hard right and hard left" political agendas.[86] In fact, some professors are now being careful not to provoke politically hard-left and hard-right students. College students are going to websites such as Professor Watchlist, Campus Reform, and College Fix to report what faculty members say in their classrooms or post on social media. These reports may be used to threaten and harass faculty members for expressing their views on politically sensitive issues (e.g., abortion, gun control, immigration). In some cases, college administrators have used the harassment comments against nontenured faculty on these sites to dismiss them. Overall, harassment and threats on websites have had a chilling effect on the free speech of faculty who choose to self-censor their comments for fear of being targeted for their expressed views.[87]

Trump's executive order applied the antidiscrimination law of Title VI to include anti-Semitic hate-crime acts on college campuses (e.g., painting a swastika on a Jewish student's residence hall door). Trump's executive order

(KMH Photovideo/Shutterstock)

was based on examples of anti-Semitism drafted by the International Holocaust Remembrance Alliance (e.g., accusing American Jewish citizens of being more loyal to Israel than to the United States). But this executive order was met with firm opposition from the political left claiming it is a form of potential free-speech censorship. Supporters of Trump's executive order for including anti-Semitism under Title VI argue that the censorship sensitivity standard is not applied to racism and sexism. Title VI anti-Semitic hate incidents have significantly increased in recent years, more than 200 in 2018. Three sources are largely responsible for these incidents: far left Israel haters, far right ethnic supremacists, and militant Islam. Colleges and universities that violate Title IX may face loss of federal support funds.[88]

A 2017 Cato Institute study found that current college students were more likely than the general population to believe disrespectful people should lose their free-speech rights and government should be more active in policing hate speech. A slight majority of students wanted a campus void of intolerant ideas.[84] Are today's college students less supportive of free speech? Or has an anti-speech minority made college campuses less tolerant of different views? What do you think?

Sexual Violence

Sexual violence addressed in this section includes sexual assault (including rape), sexual harassment, stalking, and other forms of forcible or coercive sexual activity.

Sexual Assault and Coercion **Sexual assault** is any sexual behavior that is forced on someone without his or her consent. At the least, the victim is made to feel uncomfortable and intimidated; at the worst, he or she is physically and emotionally harmed.[89,90] Sexual assault includes forced sexual intercourse (rape), forced sodomy (oral or anal sexual acts), child molestation, incest, fondling, and attempts to commit any of these acts. Another category of victimization is called **sexual coercion**, defined as imposing sexual activity on someone through the threat of nonphysical punishment, promise of reward, or verbal pressure rather than through force or threat of force.

According to various studies, 25 to 60 percent of men (and 15 to 25 percent of college men) have engaged in sexual assault and coercive sexual behavior.[91,92] The causes of this behavior are complex and probably include personality traits in the perpetrator as well as situational factors, including time and place of assault, use of alcohol and other drugs, and the relationship between victim and perpetrator. See the box "Who's at Risk? College Student Sexual Assault Victims" for an overview of at-risk profiles and situations.

Rape In the general U.S. population, someone is sexually assaulted every 92 seconds. One in six women will be the victim of rape or attempted rape in her lifetime. About 3 percent of U.S. men have been raped or experienced rape in their lifetime.[93] More than half of rape and sexual assault victims are under the age of 18, and one in five is under the age of 12.[93] An estimated 20 percent of college women experience rape or attempted rape during their college years; for college men, the rate is about 6 percent. The statistic for women is hotly contested due to disputes over survey methodology. Still, the rate of one in five is widely accepted by public policymakers.[87,94] First-year college women are at highest risk for sexual assault during the first 6 weeks of their first semester (discussed further in "The Red Zone").[94,95]

When a victim is younger than the age of consent, usually 18, the perpetrator can be charged with **statutory rape** whether there was consent or not. State codes vary, however, as to age of consent (the age below which the individual cannot legally consent to sexual intercourse under any circumstances), the age differential between victim and perpetrator, and the minimum age of the perpetrator. State codes also differ in age of consent for different types of sexual activities (e.g., sexual intercourse and sexual contact).[96]

Relatively few rapes are *stranger rapes,* that is, rapes committed by someone unknown to the victim. In about 80 percent of rapes and sexual assaults, the victim knows the perpetrator.[97,98] In 40 percent of cases, the perpetrator is a friend or acquaintance; *acquaintance rape* can be committed by a classmate, coworker, or someone else casually known to the victim. *Date rape,* sexual assault by a boyfriend or someone with whom the victim has a dating relationship, is a type of acquaintance rape. About 90 percent of campus assaults are committed by someone the victim knows. About 18 percent of rapes and sexual assaults are committed by the victim's intimate partner or husband.[92,93,99] Many states now allow rape charges to be brought by a woman against her husband.

Acquaintance-rape survivors are more likely to have consumed alcohol or drugs before the assault, possibly reducing their awareness of signs of aggression in the rapist or lowering their ability to respond to violence.[92,93] Sexual predators also use so-called date rape drugs—including rohypnol, gamma hydroxybutyrate (GHB), ketamine, and Ecstasy—to incapacitate their victims. These drugs typically have no color, smell, or taste, so they can be difficult to detect if mixed into a drink. Date rape drugs are very potent, and they take effect quickly—from a few minutes to half an hour after ingestion. Effects can include physical and cognitive distortion, blackouts, and loss

sexual assault
Any sexual behavior that is forced on someone without his or her consent.

sexual coercion
The imposition of sexual activity on someone through the threat of nonphysical punishment, promise of reward, or verbal pressure rather than through force or threat of force.

statutory rape
Sexual intercourse with someone under the "age of consent," usually 18, whether consent is given or not.

Who's at Risk?
College Student Sexual Assault Victims

Students found to have committed sexual assaults on college campuses have often faced little or no punishment from the school's judicial system. Student victims, however, often experience emotional turmoil from the sexual assault and perceived lack of support from the college or university. This box profiles sexual assaults by class year (both in general and at off-campus parties) and by method of assault and the likelihood that alcohol was involved.

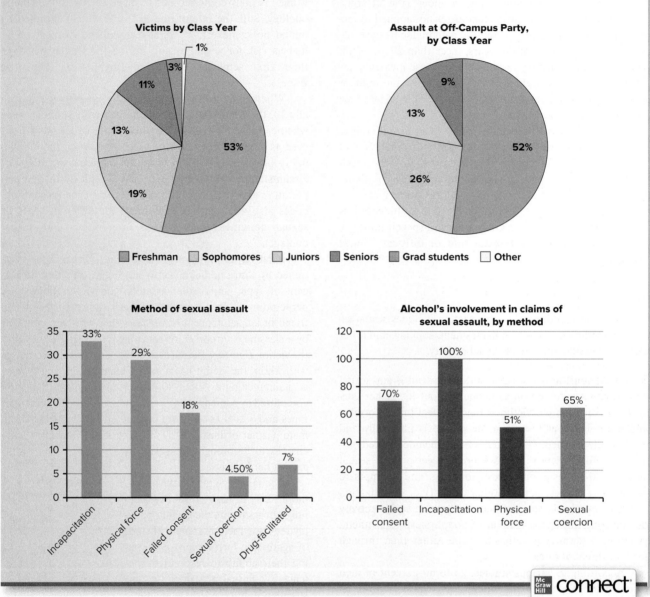

Victims by Class Year
- 53%
- 19%
- 13%
- 11%
- 3%
- 1%

Assault at Off-Campus Party, by Class Year
- 52%
- 26%
- 13%
- 9%

Legend: ■ Freshman ■ Sophomores ■ Juniors ■ Seniors ■ Grad students □ Other

Method of sexual assault
- Incapacitation: 33%
- Physical force: 29%
- Failed consent: 18%
- Sexual coercion: 4.50%
- Drug-facilitated: 7%

Alcohol's involvement in claims of sexual assault, by method
- Failed consent: 70%
- Incapacitation: 100%
- Physical force: 51%
- Sexual coercion: 65%

Source: EDU Risk Solutions. (2015). Confronting campus sexual assault: An examination of higher education claims. *EDU Risk Solutions.* Retrieved from edurisksolutions.org.

of memory. These effects can inhibit a person's ability to say no to sexual advances or to fight back if a sexual assault occurs.

The Red Zone The *red zone,* a term drawn from a campus sexual assault violence prevention program, is the period of time at college when female students are at greatest risk of sexual assault. Counseling centers, student affairs offices, and public safety centers at colleges and universities use web-based and print media to warn female students about the red zone. The zone includes the first few days or weeks of the initial fall semester as female students transition from the security of their parents' home to a less restrictive lifestyle on campus, which often includes binge drinking. For second-year females, the zone encompasses the entire first semester, when many make the move from campus

Life Stories

Heather: A Case of Sexual Assault

Heather was a first-year student in her first semester at a large university a few hundred miles from the midsize city where she grew up. During Welcome Week, her R.A. put up some flyers around her dorm floor about sexual assault, but Heather didn't stop to read them. One night during the second week of classes, Heather and her roommates attended an off-campus party where there were several kegs. Heather got very drunk and left her friends to hang out with a cute and funny junior, Tom, who was also intoxicated. She continued to drink for the next hour until she started to feel like she was going to be sick. She thought Tom was being helpful when he showed her to a bedroom at the house where he said she could rest until she felt better. But once they were in the room alone, Tom started kissing her. She tried to turn away, but she was too drunk to resist him or say anything. He then sexually forced himself on her.

Heather didn't have many people to talk to because it was only the second week of school, but one of her high school friends was a year ahead of her at the same school. Heather texted and they met up at Keisha's apartment. Heather was nervous about sharing something so personal, but Keisha quickly jumped in and said that something similar had happened to her during freshman year. Heather told her how she felt embarrassed, angry, and confused about whether she had been raped. Keisha reminded her that Tom should have stopped when she turned away from him and didn't return his advances. If she didn't report the incident, she asked, how many other girls would Tom do this to? Keisha also explained that because Heather was 18, her parents would not find out unless she told them herself.

Heather told her R.A. of the sexual assault at 10 am, about 7 hours after the alleged assault. The R.A. contacted campus police, who notified local law enforcement and the dean of students. Local law enforcement escorted Heather to the hospital for a forensic sexual assault test, about 8 hours after the alleged assault, which included a blood alcohol content analysis. Heather's BAC was 170 milligrams per 100 milliliters (mg/ml) of blood. Tom was notified of the sexual assault complaint by the dean of students that day and was given interim restrictions that included a change in his course schedule, a prohibition on visiting residence halls other than his own or eating on campus anywhere but his residence dining hall, and a ban on entering the student

union or participating in campus extracurricular activities. Tom was also to have no contact with Heather. These restrictions would be in effect until completion of a campus tribunal hearing on the sexual assault complaint. One month later, before the completion of the tribunal hearing, Tom was banned from his residence hall and allowed on campus only to attend classes.

Tom was told not to discuss the sexual assault complaint with anyone other than his attorney and family. His family and attorney helped Tom appeal the interim restrictions, but the appeal was not successful. Tom decided to reach out by e-mail to a student group that helps minority students in legal situations. In his e-mail, Tom described what had happened between him and Heather. The university administration received a copy of Tom's e-mail and viewed it as a violation of their privacy decree. Tom was then banned from campus and had to cancel all his courses. Tom was later found not guilty of sexual assault by the campus tribunal. But he was charged with failing to comply with the university's gag order (by sending an e-mail with Heather's name) and suspended from the university for 1 year. This expulsion also made it difficult for Tom to be admitted to a different university.

Local law enforcement dropped Heather's sexual assault case based on her alcohol toxicology report. Her BAC was 170 mg/ml of blood. Legal intoxication level is 100 mg/dl, and 250 to 400 mg/dl is considered sleep or stupor. But alcohol toxicology reports post sexual assault are problematic. The body excretes alcohol at the rate of 10 to 20 mg/ml/hour. For example, a reading of 100 ml taken 8 hours after an assault may mean that the peak BAC at the time of the assault could have been 260 ml, which is three times the legal intoxication level and very close to the low end of potential blackout from intoxication. Law enforcement does not typically take into account alcohol pharmacokinetics, that is, how the body absorbs and eliminates alcohol.

- Did it matter that Heather was intoxicated? Were you surprised that law enforcement did not consider alcohol pharmacokinetics in assessing Heather's alleged assault?

- Given that both Tom and Heather were very intoxicated, is he guilty of rape according to your college's affirmative consent policy?

- What is your college's policy on reporting sexual assaults? Do you think the policy is appropriate? Why or why not?

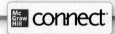

---

housing to sororities or off-campus apartments.[94] See the box "Life Stories: Heather: A Case of Sexual Assault."

Although sexual assault is a serious health problem on many college campuses, college students sometimes prefer to call it "unwanted sex" and not sexual assault, perhaps because the victim is often acquainted with her assailant.

These safety tips for college students from the Rape, Abuse, and Incest National Network (RAINN) are particularly important for the red zone years[93]:

- Trust your instincts. If you feel unsafe in any situation, go with your gut.

- Avoid being alone or isolated with someone you don't know well.

- Get to know your surroundings and learn well-lit routes to your residence.

- Don't put information about your whereabouts on your Facebook page or in your voicemail message.

- Form a buddy system when you go out. Arrive and leave with friends, and check in with each other throughout the evening. If you suspect a friend has been drugged, call 911.

- Always lock your door, and don't let strangers into your room.

- Practice safe drinking. Don't accept drinks from people you don't know, watch while your drink is being prepared, and don't leave your drink unattended.

- Don't go out alone at night. If you'll be walking home at night, arrange to walk with a friend or in a group, or use the campus security escort system if there is one.

Male Rape In about 3 percent of completed and attempted rapes in the United States, the victim is male. Like women, men are reluctant to report that they have been raped. They may feel embarrassed or ashamed, or they may not want to believe they have been raped.[93,99]

Law enforcement officers, health care providers, and social service agencies may be less supportive of male rape victims than of female rape victims because of similar misperceptions and misinformation.[93] The law is clear, however, in defining forced penetration as rape or sodomy. Male rape victims require the same level of medical treatment, counseling, and support as female victims.

Effects of Rape Rape is a crime about dominance, power, and control. For many victims, the effects of rape can be profoundly traumatic and long-lasting. Physical injuries usually heal quickly, but psychological pain can endure.

Victims often experience fear, anxiety, phobias, guilt, nightmares, depression, substance abuse, sleep disorders, sexual dysfunctions, and social withdrawal. They may develop rape-related posttraumatic stress disorder, experiencing flashbacks and impaired functioning. Between 4 and 30 percent of victims contract an STI from the rape, and many worry that they may have been infected with HIV.[92,93,95] Some state laws now mandate HIV testing of an alleged rapist if the victim requests it.

Many victims blame themselves for the rape, and our society tends to foster self-blame. Myths about rape include the false beliefs that women or men who are raped did something to provoke it, put themselves in dangerous situations and so deserved it, or could have fought off their attacker. The fact is that no matter what a person does, nobody ever has the right to rape.[100]

What to Do If You Are Raped There is no one way to respond to rape that works in all cases, and authorities recommend that you do whatever you need to do and can do to survive. No matter how you respond, remember that your attacker is violating your rights and committing a crime; rape is not your fault.

After the rape, seek help as soon as you can. Law enforcement stresses that forensic evidence used in rape kits must be collected within 72 hours after the assault. If you choose to call the police, there is a better chance that the perpetrator will be brought to justice and will be prevented from raping others. The police will probably take you to the hospital, where you will be given a rape exam and treated for your injuries. You should also contact your local Rape Victim Advocacy Program (RVAP) or the Rape, Abuse,

and Incest National Network (RAINN). These organizations can inform you of your rights under the Campus Sexual Assault Victims' Bill of Rights (an amendment to the Clery Act; see the next section) and provide advocate support during campus and local law enforcement investigations.

Rape counseling is critical to your recovery from the attack. Talking about the rape, either one-on-one with a rape counselor or in a rape survivors' support group, can help you come to terms with your reactions and feelings. Rape crisis hotlines, such as the RAINN hotline (800-656-HOPE), are available when you need immediate help, although research suggests an increasing reluctance among young people to use the phone to discuss sexual assault. It takes time to recover from rape, so be patient and take care of yourself.

Forensic rape kits may collect sexual assault information, but less than 14 percent of emergency rooms have trained professionals to collect forensic evidence. There is also a significant backlog of untested rape kits. This problem is particularly acute in rural hospitals. Many states are now using software that enables survivors to track their rape evidence kits. By law these kits are preserved for 55 years.[101]

Campus Response to Sexual Assault Complaints Four in five college women who are sexually assaulted do not report their attacks to campus police, and as few as 5 percent report it to local law enforcement. About 26 percent of college students feel the incident was a personal matter, 20 percent are afraid of reprisal, about half feel the university would not conduct a fair investigation, a significant number are concerned that the college would not protect confidentiality, and a significant number feel embarrassed by the sexual assault.[102,103]

Federal laws have recently been passed to address the way colleges handle sexual assault cases. A 1992 amendment to the Clery Act, the Campus Sexual Assault Victims' Bill of Rights, requires college administrators to provide justice, medical treatment, and psychological counseling for crime victims and survivors. They must inform victims of the outcomes of disciplinary action and of their options to notify law enforcement and change their academic and living situations. This law also requires colleges to promote educational awareness programs about sexual assault and to facilitate reporting of sexual assaults. Amendments made in 2008 protect victims and whistleblowers against retaliation. The Campus Sexual Violence Elimination Act (the Campus SaVE Act) was implemented in 2014.

Together, these laws place colleges and universities in a challenging position to ensure that victims and alleged offenders' rights are protected, unbiased investigations are conducted, adjudication hearings are fair, and "deliberate indifference" charges are avoided when sexual violence incidents are reported that would place the institution at risk for civil liability under Title IX, which makes gender discrimination unlawful. Colleges not complying with Title IX risk reduced federal funding.[90,95] In response, many colleges have

Public Health Is Personal

College Grievance Procedures for Sexual Violence Cases

Recommendations from the Obama administration (the Dear Colleague letter) to colleges and universities included using the "preponderance of evidence" standard to adjudicate sexual violence cases rather than the "clear and convincing" standard. Preponderance of evidence for a guilty decision by a college or university grievance panel means the panelists must believe it is 50.1 percent likely the student committed an act of sexual violence. The clear and convincing standard uses "highly probable" or "reasonably certain" as a criterion to adjudicate sexual violence cases (98 to 99 percent certainty of guilt). Preponderance of evidence is used for violations of civil rights laws and not criminal laws. In other words, the new criterion cancels the presumption of innocence for the accused and replaces it with the presumption that the complainant was victimized. Proponents of the preponderance of evidence standard argue that it counterbalances a long history of bias against the victim, which cultivates a campus rape culture. Opponents claim that the lower evidence standard for grievance cases violates the U.S. legal system's core concepts of fairness and due process for both the complainant and the accused.

The Trump administration revised the Obama administration's campus sexual assault policies. A core change allows colleges and universities to choose either the "preponderance of evidence" standard or the "clear and convincing" standard. The American Association of University Professors supports this action. Supporters for retaining the preponderance of evidence standard (e.g., RAINN) argue that this standard is used in civil court and thus is suitable for campus adjudication of sexual assault cases. Opponents of preponderance of evidence argue that criminal/civil court proceedings provide due process protection not present in campus tribunal adjudications: rights to discovery, cross-examination, calling of expert witnesses, specific written complaint, clear rules of evidence, and discovery protections.

Many issues surround the preponderance of evidence standard. It is a myth that colleges do not enact severe penalties for guilty decisions in sexual violence cases. Expulsion is often the punishment in incidents involving victim incapacitation or use of physical force. Probation is more likely in failed-consent cases. A fundamental issue is whether college grievance panels consisting of faculty, staff, and students should be used to "try" cases involving rape, which is a felony offense. Rape is an act that falls more appropriately under criminal law than civil law. In contrast, sexual harassment usually does not meet the standard for a criminal act and more appropriately falls under Title IX, which is broadly written and pertains to sexual discrimination. A college's deliberate indifference in responding to sexual harassment or sexual assault may be viewed as a violation of Title IX.

Colleges and universities use disciplinary tribunal panels consisting of faculty, staff, and students to adjudicate sexual assault cases. Legal experts question whether these tribunal hearings violate the due process rights of the accused and the accuser, particularly the accused. Neither the accused nor the accuser has the right to active legal counsel at the hearing, cross-examination is very limited if allowed at all, and administrators on the tribunal panel may have a conflict of interest arising from their desire to protect the university or college.

The accuser can appeal a "not guilty" decision by the tribunal, which subjects the accused to double jeopardy. Rules of evidence applied in criminal and civil cases do not apply in tribunal hearings, the accused and the accuser are not placed under oath, and formal recordings are usually not made. Tribunal panels are not effectively trained to adjudicate felony criminal acts. Many colleges and universities do not have penalties for an accuser who intentionally brings false charges, and interim penalties may be imposed on the accused, such as removal from residence halls, classes, campus dining accommodations, and campus extracurricular activities before the tribunal has reached a decision. The tribunal can have conflicting roles when it is responsible for both investigating and deciding on guilt and punishment, a common problem under the single-investigator model.

Civil rights groups like the Foundation for Individual Rights in Education (FIRE) are challenging due process violations of the accused in tribunal hearings. RAINN has urged the federal government to de-emphasize the use of college and university internal tribunals in sexual assault cases. College students accused of sexual assault and found not guilty are often stigmatized and treated with hostility at educational institutions and in future work opportunities. A finding of guilty often results in permanent suspension from the institution and jeopardizes acceptance at other academic institutions.

What do you think? Has the rush by some colleges to implement the preponderance of evidence standard unfairly tilted the adjudication process to the complainant? If so, is this shift justified by a culture of sexual violence on many college campuses? Should college tribunals adjudicate rape cases?

Sources: Heller, Z. (2015). *Rape on campus*. Retrieved from http://nybooks.com/articles/archives/2015/feb/05/rape-campus/; United Educators. (2015). Confronting campus sexual assault: An examination of higher education claims. *EDU Risk Solutions*. Retrieved from edurisksolutions.org; Johnson, K. C., & Taylor Jr., S. (2017). *The campus rape frenzy*. New York, NY: Encounter Books; Yoffe, E. (2017). The uncomfortable truth about campus rape policy. Retrieved from https://www.theatlantic.com/education/archive/2017/09/the_uncomfortable_truth_about_campus_rape_policy/538974/; Carson, S. (2018). I was raped at college. Here's how DeVos's new rules harm survivors like me. Retrieved from https://broadly.vice.com/en_us/article/d3b7gq/title-ix-betsy-devos-college-rape-sexual=assault

enacted grievance procedures that some civil rights advocates view as more favorable to complainants than to the alleged perpetrator.[95] See the box "Public Health Is Personal: College Grievance Procedures for Sexual Violence Cases."

Although some civil rights activists argue that sexual assault cases should be heard only by the criminal justice system and not by campus tribunals, it is worth remembering that criminal law is directed toward punishment, while

Title IX is directed toward maintaining gender equality. This means campus tribunal boards must take into account the survivor's physical and psychological safety during a sexual assault investigation and hearing, for example, by ensuring he or she is not living in the same residence hall as the accused, attending the same classes, or being required to speak to the person accused of the assault. Criminal courts are not held to this standard. College and university administrators face a difficult balance in protecting the survivor and maintaining a fair due process tribunal hearing. Criminal courts also have a questionable record in prosecuting sexual assaults. Only 40 percent of sexual assaults are reported to law enforcement, only 10 percent of those reported result in a felony conviction, and only 3 percent of sexual assault offenders spend even a single day in jail.[104] Although campus tribunals may do a poor job processing sexual assault cases, the criminal justice system does not appear to do any better.[105] The answer may not be removing campus tribunals for sexual assault cases but instead designing transparent investigations, hearings, and sanctions that maintain fair due process and equal protection for the accuser and the accused.

Federal directives ensure the safety of victims through "interim measures," safe accommodations that ensure the victim never has to encounter the alleged perpetrator on campus. This could mean the alleged perpetrator is removed from a campus residence hall, has classes changed, and is banned from activities, possibly from campus. Although these measures may be warranted due to the severity of the alleged incident and strong evidence against the alleged perpetrator, they have sometimes been employed by administrators in reflexive actions. Even if the alleged perpetrator is cleared during campus or local adjudication, a standing "no-contact" restraining order may be established between the victim and the accused.[103]

The fundamental right to avoid self-incrimination does not apply to the alleged perpetrator during a campus sexual assault investigation and hearing. The alleged perpetrator can be expelled if he refuses to answer questions, but whatever he says can be turned over to law enforcement authorities for criminal prosecution. Expulsion from college is a harsh penalty that can destroy an individual's future career.

The Trump administration's revisions to Title IX and sexual assaults include the following: colleges can decide whether to provide an appeal process, mediation can be used to resolve complaints between the accuser and the accused, cross-examination can be used for both the accuser and the accused, the single-investigator model is eliminated, and the college must have actual knowledge of a sexual assault allegation made to an administrative official with authority to dispense corrective action before it can be held legally responsible for failing to investigate the allegation. The Department of Education in its own projections estimated reporting of campus sexual assaults would decrease by 39 percent due to these revisions. Many colleges and universities opposed the Trump administration revisions on the grounds they shift too much legal rights to the accused student and create a direct confrontation between the accused and the accuser. Some colleges and universities petitioned state legislators to retain some of the Obama administration policies.[106]

The core tenet of the Dear Colleague letter advocated greater accountability for sexual assault investigations on college campuses on the assumption that the victim is essentially always telling the truth. Organizations like RAINN claim that only 2 to 10 percent or reported rape cases are false accusations. Empirical data on false rape accusations are challenged by groups like the Foundation for Individual Rights in Education (FIRE) and Families Advocating for Campus Equality (FACE). FIRE and FACE are strong advocates for due process rights on college campuses for both the victims and the alleged perpetrators. A 2010 study that was one of very few to analyze false rape allegations concluded, however, that more than 90 percent of rape allegations are not false.[105] This is a troubling paradox. Feminist activists argue that for a long time the judicial system and culture tended to prejudge sexual assault cases by believing male alleged perpetrators over female victims in "he said, she said" cases. But some legal experts believe the measures from the Dear Colleague letter tilted the pendulum balance too much in favor of the accuser and violate due process rights of the accused.

Pushback by male college students accused of sexual assault has made headway in federal courts. According to the National Center for Higher Education Risk Management, higher education institutions are consistently losing challenges to due process violations for sexual assault cases in federal court. If there is a bottom line to this debate, perhaps it is that during this turbulent time, the duty to dispassionately weigh the rights of the sexual assault victim and the alleged perpetrator are being legally challenged on college campuses.

What does a campus sexual predator look like? The case of Brock Turner, a swimmer at Stanford University convicted of sexually assaulting an unconscious woman after a campus party, paints an archetypal image of a white, affluent, fraternity athlete predator. The 2015 documentary *The Hunting Ground* presented a similar image of a privileged affluent male exuding white male power. But in three of the four cases focused on in the documentary, three of the accused were Black men. The question of race in campus sexual assaults has received scant attention from the Office for Civil Rights (OCR), the federal organization that enforces Title IX compliance on college campuses. Although the role of race in campus sexual assault had long been the topic no one wants to discuss, this is now changing, particularly around interracial hookups and sexual assault. See the box, "Starting the Conversation: Is the Sexual Assault Investigative Process on College Campuses Biased Against Men of Color?"

Starting the Conversation

Is the Sexual Assault investigative Process on College Campuses Biased Against Men of Color?

Is the sexual assault system used on college campuses biased against men of color? It's a sensitive question. The Office of Civil Rights (OCR) regulates higher education institutions' responses to sexual assault allegations, but it does not require that the race of the victim and the alleged perpetrator be documented in complaints. Interracial assault allegations are of particular concern. Accusations that Black men sexually assault white women are prevalent in U.S. racial history.

A potentially disturbing question is whether "morning-after" remorse may be at play in interracial relationships. Hooking up with someone of a different ethnicity, and experiencing a perceived physical or emotional injury, might lead some college women to consider a regretted encounter as a sexual assault. The challenges of considering this possibility are apparent. Since data on race and ethnicity are not collected in sexual assault complaints, it is not possible to know whether unconscious racial bias plays a role in interracial allegations.

In recent sexual assault lawsuits, male college students of color found guilty by campus tribunals and expelled from school have claimed that the tribunal process was tainted by explicit violations. Legal supporters of these students argue that college men of color, particularly foreign men of color from Africa and Asia, do not have sufficient financial resources, a network of support, and an understanding of due process rights to confront campus sexual assault charges.

The fact that college men of color are overrepresented in sexual assault complaints is raising red flags about disparate treatment. Blacks and Asians account for 7 percent of the male U.S. student population but about 40 percent of students accused of sexual assault and 42 percent of those referred to campus tribunal hearings. It is not known whether there is a systematic racial bias operating in sexual assault complaints and campus tribunal adjudications. Anecdotal evidence of disproportionate accusations suggests that racial bias may exist and should be investigated. To date, the OCR has not acknowledged the possibility of racial bias in campus sexual assault campus tribunal adjudications.

- Are white college women and men more likely to believe a white victim of sexual assault than a victim of color?

- Do you think race plays a pivotal role in the adjudication of campus sexual assault?

- Have interracial hook-ups led to morning-after remorse and contributed to false allegations of sexual assault?

Yoffe, E. (2017). The question of race in campus sexual-assault cases. The Atlantic. Retrieved from https://www.theatlantic.com/education/archive/2017/09/the-question-of-race-in-campus-sexual-assault-cases/539361/; Sexton, J. (2017). Campus sexual assault and race, the unexamined question. Hot Air. Retrieved from https://hotair.com/archives/2017/09/11/campus-sexual-assault-race-unexamined-questions.

Sexual Assault and Black Colleges Little research has focused on sexual assault disclosures at historically Black colleges and universities (HBCUs). One barrier to disclosure is the stereotypical perception of African American women as "strong Black women," that is, as self-sufficient and resilient and distrustful of social and legal support services. A cultural mandate also protects African American male offenders. The strong Black woman stereotype, if it exists, is more likely to occur at HBCUs. An Association of American Universities (AAU) report found that 26 percent of female college seniors had been victims of rape or offensive sexual touching since attending their college or university. This study did not have a representative sample of African American college women. One study found that 14 percent of HBCU women had experienced attempted sexual assault, and 10 percent completed sexual assault.[107]

The number of Black women filing campus sexual assault complaints has skyrocketed in recent years. But Black college women have faced even more racial injustice in sexual assault complaints than Black men. A 2017 study suggested that Black women are considered more sexually mature (code for hypersexual and seeking to be sexually dominated) than white women in their peer group and thus face more skepticism about being victims of sexual violence than white women. This skepticism has perpetuated racial barriers in the campus adjudication of sexual assault complaints. Fueled by the #MeToo movement, Black women are actively confronting this injustice. The inequalities faced by women and men of color in campus sexual assault adjudications cannot be ignored.[108]

Disclosure of sexual assault to informal support networks is high at non-HBCUs. Only 19 percent of stranger-rape sexual assaults and 2 percent of acquaintance sexual assault survivors pursued crisis support services after the assault. And only 5 percent of college women survivors reported their assault to law enforcement, in contrast to 14 percent of the general population. Community-based research suggests that college female survivors at non-HBCU campuses have positive experiences with both informal and formal support services. Research on African American college female survivors, though limited, suggests they experience higher levels of disregard and lower emotional support from others than do white survivors. More research is needed on African American survivors at HBCUs.[107]

Ride-sharing Services and Sexual Assault Uber provided 1.3 billion rides in 2018 in the United States and claims that 99.5 percent of its 4 million rides per day are safe. More than 3,000 sexual assaults were reported during these rides, however, including 229 rapes, of which 92 percent were charged against Uber drivers. The number may be higher since these incidents are generally underreported; Uber reports sexual assault claims to law enforcement only if the accuser insists on it.[109]

To confront this problem, Uber has increased its vetting of drivers and released a 911 emergency app. RAINN has called for cameras to be installed to record rides. Lyft, the second largest ride-hailing company in the United States, has also been accused of driver sexual assaults against passengers, although Lyft has not released national data on sexual assault incidents by its drivers. Uber has been more transparent and announced it will release sexual assault incident data every 2 years.[109]

Safety incidents, such as robbery and physical assault, can also occur in both ride-share and taxi services. Whichever you are using, observe these recommended safety tips[110]:

- Share your trip information with others, especially late at night, by using GPS notifications such as the "Save My ETA" option in Uber and "Send ETA" in Lyft.

- Request your ride while you are still indoors, to avoid lingering outside with your phone out which may attract non-ride-share drivers.

- Confirm your driver and car by checking the driver's name, car license plate, and car type (make, model, color) before getting into the vehicle. This information is provided ahead of time by the ride-share app.

- If traveling alone, always sit in the back seat.

- Check your driver's rating, which should always be at least 4.5. Drivers are fired or deactivated if their rating is below 4.5.

- Know your surroundings by tacking your route on your app's map.

Affirmative Consent   The Department of Education (DOE) has avoided setting a national standard that defines what it means to consent to sexual activity. This void has led a number of colleges to implement an affirmative consent standard that implies "yes means yes." Under affirmative consent the victim need not prove that she or he physically or verbally resisted the assailant. Currently, more than 1,400 colleges have passed an affirmative consent policy. Some states (e.g., California) have also implemented affirmative consent laws.[90,111,112] The inclusion of affirmative consent policies or state laws has become a hotly debated topic.

Higher education institutions receiving state or federal funding for financial aid are required to comply with state laws on sexual assault in their jurisdictions. State laws use a "no means no" or "yes means yes" standard for defining sexual consent. The no means no standard requires the victim to affirmatively express lack of consent verbally or by body language. Affirmative consent is a yes means yes standard that

requires both parties engaged in sexual activity to establish consent that is enthusiastic, unambiguous, and a voluntary agreement. Consent may be withdrawn at any time during the sexual activity. Lack of protest, past consent, or silence at any time during sexual activity does not constitute consent. Neuroscience suggests that there is no gender difference in perceptions of consent. It is human nature for both men and women to be influenced by what they see and hear. This means it is not unusual to reasonably miscommunicate about consent when relying on facial expressions and body movements rather than verbal cues. The point of affirmative consent is to remove gray areas that may be distorted by emphasizing explicit consent and communication. Facial expressions and body movements are not a language legally accepted for affirmative consent.[113]

Affirmative consent is not a groundbreaking policy in higher education. The National Center for Higher Education and Risk Management recommended affirmative consent as the standard for sexual assault discipline hearings in the early 2000s. This policy was already in place in more than 1,400 higher education institutions before California and New York passed their affirmative-consent laws. Proponents of affirmative consent argue that it is a needed extreme solution to an extreme problem on college campuses that perpetuate a culture of sexual entitlement. Opponents are concerned that affirmative consent trivializes the standard of consent and places innocent students (mostly men) at risk of being severely disciplined by college tribunals motivated to change a "beer and circus" image on their campus.[90]

State laws for affirmative consent are new, and there are not yet judicial decisions that frame their legality. Higher education institutions have also not faced extensive legal challenges to their affirmative consent standard. Many college students, faculty, and legal scholars, however, are raising questions about whether the affirmative consent standard violates due process rights of the accused, particularly when alcohol is involved. It is estimated that half of sexual assault cases involve alcohol. Until affirmative consent, very few of these cases made it to court. Even fewer resulted in sexual assault convictions. Many sexual assault cases are not dependent on whether sex occurred. Most often, consent is the primary focus. And alcohol complicates consent.

How intoxicated is too intoxicated for giving consent for sex? Can a man consent to sex when he is intoxicated but not a woman? How can you tell someone is too intoxicated to consent to have sex? If both parties are intoxicated, is this nonconsensual sex? What if someone said "no" to sex when sober but "yes" when intoxicated? Finding answers to these questions is difficult. Alcohol plays an important role in sex. Affirmative consent means that college students cannot pretend they have no control over the effects of alcohol. The bottom line: When alcohol is a factor, the primary responsibility to ensure consent was established will fall on the party who initiated sex. The hard and fast rule is to be very cautious in initiating sex when someone is intoxicated. Key questions to ask include: Can my partner communicate clearly? Is my partner sober enough to be coherent and give consent?[114]

Preventing Sexual Violence Rape prevention efforts need to include efforts to change the environment that promotes violence against women. That means creating a culture and a community in which sexual violence is not tolerated. Changing social and cultural norms can be a slow process, but programs like Take Back the Night and the Green Dot Strategy have taken on this challenge.

The Green Dot Violence Prevention Strategy—a program that began in the United Kingdom and is now appearing on U.S. college campuses—seeks to reduce and prevent power-based personal violence, including sexual violence, domestic violence, dating violence, stalking, child abuse, elder abuse, and bullying.[115] Rather than focusing on victims or perpetrators, as many campaigns do, it aims to mobilize the vast majority of the population who consider violence unacceptable and move them from passive bystanding to engagement and action. The Green Dot strategy addresses individual factors (such as shyness and lack of assertiveness), interpersonal factors (such as peer pressure and the well-known "bystander effect," in which everyone assumes someone else will act), community factors (by training influential members of the community to model new behaviors), and societal factors (by addressing cultural norms about the acceptability of violence).

■ Students and faculty march across the University of Alaska Fairbanks campus during a Take Back the Night march. *(ZUMA Press Inc/Alamy Stock Photo)*

Sexual Harassment Sexual harassment occurs in two types of situations: (1) a person in a position of authority, such as an employer or a teacher, offers benefits for sexual favors or threatens retaliation for the withholding of sex, and (2) suggestive language or intimidating conduct creates a hostile atmosphere and interferes with a person's work or academic performance.

Of all sexual harassment claims, the vast majority result from actions that create a hostile environment.[116] A hostile environment can be created by visual images (sexually explicit photos), language (jokes, derogatory comments, obscene e-mails), or behavior (inappropriate touching). Colleges and universities are liable under Title IX for sexual harassment perpetrated by their faculty or staff, regardless of whether the advance is accepted or rejected.

Sexual harassment can be considered discrimination. The Office for Civil Rights (OCR) and the Department of Justice (DOJ) established a blueprint that colleges and universities follow to protect students from sexual harassment, and in the 1990s and early 2000s, college and university administrators began to place considerable emphasis on the hostile-environment component of Title IX. One reason is that educational institutions receiving federal funds can be held liable if they are deliberately indifferent to sexual harassment. Under the OCR and DOJ doctrine, a person can be held liable in civil court for sexual harassment for telling a dirty joke, even if only one person was offended. Speech codes and conduct codes regulating sexual harassment incidents may be challenged as a violation of the First Amendment.[117] What do you think? Have administrators gone too far in structuring college and university speech codes?

The difference between sexual harassment and flirting depends on three factors: (1) whether the behavior is by someone who has power over the offended person that limits his or her ability to object for fear of reprisal, (2) whether the behavior puts pressure on the offended person, and (3) whether the offended person wants to end the interaction. Gender and culture differences complicate the situation. For example, men are more likely than women to misperceive friendliness as sexual interest.

If you have experienced sexual harassment, keep a written record of all incidents, including the date, time, place, people involved, words or actions, and any witnesses. If you can, speak up and tell your harasser that the behavior is unacceptable to you. If you do not feel comfortable confronting the harasser in person, consider doing so by letter.

If confrontation does not change the harasser's behavior, complain to a manager or supervisor. If that person does not respond properly to your complaint, consider using your organization's internal grievance procedures. Most colleges

sexual harassment Behavior in which a person in authority offers benefits for sexual favors or threatens retaliation if sexual favors are withheld; or sexually oriented behavior that creates an intimidating or hostile environment that interferes with a person's work or academic performance.

stalking
Malicious following, harassing, or threatening of one person by another.

cyberstalking
The use of electronic media to pursue, harass, or contact another person who has not solicited the contact.

have an administrative office where students can report incidents of sexual harassment and a procedure for doing so. Legal remedies are also available through your state's Human Rights Commission and the federal Equal Employment Opportunity Commission. If you feel your college or university administration has not satisfactorily addressed your sexual harassment complaint, you may file a discrimination complaint with the U.S. Department of Education's Office of Civil Rights.

The #MeToo movement has had a significant impact in confronting sexual harassment on the college campus. The movement was founded in 2006 but acquired a bigger foothold in 2017 when film actresses opened up about their sexual harassment. #MeToo has now become a source of solidarity for women of diverse backgrounds who have been sexually harassed. Tarana Burke, a Black activist, introduced the term "Me Too" in 2006 to bring public attention to the prevalence of sexual harassment, particularly of women of color. The underlying principle of #MeToo is empowerment through empathy.[118]

#MeToo has attempted to hold sexual harassers legally accountable for their actions not only in work environments but in the broader society as well. The courage of women who came forward to allege sexual harassment under the #MeToo banner cannot be overstated. But there is a brewing male backlash claiming the movement has become a trial by mob or a "witch hunt" in which accusation equals conviction and public shaming without due process. The backlash attempts to ask difficult questions: Aren't women also guilty of being sexual predators? Has #MeToo made relationships between men and women better or worse?[119,120]

The lack of moral and legal clarity about the difference between "sexual harassment" and "inappropriate conduct" has clouded the notion of what objectionable behavior is. Critics of #MeToo claim it has ignited a host of public accusations that can lead to expedited justice, putting some undeserving offenders in the same category as sex offenders without giving them a chance to defend themselves. The overall result, according to male critics, has been a totalitarian climate that represses sexual expression and freedom. Message boards entitled "Men Going Their Own Way" (MGTOW) and "Man-o-Sphere" are antifeminist online movements that advocate men separating from society through gender-partition policies, for example, limiting business travel with women, discouraging men from meeting with or mentoring women privately, and not hiring women. MGTOW is a community of websites that use social media broadly described as the "manosphere." Man-o-Sphere is an informal network of blogs (Reditt, 4chan) dedicated to preserving and protecting male sovereignty. Both MGTOW and Man-o-Sphere promote awareness of

how the political correctness of sex discrimination claims harms men. In other words, an unintended consequence of #MeToo has been that some men are limiting their social and professional contact with women to minimize the risk of sexual harassment claims or the the appearance of sexual misconduct.

Both men and women are concerned that false accusations may become prevalent, that women could lose out on career opportunities caused by sex segregation, and that less severe forms of sexual harassment may be categorized as far more severe offenses. Both men and women support the #MeToo movement. But some worry that the movement has gone too far, too fast. The bottom line: The future of #MeToo requires difficult conversations about sexual harassment. The male backlash has opened the door for these conversations.[121,122]

Stalking, Cyberstalking, and Cyberharassment Stalking occurs when a person repeatedly and maliciously follows, harasses, or threatens another person. Women are four times as likely as men to be victims of stalking; it is estimated that 1 in 6 heterosexual women, 1 in 3 bisexual women, and 1 in 19 men have been stalked at some point during their lifetime.[123] Prevalence rates for college students being stalked range from 12 to 40 percent, which is higher than that in the general population. It is estimated that 70 to 75 percent of stalking incidents are not reported to law enforcement or college administration.[124]

Stalking typically includes surveillance at work, school, or home; frequent disturbing telephone calls; vandalism of the target's property; physical encounters; unwanted gifts; letters; e-mails; and attempts to get the victim's family and friends to aid the stalker. Targets of stalkers live in constant fear.

Many states have passed laws to protect individuals who are being stalked, but in some cases it is difficult to arrest and prosecute stalkers without violating their rights, such as the right to be present in a public place. If you plan to report a stalker to the police, keep a written record of all dates, times, locations, witnesses, and types of incidents (personal encounters, telephone calls, e-mails).

Cyberstalking is the use of electronic media to pursue, harass, or contact another person who has not solicited the contact.[125] Online stalkers may send threatening, harassing, sexually provocative, or other unwanted e-mails to the target or attack or impersonate the person on bulletin boards or in chat rooms. College students need to be particularly cautious about Facebook stalking, especially via the Secret Admirer app and Anonymous Confessions pages. These features allow users to select "secret crushes" out of their friend's list. Some states have laws against cyberstalking, but prosecution is hampered by Internet protocols that preserve anonymity as well as by the U.S. Constitution's First Amendment protection of free speech. If you are experiencing this kind of harassment, you can contact the stalker's Internet service provider (ISP) and complain about its client; the company will often take action to try to stop the conduct.

Cyberharassment typically pertains to threatening or harassing e-mails, instant messages, blog entries, and website entries intended to torment an individual. States may have stand-alone cyberharassment statutes or language in statutes that addresses electronic communication harassment. It is important to differentiate cyberharassment from cyberbullying.[126]

Cyberbullying laws usually refer to electronic harassment or bullying among children within a school context.[127] However, cyberbullying is also a concern among college students due to their high use of social media. Female college students victimized by cyberbullying are three times more likely to meet clinical criteria for depression than the general population. The risk of depression doubles to sixfold if the bullying was in the form of unwanted sexual advances or due to a relationship break-up.[128]

About one in four women aged 18 to 24 say they have been victimized by cyberstalking, cyberharassment, or cyberbullying. Asian Americans are particularly at risk because they experience at least four times as much digital harassment or bullying as people of other ethnicities.[128,129,130]

Cyberstalking and cyberharassment also occur beyond computers and the Internet. Stalkers can track a person's location through GPS devices, audio or video recordings, or the use of malicious spyware programs. Spyware programs enable the tracker to detect the victim's online information, including keystrokes, e-mail content, and websites visited. The bottom line: Colleges need to be proactive in preventing or responding to virtual and nonvirtual stalking of and by their students.

Deepfake videos have become a cyberharassment problem. Artificial-intelligence software developed by Google and face-mapping technology are being used to create realistic fake videos and pictures. The software enables the grafting of a target's body and face onto another person's body and face and uses processing information (movement analysis) that mimics a target's voice, facial expressions, and mannerisms. Deepfake videos and pictures have commonly targeted celebrities but are now being weaponized to publicly harass and humiliate noncelebrity women. Men are also victims of deepfake videos, but most of the time these are intended as jokes and not a form of public harassment.

In addition to sexual harassment, deepfake videos can be used for blackmail attempts, phishing, and extortion scams. Deepfake videos and pictures are posted on popular websites. How-to beginner guides to creating them are available online, and the task is made easier with the use of a supply of facial images called "facesets" and sex-scene videos of women called "donor bodies."[131]

In 2018, Google installed involuntary synthetic pornographic imagery, which allows a victim to block search engines that contain deepfake videos and pictures that falsely display them as nude or in sexually explicit situations. The U.S. Advanced Research Agency has also been working on advanced technology to combat deepfake videos. Darpa's MedFor is developing an automated system that can detect deepfake videos. Although deepfake videos are very realistic, they are not perfect. Telltale signs of fake videos include lifeless or unblinking eyes, closed eyes, and jerky facial movements.[132]

Many states have passed laws to protect individuals who are being stalked, but in some cases it is difficult to arrest and prosecute stalkers without violating their rights, such as the right to be present in a public place. If you plan to report a stalker to the police, keep a written record of all dates, times, locations, witnesses, and types of incidents (personal encounters, telephone calls, e-mails).

Intimate Partner Violence

Violence in families can be directed at any family member, but women, children, and older adults are the most vulnerable. Violence between intimate partners is called **intimate partner violence or domestic violence**, which is defined as abuse by a person against his or her partner in an intimate relationship. The four types of intimate partner violence are physical, sexual, threats, and emotional abuse. This definition includes the intentional use of fear and humiliation to control another person. About 20 percent of heterosexual women, 36 percent of lesbians, and 50 percent of gay male couples were pushed or shoved by an intimate partner at some point in their lifetime. Severe intimate partner violence has been reported by one in four heterosexual women, 14 percent of heterosexual men, one in three lesbians, one in two bisexual women, 14 percent of bisexual men, and 70 percent of gay men.[133,134] Eleven percent of college women and college men report being in an abusive relationship.[27]

Cycle of Abuse Domestic violence is usually characterized by a cycle of abuse, a recurring pattern of escalating violence. Typically, tension builds up in the relationship until there is a violent outburst, followed by a "honeymoon" period in which the abuser is contrite, ashamed, apologetic, and nonviolent.[133] Often, the abuser begs his or her partner for forgiveness and promises it will never happen again. Unless the abuser gets help, however, the violence does recur and the cycle repeats itself, almost always becoming more severe (Figure 16.4). If the couple is heterosexual, the pattern is sometimes referred to as **battered woman syndrome**, but it can occur in any relationship, including gay and lesbian partnerships.

cyberharassment
Pertains to threatening or harassing e-mails, instant messages, blog entries, and website entries intended to torment an individual.

cyberbullying
Electronic harassment or bullying among children within a school context.

deepfake
Artificial-intelligence software used to create realistic fake videos and pictures that mimics a target's voice, facial expressions, and mannerisms.

intimate partner violence or domestic violence
Violence between two partners in an intimate relationship.

battered woman syndrome
The cycle of abuse in an intimate relationship, characterized by escalating tension, a violent episode, and a period of lowered tension and nonviolence.

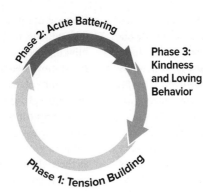

Phase 2: Acute Battering
- Batterer is unpredictable, claims loss of control.
- Victim feels helpless, trapped.
- Batterer is highly abusive.
- Victim is injured, traumatized.

Phase 3: Kindness and Loving Behavior
- Batterer is often apologetic, attentive.
- Victim has mixed feelings.
- Batterer is manipulative.
- Victim feels guilty and responsible.
- Batterer promises change.
- Victim considers reconciliation.

Phase 1: Tension Building
- Victim is compliant, tries to please batterer.
- Batterer experiences increased tension.
- Victim denies anger, minimizes threats.
- Batterer takes more control.
- Victim withdraws.
- Tension becomes unbearable.

figure 16.4   **Cycle of domestic violence.**

Research indicates that men who batter are more likely to abuse drugs and alcohol, suffer from mental illness, and have financial problems.[133] Most women who are battered eventually leave their abusive relationships, but they may make several attempts before they succeed. Battered women's shelters provide a safe haven where the woman and her children cannot be found by the abuser. They provide housing, food, and resources to help the woman start a new life. When shelters aren't available, private homes are sometimes available as safe houses, and churches, community centers, and YWCAs may also offer temporary facilities.[133]

Dating Violence Dating violence is widespread: 43 percent of college women report having experienced violent or abusive dating behaviors, and 22 percent report actual physical abuse, sexual abuse, or threats of violence.[135,136] Fifty-two percent of college women report knowing a friend who experienced an abusive relationship, including physical, sexual, digital, verbal, or controlling abuse, and 38 percent said they would not know how to help someone in an abusive relationship.[136] In response to these findings, a teen dating violence prevention organization called Break the Cycle teamed up with the National Dating Abuse Helpline to launch an initiative called Love Is Respect (www.loveisrespect.org). This initiative targets college students and provides resources to address abusive dating relationships.[137]

Studies show that individuals at risk for dating violence are more likely than others to have been sexually assaulted, to have peers who have been sexually victimized, and to accept dating violence. Perpetrators are more likely than others to abuse alcohol or drugs, to have adversarial attitudes toward others, to have sexually aggressive peers, and to accept dating violence.[136]

An important question is whether dating apps should screen for registered sex offenders. Registered sex offenders are using dating apps such as Tinder, PlentyofFish, and OK Cupid. These apps place the responsibility on its users to screen for sexual predators. The company Match Group has an estimated 35 million monthly visitors and 9 million subscribers and is currently the only dating app screening for registered sex offenders. Match.com is one of its dating apps. But it does not use this policy across its free platform, which contains about 45 dating app brands, including Tinder, PlentyofFish, and OK Cupid. Users affirm that they are not on any state or federal sex registries, but verification is not conducted. Match Group argues that risk screening is only as good as the information it receives from state and federal sex offender registries. New Jersey was the first state to mandate that dating apps disclose their screening policies and provide safety tips for users.[138]

Resources for Survivors of Intimate Partner Violence If you are concerned that someone you know may be in an abusive relationship, try talking to the person about the nature of the relationship and giving him or her information about resources available in your community. Encourage the person to maintain contact with friends and family members while getting support to leave the relationship and begin building a new life.[133] As described in the previous sections, help is available from social service agencies, educational programs, hotlines, shelters, advocacy organizations, and informational books and packets provided by national, state, and local organizations.

Coercive Control Sexual assaults, stalking, and intimate partner violence are a form of abuse known as *coercive control.* What they have in common is domination through isolation, manipulation, degradation, micromanagement, sexual coercion, and/or possibly physical violence. Although it is usually men who exert coercive control over women, victims include all genders and sexual orientations. College students may see themselves as partners, but in an ill-defined space between friendship and hooking-up relationships. For this reason, they often miss signs or ignore signs of coercive control in another, like moving too quickly to establish an exclusive relationship, blaming others for his or her own failures, having intense mood swings, holding grudges and bringing up past transgression to seek sympathy, being controlled by jealousy, and being a substance abuser.

College women are more likely to leave a coercive control relationship if it leads to physical abuse. But they are less likely to do so if the relationship involves psychological abuse or emotional abuse. These types of abuse will eventually morph into physical abuse. Classic signs that should not be ignored are being isolated from family and friends, cyberstalking, being monitored and controlled, cyberharassment, being coerced into unwanted sexual activities, and being asked for sexual pictures that can be potentially used as revenge porn. Many colleges and universities now provide education on coercive control and have revised campus conduct codes to address it. Students who feel they are in a coercive control relationship may want to consult NJ Safe and Sound, an organization that focuses on protecting individuals and families from predatory alienation and damaging coercive manipulation.[139,140]

Hate Crimes and Terrorism

Violence can occur where there are high levels of stress, bias, and perceived injustice. In most cases, however, multiple risk factors are present; very often, the perpetrator of violence is psychologically disturbed.

Hate Crimes A **hate crime** is a crime motivated by bias against the victim's ethnicity, race, religion, sexual orientation, or disability. Hate crimes tend to be excessively brutal, are frequently inflicted at random on people the perpetrators do not know, and are often committed by multiple perpetrators. There has been an increase in hate crimes in the United States since 2014. Some experts claim this increase is due to the rise of white nationalism. The Center for the Study of Hate & Extremism cites Russian meddling via social media to create racial divisiveness in the 2016 presidential election as a culprit in the increase of hate violence since 2016. The rise in hate crimes has been particularly experienced in the largest U.S. cities.[141]

Most states have laws against hate crimes, as does the federal government. Many colleges and universities have policies prohibiting hate crimes and harassment of individuals in targeted groups, as well as programs that promote cultural knowledge and diversity.[141] Hate crimes against lesbian, gay, bisexual, transgender, and queer (LGBTQ) persons have increased on campuses in recent years. Q stands for "questioning" and refers to people who are uncertain of their sexual orientation or gender identity. Many colleges and universities have specific policies forbidding violence directed toward LGBTQ students. Campus Pride's "Stop the Hate: Train the Trainer" provides social justice tools to confront hate crimes against the LGBTQ campus community.[142] The Matthew

Shepard Act was passed to expand federal hate crime law to include crimes motivated by a victim's actual or perceived gender, sexual orientation, or gender identity. Colleges also report what is called biphobia—shunning of bisexual students by support groups for gay and lesbian students. This shunning has led bisexual students to form their own support group organizations. Six states have banned the "gay and trans panic" defense used in hate crimes against LGBTQ members. This defense was used by a defendant in Wyoming's Matthew Shepard case. A victim's gender identity or sexual orientation cannot be blamed for a defendant's hate violence act.[143]

The 2016 Dear Colleague letter released by the Department of Education identified the rights of transgender students under Title IX. The Trump administration's revision of the Dear Colleague policies did not address transgender rights. Specific protected rights include[144]:

- Safe and nondiscriminatory environments
- Respect for students' chosen names and pronouns
- Ability to use restrooms, locker rooms, and housing consistent with students' gender identities, and to use gender-inclusive and/or private facilities
- Maintaining students' privacy on school records

Examples of harassment against transgender students include intentionally referring to transgender students by their birth name or wrong pronouns, asking invasive questions about a transgender student's body or gender transition, and challenging a transgender student's use of restrooms or locker rooms that are consistent with the gender identity or expression. College and university administrators, under Title IX, must take prompt action to end harassment of transgender students.

Terrorism is a form of violence directed against people or property, including civilian populations, for the purpose of instilling fear and engendering a sense of helplessness. Often, terrorist acts are committed in supposed furtherance of political or social aims. For many in the United States, the September 11, 2001, terrorist attacks on the World Trade Center in New York City and the Pentagon in Washington, D.C., remain the most traumatizing events of their lives. Colleges and universities worldwide are not immune from terrorism.

People fear events they do not understand or cannot control. Domestic and international **terrorism** fit both criteria. The 2007 Virginia Tech University mass shooting that killed 32 people was a massacre by a mentally ill former student that had ripple effects across all U.S. colleges and universities. Although they received less media attention than the

hate crime
Crime motivated by bias against the victim's ethnicity, race, religion, sexual orientation, or disability.

terrorism
Violence directed against persons or property, including civilian populations, for the purpose of instilling fear and engendering a sense of helplessness.

Virginia Tech shooting, the vehicle/knife killings at Ohio State University in 2016 are a stark reminder that college and university campuses are soft targets for terrorism.

Many campus citizens do not report suspicious behavior for several reasons, such as fear of retaliation or of being classified as a racist, or a distrust of law enforcement.[145] Some educational institutions are using phone apps for anonymous reporting to overcome these obstacles.

Preventing Violence

Although protecting yourself from violence is difficult, there are ways you can limit your risks in life; to assess how well you protect yourself from unsafe situations, complete this chapter's Personal Health Portfolio activity. Self-protection measures must, however, be part of a more comprehensive approach that addresses violence at the societal level. Current efforts to curb violence focus primarily on arresting and imprisoning offenders. Strategies are also needed that prevent violence before it occurs—that is, interventions that change the social conditions underlying violence.

The Role of Guns: Facilitating Violence
Guns contribute to the lethality of any incident involving violence. The Second Amendment to the U.S. Constitution protects the right of citizens to "keep and bear arms," a right that was important in colonial times but that may not be as important today. The gun industry—along with its powerful lobby and many clubs, organizations, and individual enthusiasts—defends the right of citizens to own guns with minimal restrictions. Some laws are in place regulating gun sales, such as the requirement for computerized background checks on persons seeking to buy guns, though the U.S. Supreme Court has deemed unconstitutional more severe restrictions, as when it overturned Washington, D.C.'s ban on handguns in 2009. Even so, one in five people avoid background checks when buying guns.[146] Some colleges are now being challenged to provide local law enforcement agencies with personal information about behavior and academic performance when students apply for gun permits. Many legal experts view this practice as a violation of the Family Educational Rights and Privacy Act (FERPA). Note, too, that background checks are not foolproof.

Proponents of gun control support banning the sale of assault guns to private individuals and other measures, including waiting periods for gun purchases, licensing of guns, and restrictions on young people's access to guns.[147] They also support the design of safer guns, such as guns with trigger locks, although gun manufacturers point out that gun owners frequently do not use the locks, and Congress has concluded that locks are effective only with children younger than age 6. The National Rifle Association (NRA) has supported the banning of bump stocks in response to the 2018

(Comstock/Getty Images)

Parkland, Florida, high school shooting and the 2017 Harvest Festival Music Las Vegas shooting. Bump stocks convert semiautomatic rifles into machine guns. But many NRA members oppose this decision. Some states are adopting "red flag" gun laws, which allow law enforcement officers to temporarily seize weapons from individuals identified as threatening, for example, due to mental illness, by family members or police.[147]

In the wake of the 2012 mass shooting at Sandy Hook Elementary School, the Obama administration commissioned the Institute of Medicine and the National Research Council to analyze the research on gun violence. The key conclusions favor neither gun-rights nor gun-control advocates:

- The United States has more firearm-related homicides than any other industrialized country, and 25 times more than other high-income countries.

- Overall, violent crime rates have declined in the past 15 years, including for homicides. But Black Americans are 10 times more likely to die by gun homicide than white Americans.

- There are 300 million guns in the United States, but only 100 million are handguns and they are used in more than 87 percent of violent crimes.

- Children are often the shooters or the victims in unintentional shootings.

- Guns are the second leading cause of death for U.S. children and teenagers and the leading cause of death for Black children and teens. Black children and teenagers are 14 times more likely than white children and teens of the same age to die in a gun homicide.

- Guns in the home are common, many children have access to these guns, and many parents have failed to have gun safety conversations with their children.

- Access to a gun in a case of domestic violence makes it five times more likely a woman will be killed. On average, 52 women are killed by a gun in intimate partner violence every year. Black women are two times more likely to be killed by a gun in intimate partner violence than white women.

- Most people who own guns say having a gun makes them feel safer.

- Denying guns to people under restraining orders saves lives.

- Technology exists to personalize guns using radiofrequency identification or biometric recognition to prevent children-caused accidental shootings and suicides, but only 43 percent of gun-owning adults in the United States are willing to purchase a childproof gun.

- Guns are often used for self-defense and safety.[148,149,150,151,152,153]

- As of August 1, 2019, there had been 251 mass shootings in calendar year 2019, and 60 people had been killed in them.[154] Mass shootings are defined by Congress as any public-place incident in which three or more people are killed, excluding the shooter. One of the high-profile mass shootings was at a Walmart in El Paso, Texas, that killed 22 people and wounded 18. The Las Vegas, Nevada, shooting that killed 58 people is the deadliest mass shooting in the United States. An important question is whether a mass shooting is an act of domestic terrorism, defined as a violation of U.S. or state criminal laws that is intended to[155]:

  - Intimidate or coerce a civilian population

  - Use intimidation or coercion to influence government policy

  - Use mass destruction, assassination, or kidnapping to influence government conduct

The association of mass shootings with the mental health of the shooter is not supported by empirical evidence. Less than 5 percent of gun-related deaths were carried out by a shooter diagnosed with a mental illness. Instead, alcohol abuse, drug abuse, and a history of domestic violence are the strongest predictors of mass shootings. The ArmaLite rifle (AR-15s) has been used in multiple mass shootings. Although it is generally illegal for private citizens to own an automatic AR-15, it is believed that 6 million to 10 million of these weapons are in circulation in the United States. The AR-15 is classified as a modern sporting rifle. Some politicians call it a "weapon of war" that should be banned.[155]

Although gun-related homicides have decreased since 1993, Blacks are still disproportionately affected by them. The CDC conjectures that Black women have been the victims of gun homicides by men who express their financial despair through hopelessness, substance abuse, and rage. Although Black Americans make up only 13 percent of the population, 22 percent of Black women who are victims of violence are killed by guns, and 94 percent know their killers. Sixty-four percent of Black women victims were wives, ex-wives, or girlfriends of their killers. The Black Lives Matter movement originated among Black women who protested racism and the unjust killing of both Black women and Black men. The March for Our Lives movement organized high school and college students to confront gun violence.[156,157]

Among organizations that support the right to bear arms is Students for Concealed Carry on Campus (SCCC), which advocates changing federal and state laws and college policies to allow gun-licensed college students to carry concealed handguns on campus. The organization argues that students may need handguns for self-defense in the event of a shooting incident and will feel safer if allowed to carry concealed guns on campus. It also points out that concealed handguns are legal in most states at virtually any locale—at movie theaters, offices, and shopping malls, to name just a few. In addition, gun proponents warn that gun-free zones are more likely to be targeted by mass shooters. The rationale is that mass shooters will avoid places that allow concealed-carry permits.[158] Opponents argue that allowing concealed guns on campus would result in a "Wild West" environment.[159,160]

State laws allowing concealed guns generally exclude concealed carry in schools, government buildings, and establishments where alcohol is sold. The American Association of State Colleges and Universities strongly opposes laws that would allow concealed guns on campus. At least 10 states allow concealed gun carry on college campuses, and 19 states ban conceal gun carry on college campuses.[160] Currently, 23 states allow colleges and universities to make their own decisions as to whether citizens can carry concealed weapons on their campuses. If states allow concealed gun carry, colleges and universities may still exclude concealed guns on their campuses. State laws on concealed carry pertain only to public colleges and universities; however, some states require private colleges and universities to take affirmative action to opt out. To date, Utah is the only state that prohibits public colleges and universities from banning concealed-gun carry.[161]

The use of guns in suicides is a serious public health problem. Mass shootings in the community and on college campuses capture the media's attention, but in fact about two-thirds of gun deaths in the United States are suicides. The U.S. gun suicide rate is almost 10 times higher than that in other high-income countries. These suicides are concentrated in states that have high gun ownership. Of all attempts at suicide, only 5 percent succeed. But in gun suicide attempts, 85 percent result in death.[152]

Suicide rates are rising among middle-aged U.S. adults, and health experts are divided on whether stricter gun control would lower the overall rate. One study suggests that suicides are often impulsive decisions, and most survivors of attempted suicide do not try again. Two-thirds of people planning suicide did so less than an hour before making the attempt. Another study found the time between deciding to kill oneself and trying to do so to be less than 10 minutes. Public health measures focused on preventing gun-related suicide include the gun industry's joining forces with public health officials to deliver social media campaigns targeting gun suicides, training health providers to screen patients for suicide risk, and creating public service announcements encouraging family and friends to provide intervention if they are concerned that a friend or loved one may be contemplating suicide.[150,162]

The Role of Media and Entertainment: Glorifying Violence Violent acts occur much more frequently in movies and television shows than they do in real life.[163,164] Repeated exposure to violence can lead to habituation and

desensitization, a raised threshold for reaction to violence and a loss of compassion. In other words, repeated exposure affects the brain. Repeated exposure to graphic images of violence also feeds the appetite for more intense violence. The greatest impact of aggressive cognitions and behaviors is more likely to fall on children and adults who are already at risk and less resilient to stress in their lives.[163,164]

Communities have organized boycotts of companies that sponsor violent and sexually explicit programs. Parents can use blocking technologies to keep their children from seeing selected television programs and Internet sites. The entertainment industry also regulates itself, primarily to avoid government regulation.[163] The National Association of Theater Owners, for example, has promised to enforce the movie rating system vigorously.

Video games have been blamed for school shootings, bullying, and violence against women. The aftermath of the 2018 Parkland shooting in Florida has led public policymakers to once again question the role that violent video games play in real-life violence. Studies affirm that violent video games can influence aggressive behavior, but there is no definitive evidence that they cause lethal violent behavior. A primary argument in favor of game makers is that players of violent video games are more than capable of differentiating reality from fantasy. Some behavioral psychologists argue that violent video games provide a catharsis and an outlet that decreases violent behavior. The bottom line: Video games are only one risk factor associated with aggressive behavior. Mental illness, adverse living environments, and gun access are also risk factors for aggression and violent behavior.[163,165] What do you think? Do violent video games contribute to violent behavior?

Self-Defense Devices Many self-defense products marketed today are wearable, lightweight, and concealable. Some examples are pepper spray in a lipstick/perfume case, defense key chains, stun guns, tasers, and rings that can activate a 110-decibel siren. Alerts and apps that can serve as a kind of "guardian angel" have included Life Button 24, Night Owls, SPOT, SOS Stay Safe, and Circle of 6. With a special cover or attachment, a smartphone can simultaneously take a picture of an assailant and disperse pepper spray. Via Bluetooth technology, a smartphone's GPS can transmit the user's exact location to law enforcement, send a medical alert to medical workers, and notify family and friends of a safety or medical emergency. Special bracelets can detect a head injury from a violent crime and assist recovery. Although self-defense technology is helpful, it is not a replacement for always being actively aware of your surroundings. Some parents concerned about campus safety have their college children download self-tracking apps on their phones such as Life 360. Although these apps may be helpful in emergency situations, some people consider them too invasive.[166]

Callisto, an app funded by Google, provides a digital portal through which students victimized by sexual assault can notify campus authorities. Students have three reporting options: (1) record, which enables them to securely store and update time-stamped information; (2) report, which reports the assault directly to campus authorities; and (3) match, which reports saved information only if someone else reports the same assailant.

Some feminist organizations are critical of these tools for focusing on the behavior of actual or potential sexual assault victims instead of taking action more directly against perpetrators and campus rape culture. App developers say apps are not "silver bullets" for ending campus sexual violence, nor are they designed to confront the larger problem of a campus rape culture.[167] Callisto, for example, provides a system to track and analyze patterns, elicit support services for the survivor, use a reporting process that is less traumatic for the survivor of a sexual assault than reporting the assault in person, and establish a documented record of the assault details. The messaging group app "bthere" utilizes location-sharing technology to help college students stay safe.

Background Checks A new strategy for protection against violence is checking the background of family friends, neighbors, and actual or potential intimate partners. For example, TruthFinder is a fee-based website that aggregates hundreds of millions of publicly available data points from criminal, traffic, and arrest records. Members can quickly search the site for public background information on anyone and find not only criminal records but also phone numbers, court records, birth dates, estimated income, current and previous addresses, and many types of licenses. A list of sex offenders located near the member's address is also provided, including mug shots and a map of their locations. Is this a scam? The truth is that TruthFinder is not much different from other subscription-based people-search websites such as Instant Checkmate, SpyFly, and BeenVerified. They provide a less cumbersome way to check public records than doing it yourself, and the information is likely to be just as accurate.[168]

The Role of Communities and Campuses: Promoting Safety Common sense suggests that safe physical environments are less conducive to criminal activity than are run-down environments. Communities where neighbors look out for one another, such as with neighborhood watch programs, are less inviting to criminals. Communities also have to support social changes that enhance economic and social stability.[169] To bring about change, some have used strategies such as cleaning up trash and graffiti and fixing broken windows, providing organized leisure activities and mentoring programs for youth, encouraging parent involvement in school activities, supporting low-income housing to curb an exodus of middle-income residents of all races, and increasing police presence in high-risk areas.[170,171]

College campuses have an important role to play in the prevention of violence, especially sexual violence. Prevention efforts in this area are undergoing major changes on many college campuses, which are moving away from awareness programs to broad community-based strategies that target the underlying issues surrounding violence.[172] The Mentors in

(John Wollwerth/Shutterstock)

Violence Prevention program takes a "bystander approach" to violence prevention in communities and schools, like that of Green Dot discussed earlier in the chapter. In this model, men are not viewed as potential perpetrators and women are not viewed as potential victims; the focus is on both as bystanders who can confront abusive peers and support abused peers. Individuals who want to take action against violence have a variety of options, from volunteering at women's shelters to supporting public policies that address the root causes of violence in our society.

Campus Security Drones

Imagine a fleet of drones hovering over a college campus 24 hours a day monitoring walking trails, secluded areas, and remote parking lots for safety. Or imagine an app from campus security that provides an Uber-Drone escort service for students leaving the campus library late at night. What about a fleet of drones armed with video surveillance and nonlethal weapons (tasers, rubber bullets, tear gas) that can be deployed quickly to protect first-response teams in the event of a campus shooting spree?

Are these science fiction scenarios? An Uber-like escort service is already operating in some cities; the start-up Go Far is based in San Francisco. Drone development is shifting from predominantly military uses to safety and security services. Safety drones are more economical than campus security officers. The opportunity to use campus drones for surveillance and safety will revolutionize campus security, but it will also raise serious questions about the need to protect privacy rights.[173]

You Make the Call
Free Speech on Campus

A controversial speaker with fascist beliefs is invited to your campus to speak. A brawl erupts at the site of a student protest outside the venue where the speech will be delivered. Some students are injured and some are arrested for causing a public disturbance. This is a scene that has become all too common on campuses where speakers address such topics as evolution, gender discrimination, religion, Planned Parenthood, pro-life or pro-choice platforms, immigration, and movements like Black Lives Matter. The escalation in hostility related to polarizing topics has led many universities to rescind invitations to public speakers who are likely to generate hostile protests. The Foundation for Individual Rights in Education (FIRE) reports more than 300 attempts by college and university administrators to do so since 2000. The American Civil Liberties Union (ACLU) claims that the escalation in hostilities from polarizing views and the reaction of administrators to aggressive outbursts has had a chilling effect on campus free speech.

Students on many campuses are categorizing offensive speech as hate speech and demanding that it be censored. In response, some campus administrators have implemented speech codes and conduct codes that may be violating free speech. Colleges and universities define hate speech as discriminatory harassment that includes oral, written, graphic, or physical acts directed at a person or group of persons based on race, color, national origin, religion, sex, sexual orientation, age, disability, or veteran status intending to be offensive, demeaning, or intimidating, or creating a hostile environment. Some campuses expand this definition to include emotional distress and threats.

The judicial system prohibits campus speech codes that restrict the First Amendment right to free speech that is based on content. A founding hallmark of colleges and universities, however, is exchange of ideas through free expression. Sometimes this may mean that uncivil, disrespectful, and offensive speech should not be suppressed. Some administrations have

Continued...

Concluded...

employed "civility police" to monitor student newspapers and faculty members' online comments and classroom remarks, and some have designated campus sanctuary locations where offensive speech is regulated. Smartphone apps can be used to report to college and university administrators comments perceived as offensive.

Colleges and universities should restrict comments that violate the law, defame others, present a legitimate threat, promote gender or racial or sexual orientation harassment, substantially invade privacy, or substantially disrupt campus operations. However, the ACLU argues that stretching speech codes to prevent wholesale use of any words and symbols that may cause discomfort or emotional distress and conducting invasive monitoring of offensive comments are violations of the First Amendment. Instead, the ACLU suggests that using forums and workshops to promote awareness and dialogue on controversial topics, diversifying at faculty and student levels, offering courses that focus on cultural diversity, and actively preventing hate speech are more viable options than censoring offensive speech.

What do you think? Do campus speech codes and monitoring of offensive comments serve a positive purpose?

Pros

- Hate speech codes prevent verbal attacks that intimidate and oppress students so they cannot compete fairly in an academic setting.
- Hate speech codes maintain the civil environment needed for fruitful academic debates.
- It is in society's best interest to prevent protests that provoke violence and disrupt essential campus operations.
- Hate speech codes protect underrepresented students when there is an imbalance of power between them and students in the majority.

Cons

- Censorship undercuts free expression on campus.
- "Political correctness" allows students to use hate speech codes to ostracize and intimidate peers who have dissenting views.
- Hate speech codes violate the fundamental right to free speech and free expression under the First Amendment.
- Hate speech codes prevent students from tolerating cultural diversity.

Sources: Uelmen, G. (2017). Campus hate speech codes. Retrieved from https://www.scu.edu/character/resources/campus-hate-speech-codes; American Civil Liberties Union. (2017). Hate speech on campus. Retrieved from https://www.aclu.org/other/hate-speech-codes; Cabranes, N.J., & Stith, K. (2017). *Campus speech in crisis.* New York, NY: Encounter Books; Andino, Y. (2019). Free speech on college campuses. Retrieved from: https://ninertimes.com/2019/02/free-speech-on-college-campuses/

In Review

How does injury affect personal health?
Unintentional injuries are the fourth leading cause of death in the United States and the leading cause of death for children and adults aged 1 to 39. Public health experts believe that injuries are preventable if people adopt behaviors that promote safety and if society takes steps to reduce environmental hazards.

What are the leading causes of injury-related death?
The top cause for all age groups is motor vehicle crashes, followed by poisoning, falls, choking, and drowning. Common causes vary by age and race/ethnicity, but males are more likely than females to die from unintentional injuries across all groups until age 80. Basic Life Support certification bridges the gap between CPR and EMT programs. E-scooter injuries are an increasing safety concern due to closed-head injuries. Wearing a helmet is a vital risk prevention factor. Interference with prospective memory, habitual memory, by parents is a potential cause of children vehicular heat stroke deaths.

How does violence affect personal health?
Many people, especially members of minority groups, are the victims of violence and of violent crimes, which include homicide, assault, robbery, and rape. Compared with other developed countries, the United States has higher rates of homicide, especially homicide committed with a firearm.

What forms does violence take in our society?
Males between the ages of 14 and 24 are the most likely to commit acts of violence. Crimes on college campuses include assaults, rapes, and, very rare but high-profile, mass shootings. Sexual violence includes sexual assault and rape, sexual harassment, and stalking and cyberstalking. Although family violence can be directed at anyone, women, children, and older adults are the most vulnerable. Violence against strangers often takes the form of hate crimes or terrorism, which is intended to create fear and helplessness in the general public. Campus sexual assault against Black women is drawing much needed attention. The issue of whether the campus sexual assault system against men of color is also being addressed. The Trump administration revised several of the core policies implemented by the Obama administration (Dear Colleague letter) to adjudicate campus sexual assault.

How is sexual harassment regulated on college campuses?
Sexual harassment on college campuses is regulated by Title IX. Deepfake video is a cyberharassment targeting women. Although men may be targeted, it is usual for joke content and

not nudity and sexual explicit videos or pictures. The #MeToo has been an important movement confronting sexual harassment of women, but there is a male backlash to #MeToo that has had the unintended consequence of sex segregation in working relationships.

How is free speech/hate speech regulated on college campuses?

Free speech on college campuses may be eroding as when it is viewed with hate speech. Speech codes and conduct codes that are too broad or vague have been struck down by the federal courts.

What are strategies to prevent violence?

Individuals can learn how to reduce their risk of encountering violence, and they can work to create safer communities and campuses and to prevent violence in society. Some public health professionals advocate reducing gun violence through a multidimensional strategy like the campaigns against smoking and drunk driving. The public can oppose the glorification of violence in the media through boycotts and monitoring what their children are watching. Communities can support neighborhood watch programs and upkeep of common areas. Many types of violence-prevention programs can be used on college campuses, including affirmative consent, although this is a controversial practice.

Personal Health Portfolio

Chapter 16   How Safe Are You?

Violence is a serious health problem on many college and university campuses. Many students who survive violent encounters are left with permanent physical and emotional scars. The purpose of this activity is to help you assess how well you protect yourself from becoming a victim of violence. Self-defense includes knowing the factors in your environment that may place you at risk for being a victim of violence. Consider the following statements and decide whether each one is always, sometimes, or never true for you.

General safety considerations	Always	Sometimes	Never
I am aware of my surroundings.			
I tell someone where I'm going whenever I leave home.			
I'm careful about giving personal information or my daily schedule to people I don't know.			
I vary my daily routine and walking patterns.			
If I walk at night, I walk with others.			
Auto safety	**Always**	**Sometimes**	**Never**
I look in the backseat before I get in my car.			
I look around before parking, stopping, or getting into or out of my car.			
I keep my car doors locked at all times.			
I have a plan of action in case my car breaks down.			
Using my mirrors I scan ahead of me and behind me for potential dangers.			
I park in well-lit areas and avoid dangerous, high-risk places whenever possible.			
If hit from behind, I drive to the nearest police station or well-lit, populated area, motioning for the person who hit me to follow.			
If I notice anyone loitering near my car, I go straight to a safe place and call the police.			
I never hitchhike.			
ATM safety	**Always**	**Sometimes**	**Never**
I avoid using ATMs at night.			
I try to take someone with me when I use an ATM.			
I look for suspicious people or activity before entering or driving into an ATM area.			
To avoid being a card-skimming victim, I inspect the card reader and the area near the keypad, and I avoid using my PIN at the gas pump.			
I take all my ATM and credit card receipts with me to avoid leaving behind personal information.			

Violence, rape, and homicide	Always	Sometimes	Never
I limit my alcohol or drug intake so I am aware of my surroundings.			
I monitor my drinks at parties.			
I refuse to be with anyone who seems violent.			
I do not allow partners to threaten or intimidate me.			
I don't stay around anyone who has a gun and is drinking alcohol or using other drugs.			
If a partner is physically or verbally abusive, I have a safety plan to end the relationship.			
Ride-sharing	Always	Sometimes	Never
When using a ride-sharing service, I confirm the name and photo of the driver and the car type before getting into the car.			
I check the driver's safety ratings using the Lyft or Uber app.			
When using Lyft or Uber I tap the options for sharing information about my ride or estimated arrival time with a family member or friend.			
If my ride-share service does not offer these options, I snap a photo of the car's license plate and send it to a family member or friend with my estimated time of arrival.			
Public transportation	Always	Sometimes	Never
While waiting for transportation, I am aware of my immediate surroundings.			
While waiting for transportation, I place myself so that I am protected from behind.			
I hold items under my arm so that they will be difficult to grab.			
While riding on buses or trains, I look aware and alert.			

SCORING

Give yourself 3 points for each "Always" answer, 2 points for each "Sometimes," and 0 points for each "Never."

Score: _____

90–99   You are probably safe as long as you continue to follow these precautions.

80–89   You may need to reexamine some of your habits and make changes to improve your safety.

79 or less   You may need to make significant changes in your habits to improve your safety.

Source: Adapted from Anspaugh, D. J., Hamrick, M. H., and Rosato, F. D. (2005). Wellness: Concepts and Applications, 5th ed., New York, NY: The McGraw-Hill Companies; Rossi, A. (2017, November 9) 10 important ride share safety tips for travelers. Retrieved from: https://smartertravel.com/ride-share-safety-tips-for-travelers/

CRITICAL THINKING QUESTIONS

1. Based on your responses to the questions, what is your risk level? Where are there areas for improvement? What are key changes that you can make to lower your risk in these areas?

2. What is your overall perception of the safety of your college campus? What are a few ways your campus and overall community can improve on safety?

Design Icons: ©McGraw-Hill Education

References

Chapter 1

1. Preamble to the Constitution of the World Health Organization as adopted by The International Health Conference, New York, 19–22 June, 1946; signed on 22 June 1946 by the representatives of 61 States (Official Records of the WHO, No. 2, p. 100) and entered into force on 7 April 1948.

2. Centers for Disease Control and Prevention. (2018). Health-related quality of life: Wellbeing concepts. Retrieved from http://www.cdc.gov/hrqol/wellbeing.htm#three

3. Badland, H., & Pearce, J. (2019). Liveable for whom? Prospects of urban liveability to address health inequities. *Social Science Medicine, 232,* 94–105. doi:10.1016/j.socscimed.2019.05.001

4. Jones, N.L., Burger, J., Hall, H., & Reeves, K.A. (2019). The intersection of urban and global health. *Pediatric Clinics of North America, 66*(3), 561–573.

5. National Academies of Sciences, Engineering, and Medicine; Health and Medicine Division; Division of Behavioral and Social Sciences and Education. (2019). Roundtable on the promotion of health equity. In W. Keenan, C.E. Sanchez, E. Kellogg, & S.M. Tracey (Eds.), *Achieving behavioral health equity for children, families and communities.* Washington, DC: National Academies Press.

6. Watts, N., Amann, M., Ayeb-Karlsson, S., Belesova, K., et al. (2018). The Lancet countdown on health and climate change: From 25 years of inaction to a global transformation for public health. *Lancet, 391*(10120), 581–630. doi:10.1016/S0140-6736(17)32464-9

7. Travert, A., Annerstedt, K.S., & Daivadanam, M. (2019). Built environment and health behaviors: Deconstructing the black box of interactions—a review of reviews. *International Journal of Environmental Research and Public Health, 16,* 1454. doi:10.3390/ijerph16081454

8. Powell, K., Wilcox, J., Clonan, A., et al. (2015). The role of social networks in the development of overweight and obesity among adults: A scoping review. *BMC Public Health, 15,* 99 6.

9. Shelton, R.C., Lee, M., Bortzman, L.E., Crookes, D.M., Jandorf, L., Erwin, D., & Gage-Bouchard, E.A. (2019). Use of social network analysis in the development, dissemination, implementation and sustainability of health behavior interventions for adults: A systematic review. *Social Science Medicine, 220,* 81–101. doi:10.1016/j.socscimed.2018.10.013

10. Raiten, D.J., & Aimone, A.M. (2017). The intersection of climate/environment, food, nutrition and health: Crisis and opportunity. *Current Opinion in Biotechnology, 44,* 52–62.

11. University of Washington School of Public Health. (2020). Population health forum. Retrieved from http://depts.washington.edu/eqhlth/

12. Woolf, S.H., & Aron, L. (2018). Failing health of the United States: The role of challenging life conditions and the policies behind them. *British Medical Journal, 360,* k496. doi:10.1136/bmj.k496

13. National Center for Health Statistics. (2019). *Health, United States, 2018.* Hyattsville, MD: Author.

14. National Center for Chronic Disease Prevention and Health Promotion. (2018). *Health equity.* Centers for Disease Control and Prevention. Retrieved from http://www.cdc.gov/chronicdisease/healthequity/index.htm

15. National Research Council and Institute of Medicine. (2013). *U.S. health in international perspective: Shorter lives, poorer health.* Panel on Understanding Cross National Health Differences Among High-Income Countries, S.H. Woolf & L. Aron (Eds.). Committee on Population, Division of Behavioral and Social Sciences and Education, and Board on Population Health and Public Health Practice, Institute of Medicine. Washington, DC: The National Academies Press.

16. Moy, E., Garcia, M.C., Bastian, B., et al. (2017). Leading causes of death in nonmetropolitan and metropolitan areas—United States, 1999–2014. *MMWR Surveillance Summary, 66*(1), SS1–SS8. doi:10.15585/mmwr.ss6601a1

17. Economic Research Service. (2020). Population and migration. United States Department of Agriculture. Retrieved from http://www.ers.usda.gov/topics/rural-economy-population/population-migration/

18. Urban Institute. (2015). What counts for America? Truth on a map. Retrieved from http://www.whatcountsforamerica.org/truthonamap/

19. U.S. Census Bureau. (2019). *Quick facts.* Retrieved from http://www.census.gov/quickfacts/fact/table/US/RHI825217

20. National Center for Health Statistics. (2016). *Health, United States, 2015: With special feature on racial and ethnic disparities.* Hyattsville, MD: Author. Retrieved from http://www.cdc.gov/nchs/data/hus/hus15.pdf#highlights

21. Peterson, E.E., Davis, N.L., Goodman, D., Cox, S., et al. (2019). Vital signs: Pregnancy-related deaths, United States, 2011-2015, and strategies for prevention, 13 states, 2013-2017. *Morbidity and Mortality Weekly Report, 68*(18), 423–429.

22. Bailey, Z.D., Krieger, N., Agenor, M., Graves, J., Linos, N., & Bassett, M.T. (2017). Structural racism and health inequities in the USA: Evidence and interventions. *Lancet, 389*(10077), 1453–1463. doi:10.1016/S0140-6736(17)30569-X

23. Devenish, B., Hooley, M., & Mellor, D. (2017). The pathways between socioeconomic status and adolescent outcomes: A systematic review. *American Journal of Community Psychology, 59*(1–2), 219–238.

24. Bor, J., Cohen, G.H., & Galea, S. (2017). Population health in an era of rising income inequality: USA, 1980-2015. *Lancet, 389*(10077), 1475–1490. doi:10.1016/S0140-6736(17)30561-8

25. Pickett, K., & Wilkinson, R. (2009). *The spirit level: Why more equal societies almost always do better.* London: Allen Lane.

26. Papanicolas, I., Woskie, L.R., & Jha, A. (2018). Health care spending in the United States and other high-income countries. *Journal of the American Medical Association, 319*(10), 1024–1039. doi:10.1001/jama.2018.1150

27. Artiga, S., & Hinton, E. (2018). Beyond health care: The role of social determinants in promoting health and health equity. Kaiser Family Foundation. Retrieved from http://www.kff.org/disparities-policy/issue-brief/beyond-health-care-the-role-of-social-determinants-in-promoting-health-and-health-equity/

28. Centers for Disease Control and Prevention. (2019). About adverse childhood experiences. Violence Prevention. Retrieved from http://www.cdc.gov/violenceprevention/childabuseandneglect/acestudy/aboutace.html

29. U.S. Department of Health and Human Services. (2019). https://www.hhs.gov/

30. DeSalvo, K.B., O'Carroll, P.W., Koo, D., et al. (2016). Public health 3.0: Time for an

upgrade. *American Journal of Public Health, 106*(4), 621–622.

31. Gase, L.N., Schooley, T., Lee, M., et al. (2017). A practice-grounded approach for evaluating health in all policy initiatives in the United States. *Journal of Public Health Management and Practice, 23*(4), 339–347.

32. United States Department of Health and Human Services. (2020). *Health People 2020*. Retrieved from http://www.healthypeople.gov/

33. United States Department of Health and Human Services. (2020). *Healthy People 2030 framework*. Retrieved from http://www.healthypeople.gov/2020/About-Healthy-People/Development-Healthy-People-2030/Framework

34. Green, L.W., & Kreuter, M.W. (2004). *Health promotion planning: An educational and ecological approach.* New York: McGraw-Hill.

35. Simons-Morton, B., McLeroy, K.R., & Wendel, M.L. (2012). *Behavior theory in health promotion practice and research.* Burlington, MA: Jones and Bartlett Learning.

36. Nutbeam, D., McGill, B., & Premkumar, P. (2018). Improving health literacy in community populations: A review of progress. *Health Promotion International, 33*(5), 901–911.

37. Centers for Disease Control and Prevention. (2019). Health literacy. Retrieved from http://www.cdc.gov/healthliteracy/index.html

38. Zikmund-Fisher, B.J., et al. (2010). Risky feelings: Why 6% risk does not always feel like 6%. *Patient Education and Counseling, 81*(1), S87–S93.

39. World Health Organization. (2017). Joint statement on public disclosures of results from clinical trials. Retrieved from http://www.who.int/ictrp/results/ICTRP_JointStatement_2017.pdf?ua=1

40. Saffery, R. (2017). Effects of the in utero environment on the epigenome. *Epigenomics, 9*(3), 209–211.

41. Green, E.D., Guyer, M.S., & National Human Genome Research Institute. (2011). Charting a course for genomic medicine from base pairs to bedside. *Nature, 470,* 204–213.

42. Tsai, Z.T., Lloyd, J.P., & Shiu, S.H. (2017). Defining functional genic regions in the human genome through integration of biochemical, evolutionary and genetic evidence. *Molecular Biology and Evolution, 34*(7), 1788–1798. doi:10.1093/molbev/msx101

43. Elkon, R., & Agami, R. (2017). Characterization of noncoding regulatory DNA in the human genome. *Nature Biotechnology, 35,* 732–746.

44. Conching, A., & Thayer, Z. (2019). Biological pathways for historical trauma to affect health: A conceptual model focusing on epigenetic modifications. *Social Science Medicine, 230,* 74–82.

45. United States Department of Health and Human Services. (n.d.). Surgeon general's family health history initiative. Retrieved from http://www.hhs.gov/familyhistory/

Chapter 2

1. Substance Abuse and Mental Health Services Administration. (2018). Key substance abuse and mental health indicators in the United States: Results from the 2017 National Survey on Drug Use and Health (HHS Publication No. SMA 18-5068, NSDUH Series H-53). Rockville, MD: Center for Behavioral Health Statistics and Quality Substance Abuse and Mental Health Services Administration. Retrieved from https://www.samhsa.gov/data/

2. Seligman, Martin E.P. (2019). Positive psychology: A personal history. *Annual Review of Clinical Psychology, 15,* 1–23.

3. Duckworth, A. (2016). *Grit: The power and passion of perseverance.* New York, Scribner.

4. Peterson, C., & Seligman, M. (2004). *Character strengths and virtues: A handbook and classification.* Washington, DC: American Psychological Association.

5. Boehm, J., Peterson, C., Kivimaki, M., & Kubzansky, L. (2011). A prospective study of positive psychological well-being and coronary heart disease. *Health Psychology, 30*(3), 259–267.

6. Seligman, M. (1998). *Learned optimism: How to change your mind and your life.* New York: Basic Books.

7. Scheier, M.F., & Carver, C.C. (2018). Dispositional optimism and physical health: A long look back, a quick look forward. *American Psychologist, 73*(9), 1082–1094.

8. Kahneman, D. (2011). *Thinking fast and slow.* New York: Farrar, Straus and Giroux.

9. Sandberg, S., & Grant, A. (2017). *Option B: Facing adversity, building resilience and finding joy.* New York: Knopf. Also available at OptionB.org

10. Feisenthal, E. (Ed.). (2019). What makes us happy. The science of happiness. *Time Magazine* (Special Edition), 30–31.

11. Morse, G. (2012). The science behind the smile. *Harvard Business Review, 90*(1/2), 84–90.

12. Seligman, M. (2002). *Authentic happiness.* New York: Simon and Schuster.

13. Rasmussen, H., & Scheier, M. (2009). Optimism and physical health. *Annals of Behavioral Medicine, 37,* 239–256.

14. Goleman, D. (2006). *Emotional intelligence: Why it can matter more than IQ* (10th ed.). New York: Bantam Books.

15. Sternberg, R.J. (1996). *Successful intelligence: How practical and creative intelligences determine success in life.* New York: Simon and Schuster.

16. Rivers, S., Brackett, M.A., Omori, M., et al. (2013). Emotion skills as a protective factor for risky behaviors among college students. *Journal of College Student Development, 54*(2), 172–183.

17. Mancini, A., Griffin, P., & Bonanno, G. (2012). Recent trends in treatment of prolonged grief. *Current Opinion in Psychiatry, 25*(1), 46–51.

18. Moss, E., & Dobson, K. (2006). Psychology, spirituality and end of life care: An ethical integration. *Canadian Psychology, 47*(4), 284–299.

19. Harvard Health Publications. (2012). Can you die of a broken heart? *Harvard Heart Letter* (blog). Retrieved from www.health.harvard.edu/blog-extra/can-you-die-of-a-broken-heart

20. Bonanno, G. (2009). *The other side of sadness: What the new science of bereavement tells us about life after loss.* New York: Basic Books.

21. Blake, J. (2017). Write to health: Journaling can enhance psychotherapeutic process. *Psychiatric News.* American Psychiatric Association.

22. Jabr, F. (2013, January 28). The newest edition of psychiatry's "bible," the DSM-5. *Scientific American.*

23. Kubler-Ross, E. (1997). *On death and dying.* New York: Simon and Schuster.

24. Mueller, P.S., Plevak, D.J., & Rummans, T.A. (2001). Religious involvement, spirituality, and medicine: Implications for clinical practice. *Mayo Clinic Proceedings, 76*(12).

25. American Psychiatric Association. (2013). *Diagnostic and statistical manual of mental disorders* (5th ed.). Washington, DC: American Psychiatric Association.

26. Giedd, J.N. (2015). The amazing teen brain. *Scientific American, 312*(6), 33–37.

27. Griffen, L. (2018, March). The developing teenage brain. *Educational Digest,* 10–15.

28. Flora, C. (2018). Are smartphones really destroying the adolescent brain? *Scientific American, 318*(2), 30–37.

29. Howard, P.J. (2014). *The owners manual for the brain: Everyday applications for mind-brain research* (4th ed.). New York: Harper-Collins.

30. Epstein, R. (2007). The myth of the teenage brain. *Scientific American Mind, 18*(2), 55–64.

31. U.S. Department of Veteran Affairs, National Center for PTSD. (2015). Symptoms of PTSD. Retrieved from https://www.ptsd.va.gov/public/ptsd-overview/basics/symptoms_of_ptsd.asp

32. Howard, P.J. (2006). *The owners manual for the brain: Everyday applications for mind-brain research* (3rd ed.). Austin, TX: Bard Press.

33. Hansen, H., Donaldson, Z., Link, B., et al. (2013). Independent review of social and population variation in mental health could improve diagnosis in DSM revisions. *Health Affairs* (Millwood), *32*(5), 984–993.

34. *Medscape.* (2013, May). Multispeciality DSM-5 news and perspectives.

35. National Institute of Mental Health. (2016). Attention deficit hyperactivity disorder. Retrieved from https://www.nimh.nih.gov/health/topics/attention-deficit-hyperactivity-disorder-adhd/index.shtml

36. National Institute of Mental Health. (2017). Attention-deficit/hyperactivity disorder. NIMH Health Topics. Retrieved from http://www.nimh.nih.gov

37. Centers for Disease Control and Prevention. (2018). *Autism spectrum disorder*. Retrieved from https://www.cdc.gov/ncbddd/autism/facts.html

38. National Institutes of Health. (2019). Major depression. Retrieved from https://www.nimh.nih.gov/health/statistics/major-depression.shtml

39. Lin, L., Sidani, J.F., Shensa, A., et al. (2016). Association between social media use and depression among US young adults. *Depression and Anxiety, 33*(4), 323–331.

40. Boers, E., Afzali, M.H., Newton, N., & Conrod, P. (2019, July 15). Association of screen time and depression in adolescence. *JAMA Pediatrics*.

41. SAMHSA. (2015). 4.3 million Americans working full time had an anxiety disorder in the past year. Press announcement. Retrieved from http://www.samhsa.gov/newsroom/press-announcements/201505210145

42. Staff of the Mayo Clinic. (2018). *Panic attacks and panic disorder*. Mayo Foundation for Medical Education and Research. Retrieved from https://www.mayoclinic.org/diseases-conditions/panic-attacks/symptoms-causes/syc-20376021

43. National Institute of Mental Health. (2017). Schizophrenia. Retrieved from https://www.nimh.nih.gov/health/publications/schizophrenia/index.shtml

44. American College Health Association. (2011). *National college health assessment, spring*. Baltimore, MD: Author.

45. American College Health Association. (2018). *National College Health Assessment II: Reference Group Executive Summary, Fall 2018*. Silver Spring, MD: ACHA. Retrieved from https://www.acha.org/documents/ncha/NCHA-II_Fall_2018_Reference_Group_Executive_Summary.pdf

46. Centers for Disease Control and Prevention. (2018). Suicides rising across the United States. *Vital Signs*. Retrieved from https://www.cdc.gov/vitalsigns/suicide/index.html

47. Bower, B. (2016). As suicide rates rise, researchers separate thoughts from actions. *Science News, 189*(1), 22–26.

48. Anastasiades, M.H., Kapoor, S., Wooten, J., & Lamis, D.A. (2017). Perceived stress, depressive symptoms, and suicidal ideation in undergraduate women with varying levels of mindfulness. *Archives of Women's Mental Health, 20*, 129–138.

49. Seligman, M., Steen, T., Park, N., & Peterson, C. (2005). Positive psychology progress: Empirical validation of interventions. *American Psychologist, 60*(5), 410–421.

50. Barlow, D., Bullis, J., Comer, J., & Ametaj, A. (2013). Evidence based psychological treatments: An update and a way forward. *Annual Review of Clinical Psychology, 9*, 1–27.

51. Mental Health Daily (blog). (2014). Most popular antidepressants in 2014: Cymbalta, Pristiq and Viibryd. Retrieved from http://mentalhealthdaily.com/2014/08/30/most-popular-antidepressants-in-2014-cymbalta-pristiq-viibryd/

52. Pratt, L.A., Brody, D.J., & Gu, Q. (2017). *Antidepressant use among persons aged 12 and over: United States, 2011-2014* (NCHS Data Brief #283). Atlanta, GA: Centers for Disease Control and Prevention.

57. Friedman, R.A. (2014). Adolescents' black-box warning—10 years later. *New England Journal of Medicine, 371*(18), 1666–1668.

58. U.S. Food and Drug Administration. (2007). FDA proposes new warnings about suicidal thinking, behavior in young adults who take antidepressant medications. Press release. Retrieved from https://www.fda.gov/ForConsumers/ConsumerUpdates/ucm048950.htm

59. McCormack, J., & Korownyk, C. (2018). Effectiveness of antidepressants: Lots of useful data but many important questions remain. *British Medical Journal, 360*, k1073.

60. Hegerl, U., Schhonknecht, P., & Mergl, R. (2012). Are antidepressants useful in the treatment of minor depression: A critical update of the current literature. *Current Opinion in Psychiatry, 25*(1), 1–6.

61. Cooper, C.L., & Quick, J.C. (Eds.). (2017). *The handbook of stress and health: A guide to research and practice*. West Sussex: John Wiley and Sons.

62. American Psychological Association. (2017). Stress in America: Coping with change. Stress in America Survey, Part I. Retrieved from https://www.apa.org/news/press/releases/stress/2016/coping-with-change.pdf

63. American Psychological Association. (2018). *Stress in America: Generation Z. Stress in America Survey*. Retrieved from https://www.apa.org/images/stress-gen-z_tcm7-247377.pdf

64. American Psychological Association. (2017). Stress in America: Coping with change. Stress in America Survey, Part 2. Retrieved from https://www.apa.org/news/press/releases/stress/2017/technology-social-media.pdf

65. Schmidt, M., & Schwabe, L. (2011). Splintered by stress. *Scientific American Mind, 22*(4), 22–29.

66. Blonna, R. (2011). *Coping with stress in a changing world* (5th ed.). New York: McGraw-Hill.

67. Benson, H. (1993). The relaxation response. In D. P. Goleman & J. Gurin (Eds.), *Mind-body medicine: How to use your mind for better health* (pp. 233–257). Yonkers, NY: Consumer Reports Books.

68. Theadom, A., Smith, H., Horne, R., et al. (2010). Participant experiences of a written emotional disclosure intervention in asthma. *Stress and Health, 26*, 45–50.

69. Pedersen, A., Baggesen, L., Ehrenstein, V., et al. (2016). Perceived stress and risk of any osteoporotic fracture. *Osteoporosis International, 27*(6), 2035–2045.

70. Brotto, L., Atallah, S., John-Agbakwu, C., et al. (2016). Psychological and interpersonal dimensions of sexual function and dysfunction. *Journal of Sexual Medicine, 13*, 538–571.

71. Zannas, A.S. (2016). Editorial perspective: Psychological stress and epigenetic aging—What can we learn and how can we prevent it? *Journal of Child Psychology and Psychiatry, 57*(6), 674–675.

72. Leger, K.A., Charles, S., & Almeida, D.M. (2018). Let it go: Lingering negative affect in response to daily stressors is associated with physical health years later. *Psychological Science*, 1–8.

73. Kiecolt-Glaser, J. (2002). Psychoneuro-immunology: Psychological influences on immune function and health. *Journal of Consulting and Clinical Psychology, 70*, 537–547.

74. Reed, R. (2019). Stress and immunological aging. *Current Opinions in Behavioral Science, 28*, 38–43.

75. Segerstrom, S., & Hodgson, D. (2019). Psychoneuroimmunology. *Current Opinions in Behavioral Science, 28* (Special Issue).

76. Benson, H. (2006). *Stress management: Techniques for preventing and easing stress*. Cambridge, MA: Harvard Medical School Press.

77. Morilak, D., & Sandi, C. (2017). Editorial overview: Stress and behavior. *Current Opinions in Behavioral Science, 14*, iv–vii.

78. National Center for PTSD. (2018). *PTSD essentials*. U.S. Department of Veteran Affairs. Retrieved from https://www.ptsd.va.gov/professional/treat/essentials/index.asp

79. Friedman, M., & Rosenman, R. H. (1982). *Type A behavior and your heart*. New York: Fawcett Books.

80. Chida, Y., & Steptoe, A. (2009). The association of anger and hostility with future coronary heart disease: A meta-analytic review of prospective evidence. *Journal of the American College of Cardiology, 53*, 936–946.

81. Barnett, M.D., Ledoux, T., Garcini, L.M., & Baker, J. (2009). Type D personality and chronic pain; Construct and concurrent validity of the DS 14. *Journal of Clinical Psychology in Medical Settings, 16,* 194–199.

82. Beutel, M., et al. (2012). Type D personality as a cardiovascular risk marker in the general population: Results from the Gutenberg health study. *Psychotherapy and Psychosomatics, 81,* 108–117.

83. Compare, A., Bigi, R., Orrego, P. S., et al. (2013). Type D personality is associated with the development of stress cardiomyopathy following emotional triggers. *Annals of Behavioral Medicine, 45*(3), 299–307.

84. Marten, A.S., & Barnes, A.J. (2018). Resilience in children. *Children, 5.*

85. Kobasa, S.O. (1984, September). How much stress can you survive? *American Health,* 71–72.

86. Maddi, S. (2002). The story of hardiness: Twenty years of theorizing, research and practice. *Consulting Psychology: Practice and Research, 54*(3), 175–185.

87. Bartone, P.T., Valdes, J., & Sandvik, A. (2016). Psychological hardiness predicts cardiovascular health. *Psychology, Health and Medicine, 21*(6), 743–749.

88. Holmes, T., & Rahe, R. (1967). The social readjustment rating scale. *Journal of Psychosomatic Research, 11,* 213–218.

89. Segerstrom, S.C., & Miller, G.E. (2004). Psychological stress and the human immune system: A meta-analytic of 30 years of inquiry. *Psychological Bulletin, 130*(4), 610–630.

90. Eisenbarth, C.A. (2019). Coping with stress: Gender differences among college students. *College Student Journal, 53*(2), 151–162.

91. Yusfov, M., Nicoloro, J.N., Grey, N.E., Moyer, A., & Lobel, M. (2019). Meta-analytic evaluation of stress reduction interventions for undergraduate and graduate students. *International Journal of Stress Management, 26*(2), 132–145.

92. Ribeiro, I.J., Pereira, R., Freire, I.V., Bruno, G., Casotti, C.A., & Boery, E.N. (2018). Stress and quality of life among university students: A systematic review of the literature. *Health Professions, 4*(2), 70–77.

93. American Psychological Association. (2009). Stress in America 2009. Retrieved from www.apa.org/news/press/releases/stress/2009/stress-exec-summary.pdf

94. Gleick, J. (2000). *Faster: The acceleration of just about everything.* New York: Vintage Books.

95. Expedia.com. (2018). 18th annual vacation deprivation study. Retrieved from https://viewfinder.expedia.com/vacation-deprivation/

96. Kraft, U. (2006). Burned-out. *Scientific American Mind, 17*(3), 28–33.

97. Pines, A.M. (1993). Burnout: An existential perspective. In W.B. Schaufeli, C. Maslach, & T. Marek (Eds.), *Professional burnout: Recent developments in research and practice.* Philadelphia: Taylor and Francis.

98. American Psychological Association. (2015). Stress in America 2014. Retrieved from www.apa.org/news/press/releases/stress/2014/stress-report.pdf

99. Douglas, H.E., Raban, M.Z., Walter, S.R., & Westbrook, J.I. (2107). Improving our understanding of multi-tasking in healthcare: Drawing together the cognitive psychology and healthcare literature. *Applied Ergonomics, 59,* 45–55.

100. Hines, L., Sundin, J., Rona, R.J., et al. (2014). Post traumatic stress disorder post Iraq and Afghanistan: Prevalence among military subgroups. *Canadian Journal of Psychiatry, 59*(9), 468–479.

101. Velasqueza-Manoff, M. (2015, July/August). Before the trauma. *Scientific American Mind,* 56–61.

102. Mobbs, M.E., & Bonanno, G.A. (2018). Beyond war and PTSD: The crucial role of transition stress in the lives of military veterans. *Clinical Psychology Review, 59,* 137–144.

103. Holmgreen, L., Tirone, V., Gerhart, J., & Hobfgoll, S.E. (2017). Conservation of resources theory: Resource caravans and passageways in health contexts. In C. L. Cooper & J. C. Quick, *The handbook of stress and health: A guide to research and practice* (pp. 443–460). New York: Wiley/Blackwell.

104. Williams, D.R., Lawrence, J.A., & Davis, B.A. (2019). Racism and health: Evidence and needed research. *Annual Review of Public Health, 40,* 105–125.

105. Ong, A.J., Fuller-Rowell, T., & Burrow, A.L. (2009). Racial discrimination and the stress process. *Journal of Personality and Social Psychology, 96,* 1259–1271.

106. Pascoe, E.A., & Richman, L.S. (2009). Perceived discrimination and health: A meta-analytic review. *Psychological Bulletin, 135*(4), 531–554.

107. Krieger, N., Kosheleva, A., Waterman, P., et al. (2011). Racial discrimination, psychological distress and self-rated health among US-born and foreign-born Black Americans. *American Journal of Public Health, 101*(9), 1704–1713.

108. Vance, S.R., & Rosenthal, S.M. (2018). A closer look at the psychosocial realities of LGBTQ youth. *Pediatrics, 141*(5).

109. Hatzenbuehler, M.L. (2009). How does sexual minority stigma "get under the skin"? A psychological mediation framework. *Psychological Bulletin, 135*(5), 707–730.

110. Meyer, I.H. (2003). Prejudice, social stress and mental health in lesbian, gay and bisexual populations: Conceptual issues and research evidence. *Psychological Bulletin, 129*(5), 674–697.

111. American College Health Association. (2017). *National College Health Assessment II: Undergraduate Student Reference Group Executive Summary Fall 2016.* Hanover, MD: Author.

112. Verkuil, B., Brosschot, J., Korrelboom, K., et al. (2011). Pretreatment of worry enhances the effects of stress management therapy. *Psychotherapy and Psychosomatics, 80,* 189–190.

113. Vaccaro, P. (2000). The 80/20 principle of time management. *Family Practice Management, 7*(8), 76.

114. Watkins, K. (2018). The role of stress in the social-support mental health relationship. *Journal of College Counseling, 21*(2), 153–164.

115. Ornish, D. (1998). *Love and survival: 8 pathways to intimacy and health.* New York: Harper Perennial.

116. Caccioppo, J.T., & Patrick, W. (2008). *Loneliness: Human nature and the need for social connection.* New York: Norton.

117. Christakis, N.A., & Fowler, J.H. (2009). *Connected: The surprising power of social networks and how they shape our lives.* New York: Little Brown.

118. Caccioppo, J.T., & Caccioppo, S. (2018). The growing problem of loneliness. *The Lancet, 391,* 426.

119. Kennedy, G., Hardman, R., Macpherson, H., et al. (2017). How does exercise reduce the rate of age associated cognitive decline: A review of potential mechanisms. *Journal of Alzheimer's Disease, 55,* 1–18.

120. deBloom, J., Sianoja, M., Korpela, K., et al. (2017). Effects of park walks and relaxation exercise during lunch breaks on recovery from job stress: Two randomized controlled trials. *Journal of Environmental Psychology, 51,* 14–30.

121. Finitsis, D.J., Dornelas, E.A., Gallagher, J., & Janis, H. (2018). Reducing stress to improve health. In M.E. Hilliard, K.A. Riekert, J.K. Ockene, & L. Pbert (Eds.), *The handbook of health behavior change* (5th ed., pp. 243–264). New York: Springer Publishing Company.

122. Geschwind, N., Peeters, F., Drukker, M., et al. (2011). Mindfulness training increases momentary positive emotions and reward experience in adults vulnerable to depression: A randomized control trial. *Journal of Consulting and Clinical Psychology, 79*(5), 618–628.

123. de Vibe, M., Solhaug, I., Tyssen, R., et al. (2013). Mindfulness training for stress management: A randomized controlled study of medical and psychology students. *BMC Medical Education, 13*(107).

124. Holzel, B., Lazar, S., Gard, T., et al. (2011). How does mindfulness meditation work? Proposing mechanisms of action from a conceptual neural perspective.

Perspectives on Psychological Science, 6(6), 537–559.

125. Schwartz, M., & Andrasik, F. (Eds.). (2003). *Biofeedback: A practitioner's guide* (3rd ed.). New York: Guilford.

126. Powers, M., & Rothbaum, B.O. (2019). Recent advances in virtual reality therapy for anxiety and related disorders: Introduction to the special issue. *Journal of Anxiety Disorders, 61*, 1–2.

Chapter 3

1. Kiecolt-Glaser, J. K., & Wilson, S. J. (2017). Lovesick: How couples' relationships influence health. *Annual Review of Clinical Psychology, 13,* 421–444.

2. Yarbrough, M., DeFilippis, J. N., & Jones, A. (2019). *Queer families and relationships after marriage equality.* London: Routledge.

3. Thomeer, M. B., Paine, E. A., & Bryant, C. (2018). Lesbian, gay, bisexual, and transgender families and health. *Sociology Compass, 12,* e12552. doi:10.1111/soc4.12552

4. Caccioppo, J., & Caccioppo, S. (2018). The growing problem of loneliness. *The Lancet, 391,* 426.

5. Fowler, J., & Christakis, N. (2010). Cooperative behavior cascades in human social networks. *PNAS, 107*(12), 5334–5338.

6. Grant, A. (2013). *Give and take: A revolutionary approach to success.* New York: Viking Press.

7. Geiger, A. W., & Livingston, G. (2019, February 19). 8 facts about love and marriage in America. *FactTank: News in Numbers.* Pew Research Center.

8. Bialik, K. (2017). *Key factors about race and marriage, 50 years after loving vs. Virginia.* Pew Research Center. Retrieved from http://www.pewresearch.org/fact-tank/2017/06/12/key-facts-about-race-and-marriage-50-years-after-loving-v-virginia/

9. Stepler, R. (2017). Number of US adults cohabiting with a partner continues to rise, especially among those 50 and older. Pew Research Center. Retrieved from http://www.pewresearch.org/fact-tank/2017/04/06/number-of-u-s-adults-cohabiting-with-a-partner-continues-to-rise-especially-among-those-50-and-older/

10. Fowler, J., & Christakis, N. (2009). The dynamic spread of happiness in a larger social network. *British Medical Journal, 337,* 1–19.

11. Christakis, N., & Fowler, J. (2009). *Connected: The surprising power of our social networks and how they shape our lives.* New York: Little, Brown.

12. Preciado, P., Snijders, T., Burk, W., et al. (2012). Does proximity matter? Distance dependence of adolescent friendships. *Social Networks, 34,* 18–31.

13. Mayo Clinic Staff. (2016). Friendships: Enrich your life and improve your health. Retrieved from https://www.mayoclinic.org/healthy-lifestyle/adult-health/in-depth/friendships/art-20044860

14. Narr, R. K., Allen, J. P., Tan, J. S., & Loeb, E. L. (2019). Close friendship strength and broader peer group desirability as differential predictors of adult mental health. *Child Development, 90*(1), 298–313.

15. de Jong Gierveld, J., Van Tilburg, T. G., & Dykstra, P. A. (2016). Loneliness and social isolation. In A. Vangelisti & D. Perlman (Eds.), *The Cambridge handbook of personal relationships* (2nd ed., chap. 27). New York, NY: Cambridge University Press.

16. Caccioppo, S., Grippo, A., London, S., et al. (2015). Loneliness: Clinical import and interventions. *Perspectives on Psychological Science, 10*(2), 238–249.

17. Shankar, A., McMunn, A., Demakakos, P., et al. (2017). Social isolation and loneliness: Associations with functional status in older adults. *Health Psychology, 36*(2), 179–187.

18. Kuperberg, A. (2014). Age at coresidence, premarital cohabitation, and marriage dissolution: 1985—2009. *Journal of Marriage and Family, 76,* 352–369.

19. Gottman, J., & Gottman J. (2017). The natural principles of love. *Journal of Family Theory and Review, 9*(1), 7–26.

20. Fisher, H. (2016). *Anatomy of love: A natural history of mating, marriage, and why we stray.* New York, NY: Norton.

21. Bruch, E. E., & Newman, M. E. J. (2018). Aspirational pursuit of mates in online dating markets. *Science Advances, 4,* eaap 9815.

22. Christakis, N., & Fowler, J. (2009). Love the one you're with. *Scientific American Mind, 20*(6), 48–55.

23. Ansari, A. (2015). *Modern romance.* New York, NY: Penguin Press.

24. Caccioppo, J., Cacciopo, S., Gonzaga, G., et al. (2013). Marital satisfaction and break-ups differ across on-line and off-line meeting venues. *PNAS, 110*(25), 10135–10140.

25. Aditi, P. (2014). Is online dating better than offline for meeting partners? Depends: Are you looking to marry or to date? *Cyberpsychology, Behavior and Social Networking, 17*(10), 664–667.

26. Smith, A., & Anderson, M. (2016). 5 facts about online dating. Pew Research Center. Retrieved from http://www.pewresearch.org/fact-tank/2016/02/29/5-facts-about-online-dating/

27. Brown, A. (2019). Couples who meet online are more diverse than those who meet in other ways, largely because they are younger. *FactTank: News in Numbers.* Pew Research Center. Retrieved from https://www.pewresearch.org/fact-tank/2019/06/24/

28. Meyer, R. (2018). Dude, she's (exactly 25 percent) out of your league. *The Atlantic.* Retrieved from https://www.theatlantic.com/science/archive/2018/08/online-dating-out-of-your-league/567083/

29. Meltzer, M. (2017, February). Online dating: Match me if you can. *Consumer Reports.*

30. Sweetheart swindle: Avoiding an online dating scam. (2016, December 29). *Consumer Reports.*

31. Hatfield, E., Bensman, L., & Rapson, R. (2012). A brief history of social scientists' attempts to measure passionate love. *Journal of Social and Personal Relationships, 29*(2), 143–164.

32. Fisher, H. (2016). *Anatomy of love: A natural history of mating, marriage, and why we stray.* New York, NY: Norton.

33. Diamond, L. (2019). Love, desire and sexual fluidty. In R. J. Sternberg & K. Sternberg (Eds.)., *The new psychology of love* (2nd ed., pp. 138-151). Cambridge, England: Cambridge University Press.

34. Sternberg, R.J. (2019). When love goes awry (part 1): Applications of the duplex theory of love and its development to relationships gone bad. In R. J. Sternberg & K. Sternberg (Eds.), *The new psychology of love* (2nd ed., pp. 280-299). Cambridge, England: Cambridge University Press.

35. Sternberg, R. J., & Sternberg, K. (Eds.). (2019). *The new psychology of love* (2nd ed.). Cambridge, England: Cambridge University Press.

36. Sheldon, P., & Antony, M.G. (2019). Forgive and forget: A typology of transgressions and forgiveness strategies in married and dating relationships. *Western Journal of Communication, 83*(2), 232–251.

37. Tannen, D. (2010). He said, she said. *Scientific American Mind, 21*(2), 55–59.

38. National Center for Transgender Equality. (2017). Frequently asked questions about transgender people. Retrieved from http://www.transequality.org/issues/resources/frequently-asked-questions-about-transgender-people

39. Human Rights Campaign. (2019). Sexual orientation and gender identity definitions. Retrieved from https://www.hrc.org/resources/glossary-of-terms

40. Kinsey, A. C., Pomeroy, W. B., & Martin, C. E. (1948). *Sexual behavior in the human male* (reprint edition, 1998). Bloomington, IN: Indiana University Press.

41. Kinsey, A. C., Pomeroy, W. B., Martin, C. E., & Gebhard, P. H. (1953). *Sexual behavior in the human female* (reprint edition, 1998). Bloomington, IN: Indiana University Press.

42. LGBT Data and Demographics. (2019). UCLA Williams Institute. Retrieved from https://williamsinstitute.law.ucla.edu/visualization/lgbt-stats/?topic=LGBT#density

43. Kiecolt-Glaser, J. K., & Wilson, S. J. (2017). Lovesick: How couples' relationships influence health. *Annual Review of Clinical Psychology, 13,* 421–443.

44. Olson, D. H., & Olson, A. K. (2000). *Empowering couples: Building on your strengths.* Minneapolis, MN: Life Innovations.

45. Munsch, C. (2015). Her support, his support: Money, masculinity, and marital infidelity. *American Sociological Review, 80*(3), 469–495.

46. Brewer, G. (2014). Heterosexual and homosexual infidelity: The importance of attitudes towards homosexuality. Personality and Individual Differences, 64, 98–100.

47. Masci, D., Brown, A., & Kiley, J. (2017). 5 facts about same-sex marriage. Pew Research Center. Retrieved from http://www.pewresearch.org/fact-tank/2017/06/26/same-sex-marriage/

48. Rostosky, S. S., & Riggle, E. D. B. (2017). Same-sex couple relationship strengths: A review and synthesis of the empirical literature (2000—2016). *Psychology of Sexual Orientation and Gender Diversity, 4*(1), 1–13.

49. Miller, B. G., Kords, S., & Macfie, J. (2017). No differences? Meta-analytic comparisons of psychological adjustment in children of gay fathers and heterosexual parents. *Psychology of Sexual Orientation and Gender Diversity, 4*(1), 14–22.

50. Pew Research Center. (2017). Changing attitudes on gay marriage. Retrieved from http://www.pewforum.org/fact-sheet/changing-attitudes-on-gay-marriage/

51. Thomeer, M. B., Paine, E. A., & Bryant, C. (2018). Lesbian, gay, bisexual and transgender families and health. Sociology Compass. Retrieved from https://onlinelibrary.wiley.com/doi/epdf/10.1111/soc4.12552

52. Yarbrough, M., Filippis, J. N., & Jones, A. (2019). *Queer families and relationships after marriage equality.* London, England: Routledge.

53. Willoughby, B., Carroll, J., & Busby, D. (2011). The different effects of "living together": Determining and comparing types of cohabiting couples. *Journal of Social and Personal Relationships, 1–23,* published online.

54. Kuperberg, A. (2014). Age at coresidence, premarital cohabitation, and marriage dissolution: 1985—2009. *Journal of Marriage and Family, 76,* 352–369.

55. Musick, K., & Bumpass, L. (2012). Reexamining the case for marriage: Union formation and changes in well-being. *Journal of Marriage and Family, 74,* 1–18.

56. Wilcox, W. B., & Marquardt, E. (2009). *The state of our unions, marriage in America 2009.* Charlottesville, VA: National Marriage Project.

57. Archibald, M., Stewart, J., Vo, L., et al. (2017). The role of social support for women living in poverty. In A. O'Leary & P. M. Frew (Eds.), *Poverty in the United States: Women's voices* (pp. 113–132). New York, NY: Springer.

58. Sokol, K., Stevenson, M., & Braver, S. (2017). Families of divorce: A research perspective. In S. W. Browning & B. van Eeden Moorefield (Eds.), *Contemporary families at the nexus of research and practice* (pp. 18–32). New York, NY: Routledge.

59. Mark, K. P., & Lassio J.A. (2018). Maintaining sexual desire in long-term relationships: A systematic review and conceptual model. *The Journal of Sex Research, 55*(4-5), 563–581.

60. Finkel, E. J. (2017). *The all or nothing marriage: How the best marriages work.* New York, NY: Dutton.

61. Olson, D. H., & Defrain, J. (2014). *Marriage and families: Intimacy, diversity, and strengths* (8th ed.). New York: McGraw-Hill.

62. Cacioppo, J., & Patrick, W. (2008). *Loneliness: Human nature and the need for social connections.* New York, NY: Norton.

63. Nowland, R., Necka, E. A., & Caciopppo, J. T. (2018). Loneliness and social internet use: Pathways to reconnection in a digital world? *Perspectives on Psychological Science, 13*(1), 70–87.

64. Bruhn, J. (2011). *The sociology of community connections* (2nd ed.). New York, NY: Springer.

65. Smith, K., & Christakis, N. (2008). Social networks and health. *Annual Review of Sociology, 34,* 405–429.

66. Fowler, J., & Christakis, N. (2008). Estimating peer effects on health in social networks. *Journal of Health Economics, 27*(5), 1400–1405.

67. U.S. Department of Health & Human Services, Administration for Children and Families, Administration on Children, Youth and Families, Children's Bureau. (2019). Child maltreatment 2017. Retrieved from https://www.acf.hhs.gov/cb/research-data-technology/ statistics-research/child-maltreatment

68. Chan, T., Michalak, N. M., & Ybarra, O. (2019). When God is your only friend: Religious beliefs compensate for purpose in life in the socially disconnected. *Journal of Personality, 87,* 455–471.

69. Ho, D. Y. F., & Ho, R. T. H. (2007). Measuring spirituality and spiritual emptiness: Toward ecumenicity and transcultural applicability. *Review of General Psychology, 11*(1), 274.

70. Fahmy, D. (2018). Key findings about Americans belief in God. *FactTank: News in Numbers.* Pew Research Center.

71. Lipka, M., & McClendon, D. (2017). Why people with no religion are projected to decline as a share of the world's population. Pew Research Center. Retrieved from http://www.pewforum.org/2015/11/03/u-s-public-becoming-less-religious/

72. Rosmarin, D., & Wachholtz, A. (2011). Beyond descriptive research: Advancing the study of spirituality and health. *Journal of Behavioral Medicine, 34,* 409–413.

73. Masters, K., & Hooker, S. (2013). Religiousness/spirituality, cardiovascular disease and cancer: Cultural integration for health research and intervention. *Journal of Consulting and Clinical Psychology, 81*(2), 206–216.

74. Koenig, H. G. (2017). Religion and spirituality in gerontology. In M. Balboni & J. Peteet (Eds.), *Spirituality and religion within the culture of medicine: From evidence to practice* (pp. 109–128). New York, NY: Oxford University Press.

75. Paley, J. (2017). Spirituality in health care. In T. Schramme & S. Edwards (Eds.), *Handbook of the philosophy of medicine.* New York, NY: Springer.

76. Cheadle, A. C. D., & Schetter, C. D. (2017). Untangling the mechanisms underlying the links between religiousness, spirituality and better health. *Social and Personality Psychology Compass, 11*(2), 1–10.

77. Strawbridge, W. J., et al. (2001). Religious attendance increases survival by improving and maintaining good health behaviors, mental health, and social relationships. *Annals of Behavioral Medicine, 23,* 68–74.

78. Marshall, J. (2019). Are religious people happier, healthier? Our global study explores this question. *FactTank: News in the Numbers.* Pew Research Center. Retrieved from http://www.pewresearch.org/fact-tank/2019/01/31/are-religious-people-happier-healthier-our-new-global-study-explores-this-question/

79. Lewis, S. L., & Bonner, P. N. (2016). Stress and stress management. In S. L. Lewis, L. Bucher, M. M. Heitkemper, & M. Harding (Eds.), *Medical-surgical nursing* (10th ed.). St. Louis, MO: Elsevier.

80. Davis, M., Eshelman, E. R., & McKay, M. (2008). *The relaxation and stress reduction handbook.* Oakland, CA: New Harbinger.

81. Finitsis, D. J., Dornelas, E. A., Gallagher, J., & Janis, H. (2018). Reducing stress to improve health. In M. E. Hilliard, K. A. Riekert, J. K. Ockene, & L. Pbert (Eds.), *The handbook of health behavior change* (pp. 243-264). New York, NY: Springer Publishing.

82. Aaker, J., & Smith, A. (2010). *The dragonfly effect: quick, effective and powerful ways to use social media to drive social change.* San Francisco, CA: Jossey-Bass.

83. Grimm, R., Spring, K., & Dietz, N. (2007). *The health benefits of volunteering: A review of recent research.* Washington, DC: Corporation for National Community Service.

84. Carter, S. B. (2014, September 4). Helpers high: The benefits (and risks) of altruism. *Psychology Today.*

85. Hafen, B. Q., et al. (1996). *Mind/body health: The effects of attitudes, emotions and relationships.* Boston, MA: Allyn & Bacon.

86. Luks, A., & Payne, P. (1992). *The healing power of doing good: The health and spiritual benefits of helping others.* New York, NY: Fawcett Columbine.

87. Ruvinsky, J. (2011, Winter). Volunteering for number one. *Stanford Social Innovation Review, 7.*

88. Beckett, W. (1993). *The mystical now: Art and the sacred.* New York, NY: Universe Publishing.

89. Osbon, D. (Ed.). (1991). *A Joseph Campbell companion: Reflections on the art of living.* New York, NY: Harper-Collins.

Chapter 4

1. National Sleep Foundation. (2015). 2015 sleep in America poll. www.sleepfoundation.org

2. Lee, Y., Park, J., & Kim, S. (2015). Academic performance among adolescents with behavioral induced insufficient sleep syndrome. *Journal of Clinical Sleep Medicine, 11*(1), 61–68.

3. American College Health Association. (2014, Spring). National college health assessment. Reference Group Executive Summary.

4. Stocksy, T. (2018). Science says you don't need more sleep to get better grades, but here's what you do need. *Elite Daily.* Retrieved from https://www.elitedaily.com/p/science-says-you-dont-need-more-sleep-to-get-better-grades-but-heres-what-you-do-need

5. National Sleep Foundation. (2018). Sleep health index scores: 2018. https://www.sleepfoundation.org/shi

6. Huffington, A. (2016). *The sleep revolution.* New York, NY: Harmony.

7. National Sleep Foundation. (2018). *2018 sleep prioritization and personal effectiveness.* Retrieved from https://www.sleepfoundation.org/professionals/sleep-america-polls/2018-sleep-prioritization-and-personal-effectiveness

8. National Sleep Foundation. (2014). 2014 Sleep in America poll: Sleep in the modern family. Retrieved from www.sleepfoundation.org

9. Stevenson, S. (2016). *Sleep smarter.* New York, NY: Rodale.

10. Stibich, M. (2019). The relationship between sleep and longevity. *Verywell Health.* Retrieved from https://www.verywellhealth.com/sleep-duration-and-longeivty=2224291

11. Winter, C. (2017). *The sleep solution: Why your sleep is broken & how to fix it.* New York, NY: Random House.

12. Kojnis, D. K. (2015). Asthma, allergic, rhinitis, and sleep problems in urban children. *Journal of Clinical Sleep Medicine, 11*(2), 101–110.

13. Zuurbier, L. A., Luik, A. L., Leening, M. J. G., et al. (2015). Associations of heart failure with sleep quality: The Rotterdam Study. *Journal of Clinical Sleep Medicine, 11*(2), 117–121.

14. Won, S. H. (2015). Sleeping for two and the great paradox of sleep in pregnancy. *Journal of Clinical Sleep Medicine, 11*(6), 593–594.

15. Czisler, C. A. (2015). Duration, time, and quality of sleep are each vital for health, performance, and safety. *Journal of the National Sleep Foundation, 15*(1), 5–8.

16. Rosenberg, R. (2014). *Sleep soundly every night, feel fantastic every day: A doctor's guide to solving your sleep problems.* New York, NY: Demos Medical Publishing.

17. National Sleep Foundation. (2016). The connection between sleep and overeating. Retrieved from https://sleepfoundation.org/sleep-topics/the-connection-between=sleep-and-obesity/

18. Genuardi, M, Althouse, A., Sharabaugh, M., et al. (2018). Exploring the mechanisms of the racial disparity in drowsy driving. *Sleep Health, 4*(4), 331–338.

19. Matthews, E., Chenghui, L., Long, C., et al. (2018). Sleep deficiency among Native Hawaiian/Pacific Islander, Black, and white Americans and the association with cardiometabolic diseases: Analysis of the National Health Interview Survey Data. *Sleep Health, 4*(3), 273–283.

20. Chokroverty, S. (2017). *Sleep disorder medicine.* New York, NY: Springer Sciences.

21. Bianchi, M. T. (2013). *Sleep deprivation and disease.* New York, NY: Springer Science and Business Media.

22. Avidan, A. (2018). *Review of sleep medicine.* Philadelphia, PA: Elsevier.

23. Park, A. (2014, September 11). The power of sleep. *Time.* Retrieved from http://time.com/3326565/the-power-of-sleep/

24. Toni, G., & Cireeli, C. (2013). Perchance to prune. *Scientific American, 309*(2), 34–39.

25. National Sleep Foundation. (2019). Sleep and your period. Retrieved from https://www.sleepfoundation.org/articles/infographic-sleep-and-your-period

26. Lockey, S. W. (2012). *Sleep: A very short introduction.* New York, NY: Oxford University Press.

27. Laber-Warren, E. (2015, September). Out of sync. *Scientific American Mind,* 30–39.

28. Macdonald, K. J., & Kimberly, A. C. (2016). Sleep physiology predicts memory retention after reactivation. *Journal of Sleep Research, 25*(6), 655–663.

29. Toni, G., & Cirelli, C. (2013). Perchance to prune. *Scientific American, 309*(2), 34–39.

30. Zadrozny, B. (2017). 7 things you need to know about Adderall. *The Daily Beast.* https://www.thedailybeast.com/7-things-you-need-to-know-about-adderall

31. Nancy, J. (2012). *Sleep deprivation, stimulant medicines, and cognition.* New York, NY: Cambridge University Press.

32. Desmon S. (2017). More college students are using Adderall to stay up and study. *Health and Medicine.* Retrieved from http://www.futurity.org/college-students-adderall-1107612-2/

33. Panda, S. (2017). *The circadian clock.* New York, NY: Rodale.

34. Winter, W. (2017). *The sleep solution.* Danvers, MA: Crown.

35. Koch, C. (2016, September). To sleep with half a brain. *Scientific American,* 22–35.

36. Ross, C. (2019). *Why we sleep and dream.* Chandler Ross.

37. Lewis, P. A. (2013). *The secret world of sleep.* New York, NY: Palgrave Macmillan.

38. National Sleep Foundation. (2013). 2013 international bedroom poll: Summary of findings. Retrieved from www.sleepfoundation.org

39. Funderburk, J. S., Shepardson, R. L., & Marketa, M. (2015). Brief behavioral interventions for symptoms of depression and insomnia in university primary care. *Journal of American College Health, 63*(6), 398–402.

40. National Sleep Foundation. (2019). Obstructive sleep apnea and sleep. Retrieved from www.sleepfoundation.org/article/sleep-related-problems/obstructive-sleep-apnea-and-sleep

41. National Sleep Foundation. (2017). Obstructive sleep apnea and sleep. Retrieved from www.sleepfoundation.org/article/sleep-related-problems

42. Jabr, F. (2017). Blue LEDs light up your brain. *Scientific American.* Retrieved from https:www.scientificamerican.com/article/blue-leds-light-up-your-brain/

43. Bindley, K. (2013). Sleep texting is on the rise. *Huffington Post.* Retrieved from www.huffingtonpost.com/2013/02/14/sleep-texting-on-the-rise_n_2677739.html

44. Panda, S. (2018). *The circadian clock.* New York, NY: Simon & Schuster, Inc.

45. National Sleep Foundation. (2015). Sleep a luxury that college students cannot afford. *Sleep Health, 1,* 13–14.

46. National Sleep Foundation. (2019). Napping. Retrieved from www.sleepfoundation.org/article/sleep-topics/napping

47. National Sleep Foundation. (2019). Bedroom. Retrieved from www.sleepfoundation.org

48. National Sleep Foundation. (2019). Keeping you awake. Retrieved from https://sleepfoundation.org/bedroom/hear.php

49. Walker, M. (2017). *Why we sleep*. New York, NY: Simon & Schuster, Inc.

50. Prevention. (2015). 9 sleep myths that make you tired. Retrieved from http://wwwprevention.com

51. Kryger, M. H., Roth, T., & Dement, W. C. (2011). *Principles and practices of sleep medicine*. New York, NY: Saunders.

52. National Sleep Foundation. (2015). 2015 sleep in America poll: Sleep and pain. Retrieved from www.sleepfoundation.org

53. Mann, D. (2017). Pain: The sleep thief. WebMD. Retrieved from www.webmd.com/sleep-disorders/features/pain-sleep

54. Skinner, G. (2016). Can you get hooked on over-the-counter sleep aids? *Consumer Reports*. http://www.consumerreports.org/drugs/over-the-counter-sleep-aids-can-you-get-hooked/

55. National Sleep Foundation. (2017). Why soda impacts your zzz's. Retrieved from www.sleepfoundation.org

56. National Sleep Foundation. (2019). How alcohol affects the quality and quantity of sleep. Retrieved from https://www.sleepfoundation.org/sleep-topics/how-alcohol-affects-the-quality-and-quantity-of-sleep

57. Moodie, A. (2019). Bulletproof. Here's why your friends are sleeping with weighted blankets. https//blogbulletproof.com/weighted-blanket-adults-benefits/

58. Live Science. (2018). Is sleeping with a fan actually bad for you? https://www.livescience.com/63179-sleeping-fan-health.html

59. National Sleep Foundation. (2019). Sleep medications. Retrieved from www.sleepfoundation.org

60. National Sleep Foundation. (2019). Orexin receptor antagonists: A new class of sleeping pill. Retrieved from https://www.sleepfoundation.org/articles/orexin-receptor-antagonists-new-class-sleeping-pill

61. U.S. Department of Health and Human Services. (2017). Many misuse OTC sleep aids: Survey. Retrieved from https://healthfinder.gov/News/Article.aspx?is=718214&source=govdelivery&utm_source=govdelivery

62. Fisher, T. (2017). Sleep trackers aren't for everyone. Van Winkle's. Retrieved from https://vanwinkles.com/the-drawbacks-of-sleep-tracking-devices/

63. Breus, M. (2017). Understanding CBD: The calming and sleep promoting benefits of cannabidiol. The Sleep Doctor. Retrieved from https://thesleepdoctor.com/2017/08/10/understanding-cbd/

64. AAA Foundation for Traffic Safety. (2017). Fact sheet: Acute sleep deprivation and risk of motor vehicle crash involvement. Retrieved from www.AAAFoundation.org

Chapter 5

1. Wardlaw, G. M., & Smith, A. M. (2019). *Contemporary nutrition*. New York, NY: McGraw-Hill.

2. Bredbenner, C. B., Moe, G. L., Beshgetoor, D., et al. (2018). *Wardlaw's perspective in nutrition*. New York, NY: McGraw-Hill.

3. Sizer, F. S., & Whitney E. (2020). *Nutrition: Concepts and controversies*. Belmont, CA: Cengage.

4. Friedman, J. W. (2016). Debunking debating water fluoridation. *American Journal of Public Health, 106*(2), 211.

5. Schiff, W. (2016). *Nutrition for healthy living*. New York, NY: McGraw-Hill.

6. U.S. Beverage Guidance Panel. (2017). Beverage panel recommendations and analysis. Global Beverage Guidelines. Retrieved from http://www.epc.unc.edu/project/beverage/us-beverage-panel/

7. Harvard Public Health. (2019). Healthy beverage guidelines. Retrieved from https://www.hsph.harvard.edu/nutritionsource/health-drinksfull-story/

8. Spoon University. (2019). Is it better to drink water cold or at room temperature? Retrieved from https://spoonuniversity.com/lifestyle/water-temperature-cold-or-room-temperature

9. Greger, M. (2015). *How not to die*. New York, NY: Flatiron Books.

10. Gameau, D. (2014). *The sugar book*. London: Macmillan.

11. University Health News. (2019). Diving in: Are smoothies healthy? Retrieved from https://universityhealthnews.com/daily/nutrition/are-smoothies-goof-for-you/

12. U.S. Department of Agriculture. (2016). 2015–2020 Dietary guidelines for Americans. Retrieved from www.health.gov/dietary guidelines

13. Vasanti, S. M., & Huh, F. B. (2011). Sugar sweetened beverages and health: Where does the evidence stand? *American Clinical Nutrition, 94*(5), 1161–1162.

14. Liebman, B. (2015, Jan/Feb). Behind the headlines: The science may surprise you. *Nutrition Action Healthletter*, 1–7.

15. Stephanson, T., & Schiff, W. (2018). *Human nutrition: Science for healthy living*. New York, NY: McGraw-Hill.

16. Roizen, M., & Crupain, M. (2019). *What to eat when*. Washington, DC: National Geographic.

17. Holscher, H. D., Caporaso, J. G., Hooda, S., et al. (2015). Fiber supplementation influences phylogenetic structure and functional capacity of the human intestinal microbiome: A follow-up of a randomized controlled trial. *American Journal of Clinical Nutrition, 101*(1), 55–64.

18. Liebman, B. (2015, May). Cancer: How to lower your risk. *Nutrition Action Healthletter*, 1–7.

19. Berger, S., Raman, G., Vishwanathan, R., et al. (2015). Dietary cholesterol and cardiovascular disease: A systematic review and metaanalysis. *American Journal of Clinical Nutrition, 102*(2), 276–294.

20. Hendry, V., Almiron-Roig, E., Monsivais, P., et al. (2015). Impact of regulatory interventions to reduce intake of artificial trans-fatty acids: A systematic review. *American Journal of Public Health, 105*(3), 332–342.

21. Jason, W. M., Wu, H., Wang, Q., et al. (2015). Prospective association of fatty acids in the de novo lipogenesis pathway with risk of type 2 diabetes: The cardiovascular heart study. *American Journal of Clinical Nutrition, 101*(1), 153–163.

22. Bakalar, N. (2019). *The New York Times*. Retrieved from https://www.nytimes.com/2019/03/15/well/eat/eggs-cholesterol-heart-health.html

23. Rettner, R. (2015, June 19). The next trans fat: Experts predict coming food battles. *Live Science*, 43.

24. Harvard Health. (Dec 16,2019). Domultivitamins make you healthier? Harvard Medical School. www.health.harvard.edu/mens-health/do-multivitamins-make-you-healthier. Accessed July 25, 2020.

25. Mursu, J., Robien, K., Harnack, L. J., et al. (2011). Dietary supplements and mortality rate in older women: The Iowa Women's Health Study. *American Journal of Clinical Nutrition, 92*(2), 338–347.

26. Chen, O., Kamil. A., & Blumberg, B. (2015). Phytochemical composition and antioxidant capacity of whole wheat products. *International Journal of Food Sciences and Nutrition, 66*(1), 62070.

27. Hutchinson, C. (2011). Heart disease death rates drop with each added fruit and veggie serving. *ABC News*. Retrieved from http://abcnews.go.com/CleanPrint/cleanprintproxy.aspx?1296051874491

28. Cassidy, A., O'Reilly, E. J., Kay, C., et al. (2011). Habitual intake of flavonoids subclasses and incident hypertension in adults. *American Journal of Clinical Nutrition, 93*(2), 338–347.

29. U.S. Department of Agriculture. (2007). Final rule promotes safe use of dietary supplements. Retrieved from www.fda.gov/consumer/updates/dietarysupps062207.html

30. Merino, J., Guash-Ferre, M., Martinez-Gonzales, M. A., et al. (2015). Is complying with the recommendations of sodium intake beneficial for health in individuals at high cardiovascular risk? Findings from the PREDIMED study. *American Journal of Clinical Nutrition, 101*(3), 44–48.

31. Center for Science in the Public Interest. (2013, June). Six reasons to eat lean red meat. *Nutrition Action Healthletter*, 7.

32. Jabr, F. (2017). Meat of the matter: Are our modern methods of preserving and cooking meat healthy? *Scientific American.* Retrieved from https://www.scientificamerican.com/article/meat-of-the-matter-modern-methods-of-preserving-and-cooking-meat-healthy/

33. Johnson, W. (2018). Burgers grown in lab are heading to your plate. Will you bite? *Washington Post.* Retrieved from htpps://www.washingtonpost.com/national/health-science/burgers-grown-in-lab-are-heading-to-your-plate-will-you-bite/2018/09/07/id048720-b060-1

34. Thorpe, J R. (2019). What happens to your body when you stop eating meat, according to doctors. Retrieved from https://www.bustle.com/p/what-happens-to-your-body-when-you-stop-eating-meat-according-to-doctors-19223048

35. Seward, M. W., Block, J. P., & Chatterjee, A. (2016). A traffic-light label intervention and dietary choices in college cafeterias. *American Journal of Public Health, 105*(10), 1808–1814

36. Steka, B. (2016, March/April). In search of the optimal brain diet. *Scientific American Mind*, 27–33.

37. Institute of Medicine. (2011). *Examination of front-of-package symbols: Phase I and II reports.* National Academy of Sciences. Retrieved from www.nap.edu

38. Food and Drug Administration. (n.d.). FDA proposes updates to Nutrition Facts label on food packages. Retrieved from www/fda.gov/NewsEvents/Newsroom/PressAnnouncements/ucm387418.htm

39. Chen, R., Smyser, M., Chan, N., et al. (2015). Changes in awareness and use of calorie information after mandatory menu labeling in restaurants in King County, Washington. *American Journal of Public Health, 105*(3), 545-553.

40. Food and Drug Administration. (2017). Calorie labeling on restaurant menus and vending machines: What you need to know. Retrieved from http://www.fda.gov/Food/IngredientsPackagingLabeling/LabelingNutrition/ucm436722.htm

41. Goldberg, B. (2015). New York is first U.S. city with salt warning on restaurant menus. *Reuters.* Retrieved from www.reuters.com/article/2015/11/30/us-new-york-salt-idUSKBNOTJ2GV20151130

42. Cohen, L., & Sims, J. (2015). How menu labeling could spark change beyond the menu board. Retrieved from http://healthaffairs.org/2015/02/24/how-menu-labeling-could-spark-changes-beyond-the-menu-board/

43. Oaklander, M. (2012, October 19). Diet soda is doing 7 awful things to your body. *Today Show*, NBC News.

44. Center for Science in the Public Interest. (2019). 5 things to look for before you order from a menu. https://cspinet.org/sites/default/files/5-things-menu-labeling.pdf

45. Dewey, C. (2017). You're about to see a big change to the sell-by dates on food. *Washington Post.* Retrieved from www.washingtonpost.com/news/wonk/wp/2017/02/16/a-barely-noticeable-change-to-how-food-is-labeled-could-save-millions/

46. Syncht, A. (2018). Sell by? Use by? Best by? Clear labels mean less food waste. *Biz Journals.* https://www.bizjournals.com/bixwomen/news/latest-news/2018/12/sell-by-use-by-best-by-clear-labels-mean-less-food-food.html?page=all

47. Gibbons, H., McNulty, B. A., Nugent, A. P., et al. (2015). A metabolomics approach to the identification of biomarkers of sugar-sweetened beverage intake. *American Journal of Clinical Nutrition, 101*(3), 471-477.

48. Bleich, S. N., Barry, C. L., Gary-Webb, T. L., et al. (2014). Reducing sugar-sweetened beverage consumption by providing caloric information: How Black adolescents alter their purchases and whether the effects persist. *American Journal of Public Health, 104*(12), 2417-2424.

49. Schardt, D. (2017, Jan/Feb). Caffeine: More than just a pick me up. *Nutrition Action Healthletter*, 7-8.

50. The Renegade Pharmacist. (2019). What happens one hour after drinking diet coke, coke zero, or any other similar diet soda. Retrieved from https://therenegadepharmacist.com/coke-exposed-happens-one-hour-drinking-diet-coke-coke-zero-similar-diet-soda/

51. Centers for Disease Control and Prevention. (2017). Get the facts: Sugar-sweetened beverages consumption. Retrieved from https://www.cdc.gov/nutrition/datastatistics/sugar-sweetened-beverages-and-consumption

52. Smith, T. J., Wolfson, J. A., Jiao, D., et al. (2015). Caramel color in soft drinks and exposure to 4-Methylimidazole: A quantitative risk assessment. *PLoS ONE.* doi:10.1371/journal.pone.0118138

53. Malik, V. S., & Hu, F. B. (2011). Sugar-sweetened beverages and health: Where does the evidence stand? *American Journal of Clinical Nutrition, 94*5), 1161-1162.

54. Centers for Disease Control and Prevention. (n.d.). Most Americans should consume less sodium (1,500 mg/day or less). Retrieved from www.cdc.gov/Features/Sodium/

55. Zinczenko, D. (2008). *Eat this, not that.* New York, NY: Rodale.

56. Streit, L. (2019). Is black pepper good for you, or bad? Nutrition, uses and more. *Health Line.* Retrieved from https://www.healthline.com/nutrition/is-black-pepper-good-for-you#downsides

57. Heid, M. (2019). Is black pepper healthy? Here's what the science says. *Time Magazine.* Retrieved from http://www.time.com/5503520/black-pepper-health-benefits/

58. National Institute of Allergy and Infectious Diseases. (2010). Guidelines for the diagnosis and management of food allergy in the United States. Retrieved from www.jacionline.org/article/S0091-6749(10)01566-6/fulltext

59. Doheny, K. (2016). Food labels on potential allergens may confuse shoppers. *HealthDay.* Retrieved from https://consumer.healthday.com/respiratory-and-allergy-information-2/food-allergy-news-16/food-labels-on-potential-allergens-may-confuse-shoppers-716385.html

60. 173. Learning Early About Peanut Allergies. (2015). www.leap.study.

61. Mayo Clinic. (n.d.). Celiac disease. Retrieved from http://www.mayoclinic.org/diseases-conditions/celiac-disease/symptoms-causes/syc-20352220

62. Anderson, J. (n.d.). Celiac disease & gluten sensitivity. Retrieved from http://celiacdisease.about.com/od/diagnosingceliacdisease/tp.l-Am-Newly-Diagnosed-What-Questions-Should-I-Ask-My-Doctor.html

63. Tucker, A. (2019). Is gluten messing with your thyroid? *Well and Good.* Retrieved from https://www.wellandgood.com/good-food/gluten-and-thyroid/

64. Chico University Student Health. (2017). Alcohol and energy drinks: A dangerous mix. Retrieved from https://www.csuchico.edu/shs/health_education/alcohol_energy.shtml

65. Howland, J., & Rohsenow, D. J. (2013). Risks of energy drinks mixed with alcohol. *Journal of the American Medical Association, 309*(3), 245-246.

66. Sepkowitz, K. A. (2013). Energy drinks and caffeine-related adverse effects. *Journal of the American Medical Association, 309*(3), 243-244.

67. U.S. Food and Drug Administration. (2015). FDA consumer advice on pure powdered caffeine. Retrieved from www.fda.gov/FoodRecallsOutbreakEmergencies/SafetyAlertsAdvisories/ucm405787.htm

68. U.S. Food and Drug Administration. (2015). FDA takes action on bulk pure powdered caffeine products. Constituent Update. Retrieved from www.fda.gov/Food/RecallsOutbreaksEmergencies/SafetyAlertsAdvisories/ucm405787.htm

69. Centers for Disease Control and Prevention. (2017). Fact sheets: Caffeine and alcohol. Retrieved from https//www.cdc.gov/fact-sheets/caffeine-and-alcohol.htm

70. Dotinga, R. (2017). Even one high-fat meal can harm your liver: Study finds. *HealthDay.* Retrieved from https://

consumer.healthday.com/diseases-and-conditions-information-37/liver-disease-news-447/even-one-high-fat-meal-can-harm-your-liver-study-finds-718960.html

71. Power of Positivity. (n.d.). Science reveals impact of fast food on gut health. Retrieved from https://www.powerofpositivity.com/fast-food-impacts-gut-health

72. Harvard Health. (2019). Microwaving food in plastic: Dangerous or not? Harvard Health. https://www.health.harvard.edu/staying-healthy/microwaving-food-in-plastic-dangerous-or-not

73. Feeding America. (2015). Hunger and poverty fact sheet. Retrieved from www.feedingamerica.org/hunger-in-america/impact-of-hunger-and-poverty/hunger-and-poverty-fact-sheet.html

74. Aggarwal, A., Cook, A. J., Junfeng, J., et al. (2014). Access to supermarkets and fruit vegetable consumption. *American Journal of Public Health, 104*(5), 917-923.

75. Fischtner, L., Kleiman, K., Melly, S. L., et al. (2016). Effects of proximity to supermarkets on a randomized trial studying interventions for obesity. *American Journal of Public Health, 106*(3), 557-562.

76. American Council on Science and Health. (2018). Build it and they will come? Food deserts and the entry of new supermarkets. https://www.asch.org/news/2018/01/05/build-it-and-they-will-come-food-deserts-and-entry-new-supermarkets-12369

77. Laterman, K. (2019). Tuition or dinner? Nearly half of college students surveyed in a new report are going hungry. *The New York Times*. Retrieved from https://www.nytimes.com/2019/05/02/nyregion/hunger-college-food-insecurity.html

78. The Atlantic. (2019). Millions of college students are going hungry. https://www.theatlantic.com/education/archive/2019/01/college-student-hunger/579877/

79. Centers for Disease Control and Prevention. (n.d.). Recipe for food safety. *Vital Signs*. Retrieved from www.cdc.gov/vitalsigns/listeria/index.html

80. Scutti, S. (2019). CNN. The dangers of eating raw fish. Retrieved from https://www.cnn.com/2018.08.30/health/raw-fish-vibrio-vulnificus-amputation/index.html

81. Stobbe, M. (2013). Study says leafy green vegetables top source of food poisoning. Associated Press. Retrieved from http://news.yahoo.com/study-says-leafy-greens-top-food-poisoning-source-150043222.html

82. Zimmer, C. (2011). Rise of the superbug. *Newsweek, 157*(26), 11-12.

83. Intelligence for Your Life. (2017). Dry pet food can be tainted with salmonella. Retrieved from http://www.tesh.com/articles/dry-pet-food-can-be-tainted-with-salmonella

84. Centers for Disease Control and Prevention. (2015). CDC data show progress in reducing some foodborne infections in 2014. Retrieved from https://www.cdc.gov/media/releases/2015/p0514-reducing-foodborne-infections.html

85. Centers for Disease Control and Prevention. (2017). CDC data show progress in reducing some foodborne infections. Retrieved from www.cdc.gov/salmonella/reading-07-18/index.html

86. Nutrition Facts Organization. (2017). Clostridium difficile in the food supply. Retrieved from http://nutritionfacts.org/2017/03/21/clostridium-difficile-in-the-food-supply/

87. U.S. Department of Agriculture. (2017). USDA issues final rule on mandatory country-of-origin labeling. Retrieved from https://www.usda.gov/rules-regulations/cool

88. ESPN. (2019). What's lurking in your stadium food? Retrieved from www.espn.com/espn/eticket/story?page=100725/stadiumconcessions

89. Hakim, D. (2016). Doubts about the promised bounty of genetically modified crops. *The New York Times*. Retrieved from https://www.nytimes.com/2016/10/30/business/gmo-promise-falls-short.html

Chapter 6

1. The State of Obesity. (2018. Physical inactivity in the United States. Retrieved from https://www.stateofobesity.org/physical-inactivity/

2. Centers for Disease Control and Prevention. (2019). Facts about physical activity. Retrieved from www/cdc.gov/physicalactivity/data/facts.html

3. American College Health Association. (2018). *ACHA, Spring 2014 National Collegiate Health Assessment*. ACHA-NCHA Reference Group Report. Retrieved from www.acha.org

4. Newman, T. (2017). What does being physically fit mean? *Medical News Today*. https://www.medicalnewstoday.om/articles/7181.php

5. Sharkey, B.J., & Gaskill, S.E. (2013). *Fitness & health*. Champaign, IL: Human Kinetics.

6. Jancer, M. (2018). This is the effect working out has on your bones. *Tonic*. Retrieved from https://tonic.com/en_us/article/ne5zg8/this-is-the-effect-working-out-has-on-your-bones

7. Reas, E. (2014). Exercise counteracts genetic risk for Alzheimer's. *Scientific American Mind, 25*(6), 12-13.

8. Charvat, M. (2019). Why exercise is good for your brain. *Psychology Today*. Retrieved from https://www.psychologytoday.com/us/blog/the-fifth-vital-sign/201901/why-exercise-is-good-for-your-brain

9. Dow, D. (2017). Exercise: Can you trust the latest buzz. *Nutrition Action Healthletter*, 9.

10. Jacobs, D. R. (2016, September/October). How does exercise benefit cognition? *Scientific American Mind*, 72.

11. Jabr, F. (2017, January/February). Head strong. *Scientific American Mind*, 27-31.

12. Coon, T., Boddy, K., Stein, K., et al. (2011). Does participating in physical activity in outdoor natural environments have a greater effect on physical and mental wellbeing than physical activity indoors? A systematic review. *Environmental Sciences and Technology, 45*(5), 1761-1772.

13. Bassuk S. S., Church T. C., & Manson J. E. (2013, August). We all know we should exercise. *Scientific American, 764-779.*

14. Office of Disease Prevention and Health Promotion. (2019). *Physical activity guidelines*. Retrieved from HealthyPeople.gov

15. HealthyPeople.gov. (2018). P*hysical activity guidelines for Americans*. Retrieved from https://healthgov./paguidelines/second-edition/pdf/Physical_Activity_Guidelines_2nd_edition.pdf

16. Biswas, A., Oh, P. I., Faulker, G. E., et al. (2015). Sedentary time and its association with risk for disease incidence, mortality, and hospitalization in adults: A systematic review and meta-analysis. *Annals of Internal Medicine, 162*(2), 123-132.

17. American College of Sports Medicine, with Garber, C.E., Blissmer, B., Deschenes, M.R., et.al. (2011). Quantity and quality of exercise for developing and maintaining cardiorespiratory, musculoskeletal, and neuromotor fitness in apparently healthy adults: Guidance for prescribing exercise. *Medicine & Science in Sports & Exercise, 43*(7), 1334-1359.

18. American College of Sports Medicine, with Rocketto, L. (2019). ACSM releases new exercise guidelines. Retrieved from https://greatist.com/fitness/acsm-releasesnew-exercise-guidelines

19. Department of Health and Human Services. (n.d.). Physical activity guidelines (2nd ed.). Retrieved from https://health.gov/paguidelines/second-edition/pdf/Physical_Activity_Guidelines_2nd_edition.pdf

20. Berbari, G. (2019). Is it unhealthy to do cardio every day? You might be overdoing it, according to experts. *Elite Daily*. https://www.elitedaily.com/p/is-it-unhealthy-to-docardio-every-day-you-might-be-overdoing-it-according-to-experts-9851214

21. The Washington Post. (2019). New government guidelines say you can get your exercise in small doses. Retrieved from https://www.google.com/search?q=w

ashington+post%2C+new+government+guidelines+say+you+can+get+your+exercise+in+small+doses&rlz=1C1CHBF

22. Centers for Disease Control and Prevention. (2017). *HealthyPeople 2020*. Retrieved from www.cdc.gov/nchs/healthy-peope/hp2020.htm

23. NBC News. (2019). The top 2019 fitness trends and how to incorporate them into your workouts. Retrieved from https://www.nbcnews.com/better/pop-culture/top-2019-fitnesstrends[how-incorporate-them-your-workoutsncna952441

24. BodyBuilding.com. (2017). High intensity interval training: The ultimate guide. Retrieved from https://www.bodybuilding.com/content/high-intensity-interval-training-the-ultimate-guide

25. National Strength & Conditioning Association. (2017). *NSCA's guide to program design*. Champaign, IL: Human Kinetics.

26. Betuel, E. (2019). A short, power-based workout can reveal your risk of early death. Inverse. Retrieved from https://www.inverse.com/article/54862=workouts-that-canpredict-death-risk

27. eHow. (n.d.). What are the benefits of a stability ball? Retrieved from www.ehow.com/about_5061285_benefits–stability-ball.html

28. Kassel, G. (2019). What exactly is the posterior chain and why do trainers keep talking about it. *Shape*. Retrieved from https://www.shape.com/fitness/tips/what-is-the-posterior-chain-exercises

29. Frederick, A., & Frederick, C. (2017). *Stretch to win*. Champaign, IL: Human Kinetics.

30. Mayo Clinic. (2017). *Functional fitness training: Is it right for you?* Retrieved from http://www.mayoclinic.com/healthy-lifestyle/indepth/functional fitness

31. Better Movement. (2010). Why slow movement builds coordination. Retrieved from https://www.bettermovement.org/blog/2010/why=practice-slow-movement

32. Halo Neuroscience. https://blog.haloneuro.com/@HaloNeuroscience.

33. Morris, N. (2018). Could 'conscious movement' be better for you than HITT. Retrieved from https://metro.co.uk2018/11/01/could-conscious-movement-be-better-for-you-than-hitt-8096624/

34. Williams, M. H., Rawson, E. S., & Branch, J. D. (2013). *Nutrition for health, fitness & sport*. New York, NY: McGraw-Hill Higher Education.

35. Douglas, S. (2018). *Washington Post*. Retrieved from https://www.washingtonpost.com/lifestyle/wellness/the-fat-burning-heart-rate-zone-is-a-myth-how-exercise-and-weight-loss-really-work/

36. Schneider, K., & Kitchens, S. (2019). Micro-workouts: A gym, but for your toes, or your face, or your butt. *The Cut*.

Retrieved from https://www.thecut.com/2019/03/micro-workouts-toes-face-butt-ears.html

37. Fetters, A. (2015). What happened to your body by skipping the gym this winter? CNN. Retrieved from www.cnn.com/2015/03/23/health/body-skipping-by/index.html

38. Chair today, gone tomorrow. (2008). *Nutrition Action Healthletter*, 1, 3-6.

39. Levine, J. (2017). Killer chairs: How desk jobs ruin your health. *Scientific American*. Retrieved from https://www.scientificamerican.com/article/killer-chairs-how-desk-jobs-ruin-your-health

40. Duvall, J., & De Young, R. (2013). Some strategies for sustaining a walking routine: Insights from experienced walkers. *Journal of Physical Activity & Health, 10*, 10-18.

41. Pillay, J. D., Kolbe-Alexander, T. L., Mechelen, W. V., et al. (2014). Steps that count: The association between the number and intensity of steps accumulated and fitness and health measures. *Journal of Physical Activity & Health, 11*(1), 10-17.

42. Neporent, L. (2015). Myth or reality: Treadmill just as good as road running. *ABC News*. Retrieved from http://abcnews.com/Health/myth-debunked-treadmill-good-road-running/story?id=2905

43. Family Health. (2015). Are the calorie counts on exercise machines accurate? Retrieved from www.acefitness.org/acefit/healthy-living-article/59/1571/Are-the-calorie-counts-on-exercise-machines-accurate

44. Graf, D. L., Pratt, L. V., Hester, C. N., et al. (2009). Playing active video games increases energy expenditure in children. *Pediatrics, 124*(2), 534-540.

45. Baranowski, T. (2015). Are active video games useful to combat obesity. *The American Journal of Clinical Nutrition, 101*(6), 1107-1108.

46. Conde-Pumpido, T, Loos, E., Wilgenburg, W., et.al. (2018) Using an ice-skating exergame to foster intercultural interaction between refugees and Dutch children. Cogent. Retrieved from https://www.cogentoa.com/article/10.1080/233186x.2018.1538587.pdf

47. USA Today. (2018). A foolish take nearly 80 percent of Americans own smartphones. Retrieved from https://www.usatoday.com/storu/money/markets/2018/02/24/a-foolish-take-nearly-80-percent-of-americans-own-smartphones/110342918/

48. Pallarito, K. (2016). Do activity trackers like Fitbit boost health? *HealthDay*. Retrieved from https://consumer.healthday.com/fitness-information-14/walking-health-news-288/do-activity-trackers-like-fitbit-boost-health-715497.html

49. Bumgardner, W. (2019). Are apps as accurate as wearable fitness bands and

pedometers? *Very Well Fit*. Retrieved from https://www.verywellfit.com/app-fitness-ban-accuracy-3434992

50. Williams, M. H., Rawson, E. S., & Branch, D. J. (2017). *Nutrition for health, fitness and sport* (7th ed.). New York, NY: McGraw-Hill Education.

51. Reinberg, S. (2016). Cushioned shoe inserts won't guard against injury: Review. *HealthDay*. Retrieved from https://www.webmd.com/pain-management/news/20161213/cushioned-shoe-inserts-wont-guard-against-injury-review#1

52. Aschwanden, C. (2019). *Good to go*. New York, NY: W. W. Norton & Company, Inc.

53. Jam, B. (2019). Paradigm shifts: Use of ice & NSAIDs post acute tissue injuries (part 1 of 2). Physical Therapy Web. Retrieved from https://physicaltherapyweb.com/paradigm-shifts-ice-nsaidpost-acute-soft-tissue-injuries-part-1-2/

54. Carney, S. (2017). *What doesn't kill us: How freezing water extreme altitude, and environmental conditioning will renew our evolutionary strength*. New York, NY: Rodale.

55. Lapidos, R. (2019). Slow wave sleep is under-the-radar stage that's key for muscle recovery. *Well & Good*. Retrieved from https://www.wellandgood.com/good-advice/slow-wave-sleep/

56. Reynolds, G. (2016). Exercising on "smog alert" days. *The New York Times*. Retrieved from https://well.blogs.nytimes.com/2016/07/08/ask-well-exercising-on-smog-alert-days

57. Leskowski, E. R. (2017). Does air pollution make outdoor exercise risky? If you have asthma or another health problem? *Mayo Clinic*. Retrieved from http://www.mayoclinic.org/healthy-lifestyle/fitness/expert-answers/air-pollution-and-exercise

58. Preidt, R. (2016). How to exercise safely in smog. *HealthDay*. Retrieved from https://consumer.healthday.com/respiratory-and-allergy-information-2/air-pollution-health-news-540/how-to-exercise-safely-in-smog-716322.html

59. Lee, B.Y. (2020, February 29). Despite COVID-19 Coronavirus. here is why you should stop buying face masks. Forbes. https://www.forbes.com/sites/brucelee/2020/02/29/despite=covid-19-coronavirus-here-is-why-you-should-stop-buying-face-masks. Accessed May 6, 2020.

60. Reynolds, G. ((2020, April 10). Exercising outdoors with a face mask. New York Times. https://www.nytimes.com/2020/04/10/well/move/exercise-outdoors-mask-running-cycling.html. Accessed May 6, 2020.

61. Exercise Guidelines for People with Disabilities. (2017). NCHPAD. Retrieved from https://www.nchpad.org/1473/Exersie-Guidelines-for-peope-with-disabilities

62. For Inspired Lives. (2010). Overcoming disability. 3 inspiring stories. Blog. Retrieved from http://forinspiredlives.blogspot.com-2010/11overcoming-disability-3-inspiring.html

63. Thompson, W. R. (2015). Worldwide survey of fitness trends for 2016: 10th anniversary edition. *ACSM's Health & Fitness Journal, 19*(6), 9-18.

64. Move, Virginia Government. (2019). Barriers to physical activity. Retrieved from https://www.move.va.gov/download/NewHandouts/Physical Activity/P01_BarriersTOPhysicalActivity.pdf

65. Ingraham, C. (2019). Actually, you do have enough time to exercise, and here's the data to prove it. *Washington Post*. Retrieved from https://www.washingtonpost.com/business/2019/10/30/actualy-you-do-have-enough-time-to-exercise-and-heres-the-data-to-prove-it/

66. Fox, M. (2017). Can running be contagious? This study shows it may be. *NBC News*. Retrieved from http://www.nbcnews.com/health/health-news/can-running-be-contagious-this-study-shows-it-may-be

67. Rundel, A. G., & Heymsfield, S. B. (2016). Can walkable urban design play a role in reducing the incidence of obesity-related conditions? *Journal of American Medical Association, 315*(20), 2175-2177.

68. Centers for Disease Control and Prevention. (n.d.). *Physical activity resources for health professionals: Active environments*. Retrieved from www.cdc.gov/nccdphp/dnpa/physical/health_professionals/active_environments/index.htm

69 Friederichs, A. A. H., Kremers, A. P. J., Lechner, L., et al. (2013). Neighborhood walkability and walking behavior: The moderating role of action orientation. *Journal of Physical Activity & Health, 10*, 515-522.

70. Duvall J. (2012). A comparison of engagement strategies for encouraging outdoor walking. *Journal of Physical Activity and Health, 9*, 62-70.

Chapter 7

1. National Center for Health Statistics. (2018). *Health, United States, 2017: With special feature on mortality*. Hyattsville, MD: NCHS.

2. Centers for Disease Control and Prevention. (n.d.). *U.S. obesity prevalence maps*. Retrieved from https://www.cdc.gov/obesity/data/prevalence-maps.html

3. Fryar, C. D., Carroll, M. D., & Ogden, C. L. (2018). Prevalence of overweight, obesity, and severe obesity among adults aged 20 and over: United States, 1960-1962 through 2015-2016. NCHS Health E-stats. Hyattsville, MD: National Center for Health Statistics. Retrieved from https://www.cdc.gov/nchs/data/hestat/obesity_adult_15_16/obesity_adult_15_16.pdf

4. World Health Organization. (2018). Obesity and overweight fact sheet. Retrieved from https://www.who.int/en/news-room/fact-sheets/detail/obesity-and-overweight

5. World Health Organization. (2017). Report of the Commission on Ending Childhood Obesity. Implementation plan: executive summary. Geneva: WHO. Licence: CC BY-NC-SA 3.0 IGO. Retrieved from https://apps.who.int/iris/bitstream/handle/10665/259349/WHO-NMH-PND-ECHO-17.1-eng.pdf?sequence=1

6. Ogden, C. L., Carroll, M. D., Fakhouri, T. H., Hales, C. M., Fryar, C. D., Li, X., & Freedman, D. S. (2018). Prevalence of obesity among youths by household income and education level of head of household—United States 2011–2014. *Morbidity and Mortality Weekly Report, 67*(6), 186–189.

7. Centers for Disease Control and Prevention. (n.d.). Defining adult overweight and obesity. Retrieved from https://www.cdc.gov/obesity/adult/defining.html

8. Aragon, A. A., Schoenfeld, B. J., Wildman, R., et al. (2017). International Society of Sports Nutrition position stand: Diets and body composition. *Journal of the International Society of Sports Nutrition, 14*, 16.

9. Gallagher, D., Heymsfield, S. B., Heo, M., et al. (2000). Healthy percentage body fat ranges: An approach for developing guidelines based on body mass index. *American Journal of Clinical Nutrition, 72*(3), 694-701.

10. Ward, L. C. (2018). Human body composition: Yesterday, today and tomorrow. *European Journal of Clinical Nutrition, 72*, 1201-1207. https://doi.org/10.1038/s41430-018-0210-2

11. Leclerc, J., Bonneville, N., Auclair, A., et al. (2015). If not dieting, how to lose weight? Tips and tricks for a better global and cardiovascular health. *Postgraduate Medicine, 127*(2), 173-185.

12. Flegal, K. M., Kit, B. K., & Orpana, H. (2013). Association of all-cause mortality with overweight and obesity using standard body mass index categories: a systematic review and meta-analysis. *Journal of the American Medical Association, 309*(1), 71-82.

13. Piche, M. E., Poirier, P., Lemieux, I., & Despres, J. P. (2018). Overview of epidemiology and contribution of obesity and body fat distribution to cardiovascular disease: an update. *Progress in Cardiovascular Diseases, 61*, 103-113.

14. Meldrum, D. R. (2017). Introduction: Obesity and reproduction. *Fertility and Sterility, 107*(4), 831-832.

15. Broughton, D. E., & Moley, K. H. (2017). Obesity and female infertility: Potential mediators of obesity's impact. *Fertility and Sterility, 107*, 840-847.

16. Arnold, M., Pandeya, N., Byrnes, G., et al. (2015). Global burden of cancer attributable to high body-mass index in 2012: A population-based study. *Lancet Oncology, 16*(1), 36-46.

17. Masters, R. K., Reighter, E. N., Powers, D. A., et al. (2013). The impact of obesity on U.S. mortality levels: The importance of age and cohort factors in population estimates. *American Journal of Public Health, 103*(10), 1895-1901.

18. Chatterjee, S., & Davies, M. J. (2015). Current management of diabetes mellitus and future directions in care. *Postgraduate Medical Journal*. doi:10.1136/postgradmedj-2014-133200

19. Tauber, S., Mulder, L. B., & Flint, S. W. (2018). The impact of workplace health promotion programs emphasis on individual responsibility on weight stigma and discrimination. *Frontiers Psychology, 19*(9), 2206.

20. Dor, A., Ferguson, C., et al. (2011). Gender and race wage gaps attributable to obesity. George Washington University and School of Public Health. Retrieved from www.gwumc.edu/sphhs/departments/healthpolicy/dhp_publications/pub_uploads/dhpPublication_FA85CB82-5056-9D20-3DBD361E605324F2.pdf

21. Jung, F., Spahlholz, J., Hilbert, A., Riedel-Heller, S. G., & Luck-Sikorski, C. (2017). Impact of weight-related discrimination, body dissatisfaction and self-stigma on the desire to weigh less. *Obesity Facts, 10*(2), 139-151.

22. Singh, R. K., Permendra, K., & Mahalingam, K. (2017). Molecular genetics of human obesity: A comprehensive review. *Comptes Rendus Biologies, 340*, 87-108.

23. Bray, G. A., Krauss, R. M., & Sacks, F. M. (2019, June). Lessons learned from the POUNDS Lost study: Genetic, metabolic, and behavioral factors affecting changes in body weight, body composition, and cardiometabolic risk. *Current Obesity Reports*, 1-22.

24. Wang, T., Heianza, Y., Sun, D., Zheng, Y., et al. (2019). Improving fruit and vegetable intake attenuates the genetic association with long-term weight gain. *American Journal of Clinical Nutrition*. doi:10.1093/ajcn/nqz126

25. Thaker, V. V. (2017). Genetic and epigenetic causes of obesity. *Adolescent Medicine State of the Art Review, 28*(2), 379-405.

26. Yazdi, F. T., Clee, S. M., & Meyre, D. (2015). Obesity genetics in mouse and human: Back and forth and back again. *PeerJ, 3*, e856. doi:10.7717/peerj.856

27. Tomiyama, A. J. (2019). Stress and obesity. *Annual Review of Psychology, 70*, 703-718.

28. Mailing, L. J., Allen, J. M., Buford, T. W., Fields, C. J., & Woods, J. A. (2019). Exercise and the gut microbiome: A review of evidence, potential mechanisms, and implications for human health. *Exercise and Sport Sciences Reviews*. doi:10.1249/JES.000000000000183

29. Cerdo, T., Garcia-Santos, J. A., Bermudez, M. G., & Campoy, C. (2019). The role of probiotics and prebiotics in the prevention and treatment of obesity. *Nutrients, 11,* 635. doi:10.3390/nu11030635

30. Hoffman, D. J., Reynolds, R. M., & Hardy, D. B. (2017). Developmental origins of health and disease: Current knowledge and potential mechanisms. *Nutrition Reviews, 75*(12), 951-970.

31. Reilly, J. J., Martin, A., & Hughes, A. R. (2017). Early-life obesity prevention: Critique of intervention trials during the first one thousand days. *Current Obesity Reports, 6*(2), 127-133.

32. Smith, C. J., & Ryckman, K. K. (2015). Epigenetic and developmental influences on the risk of obesity, diabetes and metabolic syndrome. *Diabetes Metabolic Syndrome and Obesity: Targets and Therapy, 8,* 295-302.

33. Westerterp, K. R. (2018). Changes in physical activity over the lifespan: Impact on body composition and sarcopenic obesity. *Obesity Reviews, 19*(1), S8-S13.

34. Guss, C. E., Williams, D. N., Reisner, S. L., Austin, S. B., & Katz-Wise, S. L. (2016). Disordered weight management behaviors, nonprescription steroid use, and weight perception in transgender youth. *Journal of Adolescent Health, 60*(1), 17-22.

35. Nguyen, H. B., Chavez, A. M., Lipner, E., Hantsoo, L., Kornfield, S. L., Davies, R. D., & Epperson, C. N. (2018). Gender-affirming hormone use in transgender individuals: Impact on behavior health and cognition. *Current Psychiatry Reports, 20,* 110.

36. Loomba, L. A., & Styne, D. M. (2009). Effect of puberty on body composition: Current opinion in endocrinology. *Diabetes and Obesity, 16,* 10-15.

37. Kemp, B. J., Cliff, D. P., Chong, K. H., & Parrish, A. (2019). Longitudinal changes in domains of physical activity during childhood and adolescence: A systematic review. *Journal of Science and Medicine in Sport, 22*(6), 695-701.

38. Centers for Disease Control and Prevention. (2011). Physical activity levels of high school students—United States, 2010. *MMWR, 60,* 773-777.

39. Kwan, M. Y., Cairney, J., Faulkner, G. E., & Pullenayegum, E. E. (2012). Physical activity and other health related behaviors during the transition to early adulthood. *American Journal of Preventive Medicine, 42*(1), 14-20.

40. Girz, L., Polivy, J., Provencher, V., et al. (2013). The four undergraduate years: Changes in weight, eating attitudes and depression. *Appetite, 69,* 145-150.

41. Abrams, B., Coyle, J., Cohen, A., Headen, I., et al. (2017). Impact of preventing excessive gestational weight gain on maternal obesity at age 40 years: An analysis of a nationally representative sample. *American Journal of Public Health,* e1-e7. doi:10.2105/AJPH.2017.303881

42. JafariNasabian, P., Inglis, J. E., Reilly, W., Kelly, O. J., & Ilich, J. Z. (2017). Aging human body: Changes in bone, muscle and body fat with consequent changes in nutrient intake. *Journal of Endocrinology, 234*(1), R37-R51. doi:10.1530/JOE-16-0603

43. American College Health Association. (2018). *American college health association–National college health assessment II: Reference group executive summary Fall 2018.* Hanover, MD: American College Health Association.

44. Shao, A., Drewnowski, A., Willcox, D. C., et al. (2017). Optimal nutrition and the everchanging dietary landscape: A conference report. *European Journal of Nutrition, 56*(1), S1-S21.

45. Rahkovsky, I., Jo, Y., & Carlson (2018, June). *Consumers balance time and money in purchasing convenience foods,* ERR-251. Washington, DC: U.S. Department of Agriculture, Economic Research Science.

46. Lachat, C., Nago, E., Erstraeten, R., Roberfroid, D., Van Camp, J., & Kolsteren, P. (2012). Eating out of home and its association with dietary intake: A systematic review of the evidence. *Obesity Review, 13*(4), 329-346.

47. Hollands, G. J., Shemilt, I., Marteau, T. M., et al. (2015). Portion, package, or tableware size for changing selection and consumption of food, alcohol and tobacco. *Cochrane Database of Systematic Reviews, 9.* doi:10.1002/14651858.CD011045.pub2

48. U.S. Food and Drug Administration. (n.d.). *Nutrition labeling information for restaurants & retail establishments.* Retrieved from https://www.fda.gov/food/food-labeling-nutrition/nutrition-labeling-information-restaurants-retail-establishments

49. Ulijaszek, S. (2018). Physical activity and the human body in the (increasingly smart) built environment. *Obesity Reviews, 19*(1), 84-93.

50. Ding, D., Sallis, J. F., Kerr, J., et al. (2011). Neighborhood environment and physical activity among youth: A review. *American Journal of Preventive Medicine, 41*(4), 442-455.

51. Biddle, S. J. H., Bennie, J. A., Bauman, A. E., et al. (2016). Too much sitting and all-cause mortality: Is there a causal link? *BMC Public Health, 16*(1), 635.

52. Zick, C. D., Stevens, R. B., et al. (2011). Time use choices and healthy body weight: A multivariate analysis of data from the American Time Use Survey. *International Journal of Behavior, Nutrition and Physical Activity, 8,* 84.

53. St-Onge, M. P. (2017). Sleep-obesity relation: underlying mechanisms and consequences for treatment. *Obesity Reviews, 18*(1), 34-39.

54. Christakis, N. A., & Fowler, J. H. (2007). The spread of obesity in a large social network over 32 years. *New England Journal of Medicine, 357*(4), 370-379.

55. Zhang, S., de la Haye, K., Ji, M., & An, R. (2018). Applications of social network analysis to obesity: A systematic review. *Obesity Reviews, 19*(7), 976-988.

56. Willoughby, D., Hewlings, S., & Kalman, D. (2018). Body composition changes in weight loss: Strategies and supplementation for maintaining lean body mass, a brief review. *Nutrients, 10*(12), 1876.

57. Gudzune, K. A., Doshi, R. S., Mehta, A. K., et al. (2015). Efficacy of commercial weight-loss programs: An updated systematic review. *Annals of Internal Medicine, 162*(7), 501-512.

58. Apovian, C. M., Aronne, L. J., Bessesen, D. H., et al. (2015). Pharmacological management of obesity: An Endocrine Society clinical practice guideline. *The Journal of Clinical Endocrinology and Metabolism, 100*(2), 342-362.

59. Khera, R., Murad, M. H., Chandar, A. K., et al. (2016). Association of pharmacological treatments for obesity with weight loss and adverse events: A systematic review and meta-analysis. *Journal of the American Medical Association, 315*(22), 2424-2434.

60. Cataldi, M., Muscogiuri, G., Savastano, S., Barrea, L., et al. (2019). Gender-related issues in the pharmacology of new anti-obesity drugs. *Obesity Reviews, 20,* 375-384.

61. Nuffer, W., Trujillo, J. M., & Megyeri J. (2016). A comparison of new pharmacological agents for the treatment of obesity. *Annals of Pharmacotherapy, 50*(5), 376-388.

62. Bhandari, M., Fobi, M. A., Buchwald, J. N., & the Bariatric Metabolic Surgery Standardization Working Group. (2019). Standardization of bariatric metabolic procedures: World consensus meeting statement. *Obesity Surgery.* doi:10.1007/s11695-019-04032-x

63. Caravetto, P. P., Petry, T., & Cohen, R. (2016). Changing guidelines for metabolic surgery: Now it's the time! *Current Atherosclerotic Reports, 18*(8), 47.

64. Poddar, K., Kolge, S., Bezman, L., et al. (2011). Nutraceutical supplements for weight loss: A systematic review. *Nutrition in Clinical Practice, 26*(5), 539-552

65. Sun, N., Wu, T., & Chau, C. (2016). Natural dietary and herbal products in anti-obesity treatment. *Molecules, 21*(10), 1351.

66. Geller, A. I., Shehab, N., Weidle, N. J., et al. (2015). Emergency department visits for adverse events related to dietary supplements. *New England Journal of Medicine, 373,* 1531-1540.

67. International Size Acceptance Association. Retrieved from www.size-acceptance.org.

68. National Association to Advance Fat Acceptance. Retrieved from www.naafaonline.com/dev2/

Chapter 8

1. McLean, S. A. & Paxton, S. J. (2019). Body image in the context of eating disorders. *Psychiatric Clinics of North America, 42,* 145-156.

2. Cohen, R., Irwin, L., Newton-John, T., & Slater, A. (2019). #bodypositivity: A content analysis of body positive accounts on instagram. *Body Image, 29,* 47-57.

3. Webb, J. B., Wood-Barcalow, N. L., & Tylka, T. L. (2015). Assessing positive body image: Contemporary approaches and future directions. *Body Image, 14,* 130-145.

4. Tylka, T. L., & Wood-Barcalow, N. L. (2015). What is and what is not positive body image? Conceptual foundations and construct definition. *Body Image, 14,* 118-129.

5. Tiggemann, M. (2015). Considerations of positive body image across various social identities and special populations. *Body Image, 14,* 168-176.

6. Bell, K., Rieger, E., & Hirsch, J. (2018). Eating disorder symptoms and proneness in gay men, lesbian women, and transgender and gender non-conforming adults: comparative levels and a proposed mediational model. *Frontiers in Psychology, 9,* 2692.

7. Smith, A., & Anderson, M. (2018). Social media use in 2018. Pew Research Center. Retrieved from https://www.pewinternet.org/2018/03/01/social-media-use-in-2018/

8. Dye, H. (2016). Does internalizing society and media messages cause body dissatisfaction, in turn causing disordered eating? *Journal of Evidence-Informed Social Work, 13*(2), 217-227.

9. Carrotte, E. R., Prichard, I., & Lim, M. S. (2017). "Fitspiration" on social media: A content analysis of gendered images. *Journal of Medical Internet Research, 19*(3), e95. doi:10.2196/jmir.6368

10. Watson, A., Murnen, S. K., & Kenyon College. (2019). Gender differences in responses to thin, athletic, and hyper-muscular idealized bodies. *Body Image, 30,* 1-9.

11. Neighbor, L. A., & Sobal, J. (2007). Prevalence and magnitude of body weight and shape dissatisfaction among university students. *Eating Behaviors, 8*(4), 429-439.

12. Schaefer L. M., Thibodaux, L. K., Krenik D., et al. (2015). Physical appearance comparisons in ethnically diverse college women. *Body Image, 15,* 153-157.

13. Cramblitt, B., & Pritchard, M. (2013). Media influence on the drive for muscularity in undergraduates. *Eating Behaviors, 14*(4), 441-446.

14. Chi, K. R. (2015). Men's makeover. *Nature, 526,* S12-S13.

15. Calzo J. P., Masyn, K. E., Corliss, H. L., et al. (2015). Patterns of body image concerns and disordered weight- and shape-related behaviors in heterosexual and sexual minority adolescent males. *Developmental Psychology, 51*(9), 1216-1225.

16. Baker, A., & Blanchard, C. (2017). The effects of female "thin ideal" media on men's appearance schema, cognitive performance, and self-evaluations: A self-determination theory approach. *Body Image, 13*(22), 103-113.

17. Cheng, Z. H., Perko, V. L., Fuller-Marashi, L., Gau, J. M., & Stice, E. (2019). Ethnic differences in eating disorder prevalence, risk factors and predictive effects of risk factors among young women. *Eating Behaviors, 32,* 23-30.

18. Cheng, H. L., Tran, A. G., Miyake, E. R., & Kim, H. Y. (2017). Disordered eating among Asian American college women: A racially expanded model of objectification theory. *Journal of Counseling Psychology, 64*(2), 179-191.

19. Stein, K. F., Lee, C., Corte, C., & Steffen, A. (2019). The influence of identity on the prevalence and persistence of disordered eating and weight control behaviors in Mexican American college women. *Appetite, 140,* 180-189.

20. Watson, L. B., Ancis, J. R., White, N. D., & Nazari, N. (2013). Racial identity buffers African American women from body image problems and disordered eating. *Psychology of Women Quarterly, 37*(3), 337-350.

21. Quick, V. M., & Byrd-Bredbenner, C. (2014). Disordered eating, socio-cultural media influencers, body image and psychological factors among a racially/ethnically diverse population of college women. *Eating Behaviors, 15*(1), 37-41.

22. Voelker, D. K., Reel, J. J., & Greenleaf, C. (2015). Weight status and body image perceptions in adolescents: Current perspectives. *Adolescent Health, Medicine and Therapeutics, 6,* 149-158.

23. Mizock, L. (2016). Transgender and gender diverse clients with mental disorders. Treatment and challenges. *Psychiatric Clinics of North America, 40,* 29-39.

24. Jones, B. A., Haycraft, E., Murjan, S., & Arcelus, J. (2016). Body dissatisfaction and disordered eating in trans people: A systematic review of the literature. *Internal Review of Psychiatry, 28*(1), 81-94.

25. Soulliard, Z. A., Kauffman, A. A., Fitterman-Harris, H. F., Perry, J. E., & Ross, M. J. (2019). Examining positive body image, sport confidence, flow state, and subjective performance among student athletes and non-athletes. *Body Image, 28,* 93-100.

26. Piran, N. (2015). New possibilities in the prevention of eating disorders: The introduction of positive body image measures. *Body Image, 14,* 146-157.

27. Bassett-Gunter, R., McEwan, D., & Kamarhie, A. (2017). Physical activity and body image in men and boys: A meta-analysis. *Body Image, 22,* 114-128.

28. Joy, E., Kussman, A., & Nattiv, A. (2016). 2016 Update on eating disorders in athletes: A comprehensive narrative review with a focus on clinical assessment and management. *British Journal of Sports Medicine, 50,* 154-162.

29. Samuels, K. L., Maine, M. M., & Tantillo, M. (2019). Disordered eating, eating disorders and body image in midlife and older women. *Current Psychiatry Reports, 21,* 70.

30. Schaumberg, K., Anderson L. M., Reilly E., & Anderson D. A. (2015). Patterns of compensatory behaviors and disordered eating in college students. *Journal of American College Health, 62*(8), 526-533.

31. Ambwani, S., Shippe, M., Gao, Z. & Austin, S. B. (2019). Is #cleaneating a healthy or harmful dietary strategy? Perceptions of clean eating and associations with disordered eating among young adults. *Journal of Eating Disorders, 7,* 17.

32. McComb, S. E., & Mills, J. S. (2019). Orthorexia nervosa: A review of psychosocial risk factors. *Appetite, 140,* 50-75.

33. American Psychiatric Association. (2013). *Diagnostic and statistical manual of mental disorders* (5th ed.) (DSM-5). Washington, DC: American Psychiatric Association Press.

34. Murnen, S. K., & Smolak, L. (2019). The cash effect: Shaping the research conversation on body image and eating disorders. *Body Image.* doi:10.1016/j.bodyim.2019.01.001

35. McClain, Z., & Peebles, R. (2016). Body image and eating disorders among lesbian, gay, bisexual and transgender youth. *Pediatric Clinics of North America, 63,* 1079-1090.

36. Diemer, E. W., Grant, J. D., Munn-Chernoff, M. A., et al. (2015). Gender identity, sexual orientation, and eating-related pathology in a national sample of college students. *Journal of Adolescent Health, 57*(2), 144-149.

37. Bulik, C. M, Blake, L., & Austin, J. (2019). Genetics of eating disorders: What the

clinician needs to know. *Psychiatric Clinics of North America, 42,* 59-73.

38. Walsh, B. T. (2019). Diagnostic categories for eating disorders: Current status and what lies ahead. *Psychiatric Clinics of North America, 42,* 1-10.

39. Guerdjikova, A. I., Mori, N., Casuto, L. S., & McElroy, S. L. (2019). Update on binge eating disorder. *Medical Clinics of North America, 103,* 669-680.

40. Udo, T., Billey, S., & Grilo, C. M. (2019). Suicide attempts in U.S. adults with lifetime DSM-5 eating disorders. *BMC Medicine, 17,* 120.

41. Arcelus, J., Mitchell, A. J., Wales, J., & Nielsen, S. (2011). Mortality rates in patients with anorexia nervosa and other eating disorders. *Archives of General Psychiatry, 68*(7), 724-731.

42. Goldstein, A., & Gvion, Y. (2019). Socio-demographic and psychological risk factors for suicidal behavior among individuals with anorexia and bulimia nervosa: A systematic review. *Journal of Affective Disorders, 245,* 1149-1167.

43. Westmoreland, P., Krantz, M. J., & Mehler, P. S. (2016). Medical complications of anorexia nervosa and bulimia. *The American Journal of Medicine, 129*(1), 30-37.

44. Crow, S. J. (2019). Pharmacologic treatment of eating disorders. *Psychiatric Clinics of North America, 42,* 253-262.

45. Krebs, G., Fernandez de la Cruz, L., & Mataix-Cols, D. (2017, July 20). Recent advances in understanding and managing body dysmorphic disorder. *Evidence Based Mental Health.*

46. Plastic Surgery Statistics Report. (2019). American Society of Plastic Surgeons. Retrieved from https://www.plasticsurgery.org/documents/News/Statistics/2019/plastic-surgery-statistics-full-report-2019.pdf

47. Klimek, P., Murray, S. B., Brown, T., Gonzales, M., & Blashill, A. J. (2018). Thinness and muscularity internalization: Associations with disordered eating and muscle dysmorphia in men. *International Journal of Eating Disorders, 51,* 352-357.

48. Tod, C., Edwards, C., & Cranswick, L. (2016). Muscle dysmorphia: Current insights. *Psychology Research and Behavior Management, 9,* 179-188.

49. Zestcott, C. A., Bean, M. G., & Stone, J. (2017). Evidence of negative implicit attitudes toward individuals with a tattoo near the face. *Group Processes and Intergroup Relations, 20,* 186-201.

50. Timming, A. R., Nickson, D., Re, D., & Perrett, D. (2015). What do you think of my ink? Assessing the effects of body art on employment chances. *Human Resource Management, 56*(1), 133-149.

51. Dickson, L., Dukes, R. L., Smith, H., & Strapko, N. (2015). To ink or not to ink: The meaning of tattoos among college students. *College Student Journal, 49,* 106-120.

52. Farley, C. L., Van Hoover, C., & Rademeyer, C. (2019). Women and tattoos: Fashion, meaning, and implications for health. *Journal of Midwifery and Women's Health, 64,* 154-169.

53. Van Hoover, C., Rademayer, C., & Farley, C. L. (2017, August 14). Body piercing: Motivations and implications for health. *Journal of Midwifery and Women's Health.*

54. Khunger, N., Molpariya, A., & Khunger, A. (2015). Complications of tattoos and tattoo removal: Stop and think before you ink. *Journal of Cutaneous and Aesthetic Surgery, 8*(1), 30-36.

55. Ackerman, K. E., Holtzman, B., Cooper, K. M., Flynn, E. F., Bruinvels, G., et al. (2019). Low energy availability surrogates correlate with health and performance consequences of relative energy deficiency in sport. *British Journal of Sports Medicine, 53*(10), 628-633.

56. Mountjoy, M., Sundgot-Borgen, J. K., Burke, L. M., Ackerman, K. E., et al. (2018). IOC consensus statement on relative energy deficiency in sport (RED-S): 2018 update. *International Journal of Sport Nutrition and Exercise Metabolism.* doi:10.1123/IJSNEM.2018-0136

57. Matzkin, E., Curry, E. J., & Whitlock, K. (2015). Female athlete triad: Past, present and future. *Journal of the American Academy of Orthopedic Surgery, 23,* 424-432.

58. Tenforde, A. S., Barrack, M. T., Nattiv, A., & Fredericson, M. (2015, October 26). Parallels with the female athlete triad in male athletes. *Sports Medicine.*

59. The Body Positive. (2018). Retrieved from https://www.thebodypositive.org/

Chapter 9

1. Alcoholics. (2019). Alcohol facts and statistics. Retrieved from www.niaaa-nih.gov/alcohol-health/overview-alcohol-consumption/alcohol-facts-and-statistics

2. American College Health Association. (2018). *Spring 2-14 Reference Group Executive Summary.* National College Health Assessment.

3. National Institute of Alcohol Abuse and Alcoholism. (2019). College drinking. Retrieved from https://pubs.niaaa.nih.gov/publications/collegefactsheet/collegefactsheet.pdf

4. Highland K. B., Hersschl L. C., Klanecky A., et al. (2013). Biopsychosocial pathways to alcohol-related problems. *American Journal on Addictions, 22* (4), 366-372.

5. National Institutes of Health. (2109). Rethinking drinking. Retrieved from https://www.rethiningdrinking.niaaa.nih.gov/Q-and-As/Default.aspx

6. Statista. (n.d.). Current binge, and heavy alcohol use in the United States in 2017, by ethnicity. Retrieved from https://www.statista.com/statistics/354291/current-binge-heavy-alcohol-use-in-persons-in-the-us-by-ethnicity/

7. Mailer, D. (2014). *Race, ethnicity and impaired driving: Selected research.* Hauppauge, NY: Nova Science Pub.

8. Chartier, K. G., Karriker-Jaffe, K. J., & Cummings, C. R. (2017). Environmental influences on alcohol use: Informing research on the joint effects of genes and the environment in diverse U.S. populations. *American Journal of Addictions.* doi:10.1111/ajad.12478/abstract

9. Derm Net NZ. (2015). Alcohol and the skin. Retrieved from www.dermnetnz.org/reactions/alcohol.html

10. Beaches Recovery. (2019). Millennials and alcoholism (Infographic). Retrieved from https://www.beachesrecovery.com/rehab-blog/millennials-and-alcohol-inforgraphic/

11. Tweng, J. (2017). *iGen: Why today' super connected kids are growing up less rebellious, more tolerant, less happy--- and completely unprepared for adulthood.* New York, NY: Simon & Schuster, Inc.

12. Lewis, M. (2018). Is Gen Z the end of the alcohol industry? Booze Barristers. Retrieved from https//boozebarristers.com/gen-z-end-alcohol-industry/

13. American College Health Association. (2018, Spring 2016 data). *American College Health Association—National College Health Assessment Reference Group data report.* Retrieved from www.acha.org

14. National Institute on Alcohol Abuse and Alcoholism. (2018). NIH releases comprehensive resource to help address college drinking. Retrieved from www.niaaa.nih.gov/news-events/news-releases/nih-releases-comprehensive-resource-help-address-college-drinking

15. National Institute on Alcohol Abuse and Alcoholics. (2015). Alcohol facts and statistics. Retrieved from www.niaaa-nih.gov/alcohol-health/overview-alcohol-consumption/alcohol-facts-and-statistics

16. National Institute on Alcohol Abuse and Alcoholism. (n.d.). Fall semester---A time for parents to discuss the risks of college drinking. Retrieved from www.niaaa.nih.gov/publications/brochures-and-fact-sheets/time-for-parents-discuss-risks-college-drinking

17. HAMS Harm Reduction Network. (2017). Heavy drinking. *HAMS: Harm reduction for alcohol.* Retrieved from http://hamsnetwork.org/heavy/

18. American College Health Association. (2015, Spring 2016 data). *American College Health Association—National*

College Health Assessment Reference Group data report. Retrieved from www.acha.org

19. National Institute on Alcohol Abuse and Alcoholism. (2019). NIH releases comprehensive resource to help address college drinking. Retrieved from https://www.collgedrinkingprevention.gov/statistics/consequences.aspx

20. Alcohol Organization. (2019). The prevalence of pregaming. Retrieved from https://www.alcohol.org/guides/prevalence-of-pregaming/

21. Haas, A. L., Smith, S. K., & Kagan, K. (2013). Getting "game": Pregaming changes during the first weeks of college. *Journal of American College Health, 61*(2), 95-105.

22. Promises. (2017). Pre-drinking increases alcohol use and risky behavior. Retrieved from https://www.promises.com/articles/student-pre-drinking-increases-alcohol-use-and-risky-behavior/

23. University of Michigan Health Blogs. (2019). Tailgating and alcohol: Information to take to heart. Retrieved from uofmhealthblogs.org/general/tailgating-and-alcohol-information-to-take-to-heart/17372/

24. Lohmann, R. C. (2017). Spring break and alcohol. *Psychology Today.* Retrieved from https://www.psychologytoday.com/blog/teen-angst/201703/spring-break-and-alcohol/

25. National Institute of Alcohol Abuse and Alcoholism. (2017). College drinking. Retrieved from https://pubs.niaaa.nih.gov/publications/collegefactsheet/collegefactsheet.pdf

26. Imom. (2019). Spring break: Dangers for college girls. Retrieved from www.imom.com/spring-break-dangers-for-college-girls/#XPPOHvZFw2w

27. Preidt, R. (2015). Most Americans back ban on powdered alcohol, poll finds. HealthDay. *U.S. News and World Report.* Retrieved from http://health.usnews.com/health-news/articles/2015/06/15/most-americans-back-ban-on-powdered-alcohol-poll-finds

28. Albers, A. B., Siegel, M., Ramirez, R. L., et al. (2015). Flavored alcoholic beverage use, risky drinking behaviors, and adverse outcomes among underage drinkers: Results from the ABRAND study. *American Journal of Public Health, 105*(4), 810-815.

29. Sonde, K. (2018). Pot-infused beer has hit shelves. Is it legal? *Mother Jones.* Retreived from https://www.motherjones.com/food/2018/pot-infused-beer-has-hit-shelves-is-it-legal/

30. Tonic. (2018). This is what happens when you mix alcohol and CBD. Retrieved from https://tonic.vice.com/en_us/article/j5npp7/what-happens-when-you-mix-alcohol-and-cbd

31. College Drinking Organization. (2017). College student's guide to safe drinking. Retrieved from http://www.collegedrinking.org/students/

32. Hart, C. L., Ksair, C., & Ray, O. (2015). *Drugs, society, and human behavior.* New York, NY: McGraw-Hill.

33. Lissner, C. (2017). Are women increasingly at risk of addiction? *The Washington Post.* Retrieved from https://www.washingtonpost.com/national/health-science/are-women-increasingly-at-risk-of-addiction/2017/02/24/dfa5b98c-d2ba-11e6-9cb0-54ab630851e8_story.html

34. Drunk Driving Defense. (2015). How to calculate BAC-blood alcohol content. Retrieved from www.drunkdrivingdefense.com/resources/how-to-calculate-your-estimated-blood-alcohol-content-bac/

35. National Institute of Health. (2010). *Beyond hangovers: Understanding alcohol's impact on your health.* NIH Publication No. 13-7604. Retrieved from pubs.niaaa.nih.gov/publications/Hangovers/beyondhangovers.pdf

36. Wingert, P. (2010, November 22). Why it's so risky. *Newsweek, 14.*

37. Harm Reduction Network. (2017). HAMS: Harm reduction for alcohol. Retrieved from http://www.hams.cc/blackouts/

38. AlcoRehab. (2019). Alcohol blackout: Effects of ethanol on memory. Retrieved from https://alcorehab.org/the-effects-of-alcohol-/blackouts/

39. Breen, S. (2013). Would you smoke a beer? Why people are inhaling alcohol. *Greatist.* Retrieved from http://greatist.com/health/inhaling-alcohol-061213

40. Health Check Systems. (n.d.). Alcohol–Its effect on your body and health. Retrieved from www.healthchecksystems.com/alcohol.htm

41. Jon Barron Organization. (2019). Kids drinking hand sanitizer. Retrieved from https://jonbarron.org/article/kids-drinking-hand-sanitizer

42. Fox News. (2015). Hangover cures that actually work. Retrieved from www.foxnews.com/health/2015/04/12/hangover-cures-that-actually-work/

43. Harm Reduction Network. (2017). Hangover cures: Fact and fancy. Retrieved from http://hams.cc/hangovercures/

44. Inverse. (2019). If you're still looking for a hangover cure that actually works, this is it. Retrieved from https://www.inverse.com/article/55664-blowfish-hangover-cure

45. Disalvo, D. (2018). How long does it take for the brain to recover from drinking? Science says longer than we think. *Forbes.* Retrieved from https://www.forbes.com/sites/daviddisalvo/2018/08/27/how-long-does-it-take-for-the-brain-to-recover-from-drinking-science-says-longer-than-we-think/

46. Mozes A. (2017). Heavy drinking linked to heart change, Oktoberfest study finds. *CBS News.* Retrieved from https://www.cbsnews.com/news/heavy-drinking-linked-to-abnormal-heart-rhythm-oktoberfest-study-finds/

47. Miami CBS. (2019). Even one alcoholic drink a day can raise risk of stroke, one study says. Retrieved from https://miamicbslocal.com/2019/05/05/study-alcohol-stroke/

48. Centers for Disease Control and Prevention. (2013). Binge drinking: A serious, under-recognized problem among women. *Vital Signs.* Retrieved from www.cdc.gov/vitalsigns/bingedrinkingfemale/index.html

49. Nelson, D. E., Jarman, D. W., Rehm, J., et al. (2013). Alcohol-attributable cancer deaths and years of potential. *American Journal of Public Health, 10*(4), 641-648.

50. Chen, W. Y., Rosner, B., & Hankinson, S. E. (2011). Moderate alcohol consumption during adult life, drinking patterns, and breast cancer risk. *Journal of the American Medical Association, 306*(17), 1884-1890.

51. Cherpitel, C. J., Martin, G., Macdonald, S., et al. (2013). Alcohol and drug use as predictors of intentional injuries in two emergency departments in British Columbia. *American Journal on Addictions, 22*(2), 87-92.

52. Drug Free Organization. (2012). Almost one-fourth of suicide victims are legally intoxicated when they die. Retrieved from www.drugfree.org/join-together/almost-one-fourth-of-suicide-victims-are-legally-intoxicated-when-they-die/

53. National Institute on Alcohol Abuse Alcoholism. (2017). Alcohol use disorder. Retrieved from https://niaaa.nih.gov/alcohol-health/overview-alcohol-consumption-alcohol-use-disorder/

54. Szalavitz, M. (2013). Mental health manual changes may turn binge drinkers into mild alcoholics. *Time.* Retrieved from http://healthland.time.com/2013/01/23/revisions-to-mental-health-manual-may-turn-binge-drinkers-into-mild-alcoholics/

55. Stockwell, T., Zhao, J., Panwar, S., et al. (2016). Do "moderate" drinkers have reduced mortality risk? A systematic review and meta-analysis of alcohol consumption and all-cause mortality. *Journal of Studies on Alcohol and Drugs, 77*(2), 185-198.

56. Mercken, M., & de Cabo, R. (2010). A toast to your health, one drink at a time. *American Journal of Clinical Nutrition, 92*(1), 1-2.

57. Greenfield, T. K., & Kerr, W. C. (2011). Tracking alcohol consumption over time. National Institute of Alcohol Abuse and

Alcoholism. Retrieved from https://pubs.niaaa.nih.gov/publications/arh27-1/30-38

58. Centers for Disease Control and Prevention (2018). CDC's alcohol screening and brief intervention efforts. Retrieved from https://www.cdc.gov/ncbddd/fasd/alcohol-screening.html

59. Paschall, M. J., Antin, T., Ringwalt, C. L., et al. (2011). Evaluation of an Internet-based alcohol misuse prevention course for college freshmen: Findings of a randomized multi-campus trial. *American Journal of Preventive Medicine, 41*(3), 300-308

60. Afsaneh, E., Zarebahramabadi, M., & Mirkazemi, R. (2015). Effect of Al-Anon attendance on family functions and quality of life in women in Mashhad, Iran. *American Journal of Preventive Medicine, 41*(5), 442-448.

61. Kohler, S., & Hofmann A. (2015). Can motivational interviewing in emergency care reduce alcohol consumption in young people? A systematic review and meta-analysis. *Journal of Medicine and Health, 50*(2), 107-117.

62. Rossheim, M. E., Thombs, D. L., Wagenaar, A. C., et al. (2015). High alcohol concentration products associated with poverty and state alcohol policies. *American Journal of Public Health, 105*(9), 1886-1892.

63. Smith, K. C., Cukier, S., & Jernigan, D. H. (2014). Regulating alcohol advertising: Content analysis of the adequacy of federal and self-regulation of magazine advertisements, 2008-2010. *American Journal of Public Health, 104*(10), 1901-1911.

64. Wagenaar, A. C., Livingston, M. D., & Staras, S. S. (2015). Effects of a 2009 Illinois alcohol tax increase on fatal motor vehicle crashes. *American Journal of Public Health, 105*(9), 1880-1885.

65. Lo, C. C., Weber, J., & Cheng, T. (2013). A spatial analysis of student binge drinking, alcohol-outlet density, and social disadvantages. *American Journal on Addictions, 22*(4), 391-401.

66. Scram Systems (2019). Survey shows Americans favor alternative ways to combat drunk driving. Retrieved from htps;//www.scramsystems.com/blog/2019/05/alternatives-to-combat-drunk-driving/

67. National Highway Traffic Safety Administration and Driver Alcohol Detection System for Safety. (2011). *Fact sheets.* Retrieved from Interlockfacts.com/downloads/DADSS_NHTSA_in AllCars_1_31_11_HL.pdf

68. National Institutes of Health. (2019). Regulating the supply of alcohol beverages. Retrieved from https://www.ncbi.gov/books/NBK216427/

69. Identity Hawk. (2017). What are the penalties for college students using fake IDs. Retrieved from http://www.identityhawk.com/Penalties-for-college-students-using-fake-ids/

70. Quenqua, D. (2014). Fake ids, still coveted, are harder to get. *The New York Times.* Retrieved from https://www.nytimes.com/201/07/24/fashion/fake-ids-still-coveted-are-harder-to-get/

71. National Health Interview Survey, 2018 data. Retrieved from http://www.cdc.gov/nchs/nhis.htm

72. National Health Interview Survey, 2015 data. Retrieved from http://www.cdc.gov/nchs/nhis.htm

73. American College Health Association. (2018, Spring). National College Health Assessment. Reference Group Data Report. Retrieved from www.acha.org

74. Fagerstrom, K, Etter, J.-F., & Unger, J. B. (2015). E-cigarettes: A disruptive technology that revolutionizes our field. *Nicotine & Tobacco Research, 17*(2), 125-126.

75. Maron, D. F. (2014). Smoke screen: Are e-cigarettes safe? *Scientific American.* Retrieved from https://www.scientificamerican.com/article/smoke-screen-are-e-cigarettes-safe

76. Science Daily. (2016). Flavorings and higher voltage increases toxicity of e-cigs. Retrieved from https://www.sciencedaily.com/releases/2016/09/160919133444.htm

77. Thompson, D. (2016). Flavorings boost toxicity of e-cigarettes in lab study. *HealthDay.* Retrieved from https://consumer.healthday.com/cancer-information-5/electronic-cigarettes-970/flavorings-boost-toxicity-of-e-cigarettes-in-lab-study-715093.html

78. Change, A. Y., & Barry, M. (2015). The global health implications of e-cigarettes. *Journal of American Medical Association, 314*(7), 663-664.

79. Preidt, R. (2016). Many adults unaware that using e-cigarettes can hurt kids. *HealthDay.* Retrieved from https://consumer.healthday.com/cancer-information-5/electronic-cigarettes-970/many-adults-unaware-that-using-e-cigarettes-can-hurt-kids-715954.html

80. CBS News. "Smart" cigarette pack brings social networking to smokers: Will it help them quit? Retrieved from https://www.cbsnews.com/news/smart-cigarette-pack-brings-social-networking-to-smokers-will-it-help-them-quit

81. Dickson, E. (2019). No, secondhand vaping isn't harmless. *Rolling Stone.* Retrieved from https://www.rollingstone.com/culture/culture-news/vape-smoke-dangers-806498/

82. Lotus, J. (2019). U.S. vaping deaths rise again. Retrieved from https://www.upi.com/Top_News/US/12/2019/-vaping-deaths-rise-again/5851576780129/

83. Macpherson, A. (2018). Popcorn lung and vaping. Retrieved from https://www.vapinginsider.com/popcorn-lung-and-vaping/

84. Project CBD. (2019). Toxic vape oil additives endanger patients. Retrieved from https://www.project.org/update-toxic-vape-oil-additives-endanger-patients

85. Center on Addiction. (2019). What is vaping. Retrieved from https://www.centeronaddiction.org/e-cigarettes/recreational-vaping/what-vaping

86. Jones, B. D., & Cunningham-Williams, R. M. (2016). Hookah and cigarette smoking among African American college students: Implications for campus risk reduction and health promotion efforts. *Journal of American College Health, 64*(4), 309-317.

87. Sharma E., Beck K. H., & Clark P. I. (2013). Social context of smoking hookah among college students: Scale development and validation. *Journal of American College Health, 61*(4), 204-211.

88. Centers for Disease Control and Prevention. (2013). Hookahs. *Smoking and Tobacco Use.* Retrieved from www.cdc.gov/tobacco/data_statistics/fact_sheets/tobacco_industry/hookahs/

89. National Cancer Institute. (n.d.). Questions and answers about cigar smoking and cancer. *Fact Sheet.* Retrieved from www.cancer.gov/cancertopics/factsheet/tobacco/cigars. Accessed June 18, 2019

90. Surgeon General. (2010). *How tobacco smoke causes disease.* Atlanta, GA: U.S. Department of Health and Human Services.

91. National Cancer Institute. (n.d.). Smokeless tobacco and cancer. *Fact Sheet.* Retrieved from www.cancer.gov/cancertopics/factsheet/Tobacco/smokeless

92. Goniewicz, M. L. (2015). Electronic cigarettes are a source of thirdhand exposure to nicotine. *Nicotine & Tobacco Research, 17*(2), 256-258.

93. National Cancer Institute. (2015). Influence of tobacco marketing on smoking behavior. Retrieved from Cancercontrol.cancer.gov/BRP/tcrb/monographs/19/m19_7/pdf

94. Centers for Disease Control and Prevention. (2019). Tobacco industry marketing. Retrieved from https://www.cdc.gov/tobacco/data_statistics/fact_sheets/tobacco_industry/marketing/index.htm

95. Centers for Disease Control and Prevention. (2019). Fast facts: Smoking leads to disease and disability and harms every organ of the body. Retrieved from https://www.cdc.gov/tobacco/data_statistic/fact_sheets/fast_facts/index.htm

96. Centers for Disease Control and Prevention. (2011). Inhaling tobacco smoke causes immediate harm. *CDC Features.* Retrieved from www.cdc.gov/Features/smokeExposure

97. Surgeon General. (2019). Let's make the next generation tobacco-free. Atlanta, GA: U.S. Department of Health and Human

Services. Retrieved from https://www.hhs.gov/sites/default/files/consequences-smoking-consumer-guide.pdf

98. Centers for Disease Control and Prevention. (2011). Health effects of secondhand smoke. *Smoking and Tobacco Use.* Retrieved from www.cdc.gov/tobacco/data_statistics/fact_sheets/secondhand_smoke/health_effects/

99. Centers for Disease Control and Prevention. (2011). Tobacco use, smoking and secondhand smoke. *Vital Signs.* www.cdc.gov/VitalSigns/TobaccoUse/SecondhandSmoke/

100. Cancer Center. (2018). Double trouble: Tobacco and alcohol combine to elevate cancer risk. Retrieved from https://www.cancercenter.org/community/blog/2018/06/double-trouble-tobacco-and-alcohol-combine-to-elevate-cancer-risk

101. American Cancer Society. (2018). Annual report to the nation: Cancer death rates continue long decline. Retrieved from https://www.cancer.org/latest-news/annual-report-to-the-nation-cancer-dearth-rates-continue-long-decline.html

102. Preidt, R. (2017). Smokers unleash harms on their pets. *HealthDay.* Retrieved from https://consumer.healthday.com/general-health-information-16/pets-and-health-news-531/smokers-unleash-harms-on-their-pets-717396.html

103. Centers for Disease Control and Prevention. (n.d.). Quitting smoking. Retrieved from https://www.cdc.gov/tobacco/data_statistics/fact_sheets/cessation/quitting/index.htm

104. Stop Smoking. (n.d.). How many attempts do you need to quit smoking for good? Retrieved from www.stopsmoking-charlotte.com/how-many-attempts-do-you-need-to-quit-smoking-for-good/

105. National Institute on Drug Abuse (2018). Cigarettes and other tobacco products. Retrieved from https://www.drugabuse.gov/publications/drugfacts/cigarettes-other-tobacco-products

106. WebMd. (2016). Black box warnings removed from Chantix, Zyban. Retrieved from https://www.webmd.com/smoking-cessation/news/20161219/black-box-warning-chantix-zyban

107. Reinberg, S. (2009). Anti-smoking drugs get FDA "black-box" warning. *HealthDay News.* Retrieved from www.healthday.com/Article.asp?AID=628667

108. Martin, T. (2019). How does the stop smoking nicotine shot work? Retrieved from https://www.verywellmind.com/the-nicvax-vaccine-2825145

109. Larabee, L. C. (2005). To what extent do smokers plan quit attempts? *Tobacco Control, 14*(6), 425-428.

110. Centers for Disease Control and Prevention. (2019). Cessation materials for state tobacco control programs. Retrieved

from https://www.cdc.gov/tobacco/quite_smoking/cessation/index.htm

111. Parascandola, M. (2011). Tobacco harm reduction and the evolution of nicotine dependence. *American Journal of Public Health, 101*(4), 632-641.

112. Institute of Medicine. (2019). Ending the tobacco problem. Retrieved from sites.nationalacadmeies.org/tobacco/regulation/TOBACCO_051289

113. National Institutes of Health. (2014). *About the FSPTCA.* Retrieved from https://prevention.nih.gov/tobacco-regulatory-science-program/about-the-FSPTCA

114. Villant, A. C. (2011). Food and Drug Administration regulation of tobacco: Integrating science, law, policy, and advocacy. *American Journal of Public Health, 101*(7), 1160-1162.

115. Skeptical Cardiologist. (2017). Why doesn't the USA have graphic warning labels on cigarette packs like the Netherlands? Retrieved from https://theskepticalcardiologist.com/2017/10/08/why-doesnt-the-usa-have-graphic-warning-labels-on-cigarette-packs-like-the-netherlands

116. Inside Higher ED. (2019). Colleges mull how to handle the new popularity of vaping. Retrieved from https://www.highered.com/news/2019/01/25/colleges-mull-how-to-handle-new-popularity-vaping

117. Council of State Governments. (2017). E-cigarettes and new smoke-free policies on college campuses. Retrieved from www.csg.org//pubs/capitolideas/enes/cs32_2.aspx

118. Pires, S. F., Block, S., Balance, R., et al. (2016). The spatial distribution of smoking violations on a no-smoking campus: Implications for prevention. *American Journal of Public Health, 64*(1), 62-68.

Chapter 10

1. Substance Abuse and Mental Health Services Administration. (2018). Key substance use and mental health indicators in the United States: Results from the 2017 National Survey on Drug Use and Health (HHS Publications No. SMA 18-5068, NSDUH Series H-53). Rockville, MD: Center for Behavioral Health Statistics and Quality, Substance Abuse and Mental Health Services Administration. Retrieved from https://samhsa.gove/data/

2. Martins, S., Kim, J. H., Chen, L.-Y., Levin, D., Keyes, K. M., Cerda, M., & Storr, C. (2015). Nonmedical prescription drug use among US young adults by educational attainment. *Social Psychiatry Psychiatric Epidemiology, 50*(5), 713-724.

3. National Institute on Drug Abuse. (2018). Misuse of prescription drugs. Retrieved from https://www.drugabuse.gov/publications/research-reports/

misuse-prescription-drugs/what-scope-prescription-drug-misuse

4. Schulenberg, J. E., Johnston, L. D., O'Malley, P. M., Bachman, J. G., Miech, R. A., & Patrick, M. E. (2017). *Monitoring the future national survey results on drug use, 1975—2016: Volume II, College students and adults ages 19—55.* Ann Arbor, MI: Institute for Social Research, The University of Michigan.

5. Lipari, R. N., & Hughes, A. (2017). How people obtain the prescription pain relievers they misuse. *The CBHSQ Report.* Rockville, MD: SAMHSA.

6. American Psychiatric Association. (2013). *Diagnostic and statistical manual of mental disorders* (5th ed.). Washington, DC: American Psychiatric Association Press.

7. CMS. (2019). Prescription drug expenditure in the United States from 1960 to 2019 (in billion U.S. dollars) [Graph]. In Statista. Retrieved from https://www.statista.com/statistics/184914/prescription-drug-expenditures-in-the-us-since-1960/

8. National Institute of Drug Abuse. (2012). The science of drug abuse and addiction. *Media Guide.* Retrieved from www.drugabuse.gov/publications/media-guide/science-drug-abuse-addiction

9. Saal, D., Dong, Y., Bonci, A., & Malenka, R. (2003). Drugs of abuse and stress trigger a common synaptic adaptation in dopamine neurons. *Neuron, 37*(4), 577-582.

10. National Institute on Drug Abuse. (2016). Drug facts: Cocaine. Retrieved from https://www.drugabuse.gov/publications/drugfacts/cocaine

11. Danielson, M. L., Bitsko, R. H., Ghandour, R. M., Holbrook, J. R., Kogan, M. D., & Blumberg, S. J. (2018). Prevalence of parent-reported ADHD diagnosis and associated treatment among US children and adolescents, 2016. *Journal of Clinical Child and Adolescent Psychology, 47*(2), 199-212.

12. National Institute on Drug Abuse. (2019). Drug facts: Methamphetamine. Retrieved from https://www.drugabuse.gov/publications/drugfacts/methamphetamine

13. National Institute on Drug Abuse, Advancing Addiction Science. (2018). MDMA (Ecstasy/Molly). Retrieved from https://www.drugabuse.gov/publications/drugfacts/mdma-ecstasymolly

14. SAMHSA. (2013). Ecstasy-related emergency department visits by young people increased between 2005 and 2011; alcohol involvement remains a concern. *The DAWN Report.* Retrieved from https://www.samhsa.gov/data/sites/default/files/spot127-youth-ecstasy-2013/spot127-youth-ecstasy-2013.pdf

15. National Institute on Drug Abuse. (2016). Drug facts: Synthetic cathinones ("bath salts"). Retrieved from https://www.

drugabuse.gov/publications/drugfacts/
synthetic-cathinones-bath-salts

16. NIDA. (n.d.). Club drugs. Retrieved from
https://www.drugabuse.gov/drugs-abuse/
club-drugs

17. NIDA. (n.d.). Club drugs. Retrieved from
https://www.drugabuse.gov/drugs-abuse/
club-drugs

18. National Institute on Drug Abuse. (2019).
Overdose death rates. National Institutes
of Health. Retrieved from https://www.
drugabuse.gov/related-topics/trends-
statistics/overdose-death-rates

19. Katz, J. (2017, September 3). New count of
2016 drug deaths shows accelerated rate.
The New York Times, 14.

20. Hedegaard, H., Miñiño A. M., & Warner, M.
(2018). Drug overdose deaths in the
United States, 1999-2017. NCHS Data Brief
No 329.

21. NCHS, National Vital Statistics System.
(n.d.). Estimates for 2018 and 2019 are
based on provisional data. Estimates for
2015-2017 are based on final data.
Retrieved from https://www.cdc.gov/nchs/
nvss/mortality_public_use_data.htm

22. National Institute of Drug Abuse. (2016).
Drug facts: Fentanyl. Retrieved from
https://www.drugabuse.gov/publications/
drugfacts/fentanyl

23. Daubresse, M., Chang, H., Yu, Y., et al.
(2013). Ambulatory diagnosis and
treatment of nonmalignant pain in the
United States, 2000—2010. *Medical Care,
51*(10), 870-878.

24. National Institute on Drug Abuse. (2014).
Drug facts: Hallucinogens—LSD, peyote,
psilocybin, and PCP. Retrieved from www.
drugabuse.gov/publications/drugfacts/
hallucinogens-lsd-peyote-psilocybin-pcp

25. Pollan, M. (2018). *How to change your
mind: What the new science of
psychedelics teaches us about
consciousness, dying, addiction.* New
York, NY: Random House, Penguin Books.

26. National Institute on Drug Abuse. (2012).
Drug facts: Inhalants. Retrieved from www.
drugabuse.gov/publications/drugfacts/
inhalants

27. National Institute on Drug Abuse. (2017).
Drug facts: Inhalants. Retrieved from
https://www.drugabuse.gov/publications/
drugfacts/inhalants

28. National Institute on Drug Abuse. (2017).
Marijuana. Research Report Series.
Retrieved from https://www.drugabuse.
gov/publications/research-reports/
marijuana/letter-director

29. NIDA. (2018). Monitoring the future survey:
High school and youth trends. Retrieved
from https://www.drugabuse.gov/
publications/drugfacts/monitoring-future-
survey-high-school-youth-trends

30. Johnston L. D., O'Malley, P. M., Miech, R.
A., Bachman, J. G., & Schulenberg, J. E.
(2017). *Monitoring the future national
survey results on drug use, 1975—2016:*
*Overview, key findings on adolescent
drug use.* Ann Arbor, MI: Institute for
Social Research, The University of
Michigan.

31. National Conference of State Legislators.
(2019). Marijuana overview. Retrieved from
http://www.ncsl.org/research/civil-and-
criminal-justice/marijuana-overview.aspx

32. ElSohly, M. A., Mehmedic, A., & Church, J.
C. (2016). Changes in cannabis potency
over the last two decades (1995—2014):
Analysis of current data in the United
States. *Biological Psychiatry, 79*(7),
613-619.

33. National Institute of Drug Abuse. (2019).
Marijuana. National Institutes of Health.
Retrieved from https://www.drugabuse.
gov/node/pdf/1380/marijuana

34. National Institute on Drug Abuse. (2017).
Marijuana: What are marijuana's effects on
lung health? Retrieved from https://www.
drugabuse.gov/publications/marijuana/
what-are-marijuanas-effects-lung-health

35. National Institute on Drug Abuse. (2018).
Drug facts: Anabolic steroids. Retrieved
from https://www.drugabuse.gov/
publications/drugfacts/anabolic-steroids

36. National Institute on Drug Abuse. (2018).
Drug facts: Synthetic cannabinoids.
Retrieved from https://www.drugabuse.
gov/publications/drugfacts/
synthetic-cannabinoids-k2spice

37. National Institute on Drug Abuse. (2017).
Trends and statistics. Retrieved from
https://www.drugabuse.gov/related-
topics/trends-statistics

38. Center on Addiction and Substance
Abuse. (2017). Addiction by the numbers.
Retrieved from https://www.
centeronaddiction.org/policy/
reducing-costs-consequences-addiction

39. Brown, A.M., DeFrances, C., Crane, E., Cai,
R., & Naeger, S. (2018). *Identification of
substance-involved emergency
department visits using data from the
national hospital care survey.* National
Health Statistics Reports, CDC, No. 114.

40. National Institute on Drug Abuse. (2011).
Drug facts: Drug related hospital
emergency room visits. Retrieved from
www.drugabuse.gov/publications/
drugfacts/
drug-related-hospital-emergency-room-
visits

41. SAMHSA. (n.d.). Emergency room visits
involving narcotic pain relievers. The
CBHSQ Report. Retrieved from https://
www.samhsa.gov/data/report/
emergency-department-visits-involving-
narcotic-pain-relievers

42. National Institute on Drug Abuse. (2017).
Overdose death rates. National Institutes
of Health. Retrieved from https://www.
drugabuse.gov/related-topics/trends-
statistics/overdose-death-rates

43. Pew Charitable Trusts. (2018). More
imprisonment does not reduce state drug
problems. Retrieved from https://www.
pewtrusts.org/en/research-and-analysis/
issue-briefs/2018/03/more-imprisonment-
does-not-reduce-state-drug-problems

44. NAACP. (2015). Criminal justice fact sheet.
Retrieved from https://www.naacp.org/
criminal-justice-fact-sheet/

45. Pew (2018). https://www.pewtrusts.org/en/
research-and-analysis/issue-
briefs/2018/03/
more-imprisonment-does-not-reduce-
state-drug-problems

46. National Institute on Drug Abuse. (2011).
Topics in brief: Treating offenders with
drug problems: Integrating public health
and public safety. Retrieved from www.
drugabuse.gov/publications/topics-in-
brief/treating-offenders-drug-
problems-integrating-public-health-public-
safety

47. National Institute of Drug Abuse. (2014).
Principles of drug abuse treatment for
criminal justice aopulations - a research-
based guide. Retrieved from https://www.
drugabuse.gov/publications/principles-
drug-abuse-treatment-criminal-justice-
populations/how-effective-drug-abuse-
treatment-criminal-justice

48. NIDA. (2019). Treatment approaches for
drug addiction. Retrieved from https://
www.drugabuse.gov/publications/
drugfacts/treatment-approaches-drug-
addiction

49. NIDA. (2016). Understanding drug abuse
and addiction. Self-help drug addiction
treatment. Retrieved from https://www.
drugabuse.gov/publications/teaching-
packets/understanding-drug-abuse-
addiction/section-iv/5-self-help-drug-
addiction-treatment

50. Marlatt, G. A., Larimer, M., & Witkiewitz, K.
(Eds.). (2012). *Harm reduction: Pragmatic
strategies for managing high-risk
behaviors.* New York: Guilford.

51. Drug Policy Alliance. (2010). Reducing
drug harm. Retrieved from www.
drugpolicy.org/issues/reducing-drug-harm

52. Harm Reduction Coalition. (2017).
Principles of harm reduction. Retrieved
from harmreduction.org.

53. Project Inform. (2016). *Safer consumption
spaces in the United States: Uniting for a
national movement.* Baltimore, MD:
Project Inform.

54. Kilmer, B., Taylor, J., Caulkins, J. P., Mueller,
P. A., Ober, A. J., Pardo, B., Smart, R.,
Strang, L., Reuter, P. H. (2018). Considering
heroin assisted treatment and supervised
consumption sites in the United States.
Rand Corporation.

55. Centers for Disease Control and
Prevention. (2018). Fact sheets—Alcohol
use and your health. Retrieved from
https://www.cdc.gov/alcohol/fact-sheets/
alcohol-use.htm

56. Centers for Disease Control and
Prevention. (2019). Fast facts: Smoking

and tobacco use. Retrieved from https://www.cdc.gov/tobacco/data_statistics/fact_sheets/fast_facts/index.htm

Chapter 11

1. Herdt, G. (2018). *Human sexuality: Self, society & culture.* New York, NY: McGraw-Hill.
2. Greenberg, J. S., Brues, C. E., & Conklin, S. C. (2016). *Exploring the dimensions of human sexuality.* Burlington, MA: Jones & Bartlett.
3. Alexander, L. L. (2014). *New dimensions in women's health.* Burlington, MA: Jones & Bartlett.
4. Bartholin's gland. (2015). Retrieved from https://en.wikipedia.org/wiki/Bartholin%27s_gland
5. Whipple, B. (2015). Female ejaculation, G spot, A spot, and should we be looking for spots? *Current Sexual Health Reports, 7*(2), 59-62.
6. Bulbourethral gland Cowper's gland. (2015). Retrieved from www.healthline.com/human-body-maps/bulbourethral-cowpers-gland
7. Perlstein, D., & Stoppler, M. C. (2015). Circumcision: Medical pros and cons. Retrieved from www.medicinenet.com/circumcision_the_medical_pros_and_cons/article.htm#circumcision_medical_pros_and_cons_facts
8. Lane, K. (2019). What is "summer penis"? Doctors explain everything you need to know, & wow, it's so weird. *Elite Daily.* https://www.elitedaily.com/what-is-summer-penis-doctors-explain-everything-you-need-to-know-its-so-weird-9916650
9. Intersex Society of North America. (n.d.). What is intersex? Retrieved from https://isna.org/faq/what_is_intersex/
10. Yarber, W. L., Sayad, B. W., & Strong, B. (2016). *Human sexuality: Diversity in contemporary America* (7th ed.). New York, NY: McGraw-Hill.
11. Hutson, M. (2016, March/April). Keeping up with the Jones—in bed. *Scientific American Mind*, 13.
12. Our Bodies Ourselves. (2015). Models of sexual response. Retrieved from www.ourbodiesourselves.org/health-info/models-sexual-response/
13. Carvalho, J., Verissimo A., & Nobre P. J. (2014). Psychological factors predicting the distress to female persistent genital arousal symptoms. *Journal of Sex & Marital Therapy, 41*(1). Published online.
14. Herbenick, D., Mullinax, M., & Mark, K. P. (2014). Sexual desire discrepancy as a feature, not a bug, of long-term relationships: Women's self-reported strategies for modulating sexual desire. *Journal of Sex Medicine, 11,* 196-206.
15. Gonsalves, K. (2019). This might be why some women struggle to get turned on.

Retrieved from www.mindbodygreen.com/articles/sexual-concordance-why-some-women-struggle-to-get-turned-on
16. Lehmiller, J. (2017). Infographic: Rates of orgasm by sexual orientation and gender. Retrieved from https://www.lehmiller.com/blog/2017/2/27/inforgraphic-rates-of-orgasm-by-sexual-oritentation-and-gender
17. Rathus, S., Nevid, J., et al. (2017). *Human sexuality in a changing world.* Boston, MA: Pearson.
18. Baritchi, J., & Baritchi, D. (2013). *The little black book of sex.* New York, NY: Skyhorse Pubs.
19. Mayo Clinic Staff. (2015). Female sexual dysfunction. Retrieved from www.mayoclinic.org/diseases-conditions/female-sexual-dysfunction/basics/definition/con-200271
20. Caron, S. (2015). *The sex lives of college students.* Orono, ME: Maine College Press.
21. Wincze, J. P., & Weisberg, R. B. (2015). *Sexual dysfunction.* New York, NY: Guilford.
22. Silverberg C. (n.d.). Latex versus non-latex condoms. Retrieved from sexuality.about.com/od/contraception/a/latexfreecondom.htm/
23. Boskey, E. (2014). The hidden dangers of nonoxynol-9. Retrieved from std.about.com/od/prevention/a/n9increaserisk.htm
24. Sorrentino, R. (2016). DSM-5 and paraphilias: What psychiatrists need to know. *Psychiatric Times, 13*(11). https://www.psychiatrictimes.org
25. Iwen, M. E. (2015). Shame, sexual addiction, and consumption in American culture. *Sexuality & Culture, 19*(3), 413-425.
26. Counseling Affiliates. (n.d.). Sexual anorexia. Retrieved from www.sexaddictionhelp.com/page.asp?pageID=13&content=Sexual%20anorexia
27. Baritchi, J., & Baritchi, D. (2013). *The little black book of sex.* New York, NY: Skyhorse Pubs.
28. West, M. (2018). *Sex positions: The sex bucket list for couples: 100 sexiest positions and naughty challenges.* North Charleston, SC: Create Space Publishing.
29. Goldstein, I., Clayton, A., Aoldstein, A., et al. (2018). *Textbook of female sexual function and dysfunction diagnosis and treatment.* Hoboken, NJ: John Wiley & Sons, Inc.
30. Julian, K. (2018). Why are young people having less sex today. *The Atlantic.* Retrieved from https://www.theatlantic.com/magazing/archive/2018/12/the-sex-recission/573949
31. Top Skin Secrets. (2019). This is the one symptom you should never ignore after sex. Retrieved from topskinsecrets.com/this-is-the-one-symptom-you-should-never-ignore-after-sex/
32. Mark, K. P. (2015). Sexual desire discrepancy. *Current Sexual Health Reports, 7*(3), 198-202.

33. New York Times. (2015). F.D.A approves Addyi; a libido pill for women. Retrieved from https://www.nytimes.com/1015/08/19/business/fda-approved-addiyi-a-libido-pill-for-women
34. McGown, E. (2019). Low libido in women is more complicated than you'd think. Retrieved from https://www.bustle.com/p/low-libido-in-women-is-more-complicated-than-youd-think-18815211
35. Drugs. (2018). Addyi. Retrieved from https://www.drugs.com/addyi.html
36. Najari, B. B., & Kashanian, J. A. (2016). Erectile dysfunction. *Journal of the American Medical Association, 316*(17), 1838.
37. Danoff, D. (2017). *Ultimate guide to male sexual health.* Hillsboro, OR: Beyond Words.
38. Absolute Pharmacy. (2019). Trimix injections, dosage, side effects, instructions, cost, & where to buy them online. Retrieved from https://absoluterx.comtrimix-injections-for-ed/
39. Absolute Pharmacy. (2019). Trimix injections, dosage, side effects, instructions, cost, & where to buy them online. Retrieved from https://absoluterx.comtrimix-injections-for-ed/
40. The Sun. (n.d.). The new Viagra gel that works on erectile dysfunction in just a few minutes is to be sold in pharmacies. Retrieved from https:///thesun.co.uk/news/1754000/gel-that-works-on-erectile-in-just-a-few-minutes-to-be-sold-in-pharmacies
41. Munoz, K., Davtyan, M., Brown, B., et al. (2015). Revisiting the condom riddle: Solutions and implications. *Electronic Journal of Human Sexuality, 17.* Retrieved from www.ejhs.org/volume17/condom.html
42. Boskey, E. (2014). The hidden dangers of nonoxynol-9. Retrieved from std.about.com/od/prevention/a/n9increaserisk.htm
43. Masciotra, D. (2013). Why still so few use condoms. *Atlantic.* Retrieved from www.threatantic.com/health/archive/2013/04/why-still-so-few-use-condoms/275301
44. Weber, P. (2015). Meet the 11 condoms of the future selected by Bill Gates. Retrieved from http://theweek.com/articles/455793/meet-the-11-condoms-future-selected-by-bill-gates
45. Vedantam, S. (2015). Why is condom use suddenly dropping among college sophomores? National Public Radio. Retrieved from www.npr.org/2015/04/09/398224608/why-is-condom-use-suddenly-dropping-among-college-sophomores
46. Health News. (2019). Do we really need a smart condom? Retrieved from https://www.healthline.com/health-news/do-we-need-a-smart-condom#1
47. American College Health Association. (2018). *National College Health Assessment (ACHA-NCHA-II), Reference*

Group Executive Summary. Retrieved from www.acha-ncha.org/docs/ACHA-NCHA-II_ReferenceGroup_ ExecutiveSummary_Spring2014.pdf

48. Monto, M., & Carey, A. G. (2014). A new standard of sexual behavior? Are claims associated with the "hookup culture" supported by general survey data. *Journal of Sex Research, 51*(6), 605-615.

49. Freitas, D. (2013). *The end of sex: How hook-up culture is leaving a generation unhappy, sexually unfulfilled, and confused about intimacy.* New York, NY: Basic Books.

50. Snapp, S., Ryu, & Kerr, J. (2015). The upside to hooking up: College students' positive hookup experiences. *International Journal of Sexual Health, 17*(1). doi:10.1080/19317611.2014.939247

51. Dvorak, R. D., Kuvaas, N. J., Tess, M., et al. (2017). Are drinking motives associated with sexual "hookups" among college student drinkers? *Journal of American College Health, 64*(2), 133-138.

52. Montes, K. S., Napper, L. E., & Froidevaus, B. A. (2016). Negative effects as a moderator of the relationship between hookup motives and hookup consequences. *Journal of American College Health, 64*(8), 668-672.

53. Kenney, S. R., Thadani, V., Ghaidarov, T., et al. (2013). First-year college women's motivations for hooking up: A mixed-methods examination of normative peer perceptions and personal hookup participation. *International Journal of Sexual Health, 25*(3), 212-224.

54. Arnn, L. (2017). Why are millenials having so much less sex than their grandparents did? *The Federalist.* Retrieved from https://thefedraist.com/2017/03/15/millenials-much-less-sex-grandparents/

55. Gould, W. (2019). What is maintenance sex? It may help strengthen your marriage. *NBC News.* Retrieved from: https://www.nbcnews.com/better/pop-culture/what-maintenance-sex-it-may-help-strengthen-your-marriage-ncna956116

56. Levine, J. (2017). Is stealthing a sex crime? *Boston Review.* Retrieved from bostonreview.net/gender-sexualiy/judith-levine-stealthing-sex-crime

57. CBS News. (2011, July 21). "Sexts" all the rage among college students. Retrieved from https://www.cbsnews.com/news/sexts-all-the-rage-among-college-students/

58. Lohman, R. C. (2012). The dangers of teen sexting. *Psychology Today.* Retrieved from www.psychologytoday.com/blog.teen-angst/201207/the-dangers-teen-sexting

59. Rosin, H. (2014, November). Why kids sext and what to do about it. *Atlantic,* 64-77.

60. Foster, M. (2017). I'm a college student who makes 40K a year by sexting.

Retrieved from http://www.yourtango.com/2016287201

61. Monique, J. (2017). Sending unsolicited pictures of your penis is a form of sexual harassment: Please stop doing this. The Rott. Retrieved from https://www.theroot.com/sending-unsolicited-pictures-0f-your-penis-is-a-form-of-1802749386

62. Eberstadt, M., & Layden, M. A. (2010). *The social costs of pornography: A statement of findings and recommendations.* Princeton, NJ: Witherspoon Institute.

63. Sukel, K. (2012). *Dirty minds.* New York, NY: Free Press.

64. Ley, D., Prause, N., & Finn, P. (2014). The emperor has no clothes: A review of the 'pornography addiction' model. *Current Sexual Health Reports, 6*(2), 94-105.

65. NOLO Local Defense Lawyers. (2015). Revenge porn laws & penalties. *Criminal Defense Lawyer.* Retrieved from www.criminaldefenselawyer.com/resources/revenge-porn-laws-penalties.htm

66. Stone, S., & Supler, K. (2018). Revenge porn: College students beware. *KJK.* Retrieved from https://kjk.com/2018/07/05/revenge-porn-college-students-beware/

67. Medical News Today (2018). Aphrodisiacs: Where is the evidence? Retrieved from https://www.medicalnewstoday.com/articles/320609

68. Future of Sex (2019). How tech is transforming long-distance relationships. Retrieved from https://futureofsex.net/remote-sex/how-tech-is-transforming-long-distance-relationships/

69. Silverberg, C. (n.d.). Teledildonics. Retrieved from sexuality.about.com/od/sexandtechnology/a/teledildonics.htm

70. Hertlein, K. M., & Cravens, J. D. (2014). Assessment and treatment of internet sexuality issues. *Current Sexual Health Reports, 6*(1), 56-63.

71. Weiss, R. (2017). Sex + technology = sexnology. *Huffington Post.* Retrieved from http://www.huffingtonpost.com/robert=weiss/sex-technology-_b_281431.html

72. Burgess, M. (2015). Sex in virtual reality will be common by 2030, with robots by 2050. *Virtual Realty.* Retrieved from http://factor-tech.com/connected-world/19953-sex-in-virtual-reality-will-be-common-in-2030-with-robots-by-2050

73. *The Future of Sex Report.* (2017). Retrieved from future-of-sex.net/future-of-sex-report

74. Future of Sex. (2019). How Bluetooth sex toys closed the intimacy in my LDR. Retrieved from https://futureofsex.net/remote-sex/how-bluetooth-sex-toys-closed-the-intimacy-gap-in-my-ldr/

75. Carissimo, J., Hunt, A. H., & Bruk, D. (2014). Why sex is going to be ridiculously awesome in the future. *Buzz Feed.* Retrieved from https://www.buzzfeed.com/justincarissimo/why-sex-is-going-to-be-

awesome-in-the-future?utm_term=.xcbqGjmlL#.juQAWk9JB

76. Woodley, T. (2019). Sex-tracking wearables and the quantified self. *Future of Sex.* Retrieved from https://futureofsex.net/augmnetation/sec-tracking-wearables-quantified-self/

77. Future of Sex. (2019). The future of sex, digisexuality, sex robots, and virtual reality. Retrieved from https//futureofsex.net/robots/the-future-of-sex-digisexuality-sex-robots-and-virtual-reality/

78. Future of Sex. (2019). Designing human-like behavior in sex dolls. Retrieved from https://futureofsex.net/robots/designing-human-like-behavior-in-sex-dolls/

79. Newton, M. (2015). Is this the future of sex? Oculus rift and "teledildonics." Retrieved from moviepilot.com/posts/2015/03/10.is-this-the-future-of-sex-oculus-rift-and-teledildonics-2767624?lt_source=external.manual

80. Christina, M. (2015). The future of sexual sensing: Virtual reality, augmented reality and neurostimulation. Retrieved from http://futureofsex.net/immersive-entertainment/the-future-of-sexual-sensing-virtual-reality-augmented-realty-andneurostimulation/

81. Barnes, B. (2015). Affective computing: How empathetic devices could change your sex life. Retrieved from futureofsex.net/augmentation/affective-computing-how-empathetic-devices-could-change-your-sex-life/

82. Crystal meth and sex. (n.d.). Retrieved from http://hswquietbutdeadly.wikispaces.com/Crystal+Meth+and Sex

83. Trade. (n.d.). Crystal meth: What's the score? Retrieved from www.tradesexualhealth.com/sexual-health/sex-drugs/crystal-meth.html

Chapter 12

1. Guttmacher Institute Fact Sheet. (2018). Contraceptive use in the United States. Retrieved from https://www.guttmacher.org/fact-sheet/contraceptive-use-united-states

2. Guttmacher Report. (2019). Unintended pregnancy in the United States. Retrieved from https://www.guttmacher.org/fact-sheet/unintended-pregnancy-united-states

3. Sedgh, G., Singh, S., & Hussain, R. (2014). Intended and unintended pregnancies worldwide in 2012 and recent trends. *Studies in Family Planning, 45*(3), 301-314.

4. Blunt-Vinti, H. D., Thompson, E. L., & Griner, S. B. (2018). Contraceptive use effectiveness and pregnancy prevention information preferences among heterosexual and sexual minority college women. *Women's Health Issues, 28*(4), 342-349.

5. Finer, L. B., & Zolna, M. R. (2016). Declines in unintended pregnancy in the United

States, 2008—2011. *The New England Journal of Medicine, 374*, 843-852.

6. Joint Statement by UN Human Rights experts. (2015). The Rapporteur on the Rights of Women on the Inter-American Commission on Human Rights and the Special Rapporteurs on the Rights of Women and Human Rights Defenders of the African Commission on Human and People's Rights. Retrieved from www.ohchr.org/EN/NewsEvents/Pages/DisplayNews.aspx?NewsID=16490&LangID=E

7. Sawhill, I. V., & Guyot, K. (2019). Preventing unplanned pregnancy: Lessons from the states. Brookings Institute. Retrieved from https://www.brookings.edu/research/preventing-unplanned-pregnancy-lessons-from-the-states/

8. Christian Connections for International Health. (2015). How faith-based organizations can help reduce abortions. Retrieved from www.ccih.org

9. Sundaram, A., Vaughan, B., Kost, K., Bankole, A., Finer, L., et al. (2017). Contraceptive failure in the United States: Estimates from the 2006-2010 National Survey of Family Growth. *Perspectives on Sexual and Reproductive Health. 49*(1), 7-16.

10. Curtis, K. M., Jatlaoui, T. C., Tepper, N. K., et al. (2016). U.S. selected practice recommendations for contraceptive use, 2016. *Morbidity and Mortality Weekly Report, 65*(4), 1-66.

11. Budhwani, H., Anderson, J., & Hearld, K.R. (2018). Muslim women's use of contraception in the United States. *Reproductive Health, 15*, 1.

12. Rosenstock, J. R., Peipert, J. F., Madden, T., et al. (2012). Continuation of reversible contraception in teenagers and young women. *Obstetrics and Gynecology, 120*(6), 1298-1305.

13. Committee on Gynecologic Practice Long Acting Reversible Contraception Working Group. No 642. (2015). Increasing access to contraceptive implants and intrauterine devices to reduce unintended pregnancy. Retrieved from www.acog.org/Resources-And-Publications/Committee-Opinions/Committee-on-Gynecologic-Practice/Increasing-Access-to-Contraceptive-Implants-and-Intrauterine-Devices-to-Reduce-Unintended-Pregnancy

14. Gava, G., & Meriggioloa, M. C. (2019). Update on male hormonal contraception. *Therapeutic Advances in Endocrinology and Metabolism.* doi:10.1177/2042018819834846

15. Dicker, R. (2014). Bill Gates funds skin-like condom that could actually make sex feel better. *The Huffington Post.* Retrieved from www.huffingtonpost.com/2014/06/05/bill-gates-condom_n_5447065.html

16. U.S. Food and Drug Administration. (2019). Device classification name. Retrieved from https://www.accessdata.fda.gov/scripts/cdrh/cfdocs/cfpmn/pmn_template.cfm?id=k140305

17. Planned Parenthood. (2019). Fertility awareness. Retrieved from https://www.plannedparenthood.org/learn/birth-control/fertility-awareness

18. American College Health Association. (2018). *National College Health Assessment II. Reference group executive summary, Fall 2018.* Hanover, MD: American College Health Association.

19. Jones, R. K., Lindberg, L. D., & Higgins, J. A. (2014). Pull and pray or extra protection? Contraceptive strategies involving withdrawal among US adult women. *Contraception, 90*(4), 416-421.

20. Tyson, N. A. (2019). Reproductive health. *Obstetrics and Gynecology Clinics, 46*(3), 409-430.

21. American Society for Emergency Contraception. (2015). Efficacy of emergency contraception and body weight. Current understanding and recommendations. Retrieved from http://americansocietyforec.org/uploads/3/2/7/0/3270267/asec_ec_efficacy_and_weight_statement.pdf

22. Herrel, L. A., Goodman, M., Goldstein, M., & Hsiao, W. (2015) Outcomes of microsurgical vasovasostomy for vasectomy reversal: A meta-analysis and systematic review. *Urology, 85*(4), 819-825.

23. Patil, E., & Jensen, J. T. (2015). Update on permanent contraception options for women. *Current Opinions in Obstetrics and Gynecology, 27*(6), 465-470.

24. U.S. Food and Drug Administration. (n.d.). Essure. Permanent birth control. Retrieved from https://www.fda.gov/medical-devices/implants-and-prosthetics/essure-permanent-birth-control

25. ACOG. (2019). Benefits and risks of sterilization. Practice Bulletin No. 208. *Obstetrics and Gynecology, 133*(3), e194-e 207.

26. Lino, M., Kuczynski, K., Rodriguez, N., & Schap, T. (2017). *Expenditures on children by families, 2015.* Miscellaneous Publication No. 1528-2015. Washington, DC: U.S. Department of Agriculture, Center for Nutrition Policy and Promotion.

27. Child Welfare Information Gateway. (2018). *The rights of unmarried fathers.* Washington, DC: U.S. Department of Health and Human Services, Children's Bureau.

28. Bureau of Consular Affairs. (n.d.). Adoption statistics. Retrieved from https://travel.state.gov/content/travel/en/Intercountry-Adoption/adopt_ref/adoption-statistics.html

29. Guttmacher Institute. (2018). Induced abortion in the United States. Retrieved from https://www.guttmacher.org/fact-sheet/induced-abortion-united-states

30. Refinery29. (2019). I need an abortion – now what? An indispensable guide to laws, waiting periods & restrictions by state. Retrieved from https://www.refinery29.com/en-us/2019/01/217375/abortion-clinics-laws-map

31. Public Religion Research Institute. (2019). The state of abortion and contraception attitudes in all 50 states. Retrieved from https://www.prri.org/research/legal-in-most-cases-the-impact-of-the-abortion-debate-in-2019-america/

32. Guttmacher Institute. (2018). Induced abortion worldwide. Retrieved from https://www.guttmacher.org/fact-sheet/induced-abortion-worldwide

33. Jatlaoui, T. C., Ewing, A., Mandel, M. G., et al. (2016). Abortion surveillance—United States, 2013. *Morbidity and Mortality Weekly Report, 65*(12), 1-44.

34. Steinauer, J. (2019). Overview of pregnancy termination. *UpToDate.* Retrieved from www.uptodate.com

35. Kaiser Family Foundation. (2018). Medication abortion. Retrieved from https://www.kff.org/womens-health-policy/fact-sheet/medication-abortion/

36. American College of Obstetricians and Gynecologists. (2016). *Practice Bulletin No. 143: Medical management first trimester abortion.* Retrieved from https://www.acog.org/Resources-And-Publications/Practice-Bulletins/Committee-on-Practice-Bulletins-Gynecology/Medical-Management-of-First-Trimester-Abortion

37. Murtagh, C., Wells, E., Raymond, E. G., Coeytaux, F., & Winikoff, B. (2018). Exploring the feasibility of obtaining mifepristone and misoprostol from the internet. *Contraception, 97,* 287-291.

38. Manjoo, F. (2019). Abortion pills should be everywhere. *The New York Times.* Retrieved from https://www.nytimes.com/2019/08/03/opinion/abortion-pill.html?smid=nytcore-ios-share&fbclid=IwAR120GH652eyM3DWNhUcLghF5CvXSdoQU24dlxEiXek-I447-ArZiwrvxrw

39. Tornello, S. L., & Bos, H. (2017). Parenting intentions among transgender individual. *LGBT Health, 4*(2), 115-120.

40. Centers for Disease Control and Prevention. (2014). *National public health action plan for the detection, prevention and management of infertility.* Atlanta, GA: Centers for Disease Control and Prevention.

41. Sengupta, P., Dutta, S., & Krajewska-Kulak, E. (2017). The disappearing sperms: Analysis of reports published between 1980 and 2015. *American Journal of Men's Health, 11*(4), 1279-1304.

42. 1,000 Days. (2019). Why 1,000 days. Retrieved from https://thousanddays.org/why-1000-days/

43. Park, C., Rosenblat, J. D., Brietzke, E., Pan, Z., et al. (2019). Stress, epigenetics and depression: A systematic review. *Neuroscience & Behavioral Reviews, 102,* 139-152.

44. Centers for Disease Control and Prevention. (n.d.). Before pregnancy. Retrieved from https://www.cdc.gov/preconception/index.html

45. Palatnik, A., Cicco, S., Zhang, L., Simpson, P., Hibbard, J. & Egede, L.E. (2019). The association between advanced maternal age and diagnosis of small for gestational age. *American Journal of Perinatology.* doi:10.1055/s-0039-1694775

46. Fowler, J. R., & Jack, B. W. (2019). *Preconception counseling.* Treasure Island, FL: StatPearls Publishing.

47. Simoni, M. K., Mu, L., & Collins, S. C. (2017). Women's career priority is associated with attitudes towards family planning and ethical acceptance of reproductive technologies. *Human Reproduction, 32*(10), 2069-2075.

48. Andersen, A. N., & Urhoj, S. K. (2017). Is advanced paternal age a health risk for the offspring? *Fertility and Sterility, 107*(2), 312-318.

49. Fullston, T., McPherson, N. O., Zander-Fox, D., & Lane, M. (2017). The most common vices of men can damage fertility and the health of the next generation. *Journal of Endocrinology, 234*(2), F1-F6.

50. Eisenber, M. L., & Meldrum, D. (2017). Effects of age on fertility and sexual function. *Fertility and Sterility, 107*(2), 301-304.

51. Mameli, C., Mazantini, S., & Zuccotti, G. V. (2016). Nutrition in the first 1000 days: The origin of childhood obesity. *International Journal of Environmental Research and Public Health, 13*(9), 838.

52. Cusick, S. E., & Georgieff, M. K. (2016). The role of nutrition in brain development: The golden opportunity of the "first 1000 days." *Journal of Pediatrics, 175,* 16-21.

53. American College of Obstetricians and Gynecologists. (2018). Frequently asked questions. Nutrition during pregnancy. Retrieved from https://www.acog.org/Patients/FAQs/Nutrition-During-Pregnancy

54. Gregg, V. H., & Ferguson, J. E. (2017). Exercise in pregnancy. *Clinical Sports Medicine, 36*(4), 741-752.

55. American College of Obstetricians and Gynecologists. (2017). Update on immunization and pregnancy: Tetanus, diphtheria and pertussis vaccination. Number 718. Retrieved from https://www.acog.org/Clinical-Guidance-and-Publications/Committee-Opinions/Committee-on-Obstetric-Practice/Update-on-Immunization-and-Pregnancy-Tetanus-Diphtheria-and-Pertussis-Vaccination

56. Centers for Disease Control and Prevention. (2019). Pregnancy: Zika virus. Retrieved from https://www.cdc.gov/zika/pregnancy/index.html

57. Ramos, D. (2019). Preconception health: Changing the paradigm on well-woman health. *Obstetrics and Gynecology Clinics of North America, 46,* 399-408.

58. McCue, K., & DeNicola, N. (2019). Environmental exposures in reproductive health. *Obstetrics and Gynecology Clinics of North America, 46,* 455-468.

59. World Health Organization. (2019). Infant mortality. Retrieved from https://www.who.int/gho/child_health/mortality/neonatal_infant_text/en/

60. World Health Organization. (2018). Maternal mortality. Retrieved from https://www.who.int/news-room/fact-sheets/detail/maternal-mortality

61. Centers for Disease Control and Prevention. (2019). Pregnancy-related deaths. Retrieved from https://www.cdc.gov/reproductivehealth/maternalinfanthealth/pregnancy-relatedmortality.htm

62. Centers for Disease Control and Prevention. (2019). Infant mortality. Retrieved from https://www.cdc.gov/reproductivehealth/maternalinfanthealth/infantmortality.htm

63. Petersen, E. E., Davis, N. L., Goodman, D., Cox, S., et al. (2019). Vital Ssgn: Pregnancy-related deaths, United States, 2011-2015, and strategies for prevention, 13 states, 2013-2017. *Morbidity and Mortality Weekly Report, 68*(18), 423-429.

64. Wolf, S. H., & Aron, L. (2013). *US health in international perspective: Shorter lives, poorer health.* Washington, DC: National Academies Press, Institute of Medicine.

65. Hoyert, D. L., & Gregory, E. C. (2016). Cause of fetal death: Data from the Fetal Death Report, 2014. *National Vital Statistics Reports, 65*(7).

66. Riddell, C. A., Harper, S., & Kaufman, J. S. (2017). Trends in differences in US mortality rates between Black and white infants. *JAMA Pediatrics, 171*(9), 911-913.

67. American College of Obstetricians and Gynecologists. (2019). Prenatal genetic screening and diagnostic testing. Number 162. Retrieved from https://www.acog.org/About-ACOG/ACOG-Departments/Genetics/Prenatal-Genetic-Screening-Diagnostic-Testing

68. American College of Obstetricians and Gynecologists. (2016). Screening for fetal aneuploidy. ACOG Practice Bulletin No. 163. *Obstetrics and Gynecology, 127*(5), e123-e137.

69. Centers for Disease Control and Prevention. (2019). Breast feeding. Retrieved from https://www.cdc.gov/breastfeeding/data/facts.html

Chapter 13

1. World Health Organization. (2020). Coronavirus disease (COVID-19) pandemic. Retrieved from https://www.who.int/emergencies/diseases/novel-coronavirus-2019

2. Hansen, V., Oren, E., Dennis, L. K., et al. (2016). Infectious disease mortality in the United States, 1980-2015. *Journal of the American Medical Association, 316*(20), 2149-2151.

3. Cohen, J., Powderly, W., & Opal, S. (2017). *Infectious diseases* (4th ed). Elsevier Limited.

4. Brubaker, J. (2019). The seven viruses that cause human cancers. American Society for Microbiology. Retrieved from https://www.asm.org/Articles/2019/January/The-Seven-Viruses-that-Cause-Human-Cancers\

5. Centers for Disease Control and Prevention. (n.d.). Parasitic diseases. Retrieved from www.cdc.gov/parasites/about.html

6. Centers for Disease Control and Prevention. (1999). Achievements in public health, 1900-1999: Impact of vaccines universally recommended for children—United States, 1990-1998. *Morbidity and Mortality Weekly Report, 48*(12), 243-248.

7. Shoenfeld, Y., Agmon-Levin, N., & Rose, N. R. (2015). *Infection and autoimmunity.* Elsevier B.V.

8. Elwenspoek, M. M. C., Kuehn, A., Muller, C. P., & Turner, J. D. (2017). The effects of early life adversity on the immune system. *Psychoneuroendocrinology, 82,* 140-154.

9. Centers for Disease Control and Prevention. (2019). Outbreak of *Escherichia coli* infections linked to ground beef. Retrieved from https://www.cdc.gov/ecoli/2019/o103-04-19/index.html

10. World Health Organization. (2020). Severe acute respiratory syndrome (SARS). Retrieved from https://www.who.int/csr/sars/en/

11. World Health Organization. (2019). Middle East respiratory syndrome (MERS-CoV). Retrieved from https://www.who.int/emergencies/mers-cov/en/

12. World Health Organization. (n.d.). Global outbreak alert and response network. Retrieved from https://www.who.int/ihr/alert_and_response/outbreak-network/en/

13. Centers for Disease Control and Prevention. (n.d.). Traveler's health. Retrieved from https://www.cdc.gov/travel

14. World Health Organization. (2020). Q&A on coronaviruses (COVID-19). Retrieved from https://www.who.int/news-room/q-a-detail/q-a-coronaviruses

15. Centers for Disease Control and Prevention. (2018). *Sexually transmitted disease surveillance 2017.* Atlanta, GA: U.S. Department of Health and Human Services.

16. Kidd, S. E., Grey, J. A., Torrone, E. A., & Weinstock H. S. (2019). Increased methamphetamine, injection drug and heroin use among women and heterosexual men with primary and secondary syphilis – United States, 2013-2017. *Morbidity and Mortality Weekly Report, 68*(6), 144-148.

17. Workowski, K. A., & Bolan, G. A. (2015). Sexually transmitted diseases treatment guidelines. *MMWR Recommendations Report, 64*(3), 1-140.

18. Centers for Disease Control and Prevention. (2019). Hepatitis C. Retrieved from https://www.cdc.gov/hepatitis/hcv/index.htm

19. Behrendt, P., Bruning, J., Todt, D., & Steinmann, E. (2019). Influence of tattoo ink on hepatitis C virus infectiousness. *Open Forum Infectious Disease, 6*(3), ofz047.

20. Niijmeijer, B. M., Koopsen, J., Schinkel, J., Prins, M., & Geijtenbeek, T. B. (2019). Sexually transmitted hepatitis C virus infections: Current trends, and recent advances in understanding the spread in men who have sex with men. *Journal of International AIDS Society, 22*(suppl. 6), e25348.

21. Ahmed, K. T., Almashhrawi, A. A., Ibdah, J. A., & Tahan, V. (2017). Is the 25-year hepatitis C marathon coming to an end to declare victory? *World Journal of Hepatology, 9*(21), 921-929.

22. Fouque, F., & Reeder, J. C. (2019). Impact of past and on-going changes on climate and weather on vector-borne diseases transmission: A look at the evidence. *Infectious Disease of Poverty, 8*(1), 51.

23. Erickson, T. B., Brooks, J., Nilles, E. J., Pham, P. N., & Vinck, P. (2019, August 22). Environmental health effects attributed to toxic and infectious agents following hurricanes, cyclones, flash floods and major hydrometeorological events. *Journal of Toxicology & Environmental Health B Critical Review*, 1-15.

24. Schnitter, R., & Berry, P. (2019). The climate change, food security and human health nexus in Canada: A framework to protect population health. *International Journal of Environmental Research and Public Health, 16*(14), ii,e2531.

25. Fouque, F., & Reeder, J. C. (2019). Impact of past and on-going changes on climate and weather on vector-borne diseases transmission: A look at the evidence. *Infectious Disease of Poverty, 8*(1), 51.

26. Centers for Disease Control and Prevention. (2018). Antibiotic/antimicrobial resistance (AR/AMR). Retrieved from https://www.cdc.gov/drugresistance/index.html

27. Li, J., Xie, S., Ahmed, S., et al. (2017). Antimicrobial activity and resistance: Influencing factors. *Frontiers of Pharmacology, 8*, 364.

28. Association of American Veterinary Medical Colleges. (2015). Addressing antibiotic resistance: A report from the joint APLU/AAVMC task force on antibiotic resistance in production agriculture. Retrieved from http://aavmc.org/data/files/reports/aplu_aavmc%20task%20force%20report%20final.pdf

29. Mathew, P., Sivaraman, S., & Chandy, S. (2019). Communication strategies for improving public awareness on appropriate antibiotic use: Bridging a vital gap for action on antibiotic resistance. *Journal Family Medicine & Primary Care, 8*(6), 1867-1871.

30. World Health Organization. (2015). Global action plan on antimicrobial resistance. Retrieved from http://apps.who.int/iris/bitstream/10665/193736/1/9789241509763_eng.pdf

31. Flaherty, D. K. (2011). The vaccine-autism connection: A public health crisis caused by unethical medical practices and fraudulent science. *Annals of Pharmacotherapy, 45*(10), 1302-1304.

32. Centers for Disease Control and Prevention. (2019). MMR (measles, mumps, & rubella) VIS. Retrieved from https://www.cdc.gov/vaccines/hcp/vis/vis-statements/mmr.html

33. Centers for Disease Control and Prevention. (2015). *Epidemiology and prevention of vaccine-preventable diseases. The pink book: Course textbook*(13th ed.). Retrieved from www.cdc.gov/vaccines/pubs/pinkbook/index.html

34. Ritchie, H., & Roser, M. (2019). Causes of death. Our world in data. Retrieved from https://ourworldindata.org/causes-of-death

35. World Health Organization. (2018). The top ten causes of death. *Fact Sheet.* Retrieved from https://www.who.int/news-room/fact-sheets/detail/the-top-10-causes-of-death

36. GBD 2015 LRI Collaborators. (2017). Estimates of the global, regional, and national morbidity, mortality, and aetiologies of lower respiratory tract infections in 195 countries: A systematic analysis for the Global Burden of Disease Study 2015. *The Lancet Infectious Diseases, 17*(11), 1133-1161.

37. Centers for Disease Control and Prevention. (2017). Pneumococcal disease. Retrieved from https://www.cdc.gov/pneumococcal/drug-resistance.html

38. Centers for Disease Control and Prevention. (2019). Influenza antiviral drug resistance. Retrieved from https://www.cdc.gov/flu/treatment/antiviralresistance.htm

39. Centers for Disease Control and Prevention. (2019). Rotavirus VIS. Retrieved from https://www.cdc.gov/vaccines/hcp/vis/vis-statements/rotavirus.html

40. World Health Organization. (2019). Tuberculosis. Retrieved from https://www.who.int/en/news-room/fact-sheets/detail/tuberculosis

41. World Health Organization. (2019). Global tuberculosis report. Retrieved from https://www.who.int/tb/publications/factsheet_global.pdf?ua=1

42. Centers for Disease Control and Prevention. (2019). Tuberculosis (TB). Retrieved from https://www.cdc.gov/tb/default.htm

43. World Health Organization. (2019). *World malaria report 2019.* Retrieved from https://www.who.int/news-room/feature-stories/detail/world-malaria-report-2019

44. Wu, X., Lu, Y., Zhou, S., et al. (2015). Impact of climate change on human infectious diseases: Empirical evidence and human adaptation. *Environment International, 86,* 14-23.

45. Committee on Obstetric Practice, Immunization and Emerging Infections Expert Work Group. (2017). Committee Opinion No. 718: Update on immunization and pregnancy: Tetanus, diptheria, and pertussis vaccination. *Obstetrics and Gynecology, 130*(3), e153-e157.

46. Centers for Disease Control and Prevention. (2019). Methicillin-resistant *Staphylococcus aureus* (MRSA). Retrieved from https://www.cdc.gov/mrsa/index.html

47. Karam, A., Habibi, M., & Bouzari, S. (2019). Urinary tract infection: Pathogenicity, antibiotic resistance and development of effective vaccines against uropathogenic *Escherichia coli. Molecular Immunology, 108,* 56-67.

48. Kolman, K. B. (2019). Cystitis and pyelonephritis. *Primary Care: Clinics in Office Practice, 46*(2), 191-202.

49. Centers for Disease Control and Prevention. (2020) Sexually Transmitted Diseases. Retrieved from https://www.cdc.gov/std/default.htm

50. Centers for Disease Control and Prevention. (2019). HIV basic statistics. Retrieved from https://www.cdc.gov/hiv/basics/statistics.html

51. Joint United Nations Programme on HIV/AIDS. (2019). UNAIDS data 2019. Retrieved from https://www.aidsdatahub.org/sites/default/files/publication/UNAIDS_data_2019.pdf

52. Centers for Disease Control and Prevention. (n.d.). Sexually transmitted diseases treatment guidelines 2015. Retrieved from https://www.cdc.gov/std/tg2015/default.htm

53. Centers for Disease Control and Prevention. (2019). Post-exposure prophylaxis. Retrieved from https://www.cdc.gov/hiv/risk/pep/index.html

54. World Health Organization. (2016). *Prevent HIV, test and treat all. Progress report 2016.* Retrieved from http://apps.who.int/iris/bitstream/10665/251713/1/WHO-HIV-2016.24-eng.pdf

55. Centers for Disease Control and Prevention. (2019). HIV and pregnant women, infants and children. Retrieved from https://www.cdc.gov/hiv/group/gender/pregnantwomen/index.html

56. Centers for Disease Control and Prevention. (2019). Let's stop HIV together. Retrieved from https://www.cdc.gov/stophivtogether/campaigns/index.html

57. Centers for Disease Control and Prevention. (2019). Home tests. Retrieved

from https://www.cdc.gov/hiv/testing/hometests.html

58. Centers for Disease Control and Prevention. (2019). Laboratory tests. Retrieved from https://www.cdc.gov/hiv/testing/laboratorytests.html

59. Joint United Nations Programme on HIV/AIDS. (2019). UNAIDS data 2019. Retrieved from https://www.aidsdatahub.org/sites/default/files/publication/UNAIDS_data_2019.pdf

60. Centers for Disease Control and Prevention. (2016). Updated guidelines for antiretroviral postexposure prophylaxis after sexual, injection drug use, or other nonoccupational exposure to HIV–United States, 2016. Retrieved from https://www.cdc.gov/hiv/pdf/programresources/cdc-hiv-npep-guidelines.pdf

61. Centers for Disease Control and Prevention. (2019). Sexually transmitted diseases. Retrieved from https://www.cdc.gov/std/default.htm

62. Azze, R. (2019). A meningococcal B vaccine induces cross-protection against gonorrhea. *Clinical and Experimental Vaccine Research, 8*(2), 110-115.

63. ACOG Committee on Practice Bulletins–Gynecology. (2017). FAQ085: Cervical cancer screening. Retrieved from https://www.acog.org/Patients/FAQs/Cervical-Cancer-Screening

64. Reisner, S. L., Deutsch, M. B., Peitzmeier, S. M., et al. (2017). Comparing self- and provider-collected swabbing for HPV DNA testing in female-to-male transgender adult patients: A mixed methods biobehavioral study protocol. *BMC Infectious Disease, 17,* 444.

65. Geltzeiler, C. B., Son, J., Carchman, E. H., Lawson, E. H. et al. (2019). Anal intraepithelial neoplasia screening with anal pap test: Follow-up and corresponding histology. *Journal of Surgical Research, 5*(244), 117-121.

66. Koskan, A. M., Brennhofer, S. A., & Helitzer, D. L. (2019). Screening for anal cancer precursors among patients living with HIV in the absence of national guidelines: Practitioners' perspectives. *Cancer Causes Control, 30*(9), 989-996.

67. Meites, E., Kempe, A., & Markowitz, L. E. (2016). Use of a 2-dose schedule for human papillomavirus vaccination–Updated recommendations of the Advisory Committee on Immunization Practices. *Morbidity and Mortality Weekly Report, 65*(49), 1405-1408.

68. Workowski, K. A., & Bolan, G. A. (2015). Sexually transmitted diseases treatment guidelines. *MMWR Recommendations Report, 64*(3), 1-140.

Chapter 14

1. GBD 2017 Collaborators. (2018). Global, regional, and national age-sex specific all-cause and cause-specific mortality for 282 causes of death in 195 countries and territories, 1980—2017: A systematic analysis for the Global Burden of Disease Study 2017. *Lancet, 392,* 1736-1788.

2. World Health Organization. (2018). The top 10 causes of death. Retrieved from https://www.who.int/gho/mortality_burden_disease/causes_death/top_10/en/

3. American Heart Association. (2019). Heart disease and stroke statistics – 2019 update: A report from the American Heart Association. *Circulation, 139,* e56–e528.

4. Aghayan, M., Asghari, G., Yuzbashian, E., Dehghan, P., et al. (2019) Association of nuts and unhealthy snacks with subclinical atherosclerosis among children and adolescents with overweight and obesity. *Nutrition and Metabolism, 16, 23.*

5. Abrignani, M. G., Luca, F., Favilli, S., Benvenuto, M., et al. (2019). Lifestyles and cardiovascular prevention in childhood and adolescence. *Pediatric Cardiology, 4,* 1113-1125.

6. Rubini Gimenez, M., Reiter, M., Twerenbold, R., et al. (2014). Sex specific chest pain characteristics in the early diagnosis of acute myocardial infarction. *Journal of the American Medical Association Internal Medicine, 174*(2), 241-249.

7. Gooding, H. C., Brown, C. A., Liu, J., Revette, A. C., Stamoulis, C., de Ferranti, S. D. (2019). Will teens go red? Low cardiovascular disease awareness among young women. *Journal of the American Heart Association, 19*(6), e011195.

8. Kochanek, K. D., Murphy, S. L., Xu, J., & Arias, E. (2018). Deaths: Final data for 2017. *National Vital Statistics Reports, 68,* 9.

9. Centers for Disease Control and Prevention. (2020). Stroke. Retrieved from https://www.cdc.gov/stroke/index.htm

10. American Heart Association. (n.d.). Congenital heart defects. Retrieved from https://www.heart.org/en/health-topics/congenital-heart-defects

11. American Heart Association. (2020) My life check Life's simple 7. Retrieved from https://www.heart.org/en/healthy-living/healthy-lifestyle/my-life-check--lifes-simple-7

12. Centers for Disease Control and Prevention. (2020). Outbreak of lung injury associated with the use of e-cigarette, or vaping, products. Retrieved from https://www.cdc.gov/tobacco/basic_information/e-cigarettes/severe-lung-disease.html

13. American Heart Association. (2019). Understanding blood pressure readings. Retrieved from https://www.heart.org/en/health-topics/high-blood-pressure/understanding-blood-pressure-readings

14. American Heart Association. (2017). Heart disease and stroke statistics–2017 update: A report from the American Heart Association. *Circulation, 135*(10), e146-e603.

15. Graudal N. A., Hubeck Graudal T., & Jurgens G. (2017). Effects of low sodium diet versus high sodium diet on blood pressure, renin, aldosterone, catecholamines, cholesterol, and triglyceride. *Cochrane Database of Systematic Reviews, 4,* CD004022. doi:10.1002/14651858.CD004022.pub4

16. Rodriguez, F., & Ferdinand, K. C. (2015). Hypertension in minority populations: New guidelines and emerging concepts. *Advances in Chronic Kidney Disease, 22*(2), 145-153.

17. American Heart Association. (2019). Life's simple 7 manage blood pressure infographic. Retrieved from https://www.heart.org/en/healthy-living/healthy-lifestyle/my-life-check--lifes-simple-7/ls7-blood-pressure-infographic

18. Centers for Disease Control and Prevention. (2016). *Diabetes: Working to reverse the US epidemic.* Atlanta, GA: CDC National Center for Chronic Disease Prevention and Health Promotion Division of Diabetes Translation.

19. Stone, N. J., Robinson, J. G., Lichtenstein, A. H., et al. (2014). American College of Cardiology/American Heart Association Task Force on Practice Guidelines 2013 ACC/AHA guideline on the treatment of blood cholesterol to reduce atherosclerotic cardiovascular risk in adults: A report of the American College of Cardiology/American Heart Association Task Force on Practice Guidelines. *Journal of the American College of Cardiology, 63,* 2889-2934.

20. Smith, S. C., & Grundy, S. M. (2015). 2013 ACC/AHA guideline recommends fixed-dose strategies instead of targeted goals to lower blood cholesterol. *Journal of the American College of Cardiology, 64*(6), 601-612.

21. The 10-year risk is based on a combination of risk factors and can be calculated at http://cvdrisk.nhlbi.nih.gov/calculator.asp.

22. Viitasalo, A., Schnurr, T. M., Pitaken, N., Hollensted, M., Nielsen, T. R. H., et al. (2019, August 26). Abdominal adiposity and cardiometabolic risk factors in children and adolescents: Mendelian randomization analysis. *American Journal of Clinical Nutrition,* ii:nqz187.

23. Skulas-Ray, A. C., Wilson, P. W. F., Harris, W. S., Brinton, E. A., et al. (2019, August 19). Omega-3 fatty acids for the management of hypertriglyceridemia: A science advisory from the American Heart Association. *Circulation.* CRI:0000000000000709

24. Rehm, J. ,& Roerecke, M. (2017, June 10). Cardiovascular effects of alcohol consumption. *Trends in Cardiovascular Medicine,* ii:S1050-1738(17)30078-6.

25. U.S. Environmental Protection Agency. (2019). AirNow. Retrieved from https://airnow.gov/

26. Liu, C., Chen, R., Sera, F., Vicedo-Cabrera, A. M. et al. (2019). Ambient particulate air pollution and daily mortality in 652 cities. *The New England Journal of Medicine, 22*;*381*(8), 705-715.

27. Yusuf, S., Joseph, P., Rangarajan, S., Islam, S., Mente, A., Hystead, P., et al. (2019, September 2). Modifiable risk factors, cardiovascular disease, and mortality in 155,722 individuals from 21 high-income, middle-income, and low-income countries (PURE): A prospective cohort study. *Lancet*, ii:S0140-6736(19)32008-2.

28. Udo, T., & Grilo, C. M. (2017). Cardiovascular disease and perceived weight, racial, and gender discrimination in U.S. adults. *Journal of Psychosomatic Research, 100*, 83-88.

29. Lagraauw, H. M., Kuiper, J., & Bot, I. (2015). Acute and chronic psychological stress as risk factors for cardiovascular disease: Insights gained from epidemiological, clinical, and experimental studies. *Brain, Behavior and Immunity, 50*, 18-30.

30. Rozanski, A. (2014). Behavioral cardiology: Current advances and future directions. *Journal of the American College of Cardiology, 64*(1), 100-110.

31. Daghlas, I., Dashti, H. S., Lane, J., Aragam, K. G., et al. (2019). Sleep duration and myocardial infarction. *Journal of the American College of Cardiology, 74*(10), 1304-1314.

32. National Research Council and Institute of Medicine. (2013). *U.S. health in international perspective: Shorter lives, poorer health. Panel on Understanding Cross-National Health Differences Among High-Income Countries*, S. H. Woolf & L. Aron (Eds.), Committee on Population, Division of Behavioral and Social Sciences and Education and Board on Population Health and Public Health Practice, Institute of Medicine. Washington, DC: The National Academies Press.

33. Cobin, R. H., Goodman, N. F., & AACE Reproductive Endocrinology Scientific Committee. (2017). American Association of Clinical Endocrinologists and American College of Endocrinology position statement on menopause—2017 Update. *Endocrinology Practice, 23*(7), 869-880.

34. Williams, E. A., Pelto, H. F., Toresdahl, B. G., Prutkin, J. M., Owens, D. S., et al. (2019). Performance of the American Heart Association (AHA) 14-point evaluation versus electrocardiography for cardiovascular screening of high school athletes: A prospective study. *Journal of the American Heart Association, 8*(14), e012235.

35. Zittermann, A. (2018). Vitamin D status, supplementation and cardiovascular disease. *Anticancer Research, 38*(2), 1179-1186.

36. Ganguly, P., & Alam, S. F. (2015). Role of homocysteine in the development of cardiovascular disease. *Nutrition Journal, 10*(14), 6. doi:10.1186/1475-2891-14-6

37. Degrell, P., Sorbets, E., Feldman, L. J., et al. (2015). Screening for coronary artery disease in asymptomatic individuals: Why and how? *Archives of Cardiovascular Disease,* ii:S1875-2135(15)00186-2.

38. Tian, J., Qiu, M., Li, Y., Zhang, X., Wang, H., et al. (2017). Contribution of birth weight and adult waist circumference to cardiovascular disease risk in a longitudinal study. *Scientific Reports, 29*;*7*(1), 9768.

39. Golden, S. H., Maruthur, N., Mathioudakis, N., et al. (2017). The case for diabetes population health improvement: Evidence-based programming for population outcomes in diabetes. *Current Diabetes Report, 17*(7), 51.

40. Centers for Disease Control and Prevention. (2019). Diabetes basics. Retrieved from https://www.cdc.gov/diabetes/basics/index.html

41. Mayer-Davis, E. J., Lawrence, J. M., Dabelea, D., Divers, J., et al. (2017). Incidence trends of type I and type II diabetes among youths, 2002-2012. *New England Journal of Medicine, 376*, 1419-1429.

42. Aguilar, M., Bhuket, T., & Torres, S. (2015). Prevalence of the metabolic syndrome in the United States, 2003—2012. *Journal of the American Medical Association, 313*(19), 1973-1974.

43. U.S. Preventive Task Force. (2014). Gestational diabetes mellitus, screening. Retrieved from https://www.uspreventiveservicestaskforce.org/Page/Document/UpdateSummaryFinal/gestational-diabetes-mellitus-screening?ds=1&s=diabetes

44. U.S. Preventive Task Force. (2015). Screening for abnormal blood glucose and type 2 diabetes mellitus. Retrieved from https://www.uspreventiveservicestaskforce.org/Page/Document/UpdateSummaryFinal/screening-for-abnormal-blood-glucose-and-type-2-diabetes?ds=1&s=diabetes

45. Centers for Disease Control and Prevention. (2018). Asthma. Retrieved from https://www.cdc.gov/asthma/default.htm

46. GINA Science Committee. (2019). Global initiative for asthma management and prevention. Retrieved from https://ginasthma.org/wp-content/uploads/2019/04/GINA-2019-main-Pocket-Guide-wms.pdf

47. Gold Science Committee. (2019). Global initiative for chronic obstructive lung disease. Pocket guide to COPD diagnosis, management and prevention. Retrieved from https://goldcopd.org/wp-content/uploads/2018/11/GOLD-2019-POCKET-GUIDE-FINAL_WMS.pdf

48. Kramarow, E.A. & Tejada-Vera, B. Dementia mortality in the United States, 2000-2017. National Vital Statistics Reports; vol 68 no 2. Hyattsville, MD: National Center for Health Statistics. 2019

49. Gale, S. A., Acar, D., & Daffner, K. R. (2018). Dementia. *The American Journal of Medicine, 131*(10), 1161-1169.

50. Alzheimer's Association. (2019). Alzheimer's disease facts and figures. *Alzheimers Dementia, 15*(3), 321-387.

51. Olney, N. T., Spina, S., & Miller, B. L. (2017). Frontotemporal dementia. *Neurologic Clinics, 35*(2), 339-374.

52. Alzheimer's Disease International. (2019). *World Alzheimer report 2019: Attitudes to dementia*. London: Alzheimer's Disease International.

53. Centers for Disease Control and Prevention. (2019). What is dementia? Retrieved from https://www.cdc.gov/aging/dementia/index.html

Chapter 15

1. American Cancer Society. (2020). *Cancer facts & figures 2020*. Atlanta, GA: American Cancer Society.

2. American Cancer Society. (2019). *Cancer prevention & early detection facts & figures 2019-2020*. Atlanta, GA: American Cancer Society.

3. Krishnasamy, V. P., Hallowell, B. D., Ko, J. Y., Board, A., et al. (2020). Update: Characteristics of a nationwide outbreak of e-cigarette, or vaping, product use - associated lung injury - United States, August 2019-January 2020. *Morbidity and Mortality Weekly Report, 69*(3), 90-94.

4. U.S. Food and Drug Administration. (2019). 2018 NYTS data: A startling rise in youth e-cigarette use. Retrieved from https://www.fda.gov/tobacco-products/youth-and-tobacco/2018-nyts-data-startling-rise-youth-e-cigarette-use

5. Rodriguez-Garcia, C., Sanchez-Quesada, C., & Gaforio, J. (2019). Dietary flavonoids as cancer chemopreventive agents: An updated review of human studies. *Antioxidants, 18*(5), ii:Ee37.

6. Daniel, C. R., & McQuade, J. L. (2019). Nutrition and cancer in the microbiome era. *Trends in Cancer, 5*(9), 521-524.

7. American College Health Association. (2019). American College Health Association-National College Health Assessment II: Reference Group Executive Summary Spring 2019. Silver Spring, MD: American College Health Association.

8. Produce for Better Health Foundation. (2019). Fruits and veggies—more matters. Retrieved from www.fruitsandveggiesmorematters.org/

9. Kerr, J., Anderson, C., & Lippman, S. M. (2017). Physical activity, sedentary behavior, diet and cancer: An update and emerging new evidence. *Lancet Oncology, 18*(8), 457-471.

10. Wray, A. J. D., & Minaker, L. M. (2019). Is cancer prevention influenced by the built environment? A multidisciplinary scoping review. *Cancer.* doi:10.1002/cncr.32376

11. Brawley, O. W. (2017). The role of government and regulation in cancer prevention. *Lancet Oncology, 18*(8), 483-493.

12. Printz,C. (2019). Skin cancer prevention advocates target indoor tanning: As tanning beds increasingly turn up outside of traditional salons, experts are trying innovative approaches to curb their use. *Cancer, 125*(4), 493-494.

13. Gambla, W. C., Fernandez, A. M., Gassman, N. R., et al. (2017). College tanning behaviors, attitudes, beliefs and intentions: A systematic review of the literature. *Preventive Medicine, 105,* 77-87.

14. World Health Organization. (2019). Ionizing radiation. Retrieved from https://www.who.int/ionizing_radiation/about/what_is_ir/en/

15. McLean, A. R., Adlen, E. K., Cardis, E., et al. (2017). A restatement of the natural science evidence base concerning the health effects of low-level ionizing radiation. *Proceedings Biological Sciences, 284*(1862).

16. Miller, A. B., Sears, M. E., Lloyd Morgan, L., Davis, D., Hardell, L., et al. (2019). Risks to health and well-being from radio-frequency radiation by cell phones and other wireless devices. *Frontiers in Public Health, 7,* 223.

17. Miller, A. B., Lloyd Morgan, L., Udasin, I., & Davis, D.L. (2018). Cancer epidemiology update, following the 2011 IARC evaluation of radiofrequency electromagnetic fields (monograph 102). *Environmental Research, 167,* 673-683.

18. International Agency for Research on Cancer. (2013). Non-ionizing radiation, part 2: Radiofrequency electromagnetic fields. *IARC Monographs on the Evaluation of Carcinogenic Risks in Humans, 102.* Retrieved from http://monographs.iarc.fr/ENG/Monographs/vol102/index.php

19. World Health Organization, International Agency for Research on Cancer. (2019). *IARC Monographs on the Evaluation of Carcinogenic Risks to Humans.* Retrieved from http://monographs.iarc.fr/

20. U.S. Environmental Protection Agency. (2019). Laws and regulations. Retrieved from https://www.epa.gov/laws-regulations

21. Richardson, A. K., Walker, L. C., Cox, B., Rollag, H., Robinson, B. A., et al. (2019). Breast cancer and cytomegalovirus. *Clinical and Translational Oncology.* doi:10.1007/s12094-019-02164-1

22. Chen, C. J., Hsu, W. L., Yang, H. I., et al. (2014). Epidemiology of virus infection and human cancer. *Recent Results Cancer Research, 193,* 11-32.

23. Goldberg, M. S. (2019). Improving cancer immunotherapy through nanotechnology. *Nature Reviews. Cancer.* doi:10.1038/s41568-019-0186-9.

24. Jiang, T., Shi, T., Zhang, H. Song, Y., Wei, J., et al. (2019). Tumor neoantigens: From basic research to clinical applications. *Journal of Hematology & Oncology, 12*(1), 93.

25. Jodgins, J. J., Khan, S. T., Park, M. M., Auer, R. C., & Ardolino, M. (2019). Killers 2.0: NK cell therapies at the forefront of cancer control. *Journal of Clinical Investigation, 129*(9), 3499-3510.

26. Antoni, M. H., & Dhabhar, F. S. (2019). The impact of psychosocial stress and stress management on immune responses in patients with cancer. *Cancer, 125*(9), 1417-1431.

27. U.S. Food and Drug Administration. (2019). FDA approves third oncology drug that targets a key genetic driver of cancer, rather than a specific type of tumor. Retrieved from https://www.fda.gov/news-events/press-announcements/fda-approves-third-oncology-drug-targets-key-genetic-driver-cancer-rather-specific-type-tumor

28. U.S. Food and Drug Administration. (2017). FDA approval brings first gene therapy to the United States. Retrieved from https://www.fda.gov/NewsEvents/Newsroom/PressAnnouncements/ucm574058.htm

29. National Cancer Institute. (2017). NCI and the Precision Medicine Initiative. Retrieved from https://www.cancer.gov/research/areas/treatment/pmi-oncology

30. Lin, W. F., Zhong, M. F., Zhou, Q. H., Zhang, Y. R., Wang, H., et al. (2019). Efficacy of complementary and integrative medicine on health-related quality of life in cancer patients: A systematic review and meta-analysis. *Cancer Management & Research, 11,* 6663-6680. doi:10.2147/CMAR.S195935

31. National Center for Complementary and Integrative Health. (2018). Cancer: In depth. Retrieved from https://nccih.nih.gov/health/cancer/complementary-integrative-research

32. PDQ® Integrative, Alternative, and Complementary Therapies Editorial Board. (2019). *PDQ high-dose vitamin C.* Bethesda, MD: National Cancer Institute. Retrieved from https://www.cancer.gov/about-cancer/treatment/cam/hp/vitamin-c-pdq

33. Kolor, K., Chen, Z., Grosse, S. D., et al. (2017). BRCA genetic testing and receipt of preventive interventions among women aged 18—64 years with employer-sponsored health insurance in nonmetropolitan and metropolitan areas—United States, 2009—2014. *MMWR Surveillance Summary, 66*(15), 1-11.

34. U.S. Preventive Task Force. (2018). Breast cancer: Screening. Retrieved from https://www.uspreventiveservicestaskforce.org/Page/Document/UpdateSummaryFinal/breast-cancer-screening1

35. Capurso, C., & Vendemiale, G. (2017). The Mediterranean diet reduces the risk and mortality of prostate cancer: A narrative review. *Frontiers of Nutrition, 4,* 38.

36. Siegel, R. L., Miller, K. D., & Jemal, A. (2017). Colorectal cancer mortality rates in adults aged 20 to 54 years in the United States, 1970—2014. *Journal of the American Medical Association, 318*(6), 572-574.

37. American Cancer Society. (2019). *Cancer facts & figures 201*9. Atlanta GA: American Cancer Society.

38. American Cancer Society. (2017). *Colorectal cancer facts & figures 2017-2019.* Atlanta, GA: American Cancer Society.

39. U.S. Preventive Task Force. (2016). Screening for colorectal cancer. *Journal of the American Medical Association, 315*(23), 2564-2575.

40. American Academy of Dermatology. (2017). Sunscreen facts. Retrieved from https://www.aad.org/media/stats/prevention-and-care/sunscreen-faqs

41. Fontham, E.T.H., Wolf, A.M.D. et al. (2020) Cervical cancer screening for individuals at average risk: 2020 guideline update from the American Cancer Society. Ca: A Cancer Journal for Clinicians. https://doi.org/10.3322/caac.21628.

42. Committee on Gynecologic Practice. (2017). Committee Opinion No 716: The role of the obstetrician-gynecologist in the early detection of epithelial ovarian cancer in women at average risk. *Obstetrics and Gynecology, 130*(3), 146-149.

43. Jacobs, I. J., Menon, U., Ryan, A., et al. (2017). Ovarian cancer screening and mortality in the UK Collaborative Trial of Ovarian Cancer Screening (UKCTOCS): A randomized controlled trial. *Lancet, 387*(10022), 945-956.

44. American Cancer Society. (2020). Key statistics for testicular cancer. Retrieved from https://www.cancer.org/cancer/testicular-cancer/about/key-statistics.html

45. PDQ® Adult Treatment Editorial Board. (2019). *PDQ testicular cancer treatment.* Bethesda, MD: National Cancer Institute. Retrieved from https://www.cancer.gov/types/testicular/hp/testicular-treatment-pdq.

46. Chaturvedi, A. K., Graubard, B. I., & Broutian, T. (2019). Prevalence of oral HPV infection in unvaccinated men and women in the United States, 2009-2016. *Journal of the American Medical Association, 332*(10), 977-979.

Chapter 16

1. Levi, L., Segal, L. M., & Martin, A. (2015). *The facts hurt: A state-by-state injury prevention policy report: 2015.* Trust for America's Health. Retrieved from healthyamericans.org

2. Johns Hopkins. (n.d.). Unintentional injury statistics. Retrieved from https://www.johnhopkinsmedicine.org/health/wellness-and-prevention/unintentional-injury-statistics

3. Centers for Disease Control and Prevention. (n.d.). Ten leading causes of death and injury. Retrieved from https://cdc.gov/injury/wisqrs/LeadingCauses.html

4. National Safety Council. (n.d.). Deaths by demographics. Retrieved from https://injuryfacts.nsc.org/all-injuries/deaths-by-demographics/race-and-ethnicity/

5. National Safety Council. (2019). Vehicle deaths estimated at 40,000 for third straight year. Retrieved from htps://www.nsc.org/road-safety/safety-topics/fatality-estimates

6. National Highway Traffic Safety Administration. (2019). Speeding. Retrieved from https://www.nhsta.gov/risky-driving/speeding

7. Smart Growth America. (2019). NTSB releases full report on speeding-related crash study. Retrieved from https://smartgrowthamerica.org/ntsb-releases-full-report-speeding-related-crash-study

8. Centers for Disease Control and Prevention. (n.d.). Distracted driving in the United States and Europe. Retrieved from www.cdc.gov/motorvehiclesafety/distracted_driving/

9. Drivers Alert. (2019). 10 terrifying facts about texting and driving. Retrieved from https://www.driversalert.com/10-terrifying-facts-about-texting-and-driving/

10. Dixit, V. (2016). *One split second.* Minneapolis, MN: Wisdom Editions.

11. HG Organization. (n.d.). General theory of breath testing. Retrieved from https://www.hg.org/articleasp?id=6235

12. The Law-2. (2019). Are GPS systems a distraction for drivers. Retrieved from https://www.1800thelaw2.com/blog/navigationsystems-and-distracted-driving

13. Centers for Disease Control and Prevention. (2019). Drowsy driving. Retrieved from https://www.cdc.gov.sleepabout_sleep/drowsy_driving.html

14. Harvard Education. (n.d.). Judgment and safety. Retrieved from healthysleep.med.harvard.edu/need-sleep/whats-in-it-for-you/judgment-safety

15. Driving Tests. (2019). The ultimate list of driving statistics for 2019. Retrieved from https://driving-tests.org/driving-statistics/

16. Serious Accidents. (2019). Road rage. Retrieved from https://seriousaccidents.com/legal-advice/top-causes-of-car-accidents/road-rage/

17. Centers for Disease Control and Prevention. (2019). Fact sheets - alcohol use and your health. Retrieved from https://www.cdc.gov/alcohol/fact-sheets/alcohol-use.htm

18. Helsel, P., & Almaguer, M. (2017). Drugged driving on the rise, passes alcohol alone in fatal crashes, study finds. *NBC News.* Retrieved from https://www.nbcnews.com/news/us-news/drugged-driving-rise-passes-alcohol-alone-fatal-crashes-study-finds-n751681

19. Convergence Training. (2019). Environmental driving hazards. Retrieved from htpps://www.convergencetraining.com/environmental-driving-hazards.html

20. Centers for Disease Control and Prevention. (2019). Seat belts. Retrieved from https://www.cdc.gov/motorvehiclesafety/seatbelts/index.html

21. Arrow Head Clinic. (n.d.). 14 unbelievable car accident facts you didn't know about. Retrieved from https://www.arrowheadclinic.com/category/blog/14-unbeleivable-car-accident-facts

22. Monks, K. (2018). Are obese crash test dummies the key to preventing road deaths? *CNN.* Retrieved from www.cnn.com/2018/10/23/tech/innovation/obese-crash-test-dummies-mci/index.html

23. Centers for Disease Control and Prevention. (2019). Primary enforcement of seat belt laws. Retrieved from https://www.cdc.gov/motorvehiclesafty/calculator/factsheet/seabelt.html

24. Very Well Family. (2019). Car seat guidelines to keep your kids safe. Retrieved from https://verywellfamily.com/car-seat-guidelines-2633328

25. Extra Mile. (2019). Keeping your pets safe while driving. Retrieved from https://extramile.thehartford.com/auto/pet-car-safety/

26. Centers for Disease Control and Prevention. (2019). Motorcycle safety. Retrieved from https://www.cdc.gov/motorvehiclesafety/mc/index.html

27. American College Health Association. (2018, Spring). *National College Health Assessment II.* Retrieved from www.acha-ncha.org/reports_ACHA-NCHAII.html

28. Centra Care Health. (2019). 10 tips for helmet safety. Retrieved from https://www.centrahealthcare.com/for-the-health0of-it/childrens-health/10-tips-for-helmet-safety/

29. Pucher, J. (2016). Safer cycling through improved infrastructure. *American Journal of Public Health, 106*(12), 2089-2091.

30. Felton, R. (2019). Nearly half of electric scooter injuries in Austin were 'severe', CDC study says. Retrieved from https://www.consumerreports.org/product-safety/nearly-half-of-electric-scooter-injuries-in-austin-were-severe/

31. Carson, B. (2019). CDC finds nearly half of e-scooter injuries are to the head, 'may have been preventable' in new study. Retrieved from https://www.forbes.com/sites/bizcarson/2019/05/02/cdc-finds-nearly-half-of-e-scooter-injuries-are-to-the-head-may-have-been-preventable-in-new-study/#40b57a346b3

32. Felton, R. (2019). E-scooter ride-share industry leaves injuries and angered cities in its path. Retrieved from https://www.consumerreports.orb/product-safety/e-scooter-ride-share-industry-leaves-injuries-and-angered-cities-in-its-path/

33. Centers for Disease Control and Prevention. (n.d.). Walk this way! Taking steps for pedestrian safety. Retrieved from www.cdc.gov/Features/PedestrianSafety/

34. Centers for Disease Control and Prevention. (2019). Pedestrian safety. Retrieved from https://www.cdc.gov/motorvehiclessafety/pedestrian_safety/indes.html

35. Kimbell-Sannit, A., Hall, D., Walker, L., et.al. (2019). Pedestrians die every 90 minutes in the U.S., and low income areas are hurt the most. *Los Angeles Times.* Retrieved from https://www.latimes.com/world-national/story/2019

36. Koh, H., & Mackert, M. (2016). A study exploring factors of decision to text while walking among college students based on theory of planned behavior (TPB). *Journal of American College Health, 64*(8), 619-627.

37. Alcohol Organization. (2019). Walking drunk. Retrieved from https//www.alcohol.org//guides/walking-drunk/

38. Safety. (2019). Distracted walking a major pedestrian concern. Retrieved from https://www.safety.com/distracted-walking-a-major-pedestrian-safety-concern/

39. Hacker News. (n.d.). New cars'pedestrian-safety features fail in deadliest situations. Retrieved from https://news.ycombinator.com/item?id=21151117

40. Centers for Disease Control and Prevention. (2019). Unintentional drowning: Get the facts. Retrieved from https://www.cdc.gov/homeandrecreationalsafety/water-safety/waterinjuries-factsheet.html

41. USCG Boating. (2017). Recreational boating statistics. Retrieved from www.uscgboating.org/library-accident-statistics/Recreational-Boating-Statistics-2017.pdf

42. Boat U.S. Foundation. (n.d.). Life jackets. Retrieved from https://www.boatus.org/life-jackets/

43. Boat U.S. Foundation. (n.d.). State specific boating safety courses. Retrieved from https://www.boatus.org/free/

44. Anderson, M. (2015). *The rock climber's training manual.* Boulder, CO: Fixed Pin.

45. Green, S. (n.d.). How safe is climbing? Retrieved from http://climbing.about.com/od/staysafeclimbing/aHowSafeClimbing.htm

46. Climb the Earth. (n.d.). Is rock climbing dangerous? Statistics & how to climb safe. Retrieved from https://climbingearth.com/is=rock-climbing-dangerous-statistics-how-to-climb-safe/

47. Know Before You Fly. (2019). Retrieved from knowbeforeyoufly.org/for-recreationalusers/

48. Consumer Notice Organization. (n.d.). Home safety. Retrieved from https://www.consumernotice.org/products/home-safety/

49. Centers for Disease Control and Prevention. (2019). Fire deaths and injuries: Fact sheet. Retrieved from www.cdc.gov/ncipc/factsheets/fire.htm

50. National Fire Protection Association. (2017). Fire-related fatalities and injury. Retrieved from https://injury.facts.nsc.org/home-and-community/safety-topics/fire-related-fatalities-and-injuries/

51. National Fire Protection Association. (2019). Safety tip sheets. Retrieved from www.nfpa.org/public-ducation/resources/safety-tip-sheets

52. Consumer Notice Organization. (n.d.). Home safety. Retrieved from https://www.consumernotice.org/products/home-safety/

53. Centers for Disease Control and Prevention. (2019). Poisoning in the United States: Fact sheet. Retrieved from www.cdc.gov/ncipc/factsheets/poisoning.htm

54. U.S. Poison Control Centers. (2020). Poison statistics: National data. poison.org/poisonstatistics-national.

55. Centers for Disease Control and Prevention. (2018). Carbon monoxide poisoning. Retrieved from https://www.cdc.gov/co/default.htm

56. National Conference of State Legislators. (2019). Carbon monoxide detector requirements, laws, and regulations. Retrieved from www.ncsl.org/research/environment-and-natural-resources.carbon-monoxide-detectors-state-statutes.aspx

57. Preidt, R. (2016). Child deaths highlight choking dangers posed by grapes. *HealthDay*. Retrieved from https://consumer.healthday.com/kids-health-information-23/child-safety-news-587/child-deaths-highlight-choking-dangers-posed-by-grapes-717903.html

58. CPR Care. (n.d.). Chapter 5: Choking emergencies. Retrieved from https://cprcare.com/course/firstaid/5/

59. Kids and Cars. (n.d.). Heatstroke. Retrieved from https://www.kidsandcars.org/how-kids-get-hurt/heat-stroke/

60. Null, J. (2015). Heatstroke deaths of children in vehicles. Retrieved from http://noheatstroke.org/

61. Mason, S. (2019). 51 children died being locked in hot cars in 2018. Retrieved from https://www.nydailynews.com/neows/national/ny-hot-car-child-deaths-20190626-k5lcmxjb47ezljbisz5av6l144qe-story.html

62. Chuck, E. (2019). Technology saves kids. *NBC News*. Retrieved from https://www.nbcnews.com/news/us-news/technology-save-kids-hot-car-exists-so-why-isn-t-n1038281

63. Groves, A. (2018). What happens in your brain when kids are left in cars. *Milwaukee Journal Sentinel*. Retrieved from https://www.kidsand cars.org/2018/07/17/what-happens-in-your-brain-when-kids-are-left-in-cars/

64. Heinzman, A. (2019). When can headphones and earbugs damage your hearing? Retrieved from Https://www.howtogeek.com/409503/when-can=headphones-abs-earbgs-damage-your hearing/

65. Fischelli, M. (2017). A loud warning: Millions of people do not protect their ears. *Scientific American Mind, 316*(6), 78.

66. Simring, K. S. (2016, January/February). Six things you should know about concussions. *Scientific American Mind,* 50-57.

67. Centers for Disease Control and Prevention. (2019). TBI: Get the facts. Retrieved from htpps://www/cdc.gov/traumaticbraininjury/get_the_factsindex.html

68. Thompson, D. (2016). Brain changes seen in kids after one season of football. *HealthDay*. Retrieved from https://consumer.healthday.com/fitness-information-14/football-health-news-250/brain-changes-seen-in-kids-after-one-season-of-football-716101.html

69. UPMC Sports Mediine. (2019). Concussion facts and statistics. Retrieved from https://www.upmc.com/Services/sports-medicine/services/concussion/facts-statistics

70. Wise GEEK. (n.d.). What is mouth-to-mouth resuscitation? Retrieved from https://www.wisegeek.com/what-is-mouth-to-mouth-resuscitation.htm

71. Protrainings. (n.d.). AHA CPR course. Retrieved from https://www.procpr.org/aha-cpr/course

72. AED Universe. (n.d.). AED placement. Retrieved from https://www.aeduniverse.com/AED_placement_s/17.htm

73. Furst, J. (2019). What is first responder training? Retrieved from https://www.firstaidforfree.com/what-is-first-responder-training?

74. McEvoy, S. (2019). Are you sitting incorrectly in front of your computer? This simple change could make all the difference. Retrieved from https://www.bustle.com/are-you-sitting-incorrectly-in-front-of-your-computer-this-simple-change-could-make-all-the-difference-156!

75. Aronwitz, T. (2013). How safe are college campuses? *Journal of the American Medical Association, 61*(2), 57-58.

76. Jones, M. (2018). After Virginia Tech shooting, gun violence still claims victims on college campuses. Retrieved from www.collegiatetimes.com/news/after-virginia-tech-shooting-gun-violence still-claims-vitcims-on/article_4c27a5f2-3a98-11e8-9165-4f568030151b.ht

77. Campus Safety. (2019). College campus shooting statistics you should know. Retrieved from https://www.campussafetymagazine.com/university/college-campus-shooting-statistic/

78. Rizzo, K. (2017). Campus crime 2015: Top 10 highest reported crime rates for large colleges. Retrieved from https//lawstreetmedia.com/blogs/crime/campus-crime-2015-top-10-highest-reported-crime-rates-for-large-colleges

79. Hazing Prevention Organization. (n.d.). Hazing facts. *Hazing Information*. Retrieved from www.hazingprevention.org/hazing-information.html

80. Rich, B. (2019). Hazing in college - awareness and prevention. Retrieved from https://thebestschools.ormagazine/hazing-in-college/

81. Kaplan, E., Moseley, L., & Ortiz, E. (2017). Penn State hazing death: Felony charges dismissed, 14 frat members to stand trial. Retrieved from https;//www.nbcnews.com/news/us-news/penn-state-hazing-death-felony-charges-dismissed=14-frat-members-n798076

82. Campus Safety. (2017). Hazing prevention methods for schools and universities. Retrieved from https://www.campussafetymagazine.com/for-parents/hazing_prevention_schools_universities/

83. Hudson, D. (2017). Hate speech & campus speech codes. Retrieved from https://www.freedomeforuminstitue.org/first-amendment-cnter/topics/freedom-of-speech-2/free-speech-on-public-college-campuses-overview/hate-speech-campus-speech-codes/

84. Soave, R. (2019). Free speech isn't dead on college campuses but it might be ailing. Retrieved from https://www.realcleareducation.com/2019/04/10/free_speech_isnt_dead_on_college_campuses_but_it_might_be-ailing_110321.html

85. Gottschling, G. (2019). Trump officially signs free speech exec. order: If schools censor 'we will not give them money'. Retrieved from https:www.campusreform.org/?IF=12007

86. Nossel, S., & Friman, J. (2019). Why Trump's campus free speech order is a big risk. Retrieved from https://thefreedomebeacon.com/2019/03/21.why-trumps--campus-free-speech-order-is-a-big-risk/

87. Soave, R. (2019). *Panic attack: Young radicals in the age of Trump*. New york, NY: St. Martin's Press.

88. Gertsmann, E. (2019). Why don't universities treat anti-Semitism like they treat racism and sexism? *Forbes*. Retrieved from https:forbes.com.sites/evangerstmann/2019/12/14/why-dont-universities-treat-anti-semiticism-like-they-treat-racism-and-sexism/#3283

89. Steinhauer, J. (2014). White House to press colleges to do more to combat

rape. *New York Times.* Retrieved from www.nytimes.com/2014/04/29/us-tougher-battle-on-sex-assault-on-campus-urged.html

90. Warren, T., & Williams S. (2015). Making sense of affirmative consent, Title IX, VAWA, and Clery. *Campus Safety, 23*(6), 30, 32, 34.

91. National Center on Domestic and Sexual Violence. (n.d.). Sexual assault victimization and penetration. Retrieved from www.ncdsv.org/images/Care_SA-Vitimization=and-Perpetration-Fact-Sheet.pdf

92. Cantor, D., Fisher, B., Chibnail, S. C., et al. (2015). *Report on the AAU campus climate survey on sexual assault and sexual misconduct.* Rockville, MD: Westat for The Association of American Universities.

93. Rape Abuse & Incest National Network. (n.d.). Scope of the problem: Statistics. Retrieved from https://www.rain.org/statistics/scope-problem

94. Koller Trial Law. (2018). Retrieved from https://kollertiallaw.com/campus-sexual-assault/The campus sexual assault red zone starts now

95. United Educators. (2015). Confronting campus sexual assault: An examination of higher education claims. Retrieved from EduRisksSolutions.org

96. Age of Consent. (n.d.). What is statutory rape? Retrieved from https://www.ageofconsent.net/what-is-statutory-rape

97. RAINN. (n.d.). Perpetrators of sexual violence statistics. Retrieved from https;//www.rainn.org/statistics/perpetrators-sexual-violence

98. Bureau of Justice Statistics. (2012). *National crime victimization survey, 2012.* Retrieved from www.ojp.usdoj.gov/bjs

99. National Center for Injury Prevention and Control. (2019). The sexual victimization of men in America. *AJPH.* doi:10.2105/AJPH.2014.301946

100. Jeglic, E. L., & Calkins, C. (2016). *Sexual violence and evidence based policy and prevention.* Cham, Switerland: Springer.

101. Jaffe, A. (2018). Sexual assault survivors are forced to travel hours for rape kits and congress wants answers. Retrieved from https://news.vice.com/en_us/article/439b8q/sexual-assault-survivors-are-forced-to-travel-hours-for-rape-kits-and-congress-wants-answers

102. Reingold, R. B., & Goslin, L. O. (2015). Sexual assaults among university students: Prevention, support, and justice. *Journal of the American Medical Association, 314*(5), 447-448.

103. Yoffe, E. (2017). The uncomfortable truth about campus rape policy. Retrieved from https://www.theatlantic.com/education/archive/2017/09/the-uncomfortable-truth=about-campus-rape-policy/538974/

104. Heldman, C., & Brown, B. (2016). Campus sexual assault cases should be handled by school officials. In J. Lasky (Ed.), *Sexual assault on campus* (pp. 90-95). Farmingham, MI: Greenhaven Press.

105. Brodsky, A. (2016). Fair process, not criminal process, is the right way to address campus sexual assault. In J. Lasky (Ed.), *Sexual assault on campus*(pp. 77-84). Farmingham, MI: Greenhaven Press.

106. Carson, S. (2018). I was raped at college. Here's how DeVos's new rules harm survivors like me. Retrieved from https://broadly.vice.com/en_us/article/d3b7gq/title-ix-betsy-devos-college-rape-sexual=assault

107. Lindquist, C. H., Crosby, C. M., Barrick, K., et al. (2016). Disclosure of sexual assault experiences among undergraduate women at historically Black colleges and universities (HBCUs). *Journal of American College Health, 64*(6), 469-480.

108. Girl Interrupted. (2019). Let's be honest - race does play a role in how we discuss sexual assault on campus. Retrieved from https://girlintrrupted.com.wordpress.com./2019/04/12/lets-be-honest-race-does-play-a-role-in-how-we-discuss-sexual-assault-on-campus/

109. NBC Bay Area. (2019). Uber reports more than 3,000 U.S. sexual assaults on 2018 rides. Retrieved from https://www.nbcbayarea.com/news/local.uber-reports-more-than-3000-us-sexual-assaults-on-2018-rides2189658/

110. Rossi, A. (2017). 10 important rideshare safety tips for travelers. Retrieved from https://www.smartravel.com/risdeshare-safety-tipsfor-travelers/

111. EAB Daily Briefing. (2015). How affirmative consent is changing college culture. Retrieved from https://www.eab.com/daily-briefing/2015/03/05/affirmative-consent

112. Carle, R. (2015). How affirmative consent laws criminalize everyone. Retrieved from http://thefederalist.com/2015/03/30/how-affirmative-consent-laws-criminalize-everyone/

113. Barrett, F. (2018). Why men need to stop relying on non-verbal consent, according to a neuroscientist. Retrieved from https://time.com/5274505/metoo-verbal-nonverbal-consent-cosby-schneiderman/

114. Friedrichs, E. (2016). 5 questions about alcohol and consent you're afraid to ask, answered. Retrieved from https://everydayfeminism.com/2016/05/alcohol-and-consent-questions/

115. Wooten, S. C., & Mitchell, R. W. (2017). *Preventing sexual violence on campus.* New York, NY: Routledge.

116. Educator Insider News Blog. (n.d.). Sexual harassment on campus: What are students' rights? Retrieved from https://study.com/articles/How_to_Address_Sexual_Harassment_on_Campus.html

117. Shibley, R. L. (2016). *Twisting Title IX.* New York, NY: Encounter Books.

118. Maryville University. (n.d.). Understanding the me too movement: A sexual harassment awareness guide. Retrieved from https://online.maryville.edu/blog/understanding-the-me-too-movement-a-sexual-harassment-awareness-guide/

119. Merkin, D. (2018). Publicly, we say #MeToo. Privately, we have misgivings. Retrieved from https://www.nytimes.com/2018/01/05/opinion/golden-globes-metoo.html?moudle=inline

120. Proulx, N., Pepper, C., & Schulten, K. (2018). The reckoning: Teaching about the #MeToo movement and sexual harassment with resources from the New York Times. Retrieved from https://www.nytimes.com/2018/01/25/learning/lesson-plans/the-reckoning-teaching-about-the-mtoo-movement-and-sexual-harassment-with-resources-from-the-new-york-times.html

121. North, A. (2018). Why women are worried about #Me Too. Retrieved from https://www.vox.com/2018/04/05/17157240/me-too-movement-sexual-harassment-aziz-ansari-accusation

122. Smith, K. (2018). A male backlash against #Me Too is brewing. Retrieved from https://www.foxnews.com/opinion/a=male-backlash-against-metoo-is-brewing

123. National Center for Victims of Crime. (n.d.). Stalking. Retrieved from www.ncvc.org

124. National Center for Victims of Crime. (n.d.). Responding to stalking on campus. Retrieved from https://victimsofcrime.org/docs/default-source/src/src-campus-guide.pdf?sfvrsn=2

125. Crime Library. (n.d.). Cyber-stalking: Risk management. Retrieved from www.crimelibrary.com/criminal_mind/psychology/cyberstalking/6.html

126. Brady, P. Q., & Bouffard, L. A. (2014). Majoring in stalking: Exploring stalking experiences between college students and the general public. Crime Victim Institute, College of Criminal Justice, Sam Houston State University. Retrieved from www.crimevictimsinstitute.org

127. LaMotte, S. (2015). The health risks of cyberbullying. Retrieved from http://www.cnn.com/2015/03/02/health/cyberbullying-in-college/index.html

128. Duggan, M. (2017). Online harassment 2017. Retrieved from https: //www.pewinternet.org/2017/07/11/online-harassment-2017/

129. Stop Bullying. (n.d.). Cyberbullying tactics. Retrieved from https://www.stopbullying.gov/cyberbullying/cyberbullying-tactics/index.html

130. U.S. Legal. (n.d.). Cyber harassment law and legal definition. Retrieved from

https://definitions.uslegal.com/c/cyber-harassment/

131. Interro Bang. (2019). "Deepfake porn is being used to harass women online. Retrieved from https://theinterrorbang.com/deepfake=porn-is-being-used-to-harass-women-online/ Fake-porn videos are being weaponized to harass

132. Navarro, F. (2019). Deepfake porn videos are now being used to publicly harass ordinary people. Retrieved from https://www.komando.com/heppening-now/526877/deepfake-porn-videos-are-now-being-used-to-publicly-harass-ordinary-people

133. Love Is Not Abuse. (n.d.). Retrieved from http://loveisnotabuse.com/web/guest/home/journal_content/56/10123/193872/155832

134. Centers for Disease Control and Prevention. (2019). Preventing Intimate violence: 2019 Face sheet. Retrieved from https://www.cdc.gov/violenceprevention/pdf/ipv-factsheet.pdf

135. Centers for Disease Control and Prevention. (2019). Understanding intimate partner violence: 2019 Fact sheet. Retrieved from https://www.cdc.gov/violenceprevention/pdf/ipv-factsheet.pdf

136. Break the Cycle. College dating violence and abuse poll. Retrieved from https://ww.breakthecycle.org/dating-violence-research/collge-dating-violence-and-abuse-poll

137. Love Respect Organization. Retrieved from https;//www.loverespect.org/

138. Air Talk. (2019). Should online dating apps screen for registered sex offenders? Retrieved from https://www.scpr.org/programs/airtalk/2019/12/05/65149/should-online-dating-apps-screen-for-registered-se/

139. Cooercive Control Collective. (2018). Resource: NJ safe and sound. Retrieved from https://coercivecontrolcollective.org/news/category/Resources

140. Lassiter-Cathey, P., & Goodriend, W. (2017). *Before the boil: The early warning signs of a potentially violent relationship.* Buena Vista, IA: Institute for the Prevention of Relationship Violence, Buena Vista University.

141. Yu, Y. (2019). Explaining the numbers behind the rise in reported hate crimes. Retrieved from https://www.politifact.com/truth-o-meter/article/2019/apr/03/hate-crimes-are-increasingly-reported-us/

142. Campus Pride. (n.d.). Bias and hate crime prevention. Retrieved from https://www.campuspride.org/topics/bias-and-hate-crime-prevention/

143. Joseph, E., & Croft, J. (2019). New York bans gay and trans 'panic' defenses. Retrieved from https://www.cnn.com/2019/06/30/us/new-york-cuomo-gay--anic-trans.indes.html

144. Beemyn,G., & Windmeyer, S. (2018). The dear colleague letter on transgender students: What you need to know. Retrieved from https://campuspride.org/resources/the-dear-colleague-letter-on-transgender-students-what-you-need-to-know/

145. Weinstein, J. M. (2017). Active incident training: Preparing for the future threat. *Campus Safety, 25*(2), 30-36.

146. Preidt, R. (2017). 1 in 5 U.S. gun owners avoided background check: Study. *HealthDay.* Retrieved from https://consumer.healthday.com/public-health-information-30/gun-violence-976/1-in-5-u-s-gun-owners-avoided-background-check-study-718503.html

147. Pro Con Organization. (n.d.). Should more gun control laws be enacted in the United States? Retrieved from http://gun-control.procon.org/view.answers.php?questionID=001964$print=true

148. Wolfson, J. A., Terel, S. P., Frattarolli, S., et.al. (2016). The US public's preference for safer guns. *American Journal of Public Health, 106*(3), 411-413.

149. Mitka, M. (2016). Search for ways to reduce gun violence spurred by toll of recent shootings. *Journal of the American Medical Association, 309*(8), 755-756.

150. Pro Con Organization. (2016). U.S. gun deaths, 1999—2013: Suicides, homicides, unintentional deaths, legal intervention deaths, deaths from undetermined consequences. Retrieved from http://gun-control.procon.org/view.resource.php?resourceID=006094&print=true

151. Marcus, M.B. (2016). Many kids spend time in homes with guns, but safety lags. *CBS News.* Retrieved from http://www.cbsnews.com/news/children-parents-guns-firarm-safety

152. Every Town Research. (n.d.). Gun violence in America. Retrieved from https://www.everytownresearch.org/gun-violence-in-america

153. Charlier, J., & Mayor, P. (2018). Reducing gun violence in America: The Douzaine principles. Retrieved from https://patch.com/illinois/niles/reducing-gun-violence-america-douzaine-principles

154. Garza, A. (2019). 60 people have been killed on mass shootings in 2019 alone. Retrieved from https://time.com/5643553/2019-mass-shooting-list/

155. Greenberg, J., Jacobson, L., Valverde, M., et.al. (2018). What we know about mass shootings. Retrieved from https://www.politifact.com/truth-o-meter/article/2018/feb/14/what-we-know-about-mass-shootings/

156. March for Our Lives. (n.d.). Retrieved from https://marchforourlives.com

157. Blount, L. G. (2016). On golden vaginas and gun violence. *American Journal of Public Health.* doi:10.2105/AJPH.2016.303462

158. Lott Jr., J. R. (2016). *The war on guns.* New York, NY: Regnery.

159. Pro Con Organization. (n.d.). Concealed guns: Pros and cons. Retrieved from http://concealedguns.procon.org/

160. National Conference of State Legislatures. (2017). Guns on campus: Overview. Retrieved from www.ncsl.org/research/education/guns-on-campus-overview.aspx

161. Jackson, A., & Gould, S. (2017). 10 states allow guns on college campuses and 16 more are considering it. Retrieved from https://www.businessinsider.com/states-that-allow-guns-on-college-campuses-2017-4

162. Shute, N. (2016). A plan to prevent gun suicides. *Scientific American.* Retrieved from https://www.scientificamerican.com/article/a-plan-to-prevent-gun-suicide

163. Pro Con Organization. (n.d.). Do violent video games contribute to youth violence? Retrieved from http://videogames.procon.org

164. Topps, G. (2015, July/August). How violent video games really affect kids. *American Scientific Mind,* 41-45.

165. Goldbeck, L., & Pew, A. (n.d.). Violent video games and aggression. Retrieved from www.center4research.org/violent-video-games-can-increas-aggression/

166. Miller, M. (2016). Prevention apps may be key to stopping campus sexual assaults. In J. Lasky (Ed.), *Campus sexual assaults* (pp. 120-124). Farmingham, MI: Greenhaven Press.

167. Ressler-Culp, T. (2016). Prevention apps are not an effective way to stop campus sexual assaults. In J. Lasky (Ed.), *Sexual assault on campus* (pp. 125-132). Farmington, MI: Greenhaven Press.

168. Highya.com. (2017). TruthFinder reviews. Retrieved from https://www.highya.com/truthfinder-reviews

169. Prevent Connect. (2018). Re-envisioning community norms: Social norms change as sexual and domestic violence prevention strategy. Retrieved from www.preventconnect.org/2018/12/re-envisioning-community-norms-social-norms-as-a-sexual-and-domestic-violence-prevention-strategy/

170. Longley, R. (2019). What is the broken windows theory? Retrieved from https://www.thoughtco.com/broken-windows-theory-4685946

171. National Institute of Justice. (n.d.). Hot spots policing. Retrieved from https://www.crimesolutions.gov/PracticeDetails.aspx?ID=8

172. The Community Guide. (n.d.). Violence. Retrieved from https://www.thecommunityguide.org/topic/violence

173. Minor, J. (2016, January/February). Advances in drone technology will

revolutionize campus security. *Campus Safety,* 22-24.

Chapter 17

1. Artiga, S., & Hinton, E. (2018). *Beyond health care: The role of social determinants in promoting health and health equity.* Kaiser Family Foundation. Retrieved from http://www.kff.org/disparities-policy/issue-brief/beyond-health-care-the-role-of-social-determinants-in-promoting-health-and-health-equity/

2. National Center for Complementary and Integrative Health. (2019). Complementary, alternative, or integrative health: What's in a name? Retrieved from https://nccih.nih.gov/health/integrative-health

3. Maizes, V., Horwitz, R., Lebensohn, P., et al. (2015). The evolution of integrative medical education: The influence of the University of Arizona Center for Integrative Medicine. *Journal of Integrative Medicine, 13*(6), 356-362.

4. National Center for Complementary and Integrative Health. (2017). Frequently asked questions: Name change. Retrieved from https://nccih.nih.gov/news/name-change-faq

5. Association of Schools Advancing Health Professions. (2018). What is allied health? Retrieved from http://www.asahp.org/what-is/

6. Scutchfield, F. D., Prybil, L., Kelly, A. V., & Mays, G. P. (2016). Public health and hospitals: Lessons learned from partnerships in a changing health care environment. *American Journal of Public Health, 106*(1), 45-48.

7. Clarke, T. C., Black, L. I., Stussman, B. J., & Nahin, R. L. (2015). Trends in use of complementary health approaches among adults: United States, 2002—2012. *National Health Statistics Reports,* No. 79. Hyattsville, MD: National Center for Health Statistics.

8. Wainapel, S. F., Rand, S., Fishman, L. M., & Halstead-Kenny, J. (2015). Integrating complementary/alternative medicine into primary care: Evaluating the evidence and appropriate implementation. *International Journal of General Medicine, 8,* 361-372.

9. Crawford, P. F., Rupert, J., Jackson, J. T., Walkowski, S., & Ledford, C. J. W. (2019). Relationship of training in acupuncture to physician burnout. *Journal of the American Board of Family Medicine, 32,* 259-263.

10. National Center for Complementary and Integrative Health. (2018). The use of complementary and alternative medicine in the United States: Cost data. Retrieved from https://nccih.nih.gov/news/camstats/costs/costdatafs.htm

11. Stussman, B. J., Black, L. I., Barnes, P. M., Clarke, T. C., & Nahin, R. L. (2015). Wellness-related use of common complementary health approaches among adults: United States, 2012. *National Health Statistics Reports,* No. 85. Hyattsville, MD: National Center for Health Statistics.

12. Dydyk, A. M. (2020) Chronic pain. StatPearls. Retrieved from https://www-ncbi-nlm-nih-gov.offcampus.lib.washington.edu/books/NBK553030/

13. Nahin, R. L., Boineau, R., Khalsa, P. S., Stussman, B. J., & Weber, W. J. (2016). Evidence based evaluation of complementary health approaches for pain management in the United States. *Mayo Clinic Proceedings, 91*(9), 1292-1306.

14. National Center for Complementary and Integrative Health. (2015). Credentialing: Understanding the education, training, regulation and licensing of complementary health practitioners. Retrieved from https://nccih.nih.gov/health/decisions/credentialing.htm

15. National Center for Complementary and Integrative Health. (2020). Flu and colds, in depth. Retrieved from https://nccih.nih.gov/health/flu/indepth

16. Insufficient evidence for use of omega-3 supplementation in treating depression. (2016). Cochrane. Retrieved from www.cochrane.org/news/insufficient-evidence-use-omega-3-supplements-treating-depression

17. Santesso, N. (2015). A summary of a Cochrane Review: Probiotics to prevent acute upper respiratory tract infections. *Global Advances in Health and Medicine, 4*(6), 18-19.

18. National Center for Complementary and Integrative Health. (2019). Probiotics: What you need to know. Retrieved from https://nccih.nih.gov/health/probiotics/introduction.htm

19. Brondino, N., De Silvestri, A., Re, S., et al. (2013). A systematic review and meta-analysis of Ginkgo biloba in neuropsychiatric disorders: From ancient tradition to modern-day medicine. *Evidence Based Complementary and Alternative Medicine, 2013:* 915691.

20. Sharma, A., & Kumar, Y. (2019). Nature's derivative(s) as alternative anti-Alzheimer's disease treatments. *Journal of Alzheimer's Disease Reports, 3*(1), 279-297.

21. National Center for Complementary and Integrative Health. (2019). Herbs at a glance. Retrieved from http://nccam.nih.gov/health/ herbsataglance.htm

22. U.S. Food and Drug Administration. (2019). Dietary supplements. Retrieved from https://www.fda.gov/food/dietary-supplements

23. Job, K. M., Kiang, T. K., Constance, J. E., et al. (2016). Herbal medicines: Challenges in the modern world. Part 4. Canada and United States. *Expert Review Clinical Pharmcology, 9*(12), 1597-1609.

24. Bolan, S., Kunhikrishnan, A., Seshadri, B., et al. (2017). Sources, distribution, bioavailability, toxicity and risk assessment of heavy metal(loids)s in complementary medicines. *Environment International, 108,* 103-118.

25. De Sousa Lima, C. M., Fujishima, M. A. T., de Paula Lima, B., de Sousa, F. F. O., & Da Silva, J. O. (2020). Microbial contamination in herbal medicines: A serious health hazard to elderly consumers. *BMC Complementary Medicine and Therapies, 20*(1), 17.

26. Smith, T., Kawa, K., Eckl, V., Morton, C., & Stredney, R. (2017). Herbal supplement sales in U.S. increase 7.7% in 2016. Consumer preferences shifting toward ingredients with general wellness benefits, driving growth of adaptogens and digestive health products. *American Botanical Council, 115,* 56-65. Retrieved from http://cms.herbalgram.org/herbalgram/issue115/hg115-herbmarketrpt.html?ts=1582478598&signature=58f918842366c8d763262ad43fac5869

27. Papanicolas, I., Woskie, L. R., & Ashish, K. J.(2018). Health care spending in the United States and other high-income countries. *Journal of the American Medical Association, 319*(10), 1024-1039.

28. Clarke, T. C., Barnes, P. M., Black, L. I., Stussman, B. J., & Nahin, R. L. (2018). Use of yoga, meditation, and chiropractors among US adults aged 18 and over. NCHS Data Brief, No. 325. Hyattsville, MD: National Center for Health Statistics.

29. Hall, A., Copsey, B., Richmond, H., et al. (2017). Effectiveness of tai chi for chronic musculoskeletal pain conditions: Updated systematic review and meta-analysis. *Physical Therapy, 97*(2), 227-238.

30. Nyman, S. R., & Skelton, D. A. (2017). The case for tai chi in the repertoire of strategies to prevent falls among older people. *Perspectives in Public Health, 137*(2), 85-86.

31. National Center for Complementary and Integrative Health. (2017). Tai chi and qi gong: In depth. Retrieved from https://nccih.nih.gov/health/taichi/introduction.htm

32. Duarte, L., Goncalves, M., Mendes, P., Matos, L. C., Greten H. J., & Machado, J. (2020). Can qigong improve attention in adolescents? A prospective randomized controlled trial. *Journal of Bodywork and Movement Therapies, 24*(1), 175-181.

33. Yang, H., Wu, X., & Wang, M. (2017). The effect of three different meditation exercises on hypertension: A network meta-analysis. *Evidence-Based Complementary and Alternative Medicine.* doi:10.1155/2017/9784271

34. Zou, L., Sasaki, J. E., Wang, H., et al. (2017). A systematic review and meta-analysis of

Baduanjin Qigong for health benefits: Randomized controlled trials. *Evidence-Based Complementary and Alternative Medicine.* doi:10.1155/2017/4548706

35. Madden, K., Middleton, P., Cyna, A. M., et al. (2016). Hypnosis for pain management during labour and childbirth. *Cochrane Database Systematic Review,* CD009356.

36. Sawni, A., & Breuner, C. C. (2017). Clinical hypnosis, an effective mind-body modality for adolescents with behavioral and physical complaints. *Children (Basel), 4*(4).

37. National Center for Complementary and Integrative Health. (2017). Hypnosis. Retrieved from https://nccih.nih.gov/health/hypnosis.

38. American Osteopathic Association. (2020). Osteopathic medicine. Retrieved from http://www.osteopathic.org/Pages/default.aspx

39. National Center for Complementary and Integrative Health. (2019). Chiropractic: In depth. Retrieved from https://nccih.nih.gov/health/chiropractic/introduction.htm

40. National Center for Complementary and Integrative Health. (2019). Massage: What you need to know. Retrieved from https://nccih.nih.gov/health/massage/massageintroduction.htm

41. Smith, C. A., Collins, C. T., Levett, K. M., Armour, M., Dahlen, H. G., Tan, A. L., et al. (2020). Acupuncture or acupressure for pain management during labour. *Cochrane Database of Systematic Review, 7*(2), CD009232. doi:10.1002/14651858.CD009232.pub2.

42. Wang, Y., Zhishun, L., Peng, W., Zhao, J., & Liu, B. (2013). Acupuncture for stress urinary incontinence in adults. *Cochrane Database of Systematic Reviews, 7.*

43. Zhang, G. C., Fu, W. B., Xu, N. G., et al. (2012). Meta analysis of the curative effect of acupuncture on post-stroke depression. *Journal of Traditional Chinese Medicine, 32* (1), 6—11.

44. Vickers, A. J., Cronin, A. M., Machino, A. C., et al. (2012). Acupuncture for chronic pain: Individual patient data meta-analysis. *Archives of Internal Medicine, 172*(9), 1444-1453.

45. National Center for Complementary and Integrative Health. (2017). Accupuncture. Retrieved from https://nccih.nih.gov/health/acupuncture/introduction

46. National Center for Complementary and Integrative Health. (2017). Acupuncture: In depth. Retrieved from https://nccih.nih.gov/health/acupuncture/introduction

47. National Center for Complementary and Integrative Health. (2018). Reiki: In depth. Retrieved from https://nccih.nih.gov/health/reiki-info

48. National Center for Complementary and Integrative Health. (2019). Homeopathy. Retrieved February 12, 2020 from https://nccih.nih.gov/health/homeopathy

49. National Center for Complementary and Integrative Health. (2019). Naturopathy. Retrieved from https://nccih.nih.gov/health/naturopathy

50. National Center for Complementary and Integrative Health. (2019). Traditional Chinese medicine: What you need to know. Retrieved from https://nccih.nih.gov/health/whatiscam/chinesemed.htm

51. National Center for Complementary and Integrative Health. (2019). Ayurvedic medicine: What you need to know. Retrieved from https://nccih.nih.gov/health/ayurveda/introduction.htm

52. Ratini, M. (2019) Traditional Chinese medicine. WebMD Medical Reference. Retrieved from https://www.webmd.com/balance/guide/what-is-traditional-chinese-medicine#

53. International Classification of Diseases (ICD-11). (2019). World Health Organization. Retrieved from https://www.who.int/classifications/icd/revision/en/

54. The World Health Organization's decision about traditional Chinese medicine could backfire. (2019). *Nature, 570,* 5. doi:10.1038/d41586-019-01726-1

55. National Center for Complementary and Integrative Health. (2016). Traditional Chinese medicine: In depth. Retrieved from https://nccih.nih.gov/health/whatiscam/chinesemed.htm

56. Ratini, M. (2019) What is ayurveda? WebMD Medical Reference. Retrieved from https://www.webmd.com/balance/guide/ayurvedic-treatments#2

57. National Center for Complementary and Integrative Health. (2019). Ayruveda: In depth. Retrieved from https://nccih.nih.gov/health/ayurveda/introduction.htm

58. Bolan, S., Kunhikrishnan, A., Seshadri, B., et al. (2017). Sources, distribution, bioavailability, toxicity and risk assessment of heavy metal(loids) in complementary medicines. *Environment International, 108,* 103-118.

59. National Center for Complementary and Integrative Health. (2019). Homeopathy. Retrieved from https://nccih.nih.gov/health/homeopathy

60. National Health and Medical Research Council. (2015). *NHMRC Information Paper: Evidence on the effectiveness of homeopathy for treating health conditions.* Canberra: National Health and Medical Research Council.

61. National Center for Complementary and ntegrative Health. (2017). Naturopathy. Retrieved from https://nccih.nih.gov/health/naturopathy.

62. Koithan, M., & Farrell, C. (2010). Indigenous Native American health traditions. *Journal of Nurse Practice, 6*(6), 477-478. doi:10.1016/j.nurpra/2010.03.016

63. Indian Health Service. (n.d.) Office of Urban Indian Health Programs. Retrieved from https://www.ihs.gov/urban/history/

64. Indian Health Service. (n.d.) About HIS. Retrieved from https://www.ihs.gov/aboutihs/

65. National Center for Complementary and Integrative Health. (2019). Be an informed consumer. Retrieved from https://nccih.nih.gov/health/decisions

66. U.S. Census Bureau. (2019). Income, poverty and health insurance coverage in the United States. Retrieved from https://www.census.gov/newsroom/press-releases/2019/income-poverty.html

67. Fehr, R., & Cox, C. (2019). How affordable are 2019 ACA premiums for middle-income people? The Henry J Kaiser Family Foundation. Retrieved from https://www.kff.org/health-reform/issue-brief/how-affordable-are-2019-aca-premiums-for-middle-income-people/

68. The Henry J Kaiser Family Foundation. (2013). Summary of the affordable care act. Retrieved from http://kff.org/interactive/implementation-timeline/

69. Guttmann, A. (2020). Most advertised drugs on U.S. TV 2019. Stastisa. Accessed at https://www.statista.com/statistics/639356/tv-advertise-drugs-usa/

70. Reichel, C. (2018). Direct-to-consumer drug advertising spikes demand. Journalist's Resource. Retrieved from https://journalistsresource.org/studies/government/health-care/direct-to-consumer-prescription-drugs/

71. Organization for Economic Co-Operation and Development. (2020). Health expenditure and financing. Retrieved from https://stats.oecd.org/Index.aspx?DataSetCode=SHA

72. Cha, A. E., & Cohen, R. A. (2020). Problems paying medical bills, 2018. NCHS Data Brief No 357. Retrieved from https://www.cdc.gov/nchs/products/databriefs/db357.htm

73. Papanicolas, I., Woskie, L. R., & Ashish, K. J. (2018). Health care spending in the United States and other high-income countries. *Journal of the American Medical Association, 319*(10), 1024-1039.

74. Centers for Disease Control and Prevention. (2019). Health, United States, 2018. Retrieved from https://www.cdc.gov/nchs/data/hus/hus18.pdf

Chapter 18

1. Miller, G. T., & Spoolman, S. (2018). *Living in the environment.* Belmont, CA. Wadsworth/Cengage Learning.

2. Lenn Tech. (n.d.). Specific questions on water quantities. Retrieved from https://www.lenntech.com/specific-questions-water-quantities.htm

3. United States Geological Services. (n.d.). How much water is there on earth? Retrieved from https://www.usgs.ogv/special-topic/water-science-school/science/how-much-water-there-earth/qt-science_center_objects=0#qt-science

4. U.S. Environmental Protection Agency. (n.d.). Ground water: Drinking water: Frequently asked questions. Retrieved from www.epa.gov/ogwdw

5. Castelo, J. (2018). Causes of water conflict: Past wars and future predictions. Retrieved from https://worldwaterreserve.com/water-crisis/causes-of-water-conflict/

6. Optimist Daily. (2019). We've never been closer to sustainable desalination technology. Retrieved from https://www.optimistdaily.com/2019/06/weve-never-been-closer-to-sustainable-desalination/technology

7. Tietenberg, T., & Lewis, L. (2019). *Natural resource economics.* New York, NY: Routledge, Taylor & Francis Group.

8. Christensen, N., & Leege, L. (2016). *The environment and you.* Stamford, CT: Pearson Learning.

9. Better Meets Reality. (n.d.). What is a water footprint, & virtual water? (in products, food, etc.). Retrieved from https://www.bettermeetsreality.com/explaining-the-water-footprint-virtual-water-in-products-food-more/

10. Environmental Pollution Centers. (n.d.). What is water pollution? Retrieved from https://www.environmentalpollutioncenters.org/water/

11. Szymanowska, G. (n.d.). "Flesh-eating" bacteria: Here's how you can avoid contracting necrotizing fasciitis. Retrieved from https://news.yahoo.com/flesh-eating-bacteria-heres-avoid-185105585.html

12. Chodosh, S. (2018). Why you should think twice before getting into a pool. Retrieved from htps://www.popsci.com/pool-germs

13. Smith, M., Bosman, J., & Davey, M. (2019). Flint's water crisis started 5 years ago. It's not over. Retrieved from https://www.nytimes.com/2019/04/25/us/flint-water-crisis.html

14. Lenn Tech. (n.d.). Drinking water FAQ frequently asked questions. Retrieved from https://www.lenntech.com/applications/drinking/faq/drinking-water-faq-.htm

15. U.S. Centers for Disease Control and Prevention. (n.d.). Health effects of PFAS. Retrieved from www.atsdr.cdc.gov/pfc/health_effects_pfcs.html

16. Centers for Disease Control and Prevention, Division of Oral Health, National Center for Chronic Disease Prevention and Health Promotion. (n.d.). FAQs for dental fluorosis. Community water fluoridation. Retrieved from www.cdc.gov/fluoridation/safety/dental_fluorosis.htm

17. Cunningham, W., & Cunningham, M. (2017). *Principles of environmental science.* New York, NY: McGraw-Hill Education.

18. Rosane, O. (2019). 7 million more Americans breathe unhealthy air since last "state of the air" report. Retrieved from https//www.ecowatch.com/air-pollution-americans-2635507557.html

19. Carnegie, D. (2018). What are greenhouse gasses? Retrieved from https://www.thoughtco.com/what-are-greenhouse-gasses-1203888

20. World Atlas. (n.d.). What is the ozone layer. Retrieved from www.worldatlas.com/articles/what-is-the-ozone-layer-shield.html

21. Climate Hot Map Organization. (n.d.). Global warming effects map - effects of global arming. Retrieved from www.climatemap.org

22. Pierre-Louis, K. (2019). Brace for the polar vortex: It may be visiting more often. Retrieved from https://www.nytimes.com/2019/01/18/climate/polar-vortex-2019.html

23. Popular Science. (n.d.). The polar vortex is running wild and it may not be because of climate change. Retrieved from https://www.longroom.com/discussion/1364098/the-polar-vortex-is-running-wild-and-it-may-not-be-because-of-climate-change

24. Intergovernmental Panel on Climate Change. (n.d.). AR Synthesis Report: Climate change 2022. Retrieved from https://www.ipcc.ch/report/sixth-assessment-report-cycle/

25. National Oceanic and Atmospheric Administration. (2019). Carbon dioxide levels in atmosphere hit record high in May 2019. Retrieved from https://phys.org/news/2019-06-carbon-dioxide-atmosphere-high.html

26. National Geographic (2018). Environment. Retrieved from https://www.nationalgeographic.com/environment/2018/10/ipcc-report

27. Leahy, S. (n.d.). Off-the-charts heat to affect millions in U.S in coming decades. Retrieved from https://www.msn.com/en-us/weather/topstories/'off-the-charts'heat-to-affect-millions-in-us-in-coming-decades/ar-AAEol5u

28. Ocean Science. (n.d.). Sea level rise. Retrieved from https://ocean.si.edu/through-time/ancient seas/sea-level-rise#section_1635

29. Fourth National Climate Assessment Report. (n.d.). Retrieved from https://npa2018.globalchange.gov/downloads/

30. Union of Concerned Scientists. (n.d.). Sea level rise & global warming. Retrieved from https://www.ucussa.org/global_warming/science_and_impacts/infographic-sea-level-rise-global-warming.html

31. New York Post. (2018). Climate change is making hurricanes way more intense.

Retrieved from https://nypost.com/2018/09/17/climate-change-os-making-hurricanes-way-more-intense/

32. Idele, V. (2019). Is climate change an "existential threat" - or just a catastrophic one? Retrieved from htttps://vincentidele.com/2019/06/29/is-climate-change-an-existential-threat-or-just-a-catstrophic-one/

33. Funes, Y. (n.d.). Pacific islands declare "climate crisis" that calls for end of fossil fuels. Retrieved from https://earther.gizmodo.com/pacific-islands-declare-climate-crisis-that-calls-for-t-1836849580

34. McDonald, J. (2018). Trump wrong on change, again. Retrieved from https://www.factcheck.org/2018/10/trump-wrong-on-climate-change-again/

35. Meyer, R. (2019). California's wildfires are 500 percent larger due to climate change. Retrieved from https://www.theatlantic.com/science/archive/2019/07/climate-change-500-percent-increase-california-wildfires/594016/

36. Segerstrom, C. (2018). By the end of the century 44,000 people will die every year from wildfire smoke. Retrieved from https://www.motherjones.com/environment/2018/09/by-the-end-0f-the-century-44000-people-will-die-every-year-from-wildfire-smoke

37. Kazdin, C. (2018). The terrifying future of California wild fires: It's going to get worse. Retrieved from https://www.vice.com/en_us/article/439b9g/the-terrifying-future-of california-wildfires-its-going/to-get-worse

38. Loftis, R. (2018). As wildfires rage, Trump administration plans to slash fire science funding. Retrieved from https://www.motherjones.com/environment/2018/08/as-wildfires-rage-trump-administration-plans-to-slash-fire-science-funding/

39. Struzik, E. (2019). Here's an especially terrifying new danger from the rise in wildfires. Retrieved from https://www/motherjones.com/2019/01/heres-an-especially-terrifying-new-danger-from-the-rise-in-wildfires/

40. Zme Science (2019, July 10). By 2050, many cities will have hot weather like they've never seen before. Retrieved from Zmescience.com/science-news/cities-hote-weather-15072019

41. Plumer, B. (2017, June 1). What to expect as U.S. leaves Paris Climate Accord. *New York Times.*

42. Vicce New Photo. (2019). Southerners are scared of the climate, crisis, and their politicians are ignoring them. Retrieved from https://vicenewphoto.blogspot.com/2019/07/southerners-are-scared-of-climate.html

43. NBC News. (2020). Trump's coronavirus failures offer warnings and lessons about future climate change challenges.

Retrieved from https://www.nbcnews.com/think/opinion/trump-s-coronavirus-failures-offer-warnings-lessons-about-future-climate-ncna1195931

44. Bloomberg, M., & Pope, C. (2017). *Climate of hope: How cities, businesses, and citizens can save the planet.* New York, NY: St. Martin's.

45. Garko, M. (n.d.). The impact of what we eat on climate change. Retrieved from letstalknutrition.com/the-impact-of-what-we-eat-on-climate-change/

46. Environmental Pollution Centers. (n.d.). What is air pollution. Retrieved from https://www.environmentalpollutioncenters.org/air

47. Cool Earth. (2018). IPCC global warming special report 2018/what does it actually mean? Retrieved from https://www.coolearth.org/2018/10/pcc-report-2/

48. NASA. (n.d.). NASA ozone watch. Retrieved from https://ozonewatch.gsfc.nasa.gov/

49. CNN Wire. (2019). Air pollution ages your lings faster and increases your risk of COPD, study says. Retrieved from https://wtvr.com/2019/07/08/air-pollution-ages-your-lungs-faster-and-increases-your-risk-of-copd-study-says/

50. Environmental Protection Agency. (n.d.). Particulate matter (PM) pollution. Retrieved from https://www.epa.gov/pm=pollution

51. Enking, E. (2019). Air pollution in many national parks is as bad as in Los Angeles. Retrieved from https://grist.org/article/air-pollution-in-many-national-parks-is=as-bad-as-los-angeles/

52. Keiser, D., Lade, G., & Rudik, I. (2018). Ozone pollution in US national parks is nearly the same as in large cities. Retrieved from https://www.nationofchange.org/2018/07/19/ozone-pollution-in-us-national-parks-is-nearly-the-same-as-in-large-cities/

53. Wu, V. (2019). Cruise ship pollution - the facts. Retrieved from https://cruisepassenger.com.au/cruise-ship-pollution-the-facts/

54. Farand, C. (2017). Air quality on cruise ship deck "worse than world's most polluted cities," investigations finds. Retrieved from https://www.independent.co.uk/news/world/pollution-cruise-ships-po-oceans-higher-picadilly=circus-channel-4-dispatches-a7821911.html

55. U.S. Environmental Protection Agency. (n.d.). Smog. Retrieved from https://www.epa.vic.gov.au/your-environmental/air/smog

56. Drake, N. (2019). Our nights are getting brighter, and earth is paying the price. Retrieved from https://www.nationalgeographic.com/science/2019/04/nights-are-getting-brighter-earth-is-paying-the-price-light-pollution-dark-skies/

57. U.S. Environmental Protection Agency. (n.d.). What is acid rain? Retrieved from www.epa.gov/acidrain/what/index.html

58. USGS. (n.d.). Water as acid rain. Retrieved from https://www.isgs.gov/special-topic/water-science-school/science/water-acid-rain?qt=science_center_objects=0#qt-science_center_object

59. Environmental Protection Agency. (n.d.). Summary of the Clean Air Act. Retrieved from https://www.epa.gov/laws-regulations/summary-clean-air-act

60. NRDC. (n.d.). What is the clean power plan? Retrieved from https://www.nrdc.org/stories/how-clean-power-plan-works-and-why-it-matters

61. Chow, L. (2018). Trump EPA withdraws clean air policy opposed by fossil fuel companies. Retrieved from https://www.ecowatch.com/the-crunch-quesion-on-climate-how-can-i-help-2639095520.html

62. Newsweek. (n.d.). Trump admin wants to ease thousands of deaths due to air pollution: Report. Retrieved from https://.start.att.net/news/read/category/news/article/newsweek-trump_admin_wants_to_eraese_thousands_of_deaths_due-rnewsweek

63. Needham, L. (2019). EPA plans to make it harder for people to keep polluters out of their communities. Retrieved from https://shareblue.com/epa-plans-to-make-it-harder-for-people-to-keep-polluters-out-of-their-communities/

64. Tessume. C., Apte, J., Goodkind, A., et al. (2019). Inequity in consumption of goods and services adds to racial-ethnic disparities in air pollution exposure. Retrieved from https://www.pnas.org/content/pnas/early/2019/03/05/1818859116.full.pdf

65. Rice, D. (2019). Study finds a race gap in air pollution - whites largely cause it; Blacks and Hispanics breathe it. Retrieved from https://www.usa.today.com/story/news/nation/2019/03/11/air=pollution-inequality-minorities-breathe-air-polluted-whites/3130783

66. Little, B. (2019). The environmental toll of cremating the dead. Retrieved from https://www.nationalgeographic.com/science/2019/11/iscremation-environmentallyfrinedly.heres-the-science/

67. Shorman, J. (2019). Can you get your body vibrated into particles when you die? Maybe someday in Kansas. Retrieved from https://www.nydailynews.com/news/nationa;/sns-tns-bc birial-promcssion-20191201-story.html

68. U.S. Environmental Protection Agency. (n.d.). Mold course. Chapter 1–What molds are. Retrieved from www.epa.gov/mold/mold-course-chapter-1-introduction-molds

69. U.S. Department of Health and Human Services. (n.d.). 45 potential toxins found in household dusts. Health Finder. Retrieved from https://healthfinder.gov/News/Aticle.aspx?id=714813&source=govdelivery&utm_medium=email&utm_source=govdelivery

70. Harris, W. (n.d.). How long does it take plastics to biodegrade? Retrieved from https://science.howstuffworks.com/sciencevs-myth/everyday-myths/how-long-does-it-take-for-plastic-to-biodegrade.htm

71. Gander, K. (2017). This is how many years it takes for these everyday items to decompose. Retrieved from https://www.ibtimes.co.uk/this-how-many-years-it-takes-these-everyday-items-decompose-1650426

72. Citi.Lo. (2018). We made plastic, we depend on it, now we're drowning in it. Retrieved from https://citi.lo/2018/06/11/we-made-plastic-we-depend-on-it-now-were-drowning-in-it/

73. Joyce, C. (2019). Microplastics have invaded the deep ocean - and the food chain. Retrieved from https://www.npr.org/sections/thesalt/2019/06/06/729419975/mocroplastics-have-invaded-the-deep-ocean-and-the-food-chain

74. CSBN News. (n.d.). The surprising reason your clothes are a huge source of ocean pollution. Retrieved from https://csbnnews.com/the-surprising-reason-your-clothes-ae-a-huge-source-of-ocean-pollution/

75. The Conversation. (2019). The major source of ocean pollution you've probably never heard of. Retrieved from https://theconversation.com/the-major-source-of-ocean-plastic-pollution-youve-probably-never-heard-of-111687

76. Picheta, R., & Dean, S. (2019). Over 180 countries - not including the US - agree to restrict plastic waste trade. Retrieved from https://www.breakfreefromplastic.org/2019/05/14/over=180-countries-not-including-the-us-agree-to-restrict-global-plastic-waste-trade/

77. U.S. Environmental Protection Agency. (n.d.). Contaminants of emerging concern. Retrieved from http://water.epa.gov/scitech/cec

78. U.S. Environmental Protection Agency. (n.d.). Household hazardous waste. Retrieved from www.epa.gov/garbage/hhw.htm

79. Cunningham, W., & Cunningham, M. (2019). *Principles in environmental sciences.* New York, NY: McGraw-Hill Education.

80. U.S. Environmental Protection Agency. (n.d.). Contaminants of emerging concern. Retrieved from http://water.epa.gov/scitech/cec

81. U.S. Department of Health and Human Services. FDA cracks down on antibacterial soap. Health Finder. Retrieved from https://healthfinder.gov/News/Article.aspx?id=714549&source=govdelivery&utm_medium=email&utm_source=govdelivery

82. Environmental Protection Agency. (n.d.). Medical waste. Retrieved from https://www.epa.gov/rcra/medical-waste

83. Scutti, S. (2018). When hospitals pour drugs down the drain. Retrieved from https://www.cnn.com/2018/12/28/health/water-ph

84. Conserve Energy Future. (n.d.). Nuclear waste disposal. Retrieved from https://www.conserveenergyfuture.com/dangers-and-effects-of-nuclear-waste-disposal.php

85. Environmental Protection Agency. (n.d.). Wastes - nonhazardouse waste - municipal solid waste. Retrieved from https://www.epa.gov/epawaste/nonhaz/municipal/web/html/

86. Rubicon. (n.d.). 50 recycling & trash statistics that will make you think twice about your trash. Retrieved from https://www.rubiconglobal.com/blog-statistics-trash-recycling/

87. National Conference of State Legislatures. (n.d.). State beverage container laws. Retrieved from www.ncsi.org/research/environment-and-natural-resources/state-beverage-container-laws.aspx

88. U.S. Environmental Protection Agency. (n.d.). Recycling. Retrieved from www.epa.gov/garbage/recycle.htm

89. Rosalsky, G. (2019). Are plastic bag bans garbage? Retrieved from https://www.npr.org/secions/money/2019/04/09/711181385/are-plastic-bag-bans-garbage

90. Department of the Environment. (n.d.). Biodiversity conservation. Retrieved from https://www.environment.gov.au/biodiversity/conservation

91. National Geographic. (n.d.). Deforestation explained. Retrieved from https://www.nationalgeographic.com/environment/global-warming/deforestation/

92. Ortiz, E. (n.d.). How the Amazon fires, deforestation affect the U.S. Midwest. Retrieved from https://www.nbcnews.com/news/world/how-amazon-fires-deforestation-affect-u-s-midwest-n-1045886

93. Science Daily. (n.d.). Desert. Retrieved from https://www.sciencedaily.com/terms/desert.htm

94. Flesher, J. (2019). Trump proposes cuts for Great Lakes cleanup. Retrieved from https://www.ironmountaindailynews.com/news/local-news/2019/03/trump-proposes-cuts-for-great-lakes-cleanup/

95. Answers. (n.d.). How many wetlands have been destroyed in the US? Retrieved from https://www.answers.com/Q/How_many_wetlands_have_been_destroyed_in_the_US

96. Bennett, J. (n.d.). Ocean acidification. Retrieved from https://ocean.si.edu/ocean-life/invertebrates/ocean-acidification

97. Dixon, D. L. (2017). Ocean acidification may alter the behaviors of underwater creatures in disastrous ways. *Scientific American Mind, 316*(6), 42-45.

98. Pierre-Louis, K. (2019). World's oceans are losing oxygen rapidly, study finds. New York Times. Retrieved from https://nytimes.com/2019/12/07/climate/ocean-acidification-climate-change.html

99. Climate Interpreter. (n.d.). The effects of ocean acidification on coral reefs. Retrieved from https://climateinterpreter.org/content/effects-ocean-acidificationcoral-reefs

100. United Nations. (2019). UN report: Nature's dangerous decline "unprecedent"; species extinction rates "accelerating." Retrieved from https://www.un.org/sustainabledevelopment/blog/2019/05/nature-decline-unprecedented-report/

101. Cagle, A. (2019). How Trump could make the extinction crisis worse. Retrieved from https://earthjustice.org/blog-2019-may/how-trump-could-make-the-extinction-crisis-even-worse

102. Goodell, J. (2019). Trump's war on endangered species. Retrieved from https://www.rollingstone.com/politics/politics-news/trump-endangered-species-701847/

103. Everything Connects. (n.d.). Preserve habitats. Retrieved from https://www.everythingconnects.org/preserving-habitats.html

104. Knickmeyer, E., & Borenstein, S. (2019). Americans' energy use surges despite climate change concern. Retrieved from https://apnews.com/7d4c9cc8f8c344fb9b800a5fd9c48866

105. United States Department of Transportation. (2018). The safer affordable fuel efficient "SAFE" vehicle rule. Retrieved from https://www.nhtsa.gov/corporate-average-fuel-economy/safe

106. Shepardson, D. (2019). Four automakers strike emissions deal with California, defying Trump admin. Retrieved from https://www.huffpost.com/entry/automakers-strike-emissions-deal-california_n_5d399dede4b004b6adbbd031

107. Pro Con Organization. (2015). Will increased oil drilling help the US solve its energy crisis? Retrieved from http://alternativeenergy.procon.org/view.answers.php?questionID=001255

108. Pierre-Louis, K. (2017). There's no such thing as clean coal. Retrieved from https://www.popsci.com/coal-power-plants-cpp/

109. Plumer, B. (2017). What clean coal is - and inn't. Retrieved from https://www.nytimes.com/2017/08/23/climate/what-clean-coal-is-and-isnt.html

110. Dlouhy, J. (2019). Trump makes his biggest move yet to try to save coal plants. Retrieved from https://www.bloomberg.com/news/articles/1019-06-18/trump-s-biggest-move-to-end-war-on-coal-won-t-rescue-industry

111. Losier, T. (2019). What energy security looks lie: 90% of natural gas used in U.S. is produced domestically. Retrieved from https://www.oilandgas360.com/what-energy-security-looks-like-90-of-natural-gas-used-in-u-s-is-produced-domestically/

112. Alternative Daily. (2019). Fracking: What is it and why is it dangerous? Retrieved from https://www.thealternativedaily.com/fracking-what-is-it-and-why-is-it-dangerous/

113. American Geo Sciences. (n.d.). How many nuclear plants are there is the U.S.? Retrieved from https://americangeociences.org/critical-issues/faq/what-status-us-nuclear-industry

114. Shellenberger, M. (2018). If nuclear power is so safe, why are we so afraid of it? Retrieved from https://www.forbes.com/sites/michealshellenberger/2018/06/11/if-nuclear-power-is-so-safe-why-are-we-so-afraid-of-it/#57fe37686385

115. Hartman, D. L., Klein Tank, A. M. G., Rusticucci, M., et al. (2013). 2: Observations: Atmosphere and surface. In T. F. Stocker, D. Qin, G. K. Plattner et al. (Eds.), *Climate change 2013: The physical science basis. Contribution of Working Group 1 to the Fifth Assessment Report of the Inter-governmental Panel on Climate Change.* Cambridge, UK: Cambridge University Press. Retrieved from www.climatechange2013.org/images/report/WG1AR5_Chapter02_FINAL.pdf

116. Techcopeida. (n.d.). Smart grid. Retrieved from https://www.techcopedia.com/definition/692/smart-grid

117. Live Population. (2019). Population of United States. Retrieved from https://www.livepopulation.com/country/united-states.html

118. Fact Check Organization. (2018). Illegal immigration statistics. Retrieved from https://www.factcheck.org/2018.06/illegal-immigration-statistics/

119. Smith, K. (2019). The facts on immigration: What you need to know in 2019. Retrieved from https://www.cbsnews.com/news/donald-trump-on-immigration-topics-likely-2019-state-of-the-unition-fact-check/

120. Climate and Security. (2019). Migration and the border. Retrieved from https://climateandsecurity.org/2019/04/17/central-america-climate-drought-migration-and-the-border/

121. Werrell, C., & Femia, F. (2019). Central America: Climate, drought, migration and

the border. Retrieved from https://climateandsecurity.org/2019/04/17/central-america-climate-drought-migration-and-the-border/

122. Lin, D. (2017). What is cultural carrying capacity. Retrieved from https://www.thoughtco.com/what-is-cultural-carrying-capacity-127890

123. U.S. Census Bureau. (2017). U.S. and world population clock. Retrieved from www.census.gov/popclock/

124. Parker, K., Horowitz, J., Brown, A., et al. (2018). Demographic and economic trends in urban, suburban, and rural communities. Retrieved from https://pewsocialtrends.org/2018/05/22/demographic-and-economic-trends-in-urban-suburban-and-rural-communities/

125. McDonough, W. (2018). How cities could save us. *Scientific American, 317*(1), 44-47.

126. Smart Growth America. (n.d.). Website. Retrieved from https://smartgrowthamerica.org

127. Chars Bin. (n.d.). Ecological footprint of consumption compared to biocapacity. Retrieved from chartsbin.com/view/571

128. Association for the Advancement of Sustainability in Higher Education. (n.d.). Website. Retrieved from https://www.aashe.org/

129. Taylor & Francis. (n.d.). Today's students aren't dreaming of a sustainable future. They're working out how to make it happen. Retrieved from https://librarianresources.taylorandfrancis.com/sustainable-development-goalsonline/

130. Newkirk, V. (2018). Trump's EPA concludes environmental racism is real. Retrieved from https://www.theatlantic.com/politics/archive/2018/02/the-trump-administration-finds-that-environmental=racism-is-real/554315/

131. Strauss, V. (2019). Trump administration "wrecking ball" approach to science threatens public health and environment, report warns. Retrieved from https://news.yahoo.com/trump-administration-apos-wrecking-ball-204504664.html

132. Lynas, M. (2018). Why president Macron's u-turn is a warning for climate leaders. Retrieved from https://www.cnn.com/2018/12/31/opinions/macron-warning-climate-leaders/index.html

Index